GENERAL OF THE ARMY

George C. Marshall

Soldier and Statesman

ED CRAY

A TOUCHSTONE BOOK
Published by Simon & Schuster
New York London Toronto Sydney Tokyo Singapore

Touchstone
Simon & Schuster Building
Rockefeller Center
1230 Avenue of the Americas
New York, New York 10020

Copyright © 1990 by Ed Cray

First Touchstone Edition 1991
Published by arrangement with W. W. Norton & Company, Inc.
500 Fifth Avenue, New York, NY 10110
TOUCHSTONE and colophon are registered trademarks
of Simon & Schuster Inc.
Manufactured in the United States of America

1   3   5   7   9   10   8   6   4   2   Pbk.

Library of Congress Cataloging in Publication Data
Cray, Ed.
General of the Army: George C. Marshall, soldier and
statesman/Ed Cray.—1st Touchstone ed.
p.   cm.
"A Touchstone book."
Includes bibliographical references and index.
1. Marshall, George C. (George Catlett), 1880–1959.
2. Generals—United States—Biography.
3. Statesmen—United States—Biography.
4. United States.   Army—Biography.   I. Title.
E745.M37C73   1991
973.918′092—dc20
[B]   90-28559
CIP
ISBN 0-671-74124-1

For Diane,
Finally

ACKNOWLEDGMENTS

We gratefully acknowledge permission from the Oral History Research Office, Columbia University, to print extracts from the oral histories of Harvey H. Bundy, Lucius DeBignon Clay, Dwight D. Eisenhower, Anthony C. McAuliffe, Walter S. Robertson, and James T. Williams, Jr.; and from Yale University Library to print portions of the Henry L. Stimson Diaries contained in the Henry L. Stimson Papers, Manuscripts and Archives, Yale University Library.

CONTENTS

Foreword   *xi*

Introduction: A Place in History   *3*

PART I   THE SOLDIER

I   *A Very Simple Life*   *17*
II   *The Long Years*   *31*
III   *Remarkably Gallant Fellows*   *49*
IV   *The Steamroller*   *64*
V   *The Company of Generals*   *84*
VI   *A Very Slow Thing to Improve*   *96*
VII   *The Make*   *112*
VIII   *The Last Lessons*   *126*

PART II   THE CHIEF OF STAFF

IX   *The Island Alone*   *143*
X   *The Most Businesslike Manner*   *164*
XI   *The Common Law Alliance*   *181*
XII   *The Summer's Storms*   *197*
XIII   *Oranges, Purples, and Rainbows*   *218*
XIV   *The Throw of the Die*   *236*
XV   *The Sword Drawn*   *259*
XVI   *The Pacific Deeps*   *277*
XVII   *Modicum's Success*   *304*
XVIII *Lighting the Torch*   *320*
XIX   *A Pile of Brickbats*   *337*
XX   *The Wife's Legacy*   *354*

Part III The Victor

XXI	*A Very Vicious War*	*373*
XXII	*The Great Prize*	*385*
XXIII	*Threshers*	*402*
XXIV	*A Rainbow Discerned*	*418*
XXV	*Losses*	*438*
XXVI	*A Lesson in Geometry*	*451*
XXVII	*End Game*	*468*
XXVIII	*The Winterkill*	*482*
XXIX	*The Argonauts*	*497*
XXX	*The Battle Day Past*	*516*
XXXI	*A Second Coming in Wrath*	*533*

Part IV The Statesman

XXXII	*The Chinese Midwife*	*553*
XXXIII	*The Tiger of Peace*	*569*
XXXIV	*Going to the Yar*	*586*
XXXV	*A Fair Prospect of Success*	*607*
XXXVI	*The Crowded Days*	*627*
XXXVII	*Playing with Fire*	*644*
XXXVIII	*Active Duty*	*667*
XXXIX	*Positions Reversed*	*679*
XL	*Imperator*	*691*
XLI	*The Shatter of Icons*	*706*
XLII	*Sunset*	*726*

Notes	*737*
Bibliography	*807*
Index	*823*

Photographs appear following page 284

FOREWORD

This was surely a time of giants, of men who shaped the most momentous period of the twentieth century, the years of the first truly global war, from 1931 to 1945. Roosevelt, Churchill, and Stalin, these men who massed armies, who inspired entire peoples to profound sacrifice, had but one peer, one man admitted to their councils on equal terms: General George Catlett Marshall, chief of staff of the United States Army.

Marshall—"that civilized warrior," in Peter Wyden's apt phrase—stood amongst the titans for good reason. It was he who forged the overall strategy that was to win the war, then by force of character persuaded president and prime minister to adopt that conception. Churchill once wondered if "perhaps he [Marshall] was the greatest Roman of them all," high praise from that accomplished historian. At another time the close-guarded Marshal Stalin saw in the aloof American characteristics that compelled Stalin to insist, "I would trust General Marshall with my life."

As chief of staff, Marshall was to create and train a massive army, the largest his country has ever fielded, promoting younger officers, *his* men, to progressively higher command and vast responsibility. It was Marshall who incidentally set Dwight David Eisenhower on the path to the presidency.

Denied field command, the one prize he most wanted, Marshall was nonetheless admired by those who fought the battles. One of the most celebrated of American generals during the war, Matthew Ridgway, wrote, "The combat soldier never had a better and more understanding friend than George C. Marshall. With the burdens of a global war upon his shoulders, he never forgot the man with the rifle, the man whose task it was to kill and be killed."

On leaving Washington for the last time, that craggy veteran of seven administrations, Secretary of War Henry L. Stimson, said to Marshall, "I have seen a great many soldiers in my lifetime and you, sir, are the finest soldier I have ever known."

Yet there would be even more years of duty. The war over, and at an age when most men slip gratefully into retirement, Marshall took up a new career as a diplomat, serving a new president with the same dedication that had marked his years as a soldier. Marshall did much to shape the postwar world, seeking to moderate a Cold War even as he implemented policies and programs still in effect four decades later. Oddly, yet fitting too, it is as a diplomat, and not as a soldier, that he seems fated to be remembered best. Marshall, I believe, would have appreciated that—though he was singularly uninterested in personal honors throughout his life. No battlefield victory so exemplified the American spirit as did the generosity of the postwar Marshall Plan.

Those who worked with him at the Department of State in the postwar years were as impressed as the men who had earlier soldiered with him in the Philippines, in China, in France and the United States. His reorganization of State and his leadership "was still viewed in the department a generation later as a lost golden age of innovation and creativity," two diplomatic historians noted. "I have never gone in for hero worship," wrote senior diplomat Charles Bohlen, "but of all the men I have been associated with, including Presidents, George Catlett Marshall is at the top of the list of those I admired. . . . We knew we were working for a great man."

Taking George Marshall's measure inspired even sober men to superlatives. In granting him an honorary degree, Harvard University compared him to George Washington. Harry Truman judged Marshall "the greatest living American" and "one for the ages."

Not everyone was so in awe. Senators Joseph McCarthy and William E. Jenner, the one infamous, the other forgotten, assailed Marshall as a traitor. Less hysterical, General Albert C. Wedemeyer, like Eisenhower raised to high rank by Marshall, considered the former chief of staff "primarily a military man who had little knowledge of the complexities of the world conflict," and sorely naive about communism's threat. Admiral Charles M. Cooke, Jr., the Navy's foremost planner during World War II, dismissed Marshall's reputation with scorn, growling, "Feet of clay! Feet of clay!" Chicago *Tribune* reporter Walter Trohan—who covered many of the events in this book—considered Marshall "a political general—a general by virtue of Presidential favor."

Though such critics were few, it is in the anxious nature of biographers to wonder if their subject is truly a man for the ages. Were his fame to rest solely upon his military career, it seems likely that the memory of George Catlett Marshall would recede in time. After all, how many remember Lincoln's chief of staff during the Civil War, or even Wilson's during World War I?

But Marshall seems to have achieved more than high office.

As this book neared completion, a United States naval vessel shot down a civilian airliner over the Persian Gulf. A syndicated newspaper columnist noted a strained unwillingness in Washington to accept responsibility for the deaths of the 290 innocent passengers aboard the aircraft, then added, "I wonder what Harry Truman or George Marshall or Dwight Eisenhower would make of the American government and military today." Marshall had become an icon of integrity.

It falls also to biographers and reminiscing old men like newspaper columnist Joseph Alsop to ponder "whether we shall ever see another leader of the U.S. Army with the all-around greatness of George C. Marshall." Perhaps we shall not. The qualities of selfless public service, of self-sacrifice that he represented to the men and women of his times, are today in scarce supply. Government service appears no longer to be a great privilege. Instead, presidential confidants who can trade on their closeness to the Oval Office transmute themselves into well-paid Washington lobbyists. Ranking Pentagon officers curry favor with defense contractors who can provide lucrative sinecures for retired military men. White House staff members, military and civilian alike, conduct a secret foreign policy, arranging "deniability" for their superiors while perjuring themselves in furtherance of illegal schemes. Meanwhile, a nationally syndicated columnist identified with the administration defends a cabinet officer of less than impeccable reputation, fretting about "the lasting damage we are doing to the government and to American society by overdosing on moralism."

For just these reasons we need to recall continually George Catlett Marshall, both the man and his accomplishments—in the words of James Agee, "to praise famous men." There is, of course, Forrest Pogue's four-volume biography, truly an imposing work, but formidable and forbidding to all but the most dedicated because of its very size. Other biographical efforts have scanted Marshall's postwar years, years of a Cold War that has shaped our world since.

That is the purpose of this, the first one-volume, full-length portrait of the man. This then is a stocktaking.

Such a work would not have been possible without the aid and comfort of a number of people. Deborah Latish provided research assistance for a year. A clutch of librarians, both at the University of California Los Angeles and the University of Southern California, extended themselves to locate one more book, one more dusty government publication, one more long misplaced journal. Chief among these stalwarts were Julia Johnson, Sam Russo, and Joyce Olin of the USC library staff. Cicely Surace, library director of the *Los Angeles Times,* permitted me to use what newspapermen once called the "morgue" and professionals such as Ms. Surace have transformed into a valuable research tool. Archivist John N. Jacob of the George C. Marshall Research Library in Lexington, Virginia, again and again forwarded documents for me, ever the writer's friend; Jacob's contribution may be measured by the number of times the abbreviation GCMRL appears in the notes. To Jacob and his associates of the Marshall Library, especially Royster Lyle and Fred Hadsell, my gratitude too for their hospitality.

A pair of scholars who read the manuscript deserve special mention: the sharp-eyed Larry I. Bland, editor of the Marshall Papers for Johns Hopkins University Press; and Robert Dallek, a keen historian of diplomacy and the presidency. Their unstinting generosity exemplifies the ideal of scholarship, the sharing of hard-earned knowledge with a colleague.

I would thank as well others who read the manuscript at various times and encouraged me through the doldrums every writer knows: colleagues at the University of Southern California, A. J. Langguth, Irwin Lieb and Jonathan Kotler; and my friend Sam Adams.

My editor at W. W. Norton, Starling Lawrence, endured with something approaching resigned good humor the repeated disappointments of missed deadlines, then edited a very long manuscript with deft hand.

Finally, I would thank my daughter Jennifer, just fourteen years old when the contract for this book was signed. Many are the library hours she put in or me, fetching and photocopying. Her later analytical paper led me to an understanding of the decision to use the Nagasaki bomb. She is now, at age twenty-three, a journalist in her own right; a proud father would like to think that perhaps George Catlett Marshall influenced her life just a little.

ED CRAY

Los Angeles, 1980–88

GENERAL
OF THE ARMY

INTRODUCTION

A Place in History

The five C-54 transports droned in a clumsy echelon, shepherded by skittish fighters above and below the formation. The normally chatty fighter pilots flew silently, by direct order of the deputy Allied commander in the Mediterranean, tersely acknowledging their coded checkpoints, squinting into the glare for the telltale glint of sun on the wings of a Messerschmitt. Not every day did these cocky youngsters fly cover for the president of the United States.

Were the president not responsibility enough, from the second of the transports, the army chief of staff, George C. Marshall, and the air force commander, "Hap" Arnold, could peer out a window at any moment. Marshall might not know much about flying—none of the fighter pilots could be sure since Marshall had promoted the extraordinary growth of the Army Air Force in the last four years—but Hap Arnold certainly did. The man who screwed up here would likely find himself assigned as flight controller at Dutch Harbor, unless Marshall had a vacancy for a platoon leader at Salerno.

The fighters nestled in tightly as the formation crossed the Red Sea, ferrying president, chiefs of staff, and four dozen military planners 1,300 miles from Tehran back to Cairo.

In the first of the transports, the C-54 he himself had dubbed "The Sacred Cow," Franklin Delano Roosevelt sat strapped in his seat, reviewing the agenda for the second half of the SEXTANT conference. His lifeless legs swaddled in a gray naval blanket against the mile-high cold, he chatted affably with his closest adviser, the cadaverous Harry Hopkins. Roosevelt's trademark cigarette holder pointed skyward at a jaunty angle once more.

The president had reason to feel optimistic. He had been in his element at the Tehran Conference, dealing with two prickly ministers as he had for years soothed and cajoled Senate committee chairmen and big-city bosses. They were remarkably similar, those petty princes of American politics and the powerful ministers of great nations, each jealous of his prerogatives, proud of place, stubbornly hewing to policies dictated by tradition rather than reality. Perhaps he was no different, the president might admit privately, more visionary than Churchill about a world after war, but no less hardheaded than Joseph Stalin in fashioning the accommodations they would need to bring about that world.

Marshal Stalin had agreed during the Tehran meetings to a postwar organization of the United Nations, thus committing to Roosevelt's first priority. Stalin had also agreed to enter the war against Japan once Germany was defeated. The president's calculated teasing of the red-faced Churchill had finally cracked the Russian ice, Churchill scowling around his Havana, Stalin smiling broadly as the translator whispered into his ear. Roosevelt now believed he could get along with the distant Stalin, that he could do business with the man as the prime minister, a vocal anti-Red for decades, could not. Time enough to soothe a miffed Churchill when they sat down again in Cairo tomorrow.

This first meeting with Stalin had also settled the major military questions in the West, even if it left the political problems undecided. Roosevelt had agreed that Poland's borders were to be revised, but, as he told Stalin, there could be no public announcement of that until after the presidential elections next year, perhaps not even then. Roosevelt needed the Polish ethnic vote if he was to win a fourth term. The president's decision was practical; in any event, there was nothing either the United States or Great Britain, outnumbered two to one in divisions, could do to stop the Russians from redrawing Poland's borders as the Soviets saw fit. With the Red Army just forty miles from the Rumanian border, obviously the Soviet Union would dominate the future of that nation as well. Latvia, Estonia, and Lithuania would go the same way; Churchill had conceded in the spring of 1942 those "traditional" Russian lands to Stalin. The president could hold out only for a face-saving plebiscite in Poland; the outcome they knew before the first ballot was cast, but a vote would appease American public opinion.

At a more leisurely moment, certainly not while flying back to Cairo to resume talks with a stubborn Winston Churchill, Roosevelt might appreciate the ironies of the postwar world they were grandly parceling out. The Russians would acquire their long-sought buffer states, true colonies, in the division of the spoils. Meanwhile, France would lose much of its foreign empire, certainly Indochina, if Roosevelt's notion of self-determination prevailed. Great Britain, weakened sorely, virtually bankrupt after four years of war, surely would be forced to yield its Empire bit by bit.

In the second of the dun-colored transports, Army General George C. Marshall sat reading a paperback mystery novel. Whatever the problems the president and Harry Hopkins confronted, they were geopolitical, and the chief of staff deliberately stayed clear. His concerns were strategic or logistic, his decisions made "without considering the political consequences. That was for the politicians."

The graying soldier had secured what he most wanted, a firm date for the invasion of France: May 1, 1944. A succession of other military decisions would be resolved in light of that settled date when the Cairo meetings resumed. Meanwhile, the four-star general might just as well read the mystery unperturbed, occasionally squinting over his five-and-dime bifocals at the Mediterranean coastline below. If the general were troubled, his nominal aide, Colonel Frank McCarthy, missed the usual signs: the frown, the terse command, or the slight tic that pulled one corner of his mouth into a deceiving smile.

The three American service chiefs—Marshall of the Army; Air Force General Henry Arnold, in the seat across from him; and the Navy's Ernest King—had been sharply divided, often bickering in the weeks and months after Pearl Harbor. King favored expanding the Pacific War, a war of great fleets and small armies. Arnold argued that his bombers alone, could he but get enough of them, would end the war without the necessity of invasion. Only Marshall had never wavered from their prewar estimates: Germany could win the war without Japan, Japan could not win without Germany. Thus they must fight in Europe first, Marshall insisted, and the only way to victory against Germany was through an invasion.

By dint of cool authority, Marshall had come to be the acknowledged leader of the American Joint Chiefs of Staff. He alone had held his post since the outbreak of war. He alone had the global vision to balance competing European and Pacific theaters and commanders, the personal reputation to keep such headstrong men as Douglas MacArthur and Joseph Stilwell in line, and the sheer physical presence to convince Congress and the public the war was in good hands.

Marshall stood six feet tall, his once sandy hair precisely trimmed, his back rigid still with a second lieutenant's brace. Only an unexpected double chin betrayed his sixty-three years, and only the hand jammed casually into a pants pocket sometimes softened the military posture. As a youth, the blue-eyed Marshall had been handsome. Forty years of service had left him, if not quite handsome any longer, still dignified. Those meeting him even for the first time came away reassured by Marshall's confidence, his commanding grasp of a war waged in five theaters, and his austere manner. Somehow he seemed a man to whom one could entrust one's sons and the fate of the nation.

Marshall's dignified reserve was shattered only by a volcanic temper the general had sought all his life to curb. The explosions of what his wife called a "withering vocabulary" were fewer now, the anger transmuted to cold, stifled rages through years of sheer willful control. Rarely did Marshall erupt before subordinates; to his staff he remained formally correct, if remote, a man atop the mountain.

For those who did not know him well, Marshall's aloofness seemed the
dominating characteristic of his personality. Staff officers might be paralyzed by the chief's sharp questions, or wary of his impatient disdain
for men who were unprepared or long-winded. The brusque treatment,
the insistence upon concise policy statements, on short memoranda were
all efforts to conserve his time.

The handful who did know him, usually from long service together in
the drowsy peacetime Army, recognized another, warmer person. Marshall's secretary, Virginia Nason, knew to squeeze in five minutes with
old soldiers, regardless of rank, who had once served with the general
on the dreary posts of yesteryear.

Whether they knew him from afar or from close association, as did
Hap Arnold, they shared an almost awed appreciation of Marshall's
keen insight, and his ability to grasp the complexities of global war. "If
George Marshall ever took a position contrary to mine, I would know I
was wrong," one of the Air Force's leading planners in the prewar years
acknowledged.

Marshall was keen. Not from some brilliant intellect that took in arcane
disciplines in a single sweep, but from hard application. An indifferent
student in school, Marshall was less the brilliant innovator than a determined master of accepted military truths. Just as J. S. Bach crowned the
Baroque in music by mastering all its forms, so Marshall mastered the
innovations of others, incorporating them into his thinking. The skeptical man who once asked Arnold why he was meeting with a committee
of scientists was, three years later, personally signing for the hundreds
of millions of dollars to build the atomic bomb.

Yet for all his grasp of global war, Marshall could focus on the smallest
problem. Because some chaplains' aides were denied promotion, chaplains frequently could not get good men to assist them. Marshall ordered
the promotions. Could WPA workers be fitted from old Quartermaster
stocks so they would not ruin their personal shoes and socks working on
military posts? Fit them. On a staff memo suggesting tents be set up for
servicemen visiting overcrowded Washington, Marshall tersely ordered,
"Get results."

There are as many different styles of command as there are commanders. A MacArthur or a Patton conveyed an aura of indomitable
will. A Stilwell or an Ira Eaker led by personal example; their troops
knew they shared the privations and the dangers. Omar Bradley and
Dwight Eisenhower managed to convey their personal concern for the
men in their armies, inspiring affection. Marshall exerted command
over all these men and more by dint of his mastery of the complexities of
world war. He demanded the very best of the men he appointed to field

command or accepted on his staff. Those who failed to measure up found themselves abruptly transferred to posts where they could do no harm. The quick decision, sometimes wrong, earned Marshall a reputation for ruthlessness; only his wife knew how often pained the chief of staff was when he removed an old acquaintance from fumbling command. The very speed of modern war demanded summary judgment, however harsh it was; Marshall had too little time to agonize over decisions.

Marshall shared none of his own feelings. If he had anything approaching a confidant, it was Henry H. Arnold, the air force chief of staff. They had known each other over thirty years, since their days as infantry lieutenants in the Philippines. Old acquaintances, publicly they were "Marshall" and "Arnold," sometimes "General." Only in private did they call each other by their first names. Between the two, one young air force aide noted, there was no back-slapping, no banter or small talk "you'd expect between old pals."

The Army's chief of staff stood aloof too from the White House; Harry Hopkins was his one friend there, his buffer and advocate. Hopkins had been primarily responsible for Marshall's appointment as chief of staff in 1939, arguing until Roosevelt accepted Marshall as "the best of a bad bargain." Well into 1942, the president still had doubts about that choice, relying on Hopkins's reassurances that Marshall was the man for the job. A year later, North Africa and Sicily lay cleared of the Axis; Italy had surrendered; Guadalcanal and the Solomons, Papua and New Georgia were free of the Japanese; Attu and Kiska had been retaken. The vast Army Marshall had built in just four years had become a formidable fighting machine. Marshall no longer needed Hopkins to defend him.

Success had fed the Americans' confidence while the British grew more divided. As war minister, Churchill unfurled a new military proposal almost weekly: clear the Dodecanese and Rhodes of the Germans; put all Allied forces into Italy and drive northward "posthaste"; or strike through the Aegean Sea and link up with Tito, plunging the dagger into what the mercurial Churchill called "the soft underbelly" of Hitler's Europe. The first sessions in Cairo, spent curbing Churchill's enthusiasms, had been "the most difficult of the war," Marshall sighed. The American, sometimes with help from the British chiefs, had resisted these peripheral adventures, arguing that further Mediterranean operations would delay OVERLORD, the Normandy invasion, yet another year.

OVERLORD: no other military campaign mattered as much to George Catlett Marshall, the acknowledged architect of American military strategy. Almost two years after the United States's entry into the war, Marshall and an impatient Joseph Stalin had finally wrung from the reluctant British agreement to the Normandy landing. That left the president with yet another problem to be solved: Who would command the most complicated military operation in all of history?

Through the seven-hour flight from the capital of Iran, Roosevelt pondered that decision. The Western Allies had promised Marshal Stalin OVERLORD, but Roosevelt's "Uncle Joe" was not so easily satisfied. That promise had been made twice before and twice broken. Until a commander was appointed, "nothing would come of these operations," the Soviet premier had coldly insisted through the smoke of his favorite Camel cigarettes.

Roosevelt was irritated. "That old Bolshevik is trying to force me to give him the name of our supreme commander. I just can't tell him because I have not yet made up my mind," Roosevelt had whispered to his personal chief of staff, Admiral William Leahy. The president instead promised a decision in three or four days, after the British and American parties had returned to Cairo. Satisfied, Stalin had pledged a huge spring offensive in the East to draw off German reserves from France before D-Day.

FDR could no longer delay his decision. The unwritten rules of coalition warfare demanded that the nation furnishing the bulk of the troops also provide the supreme commander. By rights, the post was Marshall's to claim. As the foremost proponent of the cross-Channel invasion in Allied councils, Marshall had earned its command. Roosevelt and Churchill had agreed at the Quebec Conference just four months before that the army chief of staff would lead OVERLORD; Mrs. Marshall had quietly packed their belongings and secretly vacated Quarters No. 1 at Fort Myer, the traditional home of the chief of staff. Expecting that new command, Marshall himself had even hinted to a handful of British and American officers he wanted them to join him at Supreme Headquarters in London when he took command on January 1, 1944.

Now Roosevelt wavered. Word of Marshall's pending appointment had leaked to the press, triggering an outrage of editorials arguing against the shift. Some saw the change as a British ploy to have Marshall "kicked upstairs"; others protested Marshall was the only man capable of dealing with a fractious Congress no longer the President's rubber stamp. The September "hullabaloo," as Marshall called it, died after two weeks, but it had seeded vague doubts in the president's mind.

Franklin Roosevelt, thumbing through the reports before him on the folding table, needed no review, no reminder of Marshall's qualifications. The general was one of the few with the organizational skill to oversee the logistical morass that would be OVERLORD. He had the staff experience and an army reputation as a military planner dating to World War I. Most of all, he could firmly, diplomatically deal with the inherent problems of coalition warfare itself. Friction with the British and French, Russians and Poles was ever likely; as Churchill groused, "The only thing worse than fighting a war with allies was fighting a war without them."

These years of coalition warfare had transformed Marshall, unrelenting when he believed American military aims threatened, into an adroit diplomat. Roosevelt now thought his chief of staff "the best man at the conference table." Modest he might be, but Marshall understood his influence. He had also proved himself capable of dealing with the persistent prime minister, a font of oratorical energy who argued one gambit after another. "Marshall has got to the point where he just looks at the Prime Minister as though he can't believe his ears," the president confided to his son Elliott.

In a last effort to promote his Mediterranean designs a week earlier, Churchill had pressed for an invasion of Rhodes. "His Majesty's Government"—by which Churchill meant himself—"can't have its troops standing idle. Muskets must flame."

Unimpressed, the best man at the conference table fired back, "Not one American soldier is going to die on [that] goddamned beach." The Rhodes alternative came to an abrupt end.

Marshall was the obvious selection for the command of the invasion of France. Yet Roosevelt wavered, ground between the correct gesture and selfish need. The chief of staff himself remained distant, though Secretary of War Henry Stimson had long interpreted Marshall's reserve as the fading nineteenth-century precept that the office sought the man, not the man the office. Months before, when pressed by Stimson, the chief of staff had said only, "Any soldier would prefer a field command."

Hopkins and Stimson had seemingly prevailed. Two weeks earlier, before the meetings in Tehran, the president leaned to Marshall. While flying over the Tunisian battlefields of the Third Punic War, he had privately probed Eisenhower's reaction, the president arguing as much to convince himself as to persuade a very junior general the two of them could work together in Washington. "Ike, you and I know who was Chief of Staff during the last years of the Civil War but practically no one else knows, although the names of the field generals—Grant, of course, and Lee and Jackson, Sherman, Sheridan and the others—every schoolboy knows them. I hate to think that fifty years from now practically nobody will know who George Marshall was." Eisenhower swallowed hard, assuming he would soon return to Washington, probably as acting chief of staff in Marshall's absence.

"That is one of the reasons," the president continued as their plane skimmed the barren desert that had once been Carthage, "why I want George to have the big command. He is entitled to establish his place in history as a great general."

Now the president again wavered. How would he replace Marshall in Washington? No one else had the general's prestige. A *Newsweek* poll to be published that week reported that a panel of newsmen and historians had selected Marshall as the individual who had made the greatest contribution to the nation's leadership in the last two years. Marshall had received one more vote than the president himself.

Even Congress stood enthralled by the man. *Life*, the influential picture magazine of the Luce empire, had decided two months earlier that General Marshall "has no 'opposition' worthy of the name, and if one should arise, it would have to brave the wrath of the American people. The folks have confidence in this general because he never forgets the folks."

Just two men had sufficient public respect to replace Marshall in Washington without reviving rumors that unnamed "powerful forces" wanted the chief of staff "kicked upstairs." One, Douglas MacArthur, was personally and politically unacceptable; his presidential ambitions made him a loose cannon on Washington decks. The other, Dwight Eisenhower, once a junior member of MacArthur's staff in the Philippines, would be hard put to keep the imperious MacArthur in check. Furthermore, could Eisenhower compete with Ernest King, the Navy's chief of operations? A brusque and difficult man, King worked well with Marshall.

Equally important, how would Eisenhower, or anyone else, fare with Congress? Marshall's forays to the Hill to testify were brilliant campaigns in themselves; the public little realized that this war was fought first in paneled hearing rooms with penny-minded appropriations committees and only later on battlefields. Marshall had patiently enlisted congressional support by treating the members of Congress as equals, fellow soldiers in a just cause. Unlike other military men, he had never condescended to these civilians, even the dullest among them, or issued peremptory orders to them as had MacArthur during his tenure as chief of staff. Anyone but Marshall might have transformed the Senate Committee to Investigate the National Defense Program and its dogged chairman, Harry Truman, into serious impediments as the nation rushed to mobilize. Marshall's respectful treatment had turned the testy Missourian from a taken-for-granted vote on party matters into a national figure (nine votes in that *Newsweek* poll).

Constitutionally, the army chief of staff ranked well below the most junior member of the House of Representatives; but in wartime Washington, he was one of the most powerful of men. The general, however, had never engaged in partisan politics and had avoided equally savage army politics.

For all his influence, Marshall refused to grasp more power. He had deliberately rejected admission to FDR's inner circle, visiting the White House only when summoned because "it gave a false impression of his intimacy with the President." When a member of the Senate Military Affairs Committee had persisted in asking the general about navy matters and navy problems, Marshall had finally sighed, "There is no point in asking me questions about the other service. I know that Admiral King is not going to expose my deficiencies and I won't even admit that the Admiral has any." No wonder King, like Hap Arnold, wanted to keep the Joint Chiefs of Staff intact. King had bluntly said as much two weeks earlier in a conversation with the chief of staff and his likely replacement.

"You, Eisenhower, are the proper man to become the supreme commander for the Allies in Europe," King announced, heedless of Marshall's presence. King rumbled on, accepting what seemed at the time inevitable. "I hate to lose General Marshall as Chief of Staff, but my loss is consoled by the knowledge that I will have you to work with in his job."

Now Eisenhower was embarrassed. King's comment was "almost official notice that I would soon be giving up field command to return to Washington," he recalled.

Through the entire conversation, Marshall sat silently, his cocktail forgotten. Finally, as Eisenhower was to leave for dinner with the president, Marshall shrugged. "I don't see why any of us are worrying about this. President Roosevelt will have to decide on his own, and all of us will obey."

One by one the transports and their fighter cover circled the Cairo airport, then settled to the metal-shod runway. The president's plane rolled to a halt before a Commonwealth honor guard drawn up in the cold North African wind.

The airport ceremony was brief. The limousine rolled slowly past the khaki-clad troops of the British Empire: Australians, New Zealanders, Gurkhas, Senegalese, South Africans, all veterans of the successful North African campaign. Smiling broadly, the president answered the successive salutes with a wave of his hand; he enjoyed military ceremonies almost as much as did Churchill. Then the limousine picked up speed.

The presidential party thundered behind the armored car and Jeeps to the three-mile-square security zone set up around the Mena House Hotel, a mile from the Great Pyramids. The celebrated hotel had been cleared of guests to serve as a meeting hall; thirty-four nearby villas— classified as "super," "first class," and "ordinary"—housed the British, American, Chinese, and French delegations.

Scattered amid the anti-aircraft guns, searchlights, and barbed wire, Marshall, King, Leahy, Arnold, and such lesser figures as Joe Stilwell and Claire Chennault, the feuding China commanders, occupied nearby villas. This had once been the most exclusive residential neighborhood in all of Egypt, perhaps in all the Arab world. Now it was an armed camp populated by grim men waging a global war.

The Cairo Conference resumed, yet three days after promising to name the supreme commander, Roosevelt still vacillated. The president finally detailed Harry Hopkins to speak with Marshall, for if anyone could get the general to state his own preference, it would be the one man on the White House staff who called him by his first name.

Hopkins, carelessly dressed in rumpled off-the-rack suits, never bothering to tighten his tie, was the only man in Cairo Marshall might have told. A onetime social worker from Sioux City, Iowa, Hopkins lived as a guest in the White House, accepting the president's hospitality, but surrendering any private life of his own. Hopkins's very dedication had led to his unlikely friendship with the reserved George Marshall; in Hopkins, the general recognized a shared sense of public duty.

Perhaps as Marshall's friend, Hopkins could do what the president as commander-in-chief could not. Roosevelt might sometimes speak of "George," but it was a token of familiarity Roosevelt exacted of all men, even Premier Stalin. Marshall had resisted putting their relationship on a first-name basis. Roosevelt was, after all, commander-in-chief, Marshall's immediate superior; a commander in Marshall's world was not overly familiar with his subordinates.

Hopkins returned empty-handed. Marshall was noncommittal. He would remain in Washington as chief of staff, or go to London as supreme commander, whichever the president wished. "He need have no fears regarding my personal reactions," Marshall assured Hopkins.

Frustrated, Roosevelt mulled the question overnight. Confronted with his self-imposed deadline, wavering between Marshall and Eisenhower, the president invited the chief of staff to a private lunch on Sunday, December 5.

Marshall went reluctantly, ever wary of the president's seductive charm. Roosevelt brimmed with a bluff, hearty warmth that filled whole rooms. He captivated visitors with his animated monologues, robust guffaws, and the sudden whispered confidence that permitted a glimpse into the deepest secrets of government and war. Not even his kinsman Theodore Roosevelt had enjoyed the presidency more, or attacked it with greater zest.

The day before the scheduled close of the conference, president and general met in the American ambassador's well-guarded villa. Roosevelt was uncharacteristically indecisive, Marshall quite characteristically reserved.

As the president later recounted the conversation to Henry Stimson, Roosevelt urged Marshall to choose his post for the remainder of the European war. He might command the invasion or continue as chief of staff in Washington. The choice was his to make.

Marshall demurred, refusing even to estimate his own capabilities. Whatever the decision, Marshall assured the president, he would "go along with it wholeheartedly. The issue was simply too great for any personal feeling to be involved."

A soldier served where he was bid, seeking no preferential treatment, that a principle drilled into a seventeen-year-old cadet at Virginia Military Institute four decades earlier. "It is for the President to decide. I will serve wherever you order me, Mr. President," Marshall said.

Perhaps President Roosevelt only wanted it to be so, but, he later told Stimson, the chief of staff might, just might, have preferred to remain in Washington.

That night Roosevelt pondered his decision, wheeling about in his chair, deciding finally, he told Stimson, "on a mathematical basis." Eisenhower could not fill Marshall's shoes in Washington. As chief of staff, he would be familiar only with Europe, barely aware of the Pacific or the faltering China-Burma-India theaters. Nor would Eisenhower be as effective in dealing with Congress, the Navy, or MacArthur.

On December 6, 1943, just before the obligatory group photographs that informally closed these conferences, Roosevelt made his decision. His explanation to the unflinching Marshall was brief. "I feel I could not sleep at night with you out of the country."

Brief and poignant. It was, for the usually self-confident man in the wheelchair, a rare admission of his dependence upon another human being. Men such as Hopkins who had worked intimately with the president since the beginning of the New Deal and even before, since his years as governor of New York, had never heard such acknowledgment.

Marshall nodded, took out his fountain pen, and quickly jotted on a lined pad of paper: "From the President to Marshal Stalin.

"I—" He stopped, scratched that out, then started again.

"The immediate appointment of General Eisenhower to command of Overlord operation has been decided upon."

The general handed the pad to the president, who just as quickly signed "Roosevelt" in bold strokes.

Then the press and Signal Corps photographers crowded in.

What presidential speech writer Robert Sherwood considered the most difficult decision Roosevelt made during the war would dramatically alter the course of American history. Command of the Normandy invasion transformed Dwight David Eisenhower into a national hero, and ultimately led him to the White House. It also, as Roosevelt had feared, came to deny the rightful place in history to George Catlett Marshall.

PART
I
THE SOLDIER

CHAPTER

I

A Very Simple Life

They were people of substance, his father would announce, the Marshalls of Augusta, Kentucky, and Uniontown, Pennsylvania, descended from the finest families of Virginia: Talliaferros, Catletts, Champes, and, of course, from John Marshall himself, the first chief justice of the United States. George Catlett Marshall, Sr., put great stock in his genealogy, even if his youngest child, George Catlett Junior, did not.

Family genealogy bored the younger boy; his father's doting upon long-dead ancestors embarrassed "Flicker" Marshall. Having the Justice as a collateral ancestor seemed of no great consequence in Uniontown in the 1880s. "I thought that the continual harping on the name of John Marshall was kind of poor business. It was about time for somebody else to swim for the family," he told a later biographer. The pug-nosed boy was far more excited by a dubious genealogy which asserted a venture-some forebear had married the pirate Bluebeard 150 years earlier. Now there was something a boy of nine or ten could take some pride in, and he bragged about the schoolyard of his truly celebrated kinsman. George Catlett Senior was not so pleased. "Father was perfectly furious that out of all the book I had chosen Blackbeard as the only one who interested me and publicized him in town as being descended from a pirate."

Of course George Senior, peering down at the red-haired boy through his pince-nez, would not be pleased. A prosperous local businessman, part owner of 150 coke ovens and coal fields, he viewed life and his position in the community most seriously. He was a prominent Mason, a vestryman in Uniontown's Episcopal church; the Marshall family pew was well forward, and filled each Sunday. It was hard enough for the sociable George Senior to be a Democrat in a heavily Republican state; he did not also have to be known as a descendant of a pirate.

Nor did the elder Marshall relish another public embarrassment his son had brought on him. As a weekly regular at St. Peter's Episcopal

Church, young George was assigned the task of pumping the organ for Miss Fannie Howell. One Sunday, engrossed in a Nick Carter penny-dreadful, he missed a cue. "I suffered more at home after the event than from Miss Fannie," the future general noted ruefully.

His musical career aborted, "Flicker" Marshall returned to the family pew; there he sat neatly turned out in his dark blue Sunday suit, "with short trousers," an old friend recalled in a letter, "your red hair plastered down with water, looking unnaturally good and solemn, except for the twinkle in your eyes that your mother was regarding apprehensively." The boy managed to suppress the twinkle long enough to be confirmed at St. Peter's when he was sixteen. Religion and politics, the one from his mother, the other from his father, were to be abiding habits; young George would be a lifelong Episcopalian and a conservative Democrat.

If the description of the mischievous boy sitting restlessly in church seemed the stuff of romantic novels, of an idyllic small-town America fondly remembered, it was partially correct. Uniontown in this last quarter of the nineteenth century was changing from a pastoral stagecoach stop on the National Road to one of the myriad communities feeding the maw of the Industrial Revolution. Main Street had been paved, and a horse-drawn streetcar paraded back and forth, leaving George Junior a new chore: hosing the horse droppings from the street in front of his house. A gasworks was to provide fuel to heat their homes, and the Edison Electric Company to light them. George Senior was surely to be one of the prosperous beneficiaries of the burgeoning industrialization, his expanding business already producing coke for the steel mills of Pittsburgh.

Looking back almost seventy years later, George Junior, no longer the snub-nosed boy, no longer "Flicker," said wistfully, "In this life of Uniontown, I saw what you might call the end of an era because it was a very simple life and a very charming life and it had a long history behind it."

For the young lad, Uniontown had special pleasures: slow-moving Coal Lick Creek which meandered behind the red-brick house the Marshalls rented at 130 West Main Street; fishing trips on the Youghiogheny River with his father; and the grand adventures in the woods across the creek, a mile beyond Chestnut Ridge where General Edward Braddock lay buried. Out there stood Colonel George Washington's earthen Fort Necessity, overlooking the route of the first National Road out of the Cumberland Gap in Maryland into the Indian lands of the West.

Fast-industrializing Uniontown then had a history rich in local lore, stories George Senior passed on to his fascinated son, stories that left a lasting impression on the boy who would grow up to be a soldier.

Life in Uniontown also had its drawbacks. His father was strict, quick to anger, too stern perhaps for his youngest child. Marshall seemed to favor the oldest son, Stuart, six years George's senior; Stuart showed business promise as George did not. George, born on New Year's Eve, 1880, became his mother's favorite. Polarized by parental affinities, separated by the difference in their ages, the two boys were never close. In later years they rarely communicated.

The third of George and Laura Marshall's children, Marie, was four years older than George Junior. Worse, she was a girl; theirs was the familiar big sister–little brother relationship, the girl tattling on the lad, the boy pestering his sister's swains. Only in later life did Marie recall her brother with nostalgic affection.

For young George Catlett, the nurturing parent was his mother. "I was always very close to her," he wrote when he himself was in his seventies, "as her youngest child and because for some years my brother and my sister were away at school while I was at home with her. She was both gentle and firm, very understanding, and had a keen, but quiet sense of humor, which made her my confidante in practically all my boyish escapades and difficulties."

His mother's love he fondly remembered. During the long winters of western Pennsylvania, he recalled, he would sit by the fire, shattering hickory nuts with a hammer for his mother's "very famous hickory nut cakes." These were special moments for the youngster. "I always liked our fires because we . . . had what we called cannel coal and it made a soft, delightful, homelike flame." It was easier for the man to talk about the fire than his deep love for Laura Emily Bradford Marshall.

It was she who put *his* special Christmas gift in the place of honor under the tree, she who baked miniature pies especially for George, she who sent him $10 for his birthday as long as she lived. If her youngest was not her favorite of the four children she had brought into the world—the firstborn lived only six months—she treated George with the affection doted on an only child. Older brother Stuart was away at school, set upon a career in business, a younger version of his father, closer to the husband than the wife. Marie, also at school much of the time, left only George Junior as Laura Marshall's last opportunity to fulfill the nineteenth century obligation of the woman as mother and matriarch.

His father was less indulgent. Laura Marshall often shielded the youngster from her husband's scorn. Young George feared that most of all, hiding his failures when he could, sometimes with his mother's help. Thus the unbending father never learned of the young man's first and last venture into cockfighting, when George and Andy Thompson, son of the town banker, set out to match their fighting cocks in an illegal pit.

The two boys, then about thirteen, had each raised a Georgia Red, and inveigled an older friend to pit the birds—the boys considered too tender by the local cockfighting fraternity to attend the illegal activity.

Though George and Andy couldn't actually pit their birds, they still drove out to see them fight one afternoon.

The Fayette County sheriff raided the cockpit, scattering Uniontown's sporting crowd. The two boys "squirted out into the forest and got separated and hid out," Marshall recalled. Fearing arrest and, worse, his father's anger, George crept carefully through the woods toward home. Soon enough he realized someone else was working his way through the trees. "I scouted him and he scouted me" for an hour before young Marshall discovered he and Andy Thompson had been stalking each other. The two boys were the only people left in the woods.

George finally made his way home after midnight. His father was asleep, but his mother confronted the apprehensive boy, who confessed the day's misadventure. "Parts of it she thought were very funny, and I remember she laughed until she cried." George's career as a cock breeder was over; the lesson hardly needed his father's belt for emphasis.

But Mrs. Marshall could not hide the boy's indifferent progress in school; indeed, she was at least in part responsible for her son's all too evident lack of scholarly proficiency.

George's "formal" education began when he was five, under the tutelage of an eighty-year-old aunt who had come to live with the Marshall family. A woman of some education—she knew both French and Hebrew, the former for the New Testament, the latter for the Old—Eliza Stuart began weekly lessons with the boy. But Saturday morning recitations were hard, particularly when his friends were playing outside. Frustrated, rebellious as any five-year-old might be, Marshall decided, "She so soured me on study and teaching that I liked never to have recovered from it."

After a year of Aunt Eliza's Bible studies, the Marshalls enrolled their youngest son in a private school on Church Street. The classwork was undemanding, to young George's delight, but would little prepare him for the career in commerce his father envisioned for the boy.

When George was nine, his father determined to enroll the boy in Uniontown's public school. His actual placement was to be determined by an interview with the school superintendent, Professor Lee Smith. Smith asked a number of simple questions which the humiliated boy could not answer. The future general remembered the excruciating embarrassment all his life; he had publicly failed his father, who "suffered very severely."

Ill-prepared for Uniontown's public school, George floundered—mathematics, grammar, and spelling gave him particular problems—and sat terrified he would be called upon for recitation. To stand up in front of the class would be to risk making a mistake in public, to be laughed at. In that he was like his father, proud to be one of the Virginia and Kentucky Marshalls, even if a lesser member of the family. He was an average student in all but history. "If it was history, that was all right; I could star in history," he recalled. History he enjoyed, and would read all his life; Benjamin Franklin and Robert E. Lee were to become personal heroes.

The fear of failure and thus rejection lay heavy on the gangling boy—rejection from his father, from his teachers, from the girls in whom he had begun to take a tentative interest. He tried once to impress Judge Lindsay's daughter Catherine, the class spelling champion. He would strive to improve his spelling, so that he might win a place by her side at the head of the spelling-bee line. For a brief moment he was triumphant, but when he missed a word, he was relegated to the end of the line. Shamed, he never tried again.

Young George Marshall remained a student in the public school for three years out of necessity. His father had sold his coke furnaces and coal fields to Henry Clay Frick, then had invested the proceeds, some $125,000, in a Shenandoah Valley land promotion. The boom collapsed, and by December 1890 the Marshalls were suddenly in straitened circumstances.

As the young Marshall remembered, his mother "bore a very heavy burden during the great financial depression of the Nineties. She was in poor health, yet did all the work of our home and made it a cheerful place. . . ." The cook and the maid they could no longer afford. With some economizing, they could still keep the two older children in school; Stuart had just entered Virginia Military Institute, intent on studying chemistry.

The Marshalls were not destitute. Marshall had salvaged interests in a coke company and in some West Virginia coal fields. Mrs. Marshall owned property in Pittsburgh and Augusta. But the family was no longer affluent. George Junior occasionally carried home from the local hotel kitchen scraps to feed the family dogs, a "painful and humiliating" experience to the sensitive boy. He would never forget; later in life he struggled to save something, anything, from his army pay each month, and by the time he was forty-five would have made a series of prudent investments which, if they did not make him wealthy, did leave him comfortably fixed.

He would not repeat the mistake his father made. The senior Marshall sought to keep up appearances, giving his wife gifts she considered too expensive, retreating more and more into the family genealogy, grasping at legendry to shore up his faltering confidence.

There were, for young George, rare moments when he did seem to please his father. One summer, George and his closest friend, Andy Thompson, rigged a greenhouse in a vacant shed behind the Marshall home, intending to go into the nursery trade. The two wrote the local congressman, asking for the free packets of seeds the government furnished to stimulate interest in agriculture. Eventually the seeds arrived, were planted, and sprouted, but the cotton plants produced no bolls in the unkind Pennsylvania clime. Undaunted, the boys decided instead to enter a seed company's contest to name a new tomato, the $50 prize a tantalizing lure.

Sending away for the tomato seeds from Henderson & Co., the boys planted them in pots filled with soil scraped from the floor of the stable. The vines flourished in the uncommonly rich soil.

The two picked the choicest of the fruit, and sold it to a local grocer. "My father was rather contemptuous of us for selling them so cheaply," Marshall remembered. But soon enough, the grocer was asking the two aspiring nurserymen for more tomatoes, these for "one of his richest clients. We came back and reported with great glee that our stock was in great demand and particularly by this well-to-do family. Then my father told us, 'Now you set the price,' and suggested it. Well, the grocer blew up because he thought he would get them for almost nothing."

Their prize tomato the boys photographed with one of George Eastman's new Brownie cameras, and with a suggested name sent the picture off to the seed company. Soon enough, Henderson & Co. responded, praising the size and asking "our parents to write and tell how the tomato had been raised. I told my father and he was intensely interested"—"interested," not "pleased," or "proud," as Marshall recounted the great tomato contest—"and wrote to Peter Henderson. He finished by saying, however, that you couldn't tear down a stable every time you wanted to raise a tomato."

Despite the size of their product, the boys did not win the $50 prize. That went to the man who suggested the name "Ponderosa."

Just when young George Catlett—he hated his middle name—decided on a military career he could never clearly recall. The decision to join the Army, in the early part of the 1890s a slender force of 25,000 buttressed by ill-trained National Guard units, did not sit well with his parents. The Army had no great reputation; opportunities for advancement were few, and strictly governed by seniority. Merit counted for little, though that, in the eyes of George Catlett Senior would hardly affect his youngest son.

Many years later, Marshall himself suggested that he settled on a military career only after 1899 and the triumphant return from the Philippines of Company C of the 10th Pennsylvania Infantry to Uniontown:

> It was a wonderful scene, that parade. The bricks of Main Street were painted red, white, and blue, and triumphal arches erected in every block—there was even an arch of coke constructed by the Frick Company. And when the head of the procession finally appeared, the individual excitement surpassed, as I recall, even that of the splendid so-called Victory parades of 1919 in Paris and London. . . .

No man of Company C could make a purchase in this community. The town was his. He had but to command and his desires
were gratified—a medal for every soldier and a sword for each
officer. And there was a final jubilation at the fair grounds. It was
a grand American small town demonstration of pride in its young
men and of wholesome enthusiasm over their achievements. It
reflected the introduction of America into the affairs of the world
beyond the seas.

While the remembrance of the returning veterans of the Philippine
campaign was vivid enough, it does not seem likely that the demobilization of Company C or the spread-eagle oratory of that glorious day solely
determined young George's choice of a career. By 1899 and the parade,
he had already been attending Virginia Military Institute for two years,
and though VMI had no great reputation for producing army officers,
George had shown little interest in any of his subjects other than military
science.
    The decision to attend VMI, ironically, came not because of the boy's
half-formed notion he wanted to join the Army, but because he had to
go to college somewhere. VMI seemed a likely choice.
    From virtually any standpoint, West Point would have better suited.
In the first place, graduation from the academy on the Hudson River
assured a commission in the Army; there was no such guarantee for
graduates of the eight "tin colleges"—among them the Citadel, Virginia
Polytechnic, Agricultural and Mechanical of Texas, and VMI, schools
which favored military training and used regular army officers as
instructors. George would have to take a competitive exam after graduation—if he were permitted to. At the moment of Marshall's matricula-
tion, VMI would boast fewer than a dozen graduates in the United States
Army.
    Secondly, West Point was tuition-free. VMI charged $365, and the
students provided their own uniforms at a cost of another $70.
    But the route to West Point was snarled in politics. Both of Pennsyl-
vania's senators and the congressman representing Fayette County were
Republicans. George Marshall, Senior, was a locally prominent Democrat, a Bryan man still, despite President McKinley's election, not one to
give or expect a dollop of non-partisan patronage. Though the boy might
have tried to enter West Point through a competitive exam, his father
thought it unlikely young George would be permitted to take the exam,
or, if he did, that he could pass.
    VMI seemed the next best choice to young George. Marshalls for gen-
erations had attended the school; his older brother Stuart was a member
of the class of 1894. But even as he beseeched his parents to send him
to VMI, his older brother argued against it:

I overheard Stuart talking to my mother; he was trying to persuade her not to let me go because he thought I would disgrace the family name. Well, that made more impression on me than all instructors, parental pressure, or anything else. I decided right then that I was going to wipe his face, or wipe his eye.

George was to do just that. He recalled with some satisfaction sixty years later, "The urgency to succeed came from hearing that conversation; it had a psychological effect on my career."

Though the Marshall family fortunes had improved somewhat, VMI still represented a major financial burden. To pay for the boy's tuition, his mother sold a piece of property in Augusta, Kentucky. The following year, she would sell a choice lot in Uniontown on which she had hoped to build a home. (It was perhaps these two gestures which led Marshall later to conclude he had been spoiled as a child. Each of the sales represented some emotional sacrifice by Mrs. Marshall: Augusta was the Marshall family's ancestral home, and parting with the Uniontown lot meant giving up a long-held dream of owning her own home.)

Virginia Military Institute in 1897 was a venerated sham of a university when sixteen-year-old George Catlett Marshall arrived on September 11, clutching his father's letter of commendation to Superintendent Scott Shipp: "I send you my youngest and last. He is bright, full of life, and I believe he will get along well."

Founded in 1839, VMI was a place of ghosts, Confederate ghosts. "Tom Fool" Jackson had taught natural and experimental philosophy and artillery tactics here before the Civil War transformed him into "Stonewall" Jackson. At night, the stories ran, an eerie light would appear in Jackson's old classroom, and the unsuspecting cadet might stumble on the shade of Jackson chalking trajectories on the blackboard.

The cult of the Confederacy ran deep here. If the sixteen-year-old missed Stonewall's ghost, he did become a lifelong admirer of Jackson's Shenandoah campaign; in later years he would ride from battlefield to battlefield, pointing out this or that position of Blue and Gray infantry and cavalry.

From the parade ground at VMI had quick-marched 241 cadets on May 15, 1864, some as young as fifteen, to turn back a Union drive into the Shenandoah Valley. Ten of the youngsters had died, and forty-four suffered wounds in a bayonet charge that afternoon at New Market. A generation later, the corps of cadets mustered each May 15 to commemorate the battle and the deaths of the ten cadets. When the name of each of the dead boys was read, a first classman would answer the roll, "Died on the field of honor." It was an impressive ceremony, resonant with the military virtues of duty, honor and, finally, sacrifice.

Five of the ten were buried in a copse on the VMI campus. The great Robert E. Lee himself lay but a few hundred yards away in the chapel he built on the adjacent Washington and Lee campus. Stonewall Jackson's remains moldered a mile from the parade ground amid the graves of hundreds of Confederate veterans, his larger-than-life-size statue gazing southward to Dixie, as all Confederate statues must.

To this tradition-heavy place came George Catlett Marshall, Jr., "a lean and a gawky cadet, sensitive and shy; a Pennsylvania Yankee in a Southern school," a few days late due to a bout of typhoid fever.

As a fourth classman, a "rat" in military school slang, Marshall shared a room with three others, including Leonard Kimball Nicholson, heir with his brother to the *New Orleans Picayune*. Nicholson, like a number of the young men at the school, had been dispatched to VMI for a bit of polishing in the discipline mill Superintendent Shipp maintained. In Nicholson's case, it was largely wasted; he entered VMI irrepressibly buoyant, survived the four-year course, and graduated quite as jovial as he entered.

Despite Marshall's reserve, born of shyness and his fear of making a mistake publicly, Nicholson and Marshall became the best of friends. While Marshall strove to excel in matters military, Nicholson good-naturedly ignored them, even reportedly assuming demerits that rightly should have been Marshall's. Nicholson replaced Andy Thompson as the would-be soldier's closest chum, the first friend Marshall would make as an adult.

He needed such a friend, for VMI presented its own particular challenges to the sheltered youth from Uniontown, Pennsylvania. VMI under Superintendent Shipp was much more interested in military discipline than in academic distinction. That suited Marshall, for, as he would later admit, "I did not like school. The truth is, I was not even a poor student. I simply was not a student, and my academic record was a sad affair."

Learning was by rote memorization, more of Aunt Eliza's Bible studies, nothing so much as an extension of General Shipp's striving for discipline. Not for another ten years would Marshall learn how to accommodate the principles of military tactics to real terrain and real soldiers.

But young George did quickly learn how to fit in, to carefully distinguish himself in approved ways. Some three weeks after his arrival, a clutch of upperclassmen descended on Room 88 one night intent on hazing the awkward sixteen-year-old. Just why they picked on Marshall is unclear. Perhaps it was his height, almost six feet, which made him stand out. Perhaps it was his Pennsylvania accent; he was one of fourteen northerners among the eighty-two rats. Perhaps it was his self-protective aloofness, the distance he imposed between himself and all but the jovial

Leonard Nicholson. Perhaps it was only because his room happened to share the same stoop with a room full of third classmen, and he was a convenient target of opportunity.

Though Superintendent Shipp had laid down stern strictures against hazing, VMI tradition overrode VMI rules. Surrounded by upperclassmen, Marshall was ordered to squat over an unsheathed bayonet whose handle had been jammed into a hole in the floor. Some accounts credit Marshall with great strength, squatting over the naked bayonet for as long as twenty minutes. More likely it was only a short period, for he was still weakened by the typhoid fever. He collapsed, and the bayonet sliced his buttock. He narrowly missed grave injury or even death, given the quality of medical practice at the time, but the wound was comparatively slight.

Marshall must have weighed the consequences, for he never reported his tormentors. Had he done so, the upperclassmen responsible might have been expelled, but Marshall himself would have faced retribution, enough even to drive him from the school. And he was determined to succeed at VMI, to live by its code.

Marshall finished his first year at the Institute ranked eighteenth academically among a class of eighty-two. He excelled only in military matters, and, as a reward, was named first corporal for the following year. It was his first promotion, his first accomplishment on his own, and it must have done much to reassure the young man he had chosen the right profession. At the same time, he also began to look the part of the soldier. As boys of seventeen will, he had filled out, adding weight to height. He was less awkward, no longer the fumbler with two left feet on the parade ground that sloped in front of the Institute.

He left Lexington at the end of the school year half expecting to be called to service in the war with Spain. Caught up in the press-fueled excitement, these obdurate sons of the Confederacy had unanimously voted "to fight for *their* country," to volunteer when Congress on April 25, 1898, declared war. But Ambassador John Hay's "splendid little war"— not overly bloody, at least to the American volunteers, rich with heroic opportunities, and immensely popular—ended too soon. By mid-August, Spain had sued for peace.

Begun on the pretext of freeing Cuba from its harsh Spanish governors, the war with Spain transformed the United States into an imperial power. Spain ceded the islands of Puerto Rico and Guam to the United States, relinquished Cuba to an American protectorate, and, most important to young George Marshall's future, sold the Philippines to the United States for the bargain price of $20 million. It was a famous victory, and a popular one, which explained Uniontown's exhilaration the following summer with the return of the 10th Pennsylvania.

George Marshall went back to school in September, the war with Spain ended in an armistice and the even bloodier Philippine insurrection just beginning. The new first corporal at VMI fared little better academically as a third classman, but at least he was no longer a targeted rat. Further, as first corporal, with his token authority, he was immune from the brutalizing, if not the teasing, about his accent. He finished this second year ranked twenty-fifth in his class of sixty-nine, but once again had scored well in military subjects. He was appointed a first sergeant for the following year.

By now he was well accustomed to the spartan routine and rigid discipline of Superintendent Shipp's VMI. The pampered youngest son of a small-town businessman had grown into a model cadet, if not model student. He was learning, as he said later, how to manage men, to be a military officer. By the end of the summer of 1899 when he stood cheering the return of Company C to Uniontown, exulting in the sheer excitement, he was confirmed in his choice of a career. What could have seemed more glorious to a young man of eighteen than the popular acclaim heroic soldiers received? What greater reward could there possibly be for a youth with no trade and no interest in the affairs of commerce?

As a second classman, Marshall devoted increasing effort to the military aspects of life at VMI. "I tried very hard," he told his biographer, Forrest Pogue. "I was exacting and very exact in all my military duties as I gradually developed from the mild authority—almost none—exercised by the corporal to the pronounced authority of the first sergeant."

He enjoyed command, and the more command he exercised, the more confident he grew. He was succeeding on his own, wiping Stuart's eye. Though still light for his height, he also turned out for football, only to have the football season canceled after a typhoid fever scare closed the school for six weeks in the fall.

When VMI opened again, Marshall picked up where he left off. A civil engineering major, he finished the year ranked nineteenth among his forty-seven classmates. He was the unanimous choice as first captain, the highest ranking cadet officer. Though he held himself aloof from all but "Nick" Nicholson and a second roommate, "Buster" Peyton, Marshall was well enough respected to be chosen to lead the Ring Dance at VMI's annual Final Ball in June.

By any measure, Marshall's last year at VMI was a triumph. He was first captain, at age twenty sure he could lead men. As a 145-pound tackle on the VMI eleven, he performed creditably, even, according to some sources, earning All-Southern honors. Academically, he finished fifteenth in his class of thirty-three, though his standing varied widely from subject to subject. He stood twenty-eighth in German, his poorest mark, and only a bit better, twenty-sixth, in math. But he came fifth in his major, civil engineering, and third in U.S. Drill Regulations, his best ranking. As might be expected, the cadet captain received no demerits that year.

In absolute numbers, he had managed to climb from eighteenth in his class to fifteenth; but the classes shrank each year. As a consequence, Marshall was in the top 22 percent as a rat, the first 36 percent in his second year, 40 percent in his third, and at graduation, only in the top 45 percent. The more time he devoted to military responsibilities, the poorer his academic standing. He was leaving the Institute without any history or social science classes; his language studies he would later consider time wasted; not for another four decades would he feel confident in writing English. He was, simply enough, no better and no worse than the great majority of commissioned officers in the United States Army at the time.

He capped this glorious year by courting and winning a wife. Elizabeth Carter Coles, known all her life as "Lily," was from an old Virginia family. Her relatives had more than a few doubts about Marshall's Pennsylvania roots, perhaps because he was a Yankee, perhaps because of his father's business background. Lily's father, after all, had been a professional man, a doctor, and descended from a long line of plantation owners, Virginia's gentry since before the Revolutionary War.

Though Lily Coles lived literally at the gate of the parade ground, Marshall did not meet her until his last year at the school. At that, the meeting came by accident one evening, when Cadet Captain Marshall was passing the Coles' wooden Gothic cottage at 319 Letcher Avenue. The young man stopped, surprised to hear on the piano "some of the airs my mother had played to which I had become devoted."

Marshall was to return—sometimes with another cadet or two to buck up his faltering courage—though it was apparently some time before Lily invited him in. For Marshall, it was virtually love at first sight.

Auburn-haired Lily Coles had been for some few years the belle of Lexington, for too many perhaps, as she was six years older than the tall cadet captain who now sat mooning in her parlor. But the young men who had come courting before George Marshall had gone on to knock at other doors. The girlish coquette was now a full-bosomed twenty-six, an age her well-married friends considered perilously close to that of an old maid. If she offered any explanation, perhaps it was her "condition." Lily suffered from a vaguely diagnosed heart problem that limited her physical activities to drives about the countryside in her spanking little carriage.

To visit the young woman more often, George began slipping away after evening formation, in defiance of the Institute's rules. He risked much to be with Lily: his rank certainly, perhaps expulsion, and even the military career he had planned for himself. Marshall later said only,

"I was much in love." He was enamored enough that when older brother Stuart, who had sparked the comely Lily in his own time, "made unkind, unfair remarks about Lily, I cut him off my list," Marshall said primly.

If he was to marry, Marshall had to assure his ability to support a wife by securing the dreamed-of second lieutenant's commission. He was fortunate in that he was graduating just as the permanent Army was to expand to 100,000 to cope with the Philippine insurrection. The Army would take an additional 1,200 commissioned officers; one fifth of these second lieutenants were to be selected by examination. The problem was to be permitted to take the test.

Marshall turned to his father for help, apparently for the last time. While George Marshall, Sr., still considered the Army a poor choice of career, he wrote Superintendent Shipp in January 1901 for an estimate of the young man's military potential. The reply was reassuring: ". . . if commissioned in the Army, young Marshall will in all respects soon take his stand much above the average West Point graduate."

An act of political favoritism for a young man who was later to resist such moves by others paved the way. Marshall Senior wrote to a onetime Virginia Democrat who had defected both to New York and the Republican Party. John Wise was himself a VMI graduate—he had been one of the under-age infantrymen at New Market—and, more important, he had the ear of President William McKinley.

Armed with letters of commendation from Wise and Superintendent Shipp, George Junior set off alone for Washington. It was a measure of his determination, or how well he had overcome his shyness of four years earlier. He buttonholed Attorney General Philander Knox, a friend of his father's; he snared an unscheduled interview with the chairman of the House Military Affairs Committee in the chairman's home; and finally, without an appointment, he set off for the White House and President McKinley himself.

The old colored man asked me if I had an appointment and I told him I didn't. He said I would never get in, that there wasn't any possibility. I sat there and watched people, some ten or fifteen, go in by appointment, stay ten minutes, and be excused. Finally a man and his daughter went in with this old colored man escorting them. I attached myself to the tail of the procession and gained the President's office. The old colored man frowned at me on his way out but I stood pat. After the people had met the President they also went out, leaving me standing there. Mr. McKinley in a very nice manner asked what I wanted and I stated my case. I don't recall what he said, but from that I think flowed my appointment or rather my authority to appear for examination.

On September 23, 1901, still three months short of his twenty-first birthday, George Marshall reported to Governor's Island off the tip of Manhattan to begin three days of examinations. He found the test comparatively simple, he wrote Superintendent Shipp, though the geography "was catchy." (He scored 65 out of a possible 100, answering "the Rio Grande" when asked, "What river forms the greater part of the boundary between Texas and Oklahoma?") He did poorly too on international law, scoring an unimpressive 42.

Still, Marshall passed the examination comfortably, that news coming as "a very acceptable Christmas present." Assured he now could support a wife, Marshall turned to the second of his great undertakings: marriage to Lily. The lady consented.

On January 4, 1902, the euphoric young man received his commission. Nine days later, Congress confirmed George C. Marshall, Jr., of Uniontown, Pennsylvania, to be a second lieutenant in the Army of the United States. He was to be assigned to the newly organized 30th Infantry Regiment, stationed in the Philippines. The infantry assignment was a surprise—he had asked for the artillery—but he swallowed whatever disappointment he felt. After all, he had achieved the major goal.

Ordered to report to Fort Myer, Virginia, on February 13, Marshall and Lily Coles were married in a hastily arranged ceremony on the 11th in the Coles' cottage. The next morning the couple took the train for Washington, where Marshall stopped by the great rococo State, War and Navy Building hard by the White House. There he found a sympathetic officer willing to bend the rules for the newly wed, newly commissioned second lieutenant; he extended the Marshalls' honeymoon by five days.

On February 18, 1902, his youth and honeymoon over, George Catlett Marshall kissed his bride of one week and reported for duty.

CHAPTER

II

The Long Years

There was no more remote, no more dismal military outpost in 1902 than Calapan, on Mindoro Island in the Philippines. To that provincial capital the United States Army sent its newest, rawest second lieutenant, George C. Marshall, late of Uniontown, Pennsylvania, and Virginia Military Institute, to begin his military career.

Calapan huddled on the steamy northeast coast of the mountainous island, sixteen miles from Luzon across Verde Passage. Swept by monsoons, the dank forests crept toward the town, an army survey team concluding "the proximity of the forests to the coastal towns makes them unhealthy. Intermittent fever turns into typhoid. Consumption also prevails."

There were other hazards. Newcomers quickly learned to shake out their boots and inspect their uniforms for scorpions before dressing in the morning. Here and there a sign along the trails through the hardwood forest warned of crocodiles in a creek or swamp ahead. The army team had concluded Calapan was "ill-suited to long residence by the white race."

Marshall later could be philosophical about his first assignment. "There isn't anything much lower than a second lieutenant and I was about the junior second lieutenant in the Army at the time."

Neither the town of 5,600 people living in thatched huts jammed hard on a plaza and casa real copied from Old Spain, nor Company G of the 30th Infantry Regiment, were very prepossessing. The soldiers were "about the wildest crowd I've ever seen before or since," Marshall recalled.

First posted on Mindoro to put down the Filipino insurrection, the troops had remained as a token symbol of empire once the last of the *insurrectos* accepted amnesty. Since then, Company G had had little to do beyond mounting patrols for outlaws in the trackless mountains and maintaining some semblance of military discipline.

Marshall was unsure of himself, as would be any twenty-one-year-old confronting bored troops who groused they had more time in the chow line than he had in the Army. Further, nothing at VMI had prepared him for the cholera epidemic raging through the islands when he arrived, or the strict quarantine that only added to the boredom. Some 500 people would die on Mindoro before the epidemic waned in June and the company took the field again.

Relying on experienced non-commissioned officers, Marshall assumed his first command. "One day while working in a torrential rain, a tall, lanky soldier from the mountains of Kentucky paused in the middle of his shoveling job, with this comment: 'I didn't see nothing like this on that damned recruiting circular.' My old first sergeant suppressed a laugh, and flashed back the order to 'keep your mouth shut and shovel coal; that's your job.' That gave me a lasting impression of the Regular Army; what discipline meant, what dependability meant in times of difficulty."

The lanky lieutenant—having filled out, he was no longer gawky—asserted himself carefully. While searching a nearby island for reported outlaws one day, Marshall led a patrol of seven men across a deep stream in single file. From behind him, someone yelled, "Crocodiles!" and the troops stampeded for the bank, trampling the young officer. Marshall picked himself up from the water, settled his VMI parade sword on one hip, the heavy Colt .45 on the other, and sloshed to his waiting patrol.

"It wasn't a time for cussing around," he recalled. Instead, he ordered the troops to fall in, then, at the head of the column, marched them back across the stream. Once on the other side, he ordered the men to turn about, back into the water amid the crocodiles, and up the far bank in proper military fashion. Then he halted the patrol, conducted a quick rifle inspection, and ordered them to fall out. Lieutenant Marshall had restored the semblance of military discipline.

VMI had taught him to drill, and there Marshall had also discovered a capacity for leadership. But he still knew little of the day-to-day realities of army life, of troop morale and field kitchens, of barracks gambling and hidden stills, but most of all, the loneliness of an army post so far from home and Lily. He would not forget the dreariness of such isolated posts.

"In those far-off days," Marshall wrote five decades later, "the soldiers of the Regular Army got little attention or consideration from the Government or the public." A private's pay was $13 per month, with a 10 percent bonus for overseas duty—and no place to spend it in Calapan anyway.

As the youngest officer, Marshall drew duty as morale officer of "a rather gloomy, depressed command." His first effort was an organized Fourth of July field day, with foot races in the afternoon—Company G's officers put up the prize money for the first four finishers in each event—to be followed by a talent show.

Only two men entered the 100-yard dash, the first event of the afternoon. Marshall divided the prize money meant for the four fastest runners between the two. "As an immediate result, I had a wealth of competitors for the following events, and I recall that we inserted a bareback pony race—and they were wild little captured ponies. One bolted into a native thatch house, wrecking it and dropping the girls hanging out the windows of the second story to the ground amidst much excitement and the first laughter I had heard in Calapan."

At the end of 1902, Marshall and his company were transferred to Manila, a cosmopolitan city of 245,000 where Lily might have lived comfortably but for the tropical climate. Garrison duty imposed only perfunctory military duties on officers and men—the work day was usually over by the noon meal—and Marshall had afternoons and evenings to himself. His most arduous chore was a week spent posting off-limits signs on the islands of Manila Bay.

To fill the time, he took up riding, borrowing cavalry mounts at the stables and acquiring a lifelong recreation. Manila at night, just eight miles from the military reservation, offered its own attractions to the lethargic occupying army of 6,500: variety theaters with acts imported from Europe and America, fine restaurants, for officers the exclusive Army and Navy Club, for enlisted men the Colorado Saloon which served ice-cold Schlitz's Milwaukee Beer for 40 cents a draught, and the fetid whorehouses along the Pasig riverfront. Marshall apparently avoided alcohol and whores alike; despite long separations from Lily, there would be no whisper of scandal about the man.

Though only dimly aware of it at the time, Marshall was also acquiring some sense of American destiny. By presidential mandate and congressional resolution, the Philippines were to have their freedom, someday. In the meantime, the islands were to be governed by a civilian administration. Ponderous William Howard Taft was the incumbent governor during Marshall's tour of duty in the islands, a man with little patience for the Army's resistance to Philippine self-government, and less for military brutality against the natives. Listening to veterans of the insurrection and later reading official reports, Marshall came to appreciate the Army's reluctance to give up land so dearly bought. He also learned of the harsh realities of guerrilla warfare. "I remember distinctly one officer reporting that he had three men wounded in an encounter and he had burned the town down. . . . When you get abroad on a wartime basis under conditions that are extremely difficult, you are likely to do things that you would utterly discountenance at another time." Marshall would condone neither the brutality nor the continued military rule as punishment for the insurrection itself. Like most Americans of his day, he favored self-government for the islands, confident his nation would win friends through benevolence and benign leadership. The United States sought not additional territory but willing international allies, a concept underpinning American foreign policy throughout Marshall's life, and one he never questioned.

In November 1903, Second Lieutenant Marshall was posted back to the United States and to Fort Reno on the north fork of the Canadian River in what was then Oklahoma Territory. A vestige of the Army's Indian-fighting days, Fort Reno offered little more than harsh duty and an arid climate too demanding for the frail Lily Marshall. The young officer continued to live in bachelor officers' quarters, if no longer the most junior second lieutenant in the Army, still without seniority or friendships enough to gain a good posting. His wife would join him later, when she felt herself able to cope with the barren land.

Garrison duty in the Army of 1904 was a matter of undemanding routine. This was a "spit-and-polish" army, more concerned with form than substance. With virtually nothing to do, commanders imposed discipline by slavish adherence to regulations and the privileges of rank. The spotless condition of a soldier's kit or a barracks loomed in importance; it was assumed that only those men who turned out impeccable troops were either good soldiers or good leaders. It was an army that might have fared well as an honor guard for royalty, but was ill-prepared for war. There was reform afoot—Marshall was eager to be a part of it after just three years of the dreary routine—but it would not take hold for another generation.

It was from Fort Reno that Marshall set out in June 1905 on what he later considered the hardest service he would have in the Army, the mapping of some 2,000 square miles of southwestern Texas desert. (He would learn that the Rio Grande marked Texas's southern border, not the northern.) Marshall and a small detail of both soldiers and civilians set off from Fort Clark, Texas, by wagon and mule train in the hottest season of the year. They traveled between ten and fifteen miles a day, measuring distances and sketching topographical features about Langtry and Del Rio on the Pecos River bottom. Water was scarce; at one point Marshall and his packer went eighteen hours without a drink. Food was poor; he lost over thirty pounds.

At the end of August, Marshall reported to Fort Clark, weighing just 132 pounds, "burned almost black," wearing a shredded Panama hat a mule had chewed and Marshall had stitched together. "When the sergeant took in the horses, Captain [Malin] Craig met him . . . and wouldn't look at me. He didn't think I could be an officer and talked entirely to my old sergeant," Marshall recalled.

His map of the Pecos River area judged "the best one received and the only complete one" of seven drawn by teams sent out that summer, Marshall was granted four months leave. He left immediately to visit his parents in Uniontown and Lily, staying still with relatives in Albemarle County, Virginia.

To the young officer, home was a strange place; there was little trace of Flicker Marshall. Uniontown had changed as much as had the young man who had left the thriving town four years before. His parents had moved from their home on West Main Street to live in an eleven-story building Andy Thompson's father had erected on East Main. The old brick house itself had been torn down, the lot leveled and filled. The creek behind the house, in which Marshall the boy had splashed, trickled now through the trash of a fast-growing city.

In the four years friends had married and died; those who remained were familiar, yet strangers too. His father, once so formidable a figure, appeared shrunken, older, much older than his years.

Marshall walked the streets, a man out of joint with the town in which he had been born. Visiting the mother of an old friend, he came across Trip, the friend's terrier, sunning himself by a water pump.

"He paid no attention to me—he didn't bark at me—he was so old he was just indifferent. . . . That was quite a blow because Trip was one of the close companions of my youth." Even the dogs had changed.

"I talked to him quite a long time, trying to renew my youth and was very much distressed that he didn't remember me at all. After, I suppose, five or ten minutes, he took a careful sniff of me, then he sniffed at me two or three times, and then he just went crazy. He had finally gotten a scent in his old nostrils and he remembered me. That was the most flattering thing that occurred to me on that short visit home after many years of not being there." From that moment, Uniontown would be the place where he was born, but not his home.

His leave ended, Marshall, his wife, and Lily's mother together returned to Fort Reno and the dulling routine of garrison life. The young officer was restless. He had served four years, yet was still a second lieutenant fretting about the $3.50 cost of a spring bonnet for his wife. Lacking seniority, Marshall's immediate prospects of promotion were slender.

Seeking an escape from the dreary rituals of Fort Reno, and perhaps with an eye on possible promotion, Marshall had twice applied for the Army's first postgraduate training course, the United States Infantry and Cavalry School at Fort Leavenworth. While he had scored highest on competitive tests for the Leavenworth assignment, both times higher-ranking officers had snared the detail. He also wrote to VMI's aging Superintendent Shipp, perhaps at the urging of Lily and her mother who would have much preferred pleasant Lexington to drab Fort Reno, to submit his name for assignment as professor of military science and tactics. It was a measure of his discontent, of family pressure, or both, for such assignments went normally to officers with far more experience.

He was not to get the VMI assignment, then or later. Instead, on his third application, Marshall—rated "an excellent officer" by Fort Reno's commandant—found himself posted to Fort Leavenworth and the newly reorganized Infantry and Cavalry School. The school had no great reputation in an army resolutely anti-intellectual; many commanders "give the detail at Leavenworth to their regimental idiot," one instructor complained at the time. Marshall's was the only application from Fort Reno.

Regimental idiots would not do well with the revised curriculum Brigadier General J. Franklin Bell had imposed on the moribund General Service and Staff College. First as commandant of the school, then as army chief of staff, Bell strove to make the two-year program the stepping stone for higher rank. By August 1906, when twenty-five-year-old George Marshall reported, "Bell's Folly" was still to be accepted. A curriculum that eventually stressed practical application of general principles rather than rote adherence to regulation did not sit well with army conservatives, which is to say, the great majority of senior officers. There was still much numbing memorization, still much by-the-numbers thinking, but the most influential of the school's instructors, Major John Morrison, would reshape tactical thinking. A generation after his retirement, his onetime students would proudly call themselves Morrison men. And disciples.

The same conflict between older conservatives and younger reformers, who were spurred on by the Japanese success over the Russians, wracked the French and British military hierarchies. New weapons, Marconi's wireless, and the internal combustion engine were to change the nature of warfare in the next decade; changes those senior officers schooled in the nineteenth century's theory of mass over maneuverability stubbornly refused to grasp. The successive bloodbaths blindly ordered by superannuated British and French generals at the beginning of World War I would validate the reformers, but the cost would be a generation of Europe's young men.

Second Lieutenant Marshall found disconcerting the Army School of the Line, as the Infantry and Cavalry School was renamed the following year. "I wondered what was going to become of me without any preparation of any kind," he later confessed. Other first-year students, all competing to be in the top half of the class and to attend the crucial second-year general staff course, came to Leavenworth coached on the field problems. Some of the fifty-four even brought copies of classroom tests with them. "And so I knew I would have to study harder than I ever dreamed of studying before in my life."

There was plenty to goad Marshall on. He was ambitious, and to succeed in his chosen career, he needed to attend the second-year course of the Army Staff College. Only that could lead to the prestigious Army War College and senior rank.

Moreover, he was competitive. When classmates in the first weeks of September speculated who would be among the top students, Marshall was overlooked consistently. It was Stuart Marshall's jibe all over again, and the second lieutenant redoubled his efforts. "I developed a position which put me in another light to my classmates who had left me out entirely of the estimate of who was going to be in the next year's Staff Class."

Further, there was a need to prove himself to his wife and her mother. A marriage might begin with love, but it flourished with esteem. After each day's classes and field exercise, Marshall beat for his home in the married officers' quarters, to dinner with Lily and her mother, then to the waiting books. He put in long hours, went late to bed, then often awoke in the middle of the night, anxious about the score on a test he had taken, nervous about the exam coming up.

Compounding his burden, during the Christmas holidays Marshall and five other students took examinations for promotion. For five days, while other students enjoyed a break in their studies, Marshall took written tests and tramped through the mud of Fort Leavenworth plotting maps. While he waited for the results of the promotion examination, Marshall returned to the school's routine of dreary memorization in the morning, and immediate application in the afternoon.

The young man would never have a year quite as rewarding as this. He passed the promotion exam handily; his promotion to first lieutenant on March 7, 1907, "was the most thrilling moment of my life," he said later, after a lifetime of honors. The single silver bar of a first lieutenant affirmed his fitness for his chosen career five years after he had joined the Army.

In May, the newly minted first lieutenant finished the year at Leavenworth ranked first in his class; his second year at the post attending the pivotal Army Staff College was a certainty. The future appeared bright, all the more so because his marks had caught the eye of the army chief of staff, General Bell. Anxious to promote the Leavenworth concept, Bell detailed five first-year graduates, Marshall among them, to help train National Guard units during the summer.

Marshall's second year at Leavenworth proved less demanding than the first. Classes were not ranked academically, and the memorization that so froze individual initiative was replaced by exercises geared to mold future staff officers capable of advising senior commanders. Marshall concluded he garnered little he could actually use, but came away believing that at Leavenworth he "learned how to learn," how to analyze a problem and reach decisions. "We were there in the midst of transformation and we knew it."

There was innovation. Marshall attended a lecture by Major George O. Squier, head of the Signal Corps School, who announced "that two brothers, named Wright, were actually reaching the solution of flight by heavier-than-air machines. I knew nothing of this at the time, having seen no reference to it in the press, and I have never forgotten the profound impression it made on my mind." Marshall also befriended First Lieutenant Benjamin D. Foulois, dismissed as a crank by many of his instructors and classmates because Foulois insisted the "dynamical flying machine" would radically alter military tactics.

The Leavenworth year ended with a two-week horseback tour of Civil War battlefields from Bull Run to Gettysburg, with a lecture by some member of the party at each. Marshall gave the last of six at Gettysburg, a summary of the battle that doomed the Confederacy. Riding along unpaved country roads on warm summer days, pulling their horses off to give way to the occasional Buick or Pierce Arrow that sputtered past them, the mounted officers were an anachronism. Many of them never would adjust to the mechanization of slaughter those coughing automobiles and the "dynamical flying machine" heralded. An army's range and mobility would no longer be limited by how far troops could march, but how well motor transport and airplanes were maintained.

Apparently, based on his performance as an instructor with the National Guard and his class rankings, Marshall was one of five students detailed to stay on as instructors for the coming year.

Before meeting his wife for their now annual Virginia vacation, Marshall stopped by Fort Myer on July 30, 1908, to join a crowd of some 7,000 "present to see the miracle," Orville Wright's attempt to win an army contract for Wright Flyers. The diplomats, cabinet officers, and army officers cheered the fragile Flyer aloft, then marveled as a confident Wright and his passenger steadily chugged in great circles over the fort. Marshall watched from amid the carriages and motorcars scattered about the parade grounds while the two men in the wood and canvas aeroplane effortlessly traveled the required twenty miles at an average speed of 40 miles per hour.

That evening, Marshall visited his friend from Leavenworth, Lieutenant Benjamin Foulois, who had spent the morning as Wright's passenger on the flight. Marshall and a vindicated Foulois, Morrison men both, talked; Marshall ever after would support an army air service, and the airplane as a weapon of war.

The next two years at Leavenworth were to foster what became the Marshall legend. The indifferent student at VMI was apparently a gifted instructor in the classroom. He was one of a vanguard advocating major reforms, and he knew it; only military tact, demanded when his students were all senior in rank and age, dampened his zeal.

In the summers, Marshall returned to the Pennsylvania National Guard encampments, putting into practice the theories promulgated in the classroom. There too he was learning, particularly "the human reactions and from what goes to make attacks, apart from maps."

No longer a student worried about the slightest error of memorization, Marshall and his wife could enjoy the ease of garrison life at Fort Leavenworth. For the officers there were dances, which the Marshalls attended, though Lily did not dance. There were rides to hounds, and a riding hall. The young first lieutenant bought hunting dogs, and hunted; he rode constantly, and trained his own horse. It was a comfortable life, an olive drab reflection of upper-class America. The man who once spent nights studying now eased his pace, and met other officers socially, among them First Lieutenant Douglas MacArthur, attached to the fort's permanent garrison. The two men were not personally close; MacArthur's biographer William Manchester decided that they "rubbed each other the wrong way." Marshall was not by nature gregarious, nor would MacArthur's already lofty opinion of himself endear him personally to many.

It was a life that smacked much of Lily's Virginia, to which Marshall was increasingly drawn. The death of his father by stroke in September 1909 accelerated the turning away from Uniontown in favor of the gracious antebellum qualities of Albemarle County. One more tie with his childhood was severed.

Gradually Marshall came to identify "home" as seemingly unchanging Virginia, rich with the legends of the Confederacy. Lily's Aunt Sally could remember as a little girl the faint rumble of the artillery on Palm Sunday, 1865, as she attended church forty miles from Appomattox courthouse. A half-day's westerly ride led to the crest of the Blue Ridge Mountains; Marshall could look down into the Shenandoah Valley, picking out misty battlefields and campgrounds of his idol, Stonewall Jackson. A half-day in the other direction meandered the James River, where Marshall learned to canoe on waters in which Confederates and Yankees had bled to death.

It was here, with Miss Lily's relatives, in the placid foothills as beautiful as industrial Uniontown was grimy, that Marshall found ties he had missed since leaving VMI. Somewhat suspect at first—even Miss Lily's husband had to overcome his birthplace—Marshall came to cherish the easy grace of this timeless place.

In the late summer of 1910, his four years at Leavenworth ended, George and Lily used his accrued leave time to take a five-month tour of Europe. Paid as a first lieutenant $183 per month, Marshall financed the trip "on a shoestring, but we managed to cover six countries and two of them while I was on half pay." The tour was leisurely: a month in England where Marshall bicycled about the British maneuvers at Aldershot, possibly seeing more than the restricted American military attaché; two weeks in Paris; a month through the Loire Valley before spending five weeks in Florence and Rome; then on to Austria.

The couple returned to the United States, Marshall reporting in the midst of a blizzard to Madison Barracks at Sacketts Harbor, New York, on the shores of Lake Ontario. He would command Company D of the 24th Infantry Regiment just three months before friends arranged his transfer to the War Department in Washington. The Army was planning its largest peacetime maneuver, concentrating 16,000 men and the elements of three divisions along the Texas-Mexican border. The maneuvers would not only serve as a training exercise, but would remind the embattled Mexican government of Porfirio Díaz to respect American neutrality before going after rebels who lurked in Texas exile.

Marshall was assigned as assistant to the chief signal officer, his Fort Leavenworth acquaintance, Major George O. Squier. "They had taken me into the Signal Corps affair just to get me present," Marshall conceded. The assignment was ideal for a future staff officer. The Signal Corps would be using for the first-time field telephones, the Marconi wireless, and airplanes during maneuvers.

When they worked. "I turned out every morning at 5:30 in the cold of a Texas winter, to avoid a possible calamity, as the planes in taking off barely cleared my tent," he remembered. "I saw the Curtiss crash and I saw the Wright run through a horse and buggy, or rather I saw the horse run over the machine."

The maneuvers, which demonstrated the Army's absolute inability to muster quickly, ended in June, not coincidentally after Francisco Madero's revolutionaries toppled the Díaz regime. By then, First Lieutenant Marshall was on his way to Boston, requested by the governor of Massachusetts as a training officer for the state militia. His first assignment was to help plan maneuvers; Marshall's reputation as a staff officer was growing.

Duty with the Massachusetts State Militia was satisfying, Boston far more exciting than Forts Reno or Leavenworth. Yet Marshall was ambitious, and ambition compelled movement; he encouraged the new superintendent at VMI to request Marshall's assignment as commandant at the Institute. Lily and her mother, who was living with them, would prefer "a few peaceful, housekeeping years in Lexington . . . more than all the glories of war." When General Edward W. Nichols's request to the War Department was turned down, Marshall thanked the superintendent: "In any event your display of interest in me will go far towards bettering my status with the War Department."

Nichols's conversation with Army Chief of Staff Leonard Wood may have helped the budding staff officer secure his next assignment, the planning of joint Regular Army and National Guard maneuvers in Connecticut during the summer of 1912. Ordered to Washington, Marshall was to "develop the maneuver and everything connected with it, and still was tied down to the necessity of having very short marches. Four miles a day, I think, was the first march. . . . But that was the way it had to be done, because you can't take a man from behind the counter of a store and put him in heavy marching shoes the next day and expect him to be able to trudge about the country. . . ." Marshall was gaining a practical awareness of the human factors in tactical operations, a knowledge that was to set him off from other staff officers.

The maneuvers, involving more than 17,000 officers and men, were considered a rousing success; Marshall would get much of the credit. A reporter for *The New York World* described the sleepless Marshall as "the busiest man on the field."

The *World* reporter was not the only one to appreciate Marshall. Secretary of War Henry Stimson and Chief of Staff Wood turned up to observe the last of the maneuvers. Marshall's superior, Brigadier General Tasker Bliss, a future chief of staff, credited Marshall with much of the success of the field exercise. The young lieutenant was now recognized as a surpassing staff officer by the loftiest of the Army's aristocracy.

Such recognition could not save Marshall from menial duty, however. Congress had adopted a military reorganization law requiring that all officers below the rank of major serve at least two of every six years with the regiment to which they had been assigned. Because of his Leavenworth and Massachusetts guard assignments, Marshall had not put in the required two years with troops. As a result, he found himself assigned to M Company of the 4th Infantry at Fort Logan Roots, Arkansas, a tiny backwater of some 300 officers and men rotting in the humidity not far from Little Rock.

The assignment was memorable to Marshall for just one reason. Learning that there was no Christmas party planned for the children living on the post, Marshall took it upon himself to organize one. He collected money from fellow officers, then bought toys in Little Rock at bargain prices. He enlisted a soldier to play Santa Claus, and arranged to become officer of the day for three consecutive nights; thus he could take charge of the prisoners who had volunteered to decorate the post gymnasium.

With the same intensity with which he planned maneuvers, Marshall brought off the Christmas party. As a reward for their help, Marshall permitted the prisoners to pass out gifts to the excited children.

That evening, Marshall received his own Christmas gift, one he would cherish for the rest of his life. The men who had decorated the gymnasium and handed out the cut-rate gifts gathered in the guardhouse to thank Marshall. Only one of them had ever spent a Christmas at home, a soldier explained; Lieutenant Marshall had given them their first holiday party.

Company M was reassigned to Fort Snelling, Minnesota, in February 1913, then, with the newly formed 2nd Division, transferred to Fort Crockett, near Galveston, Texas, to guard the uneasy Mexican border. Marshall would not be long in Texas. He had asked for overseas service, and at the end of May he received orders reassigning him to the Philippine Islands.

"I am now paying the penalty for having had too many good things during the past seven years," he wrote General Nichols at VMI, "six years of various detached service away from troops and no foreign service in *nine* and one-half years. However, I should soon come back from the Islands with a clean slate on all counts."

Marshall reported for duty on August 5, 1913, with the 13th Infantry Regiment at Fort McKinley near Manila. It would be an assignment far different from the futile patrolling of ten years before. First of all, Lily would be with him, the two of them to make a home together in the married officers' quarters on the post. (Lily planned to spend the hot months traveling to cooler Japan.) Secondly, the nature of the Army's responsibility had changed. The Army of 1903 that had worried about *insurrectos* now was concerned about an increasingly aggressive Imperial Japan, 2,000 miles from Manila. Victory in the Russo-Japanese War in 1905 and the annexation of Korea five years later had transformed a comic-opera country into a world power. Imperial Japan looked southward to economic dominance of the Far East.

The fortified Philippines stood directly in Japan's path, a western shore of American ambition and power. Self-government for the islands still lay sometime in the indefinite future; superficially, the Philippines had become an outpost of America. Malecon Drive curving along Manila Bay had been renamed Dewey Boulevard after the triumphant admiral of 1898, yet the red-tile roofs and plastered walls of the buildings remained Spanish. The theaters imported English and American vaudevillians; the opera house was awash in Verdi, Donizetti, and Puccini, yet the walled core of the city, the Intramuros, was still the heart of Manila. The American military had only a perfunctory social contact with Filipinos, officers by and large secluding themselves on American posts or hanging about the sociable Army and Navy Club in Manila. The Marshalls would live within an insular world.

For the first six months, he stagnated, a frustrated man. At that moment, Marshall may have been the most highly trained and experienced lieutenant in the United States Army; certainly no other junior officer had planned maneuvers involving 17,000 troops. Yet he himself did not even command a company of 100 men. Worse still, his company commander,

Captain E. J. Williams, had been a student of Marshall's at Leavenworth. That would cause resentment in the most phlegmatic of men, and Marshall was not phlegmatic. Captain Williams he considered both competent and a friend—two years later Marshall would write a letter of recommendation for Williams's son who wanted to enter VMI—but the same could not be said for many of the other officers senior to the first lieutenant. Marshall was confronting the "hump," the great number of by-the-book officers commissioned during the Spanish-American War, men faithful to a system that rewarded marginal performance with security.

Perhaps out of frustration, perhaps out of spite, Marshall made a bet with another lieutenant in the regiment that the next senior officer who inspected Company M would find three minor errors during the inspection, yet miss three major faults Marshall would build into the afternoon's field exercise. Marshall won the bet. The inspecting officer gravely noted the unbuttoned blouse on one private, the soldier who had not shaved that morning, and the rifleman without a bayonet. In the afternoon, Marshall's company marched in columns of four rather than a skirmish line directly up a supposedly fortified hill; a patrol was dispatched without any instructions; and the unit was marched over open ground rather than in a ravine that would have provided cover from hostile fire. The story of the bet quickly made the rounds of the Officers' Club at Fort McKinley, then to the Army and Navy Club in Manila. If Marshall had not been a marked man before, he was now.

In January 1914, Marshall was to gain a reputation that became almost mythic as the story of the Batangas maneuvers was told and retold by veterans of the Philippines. Marshall's distant patron, former Army Chief of Staff J. Franklin Bell, now in command of the Philippine Department, had detailed the young lieutenant to serve as adjutant on the staff of an invading "White" force. For four months, his duties as adjutant were simply an annoyance, an added burden to his daily, really half day's work with Company M. But two days after the White Force and Lieutenant Marshall were landed some fifty miles south of Manila with orders to take the capital, the mock attack was in chaos.

The invading White Force's commander, "a courtly gentleman, a very nice fellow," as Marshall remembered him, simply lacked ability. When the umpires from General Bell's staff proposed the colonel's removal, lest the maneuvers collapse before they began, the lowly adjutant prevailed upon them to leave the colonel in nominal command, but to allow Marshall a free hand. It was a bold, even presumptuous suggestion, born of frustrated ambitions, yet saving the colonel's dignity; better that than a new White Force commander whom Marshall might not be able to manipulate quite so easily. General Bell's staff agreed to Marshall's suggestion that he serve as the colonel's alter ego.

More authority was to come the next morning when the White Force chief of staff fell ill and returned to Manila. Since Marshall was the only one with any knowledge of the maneuvers' plans, the hamstrung umpires suggested that Marshall step in as chief of staff; in effect, a mere first lieutenant was both the planner and the commander of the invasion force of 4,800 men.

Now came the legends: of Marshall dictating orders out of his head; of the White Force progressively sweeping inland, then defeating the defending Brown Force; of brilliant improvisations by the future staff officer, which the narrators put forward as proof that they early on recognized Marshall's potential.

One man certainly did, a fellow first lieutenant of infantry, then as later known by his West Point nickname of "Hap," Henry A. Arnold.

> My company of infantry was moving up to make an attack when we halted to rest on a trail. Under the shade of a bamboo clump lay a young lieutenant with a map spread before him. It developed he was dictating the order for the attack that was to break through the defenders' line. This youthful officer was our side's chief of staff for the maneuvers, a job any lieutenant colonel or major in the outfit would have given his eyeteeth to have. Following the young lieutenant's plans, we won.

> When I returned from the maneuvers, I told my wife I had met a man who was going to be chief of staff of the army some day.

Arnold's memory was only slightly faulty. The umpires ended the maneuvers without declaring a winner—though Marshall himself thought "we pretty convincingly licked the other side." The final report blandly praised Marshall for assuming "a severe task which he carried out successfully and for which he deserves great credit."

The legends that grew from the Batangas maneuvers were far larger than the reality, which, in military eyes, was big enough. Major (later Brigadier General) Johnson Hagood clearly, and quite erroneously, remembered General Bell calling Hagood and the rest of his staff together to cite Marshall as "the greatest military genius since Stonewall Jackson."

The maneuvers ended in a draw, and a thin, tautly wound First Lieutenant Marshall returned to Manila for a two-week stay in the hospital, his nerves worn by the strain. For the thirty-one-year-old man, the hospitalization came as a shock, some intimation perhaps of his own frailty.

Warned by his collapse from what doctors described vaguely as "neurasthenia," Marshall became a cautious, deliberate man who sought a measured pace through repeated crises. From then on, he carefully rationed his efforts, hewing closely to a work schedule that allowed him an hour's horseback ride before breakfast, tennis in the afternoons, and time to relax in the evenings. He also found time for hunting trips with two particularly close friends, "Hap" Arnold and a reserved Georgian, Lieutenant Courtney Hodges.

Caution would not render him inactive. Granted two months' sick leave, and that extended by two months' regular leave, Lieutenant and Mrs. Marshall set off for a visit to Japan, Korea, and Manchuria. Ostensibly to escape the heat of the Philippines, the couple spent a month in Manchuria as guests of the prideful Japanese Army. Marshall toured the battlefields of the Russo-Japanese War, watched Japanese troops in training, and came away with ideas to improve American use of the bayonet and the hand grenade. He also urged in a report to the Army's adjutant general the use of night attacks, a tactic the Japanese had employed successfully against the Russians.

Marshall's horizons were expanding. Well before he left for the Manchurian battlefields, he had been free with his strategic and tactical observations, an admiring Hap Arnold recalled. Now, in anticipation of the June 1916 end of his tour in the Philippines and his expected promotion to captain, Marshall angled to be attached to a French Army regiment as an observer. In Sarajevo, an archduke and his consort had been assassinated; now, as British Foreign Secretary Sir Edward Grey lamented, "The lights are going out all over Europe." But what better place for a soldier than a battlefield, posted with an army considered the finest in the world?

The Marshalls returned to the ordered, torpid life of the garrison at Fort McKinley, watching from afar as the great European powers plunged into war. President Wilson's proclaimed neutrality scotched the posting of Americans, beyond the regular military attachés, to either side; First Lieutenant Marshall would not soon be going to France.

Less than a year after his return from Manchuria, Marshall finally found himself a staff billet. Brigadier General Hunter Liggett, newly arrived in the Philippines, tapped Marshall, whom he had met first at Leavenworth and later during the Connecticut maneuvers, as his aide-de-camp.

His duties as the general's aide were barely more demanding than line service had been. It was a pleasant, relaxed life, but ultimately boring to a man of ambition; soldiers his age in Europe were carving great reputations while the United States watched cautiously, lest it be dragged into foreign entanglements. For an officer trained to lead troops in battle, here was the final frustration. At age thirty-four, Marshall had rusted for five years as a second lieutenant and nine more as a first lieutenant. His captaincy seemed poor recompense, and still remote, despite plans

for the expansion of the Army pending in Congress. Finally he wrote
the commandant at VMI, soberly, almost dispassionately, as if analyzing
a field problem, the frustration leaking through only at the end:

> The absolute stagnation in promotion in the infantry has caused
> me to make tentative plans for resigning as soon as business con-
> ditions improve somewhat. Even in the event of an increase as a
> result of legislation next winter, the prospects for advancement in
> the army are so restricted by law and by the accumulation of large
> numbers of men of nearly the same age all in a single grade, that I
> do not feel it right to waste all my best years in the vain struggle
> against insurmountable obstacles. The temptation to accept an
> absolutely assured and fairly fat living, with little or no prospect of
> reasonable advancement, is very great when you consider the dif-
> ficulties and positive dangers of starting anew in civil life at my age.
> However, with only one life to live I feel that the acceptance of my
> present secured position would mean that I lacked the backbone
> and necessary moral courage to do the right thing.

General Nichols wrote quickly to reassure "my dear Marshall" that no
one in his grade stood higher. "Now my dear fellow, I would think twice
and think long before I gave up my commission were I in your place.
You are an eminent success in your present line of endeavor, highly
esteemed by everyone who knows you and with a standing in the service
of the very highest. . . ."

Some of Marshall's frustration stemmed from the fact he was half a
world away from the Mexican border where the United States Army had
once again assembled. Victoriano Huerta and what President Wilson called
his "government by assassination" had resigned. Venustiano Carranzana,
rallying the scattered Maderos forces, replaced him. Three different
political factions skirmished across the northern deserts; the turmoil in
Mexico threatened to spill over the Rio Grande.

When Francisco Villa led his band on an opportunistic hit-and-run
raid on Columbus, New Mexico, on March 9, 1916, the Army set off in
pursuit. Brigadier General John J. Pershing led a "punitive" expedition
that for eleven months crisscrossed Mexico, futilely tracking Villa's free
company. Even outfitted with new Dodge trucks, Pershing's command
proved unwieldy, and the Army stretched to breaking in its effort to
protect an ostensibly friendly border.

His Philippine tour over in June 1916, Marshall elected not to resign
just yet, not with the recession at home, the chance of adventure in Mexico, and the possibility of the Army's reorganization and expansion. He
might have a troop command yet.

But Marshall was to see no duty with troops. Instead of service on the

Mexican border, he was ordered to the Presidio in San Francisco. Brigadier General J. Franklin Bell, once the commandant at Fort Leavenworth, had tapped his former instructor to serve as an aide. Almost as soon as Marshall arrived, he found himself up for promotion, the required examination waived because he had spent two years at the staff school. Bell would help the lieutenant make up for lost time.

The captain-to-be—Marshall's promotion would not come through until August 14—was to supervise the training of civilian businessmen volunteering for a newly created Officers Reserve Corps. Marshall would train "all the hot bloods of San Francisco" who had volunteered for a month's training so as to earn army commissions. "I saw more Rolls Royces and other fine cars around there than I had ever seen collected."

From Monterey, Marshall moved to Fort Douglas, Utah, and a second of these one-month camps, this commanded by Lieutenant Colonel Johnson Hagood. The month's stay there as Hagood's adjutant contributed significantly to the Marshall legend, for friend Hagood rendered Marshall the supreme and unheard of compliment on Marshall's efficiency report. Answering the form's routine question, would you like to have this officer under your command, Hagood wrote: "This officer is well qualified to command a division, with the rank of major general, in time of war, and I would like very much to serve under *his* command."

Despite Hagood's recommendation and warning that Marshall be promoted to "brigadier general in the Regular Army, and every day this is postponed is a loss to the Army and the nation," the captain-to-be returned to the Presidio as a mere aide to General Bell.

Throughout the summer of 1916, the nation, or part of it, had crept to an awareness that the United States could not long avoid entanglement in foreign wars. A large part of the nascent labor movement, joined by the last Progressives and shards of left-of-center political parties, opposed any American involvement; meanwhile, a probable majority of businessmen and employers favored either covert or overt entry into the bogged-down battle. Neither side could claim its motives were purely patriotic; labor, after all, would furnish the majority of men to do the fighting, and businessmen were sure to reap the benefits of increased military sales. Orders from France and Great Britain for munitions, airplane engines, and food had already turned about the business recession that had kept Marshall in the Army less than a year before.

With one hundred Americans aboard, the *Lusitania* had gone down more than a year earlier, and with it, the hopes of William Jennings Bryan, Wilson's pacifist-minded secretary of state. Seven months later, President Wilson had addressed Congress to warn of the need for preparedness if the nation was to be strong enough to assert its neutrality. Since only the German U-boat threatened United States lives and property, Wilson, in effect, was tacitly siding with the Allies against the Kaiser. Meanwhile, the president would campaign for reelection that year on the slogan, "He Kept Us Out of War."

Congress responded to the president's call by finally adopting the National Defense Act on June 3, 1916. That bill increased the Army to 220,000 men and, among other things, opened the way for Marshall's immediate promotion to captain. In short order, Congress also passed an expanded five-year naval construction program and a merchant marine bill to provide ships to carry the produce of the United States to Europe, and created a Council of National Defense, authorized to make certain those bottoms were filled with marketable goods.

Within six months, the question seemed not would the United States enter the European war, only when. On January 31, 1917, Germany informed the president it would begin unrestricted submarine warfare. Four days later, a German submarine sank the USS *Housatonic* and President Wilson broke off diplomatic relations. On March 1, the British intelligence service leaked an inflammatory telegram from Germany's then secretary of state, Arthur Zimmermann, to the German minister to Mexico, suggesting an alliance between the two countries, with Mexico to invade the American Southwest. On March 12, the United States government announced it would arm its merchant fleet. Six days later, three more American ships were torpedoed.

The decision came in a rush. The cabinet asked the president to request a declaration of war on Germany. On April 2, the man who had "kept us out of war" went before a special session of Congress seeking that declaration, proclaiming, "The world must be made safe for democracy."

Four days later, the Senate by a vote of 82 to 6 and the House of Representatives 373 to 50 adopted the resolution. The war to end all wars had been joined.

C H A P T E R

III

Remarkably Gallant Fellows

The two officers stood at the window of the shipping office, watching the slowly moving lines of troops shuffle through the drizzling rain into the covered sheds of the Hoboken dock. The younger of the two men, an infantry captain wearing the flashes of a staff officer, paced with barely contained excitement, ignored by the older colonel standing quietly at the window.

Across the street, beyond the iron fence of the former North German Lloyd Line's pier, glowering shadows stood silently in the pale yellow of the street lamps. Those sullen spectators and the unsmiling dockworkers, Germans all, looked like crew members off some submarine, the younger man thought. It was not a very encouraging prospect.

Captain George Marshall looked back to the khaki lines steadily flowing into the building to disappear into the holds of the hastily converted fruit ship *Tenadores*. The sight seemed both impressive and forbidding. Captain Marshall turned to the colonel who commanded the new port of embarkation. "The men seem very solemn."

"Of course, they are," the colonel said gravely. "We are watching the harvest of death."

Startled, Marshall quickly excused himself to seek out a less somber companion from the staff of the newly formed Combat Division. America was in the war now, and the hastily assembled men trudging up the gangplank were the nation's first tithing to the bloody stalemate on the Somme and the Marne.

Marshall had few illusions about the glory of war, or the "great adventure" some thought it. Since August 1914, the nations of Europe had fed their finest young men into the maw of trench warfare as the opposing armies locked in brutish, endless combat. Thirty-three months later, both the Allied and the Central Powers had been bled to exhaustion, an entire generation destroyed in "the hell where youth and laughter go."

England had squandered 60,000 men on a single day, July 1, 1916, to open the Battle of the Somme, and achieved nothing. The horror of Flanders' fields would haunt British generals for a generation to come, yet the savagery ran on mindlessly. Ten days after the United States declared war, the French commander-in-chief had ordered yet another offensive against the solidly entrenched German lines in Picardy, offering up 95,000 casualties and triggering a mutiny that flashed through the demoralized French Army. Whatever might be noble about war had ceased to exist.

Now the Yanks were coming, Broadway showman George M. Cohan promised, "the drums rum-tumming everywhere." Eager for fresh troops to shore up sagging morale and depleted commands alike, English and French officers waited impatiently for the promised divisions America was sending to fight in Europe for the first time in history; reinforcing their own troops, the Americans could shatter the stalemate of the Western Front. General John J. Pershing, commanding the American Expeditionary Forces, had already landed in France, soon to be followed by a great outpouring of American soldiers. The issue of freedom of the seas had propelled the United States into a war that, ironically, would be decided on land.

Captain George C. Marshall, a professional soldier, counted himself lucky to be among the first of the promised million. It had taken luck, and well-placed friends who could recommend him to the right offices of the War Department. As aide to General J. Franklin Bell, Marshall might easily have been passed over.

With the declaration of war, Marshall had accompanied his superior from San Francisco to the general's new assignment as commander of the Department of the East, headquartered on Governor's Island in New York Harbor. But Bell was struck down for a month with influenza and hospitalized at Rockefeller Hospital secretly, so as not to jeopardize his own chances for a coveted overseas assignment. In Bell's absence, Captain Marshall found himself running the chaotic Department of the East, sneaking away every other day to visit his commander and inform him of the decisions taken.

There were hundreds, for the Army was suddenly, drastically to expand after years of peacetime poverty. The most urgent problem was to set up Officers Training Camps at Plattsburg, New York, to receive the first volunteers. Marshall cut corners, and red tape, locating such supplies as blankets and mattresses as far west as Chicago, then ordering them shipped express. When the quartermaster colonel protested the expense, Marshall explained "the cost was not going to mean so much to those men freezing up there. . . . The public reaction was going to be very severe," a criticism the Army could do without just then.

The camps established, Marshall could turn to the pile of applications, and the phone calls from the politically powerful sponsors of young men who wanted to take the three-month training course and go off to whip Kaiser Bill. "Each seemed to feel that political pressure was necessary. I was trying to demonstrate that it wasn't necessary. . . . I found myself then up against ex-President Taft and others, particularly from the wealthy of New York. J. P. Morgan and Company and other firms all seemed to think they could get what they wanted right away."

The flurry of preparations in those first weeks after the United States' entry into the war was to have a profound impression on the general's aide. War had caught the Army unprepared once again. At the beginning of the Spanish-American War, troops and supplies had often gone separate ways, soldiers setting off for Cuba poorly outfitted and haphazardly equipped. The War Department had suffered newspaper attacks and public scandal over the mismanagement of supplies left on Florida docks and in freightyards while Roughriders stormed San Juan Hill.

The on-again-off-again Mexican border campaign had suffered similar problems. Four years later, the greatest of conflicts upon them, the Regular Army of 210,000 and the National Guard of 100,000 were still unprepared. Congress had declared war, but had nothing with which to fight that war.

Whatever the importance of his present duties, acting, in effect, as the commander of the Department of the East, Marshall wanted overseas duty. He narrowly missed going as a member of General Pershing's staff when Pershing decided that Marshall was still needed by the weakened Bell. The captain returned home despondent in a heavy rain after secretly escorting Pershing's staff, in ill-fitting civilian clothes, to the dock. Lily Marshall was less than impressed by the bedraggled, wet pack her husband had seen off to France. "They were such a dreadful-looking lot of men, I cannot believe they will be able to do any good in France."

With Bell's approval, Marshall did what the junior members of J. P. Morgan and Company had: he looked for a sponsor in the War Department. He once more wrote VMI's General Nichols asking him to use his influence, and Nichols's word may have helped secure the overseas posting. Or a request for him might have come spontaneously from any of a number of other officers on duty at the War Department. In any event, the man chosen to head the Army's first combat division, Major General William L. Sibert, had favorably noted Marshall's efforts at the Monterey training camp the previous summer. Sibert asked Bell to release Marshall to serve as the division operations officer.

Bell could hardly have refused. The year before, he had written on Marshall's efficiency report that the thirty-seven-year-old captain was "especially well qualified to perform the duty of chief of staff for corps or army or to command same." Bell described Marshall as "an exceptionally rapid, systematic worker. Never forgets and is capable of accomplishing much in time available. Always cheerfully willing, never excited or rushed, cool and level-headed. A good countervail for me."

Informed of his new assignment just thirty-six hours before the *Tenadores* sailed, Marshall was both rushed and excited. Not only did he have to pack his own field gear to join Sibert's division assembling in the marshy meadows outside Hoboken, but he had to arrange Lily's return to Lexington, tie up what loose ends he could for General Bell, and put his personal affairs in order.

Ostensibly the division was sailing secretly to France—after a one-day delay anchored in the middle of New York Harbor while passengers on passing excursion boats cheered the restless troops. Desperately short of training, the division's precipitous sailing was determined by political factors more than military; the division was a pledge to weary France and Great Britain, a visible token of America's entry into the war, though the unit was in no condition to enter the lines. The Army had never had a primary tactical unit larger than an inflated regiment; this "quadrangle division" was the first of its kind. Under strength at the beginning of the war, the 16th, 18th, 26th, and 28th Infantry Regiments had been tripled in size, filled out with men from other units, and marched to the dock. Many of the troops were recruits from the mountains of Kentucky and Tennessee; a sizable portion were immigrants who spoke little English. The non-commissioned officers were Regular Army, grizzled veterans of Philippine jungle and Mexican desert, a steadying influence but unfamiliar with trench warfare and more than a little contemptuous of their green commissioned officers. The division staff had come from a dozen military posts and forts all over the country; not until they assembled aboard the *Tenadores* did they learn their specific assignments. The Army was starting from the beginning, with the war already upon them, just as in 1898 and again in 1913.

The division's second lieutenants were drawn from the twenty best trainees from the Plattsburg camps. "I have never seen more splendid looking men and it makes me very sad to realize that most of them were left in France," Marshall wrote later. "I recall crossing over to New York on the government ferry with nine of them, each with a bride. I never learned of the career of two of these officers, but I do know that each of the other seven was killed fighting in the 1st Division."

With an escort of six destroyers, the first American troop convoy of the war steamed 3,000 miles through a sea of rumored submarine attacks, at least one false alarm, and one abortive attack that did no more than alleviate the boredom. On the morning of June 26, 1917, the *Tenadores*, still reeking from its former fruit cargoes, nosed into the basin at St. Nazaire.

Their arrival was sobering. Only a small crowd had gathered along the banks of the Loire River to welcome this first contingent of American combat soldiers. There were few men, and most of the women, Marshall noted, wore the black of mourning. They watched silently, as if at a funeral. "Everyone seemed to be on the verge of tears," he recalled.

Bands blaring, Frenchmen had gone off to war in August 1914 in railway cars bravely chalked: "*A Berlin*" and "*Mort aux Boches*"; they had slaughtered Germans and died by the tens of thousands themselves, yet they were mired in trenches no closer to Berlin. A year, two years earlier perhaps, there might have been cheers for *les Amis,* but not now, not after the casualties of the failed Picardy offensive. Hope of victory had faded. Those first hours in France left a lasting impression on Marshall, and an enduring sympathy for the French people.

If Marshall was moved by the plight of the French, the French military was not impressed with the American troops who followed General Sibert and his tall aide down the gangplank. Many of the soldiers wore ill-fitting uniforms; others limped in boots too large or too small. Their appearance was anything but reassuring.

Their military discipline was no better. On the second day ashore, a French general approached General Sibert's office and a lanky sentry wearing an unbuttoned jacket, a watch chain stretched across his stomach. When the general asked to see the private's rifle, the soldier obligingly handed it over, then sat down in the doorway to roll a cigarette. Embarrassed, Marshall "personally got him up, got his blouse buttoned and his rifle back. This man," he added, "was probably one of those remarkably gallant fellows who fought so hard and died so cheerfully not many months later." Word of the general's encounter ran through the French Army, the story embellished with each retelling. Believing this to be a handpicked, veteran unit, the French and British quickly concluded the Americans, like children, would have to be guided by wiser heads.

From the first moments ashore, Marshall was busy planning the move to a training ground picked out behind the quiet right flank of the front lines in Lorraine. On a ride with a French liaison officer, he also made an effort to brush up on his VMI French lessons, commenting on the pleasant morning. "*Je suis très beau aujourd'hui.*" The officer looked quizzically at Marshall, who silently retranslated his remark. "During the ensuing twenty-six months I never spoke French again except when forced to."

In mid-July, the unit, renamed the 1st Division, moved from the coast to Gondrecourt in the Lorraine, one battalion detailed to pass through Paris to take part in the Bastille Day parade. There Marshall met Captain George S. Patton, Jr., the commander of Pershing's headquarters troop, a cavalryman fascinated by France's newly deployed Renault tanks. Together they watched the parade along the Champs-Elysées. The two were impressed by the French troops, and dismayed by the comparatively shabby appearance of the small American contingent. But for the first time, they heard Frenchmen cheer *les Amis*.

From Paris, Marshall traveled to Lorraine's lush green countryside and division headquarters in Gondrecourt, ten miles west of the village of Domremy, birthplace of Jeanne d'Arc. There the division confronted new problems. Impatient French officers pressed hard to have the raw American units fed into the front lines under French and English command; just as firmly General Pershing refused. His men were not ready, and would not have sufficient training for some months. Moreover, he insisted—only the demands of harmony kept his anger in check—when the Americans did go into the line, they would fight as an American army, not as mere reinforcements to be offered up for further slaughter.

At first from afar, later close at hand, Marshall learned of these realities of coalition warfare and international politics. Not since the Civil War had the American Army had any experience in trench warfare, and the sieges of Vicksburg, Petersburg, and Cold Harbor had been bloody campaigns of attrition; since that time, the Army had built its military philosophy on a war of movement, of avoiding the Napoleonic set-piece battle. Not for nothing did professional soldiers study the fast-moving campaigns of Jackson, Sherman, and Sheridan. Fifty years later, Pershing found himself with an officer corps, like himself, averse to the grinding punishment of trench warfare, advocating vigorous maneuver by massed divisions, and aggressive training with rifle, bayonet, and grenade. Pershing was determined "to force the Germans out of their trenches and beat them in the open."

Meanwhile, the anxious French insisted on hurrying their training in defensive trench warfare, the sooner to scatter them along the front from Lorraine on the right to Flanders on the left.

Pershing just as firmly resisted. Fragmenting his army would destroy it as an offensive weapon, and run the risk of intolerable casualties. For all of the United States' patriotic flush, the nation would not long accept the numbing death tolls French and British generals had airily assumed a condition of modern warfare.

To send into battle these green troops—as few as 350 of a regiment's 2,000 men were veterans—was to risk everything. "A reverse, however small, suffered by the first American unit committed to the battle would have had a most depressing effect on all of our Allies, would have encouraged the enemy, and would certainly have given the politicians in the United States an opportunity to play hob with the Army," Marshall fretted.

Further, though Pershing could not state his exact reasons openly, America's planned thirty-nine divisions would fight only as an American Army. To put Americans under the command of French and English generals would be to submerge the United States' contribution to the war. National pride, if not international politics, would not allow this.

Privately, American officers worried too much about the French General Staff. Those commanders, royalists in spirit if not politics, deemed their troops expendable "*pour la gloire*" and treated them with supercilious condescension. Such men would never understand the American Army. Nor did they have any wish to; they were already contemptuous.

In Gondrecourt, the 1st Division's operations officer daily felt the pressure. "We were 'Exhibit A' of the AEF, and there was no 'B,' 'C,' and 'D,' " he noted with some chagrin. Struggling to train the troops in elementary military drill, General Sibert fended off the patronizing French as best he could.

Men drilled on the parade grounds in the morning, then in the afternoon ran through small unit maneuvers based on tactics evolved in the trenches since 1914. As operations officer, Marshall was necessarily involved in virtually everything, from scouting out bivouac and training grounds in the misty countryside to finding scarce automobile transportation. The first six months in France were to be his most depressing; staff officers talked of it as the Winter of Valley Forge.

His only relief from the strain was in the small Gondrecourt home where he had been billeted. His tiny room on the rue Saussi looked into a quiet courtyard with a lilac tree and the terraced garden behind the home. His landlady, Madame Jouatte, was to do much to make the gloomy winter bearable, especially after she began cooking for a small group of officers Marshall invited to form a private mess.

Madame Jouatte found her conventional home upset by the bantering American officers and their French liaison, Lieutenant Jean Hugo, a great-grandson of the celebrated novelist. At first reserved, then a cheerful if middle-age coquette, Madame treated the 1st Division officers as surrogates for her own son, a prisoner of war captured at Verdun the year before. They, in turn, were protective of her, angry at her older husband—"a scoundrel," Marshall believed—who slyly visited his mistress across town.

In August, Marshall received a temporary promotion to major. He had spent nine years waiting for his captain's bars; less than thirteen months later he had jumped another rank. Promotions came quickly in time of war, especially for a captain holding down a position usually filled by a lieutenant colonel.

That same month, Marshall and other 1st Division officers temporarily scattered among French units to observe General Henri Philippe Pétain attack along the Verdun front. Major Marshall watched from a hill as the bombardment lifted and the *poilus* heaved themselves up out of their trenches into the morning fog. Above the clouds and dust, airplanes glittered in the bright sun. It was the first and last picture book battle he would see. After that one brief moment, "battles were inextricably connected with cold and rain, and mud and gloom."

Ranging the battlefield later that morning, he encountered the first of the 10,000 German prisoners the French would bag, dirty and dusty, coughing up the green vomit induced by mustard gas. That afternoon, the excited major accompanied a unit of the Foreign Legion—"so picturesquely described by Ouida in her book, *Under Two Flags*"—during a "wonderfully spectacular" attack.

His first day in combat ended in embarrassment. Caught in a German artillery barrage as he picked his way through a tangle of barbed wire, Marshall dashed for the relative safety of the trenches. He left a portion of his pants a casualty to the wire.

He returned to the division the next day to learn that the chief of staff had been transferred and that General Sibert had named Marshall acting chief. A larger portion of the ever accelerated training fell now to Marshall. The more they trained, the more the pressure mounted, not only on General Sibert but on Marshall in turn. As Exhibit A, they played host to a steady stream of dignitaries, including in early September Georges Clemenceau, preparing to return to the premiership. In passionate, accented English, Clemenceau urged the Americans to speed their training. The situation was grave, the immediate need for the division to enter the line acute. France could not wait for the Americans to reach the highest peaks of perfection. The very course of the war was at stake, the future of France. Her troops were exhausted—like Great Britain, France could no longer replace casualties—and morale was at an ebb.

Pershing too was impatient. During a visit on October 3, 1917, Pershing asked Sibert to comment on a new maneuver developed by Major Theodore Roosevelt, Jr. Sibert himself had seen the exercise only for the first time, and fumbled his critique.

In front of the assembled staff officers, Pershing exploded. "He just gave everybody hell, and he was very severe with General Sibert," Marshall recalled. The division showed little for the time it had spent in training, the general snapped. They had not made good use of the time, and had not followed instructions from Pershing's headquarters at Chaumont.

Embarrassed for his commanding officer, fuming at the injustice, Marshall "decided it was about time for me to make my sacrifice play." The junior officer approached the general and began talking quickly. Pershing shrugged his shoulders as if to dismiss the furious major and turned away. Marshall reached out and halted the general.

"General Pershing, there's something to be said here and I think I should say it because I've been here longest."

Pershing turned back, as angry as the major confronting him. "What have you got to say?"

Marshall knew he was in deep water. But once in, "I might as well not try to float but to splash a little bit."

Splash he did. As one of his deputies wrote later, when Marshall was angry, "his eyes flashed and he talked so rapidly and vehemently no one else could get in a word. He overwhelmed his opponent by a torrent of facts."

The facts tumbled out. The inadequate supplies: men were walking around with gunnysacks on their feet because the quartermaster did not have enough large shoe sizes. The inadequate quarters: troops were scattered all over the countryside, sleeping in barns for a penny a night. The lack of motor transport: they used "Walker's Hack" and that slowed down training in the field. On the torrent ran, Marshall forgetting just what he told the commanding general, but thinking of it always as "an inspired moment."

Finally he stopped. The staff of the division stood silent, nervously looking at the ground.

General Pershing eyed the major narrowly, then huffed, "Well, you must appreciate the troubles we have."

As he turned away, Marshall fired back, "Yes, General, but we have them every day and many a day, and we have to solve every one of them by night."

The two men stalked off, Marshall back to the stunned staff, a partially mollified Pershing to his waiting automobile. Gratefully, Sibert told Marshall he should not have risked his career like that. One or more of the staff predicted the major "was finished" and "would be fired right off."

Marshall shrugged. The worst that could happen to him was duty with troops, "and certainly that would be a great success," he told Sibert.

It was to be a pivotal encounter. Pershing had found an officer who would tell him the truth rather than attempt to gloss inadequacies. Marshall himself was to discover that the general was capable of bearing criticism impersonally, of weighing it without taking offense.

The two men were to meet frequently enough, "for like the only child, we suffered from too much attention," Marshall complained. Whenever the commander of the AEF drove over from his Chaumont headquarters to prod the division along, he would find a moment to talk to the major with the sharp temper. At first distant, their relationship was to become, for men of different generations, unusually close.

On October 20, four months after arriving in France, the 1st Division loaded onto buses, detailed to move into a quiet sector of the front for training in the trenches. The division had acquired a rough semblance of military discipline, though the troops perversely refused to look the military part. They had discarded their government-issued campaign hats with the inconveniently wide brims for Belgian kepis replete with dangling gold tassles, for Alpine caps bought from French Chasseurs, or for decidedly non-regulation turbans fashioned from bathing towels. Many wore sweaters, scarves, and extra socks sent from home. The "petted darlings" of the General Headquarters staff were outraged, to Marshall's amusement. More critically—and Marshall was not amused—the troops were still wearing their summer uniforms as the cool French autumn turned into the biting cold French winter; requisitioned in July, the woolen winter clothes still had not arrived. Cold and wet, the excitement dulled by repetitive training, the division settled into the trenches.

The comparatively quiet sector exploded twelve days later. Early on the morning of November 3, German artillery laid down a barrage that cut the barbed wire in front of the narrow position manned by Company F of the 16th Infantry and tumbled in the muddy trenches. A raiding party followed the barrage into the American position, surprising the bewildered troops, making off with twelve prisoners and leaving three dead. To compound the embarrassment, division headquarters learned of the raid only after German radio stations began broadcasting news of America's first "defeat."

Marshall was the first of the officers from higher headquarters who descended on the stunned company. With the French general who commanded the area, Paul-Emile Bordeaux, Marshall picked his way through the shattered trenches and dugouts, bristling when the Frenchman hinted that the Americans had not resisted the German raid.

"I think General Pershing is going to be very much interested in that reaction of a French commander to American troops," Marshall snapped. General Bordeaux himself had ordered that the Americans were not to send out patrols in front of the wire. Without patrols, the men had felt they could not protect themselves, and with no patrols to sound an early warning, they had been surprised.

The sentences tumbled into a torrent. The general need not fear for the bravery of the Americans, whatever they might lack in technical skills or combat experience, Marshall said heatedly. With a bare show of courtesy, he declined to return to headquarters with the general, instead going off to the hospital to visit the twelve wounded men.

If the Frenchman was taken aback by the junior officer's effrontery, Marshall gave it no thought. "I was representing the division commander who was 100 or more kilometers away so my [lack of] rank didn't cut any figure with me as far as I could see. My job was to represent him and his interests; and his interests were very heavily involved here. This was the first American action and we had been surprised; prisoners had been taken, and the Germans were advertising it."

Chastened, apparently worried about Pershing's reaction were Marshall to follow through with his implied threat, the punctilious General Bordeaux arranged an elaborate funeral for the first American dead of the war. In a near eloquent tribute, Bordeaux requested that the bodies of the three dead "be left with us forever. We will inscribe on their tombs: 'Here lie the first soldiers of the famous Republic of the United States to fall on the soil of France, for justice and liberty.' "

However unsteady the 1st Division would prove during its month on the line, events on the other side of the continent were to press it into combat. In Petrograd, a reputed German agent who had adopted the alias of "Lenin" skulked about the Mariinsky Palace, his beard shaved and his bald head covered with a wig, undermining the tattered Kerensky Provisional Government. Meanwhile, the younger Lev Bronstein, known in the underground as Trotsky, harangued the restless crowds in the Arctic dark along the Nevsky Prospekt. On the night of November 6/7 (October 26 on the Old Russian calendar), their Council of People's Commissars ousted Kerensky, took control of the government, and immediately sued for peace. As the triumphant Germans began shifting some 100 divisions from the Russian to the French front, the Allies intensified their pleas for American reinforcements.

Unhappy with the pace of the 1st Division's training, blaming General Sibert for want of any other convenient scapegoat, Pershing asked the War Department to relieve Sibert. The War Department complied, if for no other reason than that Sibert was an engineer, not an infantryman.

Major Marshall was furious at what he considered the rank injustice, blaming the Chaumont headquarters staff for exceeding even Pershing in severity. Marshall and other members of the division staff complained bitterly in their mess; Marshall's outspoken criticism of the Chaumont staff was "a great mistake," he decided later. "I learned the lesson then I never forgot afterwards."

Sibert's successor, Brigadier General Robert L. Bullard, arrived in mid-December. A driving, assertive graduate of West Point, Bullard had served in the Indian campaigns in the West, fought *insurrectos* in the Philippines, and chased Villa across the Sonoran desert. He expected to whip the 1st Division into shape quickly, and prove Pershing had been correct in tapping him for the post.

Bullard had intended to install Marshall as permanent chief of staff of the division. However, when he learned Marshall had been so outspoken in his criticism of Pershing's staff and of Sibert's removal, the new commanding officer decided Marshall "had no business being the chief of staff in that state of mind. . . ." Instead, Bullard selected Colonel Campbell King, "a much more moderate person [who] didn't get 'het-up' to the extent I did," Marshall conceded.

Marshall instead would remain as the division's operations officer, his bruised feelings salved by yet another temporary promotion. Five days after the new year, he became a lieutenant colonel. War was an unpleasant business, but it had some compensations for the professional soldier.

If he lived through it. Though a staff officer, billeted in dry quarters well behind the front, Marshall's own curiosity had led him into the trenches often. He would be under German bombardment more frequently as Bullard fulfilled his commitment and the 1st Division moved to the front.

Marshall was to learn, first hand, another lesson of war as the division took up positions in the trenches ten miles east of St. Mihiel. Neatly drawn plans that considered every contingency never allowed enough latitude for the weather.

No planner could anticipate the biting cold winds of this unusually severe winter; the heavy snows that alternated with driving rains and sleet; or the great thaw that sent the Meuse River spilling from its banks to flood the low-lying farmlands.

Worst of all was the mud, gummy sludge that sucked at men's feet and turned orderly marches into seething crowds, that oozed into boots, pants and packs, that gripped wagon wheels and swallowed white-eyed mules to their bellies. Whatever the country, whatever the season, infantrymen fought in mud. The dry months were but parched interludes between onslaughts of mud. The 1st Division's infantrymen lived in it, hated it, and, finally, wearily, endured it.

St. Mihiel had been a "quiet" front, the opposing armies only occasionally mounting raids, as if German and French alike were afraid of provoking the other. Meanwhile, the troops dug deeper, and wider, until entire battalions could move in and out of the line on these excavated roadways without being observed. Here in the trenches, liberally coated with chloride of lime to expunge the odor of rotting flesh and human excrement, it was relatively safe. Beyond the barbed wire, feasting on corpses the burial parties had missed, only the rats survived.

The American sector remained still for another month, while nervous troops struggled to enlarge the caved-in shambles turned over to them, digging between false alarms of gas attacks. Walking back to headquarters one evening, Marshall himself triggered a panic when he tried out his gas mask to practice breathing freely through the canister. As he passed a column of wagons, one of the teamsters spied the tall colonel in the cumbersome mask and screamed, "My God! Gas!" The terrified drivers alternately lashed their teams and scrambled for their own gas masks, while the convoy dashed up the road.

On March 1, five days after withstanding a gas attack, the 18th Infantry Regiment successfully turned back a raiding party. "This was the first nearby encounter of American troops with the Germans. Our men fought beautifully and viciously, and covered themselves with glory," Marshall enthused.

The 1st Division was hardly seasoned, even after nine months in France; three other American divisions lagged even further in training. Yet their grace period was to end with a long-anticipated German attack timed to bring victory before American troops could weight the scales in favor of the Allied Powers.

German Chief of Staff Erich Ludendorff too was seized by a desperate timetable. In Germany, restive workers had dragged through another "turnip winter" on paltry rations and adulterated bread. Strikes had spread from city to city; police could no longer control the roving bands of angry civilians demanding food and an end to the war. Berlin was in a virtual state of siege. Ludendorff needed a victory to restore the confidence of the German people in his armies.

On March 21, the German Army struck along a fifty-mile front, splitting the British and French armies, and threatening to roll up the exposed French flank. In his daily report on March 23, Ludendorff boasted, "The English army suffered the greatest defeat in English history."

The British suffered 150,000 casualties as the German offensive "assumed the propositions of a great catastrophe," Marshall estimated. Field Marshal Haig stretched his stricken units to maintain contact with the French, and fed in his last reinforcements. The Germans slowed, then stopped; Haig's casualties had bought time for the Allied cause.

Anticipating a second thrust, on March 28 General Pershing unconditionally offered his four divisions to the gloomy General de Division Henri Philippe Pétain. "Infantry, artillery, aviation, all that we have are yours; use them as you wish." Relinquishing the control he had zealously guarded so long, Pershing was "temporarily jeopardizing his own and even American prestige . . . toward the salvage of the Allied wreck," Marshall wrote. Pershing's offer of reinforcements would allow Pétain to shift seasoned French units to patch the breach.

Pétain accepted gratefully, but for the moment moved only the 1st Division from the quiet Lorraine to Picardy. After a three-day march through green plains broken by low hills, the division moved into the line before the German-occupied town of Cantigny.

The Germans had not penetrated this deeply into Picardy before; the spring countryside lay fallow, unmarked by the war. No trenches wound across farmers' fields; no concrete strongpoints lay hidden in the sudden stands of trees dotted along the gentle hills. The 1st Division was to dig in here.

Ignoring the division headquarters tucked within the wine cellar of a nearby château, Marshall ranged the division area at night, prudently avoiding the targeted roads, reconnoitering the growing trenchworks in the pre-dawn gloom. Movement by daylight was to risk a well-registered artillery barrage.

Even division headquarters was not safe from the uncanny accuracy of German gunners. Rather than sleep in the dank wine cellar, Marshall used the boudoir of the chatelaine, but retreated to the cellar "when they began hitting this building with eight-inch shells which sounded like the end of the world."

Marshall came to understand the second eternal of combat, a constant, gnawing, half-suppressed, half-denied fear. "The daily casualty lists created a feeling in each man's mind that he had but a small chance of coming through unscathed," he wrote later. Gas and gunfire sent the division's casualty toll to 900 in the first month on line.

The French and British were too defensive-minded, Pershing fretted, too willing to absorb what they called the daily "wastage" waiting for the Germans to bleed to death first. He believed that American troops pouring into France could assure the Allied Powers victory only if they went over to the offensive.

Pershing ordered the 1st Division to take the village of Cantigny, perched on the line of hills in front of the American trenches. As tiny as the objective was—a cluster of slate-roofed houses huddling in the shadow of the inevitable spired church and a small château—Cantigny was to be a crucial attack, perhaps pivotal in the course of the war. Pershing stressed that Allied morale required American troops go into battle. A success at Cantigny would also demonstrate that American tactics could break the stalemate on the Western Front. The 1st Division would announce to the Allies and Germans alike that America was, in fact, going to determine the course of the war, on American terms.

As operations officer, Marshall did much of the planning for the attack by the reinforced 28th Infantry Regiment, detailing a precise role for each man in the assault. They spent a week rehearsing in a rear area, then returned to the trenches for the attack.

Marshall almost missed the United States' first offensive gesture of the war. Having escaped repeated shelling and gas barrages, some thirty-six hours before the 28th Infantry jumped off, he set out on a routine inspection. About a mile from headquarters, his horse slipped and rolled over twice. Marshall's left ankle, caught in its stirrup, snapped.

Badly bruised, the ankle swelling in his boot, he managed to crawl back onto the horse and return to the château. Despite the pain, he refused evacuation; the doctor instead taped the ankle and ordered Marshall to keep his foot elevated.

Marshall hobbled around on a pair of too-short crutches, or sat in the fetid wine cellar with his foot propped on a table or chair. Unable to sleep because of the pain, he worked from sixteen to eighteen hours a day for the next week. Not for some days after that, "feeling pretty seedy," would he motor with General Bullard to Beauvais where the general helped him take his first bath since the fracture.

On Tuesday morning, May 28, the 28th Infantry swarmed from its trenches, swept across the neutral No-Man's-Land, and drove the Germans from the town. The attack clicked off as smoothly as an uncontested rehearsal; the regiment suffered but seventy-five casualties.

Seven times the Germans counterattacked over the next three days. Seven times the 28th Regiment stubbornly beat back the attackers, then hunkered down to wait out the increasing artillery barrage. By the end of the week, the German lines had subsided in futile rage, but a ravaged 28th Regiment still held the town.

It had been costly. For an advance of less than a mile along a narrow mile-and-one-quarter front, the division took almost 1,200 casualties, including 199 dead. But General Pershing considered the loss acceptable, a fair price for proving his theory of a war of movement. Elated, he cabled the War Department: "Our troops are the best in Europe and our staffs are the equal of any."

Although Marshall had briefed a large press contingent, the battle for Cantigny was overshadowed in the papers by yet another German offensive. The day before the 28th finally secured the town, Ludendorff sprang yet another assault toward the Marne and Paris. For the third time in this final spring of the war, the German High Command chanced its Russian trump.

Marshal Pétain gambled as well. While the Supreme War Council in Paris loaded trucks with files to evacuate the city—this war could not continue without its paper—Pétain threw in both the untested 2nd and 3rd American Divisions.

The sight alone of the columns of trucks carrying the casual young men of the two divisions toward the Marne lifted French spirits. At Pétain's headquarters, one staff officer recalled, "all felt that they were present at the magical operation of the transfusion of blood. Life arrived in floods to reanimate the mangled body of a France bled white by the innumerable wounds of four years."

The 45,000 American soldiers and Marines of the two divisions took the brunt of the German attack at Belleau Wood and Château-Thierry with the Marne, the last barrier before Paris, at their backs. They fought recklessly in the wheatfields, dying amid the red poppies, and in dark woods where bayonets were a favored weapon. Compared to these two days of savage combat, which blunted the final German advance, the showcase battle of Cantigny seemed insignificant.

Still, for Lieutenant Colonel George Marshall, Cantigny remained memorable. It would be the last time he was to see combat as an infantryman.

CHAPTER

IV

The Steamroller

Exhausted, its ranks pocked with casualties, the 1st Division settled into a defensive line, waiting for additional divisions to join in creating Pershing's American Army. For the men in the rear, the work eased, and in the long twilights of the late spring, the staff played an endless pick-up baseball game in the courtyard of division headquarters. Marshall sat sidelined by his fractured ankle, while enlisted orderlies hooted the officer infielders, and the standoffish lord of the château, a former general himself, watched the antics skeptically. "When a high fly coincided with the bursting of a German shell in the air over the chateau," Marshall recalled, "not even one of Babe Ruth's home runs could have produced more thrills."

The spring respite before the summer's savagery gave Marshall's fracture an opportunity to heal, yet stirred a sense of restlessness too. As a staff officer, he could not be promoted to colonel, since the War Department had reserved that rank only for officers commanding troops. Others had outstripped him in the race for the brigadier general's first star. Benjamin Foulois, once Orville Wright's co-pilot, was already a general, and the month younger Douglas MacArthur was now a full colonel and chief of staff of the 42nd Division.

Marshall formally requested a transfer on June 18 to duty with troops, adding he had been on staff assignments since February 1915, "and I am tired from the incessant strain of office work." Never mind that the incessant strain of combat would be worse; Marshall wanted the crucial promotion that would put his first star within reach.

General Robert Bullard, the division commander, forwarded Marshall's request through channels, but effectively vetoed it on the ground that Marshall was too valuable to spare. "Lt. Col. Marshall's special fitness is staff work. . . . I doubt that in this, whether it be teaching or practice, he has an equal in the Army today." Despite two requests from division commanders for Marshall to serve as brigade or regimental commander, he would stay on staff duty.

The endless baseball game was suspended momentarily on the Fourth of July in favor of a dinner honoring the Americans, who were to be pulled out of the line for refitting. After French officers proposed a series of toasts to their newly blooded comrades, Marshall was hauled to his feet to reply in his best VMI French on behalf of the tipsy Americans. "I had just enough champagne to undertake this duty in a very nonchalant spirit. While the other American officers claimed my speech was verbless," Marshall managed to end "in such a grand burst of oratory" that the French corps commander leaped to his feet, embraced the flushed lieutenant colonel, and kissed him on both cheeks.

The division began pulling out of Picardy for a bivouac northeast of Paris the following day. Despite 4,400 casualties, including 766 dead, the troops were in high spirits. The successive German offensives of the spring had failed, and now the Americans—arriving at the rate of 250,000 per month—were forming.

France found leadership in the Socialist Georges Clemenceau, "the Tiger" of French politics. Disdainful of the war-weary, the new premier bustled between Paris and army headquarters, prodding generals who had settled for a defensive stalemate and low casualties after the 1917 mutinies.

As suspicious as Clemenceau's coalition cabinet was of the English— more than a few members of that "Sacred Union" believed Great Britain intended to fight only until hapless France was exhausted—the premier was fond of Americans. As a schoolteacher-journalist in Virginia he had watched Grant take Richmond in 1865; his first wife was an American. Clemenceau's affection, however, was that of a stern parent; he expected these political naifs to follow his worldly advice.

When the Americans relied on Clemenceau's kindly light to lead them, the premier was affable and affairs ran smoothly. The British were less malleable than the Americans. For months after taking office, Clemenceau had unsuccessfully urged the Allies to adopt the principle of unity of military command. For just as long, the distrustful British had resisted; France, with the most troops in the field, would by rights furnish the supreme commander. Only the near-disaster of the German spring offensives shocked the British—"bled white by frightful losses, its regimental officers shorn away by scores of thousands"—into accepting a single generalissimo to coordinate their separate military efforts. Pershing easily agreed to unity of command, repeating his earlier offer to Pétain, reserving only the right to form his long-delayed American Army once the front stabilized.

The appointment of the white-haired *Maréchal* Ferdinand Foch as supreme commander was long overdue. Through three and a half years of war, the strategy of the bickering Allies had run on uncoordinated, frequently at cross purposes. The English under Haig fought in the northwest with an eye always on the Channel ports, their escape hatch if the Germans routed the Allied armies. The French meanwhile arranged troop displacements and husbanded reinforcements to protect Paris, not only the capital, but the nation's largest industrial center.

Ludendorff had taken advantage of these disparate aims of the Allied strategists in the spring to pound at weakened British units, confident Pétain would never transfer reinforcements from the Paris sector to aid the hard-pressed Haig. With that strategy, Ludendorff had missed victory in the west only by a hairsbreadth, at the cost of 400,000 of his troops.

At sixty-seven, Foch was venerable, though no longer venerated. A week before the climactic meeting of March 26 he had been scorned as a dotard; now "he alone possessed the size and the combative energy to prevent the severance of the French and British armies." Despite France's malaise, Foch stood fixed in his belief of a war of maneuver, expounded in his 1903 *Principles of War*. To that extent, he and the Americans thought alike.

But like most generals, Foch had based his theories on the last war, the Franco-Prussian conflict of thirty years before. He had underestimated the firepower of modern weapons, especially of the machine gun, in neutralizing even massive infantry attacks. Machine gun and barbed wire had combined to produce the numbing casualty tolls of the Somme, of Passchendaele, and the Michael offensive; French, German, and British alike were scythed down by a supreme weapon of defense. Hewing blindly to Foch's textbook doctrine of the *offensive à l'outrance,* French generals had left the nation in despair and its army shattered. France by the winter of 1917 no longer had enough men to mount an attack strong enough to overcome German weaponry. Patriotic slogans and even public executions failed to stir disillusioned troops. At the same time, English tenacity had turned to stubbornness and scapegoating; the British were reduced to drafting fifty-year-olds to fill their depleted armies.

Foch, Clemenceau, and a million comparatively green American reinforcements were to change that, and Lieutenant Colonel George C. Marshall would play a key role. Still hoping for a troop command, Marshall instead was surprised on July 12 with orders transferring him to General Pershing's headquarters at Chaumont.

Marshall said a choked goodbye at 1st Division headquarters. For thirteen months they had worked closely, had risked gas and shelling together, shaping a true American army. They were the firstborn; their shared "trials and tribulations had served to bind us very close to one another. . . . Bigger problems were to come—but never again that feeling of comradeship which grows out of intimate relationship among those in immediate contact with the fighting troops." Marshall had reluctantly taken another step toward the isolation of the very powerful. Nine days later, most of the men who bid him goodbye in the courtyard of the château were dead.

Duty at the former French regimental headquarters in Chaumont seemed strange to Marshall. For a year he had worried about daily necessities for his division, about health and morale, and for the last six months grieving over daily casualty lists. With the 1st Division, he concentrated on matters of literal life and death. "Less frequent visits from critical staff officers in limousines would have met our approval," he noted sourly.

Now he was one of those intruding staff officers, well removed from troops, combat, or even the stray artillery shell. Pershing's headquarters instead concerned itself with such grand matters as the ocean tonnage and ports needed to supply an American Army that might grow to as many as 2 million men; with the production of tanks; and with minister-ial-level relations among the Associated Powers.

The opportunity to work with Colonel Fox Conner, one of the Army's true intellectuals and the AEF's chief of operations, eased the disap-pointment. New friendships helped also, particularly with Colonel Wal-ter S. Grant, also assigned to the Operations Section. The two developed a constantly joking, bantering relationship, and "the more serious the situation, the more absurdities we usually indulged in," Marshall acknowledged.

Marshall arrived at Chaumont just as the momentum of battle hung between the Central and the Allied Powers. Ludendorff's spring offen-sive had failed; the depleted divisions from the Russian front had not been enough. The Germans would try once more before Foch ordered a general counterattack; Marshall's immediate detail at Chaumont was to plan the United States' part of that combined assault. General Persh-ing wanted to reduce the St. Mihiel salient, taken four years earlier by the Germans, and an irritant ever since.

Like some dormant volcano stirring to life, the front rumbled faintly for six weeks while Ludendorff scraped up troops for a last effort, his *Friedensturm* or Peace Assault. Once more his gray-clad armies were to try to burst the aneurysm of the Marne, to draw off reinforcements from Haig's western trenches, then to attack the weakened British front. Haig recognized the German plan easily enough and proposed scattering the sixteen available American divisions all along the line. Pershing stub-bornly refused; Foch and Haig only relented when Pershing threatened to take the matter to the White House.

On the morning of July 15, six German divisions rammed across the Marne five miles east of Château-Thierry and into the unsullied wheat and cornfields on the south bank. The American 28th Infantry Regiment lay in wait there, then opened fire at pointblank range. "This enemy has coolness, one must acknowledge, but he also gave proof that day of a bestial brutality," complained one German survivor of the wheatfields. " 'The Americans are killing everyone!' Such was the terrifying word that spread through all our ranks on the 15th of July."

For three days Parisians forty-five miles away listened anxiously to the incessant thunder of this Second Battle of the Marne. On the third day, the bare remnants of Ludendorff's storm troops straggled back across the river, just as Pétain sprang his counterattack from another quarter. Five miles south of German-held Soissons, on the western side of this bulge, the American 1st, 2nd and French Moroccan Divisions with the Foreign Legionnaires Marshall had so admired drove doggedly into the German lines. At the end of the day, they had advanced six miles through the ripening wheatfields. The fighting was brutal; Marshall's old division suffered 7,200 casualties, including most of the officers who had bid their former operations officer goodbye the week before. The 2nd Division lost 4,925, one quarter of its force at the beginning of the day, but they had broken the stalemate. In Berlin, the Kaiser's chancellor, Count Georg von Hertling, pondered the military dispatches and concluded, "The history of the world was played out in three days."

Now, "wherever American troops appeared," Marshall recalled, "they were cheered and acclaimed by the French populace, truly after the fashion so frequently and erroneously described in the American press prior to this time."

A week later, the jubilant Allied commanders gathered in Paris. Sensing the German weakness, Foch laid out a succession of counterattacks from Flanders on the northwest to the Marne region.

The first of these assaults, led by 462 British tanks, sprang from the fog around Amiens on August 8, "the black day of the Germany army," as Ludendorff called it. British and Commonwealth troops forced a salient six- to seven-miles deep into Germany positions along a twelve-mile front. The Kaiser's army on the Western Front bent, then gave way, demoralized. Ludendorff gave up hope of winning the war that day. He would fight now only to preserve some position at the armistice table, to save the monarchy, and, as he saw it, the ungrateful Germany people themselves.

Seeking to turn retreat into rout, Foch revised his plans. On August 30, he proposed that Pershing limit the long-planned St. Mihiel assault, dispatch two divisions to reinforce the French Second Army, then form a new army as soon as possible for a joint attack north of the Marne.

Furious, Pershing refused. Foch's plan would strip him of his veteran divisions, effectively place them under a French commander, and leave Pershing tending a quiet sector of the front. "This virtually destroys the

American army that we have been trying so long to form," he argued. American participation in the land war would be rendered invisible.

Foch raged at Pershing's stiff-necked and seemingly uncooperative attitude. *"Voulez-vous aller à la bataille?"* he asked, the insult clear.

"Most assuredly, but as an American army and in no other way," Pershing retorted. "If you will assign me a sector, I will take it at once," he promised. For a year he had contemplated the St. Mihiel salient, promised as an American objective; George Marshall had drawn no less than four different plans to reduce that bulge. Pershing would not willingly relinquish what would be a purely American contribution to the defeat of Germany.

Foch could only relent; he needed American arms. Three days later, after what Pershing discreetly described as "considerable sparring," the *maréchal* came to a decision, one that would have a major impact on the career of newly promoted Colonel George C. Marshall. Pershing was to have his St. Mihiel battle, but with limited objectives; he was then to transfer the bulk of his divisions to the Meuse-Argonne, and, supported by the French Second Army, fight a second battle as an American Army.

This new plan was to deprive Marshall of his last chance to lead combat troops. Marine General John A. Lejeune, commanding the 2nd Division, turned up at Pershing's headquarters to ask that Marshall take over one of the 2nd Division's regiments during the St. Mihiel attack. Imploring Lejeune "to make a strong plea for me," Marshall regretfully referred them to General Conner.

Twenty minutes later, Conner and Lejeune were back. Marshall was to move, not to the 2nd Division, but to headquarters of the newly formed First Army.

Disappointed but resigned, Marshall packed his usual package of emergency rations: some chocolate bars, a box of dried figs, and several packages of cigarettes. It was hard to miss this last opportunity to command troops, to be so close to grasping that first star, yet lose it once again. If there was any comfort, it was in the knowledge that he was not the only man overlooked, or worse, cast aside in this war.

A number of Regular Army officers had not done well in France. Many were simply too old to withstand the physical demands, Marshall noted, or unable to cope with the emotional strain. Others drilled so long in the routine of the Regular Army had lost the flexibility necessary in the instant crises of combat. "The high standard of ideals and personal honor engendered in these men by practice and traditions made it particularly hard to relieve them ruthlessly in advance of their clearly evident failure," Marshall wrote in his later memoirs of the war.

The best peacetime commander might not be suited for the battlefield, Marshall had learned, while the best combat officer chafed against the rigid military routines of peacetime. He saw both, conservative and hotspur, as they passed through headquarters to and from the front. Some of those relieved, former students at Leavenworth, dropped by to say goodbye over a glass of brandy and to complain of the injustice done them. Often enough, the instructor of old silently agreed his former students deserved dismissal, yet "to discuss with an old friend the smash-up of his career is tragic and depressing at best, and more particularly when he feels that he has been treated unfairly and an honorable record forever besmirched."

Marshall himself risked the same fate. At headquarters for the First Army in Ligny, the chief of staff, Colonel Hugh Drum, detailed Marshall to draft combat instructions for the St. Mihiel offensive. Fortunately, it was easily done, for he was merely implementing his own operations plan written earlier for General Pershing. Dictating to a stenographer, juggling his own experience with the 1st Division and the dicta he had set down at Chaumont, Marshall rattled off the order. As much as he might have desired a field command, he was in his metier at headquarters.

Three days before the attack, put off until September 12, the newly promoted General Drum assigned Marshall the task of moving troops from the St. Mihiel assault to the Meuse-Argonne for Foch's offensive.

Planning the attack had been challenge enough; extricating 400,000 fighting men from one battlefield and moving them sixty miles to another was unheard of. The shaken Marshall was bearing the cost of Pershing's compromise with Foch. Ten minutes' study of a map indicated that to have the bulk of the American Army deployed to attack by the scheduled September 25 would mean pulling troops out of the St. Mihiel battle after just one day. Yet the tactical plan called for two days of advances after the infantry broke through the German lines; the practical effect was to arbitrarily limit the length of the American advance, to minimize the scope of the victory. Even with a breakthrough, there would not be enough troops to exploit the breach.

Stunned by his estimate, Marshall wandered away from the headquarters, his mind churning concern into anxiety. The entire operation was unprecedented; there was no model to follow. He could not recall a single instance in history where troops fighting one battle were to be pulled out according to a pre-set plan to immediately fight another battle.

He wandered through the small town of Ligny, trying to sort out the problem. In a very real sense, his own career hung in jeopardy. How many times had he seen other officers, with too little time and too few facilities, falter in this past sixteen months? Though good men, they had failed and been reassigned. "One man sacrifices his life on the battlefield and another sacrifices his reputation elsewhere," he thought. But "wars are won by the side that accomplishes the impossible. . . . The army with the higher breaking point wins the decision."

The more Marshall nagged at the problem, the more confused he became. He would have to pull fifteen divisions out of the line, replace them with 200,000 French troops, then move the Americans, their French-manned artillery, their supplies, field kitchens, hospitals, and headquarters, sixty miles over dreadful roads at closely timed intervals, yet keep the migration from snarling in a great tangle.

Had he enough motor transportation, the task would be simplified; but a third of the troops would have to march. There were 3,000 artillery pieces to be reshuffled; horse-drawn artillery moved more slowly than truck-drawn. Engineer, supply, ordnance, and medical units had to be spotted along the roads to provide support. Worst of all, if they were to achieve surprise, the movement would have to take place secretly, at night certainly.

Marshall returned to AEF headquarters early that evening in what he thought of as a more philosophic mood, ready to accept the risk to his reputation if not his career. Walter Grant was waiting for him, grinning at Marshall's dilemma. Grant, after all, had only the problem of redeployment of the troops on the twenty-five miles of the Meuse-Argonne front once Marshall delivered them there.

Closeted in his own office, Marshall made a few false starts at preparing the overall plan. Finally he called in a stenographer, dictating as he studied a map spread before him: "Release and readjustment of units following reduction of St. Mihiel Salient. The following order will serve as a guide. . . ."

Less than an hour later, the order was complete and the stenographer typing it. It covered not only the transfer of troops but the repositioning of those American divisions left behind and French reserves brought up to form a secure defensive position.

Marshall was simultaneously relieved and distressed. The order he had dictated seemed imperfect, yet he had nothing better to offer. He ordered the typed plan delivered to General Drum, the corps' chief of staff. Marshall himself did not want to be there when Drum and General Pershing first read it.

Marshall arrived at his office the next morning to learn General Drum wanted him to report immediately.

A solemn man, burdened equally by responsibility and his own sense of importance, Drum kept Marshall waiting for fifteen minutes. Finally he announced tersely, "General Pershing wishes to speak to you."

Drum came around from behind his desk to escort Marshall into Pershing's office. Drum knocked, and waited for the command, "Come in." As they entered, he turned to Marshall and casually remarked, "That order for the Meuse-Argonne concentration you sent over last night is a dandy. The General thought it was a fine piece of work."

So relieved was he, Marshall could not remember just why he had been summoned to see Pershing. The plan "was the hardest nut I had to crack in France," he decided. Though dissatisfied with it at first, he finally judged the plan for the Meuse-Argonne transfer his best contribution to the war.

Two days later in a driving rain, General Pershing sent his carefully husbanded, slowly built American Army on the offensive. Nine American divisions, with seven more in reserve should they be needed, followed a five-hour artillery barrage into No-Man's-Land. The Germans had held this triangular wedge since 1914, and had fortified it heavily. From concrete pillboxes radiated long communication trenches, virtually bombproof tunnels into the hillsides, and successive layers of barbed-wire entanglements.

Against this formidable obstacle, Pershing launched the bulk of his army. Only three of the divisions had been blooded. Most of the others were only partly trained; more than a few of the replacements had just two months earlier been civilians. They had never fought before as an army, division coordinating with division or with the newly organized tank corps led by Marshall's old acquaintance from headquarters, Lieutenant Colonel George Patton, Jr. Increasing the risks, Pershing had elected just a five-hour barrage from his French artillery units, this to give the Germans less time to call up reinforcements. The planners in AEF headquarters anticipated as many as 50,000 casualties—that was the normal percentage French and British generals expected from such an operation—yet Marshall realized that if they suffered that many, Pershing faced condemnation and removal.

Along with a number of other rear-echelon observers, Marshall awaited the first word of the advance. The battle just begun, the artillery units, their hot barrels turning drops of rain to steam, began pulling out for the Meuse-Argonne front according to Marshall's timetable.

The rain halted, replaced by a morning fog that hung heavy over the swampy ground. The first reports trickled in. The troops were through the wire; they had impatiently walked over the top rather than wait for engineers to blow gaps for them. (Some 800 disbelieving French officers would later visit the battlefield to view the uncut wire; the consensus held the Americans had done the "impossible" because of the size of their feet.)

The first prisoners were wandering dazed in the rear of the assault forces. German resistance had been halfhearted, the stunned troops caught by surprise. Their heavy artillery had been strung out on roads when the attack came, leading piqued French and British observers to claim the Germans were withdrawing when the assault began. Five thousand American casualties that day argued otherwise.

Though French divisions stalled at the apex of the triangular salient, the Americans attacking the twenty-five-mile-long flanks slashed forward. By noon the German commander had ordered a general withdrawal. By five o'clock, American troops had overrun both their first- and second-day objectives. It would take another ten days to end scattered resistance and round up their 15,000 prisoners, but the St. Mihiel salient was no more.

By midday on September 13, AEF headquarters rippled with excitement. The Germans had broken; American casualties were one tenth what they had anticipated. Pershing had used few of the reserve divisions, leaving a corps of fresh, if untested, men to throw into the coming Meuse-Argonne campaign. Having gained their objectives, however, combat officers impatiently halted their troops, meanwhile pressing AEF headquarters for permission to renew the advance. Had not the attack been sharply curtailed so as to begin the removal of troops to the Meuse-Argonne, Marshall believed, American soldiers that afternoon would have marched to the outskirts of Metz, some thirty miles from their jumping-off point.

That night Marshall and Grant argued against renewing the attack the next day. Worrying about the redeployment of troops for the Meuse-Argonne, the two men insisted the assault had lost its momentum. German reinforcements had finally arrived, and the new front lay just outside the range of German artillery in well-fortified Metz. They were better off here than under the walls of the city. Pershing had no choice; his pledge to Marshall Foch required they break off the attack and switch to the Meuse-Argonne.

For the next ten days, Marshall shepherded the movement of some 600,000 men and 900,000 tons of supplies and ammunition from the St. Mihiel sector to and from the new front. It was a massive undertaking, the largest military logistics problem of the war. The long convoys of trucks, horse-drawn wagons, and buses splashed through intermittent rains, moving by night to escape detection. When the narrow lanes clogged with traffic and the pitted roads crumbled under the heavy vehicles, military police and engineers stepped in to keep the muddy flow of troops oozing toward the Meuse-Argonne concentration.

Despite the snarl along the dark highways, at headquarters Marshall and his French liaison officers cooperated smoothly. "It was my fixed policy to make every minor concession without question," Marshall explained, "which usually resulted in settling the more important matters to our advantage."

There were hundreds of modifications to Marshall's original plan.

Closely timed schedules shredded as trucks broke down and were tumbled off the road to clear the way. Units found themselves on the wrong route, unable to turn back in the face of the endless columns behind. Ill-fed horses pulling wagons collapsed in mid-stride, blocking traffic. The incessant drizzle and fog mired the columns, the weather a mixed blessing since it also obscured German observation.

The secrecy held. Marshall took the opportunity one night to have an aching tooth filled by a curious army dentist who sought to pump him about the massive troop concentration. "I rather feared to be too uncommunicative, lest he register his disappointment in my mouth," Marshall wryly admitted. His dental appointment and interrogation alike ended when a lone German aviator lofted a bomb into a nearby courtyard. "The explosion almost resulted in the loss of my tongue, as the dentist was a trifle gunshy and I was none too calm."

AEF headquarters moved to the middle of the concentration area, Marshall setting up his desk on the second floor of the town hall of the village of Souilly. Just outside the *mairie* ran the Sacred Way, the vital lifeline Pétain had used to supply beleaguered Verdun two years before; Marshall himself shared the office from which Pétain had directed the battle. Marshall judged the small village depressing, its single road choked with traffic day and night.

Men and weapons rumbled northward, taking up positions along the line. By the night of September 24, the assault units were in place, the supply depots scattered to the rear, the last artillery pieces scheduled to arrive just hours before the opening bombardment began.

Improvising freely on the plans he had drawn up, relying on a dozen other officers to make necessary changes at thirty-seven railheads and a hundred villages along the routes of march, Marshall monitored the great shift.

"Despite the haste with which all the movements had to be carried out," he wrote with understandable pride eight days after the armistice, despite "the inexperience of most of the commanders in movements of such density, the condition of the animals and the limitations as to roads, the entire movement was carried out without a single element failing to reach its place on the date scheduled, which was, I understand, one day earlier than Marshal Foch considered possible."

Though disappointed that he was not leading troops in this massive autumn offensive, Marshall could take some rueful comfort in a temporary nickname, "Wizard," acquired as a result of the secret troop movement. Even the profoundly critical English were impressed. The London *Times*'s influential military correspondent, Colonel Charles Repington, wrote: "Few people in England know that this operation was preceded by one of the most interesting and difficult Staff operations of the war. . . . It was a fine piece of Staff work and no other Staff could have done it better."

Still preoccupied with that transfer, Marshall did not get around to studying the plan for the Meuse-Argonne offensive until the night of September 25. The next morning, nine American and French divisions, supported by 2,700 artillery pieces and 189 tanks, would begin a drive over the treacherous floodplain between the Meuse River on the right and the Argonne Forest on the left.

The combined American and French thrust northwestward toward Sedan and the vital east-west rail line that ran through Mezières was to be coordinated with three other offensives stretching to the English Channel.

Of the four attacks, the American and French assault between the Meuse and the forest was the most critical. If they drove far enough north, Allied artillery could interdict or destroy the rail lines supplying most of the 1 million Germans in northwest France. That would severely weaken the already strained German defense, while impeding any retreat.

This too had been German-held territory for four years, and for four years well fortified. The German General Staff had laid out three successive defensive lines blocking the valley of the Meuse. In a space of just thirteen miles, the Germans had extended first the Hagen, then behind it the Kriemhilde, and finally the partially complete Freya *stellungen*. To man these lines named after the gods of the Niebelungenlied, Ludendorff eventually assigned fully one third of his forces.

The thirty miles of terrain between the Allied front and Sedan was ideally suited for the defenders. Earlier ravaged by the fighting around Verdun, once placid farms had become tortured wastelands of water-filled shellholes and splintered trees. The valley itself was dominated by a series of fog-shrouded heights, topped by 1,200-foot Montfaucon, all thickly reinforced by German veterans.

At two-thirty on the morning of September 26, Pershing's artillery opened the battle, concentrating on a four-mile-wide sector. The Germans were taken by surprise, unaware of the massive shift from the St. Mihiel sector to this new front. Once again the green American troops walked over the wire and raced into the collapsed German trenches.

Early reports were confused, but by noon AEF headquarters realized the assault had cracked through the defenders. In the Argonne Forest, three American divisions advanced over 2,000 yards. On the other side of the front, III Corps had driven beyond Hagen, and bypassed the dominant heights of Montfaucon in the center. Pershing lashed his commanders, forbade excuses, and stiffened the flagging; they had to press the attack.

By noon of the 27th, II Corps had fought its way to the heights of pivotal Montfauçon, and evened out the front. Then the assault began to slacken. On the first day, they had outrun their artillery support and supplies; on this second they had failed to exploit their successes, in large part, Marshall concluded, due to the inexperience of young officers who could not gather their men after an initial success to renew the attack.

Resupply became crucial. There were simply not enough roads across the battlefields, and those few were clogged for ten kilometers in each direction, Marshall noted. The wounded suffered the most, enduring "long and what must have been agonizing delays" waiting for the unending trains of ambulances to move southward out of the carnage.

They had anticipated the road problem; supplies of crushed rock and engineers stood waiting, but unable to get through. Meanwhile ammunition trains and support units stood locked in colossal traffic jams behind the front.

London and Paris were laced by rumors of an American failure on the battlefield. Soon enough newspapers were reporting a nonexistent "disaster," Marshall grumbled. Pershing now had to deflect yet another political attack. A British delegation demanded the transfer of Pershing's divisions to the British sector where they would fight under experienced commanders. Marshal Foch meanwhile mulled a plan to insert a French army in the middle of the American, and give overall command to the French. The question was no longer could the Allied Powers win, but who would get the credit for the victory.

Even when Pershing renewed the attack, the criticism was to continue. "The propaganda built out of this incident grew by leaps and bounds," Marshall wrote after the war, "and like a snowball it continued to gather weight and size after the Armistice, apparently with the object of depreciating the American effort in order to weaken Mr. Wilson's powerful position at the opening of the Peace Conference in Paris."

By midday of the 28th, the American advance had halted. The inexperienced field commanders had lost contact with their scattered units, making a coordinated attack all but impossible. At the same time, German resistance had stiffened.

The American divisions, especially the inexperienced ones, had taken heavy casualties; many of the men were suffering from "more a nervous exhaustion than a physical," Marshall recalled. No one in the untested divisions knew what to expect; close order drill could never prepare soldiers for the realities of combat. The troops had fought well, but commanders had missed opportunities to press the attack; only realistic field training or combat experience could have taught the young officers and non-commissioned ranks how to exploit small advantages. They had had none.

The squandered opportunities in those first days of the Meuse-Argonne infuriated Marshall. Five years later, writing his own memoirs of the war, Marshall barely suppressed his anger. "Everywhere on the battle-field individuals were paying the price of long years of national unpre-paredness. They paid with their lives and their limbs for the bullheaded obstinacy with which our people had opposed any rational system of training in time of peace, and with which the Congress had reflected this attitude."

For two days the armies heaved at each other, the Germans giving ground grudgingly. Even as he fended off French critics, Pershing sub-stituted three veteran divisions for the green, lagging units in the center of the American line. Once again Marshall was to do the planning, this time to arrange the overnight transfer of some 140,000 troops.

Speed was all. The German situation had become precarious; any timely effort would send the Central Powers hurtling into chaos. On October 1, the commander of the German units in the Ardennes told his weary soldiers, "The fate of a large portion of the western front, perhaps of our nation, depends upon the firm holding of the Verdun front. The Fatherland believes that every commander and every soldier realizes the greatness of his task and that everyone will fulfill his duties to the utmost." Despite General von der Marwitz's brave words, a sense of doom had seeped into his order of the day.

Marwitz's foreboding reflected the gloom at Ludendorff's headquar-ters in Spa. Two days earlier, Bulgaria had signed a hasty armistice. Turkish troops were in wild flight from the British in the Middle East. The emperor Karl of Austria had threatened to seek a separate peace.

Ludendorff the imperious had tearfully proposed to the Kaiser they seek an armistice through President Wilson. The only question now was whether the Kaiser would be forced to abdicate as a condition of the armistice, surrendering Germany to anarchy.

Even as the German note reached the White House, the nine Ameri-can divisions gathered themselves for a new offensive.

Despite criticism from Paris, despite their mistakes, the Americans had driven much farther than the faltering French Army on their left. Con-sequently, the American left flank hung in the air, the gap growing as the American 77th Division on the extreme left inched forward. Small units of combat-wise German infantry were quick to take advantage, slipping behind two understrength battalions of the 308th Infantry Reg-iment and cutting off this "Lost Battalion" in the tangle of the Argonne Forest.

For five days, the 555 men of the 1st and 2nd Battalions under Major Charles Whittlesey held a surrounded defense perimeter while news-men reported their gallant stand from afar. Though this was no more than a minor skirmish, the publicity embarrassed Pershing, seeming to mark the American soldier as gallant but inept.

While the Lost Battalion captured headlines, Pershing massed his armies. He now had more than a million men crammed along a front no more than twenty miles wide. From sheer mass, Marshall's old division, the 1st, overwhelmed the German trenches on October 4, then burst into the rear of the defenses. Other units followed to exploit the breach, pouring through in sweeping arcs that cut off the entrenched Germans. The 1st Division in a second surge finally punched through to relieve the decimated Lost Battalion on October 7. Major Whittlesey, a Wall Street lawyer but eighteen months before, stumbled from the forest a national hero with 194 men left in his command.

The Germans in the Meuse Valley and Argonne Forest buckled. The army Pershing had so jealously hoarded ignored its losses to push in on the increasingly demoralized defenders. Only after eight days did the American assault begin to slacken, the divisions scattered, their supply lines stretched to the breaking. Pershing was finally forced to suspend the attack. His army had pushed twelve miles north in forty-seven days; the once narrow front stretched ninety miles in a curving line from northwest to southeast. Casualties were heavy; the 1st Division alone had 9,000 dead, wounded, and missing. Only one quarter of the men who had marched off the *Tenadores* with Marshall sixteen months earlier were still carried as effectives. Other divisions were as badly stricken; altogether, Marshall had to arrange for the transport to the rear of 176,000 wounded and ill.

Pershing's suspension of the assault in mid-month became pretext for renewed political maneuver. France wanted revenge for four years of war on its soil; Clemenceau considered Wilson's unilateral negotiations on the eve of triumph a threat to French and English hegemony in a postwar Europe. The idealistic Wilson—"a dangerous visionary," according to the chief of the Imperial General Staff, Field Marshal Sir Henry Wilson—hoped to negotiate an equitable armistice rather than a harsh peace dictated by arms.

Prodded by Clemenceau, Foch sent a peremptory order relieving Pershing of command of his army and transferring him to a quiet sector of the front. Foch's order would never do, snapped the French liaison officer to Pershing, Colonel Jacques de Cambrun. "It would be a fatal blunder and would forever obliterate the part America had taken in the war," that descendant of Lafayette advised Pershing. Watching from afar, Colonel Marshall concluded "certain of our Allies . . . feared American prestige on the battlefield."

The American commander drove to Marshal Foch's headquarters and confronted the old man. Each of Foch's arguments Pershing beat down in an angry confrontation both men realized was political, not military. Stripping Pershing of command would also deprive President Wilson— now scorned by the sputtering British chief of the Imperial General Staff as "a vain, ignorant, weak ASS"—of the prestige necessary to negotiate a truce.

Yet removing Pershing might provoke the Americans with their 2 million soldiers to abandon the war. Foch had no heart to stand up to the stubborn Pershing. He withdrew the order, then wearily acceded to Pershing's own proposal that the Americans form a second and third army for independent operations.

The Allied forces gathered for what their commanders confidently believed would be the final campaign. Pershing split his divisions into two independent armies and assigned the First Army to General Hunter Liggett. Liggett as quickly snatched his former aide-de-camp, Colonel George Marshall, to be assistant chief of staff for operations, a position that normally called for a brigadier general's rank. Marshall was to have immediate responsibility for planning the final assault of the war.

Set up once again in Souilly, Marshall discovered an unoccupied bedroom in the curate's home. He settled in, inviting friends passing through the town to sleep there. More than once he shared his bed with an equally worn-out officer. Up before dawn, they would be gone without a word to their still sleeping host. It was a strange life, he thought, appropriately part of the blurred weeks of constant gain, thick mud, hasty improvisations, growing elation, then, finally, exhaustion.

At work, Marshall prepared first a plan of attack for the entire American sector west of the Meuse River. It was to be a "steamroller operation" on distant objectives rather than another of the nibbling advances favored until now by the battle-weary French and British.

Foch set November 1 for the final attack, covertly racing against President Wilson's effort to arrange an armistice. Meanwhile, the new German chancellor, Prince Max of Baden, sought some method of preserving the monarchy. The Kaiser himself wavered, one day ready to resign, the next proclaiming, "A successor of Frederick the Great does not abdicate."

When in mid-October the Allied convergence slowed, Ludendorff momentarily regained his poise. Blustering that politicians were selling out the German Army, he promised to fight on, loyal to the Kaiser. Millions of German soldiers, including a battle-wise corporal from Munich, Adolf Hitler, clutched to the general's excuses as an explanation for the looming defeat.

At five-thirty on the morning of November 1, the American Army broke the comparative calm with an attack along an eighteen-mile front. Assault troops staved in the German defense, plunged through, then fanned out into the countryside. Within two hours, Marshall had reports of a costly success. The infantry had taken casualties unnecessarily because they lacked tank support. "Here was a commentary on the price of unpreparedness to be paid inevitably in human life," Marshall wrote bitterly. "With America the master steel-maker of the world, American infantrymen were denied the support and protection of these land battleships."

By nightfall, German resistance had fragmented. The First Army's advance seemed limited only to how far an infantryman could walk in the daylight hours. The next day, the advance continued, correspondent Thomas Johnson reporting, "Staff officers in the front room of the Souilly *mairie* almost capered before the wall map as the thumbtacks and red string went forward to places that had seemed once as far away as Berlin. The drawn, sleepless face of Colonel George C. Marshall, chief of operations, lighted up as he went over with us the colored lines on his own map and talked with happy sureness of where we would be the next day."

Pressed by the Americans, the Germans began a general retreat. As the line buckled, the nation's will to resist shattered. Sailors mutinied in Wilhelmshaven. In Kiel, sailors and workers formed ad hoc soviets under the direction of German Socialists. First Berlin and Munich succumbed to anarchy, then virtually every city in Germany. In the face of collapse, armed gangs roaming unhindered on the streets of his capital, Kaiser Wilhelm dug in his heels: "I have no intention of quitting because of a few hundred Jews and a thousand workmen." Two more scapegoats had been identified.

Yet even as the war seemed to wind down, George Marshall was drawing up plans for yet another assault, one that was to reverberate for the next three decades.

Directly ahead of the advancing American armies lay the city of Sedan, taken by the Germans four years before. For the French, the city held an emotional significance far beyond its military importance: Germany had administered a crushing defeat to the French Army here in 1870. Marshal Foch had intended the French Fourth Army on the left of the Americans to recapture the city, and had revised the boundary between the two Allied forces to give the lagging French that objective.

Reviewing the battlefield situation on the afternoon of November 5 with Pershing's operations officer, Fox Conner, Marshall concluded he would have to pivot the left wing of his First Army out of the path of the trailing French. Perhaps aware of Foch's attempt to dismiss Pershing, certainly conscious of French contempt for the American soldier, Conner suddenly announced: "It is General Pershing's desire that the troops of the First Army should capture Sedan, and he directs that orders be issued accordingly."

Conner told Marshall to issue the order. Laughing, Marshall asked, "Am I expected to believe that this is General Pershing's order when I know damn well you came to this conclusion during our conversation?"

Conner ignored the question. "That is an order of the commander in chief, which I am authorized to issue in his name. Now get it out as quickly as possible."

With both General Liggett and his chief of staff, Hugh Drum, absent, Marshall was reluctant. He proposed they wait an hour.

Five minutes before the six o'clock deadline, Drum returned; he hastily approved the order, then added a single sentence at the end: "Boundaries will not be considered binding."

Drum's one-sentence addition—of which Marshall approved—served as a goad to zealous officers who needed none. The corps commanders in the First Army took the order as the starting gun in a race to capture Sedan.

Brigadier General Frank Parker sent his 1st Division in five columns on a route march across the front of the 42nd and 77th Divisions on his left. By early morning November 7, even as Germany's representative to the armistice meeting sought to contact Marshal Foch, elements of the American 1st and 42nd Divisions were snarled on the country roads leading to Sedan. Wrapping himself in the decidedly non-regulation muffler his doting mother had sent, Douglas MacArthur, a brigade commander in the 42nd, went forward to investigate the reports of strange troops in his sector.

MacArthur, his garrison cap set at a rakish angle, did not get far. A 1st Division patrol led by a young lieutenant came across MacArthur in the forward area, studying a map, wondering what had gone wrong.

Spying MacArthur's bizarre uniform—"senior officers," MacArthur blandly fibbed, "were permitted to use their own judgment about such matters of personal detail"—the lieutenant mistook the brigadier general for a Germany officer. Who else but the Hun carried a riding crop, or wore high polished boots and a crushed hat? The lieutenant placed the sputtering MacArthur under arrest.

He would not stay long arrested; once identified, he was quickly released with apologies. But such patches on his pride would not soothe what his biographer, William Manchester, called "MacArthur's paranoia." MacArthur, already denied both a division command and the Congressional Medal of Honor, attributed this latest humiliation to "the enmity on the part of certain senior members of Pershing's GHQ staff." He vowed to someday deal with those he derided as "the Chaumont Crowd." (Years of what Marshall considered senseless bickering between MacArthur and the Chaumont cadre would follow. Though one of the Chaumont staff himself, Marshall "didn't have much patience with it, but I wasn't the one receiving the animosity.")

The French would retake Sedan after Pershing generously deferred to them and ordered his divisions to turn aside. Even then Marshall was planning further attacks from the east bank of the Meuse. New York newspaperman Damon Runyon dropped into the Souilly operations room and listened to "a mild-looking, retiring man" discuss Stonewall Jackson's use of infantry. "This man Marshall," Runyon cabled the Hearst newspapers, "is Chief of Operations of Liggett's forces. It was Marshall who had much to do with planning of operations against Sedan, and he turned to the Great Master of Infantrymen for the general scheme. 'Drive the infantry' was the word."

The following day, Marshall learned he was to be transferred to become chief of staff of a new corps, a post that called for promotion to brigadier general. It was a fillip on the expected news of the armistice for the excited officers in the mess. The German representatives were meeting with Marshal Foch in a French railroad car on a siding in the Compiègne Forest. The collapse of the German government and with it the last opposition by its army appeared imminent. The ad hoc Workers and Soldiers Committees openly broadcast calls for peace; a group of German women appealed by radio directly to the women of the United States, asking an end to the fighting. The only question was the possible terms of the armistice, a subject the officers of the mess thrashed out to their own satisfaction between champagne toasts. Both the French attaché and an observer from the British Army weighed the distribution of Germany's colonies among the Allies, to Marshall's amusement. "We had no thought of colonies, but they thought of little else."

When the French attaché magnanimously suggested the United States take possession of Turkish-held Syria, Marshall declined on behalf of his government. "America is opposed to any colony that has a wet or a dry season, and an abnormal number of insects." However, he added on a whim, Bermuda might do nicely. Quite certain the United States' real reason for entering the war lay revealed, the Englishman protested America had no claim on that island. The champagne had taken its toll.

Along the front, the fighting continued sporadically, the troops on both sides concerned only with survival. Berlin had slipped into anarchy; the red flag of the soviet committees flew everywhere. The army itself was out of provisions; hungry soldiers short of ammunition would no longer fight. It was finished. The Kaiser would have to abdicate if only to save Germany from revolution.

Early on the morning of Sunday, November 10, Kaiser Wilhelm II motored into exile in neutral Holland. That day the front gradually fell silent. After a night spent toasting the impending armistice, Marshall dropped into bed at 2:00 a.m. on the morning of November 11. Awakened twice to deal with the movement of four divisions needed for planned drives into Luxembourg, Marshall did not get up for breakfast until ten o'clock that morning. He learned for the first time that the armistice signed on a rail siding in the forest of Compiègne was to go into effect at 11:00 a.m.

A half-hour afterwards, he was in the mess for a late breakfast. Their usual discussion of what should be done to Germany ended abruptly as an unexpected last bomb exploded in the garden, no more than ten yards from where they were sitting. The concussion sent the diners tumbling. Marshall ended up on the floor, an angry bump on his head. Only the thick stone walls of the house had saved their lives. Moments later, a young aviator rushed in, apologizing repeatedly; a bomb stuck in its rack had shaken loose just as he was about to land on the other side of the headquarters building. By the narrowest of margins Marshall had escaped the casualty list in the last moments of the war.

The eleventh hour of the eleventh day of the eleventh month came quietly. In Paris, Marshal Foch shook Clemenceau's hand. "My work is finished. Your work begins," the old soldier warned. Here and there along the front lines from the Channel to the Moselle, a few men cheered. Others wandered shyly into No-Man's-Land to see the face of the enemy. Most sat silently in their trenches, disbelieving, grateful to have survived. The war to end all wars had worn itself out.

CHAPTER

V

The Company of Generals

The offer came suddenly, though not as a great surprise. For the past six months, Colonel George Marshall, the nominal chief of staff of VIII Corps, had performed a series of thankless tasks for General Pershing: organizing the occupation of various German cities along the French border; devising plans for a wider occupation of that sinking country if the German Army refused the armistice; giving morale talks to troops wanting only to go home, to be quit of France, the Army, and endless, pointless training.

The Pershing assignments were routine work for a restless career officer. George Marshall was thirty-nine, still only a temporary colonel, outranked at war's end by men once his junior, men who had held troop commands while he filled repeated staff positions. General Pershing in October 1918 had nominated Colonel Marshall for his first star—faint consolation that—but Congress had delayed a vote on the promotions, the war had ended abruptly, and the need for yet another general in an army that would certainly be demobilized was unclear.

Detailed in late April 1919 to Metz to receive the French Legion of Honor, Marshall barely hesitated when a member of Pershing's staff abruptly asked, "How would you like to be the General's aide?" At the end of the ceremony, he accepted.

His reasons were unclear, beyond frank admiration for Black Jack Pershing; later in life he would argue all his years as an aide were a handicap to his career. Perhaps the motive was no more than a desire to remain in the cockpit of international affairs. Once returned to the States he could look forward to little more than routine troop assignments on isolated posts; his permanent rank of major would qualify him for command of a battalion, if that.

Pershing already had an aide to handle his crowded social calendar. The general wanted Marshall for other, more important duties, as an adviser or personal chief of staff. Marshall might not have his first star, but, at Pershing's side, he would be closer to the very core of the Army than many who did.

The man who was to be Pershing's aide-de-camp for the next five years was not the officer who had earlier served Generals Liggett and Bell as an aide. The responsibilities were greater, and he had developed a nervous tic that pulled the corner of his mouth into a strained smile when he was under pressure; it would never entirely disappear. The past eighteen months had taught the tight-lipped colonel a grim lesson about the carnage that was war. "There is nothing romantic, dramatic, or satisfying in modern conflict. It is all horrible, profoundly depressing," he warned a later audience. Combat produced "hideous losses," often at night, inglorious deaths without heroics. Only once had he glimpsed anything approaching the grandeur of massed armies, those tidy set pieces beloved of generals and authors of tactical manuals. "It always seemed that battles were inextricably connected with cold and rain, and mud and gloom." As valuable as military training might be to a man, "ten minutes of combat was ten minutes too much."

War was no longer a festive march for triumphant heroes returning to Uniontown when Colonel Marshall visited the battlefield where Colonel Jimmy Shannon had been killed. "We had been friends for years in the old Army," Marshall wrote after the armistice with a quaint appreciation of nineteenth-century manly virtues, "and he was always my ideal of a Christian gentleman. Very religious, but most unobtrusively so, a jolly companion, an unusually fine athlete, gentle with his horses, and a perfect model of a husband and father. I don't recall any tragedy of the war that so distressed me as the news of his death."

The Jimmy Shannons lay in France, "while others much less worthy were to survive." Out of the carnage grew a skeptic's special pain. The rows of white crosses in the American Cemetery at Romagne made Marshall reflective, unloosing "perplexing thoughts regarding the bickerings of the Peace Conference then in session in Paris."

Marshall's postwar disillusionment was no more than that of his countrymen. The war had cost the nation the lives of 116,708 men and women, as well as $23.5 billion. Yet the sacrifices had yielded nothing in the face of the prior secret treaties among the European allies, and Clemenceau's unrelenting effort to transform an armistice into a German defeat. Peace, the Tiger coldly insisted, was "the continuation of war by other means."

America's anger was palpable. Even the once internationalist *New Republic* recoiled in distaste: "Americans would be fools if they permitted themselves now to be embroiled in a system of European alliances. . . . The peace cannot last." Wilson the naive had been gulled by the sharpers Clemenceau and Lloyd George.

Wilson would bring home only the proposed Covenant of the League of Nations, little enough, and that the Senate rejected in a spasm of isolationism. Intent on demobilizing a hugely expensive army, Congress hunkered down behind the barriers of two vast oceans and repudiated foreign alliances. The Senate's "Irreconcilables" saw only a noble United States confronted by cynical diplomats from the decaying Old World. Those sentiments, widely shared across the country, would permeate American policy, foreign and domestic, for the next two decades.

Pershing understood that army policy would have to adapt to public opinion. In selecting Marshall as his aide, he recognized a man to help shape that different army. Marshall had emerged from the war the rare soldier. His service with troops had taught him the alternating boredom and terror that was the combat infantryman's life. At the same time, as a staff officer he had gained a larger perspective, one that permitted him knowing judgments on both the principles of command and public policy.

This was the sober man who reported to Pershing's Chaumont head-quarters in mid-April 1919. He found himself tending to the details of moving a two-million-man army and its equipment home from France. Much of his work was undemanding, no more than obligatory ceremonial festivities that filled afternoons and evenings in Paris from July on. Pershing and his staff stayed in the sumptuous home of American lawyer-financier Ogden Mills, and there Marshall met a string of men already prominent in American business affairs or soon to be. Pershing fancied their company; one of his aides, Colonel Willard Straight, had been a partner in J. P. Morgan and Co., and even after Straight's death in the influenza epidemic of December 1918, the general maintained close ties with the House of Morgan.

Not long after joining Pershing in Paris, Marshall met the cautious Dwight Morrow, senior partner of that bellwether banking firm. After the discreet inquiries that marked his firm's manner of doing business, Morrow tendered the tall colonel a position with the Morgan bank. Marshall seemingly gave the offer and the $30,000 annual salary little consideration before turning it down. Nonetheless, he remained friendly with the Morgan people, and especially with budding industrialist Edward Stettinius, Jr., son of a Morgan partner then serving as a dollar-a-year assistant secretary of war. Ed Stettinius and George Marshall would remain lifelong friends, Stettinius managing Marshall's modest investment portfolio from 1921 on.

On Bastille Day 1919, Pershing led the reluctant remnants of the AEF still in France on a grand Victory Parade. Hundreds of thousands of excited Parisians cheered the marchers from the Place de l'Etoile, down the Champs-Elysées, then wheeling left past the Madeleine hung with crimson drapes between its grimy columns, and on to the Place de l'Opéra and the reviewing stand at the Place de la République.

For Colonel George C. Marshall, the cheering was tinged with pathos. Marshall himself felt no exultation, only a vague sorrow perhaps triggered by the thousand blinded and maimed veterans who hobbled at the head of the parade. "As long as I live," he told a young American friend later, "I will never forget the faces I saw that day. . . . Because France was the actual battlefield, I don't suppose there was a single person there who had not lost someone dear." *La gloire* had its price.

London followed, in a week-long social whirl surrounding that city's Victory Parade on July 19. Marshall the aide accompanied Pershing to many of the formal, government-sponsored events, meeting among others the king and queen, platoons of lesser royalty, and Great Britain's secretary of state for war, Winston Churchill. As a relatively young, quite handsome American, Marshall found himself dancing into the early mornings with a cluster of England's reigning beauties.

Marshall's military responsibilities were no heavier than sorting out medals for various British officers or reviewing a selected American regiment with Pershing, the Prince of Wales, and Churchill. (The rosy-cheeked cabinet minister, acknowledging the ratification of the Eighteenth Amendment, growled, "What a magnificent body of men never to take another drink.") The absence of military duties left ample time for balls, afternoon tennis, late evening dinners with attractive women, fireworks displays, and formal receptions.

Cast among royalty, managing even to tramp on the foot of the king of Portugal, Marshall remained poised and unimpressed. The jewels and tiaras on the richly gowned women "were so massive that they did not make much appeal to me as they looked like glass. Pearls were as common as beads," he wrote Lily.

Marshall had one bad moment during the eight days of triumph in England. Having prudently chosen a docile horse from the string furnished by the British Army for the Victory Parade, the colonel had to swap mounts with General Andre Brewster whose chosen horse was fractious. "For eight miles I had the ride of my life," the beast trying to kick spectators, rearing and prancing sideways while Marshall struggled to keep his place in the long column. Just as they entered Admiralty Arch, the horse reared, lost its footing, and fell over backwards. Marshall tumbled clear, rolled three times to escape the flailing hooves, and remounted with the animal still on the ground. "As it turned out, I entered the Arch on a horse, and came out of it on a horse—and did not even lose my place in the line-up." He would long savor that moment of equestrianship, while ruing the broken bone in his hand, and the embarrassment of his spill before thousands of onlookers.

Briefly returned to France, Pershing and his entourage toured battlefields, then left for yet another round of ceremonies in Italy. By now the festivities had begun to pall; Marshall yearned for home and Lily.

On September 1, Pershing, his staff, and selected members of Marshall's old division, the 1st, finally sailed from Brest for New York and the last parades. A news photo of Pershing and his three aides standing on the promenade deck of the liner *Leviathan* captured an amused Marshall, reserved in comparison to the beaming, gesticulating commander of the victorious American Expeditionary Forces.

If the general's personal aide was publicly self-effacing, in private their relationship was something else. Pershing expected Marshall to speak out, to advise, and, if he thought it necessary, to criticize. Marshall did so, discovering in the AEF commander a rare personal objectivity. "I have never seen a man who could listen to as much criticism. . . . You could say what you pleased as long as it was straight, constructive criticism." Other men had influenced him, but in Pershing Marshall found a personal model. "General Pershing as a leader always dominated any gathering where he was. He was a tremendous driver if necessary, a very kindly, likeable man on off-duty status, but very stern on a duty status."

With Pershing assigned to Washington, the Marshalls went house hunting, eventually taking an apartment at 2400 Sixteenth Street, Northwest, a clublike residential hotel favored by such semi-permanent residents of the city as congressmen and military officers. Washington in those smugly content days of the American Century was slow-paced, a town of carriages and liveried "Nigras" still, its life ordered and serene. Even the long, guarded convalescence of President Wilson from a stroke, which left the nation effectively governed by the president's wife, hardly disturbed the city.

In Washington, the colonel and his lady settled down to the longest period of shared domesticity of their married life. These would be comfortable years, rich with friendships and the discovery of a young friend who brought a new quality to their marriage. It was at 2400 Sixteenth Street that the colonel first met eight-year-old Rose Page, daughter of a University of Virginia professor appointed by President Wilson to the United States Tariff Commission. The Marshalls struck up an ever-deepening relationship with the child, one that led him first to become her godfather, then a lifelong friend. Rose idolized the Marshalls, understandably, for here was a tall, handsome officer, married to a generous "Titian goddess," who paid special attention to a child all but lost in a world of adults. Young Rose discovered, however, there was a quid pro quo for Colonel Marshall's courtly company on walks to Rock Creek Park, rides in the Marshalls' new Model T, or visits to their tidy apartment; he expected strict decorum from a high-spirited, inquisitive girl.

When Rose innocently passed along the delicious news picked up in the marble lobby that "a voluptuous young Cuban woman" staying at 2400 was Brigadier General Douglas MacArthur's "sweetheart," Marshall exploded. "Don't you ever repeat talk like that again!" He did not know if it were true; neither did anyone else. He wasn't interested in gossip and expected Rose to respect that.

The girl broke into tears. Marshall, abruptly chastened, curbed his anger, explaining gently, "Careless talk might unfairly and seriously injure a person's reputation."

As Rose Page remembered the Marshall of these inter-war years, he was dashing in a manner her professorial father could not be. "Courtesy was one of Colonel Marshall's irrevocable rules for personal conduct." "The Colonel," as she called him, was chivalrous to women; in turn they valued him as an amusing dinner partner in 2400's gold and white dining room, a "capital raconteur" who did not like to be interrupted when he was talking. For all his popularity, he was "a homebody," devoted to a charming wife who was "a raving beauty."

Marshall lavished a hundred little attentions on Lily, Rose recalled in later years. "He fetched and carried. He planned little surprises. He was ever solicitous about her health and comfort. He relieved her of mundane financial budgeting and any like chores and decisions, and if he teased her, he paid her innumerable little compliments. . . . He gave her his unremitting consideration, smoothed the path before his queen and led her by the hand."

Lily, more capable than her husband allowed her to be, accepted it all with some humor. "George just naturally has to look after me," Lily once told the young Rose. "It's his pleasure, bless his heart. You too. Haven't you noticed how he absolutely has to take care of us fragile females?"

Young Rose was one of the few to penetrate the Marshalls' closely held domestic preserve. The colonel made friendships readily enough, but the couple had relatively few intimates to whom they opened their home. Surprisingly, since he had never sought to curry favor, many of those closest were senior to Marshall in age and rank: John McAuley Palmer, and Pershing himself, then another future chief of staff, John Hines. Marshall might warm to the camaraderie of the mess, or enjoy mixing with other officers at a post dance, but there was none with whom he discussed personal or family affairs. The bounds of rank, coupled with his own reserve, held him more firmly than most professional soldiers.

From Pershing, the colonel so stern on duty learned to unbend at other times, though he often chided high-spirited Rose for her frequent lapses of behavior. He could even coax General Pershing during a visit to the commander's quarters at Fort Myer to allow the girl a ride on Pershing's celebrated horse Jeff.

Rose recalled an enchanting memory of a dignified general and sober colonel entertaining a delighted child. "Pershing led Jeff at a walk around the lawn while I sat on his back, shouting, 'Advance, men! Courage!' and other soldierly commands out of my story books, and each time we passed Lily watching from the veranda, I gave her a smart military salute.

"General Pershing, Jeff and I made three or four circles around the
lawn before we returned to Colonel Marshall.

" 'We won the battle,' the General reported and they both laughed."

Rose became the child the Marshalls, in deference to Lily's heart condition, had never had. Marshall's affection for the girl even led him to
write poetry for her.

> A little girl I strive to please
> Is very shy, but likes to tease
> And tell all sorts of funny jokes
> About all kinds of curious folks.
>
> She likes to ride and dance and coast
> But better still to butter toast
> And smear it deep with honey sweet
> And sit and eat and eat and eat.
>
> I think some time along in spring
> She'l [sic] eat so much of everything
> Her dresses all will spread and split
> And open out to make a fit.
>
> And then perhaps she'l look right thin
> With strips of dress and streaks of skin
> I think she'l look real odd like that
> With nothing whole except her hat.

Pershing and Marshall, despite their matched austerity, developed a
warm friendship, Pershing paternal, Marshall protective. By the end of
1920, Marshall, speaking too for Lily, could write Pershing, "We both
send you our love," an unusual ending for a letter from an aide to a
General of the Armies, the highest ranking officer in United States history.

Service as Pershing's aide offered another benefit, a professional
sophistication few other officers could match. Marshall found himself
thrust, like it or not, into army politics, for Pershing's return to the United
States was less than a happy moment for Army Chief of Staff Peyton
March. A permanent major general, March held four-star rank only so
long as he served as chief of staff. Worse still from March's point of view,
Pershing's rank was not only permanent but he had become a four-star
general first and had seniority. The result was a command snarl of sizable egos.

Less stiff-necked men might have overcome the organizational anomaly, but neither general would yield the prerogatives he thought his due.

Complicating their relationship, President Wilson had used Pershing as his personal representative in France, often enough on purely political matters, thus boosting Pershing's prestige at the expense of the chief of staff. Pershing had treated March, his former artillery instructor in France, as merely the head of the logistical system for the AEF. When Pershing ignored or, worse, disdained strategic and military advice from the chief of staff, March could only sputter in rage.

March's anger was considerable, and unmitigated by any sense of diplomacy. Knowing both men, Marshall was to conclude later that March, "a master administrator," had a capacity for "antagonizing everybody"; March "almost ruined himself by his bitterness. . . ."

An ocean had separated the two egos until Pershing's triumphant return to America. Inevitably these two roosters strutting about Washington's cockpit would clash.

They squared off first on an issue simmering since the armistice, a major military reorganization bill. Congress was intent on deflating the swollen wartime Army to peacetime size; Secretary of War Newton Baker and March acceded to political realities, but sought to incorporate within the bill some of the lessons hard learned in France.

The two men conceived a plan for a standing army of 500,000 men, organized into division cadres that would train raw recruits in time of war. The bill would create a heavy drain on the treasury, at a time when victorious America intended to retreat to its continental fastness.

The Republican-dominated Congress pushed for a less costly program, and found the germ of it in congressional testimony given by Marshall's close friend, Colonel John McAuley Palmer. Palmer had served as a brigade commander in France, and was nominally one of Pershing's Chaumont men. A longtime student of army organization, he had been recalled to the War Department shortly after the armistice to analyze the military's future requirements. His criticism of the March-Baker bill before the Senate Military Affairs Committee was erroneously considered Pershing's voice from afar. March was less than delighted; Palmer would be denied promotion.

March was even less pleased after Pershing himself testified from October 31 to November 2, 1919, before the joint congressional committee on military affairs. Prompted by Marshall and Fox Conner, Pershing elected to support a plan similar to that which Palmer was drafting for Senator James Wadsworth. Chairman of the Senate Military Affairs Committee, Wadsworth wanted none of the expensive March plan, preferring instead a bill—to use Palmer's words—"in harmony with the genius of American institutions." Pershing agreed. A standing army of approximately 300,000 men would be large enough, he testified, its job to be the recruitment and training of the National Guard and reserves. To speed up mobilization, and to create the standing reserve, Pershing advocated eleven months of universal military training followed by a four-year reserve obligation. Only such a citizen army comported with American tradition; by inference, the March-Baker proposal, with its larger standing army, smacked of hated Prussianism.

Pershing's testimony crushed the March bill. In late 1919, Pershing's scheme was more politic, far better attuned to the public mood, fitting indeed for a possible Republican presidential nominee.

As the man who won the war, Pershing was presidential timber. Influential men in the GOP, notably Charles G. Dawes of Chicago's Central Republic Bank, liked Pershing's fiscal conservatism, and dropped hints. Unofficial delegations turned up to urge the general into the race and to fuel that grandest of American ambitions.

Almost alone of those around Pershing, George Marshall disapproved of the general's entry into the campaign; at one point he even dismissed one of the ad hoc state delegations come to beg Pershing's open candidacy. Pershing knew little of partisan politics, Marshall argued. Inevitably, the general would be compromised, as was Grant before him, sullying his achievements as a soldier. Pershing the war hero was honored; Pershing the presidential candidate was a threat to American democracy.

Through the first months of 1920 Pershing listened to more flattering tongues. By June he was poised to accept a draft from the Republican delegates gathered in Chicago. With a deadlock looming, the party professionals instead maneuvered the nomination of another compromise candidate, Ohio Senator Warren Gomaliel Harding, on the tenth ballot. Pershing's presidential posturing was ended.

Detailed by Pershing, Marshall meanwhile spent that summer of 1920 on a War Department committee, chain-smoking Chesterfields, arguing for a reduction in the size of the standard infantry division. Based on their experiences in France, a number of reformers had proposed cutting the 28,000-strong division with four infantry regiments to a three-regiment organization of 17,000 men. The smaller division would provide greater flexibility; what it lacked in mass, it gained in mobility. The "triangular" division of three regiments also gave the commander tighter control of his units, a lesson Marshall had learned with the first American offensive at Cantigny.

A mere permanent major among generals, Marshall was both outranked and outvoted on the committee. General Hugh Drum, his old companion from the First Army, led the opposition and scotched the proposal.

Perhaps out of frustration with the committee's conservatism, Marshall wrote one of his few professional articles that fall. It was a routine piece for *Infantry Journal,* distinguished not so much for bold thinking as for its commonsense arguments that the Army "profit by war experiences."

The frustrations would be different after July 1, 1921, when newly elected President Harding appointed General Pershing to succeed March as chief of staff. From their ornate offices in the State, War and Navy Building next to the White House, Pershing set about instituting the reforms embodied in the Wadsworth bill, Marshall playing a key role. "General Pershing," he explained, "had a way of sending most all of these things into me and nobody knew about it, and all he would put on the paper was 'Colonel M.' Then it was up to me to take a look at it and tell him what I thought. But that was never betrayed outside of the office, that I was put into this position of maybe criticizing my superiors."

Marshall's advice came frankly. On one occasion he criticized Pershing and his deputy, General James Harbord, for proposing changes in a procedure March had earlier instituted. When Marshall disagreed, Pershing slammed his palm down on the desk and roared, "No, by God, we will do it this way!"

Unruffled, Marshall warned, "Now General, just because you hate the guts of General March, you're setting yourself up—and General Harbord, who hates him too—to do something you know damn well is wrong."

Pershing looked narrowly at the colonel, and said, "Well, have it your own way."

Years later Marshall could recall that confrontation with admiration. "General Pershing held no griefs at all. He might be very firm at the time, but if you convinced him, that was the end of that. He accepted that and you went ahead."

These years as personal aide to the army chief of staff were to be the most valuable of Marshall's career. He accompanied his chief to the White House, sitting in on long conversations with President Harding. Through Pershing he met and befriended Charles Dawes, who discussed government monetary policies with him, and Bernard Baruch, the shrewd Wall Street speculator turned into a political sage by *New York Tribune* editor Herbert Bayard Swope's fulsome editorial acknowledgments. He dealt with numbers of congressmen on the two military affairs committees, acquiring a sense of political realities and a knowledge of the legislative process not taught in civics books. However much he personally stood aloof from partisan politics, he understood politics and politicians far better than most military men, certainly far better than he ever let on.

Word of Marshall's function as the unofficial deputy chief of staff quietly circulated about Washington, enhancing his wartime reputation as a wizard of military efficiency. Pershing turned ever more responsibility over to Marshall when the chief of staff left on his annual trip to visit Paris and his mistress. Reading the flow of paper in and out of the office, Marshall came to scan the entire army establishment. He reviewed personnel files, identifying many younger officers who would later rise spectacularly with his backing. He watched, fretted, even grew angry as Congress reneged on its commitment to an army of 300,000.

Rushing to "normalcy," Congress was dominated by concern for "the war debt, high taxes, and their reduction. Economy is demanded by public opinion; everybody loathes war; and a reduction of the military establishment is the easiest political makeshift for immediate retrenchment," Marshall pointed out in a short address to the private Headmasters Association meeting in Boston in 1923. Within two years of the passage of the Army Reorganization Act, Congress had halved the military.

This move to a smaller army fitted neatly a new concept in national political life, deliberate isolationism. Once a hallmark of Progressives alone, the rejection of "foreign entanglements" stood paramount in the minds of most politicians. The United States had demonstrated its strength in the Great War while all of Europe had crumbled; American institutions were, moreover, far superior to the decay of the Old World. Embittered America turned inward, xenophobic. From Louisiana north to Wisconsin, reborn klaverns of white-robed men denounced Catholics, Jews, and blacks—the foreigners, they asserted, who had weakened the strain of self-reliant Anglo-Saxons that had made America great. In Washington, Congress adopted a succession of immigration laws with ever more restrictive quotas based on national origin, favoring always northern Europeans. Immigration fell from 800,000 annually to 164,000 by decade's end.

Complementing this turn inward, there lurked an anti-military streak. With America seemingly safer from attack behind the fastness of two oceans, a large standing army was unnecessary. The Regular Army was progressively reduced to its prewar size, and yet there was still dissatisfaction; when congressmen complained there were too many military men in Washington—the Army's general staff numbered about seventy-five—the chief of staff ordered his men to wear civilian clothes while on duty.

For Marshall, there were also personal disappointments. Reform and promotion alike came slowly to a retrenching army burdened by budget strictures and top-heavy officer lists. Only a temporary colonel, Marshall appeared stuck at the permanent rank of major, his promotion to permanent lieutenant colonel and a field command blocked by an ever parsimonious Senate Military Affairs Committee. Marshall estimated he would have to wait as long as five years before retirements in the ranks above him permitted his own advancement and transfer to that all-important command of troops.

With Pershing's assumption of the chief of staff's office, the general took over Quarters No. 1 and his aide No. 3 at Fort Myer across the Potomac River. The Marshalls slipped easily into the grave round of courtesy visits in official Washington and less formal parties among close friends on the post. Brigadier General John Hines, a friend from the 1st Division's earliest days in France, and his wife motored with them to parties in the Marshalls' new Oakland automobile. Because Lily found cigarette smoke oppressive—or because she enjoyed driving herself—she and Mrs. Hines often left early, leaving their husbands to find their way home later. Marshall rode horseback almost daily, picking favorite mounts from the stable at Fort Myer, sometimes luring General Drum from his desk with the promise they would ride with one or another young woman Marshall had invited.

Marshall drew closer to General Pershing as well. When Marshall's bedridden mother moved into a Washington hotel, he visited her almost daily, sometimes twice daily, on occasion bringing General Pershing along. The visits were another bond between the two men, Pershing a surrogate father to Marshall—who had respected but never felt close to his own father.

Left with time to fill, Marshall decided to follow the lead of both Generals Pershing and Harbord, each writing his memoirs under contract to a publisher, and to set down his own impressions of the war before they faded. Unlike his seniors, he began his manuscript as a private effort, working on it intermittently, only near the end of his tour as Pershing's aide venturing to show the typed pages to a publisher. When the publisher asked for revisions, Marshall put it aside as unworthy; he never had a high regard for his capacity as a writer. (The *Memoirs of My Service in the World War* would not be published until 1976.)

The pleasant years as Pershing's "Colonel M."—at the very center of the Army Marshall had made his life—stretched to 1924. Then, confronted with Pershing's imminent retirement, and finally promoted to the permanent rank of lieutenant colonel, Marshall applied for the troop command he would need to further his career. The chief of staff undoubtedly discussed Marshall's next posting with the chief of infantry, who would actually make the assignment; a general was expected to help his aide along. Certainly this most junior of lieutenant colonels was well rewarded.

After a farewell luncheon hosted by General Pershing, Marshall, his wife, and Lily's mother boarded the army transport *St. Mihiel* in New York Harbor on July 12, 1924. Their destination was the crack 15th Infantry Regiment, stationed in that choicest of overseas assignments, Tientsin, China.

C H A P T E R

VI

A Very Slow Thing to Improve

Once awesome China groaned in anarchy as the transport carrying Lieutenant Colonel and Mrs. George Marshall docked on September 7, 1924, at the port of Chinwangtao. Marshall was to take over as executive officer of the 15th Infantry Regiment, one of five foreign military units that policed the Peiping-to-Mukden railroad and guarded the property of their respective nationals in the riverport city of Tientsin.

The foreign detachments in Shanghai and Tientsin, sixty miles up the Hai River from the coast, had been imposed on the weak Peiping government after the Boxer Rebellion of 1900. The United States had declined its own territorial concession for a decade until 1911; then it had dispatched two battalions of the "Can Do" 15th Regiment to Tientsin, astride the crucial railroad, punctiliously paying rent rather than carving out a concession of its own. With the outbreak of the world war, the United States had assumed the vacated German concession, and the 15th had settled into the brick barracks of one of the most coveted of overseas duty stations. Morale among the 850 officers and men of the United States Army Forces in China was superior, consistent with the venereal disease rate, perennially the highest in the Army.

This was a veteran unit of "fine old soldiers," the new executive officer decided. Many of its privates had been regimental sergeants major during the war, its ranking non-commissioned officers former captains and majors who had taken reductions in rank in order to stay in the service until they were pensioned out. The handpicked officers lived in sumptuous style, attended by staffs of Chinese servants. A ten-room house with ample servants' quarters rented for $15 American; the requisite staff of four or five servants, amahs, and handymen cost an additional $35 to $50. Beyond that, the *Infantry Journal* warned the China-bound officer, "In the course of a tour in China his wife, if he has one, invariably accumulates a rather impressive store of rugs, silver, linen, lingerie, embroideries and other impedimenta that would be utterly beyond his means if priced on Fifth Avenue."

Certainly Lily Marshall was not to be denied. To their "awfully nice house" hard by the military compound on the former Kaiser Wilhelm-strasse, Lily brought a profusion of new purchases. "We quite adore it over here and find life so easy. Many servants and much liquor make things *so* simple," she wrote another former Pershing aide. "We are actually accumulating some lovely things for our house—rugs—old mellow lacquer—some good screens and brocades—linen, etc. Viewed merely as a three-year shopping trip, our tour here would be well worthwhile."

Lieutenant Colonel Marshall was just as delighted with his assignment. After five years as Pershing's aide, he was back with troops, carrying a swagger stick when not armed with the useless ceremonial sword the 15th required of its officers.

As acting commander for his first two and a half months in China, Marshall was immediately tumbled into the middle of yet another civil uprising. Sun Yat-sen's revolution of 1911 had splintered, his Kuomintang withdrawing south of the Yangtze River while three powerful warlords scrambled for power in the north.

Sometime bandit Marshal Chang Tso-lin, the dominant military figure in Manchuria, had marched against rival Marshal Wu Pei-fu, who held Peiping and with it symbolic control of the government. The balance of power between these two lay with Feng Yu-hsiang, the "Christian General," a convert who religiously did what was best for Feng Yu-hsiang. Westerners favored Feng because of his religion, even if he did baptize his recruits en masse with a fire hose; it was the thought that counted.

With three private armies roaming the province of Chihli, Marshall, the 15th Infantry, and the four other concessionaires were on guard. Marshall's command was charged with barring any Chinese but domestic workers from the former German concession and maintaining communications between the American Consulate in Peking and the sea, some 135 miles away.

National policy, not to mention overwhelming odds, dictated tact rather than bluster, diplomacy rather than force. The United States saw no greater mission in China than benevolent paternalism; it sought no special privileges and had even used half of its $25 million in Boxer reparations to educate Chinese students. Americans viewed China as a vast country, teeming with hordes of heathens, ravaged by periodic famine and constant pestilence; American good works were to cure all three conditions while American businessmen profitably introduced the wonders of twentieth-century industry.

This peaceable-kingdom attitude was to garner for the United States great respect and moral authority among the Chinese intelligentsia and middle class. But it also required that the 15th Infantry fulfill its mission

with no greater weapon than a persuasive tongue. As Captain Matthew
B. Ridgway recalled:

> A Chinese force of twelve thousand men, soldiers of Chang Tso-
> lin, were reported to be marching toward the restricted zone. I was
> told to take as many men as I thought I would need to go out and
> divert them. Since not all the forces of the 15th, and the British
> regiment combined, could have done much about "diverting" a force
> of twelve thousand if they had chosen to come in, I picked two men
> to go with me. This was sufficient, I felt, to carry out my instruc-
> tions, which were to use "bluff, expostulation, or entreaty," but under
> no circumstances to fire unless I was fired upon.

When the "tan snake" of the warlord's column skirted the city and
contact with Ridgway, the young captain reported to Lieutenant Colonel
Marshall. "He merely nodded. It was a routine contact."

Just eleven days after arriving in China, Marshall took time to write
General Pershing. Thousands of Chinese troops had passed through the
city for a week or more. The vital railroad was blocked for a hundred
miles. The Chinese quarters of Tientsin were to go under martial law.
"Altogether, I find things very interesting," he noted with cool under-
statement.

Marshall then added a sentiment he would have found difficult to
express in person: "I must confess that I have a hard time remembering
that everything I do is not being done directly for you. My five years
with you will always remain the unique experience of my career. I knew
I would treasure the recollection of that service, but not until I actually
landed here and took up these new duties—not until then did I realize
how much my long association with you was going to mean to me and
how deeply I will miss it."

For the three years of Marshall's tour in China, there would be repeated
alarms and excursions—outbreaks of violence as the Kuomintang struggled to power in the south once again, repeated anti-foreign demonstra-
tions and student strikes. Except as an observer, Marshall was little
involved. China, despite its fascinations, was for Marshall merely another
overseas duty station; it was not, as some 15th Infantry men perceived
it, a second home.

Reverting to executive officer with the arrival of a permanent commander, Marshall settled into the garrison routine. Despite his indifferent record as a student of French, he determined to learn the far more
complex language of China at the regimental language school. If he had
to negotiate rather than shoot his way out of trouble, he needed to learn
Chinese in the four-hours-per-week classes. By the end of January 1925,
he could report confidently to Pershing, "Evidently my Chinese will be

much better than my French." Three months later, he could discuss treaty rights "with a fair degree of fluency." By the middle of July, he wrote former Pershing aide John Hughes with understandable pride, "Now I can carry on a casual conversation in Chinese with far, far less difficulty than I ever could manage in French. And I can understand even the wranglings and squabbles of the rickshaw men." He would complete the regiment's two and one-half year course in just eleven months.

Marshall as executive officer of the regiment was once more at a desk, still administering details, but more knowledgeable than ever on how to get things done the "Army way." Acknowledging he was "stepping out of prescribed channels," he wrote his old friend and new chief of staff, General John Hines, to complain of the hours officers of the regiment spent on courts-martial. Recent changes in the procedure were "harmful . . . squelching the soldierly spirit and developing a tribe of legal quibblers." With something of an eye on his own personal circumstance, he groused that "administrative work is also a heavy handicap on training."

Despite the paperwork, Marshall found time to train a Mongolian pony, then rode eight to twelve miles each morning capped by a mile loop at top speed on the Tientsin race course. He played squash in the afternoons, and tennis at the American Club on Woodrow Wilson Street in the compound. He sought to organize an informal cavalry troop mounted on the small ponies and staged mounted hunting parties.

Meanwhile, he maintained a steady correspondence with Pershing and the new chief of staff. His letters included chatty exchanges of family news, his observations on Chinese politics, and, in one instance, a request of General Hines to visit "that farm home where all the orphan kids hold out" to extend "that very kindly and motherly woman my regards."

Although Lily and her mother remained isolated in the American enclave, unconcerned about the churn of revolution beyond the compound walls, Marshall watched carefully.

"During the last few days," he wrote General Hines in mid-1925,

> a serious anti-foreign sentiment has developed due to the Shanghai student movement and its consequences. To a certain extent, it matters little what the justice or injustice of the affair happens to be. The fact is, that regardless of the merits of the case, the Shanghai student riot has caused a widespread, and as a rule, unreasoning anti-foreign feeling to develop. I suppose it will die down but it must be accepted as a forerunner of definite demands by China for the removal or at least modification of many provisions of the present treaties.
>
> There would be absolute justice in these demands of the Chinese, if they had any form of stable government to guarantee the fulfill-

ment of their obligations under more normal treaty relations. But, unfortunately, there is neither a central nor a stable government; there are merely strong men, or clever men, temporarily acting virtually as dictators.

Six months later he wrote General Pershing that the Chinese puzzle was almost impossible to solve. "There has been so much of wrong doing on both sides, so much of shady transaction between a single power and a single party; there is so much of bitter hatred in the hearts of these people and so much of important business interests involved, that a normal solution can never be found."

Unlike the 15th's newly arrived Major Joseph Stilwell, Marshall—despite his sympathy for the Chinese people—made no special effort to immerse himself in the culture. Stilwell, once intelligence officer with Marshall in the 1st Division, was beginning his second tour in China when he joined the unit as battalion commander in September 1926. "We all felt we were going home," his wife Winifred had written as the family boarded the transport for China.

The eight months Marshall and Stilwell were to serve together in China welded a lasting professional and personal bond between the two. Stilwell was one of the few close enough to call Marshall by his first name, yet the two made an oddly matched pair. Stilwell was as impolitic as Marshall was circumspect. Stilwell larded his conversation with the profanities of a frustrated muleskinner; Marshall confined himself to the infrequent angry "damn." Marshall rode horses, an animal Stilwell deemed "all prance and fart and no sense." No aristocratic riding horse for him; Stilwell the splenetic preferred cross-country running or long marches. The occasional game of tennis with an equally competitive player like Marshall satisfied.

Physically too they were an odd pair, hawk-nosed Stilwell gaunt and slumped, standing three inches shorter than the ever upright Marshall. Marshall looked the officer's part; Stilwell barely bothered with his uniform, and frequently cast off parts of it when he left the cantonment and the watchful eye of the regimental commander.

Intellectually, however, these two friends were much alike, pragmatic rather than philosophical. The war had taught them the same lesson: battlefield conditions demanded officers who were flexible, not men who went by the long-outdated field manual. Both were impatient with anything less than the highest performance, in themselves and in others. For all his profanity and a caustic tongue that would earn him the enduring nickname of "Vinegar Joe," Stilwell was modest about his own accomplishments, a personal quality Marshall appreciated above most. In Stilwell, Marshall also saw the ideal infantry officer, a man who shared the privations of his troops, who earned their respect through his leadership. If Stilwell's battalion was to take a twenty-mile training march, Stilwell walked at the head the full distance.

Marshalls and Stilwells exchanged visits beyond the ritual afternoon teas; Marshall spent a good deal of time playing with the Stilwell children. For Stilwell, and the younger Captain Ridgway, service with Marshall in the 15th Infantry was to be fateful.

These were pivotal years for China as well. The civil war had flared anew in the south. Sun Yat-sen had died in March 1925, politically intestate. His Kuomintang, soon to be renamed the Nationalist Party, fell to a younger, Moscow-trained officer, Chiang Kai-shek, and his adroit Russian political adviser, Mikhail Borodin. Vowing to expel all foreigners, Chiang marched across the Yangtze River, carrying the Nationalist cause to the gates of Shanghai by the end of 1926. Chiang had become a potential rival of the wary northern warlords.

As the end of his three-year tour of duty in China approached, once again Lieutenant Colonel Marshall confronted the question of his next assignment. There were few choices, he confided in a long letter, perhaps the most revealing that survives, to the superintendent of VMI. Three years before he had been asked to take the post of assistant commandant of the Infantry School at Fort Benning, Georgia, but, anxious for duty with troops, he had declined. That offer renewed, then withdrawn, Marshall had instead accepted an invitation from Major General Hanson Ely, another of Pershing's Chaumont men, to lecture at the Army War College in Washington. It was not all he could have asked for, but it was a form of professional recognition, particularly as he was not even a graduate of the War College.

To Brigadier General William H. Cocke's hint that he might retire as superintendent of VMI in favor of Marshall, the lieutenant colonel answered:

As for me, I would never consider throwing up my army career for the uncertainties of your job, unless financially independent. My ideas and methods would too probably arouse the restricting hand of a board of visitors, and I would never willing[ly] place myself in the position of being wholly dependent financially on their good will. As a retired officer, my status would be a little different but that does not happen to be the case. This may seem a strange point of view for one accustomed to the restrictions of army life. But it has been my good fortune to have had a number of jobs where I could pursue a pretty independent course, at least I did pursue such a course. Fortunately for me, the results usually justified the methods, though some of the "old boys" seemed to think I was walking the plank, until the seal of approval was stamped on the enterprise. Of course, I made it my business to be as quietly and unobtrusively independent as the work permitted and went always a considerable distance out of my way in order to be considerate of the opinions and persons of the older officers. But this is merely one way of the world.

Marshall was to cope with worries greater than his assignment in the months to come. Their household goods crated for the long journey home, the Marshalls sailed from China in May 1927. Lily did not feel well; even a slow-paced cross-country drive from San Francisco, and a two-week visit in Lexington, failed to perk her up. Late in July, they moved temporarily into the Washington apartment of Brigadier General John McAuley Palmer, on duty at the Panama Canal; there Marshall nursed his wife, while preparing his lectures for the coming term at the War College.

Lily's condition worsened. Early in August, she entered Walter Reed Hospital for tests. Her chronic heart problem, doctors determined, was aggravated by a goitrous thyroid that required an operation. But Lily grew feebler in the hospital, eating little, and steadily weakening. Rather than operate, doctors sent her home with her husband; he was responsible for building her resistance to the point where they could operate.

Marshall took his weakened wife first to the Palmers' apartment, then finally to their white-columned quarters at the War College, "the pleasantest house we have had in the Army." Lily was determinedly optimistic; the doctor had assured her the operation would leave but a small scar and that easily masked by a necklace. "A heart is a very slow thing to improve, but I pray that I may be back in my own house at the War College before so very long," she wrote in a note to Pershing, thanking him for flowers he had sent.

Two weeks with her doting husband in the white-pillared home on the parade grounds helped Lily. She gained nine pounds, but remained weak, unable to sit up, struggling for breath through a windpipe strangled by the goiter. She returned to the hospital on August 21 for a thyroidectomy the following day.

The operation went slowly, and was far more delicate than the surgeon had anticipated, the goiter grown deep into her chest. The anxious Marshall was not permitted to see his sedated wife for thirty-six hours. For all the reassurances of the doctors, she seemed in very serious condition, leaden with morphine; his visits were limited to but a few moments for the next five days. She improved slowly, but two weeks later, Lily was able to write her aunt, "I believe if I had had any notion beforehand what it would be like I might not have had the courage to face it. . . ."

She looked forward to going home. Her husband, teaching all day long, had done little to unpack their belongings. He was "just sort of picnicking" amid the open packing crates, Lily fretted. She so looked forward to his daily visits to relieve the hospital's routine. "George is so *wonderful* and helps me so. He puts heart and strength in me."

Early on the morning of September 15, the doctor told Lily she could go home the following day. Delighted, she began a letter to her mother. Then very quietly, Elizabeth Coles slumped over, her fluttering heart finally silent. The last word she wrote was "George."*

Summoned to the telephone from a lecture hall, Marshall "spoke for a moment over the phone, then put his head on his arms on the desk in deep grief," a guard at the War College recalled. "I asked him if I could do anything for him, and he replied, 'No, Mr. Throckmorton. I just had word my wife, who was to join me here today, has just died.'"

Marshall was stricken. He wandered numbly about the house they had so anticipated furnishing with their Chinese trophies. He slept only fitfully in the great four-poster bed they had shared for so long. To sixteen-year-old Rose Page, the child he had befriended seven years earlier, he blurted, "Rose, I'm so lonely, so lonely." With a young girl he could let down his carefully guarded reserve.

General Pershing, who had lost his wife and three daughters in a fire, wrote a formal condolence, aware how little such notes helped. "No one knows better than I what such a bereavement means, and my heart goes out to you very fully at this crisis in your life. It is at such moments that we realize that our reliance must be placed in the Father who rules over us all."

Still controlled, the act of writing itself a restraint, Marshall responded:

> The truth is, the thought of all you had endured gives me heart and hope. But twenty-six years of most intimate companionship, something I have known ever since I was a mere boy, leave me lost in my best efforts to adjust myself to future prospects in life. If I had been given to club life or other intimacies with men outside of athletic diversions, or if there was a campaign on or other pressing duty demanding a concentrated effort, then I think I could do better. However, I will find a way.

Despite his pain, after Lily's funeral Marshall showed no outward sign of grief, Rose Page remembered. To the young lady he gave many of Lily's personal effects, the hand-embroidered lingerie smelling of sachet she had brought home from China, strands of pearls, a fur stole, and a

---

*The death certificate, dated September 16, 1927, noted the cause of death as "myocarditis, chronic with auricular fibrillation—goiter, adennomatus, toxic secondary/contributory." It listed her age as forty-four, a last gesture by Marshall to his wife's pretense that she was younger than her forty-seven-year-old husband. Lily was probably fifty-three at the time of her death.

Chinese wrap with billowing silk sleeves. "She used to wear it pouring tea," Marshall recalled wistfully. "She always managed to reach for things so the butterfly sleeves would show."

Memories pressed hard on him. What he needed, Marshall told Rose Page, was a change in assignment, a job that would occupy him both mentally and physically. Restless, yet pinned to a classroom at the War College, he confided later to a friend, "I thought I would explode."

The Army rallied to its own. Chief of Staff Charles F. Summerall, under whom Marshall had served in the closing days of the war, offered his onetime operations officer a choice: he might stay at the War College; transfer to Governor's Island, New York, to serve as chief of staff of a corps; or accept the newly vacated post of assistant commandant of the Infantry School at Fort Benning, Georgia.

As he mulled the choice, the newly appointed governor-general of the Philippines, Henry Stimson, extended an offer to take Marshall back to the islands as his aide. A Wall Street lawyer and devoted internationalist at a time when such sentiments were decidedly out of favor, Stimson had served in one capacity or another with every administration since William Howard Taft's. During the war he had been commissioned in the field artillery—he still asked that subordinates address him as "Colonel"—and had met Marshall at the General Staff School in France. "I have never forgotten the impression of efficiency you made on me when you came to the school at Langres and I had the pleasure of talking to you. . . ." Stimson wrote. Though flattered, Marshall declined the offer; were he to be an aide for the fourth time "to the army at large I would be convicted of being only an aide and never a commander."

Instead, Marshall selected the Infantry School. As assistant commandant, he would have virtually full charge of the Academic Department and control of the curriculum. It was an ideal assignment.

He and his select faculty were to teach company-grade officers small-unit tactics and to train enlisted men to become training cadre themselves in the event of mobilization. They were also to experiment with new infantry tactics and techniques. He could implement theories nurtured since the war, seeking ways to alleviate the rigid, by-the-numbers operational thinking that hobbled so many military men. Moreover, he could expand upon Pershing's concept of battle based on firepower and maneuverability, a concept that had too often faltered during the war because of the inadequacies of these very company-grade officers. The assignment would be a challenge professionally, and his involvement an antidote for his grief.

In just short of five years, Marshall would manage to thoroughly revamp both the instructional style and the tactical concepts taught the 150 lieutenants and captains in each year's class. "We bored from within without cessation during my five years at Benning."

It was slow work, but satisfying. His quarters—a home built in 1850 and now well planted with flowers, a grape arbor, and the obligatory magnolia of southwest Georgia—were attractive, if far larger than a childless widower needed. In all, it was the nicest home he had had in the Army, he decided, and it was there he would first indulge his enduring interest in gardening. He also made time for early morning rides along trails that followed the Chattahoochee River bottom. Benning "was magical with its atmosphere of youthful vigor."

The work helped fill the hours of lingering loneliness. Infantry training when Marshall arrived at Fort Benning was modeled upon the American experience in the war, "a very special form of fighting, one of static or siege warfare," he pointed out in a lecture at the school. The Army would do better to train its young officers for the opening campaign of a war, that first aggressive thrust by an enemy increasingly motorized, with aircraft rather than cavalry to scout ahead. Then there were no settled lines, no well-mapped trenches, no elaborate telephone networks, as the 1st Division had found when it first entered the lines in France.

> . . . Picture the opening campaign of a war. It is a cloud of uncertainties, haste, rapid movements, congestion on the roads, strange terrain, lack of ammunition and supplies at the right place at the right moment, failures of communications, terrific tests of endurance, and misunderstandings in direct proportion to the inexperience of the officers and the aggressive action of the enemy. Add to this a minimum of preliminary information of the enemy and of his dispositions, poor maps, and a speed of movement or in alteration of the situation, resulting from fast flying planes, fast moving tanks, armored cars, and motor transportation in general. There you have warfare of movement such as swept over Belgium or Northern France in 1914, but at far greater speed. That, gentlemen, is what you are supposed to be preparing for.

In bringing about the contemplated reforms, Marshall's first problem was to indoctrinate his staff of eighty instructors in the new order of things. "I found that the technique and practices developed at Benning and Leavenworth would practically halt the development of an open warfare situation, apparently requiring an armistice or some understanding with a complacent enemy," Marshall dryly observed. He insisted his fire-and-maneuver exercises be practical, and student initiative encouraged; no more would they be handed lengthy field orders and expected to march their men mindlessly from paragraph one, section one, through paragraphs two, three, and four.

Striving to simplify, he demanded that his instructors "expunge the bunk. . . ." To mobilize for war, he insisted, "We must develop a technique and methods so simple and so brief that the citizen officer of good common sense can readily grasp the idea."

While some on the faculty stood ready to adopt Marshall's reforms, many were reluctant. Those who would not adapt he quickly replaced with more flexible men.

The turnout of conservative faculty was to give rise in time to two army legends: that Marshall was ruthless in his personnel assignments; and that the Infantry School in the five years of his tenure was to be the breeding ground of army commanders during World War II. There was enough truth in both legends to give them rich currency. Marshall was demanding, and while he may have kept the whispered black book, he took pride in his "wicked memory." He was not one to forget either an outstanding or an inept performance. Some 150 of the students and instructors at the Infantry School during Marshall's years as assistant commandant became generals in the next twenty years. Two of his instructors, Lieutenant Colonel Joseph Stilwell and Major Omar Bradley, were among the leaders in what old army men would call the Benning Revolution.

Combat experience was not the major factor in Marshall's choice of instructors. He was more interested in the men themselves. Bradley was "conspicuous for his ability to handle people," and Stilwell, "a genius for instruction, [was] qualified for any command in peace and war," Marshall wrote on their fitness reports. Most important, both shared Marshall's "move, shoot and communicate" policy, and both had an enduring concern for the men in the ranks that would make them the most respected of commanding generals.

From Marshall, Bradley recalled, he learned "the rudiments of effective command. After once having assigned an officer to his job General Marshall seldom intervened." If a man performed, you left him alone. If not, you either bucked him up or sacked him.

While he filled his days with the ongoing Benning Revolution, the nights and weekends continued to hang heavy on him. A year after Lily's death, he confessed to the visiting Rose Page, "I hate to let you go. I dread returning to an empty house." For twenty-six years Lily had served as his lodestone. Where she was was home, however often they moved, however often they were parted. This place could not be *their* home; he could not quite make it his. At night, he rattled about the house adorned with photographs of Lily. By day he left early to ride, or went hunting, played tennis, and organized fox hunts or amateur theatrical presentations with two other China hands, Stilwell and Major E. Forrest Harding.

Marshall strove not to be alone. Long visits by his sister Marie after their mother died in October 1928, and a succession of guests like Rose Page filled some of the hollow hours. The once taciturn aide became a compulsive conversationalist, as if he could charm his guests to stay a bit longer. He played with the Stilwell children, and invited other young-sters to refreshments in this large and empty house. He even joined the Rotary Club, driving to town in the chauffeured Cadillac the Army pro-vided assistant commandants.

Loneliness was only one of Marshall's concerns. His nervous tic had reappeared. He lost weight, enough so his face appears drawn in con-temporary photographs. He developed a recurrent thyroid condition that triggered an irregular pulse. Such an arrhythmia, if picked up by an army doctor during the required routine examination, would be enough to have him retired. Even whispers of a medical problem might bar him from desirable postings.

Marshall anxiously turned to Lieutenant Colonel Morrison C. Stayer, a medical doctor whom the assistant commandant had earlier appointed to head his supply section at the school. Stayer ordered Marshall to give up cigarettes and Scotch, confidentially prescribed pills for the irregular heartbeat, and privately monitored Marshall's health for the next decade.

Sometime in the spring or early summer of 1929—neither troubled to set down the date—Marshall received an invitation to dinner in nearby Columbus, Georgia. It was to be a small gathering: the hosts, Mr. and Mrs. Tom Hudson, Marshall, and an old college friend of Mrs. Hudson's who was visiting Columbus. The out-of-town visitor was also bringing her seventeen-year-old daughter.

Katherine Tupper Brown had accepted the invitation to dinner some-what reluctantly. Even Mrs. Hudson's assurance that her dinner com-panion was to be "a very interesting officer from Fort Benning" was of little allure to the widow of a year. Her husband, a successful Baltimore lawyer, had been murdered by a dissatisfied client in June 1928, leaving Mrs. Brown and their three children. Their oldest child, Molly, had taken her father's death particularly hard; mother and daughter had spent the winter in Honolulu comforting each other. Before returning to their Baltimore home, Katherine and Molly Brown had accepted an invitation to visit the girl's godmother in Columbus.

Marshall arrived first, and was standing by the fireplace when Mrs. Brown entered the room. "My first impression was of a tall, slender man with sandy hair and deep-set eyes," the widow recalled. She was imme-diately impressed, the more so when he declined a drink.

"You are a rather unusual Army officer, aren't you? I have never known one to refuse a cocktail before," she teased.

Amused, Marshall asked how many army officers she knew.

"Not many," she confessed.

Through the rest of the evening, the two dinner companions bantered back and forth between amusing stories Marshall spun. Mrs. Brown was taken with this army officer, his "way of looking right straight through you," and his imposing stature. When her daughter Molly left early with a young companion, Marshall asked if he might take Mrs. Brown home.

Having assured her he knew the Blanchard residence where Mrs. Brown was staying, Marshall spent an hour driving the streets of the small town of Columbus, while the two of them chatted.

Finally Mrs. Brown asked, "How long have you been at Fort Benning?"

"Two years," the colonel answered.

"Well, after two years, haven't you learned your way around Columbus?"

"Extremely well, or I could not have stayed off the block where Mrs. Blanchard lives."

Widow and widower were attracted to each other, Marshall as smitten as a sober man of forty-eight might be. The following day he invited Mrs. Brown to a reception at the post, then sent an army car to make sure she came. Marshall monopolized her at the reception, and by the end of the day, with Mrs. Brown soon to leave for her home in Baltimore, they had agreed to exchange letters.

Their mutual attraction was understandable. The colonel was gravely dashing, a handsome man in her eyes, experienced in a way her husband, Clifton, had not been. Marshall was no less charmed by the widow, a woman of independence so unlike the devoted Lily.

Katherine Boyce Tupper Brown was a few months short of her forty-seventh birthday when she visited Columbus in 1929. Born in Harrodsburg, Kentucky, the daughter of a Baptist minister, niece of two others, Katherine had displayed unusual determination in leading her own life. She had graduated Hollins College near Roanoke, Virginia, then persuaded her reluctant father to let her enroll in the American Academy of Dramatic Arts in New York. After two years of work there, intent on further stage studies in London, she and her sister talked their ever less enthusiastic father into subsidizing their overseas adventure. When the determined young actress succeeded in winning a place in a touring English repertory company—warned she would have to learn to speak "English"—her allowance stopped. At the beginning of her second season, after hours of diction lessons, she was promoted to leading lady, playing both Shakespearean and Restoration heroines in the provinces.

It was hard work, and far less glamorous than a would-be Sarah Bernhardt might have wanted. She collapsed at the start of her third season; doctors in Newcastle-on-Tyne's hospital concluded she was suffering from tuberculosis of the liver.

Katherine and her sister returned home, where a Baltimore specialist decided the budding actress was suffering only from exhaustion. He recommended a rest in the Adirondack Mountains. When a friend from childhood, Clifton S. Brown, asked the hazel-eyed Katherine to marry him, she demurred. Still intent upon a stage career, she instead joined Richard Mansfield's celebrated theatrical company in Chicago.

She collapsed a second time after a handful of performances, and fled again to the Adirondacks. When Brown proposed a second time, the young woman acceded. The decision to give up her dream tormented her; for two years she was unable even to enter a theater, she told Marshall's biographer, Forrest Pogue.

As time passed, the disappointed actress settled into a comfortable life as the wife of a successful attorney. The Browns had three children: Molly, Clifton Junior, and Allen. They purchased a home, and Mrs. Brown used some of her own money to buy a summer cottage on Fire Island, one of the first of those to make this a haven for writers and artists. If she had sacrificed the excitement of the theater, she had gained the settled security of the affluent middle class. Then her husband was murdered.

For a second time the world she had carefully erected came apart. While she enjoyed a comfortable income from her late husband's investments, the onetime actress, then dutiful wife was now attempting to paste together a new life. She did not expect to remarry, she told Marshall. He echoed her feelings.

The assurances were shallow defenses for two people who had each deeply grieved. During the summer, they exchanged letters, Marshall going so far as to arrange another invitation for the comely Mrs. Brown to visit in Columbus. When the lady did finally accept, the following spring, Marshall once again monopolized her evenings.

By the end of the visit, Mrs. Brown thought of them as "tentatively engaged," her hesitation that of a woman unsure of her children's acceptance of a stepfather. Molly liked the man she had taken to calling "Colonel"; her younger brother Clifton, fifteen, appeared understanding, if not enthusiastic. Mrs. Brown worried most about twelve-year-old Allen's reaction.

She decided to ask Marshall to visit her on Fire Island during the summer, to spend time with her children. Young Allen was at first dismayed, telling his mother, "I don't know about that, we are happy enough as we are." The next morning, the boy recanted. "It is all right, Mother, about your asking Colonel Marshall." He wrote a note to the colonel, solemnly assuring him, "I hope you will come to Fire Island. Don't be nervous, it is OK with me." It was signed, "A friend in need is a friend indeed. Allen Brown."

Marshall spent five weeks with the Brown family on Fire Island during the early summer of 1930. By the time he left for a Wyoming hunting trip at the end of July, they had agreed upon an October 15 wedding date.

They planned a quiet family wedding in Baltimore, Marshall deliberately asking only General Pershing to stand up with him. No one else in Washington was invited, he wrote the general, for "we hope to do this thing as quietly as possible."

It was not to be. When word leaked out that the celebrated AEF commander would be present at Emmanuel Episcopal Church, large crowds, far outnumbering the wedding party, turned out to see the hero. The crush at the railroad station after the ceremony was even greater. Few "quiet" weddings are quite as tumultuous.

With coaching from her husband, Katherine Tupper Brown Marshall accommodated herself to life on a military post. Her husband, his home once more a haven, picked up his old routine.

Shortly after the wedding, Pershing asked Marshall to review the manuscript of his memoirs to be published the following year. Marshall read it, ever the protective aide, with an eye out for "any portion which would give rise to acrimonious debate." Tactful he might be, but he would not duck all controversy. "I suggest you point out the real difficulty," he advised Pershing, "which was a collection of old officers at the head of every [American] division, who had ceased mental development years before."

On a hasty trip to Washington to read a draft of the manuscript, the colonel met for the first time a promising young officer, Major Dwight Eisenhower, who had edited the revision.

Eisenhower knew a good deal about Marshall before the two ever met. Stationed in Panama for two years, Eisenhower had fallen under the influence of the scholarly Fox Conner, already predicting that the harsh Versailles Treaty would lead to a second world war. Conner had recommended Eisenhower seek an assignment with Marshall. "In the new war we will have to fight beside allies and George Marshall knows more about the technique of arranging allied commands than any man I know. He is nothing short of a genius," Conner advised.

The genius recommended that Pershing reject Eisenhower's revision of the manuscript. Impressed with the younger man, however, Marshall offered him a position on the Infantry School faculty. Eisenhower, with prior orders to another posting, had to decline.

Marshall by 1930 had reached a level of influence few officers below the rank of general could claim. His home life was full again, his work at the Infantry School rewarding, his reputation within the Army secure, however slow promotions were to come in a peacetime army suddenly confronting the Great Crash and savage budget cuts.

Because army regulations required that officers below the rank of brigadier general perform duty with troops at least one in every five years, the Infantry School commander, Brigadier General Campbell King, on April 25, 1931, issued a special order nominally assigning Marshall to the 24th Infantry at Fort Benning "for duty with troops, in addition to his other duties." King's order was a bureaucratic evasion of a bureau-cratic rule, but it permitted Marshall, the ostensible second-in-command of a regiment, to supervise a year of joint armor-infantry tactical exer-cises at the school. Marshall's infantry revolution had spread to a second branch.

Marshall was a contented man. The colonel and his lady rode eight to ten miles every afternoon. Marshall played tennis and took longer rides at other times. He and young Allen, growing closer, went hunting for wildcats on the reservation. With real affection, he welcomed Molly and a girl friend, who filled the house with their friends for a month.

Marshall was less driven or turned inward. There crept into his letters a new thoughtfulness of others. When his sister's husband suffered a nervous breakdown, the Marshalls invited him to recuperate in their home. He wrote Pershing asking that the retired general of the armies put in a word with the chief of staff on behalf of an elderly colonel's promotion. He forwarded certificates for Thirty-second Degree Masonry to the general at the request of two "fine old soldiers, master sergeants" who wanted Pershing's signature on the documents. On behalf of an over-age lieutenant with whom he had served in China, Marshall suc-cessfully petitioned that the junior officer be permitted to attend the vital Command and General Staff School at Leavenworth. Lily's death, his grief, his marriage to Katherine—something had loosened a gener-osity of spirit and spurred a willingness to seek favors for others.

At the close of the school year in June 1932, Marshall was routinely reassigned to Fort Screven, Georgia, "an unimportant station" in the Army's scheme of things, but one, he wrote Pershing, which "at least keeps me away from office work and high theory." Marshall was to take command of one battalion of the 8th Infantry stationed at the post on Tybee Island, some eighteen miles from Savannah. Marshall left the Infantry School with an enthusiastic benediction for his "splendid work" in the commanding officer's annual report:

> Under his direction each year has witnessed a steady and marked improvement in the subject matter covered, as well as the methods of instruction in the school. The present high standard attained is due to his energy, his foresight and his very unusual qualifications.

It was but another in a long string of such commendations. It set him no closer to the coveted first star. If that promotion did not come soon, George C. Marshall risked forced retirement as a superannuated colo-nel.

C H A P T E R

VII

The Make

Wall Street's bravado of October 1929 had vanished. Now even the affluent men who so confidently had waved aside the successive crashes as a
temporary pause in the march to continuous prosperity were screwed
tight. Gone too was the superheated excitement of the twenties, replaced
by a gray pessimism and the insecurity of men who waited fearfully for
pink slips in their pay envelopes.

A once proud army had been reduced to a budget-starved anti-riot
force. President Hoover sent a secret message to Republican leaders in
the Senate in June 1932 asking them to delete army and navy enlisted
personnel from a proposed 10 percent pay cut for all government
employees; he did not want to have to rely on a military unhappy with
lower wages in case of internal disorder. Congress cut anyway.

The Army's new chief of staff, Douglas MacArthur, continually reviewed
War Plan White, the mobilization to suppress domestic rebellion. To the
anxious men in the White House, the threat was real. Dynamite wars
and night ambushes wracked the dark and bloody ground of Harlan
County, Kentucky, through the bitter winter of 1931. Miners in West
Virginia had broken into company stores, stealing food and supplies for
their families after the mines closed. In Oklahoma, dirt farmers and the
unemployed rioted for food. Miners and scabs fought pitched battles in
southern Illinois; the nervous governor had called out the National Guard.

The tension spread to Washington itself, when 20,000 rag-tag members of the Bonus Expeditionary Force marched on the capital, seeking
early payment of their veterans' bonuses. President Hoover sat silent in
the White House, then on July 28, 1932, ordered the Army to disperse
the marchers and their families squatting peacefully in a "Hooverville"
thrown up at Anacostia Flats.

That night, a tight-lipped president watched from the Lincoln Study as the shacks burned. The crimson glow lighted the Capitol, and doomed Hoover to one term.

MacArthur defended his troops, asserting the "mob" smelled of "the essence of revolution." The *Washington News* was closer to the mark: "What a pitiful spectacle is that of the great American Government, mightiest in the world, chasing unarmed men, women and children with Army tanks. If the Army must be called out to make war on unarmed citizens, this is no longer America."

Herbert Hoover, radiating defeat and the paralysis of will that had affected his administration, merely went through the motions of campaigning that fall. Dismissed earlier by the lordly columnist Walter Lippmann as a "kind of amiable boy scout," Franklin Delano Roosevelt swept into office in a landslide.

In the capital for a meeting of the Civilian Military Education Fund, Marshall watched Roosevelt's inauguration parade on March 4, 1933— and was caught short himself after lending an acquaintance five dollars when the new president suddenly announced a bank holiday the next morning. Otherwise temporary Colonel George C. Marshall was yet untouched by the social cataclysm of the Depression. The Marshalls were comfortably established. They were able to live on his reduced pay as a lieutenant colonel, while Mrs. Marshall enrolled her children in private schools and sent Molly on a year-long, round-the-world trip.

The younger officers and enlisted men of Marshall's new command in the 8th Infantry were not as fortunate. Congress had mandated furloughs without pay, and a freeze on pay raises with promotions and seniority. The practical effect was to reduce a second lieutenant's monthly salary to $119, almost one fifth less than he might have received twenty-five years earlier. The ranks were even harder hit; privates suffered reuctions in pay as high as 44.7 percent, sergeants from 20 to 23 percent.

In his first months at Fort Screven, the new regimental commander worked to alleviate the straitened circumstances of his 400-man battalion. He personally oversaw the laying out of vegetable gardens and the erection of chicken coops and hog pens to help feed the families of the troops. He ordered the mess officer to prepare larger portions of the midday meal, then permitted his men to buy at cost hot meals to take home to their families; ten cents would feed a soldier's family regardless of size that summer at Fort Screven. "We ate this mid-day dinner ourselves until the custom was well-established," Mrs. Marshall recalled, "so that he might know what the men were getting." The colonel's presence would throttle any prideful resistance to "taking charity" as well.

Meanwhile, he began dressing up the post. On his morning horseback tours he noted places where planting or a paintbrush would improve appearances. When the commanding officer and his lady began tidying up the yard around their cottagelike home, younger officers too decided to plant grass, shrubs, and flowers. No detail—including the scuffed tennis shoes of young women on the courts—slipped his ken. He managed the tiny post, a younger officer observed, "as would a Southern planter his domain."

Before he had finished his first year at Screven, an inspector general noted that despite the grave financial condition of younger officers, Marshall deserved a commendation "for the efficient and economical administration of his duties and the high state of morale of his command."

Marshall's responsibilities were to expand vastly with the election of Franklin Roosevelt. Inaugurated on March 4, having declared the bank holiday on the 5th, on Sunday night, March 12, Roosevelt broadcast the first of his Fireside Chats. Sixty million Americans listened to their president explain the banking crisis in everyday language, and found hope. In one week," columnist Walter Lippmann wrote of the amiable Boy Scout, "the nation, which had lost confidence in everything and everybody, has regained confidence in the government and in itself."

Two days later, the president told adviser Raymond Moley of a scheme that would put unemployed young men into conservation work in the national forests. Within a week that proposal went to Congress, calling for the creation of a Civilian Conservation Corps (CCC).

The plan was complex. The Labor Department was to recruit the volunteers. The Army was to train them. Agriculture and Interior would supervise the actual work. By March 31, the president's concept was law, passed in the rush of remedial legislation celebrated as the Hundred Days.

The Army took the lead in the CCC, and thus restored some of the luster lost during the expulsion of the BEF from Anacostia. The president wanted action—250,000 young men in the training camps by summer—and action he would get. By the end of July, the Army had created 1,468 work camps across the country and had settled the 250,000 young men, 25,000 world war veterans, and another 25,000 foresters and woodsmen in them.

The chores assigned the young men ranged from planting 200 million trees in a vast soil conservation effort, to cutting fire breaks, to cleaning streams, beaches, and historical battlefields, building small reservoirs, coffer dams, and fish ponds, and refurbishing roads, bridges, and trails in national parks.

To do all this, eighteen- to twenty-five-year-olds on relief were to be shipped to training camps set up by the Army. There they would be "inducted" for periods ranging from six months to one year, taught simple job skills, fed and housed, given medical treatment, then sent into the woods to work.

Many army men had grave reservations about such salvage work. Almost 10 percent of the CCC volunteers were blacks and all of them were poor, keen irritants to a caste- and status-bound army establishment. Training the unemployed in simple health care and discipline merely to cut trees offended some professional soldiers.

The concept appealed to Marshall. Notified Screven would be responsible for 500 recruits, Marshall threw himself into the CCC work, setting up seventeen camps in South Carolina and northern Georgia for 4,500. When the corps commander asked for more men to staff other hastily organized receiving stations, Marshall dispatched most of his officers and ran Screven with first sergeants.

The lieutenant colonel was deeply involved in CCC training in May 1933 when he learned that his promotion to the permanent rank of colonel had finally come through. It had taken ten years, "a long wait for one grade," he wrote Pershing, half in resignation, half in relief. With the promotion came a transfer to Fort Moultrie, South Carolina, and command of the full 8th Infantry Regiment.

By then the new colonel had concluded that the CCC mobilization was "a splendid experience for the War Department and the Army," a trial run for Mobilization Day in the event of war. The Army had far surpassed its World War I record, but, Marshall cautioned Pershing, the War Department "has got a lot to learn about decentralization and simplicity."

As commander of the 8th Infantry, the colonel filled his days with the CCC while his wife set about restoring the run-down commanding officers' quarters of this post in the middle of Charleston Harbor. The satisfactions for Marshall were large. He not only was in command of a regiment, but that understrength outfit was busy with a task far more vital and interesting than the routine chores of garrison life.

In the next months he set up an additional fifteen CCC camps in South Carolina, staffed them, then supervised the mobilization of the volunteers to fill those camps. This was rewarding work personally, watching the often sullen, malnourished young men regain confidence and health. Later, when the press of the mobilization eased, Marshall would institute remedial education programs and expand health care services. They were reclaiming young men who would otherwise have drifted into lifelong poverty.

Marshall enthusiastically praised the CCC publicly as "the greatest social experiment outside of Russia." To make the experiment succeed in South Carolina and northern Georgia, he could be "pretty ruthless about getting rid of the poor fish" among the officers. "I made it unmistakably clear to the captains that their continuance on this duty would depend entirely on the efficiency of their companies, the administration of the camp, excellence of the mess, morale of the men and work done in the woods. . . . I would be compelled to protect the interests of 200 boys, rather than one reserve officer."

The War Department too discovered the benefits of the popular CCC, which was to enroll 2.5 million men in its ranks before it was ended. Quite quickly the onerous and distasteful work, as the acting chief of infantry had described it, put an end to congressional discussions of cutting the regular officer corps by another 4,000. Chief of Staff Douglas MacArthur publicly suggested the CCC volunteers could be the trained nucleus of the enlisted reserve created by the half-forgotten Army Reorganization Act; such pacifist-minded figures as Reinhold Niebuhr and John Dewey lobbied that to a sudden death in the White House. Assistant Secretary of War Harry H. Woodring proposed the Army take control of the entire program, from training through service, creating "economic storm troops." Woodring suffered Roosevelt's reprimand; the president wanted nothing smacking of war talk. The new chancellor of Germany, Herr Hitler, had pulled his country from the League of Nations, condemned the inequities of the Versailles Treaty, and announced a military rearmament effort.

Colonel Marshall was deeply engrossed in the CCC work and refurbishing Fort Moultrie when he suddenly received orders in October 1933 transferring him to Chicago as chief of staff of the National Guard's 33rd Division.

The change of assignment came as a shock; the Marshalls had anticipated at least a two-year tour of duty at Moultrie in a delightful home looking out on the ocean. Even as the orders arrived, a van of Katherine's antique furniture awaited unloading before their repainted quarters.

Professionally, the blow was even worse. He was to be removed once more from a troop command, the way of promotion. Moreover, he would not be with Regulars but with the National Guard, which, for all its influence in state politics, was still considered no more than a dumping ground for poor officers. Finally, the Marshalls would be moving from a comparatively small post, offering ample outdoor pleasures, to the nation's second largest city. Just when it appeared he was on his way to that first star, he had been shunted aside.

Marshall had been assigned to the 33rd Division at the request of its commander, Major General Roy D. Keehn, a man of influence in Washington by virtue of his civilian job as attorney for William Randolph Hearst's interests in Chicago. In addition, he was prominent in Democratic Party politics and within the nationwide National Guard Association. When Robert W. McCormick's powerful *Chicago Tribune* had charged Keehn's division was not capable of coping with expected strikes in the mines of southern Illinois or with massive hunger marches that winter, party, Army, and administration moved decisively to choke off the bad press.

Keehn had asked for a new chief of staff to improve the division's shoddy training and performance. Chief of Staff MacArthur selected Marshall's name, despite the notation that the new colonel preferred to stay at Moultrie. MacArthur wired Keehn, suggesting Marshall: "He has no superior among Infantry colonels." Keehn looked no further.

For the first time in his career, Marshall sought special consideration. Detached service once more, after a long stint at Fort Benning, would be detrimental to his career, he argued in a letter to MacArthur. He asked to remain with his regiment.

In what Marshall thought "a very sympathetic manner," MacArthur only reaffirmed the colonel's transfer.

His career stalled, the frustrated Marshall reported as chief training officer of the Illinois National Guard. "Those first months in Chicago I shall never forget," Katherine Marshall wrote later. "George had a grey, drawn look which I had never seen before, and have seldom seen since." By December, his enthusiasm had returned, she recalled, but some bitterness remained during his entire tour in the city.

His hopes for the first star dwindled. When Rose Page visited, she asked how long before her beloved "Colonel" would be army chief of staff.

"Well, Rosie, it looks now as if I never will," he acknowledged. "If I don't make brigadier general soon, I'll be so far behind in seniority I won't even be in the running."

Angered by his doubts, the young woman scolded him. Marshall leaned over and kissed her. "Thank you for your confidence." He had little himself.

Though the National Guard had been called out during the fall and winter of 1932, the threatened civil disorders and the hunger strikes of 1933 never materialized. Chicago remained a grimy city weighted by Depression. Just half of its wage earners were employed; the city's welfare efforts had dried up with the adjournment of a heedless state legislature in Springfield.

For Marshall personally, there were few friends; Chicago contained no companions from former assignments until Major General Frank R. McCoy took command of the VI Corps Area, headquartered in the city. The McCoys rented an apartment across the hall from the Marshalls and the two couples spent frequent evenings together. Frances McCoy and Katherine Marshall also went bargain-hunting at auctions, "but the only trouble is, they usually come back with something other than what they went after. We drew a pool table in one of the recent events," Marshall complained good-naturedly.

With the companionship of the McCoys, Marshall's depression gradually lifted. Within months the demanding colonel had organized instruction courses for officers and senior enlisted men of the lackluster division and installed tactical exercises. By the summer of 1934, he had turned the division around; army examiners rated the unit satisfactory or better in all departments, the first such passing grade the division had earned in years.

The demands upon a senior instructor of the National Guard were not burdensome. Even the sense of urgency, which had compelled his assignment to Chicago, had evaporated. Plan White for civil insurrections went back into the War Department's vaults. Marshall found time to ride horses available at the armory, and to go hunting on at least one occasion with newly elected Representative Scott Lucas, a colonel in the division.

However slow the pace of national recovery—the gross national product would not surpass 1929's record until 1940—the Marshalls lived comfortably. They had full-time help, "our colored man"; Molly, back from her world cruise, managed the house. They spent a large part of the summer at Fire Island, the colonel joining his family after the obligatory summer maneuvers, while young Allen, a student at the University of Virginia, worked as a lifeguard.

Through it all, Marshall had but one concern: timely promotion. There was little doubt he would eventually be nominated for his first star; simple seniority would assure that in due course. For Marshall, the question was whether he would be promoted soon enough to be eligible for a second star and the chief of staff's position. The Army's unwritten rule held that a prospective chief of staff must have four years to serve before he reached the mandatory retirement age of sixty-four. Dozens of good men had been passed over, yet even Pershing, who favored promotion on merit rather than age, felt the four-year rule sound.

Marshall's frustration burst his usual reserve. "Two or three BG [brigadier general] vacancies now exist," he pointed out to Pershing late in 1934. "I want one of them. As I will soon be 54 I must get started if I am going anywhere in the Army."

Promotion was ostensibly based on seniority alone, but politics both military and civilian could speed a favored officer along. Marshall had influential friends willing to drop a quiet word on his behalf; unsolicited, Generals George Van Horn Moseley and Johnson Hagood had already braced Roosevelt's Secretary of War, George Dern. Lack of professional recognition was not the barrier, either; a seniority system that promoted deadwood blocked Marshall's advancement. "I have had the discouraging experience of seeing the man I relieved in France as G-3 of the army, promoted years ago, and my assistant as G-3 of the army similarly advanced six years ago," he complained to Pershing. "I think I am entitled to some consideration now."

Rather than solicit letters from senior officers on his behalf, for "such letters as a rule do not mean much, because the War Department is flooded with them," Marshall asked the former AEF commander only to present the colonel's efficiency reports since 1915 to the Secretary of War. "I am prepared to gamble on my written record in the War Department before, during and since the war, for I have been told no one else in the list of colonels can match mine."

Pershing, whose name alone opened doors, went one better; he spoke to the president of the United States. On May 24, 1935, Franklin Delano Roosevelt sent a memorandum to his Secretary of War:

> General Pershing asks very strongly that Colonel George C. Marshall (Infantry) be promoted to Brigadier.
>
> Can we put him on list of next promotions? He is fifty-four years old.
>
> F.D.R.

Even the president's request would not help. Either Dern, MacArthur, or the selection board kept Marshall from the 1935 list. Discouraged, he wrote Pershing, "I can but wait, grow older, and hope for a more favorable situation in Washington."

Pershing pressed his suit at the White House and War Department, learning that MacArthur intended to appoint Marshall as chief of infantry. While that appointment carried with it a major general's star, it was not expected to open for two years. Further, it was a staff position and the staff did not produce chiefs of staff; they came from field commands.

Pershing then turned to John Callan O'Laughlin, publisher of the authoritative, if unofficial, *Army and Navy Journal*. O'Laughlin buttonholed MacArthur on behalf of Pershing's "outstanding man," then reported that the chief of staff still wanted Marshall to wait for the chief of infantry slot. But, to please his old AEF commander, MacArthur would recommend Marshall for promotion when the Secretary of War returned from a tour of the Philippines.

MacArthur never had an opportunity to speak to Dern. President Roosevelt abruptly announced on October 2 that MacArthur, already held over in the chief's office for a year, was to become military adviser to the planned defense force of the newly established Commonwealth of the Philippines. The new chief of staff would be Malin Craig.*

---

* MacArthur had earlier accepted the Philippines assignment at White House urging, yet the president's unexpected announcement was a calculated slap. FDR had delayed almost

Craig's appointment seemed at first to create just the more favorable situation in Washington Marshall had hoped for. The two men were friends of thirty years' standing. It was cavalry Captain Malin Craig to whom Second Lieutenant Marshall reported at the end of the long-ago mapping expedition along the Pecos River bottom. Craig and Marshall had served together in France as members of Pershing's headquarters staff, and Craig just the year before sat on a selection board that had recommended Marshall for his first star.

However much the new chief opposed the practice of appointment by seniority alone, however much he wanted Marshall promoted, Craig could not prevail on this year's board to advance the colonel by jumping files. Marshall's disappointment was all the more keen, he confessed to Pershing. "Every one of these men made was junior to me—in position—in France. . . . I'm fast getting too old to have any future of importance in the army."

In April 1936, his former Chicago apartment mate General Frank McCoy and Major General Charles Herron, a friend since their Leavenworth days together, arranged for Marshall to meet privately with Secretary of War Dern. Dern had already "heard from many sources," he told Katherine Marshall, "of the brilliance of my husband's work." The unrecorded conversation between Dern and Marshall was decisive; in May, Pershing wrote the colonel that the first star, delayed for sixteen years, was "positively and definitely" to come in September.

Marshall received formal notice in August, and his reassignment, as commander of the Fifth Brigade of the 3rd Division stationed at Vancouver Barracks, Washington, on October 1. Thirty-four years of achievement capped by three years of insistent lobbying on his behalf had finally won for Marshall the coveted star. Neither accomplishment nor pressure had meant much more than accelerating Marshall's promotion by little more than a month. On November 1, 1936, the two colonels immediately below Marshall on the seniority list duly received their promotions.

Marshall had taken the last hurdle, and was back with troops. Perhaps any post would have looked beautiful to the newly minted general, but historic Vancouver Barracks across the Columbia River from Portland offered special attractions when the Marshalls arrived after a cross-coun-

------

a year in picking a successor for MacArthur as chief of staff, to make certain that MacArthur's choice of a malleable successor would not have the requisite four years to serve. MacArthur had antagonized Roosevelt with his arrogance and self-aggrandizement, as well as public appeals to Congress for larger military budgets. Roosevelt once considered MacArthur and Louisiana Senator Huey Long "the two most dangerous men in the United States today." The Kingfish was dead, assassinated by a Louisiana doctor on September 8, 1935; the general now was to be placed safely out of the country, with no surrogate in his place. See Schlesinger, *Crisis,* pp. 417–418, and Petillo, pp. 170–174.

try tour in their new Packard. Their much-remodeled Queen Anne house with its witch's-cap tower was "palatial" in size. From her bedroom window Katherine could see snow-covered Mount Hood, an hour and a half's drive away. Fir trees bounded the parade ground and the airfield beyond; a venerable cherry tree flourished in the front yard of the Marshall's home, along with more than sixty varieties of roses planted by successive commandants. "All is in delightful contrast to the institution-like appearance of many army posts," Marshall wrote enthusiastically.

Equally enticing were the thirty-five CCC camps for which he was also responsible, each set in an idyllic surrounding. He could often combine his inspections through the CCC camps of Oregon and southern Washington with fishing for steelhead salmon; at home, he fished for dinner in the Columbia River which bordered the airfield.

The CCC's progress was gratifying, the education aspects of it especially satisfying. "This matter of schooling," he wrote in his comments about one inspection tour in June 1937,

> outside of the forestry, soil conversation, or other work of the companies, is in my opinion the most important phase of the CCC program at the present time. The work in the woods, on the trails or otherwise, is the justification for the camps; but their primary purpose is to fit young men, now out of employment, to become more valuable and self-supporting citizens. On every side it has become glaringly apparent during the past two years of business revival, that hereafter the unskilled man will have a desperately hard time succeeding, much harder than ever before.

Marshall also made special efforts to find jobs for CCC graduates. Many would stay in the Northwest, launched with jobs Marshall found for them, rather than return to their homes.

The new general's paternalism extended to a number of junior officers, especially those who like himself were stagnating "with brilliancy and talent damned by lack of rank to obscurity." He corresponded with these younger men, somewhat stiffly, as if awkward in the trust and respect these self-styled "Marshall's men" accorded him. He exchanged organizational and tactical theories, advocated reforms, or often offered a sympathetic ear to their complaints. Even with his first star, he was still very junior himself, and could do little "to help unblock a system which leaves men like yourself to languish," he wrote one future major general, then a mere captain.

As pleased as he was with his new assignment, Marshall had one grave concern. Just before he left Chicago, his thyroid began troubling him; his normal pulse of 72 irregularly shot up to 100. Marshall gave up smoking, gained weight, and saw private doctors in Portland in December 1936. The diagnosis was pressure from an enlarged thyroid, a condition similar to Lily's almost a decade before.

The diagnosis confirmed at the Army's Letterman General Hospital—Marshall went there only after confidential assurances that an operation would provide a complete cure—in mid-February 1937, he underwent a subtotal thyroidectomy. He spent five weeks in the hospital before returning to duty, twelve pounds heavier, his pulse back to normal, confronting a tendency to gain weight for the first time since his college days. "I am in splendid shape now, registering normal in every respect—except probably, you would say, in some of my personal idiosyncrasies, which no operation could alter," he wrote a Chicago friend.

Lest rumors undermine his career, Marshall was at some pains to demonstrate for the next months he had fully recovered. He spent a month on maneuvers in May, but gingerly extending himself so as to make sure there were no relapses. He rode, and as the year went on, played tennis with Molly and younger officers on the post.

If there were any lingering doubts about his fitness, they should have been dispelled on June 20, 1937, when three Russian fliers, making the first non-stop transpolar flight from Moscow to the United States, unceremoniously settled on the airfield just beyond the parade ground of Vancouver Barracks.

The three weary pilots appeared on the Marshalls' doorstep at eight-thirty on a Sunday morning, unwashed, unfed, and, for the moment, unfêted. Marshall posted guards around his house and in front of the bedrooms in which the officers slept while sixty or more newspaper reporters and photographers clamored for interviews with the sudden celebrities. Marshall knowingly fed the reporters information; his years with Pershing had trained him well. By that evening, the Russian ambassador and his staff of six had arrived, Marshall had routed out tailors and dry goods merchants to provide civilian clothing for the pilots, had taken fourteen phone calls from Moscow, and entertained the unexpected guests.

The following day, Marshall mounted a parade in the pilots' honor, then accompanied them to a hastily arranged Portland Chamber of Commerce luncheon. By evening, fliers, ambassador, and staff were on their way to Washington. The visit had generated the first nationwide publicity Marshall received—and reminded a handful of military planners that the modern airplane could leap America's defensive water barriers.

Marshall himself was to follow the Russians to Washington soon enough. Army Chief of Staff Malin Craig was emphatically pressing the White House to increase military appropriations, to upgrade an army that ranked just nineteenth in size in the world, behind such powers as Bulgaria and Portugal. Craig felt a special urgency, for any reading of European politics, as the United States military attaché in Poland wrote Marshall informally, suggested "though no one wants a war there is a general conviction that a German attack must be faced before many years."

Herr Hitler had begun rearming Germany in March 1935, the Allies of old raising only feeble diplomatic response to Germany's defiance of the Versailles Treaty. The following year Hitler sent a token three battalions into the Rhineland, demilitarized by the treaty; as he had anticipated, Britain and France did no more than telegraph limp protests. In October 1936, Hitler and Italian premier Benito Mussolini reached a secret agreement aligning their foreign policies in "an axis round which all European states animated by the will to collaboration and peace can also collaborate." War came to Europe once more—less than eighteen years after the bloodiest conflict in recorded history—when General Francisco Franco and his Spanish Moroccan legions marched in July 1936 against the Socialist government of Spain. Italy, emboldened by its conquest of hapless Ethiopia and a desire for empire, joined Germany in supporting Franco's Nationalists; only the Soviet Union openly rallied to the Loyalists, while France covertly sent supplies to the government. On the plains before Madrid the Russians experimented with the massed tank attacks of the blitzkrieg while in the skies over the Basque city of Guernica Germany's "volunteer" Condor Legion tested its new Junkers bombers.

Half a world away, Japan expanded its incursions into China, despite the amalgamation of warlords under the leadership of Chiang Kai-shek. On the night of July 7/ 8, 1937, soldiers of the Imperial Army demanded the right to search a suburb of Peking for the alleged murderers of a Japanese soldier, then marched across the Marco Polo Bridge into the capital. Within days Japanese reinforcements had landed, and before the end of the month troops of the Kwantung Army had taken first Marshall's old post at Tientsin, then Peking. Meanwhile, Japan joined Germany in an "anti-Comintern" agreement, squeezing the nervous Soviet Union between two increasingly aggressive powers.

The United States was no more effective than Great Britain and France had been in dousing the fires of war. Twice the State Department offered its "good services" to negotiate the Sino-Japanese disputes; twice its offer was rejected. At the end of a week-long political tour of the West—on which Brigadier General Marshall met Franklin Delano Roosevelt for the first time since 1928—the president proposed a "quarantine" to contain "the epidemic of world lawlessness. . . ." But the president had no plan, and the hostile press reaction assured none would be forthcoming; Roosevelt could not yet risk his political capital. Ground between the prevailing public sentiment favoring isolationism and the influence of big business in Congress, Roosevelt could do little more than enforce the successive Neutrality Acts Congress passed—however onerous they were

to him. Strong Catholic sentiment, especially in the Midwest, transformed the Spanish Civil War into a crusade against godless communism. Ethiopia's Haile Selassie elicited sympathy, but could not deliver
votes to match the Italian precincts of Chicago and New York. The president could muster little support for a more active policy; press and public wallowed in delusion. The interests of the United States and Japan
did not conflict, the influential Walter Lippmann decided in a newspaper column in December 1936. The Philippines were a "strategic trap"
that would snare the United States for years, he wrote. The wisest course
was to withdraw, leaving the Navy to sweep the Pacific of threats to the
West Coast while the British fleet guarded the Atlantic.

Far removed from war in Spain or China, fishing the salmon streams
of the Pacific Northwest, Marshall would soon be deeply involved with
the looming conflict. Chief of Staff Malin Craig had told Marshall late in
1936 that he could expect to be transferred to Washington for duty with
the War Department.

The War Department lumbered to life. Major General McCoy asked
Marshall if he would be interested in assuming command of his old division, the 1st; Marshall accepted, though he doubted he had seniority
enough to get the assignment. At the same time, he turned down yet
another bid to assume the superintendency at VMI, in part because of
money—retirement before he made major general would cost him $2,000
per year for the rest of his life. But Marshall also believed the achievements of a Pershing were within his reach. To accept the VMI post meant
"abandoning the possibilities of the next eight or nine years, so far as
that pertains to a professional soldier. With the world in its present turmoil no one can prophesy what the outcome will be, and as I made my
life occupation that of a soldier I hesitate to take any decision which
might leave me eliminated at the critical moment."

Official word of his transfer to Washington came in May, ending "the
two happiest years of my life," as Katherine put it. He was to report to
the War Plans Division in Washington on July 1, 1938.

Both personally and professionally, the transfer was a setback. Once
again he would be at a desk, Marshall sighed. "I am a country boy who
rides every morning before breakfast, walks in the woods every evening,
or runs about the mountains or down the sea coast inspecting and playing."

The transfer would not necessarily aid his advancement. Marshall still
confronted "the more prosaic problem of how-to-get-to-be a major general before I am too old or too junior in rank to amount to much of
anything." He had reason to worry. Craig had told him privately War
Plans was only a temporary slot, to give him some background before
Craig elevated him later to deputy chief of staff. As lofty as that position
appeared, it did not assure advancement to the chief's office; only one

of the previous eleven deputies had made the jump since the post was created in 1921. Moreover, at age fifty-seven, he had but one more chance to become chief of staff, when Craig retired in 1939. After that, he would lack the requisite four years to serve before he too reached mandatory retirement.

Marshall was going to Washington with as broad a training an officer could receive in the military. He had thirty-six years in uniform, and, despite his recurrent staff positions, had served with troops more than fourteen years, as lieutenant, major, lieutenant colonel, colonel, and brigadier general. Oddly, for a man so closely linked to professional education, he had himself attended only two years of army schools, from 1906 to 1908 at Fort Leavenworth. He had never attended the prestigious War College, though once assigned there as an instructor.

This blue-eyed general with a gaze that drilled incompetents had few illusions about the Army and its present capacities. They were still fumbling their way to the smaller triangular division upon which an entirely new concept of land warfare was to be based. Even at the platoon and company level, those actual fighting units that won battles, "much, a tremendous amount . . . taught at Benning will not hold water as a practical proposition in a warfare maneuver." The Air Corps existed as an underappreciated, underutilized force, yet to learn about close support of infantry, fascinated instead with bombers. Logistics, from industrial procurement down to the company supply room, was a paper-choked channel that grudgingly washed up shoddy clothing and tools. As a young officer on a mapping trip three decades earlier, he had needed fourteen signatures to get rations for his men; that had hardly changed. Intelligence from General Staff to battalion level was a scorned dumping ground for misfits and time-servers.

There were plenty of those in all branches, often in high places, "conservatives" as he thought of them, resistant to reform. "I am coming more and more to find, in the Army, that if a thing has not been done it is tremendously hard to get anyone today in favor of doing it. . . ."

Marshall differed too from other army officers in his willingness to rely on younger men, even enlisted men. "We are so damned conservative in peace as to who can do what," he complained, "that we seldom do otherwise; and the hour war is declared we take a boy out of high school and give him a couple of thousand men."

In the Great War Marshall also had learned civilians could assume military responsibilities; Wall Street lawyers might heroically lead "Lost Battalions." He had served two tours with the National Guard and knew its worth. He had set up dozens of CCC camps, mobilizing unlikely youths into effective work forces, no more than a mass call-up in time of war would require. And no one knew better that the most promising men did not always wear high rank in the Regular Army.

CHAPTER

VIII

The Last Lessons

Washington sweltered in the humidity of a Potomac summer when George Marshall, in wilted suit and straw boater, reported for duty at the War Department on July 7, 1938. He was to spend three months in the War Plans Division familiarizing himself with the plans and budgets of a skeletal army battling cautious president and niggardly Congress for appropriations to ready itself for war.

Craig himself was to retire a year later and wanted Marshall to succeed him; the transfer to Washington was calculated not only to give Marshall a grasp of current War Department planning, but to introduce him to the one man whose opinion mattered in the selection of the next chief, the president of the United States. Craig also needed help, he privately admitted. "Thank God, George, you have come to hold up my trembling hands," Craig greeted his friend from AEF days.

However meteoric Marshall's sudden ascension appeared, it also posed a problem, for Craig and Marshall alike. As deputy chief of staff, Marshall would be giving orders to three dozen generals senior to him, a sticking point in an army bound by protocol. Those orders would be obeyed, but the resentment could corrode Marshall's support from the military establishment and undermine his candidacy for the chief of staff post.

Marshall took up his duties in a War Department scored by rivalries. The Air Corps' younger officers were impatient with the earthbound generals who ran the department, those generals scornful of both air-power and the young men who argued the bomber would change the nature of warfare. Army-Navy cooperation rested on a 1903 agreement both the lordlings of seapower and war disdained. Craig owed his trembling hands to his two immediate superiors, new Secretary of War Harry Woodring and the assistant secretary, Louis Johnson. Woodring, who had succeeded George Dern in 1936, and the outspoken Johnson agreed on little more than the choice of Marshall as Craig's successor.

Woodring was a turn-of-the-century farmlands progressive, a former governor of Kansas whose social insularity compelled him toward isolationism. Wary of the president's *realpolitik,* Woodring recognized that he had risen to the top post with Dern's death only because Roosevelt believed an isolationist in that position would dampen the suspicions of a hostile Congress.

FDR intended to placate the right wing, not capitulate to it. To balance Woodring, Roosevelt installed as assistant secretary Louis Johnson, a former national commander of the American Legion and irrepressible spokesman for preparedness. Johnson was a headstrong political brawler who openly, repeatedly clashed with his nominal superior.

The two men bickered through this congressional election year, President Roosevelt unwilling or unable to relieve either without undercutting his party in Congress. Instead he left the two to squabble, grinding fine Malin Craig between them. "I shall never forgive Washington," Mrs. Craig threatened, as she explained to Katherine Marshall the toll the chief of staff's job had taken on her husband.

Marshall intended nothing more than to walk a fine line between the two. He burrowed into the War Plans Division while his wife and Molly, accompanied by the general's enlisted orderly, escaped their home at 2118 Wyoming Avenue for Fire Island. The summer and their ocean-side vacation ended simultaneously in a hurricane that rammed through the East Coast and Fire Island on September 21.

First news reports stated the island had been hit hard, the casualty toll high. Unable to reach the cottage by telephone, Marshall quickly commandeered an Air Corps bomber and pilot. They flew northward, along the track of the hurricane, flying in low over the resort in the storm-whipped Atlantic. From the air he could see the small cottage still stood, though many of the neighboring homes had been smashed by the 90-mile-an-hour winds, or blown off their foundations into the leeward bay.

Unable to land on the island, the pilot flew to Mitchel Field on Long Island where he and the worried general exchanged their bomber for a smaller, two-seat, open trainer. Flying back to the island, the pilot picked his way to a landing on the debris-strewn beach. Still in flying togs and goggles, Marshall hurried to the battered cottage.

"In the doorway stood a weird apparition," Mrs. Marshall recalled. "It looked like a deep-sea diver." She, her sister, and Molly had spent a sleepless, miserable night, exhausted but safe under the guard of Marshall's orderly.

"Can't you speak? Say something!" the goggle-eyed apparition commanded.

"Is that you? Why, you are the most beautiful thing I ever saw in my life!" she gasped.

Grinning relief, Marshall turned to the waiting orderly. "Sergeant, order another hurricane."

Not all of Marshall's anxieties were so quickly erased. Having appointed himself manager of Marshall's ascension to the chief of staff post, Assistant Secretary Johnson and his none-too-subtle efforts provoked a wallow of speculation in a town that relished gossip. "Rumor is destroying me, I fear," Marshall worried in a letter to General Pershing, the one man to whom he could reveal himself. "I am announced by Tom, Dick and Harry as deputy chief of staff to be, the assistant secretary makes similar announcements. Probably antagonizing Woodring and Craig."

As part of his campaign, Johnson arranged for Marshall to address the state convention of the American Legion in Johnson's hometown of Clarksburg, West Virginia. If Marshall was reluctant to become so visible an army spokesman, he could hardly refuse for fear of alienating Johnson.

In an address to the convention of world war veterans, Marshall argued for military preparedness, a theme that would run through his public statements for the next two years. It took time—as long as five years—to design a new fighter or bomber, and another year to put that design into production. The manufacture of even such comparatively simple items as bombs required a year, artillery pieces longer. While the first appropriations of necessary dies and jigs had been made the previous year, manufacturers were critically short of machine tools to take on defense contracts. Preparedness must begin now. And it was costly. "We never have, nor can we get, money enough to buy everything. . . ."

By the end of September 1938, the $250 million War Department budget appeared even less adequate. Hitler mobilized Germany's thirteen divisions over the protests of his General Staff, then demanded that Czechoslovakia return the German-speaking Sudentenland and Ostrava to Germany. Those border provinces, carved out of the Kaiser's reich at the end of the world war and awarded to the newly created nation of Czechoslovakia, were the last territorial claims Hitler had in Europe, or so the German chancellor assured the world.

The Czech Army mobilized. France directly and Great Britain indirectly were pledged to defend the Czech borders; twenty years after the armistice the specter of war again shadowed Whitehall and the Quai d'Orsay.

But the victors of World War I had neither the desire nor the will for a second. Rather than stand up to Hitler's threat, Chamberlain and French Premier Edouard Daladier brought pressure on hapless Czechoslovakia to surrender the claimed territory, and with it the nation's border defenses.

Lacking French and British military aid, the Czechs were left to twist slowly in the wind. At a hastily summoned two-day conference in Munich's Fuehrerbau, the two ministers met with Hitler and Mussolini, while a delegation of Czechs waited anxiously in an anteroom to learn the fate of their nation. The French and British agreed to Hitler's "last" demand.

The much relieved Chamberlain returned to London triumphant, appearing on the balcony at 10 Downing Street to tell a cheering throng he had secured "peace with honor. I believe it is peace for our time." In Paris, applauding crowds met Daladier; the Chamber of Deputies approved the Munich agreement 535 to 75. The House of Commons, despite Winston Churchill's assertion that the settlement was "a disaster of the first magnitude," approved Chamberlain's pact 366 to 144. If the prime minister was an appeaser, so too were majorities in both France and Great Britain.

Through the month-long crisis, official Washington watched and waited. Publicly, the president said he shared the universal "sense of relief," and wired Chamberlain, "Good man." Privately, he told the cabinet that Britain and France would "wash the blood from their Judas Iscariot hands." The League of Nations had been done in by ineffectual dithering over Japan's invasion of Manchuria, then Italy's attack on Ethiopia. Now the Versailles Treaty and Europe's intricate web of mutual defense treaties had collapsed. Hitler's territorial assurances notwithstanding, back bencher Winston Churchill warned Germany would return for more. Munich was "only the beginning of the reckoning."

The Munich crisis triggered a worldwide rush to armament. President Roosevelt hinted on October 11 he would seek another $300 million for national defense. Just how the money would be spent, if it was appropriated, the president determined on the night of October 14, 1938, when he met with his ambassador to France, William C. Bullitt.

Briefed by French intelligence, Francophile Bullitt came to the White House sounding alarms. The Germans "would be able to bomb Paris at will"; France had but seventeen modern airplanes, he told the president, and desperately needed all the United States could build. The two men talked late into the night; by the time Bullitt left, Roosevelt the secret interventionist had become an airpower advocate.

The next day, FDR told reporters he would seek $500 million in additional defense funds, and ordered Assistant Secretary of War Johnson—Woodring was absent from Washington—to prepare plans for a major expansion of the Air Corps. The president casually settled upon the production of 15,000 planes a year.

The president's order was one to make the General Staff break out in a cold sweat. Aircraft were needed, but so too were modern tanks, artillery, anti-aircraft guns, and a thousand other tools of war. Disproportionate expenditures for planes would not prepare the Army to defend American shores.

Craig moved to call a meeting of the War Council, but Johnson interfered. There was no deputy chief of staff, the one man most responsible for the Army's budget, Johnson pointed out, and there had been none for two weeks, since Major General Stanley Embick assumed command of the IV Corps in Atlanta. Never mind that Marshall was junior to so many generals, as Craig had agonized; Johnson wanted Marshall appointed immediately to the vacancy. If not, Johnson would cancel the meetings of the council until it was done. Given a direct order, one that would mute criticism of Marshall as overweening, the chief of staff left the office briefly, and returned to say the orders had been issued. Marshall was now the Army's foremost budget expert.

He anticipated problems. The day of his elevation he wrote Major General Keehn of the Illinois National Guard, "I fear that this will carry with it a great deal of grief, because it will be my job to struggle with the budget. . . ." It would be "a continuous matter of robbing Peter to pay Paul. In one sense, the Army runs on a shoe-string," he complained to another.

Marshall immediately confronted the question of meeting the president's call for a massive increase in airpower. "What are we going to do with 15,000 planes?" Craig fumed. Who would fly them, and from what fields? Where were the ground crews to maintain them? Craig, Marshall, even the newly named chief of the Air Corps, Brigadier General Henry "Hap" Arnold, favored a balance between ground and air forces, between weapons and barracks, airfields and training facilities.

Marshall had little detailed knowledge of Air Corps problems when he arrived in Washington in July 1938. He deliberately set out to learn what he could, taking a week-long, 8,000-mile flying tour of aircraft factories and Air Corps installations. Across the country Marshall listened to the complaints of mostly younger men frustrated by the lack of representation on the General Staff, by the lack of interest in Air Corps problems by the War Department itself. He returned to Washington aware of construction snarls in industry, of the shortage of training planes, and acutely conscious of the lack of either a tactical or strategic concept in the use of airplanes.

Marshall proposed a number of reforms planned to give the Air Corps parity with the fast-developing air forces of Europe. Though he never accepted the "victory through air power" concept, Marshall was to become one of the three men outside of the Air Corps itself Hap Arnold believed most helpful in building the vast squadrons to come.

In a speech at the Air Corps' tactical training school at Maxwell Field, Alabama, Marshall cautioned the young pilots, "Military victories are not gained by a single arm—though the failures of an arm or service might well be disastrous—but are achieved through the efforts of all arms and services welded into an Army team."

Because of the United States' geographical location, Marshall continued, no one could predict who would be the enemy in the next war, where it would be fought, and even with what weapons. The only sensible policy for the War Department then was to maintain a balanced force to defend the nation. (In truth, Marshall remained an infantryman at heart. In a speech on March 3, 1939, he detailed a long list of military innovations that supposedly would dominate the battlefields of history: chariots, then elephants, the mounted hordes of Genghis Khan, armored knights, artillery, tanks, and now the airplane. "But in all these struggles, as the smoke cleared away, it was the man with the sword, or the crossbow, or the rifle who settled the final issue on the field.")

"A balanced force" became the watchword for the War Department as it struggled to shape a $500 million budget for supplemental military appropriations in 1939. A balanced force also set Craig and Marshall on a collision course with the equally firm-minded president.

On November 14, FDR summoned Johnson, Craig, Marshall, and Arnold to the White House for a discussion of the 15,000-airplane procurement plan. Waiting in the president's office, in addition to Roosevelt, were the secretary of the treasury, Henry Morgenthau; his solicitor Herman Oliphant; Solicitor General Robert H. Jackson; and Works Progress Administration director Harry Hopkins, New Dealers all, men who wanted what the president wanted, because the president wanted it. One man was conspicuously absent: Secretary of War Woodring. Roosevelt would not miss Woodring's isolationist opinions.

The president "did the major portion of the talking," Marshall recalled. Sitting behind the large desk strewn with mementos, gifts, and knick-knacks, FDR quickly dismissed the Army's proposal for a balanced force. "A well-rounded ground army of even 400,000"—authorized strength now stood at 174,000—"could not be considered a deterrent for any foreign power whereas a heavy striking force of aircraft would." As Hap Arnold rephrased it, Hitler would not be frightened by new barracks in Wyoming.

For the first time since the Holy Alliance of 1818, the New World faced possible attack, Roosevelt continued, "This demands our providing immediately a huge air force so that we do not need a huge army. . . ." Besides, sending American boys to defend South America was not possible politically. "Had we had this summer 5,000 planes and the capacity immediately to produce 10,000 per year . . . Hitler would not have dared to take the stand he did."

Talking steadily, stopping only to fit another cigarette to the holder, Roosevelt proposed an air force of 20,000 planes and production capacity of 24,000 per year. Because Congress was sure to trim that gargantuan figure, the president ordered Craig to begin planning for a fleet of 10,000 planes. Four fifths of these were to be built in existing airframe factories; the Works Progress Administration was to build seven more installations, two to be placed into immediate production, the remaining five held as reserve capacity.

When the president had concluded, he asked each of the men in the room for their opinion. "Most of them agreed with him entirely, and had very little to say, and were very soothing in their comments," Marshall remembered. Finally, the president turned to the deputy chief of staff sitting on a lounge against the wall, and asked, "Don't you think so, George?"

Irritated by what seemed the president's glib, even irresponsible presentation, then by the presumed familiarity, Marshall replied coldly, "Mr. President, I am sorry, but I don't agree with that at all."

Startled, the president looked at Marshall, then abruptly dismissed the meeting. Just as in 1917, when he challenged General Pershing, George Marshall once more had bearded the lion.

As they filed from the president's office, "they all bade me good-by and said my tour in Washington was over," Marshall recalled.

Arguing for a balanced force, Marshall discovered, was militarily and personally expedient at the same time. The fewer planes produced in the United States, the more those aircraft appeared to be defensive weapons; thus Marshall appeared as a non-interventionist, a man of Woodring's mettle. Yet he could equally well appear as favoring increased armaments for other branches of the Army, a position Johnson advocated. Among the military decision makers, President Roosevelt stood alone, but then his was the only vote that counted.

If Marshall was on soft ground with the president, both he and Johnson ignored it. The day after the White House meeting, the assistant secretary ordered Chief of Staff Craig to prepare budget estimates for a major rearmament of a balanced force. Johnson hoped to piggyback increased funding for ground troops with the boost in Air Corps appropriations. Preparing that budget, then putting it in the form of a draft bill, fell to Marshall.

Here was another burden in what Marshall considered "the most pressing job in the W.D.," as he conceded in a letter to his personal doctor, Colonel Morrison C. Stayer.

The pressure of managing the emergency appropriations bills, of apportioning funds between the competing branches, of lining up support in Congress and testifying repeatedly before various committees had exacted a toll. Stayer began visiting Washington and his secret patient in late 1938, prescribing medicine for the recurrent arrhythmia of Marshall's heartbeat.

As the time of his annual physical examination approached, Marshall grew more cautious. On Morrison's advice, he planned to take the medication for a week prior to the physical, and rest the morning before.

It was not to be. While eating lunch in the chief of staff's office, Craig suddenly recommended that Marshall not wait for his scheduled appointment, but instead squeeze in the physical that afternoon. They would be busy for some days to come with the president's emergency appropriation bill, Craig said between bites on a sandwich. The chief of staff promptly picked up the telephone and made an immediate appointment. A half hour later, the deputy chief of staff was on his way to Fort Myer.

Marshall may well have driven across the Potomac River more agitated than he let on. He had been on Stayer's medication for just one day. The quiet morning before the planned physical had not materialized; instead, they had spent "a tumultuous morning, with much emphatic argument." Suddenly, after thirty-seven years, with the great prize of the chief of staff's office so close, he risked being washed out for medical reasons.

The physical examination was as thorough as Marshall could recall. "I do not know yet how I got by," he wrote Stayer with obvious relief. The doctor noted a slight irregularity in Marshall's pulse prior to exercise, but none afterwards. "If you wrote your own ticket, you could not beat that," the examining physician concluded.

The irregularity of the pulse the doctor attributed to smoking, until Marshall said he no longer smoked. Instead, Marshall suggested, "It was due to too much desk and too little exercise of the type to which I had been accustomed." The doctor agreed, adding that Marshall would have to fight "desk belly." The general would hear no more about his irregular pulse.

Relieved, Marshall returned to his new office in the Munitions Building on Constitution Avenue to line up political support for the huge budget increase—and discovered an improbable ally in the White House itself.

Harry Hopkins was arguably the most hated man in Washington, and probably the second most powerful. Even his sometime rival, Secretary of the Interior Harold Ickes, conceded as much, if only to his private diary. "Harry Hopkins is described as the person who is closest to the President and there is no doubt that this is the fact. He is extraordinarily close. He all but lives in the White House and he seems to be in the complete confidence of the President."

Tall, lantern-jawed, Hopkins was a demanding taskmaster who had ramrodded the New Deal's Emergency Relief effort and the CCC, then had taken charge of the Works Progress Administration. Born in Sioux City, Iowa, in 1890, a social worker by training, Hopkins had worked his way through a succession of public welfare jobs, eventually winding up in New York City as director of the Tuberculosis and Health Association. It was there he met New York's future governor, Franklin D. Roosevelt. Roosevelt, the Hudson River patrician, genial and elegant, took an instant liking to Hopkins, the son of a harness maker, blunt, sarcastic, looking like "something of the ill-fed horse at the end of a hard day."

Hopkins was a hard-boiled visionary who had spent his entire life working on behalf of that "one-third of the nation" the president later described as ill-nourished, ill-clad, and ill-housed. (The phrase itself was Hopkins's.) With the national economy paralyzed, New York Governor Roosevelt in 1931 had appointed the hard-driving Hopkins as director of the state Relief Administration. Hopkins was to manage a work relief program that spent $140 million in just two years, an effort that validated the governor's concern for the poor, and more than any other turned him into a serious presidential candidate.

That $140 million would be the merest beginning. As head of the Federal Emergency Relief Administration, the former social worker administered $8.5 billion in a bewildering array of federal relief efforts. He became "history's greatest spender," one magazine decided.

Hopkins was also impious, impolitic, and impassioned. Not one to suffer fools, the man Winston Churchill would later dub "Lord Root of the Matter" for his ability to clearly define problems and propose solutions, scored his critics as "too dumb to understand."

Probably no man in Washington was more disliked. "He was generally regarded as a sinister figure, a backstairs intriguer," his friend Robert Sherwood wrote. Yet the "strange, gnomelike creature," as the equally salty Joseph Stilwell described him, got things done. Now.

Looking ahead to the 1940 election, FDR seriously considered tapping Hopkins to run on the party ticket. In mid-1938, the president began inviting Hopkins to sit in on White House meetings on a wide range of topics; in December of that year, the president appointed him secretary of commerce, on the theory that familiarity would erase some of the animosity the conservative business community held toward the man.

Hopkins was to be the War Department's most important ally in putting forward Marshall's balanced-force budget. Marshall had earlier talked with Hopkins, knew the lanky man in the ill-fitting suits had the president's ear, and that Hopkins had secretly arranged to divert WPA funds to buy $2 million in machine tools necessary for the production of small arms ammunition. Moreover, with Hopkins's approval, some $250 million in CCC funds had gone toward construction on military posts, especially barracks for CCC volunteers, buildings the Army would need for a mass mobilization, but buildings Congress had refused to fund over the years.

In the last week of 1938, Hopkins telephoned Marshall, asking to visit the deputy chief. Instead, Marshall deferentially chose to meet Hopkins at the Department of Commerce. There the two men discussed the bal-

anced-force concept, Hopkins asking the keen questions that so terror-
ized bureaucrats, Marshall answering precisely, tersely.

Though relatively brief, their private conversation apparently left each
man profoundly impressed with the other. Marshall's description of the
woeful state of the Army and the nation's defenses, especially in anti-
aircraft weapons, alarmed the secretary. To Hopkins's urgings that Marshall take his care for a balanced force directly to the president, Marshall
demurred. He was not yet chief of staff, lacked that titular authority, but
more importantly, did not have the president's confidence. Marshall
preferred that the influential Hopkins deliver the message.

The resolution came in the last days of 1938 at a second meeting in
the White House, with the president working over his annual State of
the Union address. FDR began the meeting by complaining that the Army
was offering him everything except the airplanes he wanted. Hopkins,
Johnson, Craig, and Marshall, one after the other, countered: Airplanes
without trained pilots, crews, and ground support would be useless. Even
if they were to sell planes to Great Britain and France—and the Neutrality Act barred such sales at the moment—they lacked hangars to
store the planes and test pilots to check them out prior to delivery. In
the end, the president yielded; he would ask Congress for an emergency
defense appropriation of $552 million, $180 million of that budgeted
for 3,000 of the airplanes Roosevelt wanted "to impress Germany."

Hopkins's aid to Marshall continued as the two men crossed the
boundary between colleague and friend in the next months. From "Mr.
Secretary" and "General," they became "Harry" and "George," a rare
concession that Marshall would not permit even the president of the
United States. Each perceived in the other a quality of selflessness, a
dedication to a larger cause, in Hopkins's case a commitment that would
ultimately ruin his health. For all their seeming dissimilarities—Hopkins
casual, Marshall precise; Hopkins the political operator, Marshall the
good soldier; Hopkins in threadbare suits bought off the rack, Marshall
in fashionable civilian clothes or well-pressed uniform—they were much
alike in ways they deemed important. Both men were, at heart, reformers. They also shared a pleasure in their accomplishments with the CCC.
Both had a capacity to distill great amounts of information into a succinct, cogent statement of a problem. Both were unimpressed with either
exterior appearances or mere rank; neither man had patience for
incompetents.

Through a series of discussions in the early months of 1939, Marshall
continued Hopkins's military briefing, stressing the need for preparedness in the event of war. The muddles of 1898, when food rotted on the
docks of Florida and needed equipment never reached the troops, could
not be repeated against a modern, well-equipped enemy. The Great War's
year-long delay in fielding even a single American division in France was

time they would not have in an age of airplanes and fast-moving tanks. Yet the structure of the nation's next mass mobilization existed only on paper; facilities and equipment, not to mention modern weapons, simply did not exist. Despite three years of record military spending, they were no better than half-equipped to mobilize the 1 million men called for on M-Day. Even then it would take them eight months to put all million into the field. Facts, figures, timetables, Marshall carried them all in his head and delivered them precisely, coolly.

Hopkins understood now that they were working against time. Hitler's military budget had steadily increased to 18.4 billion marks this year, 60 percent of the national budget. The German military had been able to outfit its divisions with the most modern equipment and weaponry. No one doubted German intentions any longer; the only question was when the blow would fall. From Berlin the United States military attaché wrote privately to Marshall, "We have lived more or less on a volcano here and the strain on one's nerves has been tremendous."

Halfway around the world, Japanese troops had continued their advances in China, and gained control of the lower Yangtze. The Japanese Foreign Ministry had proposed a "new order" for the Far East, one that would bind together Japan, China, and Manchuria economically— and make colonies of Southeast Asia, the Philippines, and Indonesia.

In Europe, German soldiers crossed into the remainder of quartered Czechoslovakia on March 15, 1939. Four days later Hitler annexed the city of Memel in Lithuania, then demanded the Poles cede the Free State of Danzig. Italy blustered about its border with France, demanding territorial concessions, then invaded tiny Albania. French Foreign Minister Georges Bonnet, once as eager as any to appease Hitler, lamented, "It is five minutes before twelve."

Neville Chamberlain abandoned his tattered policy of appeasement, and asked Parliament on April 26 to authorize military conscription. "Nothing would so impress the world with the determination of this country to offer firm resistance to any attempt at general domination."

President Roosevelt could only watch in frustration. Neutrality laws could operate unfairly, he had lectured a hostile Congress in his State of the Union address on January 4. The democracies "cannot forever let pass, without effective protest, acts of aggression against sister nations— acts which automatically undermine us all. . . . We have learned that when we deliberately try to legislate neutrality, our neutrality laws may operate unevenly and unfairly—may actually give aid to an aggressor and deny it to the victim. The instinct of self-preservation should warn us that we ought not to let that happen anymore."

Three months later, Roosevelt told reporters the Neutrality Act had to be revised. As he complained privately to Senator Tom Connally of the Foreign Relations Committee, "If Germany invades a country and declares war, we'll be on the side of Hitler by invoking the act. If we could get rid of the arms embargo, it wouldn't be so bad." FDR had learned the harsh lesson of neutrality in Spain, where the Nationalists had driven the last of unaided Loyalists across the French border, and Francisco Franco promptly joined the Anti-Comintern Pact with Germany, Italy, Japan, and Hungary.

Despite odds he calculated as but one in five, President Roosevelt appealed in a worldwide broadcast to Hitler and Mussolini to ease the "constant fear of a new war." Would they assure peace by respecting the borders and territories of thirty-one nations for the next ten years? Hitler, who had already fixed the date for the invasion of Poland, and Mussolini both flatly rejected Roosevelt's approach.

With some satisfaction, California Senator Hiram Johnson, reflecting the prevailing Republican view, decided, "Roosevelt put his chin out and got a resounding whack. I have reached the conclusion there will be no war." The president, Johnson rumbled on, wanted "to knock down two dictators in Europe so that one may be firmly implanted in America." Congress might appropriate millions for defense, but not one cent for Roosevelt's foreign adventures.

The world had gone mad in that spring of 1939 as FDR turned to the question of a successor to Chief of Staff Malin Craig. Craig was to take his terminal leave at the end of June, formally retiring on August 31. The president would select Craig's successor from the list of senior officers with at least four years to serve before they reached the mandatory retirement age of sixty-four.

Thirty-three generals outranked Marshall on the Army's seniority lists before this four-years-to-serve rule was applied. With the superannuated pared from the roll, Brigadier General Marshall ranked fifth in seniority behind Major Generals Hugh Drum, John L. DeWitt, Frank Rowell, and Walter Krueger. Official Washington and much of the press considered Drum the likely choice.

At eighteen the youngest lieutenant in the United States Army, Drum had held a succession of key posts through his career. During World War I he was Marshall's superior as chief of staff of the I Corps. Promoted to brigadier general in 1922, he was a major general by 1930, while Marshall was still a lieutenant colonel. In just the last ten years he had served as inspector general of the Army, as deputy chief of staff for MacArthur, as commander of the Hawaiian Department, and finally as commander of the prestigious II Corps headquartered on Governor's Island in New York Harbor. At every turn he led Marshall, indeed, everyone on the eligible list.

Drum sorely wanted the Army's highest rank, and had campaigned vigorously for the appointment. He had been considered in 1930, only to be passed over for MacArthur; he had been on the list again in 1934, only to be frustrated when the president held MacArthur over for a year; then he had lost out to Craig in 1935.

This would be his last try for the chief of staff's post. He curried newsmen, prompting fulsome articles in national magazines. He asked influential visitors to write the president on his behalf, lined up politicians, and solicited others for endorsements. Drum had secured at least one major supporter beyond the Army, Postmaster General James A. Farley, twice the president's national campaign manager. Army circles considered Farley's endorsement a virtual guarantee that Hugh Drum would finally reach the pinnacle.

Marshall had significant support himself. Woodring, Johnson, and Craig all favored his selection, though Marshall feared if either the feuding Woodring or Johnson publicly announced for him, the other would find an alternative candidate. Craig claimed no influence at the White House other than that which his office conferred, but his backing implied Marshall would be acceptable to the Army at large. Pershing supported him, carrying the ghostly endorsement of military tradition. Marshall's long years with the National Guard and the Reserve Officers Training Corps garnered him support from those politically powerful sources as well. Beyond these, Marshall knew a number of senators and representatives, notably South Carolina's Senator James F. Byrnes, a staunch New Dealer with access to the White House. "My problem," he wryly told his young friend Rose Page, "is not lining up backers, but stopping the well-wishers who want to intercede for me."

In calculated contrast to Drum, Marshall wanted no overt campaign on his behalf. The very fact he had been appointed deputy chief of staff "while a brigadier general, junior to other generals of the general staff, makes me conspicuous in the Army. Too conspicuous, as a matter of fact." Rather, he wrote Leo A. Farrell, the political editor of the *Atlanta Constitution,*

> My strength with the Army has rested on the well known fact that I attended strictly to business and enlisted no influence of any sort at any time. That, in Army circles, has been my greatest strength in this matter of future appointment, especially as it is in strong contrast with other most energetic activities in organizing a campaign and in securing voluminous publicity. Therefore, it seems to me that at this time the complete absence of any publicity about me would be my greatest asset, particularly with the President. And the Army would resent it, even some of those now ardently for me.

Any press attention troubled him. Stories in Hearst's *New York Mirror* speculating on the next chief of staff made him fretful. In January he declined a prestigious speaking engagement, confidentially explaining he desired to avoid publicity; talk of his becoming chief of staff was "distasteful and I think equally harmful."

Most of all, he wanted nothing smacking of a campaign. Outside pressure was an irritant and merely stiffened resistance, Marshall cautioned Colonel Stayer, who was himself seeking a transfer. That advice was a cautious prescription for his own campaign.

He might not have worried. So long as Marshall did not himself encourage either the publicity or the recommendations, Franklin Delano Roosevelt gave little thought to what appeared in the newspapers about the chief of staff's successor. A canny politician himself, Roosevelt recognized an orchestrated campaign when he was its target.

For all of Drum's qualifications, and his effort, he made little headway. The presumably influential support of James Farley counted for nothing since the president considered Farley a poor judge of anything beyond practical politics.

In addition, Drum's unusually high opinion of himself damaged his chances. Capable and hardworking he was, but Hugh Drum was also pompous, stuffed with self-importance. The president disliked such graceless pretensions.

Marshall meanwhile had the persistent backing of Hopkins, the resident Rasputin. If Marshall remained his own man, no matter; all three of the president's closest friends and advisors, speech writer Sam Rosenman, Secretary of the Treasury Henry Morgenthau, and Hopkins, were men who spoke their minds, frequently profanely.

Some combination of Pershing's endorsement and Hopkins's insistence decided the matter. On Sunday, April 23, 1939, the president summoned Brigadier General George Catlett Marshall to his second-floor study in the White House. Roosevelt had made his choice of a new chief of staff.

Their conversation amid the president's forty stamp albums and stacks of dealers' catalogues was brief, Marshall recalled. The president, as usual, did most of the talking during the half-hour interview. The new appointee managed to outline some of his own conceptions of the nation's defense problems, but "in very sketchy form." Marshall told the president he wanted to be able to speak his mind, and it would not always be palatable.

"Is that all right?" the soldier asked.

"Yes," the commander-in-chief replied from behind the row of stamp albums.

"You said 'yes' pleasantly, but it may be unpleasant," Marshall warned.

Roosevelt smiled as the new four-star general stood up. "I feel deeply honored, sir, and I will give you the best I have," Marshall promised.

This would be no easy task, Marshall realized. The president had selected him, the general believed, with little confidence, only as "the best of a bad bargain" among officers with little vision and less interest than Roosevelt in airpower. It was not precisely the promotion on merit alone he had coveted, but he had nonetheless gained the Army's highest rank. He would have to earn the president's respect.

At Marshall's request, the White House delayed the announcement of his appointment until April 27, when he was safely beyond the reach of Washington reporters on an inspection tour. Flying between Dayton and Denver, he wrote a brief note to Leo Farrell of the *Atlanta Constitution* to thank him for his unflagging support.

The next chief of staff of the Army of the United States added a hasty last line: "I will need your prayers for the next few years."

PART

II

THE CHIEF OF STAFF

C H A P T E R

IX

The Island Alone

They had a special reason to celebrate. The following morning, Brigadier General George C. Marshall was to be sworn in as chief of staff,
putting on the temporary rank of four stars that went with the Army's
highest office. Even if the ceremony was only a formality brought on by
Malin Craig's retirement, here was a moment for the Marshalls to savor.

The couple looked forward that August 31, 1939, to a pleasurable
evening at the home of Justice and Mrs. Harlan Stone, drinks—Marshall
would nurse a well-watered highball—dinner, and conversation, no doubt
about the unsettling news from Europe. Germany and the Soviet Union
had concluded a non-aggression pact the week before. Poland stood nervously defiant between those unlikely allies. France and Great Britain
had mobilized; Poland had called up its reserves. Perhaps the Army's
new chief of staff had secret word just how close Europe was to war, but
the Stones and their guests knew better than to ask.

The telephone call came midway through the dinner. The general
excused himself momentarily, then returned to the table grim-faced. The
duty officer in the Munitions Building had called to inform him that
Hitler had massed the Wehrmacht at the Polish frontier, apparently to
reinforce his demand for the return of Danzig to Germany. With Britain
and France pledged to protect Poland's borders, a second great war in a
generation loomed.

The second telephone call awakened the chief of staff at three o'clock
in the morning. German dive bombers had attacked Warsaw. Marshall
hung up the telephone and turned to his sleepy wife. "Well, it's come,"
he told her, and began dressing.

When he returned to Fort Myer late on the night of September 1, he
was officially chief of staff of the seventeenth largest army in the world,
sworn in during a hasty ceremony by Secretary of War Woodring in the
middle of a tumultuous day.

Marshall's installation came as a relief to long-stalled younger officers, particularly Colonel George S. Patton, Jr., who went so far as to send the new chief a set of insignia ordered from a New York jeweler. Marshall accepted "that whole firmament of stars" stiffly, perhaps aware that the wealthy Patton was anxious to ingratiate himself.

In contrast to the Army's acceptance, Washington and the reporters who covered the newly awakened village knew little about the chief of staff. More importantly, neither did the president; FDR had relied on Harry Hopkins's recommendation in naming the chief of staff. As Marshall himself realized, "I had not been proven. He appointed me without any large war experience, except being with General Pershing in the first world war. . . ." Though no one else on active duty had any greater experience, "it was quite a while before he built up confidence in me. . . ."

For his part, the new chief of staff had little more regard for the president. Roosevelt appeared mercurial, even slippery, a man to gloss over problems such as the "sorry state of the War Department" with its ongoing squabble between Secretary of War Woodring and the assistant secretary, Louis Johnson. As an administrator, Roosevelt improvised freely, violating the rules Marshall held sacrosanct: tables of organization, channels of communication, fixed authority, and final responsibility. Only later would Marshall appreciate the president's nerve and his true leadership capacities.

More than unfamiliarity separated these two men. A president who joked with his staff, teased his cabinet officers, and bantered with friendly newsmen during twice-weekly press conferences would not appeal to the formally correct soldier. Marshall deliberately kept his relationship with his commander-in-chief distant, refusing even to laugh at the president's jokes; laughter only encouraged Roosevelt to filibuster his way around difficult questions needing immediate answers. Moreover, to be on a first-name basis with the president would be to misrepresent their relationship, Marshall felt.

The general also grappled with other problems. The Woodring-Johnson feud, isolationist versus internationalist, left the chief of staff without firm civilian policy direction. The lack of presidential guidance, in fact, the seemingly aimless leadership as the threat of war grew over that last summer of fretful peace, frustrated Marshall. The token military appropriations for a force of just 174,000 officers and men held them well below the authorized strength of the Army Reorganization Act, now almost two decades old. That was the big problem he confronted; the petty irritants he could overlook, as he had when dealing with French officers during the Meuse-Argonne transfer so long ago. "I never haggled with the president," Marshall explained later. "I swallowed the little things so that I could go to bat on the big ones. I never handled a matter apologetically and I was never contentious. It took me a long time to get to him. When he thought I was not going for publicity and doing things for publication—he liked it."

Insulated from partisan politics—like most military men of that day Marshall had never even voted—he had only the most general understanding of either political realities or political possibilities. Roosevelt would lead, but only when he recognized the public was ready to follow. To rush into preparations for war when the threat seemed so remote, so purely a European business, was in Roosevelt's view to risk permanent loss of a public mandate when it would be needed.

Furthermore, the president was not only commander-in-chief, he was also leader of a political party in an election year. At the moment, he did not know if he could run again. The load was grueling, he told his visiting ambassador to the Court of Saint James, Joseph Kennedy. "I'm tired. I can't take it. What I need is a year's rest. . . . I just won't go for a third term unless we are in war." Then, remembering the strongly isolationist sentiments of the ambassador, Roosevelt added, "Even then, I'll never send an army over. We'll help them, but with supplies."

The coming of war in Europe had little impact on most Americans. The stock market jumped four points on September 1 with the Stuka assault on Poland, investors anticipating a rush of defense orders. Within days, shipyards had splashed camouflage paint on English, Danish, and Norwegian freighters. American ships blossomed with large Stars and Stripes painted on the hull; sardonic merchant mariners judged them "bullseyes."

Europe remained remote, despite the dire news. Within days the German Panzers had slaughtered the foolhardy Polish cavalry while the Luftwaffe obliterated Polish air forces. Day by day the Wehrmacht drove eastward. Poland was dying as forlorn guides at the Polish pavilion at the New York World's Fair urged visitors to enter the essay contest, "I would like to visit Poland because . . ." First prize was a vacation in Warsaw.

Through the summer the president had urged revision of the Neutrality Act, which barred the sale of arms to belligerents. On September 3, just hours after France and Great Britain declared war on Germany, Roosevelt took to the radio for another of his Fireside Chats.

"This nation will remain a neutral nation," he assured his unseen audience. But to a flexible president, the concept of neutrality might be flexible too. "I cannot ask that every American remain neutral in thought. . . . Even a neutral has a right to take account of facts. Even a neutral cannot be asked to close his mind or conscience."

The coming of war did what presidential exhortation could not. Within a week of the German invasion, the White House had a sense that congressional opposition to neutrality reform was shifting. For the first time, congressmen and senators could vote not only their district, but their conscience. A *Fortune* magazine poll indicated as many as seven out of ten Americans now favored selling munitions to England and France—on a cash and carry basis.

On September 13, the president called a special legislative session to consider revision of the Neutrality Act. Strict neutrality aided the aggressors, the president argued as the Red Army marched across Poland's eastern provinces to link with the Wehrmacht along the Bug River. Organized resistance in Poland shriveled while isolationists Charles A. Lindbergh and the influential radio priest Father Charles Coughlin exhorted their followers to avoid foreign wars. Privately, the White House encouraged a countercampaign by a Non-Partisan Committee for Peace Through Revision of the Neutrality Act.

Marshall's own sense of urgency increased with events in Poland. His army had languished since the 1918 armistice, starved first by a complacent Congress, then by administrations concerned more with domestic than foreign affairs. Not only was this army understrength—only four of its nine infantry divisions could muster even half of the troops that tables of organization called for—it was poorly equipped. The bolt-action 1903 Springfield that served as the basic infantry rifle was obsolescent. Artillery dated from the first war; mortars, machine guns, and the automatic rifle were of similar vintage. Army Ordnance had designed or approved newer weapons, but Congress had not appropriated procurement monies.

Virtually everywhere Marshall looked he discovered the inadequacies that made the Army a poor match for the Wehrmacht if war came. Mechanization and especially infantry-tank tactics and training had not yet recovered from the setback delivered when Chief of Staff Douglas MacArthur in 1931 ordered early experiments abandoned. The Air Corps had fared no better, for while aircraft design and performance improved dramatically during the interwar period, procurement had not kept pace. Plans for a succession of new bombers, dive bombers, and pursuit planes were complete, but only two, the Boeing B-17 bomber and the Curtiss P-40 fighter, had gone into production. Early models of these aircraft, as the British would discover, were unsuitable for combat, lacking sufficient armoring for the crews and self-sealing gas tanks.

Organizationally, Marshall's army was an unstitched patchwork. Some 45,000 of its 174,000 enlisted men were stationed in Panama, the Philippines, and Hawaii. The balance was scattered among more than 100 stateside posts and camps. The lack of motor transportation made it impossible to bring entire divisions together for maneuvers. Corps and general headquarters command units existed only on charts in the Munitions Building.

The appropriations bill for fiscal 1940 had increased the authorized troop strength to 210,000, but the new troops were entirely absorbed by the Panama Canal command and the Air Corps. The parallel increase to an authorized strength of 5,500 airplanes was also an encouragement, but the planes did not exist as of September 1, 1939, and the invasion of Poland.

In that first week of war, President Roosevelt declared a state of national emergency. Yielding to Marshall, he authorized the expansion of the Army by another 17,000 men, and the National Guard to 235,000. He also approved $12 million in emergency funds to buy desperately needed trucks. Still, the Army was no more than "that of a third-rate power," Marshall warned.

Barely settled in Quarters No. 1 at Fort Myer, Marshall moved quickly. He approved Malin Craig's long-shelved plans to reorganize World War I's cumbersome quadrangular division into a three-regiment, triangular configuration. Where once he had three serviceable if unfilled divisions composed of twelve regiments, he now had five made up of fifteen—all understrength.

"Time—time more than anything else" was the dominant factor now, the chief of staff fretted. Everything they needed—the Garand semi-automatic rifle, heavy machine guns, even cannons for the new Stuart tank—required a year or more to produce. "A billion dollars the day war is declared will not buy ten cents worth of such material for quick delivery," he told an interviewer for *The New York Times.*

Time and immediate supplemental appropriations he would not get. While the president groped for a coalition to repeal the Neutrality Act before Hitler turned to the West, the White House would hear no appeals from the War Department; larger appropriations for ground forces implied that Roosevelt would send America's sons to fight in Europe. Mere sales of armaments could be justified as good works and good business.

The surrender of hapless remnants of a once proud Polish Army on September 12 and the uneasy truce that settled over Europe seemingly removed some of the urgency in any event; public and congressional opinion, so eager to build up defenses at the first part of the month, began to flag by the end of September.

Poland lay subdued, divided between Germany and the Soviet Union. Russian troops reoccupied the old czarist provinces of Latvia, Estonia, and Lithuania, creating an additional buffer between Germany and the Soviet Union. The French Army and British Expeditionary Force waited restively along the French frontiers as Europe settled into the tense interlude known as the Phony War. Wary of public opinion, the president hewed to his first priority, revision of the Neutrality Act, which prevented the United States from supplying those who were to do the fighting. While Congress debated repeal, Roosevelt cautiously curtailed expansion of the Army by one half and suspended White House consideration of the 1941 military budget. "Have you noticed that . . . I have been trying to kill all war talk?" he wrote Chicago newspaper publisher Frank Knox, the Republican vice-presidential nominee of three years before.

The drone of congressional debate turned to outrage on October 9 when the German pocket battleship *Deutschland* intercepted the American cargo ship *City of Flint* en route to Great Britain. The steamer was carrying contraband tractors, fruit, and grain, the German captain claimed as he put a prize crew aboard the unarmed freighter. Like the mistimed naval depredations of World War I, the *City of Flint* incident tipped public opinion in favor of repeal of the act.

For another month isolationist senators fought a rearguard battle against any revision. On October 27, the Senate approved a compromise revision of the Neutrality Act, 63–30. The next day an unyielding Secretary of War Woodring assured the nation, "There is no man in public office today who is more determined than your Secretary of War that your sons and my sons shall not march forth to war." So reassured that revision was merely good business and not a declaration of war, a week later the House too voted for revision, 243 to 181. America could sell arms to belligerents on a cash and carry basis.

Through the fall, Marshall's efforts to increase the pace of the nation's rearmament remained low-key, hobbled by respect for the constitutionally mandated role of the president as commander-in-chief. Moreover, he was caught between the feuding Woodring and Johnson.

The chief of staff tried to remain neutral. Demanding loyalty himself, he was prepared to give it, Marshall told the irritated secretary of the treasury, Henry Morgenthau. "Everybody in town is shooting at Woodring and trying to put him on the spot and I don't want to see him get on the spot. Everybody is trying to get him out of there and I am not going to be a party to it."

Marshall's impartiality infuriated Assistant Secretary Louis Johnson, who believed he had a claim on the chief for supporting Marshall for that post. Strong-willed, petulant, and ambitious, Johnson had maneuvered himself to the leadership of the American Legion, and with that organization's backing had secured the assistant secretariat. Now he wanted to be secretary, and was calling in his political debts.

When Johnson reproved Marshall, the chief of staff snapped, "Listen, Mr. Secretary, I was appointed chief of staff and I think you had something to do with it. But Mr. Woodring [is] Secretary of War and I owe loyalty to him. . . . I can't expect loyalty from the Army if I do not give it."

With the civilian leadership of the department at loggerheads, Marshall had no effective entrée to the White House. The influential Harry Hopkins, so helpful earlier, was hospitalized for treatment of hemochromatosis, failure of the intestines to leach nutrients from food. The president meanwhile seemed little interested in the Army's problems.

The chief of staff confronted not only Roosevelt's seeming indifferent, but a president who considered himself a navy man. A lifelong sailor, Roosevelt had served as assistant secretary of the navy during World War I. He understood the fleet, knew its ships and men, and even took a hand in its day-to-day administration. Yet if Chief of Naval Operations Harold Stark was irritated, he still had ready access to the White House and to a president more than happy to discuss navy problems. Marshall stood outside the president's circle, because he was in the Army; because he deliberately refused to cultivate FDR's friendship; because he was a formal, austere man distancing himself from an administration that ran on improvisations, good humor, and political cunning.

In one sense he was fortunate, for the president left the chief of staff alone to deal with the emergency. Still there was much to do, and too few of them to do it. Despite Marshall's widely quoted assertion that "nobody had an original thought after 3 p.m.," he often worked long hours in these hectic months following the German invasion of Poland.

A man of routine and habit, he attempted to follow a schedule even as the situation in Europe worsened. He rose at 6:30 a.m., and was at the breakfast table by seven. A half hour later he was at his desk in the Munitions Building. He often recrossed the Potomac in his chauffeur-driven staff car for lunch, frequently now with guests; the cook grew adept at stretching meals for two into repasts for four.

Marshall expected his household to run with drill-like precision. Alerted by a secretary as the chief of staff left the building, Marshall's cook had lunch waiting for him. "I walk right to the lunch table . . . from the car, and then I have a half hour or more to relax in a more restful atmosphere than here at the office or at the Army and Navy Club," he wrote Malin Craig. If he had no guests, he would nap on a chaise-longue in the second-floor sun room. Acutely conscious of his health, Marshall sought to conserve his energy.

Whenever he could, but never before the basket of papers on his desk had been emptied, Marshall left at four o'clock. Before nightfall he went riding with Molly; in the summer of 1940 he began to take Katherine for a picnic dinner on a lazy canoe ride down the Potomac or on leisurely walks through peaceful Arlington Cemetery. He kept his entertainments simple: dinner with the handful of personal friends to whom he was closest; biweekly visits with the elderly Pershing at the general's suite in the Hotel Carleton or at Walter Reed Hospital. The Marshalls attended movies at the post theater where seats were reserved for him in case he should turn up; westerns were certain to lure them from Quarters No. 1. Whenever he could, he avoided formal social gatherings, attending as few as possible and leaving early, his highball unfinished. In gossiping

Washington, it only added to his reputation for austerity; columnists had already noted he drove his own car when off-duty and had refused to adopt the beribboned, comic-opera dress uniform designed by his predecessor. Katherine Marshall had also ordered the two cannons removed from the front lawn of their home. The only symbol of the chief of staff's residence in Quarters No. 1 was a small brass plate on the door, a souvenir of his Tientsin service, that read in Chinese characters: "Marshall, Officer of the Beautiful Country's Army."

Conscious of her husband's need for a retreat, Katherine in the spring of 1940 bought a colonial house in Leesburg, Virginia, as a weekend and summer home. Though Dodona Manor, built in 1786 by a nephew of George Washington, was but thirty-five miles from Washington, it was some months before the busy general was able to break away to see the brick house with its fluted columns and front portico. When Marshall finally made his way to the small town in the foothills of the Blue Ridge Mountains, he apparently discovered—as Katherine had guessed—his long-desired haven, what for him would be home. Amid the elms and oaks that towered over the white house at the edge of town, he was to spend frequent weekends, puttering about the four acres, pruning trees. He began a noisome compost pit that would rival the virile properties of his boyhood stable; he eventually laid in a splendid garden that yielded beets "no one would eat," Katherine teased; birds got the raspberries before the Marshalls did. It was a satisfying refuge from the realities of the Munitions Building.

At Dodona Manor or Fort Myer, the chief generally retired at ten o'clock. He discouraged telephone calls from the War Department after dinner; two duty officers screened messages, decided which were to be relayed to the chief of staff immediately and which would wait. They tended to err on the side of delay.

As work in the War Department piled up, Marshall sought ways to handle the flow of paper. Sixty or more men reported directly to him, far too many, he told a luncheon guest. He would prefer just three or four deputies to whom were funneled all documents. While he could summarily order a reorganization, the blow to morale "would do much more harm than good would be accomplished from an organizational standpoint. The men who would be relieved and retired have given the best they had to the army."

Those who reported to him were expected to be prompt and succinct. The unprepared would find themselves on the way to new posts; the longwinded he cut off. He insisted memoranda be terse; staff officers learned how to write letters and reports, just as Marshall had earlier for Pershing, needing little editing before the chief of staff signed them. Only by the strictest of personal discipline, and by shifting large amounts of work to others, could he possibly keep pace.

His hardworking staff tended to hold him in awe, or fear, or both. Those who performed well—among them Omar Bradley, Maxwell Taylor, J. Lawton Collins, Walter Bedell Smith, and Orlando Ward—he marked for promotion. Less competent officers found themselves reassigned and forgotten.

Marshall was swift in his judgments, and an opinion once formed about an individual rarely changed. Those who sought preference he deliberately held back; fawning George Patton was to wait a full year before Marshall arranged his transfer from the cavalry to the tanks corps and awarded him a first star.

In dealing with his staff, in assigning officers to new tasks, his constant effort was to encourage independent thought. "Whenever I find these fellows who seem to have ability and a certain amount of disagreement with what we are doing, I am always interested in seeing them, and getting first hand impressions," he advised.

Marshall intended to overhaul the ossified army he commanded. He arranged the assignment of old friend Brigadier General Lesley J. McNair as the reform-minded commandant of Leavenworth's hallowed Command and General Staff School and instructed him to immediately revise the outmoded tactical training. "We must be prepared the next time we are involved in war, to fight immediately, that is within a few weeks, somewhere and somehow," he wrote McNair. They could expect "open warfare will be the rule rather than the exception," and it was for that Leavenworth had to train its students. The first days were critical; they had to "survive the first three or four months" before they could complete mobilization of the troops necessary to defend the continental United States.

Such internal reform he could accomplish with his own devices. Building the Army to adequate strength required White House and congressional cooperation. As the "sitzkrieg" wore on through the winter of 1939–40, Marshall waited impatiently. It was out of their hands, he advised his congressional liaison office in February 1940. "Events in Europe will develop in such a way as to affect congressional action." Marshall however came as close to pleading as his pride would permit on February 23 in an appearance before the House Appropriations Committee. "If Europe blazes in the late spring or early summer," he warned, "we must put our house in order before the sparks reach the Western Hemisphere."

His appeal fell on parsimonious men eying the June primaries. The committee trimmed by 10 percent the president's request of $850 million for the Army, chopping funds for an air base in Anchorage, Alaska, and leaving only 57 of the 166 airplanes Marshall sought in the budget.

Six days later, the Wehrmacht invaded Norway and Denmark. The Phony War had ended.

Increasingly nervous, Marshall had sought to get at least the $12 million for the Alaskan air base restored. In desperation, he turned to an old acquaintance, Bernard Baruch, the head of the war mobilization effort during the first war, more recently the self-styled park bench sage and influential "elder statesman number one" of Washington. Baruch was a demanding ally; his advice, freely given, was to be counted the wisest of counsel even when it was, frequently, useless. Baruch had tried Pershing sorely, not to mention a succession of presidents, but Marshall needed him now.

"The Army has never gotten its real story over," Baruch told Marshall. He suggested a private dinner with a handful of pivotal senators invited by James Byrnes, Marshall's acquaintance from Fort Moultrie, now one of the New Deal's spokesmen in the upper house. On the night of April 10, with Denmark's surrender the afternoon headline, Marshall, Baruch, Byrnes, and a handful of the Senate's leaders sat down to dinner and dealing.

The meeting lasted well into the early morning hours. After first suggesting that Baruch discuss the Army's needs, Marshall interrupted, moved by a passion Baruch had not seen before in the chief of staff. Marshall spoke eloquently, heatedly, of shortages and more shortages, of the lack of weapons, transportation, of even such elemental requirements as blankets. On and on he went, until suddenly the catalogue was ended. Exhausted, Marshall confessed, "I feel culpable. My job as Chief of Staff is to convince you of our needs and I have utterly failed. I don't know what to do." He looked from one to another of the stone-faced legislators.

Colorado's Democratic Senator Alva Adams, a leader in Senate caucuses and the man Marshall most hoped to convince, sat silently for a long moment. Then he nodded, his decision made. "You get every God damn thing you want," he promised.

Not everything, though Baruch decided that meeting was "a turning point in convincing such critics as Senator Adams of the urgent need for speeding the rebuilding of our defenses."

The speed was only relative. Appearing before the Senate subcommittee weighing the president's request for supplemental appropriations on May 1, Marshall suppressed his own sense of urgency to placate skeptics on the panel. Arms purchases were prudent now, "before we become involved in a real emergency," he advised. They might ponder the fact that the United States at that moment had fewer anti-aircraft guns than the British had mounted to defend just the City of London.

"I am more of a pacifist than you think," Marshall assured the subcommittee. "I went through one war, and I do not want to see another. My idea, however, as to the sound basis for peace may differ from others'."

Sitting at the end of the committee table, the senator from Missouri interrupted. "General, I think that all of us who were in it feel that way," said Harry S. Truman, a former field artillery captain in France.

"I saw it from the start, and I do not want to see it again," Marshall reiterated. ". . . I say this in all sincerity. I do not believe there is a group of people in the United States who are more unanimous in their earnest desire to avoid involvement in this ghastly war than the officers of the War Department. There is not the slightest thought in any of our minds of trying to utilize this emergency to aggrandize the Army, or of making exorbitant demands to put something over, as it were, under the pressure of the situation. We occupy most of our time trying to find some more economical method of improving the national defense, and the unanimous opinion of the officers I have talked with and come in contact with in the War Department is that we must do everything possible to make it that much more certain that we will not be drawn into this world tragedy."

Two weeks later, the Senate subcommittee was still dithering about restoration of the House of Representative cuts, spending hours scrutinizing the number of dentists' chairs the Army needed, even questioning the architect's designs for a new army building in Washington. But the Senate's mood had shifted; Senator Carl Hayden of Arizona felt compelled to "state for the record" that his subcommittee "was anxious and willing to undertake what the War Department wanted. . . ."

Marshall still had to convince the White House of the Army's inadequacies, of the necessity for a balanced force. With Hopkins hospitalized, the chief of staff turned to the second of the president's close friends, fellow Hudson River squire Henry Morgenthau, secretary of the treasury.

Morgenthau had known FDR for a quarter century, since he first became a gentleman farmer on his 1,000 acres near Fishkill, New York, then publisher of the influential *American Agriculturalist*. The two discovered their mutual love of the Hudson River Valley, and became constant companions. Morgenthau had taken on a variety of chores in Albany for Roosevelt the governor, and had come along to Washington in the first days of the New Deal, ultimately filling the sensitive post of secretary of the treasury. Morgenthau and Hopkins were the two men the president most trusted to handle difficult tasks.

Morgenthau had gained some sense of defense needs while coordinating British and French aircraft purchases in the United States. He wanted the full picture, for the mistake until now, he told Marshall, had been in "feeding the President little pieces here and little pieces there."

They met in Morgenthau's office on May 11, one day after Luxembourg, Belgium, and the Netherlands became the sixth, seventh, and eighth nations to fall to Hitler since the *Anschluss*. Neville Chamberlain's government had fallen; the discredited prime minister had bowed out in favor of a new coalition cabinet headed by Winston Churchill. Churchill immediately pledged his government to "victory at all costs, victory in spite of all terror, victory however long and hard the road may be." As for himself, he could offer only "blood, toil, tears and sweat."

As newswires clattered the debacle in the Lowlands, Marshall sketched for Morgenthau the Army's present mobilization plan. It called for a total of 1.25 million men under arms, combat-ready, within six months of M-Day. At the moment they had less than one quarter of that number on active duty, and only 75,000 could be said to have modern weapons. At best, a War Department report on the president's desk that day noted, they could equip 500,000 men with any arms at all. They needed everything, but the shortage of modern fighters and bombers was especially acute.

"I don't scare easily," Morgenthau said. "I am not scared yet."

The immediate cost, Marshall estimated, was an additional $650 million, more than twice the Army appropriation the president had asked in January. "It makes me dizzy," Marshall acknowledged.

"It makes me dizzy if we don't get it," Morgenthau retorted.

Airplanes alone would be insufficient, Morgenthau realized. He agreed to be Marshall's advocate when the president reviewed the "basic war plans" in two days, but urged Marshall to speak out himself. "Stand right up and tell him what you think. . . . There are too few people who do it and he likes it."

The subsequent White House meeting of May 13, 1940, was pivotal, Marshall believed, "an incredible performance," he later decided. The War Department delegation of Woodring, Johnson, and Marshall was sharply divided. Johnson favored the president's airplane plan, now fixed at an unheard-of 50,000-plane capacity per year, that figure plucked as casually from the president's fancy as Marshall's closely figured budgets were carefully drawn. Secretary Woodring, disapproving of any mobilization, sat silent.

Morgenthau opened the meeting, only to run into the president's feigned disinterest, then disdain. FDR joked, teasing his old friend, ever the harbinger of gloom; he talked on, dominating the meeting, rambling to deflect the secretary's appeal. Finally the president said no.

"Well, I still think you are wrong," Morgenthau insisted.

"Well, you filed your protest," the president snapped.

The meeting wound on inconclusively. Just as Roosevelt was to dismiss them, Morgenthau asked him to hear out the chief of staff.

"I know exactly what he will say," Roosevelt demurred. "There is no necessity for me to hear him at all."

The control Marshall so prided himself upon snapped. The chief of staff stood seething in the cold fury subordinates had learned to fear. "Mr. President, may I have three minutes?"

The words spilled out, precisely at first, then in a rush of frustrations. Barracks, rations, weapons, all in short supply. New artillery and anti-aircraft guns designed but not in production. Headquarters units unorganized, leaving this an army that could effectively throw no more than 15,000 men into combat at a time. The Germans had 2 million men in 140 divisions massed in the West. What were their five against that horde? On and on, well past the three minutes he had asked for, the chief of staff ticked off his army's deficiencies.

Two decades earlier he had confronted General Pershing in the muddy field of Gondrecourt; now he challenged the president of the United States. National policy remained vague, rudderless. They lacked coordination in their defense purchases; the Army and the Navy could not even agree to purchase the same brooms. There were no clear priorities: was steel for new naval vessels more important than steel for tanks? Military production was an afterthought of big business; at the moment, only the E. I. duPont powderworks might be described as on a war footing, and only because of British orders for smokeless powder. The United States was no more than a step ahead of the pace set prior to World War I, when it had taken them eighteen months to organize a field army. Hitler was not going to permit them such a leisurely schedule. Finally, his anger dissipated, Marshall subsided, "If you don't do something . . . and do it right away, I don't know what is going to happen to this country."

There was a long silence. "He stood right up to the president," a delighted Morgenthau chortled in his diary that night.

Just a month earlier, Marshall had been unable to get $12 million for an airfield in Anchorage, Alaska. Now President Roosevelt, plainly stunned by the chief of staff's vehemence, was asking Marshall to return the next day to discuss a supplemental army appropriation of $657 million. Morgenthau estimated the general might get three quarters of what he said the Army needed.

That meeting was the turning point, Marshall later decided. As the president worked over the chief of staff's requests on May 14 and 15, German troops crossed the Belgium border into France, driving toward Sedan; haunted names of World War I battlefields datelined the news from Europe once again. Panzer General Heinz Guderian's tanks pivoted westward, racing for the English Channel to close the noose on the British Expeditionary Force in Belgium; 200,000 men, the very heart of the British Army, began a grudging, punishing retreat to a small resort on the sea, Dunkirk.

While Roosevelt balanced congressional reaction to the news bulletins against the size of the supplemental appropriation, the newly installed British prime minister sat at his desk on the second floor of Number 10 Downing Street writing the president:

> As you are no doubt aware, the scene has darkened swiftly. The enemy have a marked preponderance in the air, and their new technique is making a deep impression upon the French. . . . The small countries are simply smashed up, one by one, like matchwood. We must expect, though it is not yet certain, that Mussolini will hurry in to share the loot of civilization. We expect to be attacked here ourselves, both from the air and by parachute and air borne troops in the near future, and are getting ready for them. If necessary, we shall continue the war alone and we are not afraid of that. But I trust you realise, Mr. President, that the voice and force of the United States may count for nothing if they are withheld too long. You may have a completely subjugated, Nazified Europe established with astounding swiftness, and the weight may be more than we can bear.

The prime minister asked for American aid "with everything short of actually engaging armed forces." The immediate needs were the loan of forty to fifty destroyers of World War I vintage to keep the sealanes to North America and the Middle East open; "several hundred of the latest types of aircraft"; anti-aircraft guns and ammunition; steel and other raw materials. In addition, he wrote, "I am looking to you to keep that Japanese dog quiet in the Pacific, using Singapore in any way convenient."

Churchill's message underscoring the importance of airpower in this new war of maneuver apparently confirmed the president in his decision to ask Congress for $300 million to fund production capacity for 50,000 airplanes a year. But Great Britain's other needs, desperate as they were, would have to compete with Marshall's. Roosevelt settled on a supplemental appropriation request on May 15, seeking only the bare minimum for a "thoroughly rounded Army": 200 new B-17 bombers; supplies to equip 1.25 million men on M-Day; and funds for the training of more pilots. The total, including another $250 million for the Navy, came to $1.8 billion.

"I know you can get them to accept it; they can't evade it," Marshall reassured the president. The chief of staff himself drafted the president's message to Congress that would accompany the request on May 16.

Congressional resistance wilted before news reports from Europe. German troops marched into the Belgian port of Antwerp and the French cathedral city of Amiens on May 17; in a week Guderian had accom-

plished with massed armor what Ludendorff's infantry had failed to gain
in four years. The Wehrmacht rammed a fifty-mile-wide gap in the lines
of a French Army believed by many Americans to be the best in Europe.
Those British and French troops still in unit formations fought through
to the Channel.

On May 26, the British began evacuating the troops who had made
their way to the coast. Cloudy weather obstructed Luftwaffe bombers as
a motley fleet of Royal Navy warships, ferry boats, and privately owned
vessels began boarding weary men from the beaches and quai. Through
eight days of round-the-clock rescue efforts, the fleet managed to save
from captivity 225,000 British and 113,000 French soldiers. As gallant
as the effort was, it was equally costly. The Royal Air Force lost 180
aircraft; French and British soldiers left behind 11,000 machine guns,
2,400 artillery and anti-aircraft guns, and 75,000 vehicles. The chief of
the Imperial General Staff, Sir Edmund Ironsides, watched the hollow-
eyed survivors entrain from the Channel ports in England and groaned,
"This is the end of the British Empire."

As England in 1588 awaited the Spanish Armada with a "militia of
Dogberries, Bottoms, Mouldies, Shadows, Warts, Feebles and Bullcalfs,"
so half-armed Great Britain in 1940 confronted Hitler. The French Army
crouched demoralized in hastily dug defense positions north of Paris as
Prime Minister Churchill promised Commons on June 4:

> We shall defend our island, whatever the cost may be. We shall
> fight on the beaches, we shall fight on the landing grounds, we shall
> fight in the fields and in the streets, we shall fight in the hills. We
> shall never surrender! And even if, which I do not for a moment
> believe, this island or a large part of it, were subjugated and starv-
> ing, then our empire beyond the seas, armed and guarded by the
> British fleet, would carry on the struggle until in God's good time
> the New World, with all its power and might, steps forth to the
> rescue of the old.

Churchill had little more than words to fling at Hitler. France's premier, Paul Reynard, appealed for fighter planes. Churchill declined; he
preferred to hoard his air force for the coming invasion, rather than
expend it in a futile gesture to a doomed ally. Marshal Pétain, the revered
hero of Verdun a generation before and now vice-premier, told the cabinet, "An armistice is, in my view, the necessary condition for the survival
of eternal France."

Confronted by the disaster in Europe, Congress abruptly opened the
public purse to defend the continental United States. Within two weeks
of the president's supplemental appropriations request, both House and
Senate had voted $1.5 billion, $300 million *more* than the president had

sought. It took but another four weeks to authorize an additional $1.7 billion in June after "the almost incredible events of the past two weeks."

Marshall's major problem now was not so much the lack of modern equipment, but keeping what he had. Almost daily he confronted the president's insistence that the United States provide some of the arms Churchill's purchasing agents sought.

Churchill's plea for arms "has a tragic similarity to the pressure for American men in 1917," Marshall confided to Morgenthau, but Marshall of 1940 was less sure than was Pershing of 1917–18. Reflecting the widespread military opinion that England would not hold, Major Walter Bedell Smith, a member of Marshall's handpicked personal staff, warned the chief: "If we were required to mobilize after having released guns necessary for this mobilization and were found to be short . . . everyone who was a party to the deal might hope to be hanging from a lamp post. . . ."

Marshall himself had doubts whether Churchill's island alone could withstand assault. The Wehrmacht's campaigns in Poland, in Denmark and Norway, through the Low Countries and then into France were disciplined, well-coordinated efforts linked by radio, and supported by efficient engineering and supply units. "The tanks made the holes, the planes ran beautiful interference, and the infantry carried the ball," Marshall, the onetime VMI football player, told journalist A. J. Liebling. Thus far the British Army had demonstrated nothing more than a capacity for the orderly retreat, the most difficult of all military maneuvers, but not one to win battles or wars.

Well before the Dunkirk evacuation, Marshall chose caution. If England collapsed, even with American airpower, the United States would be half-armed, he argued. On May 18, he warned Morgenthau against "submitting" to British requests for aircraft.

Yet his decision troubled him enough that he repeatedly sought to rationalize his no-aid stance. In a heated discussion with the secretary of the treasury on May 22, 1940, Marshall asked Air Corps Chief of Staff Hap Arnold what it would mean to release 100 of his newest aircraft to the British. A hundred planes, Arnold estimated, would replace but three days' combat losses at present rates, while setting back Arnold's training program by six months. The United States had just 260 pilots qualified to fly its combat-worthy air force of 160 fighters and 52 bombers. Obsolete bombers he could let go, but release of the new B-17s Churchill sought would seriously hamper North American defense.

As the Dunkirk evacuation began, Marshall relented in part, prodded perhaps by a May 29 cable from London asking for pistols and submachine guns "required to meet parachute attacks expected in the early future." In army warehouses reeking of Cosmoline lay half a million Enfield rifles, hundreds of artillery pieces, mortars, and machine guns, all of World War I vintage. The weapons, though obsolescent, might bolster British defenses.

It was no longer a matter of conscience, but of Great Britain's survival, and the survival of its fleet to protect the Atlantic Ocean. At first Marshall hoped Secretary Woodring would yield to White House pressure; later the general ignored Woodring's protests and on June 3 approved a long shopping list of weapons presented by the British. To complete the transfer, Marshall used a loophole in the Neutrality Act stretched wide by Attorney General Francis Biddle. Though the law barred government sales to belligerents, the Army could sell the arms to United States Steel Exporting Co. That private firm, responsible to Marshall's friend Ed Stettinius, would do what the government could not. Once again Marshall had creatively avoided an onerous rule. By June 11, stevedores were loading the long-warehoused World War I weapons and supplies of ammunition on British bottoms.

No single shipment could slake Britain's need. Marshall and his staff were to devote thousands of hours over the next two years resupplying the British Army. For Marshall and Stark, the problem of conscience would be compounded the following month when Congress, suspicious of President Roosevelt's intentions, adopted a bill requiring the two service chiefs to certify that goods sold overseas were not essential to national defense.

His task of readying the Army for war now more difficult than ever, Marshall spent long hours at his richly carved desk once used by the legendary Philip Sheridan. Weekends blurred into weekdays, especially for his hard-pressed staff. (Marshall had a habit of assigning tasks late in the day, either forgetting or heedless that his staff would have to work through the night to have the finished report on his desk the next morning. Occasionally he would comment that the drained men around him needed to get out and exercise, to spend some time in the sun.)

Marshall himself could spend only two days away from Washington when stepson Allen, working for a small radio station in Poughkeepsie, New York, married late in June. Concerned until then that the young man had not settled on a permanent line of work—radio seemed rather insubstantial—Marshall thought the new bride would be a "splendid stabilizer" for the boy he had accepted as his own son.

Allen's wedding was but a brief interlude in a month of tension. The end of France was near. Paris fell on June 14. From the temporary capital of Bordeaux, Pétain asked for an armistice. In Great Britain, a little known French general, Charles de Gaulle, broadcast reassurance to his countrymen: "France has lost a battle. But France has not lost the war."

The rush of events in Europe during June convinced President Roosevelt he must run for a third term. Until now he had waffled, mindful of the two-term tradition, yet worried that his successor, Republican or

Democrat, would not stand with Great Britain. The threat of a triumphant Germany commanding the Atlantic while upstart Japan ranged
the Pacific impelled him to run once more.

To do so, he had to put his own house in order, beginning with the
cabinet. As early as September 1939, he had weighed finding posts for
the 1936 Republican ticket, Alfred Landon and Frank Knox, to create a
bipartisan cabinet in time of war. Landon flatly declined to be FDR's
"catspaw," but Knox, the internationally minded publisher of the *Chicago Daily News,* told the president on December 10 that he would take
the offered post of secretary of the navy when public opinion recognized
the emergency.

Secretary of War Woodring's resistance to British aid early in June
sealed his fate. To replace him, the president turned at the suggestion
of Supreme Court Associate Justice Felix Frankfurter to Henry L. Stimson, former secretary of state under Herbert Hoover. On June 19, Roosevelt telephoned Stimson at his apartment in New York's Pierre Hotel.
Stimson was needed once more in Washington where "everybody is running around at loose ends," the president said. Stimson "would be a sta-
bilizing factor in whom both the Army and the public would have
confidence." At age seventy-two, Stimson might have declined the offer
with good reason. Instead, he discussed the appointment with his wife,
then called the White House to accept.

The appointments represented a shrewd political move. Bipartisanship muzzled at least some Republicans who otherwise would be quick
to charge the dismissal of Woodring as another Roosevelt step to war.

Both Woodring, who chose to resign rather than be dismissed, and
Assistant Secretary Louis Johnson were furious with Stimson's appointment, the one for his ouster, the other for the denied promotion, promised "not once but many times" by the president. Smarting from the
dismissal, Woodring told the hometown *Topeka Capital* he was the victim
of "a small clique of international financiers who want the United States
to declare war and get into the European mess with everything we have,
including our manpower. . . . They don't like me because I am against
stripping our own defenses for the sake of trying to stop Hitler 3,000
miles away."

Both Woodring and Johnson believed Marshall had influenced the
president's decision; fourteen years later Woodring wrote that Marshall
"would sell out his grandmother for personal advantage; that he would
sell out his policies, beliefs, and standards to maintain his political and
military position with the powers that be." In fact, Marshall had nothing
to do with the shift, however relieved he was to have the Woodring-
Johnson feud behind him.

Henry Stimson was all Woodring was not. A Yale graduate who had
gone on to Harvard Law School, Stimson was of that nineteenth-century

social class that considered leadership an obligation and a right. Secure themselves, and well placed, men like Stimson—who had served every president since William Howard Taft—moved easily back and forth from their law offices, banks, and corporate boardrooms to government positions, emulating the British upper classes as they went. Even Stimson's recreations were those of the British gentry: riding to hounds, three- and four-day weekends for multitudes of guests on his Long Island estate, or polite croquet matches on the lawns of his Washington home, Woodley.

Fresh from Harvard, Stimson had joined the influential Wall Street law firm headed by sometime cabinet officer and diplomat Elihu Root, and within two years had been elected a partner. As United States Attorney for the prestigious Southern District of New York, in 1906 he had taken on the young Felix Frankfurter as a deputy. The two men had remained close through the years, Frankfurter the upwardly mobile Jewish Democrat, Stimson the Presbyterian Republican, member of Yale's Skull and Bones, pillar of New York's select Century Club.

In snaring Stimson and Knox for his cabinet, Roosevelt was enlisting the internationally minded wing of the Republican Party, a faction alienated by the GOP's isolationism since the end of World War I. As far as Stimson was from the isolationist wing of his own party, that worldly Wall Street lawyer was close to the privately held views of Franklin D. Roosevelt. Knox's paper similarly had called for rearmament in a page-one editorial and the former Rough Rider himself had demanded all-out aid for the French and British short of sending troops to Europe. To men such as these, partisanship never interfered with public duty.

For all his experience as a diplomat, most recently as Herbert Hoover's secretary of state, Stimson cherished a special passion for the Army. As secretary of war from 1911 to 1913, Stimson had acquired the nickname of "Light Horse Harry," in part for his habit of riding daily, in part for the speed with which he worked. He had served at the age of fifty as colonel in the 31st Field Artillery during World War I; he still preferred to be addressed by the comparatively lowly rank of "Colonel" rather than "Mr. Ambassador" or "Mr. Secretary."

As secretary of war, once more the civilian head of the Army he loved, Stimson brought to the Munitions Building the flinty integrity of "a new England conscience on two legs." One wary colonel, confronted by Stimson's majestic rectitude, left the new secretary's office muttering, "I never heard the Lord God speak before."

This croquet-playing crony of Secretary of State Cordell Hull recruited three civilian deputies, internationalists like himself, influential and sophisticated: Robert A. Patterson, a federal judge who resigned from the bench to take Johnson's position; John J. McCloy, at first an expert in subversive activities, later an assistant secretary; and Robert A. Lovett, a navy flier during the first war and more lately a Wall Street investment banker, who was to be assistant secretary for air.

All were military-minded. An infantryman in the first war, Patterson had killed two Germans in close combat while on a patrol in No-Man's-Land. He still wore the belt taken from one of the bodies.

Stimson and Marshall knew each other largely by reputation. They had met in France during the war, and Stimson had later included Colonel Marshall on a private list of the best officers in the Army. About the War Department itself, Stimson and his assistants were less sure. Stimson's candid diary for the last six months of 1940 contained no less than sixteen entries regarding organization problems, in particular the inadequacies of the intelligence service. Lovett, a man of wry wit, decided the General Staff was so heavy with deadwood it was a fire hazard.

Marshall took pains to accommodate his new secretary, each of them sensitive to the peculiar triangular relationship of the chief of staff, the secretary of war, and the president. Stimson held the secretary's role to be military adviser to the president; communication between the War Department and the White House was to receive his "critical attention," he insisted. When Marshall pressed him, however, Stimson reluctantly agreed that the president "should have the constant right to consult" the chief of staff directly.

Each respecting the other's position, Marshall and Stimson were to work out a pragmatic modus operandi. They communicated frequently through "the door that was always open" between their adjoining offices in the Munitions Building, and though President Roosevelt frequently by-passed the secretary to talk directly with the chief of staff, Marshall briefed Stimson after each visit to the White House. When Stimson later complained he felt removed from strategic planning, Marshall immediately invited him to attend the daily military staff meetings. Stimson would never change his first assessment of Marshall as "always anxious to help . . . very loyal and faithful."

In deferring to Stimson, Marshall was acknowledging what he termed "the wisdom of the founders of our government in subordinating the military to the civilian authority." That conviction anchored his relationship with Stimson. Deferential to the office and the man alike, Marshall later said his only disagreements with Stimson came when the secretary asked for Marshall's opinion on what the chief of staff believed were purely civilian questions. "It will be made by the civilian head," Stimson retorted, "when he has had the benefit of the military head, of his military alter ego's best judgment."

For all that might have separated the two men, they shared a binding sense of duty. Stimson neither needed nor sought further honors, and he risked ignominious removal if the Republicans captured the presidency in November. He might have lived on in semi-retirement, idly following world affairs from the porch of his Long Island mansion, Highhold. Instead, he had accepted his president's summons, ignoring the partisan implications, to be of service in time of crisis.

The Stimson and Knox appointments were announced as the GOP gathered in Philadelphia for its nominating convention. The news shook the delegates. Senator Robert Taft charged: "Their selection indicates that the Democratic Party is rapidly becoming a war party."

Prime Minister Churchill, scrambling to meld his Dogberries and Feebles into an island defense, could only hope it was true. Across the Channel, just six minutes' flying time from the limestone cliffs of Dover, the Luftwaffe was scraping airfields out of French farmland. In the evenings, Londoners could hear an earnest children's choir on Berlin Radio singing a new song, *"Wir Fahren gegen England"*:

> So give me your hand, your pretty white hand,
> For tonight we march against England.

CHAPTER

X

The Most Businesslike Manner

Through July, August, and September 1940, Great Britain endured. Pummeled almost nightly by three Luftflotten totaling 2,800 bombers and covering fighters, the island absorbed an onslaught Reichsmarschall Hermann Goering had promised would leave it hapless.

Despite fifty-seven consecutive nights of bombing, people in sandbag-muffled London gamely went about their daily business. The Blitz wore on, Secretary of War Henry Stimson wrote in his diary in early September, "but all reports indicated that the morale of the British is holding out. . . . It is very interesting to see how the tide of opinion has swung in favor of the eventual victory of the British. The reports of our observers on the other side have changed and are quite optimistic."

Though Great Britain had weathered one summer's crisis, Stimson and President Roosevelt recognized that next spring would bring a renewed threat. American aid was critical.

Through the summer Roosevelt had kept one eye on the November elections—Harry Hopkins had manipulated a third-term "draft"—and with the other eye followed the progress of the German Army on a map set up in the Oval Office. Whatever he proposed to supply the British, he had to reckon with public opinion and the isolationist bloc.

The isolationists were formidable, especially in the Republican Party, led by an Old Guard of men whose bullish patriotism blinded them to new realities. They were joined by the privileged, who scorned Roosevelt as a traitor to his class, who opposed aid to Great Britain merely because *that man* sought it.

Elsewhere there were also powerful voices: the Radio Priest, as Father Charles Coughlin called himself, broadcasting from Detroit to an audience of millions across the country; the idolized Charles A. Lindbergh, ostensibly a non-political expert on aviation, in actuality an awed Germanophile; and such influential men as Wall Street attorney John Foster Dulles.

Bonded together as America First, they formed the core of opposition to both Roosevelt's reelection and aid to the Allies. At least 40 percent of the public in spring 1940, the Gallup Poll reported, believed aid to Britain and France a mistaken first step toward direct American involvement in Europe's war. In early June, public opinion churned by a massive public relations struggle was about evenly divided—on aid and the presidency alike.

Like France and the Lowlands, the isolationists too were crushed in the assault of Hitler's Panzers. "Two months ago," one Republican strategist warned in mid-June, "an isolationist was a sound fellow who minded his own business." With the fall of France, an isolationist had become "one who believes we have no interest in the European mess and is willing to sit back and watch Nazi aggression conquer the world by terror."

In Washington, a chief of staff increasingly sensitive to political realities also weighed the public mood. Learning quickly, Marshall timed what he termed a great many proposals with the actions of Hitler's government. He would wait the right moment to seek funding, meanwhile dealing with internal War Department problems.

Emboldened by President Roosevelt's call for the production of 50,000 aircraft, young Air Corps officers argued that great bombers alone would determine the outcome of future wars. Their partisans in Congress and the press assailed Marshall's "outmoded" concept of balanced air and ground forces. The chief of staff asked for such mundane items as barracks and blankets, neither of which won wars nor would impress Hitler, while the president sought bombers. Still Marshall refused to back down. If the United States went to war, the issue would be decided in a great land battle, not in the air, he believed. He wanted no repetition of the Spanish-American War's massive supply snarls, or the lack of winter clothing that confronted Pershing in France were *his* army sent into the field. Furthermore, Marshall asked pointedly, what good were airplanes when they lacked pilots to fly them?

Marshall did not oppose a build-up of the Air Corps as such. He insisted, however, that it come about rationally, coordinated with the needs of other branches. Both the chief and the younger flying officers could look to the European war for proof of their arguments.

Airpower would be essential, Marshall acknowledged. In the early months of 1940, he had reviewed a staff proposal calling for 54 air groups, some 5,000 planes, with all the training facilities, landing fields, air bases, and technical installations needed to support such an air fleet. After listening to young Major Laurence Kuter's presentation, Marshall asked only, "Why is this a fifty-four group program? Why not fifty-six, or sixty-four, or more?"

Surprised, Kuter said no one had ever asked him that question before. Fifty-four groups was all the Air Corps could effectively manage at the moment, he replied.

Marshall nodded. "The program is approved. Let's get on with it."

For all he had accomplished, Marshall could take no satisfaction in the pace of rearmament. Accepting an honorary degree in June 1940 from Pennsylvania Military College, he told the graduates the nation had begun preparing for war and was now far more advanced than it had been in 1917. But how much further along to the prescribed Protective Mobilization Force would they be had Congress funded the peacetime Army conceived in 1921? "Then there was plenty of time and little money, and now there is plenty of money and very little time."

As Marshall anticipated, events in Europe opened the Treasury as domestic appeals could not. Admiral Harold Stark, chief of naval operations, would place the largest naval procurement order in history before the end of summer, calling for construction of 210 ships, including twelve aircraft carriers and seven battleships. By mid-year, the total army and navy appropriations would top $17 billion, more than nine times the 1939 figure.

The Army's appropriations were to pay for a multi-layered preparedness program. Marshall sought to equip a combat-ready ground force of 1 million men, while simultaneously stockpiling "important long [lead] time items" such as tanks and anti-aircraft guns sufficient for an army of 2 million. At the same time, army procurement was to build up an industrial base to supply an army of 4 million men.

The program was ambitious, but suddenly possible. Congress cheered when the president sought funding for his 50,000 airplanes, sending FDR back to the White House contemplating yet another $4 billion appropriation for defense. An economy that had resisted all the ministrations of Roosevelt's "Dr. New Deal" would dramatically turn about with the cures of "Dr. Win-the-War."

These weapons of war would be important, when deliveries began, but they raised the question of expanding the Army from its authorized 255,000-man strength. Even the most isolationist of officeholders could rationalize a vote for arms purchases or military construction; that added to the local economy. Manpower levies on the other hand subtracted men from their families, wage earners from the community, and votes from election returns.

For just that reason, President Roosevelt refused to advocate conscription; any such move would inevitably appear to be the first step to sending American boys to rescue the British Empire. The president wanted to appear to be " 'attacked' for inactivity and thus 'goaded' into action by public demand." Roosevelt's briar-patch gamble rested on the expectation that public opinion would veer toward mobilization before the nation found itself at war, without an army to defend it.

Instead, the nation's first peacetime conscription bill sprang from one of the more remarkable, if little remembered men of his time, Grenville Clark. Once Henry Stimson's law partner, Clark had advocated military preparedness since World War I and the Plattsburg experience. In the spring of 1940, as the "sitzkrieg" exploded into war, Clark approached Marshall with a model selective service bill, seeking the chief of staff's support.

Marshall declined to endorse the bill introduced at Clark's behest by New York Republican Congressman James Wadsworth and Democratic Senator Edward R. Burke of Nebraska. As chief of staff, he was technically independent of the "political" executive branch, free to render such professional judgments as he considered in the nation's best interest. Nonetheless, to support the bill risked a White House confrontation over the president's calculated strategy, and squandering his modest influence with FDR. However much he wanted to increase the size of the Army's long-planned Protective Mobilization Force, however certain the eventual passage of a draft bill, Marshall's first priority was to build up stocks of supplies for those draftees. He too needed time.

Two other political considerations figured in his decision: endorsement of a bill Democratic floor leader James Byrnes said did not have a "Chinaman's chance" in the Senate would undercut his growing authority with Congress. Finally, he was acutely aware that his backing of a draft bill would be widely interpreted as a move to increase his own power. The Burke-Wadsworth bill, one senator had already complained to Marshall, was "one of the most stupid and outrageous things that *'the generals'* had ever perpetrated on Congress."

Marshall preferred to make haste slowly. An immediate draft would force him to strip his five partially mobilized, triangular divisions of men to train the inductees. The Army would be left, literally, with no effective infantry. Instead of an immediate draft, he favored an enlarged volunteer army of 375,000, the 120,000 new recruits used to bring the nine planned infantry divisions to full strength.

Draftees would require clothing, vehicles, weapons; even housing was in short supply. To outfit the new troops now, Marshall would be forced to strip National Guard units across the country, just when increased training had measurably improved their combat efficiency. By terms of the long-standing mobilization plan, those 241,000 guardsmen needed further training, not abandonment in favor of raw levies.

Undaunted, Clark pressed on, riding the crest of events in Europe. The appointment of his law partner Henry Stimson on June 20, 1940, as secretary of war gave him a dedicated ally lobbying effectively within the administration. Stimson set to clearing away the opposition to the draft bill.

While Washington sweltered in the heat of the hottest July in memory, Stimson first dissuaded the president from openly backing Marshall's volunteer-only plan, arguing it was inadequate. The president's endorsement of a volunteer army, however appealing the plan was politically, would give anti-draft legislators a weapon with which to beat the Clark bill to death.

Stimson and Clark together convinced Marshall on the morning of July 8 that his all-volunteer army would not be sufficient. Even as they talked, enlistments lagged. Compulsory service was the only solution in a period of crisis, and Clark's plan for a national lottery "the only fair, efficient and democratic way to raise an army."

Marshall needed little urging. He wanted civilians to initiate proposals to conscript civilians for service in his army. If he led off, he later acknowledged, "I would have defeated myself before I started and I was very conscious of that feeling." If the initiative came from civilians, however, the army chief of staff "could take up the cudgels. . . ."

At least some of their manpower problems might have been eased were Marshall and Stimson less men of their times. Approximately 10 percent of the nation's population was black, generally undereducated and greatly underemployed. Many sought to enlist but encountered quotas and discouragement.

Black troops had served in segregated units since the Civil War, occasionally with distinction, but usually under white officers. During the first war, President Wilson had yielded to political pressure and appointed some black junior officers to serve with the 92nd Division (colored), as the Army formally designated it. They had not done well, General Pershing noted, "owing to the lower capacity and lack of education of the personnel" and because they themselves were hastily trained.

Marshall, unquestioning, shared Pershing's opinion. Never overtly hostile to blacks, he was instead patronizing. In at least one letter, written in 1941 to a childhood friend, he referred to a "darkey soldier." While such an attitude was hardly cruel bigotry, it would do nothing to enlarge the limited role assigned to black troops by men like Marshall.

Reflecting the society at large, magnifying that society because of the high percentage of southerners in uniform, the Army was a segregated institution. How else when even the Red Cross labeled blood plasma "colored" and "white"?

Marshall saw no irony, only a righteous sense of even-handed treatment in the Army's separate but equal policy. He assured one complainant that four black soldiers had suffered no discrimination when compelled to eat at a separate table in the kitchen at a California air base.

White cooks and mess attendants customarily eat in the kitchen, and the food and service are the same as those provided in the main dining room. It is felt that no discrimination was intended.

Upon the arrival of twenty additional negro soldiers at the school on October 4, all were fed in the main dining room with white troops. Since October 10 a separate dining room and mess hall has been provided for them.

Discrimination in the Army against men of any color or race is not sanctioned by the War Department, and I thank you for bringing this matter to my personal attention.

The Army's separate but equal policies produced waste. When Senator Joseph O'Mahoney of Wyoming pointed out that Negroes were turned away from the Air Corps, Marshall responded,

It has been the policy—and I think it is a necessary one—that we do not have mixed units. . . . I have had the question asked me why, in advertising for recruits, more effort was not made toward procuring colored recruits. As a matter of fact, the usual reenlistments for the white organizations have been on the basis of about 40 percent; for the colored organizations they are about 80 percent reenlistments. All colored units have a waiting list. We do not have to make any effort to recruit for those units.

No one proposed creating additional black units, even though white enlistments continued to lag.

Other policies might change, however. The fall of France had galvanized public sentiment in favor of preparedness, and the draft bill once given only a "Chinaman's chance" appeared now a good bet.

Still FDR raised no public voice in support of the bill. At the same time, he permitted Marshall to quietly lobby individual congressmen. "The Army played politics," Marshall candidly admitted in a later interview.

Not until July 31, with the Luftwaffe swarming the skies over England, did the president sanction administration support of the draft bill. Stimson immediately issued a statement advising Congress, "We've got to very radically revise our prejudices about our first line of defense. A prudent trustee must take into consideration that in another thirty days Great Britain may be conquered and her fleet come under enemy control. Across the Pacific there is a powerful Japan in sympathy with Italy and Germany."

With the president's approval, Marshall endorsed the Selective Service bill in testimony before the House Committee on Military Affairs on the afternoon of July 24, 1940. Testifying in the swelter of the high-ceil-inged hearing room, Marshall warned the committee, "We cannot afford, under the present conditions, to speculate with the national defense. We certainly are not doing too much, but I think it would be far, far better that we do too much . . . than that we underrate the hazard of the very critical situation in the world at the present time, as it affects us."

Was not the Army asking for too much—1.4 million men to serve eighteen months—Congressman R. Ewing Thomason demanded.

"I might say my relief of mind would be tremendous if we just had too much of something besides patriotism and spirit," Marshall sighed.

Masking his impatience with politic gestures, Marshall acceded to a series of amendments the White House believed necessary to get the draft bill adopted. The first trimmed the term of service from eighteen to just twelve months, with a clause permitting extension if Congress were to declare a state of national emergency. Marshall also accepted an amendment limiting the number of inductees to 900,000 per year, thus avoiding a drain on the national economy some congressmen feared. Finally, to appease isolationists, he silently accepted another amendment barring use of draftees outside the western hemisphere.

Speaking candidly, with some deference always, Marshall appeared repeatedly before congressional committees through the summer. His sober demeanor deflected charges he was an alarmist. His frankness guaranteed he was not merely the president's henchman.

On August 7, with a torpid Congress seemingly stunned by the record heatwave of that summer, Marshall took a bold step, one that had the effect of establishing his reputation as a professional rather than a polit-ical soldier. Appearing before the crucial Senate Appropriations Com-mittee's military subcommittee, the chief of staff asked for a second supplemental military appropriation of $4 billion. The Army's portion of the money was to be used, he candidly told the senators, to outfit and house the long-planned Protective Mobilization Force of 1.2 million men and 800,000 reserves. For the moment his Army and National Guard together mustered only a quarter of that; the additional manpower he hoped to secure through the draft, pending in Congress. They had to act now, even before approval of the Selective Service bill, if the Army was to be ready for the first call-up. "The weeks have come and gone and we have been unable to make a start" on construction, he reminded the senators.

Marshall made no attempt to soften the blow, relying instead on can-dor. "I think it is tragic that we find ourselves in a situation which requires the spending of these colossal amounts of money for purely a war-mak-ing purpose," he told the senators.

"I think it is indeed unfortunate that the so-called enlightened peoples of the world should be engaged in devoting such a large part of their resources to nonproductive, war-making purposes."

Marshall would not flinch from responsibility. Neither would he permit the senators to slip the burden. "We must meet the situation that is facing us, and I see no way of doing that except by preparing. Huge sums of money must be spent, but that spending must be done in the most businesslike manner possible. There must be no undue waste. Hasty and ill-considered expenditures must be avoided."

In speaking so frankly, Marshall risked appearing presumptuous, as if assuming the Selective Service bill, wending its own way through the Congress, would be adopted. Because legislators resented assumptions of how they might decide an issue, the general could destroy his growing rapport with Congress, and with it his own effectiveness as chief of staff.

He might have ducked the issue entirely, putting off the funding request until passage of the draft bill. That strategy assured delaying inductions until facilities could be built for the draftees.

Isolationist Senator Gerald P. Nye, who had built an international reputation investigating World War I's munitions industry, deemed the bill hasty. "Of course, General, we can entertain a hope that developments abroad in the next few months will be such that we can abandon a considerable part of this program, can we not?"

The general shook his head. "Senator, I am sorry that I cannot entertain any such hope at present. My fear is not that I am recommending too much but rather that I may find at some time in the future that I recommended too little. In fact, if I could feel now that I might expect some day to face an investigation for having recommended too much, my mind would be more at rest than it is at present."

Marshall spoke bluntly, refusing to temporize. The Protective Mobilization Force was but a "first essential requirement. It would furnish the covering force behind which we would have to prepare additional forces for a larger effort to maintain the integrity of the Western Hemisphere." A planned army composed of 27 infantry divisions, two armored divisions, six cavalry divisions, and an Air Corps of 11,000 planes would still "be inadequate to wage a successful war with a fully prepared foreign power."

Persuaded by Marshall, the subcommittee voted its do-pass to the appropriations bill just as the end of the heatwave released Congress from lethargy. At the same time, public opinion polls reported that seven of ten Americans now favored the draft, and deemed preparedness the best defense in the current crisis. Then Wendell Willkie, the independent who had become the Republicans' presidential nominee, surprisingly endorsed the concept of selective service, and thereby removed the bill from partisan dispute. That slow, inefficient thing termed a democracy had reached a decision; suddenly, America determined to arm, and on August 27, both houses of Congress authorized the call-up of the National Guard for one year.

The Army's affairs would improve even more. On September 14, the House of Representatives turned back a last effort to postpone the draft until after the election, and adopted the Senate version of the Burke-Wadsworth bill. Two days later, the first of the federalized National Guard units reporting for duty, President Roosevelt signed the Selective Service Act. The measure that would form the basis for the United States' war effort was law.

On Wednesday, October 16, 16,316,908 men between the ages of twenty-one and thirty-six lined up for "R-Day" at schools, public buildings, and churches to enroll in what *The New York Times*'s Cabell Phillips called "an historic muster." The draft swept democratically across economic and social class lines. The president's second son, Franklin Delano Junior, turned up to register at an Indianapolis firehouse, listing his occupation as "unemployed." The intervention-minded son of the isolationist Ambassador Joseph Kennedy, twenty-three-year-old John Fitzgerald Kennedy, registered in Stanford, California, where he was spending a year in pre-law and racing his red Buick convertible about the Bay Area. FDR Junior, John Kennedy, and each of the other 16,316,906 men who signed up on Registration Day was assigned a number from 1 to 6,175 by his draft board. That number was to govern the lives of an entire generation.

Thirteen days later, a blindfolded Secretary of War Henry Stimson dipped a ladle carved from a beam taken from Independence Hall into a huge glass bowl containing bright blue capsules. He handed the first containing its fateful number to President Roosevelt, who opened it and read, "One hundred fifty-eight."

On paper at least, Chief of Staff George Marshall finally had his army: 500,000 were Regulars, 270,000 were from the National Guard, and 630,000 were to be draftees, inducted at the rate of 20,000 to 50,000 per month over the next year. Together they would form five Regular Army and four National Guard divisions, all at full strength finally; two cavalry divisions; one experimental, barely equipped armored brigade; an air force with 5,000 planes; and support troops. At the end of October 1940, the first 16,000 draftees reported to twenty-nine induction centers set up across the country. Ten million more would follow in the next five years.

Mobilization aggravated Marshall's supply problems in the fall and early winter. Continued British requests for ever more armaments jeopardized his caches and left the chief of staff confronting the president.

When Great Britain requested delivery of fifteen B-17s earlier disdained in favor of the Royal Air Force's Lancaster bomber, President Roosevelt suggested to Marshall he comply. The new bombers thus could be tested under battle conditions, Roosevelt recommended; surely that was essential to America's defense.

Marshall bridled. Congress had charged him with the responsibility of certifying that military equipment was not essential to the Army before it could be released to the British. Marshall agonized. "I was a little ashamed of this," he acknowledged later, "because I felt that I was straining at the subject in order to get around the resolution of Congress." Marshall strained, finally accepting whatever rationalization was necessary to provide the British with the fifteen bombers.

Still the president wanted more than tokens. Advocating an "even Stephen" division of bombers as they came off the assembly line, FDR summoned a White House meeting on September 27. State, Treasury, Army, Navy, they gathered in the Oval Office.

Marshall did the talking for the Army, the secretary wrote in his diary that night. "And he did it well. We had only 49 bombing planes fit for duty outside of those in the insular possessions—the garrisons of Panama and Hawaii—and the president's head went back as if someone had hit him in the chest when this fact was brought out."

They were dusting empty shelves, yet the British need was acute. In mid-October, the British Purchasing Commission presented a shopping list of supplies necessary to outfit ten divisions by the end of 1941. Moreover, Great Britain wanted to increase its airplane orders from 14,000 to 26,000 of all types. None of this would have been beyond American industrial capacity, but for the U.S. Army's own swelling needs.

Marshall was to constantly reevaluate his commitment to arming the British in light of international developments. As the Battle of Britain waned, Marshall grew more optimistic. But the September 27, 1940, announcement that Japan had affiliated with the Berlin-Rome axis stirred new anxieties in him. Germany and Italy posed no immediate threat to the United States, but assertive Japan could easily move on the Philippines if provoked by American opposition to Japanese economic expansion.

For the moment, Marshall had not the forces to prevent Japanese expansion anywhere. The secretary of war, once a governor general of the islands, had declined to approve an increase in the number of Philippine Scouts a month earlier. The increase would be far too small to make any difference should Japan attack the Philippines.

Marshall's only option in the face of a looming threat from Japan was to urge the president not to take any action that might provoke the Japanese to attack the Philippines until the Army was better equipped and trained. For the next year Marshall would find himself pitted against Secretary of State Cordell Hull petulantly urging strong counters to Japanese territorial ambition. Heeding Hull one day, booming welcome to Marshall the next, President Roosevelt played for time in the Far East.

Like the president, the chief of staff was capable of the clever stratagem, however much he preferred to deal openly. A combination of overt and covert tactics during these months wrought what may well have been Marshall's greatest contribution to the United States Army.

During a recess in the Senate appropriations hearings of August 7, Marshall delayed his return to the Munitions Building to talk privately to Senator Byrnes about a pressing problem. If he was to build an army for war, Marshall explained, he had to have troop leaders fit for combat. Now he was stymied. Four months earlier, he had appeared before the House Military Affairs Committee seeking a bill that would permit the War Department to promote younger officers by retiring older men no longer fit for field service. Marshall meant to wipe out the dreaded hump.

The Army was different from civilian life, Marshall had told the committee. "One does acquire experience and judgment with the years, but also, unfortunately, we lose the resiliency of tendons and muscles. . . . We may have the wisdom of the years, but we lack—I know I do in many respects—the physical ruggedness of more youthful days."

In the first war, Marshall continued, he had seen twenty-seven of the twenty-nine divisions sent into combat, "and there were more reliefs of field officers, those above the grade of captain, due to physical reasons than for any other cause."

A second war now loomed; Marshall needed younger officers commanding regiments and battalions, yet was stuck with superannuated colonels waiting eventual retirement.

The House committee had been unmoved, Marshall told Byrnes. Those older officers had longstanding ties with congressmen, and fought back; a sympathetic Chairman Andrew J. May of Kentucky held the bill in committee. "I was accused of getting rid of all the brains in the Army," Marshall later said. "I couldn't reply that I was eliminating considerable arteriosclerosis."

Byrnes agreed to help. When the appropriations bill came up for Senate consideration, he inserted an innocuous-sounding amendment drafted by the War Department: "In time of war or national emergency determined by the President, any officer of the Regular Army may be appointed to higher temporary grade without vacating his permanent appointment." (The president had declared a "state of unlimited national emergency" on May 27, 1940.)

Byrnes's amendment passed easily, and became law with the adoption of the Second Supplemental Appropriation Act of 1940. Chairman May not only voted for the amendment, but did not learn he had been effectively outmaneuvered for some days. The chief of staff would have to spend a considerable amount of time soothing May's injured pride.

Vested with the authority to promote the younger men he considered deserving, Marshall set about making vacancies for them. He created a "plucking committee" of six retired officers headed by former Chief of Staff Malin Craig and assigned them the task of reviewing the efficiency ratings of older officers. They were to weed out the worst, he instructed, to make room for younger men.

No action by Marshall would cause as much bitterness as his creation of the plucking board. In its first six months, the panel removed 195 captains, majors, lieutenant colonels, and colonels; in the next five years it would ticket 500 colonels for immediate retirement. (Marshall agreed in a later interview that the board had been "ruthless," but defended the retirements as necessary. Even years later, those officers forced into retirement without promotion to the rank of brigadier general, and their wives, could not mention Marshall's name without a curse.)

Marshall himself was to turn sixty at the end of the year, reaching the age he had established for mandatory retirement of older officers no longer able to stand the strain. Should not he too be subjected to the same standard, he wondered.

Even before Malin Craig's review board began its work, the chief of staff paid one of his infrequent visits to the White House. After explaining the amendment, and no doubt preparing the president for the public outcry that would surely follow the enforced retirements, Marshall offered his own resignation to FDR.

Roosevelt, himself fifty-eight, made no comment. He could afford to wait. If the press rallied to the superannuated colonels and turned its editorial fire on the president, FDR would be able to announce Marshall's own resignation as both an example for others to follow and a propitiating sacrifice.

After two weeks, with only the anti-New Deal McCormick and Patterson papers sounding alarms, and still no word from the White House, Marshall called Harry Hopkins.

Hopkins was amused. "The President just laughs at you," he told the chief of staff. "He says no politician ever resigns a job and that's just talk."

Not to Marshall. A second time he marched to the White House to offer his resignation. This time he suggested he train his successor for two or three months, and then step down. A second time the president listened impassively.

McCormick's *Chicago Tribune* and Cissy Patterson's *Washington Times-Herald* found no support elsewhere. Their editorial protest sputtered impotently; the retired colonels were forgotten. Once more Hopkins explained by telephone that the president had ignored his chief of staff's offer to retire. Marshall would stay on.

As the plucking board set to work, Marshall meanwhile drew up the first list of promotions to submit to the president. In a year of decisions vital to the nation's rearmament, none would be more important than the selection of the Army's new leadership. Marshall would be shaping, as had Pershing before him, an army in his own image.

Though he relied mainly on his prodigious memory for both success and failure, Marshall checked at least some of the names with his old mentor, General Pershing, during biweekly visits to the old man's suite at Walter Reed Hospital. The recommendations then went to Stimson for review.

Over a weekend at Highhold, the secretary and Marshall's old friend from Chicago, retired General Frank McCoy, examined the service records of each of the chief of staff's nominations. Stimson was delighted, he noted in his diary, for Marshall had tapped "several men whom McCoy and I knew to be good war men and yet who might have not have had as good a record on paper."

The first list of hundreds to come bumped seventy-nine colonels and two lieutenant colonels to the rank of brigadier general. While a number were to achieve distinction as combat commanders, the majority of the promotions went to men who would provide the training and logistical spine of the new army Marshall was building. Throughout, Marshall maintained, "I have been absolutely cold-blooded in this business."

For every bitter colonel jumped by younger men, there was a more vigorous and delighted officer. Robert L. Eichelberger's happily weeping wife showed him the telegram announcing his promotion. The following day, George S. Patton, who had privately feared his age would count against him, wired Eichelberger: "At last they have had sense enough to promote the two best damn officers in the U.S. Army."

The question of senior commanders addressed, Marshall took on the problem of providing the junior officers necessary to lead the expected draft levies. That matter was to provoke the first major clash between the chief of staff and the secretary of war, even as it raised once again the unresolved issue of who set policy for the War Department, the military chief or the civilian secretary.

Stimson and his closest advisers, Judge Patterson and Grenville Clark notably, favored the Plattsburg system of World War I, copied from the British. Commissions would go to college graduates after a short period of military training.

Marshall had once supported the concept, but had recently changed his mind. He never explained precisely what inspired his conversion. Perhaps his own experience with the CCC during the grim years of the Depression made him realize the injustice and the wastefulness of a system that structurally favored those who could afford to attend college. Certainly leadership did not flow from a diploma. Moreover, the prospective draft was to be democratic in operation; the resulting army could not be led by a social elite if it was to reflect the best of a democracy.

Instead, Marshall endorsed a far broader selection process in which

Regular Army cadres would tap exceptional men from the ranks for further training at Officers Candidate School. Both Regular Army enlistees and Selective Service draftees, when they came, were to be eligible. Direct commissions for the favored, the socially conscious Navy's favored method, were to be limited. Marshall would bend only to offer a slight compromise: college men would have their commissions confirmed only after taking basic training. At least, he argued, they would have had a taste of the enlisted man's lot, and thus would be more sensitive to the needs of the troops.

The secretary of war could be as rigid as his chief of staff. When Stimson held out for the Plattsburg system of direct commissions, Marshall exploded. "I tell you I am going to resign the day you do it!"

Stunned as much by the vehemence as the threat itself, Stimson backed down, to the irritation of Patterson and Assistant Secretary of War John J. McCloy. They insisted the General Staff's opposition was "simply a mark of incompetence and narrowmindedness." Marshall had prevailed, but threats alone would not resolve the larger question of who set policy for the War Department. The issue would rise again.

In pressing the Officers Candidate confrontation, the chief of staff was groping his way to shaping a vast citizen army, democratically selected by a random draft. Its combat leaders, the platoon, company, and battalion commanders, were to be chosen not by social privilege as in armies of the past but by personal qualifications. The Army he envisioned required a new form of discipline as well, one that discarded the "monotonous drilling, which, to be honest, achieved obedience at the expense of initiative. It excluded 'thought' of any kind."

That would not do in Marshall's new army. He wanted military discipline to grow out of "respect rather than fear; on the effect of good example given by officers; on the intelligent comprehension by all ranks of why an order has to be and why it must be carried out; on a sense of duty, on *esprit de corps.*"

Marshall had seen discipline based upon blind obedience in wartime, and had seen it fail with the abortive mutiny in the Fifth and Sixth French Armies in 1917. He had also seen the destruction of morale by officers insensitive to the needs of their men, and whole armies that sought to substitute rigid discipline for the will to win. "It is morale that wins the victory," he argued. "It is steadfastness and courage and hope. It is confidence and zeal and loyalty. It is élan, *esprit de corps*, and determination. It is staying power, spirit which endures to the end. . . ."

The great destroyers of morale—inadequate creature comforts, boredom, and a sense of unfair treatment—Marshall sought to alleviate. He encouraged experiments in the design of uniforms, including a change from World War I's steel helmet to the ubiquitous, all-purpose "pot" of World War II that would cut down on neck and head wounds. More than one field commander was sharply rebuked for the poor quality of his mess after an inspection by the chief of staff. When Marshall discovered on another trip that units were short of clothing, he tersely dismissed the Quartermaster's excuses in Washington, "I am interested in the soldier having his pants."

The shortage of recreation facilities led him to make an unannounced visit in civilian clothes to a small town in the South inundated with idle troops from the nearby army post. Troops swarmed through the town, taxing the small restaurants, crowding the streets as they wandered away a rare day of leave. Forced to wait four hours for a seat at a lunch counter, and then served "some warmed-over biscuits and things of that sort," Marshall returned to Washington to establish a committee to plan recreational activities for his army. Out of that directly grew the United Services Organization, more familiar as the USO, a joint military-civilian enterprise that was eventually to become the largest theatrical booking agency in the world, and manager of an equally impressive number of recreational centers for troops on passes.

Marshall made it a part of his routine to spend perhaps twenty minutes a day reading through letters of complaint from parents and soldiers alike, answering them himself, or forwarding them to commanders with orders that the matter be corrected. He would not remove all the injustices, nor correct all the grievances, but his example was meaningful. Even a private soldier in this democratically selected Army of the United States was to have the right to petition for a redress of grievances.

The accelerating pace of military mobilization took its toll on the man responsible for the build-up. Marshall worked long days, his four o'clock quitting time ignored, his weekends in Quarters No. 1 interrupted by telephone calls or additional hours in his office over the entryway of the Munitions Building. Despite delegating responsibility, too many questions came to his desk for decision—the timing of legislation, the curbing of presidential enthusiasm for airpower alone, the wooing of key legislators and influential newsmen. Unable to put aside his anxieties at night, he slept poorly.

Mrs. Marshall became concerned. Aware that her husband—who still followed the fortunes of VMI's football team—had hoped to squeeze in time to attend one game that season, she paid a call on Secretary Stimson. The result was one of the more unusual orders issued by the War Department:

The President of the United States directs that General George C. Marshall during the period between Friday, October 11th, and Monday, October 14th, shall visit the city of Charlotte, North Carolina, for the purpose of making a report upon the comparative skill and valor of the football teams of Davidson and Virginia Military Institute.

During said period he shall be under the exclusive control and direction of Mrs. Marshall and shall be protected against all interruptions, particularly by members of the War Department and of the Congress.

By virtue of the Secretary of War's order, Marshall saw the game. VMI won, 13 to 7.

Marshall returned to a Washington caught up in the 1940 presidential election campaign. Republican nominee Wendell Willkie, who had defused aid to Britain as a partisan issue by endorsing it, suddenly changed course. Trailing in the polls, unable to make capital of the third-term issue, Willkie succumbed to the urgings of party professionals and abandoned the concept of a bipartisan foreign policy.

The United States would be involved in the war within five months were Roosevelt reelected, Willkie charged. The sons of American mothers were already on the boat; wives and sweethearts would be heir to wooden crosses; American boys would die defending Great Britain's cowering Empire. By constant repetition, Willkie stirred fears across the country, and dramatically reversed the polls. Alarmed messages from Democratic National Headquarters pleaded for FDR to pledge to stay clear of foreign wars. If he did not, the Democratic ticket would lose. By the end of October, when the first draft call underscored Willkie's charges, the Republican candidate had closed to within four percentage points of the president. Perhaps for the first time in his political career, Roosevelt himself became rattled.

On a campaign train to Boston, he bowed to pleadings of party regulars. Into the draft of a speech he was to give that night, FDR inserted a pledge "addressed to you mothers and fathers . . . I have said this before, but I shall say it again and again and again: Your boys are not going to be sent into any foreign wars."

On election night, Roosevelt took refuge in his home at Hyde Park to await the outcome. Willkie ran well in early returns, mostly from the Republican Northeast, but by 10:00 p.m., Roosevelt had rolled up a safe margin. His tie loosened, the president sat at the dining-room table noting the state-by-state totals as they were reported, laying down his pencil only when he had marked up 27.2 million votes to Willkie's 22.3 million. The Republican had carried only ten states, but the margin was the smallest since Woodrow Wilson's narrow defeat of Charles Evans Hughes in 1916. The Boston speech with its reassurance had been enough to stem Willkie's rush.

In London, a relieved Winston Churchill composed a telegram at his desk in the underground war room three stories below Storey Gate. "I did not think it right for me as a foreigner to express any opinion upon American politics while the election was on but now I feel that you will not mind my saying that I prayed for your success and that I am truly thankful for it."

The king's first minister sorely needed Roosevelt's support. Winter's overcast skies had given Londoners some respite from the Blitz, though the Luftwaffe managed to drop some 4,300 tons of bombs on England in December. The submarine assaults in the North Atlantic had increased through the year; U-boats had already sunk 4 million tons of shipping, choking off part of the vital supply line to Great Britain. "It is now very clear that England will not be able to hold out very much longer against it unless some defense is found," Stimson confided to his diary.

The few bright spots for the Allies were all in peripheral actions. Greek forces had rallied to drive invading Italians back into Albania. In Egypt, the British Western Desert Force outflanked an Italian army at Sidi Barrani, capturing 38,000 Italians and Libyans. Yet the power of the Wehrmacht stood untouched, arrayed along the Channel facing the Dover coast. London and Washington expected Hitler's Operation Sealion in the spring.

On December 16, Stimson and Marshall met with Secretary of the Navy Knox and Admiral Stark to assess the year's accomplishments. The four men agreed "this emergency could hardly be passed over without this country being drawn into the war eventually," Stimson wrote in his diary. A growing minority of Americans concurred, whatever their hope that the United States could stay out of the conflict.

XI

The Common Law Alliance

The PBY slipped out of the Caribbean sky to land with a plume of spray in the blue-green waters alongside the USS *Tuscaloosa*. As a launch churned toward the plane, a member of the flight crew in a bright yellow life vest handed over the sealed pouch containing the White House mail for President Roosevelt.

Aboard the cruiser, the vacationing president waited for the deck officer to deliver the daily pouch. For a week Roosevelt had rested, joked with the three newsmen from the press associations, and sometimes fished—with poor luck. The campaign was over; ostensibly he was relaxing with nothing more on his mind than the quality of the Cuban cigars they had purchased at Guantanamo Bay. The president had spent this week of leisure "refueling." Now a letter from Winston Churchill in the mail bag would turn his attention back to the reality of a European war.

Dispatched on December 7, 1940, the coded telegram "was one of the most important I ever wrote," Churchill decided, a plea to an ally committed in heart, if not hand.

Great Britain desperately needed to replace the shipping lost to German U-boats, Churchill wrote. Only the United States could build the 3 million additional tons the prime minister calculated were necessary. Another 2,000 aircraft a month were required, the bulk to be heavy bombers, he advised. Further, British war plans called for a Commonwealth army of fifty divisions eventually, an army that could not be equipped without "expanding to the utmost American productive capacity for small arms, artillery, and tanks."

Churchill then turned to the real reason for his letter. Great Britain was fast approaching the point when it would no longer be able to pay for the military supplies, the ships, and the aircraft it needed. Simply enough, Churchill wrote, the United States could not continue to demand "cash and carry."

The president returned to Washington on December 16 having conceived a new plan to aid Great Britain, a proposal that would bind the two nations into a pact presidential speech writer Robert Sherwood called "the common law alliance." At his press conference the next day, the president floated a meandering statement arguing "the best immediate defense of the United States is the success of Britain in defending itself."

Roosevelt suggested the nation try "something brand new." The United States would supply Great Britain with the material it needed; the British would repay the loan "sometime in kind."

The idea was really not so far-fetched, the president said lightly. "Suppose my neighbor's home catches on fire, and I have a length of garden hose four or five hundred feet away. If he can take my garden hose and connect it up with his hydrant, I may help him to put out his fire." The fire out, the neighbor returned the hose, or if perchance the hose was damaged, merely replaced it.

"With that neighborly analogy." Sherwood later wrote, "Roosevelt won the fight for Lend Lease."

Twelve days later, in a Fireside Chat broadcast nationally over the three radio networks from the diplomatic reception room at the White House, the president stepped up his campaign:

"The Nazi masters of Germany have made it clear that they intend not only to dominate all life and thought in their own country, but also to enslave the whole of Europe, and then to use the resources of Europe to dominate the rest of the world."

Speaking easily in the resonant voice that had reassured the nation since 1933, the president renewed his pledge to keep the United States out of the war, "if we do all we can now to support the nations defending themselves against attack by the Axis. . . .

"There is no demand for sending an American Expeditionary Force outside our own borders. There is no intention by any member of your government to send such a force."

Instead, the United States should expand its industrial base, to provide the weapons for Britain. "We must be the great arsenal of democracy. For us this is an emergency as serious as war itself. We must apply ourselves to our task with the same resolution, the same sense of urgency, the same spirit of patriotism and sacrifice as we would show were we at war."

A week later, the now decisive president stood at the rostrum in the House of Representatives, his legs locked in the ten-pound braces that held him upright, smiling broadly and waving at familiar faces in the crowded chamber. In the gallery, his wife sat with Princess Martha of Norway, exiled by the German invasion to Bethesda, Maryland, a reminder, if any were needed, of the menace of Hitler's Germany.

America was threatened as at no time in its history, the president told the Congress. "In times like these it is immature—and incidentally, untrue—for anybody to brag that an unprepared America, single-handed, and with one hand tied behind its back, can hold off the whole world." Sitting in the front row next to the cabinet and Supreme Court, Army Chief of Staff George Marshall might have nodded agreement, or sighed wistfully for even one free hand.

The president's speech gathered momentum as he turned to his vision of a future world "founded upon four essential human freedoms:

"The first is freedom of speech and expression—everywhere in the world.

"The second is freedom of every person to worship God in his own way—everywhere in the world.

"The third is freedom from want—which, translated into world terms, means economic understandings which will secure to every nation a healthy peacetime life for its inhabitants—everywhere in the world.

"The fourth is freedom from fear—which, translated into world terms, means a world-wide reduction of armaments to such a point and in such a thorough fashion that no nation will be in a position to commit an act of physical aggression against any neighbor—anywhere in the world."

The first step toward that future world came four days later. House Bill 1776—the number was no accident—was introduced on January 10, the Lend-Lease bill drafted in the Treasury Department titled "A Bill to Further Promote the Defense of the United States, and for Other Purposes." Under terms of the bill, the president could sell, transfer, lend, lease, or exchange any material he decided was necessary for American security. The president would determine the repayment schedule.

Public opinion, by a 4-to-1 margin, had turned in favor of the measure; isolationists like Senator Burton K. Wheeler could only protest futilely, "The result of lend-lease will be to plow under every fourth American boy." The House adopted the bill 260 to 165 on February 8; the Senate followed suit a month later, 60–31. Within hours of signing the measure on March 11, 1941, President Roosevelt requested $7 billion to finance the first Lend-Lease production.

Lend-Lease, in Churchill's phrase that "most unsordid act," was to supplement army and navy appropriations, already set at $10.8 billion for fiscal 1942, and certain to increase. Because the Lend-Lease Act expanded the industrial base of the Army's mobilization effort, both Secretary of War Stimson and the chief of staff strongly favored it. Further, the act required the British to coordinate orders through the War Department, rather than compete with the Army. Stimson considered the act "a declaration of economic war"; Marshall lobbied pivotal senators in a private meeting prior to Senate passage with what Stimson called "a ripping speech." Though the chief of staff might speak solely as a professional soldier of armaments, raw materials, divisions, and corps, in the context, Marshall's advocacy was a political act. Only his arm's-length, seemingly objective analysis saved him from partisanship.

Eventually, the Lend-Lease Act would ease the supply problem, for increased military orders would expand production capacity. But it would take time. Supplies for the British would not increase substantially before 1942, the War Department estimated. Until then, the president would preside over what Winston Churchill called "their hungry table." Even the appointment of Harry Hopkins as Lend-Lease administrator could not still grumbling in the War Department that scarce tanks, trucks, and artillery pieces that might have equipped U.S. divisions funneled instead to the British. This was the winter of army discontent.

The workday in the adjacent Munitions and Navy Buildings on Constitution Avenue stretched longer into the night. Swarms of green-jacketed files sailed from Marshall's office; the "green hornets" pinned staff officers to their desks, upsetting assignations, marriages, and golf dates alike.

From the morning intelligence report to the handful of obligatory social events he could not politely avoid, Marshall's day was full. What his wife remembered as "an endless chain of midday luncheons at our quarters" filled even the noon hour. After lunch, Marshall would slip off for a fifteen-minute rest stretched out on the chaise-longue in the sun porch, whispering a request to his wife as he left that she entertain their guests.

Christmas 1940 was one of the few free days the chief of staff could manage that winter, and his presence at Quarters No. 1 was obligatory. His stepdaughter, Molly Brown, was married in a formal wedding, given away by the chief of staff to James Winn, Jr., a captain in the field artillery stationed in Panama. The formal wedding, with its arch of crossed swords held by the groomsmen after the reception, was the first wedding ever in the chief of staff's quarters, and the last time the Marshall family would be under one roof together.

Such moments of respite were rare, and fondly remembered. The chief of staff carried too many burdens, however much he sought to delegate authority. The army mobilization effort had already fallen behind schedule. Winter had slowed the construction of barracks for the 50,000 draftees Marshall had hoped to induct each month. The War Department had delayed the levies for weeks until additional housing could be built.

The rush to construction had already produced the waste about which Marshall had warned Congress. Now there would be even more. The War and Navy Departments were shy of men with logistical experience. For long, lean years they had dealt with only a handful of familiar contractors, monitoring production casually. Suddenly, the military had billions to spend, and industry, once loathe to expand for anything so transitory as munitions production, was clamoring for the lucrative cost-plus contracts.

Congress had authorized $64 billion for army and navy appropriations during 1940 and 1941, another $7 billion to fund the first year of Lend-Lease, and $3 billion in loans to private industry to expand capacity. Less than one third of that had actually been contracted, for industry was simply unable to gear up fast enough. Still, by mid-1941, the services were taking delivery on $2 billion in armaments each month.

The industrial mobilization was, in some instances, staggering. Chrysler's Tank Arsenal, built on a cornfield in the spring of 1941, would be producing 100 M-3 tanks per week before fall. In another year, monthly airplane production would equal the entire 2,500-plane production for all of 1939. By the spring of 1942, military and naval planners estimated, America's "arsenal of democracy" would be producing armaments enough to supply both Britain and America.

Waste was the inevitable consort of hasty mobilization. Chrysler's M-3 tanks were delivered, though the Army could not explain why, with police sirens. The new P-40 engine was balky and so underpowered that the Army's first-line pursuit plane was obsolete before it was produced. Shortages also prompted a form of panic procurement. The government simply gave $250 million to obdurate Reynolds Metals to build an aluminum plant, the profits from which would enrich corporate stockholders.* Profits were huge; half of all defense contractors were scoring 40 percent or more on investment.

Learning of waste in the hurry-up construction at Camp Leonard Wood in his home state, an unsung senator from Missouri was riled. But then Harry S. Truman riled easily when he thought people like his neighbors were being gouged or flimflammed. A prairie populist at heart, Truman had spent his first term in the Senate as a dutiful New Deal vote. No more. Reelected in 1940 despite a machine- and presidential-backed rival in the Democratic primary, Harry Truman had "been through hell three times with his hat off." Now he intended to be a senator in his own right.

Truman first made a 30,000-mile trip in the family Dodge through the South and Midwest, sniffing out charges of favoritism in the awarding of defense contracts. He heard again and again how big companies inevitably won contracts, while qualified small businesses were left stand-

---

*One heralded defense effort, a government-promoted aluminum scrap drive, saw housewives contributing 70,000 tons of pots and pans to build fighters and bombers. Scrap dealers bought it up. "They melted it down, refined it, and it reappeared—as pots and pans: Only virgin aluminum was good enough for modern planes. Unwittingly, American housewives went out and bought back what they had given away."—Perrett, *Days of Sadness, Years of Triumph.* p. 194.

ing hat in hand. Unannounced, he turned up at military posts under construction, noting the wastage, the padded payrolls, and the sweetheart contracts with their incentiveless, cost-plus guarantees.

Truman, who could be a "goddam contrary cuss," returned to Washington determined to investigate the entire military procurement effort. To senior senators he explained he intended no witch-hunt, and since he had just been reelected, needed no publicity either. He was angry. "Every ten cents that was spent for those work relief projects, the WPA and PWA and those [sic], every dime was looked into, and somebody was always against spending a nickel that would help poor people and give jobs . . . to the men that didn't have any. But the minute we started spending all that defense money, the sky was the limit and no questions asked."

An artillery captain in the first war, still proudly carrying his green registration card as a reserve officer, Truman had little respect for army brass. "No military man knows anything at all about money," he groused; someone had to check greed masking as patriotism.

Truman's committee was set up—after White House approval—with a meager appropriation of $15,000 to forestall a similar move by an anti-Roosevelt member of the House. In short order the Special Committee to Investigate the National Defense Program became known in Washington as the Truman Committee, determined, low-key, and inevitably correct in its carefully researched findings.

Initially apprehensive that the Truman Committee might attempt to run the war from Capitol Hill, Marshall decided to treat it as he had all other congressional bodies, with deference and candor. "It seems to me that a free and easy and whole-souled manner of cooperation with these committees is more likely to create an impression that everything is all right in the War Department, than is a resentful attitude, and that it must be assumed that members of Congress are just as patriotic as we. . . . I do not believe that we should adopt an attitude of official nervousness," the chief of staff instructed.

From his first appearance before the committee on April 22, 1941, Marshall was cooperative, frank, and insistent upon his ultimate responsibility for all army decisions. It was the beginning of a mutually respectful relationship between the soldier and the senator. "I got to know General Marshall really well," Truman explained, "and I got to know that you could depend on every word he said, that he just never would lie to you, and that he always knew what he was talking about."

The distant, cool Marshall and the feisty, strong-willed Truman, dapper as only a failed Kansas City haberdasher could be, slowly perceived in each other common traits: a willingness to shoulder responsibility; a passion for history (the self-educated Truman was exceptionally well read); and a deeply rooted patriotism that produced not flag-waving oratory but an unshakable commitment to the principles embodied in the Constitution. Truman was, more overtly, an outspoken advocate of the "little man" still struggling out of the Depression; he was, after all, a politician. But even there Marshall shared the sentiment. None of this was instantly clear; there was no sudden recognition of identical values between the two. Marshall's reserve prevented any such flash of insight. For some time the War Department was to treat the methodical, dogged Truman with wary cooperation and formal courtesy, realizing only belatedly that the committee protected the Army from far wilder and even irresponsible attacks.*

For the Army and its chief of staff, this was to be a time of adjustment. They would be dealing with vast sums of money, amounts neither Congress nor the War Department well understood. How those fortunes would be spent remained unresolved even as a delegation of British military planners slipped unannounced into Washington for talks with army and navy staff members. Over the next two months, the meetings on joint operations, "should the United States be compelled to resort to war," were kept secret, as much in the interests of domestic politics as the necessity for military security.

President Roosevelt laid out the general American position prior to the talks. In a long White House meeting on January 16, 1941, with Secretaries Hull, Stimson, and Knox, Admiral Stark and Marshall, the president estimated there was a one-in-five chance that Germany and Japan would together launch a surprise attack on the United States. If that were to happen, the United States must continue to supply the British, hoping to buy time. With luck, they might have eight months before Britain collapsed and the enemy could turn to the United States. Marshall's minutes of the meeting detailed the presidential directives:

> That we would stand on the defensive in the Pacific with the fleet based in Hawaii . . . that there would be no naval reinforcement of the Philippines; that the Navy should have under consideration the possibility of bombing attacks against Japanese cities.
>
> That the Navy should be prepared to convoy shipping in the Atlantic to England, and to maintain a patrol off-shore from Maine to the Virginia Capes.
>
> That the Army should not be committed to any aggressive action

---

*Truman's committee uncovered, among other things, enormous profiteering in the rental of construction equipment; the knowing construction of defective bombers; the installation of faulty Curtiss-Wright aircraft engines with the connivance of army procurement officers, two of whom were convicted of fraud; and heavy assessments upon non-union workers by construction unions for the privilege of working. In all, Truman claimed the committee saved taxpayers some $15 billion.

until it was fully prepared to undertake it; that our military course must be very conservative until our strength had developed. . . .

These presidential stipulations came from no sudden burst of strategic brilliance, but from the accumulation of successive war plans conceived since the end of the Spanish-American War. As early as 1904, army and navy staff officers had begun work on a series of color-coded war plans, BLACK in the event of war with Germany, RED for Great Britain, ORANGE for Japan, and so on through an artist's palette of growing files.

The Navy took major responsibility for devising the plan for a war with ORANGE, which both services believed would be fought by rival fleets stalking each other across the vastness of the Pacific. Army participation in that possible Pacific War was limited to defending the Philippine Islands, especially vital Manila Bay with its harbor facilities.

In the years after World War I and Germany's enforced disarmament, military and naval planners considered only Japan and Great Britain as potential major enemies. Were these two powers, linked formally in an alliance from 1902 to 1921, to wage a two-ocean war against the United States, the planners decided America would necessarily fight first in the Atlantic, leaving the far-off Japanese for later. From 1919 on, the United States was to hew fast to the Atlantic-first policy.

Not until November 1933 did the War and Navy Departments' Joint Board reconsider the skimpy BLACK plan dealing with Germany. Noting the resurgence of German militarism, and the increasing economic and political influence of German expatriate colonies in South America, the planners reconsidered the possible alliance of enemies. Were Germany, Italy, and Japan to wage war as allies, the planners decided, "there can be no doubt but that the vital interest of the United States would require offensive measures in the Atlantic," making it "necessary to assume a defensive attitude in the Eastern Pacific."

Rushing to keep pace with events, on June 30, 1939, the Joint Planning Committee began to prepare five contingency plans for coalition war. As tints of RED, ORANGE, BLACK, GREEN, PURPLE, and BLUE, these new RAINBOW plans hinged on the assumption that Germany, Italy, and Japan would wage war against the United States.

By spring 1940, events in Europe had overtaken the scribblers in Washington. As German troops marched into Copenhagen and Oslo, the Joint Planning Committee warned Marshall and Chief of Naval Operations Stark of "an ever present possibility of the United States being drawn into the war" and "forced to defend, without allies, the integrity of the Monroe Doctrine and [American] interests in the Pacific."

A month later, the planners were urgently drafting yet another paper to cope with the most likely of situations, a war in which the United

States alone defended the hemisphere, fought in the eastern Atlantic, and meanwhile held the Japanese at bay in the Pacific.

Their greatest concern was the combined fleets of Germany and Italy, joined by captive France and Great Britain, ranged in the Atlantic against the United States while the resurgent Japanese sallied into the Pacific. Assuming the worst possible case—Axis possession of all French, British, Dutch, and Danish colonies, Japan demanding the entire Far East for its sphere of influence, the Soviet Union neutral—the planners conceived a predominantly naval and aerial war. To Japan they conceded the Philippines and Guam until reconquered later. The United States was to defend the American hemisphere, extend control of the sea to the western Pacific and eastern Atlantic, and finally to invade western Africa and thereby remove any threat of a cross-Atlantic invasion of Brazil.

The RAINBOW planners were not optimistic that the United States standing alone could achieve anything more than an armistice against the combined forces of Germany, Italy, and Japan. The best that could be hoped would be terms "favorable" to the United States, they concluded. A clear-cut victory could only be achieved in partnership with the British Commonwealth.

By June 1940, with the British Expeditionary Force driven from Dunkirk, Britain's survival could no longer be assumed. Two factors pressed hard on the president: "First, that America must at once and with the greatest possible speed arm itself with all the new machinery of war. Second, that the chief hope upon which America could rely for the necessary time required to carry on this rearmament program was the continuance of the British resistance to the Nazi. . . ."

The military planners wobbled in their estimates of Britain's chances of survival throughout the grim summer and fall of 1940. Only after the Blitz abated did they feel secure in assuming the United States would have a major industrial nation as an ally. With that they completed their planning.

Admiral Stark—who urgently needed guidance to make fleet dispositions—forwarded four strategic options to the White House on November 20, 1940. In a two-ocean, global conflict, the United States could: (A) defend only the western hemisphere; (B) focus on the Pacific, ignoring the Atlantic; (C) split military and naval forces to wage a two-ocean war; or (D) concentrate on Europe, fighting a defensive war in the Pacific.

The immediate question was Great Britain's beleaguered status. Even if Germany failed to conquer the British Isles, an isolated England might still lose the war; the tight little island was vulnerable to blockade.

"Alone, the British Commonwealth lacks the manpower and the material means to master Germany," the planners continued. American naval assistance was "unlikely to *assure* final victory for Great Britain." Naval plus air operations might, but "its certain accomplishment depends upon her [Great Britain's] ability to effect a successful land offensive against Germany and Italy."

The United States was not to "willingly engage in any war against Japan," the planners warned, but if attacked, the nation should declare war on all three Axis powers. According to Plan D, the Army and Navy would then "restrict operations in the Mid-Pacific and the Far East in such a manner as to permit the prompt movement to the Atlantic of forces fully adequate to conduct a major offensive. . . ."

In proposing to aid Great Britain, the military planners were hardly naifs led by the cynical British into carrying the brunt of the battle in defense of the Empire. "British leadership has not had the competence in any sphere that would justify our entrusting to it the future security of the United States," the memorandum warned the president. If the United States was to go to war, it should insist on "full equality in the political and military direction" of that war. They had learned the costly lesson of World War I. "No important allied political and military decisions should be reached without clear understandings between the nations involved as to the common objectives of the participation; the strength of the contingents to be provided in any particular theater; the proposed skeleton plan of operations; and desired command arrangements."

From among the four war plans, Stark and Marshall recommended the fourth option, what became known by the military alphabet name as Plan Dog. President Roosevelt declined to settle formally on any of the particular choices, but did assent to the suggestion that United States and British military planners hold exploratory talks centered on Plan Dog. There was to be no commitment of American military involvement, unless the United States was attacked, the president cautioned. He wanted as much maneuvering room as the Axis would give him, seeking time for public opinion to come around.

Roosevelt himself did not meet the British delegation when it arrived, wearing civilian clothes, in January 1941. Marshall and Stark also stood at arm's length, attending only the opening session tucked away in a conference room in the Public Works Building. The vaguely labeled "American-British Conversations," or ABC-1, were to be exploratory only, Marshall advised the group. Sensitive to accusations that the president and the military were "backing the United States into war," Marshall later insisted, "I don't feel that in any way we committed the United States to take specific military action unless we were attacked."

The British representatives were to be keenly disappointed; they considered American strategic thinking "muddled." They failed to grasp that the Americans were not confused at all, but were fixed upon national interest and the principle of hemispheric defense first. Further, American plans were larded with a skepticism of Great Britain's military capacities. Understandably on the defensive when the war began, the

British in the sixteen months since had shown no special talent for offensive operations either.

Two months of ABC-1 produced only the most general agreement on strategic areas of responsibility; unity of command; the integration of United States naval forces into Atlantic and Mediterranean operations; and, most specifically, allocation of expanded aircraft construction in the United States to Great Britain. As vague as that was, President Roosevelt still avoided formal approval of the concluding paper, yet the exchange of opinions and the short list of conclusions "provided the highest degree of strategic preparedness that the United States or probably any other nonaggressor nation has ever had before entry into war."

Far more important, ABC-1 opened the way for a continuing exchange of scientific research and intelligence data. Great Britain was shortly to deliver plans for its far-seeing radar, which had provided the Royal Air Force the secret key to victory in the Battle of Britain; blueprints for an artillery proximity fuse; summaries of the promising atomic research conducted in British laboratories; advice in counterespionage and secret operations; and, ultimately, the closely guarded intercepts of broken German codes known as BONIFACE or ULTRA.

The next months would give American staff officers little to build trust in their British allies. The Commonwealth troops had routed the Italians in Libya and the Horn of Africa, but no one in Washington held the Italian Army in high regard. Great Britain had reinforced Greece with tanks and planes badly needed in North Africa, only to see both theaters disintegrate. Hungary, Bulgaria, and Rumania had gone over to the Axis; Yugoslavia's capital of Belgrade fell to the XLVI Panzer Corps on April 12. Eight days later, Greece finally capitulated to Germany, though resistance would continue for another month. On May 20, in the most spectacular operation of the war, German paratroops and glider-borne soldiers invaded the island of Crete, bagging 45,000 British and Greek defenders. In New York, before an America First rally, Charles A. Lindbergh warned that Great Britain was left only "one last desperate plan . . . to persuade us to send another American expeditionary force to Europe and to share with England militarily, as well as financially, the fiasco of this war."

Short of that expeditionary force, the United States was already at war, albeit unofficially. Navy and Coast Guard vessels patrolled from 500 to 1,000 miles into the North Atlantic at the president's orders, covering convoys of merchant ships bound for Britain's northern approaches. On April 10, one of those ships, the USS *Niblack,* fired the first shot in anger, an ineffectual depth charge launched at a German submarine that had sunk a Danish freighter. On May 21, a U-boat torpedoed the SS *Robin Moor* in the South Atlantic, the first American ship to go down.

In a radio address heard by 85 million Americans six days later, the president reiterated his pledge to give "every possible assistance to Britain and to all who, with Britain, are resisting Hitlerism. . . . All additional measures necessary to deliver the goods will be taken."

Building to the announcements that had made his earlier radio addresses so riveting, the president warned, "Our Bunker Hill of tomorrow may be several thousand miles from Boston." To reassert the doctrine of freedom of the seas, and to preserve the independence of the western hemisphere, he announced, American armed forces would be permitted to repel attacks. "Therefore," he concluded, "I have tonight issued a proclamation that an unlimited national emergency exists and requires the strengthening of our defense to the extreme limit of our national power and authority. . . ."

Having boldly led, Roosevelt once again temporized, aware just how limited his resources were. The Navy resisted transferring more than a quarter of the Pacific Fleet to the Atlantic for fear of leaving Hawaii unguarded. The Army found itself unable to provide sufficient troops to garrison Alaska, let alone the division the president wanted to send to Iceland. General Marshall and Admiral Stark saw the nation unprepared for war before March 1942, at the earliest.

Even that estimate gave them only the narrowest margin, Marshall stressed. Training and logistics—the mundane business of designing, manufacturing, shipping, and distributing the materiels of war—remained his greatest concerns.

Neither the Navy nor the president shared those worries. Readiness for war in the president's opinion was a cavalier command for "clouds of warplanes." The Navy considered war preparation a given number of ships of the line, preferably battleships. Neither gave much thought to logistics, and especially to the prosaic infrastructure that transported munitions, food, replacement parts, clothing, and manpower to fighting fronts. "The naval thinking," Marshall told White House confidant Robert Sherwood, "simply did not comprehend the necessity for gigantic supply trains across thousands of miles of ocean which would establish and maintain tremendous bases of supply for operations that would penetrate hundreds of miles into hostile interiors." The Navy penetrated no interiors; its logistics problem ended "on the hostile shoreline." The fleet would be supplied from home bases.

Aware of the logistical snarls that had hampered the Army's performance in two previous wars, Marshall could not so easily ignore such unglamorous business. Neither could he dismiss the urgency of his own department's reorganization.

Marshall—who had once removed eighteen men from a staff of forty-four when he took over as operations officer of I Corps in France— found a similarly lean staff impossible in a mobilizing War Department. In 1938, he had served as Malin Craig's lone deputy chief of staff. Two years later, Marshall himself had three deputy chiefs, all overstrained: "Hap" Arnold for the revamped Army Air Force; Richard C. Moore for supply; and William Bryden for personnel, intelligence, and organization. Each of them had a dozen or more officers from lieutenant to colonel fielding the green hornets that swarmed from the chief of staff's office. The General Staff's secretariat, once one officer and a civilian chief clerk who handled all War Department papers, quadrupled, then quadrupled again. Marshall, who used the post of assistant secretary as a proving ground for promising officers, now had a secretary and four assistants. That group, responsible for all correspondence and reports to and from the chief of staff and the secretary of war, included by the end of 1940 a future army commander, a corps commander, a division commander, and a theater chief of staff. One of the four, Major Walter Bedell Smith, had already proved his enterprise when he plumped for a light, rugged utility vehicle brought to the War Department by a civilian auto designer in 1939. Smith's General Purpose Vehicle, the ubiquitous Jeep, was to be one of the five "most valuable pieces of equipment" produced for the wartime Army, senior officers later decided.

Marshall's War Department no longer fit easily into the four-story Munitions Building. Four blocks long, connected by a second-floor overpass to the identical Navy Building, the stucco structure had been erected as "temporary" quarters during World War I. Two decades later, it was still in service, clerks piled upon clerks, carpenters continually nailing up plywood partitions for ever smaller offices, mailmen pedaling its corridors on oversized tricycles to make deliveries. The quarters were cramped and poorly lighted; only Marshall and Secretary Stimson could claim private offices. Even deputy chiefs doubled up with lower ranks. Civilian clerks and secretaries shared space with army officers, the military men in mufti distinguishable only by the rigid set of their spines. One officer newly assigned to the graceless building on Constitution Avenue felt overwhelmed, lost "at the dead center of the control of a vast machine."

Surrounded by the turmoil, Marshall struggled to organize the staff frenzy, though all of his rank could not persuade the General Services Administration to perform such a simple chore as cleaning the main entrance directly below his office. Despite the tumult about them, the chief of staff impressed newly assigned Major Paul Robinett as "the most self-contained individual I have ever encountered." It was the way of self-preservation. Marshall managed to get through the day's meetings and the unending reports that flowed upward only by hewing to a strict schedule.

He began at 8:00 a.m. by reading the secret contents of the locked pouch from the intelligence division, then handling the day's correspondence, dictating replies or editing letters drafted for his signature. His desk clean by 10:00 a.m., he turned to his appointment calendar and the file of deputies waiting nervously outside his office. Those meetings were usually brief, Marshall giving each one in turn his undivided attention. Staff officers reporting on military problems sat in chairs in front of his desk. On less urgent matters, or with old friends, he and his visitor would share a worn leather sofa. "He would seem to have all the time in the world," one frequent visitor about this time remembered, though "I never found myself believing that you would ever wish to remain in his presence one minute after he became bored. You would probably just feel it."

Despite the misleading sign on the door to his office—"When you open this door, walk right in, regardless of what is going on inside"—Miss Virginia Nason closely guarded her chief. The only interruptions came from the secretary of war, Henry Stimson, who would put his head through the door that connected their adjoining offices. Stimson found the personal chat more efficient than the formal exchange of opinions in memoranda.

The day was tightly scheduled. An unexpected call to the White House or to visit a legislator might mean the cancellation of a half-dozen appointments. Marshall kept to his daily schedule only by insisting on brevity and concision.

"Nothing irritates him more," a fellow staff member advised newcomer Robinett, "than long, involved writing or oral presentation." Robinett, who managed to pare one such bulky document, proudly recalled Marshall's approval: "Thank goodness, someone can cut things down!"

Robinett was just one of the many promising officers Marshall transferred to the staff with a mandate to prod the Army into readiness. Recently promoted to the rank of major, Albert C. Wedemeyer found himself ordered to Washington after instructing at the Army's Command and General Staff School at Leavenworth. Two years before, fresh from the German War College, Wedemeyer had returned from Berlin to spend much of a day with Marshall discussing Wedemeyer's conviction that the Germans "would never fight a trench war again. It must be a war of mobility." The United States would have to be prepared, with armor and armored personnel carriers, and close air support of infantry. The Germans had developed special aircraft to serve as "artillery" for fast-moving armored columns on the attack. The United States had nothing comparable, and nothing planned.

Once in Washington, Wedemeyer became a Marshall favorite, though it was some time before the chief of staff, whose memory awed legislators, could remember his name. Wedemeyer became "that long-legged major in War plans"; Major Anthony McAuliffe, another of the Army's brighter young officers, was "that blue-eyed major in G-4." The foible softened the hard edge of a man who first appeared to younger men as "very severe, a cold sort."

Marshall relied on these younger men to free the War Department from the plodding conservatism of the past. "No one was willing to take a chance," McAuliffe recalled; decades of pinch-penny appropriations imposed on an archaic command structure had paralyzed initiative.

Rank vouchsafed no special wisdom in Marshall's War Department. As head of research and development for the supply component, McAuliffe recommended the Army stop producing the 37-millimeter anti-aircraft gun in favor of the Swedish-British 40-millimeter Bofors gun. Called in by Marshall with the furious chief of ordnance, Major General Charles "Bull" Wesson—"and they didn't call him 'Bull' for nothing"—McAuliffe found himself defending his recommendation. "A major argued with this major general the merits of the case, and General Marshall supported me."

The younger officers found it a heady moment, their ideas valued as the Army raced to prepare for a war they "were almost sure" would come. Criticism could extend to Marshall himself. On his first meeting with the chief of staff, Air Force Colonel Joseph T. McNarney presented a carefully conceived plan for Marshall's review. The general skimmed it quickly, then suggested a change.

"Jesus, man, you can't do that!" the outspoken McNarney blurted.

Marshall eyed him narrowly, but said nothing. Outside the chief of staff's office, the secretary of the General Staff reassured the shaken, embarrassed McNarney. "Don't worry. He likes for people to speak up."

As much as he was able, Marshall attempted to maintain a personal contact with the growing Army. He read all letters addressed to him personally, at least until the beginning of 1941 when the flow became overwhelming. Then he read samples of that mail, still trying to reach across the burgeoning bureaucracy that was the War Department's General Staff. He often drafted his own replies, then sent them to the staff secretaries for their editing. Nor did the chief "resent our suggestions," Robinett confided to his diary, not realizing the young majors were serving in a capacity Marshall had once held for an earlier chief of staff. Robinett was impressed with Marshall's memory, his political sense, and what an old friend had once described as Marshall's "golden streak of imagination."

Marshall was "a consummate Army politician," Robinett decided after two weeks in the dimly lighted Munitions Building. "He indicates clearly that he prefers not to cross swords with individuals but prefers to let them down gracefully, if at all. . . . He certainly is smarter than any of his contemporaries known to me."

For all his acumen, Marshall had not yet grasped the sheer complexity of the army he was resuscitating, nor how large it would grow if the United States declared war. Another member of the secretariat, Omar Bradley, noted, "I often shudder at some of the antiquated precepts that underlay our thinking. The quaintest by far was the notion that after we had trained a force of four field armies (over a million soldiers), Marshall himself would lead it, perhaps to Europe, as Pershing had led the American Expeditionary Force to France in 1917." For eighteen months the General Headquarters of this putative expeditionary force duplicated the efforts of planners in the Munitions Building, snarling authority and communication into a grand bureaucratic tangle.

All of their problems were compounded by the chief of staff's anxiety that the first selectees of the previous October would begin returning to civilian life in September. The Army of 1.5 million nurtured so painfully was about to evaporate, unless an unheeding Congress mustered a rare political courage.

CHAPTER

XII

The Summer's Storms

Precisely at 0300 hours, in the first light of a northern dawn, the two squads of uniformed soldiers stepped off from the opposite ends of the truss bridge spanning the Bug River. Ten yards from the barrier and the white line painted across the roadway, they stopped, subalterns in German and Russian snapping commands to change the guard. The guards relieved, the two squads presented arms, then retreated toward the darkness of the opposite banks. Suddenly the Germans turned, leveled their Schmeisser machine pistols, and opened fire. The Russian guards crumpled onto the roadway; they were the first of 20 million who would die in the Great Patriotic War.

Out of hidden vehicle parks on the German side clanked Army Group Center's columns of armored cars, motorcycles, and tanks, rolling over the bridge into Brest-Litovsk in Russian-held Poland. North and south, coordinated army groups protected by 1,800 planes brushed aside the thinly held defenses, the blitzkrieg slashing eastward in the early morning of Sunday, June 22, 1941. Three million troops, led by 3,580 tanks, surged across the Polish border in a three-pronged attack aimed at Leningrad, Moscow, and Kiev. Hitler's Operation Barbarossa achieved complete tactical surprise, rolling up incredulous Soviet defenders along a front that stretched within two weeks from the Baltic to the Black Sea.

The greatest military assault in history came as a bolt of lightning out of a summer sky, anticipated but startling for all that. It stunned Marshal Joseph Stalin, who had chosen to ignore repeated, authoritative warnings that Hitler intended to violate their non-aggression pact. Stalin withdrew in a daze to his dacha outside Moscow, refusing telephone calls for a week while his government and army disintegrated.

Within seventy-two hours of the attack launched across the Brest-Litovsk bridge, 2,000 Russian combat aircraft, the core of the largest air force in the world, had been destroyed by faster Luftwaffe fighters and bombers.

By July 1, the Wehrmacht had swept over the Baltic states, driving on Leningrad. A week later Panzer divisions crossed the 1939 Polish-Russian border.

The thunderclap of Barbarossa reverberated in Whitehall and the White House. Winston Churchill immediately promised aid to the Soviet leader, explaining privately if the devil himself joined the battle against Hitler the prime minister would manage a good word for him in Commons. Well he might, for Hitler's turn east surely saved Britain from invasion this year.

In Washington, President Roosevelt temporized as War Department reports ticked off the daily roll of Russian defeats. Military intelligence, backed by both Stimson and Marshall, estimated the Soviet Army might hold out "a minimum of one month and a maximum of three months." Virtually the entire department staff wrote off the Soviet Union as "formidable only because of her size." Only an "act of God" could save that country. The chief of staff himself thought Soviet military leaders, not a Supreme Being, might save the day, if they "were wise enough to withdraw and save their army, abandoning their people, if necessary," and sabotaging the oil fields left undefended.

In mid-July, as the Wehrmacht halted to regroup 250 miles inside the Soviet border, President Roosevelt formally ordered the War Department to furnish military supplies to the Red Army. Already strapped for equipment to arm Britain, Marshall bridled when Soviet Ambassador Constantine A. Oumansky imperiously demanded the Army yield first call on munitions, especially vitally needed aircraft. Oumansky's demands, coming on top of escalating British requirements that alone set back the United States' mobilization timetable, infuriated the chief of staff.

In a memorandum to Secretary of War Stimson, Marshall complained: "In the first place our entire Air Corps is suffering from a severe shortage of spare parts of *all* kinds. We have planes on the ground because we cannot repair them ... Mr. Oumansky and his Russian associates were informed of this. . . . If any criticism is to be made in this matter, in my opinion it is that we have been too generous, to our own disadvantage, and I seriously question the advisability of our action in releasing the P-40's at this particular time. I question this even more when it only results in criticism. . . ."

Some part of Marshall's objection to aiding the Red Army lay in his estimate of the Soviet capacity to resist. By July 23, with the Wehrmacht girding for a second thrust, German troops had swept over 720,000 square miles of Russian soil, an area only slightly smaller than the United States from the Atlantic to the Mississippi River. Germany had suffered 30,000 dead, but it had more than ample reserves to make up the losses. The Soviets had taken an estimated 5 million casualties, including more than 1 million dispirited soldiers milling about in prison compounds.

Further, the American military attaché in Moscow, Major Ivan Yeaton, severely restricted by Russian xenophobia, had few contacts beyond the capital. His reports to Washington reflected a forbidding sense of imminent collapse, and left Marshall to wonder just how much scarce material he should waste on the Soviet Union.

Marshall was no anti-Communist ideologue. At best, or worst, he shared the professional soldier's conservative dislike for announced Communist goals, and an abiding disdain for the Russian military, czarist or Communist. Defeat at the hands of the Japanese in 1905, then by the Germans in 1918, then mutiny in the ranks during the Revolution, all that in Marshall's eyes marked the Russian soldier as poor stuff. The past month's events only reinforced that feeling.

At the same time, Marshall did not share the plague-on-both-houses opinion of some of his staff that Nazis and Communists should be permitted to fight unaided until each bled the other to death. If he did not recognize it immediately, he would soon come to the conclusion Churchill and Stalin had reached independently: neither of their nations could beat the Germans alone or in combination. "The only thing that could defeat Hitler," the Soviet premier told Harry Hopkins in the Kremlin on July 31, "perhaps without ever firing a shot, would be the announcement that the United States was going to war with Germany."

Hopkins's coded report on August 1 of two long talks with Stalin in the Kremlin apparently hardened President Roosevelt's resolve to aid the Soviets. Whatever supplies they could furnish the Russians would help assure the Red Army's survival through the winter, thus buying time for Great Britain, the president reasoned.

Though he would never release enough materiel to satisfy either the president or the Russians, Marshall was to come around. Presidential directive commanded him, of course, but equally important were the unrecorded discussions Marshall had with Hopkins. If nothing else, Hopkins was able to counterbalance the unwavering pessimism of Major Yeaton's reports to Washington.

On September 29, 1941, Marshall appeared before a House of Representatives appropriations subcommittee in support of additional Lend-Lease funding. Defending the concept, the chief of staff argued calmly, "The estimates now before you make no specific provision for aid to Russia and while we have not a great deal we could provide at this time, what little we do to keep the Russian army in the field aggressively resisting the Germans is to our great advantage. . . .

"It is axiomatic that anything that can be done to keep Russia fighting makes a mighty contribution to what we all are endeavoring to bring about—an early termination of the war by the destruction of the German war machine, through attrition or dispersion, through defeat or by the collapse of the German government."

Subcommittee chairman Clarence Cannon asked if generous appropriations would shorten the war, and make it less expensive in the long run.

"We certainly will not shorten it by delays," the chief of staff responded.

Should the United States, Cannon asked, proceed "with the use of every resource and with as little delay and little parsimony as possible?"

"That is an excellent statement of the way I feel about it, except the last three words: 'As little parsimony as possible'; I think with 'as much efficiency as possible.' "

The constant drain of armaments through the Lend-Lease pipeline, exacerbated by Soviet needs, frustrated Marshall. More than ever, weapons needed for his own divisions were going overseas, to Britain, to the USSR, now also to China.

As early as May 1941, the chief of staff had ordered his planners to draw up a "clearcut strategic estimate of our situation from a ground, air and naval viewpoint." That document he intended to use to try to bring some order to the scramble for military supplies between the British and his own G-4. Now, with the Russians and Chinese also demanding a share of American production, a coherent industrial mobilization plan was more than ever needed. By July, when President Roosevelt finally agreed such a study was necessary, Marshall's War Department was well launched on the industrial plan that would become known as the Victory Program.

The task of preparing that document fell to young Major Wedemeyer, one of the Army's new generation of intellectuals, tutored by his father-in-law, Major General Stanley D. Embick. Wedemeyer, born of German parentage in Nebraska in 1897, came away from those talks with Embick primed with "the intrigues, machinations, and shortsighted national aims that motivated the representatives of Britain, France, and Italy" at Versailles. Those discussions with Embick, plus his schooling at the German War College, had left the major a committed anti-Communist. Thus Wedemeyer, skeptical of one ally and hostile to another, found himself drafting the mobilization plan that would defeat the nation, Germany, for which he felt the closest familial and personal ties.

Wedemeyer's Victory Plan was intended to advance some comprehensive national estimate of the men and equipment necessary to defeat both Germany and Japan. To Wedemeyer, then ultimately to Marshall fell the task of rectifying entirely different strategies of army and navy planners. The Navy argued that air- and seapower would wear down the Axis by blockade and bombing; as the Navy saw it, American land armies would fight only where the Germans could not mass their troops in overwhelming numbers. Perhaps the Army would need a million men in France, the Navy estimated, about half the number shipped overseas during World War I.

Neither did the Navy see great need for building its own forces; a total strength of 1.3 million men, including somewhat more than 160,000 Marines, would be sufficient, its planners calculated. At no time would the American industrial base be required to go over onto a full wartime footing.

The Navy's "victory-on-the-cheap" plan had at least a public relations appeal to newspaper correspondents and legislators. Wedemeyer was not persuaded. He calculated that most nations at war mobilized about one tenth of the adult male population. If the United States, with a population of 135 million, shifted women into defense work, the country could put 13.5 million men under arms. That seemed the ceiling; he estimated army-navy needs as 8 percent of the population, or 10.8 million men. Of these, 2 million would be in the Navy and Marines, 8.8 million in an army composed of 215 divisions—the German Army had 300—and the bulk of those divisions to be armored or motorized. Air Force planners estimated a fleet of 63,467 planes of all types.

Wedemeyer's final draft was based on certain priorities tacitly set by White House acceptance of Plan Dog the previous November. National military objectives were, first, the preservation of the integrity of the western hemisphere; then "prevention of the disruption of the British Empire"; followed by prevention of any further Japanese advances in the Far East; and finally, "eventual establishment in Europe and Asia of balances of power which will most nearly ensure political stability in those regions and the future security of the United States; and, so far as practicable, the establishment of regimes favorable to economic freedom and individual liberty."

These national policies, the joint planners warned, "can be effectuated in their entirety only through military victories outside this hemisphere, either by the armed forces of the United States, by the armed forces of friendly powers, or by both."

Contrary to the British plan put forward at the ABC-1 talks, American military and naval planners argued that Germany could not be defeated without the entry of the United States into the war, and then offensive use of the armed forces in the eastern Atlantic, in Europe, or in Africa.

While the planners preferred to fight in only one theater, if Japan did go to war, the United States was to shoulder the German wheel, *"while holding Japan in check pending future developments."*

Wedemeyer's final plan of September came down heavily in favor of a large land army, for "naval and air forces seldom, if ever, win important wars. It should be recognized as an almost invariable rule that only land armies can finally win wars."

Navy planners dissented, considering a major land offensive against the German Army out of the question in the near future. They opted instead for the British strategy of blockade, subversion, and peripheral attrition. If that strategy failed, Wedemeyer countered, they would eventually have to "come to grips with the German armies on the continent of Europe. Consequently, the Army feels that the equipment of land armies necessary to meet this contingency should be provided as a part of the over-all production requirements." If they failed to provide for it now, the Army would not be ready when it was needed.

The formation of such large armies and navies depended entirely upon the conversion of industry to war production. The Victory Program envisioned a massive effort that threatened severe dislocation of the civilian economy if not implemented with care. Men with particular skills, doctors and engineers especially, would be in short supply; women would necessarily take over jobs on production lines heretofore considered for men only. Non-essential industries that could not convert to military production would suffer most, requiring workers to find new jobs, and even to relocate; as many as 4 million would move in the next four years. Smaller communities dependent upon a handful of industrial employers would be hardest hit if those firms could not convert. Pushed to its fullest, mobilization could cripple the entire civilian economy, undermine public health, and corrode the education system as well. For the next four years, Marshall would watch closely the impact of the mobilization upon the national economy. He "was very worried about the need for speed in defeating Germany, 'before our very institutions melt under us,' " he told a young member of the General Staff, Colonel Dean Rusk.

The first institution to melt, ironically, might well be the Army itself. From the first months of spring 1941, Marshall had sought with increasing urgency, even a sense of desperation in the face of House opposition, to secure passage of an extension to the draft. By late June, he recognized "his efforts had failed utterly," and the Army of thirty-three skeletal divisions fashioned over the last year would begin to evaporate before the end of September.

By training and inclination Marshall was a team player, the good soldier who followed orders. His dissenting opinions he registered in confidence; win or lose in the White House, he did not go to the press. That characteristic more than any other had fostered the president's trust.

But now the White House seemed frozen, unable to bring itself to endorse extension of the term of service, unable to save the Army so painstakingly created in the last year. Marshall felt compelled to act, to do something, even at the risk of further dividing a nation torn between intervention and isolation. "The virtual demobilization of the Army," he told his wife, "would invite future disaster."

Marshall reached a major decision while horseback riding along the grassy bank of the Potomac one afternoon in late June. Recalling he had not issued the chief of staff's annual report to the secretary of war the previous year, he decided to write a concise account of his stewardship since July 1, 1939, when he became acting chief of staff. With proper press attention, the report could alert the public to the peril as seen by the responsible army officer, yet not seem partisan.

The forty-page report detailing the state of the Army and the looming threat of demobilization rested heavily on Marshall's growing reputation as a professional without party bias. By not allowing White House review before its release, Marshall put distance between himself and the president—even at the risk of Roosevelt's irritation. At the same time, he was taking responsibility, deflecting criticism from a president who believed himself already too far in front of public opinion.

Marshall's first biennial report detailed the eightfold growth since 1939 of a green, still ill-shaped army. There were twenty-six infantry divisions, one motorized infantry division and four armored divisions modeled after the German Panzer, and two cavalry divisions, with no less than 20,000 newly purchased horses. Mountain, ski, and paratroop divisions, all innovations of European armies, were under study.

Most of these units struggled to maintain any semblance of combat efficiency. "Only a small portion of the field army is at present equipped for extended active operations under conditions of modern warfare," the report noted.

In a section tersely written in a style that bears Marshall's personal imprint, the report noted, "It is vital to the security of the nation that the hazards of the present crisis be fully recognized. . . . There are legal restrictions on the use of the armed forces which should be removed without delay. Events of the past two months are convincing proof of the terrific striking power possessed by a nation administered purely on a military basis. Events of the past few days [the German successes in Russia] are even more forcible indications of the suddenness with which armed conflict can spread to areas hitherto considered free from attack."

Three things Marshall's report asked of the nation, and more specifically, of Congress: the end to the congressional restriction on draftees serving beyond the continental limits; retention of the National Guard on active duty; and unlimited extension of the draftees' terms of service.

The report was candid, sober, even painful to a nation huddled behind its ocean barriers. Yet for all his apparent candor, Marshall could not reveal just how threatened was the nation. Since August 1940, army cryptographers had been reading the most secret Japanese diplomatic messages almost as fast as the diplomats to whom they were addressed. The cables, code-named MAGIC, yielded unmistakable proof of the Japanese Imperial Council's aggressive intent in Southeast Asia and the oil-rich Dutch East Indies.

Within hours of the report's release to the press—Marshall still had something to learn about both public relations and congressional politics—House and Senate leaders were angrily telephoning the White House, demanding to know why they had been put on the spot. The president, equally surprised, could only soothe House Speaker Sam Rayburn with assurances that the chief of staff had acted on his own.

Marshall had neglected to issue a press release with the report, one that underscored his major points. Instead, reporters and administration opponents focused on the implication that by asking removal of the ban on overseas service Marshall was seeking permission to create another American Expeditionary Force.

This statement, thundered California's Hiram Johnson, ranking minority member on the Senate Foreign Relations Committee, sought to alter the one-year contract made by the Selective Service Act. "Worst of all, it apparently contemplates the taking of our boys across the water to fight a foreign war." Johnson wanted no Americans used "for making the world safe for communism." Instead, he "would place Stalin and Hitler enclosed in an elevated cage and let them fight it out."

Even moderates backed away from the biennial report, fearing contamination. Alva Adams, so patiently wooed earlier by the chief of staff, remarked sardonically that American boys "do not come under the Lend-Lease Act"; Congress had no right to transport American boys "to participate in foreign wars in which we have no part."

Any hope Marshall might have nurtured for a reasoned change in public opinion was trampled by a rush of hostile editorials after unguarded comments by the two embattled British commanders in the Middle East. On July 5, the day after *The New York Times* ran long excerpts from Marshall's biennial report, General Archibald Wavell told a *Times* reporter, "Undoubtedly we shall need manpower if the war continues long enough, and I have no doubt it will. We shall have to have planes, tanks, munitions, transports and, finally, men." His thinned forces retreating before the Afrika Korps, Wavell added ominously, "The sooner the better."

Wavell fitted the noose; two days later "the Auk" pulled the trap. General Claude Auchinleck, Wavell's successor as Middle Eastern commander, stirred bitter memory. "We certainly are going to need American manpower, just as we did in the last war."

The biennial report and the comments of the two British generals only confirmed Roosevelt's opponents in their suspicions of the man. Like Representative Hamilton Fish, they divined "a gigantic conspiracy" to involve the country in global war. The America First Research Bureau decided, "There seems no justification for the proposed resolutions, unless military ventures into foreign lands are planned."

Marshall, Stimson, and the president could only gnash their teeth. The immediate result was Marshall's painful decision to drop his request that congressional restrictions on the use of American troops overseas be lifted. He would have to cannibalize two army divisions in order to form a single unit of enlistees to relieve the volunteer 1st Marine Division in its temporary occupation of Iceland. (The president on June 7 had ordered the Marines to that vital Danish-owned island in the mid-Atlantic to preempt a German occupation.)

Roosevelt was "again afraid of fear itself," one of his closest advisers noted. The president was drifting once more in the face of events, waiting for public opinion to catch up with him, unwilling to authorize convoying of merchant vessels in the North Atlantic despite grievous losses to U-boats, unwilling to push for the draft extension. But Marshall could not wait if Congress were to act before the first draftees began going home.

More clever than bold, President Roosevelt convened a long strategy meeting at the White House on July 14, 1941, bringing together congressional leaders from both parties for a secret briefing by the chief of staff. Marshall repudiated any thought of another expeditionary force on the Pershing model, though he warned the legislators he might need small task forces to take and hold the Azores and Cape Verde Islands if Germany were to seize Spain and Portugal. Moreover, Nazi influence in South America, especially coup-prone Brazil, might require garrisoning defensive positions in Venezuela and Colombia to protect the Panama Canal.

The legislators listened, but made no commitments. Marshall's presentation was sobering, but it would not change the political equation. Significant numbers of isolationist Republicans and alienated Democrats, enough to make passage a dicey bet, would vote against the measure if only to embarrass the president.

To deflect some of that criticism, the president and Henry Stimson decided that Marshall should personally lead the fight for extension of the draft. The president himself would give one radio address to cover their flank by firming public support as best he could; at the moment, only a bare majority of the public believed a draft extension necessary.

The chief of staff was the only choice possible. In his two years in Washington, he had achieved a considerable reputation, just as the president—the economic crisis and his New Deal reforms behind him—lost favor. Stimson had not the energy, his assistants, Patterson and McCloy, not the reputation.

Marshall it would be, agreed Speaker of the House Sam Rayburn, the North Texas Democrat with thirty years' experience in the House. "Of all the men who ever testified before any committee on which I served, there is no one of them who has the influence with a committee of the House that General Marshall has." Rayburn, the shrewdest of vote-counters on the Hill, had good reason to admire Marshall. The chief of staff, after all, had put over the peacetime draft the year before despite Rayburn's certain prediction that the votes were not there.

Marshall testifying, Rayburn told the others, could convince legislators to uncharacteristically put aside their ingrained partisanship. "We just remember that we are in the presence of a man who is telling us the truth, as he sees it. . . ."

The truth this year was unpalatable, awkward, and unnerving. The world slipped deeper into global war, the fighting already more widespread than that of the 1914–18 conflagration. Yet the United States found itself naked before its enemies, its army scheduled to wither away beginning on September 1 when the first Guard units demobilized. Draftees would be discharged beginning November 1.

The White House could not offer much support. The president was no longer the all-powerful political force of eight years earlier. A Congress once cowed by fear of economic collapse had acceded to Roosevelt's reforms, however "socialistic" they seemed in retrospect. Eight years later, the business and financial structure of the nation functioned once more, and those same legislators were embarrassed by their earlier lack of faith. Many resented Roosevelt for acting when they stood paralyzed.

Moreover, the vital Roosevelt had upset the balance of power in Washington. Congress since 1933 had steadily ceded authority to a newly activist executive branch with its myriad of alphabetic agencies and brash young reformers. Congress, by comparison, seemed old, more than a little tired. Here was reason to resent that man in the White House, crippled yet so vigorous. Anti-Roosevelt sentiment alone might kill the draft extension.

In publicly advocating an extension of service, Marshall found himself virtually alone. Few legislators would openly support extension; a congressional aide noted, "In forty years on the Hill he had never seen such fear of a bill."

With good reason. Morale in Marshall's army was shattered. Draftees who thought they would serve only one year found themselves facing indefinite extensions. Ignoring the clause in the original Selective Service Act that provided for extensions "whenever Congress has declared that the national interest is imperiled," the draftees chalked "O.H.I.O." (Over the Hill in October) on barracks walls. They no more than their parents understood the crisis; no more than Senator Johnson did they think it necessary to fight for Great Britain, let alone the Soviet Union. Even those who might have understood the larger issues found their ideals mocked by military training that substituted trucks for tanks and stovepipes for artillery pieces on maneuvers.

Strategically, Marshall and his legislative liaison decided to try the Senate first. Only one third of the members would be up for reelection the following year and therefore would be overly sensitive to current public opinion. Further, South Carolina's James Byrnes was a canny majority leader, a successful floor manager of more than one problematic bill.

Testifying before the Senate Military Affairs Committee, Marshall neatly disassociated himself from the White House, at the same time appearing once more in full candor:

"It may clarify the atmosphere for me to explain that I made the specific recommendations regarding the extension of the twelve-month period of service . . . purely on the basis of a military necessity for the security of the country. The commander-in-chief, that is, the president, had no knowledge that I was going to make them. My report was submitted to the secretary of war and at the same time was released to the press. The recommendations were dictated by military necessity. I tried to keep as wide a separation as possible between military necessity, the sole basis for my recommendations, and political considerations which are matters for the decision of the president and the Congress."

Time was passing. It was now the middle of July, and the first draftees would be released in September, the cool soldier in his neatly tailored summer suit told the senators. They were working against time.

"We have seen nation after nation go down, one after the other, in front of a concentrated effort, each one lulled, presumably, into negative action, until all the guns were turned on them and it was too late."

According to the terms of the draft act, once a draftee finished his year of active service, he was to be transferred to the reserves, subject to recall. His period of active duty could only be extended if Congress declared the national interest imperiled.

"In the opinion of the War Department"—again Marshall was shouldering all responsibility—"such a situation now exists. The president has deemed it expedient to declare an unlimited national emergency concerning civil functions, and the War Department and I personally now believe it to be urgently necessary in the public interest for Congress to declare the existence of a national emergency."

He could not say it more forcefully. Recalling his earlier testimony that he would prefer to be investigated for overspending than for not having spent enough, Marshall added, "We must not make the mistake of going on the short side. The hazards are too great. We cannot speculate with the security of this country."

Passage of the resolution would create a unified army, with all its members subject to the same consideration. At the moment, Marshall's personnel division had to contend with three different categories of service, scraping for Regular Army volunteers to fill out units going overseas. When there were not enough, the units went short-handed, or were not sent at all.

Did the chief of staff anticipate increasing the size of the Army, California's Sheridan Downey asked.

Marshall sought no further increase now, but resisted being "committed indefinitely." The situation remained fluid, volatile. President Roosevelt, he assured them, was a throttle on any grandiose expansion. "The president has been against tremendous increase, if it were possible to avoid it. He has always demanded convincing proof of the necessity of the increase."

Building up the Army was the best assurance the United States might avoid war. "It has been our determination to bring the Army to such a state of efficiency that nobody would dare to interfere with our freedom of action."

Marshall's testimony was adroit. He cast the president in the guise of a conservative with no desire to approve the army appropriations Marshall sought. If that risked stirring the faint fears of a standing army, the general himself stood as the strongest assurance there would be no usurpation of civilian powers by strutting brass. At the same time, he gently reminded the senators of their ultimate veto power, and credited their cooperation in passing successive defense appropriation bills.

One by one Marshall won over the committee members, but not without accepting an amendment that barred the president from extending the terms of service beyond another eighteen months. In time, the Senate would follow the committee's do-pass recommendation, voting 54–30 on August 7 to proclaim a national emergency.

The House of Representatives, slow, balky, with party discipline forgotten on a bill of such gut-wrenching importance, would prove more difficult. Anti-Roosevelt feeling ran stronger here. Furthermore, Republicans held a larger bloc of votes, and had cast them repeatedly against crucial preparedness bills in the past.

Raw partisanship corroded the debate. Minority leader Joseph W. Martin described the draft extension as an issue that might "blow us back to the commanding position the Republican Party had enjoyed in the 1920s." Martin, who privately claimed to favor the resolution, would abandon principle for whatever partisan advantage he could squirrel from the crisis.

Mustering what support he could for the resolution in the House, Marshall turned to his old ally, Representative James W. Wadsworth. That sponsor of the Selective Service Act in the House a year earlier convened a meeting at the Army and Navy Club of forty fellow Republicans who, Wadsworth believed, might be persuaded to vote aye. For five hours, finishing only at midnight, Marshall pleaded, first logic, then patriotism. Only a handful came around, "willing to risk their seats to vote the extension. A few told him they would support the measure although it would cost them re-election. Deeply moved by their action, he resolved, if his help was needed, to go on the platform when they ran in 1942 and defend their patriotism."

Finally, one of Wadsworth's guests shrugged. "You put the case very well, but I will be damned if I am going along with Mr. Roosevelt."

Stunned, Marshall snapped angrily, "You are going to let plain hatred of the personality dictate to you to do something that you realize is very harmful to the interest of the country."

The lobbying wore heavily on the chief of staff. Leaving Capitol Hill one afternoon in that tense summer, he leaned wearily back in the staff car, closed his eyes, and murmured, "If I can only keep all personal feelings out of my system, I may be able to get through with this job."

How to defuse fear of the president without appearing to oppose the president? Testifying in secret session before the House Military Affairs Committee, Marshall again carefully asserted he alone had authorized the biennial report and its recommendations. The conclusions "were based on military necessity only, and I was especially concerned that they be made in a manner that was clearly nonpolitical."

Speaking without notes, his voice intense, Marshall asked the committee members to recognize the realities of a world at war. "Are the national interests imperiled? Does a national emergency exist? As I said before and as I say now again, in my opinion a national emergency decidedly does exist; in the opinion of the War Department, it does; in the opinion of the president, it does."

The urgency of the moment laces Marshall's words even on the printed page. "The declaration of an emergency does not create it. An emergency exists whether or not the Congress declares it. I am asking you to recognize the fact—the fact that the national interest is imperiled and that an emergency exists. I am not asking you to manufacture a fact."

His major concern, he told the panel, was "over temporizing, over expediency, over a patchwork solution, when direct action is so clearly indicated."

Marshall had accepted the one-year term of service a year earlier not "from cold military reason" but for "plain political expediency." Now he was back, seeking not expansion of the Army, he reminded the representatives, but only a longer training period. As long as the size of the Army remained fixed by congressional appropriations at present levels, they would have to discharge into the reserve trained men to make way for new trainees. That left them with two half-trained groups, one on active duty, the other in the reserves.

House Republicans and some anti-administration Democrats floated a counterproposal, one that would shift responsibility for extending the term of service from the Congress to the president. Under terms of the Selective Service Act, draftees could be discharged into the reserve, then as members of the reserve called back by the president onto active duty for another twelve months.

Confronted by that plan, Marshall characteristically argued against it. "I think it would be most unfortunate to do that at this time because the soldier would feel that he had been victimized by a maneuver, by sharp practice, under the cover of the law."

Even with his army at stake, Marshall could not bend on a matter of principle. "I want to go right straight down the road, to do what is best, and to do it frankly and without evasion. I think it would have a most unfortunate effect on morale if we adopted the other method. We would give our men the feeling that we were taking some unfair though legal advantage of them."

The House called the question on August 12 amid a flurry of last-minute lobbying and reports of Democratic defections. Before a tense gallery crowded with Mothers for America and American Firsters, the House of Representatives voted 203–202 in favor of the resolution to extend the term of service. By a single vote, Marshall's, America's Army had been saved.

The victory was Marshall's, made possible by Representative Wadsworth and the twenty-one GOP votes he was able to keep in line. Democrats split 182 for the resolution, 69 against. The Republicans voted 21 for, 133 against.

The chief of staff would not be in Washington at the moment of his great political victory. Instead, he was 1,000 miles away, aboard the USS *Augusta,* anchored in the Arctic-green waters of Ship Harbor in Placentia Bay, Newfoundland. At the orders of the president, Marshall, Arnold, Stark, and the commander of the Navy's Atlantic Fleet, Ernest J. King, had all slipped separately from the capital. The president too was gone, ostensibly cruising in the presidential yacht *Potomac* off Martha's Vineyard. Roosevelt had evaded his ever present guard of wire service reporters, leaving behind a faint look-alike to lounge smoking on the afterdeck and wave grandly at sailors who cruised nearby under the watchful eye of a Coast Guard cutter. Roosevelt, however, was neither fishing nor relaxing. Instead, he had secretly transferred from *Potomac* to *Augusta,* Admiral King's flagship, then sped north by northwest at flank speed to meet with Winston Churchill.

The suggestion to meet at what would later be called the Atlantic Conference had come from the prime minister. Hoping to involve the United States more deeply in the struggle against Hitler, Churchill sought to prepare a joint declaration of war aims. Such an announcement would merely underscore the fait accompli—the Atlantic patrols, the occupation of Iceland that freed a British division for combat duty, the growing resupply of Great Britain's military forces. Roosevelt had set two preconditions for the meeting: the United States would agree to no economic and territorial deals for a postwar world; and there were to be no embarrassing questions raised at the forthcoming conference about United States entry into war.

Awaiting Churchill's arrival, the president fished amid the small battle fleet surrounding *Augusta* while his party of advisers grumbled about the foul weather and close quarters. For two days they sought some agreement among themselves on their military and naval position, hampered by Roosevelt's reluctance to commit himself.

They had made little progress by August 9 when the great hulk of the Royal Navy's newest battleship, *Prince of Wales*, steamed up the channel in a drizzling rain, breaking out of the fog as if bringing the sunlight with her. Her crew assembled on the deck, the band playing, the Royal Marine guard drawn up, and the king's first minister—in the uniform of an Elder Brother of Trinity House—on the bridge, the battleship grandly anchored astern *Augusta*.

To the piping of the boatswain's whistle, Winston Churchill and his party came aboard the American cruiser, the prime minister beaming at the salute. Passing the rows of officers drawn up on the deck, Churchill crossed to the president, standing with the aid of his son Elliott. President and prime minister shook hands.

It was a historic meeting, the first of nine wartime conferences.* The two men chatted for a moment, instantly on a first-name basis, then began the introductions of their mutual staffs.

Churchill had brought to Placentia Bay a large staff as well as the haggard Harry Hopkins, returning from Moscow and London. Churchill's party included General Sir John Dill, chief of the Imperial General Staff; Admiral of the Fleet Sir Dudley Pound, the first sea lord; Air Vice Marshall Sir Wilfrid Freeman; Permanent Undersecretary of State for Foreign Affairs Sir Alexander Cadogan; and his scientific adviser, Professor F. A. Lindemann, first and last Viscount Cherwell. Each of these men had an array of deputies, all at the ready with position papers and supporting studies.

The American delegation was small, and certainly unprepared even to record the momentous meeting. Besides Hopkins, Roosevelt had summoned Assistant Secretary of State Sumner Welles, a polished diplomat already concerned with reports that Great Britain had made secret deals with the Greek and Yugoslav monarchs in return for wartime support; Averell Harriman, the Lend-Lease expediter in London; and the three military chiefs, Marshall, Stark, and Arnold, all looking somewhat stiff, as if unaccustomed to their long-mothballed uniforms. In contrast to the British staff, ranked three deep, the Americans had brought few

---

* In order, they were: Placentia Bay, August 1941; Washington (ARCADIA), December 1941 to January 1942; Casablanca (SYMBOL), January 1943; Washington (TRIDENT), May 1943; Quebec (QUADRANT), August 1943; Cairo (SEXTANT) and Tehran (EUREKA), November–December 1943; Quebec (OCTAGON), September 1944; and Yalta (ARGONAUT), February 1945. President Roosevelt died three months before the last wartime conference at Potsdam (TERMINAL) in July 1945.

aides and no planners. Elliott Roosevelt found himself dragooned into taking notes of military discussions.

The British prime minister and the American chief of staff were meeting for the first time since 1919 and the victory celebration in London. Each had changed over those twenty-two years. They were no longer quite the spirited—in Churchill's case, the irrepressibly spirited—innovators of their middle years. The once lean Briton, who would be sixty-seven at the end of November, had thickened, grown into that cross between a cherub and a bulldog English editorial cartoonists had been drawing since the first war.

Roosevelt and Churchill were meeting as equals, though in fact, they were not. As president of the United States, FDR was a head of state. As prime minister, Churchill was merely a head of government, responsible both to his king and a coalition cabinet of considerable power.

The military delegations were not so well matched. The British had had almost two years' experience in modern warfare. Despite that edge, the American military group, at least in Marshall and Stark, had more experience in the realities of coalition warfare than the British gave them credit for. Marshall had dealt with the demanding French for twenty months during World War I, and his three years in Tientsin had given him a first-hand view of European colonialism. He had come away with something of a distaste for the British, at least those manning the Empire's outposts who seemed to be more imperial and stiff-necked than relatives at home.

Chief of Naval Operations Harold Stark, known throughout the Navy by his academy nickname "Betty," agreed with Marshall that they needed to jointly plan with the British. As aide to Admiral William S. Sims, Stark had been caught up in the frenzy and futility of efforts to integrate operations of the two fleets in 1917–18. Confronting an undeclared war a generation later, Stark insisted upon coordination before the inevitable.

Stark's problem was Roosevelt's evasiveness. "To some of my pointed questions, which all of us would like to have answered, I get a smile or a 'Betty, please don't ask me that!' Policy seems something never fixed, always fluid and changing," Stark wrote a friend just weeks before.

Every bit the introspective planner his nickname and wire-frame glasses suggested, Stark could only bide his time and temper. He was unable to give guidance to the commander of his Atlantic Fleet, Admiral Ernest J. King. King needed that guidance; on taking over his flagship in April, he had discovered the locked safe in the captain's cabin contained just one strategic plan—for a war with Mexico.

But King would not be landing Marines at Vera Cruz or shelling Tampico. His squadrons, bolstered with ships from the much larger Pacific Fleet, were limited to "patrolling," permitted only to seek out German *unterseebooten* and report their location to the British. At the same time, American-owned freighters were barred from carrying war goods to the British; thus the merchant navy was neutral, the warships a little bit pregnant. The president intended no change until he believed the American public committed to the inevitability of war.

Britain, however, could not wait indefinitely for a surer American hand. Merchant losses totaled 5.7 million tons by June; English shipyards could replace only 800,000 tons annually, and Churchill had already asked the president to order accelerated production of freighters and tankers. Here at Placentia Bay, Churchill intended to ask the president to increase the Atlantic Fleet's role.

The delegations had different goals in mind. "Watch and see if the PM doesn't start off by demanding that we immediately declare war against the Nazis," the president said to his son. He had no such intention, preferring only a general statement of mutual war aims, nothing so much as a flag of propaganda around which to rally the nation.

Keeping his advisers ill-advised was one method of assuring they would not find common military cause with their opposite numbers on the British side. "I think the best answer to those who feel that we were planning the war in detail ahead of time would be the fact that we had so little basis for planning at the time of the meeting on the *Augusta*," Marshall said later.

Early in their conversations, Marshall and Sir John Dill, chief of the Imperial General Staff, took a liking to each other. At lunch that day on the *Augusta*, then during a courtesy visit to the *Prince of Wales*, the two chatted, no doubt probing, each discreetly taking the measure of the other.

Dill, whose very thinness made him appear taller than he was, had the look about him of a man beset by too many problems. Command of the British armies since June of the previous year had left him hollow-eyed and pale, with thinning hair brushed smartly to his skull. His disarming sense of wry humor remained intact.

Marshall was to discover in Dill "charm and real goodness." Dill possessed the modesty and selfless judgment that to Marshall were the hallmarks of a professional. Later he would learn, through others of course, of Dill's resilience, his wearying acceptance of Churchill's abuse because Dill advocated caution in the face of the PM's demands for bold military strokes. Jack Dill was tired, but determined to stay the course.

At dinner on the first evening, Churchill began his campaign. He launched into a long, detailed review of the war, dazzling in its brilliance, Elliott Roosevelt thought, optimistic, as resolute over brandy and cigars as he was in the House of Commons. Britain might lose battles, he conceded, "but Britain always wins the wars."

The president listened, asking the occasional question, his diffidence only stirring Churchill to further oratory. "The Americans *must* come in at our side! You must come in if you are to survive!" Churchill finished.

Great Britain needed all America could produce—ships, planes, tanks, ammunition—and men as well, the prime minister acknowledged. The first chore, even short of the declaration of war that Roosevelt refused to seek, was the protection of all ships in the North Atlantic. Great Britain was doomed without that assistance.

If America took over convoying responsibilities from North America to the northern approaches, British warships released from that duty by the Atlantic Fleet could be moved to the Mediterranean and especially the Far East. Japan's looming move southward threatened them all, the American Philippines, Britain's Malayan Peninsula with the large base at Singapore, and the Dutch East Indies, probably the greatest prize of all with its oil and rubber.

The following morning, a destroyer pulled alongside the *Augusta,* took the president and his small party aboard, then backed gingerly to the *Prince of Wales.* Once again the president insisted on walking, one hand tense on the rail of the gangplank, the other on his son's arm, taking the salute, then grinning broadly as he sank into the chair set up for him on the quarterdeck.

Churchill himself had arranged the worship service in the hazy sun that morning, turning it into an emotional appeal for unity. American and British crewmen stood mingled under the aft guns; flags of both nations draped the altar; American and British chaplains led prayers before the superstructure still marked by the scars of the ship's fight with the *Bismarck* earlier that year. The lesson was from Joshua, the first chapter: "There shall not any man be able to stand before thee all the days of thy life: as I was with Moses, so will I be with thee: I will not fail thee, nor forsake thee. Be strong and of a good courage." The service concluded with three hymns, "Onward Christian Soldiers," "O God, Our Help in Ages Past," and "Eternal Father." The "deeply moving expression of the unity of faith of our two peoples" left Churchill's eyes moist. "It was a great hour to live."

The unity of the morning would be tested that afternoon when the conferees broke up into smaller groups. Roosevelt and Churchill exchanged strong words when discussing the joint declaration to be issued when they parted. Roosevelt insisted on including an assurance "that these military and naval conversations had in no way involved any future commitments between the two governments." He needed such a clause to forestall isolationist charges of secret deals. Churchill argued against the assurance as "deeply discouraging to the population of the occupied countries," as well as a serious blow to British morale.

Below decks, Assistant Secretary of State Welles and Foreign Minister

Cadogan were attempting to work out a strong declaration to be issued to the Japanese by the American, British, and Dutch governments, warning that any further encroachment in the southwestern Pacific would compel the three nations "to take countermeasures even though these might lead to war. . . ." Churchill was especially anxious to secure American endorsement of these declarations. A Japanese attack could "be almost decisive," crippling Great Britain's ability to wage war, Churchill later told Welles. Roosevelt would not be pushed; there would be no joint warning for the moment.

The military chiefs were hardly getting on any better. The British had come prepared with a proposed outline of general strategy to defeat Germany and Italy. The British paper began with a careful defense of the Middle East campaigns, already questioned by Hopkins in his earlier conversation with the prime minister. Of the Americans, it asked two things: more supplies, especially tanks; and the use of United States troops to occupy North West Africa before the Axis did. Such a modest effort, a token really, considering America's vast resources in men and industry, would allow the British to bring the Axis down, Dill asserted.

The strategy proposed by the British team for the *coup de main* was a combination of blockade, bombing, then insurrection in the captured nations on the continent. Only when Hitler's fortress had been ringed by peripheral attacks, weakened from within by bombing and uprising, would the Allies mount a conquering force to march into Berlin.

Air Corps General Arnold was pleased with the emphasis the British had placed upon bombers. Stark and King were both skeptical of the plan because it undervalued the difficulty of keeping the vital North Atlantic lifeline open.

Marshall was profoundly dismayed by the British plan. Instinctively, without study, he doubted Germany could be brought to its knees without a full-scale land battle. That would require invasion of the continent, most likely from Great Britain, and the defeat of the German Army. A peripheral strategy such as the British proposed, combined with attrition of the German homeland, might succeed, but it would take years longer, and ultimately would be more costly in blood and materiel than the United States might be willing to bear.

Agreeing to nothing, forbidden by the president to discuss war plans, the Americans offered to take the British paper back to Washington for staff study. In the dryly underwritten opinion of the official British historian, "It seemed likely that these would be critical." With previous presidential permission, the Americans agreed to only one British proposal, the most important to them for the short term, the convoying of all shipping, including British, from Newfoundland to Iceland.

For their part, the British were stunned by the American concentration on defense of the western hemisphere, deciding at that moment that the United States military planners lacked an appreciation of global strategy. Defense of the somnolent Panama Canal when the threatened Suez was the great prize in the war seemed misguided at best. Dill came away disappointed in Marshall's seeming lack of interest in grand strategy; the American spoke only of production and mobilization rather than operations.

The differing war aims set the strategists in conflict. American planners did not lack for strategic wisdom; they simply did not share the British goals. Churchill, Dill, and their colleagues were intent upon saving the Empire, American planners would later point out. The United States might be drawn into war to protect its own interests, but it would not fight to preserve only British territories for British exploitation.

Moreover, the British were to learn with a dismay that matched Marshall's own, the United States was woefully armed. While the production of light and medium tanks would reach 1,400 a month in early 1942, at the moment, Marshall had just 40 to be shared by his four armored divisions. Replacement of British losses in the Middle East and Greece had absorbed all current production.

The prime minister spoke of warnings to the Japanese when the American garrison in the Philippines had no more than a single battery of four anti-aircraft guns to protect the city of Manila.

The manpower situation was no better. An occupation of North Africa, even of Dakar, nearest the Horn of Brazil, clearly would strain the Americans. Admiral Ernest King had embarrassed General Marshall before the British merely by asking when the Army would relieve the last of the Marines garrisoning Iceland.

A second round of talks the following day achieved little. Marshall and Stark, in fact, were more parsimonious than they had been in the past. A British request for 6,000 more bombers than the United States was producing this year only provoked irritation. Such British orders, uncoordinated with American, had already snarled the procurement of too many items. To placate their providers, the British conferees agreed to overhaul their purchasing commission in Washington with an eye to greater coordination. The Americans' niggardly manner was something of a ploy, designed to probe "the exact status of British war potential" for the president.

In one sense, the American party came away from the conference more than a little impressed. They had been, in the football term, outplayed in every facet of the game. At dinner in their dress uniforms, the British staff appeared "so resplendent as to put us Americans . . . to shame." When the president had served roast chicken on Saturday night, Churchill had arranged a menu for Sunday that included grouse shot on the Scottish moor just before sailing. More importantly, and it was a lesson Marshall learned well, the British had come prepared. Their disagreements between government and military, between the services themselves, were ironed out in advance, or at least papered over with formidable studies that obscured the issue; the British never admitted dispute outside their councils. British staff work was not necessarily better, Marshall realized, only more comprehensive. If anything, he judged British policy to be shortsighted, focused on British war aims, and nothing so grand as the American theory.

This first wartime conference resulted in few understandings and only one public document, a lofty Atlantic Charter stating their mutual war aims. The charter renounced any Anglo-American territorial interests; denounced any imposed governments or boundary changes; advocated self-determination for all nations; urged equal access to trade for all; pledged a peace that assured freedom from fear and want, freedom of the seas, disarmament of Germany, Italy, and Japan, and an end to the crushing burden of armaments; and called for the creation of a permanent system of general security.

Roosevelt had his statement of war aims. Churchill had a document that publicly bound the two nations together in common cause.

Tuesday afternoon, the *Prince of Wales* slipped her mooring and headed down channel while the band played "The Star Spangled Banner" in salute. *Augusta*'s band responded with "Auld Lang Syne" as the British battleship churned toward the open sea. Four months later, Japanese bombers would send that splendid relic of Empire to the bottom of the South China Sea with the loss of almost half her crew.

C H A P T E R

XIII

Oranges, Purples, and Rainbows

The Year of the Dragon gave way to the Year of the Snake. Aboard the massive battleship *Nagato* anchored in ironclad serenity in Hiroshima Bay, Admiral Isoroku Yamamoto, commander in chief of the Japanese Combined Fleet, weighed his plan conceived late in December 1940. A bold thinker, Yamamoto intended to radically revise traditional naval strategy, to shift the *Kantai Kessen* or Great All-Out Battle from the western Pacific eastward, to change its character from a defensive sea encounter fought near the Japanese homeland to an offensive strike at the enemy wherever its fleet might be.

The stocky, thick-chested admiral, then sixty-four, had no great desire for that battle, or for the long war he knew would inevitably follow. As a Harvard undergraduate, then as naval attaché in Washington, he had seen the massive power of American industry, and the vast natural resources that Japan lacked. The younger officers on the Naval General Staff, so cocky, so certain of victory, could boast of Japan's growing naval power, but Admiral Yamamoto was not so deluded. If war came, he wrote a former classmate at the naval academy, "I shall run wild for the first six months or a year, but I have utterly no confidence for the second or third year."

Like so many senior naval officers, Yamamoto wanted to avoid that conflict. Yet if it came, if Japan's claims upon Southeast Asia and the resources of the Indies were rebuffed and his country thereby doomed to the status of a second-class power, the admiral would fight. He had already asked for command of the fleet that sought out the American Navy according to his plans.

Yamamoto's conception was simple: a preemptive strike upon the American fleet anchored in Pearl Harbor. Two to four aircraft carriers were "to launch a forced or surprise attack with all their air strength, risking themselves on a moonlight night or at dawn." Then in direct support of invasion forces moving toward Malaya and the Dutch East Indies, "a forestalling and surprise attack on enemy air forces in the Philippines and Singapore should definitely be made almost at the same time as the attacks against Hawaii."

The key was the elimination of America's Pacific Fleet before it could strike a flank attack on Japanese forces moving toward Southeast Asia. The British had proved such an aerial assault possible; twenty obsolete biplanes carrying special torpedoes had flown off the carrier *Illustrious* on the morning of November 11, 1940, then at an altitude of just 35 feet swooped upon the Italian fleet anchored in the naval roadstead on the Ionian Sea at Taranto. The torpedos slipped under nets across the mouth of the harbor and struck no less than three battleships. Half the effective force of the Italian Navy was in repair. Control of the eastern Mediterranean had passed to the British at a cost of two planes in this, the first successful attack on warships by carrier-launched planes.

To perfect his plan, Admiral Yamamoto turned to Commodore Minoru Genda, a brilliant advocate of naval airpower who had long argued for massed air attacks on surface ships rather than the classic sea war between hulking battleships. Genda set to work solving two problems: how to deploy large numbers of attacking bombers in the narrow confines of Pearl Harbor, and the development of a torpedo, like the British, effective at short range in shallow waters.

Yamamoto considered his a contingency plan, in case diplomacy failed to secure the Greater East Asia Co-Prosperity Sphere Japan prized. He much preferred the peaceful way, even in the face of the Americans' provocative behavior.

First the Americans had decided not to renew the twenty-year-old Treaty of Trade and Navigation with Japan. Though trade had not been injured, the non-renewal on the grounds of Japan's continued war with an American ally, China, set the two nations on a diplomatic collision course.

Then the United States had announced an embargo on aviation fuel shipments and Number 1 grade scrap iron used to make steel. Japan might still buy crude oil, but its refinery capacity was small, too small to meet the projected need of a nation mobilizing its armed forces. Successive restrictions on other raw materials President Roosevelt said were used in the bombing of the Chinese only made matters worse.

Such embargos were tokens of America's emnity, and signals to the expansion-minded that Japan's future lay with the Axis. Prodded by impatient army leaders, a new premier, Prince Fumimaro Konoye, installed the former chief of staff of the bellicose Kwantung Army as Minister of War. The ascension of the man known as "Razor Brain," General Hideki Tojo, was an ominous setback for the peace party in Tokyo.

The new foreign minister, Yosuke Matsuoka, quickly concluded a Tripartite Pact with Germany and Italy. By terms of the agreement approved on September 26, 1940, Germany and Italy were to hold sway in Europe, Japan to dominate "a new order in Greater East Asia." Further, the three signators agreed to "undertake to assist one another with all political, economic and military means when one of the three Contracting Parties is attacked by a power at present not involved in the European War or in the Sino-Japanese Conflict."

Japan's New Order was to stretch from the mid-Pacific to New Zealand and Australia, across the Malay Peninsula to swallow Indochina, Burma, Thailand, and India. The home islands, Korea, Manchuria, and China were to be the core of the largest empire the world had ever known.

Japan first meant to secure the center, or at least to isolate the enfeebled Nationalist armies of Chiang Kai-shek. In July 1940, Japanese pressure forced the British temporarily to close the one-lane road through the Yunnan Mountains over which traveled the meager supplies Chiang could secure in the West. The threat to China mounted when Vichy France, at German orders, yielded to Japan the right to maintain troops and airfields in the northern portion of French Indochina. A second arm of the pincers thus closed on Chiang, paralyzing his lethargic divisions by mere threat of assault.

The broad outlines of Japanese policy stood out clearly enough in Washington. The precise details would flow from the work of the son of an immigrant sewing machine salesman in the Pittsburgh area.

Since 1918 the largely self-taught William F. Friedman had been the one-man core of a small code section tucked away in the Munitions Building, devising secure systems for the Army and cracking the codes of other nations. In February 1939, Friedman's team of cryptanalysts— the word itself coined by him—began work on a new Japanese diplomatic code. Eighteen months later, the day after his forty-eighth birthday, he decoded his first complete message transmitted in the code they had nicknamed "Purple." Friedman had pulled off one of the two great intelligence coups of the war. From September 25, 1940, the Japanese had no diplomatic, and few military secrets from the United States. The intercepted messages, code-named MAGIC in the War Department, were to be one of the most tightly held secrets of the war.

Intercepting, decoding, and translating the Japanese signals was a joint venture of the Army's Signal Intelligence Service and the Navy's OP-20-G. The process was neither simple nor speedy, though SIS had grown from a bare dozen people to well over 300 in the last year. Friedman had built just eight of the Purple machines; four more with their "intricate rat's nest of wiring," were on order. Under close guard, four of the machines were in Washington, two each assigned to the Army and Navy.

Another was in the Philippines, the remaining three in London, where the British monitored Japanese signals as well.

Even with eight machines at work, the cryptanalysts were busy. An average of twenty-six signals in the diplomatic code arrived from the listening posts each day. The messages not only had to be decoded into Japanese, but then translated, no small problem. Both services were short on men or women with sufficient knowledge of Japanese culture and language to precisely, delicately translate the nuances of formal diplomatic language. To solve some of the backlog, the Army took responsibility for messages originating on even-numbered days in Tokyo, the Navy the odd.

Beyond those working in the closely guarded code rooms, at Marshall's orders access was severely limited to MAGIC. Five army people alone saw the original translations; the list of navy recipients was no longer. "Need to know"—as determined entirely by Marshall and Stark—governed admission to this inner circle in the interest of protecting the secret of MAGIC. Distribution overseas was limited to MacArthur and three members of his staff in Manila, and a similar handful of British officers in Singapore.

All-knowing MAGIC had secretly followed the negotiations of the Tripartite Pact from afar. Announcement of the treaty's signing on September 26, 1940, led Secretary of State Hull to issue a warning to American civilians to leave the Far East "in view of abnormal conditions in those areas."

Those abnormal conditions, and especially the increased threat to China, provoked a Roosevelt gesture of disapproval. The Treasury Department on his orders tightened the embargo by adding vital copper, brass, bronze, zinc, nickel, and potash to the list of proscribed materials.

Prime Minister Konoye groped for an accommodation with Washington on the Chinese question by changing ambassadors. Twice his choice turned the offer down, and only with the added urgings of moderate naval officers and industrialists who feared war with the United States did retired Admiral Kichisaburo Nomura agree to take up the portfolio.

At another time, Admiral Nomura might have been the ideal ambassador of peace. Nomura, tall by Japanese standards at six feet, liked the United States and spoke English well, though deliberately, as if relearning it. During World War I, he had served as naval attaché in Washington and had befriended Assistant Secretary of the Navy Franklin Delano Roosevelt. The admiral also had a number of other friends in the United States, especially among naval officers.

Nomura was now sixty-four, blinded in his right eye, partially deaf, and crippled with a limp—all the result of a bomb thrown by a Chinese Nationalist in Shanghai in 1932. He was also burdened by the certainty that the Imperial Conference meant to go to war if necessary to expand the Co-Prosperity Sphere in Greater East Asia. Later, in recalling his futile eleven-month ministry, he would recite the Japanese proverb: "When a big house falls, one pillar cannot stop it."

Four days after Nomura departed for Washington in January 1941, United States Ambassador Joseph Grew passed on persistent, "fantastic" reports circulating in Tokyo that Japan had begun planning an attack on Pearl Harbor. The following day, Foreign Minister Matsuoka told a budget committee of the Diet that Japan must dominate the western Pacific. "I wish to declare," the pugnacious, outspoken Matsuoka said, "that if America does not understand Japan's rightful claims and actions, then there is not the slightest hope of improvement of Japanese-American relations."

In the War Department, the chief of staff watched these Far Eastern developments with wary eye fixed on their Pacific bases. Nine months before, he had visited the Hawaiian Islands to observe an army alert. He returned to the United States satisfied, perhaps lulled, his official biographer concluded, by the Army's defenses on the island. Marshall judged the Hawaiian Department in "excellent shape," lacking only some anti-aircraft weapons. He would dispatch an anti-aircraft regiment to plug that hole in the defense.

An island chain lying 2,000 nautical miles from the mainland athwart the Tropic of Cancer, Hawaii and especially the Big Island of Oahu sat as a volcanic outpost of American seapower. Fortified and refortified over the years, the naval base at Pearl Harbor was the linchpin in any defense of the Pacific. From here, rather than its home port of San Diego, the Pacific Fleet would sortie in the event of war, and here it would return for refitting and repairs. The Army's responsibility, Marshall instructed the new Hawaiian Department commander in February 1941, was "to protect the base and the naval concentration. . . . Fullest protection of the fleet is *the* rather than *a* major consideration for us."

The Navy too was reviewing the defenses at Pearl Harbor. On January 24, 1941, Knox wrote to Stimson that the "dangers envisaged in their order of importance and probability are considered to be: (1) air bombing attack; (2) air torpedo plane attack; (3) sabotage; (4) submarine attack; (5) mining; (6) bombardment by gun fire." Because air defense was primarily an army responsibility, Marshall moved to beef up the paltry fighter plane complement. By stripping squadrons in the United States, reducing them to just three planes each, Marshall was able to round up by March 15 another thirty-one of the obsolescent P-36s. He was down to "seed corn, and that left us nothing back here at all," he wrote Stark. It slowed pilot training, he noted later, but the shipment gave Brigadier General Frederick L. Martin, the Air Corps commander in Hawaii, the nucleus of a defense force. Another fifty of the faster P-40s, plagued with engine failures early in the year, would follow in October 1941, when production reached a total of eight per day.

Weapons could not assure invulnerability. For a decade or more the Navy War College had studied the possibility of a surprise attack on the islands, concluding again and again the Japanese would launch an attack from the air when their carriers were less than 500 miles to the north or northwest of the chain. In January 1938, a War Department estimate of the islands' defenses stipulated ORANGE would attack without warning if war came, adding, "There can be little doubt that the Hawaiian Islands will be the initial scene of action."

Three years later, Air Corps General Martin joined the naval air commander in a report to Washington on March 31, reiterating, "In the past ORANGE has never preceded hostile actions by a declaration of war. A successful, sudden raid against our ships and naval installations on Oahu might prevent effective offensive action by our forces in the western Pacific for a long period. . . . It appears possible that ORANGE submarines and/or an ORANGE fast raiding force might arrive in Hawaiian waters with no prior warning from our Intelligence service." The two airmen reminded their superiors: "It appears that the most likely and dangerous form of attack on Oahu would be an air attack. It is believed that at present such an attack would most likely be launched from one or more carriers which would probably approach inside of 300 miles."

Keeping the Hawaiian Department on the mark, in a state of partial if not full alert, was critical. That was the major factor in Marshall's selection of Major General Walter Campbell Short to replace the retiring Charles D. Herron in February 1941.

An Illinois native, Short had joined the Army in 1902, after graduating the state university. He met the future chief of staff at Fort Reno four years later, then soldiered in the Mexican campaign. Like Marshall, he had served with the 1st Division in France, winning a Distinguished Service Medal for his efforts during the St. Mihiel and Meuse-Argonne campaigns when he trained "machine gun outfits at every available opportunity during rest periods." Like Marshall too, he did not return to the United States until after the victory celebrations in Paris and London. He had pulled two routine tours in Washington during the interwar period, attended the War College, taught at Leavenworth, and earned his first star in 1937. He was "old Army" at age sixty-one, unimaginative and conscientious, a man drilling his way doggedly through the book. Those who had served with him thought him a decent sort, if cool and authoritarian. Much of his career devoted to teaching and training, he was just the man to bring the Army's largest overseas garrison up to full alert, Marshall believed.

In a letter of instruction to Short, Marshall laid out his "impression of the Hawaiian problem" on February 7. The "real perils [are] the risk of

sabotage and the risk of surprise attack by Air" from the "Japanese car-
rier-based pursuit plane." Complaints of the new Pacific Fleet commander, Admiral Husband E. Kimmel, about the state of the Army's air
defenses were to be handled tactfully. "What Kimmel does not realize is
that we are tragically lacking in this materiel throughout the Army and
that Hawaii is on a far better basis than any other command in the Army."

Short was instructed to cooperate fully with Kimmel, to put aside "old
Army and Navy feuds engendered from fights over appropriations." True,
"Mustapha" Kimmel was a difficult man, sometimes even tactless, but
the closest cooperation between the services was necessary. "We must be
completely impersonal in these matters, at least so far as our own nerves
and irritations are concerned," Marshall cautioned in a rare personal
aside to his usually formal correspondence. "Fortunately, and happily I
might say, Stark and I are on the most intimate personal basis, and that
relationship has enabled us to avoid many serious difficulties."

Once Short was in place and the island's air defense reinforced, Hawaii
slipped from Marshall's close attention. The air units had been strengthened, the anti-aircraft batteries increased by one third. New radar would
be shipped by June, giving the Army an all-seeing eye 130 miles to sea,
day and night. "The hazards are too great" for the Japanese to risk an
attack on the fortified island of Oahu, he concluded.

The airplane was to be the backbone of Hawaiian defenses, for Marshall's faith in the new B-17 and B-24 bombers was that of the converted
true believer. When President Roosevelt as early as April 23, 1941, decided
to retain the Pacific Fleet in Hawaii rather than transfer it to the North
Atlantic, a disappointed Marshall told Stimson, "With our heavy bombers
and our fine new pursuit planes, the land forces [alone] could put up
such a defense that the Japs wouldn't dare attack Hawaii. . . ." Sabotage
remained a bigger problem in Marshall's mind. "It would be highly
desirable to set up a military control of the islands prior to the likelihood
of our involvement in the Far East," Marshall wrote in an aide-memoire
for the president early in May.

Three weeks later, General Short confirmed Marshall in his opinion,
reporting a combined army-navy exercise in which Short's bombers located
imaginary Japanese carriers 250 miles at sea, then bombed them "just as
one carrier was in the act of sending a flight of planes off her decks,
maneuver authorities said."

Bombers then were to be the guarantee of the island's defense, Short
was confident. "Here in Hawaii we all live in a citadel or gigantically
fortified island."

The reinforcement of Hawaii was coming none too soon, for events in
the Pacific loomed ominous. Early in February, the British Admiralty
advised the American military attaché in London that it had reason to
believe Japan planned a large-scale offensive in either Indochina, the

Malay Peninsula, or the Indies, perhaps in all three places, by the 10th. Though the Admiralty revised its estimate of the timing, Prime Minister Churchill on February 15 cabled Potus, President of the United States:

> Many drifting straws seem to indicate Japanese intention to make war on us or do something that would force us to make war on them in the next few weeks or months. I am not myself convinced that this is not a war of nerves designed to cover Japanese encroachments in Siam and Indochina. However, I think I ought to let you know that the weight of the Japanese navy, if thrown against us, would confront us with situations beyond the scope of our naval resources.

Churchill estimated the Japanese would first strike for the oil fields of the Dutch East Indies, then attack Singapore. Raids on New Zealand and Australia would force the withdrawal of those Dominion troops from the Middle East to protect their homelands. Japanese raiders in the western Pacific and Indian Oceans would force the British to send the Mediterranean Fleet in pursuit—sacrificing at least the eastern end of that once British sea to the Axis.

Churchill doubted the Japanese would wish to fight both the United States and Great Britain simultaneously, "but no one can tell. Everything that you can do to inspire the Japanese with fear of a double war may avert the danger. If however they come in against us and we are alone, the grave character of the consequences cannot easily be overstated."

However much Roosevelt, Churchill, and the moderate faction in Tokyo wished to avoid hostilities in the Pacific, the militant General Tojo and Foreign Minister Matsuoka determined otherwise. On February 25, Matsuoka cast a covetous eye upon Oceania, proclaiming, "This region has sufficient natural resources to support 600,000,000 to 800,000,000 people. I believe we have a natural right to migrate there." On March 10, Vichy France succumbed to Japan's demand for a monopoly on rice produced in Indochina, and the use of the airfield at Saigon. Three weeks later, Japan proclaimed a similar monopoly on rubber exports from Thailand and Indochina. The threatened Netherlands East Indies opted for appeasement, grudgingly, yielding a portion of its vital raw rubber crop to Japanese buyers. In June, Japan turned back to Indochina, demanding Vichy grant the use of eight army and navy bases in that Southeast Asian colony. Indochina was the key to Japanese expansion; if Vichy, the nominal puppet of Japan's ally, denied use of those bases, the cabinet resolved, "We shall attain our objective by force of arms."

The Japanese game was cunning, and solely its own. Matsuoka turned aside Hitler's urgings that the Japanese attack the British in the Pacific and bring about precisely that scenario Churchill most feared. In a meeting in Berlin on April 4, Hitler assured the Japanese foreign minister that the Americans posed no threat, that Germany would declare war on the United States if Japan went to war.

Japan was not to be rushed. Matsuoka instead negotiated a treaty of neutrality with the Soviet Union, assuring each of the mutually suspicious signatories a protected flank. The Imperial Army could redeploy troops in Manchuria southward.

On June 25, the Japanese war cabinet ratified Admiral Yamamoto's Pearl Harbor strategy. Naval exercises in the previous two months had confirmed the feasibility of the overall plan and the air assault devised by Commander Genda. Those remaining admirals opposing a war with the United States either fell into line or found themselves ostracized. The navy was to stage a preemptive strike on the American Pacific Fleet while the army invested the first outposts of the Greater East Asia Co-Prosperity Sphere.

Washington learned of the decisions in Tokyo on July 14. Japanese officials using the vulnerable Purple code radioed from Canton to Tokyo acknowledgment of earlier orders:

> We will endeavor to the last to occupy French Indo-China peacefully but, if resistance is offered, we will crush it by force, occupy the country and set up martial law. After the occupation of French Indo-China, next on schedule is the sending of an ultimatum to the Netherlands Indies. In the seizing of Singapore the Navy will play the principal part. . . . We will once and for all crush Anglo-American military power and their ability to assist in any schemes against us.

The Purple decrypt made U.S.-Japanese discussions all the more difficult. One American ally, China, was immediately threatened, two others, Britain and the Netherlands, placed in jeopardy. With both the United States and Japan seeking to avert an immediate crisis, each for its own reasons, into the fragile Washington negotiations cruised the vacation-bound American motorist.

Late in the spring of 1941, largely because of the lack of available tankers, oil supplies began to run scarce on the Eastern seaboard. The shortage was posted first on gasoline prices at service stations, just as drivers began thinking about vacation travel, then in dire warnings from oil executives of a scarcity of heating oil come winter. The public protest was sharp.

Reacting to the outcry, the president imposed an embargo on foreign oil shipments from Eastern and Gulf of Mexico ports except to Britain. The only other major customer was Japan, buying oil on East and West coasts to build up its reserves.

At the urging of Marshall and Stark, still bargaining for time, President Roosevelt declined to impose a total ban on oil exports to Japan. "The Japs are having a real drag-down and knock-out fight among themselves and have been for the past week—trying to decide which way they are going to jump—attack Russia, attack the South Seas (thus throwing in their lot definitely with Germany) or whether they will sit on the fence and be more friendly with us," Roosevelt wrote to his petroleum administrator. "No one knows what the decision will be but, as you know, it is terribly important for the control of the Atlantic for us to help to keep peace in the Pacific. I simply have not got enough Navy to go around and every little episode in the Pacific means fewer ships in the Atlantic."

The partial ban on oil inadvertently became total in response to Vichy's yielding bases to Japan in Indochina—proof of Japan's "policy of force and conquest," in Roosevelt's words. On July 25, an executive order issued from the Summer White House at Hyde Park announced the freezing of all Japanese assets in the United States. The instant effect was to end all remaining trade between the two countries.

The freezing of Japanese assets forced the issue. In Tokyo, the Naval General Staff weighed the eighteen-month supply of oil on hand against the still incomplete training of Genda's squadrons. The longer they postponed a decision, the less oil Japan would have to follow up a victory at Pearl Harbor. The enforced compromise settlement they sought, with the Pacific divided between the two nations, would be harder to achieve if they delayed. The decision was to rush the pilots' training.

The announcement of the freeze marked one of the few times the president was to disregard the advice of his two military commanders. Both Marshall and Stark had argued against it, asking for more time to build their defenses, aware that oil-poor Japan would feel all the more impelled to go to war to secure the black lifeblood of a modern military machine.*

The night before the president's announcement, Marshall and Stark radioed word of the economic sanctions to Admiral Kimmel and General Short on Oahu. "CNO and COS do not anticipate immediate hostile reaction by Japan through the use of military means but you are furnished this information in order that you may take appropriate precautionary measures against possible eventualities." The following day, Marshall recalled Douglas Arthur MacArthur to active duty. The decision had been long weighed, long delayed.

---

*Oil played the crucial role in precipitating the timing of war. As far back as 1918, Clemenceau had walked about Versailles muttering, "Oil governs everything," while the Associated Powers divided up the postwar world. By World War II, the Allies controlled 86 percent of the world's oil supplies.

Each Japanese diplomatic ploy had compelled the War Department to reevaluate its position, to attempt to conjure a Pacific defense out of little more than broomstick rifles and stovepipe cannons. So it was that General Douglas A. MacArthur, United States Army, Retired, living in the sumptuous six-room penthouse atop the Manila Hotel, returned to active duty.

MacArthur had angled for the assignment. Great things were afoot, yet he was effectively sidelined as military adviser to the Commonwealth of the Philippines. He was "field marshal of a state and an army neither of which has, as yet, independent existence," as General Pershing noted. With MacArthur's offer to the president to become Philippine high commissioner ignored, the general was left "a more or less ridiculous" figure.

On February 1, 1941, MacArthur wrote a thinly disguised reminder of his availability to the chief of staff, his former subordinate. MacArthur's letter detailed a projected fight for the archipelago. His forces, he wrote Marshall, would "provide an adequate defense at the beach against a landing operation of 100,000, which is estimated to be the maximum initial effort of the most powerful potential enemy." Still Washington remained silent.

Six weeks later, he tried another gambit. In a letter to FDR's press secretary, Steve Early, an old friend, the retired general again suggested he be appointed high commissioner:

> I hold the complete confidence of the Filipinos, having served here during four different tours, a total period of twelve years. I know local conditions, especially military and naval affairs, as possibly no one else does.
>
> From Vladivostok to Singapore I am thoroughly familiar with the most intimate details, political, military and commercial. I have a personal acquaintance with everyone of importance in the Orient and I believe no American holds the friendship and respect of this part of the world more than myself. In the present situation these are assets which the president might utilize in his co-ordination of the Pacific problems. I can respond to any call here or elsewhere.

MacArthur closed with fulsome praise for Roosevelt, "not only our greatest statesman but what to me is even more thrilling, our greatest military strategist."

This time he received an answer. The president's military aide, Major General Edwin Watson, assured the restless MacArthur that "in all discussions as to the availability of various active and retired officers, your name is always outstanding and most seriously considered."

Marshall did discuss MacArthur's future role with the secretary of war. On May 21, Stimson wrote in his diary, "Marshall incidentally told me that in case of trouble out there they intended to recall General Mac-

Arthur into service again and place him in command." Until then, he would be informed of all army planning.

Half-promises would not soothe MacArthur's ambition. He tried a new tack. He made reservations, then wrote Marshall on May 29, with a copy to Early, saying he was going to resign as military adviser to the Philippine government and return to the United States. MacArthur won.

On June 20, Marshall replied that he and Stimson had discussed MacArthur's role three months earlier and

> It was decided that your outstanding qualifications and vast experience in the Philippines make you the logical choice for the army commander in the Far East should the situation approach a crisis. The Secretary has delayed recommending your appointment as he does not feel the time has arrived for such action. However, he has authorized me to tell you that, at the proper time, he will recommend to the President that you be appointed. It is my impression that the President will approve his recommendation.

The Japanese incursions into Indochina and the resulting freeze of Japanese assets in the United States decided the matter. On July 27, Marshall cabled MacArthur in Manila he was to take over a newly formed United States Army Forces in the Far East (USAFFE). His command would consist of 10,000 Regular Army officers and men, 12,000 crack Philippine Scouts trained by American troops, and twelve half-formed, underequipped, and poorly trained Philippine infantry regiments. He was authorized to spend $10 million on defenses. MacArthur was no longer a bystander, but once more in the pit.

Still, there was the problem of MacArthur's rank. Recalled at his permanent rank of major general, he was on the next day "given the rank of lieutenant general, although my retired rank was that of a full general," he complained. Such presumed slights—federal law provided for just one full general in the Army, the chief of staff—chipped away at MacArthur's always fragile sense of ego.

MacArthur's appointment as commander of USAFFE was to provide the chief of staff with irritants aplenty once their initial enthusiasm wore off. But to ignore MacArthur in a time of national emergency was unthinkable. At sixty-one, he was still vigorous, the father of a three-year-old son born to his second wife, a woman twenty years his junior. He was the heir of a great military tradition, son of a Medal of Honor-winning father. Guided first by father, then by doting mother, Douglas MacArthur had held virtually every post of honor the United States Army could offer. He had, he once thought, climaxed a distinguished military career with a five-year tour as chief of staff, longer than any man in history.

War now threatened in the Far East. MacArthur, an adopted child of the Orient, could not be permitted to remain in retirement, especially were he to return to the United States. A genuine hero, a favorite of the conservative press and a man with active political contacts in the Republican Party, MacArthur in America would be the cuckoo in the nest.

Then and later, MacArthur was to prove difficult. Once chief of staff himself, he found it impossible to subordinate himself to a man who had been a mere colonel under his command. Moreover, the War Department in MacArthur's judgment was staffed with civilians in uniform who toadied to the president, who favored accommodation with the Russians, who overruled his sound military-political decisions—three great errors MacArthur could not condone.

MacArthur's arrogance, his currying of publicity, his very theatricality made the man a prickly subject in the Munitions Building. "I think Stimson was impatient of MacArthur because Stimson was a Marshall man and Marshall had a lot of trouble with MacArthur, too. So Stimson would share the impatience of the general staff," decided Harvey Bundy, a Boston Brahmin called to service in the War Department. That Beacon Street lawyer concluded MacArthur "was an opera star and everything had to be his way."

Perhaps, as Marshall's official biographer decided, the differences between the opera star and the chief of staff "lay more in their temperaments and styles than in ancient quarrels and fancied injuries." MacArthur's biographers, even those with a critical eye for their subject, on the other hand credit some personal ill-feeling between the two men for the difficulties that would come. For all of Marshall's deference to him, MacArthur was to complain frequently to his staff of presumed slights; his own sense of self-esteem magnified any field commander's natural belief that his theater was the most needy, the most important, and the most slighted. For all of Marshall's efforts to supply men and munitions to the Philippines commander, MacArthur blamed shortfalls not on higher priorities elsewhere, but on personal bias, on "secret plans and commitments to Britain and Russia," on anything but the reality. If their antagonism was one-sided—the chief of staff did have an ability to personally distance himself from issues—it was no less real.

The two men began cordially enough, MacArthur fired with his grand plans, the chief of staff straining to provide the troops and weapons MacArthur sought. Fourteen companies of infantry arrived on September 26 aboard the chartered *President Coolidge*. More than 450 officers to train the Filipino regiments followed, then a tank battalion, then the understrength 4th Marine Regiment from Shanghai.

By October, MacArthur was radiating an optimism that would spread as a contagion in Washington, 10,000 miles away. His recall had inspired the Philippines, the Netherlands East Indies, Malaya, and China to "complete jubilation," he wrote. "It was the sign they had been waiting for." With his new army, almost 200,000 strong when fully mobilized, MacArthur was "confident that we can successfully resist any effort that may be made against us." The War Department had offered him "splendid support," he added, and "no field commander could have received better support from a chief of staff than I have from Marshall."

If his defenses had a weakness, it was in the air, the new Far East commander reported to Washington. Reinforce his air force and he could indefinitely hold the islands in the event of Japanese attack, until relief convoys fought their way through, he pledged. It was a brave conception, a brass-bright piece of optimism in the gloom of defeats elsewhere.

At Marshall's orders, General Arnold allocated to the Far East Air Force four bomber groups of 70 planes each, and 260 fighters. Despite standing agreements to supply the British, not to mention training needs, MacArthur was to have priority. Arnold began transferring air groups from the Hawaiian Islands and Panama, then earmarked for the Philippines 165 of the 220 B-17s to be delivered from factories before February 1, 1942. By December 1, MacArthur's air arm included half of all heavy bombers and one sixth of all fighters the Army had overseas.

Those air reinforcements and MacArthur's pledge were pivotal in Marshall's ordering a revision of the Army's longstanding Pacific strategy. First informed of the tentative agreement on RAINBOW 5 in early October, MacArthur protested the planners' decision to fight only a holding action in the Philippines by defending Manila Bay. In part, MacArthur's objection was motivated by a refusal to accept what inevitably would be a defeat if large forces invaded. In part, his objections were spurred by pride. Added to that was what his biographer termed MacArthur's "overconfidence and unjustified optimism as to the abilities of himself, his staff, and the untried Filipino soldiers." But a bigger part of MacArthur's criticism of RAINBOW 5's "citadel" notion was a burgeoning confidence in the ability of heavy bombers to attack and sink an invasion fleet. MacArthur instead boldly proposed an all-out defense of a Philippine bastion of 7,100 islands with a coastline 10,850 miles long.

Logic might have insisted otherwise, but Marshall and Stimson alike were willingly seduced. Marshall had served two tours in the islands, and felt some of the paternal fondness for the Filipino common in the Regular Army. Stimson too had close ties with the protectorate. As governor-general of the islands from 1927 to 1929, he had encouraged economic development, modeling himself as a benign father figure to Filipino independence. Later, as secretary of state, he had taken a strong stand against Japanese aggression in Manchuria, partly on the ground that Japanese expansion there inevitably foreshadowed the loss of the Philippines.

As in all seductions, delusion played a part. Marshall and Stimson were dazzled by inflated estimates of the performance of improved B-17s the Boeing Aircraft Company was now producing. As MacArthur argued, airpower suddenly seemed an alternative to reinforced land units; any ground troops they sent were virtual hostages should war come. Bombers ferried over a new route that circled the Japanese-mandate islands in the mid-Pacific were an offensive weapon that tipped the balance in their favor.

However misplaced his trust, Marshall ordered the Philippines defended. The joint planners revised RAINBOW 5 in early November to incorporate an all-out defense of the islands, from southern Mindanao to northern Luzon, 800 miles away.

At home, the pace of rearmament quickened. The chief of staff, once so conscious of his heart murmur and Morrison Stayer's advice to make time to relax, could not escape the Munitions Building. Questions pursued him.

In early September, the Marshalls finally managed to slip away to Leesburg for the first time since the Fourth of July. The general was looking forward to a chore he found gratifying, pruning his apple trees.

No sooner had he climbed to the dead branch of a tree with rope and saw in hand than the telephone rang. The duty officer at the Munitions Building was calling to report a German raider sighted in the Caribbean. Marshall immediately called the president in Hyde Park, asking him to secure permission from exiled Queen Wilhelmina of the Netherlands to implace coastal guns and aircraft near the vital refineries at Aruba and Curacao. That done, back he climbed to the dead limb.

A second time the telephone rang, and a second time Marshall picked his way to the ground to take the president's call for more information. Marshall dictated a proposed radiogram to the queen, then returned to the tree.

Finally, straddling the trunk once more, he began sawing. He was halfway through the dead limb when the telephone rang a third time. "General Marshall," his orderly called, "War Department calling." War Plans wanted instructions on the refinery's defense.

Marshall sat there high above the garden for a moment, sighing in frustration, then yelled to his orderly: "Call the car. I am leaving for Washington." The dead limb hung there forgotten through the winter.

Marshall had more urgent concerns as muggy August turned to muggy September. Virtually alone, the chief of staff had argued in the White House and beyond that a second world war could end decisively only with huge land armies eventually colliding in western Europe. His was the politically unpalatable, costly conflict, with none of the lower-risk, lower-casualty appeal of a naval or air war, certainly none of the glamour. Blockade and bombardment alone, he stressed, would eventually sap German will, but were Germany's armies left essentially intact, they would remain a threat to peace. The chief of staff found himself fending off foreign ally and American Navy alike, each coveting the materiel an invasion army, a large army, would need.

Washington Post columnist Ernest K. Lindley and the influential syndicated columnist Walter Lippmann got wind of the debate over "the case for a smaller army." American power, Lippmann wrote in a September column, lay "on the seas and in the air and in the factory—not on the battlefields of Europe and Asia. . . . Our most effective part in this war is now, and for any predictable future, to help hold the seas and to be the arsenal of those fighting aggression."

With England safe from immediate danger of invasion, the 1.5-million-man Army Marshall had brought into being was no longer necessary, Lippmann decided. Instead, he proposed shrinking the Army to increase its efficiency, while putting more money into Lend-Lease and the Navy.

The British, the Navy, even the Air Corps he had sponsored pressed Marshall hard. "The British, for example, were very intense in their efforts to get more metal, to get more tanks from us, to get more weapons from us—and they opposed a lot of our proposals—particularly my proposals," Marshall acknowledged. "I notified the British—their representatives—confidentially once or twice—that if they didn't stop this business I would have to come out and pillory them publicly."

Summoned to the White House on September 22, the chief of staff carried with him a four-page aide-memoire arguing his case, militarily, politically, morally. Noting that they had just secured passage of the draft extension, "to sound an alarm and an all-clear at virtually the same time can only add to national confusion and disrupt the national unity we are struggling to achieve." To disband the Army so painstakingly built was "wholly reckless." Marshall then, apparently for the first time, acknowledged the inevitability of American forces fighting in Europe, of the isolationist dread, an American Expeditionary Force. "British manpower alone is insufficient to accomplish complete victory and to protect their interests as well as ours. Military opinion including that of the British high command itself as expressed in off-the-record statements has frequently pointed out that while materiel assistance alone from the U.S. in sufficient quantity may enable them to maintain a stalemate, active American participation will ultimately be needed for a decisive victory within a foreseeable time."

The chief of staff prevailed for the moment. Even so, his insistence that they prepare for a future land war grew more difficult as the war at sea intensified from patrolling, to convoying, to armed defense.

In the abstract, Americans favored freedom of the seas, yet hoped for a deliverance from evil in Europe. At the same time, public sentiment overwhelmingly favored support for China in its now three-year-old struggle with Japan. The ambivalence lay rooted in history.

Since the turn of the century, Americans had viewed China and the Chinese with equal parts protective benevolence and Christian charity. Through missionaries and evangelical fervor, William Jennings Bryan had proposed building "a new Chinese civilization . . . founded on the Christian movement." Forty years later, Nebraska Senator Kenneth Wherry had pledged, "With God's help, we will lift Shanghai up and up, ever up, until it is just like Kansas City." All China seemed fertile ground for Christianity and good works. Was not Chiang Kai-shek himself a Methodist, and his beautiful wife educated in the United States? Sympathy for the embattled Chinese ran high, fostered by Henry Luce's *Time* and *Life,* by Pearl Buck's best-selling *The Good Earth* and Alice Tisdale Hobart's *Oil for the Lamps of China.*

A pro-Chinese public grew ever more impatient with the administration's caution in the Far East. Editorial writers across the country demanded some action that would slap down the upstart "Nips," to step in and put them in their place. Most Americans believed the United States could do it with one hand tied behind its back.

Such naivete and ambivalence disturbed Marshall and Stimson, particularly the national lack of resolve. The defense effort "will function as far as the sentiment of the people will spur it on," Stimson told an airport press conference in Denver in August. Speaking for himself and the chief of staff at his side, Stimson added: "It is not functioning the way we should like to see it. If there was the same sharp objective that we had twenty-three years ago, there would be a different story."

Without clear purpose, their army of civilians oozed discontent. "O.H.I.O." threatened from barracks walls. *Time* magazine determined, through Henry Luce's delphic powers, that two thirds of the Army was suffering a morale problem. Its companion magazine, *Life,* interviewed 400 men in five National Guard divisions and reported half said they would desert in October, when their one-year call-up was ended. *Life* quoted one private: "To hell with Roosevelt and Marshall and the Army and especially this goddam hole and the Germans and the Russians and the British. I want to get the hell out of this hole." A reporter for the *Nation,* a magazine as opposed to intervention as *Time-Life* favored it, found similar sentiments in a Times Square poll of men in uniform.

Marshall's own spirit suffered as well. The change that had overtaken his army, he wrote Bernard Baruch a week after the House vote on extension, was "quite tragic." The long debate had undercut morale. "Individual soldiers were taught to feel sorry for themselves."

Even as he wrote to Baruch, his resolved stiffened once more:

I have always felt surprised that in our democracy we were able to achieve a selective service system late last summer, but I guess it was hoping too much to think that we could continue the strenuous preparation to meet this emergency without great difficulties. There is no more delicate problem than troop morale, and with such a slender margin of public approval to back us, it is no easy matter to build up the highly trained and seasoned fighting force that we must have available as quickly as possible. However, we are going to do it if too many of us do not lose our tempers.

Marshall was to lose his, lashing out against "misinformed individuals" in a speech before the American Legion in September. "It is impossible to develop an efficient army if decisions purely of a military nature are continuously subjected to investigation, cross-examination, debate, ridicule and public discussion." For perhaps the only time in his career Marshall forgot he was a soldier in a democracy. It was a token of his own anxiety and weariness.

Out of that anxiety, Marshall wrote to the president on September 6:

While the troops in 90 percent of the organizations have weathered the storm in excellent shape—as a matter of fact in every instance where we have had good leadership in the higher command— nevertheless the home influence presents a continuing difficulty. Parents have been so confused as to the facts or logic of the situation and so influenced by what they read of a critical nature that something must be done to bring them to an understanding of the national emergency and of the necessity for a highly trained Army.

The president wrote "Dear George" a tart reply:

In effect you say: (a) The boys in camp are O.K. (b) The parental influence hurts the morale of many of them. (c) Please, Mr. President, do something about this weakness on the part of the civilian population. Got any ideas?

While Marshall agonized, over Toso Bay on the southern coast of Shikoku, Japanese naval pilots completed practice for an attack that would inadvertently eliminate that worry. On November 5, 1941, the Naval General Staff ordered preparations for war to be completed. Two days later, Admiral Yamamoto issued his combined fleet operations order: "The Task Force will launch a surprise attack at the outset of the war upon the U.S. Pacific Fleet supposed to be in Hawaiian waters, and destroy it. . . . The date of starting the operation is tentatively set forth as December 8, 1941."

C H A P T E R

XIV

The Throw of the Die

Ambassador Joseph Grew's telegram from Tokyo weighed heavily on the seven men gathered in the president's office of the White House. "Action by Japan which might render unavoidable an armed conflict with the United States may come with dangerous and dramatic suddenness." Grew, a cool observer with reliable sources, confirmed what they suspected.

Dammit, it was fish-or-cut-bait, Secretary of State Hull insisted, lapsing into the Tennessee mountain vernacular of his youth. Further ultimatums to Japan, warning against a move to the south, would do no good if the Army and Navy would not back the threat.

The discussion had gone on for more than an hour now, Marshall and Stark protesting, arguing not against Hull, a weary and petulant man after all, but to sway the only one in the room whose vote counted, the president of the United States. Any diplomatic ploy gave them time, the two service chiefs argued. They needed to delay a break with Japan as long as possible, "because of our state of preparedness and because of our involvements in other parts of the world," Marshall warned.

Time. In just another month MacArthur would have enough bombers to make an invasion hazardous. Marshall estimated 100 of the B-17s and new four-engine B-24s would be a deterrent to any Japanese convoy moving southward. Granted, they were taking a "calculated risk" dispatching those bombers immediately, without additional fighter support, but the gain was worth the gamble. By March 1, Marshall calculated, General MacArthur would have received sufficient reinforcements and time to train his Filipino regiments to defend the islands against any invasion the Japanese might mount.

An ultimatum to the new Japanese cabinet as Hull and Stimson urged would set off that powder magazine. On October 18, the Konoye government had fallen, toppled by the militants surrounding Minister of

War Hideki Tojo. In Prince Konoye's place, Tojo now sat, both prime minister and minister of war. Intent on control of Southeast Asia and thereby outflanking China, Tojo would make no strategic concessions.

Konoye's ouster had left Japanese Ambassador Nomura floundering. The Americans had proved anything but conciliatory in the nine months he had been in Washington, and the new cabinet had provided no alternative strategy. It was as if the Foreign Ministry no longer cared what happened. Disheartened, Nomura cabled Tokyo in the compromised Purple code, "Now that I am a dead horse, I do not want to continue this hypocritical existence, deceiving myself and other people."

Nomura's discouragement sharpened Marshall's anxiety this November 5. Militarily they were still in poor shape, the Navy hardly better, Marshall and Stark concluded in a joint evaluation of their readiness. "At the present time the United States Fleet in the Pacific is inferior to the Japanese Fleet and cannot undertake an unlimited strategic offensive in the Western Pacific." Nor would that situation soon improve. Only if the United States were directly attacked or the Japanese moved on strategic Thailand or into the Gulf of Siam should they go to war, Marshall insisted.

The president considered a warning to Japan that any such step would be inimical to United States-Japanese relations, then at Marshall's urging, discarded the notion. Instead, he adopted the chief of staff's suggestion that they increase aid to China, if it could be spared from shipments to Russia and Great Britain. The aid was no more than a bribe to the Nationalists; Chiang's armies used little enough of it to actually fight the Japanese.

Meanwhile, Marshall suggested, they might offer token compromises to Japan, "minor concessions which the Japanese could use in saving face. These concessions might be a relaxation on oil restrictions or on similar trade restrictions."

The president was caught in an inexorable squeeze. His diplomats were pessimistic that war could be avoided, short of a humiliating capitulation to Japanese blackmail. Repeated MAGIC intercepts supported their arguments. At the same time, his military chiefs were pleading for more time to prepare for war.

Roosevelt opted to play for time. Hull was to keep the Nomura talks alive, to "strain every nerve to satisfy and keep on good relations" with the Japanese. "Let us make no move of ill will. Let us do nothing to precipitate a crisis."

While the president groped for a plan—he considered a six-month truce during which the United States and Japan would move no troops— Japan pressed its initiative. With the emperor's tacit agreement, an Imperial Conference approved two proposals to be forwarded by Admiral Nomura to the United States. These were to be the "last effort" at negotiation, Proposal A to be presented to the president first, Proposal B to be extended only if Proposal A produced no significant movement. "This time we are showing the limit of our friendship," Tokyo advised the disheartened Nomura in Washington. "This time we are making our last possible bargain. . . . The success or failure of the pending discussions will have an immense effect on the destiny of the Japanese Empire. In fact, we gambled the fate of our land on the throw of this die."

A message the following day gave Nomura a November 25 deadline to complete negotiations "because of various circumstances." To stiffen the man, Tokyo was dispatching a second envoy, Saburo Kurusu, who was to present the fallback Proposal B.

Nomura met on November 7 with Hull. The Secretary's cool manner—he had, through MAGIC, already read the text of the proposal—led Nomura to request a meeting with the president. On November 10, Roosevelt personally accepted the proposal, a harsh restatement of existing Japanese demands coupled with modest concessions. Japan would indefinitely maintain a garrison in North China, Mongolia, and on Hainan Island, withdrawing other troops from occupied China once peace was restored between those two nations. Japanese forces in Indochina would be withdrawn once the Chinese war was settled. Meantime, Japan intended to honor the Tripartite Pact.

There was little to discuss. The Japanese concessions were illusory, MAGIC had revealed; troop withdrawals from China "would be out of the question."

Even as the tired Admiral Nomura limped his way to the president's office on November 10, his onetime colleague aboard the flagship aircraft carrier *Akagi,* Vice Admiral Chuichi Nagumo, was issuing Striking Force Operations Order No. 1. The ships of *Kido Butai*—the First Air Fleet of six aircraft carriers with 378 airplanes, two battleships, two heavy cruisers, a light cruiser, nine destroyers, three submarines, and seven oil tankers—were to rendezvous at Hitokappu Bay on Etorofu Island in the Kuriles. The "various circumstances" had been set in motion.

However badly fared the negotiations between Tokyo and Washington, Marshall was gaining time, and some sense of optimism. On Saturday morning, November 15, he held an unusual press conference for seven reporters, pledging them to secrecy. What he had to tell them, he said with some embarrassment, was not for publication, but for their guidance only. Otherwise what they wrote could inadvertently foul military strategy.

"The United States is on the brink of war with Japan," the general calmly told the reporters. Despite diplomatic negotiations—a newly arrived ambassador, Saburo Kurusu, was meeting that day for the first time with Secretary of State Hull—Marshall held little hope for the outcome.

"Our position is highly favorable in this respect," he explained. "We have access to a leak in all the information the Japanese are receiving concerning our military preparation, especially in the Philippines. In other words, we know what they know about us, and they don't know that we know it."

Standing before a large map of the Pacific, pointing to it occasionally, the chief of staff bared the American strategy. The United States was preparing for an offensive war in the Philippines, massing on airfields there the largest concentration of bombers anywhere in the world. By the end of February, he expected to have a total of 165 of the Air Force's newest bombers in the Philippines. Shiploads of other weapons, the new self-propelled 75-millimeter guns and 105-millimeter artillery pieces, tanks, and a squadron of dive bombers, were either landed or en route. "The danger period," Marshall cautioned, "is the first ten days of December." After that period, MacArthur would have enough men and weapons "to make an attack by the Japanese extremely hazardous."

This information was to be leaked quietly to the Japanese during diplomatic talks. "If it got out publicly," Marshall explained—and two attempts to publish word of the bomber reinforcement had been "thwarted," he added without explanation—"the Army fanatics in Japan would be in a position to demand war immediately, before we were better fortified." If only Nomura and Kurusu were told, they could say to the Imperial Council, "Look here. These people really mean to bomb our cities, and they have the equipment with which to do it. We'd better go slow."

Were war to come, Marshall continued, the United States would "fight mercilessly. Flying Fortresses will be dispatched immediately to set the paper cities of Japan on fire. There won't be any hesitation about bombing civilians."*

Bombers in the Philippines, Marshall told the numbed reporters, would bomb Japan, then fly on to Vladivostok, perhaps to China. Landing fields had not been arranged, but Marshall said he was certain the Russians would agree.

The war would be fought throughout the Pacific. The map to which he occasionally pointed was marked with semicircles radiating out from United States possessions. Those lines represented the range of American bombers; the Japanese-held islands of the Pacific all fell within the semicircles. So too the cities of the China coast that Japan had seized.

---

*Though both Germany and Great Britain were bombing the other's civilian populations, Marshall was announcing a fundamental change in American policy. In 1917, President Woodrow Wilson wrote his White House adviser, Edward House, "I desire no sort of participation by the Air Service of the United States in a plan . . . which has as its object promiscuous bombing upon industry, commerce or populations in enemy countries disassociated from obvious military needs to be served by such action." The origins of Marshall's shift from Wilsonian idealism remain obscure forty years later. Wilson is quoted in May, *The Ultimate Decision*, p. 130.

"The Grand Strategy," *Time* magazine's Robert Sherrod wrote in his notes that Saturday morning, "does not include the use of much naval force. Marshall indicates that he believes U.S. bombers can do the trick against Japanese naval strength and against Japanese cities 'without the use of our shipping.'" Perhaps out of desperation, Marshall had become a convert to the offensive use of the bomber; upon that rock he intended to build a defense of the Philippines, a certain Japanese target when war came.

Ambassadors Nomura and Kurusu were also grasping at slender reeds. Proposal B was hardly better than the rejected Proposal A. Japan offered to withdraw troops from southern Indochina but was free to move on China; neither the United States nor Japan would move troops into the South Pacific or Southeast Asia; both nations would cooperate in securing a share of oil and rubber for Japan from the Dutch East Indies; the trade embargo was to be lifted; and the United States was not to interfere with Japan's efforts to end the war in China.

While the president stalled, ostensibly mulling the Japanese offer, Marshall and Katherine took the weekend to escape Washington and relax at the cottage of Edward Stettinius at Pompano Beach.

Both Marshall and his wife sorely needed the Florida trip. In early October, Katherine had slipped on a rug in the sun porch and slammed into the edge of the table. The four broken ribs were slow to heal despite Katherine's restricted schedule. The general too was tired, more than he had realized. He even considered a recuperative sojourn at the army hospital in Hot Springs, Arkansas, "to stay there ten days or two weeks and give myself an opportunity to rest up." That plan was tentative, he advised the hospital commanding officer, depending upon "the international situation and the president's desires. . . ."

It was not to be. The chief of staff returned to Washington on Monday, November 24, to find Admiral Stark waiting with an alert he intended to send to his commanders in Manila and Pearl Harbor. Two days before, navy cryptanalysts had broken into yet another signal from Tokyo to the anxious ambassadors in Washington. The cabinet had agreed to extend the deadline for negotiations from November 25 to November 29. "After that, things are automatically going to happen."

What "things," neither Stark nor Marshall knew for certain. Marshall concurred in Stark's alert.

TOP SECRET

Chances of favorable outcome of negotiations with Japan very doubtful. This situation coupled with statements of [Japanese] government and movements of their naval and military forces indicate in our opinion that a surprise aggressive movement in any direction including attack on Philippines or Guam is a possibility. Chief of staff has seen this dispatch, concurs and requests action addressees to inform senior army officers their areas. Utmost secrecy necessary in order not to complicate an already tense situation or precipitate Japanese action.

That evening, the president cabled to Winston Churchill the text of an American counterproposal to the Japanese. By its terms, neither Japan nor the United States was to move aggressively anywhere in Asia; Japan was to withdraw from southern Indochina and hold its force level in the north, all in exchange for a resumption of trade between the United States and Japan. There was no mention of China, cut adrift in the interest of buying time for Marshall and Stark.

"It seems to me a fair proposition from the Japanese but its acceptance or rejection is really a matter of internal Japanese politics," Roosevelt cabled. "I am not very hopeful and we must all be prepared for that trouble, possibly soon."

While Roosevelt and Hull groped for a saving compromise, halfway around the world, in the cold half-light of a dawn snowfall, the ships of *Kido Butai* secretly slipped anchor in Hitokappu Bay. It was 6:00 a.m. Wednesday, November 26, Tokyo time, 10:30 in the morning of November 25 in Pearl Harbor, and 4:00 in the afternoon of November 25 in Washington.

This would be a long day in the capital. At noon, the president met once more with his War Cabinet of Hull, Stimson, Knox, and the two service chiefs, Marshall and Stark. For an hour and a half they reviewed the situation in the Far East. The secretary of state gave a lengthy estimate, his lisp the more pronounced with his fatigue and frustration. "The Japanese are already poised for attack," he reminded them. "The Japanese leaders are determined and desperate. They are likely to break out anywhere, at any time, at any place. . . ." Surprise would be a factor in their plans.

"These fellows mean to fight; you will have to be prepared," he said pointedly to Marshall and Stark.

There was little time left to them. The assault could come as early as the following Monday, December 1, the president estimated, "for the Japanese are notorious for making an attack without warning. The question is how we should maneuver them into the position of firing the first shot without allowing too much danger to ourselves."

Much of the discussion that afternoon in the president's office centered on their estimate that Japan would strike first at the weakened British or Dutch. Hull had a message in hand from the American consul in Hanoi relaying a report the Japanese intended to attack the Isthmus of Kra, the narrow neck of the Malayan Peninsula on December 1. Would such an assault be justification for the president to ask Congress for a declaration of war? If American interests were not directly threatened, would Congress vote it? And what would the public response be? Marshall particularly worried that anything short of wholehearted endorsement would be crippling to the war effort.

The meeting broke up inconclusively, the six participants apprehensive and uncertain. Marshall returned to the War Department to find yet another MAGIC intercept waiting him. Five Japanese divisions had been embarked in Shanghai on a convoy sighted south of Formosa. Their destination was unknown, the chief of staff's intelligence officers said: Singapore, the Indies, even the Philippines. Any one of them, or any combination of these, could be the destination. Equally possible, those troops could be reinforcements for Indochina, a less hostile move than an attack on the Allies, but a worrisome threat to China.

Whatever its destination, the very massing of this convoy overturned Marshall's calculations. "The first Japanese attack was going to be directly south," Marshall recognized. "That would be the main campaign, and the Philippines, of course, would become involved in it." Lightly held Guam, no more than a stop on the Pan American clipper route, and Wake Island would fall almost immediately as the Japanese attempted to set up a defensive screen against the Pacific Fleet in Hawaii.

Marshall immediately discussed the report of the sighting of the Japanese convoy with Stark. The two decided to make a last appeal to the president to stall for time. Marshall also directed the chief of the War Plans Division, Brigadier General Leonard Gerow, to prepare a special warning to MacArthur. Gerow was to make clear, Marshall instructed him, that the president had specifically ordered that the United States not commit the first overt act of war. MacArthur need not wait for a declaration of war, Marshall ordered, but was to move once "actual hostilities" began.

As Marshall and Gerow drafted MacArthur's instructions, the president and Cordell Hull met in the White House. No one reading the daily newspapers could miss the fact that Japanese-American relations were fast deteriorating, but only those two realized how little time they had left before negotiations ended in stalemate.

Confronted with the army intelligence report of the convoy bearing south of Formosa, Roosevelt "fairly blew up," Hull told Stimson. Here "was evidence of bad faith on the part of the Japanese," if any were needed by these avid readers of MAGIC. "While they were negotiating for an entire truce—an entire withdrawal [from Indochina]—they should be sending this expedition down there to Indochina."

Each hour the slow Japanese convoy steamed southward brought it closer to the tripwire stretched across the Gulf of Siam. They had no formal agreement with the British, no more than a consensus within the

War Cabinet that, as Marshall put it, "the moment the Japanese moved into the Gulf of Siam that was a definite offensive act which would result in a catastrophe for us in the Philippines, and for the British in Singapore, unless we definitely resisted it."

The Japanese had forced the issue. Without consulting Marshall and Stark, Roosevelt and Hull determined "to kick the whole thing over." Hull would present the Japanese ambassadors a stiff "Ten-Point Plan" to serve as a basis for negotiations.

Perhaps they might have kept negotiations alive a bit longer, as the two service chiefs so fervently wished; Hull himself thought there was only a one-in-three chance of it. But the new Ten-Point Plan with its demand that Japan withdraw from China, then negotiate a peace with Chiang, would be unacceptable to the Japanese cabinet. For all practical purposes, the president and his secretary of state agreed, negotiations were at an end. War was "possible at any moment." Hull could argue that the Ten-Point Plan was no more than "any peaceful nation pursuing a peaceful course" might accept, but he was no longer dealing with such a country.

Hardly bothering to mask his anger at what he considered the deceit of the two Japanese envoys, Hull effectively ended negotiations at five o'clock on the afternoon of November 26. Nomura and Kurusu received the unbending Ten-Point Plan with sinking hopes. The Japanese argued with the secretary, in undiplomatic fashion, "but Hull remained solid as a rock," Nomura reported to Tokyo.

Thursday the 27th was "a very tense, long day" for Stimson. Marshall was out of town, observing the last day of maneuvers along the Peedee River in North Carolina. Though the chief of staff had approved radio alerts to the Pacific commanders, Stimson felt his absence "very much." The secretary worried that Stark was, "as usual, a little bit timid and cautious when it comes to a real crisis, and there was a tendency, not unnatural, on his part and Gerow to seek for more time."

Early in the morning Stimson called Hull to ask if the secretary had, in fact, broken off negotiations. Perhaps with some petulance, certainly with some chagrin, Hull said, "I have washed my hands of it and it is now in the hands of you and Knox, the Army and the Navy."

A report tracking the southbound Japanese convoy in hand, Stimson called the White House. The president affirmed that negotiations appeared doomed, and gave permission to Stimson to send a warning to MacArthur "to be on the *qui vive* for any attack and telling him how the situation was." Stimson took a last cautious step, telephoning Hull to elicit a grudging admission that the Japanese might reopen the negotiations.

Working from Marshall's original alert drafted the morning before, Stimson and Gerow rephrased the order:

Negotiations with Japan appear to be terminated to all practical purposes with only barest possibilities that Japanese Government might come back and offer to continue. Japanese future action unpredictable but hostile action possible at any moment. If hostilities cannot, repeat cannot, be avoided, the U.S. desires that Japan commit the first overt act. This policy should not be construed as restricting you to a course of action that might jeopardize the successful defense of the Philippines.

Stimson decided to send the same message to the Presidio at San Francisco, to Panama, and to General Short in Hawaii. Those three radiograms contained a significant addition to the alert: "Prior to hostile Japanese action you are directed to take such reconnaissance and other measures as you deem necessary *but these measures should be carried out so as not repeat not to alarm civil population or disclose intent.*"

The last caution flowed from their suspicion of "the large numbers of Japanese inhabitants," Stimson said later. He wanted nothing "to alarm the civil population and thus possibly to precipitate an incident and give the Japanese an excuse to go to war and the chance to say that we had committed the first overt act."

Though he had not included such a caution, Marshall later concurred in its addition. If the Japanese could create a situation, "however unjustified, however illogical," that might lead "at least a portion of the people to believe that our overt action had forced them into an act of war," the United States would begin the fight a divided country, "a terrible tragedy in a war situation."

Timid or no, Admiral Stark that afternoon made one last plea at the White House for a delay. In a joint memorandum he and Marshall had previously approved, they argued that Thailand, the Burma Road, and the Philippines were the most likely targets of Japanese aggression.

"The most essential thing now, from the United States' viewpoint, is to gain time," the joint planning memorandum stressed. They were reinforcing the Philippines, with two convoys en route and a third scheduled to sail from the United States on December 8.

"Precipitance of military action on our part should be avoided so long as consistent with national policy. The longer the delay, the more positive becomes the assurance of retention of these islands as a naval and air base." If the islands remained in American hands, the Japanese would be hindered from moving southward by the threat on their flank. Again, Stark and Marshall recommended the nation go to war only if United States, British, or Dutch territory were attacked.

The president barely considered the memorandum. Matters were out of his hands now. Stimson's alert reflected the reality they confronted.

In Hawaii, General Short read not only that warning on November 27 but two others: one from Stark to Mustapha Kimmel bluntly beginning, "This dispatch is to be considered a war warning," and another from Army G-2 reminding Short to institute precautions against sabotage.

Well to the west of Short's headquarters at Fort Shafter, steaming in the little traveled North Pacific, the First Air Fleet silently bore eastward at 14 knots through calm seas. Aboard the flagship *Akagi*, Commodore Genda refined his attack plan while his pilots studied large-scale models of Pearl Harbor.

On November 28, the chief of staff returned to the War Department to find reports from his four Pacific commanders noting their response to the alert sent by Stimson the day before. General Short had ordered an Alert Number One, a deployment of guards to prevent sabotage, and the massing of parked aircraft wing to wing so that they could be more easily guarded. No one in the War Department—not Marshall, not Gerow who later attempted to assume all responsibility, not Sherman Miles of the intelligence office—recognized that Short had not gone on full alert and ordered aerial reconnaissance.

Marshall's attention was fully fixed on MacArthur. He read the Far East commander's report, then radioed a satisfied, even quietly elated acknowledgment: "The Secretary of War and I were highly pleased to receive your report that your command is ready for any eventuality and that you and [Admiral Thomas] Hart have worked out plans for the effective coordinated employment of all United States forces in the Philippines. There is no, repeat no, improvement in the international situation."

A growing pile of MAGIC intercepts awaited Marshall on Friday morning, November 29. The most critical appeared to be a telegram from Japanese Foreign Minister Shigenori Togo to Nomura describing Hull's Ten Points as a "humiliating proposal," unsuitable for further negotiations. Togo added an instruction: "However, I do not wish you to give the impression that the negotiations are broken off. Merely say to them that you are awaiting instructions. . . ."

A second intercept decoded a Foreign Ministry message to Nomura in Washington advising that in the case of a threatened rupture in diplomatic relations, Tokyo's daily overseas news broadcast would carry a special "weather report." If Japanese-American relations were in danger, the report to be broadcast a total of seven times in the program would be "*higashi no kaze ame* (east wind, rain)." If Japan-Soviet relations were to end, it would be "north wind, cloudy," and if British, "west wind, clear."

Marshall was not especially alarmed by the weather-code advisory. Even if Japan broke relations, it did not necessarily mean war. Great things had been accomplished between nations without formal relations, he pointed out. Stark was less convinced. From then on, navy monitors were to pay special attention to the news broadcast, hoping to pick up the telltale warning.

At noon that Friday, FDR's War Cabinet met once again in the White House. The meeting centered on estimates of public support for a war begun without direct attacks on American possessions. A long discussion followed, Stimson arguing the Japanese must be forced to pull back, Marshall still urging conciliation to buy time. Furthermore, the chief of staff argued, a hard line on China would inevitably lead to American involvement on the mainland; Marshall had no confidence the public would support a war solely on behalf of a foreign state.

President Roosevelt decided upon two moves: one, a secret, personal appeal through Ambassador Grew to the emperor, thereby circumventing the bellicose Imperial Council; and the second, an address to both houses of Congress that would explicitly inform the public of the danger in the Far East. The one might soothe feelings in Tokyo; the other would surely rasp on Japanese sensibilities.

With the knowledge that Tokyo would not reply to the Hull proposal for a few days, Roosevelt elected to spend a delayed Thanksgiving weekend with the patients at Warm Springs Foundation. The president was en route to Georgia when shortly before 5:00 p.m. on December 1, Tokyo time, the limousines converged on the gates of the Imperial Palace. One by one, the formally dressed industrialists and government ministers in swallowtail coats, generals and admirals in their sumptuous uniforms made their way across the immaculately groomed inner courtyard to the lacquered conference room.

Not everyone in Room East of the Imperial Palace favored war. The emperor, who had raised grave questions three months earlier, sat silent, only nodding with each speaker. Elements of the navy, though its fleets were already steaming to strike east and south, still doubted the wisdom of war with such an industrial power as the United States.

The general known behind his back as "Razor Brain," Prime Minister Hideki Tojo, bowed toward the emperor three times, then opened the meeting. "With the permission of the emperor, I will take charge of the proceedings today." A bad sign for the peace party.

Submission to Hull's Ten Points, Tojo told the solemn men in the exquisite politesse of formal Japanese, "would not only deprive Japan of her authority and forestall her efforts for the successful settlement of the China Incident, but would also jeopardize her very existence." A nervous man, given to coffee and chain-smoking, Tojo continued: "Matters have now reached the point where Japan, in order to preserve her empire, must open hostilities against the United States, Great Britain and the Netherlands."

They could still avert war if the United States backed down and offered "just terms," Tojo assured the conferees. He wished a vote ratifying the plans already set in motion, to inform the emperor of the national will.

It was done. One by one, the men in the swallowtail coats and splendid uniforms rose, bowed to the throne, then answered, "*Hai.*"

An elated Tojo pronounced benediction. War waited only for the emperor's nod. The following day, Tokyo flashed word to its naval expeditions bearing down on Palau, the Pescadores, the Gulf of Siam, Midway, Kwajalein, Guam, the Malay Peninsula, and the Netherlands East Indies: "Our empire has decided to go to war against the United States, England, and Holland early December." The message was received at 5:00 p.m. December 2 on the great battleship *Nagato*, flagship of Admiral Yamamoto. The man who had conceived the bold opening strike a year earlier, Yamamoto dictated a coded message to the fleet his plans had brought forth.*

Three hours later, with the First Air Fleet approximately 940 miles north of Midway, a signal officer brought an opaque one-line message to the bridge of *Akagi*. Admiral Nagumo understood the prearranged code instantly: "*Niitaka yama nobore ichi-ni-rei-ya.* (Climb Mount Niitaka, 1208)." X-Day, the day of the attack on Pearl Harbor, was December 8, Tokyo time, Sunday, December 7 in Honolulu.

Now came the firebrands' time of tension. According to Admiral Yamamoto's battle plan, if discovered by the Americans any time in the next three days, the fleet was to turn back. After that, they were to fight their way through to the enemy fleet.

President Roosevelt abruptly broke off his long weekend at Warm Springs and, at the request of the secretary of war, returned to Washington on December 1. The hard-pressed cadre of cryptanalysts and translators had laid open a vital transmission in the Purple code from Japan's ambassador in Berlin to Tokyo. Baron Oshina was reporting that German Foreign Minister von Ribbentrop urged Japan to strike against the Americans and British. Ribbentrop offered by way of encouragement a definite commitment: "Should Japan become engaged in a war against the United States, Germany, of course, would join the war immediately."

Tokyo, in response, advised the ambassador that American-Japanese negotiations "now stand ruptured, broken." The ambassador was directed to secretly tell Hitler and Ribbentrop "that there is extreme danger that war may suddenly break out between the Anglo-Saxon nations and Japan through some clash of arms and add that the time of the breaking out of this war may come quicker than anyone dreams."

---

*Though United States cryptanalysts had broken into at least two lower-ievel Japanese Army codes, and the Navy's OP-20-G was close to cracking the Imperial Navy's most "secure" code, prior to Pearl Harbor the Americans could not read the highest military codes and missed these messages.

In the Munitions Building meanwhile, Marshall and Stimson discussed the Tokyo-Berlin exchange, and the question of including China in any warning sent to the Japanese government. Marshall argued against throwing a protective blanket over China; the Asia mainland would bleed American military might, would sabotage the long-standing war plans, and virtually guarantee a stalemate in Europe, he argued. Stimson cooled in his advocacy. "Perhaps his position is safer," Stimson admitted in his diary.

In the basement of the Munitions Building, near the closely guarded rooms in which William Friedman's MAGIC team worked, Colonel Rufus Bratton, the head of Army Intelligence's Far East Section, told his staff, "Something is going to blow in the Far East soon." They would remain open around the clock from now on.

The ratchet tightening, Marshall sought as best he could to rush preparations. Still beset by a clumsy command structure, by staff members who issued orders through the chief of staff's office but had no effective means of assuring compliance, Marshall found himself struggling with details. A note on December 2 to Betty Stark asked the chief of naval operations to take a look at the prospective menu for troops in Iceland. "Thanksgiving failed to provide much of a meal and it looks as though Christmas may be a similar fiasco." To the commander of the 8th Infantry at Fort Jackson, South Carolina, he whipped off a sharp rebuke for unloading his worst troops on an infantry detachment bound for British Guiana. "I want to know who is responsible," the chief of staff's letter snapped. Throughout the entire period of crisis, and no doubt contributing mightily to his fatigue, Marshall attended to such small matters, including the promotion of one of his house orderlies from private to staff sergeant and his horse orderly from corporal to sergeant in the interest of fairness. "Anyone who stays with me loses heavily in rank if he belongs to the negro personnel. It is, therefore, difficult to hold a good man in contentment." Stimson had discussed with him the needed army reorganization, but even that would take too much of his time.

Wednesday, December 3, was ominous. MAGIC turned up information that the Japanese diplomatic service had ordered its embassies and consulates from London to Batavia to destroy their code machines and ciphers. An FBI wiretap on the Japanese Consulate in Honolulu revealed that the consul general was also burning classified papers. The destruction of the code machines, G-2 insisted, was a sure indication that Japan intended to break off diplomatic relations.

If that break meant war—and there had been repeated reminders in Washington that the Japanese would attack without warning—just where would the blow fall? Marshall remained certain the Philippines were the main target, a conviction reinforced by reports that a single Japanese reconnaissance plane had flown over Clark Field and Manila the day before.

Thursday, December 4, brought a shock from the Midwest. Under two-inch-high banners, the *Chicago Tribune* and its sister paper, the *Washington Times-Herald,* revealed: "Tribune Has War Plans." An unidentified air force colonel had leaked to Senator Burton Wheeler a copy of the secret Victory Program prepared during the summer and finally approved in September. That isolationist-minded senator in turn passed the document on to *Tribune* reporter Chesly Manley. Manley had the biggest story of his career, the complete mobilization plan of the United States in the event of war.

The leak was unnerving, a perfect provocation for Japan. In Stimson's opinion, "nothing more unpatriotic or damaging to our plans for defense could very well be conceived."

There was more frustration that Thursday for the chief of staff. A flight of thirteen B-17s intended to reinforce the Philippines had been held up on the West Coast for two and a half weeks because of headwinds that would have made the 2,400-mile flight to Hawaii perilous. Marshall dispatched Hap Arnold to the West Coast on December 4 to get the flight off; a major general might have command over the winds.

In Honolulu, Admiral Kimmel approved an order to send the carrier *Lexington* with a large escort to deliver a squadron of Marine planes to reinforce Midway. They were to sail the following day and deliver the aircraft on December 7.

On Friday, December 5, navy monitors reported hearing a weather bulletin on Tokyo's overseas news broadcast. But the message, "North wind, clear," did not fit any of the prearranged codes sent earlier to Nomura. Navy intelligence persisted, however, passing word that the weather report implied Japan would break off relations with Great Britain.

At Oahu, *Lexington* dropped its lines and steamed out of Pearl Harbor, the last of Admiral Kimmel's three aircraft carriers to go to sea. A second task force composed of the cruiser *Indianapolis* and five destroyer-minesweepers followed, bound for scouting duty in the mid-Pacific.

About the same time, the destroyers *Selfridge* and *Talbot* picked up an underwater sonar contact five miles off of the channel leading into Pearl Harbor. *Talbot* asked permission to drop depth charges. Squadron leader *Selfridge* refused, dismissing the contact as only a large blackfish. *Talbot*'s commander snorted, "If this is a blackfish, it has a motorboat up its stern."

Saturday's winds blustered through Washington, a harbinger of winter. Stimson, Marshall, Intelligence chief Sherman Miles, and Gerow met repeatedly that morning, in the secretary's or the chief's office. "As the morning went on," Stimson noted, "the news got worse and worse and the atmosphere indicated that something was going to happen." Something. But what? Ambassador John G. Winant in London had relayed a British report that not one but two Japanese convoys had rounded the southern point of Indochina, churning slowly toward Bangkok and the Kra Isthmus. At their current speed, they would arrive there in fourteen hours, sometime before dawn in the Far East.

The report only heightened their concern for the Philippines. Even at the risk of its being attacked en route to Manila, Marshall ordered Arnold to get the flight of thirteen B-17s at Hamilton Field airborne.

About 11:00 a.m. in Washington, 5:30 a.m. Honolulu time, Admiral Nagumo's First Air Fleet, still under strict radio silence, steamed 600 miles north and somewhat west of Oahu. In running seas with the wind stiffening to 20 knots, the fleet refueled for the last time before launching its aircraft. There was no more vulnerable moment than this, Japanese naval planners had projected. Hawaii lay beyond their range, but the fleet was well within range of B-17 reconnaissance planes. They did not know that General Short had ordered no reconnaissance, assuming that to be the Navy's responsibility. The two-plane navy patrols, sent out dutifully each dawn, had a range of only 300 miles.

In the early afternoon of December 6, Colonel Bratton passed on to General Miles yet another intercept from Togo to Nomura. The Foreign Ministry was about to send Japan's reply to the Hull Ten-Point Plan. Nomura was to keep the fourteen-part message secret until told to deliver it. "The situation," Togo advised unnecessarily, "is extremely delicate." Bratton personally delivered copies of this pilot message to Hull, Stimson, Marshall, and Gerow.

The first thirteen parts of the message had already been picked up in Bainbridge, Washington, by navy monitors; the individual parts were relayed to the Navy Department beginning at 11:45 a.m. In little more than three hours, cryptanalysts were working to decode the long message.

Six hundred miles due north of Oahu, the six carriers in two columns and the accompanying escorts of the First Air Fleet turned in a great arc, bearing due south. At 11:40 in the morning Honolulu time, 5:10 in the afternoon in Washington, *Akagi* ran up the ensign that had flown from the Japanese flagship during the Battle of Tsushima almost four decades before. From *Akagi* blinkered the admiral's message to the other ships of his fleet: "The rise and fall of the Empire depends upon this battle. Every man will do his duty."

At approximately the same moment, President Roosevelt decided to send a last appeal to the emperor. Withdrawal of Japanese troops from Indochina was the only way to peace. He urged the emperor to "give thought in this definite emergency to ways of dispelling the dark clouds. I am confident that both of us, for the sake of the peoples not only of our own great countries, but for the sake of humanity in neighboring territories, have a sacred duty to restore traditional amity and prevent further death and destruction in the world."

Roosevelt had little hope. "This son of man has just sent his final message to the Son of God," he told guests at the White House shortly after the message went off at 9:00 p.m.

While the president entertained that Saturday evening, navy cryptanalysts worked at the multi-part Japanese message. With the help of William Friedman's Purple team, they produced copies of the fifteen-page document for distribution to their lists of recipients.

Though the last part would not be radioed to Nomura from Tokyo until the next morning, Lieutenant Commander Alwin D. Kramer of Navy Intelligence began delivery to the names on his list. Admiral Stark was at the National Theater attending a performance of Sigmund Romberg's *The Student Prince,* so Kramer instead made his first call at the White House Office Building.

The long message placed in the president's locked pouch, a young naval aide carried the bag to Roosevelt waiting in his second-floor study. Harry Hopkins slowly paced the room as the president read for the next ten minutes. It was about ten o'clock.

The thirteen parts were an argumentative, even querulous review of the past eleven months of negotiations between the two countries. Naturally enough, the message put the best gloss possible on the underlying Japanese aggression in mainland Asia. "It is the immutable policy of the Japanese Government to ensure the stability of east Asia and to promote world peace, and thereby to enable all nations to find each its proper place in the world.

"Ever since the China affair broke out owing to the failure on the part of China to comprehend Japan's true intentions, the Japanese Government has striven for the restoration of peace. . . ." The United States and Great Britain, the note continued, were obstructing Japanese efforts toward the stabilization of East Asia, and attempting to "frustrate Japan's aspiration to realize the ideal of common prosperity in cooperation with these regions." Meanwhile, those two countries and the Netherlands East Indies had "strengthened their military preparations perfecting an encirclement of Japan, and have brought about a situation which endangers the very existence of the empire."

Hull's proposal of November contained "certain acceptable items" dealing with the resumption of trade between the two countries, Part Thirteen of the memorandum acknowledged. But the Hull offer "ignores Japan's sacrifices in the four years of the China affair, menaces the empire's existence itself and disparages its honour and prestige. *Therefore, viewed in its entirety, the Japanese Government regrets that it cannot accept the proposal as a basis of negotiations."*

The language of the memorandum was sharp, unusually hostile for a diplomatic message. Yet it ended in mid-air. The last part, still awaiting transmittal in Tokyo, would provide the dénouement: an end of negotiations, or the breaking of diplomatic relations perhaps, or even an entirely new proposal upon which to negotiate. Meanwhile, the Japanese had a fleet at sea, heading for Indochina. Chiang was in parlous state; Japan would not ease its pressure waiting for some new overture from America to reopen talks.

Short of the United States conceding Japan's right to wage war in China, the two nations had no real basis upon which to negotiate. Inevitably, Japanese aggression would carry that nation into the Gulf of Siam, threatening Thailand, Singapore, and the Philippines.

When the president finished reading the document, he handed it without comment to the pacing Hopkins. While Hopkins read through the sheaf, Roosevelt pivoted his wheelchair, turning his back on Hopkins and the naval aide.

The president spun about as Hopkins handed back the papers. "This means war," the young naval lieutenant heard Roosevelt say. Hopkins agreed. The two discussed the deployment of Japanese forces in the Pacific, especially in Indochina. It was too bad, Hopkins mused, that war was going to come at the convenience of the Japanese and the United States could not strike the first blow.

The president shook his head. "No, we can't do that. We are a democracy and a peaceful people. But we have a good record," he added, his voice rising.

A good record. Were an attack to come, the United States would have clean hands, leaving the isolationists without effective argument against American intervention on the side of the British or Dutch. The president considered calling Admiral Stark, but decided against it when the aide told him the admiral was at the National Theater. If the chief of naval operations were paged by the president, or left suddenly, it might cause "undue alarm," FDR decided.

Not until eleven-thirty that night did the president reach Admiral Stark at his home on the Naval Observatory grounds. The two men agreed that nothing in the message "required action." Since they had already determined the Japanese were "likely to attack at any time in any direction," the thirteen-part message was no more than another confirmation.

As the president and Hopkins discussed the message, Lieutenant Commander Kramer continued on his rounds. He delivered a copy of the message to the secretary of the navy at his apartment at the Hotel Wardman Park. Knox spent some twenty minutes reading it carefully, then told Kramer to join him the next morning at ten for a meeting with Secretary Hull at the State Department. Finally Kramer and his chauffeur-wife drove to the Arlington, Virginia, home of the director of Naval

Intelligence, Commodore Theodore Wilkinson. Wilkinson was entertaining General Miles and the president's naval aide, Captain John R. Beardall, among others. Kramer, Wilkinson, Miles, and Beardall went off to a closed room and read the message. They concluded "it certainly looked as though the Japanese were terminating negotiations."

Meanwhile, Colonel Rufus Bratton was making deliveries to the recipients on the Army's list. Told by Signal Intelligence there was little likelihood the indicated fourteenth part would be in that night, Bratton took a copy to the State Department duty officer with instructions to deliver it to Secretary Hull. General Miles called Bratton at home, the two men agreeing the message had little military significance. They decided there was no reason to bother the chief of staff. They would wait until the fourteenth part was in to show it to Marshall. He would be in the next day for an unusual Sunday afternoon meeting at the White House.*

Official Washington all but closed down for the night as Kramer and Bratton turned in. At 2:38 a.m. Washington time, the Navy's monitoring station in Bainbridge began intercepting a series of five messages from Tokyo intended for the Japanese Embassy on Massachusetts Avenue. The first was the concluding fourteenth part, the next two notes of gratitude to the ambassadors and the embassy staff for their efforts "in coping with the unprecedented crisis."

At 4:37 a.m., the fourth of the series instructed Nomura: "Will the ambassador please submit to the United States government (if possible to the secretary of state) our reply to the United States at 1:00 p.m. on the 7th, your time." The last of the series ordered the embassy to destroy the remaining cipher machine, the codes they had used, and all secret documents.

Forwarded by teletype to Washington, the five messages were decoded in OP-20-G by 7:00 a.m. Washington time. Two hours later, Army Intelligence had translated them, ready for delivery.

---

*Various historians have questioned Marshall's whereabouts on the night of December 6, 1941, as if his failure to read the thirteen parts then were pivotal. Yet there is no evidence that Marshall would have seen in it what the president, Hopkins, the secretary of the navy, the heads of both Army and Navy Intelligence, and two of MAGIC's most knowledgeable Japanese experts all had not. Marshall stated he was at home that night, for his wife's appointment book showed nothing, and "they were leading a rather monastic life" due to Katherine's mending ribs. Neither had he seen the films—about his only source of entertainment, he said—that played that night at the Fort Myer theater. See his testimony in *Pearl Harbor Attack*, II, pp. 925–26. Toland's *Infamy*, p. 302, makes much of the fact that the *Washington Times-Herald* of December 7 reported the chief of staff had attended a dinner at the University Club where Marshall was awarded a "vote of confidence." The general may well have attended without Katherine—hence that engagement was not on his wife's social calendar—but left early, as was his custom. So he might well have been at home, as he recalled, for much of the evening. The *Times-Herald* story might be questioned in that weekend editors, understaffed, often used press releases as the basis for news stories without checking them out.

Sunday morning dawned warmer, gentling the last days of fall. Marshall woke at Quarters No. 1 about 7:30 a.m., thankful after a grueling week that no call from the War Department had summoned him in the middle of the night. An uninterrupted sleep, even with aides screening his calls, was a rare thing these days.

The chief of staff ate breakfast about eight o'clock, an hour later than on weekdays, and looked at the Sunday papers. A man of habit, he then called the stable for his mount, intent on his usual Sunday morning ride. Normally he rode along the Virginia bank of the Potomac River as far as the government experimental farm where since September construction crews had been excavating the site of a mammoth five-sided structure to house the War and Navy Departments. The entire ride usually lasted about fifty minutes, at a trot and a canter along the riverbank, at a full run on the experimental farm.

Shortly before 9:00 a.m., about the time Marshall mounted his horse, Colonel Bratton sat reading the entire memorandum from Tokyo to Secretary Hull in his office in the Munitions Building. He was interrupted by arrival of the message asking Nomura to deliver the entire fourteen parts to the secretary of state at 1:00 p.m. The specific deadline set off Bratton's personal alarm. Diplomatic activity on Sunday was rare, but the stipulation of an exact hour suggested Tokyo was coordinating Nomura's response with other Japanese moves. Bratton was instantly convinced "the Japanese were going to attack some American installation in the Pacific area."

Bratton immediately sought someone with authority to order an alert, authority he lacked. Neither the chief of staff nor the chief of the War Plans Division were in, he learned. Nor was General Miles, head of Army Intelligence. Bratton telephoned General Marshall's quarters at Fort Myer.

An orderly at the red-brick Quarters No. 1 explained Marshall was riding. Bratton asked him to find the general instantly, to give him a message to call Bratton immediately on a "vitally important" matter. Speaking guardedly, protective of the secret of MAGIC, Bratton could say no more.

Somehow he failed to communicate his urgency; the orderly sent no one after the chief of staff. It was nearly ten-thirty when Marshall returned the call. Bratton explained he had "a most important message" that Marshall must see at once. When he offered to bring it to Fort Myer, the chief of staff said, "No, don't bother to do that. I am coming down to my office. You can give it to me then."

While Marshall showered, Stimson, Knox, and Hull gathered to discuss the Japanese threat in the Gulf of Siam. They were tense, aware "everything in MAGIC indicated they had been keeping the time back until now in order to accomplish something hanging in the air. . . ." The secretary of state was agitated by the tone of the first thirteen parts, and particularly alarmed by the tenor of the last, Stimson noted. Hull was "very certain that the Japs are planning some deviltry and we are all wondering where the blow will strike."

Marshall arrived at the War Department sometime around 11:00 a.m. Shortly after he sat down at his desk, General Miles and Colonel Bratton handed over to him the full text of the Japanese memorandum. Marshall began reading the fourteen parts, slowly, some of the more opaque sections a second time, while Bratton waited anxiously, wanting to call the general's attention to the one-o'clock message clipped to the end of the memorandum.

A man not to be interrupted, Marshall read on, looked at the attached deadline message, and asked the two intelligence officers what they thought it meant. The colonel could not be specific, but he was convinced the rider indicated some aggressive Japanese move in the Far East timed for 1:00 p.m. General Gerow and the chief of the Pacific Affairs Section of War Plans, Colonel Charles Bundy, agreed. They had less than two hours.

On board the six carriers of the First Air Fleet, practiced deck crews swiftly armed the torpedoes and topped off gas tanks. Aboard *Akagi*, the watch officer listened to the early morning program on radio station KGMB for any hint that Honolulu was on alert. "The Honolulu radio plays soft music. Everything is fine," the leader of the first wave of torpedo bombers announced with a grin.

The time, the specific time of the one-o'clock message, had "some definite significance," Marshall told the group of officers in his office. It was now 11:40 a.m., 6:10 a.m. in Hawaii. Marshall pondered a moment, then reached for his telephone.

Betty Stark had seen the one-o'clock message too, he told Marshall. "What do you think about sending the information about the time of the presentation on to the various Pacific commanders?" Marshall asked.

Stark hesitated. They had already sent warnings, Stark even more than Marshall. Another might merely confuse them. Marshall told Stark he was going to send another message.

The chief of staff scrawled in pencil on a plain lined pad:

The Japanese are presenting at 1 P.M. Eastern Standard Time, today, what amounts to an ultimatum. Also they are under orders to destroy their code machine immediately. Just what significance the hour set may have we do not know, but be on the alert accordingly.

Marshall handed the message to Colonel Bratton with instructions to dispatch the alert to the Philippines, Hawaii, and Panama. Just as Bratton reached the door, the telephone rang. Stark had reconsidered. He would go along with Marshall's alert. The chief beckoned Bratton back.

Stark asked Marshall if his communications system was rapid enough, given the short deadline. If not, he could use the Navy's. Marshall declined, assuring Stark the army system would get it out in time.

Marshall then added a final line to the message, telling his commanders to advise their naval opposites of the contents of the message.

As Bratton left with the alert, Gerow called out: "If there is any question of priority, give the Philippines first priority."

While Marshall talked with Stark and drafted the alert, some 220 miles north of Honolulu, two scout planes darted from the cruisers *Tone* and *Chikuma* into the cloudy sky. Twenty minutes later, the warships of the First Air Fleet turned east, into the wind, increasing their speed to 24 knots.

The rising seas delayed the takeoff twenty minutes as the carriers pitched in the steep swells. Then the first of the Zeros that would provide cover for the fleet raced down the flight deck of *Akagi*, dipped toward the ocean, and struggled aloft into the ominous sky. The balance of the first attack wave—forty-three fighters, forty-nine bombers, fifty-one dive bombers, and forty torpedo planes—followed, circling high over the fleet, then turning south. It was 6:20 in the morning in still sleeping Pearl Harbor, 11:50 a.m. in Washington.

Colonel Bratton half-ran, half-walked to the Message Center. He had little more than an hour before the 1:00 p.m. deadline, and an order from the chief of staff to get out the alert "at once by the fastest safe means." That ruled out the telephone, for though the conversations were scrambled electronically, they distrusted the security of the system. Marshal himself had ruled out the telephone for fear the Japanese were tapping the underwater cable and unscrambling the conversations. If they were, they could claim the alert a hostile act, but more importantly they would quickly figure out just how the United States had learned of the deadline. The secret of MAGIC had to be protected.

At the Message Center, Bratton dictated Marshall's scrawled message to the code clerk, then returned to Marshall's office. Within minutes he was back, ordered by the chief of staff to find out how long it would take for delivery. Thirty or forty minutes, Colonel Edward French assured Bratton.

As Bratton tried to clarify the status of the messages in Washington, the USS *Antares* hovered off the narrow channel leading into Pearl Harbor, waiting for a tug to lead her in. Some 1,500 yards to starboard, *Antares*'s skipper spied the conning tower of an unfamiliar submarine, "obviously having depth control trouble." *Antares* radioed the sighting to the destroyer *Ward*.

Ward went to general quarters at 6:40 a.m., bearing down on the crippled submarine. At a range of 50 yards, the destroyer opened fire. Struck at the base of the conning tower, the submarine heeled over. A salvo of depth charges bracketed the stricken submarine.

Ward had taken first blood.

Within minutes, the *Ward*'s captain, William W. Outerbridge, radioed his sighting and an attack report. It was shortly after 7:00 a.m. before Admiral Kimmel, dressing for a round of Sunday golf with General Short, learned of the attack by telephone. Skeptical, for too many skittish seamen had spotted too many nonexistent submarines in recent months, Kimmel ordered that the report be verified. Until the sighting was confirmed, they would not notify the Army.

While the Navy's duty officer sought to contact *Ward*, the Message Center in the Munitions Building dispatched Marshall's scrawled alerts. The first message, to Panama, went by radio at noon, the second, to MacArthur, five minutes later. A third was dispatched at 12:11 p.m. to the commanding general of the Fourth Army in San Francisco. The message intended for General Short in Hawaii could not go by radio because of atmospheric conditions, French learned. Radio communications with the island had gone sour about 10:20 that morning.

French elected instead to use the regular commercial facilities of Western Union and RCA. The Army had only a 10-kilowatt-strong radio signal; RCA's San Francisco office, which handled high volumes of trans-Pacific communication, had a 40-kilowatt transmitter, powerful enough to break through the static.

On Oahu's northern shore, 230 feet above the surf of Kahuku Point, the single mobile radar unit Secretary of War Stimson had rushed to the Hawaiian Department was preparing to shut down. It was 7:00 a.m. locally, 12:30 p.m. in Washington, and the three-hour daily shift General Short had ordered was at an end. Suddenly Private Joseph L. Lockard spotted on the small screen "the biggest sightings he had ever seen." The flight, probably more than fifty planes, Lockard and another private agreed, was then 132 miles north of the island. The two enlisted men followed the flight in, finally deciding, technically off-duty or not, to relay the tracking to the Air Force's Information Center.

Lieutenant Kermit Tyler dismissed the telephoned report, first assuming it was a navy flight off a carrier, then remembering he had heard that a flight of B-17s was due in from California this morning. Tyler told the two radar operators, "Well, don't worry about it." It was 7:20 a.m.

Marshall's alert to General Short at Fort Shafter arrived in Honolulu at 1:03 p.m. Washington time, 7:33 local time. Because the teletype line between RCA and Fort Shafter was temporarily out of order, a clerk assigned the coded telegram to a messenger for delivery. Messenger Tadao Fuchikami picked up the envelopes for the Fort Shafter area and set off on his motorcycle.

Homing in on KGMB's morning music program, the first wave of Japanese bombers was then thirty-five miles north of Kahuku Point. The two enlisted men at the radar station casually followed the blips to a range of twenty miles before interference broke up the reflected signal. It was 7:39 a.m., 1:09 p.m. in Washington.

The chief of staff left the Munitions Building for lunch at Fort Myer after gathering up the file of papers he intended to take to the White House for the scheduled 3:00 p.m. conference. He was at Fort Myer when Commander Mitsuo Fuchida flew over the north shore of Oahu, shoved back the canopy of his cockpit, and fired a single flare as a signal to his squadrons.

The first wave of bombers sped across the island, the Koolau Range on its left, the Waianae on its right, over Schofield Barracks and Wheeler Field, bearing down on the Pacific Fleet snugged in the oily waters of Pearl Harbor on a quiet Sunday morning.

C H A P T E R

XV

The Sword Drawn

The first report of the attack made its way to the White House about an hour after Admiral Yamamoto's bombers struck the naval anchorage at Pearl Harbor. Monitoring stations on the West Coast, Secretary of the Navy Frank Knox told the president at 1:40 p.m. Washington time, had picked up a signal from Hawaii advising local commanders they were under Japanese attack, and adding the advisory, "This is no drill."

Presidential adviser Harry Hopkins suspected a mistake. Japan surely was going to strike southward, to Indochina. The president disagreed; the surprise attack on Pearl was "just the kind of unexpected thing the Japanese would do, and that at the very time they were discussing peace in the Pacific they were plotting to overthrow it."

Some forty minutes later, Admiral Stark called from the Navy Building to confirm the report. Stark lacked details; he knew only there had been some damage inflicted to the fleet, and some loss of life. He expected to have further details when the president met with them at 3:00 p.m. Washington time.

This first wartime meeting of the president's War Cabinet in the study on the second floor of the White House was strained. They were in it now, well before they were ready militarily. But the Japanese attack had eliminated a political problem: there could be no congressional resistance to a declaration of war against the Japanese. If Hitler fulfilled his promise to declare war on the United States in support of his ally Japan—MAGIC intercepts had reiterated the pledge of the Tripartite Pact—the issue would be joined cleanly.

There was little they could actually do at the meeting. As damage reports from Hawaii trickled into the White House, "Betty" Stark became increasingly agitated. *Arizona* had been hit in the forward power magazine and was burning out of control. The adjacent *Tennessee* could catch fire at any minute. *California* was down at the stern, burning, abandoned at the captain's orders. *West Virginia* was sinking, her captain dead, her survivors aboard the damaged *Tennessee* fighting the fires there. *Oklahoma* had taken four torpedoes and capsized in the shallow waters, her encrusted steel bottom obscenely exposed to the smoke-blackened sky. *Nevada, Maryland,* and *Pennsylvania* had been damaged. The very backbone of the battleship navy lay broken in the garbage-fouled waters about Ford Island, and with it the dreams of two generations of navy men.

Three cruisers and three destroyers were holed or burning, two auxiliaries damaged, and two more sunk. Strafing Japanese fighters and high-level bombers had destroyed ninety-two planes at adjacent naval air stations and damaged another thirty-one. Wheeler and Hickam Fields had been heavily hit, with three hangars destroyed at each. A total of 347 of the 394 aircraft in the islands lay smoldering, wing tip to wing tip. Casualties were heavy, the telephone calls indicated, though just how severe no one knew.*

Within minutes of the announcer's bulletin interrupting the Sunday broadcast of the New York Philharmonic, knots of anxious people gathered outside the White House. Occasionally they sang "God Bless America," their thin voices filtering through the cold winter afternoon to the second-floor study. Grace Tully, the president's longtime secretary, assumed responsibility for the incoming reports, taking the calls from the War and Navy Departments on the telephone in the president's bedroom, then relaying them to the men in the adjacent study.

Admiral Stark grew increasingly agitated as the toll mounted, his voice revealing a "shocked disbelief," Miss Tully recalled later. The mild-mannered Stark was moved near to tears by the death of the great battleships he had loved. The president seemed the calmest of all those in the crowded room, "but there was a rage in his very calmness," she added. That rage focused on the stricken admiral. The president—a navy man, after all—would later tell Secretary Stimson he now understood why Stark's nickname was Betty. "I suppose it was either that or Emily, and Betty seemed more appropriate." Stark's days as chief of naval operations were numbered.

Marshall remained cool even as the damage reports turned hysterical. Speaking to the president by telephone long after the Japanese planes had returned to their carriers, Hawaii Governor Joseph B. Poindexter suddenly shrieked, "My God, there's another wave of Jap planes over Hawaii right this minute!" Equally unreliable reports of landings by Japanese troops, of enemy fleets steaming toward an unprotected West Coast, of massive sabotage by a Japanese fifth column in Hawaii, of bombings in half a hundred locations in California; of Oahu invaded, all reminded

---

*The final report of the congressional Pearl Harbor Investigating Committee listed 2,304 killed, 1,109 wounded, and 22 missing in action.

the chief of staff of the first war. "We're now in the fog of battle," he cautioned.

Calmly Marshall reviewed troop dispositions with the president. The Panama Canal was on the alert. General MacArthur in the Philippines had been in touch with the War Department; he too was alerted. Yes, Marshall agreed, they could mount guards around defense plants. The president bridled when Marshall insisted he was also posting guards around the White House; Marine and army guards showed up nonetheless. (Both the president and Mrs. Roosevelt considered the two .90mm anti-aircraft guns posted on the roof of the White House in the next few days to be a crowning idiocy.) That much taken care of, Marshall was impatient to be away. They were at war and there was much to do.

The meeting broke up only after Prime Minister Churchill telephoned the president.

"What's this about Japan?" Churchill asked Roosevelt.

"They have attacked us at Pearl Harbor," the president replied. "We are all in the same boat now."

In one stroke, the Japanese had solved Roosevelt's greatest political problem, bonding the American people together as nothing else could have done.

As Marshall and Secretary Stimson left the White House, the president began a draft of the war message he intended to deliver the next day to the Congress. Dictating to Miss Tully, he started: "Yesterday comma December 7 comma 1941 dash a date which shall live in world history—" Later he would change the draft to read "a date which shall live in infamy."

Marshall and Stimson returned to a War Department awash with rumor and confusion. Guam and Midway Islands were under attack, Hong Kong, Bangkok, and Singapore bombed. Britain reported Malaya had been invaded. Planes from a Japanese carrier force had struck the Philippines; worse yet, they had apparently surprised the bulk of MacArthur's small air force on the ground four hours after MacArthur had word of the Pearl Harbor attack. The news from Manila left Marshall in a cold fury. He could not conceive how the Japanese strikes had come as a complete surprise. Short and MacArthur had been put on the alert, yet did not follow orders. "They were careless and overconfident—a fatal mistake."

The chief of staff was particularly angry with MacArthur. Long after the attack, he still fumed about the Philippine commander's failure to defend his airfields. "Four hours, and our aircraft were still on the ground in the open—perfect targets. I sweated blood to get planes to the Philippines. It is inexplicable."*

---

*In his autobiography, *Reminiscences*, MacArthur says only, "Our fighters went up to meet them, but our bombers were slow in taking off" (p. 127). He does not state that he failed to alert his command after learning of the Pearl Harbor attack.

The loss of the aircraft was particularly galling. They were beginning the war with no more than 1,100 combat-worthy planes. Of these, only 159 were four-engine bombers. The most advanced fighter the Air Corps had was the obsolescent P-40; army pilots had dubbed the new twin-engined "Marauder" bomber the "Murderer" for its quirky handling characteristics.

There were few planes on the mainland with range enough to even fly patrols that would give them sufficient warning should the next Japanese move be on the West Coast. Even now there was a report of a Japanese fleet just off the coast of California. Marshall drove back to the Munitions Building fully expecting reports of nuisance raids at least; defense plants, especially the aircraft factories in the Los Angeles area, would have to be heavily protected with anti-aircraft guns and camouflage.

At that moment, Marshall did not realize and probably only a handful of younger, air-minded naval officers knew that the bombers of the First Air Fleet had done the United States Navy a great service. The burning hulks at Pearl Harbor represented more emotional than actual losses. The four carriers based at Pearl Harbor had been on sorties when the Japanese struck and had escaped harm. Of the battleships that had been hard hit, only two were a total loss—and one, the *Utah*, was a decommissioned target ship. Despite the dreams of admirals, vulnerable battleships would not figure importantly in any Pacific engagement; submarines and airpower would carry the brunt of the sea war,

Monday, December 8, dawned cold, the winter wind gusting raw and wet. Across the street from the White House once more grim-faced crowds gathered silently to catch a glimpse of the president as he left for the Capitol and his midday speech. In the gloomy Munitions Building, the news was all bad. MacArthur seemed to be putting up a defense, but, with the loss of the aircraft and the fleet at Pearl, "we should be unable to reinforce him probably in time to save the islands," Marshall told Stimson. The immediate problem was to divert four-engine bombers intended under Lend-Lease for the British to bolster the defense of the Hawaiian Islands should the Japanese return.

The blow had fallen, and in that there was some relief. By the second day of war, a certain calm had taken hold on the second floor of the Munitions Building. Told by an assistant secretary that a Japanese fleet was thought to be bearing down on San Francisco, Stimson "thanked him for telling me but suggested that I didn't know anything that I could do to prevent it." They had little to throw at a threatening Japanese fleet wherever it turned up. Marshall was still trying to muster his army, discovering in the process that the War Department was a poor command post.

It was also a terribly overburdened command post. From the first, Secretary Stimson pressured the chief of staff to add personnel and delegate responsibility. He was carrying two burdens now, Stimson argued, one strategic, the other organizing the training of the Army the United States would put in the field. In fact, there was a third evolving, one neither man quite understood at the time: the diplomatic. Marshall was called upon to advise Undersecretary of State Sumner Welles about the South American republics declaring war on Germany and Japan. Marshall cautioned against it on the ground that the United States lacked the manpower and materiel to defend those countries against possible Axis retaliation.

Marshall needed help, Stimson insisted. The secretary recommended on December 11 that the chief of staff tap smart, young men, mentioning Brehon Somervell, Jacob Devers, and Mark Clark. Marshall already had his eye on all three; he was especially keen on Somervell, a dapper, energetic man capable of charm when he chose to be charming, but a man with no patience for incompetence. Efficient "Bill" Somervell was to become the first of the Army's technocrats, serving as the War Department's G-4, or head of supply; then as commander of Army Services of Supply. To deliver the $120 billion in clothes, food, armaments, and other supplies called for in the Victory Plan, Somervell took responsibility, frequently without authorization. Marshall was later to turn back requests from more bureaucratic-minded men that he curb Somervell's take-charge attitude, asserting "he spent his whole life lighting fires under generals and that when he got a self-starter, he wasn't going to change him."

Tapping younger officers such as these, the chief of staff was to gain a reputation as a "genius at picking men" for responsible positions both in the field and in the War Department. Some men served with distinction in both places, none more successfully than a fifty-year-old, newly minted brigadier general from Fort Sam Houston, Texas.

George Marshall had met Dwight David Eisenhower just twice. But in the tightly knit Army of the years between the wars, he heard much about the younger man's career.

It was a career of a late bloomer that paralleled Marshall's own. An indifferent student at West Point—sixty-fifth in a class of 165—Eisenhower had fallen under the sway of Fox Conner after graduation. Assigned to the somnolent Panama Canal from 1922 to 1924 and seeking to fill empty days, Eisenhower took to borrowing books recommended by Marshall's old friend. Conner and Eisenhower spent evenings together, the junior officer expanding under the tutelage of one of the Army's true intellectuals. The time spent as the general's executive officer became for Eisenhower "a sort of graduate school in military affairs. . . ." Conner talked long about the lessons of the first war, predicting that a second would arise inevitably from the harsh peace of Versailles, and discussing how it should be fought. From Conner, "Ike" Eisenhower learned of the necessity for a single unified command, and the Allies' need to put aside nationalistic considerations in waging war. From Conner, too, Eisenhower first learned of Lieutenant Colonel George C. Marshall, a man "nothing short of a genius," who knew "more about the techniques of arranging allied commands" than anyone Conner had met.

The general became the young officer's sponsor, seeing to it that Eisenhower attended the Command and General Staff School at Fort Leavenworth. There Eisenhower finished first in a class of 275, that alone enough to mark him as a man with a future in the Army. Eisenhower's success or Fox Conner's advocacy led him to Washington, where he served as aide to General Pershing, helping the old man to write his memoirs of World War I; Marshall had met him then. The Army War College, and later the Army Industrial College—Eisenhower had gone on to get his staff ticket punched in all the right places. He had served MacArthur in the office of the chief of staff, then accepted MacArthur's invitation in 1935 to go with him to the Philippines as assistant military adviser to the commonwealth. That Eisenhower, clearly a disciple of Pershing's "Chaumont crowd," could garner MacArthur's favor was proof enough of Ike's winning personality.

Eisenhower had turned down MacArthur's request that he serve a second four-year tour of duty in the Philippines, choosing instead to return to the States and the 15th Infantry at Fort Ord, California. It was there on the beaches of Monterey Bay, during an amphibious exercise, that the chief of staff, on an inspection tour, met Lieutenant Colonel Eisenhower for the second time.

More than a year would pass before the two met again. By then Eisenhower, as chief of staff for the "winning" Third Army during the maneuvers of September 1941, had distinguished himself by planning the successful assault. That resulted in a temporary promotion to colonel, and hope for a regiment.

Five days after Pearl Harbor, Eisenhower received a call from the secretary to the General Staff, Colonel Walter Bedell Smith, an old friend. "The chief says for you to hop a plane and get up here right away." Orders would follow.

Marshall was at his desk in the office over the entrance to the Munitions Building when Eisenhower reported for duty Sunday morning, December 14. The chief of staff immediately plunged into a crisp outline of the Pacific situation.

The Navy lacked the vessels to mass a task force powerful enough to punch through to the Philippines, he stated. Repair facilities at Pearl

Harbor had been severely damaged; no one could say when the fleet would be back to strength. The four carriers now at sea had to be held back for reconnaissance and defense of the otherwise unprotected Pacific Coast.

Hawaii had been badly hit; reinforcement of the islands took precedence over everything else lest the Japanese return with an invasion force. In the Philippines, Marshall continued, MacArthur's armed forces amounted to 30,000 men. Eisenhower probably had a better idea of their quality, since he had trained them, than did the chief of staff. They had managed to beef up MacArthur's air strength, including 35 B-17s and 220 fighters. That force had been badly hit; how badly Marshall didn't know.

Having detailed the situation in the Far East, the chief of staff abruptly asked, "What should be our general line of action?"

Taken aback, Eisenhower asked for a few hours. "All right," Marshall snapped, turning to the next document on his desk.

Eisenhower found his way to a vacant desk in the War Plans Division, pondering the dilemma. The big question was the Navy's lack of enthusiasm for a relief convoy. It was understandable; just four days before, land-based bombers flying from Saigon had attacked and sunk in ninety-minutes the Royal Navy battleship *Prince of Wales* and the battle cruiser *Repulse* off Malaya. The day of the battleship, so massive, seemingly so formidable, had ended—and with it any projected early relief of the Philippines.

Such logistical realities governed everything but public opinion, Fox Conner's disciple noted. The United States simply could not turn its back on its "Filipino wards," he concluded. Regardless of the cost, they were obligated to attempt to reinforce the beleaguered islands.

By early afternoon, Eisenhower was back in the chief of staff's office. "General," he said firmly, "it will be a long time before major reinforcements can go to the Philippines, longer than the garrison can hold out with any driblet [of] assistance, if the enemy commits major forces to their reduction. But we must do everything for them that is humanly possible. The people of China, of the Philippines, of the Dutch East Indies will be watching us. They may excuse failure but they will not excuse abandonment. Their trust and friendship are important to us. Our base must be Australia, and we must start at once to expand it and to secure our communications to it."

Marshall nodded. "I agree with you. Do your best to save them."

With that, Marshall named Eisenhower chief of the Philippines and Far Eastern Section of the War Plans Division. He leaned across the carved wooden desk, fixing Eisenhower with "an eye that seemed to me awfully cold," and announced, "Eisenhower, the department is filled with able men who analyze their problems well but feel compelled always to bring them to me for final solution. I must have assistants who will solve their own problems and tell me later what they have done."

Eisenhower had passed a critical first test. Virtually any staff officer could add a column of military assets; it took one of Fox Conner's favorites to understand the equally crucial, intangible elements such as civilian morale or the good feeling of allies.

As Eisenhower guessed, the chief of staff and the secretary of war had already reached the same conclusion. They too had served tours in the islands, Marshall twice, Stimson as governor-general; neither could give up the Philippines without a struggle. That afternoon Stimson secured the president's agreement to the general strategy during a visit to the White House. The president immediately ordered the Navy to cooperate.

Navy Secretary Frank Knox returned to Washington the following day after a hasty inspection trip to Pearl Harbor. The damage was not as bad as first feared, Knox told the president; at least three of the patched battleships were already at sea and three more could be refitted, though it would take time.

Hardly mollified, the president decided to appoint a commission to investigate the Pearl Harbor attack, and to fix blame on the commanders responsible. There was plenty of blame to go around, both Knox and Stimson agreed. Though both branches of the service had been remiss, the two secretaries were anxious to avoid intramural squabbles between their departments. Stimson recommended the president appoint Supreme Court Justice Owen J. Roberts to head that investigation.

In the meantime, the president himself intended to take measures to put some drive into their command. He was ordering the relief of both Admiral Kimmel and General Short, the two commanders in the Hawaiian Islands. They were to return to the United States for the Roberts investigation. Then he intended to divide the burden "Betty" Stark carried by naming a commander in chief, United States Fleet. The new COMINCH was to be hard-bitten Ernest J. King, who took secret pride in the fact that his crews proudly considered him "the toughest sonovabitch in the entire U.S. Navy."

King was to have supreme command of the fleets at sea, directly responsible to the president, Roosevelt insisted. Stark as chief of naval operations was to preside over the development of long-range war plans, King over "current" war plans. The mild-mannered Stark had been effectively removed from direct command while still retaining the title. In the interest of civilian morale, it would not do to turn out the chief of naval operations as an incompetent, but Admiral King now sat at the president's right hand.

The great American giant was stirring. In London as well as in Washington there was a sense of relief. The bombing of Pearl Harbor and

Hitler's declaration of war had brought the United States into the war, more than twenty-six months after Germany and the Soviet Union attacked Poland. For a year and a half Great Britain and the Commonwealth stood virtually alone, parceling out men and equipment in an unsuccessful effort to slow the German advance. Now the United States with its great manpower pool and its awesome industrial might was a partner. Churchill went to bed the night of December 7 a happy man. The next day he would secure a declaration of war upon Japan from the House of Commons.

If Churchill had one canker eased, another festered: could he count on the United States to follow the agreed-upon war plan that placed Europe first on the military agenda? Public opinion in the United States might compel the president to avenge Pearl Harbor immediately— regardless of RAINBOW 5 and Plan Dog.

Roosevelt and Churchill met on December 22 in Washington where Churchill and his entourage arrived after an eight-day voyage on the new battleship *Duke of York*. They met, as Churchill proposed, to review the entire war plan in light of "reality and new facts," a euphemism for the staggering succession of blows they had absorbed since December 7. Thailand had succumbed without a struggle. The Japanese had taken the Gilbert Islands and Guam; an unopposed invasion force was ashore in northern Luzon, another in the southern part of the island. Wake Island's defenders had run out of water and ammunition, and sat waiting the last assault against their sandbagged positions. British troops in Malaya were in retreat, Hong Kong was under attack, and yet another invasion force steamed toward Borneo.

Churchill was to stay more than three weeks for this conference, which he had code-named ARCADIA. As the president's guest, Churchill and a bustling entourage turned White House routines topsy-turvy. The prime minister worked far into the night, then slept the morning away in the second-floor bedroom across from Hopkins's in the East Wing. Late to rise, he spent the first part of his day reading dispatches and drafting replies while writing against a board propped across his thighs in bed. He rose to dress for lunch with the president, frequently in the Monroe Room where the prime minister had set up his traveling map room. He might nap in the afternoon, but was in full stride by the cocktail hour. From then into the late night he was the expansive, winning guest, telling stories, wooing his host. He even charmed the White House staff to culinary accomplishments beyond the dreary; Robert Sherwood, a frequent dinner guest in the White House during those years, considered the food always better when Churchill visited. So too the wine.

Churchill and the chiefs of staff he brought with him met with their opposite numbers in formal sessions twenty times during ARCADIA. At least eight of the sessions were devoted to the geopolitical aspects, with

Roosevelt and Churchill carrying the brunt of the discussions while cabinet officers and military men contributed technical information.

Churchill arrived in Washington aware "the war against Japan would loom large in American eyes," and aware too that they would have to tread warily in the face of American public opinion. At the first general meeting of the two leaders and their military staffs, held at the White House on December 23, Churchill proposed a six-point strategy:

(a) The realisation of the victory programme of armaments, which first and foremost requires the security of the main areas of war industry.

(b) The maintenance of essential communications.

(c) Closing and tightening the ring around Germany.

(d) Wearing down and undermining German resistance by air bombardment, blockade, subversive activities and propaganda.

(e) The continuous development of offensive action against Germany.

(f) Maintaining only such positions in the Eastern theatre as will safeguard vital interests while we are concentrating on the defeat of Germany.

For the next twelve months, the British suggested, they should marshal their forces for a land offensive against the Germans or Italians. Meanwhile American and British bombers based in England would increasingly raid Germany. Their navies and merchant marine would provide war materials for the Soviet Union and would blockade Germany. In addition, the Allies would promote underground resistance movements on the continent.

Though the British doubted they could conduct any large-scale invasion before 1943, they argued it was essential to mass a force ready to conduct a limited, opportunistic adventure on the mainland should Germany suddenly collapse. (Without that force, the Soviet Union would be able to race unopposed to the English Channel.) Churchill himself suggested the goal for 1943 was "the mass invasion of the continent," though his chiefs of staff thought a later date more likely.

The ARCADIA conversations between the two government leaders ran easily, Churchill holding forth at length, Roosevelt deferring in the interest of good manners to his guest. The military chiefs said little in the general sessions, though a wary Marshall feared Churchill's persuasive tongue would win too many concessions from Roosevelt. The president did insist on one point—the need to get United States troops into combat somewhere across the Atlantic as soon as possible. It would have a telling effect on the German public, not to mention the impact on the morale in the United States, he insisted.

The prime minister essentially outlined what the British chiefs of staff considered to be a supple, opportunistic strategy, one that made no early commitments but took advantage of the situation. It was also to be a peripheral strategy, one that avoided the killing blow until Germany had been bled, then bled again. For a nation with a relatively small population, such a low-casualty option was vital.

Though they offered no counter of their own, the American chiefs of staff were skeptical of the British plan. The peripheral strategy favored British interests, notably protecting the Empire and restoring the Mediterranean to de facto British sovereignty. It was also a cautious policy, one that could provoke an impatient American public to demand alternative action in the Pacific. Moreover, Churchill might say he "did not foresee the necessity for very large armies to be shipped overseas from the United States," but the American chiefs had serious doubts. The Third Reich would not collapse because Britain nibbled upon the edge of the cracker.

Whatever their reservations about the particulars of the British position, the American chiefs of staff and the president agreed on the crucial principle of a Europe-first strategy.

Arcadia was not only to shape grand strategy, but, as it happened, to bind the two delegations in a web of personal friendships that made possible the execution of that grand strategy. The most important were the warm relationships that grew up between Roosevelt and Churchill, between Harry Hopkins and the prime minister, and, unexpectedly, between the reserved Marshall and the equally severe Sir John Dill.

That POTUS and Former Naval Person got on so well could have been expected. Both were outgoing, expansive men, politicians after all. They ate lunch together all but one of the fourteen days that Churchill stayed in the White House, and if they spent some of those lunches privately thrashing out disagreements, they also made time for the anecdotes and reminiscences of two men who hugely enjoyed each other's company. Churchill took to pushing Roosevelt's wheelchair from room to room on the second floor of the White House. The ease of their relationship led to an anecdote only partially denied by a Churchill intent on preserving his dignity.

The president wheeled into Churchill's bedroom one afternoon to discover the prime minister stalking the room in the nude, puffing on a cigar as he dictated to a male secretary. As Roosevelt spun about to leave, Churchill called him back, adding, "The prime minister of Britain has nothing to conceal from the president of the United States."

Less expectedly, Marshall and Field Marshal Sir John Dill struck it off. The former chief of the Imperial General Staff, Dill had been replaced by Churchill just weeks before, worn out after carrying two burdens for the past eighteen months. He had not only managed to rebuild the British Army after Dunkirk, but had done so while watching helplessly as his wife died of a wasting illness.

In the best of times Dill had little taste for argument, and none for the impractical military schemes Churchill fabricated almost weekly. Like so many of the British officers blooded on the Somme during the first war, Dill was a cautious tactician, determined to avoid the sort of bold strokes Churchill favored. "Jack" Dill's army friends might whisper doubts among themselves whether he had the iron will to stand up to the prime minister, but they had only kind words for him personally. Indeed, their criticism that Jack Dill was *too* kind more than anything else probably determined his future—assigned to duty in Washington as Churchill's military liaison.

Courteous and reserved, in that sense like Marshall himself, the balding Dill was hardly as aloof as the American general. He also had a droll sense of humor; asked shortly after he became Churchill's man in Washington just what his job was, Dill confessed he did not know, but "at least he provided neutral ground on which the American army and navy could meet."

Shared interests bonded the two men together. Both enjoyed riding horseback. Dill also had studied Civil War strategy and the classic Valley of the Shenandoah campaign. Together the two men were to steal a few hours to visit the Civil War battlefields in the Washington vicinity, marking the paths of Union and Rebel forces. In the battles of the past they found a means to deal with the battles of the present.

Joined later by his second wife Nancy, Dill was to live at Fort Myer in quarters that Marshall made available to them. The Dills became frequent visitors of the Marshalls in Quarters No. 1. The two couples played bridge sporadically, with no great interest in the outcome; the companionship was the most important aspect of those friendly evenings. Theirs was a close friendship the more cherished because it came at a time in their lives when most men would conclude such new relationships were unlikely.

This friendship between the two was to become pivotal in the conduct of the war. Like Marshall, Dill was selfless. Beyond personal ambition, neither man sought favor or publicity. Once each recognized this trait in the other, "they could examine every case without risk of the conclusion being affected by any consideration smaller than the merits of it," the British ambassador later wrote. Marshall came to discuss the most sensitive matters with Dill, sure that the field marshal would report fairly what Churchill needed to know of American intentions, and keep to himself what the prime minister did not need to know. Dill was to become an informal conduit of great importance during the trying months to come.

There were those on both sides who doubted the wisdom of the informal arrangement Marshall and Dill fashioned between them. Some years later one American planner complained that Marshall told Dill too much. British senior staff members groused that Dill was far too sympathetic to the American position on overall strategy and Lend-Lease. Still, with frankness and mutual sympathy, they avoided problems and smoothed over disagreements.

Fresh from the austerity of wartime London, Dill was nonplussed by the affluence he found in Washington in its first Yuletide of the war. "This country is the most highly organised for peace you can imagine," he wrote his successor as chief of the Imperial General Staff, Field Marshal Alan Brooke. "Everything is done on a grand scale. I have never seen so many motor cars, but I have not seen a military vehicle. . . . And yet amid all this unpreparedness the ordinary American firmly believes that they can finish off the war quite quickly—and without too much disturbance. . . . Never have I seen a country so utterly unprepared for war and so soft."

The holiday was crowded for military and civilians alike. The Marshalls served a midday Christmas dinner for the British ambassador and members of the British chiefs of staff—all of whom would have a second such meal at the White House in a formal dinner that night. Marshall surprised Dill with a birthday cake decorated with small silk flags of their two nations; the British field marshal was moved that the American chief of staff had taken the time to learn of his birthday. This was, he said, the first birthday cake he had had since his childhood.

The day after Christmas, Churchill formally published the banns of their alliance in a speech before the United States Congress. Many of these men had been staunch isolationists all their lives. Others, on principle, were suspicious of the Empire and its colonialists. Roosevelt and Hopkins had worried about the prime minister's reception; Churchill too had fretted about his address before the joint session. Despite his anxiety, or perhaps because of it, Churchill gave an emotional address, but won that audience of politicians with an almost off-handed comment, "I cannot help reflecting that if my father had been American and my mother British, instead of the other way around, I might have got here on my own." The roar of laughter and applause effectively ended all congressional doubts of the man or his cause. At the end of his address, a moist-eyed prime minister responded to the cheers with his trademark V-for-Victory sign; the sober chief justice of the United States, Harlan F. Stone, returned the salute. With such gestures were the two countries bound together.

The cordial unanimity on the Hill and in the White House did not necessarily extend to the new Federal Reserve Building across Constitution Avenue from the Munitions Building. There the chiefs of staff of both nations had quickly affirmed the "Europe-first" concord. Beyond that they could not agree.

The United States was at war, yet, Dill noted, "this country has not—repeat not—the slightest conception of what the war means, and their armed forces are more unready for war than it is possible to imagine." A week before the British arrived, a House of Representatives committee had refused to approve a bill to lower the draft age to eighteen. Strategic planning was nonexistent in British terms, with no regular meetings between the president and his chiefs of staff. "The whole organization belongs to the days of George Washington," Dill added.

Marshall was to take the first step toward modernizing the combined war effort the day after Churchill's address. The general pressed hard in a series of meetings for what he later described as "one of his major contributions to the winning of the war," the concept of unified or supreme command in the field.

"I am convinced," the army chief of staff told the officers assembled in the crowded conference room on December 26, "that there must be one man in command of the entire theater—air, ground and ships. We cannot manage by cooperation. Human frailties are such that there would be emphatic unwillingness to place portions of troops under another service. If we can make a plan for unified command now, it will solve nine-tenths of our troubles."

Specifically, Marshall wanted two groups of staff officers, British and American, to provide "a controlled directive" with a single theater commander implementing that directive. As Marshall pointed out, and it was an argument he would repeat often in the next days, "We had to come to this in the first world war, but it was not until 1918 that it was accomplished and much valuable time, blood, and treasure had been needlessly sacrificed."

Marshall made little headway with the British chiefs, unprepared and therefore wary of the American's proposal. Instead he was to turn to his newest planner, Ike Eisenhower, to draft a model letter of instruction to a prospective theater commander. Marshall deliberately chose the sweeping Far Eastern area, the only theater in which troops of both nations were presently fighting; he named it ABDA, an acronym for Australian, British, Dutch, American.

As a sweetener, Marshall suggested that General Sir Archibald Wavell be named supreme commander of ABDA. He was battle-tested and had handled large bodies of troops. He knew India, and offered the best prospect for preserving that jewel for the imperial crown. Yet Marshall's solicitude only increased British suspicions. Throughout the Far East, in

Indochina and even on the Indian subcontinent, the Allies faced reversal after reversal; Wavell would be a convenient scapegoat for the disasters certain to come.

The following morning, Marshall persuaded the president of the wisdom of a single commander. At a midday meeting in Admiral Stark's office in the Navy Building, he won over the admirals; first King assented, then one by one the ranking officers of the fleet agreed.

Marshall now confronted the British chiefs with a unified front of his own. On the afternoon of the 27th, he pressed the issue, against the opposition of Britain's senior service; the Royal Navy, bearers of Drake's and Nelson's tradition, took no orders from soldiers. Marshall persevered, pointing out that the Japanese in the Pacific had a unified command; they would need a similar structure to match the Japanese. Nothing was worse than what they had.

The British resistance turned suddenly to criticism of the command concept as too restrictive. Marshall conceded he had sought a palatable compromise; they could strengthen the supreme commander's authority. Stark chimed in, urging that they immediately accept the principle, and make necessary revisions later. Agreement came quickly then.

The session broke up in a mood of elation. One of the British naval planners rushed to the door to shake hands with Marshall, then put his arm around the surprised chief of staff. Dill followed, throwing his arm around Marshall's shoulder. However unlikely the picture, it was for the usually standoffish Marshall a moment of supreme accomplishment, enough to make him recall with pride the comradeship years later.

Still Marshall needed Churchill's assent. Hopkins stepped in to arrange a meeting on the morning of December 28. The pajama-clad Churchill received Marshall while still in bed, working at the red leather box of dispatches that had come in during the night.

Marshall paced back and forth in the big bedroom, arguing for the principle of a unified command. Churchill scowled, took notes, and gruffly brushed aside the chief of staff's arguments. What would an army officer such as Wavell know about naval warfare, he asked?

"What the devil does a naval officer know about handling a tank," Marshall shot back. That was not the issue. The issue was unified command, of one man coordinating the land, sea, and air effort in his theater. "I told him," the chief of staff recalled, "I was not interested in Drake and Frobisher, but I was interested in having a united front against Japan, an enemy which was fighting furiously. I said if we didn't do something right away we were finished in the war."

Churchill interrupted their discussion to take one of his twice-daily baths, emerging from the bathroom some minutes later swathed in a towel, still scowling, still resisting, warning Marshall he "would have to take the worst with the best."

Yet Marshall had prevailed. Churchill admired what he described as the "broadmindedness" of the plan. He recognized too that President Roosevelt, from whom he would need concessions in the future, favored the Marshall concept. That evening he told his grim-faced military chiefs he was accepting the plan. Wavell would command ABDA with an American as his deputy, taking his general orders from a combined group of military chiefs. Those chiefs, in turn, would be responsible to the president and prime minister.

The concept of a unified command was but one of the battles Marshall won at ARCADIA. Usually courteous, always diplomatic, Marshall would not hesitate to disagree with the president, the prime minister, or the British military delegation whenever he felt strongly enough about an issue. When Harry Hopkins and Max Beaverbrook, the British minister of production, settled on a plan to install a civilian board to allocate war production, Marshall exploded. Such a board would give an effective veto power to military plans already approved by president and prime minister simply by favoring one plan over another in allocating materials. Allocation was a military matter, to be left with the chiefs of staff; if it were not, he told the president, he would not "accept the responsibilities of his office."

A man interested in power might have argued with Marshall. Hopkins reversed himself, then persuaded the president that Marshall was correct in his stand. The three of them in turn worked on Churchill, Beaverbrook, and the British staff officers. One by one they fell into line, agreeing to try Marshall's alternative for a month. Marshall's alternative would stay in place for the entire war.

On the second floor of the White House, they had focused their attention on the creation of a unified field command—and the naming of Wavell. In fact, the unified staff command they set up in Washington was to be equally important, and for the Americans even more revolutionary.

The British already had a supreme staff made up of the chiefs of the three services. They proposed detailing to Washington for the course of the war representatives of each of those commanders. Those senior officers would sit with the American chiefs on a Combined Chiefs of Staff, directing the strategic course of the war.

The Americans, however, had no formal organization equivalent to the Imperial General Staff. That situation Marshall later moved to address by suggesting to the president that Hap Arnold simply be included in a statement by the president naming his military advisers. Arnold thereby became a member of the American-British Combined Chiefs of Staff so that each nation had military, naval, and air corps representation.

Subordinate in rank and command to Marshall, Arnold would also serve as an equal on the American Joint Chiefs of Staff; the practical result was the elevation of Arnold at Marshall's behest to co-equal status with Marshall, and de facto recognition of the Air Corps as a separate branch of service.

The secret conferences during this first week of ARCADIA organized the Anglo-American war effort. Roosevelt meanwhile planned to announce the wartime alliance of an even larger group of "associated powers," including the Soviet Union.

The international alliance meant much to him, less to Churchill. Roosevelt had tinkered with the draft of the declaration of unity through the week while the State Department lined up concurrences from the European governments in exile and those Latin republics that had declared war. Concerned the officially atheistic Soviet Union might balk, the president himself secured approval from the Russian ambassador for inclusion among the war aims a freedom of religion clause inadvertently omitted from the Atlantic Charter. On New Year's Day, Roosevelt gave the draft a last gloss, substituting for "Associated Powers" the words "United Nations."

It had been a long week. The newly named United Nations had pledged unity, in word if not in deed. Great Britain and the United States had agreed on a general strategy. By the beginning of the New Year, with Marshall established as the dominant member of the Combined Chiefs of Staff, they were deep into planning a global war.

The question, as Churchill put it later, was not *whether* to implement the Atlantic-first strategy, but *how* to do so. The American concept of war was based on coming to grips with the enemy army and destroying its capacity to make war. It was a concept based on overwhelming force, of crushing opposition. The British, in keeping with their smaller population and sprawling colonial interests, favored what the Imperial General Staff thought of as a more supple or flexible strategy, one that bled the enemy to death, or so weakened it that the outcome of the final battle was a foregone conclusion.

The British peripheral strategy, American planners objected, was "motivated more largely by political than by sound strategic purposes. It seems to me persuasive rather than rational," as General Embick told the chief of staff. Joseph Stilwell, the man Marshall had tapped to lead the first American assault overseas, complained "the Limeys" had "sold Roosevelt a bill of goods"; Churchill and all the staff officers with their impressive leather dispatch boxes had the president's ear, "while we have the hind tit," Stilwell complained to his diary. Confronted with a farrago of Churchill's strategic options, the War Plans Division took it as its mission to prevent "the ineffectual bleeding away of Army strength in pursuit of British-sponsored projects."

Marshall was more trusting of the British. In his mind there was "too much anti-British feeling on our side; more than we should have had. Our people were always ready to find Albion perfidious," he said later.

To the American military staff, no Churchillian plan forwarded to Washington seemed more self-serving than GYMNAST, a combined British-American invasion of French North Africa. A preemptive strike, designed to deny that area to the Germans, GYMNAST had the added advantage in Roosevelt's eyes of putting American troops into battle quickly. Stilwell, rated the best of the Army's corps commanders, found himself ordered to Washington where he was informed he was to command an immediate landing on the coast of French West Africa. Taking out the Vichy French submarine base at Dakar, he was told on the morning of December 24, would remove the threat of an Axis invasion of South America.

That afternoon, an irritated Stilwell learned, Dakar was out. Marshall had concluded an invasion there ran too many risks. No one knew just how the French would react, whether the colonial troops would rally to the Allied cause or would remain loyal to Vichy and its German patrons. If the acutely political French Army sided with Vichy, the Americans would lack the strength to force a landing.

Stilwell could only throw up his hands. "Nobody knows where I am going."

Or if he would go anywhere at all. The shortage of shipping was critical. They could put ashore a single Marine division of 11,000 men by March 3, but reinforcements would arrive only after the ships made a round-trip voyage of forty-five days.

So short of vessels, they could not gamble the Dakar enterprise on the mood of Vichy troops or their mercurial commanding officers, Marshall argued. "Failure in this first venture would have an extremely adverse effect on the morale of the American people."

Roosevelt agreed, but he also "considered it very important to morale to give the people of this country a feeling that they are in the war, to give the Germans the reverse effect, to have American troops somewhere in active fighting across the Atlantic."

One felt the need to go slow, the other to go fast. Events in the Pacific would settle their disagreement.

C H A P T E R

XVI

The Pacific Deeps

It took all of Marshall's studied willpower to keep his eye fixed firmly on Europe in those first weeks of the new year. Even as they laid plans for future attacks on the continent, the situation in the Far East was rapidly disintegrating. MacArthur had declared Manila an undefended open city and retreated to Bataan peninsula and the fortified island of Corregidor commanding Manila Bay. Japanese troops had cracked the British defense line in Malaya. Another Japanese invasion force had landed at Brunei Bay in Borneo, yet another in the Dutch East Indies. The defense lines hastily drawn on maps bowed under assault, then gave way. Nothing the Americans and British did in those first weeks of war seemed adequate to stop the surprisingly effective Japanese forces.

The year would be "the darkest, most humiliating and bloodiest in our history," Marshall recalled through his wife's reminiscences. He took to twilight walks with Katherine, laying out the problems he confronted daily in the Munitions Building. "I was listening to a man steeling himself to carry a burden so tremendous in magnitude and so diverse in its demands that it was difficult to comprehend how one man could carry it alone," Mrs. Marshall later wrote. She said little on these walks through darkened Arlington back to Quarters No. 1. "I had the feeling he was really talking to himself. It was as though he lived outside of himself and George Marshall was someone he was constantly appraising, advising and training to meet a situation."

The dispassionate assessment was all part of the chief of staff's effort to manage a global war beyond any individual's management. "I cannot afford the luxury of sentiment, mine must be cold logic. Sentiment is for others," he explained to her. "I cannot allow myself to get angry, that would be fatal—it is too exhausting. My brain must be kept clear. I cannot afford to appear tired. . . ."

To his staff, to the press, to the public, Marshall appeared decisive.

Dwight Eisenhower described his chief in those grim months as firm, refusing to consider failure, with that resolution alone instilling the War Department with energy and confidence.

Such self-control took its toll, however flinty or unfeeling he seemed to subordinates. "I get so tired of saying 'No,' it takes it out of me, I am really thankful when I can say 'Yes,' he told his wife. Attempting to reorganize the War Department in that dark winter, Marshall acknowledged, "It is not easy to tell men where they have failed. . . . My days seem to be filled with situations and problems where I must do the difficult, the hard thing."

Confronting a global war, Marshall pressed his effort to reorganize the clanking machinery of the War Department. His moves were drastic, rammed through by Joseph McNarney, another of the newly minted generals Marshall had raised from anonymity. McNarney was both blunt-spoken and tough-minded. The combination of traits achieved results, but hardly endeared him to often senior men who found their authority trimmed or eliminated entirely by the chief of staff's henchman. Some of those whom McNarney moved aside in the first reorganization of the War Department since 1903 blamed Marshall for insensitivity; others sadly, dutifully, accepted what they could not themselves avert.

Marshall's plan was designed to create "some kind of organization that would give the chief of staff time to devote to strategic policy and the strategic aspects and direction of the war." Too many people reported to him; too many people had to approve too many documents before the War Department lumbered into action.

The major change in Washington was to eliminate the fiefdoms of the chiefs of infantry, cavalry, field artillery, and coast artillery. Each of those major generals jealously guarded his branch of service and his personal prerogatives. Intent on creating an army rather than a collection of separate services, Marshall was slicing away satrapies of power.

McNarney's "Soviet Committee," as the bitter chiefs of service called it, was "not a voting committee, not a debating society," he announced summarily. Its task was to draft the necessary directives to get the reorganization accomplished.

That reorganization stressed efficiency, and with it, increased authority to the men immediately below Marshall. Once, some sixty officers had access to the chief of staff; the new plan cut that to just six—though Marshall frequently reached into the lower ranks to hear out the proposals of younger men with good ideas.

The new Army comprised three commands: the army Ground Forces, commanded by Marshall's longtime friend from the first war, Lesley McNair; the Services of Supply under Brehon Somervell; and Hap Arnold's Army Air Forces. Marshall kept as his command post only a reorganized War Plans Division, renamed the Operations Division.

In simple terms, McNair was to have responsibility for molding the ground troops into a fighting army. Arnold had the same authority for the air. Somervell, who was to become one of the most influential men in Washington if not in the country during the next four years, had responsibility for all procurement, supply, and support services, including recreation and morale, military justice, even mail delivery. Somervell, like McNarney a hard taskmaster, was also a cunning empire builder; still Marshall defended him as "one of the most efficient officers I have ever seen. And he got things done in Calcutta as fast as he did in the meadows there around the Pentagon."

Even as he set afoot this massive reorganization, Marshall was pondering yet another shift in the command organization. Marshall's suggestion that the Joint Chiefs of Staff be reorganized would be one of his more enduring accomplishments.

Sometime late in February 1942, Marshall realized that Admiral King had won the intramural scramble for power within the Navy Department. Betty Stark was going to yield the title of chief of naval operations, or have it taken from him. If Stark were transferred to London as naval liaison, as word around the Navy Building had it, the Joint Chiefs of Staff would be left with two army members, Marshall and Arnold, and just one navy member. Ever suspicious of the Army, opposed to the concept of unified command, King would be all the more distrustful.

Marshall proposed that the president name retired Admiral William D. Leahy, a former chief of naval operations, to be the president's personal chief of staff. Bearing that title, Leahy would also serve as the chairman of the Joint Chiefs, and give each of the two services two votes on the panel.

Leahy's selection was deliberate. A navy man it had to be, not only to equalize the representation, but to quiet King's fears of army domination. Leahy was, by reputation, "entirely impersonal and a man of good judgment," Marshall explained later. A bit of checking convinced him that Leahy would be a fair chairman. More than that he could not ask.

Marshall was gambling this retired admiral could or would put aside his lifetime career in the Navy and his friendship with the president. The grandson of Irish immigrants, Leahy had graduated from Annapolis in 1897. He had served as an engineering cadet on the battleship *Oregon* when she made a celebrated dash from Bremerton, Washington, around Cape Horn in time to take part in the battle that destroyed the Spanish Atlantic Fleet off Cuba. By the first world war he had risen to command of a troop transport, then began an alternation between staff and fleet commands. Up the ranks he climbed, finally spending two and a half years as chief of naval operations before his retirement in July 1939.

Leahy then served two terms as governor of Puerto Rico, acquitting himself so well that the president tapped him to be ambassador to France. Leahy's main task was to do what he could to curb Marshal Pétain's collaboration with Hitler. It was a futile assignment. The Vichy government cowered in its corner of Metropolitan France.

By advocating Leahy for the job of presidential chief of staff, Marshall was once more creatively bending the rules to suit his needs. The Joint Chiefs, created without legislative authority, were to have an equally extralegal chairman. Moreover, that chairman would actually hold down a job, chief of staff to the president of the United States, that did not exist.

President Roosevelt was evasive. Leahy was well placed in Vichy France, doing good service at that peephole into the Axis world. Furthermore, having a chief of staff in the White House would infringe on Roosevelt's own authority as commander-in-chief.

"But you are chief of staff," Roosevelt protested.

"Mr. President, I am only chief of staff of the army and, in a sense, of the army Air. There is no chief of staff of the military services."

"Well, I am the chief of staff," Roosevelt replied. "I'm the commander-in-chief."

That job was too great for one man, Marshall insisted. It was a "superman job and I didn't think that even the exaggeration of the powers of Superman would quite go far enough for this," Marshall explained later.

Frankly displeased with Marshall's idea, Roosevelt delayed acting on it for five months. Only with Marshall's repeated urgings did the president finally name Leahy as his personal chief of staff, then would use him far more than Marshall had ever intended on political matters. Still, Leahy did assume the duties of chairman of the Joint Chiefs, a post Stimson believed Marshall himself was best suited for, but a post Marshall knew that King would not want him to hold.

However slow the reorganization of the War Department and the formation of the Joint Chiefs of Staff, the Japanese would not permit them such stately mobilization in the Far East.

"Time—even days—is the pressing factor," Marshall warned his staff in early January. The Japanese tide rolled southward while the United States sought to organize itself for war. There were too few capable men and too many Hugh Drums.

Marshall's superior during the first war and his major rival for the chief of staff position two and a half years before, Hugh Drum was the ranking three-star general in the Army. Nothing since had diminished his excellent opinion of himself. As commander of the First Army with headquarters on Governor's Island, New York, Drum also impressed reporters and politicians alike with his military bearing.

Drum had come down to Washington at White House invitation, bringing a large staff with him, ready to be the John Pershing of World War II and lead the United States' first overseas expeditionary force.

The president's proposal that he go to China was something less than that, even if he were to carry the grand title of chief of staff to Generalissimo Chiang Kai-shek.

Fractious China appeared a backwater of the war; reputations would be broken there, not made. Politics, not strategy, dominated all discussions of China. The president wanted to prop up Chiang as a world leader, thereby adding weight to the newly signed United Nations Declaration. Scornful of China's military potential, the British were willing to accede to Roosevelt's plan only so long as support for Chiang was confined to the moral. The president wound a crooked way, making loans available, sending such aid as could be diverted from Great Britain and Russia, encouraging the organization of the volunteer Flying Tigers air group, and prodding the reluctant Chiang to use his troops against the Japanese.

Drum was even less enthusiastic after a series of briefings in the Munitions Building. Drum proposed instead he take command of a major build-up of ground and air units through the entire Southeast Asian area.

Marshall and Drum met alone on January 8. Both men were edgy. Marshall brusquely dismissed Drum's counterplan; there would be no build-up in the area, he said, if only because he doubted the British would agree to it.

Struggling to salvage his plan or his pride, Drum suggested his proposal might serve as a basis for a future build-up. Marshall coldly brushed that aside as well. The British would never agree to anything dealing with China or India, he snapped.

Drum grew angry. The China mission was limited, he insisted, and, worse, posed "certain inconsistencies and indignities relative to command arrangements." They had to increase the American presence in China and give greater authority to the head of the mission, he argued.

Marshall lost control. Dammit, they were at war. He expected his officers to put aside their personal ambitions, he shouted at the red-faced Drum. China, however confused the situation, however fraught with political pitfalls, however impossible a challenge, was a job that needed the doing.

Drum pressed his plan, but he had lost the argument. And the posting.

Suddenly cold once more, his temper in check, Marshall announced he would recommend against Drum's appointment.

Drum would twice appeal over Marshall's head to Stimson. Given his experience, Drum insisted in a letter to the secretary, he "would be more valuable to the country . . . with a mission involving larger responsibilities than those contemplated by the memorandum of the General Staff." Drum frankly feared he "would be lost by being involved in the heart of China in a minor effort of little decisive consequence." Put off by Drum's personal ambition, the secretary of war began casting about for someone else. His search lasted only a few hours.

Marshall had not originally intended to send Joseph Stilwell to China; the chief of staff had called Stilwell to Washington to plan GYMNAST, expecting he would then lead that invasion of North Africa. But the more Stilwell worked on the "crazy scheme," the less likely it appeared they would be able to transport enough troops to assure its success. Well before the end of the ARCADIA conference, the plan was marked down as too risky, something for the future. Stilwell himself had no faith in its success or its purpose. "The means are meager, the transport uncertain, the consequences serious. A few lucky hits will jeopardize the whole affair."

Stilwell knew that Stimson and Marshall had ticketed Drum for China. Aware of the difficulties of the China command as few army men were, with no taste for court politics, Stilwell wanted no part of it. "Me? No, thank you," he wrote in his frequently salty diary. "They remember me as a small-fry colonel that they kicked around. They saw me on foot in the mud, consorting with coolies, riding soldier trains."

As military attaché and as a battalion commander with the 15th Infantry in Tientsin, Stilwell had served ten years in China. He and his wife Winifred fondly considered that country a second home. He spoke Mandarin, and swore capably in enough dialects to make himself understood in much of China. Most of all, he had developed a deep respect, even an affection, for the long-suffering, long-enduring Chinese peasant. Neither affection nor respect, however, extended to the president of China, Chiang Kai-shek, "Peanut" to Stilwell's diary, and "an ignorant, illiterate, superstitious, peasant son of a bitch" to reporter Teddy White.

With Drum erased, no one else qualified for the Chinese command other than Stilwell, who was then busily drafting memos advising against undertaking his own GYMNAST plan. Once a tactical instructor under Marshall at the Infantry School, Stilwell was ideal for the task of transforming the warlords' mercenary bands into a modern army. "Joe, you have twenty-four hours to think up a better candidate. Otherwise it's you," Marshall warned him. Stilwell could recommend no one.

A conversation on January 13 with Stimson in the Secretary's home overlooking Rock Creek Park clinched Stilwell's assignment. Stimson was impressed with Stilwell's straightforward attitude and his knowledge of China. What did Stilwell think of the China assignment, Stimson asked.

Stilwell, who saw his command of the first American combat force slipping away, swallowed hard. "I'd go where I was sent," he replied.

Even to China, where he would simultaneously hold down three jobs as chief of staff to Chiang, as commanding officer of the few American forces in China, and as Lend-Lease administrator. The China post required a man with enormous tact, a taste for diplomacy, and great patience. Stilwell, who may well have been the best combat commander in the United States Army, had none of these skills. Not for nothing was he known as "Vinegar Joe."

Stilwell arrived in Chungking on March 6, 1942, with China under siege. The Fifteenth Japanese Army had sliced across Burma, capturing the port city of Rangoon. The Japanese had then swung northward through the tropical rain forests of three river valleys, driving British and colonial troops before them. Each day's fighting brought them closer to the China-Burma border and the vital railhead at Lashio, where the torturous, twisting Burma Road supplying China began.

Five days after his arrival, Stilwell left Chungking, hoping to set up blocking positions in the Burmese jungle with a hodgepodge of British, Burmese, Indian, and Chinese troops. Stilwell ranged the front, mustering what resistance he could, but also watching his Chinese divisions melt away before they suffered casualties. Only later would he discover that Chiang himself had ordered his commanders to avoid losses, to retreat, despite Stilwell's orders.

The May monsoon saved what was left of the retreating Allied forces. Stilwell himself led to the safety of India a group of 114 men. Stilwell, lank before he ever left the United States, trekked into India twenty pounds lighter, yellowed with jaundice, "looking like the wrath of God and cursing like a fallen angel."

Flown to Delhi and the plush Imperial Hotel, Stilwell consented to hold a press conference. For ninety minutes he bluntly discussed the Burmese campaign, ticking off the reasons for the debacle. He closed the conference with a simple, truthful statement that more than anything else sobered the American people, and steeled them for what was to come.

"I claim we took a hell of a beating," Stilwell told the reporters. "We got run out of Burma and it is humiliating as hell. I think we ought to find out what caused it, go back, and retake it."

Stilwell's unflinching assessment shattered American complacency, the arrogance of one-American-is-worth-ten-Japs, and the pervasive reluctance to make material sacrifices. The nation finally was going to war.

As humiliating a defeat as Burma was, from the first days of the war nothing occupied the War Department more than the crumbling situation in the Philippines. Marshall, Stimson, the host of other men who had served in the islands and considered the Filipinos American wards, wanted to help, yet had no way of pushing reinforcements through to the islands without navy cooperation. "Ships! Ships! All we need is ships!" the frustrated Eisenhower complained to his diary on January 12, 1942.

Competing political goals complicated the problem for army planners. They had neither enough men or equipment to meet all their needs. Against the Philippines they had to balance both the build-up of forces in Great Britain and GYMNAST—and the implicit pledge to the British those plans represented. Still, an invasion of Hitler's Europe was far off; the crisis in the Philippines was immediate. Then they had to weigh the contribution any reinforcements would be able to make to MacArthur's beleaguered forces. The additional troops and material they could scrape together might prolong the fight, if they could be delivered to the islands, but would not be enough to turn back the Japanese tide. Those troops would be sacrificed in a lost cause.

Geopolitical reality made no dent in the Philippines, where Mac-Arthur wavered between tactical brilliance and vainglory. The Philippine commander, returned to the rank of four-star general by President Roosevelt on December 19, managed to withdraw 80,000 American and Filipino troops from a Japanese pincers—but failed to bring along sufficient food. Now dug in on the peninsula of Bataan dangling into Manila Bay, his troops on half-rations, MacArthur from his Corregidor headquarters radioed repeated pleas for relief.

Marshall dispatched what supplies he could even as the Japanese tightened their ring around the archipelago. Two further shiploads of pursuit planes and flights of bombers were held up in Australia, flight officers unwilling to risk their destruction before they even reached MacArthur. Admiral Stark refused Marshall's request to use an aircraft carrier to ferry the planes to the Philippines; Stark and King needed their carriers around which to reorganize the stricken Pacific Fleet.

By mid-January, Marshall was grasping at straws. He arranged to send the pugnacious former Secretary of War Patrick J. Hurley to Australia with orders and cash enough to ram supplies through to the islands. At Marshall's orders, Hurley offered merchant captains handsome fees to risk their vessels and their lives while running the Japanese blockade. Hurley found six, three of whom weaved a course to Mindanao and unloaded 10,000 tons of food, ammunition, and medical supplies. A relay of submarines also brought food to the wasting defenders of Bataan, but too little and much too late. What scant aid they delivered mocked their very effort; Hurley, whose admiration for MacArthur bordered on idolatry, could do nothing to aid his friend. "We were out-shipped, out-planed, out-manned and out-gunned by the Japanese."

From Corregidor, "the Rock" that dominated Manila Bay, MacArthur issued proclamations promising help was on the way. The ragtag Filipino and American troops dug in on Bataan waited for reinforcements that would never come, reduced to brave desperation. On half-rations, using old ammunition that often misfired, they held a defense line across the peninsula for three weeks before weary Japanese troops broke through. On January 23, MacArthur reported to Marshall he intended to retreat to his second line when "all maneuvering possibilities will cease. I intend to fight it out to complete destruction." In case of his death, he

The Marshall home in Uniontown, Pennsylvania. *George C. Marshall Research Foundation.*

George C. Marshall, third from left in the front row, with Virginia Military Institute Cadet Staff, 1901. *George C. Marshall Research Foundation.*

Wedding party at Pendleton—Coles House, Lexington, Virginia, February 11, 1902. Left to right: Marie Marshall, Elizabeth Carter Coles, George C. Marshall, Stuart Marshall, Mr. and Mrs. George C. Marshall, Sr., and Mrs. Walter Coles (Elizabeth Pendleton Coles). *George C. Marshall Research Foundation.*

Second Lieutenant George C. Marshall in dress blues before graduation from Staff College, Fort Leavenworth, Kansas, 1908. *George C. Marshall Research Foundation.*

General Pershing and staff at the State, War, and Navy Building, Washington, D.C., 1919. Left to right: Colonel Aristides Moreno, Lieutenant Colonel Albert S. Kuegle, Major General Fox Conner, Colonel George C. Marshall, General John J. Pershing, Colonel John Quekemeyer, Major General Andre Brewster, and Major Robert C. Davis. *George C. Marshall Research Foundation.*

Colonel George C. Marshall, aide to General John J. Pershing, Chaumont, France, 1919. *George C. Marshall Research Foundation.*

Marshall and instructors at the Fort Benning Infantry School, Georgia, ca. 1930. First row (left to right): M. C. Stayer, J. W. Stilwell, George C. Marshall, W. F. Freehoff, and E. F. Harding. *George C. Marshall Research Foundation.*

George and Katherine Marshall during a fishing trip along the Metolius River, Oregon, 1938. *George C. Marshall Research Foundation.*

Photograph of General Marshall taken in the summer of 1938 when he was assistant chief of staff. After he became chief of staff, in September 1939, three more stars were added to the negative and the photograph was continued in use. *U.S. Army Signal Corps.*

Katherine Tupper Marshall, 1939. *George C. Marshall Research Foundation.*

Marshall and his stepchildren picnicking at Fire Island, Summer
1939. Left to right: Allen, Molly, and Clifton Brown. *George C.
Marshall Research Foundation.*

Marshall on an early morning ride with his dog, Fleet.
Fort Myer, Virginia, 1941.
*George C. Marshall Research Founda-
tion.*

Roosevelt and Churchill, with Marshall and Admirals King and Stark, at Placentia Bay, August 1941. *George C. Marshall Research Foundation.*

Marshall arriving to testify before the Joint Committee on the Investigation of the Pearl Harbor Attack, December 1945. *George C. Marshall Research Foundation.*

Salisbury Plain, England, April 1942. Left to right: Sir Bernard Paget, General, later Field Marshal, Bernard Montgomery, General Robert McClure, Marshall, unidentified, and Prime Minister Winston Churchill. *George C. Marshall Research Foundation.*

Field Marshal Sir John Dill and George C. Marshall at Lee Mansion, Arlington, Virginia, April 28, 1942. *Abbie Rowe—Courtesy National Park Service.*

Marshall and Eisenhower hold an informal press conference at Allied Headquarters, Algeria, North Africa, June 3, 1943. *George C. Marshall Research Foundation.*

Marshall visits General Douglas MacArthur at MacArthur's headquarters, Goodenough Island, off the northern coast of Papua, New Guinea, 1943. *George C.
Marshall Research Foundation.*

Left to right: Admiral Ernest J. King, Admiral William Leahy, President Franklin D. Roosevelt, General George C. Marshall, and Major General L. S. Kuter in conference aboard a warship. Malta Conference, February 2, 1945. *Signal Corps, Frank McCarthy.*

Marshall, Lieutenant General Mark J. Clark, and Lieutenant General Lucian K. Truscott, Jr., tour the Italian front, February 14, 1945. *George C. Marshall Research Foundation.*

A final discussion between Mao Tse-tung and Marshall prior to his departure from China in 1946. *George C. Marshall Research Foundation.*

Secretary of Defense George C. Marshall and Secretary of State Dean Acheson converse at table during an informal luncheon in the Pentagon Building, October 12, 1950. *George C. Marshall Research Foundation.*

Washington, D.C. Prime Minister Clement Attlee (seated right) of Great Britain conferring with President Harry S. Truman (seated left) in the president's office at the White House, with Dean Acheson and Marshall standing behind them. December 6, 1950. *George C. Marshall Research Foundation.*

Marshall on tour of front-line command posts in Korea. Seated behind him are Major General Matthew B. Ridgway and Lieutenant General James H. Van Fleet. June 8, 1951. *George C. Marshall Research Foundation.*

advised Washington, his chief of staff, Richard Sutherland, was to succeed him.

MacArthur's "most flamboyant radio" irritated the Philippine commander's former aide, Dwight Eisenhower. MacArthur was in many ways "as big a baby as ever. But we've got to keep him fighting," he wrote in his diary.

To Eisenhower's chagrin, the retreat on Bataan became MacArthur's apotheosis. "The public has built itself a hero out of its own imagination," Eisenhower confided to the privacy of his diary. With little good news to report, the press had fastened on MacArthur as the "Lion of Luzon," bravely, cannily fighting off superior hordes of Japanese invaders. Republican Party publicists, who saw the general as the GOP's presidential nominee in 1944, happily fed the myth. In Congress, conservatives of both parties took the floor to demand MacArthur's recall and promotion to generalissimo in command of both Army and Navy. The president did not intend to go that far, but he did cooperate with the War Department in using MacArthur and the legend of Bataan to perk up civilian morale. An unremitting diet of defeats, setbacks, and losses had sapped public support for the war, provoking a defensive apathy or a callous indifference.

A young radio reporter returning to the United States early in 1942 was angered by the air of unreality he sensed about him in New York. Despite rationing and shortages, "there was money to burn, and it was burned in a bright, gay flame," Eric Severeid recalled. The black market came to America; rationed gasoline and tires were available to those with cash. Men's pants lost their cuffs, and suits their vests, yet buyers willingly paid three times the prewar price. The nation learned a new word, "ten percenters," the fixers who introduced buyer and seller. There were plenty of both. The government would place $100 billion in military orders during the first six months of the year.

Disdainful of a Congress that "alternately dozed and shouted," of FBI agents sniffing out "subversives," of banner headlines trumpeting daily victories, Severeid still found "great men around who required neither profit nor adulation to hold them to their duty." First in his mind there was the president, alternately irritating, disappointing, and captivating, "a man who would surely stand near Washington and Lincoln." After Roosevelt there was Marshall, "a hulking, homely man of towering intellect, the memory of an unnatural genius, and the integrity of a Christian saint. The atmosphere of controlled power he exuded made one feel oneself a physical weakling, and his selfless devotion to duty [was] beyond all influences of public pressure or personal friendship. . . ."

Severeid's opinion was somewhat more lofty than Marshall wanted or deserved. The chief of staff was keenly aware of public opinion and at times deliberately sought to mold it. At Marshall's instigation, President

Roosevelt approved the award of a Medal of Honor to MacArthur; Marshall personally wrote the citation recognizing MacArthur's "heroic conduct of defensive and offensive operations on the Bataan Peninsula." To Stimson, the chief of staff explained that awarding the medal "will meet with popular approval, both within and without the armed forces, and will have a constructive morale value."

MacArthur himself happily fed the public appetite for news of its hero, issuing what Stimson sourly called "magniloquent communiques" that spoke of "MacArthur's troops" or "MacArthur's flank." Meanwhile MacArthur fired off repeated requests for reinforcements to the War Department, demanding that the longstanding war plans be revised, that the Europe-first strategy be abandoned, even suggesting that the Soviet Union be asked to open a second Pacific front. MacArthur's "flood of communications" suggested to Eisenhower "a refusal . . . to look facts in the face, an old trait of his." MacArthur was "jittery," Eisenhower concluded. The former chief of staff was also imperious, informing Marshall he expected his radiograms to be shown to the president, quite as if he were head of a separate state. Aware that any theater commander considered his theater to be both the most important and the least supported, Marshall held his temper. The president saw each of MacArthur's ever more demanding pleas for relief.

The worse the plight of the Philippines, the more time and emotional energy Washington poured into the futile campaign. The islands were already written off strategically—as War Plan Orange had long since decided. Stimson, Marshall, and Eisenhower, Philippine veterans all, might wish it to be otherwise; they might sometimes waver, but nothing now would change that reality; they could only put on it the best face possible.

Events of these dark months of early 1942 were to change Marshall's opinion of FDR. Since July 1, 1939, Marshall had watched as Roosevelt slipped hard decisions, waiting for public opinion to catch up with events. Now it fell to the president to make the hardest decision, to consign "a brave garrison to a fight to the finish," as Stimson put it. Roosevelt had to order that they fight on in the Philippines, to bargain their lives for the vaguest concept of national honor, an honor that would figure in a far-off, postwar settlement.

The United States had promised the Philippines their independence, and "so long as the flag of the United States flies on Filipino soil as a pledge of our duty to your people, it will be defended by our own men to the death," the president stated in a message to the Philippine president, Manuel Quezon. The Filipino units could lay down their arms, but MacArthur's troops would fight on until further resistance was useless.

Roosevelt had made his decision as a commander-in-chief "without flinching." Marshall was impressed. "I immediately discarded everything in my mind I had held to his discredit," Marshall later told his biographer. "Roosevelt said we won't neutralize. I decided he was a great man."

The situation in the Far East continued to crumble. On February 15, in a move that signaled the end of Britain's storied Empire east of Suez, Lieutenant General Arthur Percival surrendered Singapore "the impregnable." The capitulation of the fortress that stood as a symbol of British power from India to Australia marked "the greatest disaster to British arms which our history records," Churchill keened.

That night the president and Harry Hopkins summarily revised American military priorities. First, the United States was to take primary responsibility for supplying Australia and New Zealand, and reinforcing the Netherland East Indies. Men and materiel were to be aboard ship before March 31, and "supporting supplies of men and material to compensate for attrition rate to follow regularly," Hopkins noted in a memorandum of the meeting. The memorandum's list of twelve primary and three secondary priorities barely acknowledged Europe and the planned build-up of forces in Great Britain for an invasion of the continent. To shore up the sagging ABDA command, Roosevelt was summarily suspending all their war plans. The War Department was left only with gallows humor. Transferring to the command of a division, Leonard Gerow, the head of the War Plans Division, told his successor, Dwight Eisenhower, "Well, I got Pearl Harbor on the book; lost the Philippine Islands, Singapore, Sumatra and all the NEI north of the barrier. Let's see what you can do."

The fall of Singapore was to begin one of the worst weeks of the war for the Allies, presidential adviser Robert Sherwood later wrote. The Japanese invaded Bali, then Portuguese Timor at the eastern tip of the East Indies. On February 19, Japanese carrier planes swooped down on the port of Darwin in Australia, sinking more than a dozen ships, destroying the harbor and the accumulated supplies, and ending any hope of supplying besieged Java. Meanwhile Allied troops were withdrawing in Burma and seeking to escape from Sumatra.

By February 25, the first of George Marshall's unified commands was a shambles. The Combined Chiefs of Staff in Washington agreed to put the misbegotten ABDA command out of its misery.

The western portion of that command was to be given over to the Lion of Luzon, Douglas A. MacArthur. Though MacArthur had talked of going to his death on Corregidor—his wife and son perishing too in sutteelike immolation—neither the president, Stimson, nor Marshall intended to let that happen. MacArthur's capture or death on the Rock would be a psychological victory of major proportions for the Japanese. At the same time, it would provoke criticism of the nation's military leadership among MacArthur's supporters on the Hill. Despite Dwight Eisenhower's conviction that Marshall was reacting to public opinion rather than military necessity, MacArthur, his family, and the civilian leaders of the Philippines had to be withdrawn.

On the advice of one of MacArthur's World War I colleagues and of Patrick Hurley in Australia, Marshall drafted a direct presidential order transferring MacArthur to Australia. As part of a hasty reorganization of global responsibilities, MacArthur was to assume command of a newly created Southwest Pacific theater carved from the western portion of shattered ABDA.

MacArthur's transfer to Melbourne was as much a political as a military move. Having lost faith with Great Britain's war leadership, Australian Prime Minister John Curtin had cabled Washington asking that MacArthur take command of the defense of Australia. Only Roosevelt's agreement to assign MacArthur and his pledge to send immediate reinforcements had kept Curtin from withdrawing his Diggers from the British Eighth Army in North Africa.

With an airy wave of his cigarette holder, the junior member of the alliance was assuming practical leadership of the Allied war effort.

On March 7, President Roosevelt cabled Prime Minister Churchill a proposed redivision of operational responsibilities. The United States, Roosevelt suggested, would take over all operational responsibilities in the Pacific area. The supreme commander in the Pacific would be an American—MacArthur, in fact—with local Australian, New Zealand, and Dutch commanders reporting to him.

"The middle area" would stretch halfway around the world, from British Malaysia across the Indian Ocean, through the Middle East, and across the length and breadth of the Mediterranean. Great Britain was to have responsibility for all operational matters in this vast theater.

The third area was to include both an operating theater, the Atlantic Ocean, and a concept, "definite plans for an establishment of a new front on the European continent." Both nations would share responsibility for this theater.

The president's plan had the advantage of more closely conforming to geopolitical realities, in effect creating spheres of influence. The Pacific was to be an American pond, the "middle area" a British dominion. They would share influence in Europe where both had substantial economic interests.

Roosevelt's proposal dealt Marshall two severe setbacks: there would be no unity of command in the Atlantic area; and any emphasis on the Pacific inevitably would come at the expense of the Europe-first strategy, at least temporarily. The chief of staff could only swallow his anger as the carefully husbanded combat troops were scattered by presidential directive over the Pacific. Of the 132,000 American troops shipped overseas in the first months of the year, all but the 20,000 sent to garrison Iceland and Ireland were assigned to the Pacific.

In ordering troops to the Pacific, Roosevelt seemed too solicitous of navy needs. Eisenhower groused in his diary, "The navy wants to take all the islands in the Pacific, have them held by army troops, to become bases for army pursuit and bombers. Then the navy will have a safe place to sail its vessels. But they will not go farther forward than our air can assure superiority. The amount of air required for this slow, laborious and indecisive type of warfare is going to be something that will keep us from going to Russia's aid in time." (The Navy was no more complimentary of army planning. King complained the "War Department is just like the alimentary canal. You feed it at one end, and nothing comes out at the other but crap.")

The March 7 realignment of spheres also had the effect of undercutting the second of Marshall's most dearly held precepts, unified command and its implicit notion of consultation and cooperation. In the Pacific, the United States would make all decisions. An advisory council with representatives of Australia, New Zealand, the Netherlands, and China was to sit in Washington, but it had no authority. The councils of war were hollow chambers.

On Corregidor, the man who was to command the Southwest Pacific theater settled upon his escape plan. To Major General Jonathan Wainwright, known as "Skinny" since his youth, now made gaunt by reduced rations, MacArthur pledged: "If I get through to Australia you know I'll come back as soon as I can with as much as I can. In the meantime you've got to hold." If Wainwright was still across the bay on Bataan peninsula when he returned, MacArthur added, he would promote him to lieutenant general.

At 8:00 p.m. on March 11, MacArthur, his wife Jean, their son Arthur, just shy of his fourth birthday, the child's Chinese amah, and MacArthur's aide slipped aboard torpedo boat PT-41 idling alongside the gutted South Dock at Corregidor. The boat eased its way through a minefield, joined three others carrying MacArthur's staff of fifteen, and raced for the southern channel.

Thirty-five hours later, Lieutenant John D. Bulkeley guided his weathered craft alongside the Del Monte plantation docks in northern Mindanao. Within a week MacArthur was in Adelaide, Australia, seething because the divisions he believed poised to retake the Philippines simply did not exist. There he released a statement to the press calculated to force the president and the War Department to end the fast-fading Europe-first strategy:

"The President of the United States ordered me to break through the Japanese lines . . . for the purpose, as I understand it, of organizing the American offensive against Japan, a primary object of which is the relief of the Philippines. I came through and I shall return."

MacArthur had escaped from the Rock, leaving behind more than

75,000 American and Filipino troops on Bataan, some 15,000 more on Corregidor, and as many as 20,000 on the outlying islands of the archipelago. He had deliberately divided authority among four commanders, intending to direct the defense himself from Australia. Marshall would have none of it; MacArthur, the chief of staff insisted in a meeting at the White House, could not control a battle raging 4,000 miles from his new headquarters in Melbourne. Moreover, a theater commander, even a MacArthur should not devote too much of his attention to any one sector, but try to see the entirety.

The president agreed. MacArthur, not ready to take on the president, could only concur. But Wainwright's appointment as commanding general of the United States Army in the Far East would continue to rasp MacArthur's pride.

No matter who commanded the Philippines, the defense there was doomed. Four out of five troops were suffering from malaria, three quarters had dysentery, and more than a third beriberi. Ammunition and food stocks alike were depleted, morale reduced to a grim combination of bravado and resignation.

On April 3 a fresh Japanese division launched an assault on Bataan, rooting the worn defenders out of their trench lines with a five-hour artillery barrage. (By one of the fine ironies of history, Lieutenant General Akira Nara, commander of the 65th Brigade, and Major General Vicente Lim, commanding the 41st Philippine Infantry, had attended the Infantry School at Fort Benning in 1928 when Colonel George Marshall was assistant commander.) As the American and Filipino troops gave ground, from far-off Australia MacArthur ordered a counterattack to recapture a supply base lost earlier. It was a textbook move, failing to account for either the quality of his troops or the strength of the reinforced Japanese units.

On the morning of April 8, Wainwright passed along MacArthur's order to the Bataan command. Wainwright could only add sadly, "God help you all over there."

On Bataan that night Major General Edward P. King concluded his scattered forces could no longer even delay the Japanese, let alone counterattack. He decided to surrender, telling his staff, "I have not communicated with General Wainwright because I do not want him to be compelled to assume any part of the responsibility."

Two thousand of Kings' troops escaped in small boats to Corregidor as their comrades surrendered their weapons. Some 35,000 surviving Americans and Filipino scouts would begin a "Death March" into forty-one months of captivity; as many as 10,000 would not survive the savagery of the first weeks.

Now only Corregidor remained. For three weeks the Japanese shelled the three-mile-long island with 200 guns from dawn to midnight, reducing the defenses by blasting rock and concrete to pieces. Marshall, the chief of staff, had nothing to offer—no relief, no supplies, no food. Words alone he could send, praising Corregidor's "hardihood, courage and devotion to duty," and conveying "special commendation and gratitude of the War Department to the nurses on Corregidor whose service is a source of inspiration to all of us."

Wainwright radioed Marshall on May 3 that he estimated they had a less than even chance of beating off an assault. Three days later, a Japanese landing party forced its way onshore in darkness, fighting 550 yards across the island's waist. That night, his garrison pinned into isolated pockets, water supplies almost gone, ammunition expended, a remorseful Skinny Wainwright radioed Marshall: "Please say to the nation that my troops and I have accomplished all that is humanly possible and that we have upheld the best traditions of the United States and its Army. . . . With profound regret and with continued pride in my gallant troops I go to meet the Japanese commander."

In Washington, the head of Operations Division, Dwight Eisenhower, wrote in his diary, "Poor Wainwright! He did the fighting in the Philippine Islands, another got such glory as the public could find in the operation." MacArthur in Melbourne was the hero. "Yah," Eisenhower snorted.

George Marshall grieved. He of all people understood the nation's, the Army's, his own complicity in the futile stand in the Philippines. Strategic decisions made decades before and years of underfunding had foredoomed the islands. Marshall could only make token amends.

He recommended to MacArthur that Wainwright receive the Medal of Honor. MacArthur refused to endorse the award, insisting, "Wainwright's actions fell far short of those needed to win the award, and that if he received it the action would constitute an injustice to others who had done far more than the Philippine commander." (Thwarted by MacArthur's shabby stand, Marshall waited until the end of the war to secure for Wainwright the medal. In the meantime, he added Wainwright's name to a list of officers receiving permanent promotion, though Wainwright was in a Japanese prison.)

Six months from the beginning of hostilities, War Plan ORANGE had projected, a relief convoy could break through to an embattled Philippine garrison. Corregidor, once deemed "the Gibraltar of the Pacific," surrendered five months to the day after Pearl Harbor. War Plan ORANGE lay amid the hulks sunk in the oily waters of Pearl Harbor.

The Europe-first concept barely drew breath. Hints from Moscow suggested the reeling Soviet Union might sign a separate peace with Hitler. Churchill and Roosevelt groped for some strategic agreement between themselves. Allied fortunes had reached low ebb.

XVII

Modicum's Success

The chief of staff's anger was tightly controlled, but all the more intense for that. Churchill's telegram of the day before was nothing more than an appeal for further dispersion of their already scattered forces, the chief of staff fumed. Send a division to New Zealand, send another to Australia. Churchill would accept a delay of the garrisoning of Northern Ireland, the prime minister informed the president in the March 4 message, if it resulted in more troops for Australia. They could regain lost territory in 1943 or 1944, "But meanwhile there are very hard forfeits to pay."

Confronting the president, Secretary of War Stimson supported Marshall. Better to put troops into Great Britain, he advised, even their raw divisions, thereby posing a threat to Hitler's western flank and boosting British morale at the same time.

Marshall and Stimson left the White House that afternoon of March 5 convinced the president retained his commitment to the Atlantic-first strategy. King was not enthusiastic—the Navy would never be—but he and Arnold had abided by their earlier strategic decision to deal with Germany before Japan.

Three days later they were again at the White House, reviewing the president's plan to divide the world into three strategic areas: the Pacific, the Middle East and Asia, and Europe. Stimson and Marshall were encouraged. The president had taken the initiative from Churchill, who would have turned their war plans into nothing more than a "defensive operation to stop up urgent rat holes," Stimson grumbled. Most important, Roosevelt cabled Churchill that he was interested in the establishment of a new front that summer. A second front would relieve pressure on the hard-pressed Soviet Union, which was doing more to defeat Germany than the United States and Great Britain combined, the president pointed out with some asperity.

Still, the pressure to disperse Marshall's hastily trained divisions mounted in Washington. MacArthur fleeing the Philippines called for immediate reinforcements to recapture that archipelago. The Navy wanted troops with which to garrison every atoll along the shipping lanes to Australia, then more to launch an amphibious assault in the Solomon Islands. The Middle East and Indian theaters needed bolstering, for if they lost the Middle East they ran the risk of losing the war, the new head of the War Plans Division, Dwight Eisenhower, wrote in his intermittent diary. Eisenhower was prepared to recommend the transfer to the Middle East of George Patton's 2nd Armored, about to begin training in California's Mojave Desert. It was all they could offer.

Confronted with the conflicting demands, Eisenhower exploded, slashing his anger across a page of his diary, then repenting the next day and cleaning up the language. "Anger cannot win, it cannot even think clearly," he noted in the revised entry.

> In this respect Marshall puzzles me a bit. I've never seen a man who apparently develops a higher pressure of anger when he encounters some piece of stupidity than does he. Yet the outburst is so fleeting, he returns so quickly to complete "normalcy," that I am certain he does it for effect. At least he doesn't get angry in the sense I do—I blaze for an hour!

The tension on the second floor of the Munitions Building mounted through March. Marshall "had a rather rambunctious interview" with the arms-seeking Australian foreign minister. Stimson got into a stiff argument with Sir John Dill after a dinner at the British Embassy about the possibilities of offensive action in Europe. Dill's lack of enthusiasm provoked the secretary to a show of diplomatic bad manners in front of the ambassador's guests. Winning the argument outweighed any sense of chagrin Stimson might have felt for the lapse of etiquette.

By March 24, Marshall's throttled anger had turned inward to become depression. The following day he was to present to the president a plan for a summer offensive, yet he had few troops to throw into the campaign, too few planes to support it, too few ships to supply it. Even the theater was undetermined, and whatever they adopted, it would surely drain men from any cross-Channel operation in 1943, he explained to Stimson.

The meeting on March 25 of FDR's War Cabinet—Stimson and Marshall for the Army, Arnold for the Air Force, Knox and King for the Navy, Harry Hopkins and the president—began badly. The president opened the discussion, proposing the "wildest kind of dispersion debauch," grandly suggesting operations in the Mediterranean and the Middle East with what Marshall called "his cigarette-holder gesture." At first taken aback, Marshall and Stimson managed finally to guide the president back to the Atlantic and a plan completed only that morning by the War Plans Division.

Dwight Eisenhower's memorandum argued in favor of implementing the Europe-first strategy with BOLERO, a build-up of American forces in the British Isles. BOLERO rested on simple fundamentals: the build-up in Great Britain prevented the dispersion of their forces elsewhere, and simply because of proximity pointed to their fighting first on the continent.

A build-up in Great Britain, Marshall told the War Cabinet, would put American forces at the closest possible point to France, a mere twenty miles across the Straits of Dover. The island, moreover, provided ample airfields for both bombers and fighters necessary for air superiority and the success of any invasion.

BOLERO also made it possible to concentrate their few naval escorts within the vital North Atlantic sealane, and thereby protect not only troopships but merchant vessels carrying the food and Lend-Lease supplies England and Russia needed. The build-up in the British Isles had an added advantage of posing a threat to France, small now, but one that would grow, and one that Hitler dare not ignore. Even if they did not actually invade France, they would thus help the Soviet Union by pinning German troops to the western shore.

Roosevelt hedged, tentatively agreeing they might present the plan to the Combined Chiefs of Staff sitting permanently in Washington. He ordered another review the following week.

On April 1, they met once again at the White House to hear Marshall's presentation of a more detailed BOLERO and two corollary offensives that flowed logically from it. A build-up, Marshall and Eisenhower realized, in itself would not bring down Hitler. SLEDGEHAMMER and ROUNDUP would put into combat the forces massed in the British Isles.

ROUNDUP envisioned a cross-Channel attack in the spring of 1943, by which time there were to be no fewer than thirty American and eighteen British divisions poised to invade France. They would be supported by 1,500 American fighters and 1,000 bombers, in addition to what the British air forces could provide. ROUNDUP was the child of American strategic doctrine, of striking directly at the enemy, defeating his army, and thereby destroying his ability to wage war.

SLEDGEHAMMER was, in contrast, conditional, a premature ROUNDUP. It depended on either of two developments: the sudden collapse of Nazi Germany; or the threat that resistance in the Soviet Union would fold. In either case, by September 1942 they could put across the English Channel five divisions, one and a half of them American. If Germany collapsed, SLEDGEHAMMER was to liberate as much territory as possible before the Russians poured into western Europe; if the Soviets weakened, a sacrificial invasion of France was to draw off German troops from the Russian front for as long as possible.

For two and a half hours they discussed the enlarged proposals around the long table in the Cabinet Room. Marshall carried much of the discussion, Stimson and Hopkins holding Roosevelt to the Atlantic-first strategy.

Near the end of the meeting, Hopkins pointedly turned to Admiral King. "I want to be sure that everybody is in accord with this program. Admiral King, do you see any reason this cannot be carried out?"

"No, I do not," King replied, neatly forced to endorse a plan no Pacific-minded admiral could embrace with enthusiasm.

They were agreed then. Roosevelt promptly instructed Hopkins and Marshall to present the plan to Churchill in London. Here was a decision, finally, Stimson believed would "mark this day as a memorable one in the war."

The presidential mission, given the code name MODICUM, was small in size; neither Marshall nor Hopkins cared at all for the trappings of high office. Hopkins only barely tolerated the personal doctor assigned to him at Roosevelt's order. Colonel Wedemeyer, now recognized as the foremost advocate of Europe-first in the War Plans Division, was to serve double duty as Marshall's aide and as a proponent of the plan they were carrying with them. Marshall traveled in civilian clothes as Mr. C. G. Mell, Hopkins as A. H. Hones, and Wedemeyer as J. E. White.

Their Boeing B-14 Flying Boat lumbered into the air over Chesapeake Bay on April 4, off on a leisurely 150 mph transatlantic flight that would take them first to Bermuda. A two-day layover there to repair an engine gave the weary Hopkins a needed rest.

Ignoring the president's order to "put Hopkins to bed and keep him there under 24-hour guard," Marshall instead took him fishing. Hopkins returned to their hotel a happy man. He had caught fish big and little; Marshall had caught nothing. The MODICUM party dined in their hotel room that evening on Hopkins's catch.

Marshall had a long time to weigh his looming responsibility during the twenty-hour flight from Bermuda to Lough Erne in Northern Ireland. He read bits and pieces of two books on the flight, H. G. Wells's *Outline of History,* in one of the new paperback publications, and Sir William Robertson's scathing critique of military folly, *Soldiers and Statesmen.* Wells offered a broad gauge of world history, Robertson a chapter on World War I's disastrous Gallipoli expedition. That abortive attempt to force the Dardanelles at the eastern end of the Mediterranean had cost one of its staunchest proponents, Winston Churchill, his post as first lord of the Admiralty.

Twenty-seven years later the chief of staff of the United States Army was traveling 3,000 miles in a heaving, creaking Flying Boat to meet with

Prime Minister Churchill. It was a difficult assignment, Marshall's first as a principal spokesman for national interests. While Hopkins was to take the lead in the political or diplomatic discussions with Churchill, such questions were always tightly intertwined with the strategic; Marshall would inevitably be drawn in. At the Atlantic Conference, then at ARCADIA, he had served as an adviser to the president. Now he was flying to London to dissuade Winston Churchill from the beliefs of a lifetime.

The MODICUM party arrived in London on April 8, Marshall's first visit to the British capital since the delirious victory celebrations of another war. The chief of staff was struck with the contrast between a Washington that five months after Pearl Harbor had yet to acknowledge the sacrifices necessary to victory and a grimy London pockmarked with bomb craters and gutted buildings, sandbagged against Luftwaffe attack and ever alert for air-raid sirens.

Marshall and Hopkins met Churchill forty feet beneath Great George Street in the cramped underground bunker from which the prime minister directed the Empire's war. Marshall laid out their proposed war plan. Churchill listened, lukewarm to SLEDGEHAMMER and ROUNDUP, but offering far less resistance than Marshall had anticipated.

Any satisfaction was premature, he would learn. This first visit to London was to teach him a frustrating lesson: no battle with the prime minister stayed won, but had to be fought and refought against dogged resistance. He was to have "hectic scenes" with the prime minister, the general later acknowledged.

Marshall made even less impression on the chief of the Imperial General Staff, Field Marshal Sir Alan Brooke. The field marshal had little patience for either the Americans or their plan. Born into the "fighting Brookes," an Anglo-Irish family with a long military tradition, Sir Alan was a man of icy precision and immaculate dress. Then fifty-seven, three years Marshall's junior, Brooke was spindly-legged and slope-shouldered; that appearance and his delight in bird watching belied his combat experience. As an artilleryman he had served with distinction in World War I, reaching the rank of lieutenant colonel. Between the wars he had served as an instructor at the Staff College in Camberley and the Imperial Defence College. In the years immediately prior to the outbreak of war he had set up Britain's anti-aircraft defenses, then led the II Corps of the British Expeditionary Force in France. He had neatly extricated his men at Dunkirk, and assumed command of the hastily assembled Home Forces. In December 1941, Brooke had replaced Marshall's new friend, the exhausted Sir John Dill, as chief of the Imperial General Staff.

It was perhaps that circumstance, Marshall's biographer, Forrest Pogue, noted, that unconsciously prejudiced the chief of staff against his British opposite number. "Brooke made an unfavorable impression on Marshall," Hopkins reported to the president. "While he may be a good fighting man, he hasn't got Dill's brains," Marshall had determined.

Nor did Brooke have Dill's charm. A man of few words, Brooke conveyed an air of haughty disdain not always intended. In Marshall's case the feeling was initially real, if masked in the interests of politeness and cooperation between allies. The American was "a pleasant and easy man to get on with, rather over-filled with his own importance. But I should not put him down as a great man," Brooke noted in his diary.

Brooke and his colleagues would never muster much admiration for Marshall as a global strategist. "He had old-fashioned ideas of always wanting to get straight at the enemy regardless of over-all strategic requirements," Churchill's personal chief of staff, General Hastings Ismay, complained later.

Marshall's arrival in London coincided with yet another distracting turn of events. A Japanese naval force had sliced into the Bay of Bengal and attacked first Columbo, then Trincomalee in Ceylon, sinking a British carrier, two cruisers, and two merchant ships. The Japanese raid underscored the constant British fear that Germany and Japan would link up in the Middle East and thereby doom the Empire. Additional American ships would be needed to flush the Japanese from the Bay of Bengal and preserve the sea route to India.

Meantime, Premier Stalin was pressing for more aid, but especially for a second front in France. German armies threatened Sebastopol and with it the entire Crimea; Moscow hinted of a withdrawal to the Urals, a move that foreshadowed an end to effective Soviet resistance. A Russian propaganda campaign had fueled British criticism of Churchill's conduct of the war, and especially of the lack of a second front. No less than Roosevelt, Churchill had to pay heed to public opinion.

Although Churchill quickly agreed "in principle" to the concept of SLEDGEHAMMER and ROUNDUP, Marshall realized that British concurrence was something less than wholehearted. When Marshall argued that an invasion of France was the quickest way to end the war, Brooke had snapped, "Yes, but not the way we want it."

Their major problem, Brooke insisted, was naval. German submarines had sunk 1.2 million tons of shipping in the first four months of the year; more than half of the torpedoed ships were tankers. Without merchant ships, there could be no effective build-up in the British Isles, and certainly no relief to the Russians via the hazardous Murmansk run.

Even if they managed to defeat the U-boats and restore their merchant fleets, another problem loomed: they lacked landing craft. After meeting Lord Louis Mountbatten, whose experimental commando raids along the French coast provided the Allies' sole amphibious experience, Marshall abruptly asked, "How can I get into this game as soon as possible?"

"Double all the orders you've already given for landing craft," Mount-batten replied grandly.

"Right," Marshall said, ordering Wedemeyer to send a cable.

There was more, Mountbatten said smoothly. British tactical exercises made it clear that they could not coordinate more than twenty boats at any one time. Working with the small landing craft then available, they could not ferry ashore any more than 600 men at one time, little more than a battalion. What they needed were larger landing craft—Mount-batten had plans for an LCI or landing craft (infantry) capable of car-rying 250 infantrymen for 48 hours. Twenty of these vessels could land 5,000 men in a single wave.

"How many would you like?" Marshall asked.

"Let's say, three hundred," Mountbatten speculated.

"That will mean 150 for you and 150 for us," the chief of staff said. Another cable to Washington settled that.

Such generosity seemed mere prodigality to the hard-pressed Britons, who already considered American production quotas like 50,000 aircraft annually sheer bravado. It was another reason to be wary of the Ameri-can chief of staff, the more so since British regulars considered Mount-batten, a cousin of the king or no, to be an unsound dreamer.

Still Marshall's matter-of-fact manner, the lack of any hint of boastful-ness reassured the British chiefs. By April 15, Brooke was ready to con-cede the American "a good general at raising armies and at providing the necessary link between the military and political worlds, but his stra-tegical ability does not impress me at all. In fact, in many respects he is a very dangerous man whilst being a very charming one."

Marshall had spoken frankly with Brooke, candidly laying out his immediate problems in Washington. King and MacArthur were calling for forces with which to launch offensives in the Pacific. "To counter these moves Marshall has started the European offensive plan and is going one hundred per cent all out on it," Brooke noted in his diary. "It is a clever move which fits in with present political opinion and the desire to help Russia."

Brooke himself harbored grave reservations about any invasion of France, either the sacrificial offering of SLEDGEHAMMER or ROUNDUP's permanent beachhead. Marshall's plan, the chief of the Imperial Gen-eral Staff grumbled, did not go beyond getting ashore. "I asked him this afternoon—Do we go west, south or east after landing? He had not begun to think of it," Brooke sniffed. Mountbatten even doubted they could maintain a beachhead without more air and naval support than they would be able to muster.

Neither had Marshall considered the strategic implications of a cross-Channel assault, Brooke complained to his diary. "The plans are fraught with the gravest dangers. . . . Should Germany be getting the best of an attack on Russia, the pressure for invasion of France will be at its strongest, and yet this is just the most dangerous set of circumstances for us."

Despite his rhetorical fanfares celebrating their "noble brotherhood of arms," despite his agreement "in principle," Churchill too doubted the wisdom of any cross-Channel adventure, and especially of a sacrificial SLEDGEHAMMER. At that moment, the sacrifice would largely fall upon Great Britain; the United States would not be able to transport more than a division and a half for any cross-Channel operation until September.

Churchill instead privately preferred either his own plan for an invasion of northern Norway, code-named JUPITER, or a revival of GYMNAST, the assault of French North Africa. His chiefs of staff—Brooke especially—vehemently opposed the Norway adventure, and nurtured only a bit more enthusiasm about North Africa. Churchill would first have to bring Brooke around before presenting it to the Americans.

In an all-night session with Marshall two days before the MODICUM party left for home, Churchill gave guarded consent to "offensive action in 1942, perhaps, and in 1943 for certain." To the members of the Imperial General Staff, however, he later emphasized he would have no bloodbaths such as Great Britain had endured in World War I. "The shadow of that lost generation, one million men of the British Empireogne)who had died so needlessly, continually darkened our counsels," General Sir Leslie Hollis later recalled.

British reserve interfered with frankness, suggested Churchill's personal chief of staff, General Hastings Ismay. "I think we could have come clean, much cleaner than we did, and said, 'We are frankly horrified because of what we have been through in our lifetime—60,000 in a day, the 1st of July 1916, 60,000. . . . We who survived had got that into our minds: "Never again." We are not going into this until it is a cast-down certainty.' "

Yet no such caution crept into their midnight discussions, "Pug" Ismay wrote with some regret. "Our American friends went happily homewards under the mistaken impression that we have committed ourselves to both ROUNDUP and SLEDGEHAMMER." When the British finally did reject SLEDGEHAMMER, the Americans "felt that we had broken faith with them."

Aware certainly of British reservations, Marshall and Hopkins left for Northern Ireland to visit the first American troops to begin training in the British Isles. With reporters at his elbow, Marshall promised a group of young officers, "The time of action is near."

Just prior to their departure, Marshall and Hopkins stopped in a fishing village on the Scottish coast. From a local inn, Mr. A. H. Hones and Mr. C. G. Mell sought to place a telephone call to the president of the United States. Only a second call to a Scotland Yard official who knew their code names prevented the alert local police from arresting the two as spies or, worse, drunks. The next day, Messrs. Mell and Hones were safely airborne for Washington. They were returning home to the sound of one hand clapping, a vague agreement on a military offensive for which Marshall had no plan and his ally no enthusiasm.

The city to which Marshall returned at the end of April 1942 was gripped in an emotional hangover. On April 18, sixteen B-25 bombers launched from the carrier *Hornet* 800 miles at sea swept in at low altitude to bomb Tokyo, Yokohama, Kobe, and Nagoya, then fly on to land in China. The bombers led by Lieutenant Colonel James H. Doolittle caused little damage, but did embarrass the Japanese military, which had promised to protect the home islands from American attack. (Humiliated and threatened, the Japanese cabinet decided to consolidate the territorial gains already made, rather than further expand the empire by conquest; in effect, the Doolittle raid had an impact far greater than the actual bomb damage.)

Euphoria seized the United States; America had struck back. Then came the letdown: what if Japan chose to retaliate? The West Coast, seeing itself undefended, demanded reinforcements anew. The alarm spread to Washington where anxious navy officers realized that a radio silence had fallen over the Japanese fleet, a sure sign of an imminent operation.

Here the chief of staff returned at the end of April, believing he had agreement on the Allies' first offensive. Waiting for him was yet another request from the Soviet Union for Lend-Lease assistance. This time the Russians wanted transport aircraft, planes that would be needed if there were to be any cross-Channel attack that summer.

MacArthur also clamored for reinforcements; two British divisions and a British aircraft carrier would do nicely, he told the admiring Australian prime minister, John Curtin. Curtin immediately relayed the out-of-channels request to London, prompting Churchill to send a stiff note to Roosevelt asking "whether General MacArthur has any authority from the United States for taking such a line?"

Marshall wrote a sharp reproof to MacArthur, the more stinging for its didactic tone:

> ... It is realized that you are not concerned in the nature of communications passing between the two prime ministers but where these take form of definite request for reinforcements for Southwest Pacific area they create confusion unless originated by you as supreme commander and transmitted directly to the U.S. War Department which acts as executive for U.S. Joint Chiefs of Staff in controlling that area. . . . It is requested that all communications to which you are a party and which relate to strategy and major reinforcements be addressed only to the War Department.

Meanwhile, Marshall had to fend off other raids on his small stocks. An offhand remark by FDR had been interpreted by his naval aide as an order to provide MacArthur with no fewer than 1,000 combat aircraft and 100,000 troops on a priority basis. Marshall's staff estimated that the increases so casually ordered by the president would necessitate cutting the number of troops scheduled for deployment in Great Britain by 50,000, and halving the number of air squadrons there. King also was requesting soldiers to protect Pacific bases and 500 aircraft to fly antisubmarine patrols over the Atlantic.

On May 4 Marshall directed a personal memorandum to the president, noting how difficult the negotiations in London had been, and how precarious was British approval. Diversions of material to other theaters threatened SLEDGEHAMMER and ROUNDUP, he stressed. For his part, he was willing to run risks in the Pacific in order to mount an early offensive on the continent.

He received no answer. Two days later, the chief of staff pressed the issue with a position paper recommending the president choose between the continued build-up in the British Isles and sending reinforcements hither and yon. If SLEDGEHAMMER was not their primary consideration, he suggested it be abandoned completely.

> We must remember that this operation for 1942 depends primarily upon British forces and not our own. They have far more at stake than do we and are accepting very grave hazards to which our own risks are not comparable. They have accepted the "Bolero" project with a firm understanding that it would be the primary objective of the United States. If such is not to be the case, the British should be formally notified that the recent London agreement must be cancelled.

Marshall's stern lecture brought the president up short. That same day Roosevelt replied, "I do not want BOLERO slowed down." Marshall once more had his mandate.

While such immediate concerns kept the chief of staff preoccupied, they did permit his wife to finish a project of her own intended as a surprise for her husband.

Katherine Marshall had purchased Dodona Manor in Leesburg, Virginia, two years earlier, but she and the general had spent only occasional weekends in the early colonial house once owned by a nephew of George Washington. The chief of staff had enjoyed working in the overgrown yard on the rare days he could get away, but they had done nothing to make the house truly theirs.

As soon as she learned her husband would be going to London, Katherine plunged into the task of remodeling Dodona Manor. The work took a week longer than she anticipated, and ran over the estimates, she noted with some apprehension, but the newly landscaped, refurbished home was ready by the first week in May.

Together they drove the thirty-five miles from Washington on a spring afternoon, turning from the undulating road onto their property just at sunset. Sighing in contentment, Marshall parked their car in the gravel driveway in front of the new garage. He walked about, noting the many changes in the yard and on the exterior. Finally he turned to his wife and said in a husky voice, "This is home, a real home after forty-one years of wandering."

On the drive back to Fort Myer, Katherine confessed the job costs had gone over estimates. "All I ask is, when you look them over be easy on me. Remember your testimony before the investigating committee of the Senate on the construction of camps. It costs more to do things in a hurry." The chief of staff assured her he planned no investigation of the costs.

Marshall was to have little opportunity to escape Washington for quiet Leesburg in the next months. Already beset with the organization of an army growing by 300,000 men and women every thirty days, he found himself grappling with knotty geopolitical questions posed by the White House.

Logistics shaped strategy, and strategy international relations. A shortage of shipping limited the number of divisions the War Department could dispatch to Great Britain. Any cross-Channel invasion prior to April 1943 would necessarily require that the British furnish a majority of the troops put ashore. Even if the United States could move more divisions to England, a scarcity of landing craft would prevent them from putting those additional men ashore in France.

On May 6, Eisenhower returned from a meeting with navy procurement officers, put out about their indifference to the construction of landing craft. "How in hell can we win this war unless we can crack some heads?" he complained in his diary.

The shortage of shipping, and especially of tankers, grew worse during the second quarter of the year. German U-boats roamed virtually unhampered in the Caribbean and Atlantic, plucking off unprotected merchant vessels. (The Navy, to Marshall's dismay, insisted that individual merchant ships stood a better chance of getting through to Great Britain than did convoys that would attract large numbers of submarines.) Lost tonnage surpassed the half-million mark in March, then again in April and May before the Navy agreed to convoy merchant vessels.

Eventually they would be able to make up the losses, Bill Somervell's procurement officers calculated. If industry met production schedules laid down in the Victory Program, the shortage of shipping, indeed, the shortage of most military supplies would ease by the end of the year.

The military had placed orders for 60,000 planes to be delivered in 1942, for 45,000 tanks and 8,000,000 tons of merchant shipping. The following year the Victory Program called for 125,000 aircraft of all types, 75,000 tanks, and 10,000,000 tons of shipping. No one scoffed now at calls for 50,000 aircraft.

The costs of modern war, of equipping an army whose authorized strength had reached 5,000,000, were beyond anything the nation had known. The War Department spent $30 million to equip one of its new armored divisions, and $10 million for an infantry division. Military procurement would cost taxpayers $160 billion before the year was out.

Marshall watched the totals closely, though there was little he could do to keep them from soaring beyond true comprehension. He later told and retold the story on himself of then-Brigadier General Leslie R. Groves, the military director of the atomic bomb project, requesting Marshall's approval of $100 million in expenditures. The chief of staff, busy writing when Groves arrived, kept the general waiting. When Marshall finally laid down his pen, he scanned the $100 million request, approved it, and handed it back. As Groves was about to leave, Marshall volunteered, "It may interest you to know what I was doing. I was writing the check for $3.52 for grass seed for my lawn."

The chief of staff was also aware of the social impact such monumental spending produced. Military contracts had spawned hundreds of new businesses, all looking for workers; even as the Army drained the manpower pool, newspapers carried help-wanted ads seeking to entice retirees back to work, offering top wages for "100 percent war work." In 1937, one estimate had it, only six firms in the United States were capable of building seagoing vessels of longer than 400 feet. By 1942, that number had grown to sixty—all at full capacity, all of them competing for workers. American women set aside potholder and steno pad in favor of a welder's torch to build the 1,400 Liberty Ships on order by June 1942. (Rosie the Riveter helped some yards achieve phenomenal production records; at a time when the national average for completing a 10,000-ton Liberty Ship was 150 days, Kaiser Industries was doing it in 72. As a promotion stunt, in October that company would launch a merchant ship ten days after its keel was laid.)

The shortages of skilled workers, already acute, would only get worse as the mobilization continued; Marshall had proposed drafting eighteen-year-olds, and building the Army to 9 million. Hospitals, schools, and government agencies particularly suffered in the competition for workers. According to one younger staff officer, the chief of staff stressed the need to win the war "before our very institutions melt under us."

Despite Eisenhower's complaint that too many people in government still believed the United States could merely spend its way to victory, slowly the nation was gathering itself for war. Food rationing started on

May 4, 1942, beginning with sugar. Butter, coffee, then meat would follow soon after. Gasoline rationing tightened, far short of English austerity, but angering mobile Americans nonetheless.

The quickening pace of national mobilization alone would have made Marshall a major figure in wartime Washington. In addition, the president himself was turning more often to his chief of staff. At another time, the diplomatic visit of Vyacheslav M. Molotov would not have involved Marshall, but in late May 1942, the stolid, unyielding Soviet foreign minister was coming to Washington to demand a second front.

Through a bitterly cold winter, the Soviets had held the Germans at bay. With the thaws of spring, the Russians had mounted a spoiling attack on Kharkov but faltered. The Wehrmacht's counterattack bagged tens of thousands of Russian prisoners. Kerch fell, opening the agriculturally vital Crimea to the invaders. Once more there were whispers that the Soviet Union would abandon the war; once more London and Washington talked of inducements to keep the Russians in the fight.

Winston Churchill had unilaterally determined upon one inducement: secret recognition of the Soviet Union's 1939 borders. The move, in effect, ceded Latvia, Estonia, and Lithuania to the Russians, and granted to them a portion of Finnish Karelia and all of eastern Poland. Recognition of the prewar borders—there was no way they could compel the Soviets to relinquish the territory anyway—would be a cheap price to pay for continued Soviet resistance, Churchill stressed. Roosevelt objected to the territorial concessions, arguing such a secret treaty would annul the Atlantic Charter's assurance of self-determination.

Roosevelt, not Churchill, would have to deflect Molotov. The people's commissar for foreign affairs was making the hazardous flight from Moscow to the West intent on garnering some diplomatic concession; the border realignment Churchill had offered, or an immediate second front to relieve pressure on the hard-pressed Russian Army, or increased Lend-Lease aid. The onetime economics student who had taken the name "Hammer" in his underground years arrived in Washington on Friday, May 29, with a loaf of black bread, a sausage, and a pistol tucked in his suitcase.

President and people's commissar made little progress in preliminary meetings that afternoon and evening. The need for interpreters cramped Roosevelt's casual style, while the Bolshevik eyed all westerners with unrelenting suspicion. The two men barely warmed to each other.

The following day the president invited Marshall and King to the White House to discuss the second front issue. Molotov stated the Russians were "reasonably certain they could hold out" against the German armies preparing for a summer offensive. To prevent Germany from tipping the balance in its favor, the foreign minister asked the United States and Great Britain to open a second front that would draw off at least forty

German divisions. Staring fixedly through the pince-nez glasses that only emphasized his impenetrable formality, Molotov "declared his government wanted to know in frank terms what position we take on the question of a second front, and whether we were prepared to establish one. He requested a straight answer," the American translator stated in his notes.

Roosevelt turned to Marshall. "Were developments clear enough so that we could say to Mr. Stalin that we are preparing a second front?"

"Yes," the general replied without hesitation.

With his chief of staff's assurance, the president authorized Molotov to inform the Soviet premier that the United States expected the formation of a second front in 1942.

Marshall had questions of his own. The problem, the chief of staff explained frankly, was neither troops nor equipment, but shipping. They lacked the vessels to both provide Lend-Lease aid in the quantities the Soviets had asked and complete the BOLERO build-up prior to an invasion of the continent. The Murmansk run was particularly deadly, he noted; a recent convoy had lost a third of its ships to German bombers based in Norway.

"What do you want, the second front or Murmansk?" Marshall demanded. "It isn't possible to provide both."

The general waited for Molotov's interpreter to relay in Russian Marshall's comments and question for the foreign minister. He then turned to the American translator, Professor Samuel Cross. Had the Russian interpreter repeated the general's words fully?

No, Cross responded. Then, Marshall ordered, Cross was to tell the Russian to repeat Marshall's comments fully. A second and third time the interpreter abbreviated the general's remarks, and twice more Marshall insisted "his word be translated and passed fully and exactly to Mr. Molotov." Narrow-eyed, Molotov listened to Cross's instructions to the Russian interpreter; Marshall learned later the Russians valued his straightforward manner, equating it with blunt honesty.

At lunch that day, the president handed his Russian visitor a list of 8 million tons of supplies the United States would make available to the Soviets through Lend-Lease in the last six months of 1942. The United States could ship but 4.1 million tons because of the shortage of vessels, he added.

Even those limited shipments would upset timetables for a second front in 1942, Marshall and King worried. In an hour-long conference on Sunday, May 31, the two chiefs of staff reviewed their worldwide commitments, concluding with Harry Hopkins that they could not provide even the tonnage promised Molotov the day before.

Roosevelt now was concerned. The pledge to Molotov "was a little vague and the dangerous situation on the Russian front required that he, the president, make a more specific answer to Molotov in regard to a second front." When the president proposed they assure Stalin of the opening of a second front in August, Marshall reminded him that the British would resist. The chief of staff urged that Roosevelt delete any mention of a date for a cross-Channel operation; the president insisted they pledge a second front sometime "in 1942."

Subdued by Marshall's arguments of the previous day, Roosevelt was to strike a hard bargain of his own with the increasingly agitated Molotov on the last day of their talks. "The chiefs of staff suggested that, in order to speed up initiating the second front, your government, with this situation in mind, reconsider the Lend-Lease list which you have submitted, remembering that, of the 4,100,000 tons which we planned to ship during the year commencing July 1st, only 1,800,000 consist of material immediately ready for use for military purposes on the Russian front this summer. The rest is mostly raw materials and other items for production of material which would not be ready for use until next year." They would ship all the tanks, planes, and trucks—3,000 trucks a month, the president promised—but withhold the raw material to free shipping for a second front. "The Soviets could not have their cake and eat it too," he concluded.

"The second front would be stronger if the first front still stood," Molotov replied bitterly. Logistical reality had reduced him to futile protest.

Marshall emerged from his first dealings on a diplomatic level with enhanced stature. With Hopkins, he had assumed some of the burden that normally was the president's, acquitting himself well. Beyond that, his straightforward manner had impressed the Russian minister. He had promised no more in private than he had in public—when concessions made in secret to be disavowed later would have made Marshall's task easier.

The day Molotov arrived in Washington, the army chief of staff flew to West Point to address the graduating class. War had come to the United States, and American soldiers were scattered "throughout the Pacific, in Burma, China, and India. Recently they struck at Tokyo. They have wintered in Greenland and Iceland. They are landing in Northern Ireland and England, and they will land in France," he promised.

Reporters covering the ceremony played up the chief of staff's pledge of a second front, only incidentally mentioning an even more portentous promise. "We are determined that before the sun sets on this terrible struggle our flag will be recognized throughout the world as a symbol of freedom on the one hand and of overwhelming power on the other," the chief of staff told the graduating class. Marshall's words in private the next day in the White House underscored his public remarks. If he was vague about the date of a second front, he was sure that it would soon take place.

People's Commissar Molotov would leave Washington with the promise of a second front in 1942. Two weeks later, Winston Churchill was to scuttle that cross-Channel operation.

C H A P T E R

XVIII

Lighting the Torch

Winston Churchill was tormented by ghosts. Each time he stood in the Commons, he saw "the faces that are not there," faces of men dead in the muddy fields of Flanders in the first war. The vision pressed on him. Never again must Great Britain lock in pitched battle against Germany on the continent.

In mid-June 1942, those ghosts accompanied the prime minister to Washington. Chief of Staff George Marshall noted that Churchill seeped "discouragement and new proposals for diversions." Those same ghosts impelled the prime minister to fly on to Hyde Park and an immediate meeting with the president of the United States.

On this warm Saturday in June, the president drove his convertible with the manual controls about his Hyde Park estate, the prime minister at his side, the two of them discussing the Allies' precarious position. The Wehrmacht had taken virtually all of the Crimea and had begun shelling the last Russian positions in Sevastopol. In the Kharkov region the Russian attack had worn itself out, and now a German counterattack was pressing eastward. The Soviets were demanding ever more Lend-Lease supplies, yet the Murmansk run was increasingly costly; only fifty-eight of eighty-four ships got through in April and May. In Libya, General Rommel had sprung a trap on the British Eighth Army, sending those remnants of the Empire reeling back toward the Egyptian border; only the garrison at Tobruk barred Rommel's path to the Suez Canal.

The situation in the Far East was, if anything, worse. But for scattered guerrilla bands, opposition in the Philippines had ended. Stilwell had escaped from Burma, but Japanese troops were pushing into northern India. The northeast coast of New Guinea, the last barrier before Australia, was virtually in Japanese hands.

There had been but one bright spot, the defeat of the Japanese fleet at Midway, a victory by the narrowest of margins and the greatest of luck, but a resounding victory nonetheless. Warned by decoded MAGIC intercepts, the United States Navy had sought the Japanese in the central Pacific with the carriers *Hornet, Yorktown,* and *Enterprise.* Their dive bombers had sunk four Japanese carriers and a heavy cruiser, the very heart of the great striking force of the First Carrier Fleet. Despite the loss of the *Yorktown* and a destroyer, those dive bombers had tipped the balance of naval power in the Pacific.

The two men sitting alone in the convertible on the bluffs overlooking the Hudson River discussed a report the president had received from his science adviser two days earlier. Vannevar Bush had written that his Uranium Committee concluded it was possible to build a nuclear bomb; he recommended the United States take up the task. The day before, Roosevelt had given his approval. The War Department would administer the budget of $100 million.

Together the two men returned to the house for lunch. There in the stuffy little study off the portico, Churchill finally turned to the problem that had brought him to the United States for the second time in six months, the ghosts of the House of Commons.

His military staff, Churchill told the president, had not been able to fashion a plan to invade France that had any reasonable chance of success. They had too few landing craft, enough to land only 4,000 men at a time. In addition, they were not certain they would be able to establish air superiority over the invasion beaches; without it, any landing was foredoomed. Failure on their first joint venture would be costly, and the British Empire, already bled white, would bear the brunt of it, Churchill added. Failure too—though there was no need for him to mention it to so astute a politician as the president—would surely cost Churchill his post as prime minister; the very people in London clamoring most loudly for a second front to relieve pressure on the beleaguered Soviets would be the first to cry for Churchill's head when the diverting attack failed. There was already grumbling about the conduct of the war.

As president and prime minister talked in Hyde Park that Saturday afternoon, their military chiefs stewed in the heat of a stifling Washington. Both George Marshall and Alan Brooke fretted about Churchill's influence upon Roosevelt. Marshall was especially concerned with the diversionary schemes the prime minister might put forward, plans that would inevitably delay BOLERO and the invasion of France next summer. Churchill could be seductive if wrongheaded.

The diversionary threat was very real, Brooke and Marshall realized. Though Marshall had returned from London in April with what he believed was a British commitment to the BOLERO build-up and an invasion of the continent, since then there had been hints the agreement was half-hearted. Marshall told some of his staff that the British "seemed to have agreed in London to our planning concepts with their tongues in their cheeks."

Now it appeared that—as Stimson put it—the president also "was going to jump the traces." Two days before the prime minister's arrival, Roosevelt had raised the question of an invasion of North Africa to relieve pressure on the Russians. Despite the opposition of both Marshall and Stimson, the president had ordered them to "get to work on this proposition." A landing in North Africa would divert resources from BOLERO, and mean postponing the invasion of the continent in 1943.

Meanwhile, the prime minister had in the last two weeks revived JUPITER, the invasion of Norway. On that the British and the American generals were agreed; the prospect of landings in the north was even worse than the North African venture.

Brooke, who was gradually warming to Marshall, discovered they "were pretty well of the same accord as to the general outlook." BOLERO and ROUNDUP they could agree upon, though Marshall wanted the invasion of France in 1943 and Brooke preferred to postpone it until the Wehrmacht had been sorely depleted. The two military men could also agree that Norway and French North Africa made little strategic sense. Each had his own reasons: Marshall feared a North African operation this year would postpone the invasion of France to 1944; Brooke preferred to reinforce the embattled Eighth Army in Egypt and lift the air siege of strangled, vital Malta.

For almost two days Churchill had inveighed against BOLERO-ROUNDUP. What forces did they have to mount an attack? How many landing barges? How much critical air support could they provide? Where even would they land? Did Marshall have a plan? Who would command the enterprise? Most important, Churchill asked rhetorically, "Can we afford to stand idle in the Atlantic theater during the whole of 1942? Ought we not to be preparing within the general structure of BOLERO some other operation by which we may gain positions of advantage, and also directly or indirectly to take some of the weight off Russia?"

Churchill had taken up GYMNAST—the invasion of North Africa—"knowing full well, I am sure, that it was the president's great, secret baby," Secretary of War Stimson confided to his diary.

Intrigued, enticed, on Saturday night the president had ordered his chief of staff to meet them at the White House the next morning with answers to Churchill's many questions.

Roosevelt and Churchill returned by private train early Sunday morning, then convened Marshall, Brooke, and "Pug" Ismay for a daylong conference. For years after, the men who were there would think it one of the most important of the war.

Marshall came to the White House disarmed. He had never advocated

SLEDGEHAMMER as anything more than an emergency operation to relieve pressure on the Russians; as such the troops involved might be sacrificed if they could draw off enough German troops from the Eastern Front.

That proposition collapsed quickly. The Germans already had as many as twenty-five divisions in France, five or six times the number the Allies could force ashore. They might attempt the amphibious landing, but the cost would be high and the Russians would garner no relief.

For all practical purposes, SLEDGEHAMMER was dead by noon. Britain would have no part of it and the United States had too few troops ready to mount the operation alone.

But if not SLEDGEHAMMER, then what? Only later would the chief of staff recognize his miscalculation. "We failed to see that the leader in a democracy has to keep the people entertained. (That may sound like the wrong word, but it conveys the thought.) The people demand action," Marshall explained.

Shortly after lunch, Marshall received a message which he carried into the second-floor study. He silently handed the pink slip of paper to the president, who skimmed it before passing it on to the prime minister.

"Tobruk has surrendered with 25,000 men taken prisoner," Churchill read, wincing.

It was a bitter moment for Churchill. "Defeat is one thing, disgrace is another," he wrote later. In a single day, Rommel had punctured the defense perimeter thrown up around the vital Libyan port, and pushed his armor and infantry into the breach. The Germans and Italians had captured enough supplies and vehicles to refit the resurgent Afrika Korps. Meanwhile, the Eighth Army straggled in retreat toward the Egyptian frontier, leaving the road to Cairo thinly defended.

After a heartbeat's silence, the president asked quietly, "What can we do to help?"

"Give us as many Sherman tanks as you can spare, and ship them to the Middle East as quickly as possible," Churchill requested.

Marshall's response was even more generous. He offered to send the 2nd Armored Division to Egypt though that division would require tanks stripped from other newly formed units. "It is a terrible thing to take the weapons out of a soldier's hands," the chief of staff told the prime minister, but "if the British need is so great they must have them." Within minutes Marshall had ordered Major General George Patton to prepare his division for shipment overseas.

In the next four days they would reconsider committing the division, which could not arrive in time to aid the British Eighth Army. Marshall instead proposed delivering 300 of the new Sherman tanks and 100 howitzers; Churchill accepted the offer. (When one of the ships delivering the tanks and guns was sunk by a submarine, Marshall immediately made good the loss by dispatching another seventy tanks.)

Many in the War Department considered these offers to shore up the sagging Middle East wasteful. A number of senior officers nursed grave reservations about British strategy, and had little respect for the generalship of their Allies. Staff planners resented the British expectation that Washington would defer to whatever strategies emerged from Whitehall. The Brits, after all, had little experience in offensive warfare. "The British Army," wrote Albert Wedemeyer, "aside from the small forces engaged in North Africa, was surely no more combat-effective than our own."

Whatever the reservations in the Munitions Building, the Americans' generosity in the wake of the Tobruk debacle—though Marshall never described it as such—impressed the shocked British delegation. "I always feel," Brooke later told his biographer, "that the Tobruk episode in the president's study did a great deal towards laying the foundations of friendship and understanding built up during the war between the president and Marshall on the one hand and Churchill and myself on the other."

Generous it may have been, but the proffered aid was compelled by Erwin Rommel's success. Concerned about the steady retreat of the British across North Africa, the president asked the Joint Chiefs for an estimate of what would happen if Rommel's forces rolled on to Cairo. Alexandria would fall too and with it the entire Middle East, the planners replied. Turkey would be next to go, caught in a giant pincers at the eastern end of the Mediterranean. If Egypt fell, Marshall warned, the Allies should not attempt to defend anything east of the Canal. "A major effort in this region would bleed us white."

The German threat to close the Suez Canal and thereby cut the British Empire in half dominated their talks through the night. Late that Sunday, June 21, Roosevelt suddenly suggested the United States place an American army to fortify the Middle East. Marshall was taken aback; it was so contrary to everything they had been planning for, he told the president, that he refused to discuss it at that hour of the night. Churchill averted an argument between soldier and commander-in-chief; he agreed such a move would be helpful, but he had no intention of asking for such aid. Marshall coldly asked to be excused, thus closing the subject as abruptly as it had been opened.

In search of compromise, General Ismay drafted a statement on offensive operations for the balance of the year. Ismay, "a perfect oil-can," gave with one hand while taking away with the other.

Operations in Western Europe in 1942 would, if successful, yield greater political and strategic gains than operations in any other theatre. Plans and preparations for the operations in this theatre are to be pressed forward with all possible speed, energy and ingenuity. The most resolute efforts must be made to overcome the obvious dangers and difficulties of the enterprise. If a sound and sensible plan can be contrived, we should not hesitate to give effect to it. If on the other hand detailed examination shows that despite all efforts, success is improbable, we must be ready with an alternative.

Ismay adopted as an alternative for 1942 Roosevelt's "secret baby," the invasion of North Africa code-named GYMNAST. It looked appealing, for a landing in Rommel's rear would place the rampaging Germans between hammer and anvil. Marshall argued against GYMNAST for the next three days, extracting from the British and the president an agreement to study GYMNAST further.

They had postponed a decision, but the president's gaze had wandered afield. Stimson raged in his diary, "The president was in his most irresponsible mood. He was talking of a most critical situation and in the presence of another government with the frivolity and lack of responsibility of a child."

That threat momentarily abated, Marshall escorted the British party to a field demonstration by three divisions training at Fort Jackson, South Carolina. The chief of staff had scheduled the exercises, which included a paratroop drop by 600 troops, in order to impress upon his visitors the Americans' ability to mass-produce combat units. The show delighted the prime minister; the bird watcher in Brooke was more impressed by a Kentucky cardinal he saw the day before than he was with the training of the men. They had a lot to learn about war against the Hun, Brooke commented. Churchill was more enthusiastic. "You're wrong. They are wonderful material and will learn very quickly." Both men were right.

Churchill was to return to London to fend off a motion of no confidence in the House of Commons. Unhappy with the course of the war, members of the opposition had called for the appointment of a professional soldier or sailor to head the War Cabinet. Disgruntled London newspapers also called upon Churchill to step down. The prime minister retaliated in Commons with a brilliant speech, one rich in the artful scorn of British debate. With that he scored a resounding victory, 475 to 25, but the very fact that a motion of no confidence had been placed on the Order Book suggested he would need a military victory, and soon, to remain in office. It was one more reason why there could be no sacrificial SLEDGEHAMMERS, even if a German offensive toward the Volga River and the Caucasus Mountains broke the back of Soviet resistance.

On July 8, Churchill informed Washington, "No responsible British general, admiral, or air marshal is prepared to recommend SLEDGEHAMMER as a practicable operation in 1942." Even if they managed to get ashore, Churchill's telegram insisted, "all our energies would be involved in defending the Bridgehead."

Instead, Churchill recommended the North African invasion as offering "the best chance for relief to the Russian front in 1942. This has all along been in harmony with your ideas. In fact it is your commanding idea. Here is the true second front of 1942."

Marshall was livid. After a private discussion with Admiral King, at the July 10 meeting of the Joint Chiefs of Staff Marshall posed two questions: should the United States also opt for North Africa; and, were the British sincere about ROUNDUP in 1943? Unless the British were truly committed to it, the invasion of France in 1942 or 1943 would be impossible.

The chief of staff then proposed an alternative, a massive redirection of their strategy. If the British continued to resist the invasion of France, he suggested, "the U.S. should turn to the Pacific for decisive action against Japan."

Ernest King happily agreed. King did not like the North African operation at all: it would force them to transfer aircraft carriers to the Atlantic, possibly upsetting the hard-won balance of naval power. Moreover, the victory at Midway and the retreat of the sorely wounded Japanese carrier fleet to home waters opened the way for an American counterstroke.

For the past month General MacArthur and Pacific Fleet commander Chester Nimitz had been jockeying for command of that first American offensive in the Pacific. Both favored hitting the Solomon Islands. As the farthermost point of the Japanese advance, it was the logical place to strike. They could not agree, however, on which of the two should command the campaign, and just which of the Solomon Islands they should target.

Admiral Nimitz argued that he commanded the Marines who would make the assault, the transports that would ferry them, and the combat vessels that would protect the invasion fleet. MacArthur, for his part, insisted on his territorial prerogative; the Solomon Islands were well within his Southwest Pacific area.

MacArthur also put forward the bolder plan, proposing the Navy lend him the 1st Marine Division as well as the ships to strike at Rabaul, the fortified Japanese base on the northern tip of New Britain. Capturing that island would sever the entire Solomons tentacle from the Japanese octopus and end the threat to Australia at the same time, MacArthur argued.

"Savvy" Cooke, Admiral King's chief of staff, pressed a more cautious plan, one that would not bring the Navy's too few carriers within range of land-based Japanese planes. Cooke, as iron-willed as the chief of naval operations himself, preferred to move from island to island up the Solomon chain, leaving no Japanese threat in their rear.

Neither man, neither service would yield. For a week Marshall and King sought a solution between themselves. Or the general did. King remained obdurate, even threatening to undertake a campaign in the Solomons without army support.

To MacArthur, Marshall suggested that the Army fight the Japanese rather than the Navy. To King—who privately believed that Marshall "would do anything rather than disagree with MacArthur"—the chief of staff proposed a compromise.

The two chiefs agreed on June 30 to a three-part plan: the Navy would first command an operation to seize the Santa Cruz Islands and Tulagi in the Solomon chain. Then the Army would take control of Task Two to clear the northeast coast of New Guinea and launch Task Three, an assault on Rabaul.

To straighten out the jurisdictional squabble, Marshall agreed to redraw the boundary between the Navy's Pacific theater and MacArthur's Southwestern Pacific area. The bulk of the Solomons would shift from army to navy jurisdiction.

In Melbourne, Douglas MacArthur seethed from this slight at the hands of old enemies. To friendly news correspondents assigned to his headquarters, he described grand schemes for a single unified Pacific Command scuttled by pusillanimous staff officers in far-off Washington. For months, Secretary Stimson later complained, American newspapers reported the Pacific had been divided "at the behest of the navy for the purpose of belittling MacArthur."

On July 10, Marshall and King ordered their field commanders to prepare for the first task, the invasion of Tulagi and a second target, Guadalcanal, where the Japanese had begun building an airfield. MacArthur, who just weeks before had advocated the bold strike at Rabaul, suddenly grew cautious. Hastily built Japanese airfields throughout the Solomon chain forced them to build up their own air forces and naval support. "Savvy" Cooke snorted his disdain; if anything, they had to move quickly before the Japanese advance positions were so reinforced that they would make any Solomons campaign prohibitively costly.

The decision rested with the army chief of staff. If the Solomons fell to the Japanese, New Guinea would be next, and the way opened to Australia. There was little standing between the Japanese and dominance of the western Pacific. Against that Marshall balanced the realization that any concerted campaign in the Pacific inevitably meant the postponement of the invasion of France. Providing the necessary materiel in the Pacific, especially airplanes, would work against ROUNDUP in 1943.

Political realities dictated Marshall's decision. Virtually undefended Australia could not be permitted to fall. Strategically, it would be a grave loss, but psychologically an even worse blow. Undoubtedly the loss of that Anglo-Saxon country to "the Yellow Race" would bring down the Churchill government, and with it who knew what consequences.

At the July 10 meeting of the Joint Chiefs of Staff, Marshall not only proposed they adopt a Pacific-first strategy, but threw his support behind the navy position. He agreed they were to go ahead with Task One, the seizure of Guadalcanal and Tulagi at the western end of the Solomons. Planning was to go forward on Tasks Two and Three.

Marshall was playing his Pacific trump.

That afternoon King and Marshall dispatched a memo to President Roosevelt, who had escaped the humidity of Washington for a weekend at Hyde Park. Their memo scored the North African invasion as "both indecisive and a heavy drain on our resources. . . . If the United States is to engage in any other operation than forceful, unswerving adherence to full BOLERO plans, we are definitely of the opinion that we should turn to the Pacific and strike decisively against Japan; in other words assume a defensive attitude against Germany, except for air operations; and use all available means in the Pacific."

Later Marshall would describe his Pacific proposal as "a bluff." If so, he deluded the normally astute secretary of war. The British persisting in their "fatuous defeatist position," Stimson wrote in his diary, the Pacific ploy would be better than a half-hearted European gambit.

If bluff it was, the president smelled it out. On Sunday morning, July 12, FDR telephoned from Hyde Park to demand a comprehensive outline of the Pacific alternative. He expected it to be delivered by airplane that afternoon.

The response was a limp, hasty paper acknowledging that they still had no plan for offensive operations in the Pacific. On Tuesday, the president responded with a message to Marshall that tagged the Pacific alternative as "something of a red herring." The president even recommended "the record should be altered so that it would not appear in later years that we had proposed what amounted to the abandonment of the British."

The following day, FDR brushed aside Stimson's defense of the Pacific alternative as petulance, "taking up your dishes and going away." Stimson conceded the point but insisted it was necessary to move the British to reason.

The president was somewhat more charitable with Marshall later in that morning of a tense day at the White House. Roosevelt understood Marshall's frustration. Three times the British had seemingly agreed to an invasion of France and three times they had backed away from the commitment. In the meantime the British were proposing strategies of their own that would do little to shorten the war, Marshall's planners argued, but much to preserve the Empire. It was time to "fish or cut bait."

The president himself still favored the build-up in Great Britain preparatory to the invasion of France next year, he assured his chief of staff. He too wanted a firm decision, and had decided to send Marshall, King, and Harry Hopkins to London to thrash it out. They were to leave the following day. (To announce their coming, undoubtedly with Marshall's tacit assistance, Field Marshal John Dill sent off a telegram to Churchill warning that without a pledge of devotion to BOLERO, "everything points to a complete reversal of our present agreed strategy and the withdrawal of America to a war of her own in the Pacific. . . .")

That night at dinner in the White House, the president checked Marshall's gambit. "My main point," Roosevelt instructed Hopkins, "is that I do not believe we can wait until 1943 to strike at Germany. If we cannot strike at SLEDGEHAMMER, then we must take the second best—and that is not the Pacific."

While they were in London—and he wanted a final decision within the week—they were to decide upon "a specific and definite theater where our ground and sea forces can operate against the German ground forces in 1942. The theaters to be considered are North Africa and the Middle East."

Of the two, the president favored North Africa, for it would be solely an American operation, an offensive move designed to deprive ports and territory to the Germans rather than merely aiding the British defense of Suez.

At noon on July 16, Hopkins, Marshall, King, and a small group of aides boarded an olive drab TWA Stratoliner at National Airport. They landed early on the morning of the 18th at Prestwick in Scotland, where heavy fog grounded their plane. Waiting for them stood the prime minister's private train and an engineer with instructions to deliver the party to the prime minister's country estate, Chequers, for the weekend.

It was a divided group of Americans standing in the Scottish fog, "a queer party," Brooke noted in his diary. "Hopkins is for operating in Africa, Marshall wants to operate in Europe, and King is determined to stick to the Pacific."

Ordered by the president to go directly to London, and anxious to unify their position, Marshall ordered that the train deliver them to the capital rather than to Chequers. It was important that they talk immediately with the handful of American planners already in London and especially with the newly named commander of the American European Theater of Operations (ETO), Dwight Eisenhower.

Less than a year before, temporary Colonel Eisenhower had been chief of staff of the Third Army in San Antonio, Texas. He had been summoned in the aftermath of Pearl Harbor to the War Plans Division, where for six months the chief of staff had taken his measure. They had met daily, frequently hourly in times of crisis, Eisenhower's staff preparing plans and position papers for his chief, adapting himself to Marshall's thinking and personal style. The months in Washington had been a "tough, intensive grind," he wrote a friend, but worth it all. He had gained Marshall's confidence, which meant much to him because "the chief is a great soldier." In Marshall he saw too the qualities necessary for high command; Marshall was "quick, tough, tireless, decisive and a real leader. He accepts responsibility automatically and never goes back on a subordinate." All that Eisenhower admired, and admiring it had adopted as his own. To a large extent, Eisenhower had come to be Marshall's protégé; command of the renamed, reorganized Operations Division of Marshall's War Department was the cap upon Fox Conner's tutelage of two decades before.

Still, Marshall's decision to appoint the man everybody but the chief of staff called "Ike" to command a new American theater of operations in Europe came as a surprise. Weeks before, Marshall had told Eisenhower that "the men who are going to get the promotions in this war are the commanders in the field, not the staff officers who clutter up all of the administrative machinery in the War Department and in higher tactical headquarters." It had not been that way in the first war, and he intended no repetition.

Turning to Eisenhower himself, Marshall snapped, "Take your case. I know that you were recommended by one general for division command and by another for corps command. That's all very well. I'm glad they have that opinion of you, but you are going to stay right here and fill your position, and that's that!"

Impulsively, Eisenhower blurted, "General, I'm interested in what you say, but I want you to know that I don't give a damn about your promotion plans as far as I'm concerned. I came into this office from the field and I am trying to do my duty. I expect to do so as long as you want me here. If that locks me to a desk for the rest of the war, so be it!"

Now flushed with resentment, Eisenhower stalked to the door, "a long march from where he was sitting," Eisenhower recalled. Somewhat sheepish, he turned toward Marshall. "I had to grin a little bit at my own childishness. A tiny smile quirked the corner of his face." Eisenhower had passed another test.

Some days later, Eisenhower had reported to Marshall on an inspection he had made of the American command in Great Britain. They lacked what Eisenhower called punch, a sense of urgency. Eisenhower was particularly irritated that the officers were wearing civilian clothes on leisurely weekends. Eisenhower recommended the commander of the European Theater of Operations be replaced.

Who did Eisenhower have in mind, Marshall asked casually. Eisenhower recommended Major General Joseph McNarney, now Marshall's deputy chief of staff, a man who could crack heads or crack whips as needed. Marshall dismissed the suggestion. McNarney was needed in Washington.

On June 8, Eisenhower was back with a draft of a directive for the commanding general of the ETO, whoever it might be. Eisenhower advised Marshall to read it carefully since it provided for a unified command of all American forces, military, naval or air, assigned to Europe.

"I certainly do intend to read it. You may be the man who executes it. If that's the case, when can you leave?"

Eisenhower was stunned. Marshall had said nothing, dropped no hint. Instead he had watched Eisenhower closely, measuring his performance, deciding finally on the genial Eisenhower because of the man's ability to get along with people.

This was no impulsive decision. Marshall had thought long about Allied cooperation; he insisted the greatest hazard was that "we would lick ourselves," as he told the Australian ambassador to the United States. Eisenhower's affability would go far to ensure the success of the command. "His faculty for getting along well with top brass—Americans and Allies alike—and his immense popularity with the troops were extremely important," he explained later.

Admittedly flabbergasted, Eisenhower marveled in his diary, "It's a big job; if the United States and the United Kingdom stay squarely behind BOLERO and go after it tooth and nail, it will be the biggest American job of the war. Of course, command now does not necessarily mean command in the operation"—Eisenhower expected Marshall would eventually take charge of the invasion—"but the job before the battle begins will still be the biggest outside of that of the chief of staff himself."

Having made his choice, Marshall permitted Eisenhower to select his immediate subordinates and staff. The new ETO commander named two men: Walter Bedell Smith, then secretary of the General Staff; and Mark W. Clark, by consensus the outstanding infantry officer after Joseph Stilwell. Clark had previously recommended Eisenhower for the European post; now Eisenhower was returning the compliment. "It looks as if you boys got together," Marshall said with a smile. "How soon can you go?"

Instinctively Clark looked at his watch.

"Never mind," Marshall sighed. "That's soon enough."

Three weeks later, barely established in the apartment building at 20 Grosvenor Square that had been converted into his headquarters, Eisenhower was to welcome the men who would determine the mission of his newly created European Theater of Operations.

The chief of staff's party swept into Claridge's, one of the most distinguished of London hotels, whose fourth floor had been hastily converted into a temporary if elegant military headquarters. Army sentries stood before fifteen of the suites, a Marine at the sixteenth, Admiral King's. Marshall immediately launched a round of meetings with Eisenhower and the military planners in his headquarters. One of them, Lucian Truscott, recalled the intensity of that weekend:

> I opened the door and entered. General Marshall spoke from the bathroom. "Sit down. I am dressing. I will be with you in a few minutes." He came out shortly, greeted me, and continued with his dressing while he talked. He asked how I was. How the job was going. About each of the officers who had accompanied me. What our activities were. What I thought of Mountbatten. About British organization and methods. About other British officers. About British people.

Through Scotch-and-sodas and dinner in Marshall's suite, the questioning continued. ". . . I was being subjected to the most thorough examination and in the most charming manner that one can imagine. For every activity since my arrival, every personality, every impression, views concerning the British, their attitude toward the plans. Nothing was overlooked. I could well understand the expression 'pick your brains.' "

From Truscott, the chief of staff learned that younger planners from both nations believed they could hold a beachhead on the Cherbourg peninsula through the winter. They had proposed SLEDGEHAMMER be transformed from a sacrificial offering into a foothold for ROUNDUP; senior advisers to the British chiefs of staff had killed that idea.

Marshall had an alternative to defeat. For the next three days, the chief of staff futilely pressed the British chiefs for an immediate invasion of France, confronted by the president's insistence upon an offensive in 1942. Marshall was to absorb a bitter lesson in London, as he acknowledged later. "In wartime, the politicians had always to appear to be winning, or taking steps to win that war. They could not use 1942 merely to prepare for the offensives of 1943 or 1944; they must not be charged with fighting another 'phony war.' "

It was perhaps some measure of Marshall's residual anger fifteen years later that he blamed his predicament on the politicians alone. Eisenhower, who was charged with drafting a viable SLEDGEHAMMER, spread the responsibility more widely. He noted in his diary that the Allies must take the offensive. "The British and American armies and the British and American people need to have the feeling that they are attempting something positive. We must not degenerate into a passive and mental attitude."

Marshall was in an untenable position. Promoting an immediate invasion, he was, in fact, arguing to preserve 1943's ROUNDUP and coming to grips with the German military machine on the continent. Any other operation in 1942, in North Africa, in the Middle East, in Norway, would drain troops needed for the invasion of France and force postponement of the cross-Channel attack to 1944. Meanwhile the Navy and MacArthur alike clamored for a Pacific offensive; any operation there would also come at the expense of ROUNDUP.

Early invasion of the continent, he knew, had little chance. At one point in the discussions, Professor F. A. Lindemann, Churchill's science adviser and all-subject sounding board, turned to Marshall and said, "It's no use. You are arguing against the casualties on the Somme."

On Wednesday, July 22, the British chiefs of staff flatly rejected SLEDGEHAMMER. Eisenhower was despondent, suggesting this might become the "blackest day in history." He himself was "right back to December fifteenth," when he reported for duty in Washington.

Defeated by Churchill's ghosts, Marshall wired the White House for instructions.

The president's reply restated their orders of the 17th. He wanted American ground troops in action against the Germans in 1942. (On Hopkins's recommendation, he would later set a deadline prior to October 30, in part because the Russians were in desperate shape, in part because the Democratic Party needed a lift before the November 3 congressional elections.)

Roosevelt listed five possible operations in order of priority: (1) an invasion of North Africa with French possessions as the target; (2) the original GYMNAST, which would put American and British troops into Tunisia at Rommel's rear; (3) Churchill's Norwegian plan; (4) a joint British-American breakout from Egypt; or (5) a land campaign from northern Iran into the Caucasus to aid the Russians.

With the president's reply in hand, Marshall sat down in his suite at Claridge's on the morning of July 24 and began drafting a proposal for "the least harmful diversion." His problem was "that we didn't have much and that much of what he had was in an amateurish stage—particularly Air." Marshall completed his proposal for a North African invasion—one that combined Roosevelt's first two options—just as King walked into the room. To Marshall's surprise, King accepted the plan "without a quibble. Usually he argued over all our plans."

Presenting his plan to the British chiefs of staff, Marshall warned that the North African invasion would in all likelihood make a 1943 ROUNDUP impractical. The best they could hope to accomplish was "a defensive, encircling line of action for the Continental European theater, except as to air operations." ROUNDUP, the big, inevitable invasion, would come in 1944, if the Germans had weakened.

It fell to a momentarily relieved Alan Brooke to present the Marshall proposal to the War Cabinet. Things went wrong from the start, Brooke recalled. The problem was Marshall's conclusion that the North African invasion would postpone ROUNDUP. "They didn't want it used against them politically if they prevented ROUNDUP in 1943, thus delaying the freeing of Europe," Marshall told his biographer, Forrest Pogue, in 1956.

When the cabinet refused to accept that wording, Marshall balked. "I blew the hell out of that and said unless the cabinet agreed I wouldn't go along."

Brooke, who had prevailed in the shaping of Allied strategy, knew when to bend. Any change would have been fatal, Brooke warned the cabinet ministers on July 25. "The Americans had gone a long way to meet us, and I should have hated to have to ask them for more." The War Cabinet approved the Marshall proposal.

The triumphant prime minister stepped in to rename the modified North African invasion, selecting the code word TORCH. Even years later Churchill could not contain himself. "All was therefore agreed and settled in accordance with my long-conceived ideas and those of my colleagues, military and political. . . . At every point except one [JUPITER] the plans I cherished were adopted."

By transatlantic cable on July 25, Roosevelt approved the plan. Only one decision remained, the selection of a commander for the operation. That officer would actually have three responsibilities: planning TORCH, then carrying it out, meanwhile continuing to prepare for the invasion of France.

Because the United States would furnish the bulk of the troops and vessels involved in the North African invasion, the unwritten rules of coalition warfare required that an American be supreme commander. The prevailing sentiment, repeatedly expressed by Admiral Mountbatten in London and Sir John Dill in Washington, favored Marshall as supreme commander of any joint operation. Since Marshall could not be immediately available, King nominated Eisenhower as his temporary surrogate.

The chief of staff returned to his hotel suite and promptly sent for Eisenhower. The general arrived while Marshall was in the toilet. Through the closed door Marshall shouted that Eisenhower was to plan the North Africa invasion and that both King and he favored Eisenhower for command of the operation.

Marshall preferred that the same man plan both TORCH and ROUNDUP to avert competition for scarce divisions and weapons between the two operations. The Combined Chiefs of Staff agreed that the unnamed supreme commander could have a deputy in London to do the planning; that deputy would then command the North African invasion. As the date for ROUNDUP neared, the Americans would name the supreme commander for that invasion. (At Dill's prodding, Churchill telegraphed

Roosevelt a week later: "It would be agreeable to us if General Marshall were designated for Supreme Command of ROUNDUP and that in the meantime General Eisenhower should act as his deputy here.")

The essential business concluded, the Americans were impatient to return to Washington. Still there remained one ally to be dealt with, the stiff-necked, self-pronounced leader of the Free French, Charles de Gaulle.

This first meeting between the two almost foundered on protocol. De Gaulle considered it only proper that the Americans call upon *him* as head of a foreign government; the Americans did not wish to appear to be supporting de Gaulle politically. The Frenchman yielded only after it was pointed out both Marshall and King wore four stars while de Gaulle could boast but the equivalent of two.

Accompanied by an aide and a translator, the 6 foot 4 inch de Gaulle visited Marshall in the makeshift military headquarters set up on the fourth floor of Claridge's. Apparently expecting a private meeting, de Gaulle instead discovered Marshall had invited King, Eisenhower, Eisenhower's new chief of staff, Walter Bedell Smith, and Mark Clark to sit in. De Gaulle was not meeting Marshall as an equal, a fellow leader of the United Nations, but as no more than a general with nominal authority over troops scattered halfway around the world. Even the bottle of champagne King had ordered did nothing to warm their discussion.

The conversations were frosty, the Americans careful not to say anything that might be construed as political support of the Frenchman, who wanted just that endorsement more than anything. De Gaulle broke an awkward silence by offering a review of the Free French resources.

De Gaulle claimed troops loyal to him were scattered across Africa, in the eastern Mediterranean, and on a handful of Pacific islands. He was particularly concerned that nothing interfere in the Pacific with the maintenance of French sovereignty. The Free French everywhere would welcome the opening of a second front, de Gaulle asserted. What could the army chief of staff tell him, the Frenchman asked.

Marshall and King responded vaguely. "Neither of them told him as much as he could have learned by reading the morning paper," a sardonic Mark Clark noted.

Realizing there was nothing to be gained here, de Gaulle rose stiffly, shook hands, and left. The "discussion"—the quotation marks are in the French minutes of the meeting—had lasted a bare half-hour. De Gaulle, a man of enormous and prickly pride, would not soon forget what he considered this slight to the leader of Free France.

For the army chief of staff, this second visit to London in four months had not been a great success, either strategically or diplomatically.

It remained only for the president to scuttle whatever Marshall might have hoped to salvage from this London wreck. After a round of discussions when they returned to Washington, FDR flatly ruled "that TORCH would be undertaken at the earliest possible date . . . that this operation was now our principal objective and the assembling of means to carry it out should take precedence over all other operations. . . ."

The president as commander-in-chief had made the pivotal strategic decision of the war the Allies would fight. He made it while ignoring the advice of his military chief of staff. He made it for political reasons. He made it without weighing the risks, while ignoring the certain diplomatic repercussions.

For all intents and purposes, BOLERO was dead and with it ROUNDUP in 1943. They were embarking instead on a campaign, the invasion of North Africa, that would only marginally aid in the defeat of Hitler's Germany. Meanwhile King siphoned men and materiel to the Pacific, and MacArthur demanded a share of their scarce resources. Marshall's strategic concept had been junked.

A Pile of Brickbats

Two hundred feet below the surface of the granite sentinel his British hosts called "Gib," Lieutenant General Eisenhower nervously waited word from his three task forces. So far, only one ship was reported torpedoed; more than 330 vessels had slipped unnoticed through the Straits of Gibraltar. Still Eisenhower paced. Spain seemed ominously quiet; German observers across the border must have spotted the unusual activity at the Gibraltar airfield, must have sensed that something was afoot. Just now, Marshall's insistence they put a force ashore in Casablanca, outside the Straits, seemed wise. If Spain threw in with the Axis, George Patton's three divisions in Morocco could maintain an overland line of communication with the invasion forces in Algiers and Oran.

Eisenhower marked the hours tensely, chain-smoking his daily four packs of Camels. Early the next morning, American and British troops under his command would launch a coordinated, three-pronged assault on French possessions in North Africa—at Casablanca on the west coast of Africa, at Oran and at Algiers on the Mediterranean coast. More than 107,000 men would go ashore, prepared to fight a war or be welcomed as liberators. No one knew which to expect.

There had never been an amphibious operation so ambitious in all the history of warfare. More than 500 vessels in four convoys had converged in the Atlantic Ocean off the northern coast of Africa. From the convoys would spill three coordinated landings on beaches stretching 650 air miles from Casablanca on the Atlantic coast to Algiers on the Mediterranean. The sheer size of TORCH made the ports in North Africa too small and the roads and narrow-gauge railways inadequate to maintain the first American army to fight in the theater.

Eisenhower was fiercely proud of the team he had put together in the previous six months to plan this first joint American-British offensive. As Allied commander-in-chief, he had insisted that his staff officers put aside both the traditions of their services and the prejudices of nation-ality to get the job done. Those who could not adapt to his first rule of coalition warfare found themselves summarily replaced. All of official London had heard the story of the usually good-natured Eisenhower furiously dispatching a staff officer back to the United States for calling a co-worker a "British son-of-a-bitch." The slur on his paternity was acceptable; the scorn for his nationality was not.

The British had cooperated fully, at Eisenhower's suggestion going so far as to rewrite the orders placing the commander of the British Expe-ditionary Force under Allied command, and restricting his right to appeal to the War Cabinet. As supreme commander, Eisenhower held more authority than had Foch during World War I.

In tapping Eisenhower for the assignment, Marshall had stressed repeatedly the need for a unified command; Eisenhower, the first to exercise that command, wanted his mentor to know he had faithfully followed through. ". . . I truly believe that we have established a pattern for Combined Staff operation that might well serve as a rough model when expeditions of this nature are undertaken in the future," Eisen-hower wrote Marshall on the eve of TORCH.

They still had so much to learn—about the troops, their officers, their training for combat, their weapons. This was the first American opera-tion against hostile troops since the Argonne offensive a quarter century before. The six American divisions assigned to TORCH had never been in battle. None of them had even existed as more than skeletal cadres three years earlier; since their formation they had been repeatedly stripped of experienced men for newer divisions, then rebuilt. How would they respond? How, for that matter, would Eisenhower himself, without a day in combat, do?

Senior British officers had their doubts about these green troops and equally inexperienced commanders. One did not know what war was until one had fought the German, they assured each other with knowing winks. The Americans were not yet "blooded."

Aware of the whispered criticism, Eisenhower had defensively explained to Marshall, "Unfortunately, the estimated worth placed upon our Army by many observers is often established by outward appearances. . . . I have found a very high degree of efficiency in performance of duty [but] the appearance and rather careless attitude of many of our men when on pass create an unfortunate effect." Among the British, Churchill alone defended the Americans' fighting abilities.

For all the risks, Roosevelt and Churchill each had his own motive for pressing the North African venture. Roosevelt had one eye cocked on the November 3 mid-term congressional elections and public opinion polls, which since May had showed the Democrats slipping in popularity.

His hands poised in mock prayer, the president urged Marshall, "Please make it before Election Day." A timely offensive would help to restore Democratic fortunes.

Churchill wanted TORCH because he had taken on "a somewhat raw job"—explaining to Marshal Stalin why there would be no landing in France that year. His task would be a bit easier if he could fly to Moscow with TORCH as a token gift.

The first step to solidifying TORCH was to select a commander for the operation. Churchill recommended that Marshall be named supreme commander of ROUNDUP, the 1943 invasion of France; he proposed that Eisenhower, as commanding general of United States Forces in the European theater, be responsible for planning and executing the smaller North African operation. Roosevelt approved Eisenhower's nomination.

On August 14, Eisenhower radioed Marshall to inquire tactfully about the chief of staff's future place in the European command structure. Marshall replied with what must have been some embarrassment, "Just why the president has given no expression of his view or concurrence I do not know, but I must not under any circumstances in any way be put in the position of seeking his favorable action, or even of suggesting that he make a decision."

Eisenhower pressed ahead with TORCH planning, though Marshall remained wary of British ambitions and overcommitment in the Mediterranean.

The British strongly favored a bold stroke, one that landed troops well to the east. A *coup de main* to seize Tunisia before German and Italian reinforcements could flow across the Sicilian straits would squeeze Rommel's forces between invaders and the British Eighth Army in Egypt.

Marshall said no. French colonial reaction to an invasion force—certainly hostile to the British, perhaps less so to the Americans—might render their line of communication precarious. Axis air and submarine forces might cork the Straits of Gibraltar. Or Spain and Spanish Morocco, with or without German pressure, could pull a drawstring tight around the Straits, bagging a large invasion fleet and Allied army inside the Mediterranean.

Marshall inclined toward a cautious plan, one that involved a landing in the Casablanca area of French Morocco, outside the Straits. The Allies then would move overland toward Tunisia, consolidating their gains.

With something verging on horror, the British argued against Marshall's "outside" plan. It would take months to advance the 1,000 miles and more from Morocco to Tunisia, months in which the Germans and Italians would be able to reinforce their African army. With that delay would go control of the vital mid-Mediterranean.

What Eisenhower came to call "the transatlantic essay contest" raged for two months after Roosevelt's decision for TORCH. Marshall, so vigorous in support of the bold SLEDGEHAMMER concept, now was cautious; Alan Brooke, so conservative when considering an invasion of the continent, now advocated the bold strike. Their *bouleversement* stemmed from each man's concept of the proper strategy to defeat the Axis: Brooke favored opportunistic operations in the Mediterranean littoral, Marshall the heartland offensive. Brooke and his colleagues considered American strategy naive; Marshall and his planners suspected British strategic concepts were as much concerned with preserving the Empire as defeating Hitler and Mussolini.

A landing in Morocco with troops from the United States also had the advantage, in Marshall's unspoken opinion, of slowing the movement of troops to TORCH from the BOLERO build-up in the British Isles. TORCH barred an immediate invasion of Europe, but there was always 1943, if Marshall could hold down the North African commitment.

President Roosevelt aside, there was little sentiment for TORCH in Washington. As the Imperial General Staff's chief planner put it, "The hearts of the Americans were not really in this business." The War Department staff gave Ike's first plan only a 50 percent chance of success, the chief of staff wrote Eisenhower in mid-August. Marshall himself considered that judgment "immediate and artificial," he added.

Eisenhower was no more content than Marshall. His plans were "just a God damned mess," but they were the best he could do with the available forces. "So far as he was concerned, he had received the order to carry out the operation and he would carry it out even if he had to go in himself with only two squadrons."

Putting the best face on it he could, Eisenhower gave TORCH "a fair chance" of success if Spain stayed neutral and the French put up only token resistance. George Patton, who would lead the Morocco assault, estimated "it was better than even money we could land, but a poor bet we could get Tunis ahead of the Boches."

The prospects looked no better after August 19 when a force of 6,000 Canadian and British commandos with a platoon of American Rangers raided the French coastal resort of Dieppe. The raid, planned to test amphibious tactics and vehicles, ended disastrously. Without a supporting naval barrage, without dominance of the air, the landings stalled on the beaches. The Canadians reported 66 percent casualties; equipment losses were severe.

As the new commander-in-chief of the Allied Expeditionary Force, Eisenhower was understandably insecure. A very junior officer, he had been promoted over the heads of hundreds of his seniors, many with outstanding qualifications. How not feel just a bit uncomfortable when George Patton, who outranked Eisenhower on the Regular Army list, had only two stars to Ike's three? (Patton accepted the indignity because

Ike was an old friend, but resented the even more rapid rise of Mark Clark to major general and deputy commander of the operation.)

Some of his insecurity Eisenhower eased by writing weekly letters to Marshall. Writing was perhaps something like talking through a problem; it was also a way of assuring Marshall that his surrogate remained the faithful servant. In his first letter, Eisenhower promised: "I shall try to apply your dictum—'Persuade by accomplishment rather than by eloquence.'"

Eisenhower's repeated assurances verged on the obsequious. "Whenever I'm tempted to droop a bit over the burdens cast upon us here, I think of the infinitely greater ones you have to bear and express to myself a fervent wish that the army may be fortunate enough to keep you until the final victory is chalked up."

Eisenhower's deference provoked Marshall to reiterate that he, Marshall, wanted their relations on the "frankest possible basis." Eisenhower instead had tried to please the chief of staff, a man who disliked that in subordinates. "When you disagree with my point of view," Marshall instructed, "say so, without an apologetic approach; when you want something that you aren't getting, tell me and I will try to get it for you. I have complete confidence in your management of the affair, and want to support you in every way practicable."

Eisenhower continued to feel his way gingerly with Marshall for some months. Though he picked his own commanders, Ike passed over men he knew Marshall did not favor, and accepted one man with reservations only because he had been put forward by the chief of staff.

Even as he tutored his London surrogate, Marshall groped for a compromise between the British and American positions. It was a measure of his influence by this time that Marshall was able to convince Roosevelt, who favored bold action, to accept a more conservative plan.

Success in this first American effort in Europe was vital, Marshall reminded FDR. "A failure of SLEDGEHAMMER, for which the public has been adequately prepared, could have been accepted, but failure in TORCH would only bring ridicule and loss of confidence."

Marshall proposed they make two landings only, "outside" at Casablanca and "inside" at Oran. Instead, Roosevelt as commander-in-chief suggested a three-pronged attack on Casablanca, Oran, and Algiers. The British, however, would have to supply the shipping for the Algerian venture they wanted so badly.

For ten days Roosevelt and Churchill haggled by radio before hammering out a compromise. The British agreed to the Casablanca landings; Marshall, in turn, accepted first-day assaults on Oran and Algiers, then follow-up attacks on Philippeville and Bone, 260 air miles closer to Tunisia, within a week of D-Day.

Finally on September 5, little more than two months before the date set, Roosevelt cabled: "Hurrah!"

Churchill, now resigned to a landing at Casablanca, replied: "Okay, full blast." The transatlantic essay contest had ended.

It took longer to settle upon a Pacific strategy, but there the chief of staff was dealing not with a head of government, Churchill, but with a nascent political force, Douglas MacArthur.

During the first days of July 1942, Marshall and Admiral King had divided responsibility for operations in the Pacific. Admiral Nimitz was to launch the opening offensive, then would pass command to General MacArthur for the second and third tasks. The Navy would be responsible for the amphibious landings in all phases; King adamantly refused to let MacArthur, or any other soldier, have command of his aircraft carriers.

The pact was the best Marshall could negotiate, and tenuous at that. "King never lets up," Arnold complained to Stimson early in September. "He has not receded one inch from any of his demands upon us. . . ." Only too aware of King's willingness to go it alone, Marshall cautioned MacArthur that friction with the Navy could unravel the unprecedented unity of command the Joint Chiefs had hammered out in Washington.

Word that the Japanese were constructing an airfield on Guadalcanal, one of the larger of the Solomon Islands, forced an immediate revision of their targets. The Navy would take out both Tulagi and Guadalcanal in the first phase, denying the Japanese airfields that would give them control of the surrounding waters. Meanwhile, MacArthur was to plan the follow-up campaigns.

Once so confident, MacArthur clamored for increasing reinforcements, and especially for aircraft to defend his Southwest Pacific area. The Japanese had landed 16,000 elite troops at Buna on the northern coast of New Guinea and sent them through the rain forest and steep mountains toward Port Moresby on the southern coast. Outnumbered Australian defenders fought a dogged rearguard action on the tortuous Kodoka Trail, grudgingly giving ground. No training had prepared them for fighting in almost continuous rain or in deep mud that swallowed men to the waist; nothing could prepare them for jungle rot, malaria, typhus, and dysentery. The Japanese inched over the mountains, slowing each day, but drawing nearer to Port Moresby, the last Allied outpost before northern Australia.

A gloomy Douglas MacArthur in Brisbane wrote off New Guinea. To a visiting Hap Arnold, MacArthur complained that the Japanese were better infantrymen than the Germans, that he lacked the troops to prevent another Japanese breakout, that the Australian troops would not make even good militiamen.

On and on MacArthur rambled. The Japanese could extend their advance any time they pleased, and dominate the Pacific for a hundred years to come. The Navy was incapable of stopping the Japanese—this opinion coming more than two months after Midway. MacArthur was more than ever sure that Japan posed a bigger threat to the United States than Germany.

Arnold listened, troubled by MacArthur's appearance, and wrote in his diary, "[he] gives me the impression of a brilliant mind—obsessed by a plan he can't carry out—dramatic to the extreme—much more nervous than when I formerly knew him. Hands twitch and tremble—shell shocked."

Fearing the worst, already making excuses, MacArthur did not recognize the turn of the tide when it lapped over his shoes. On September 7, Australian troops and American combat engineers defeated a Japanese force at Milne Bay on the eastern end of New Guinea, blunting one of the pincers' prongs closing on Port Moresby. Four days later, outnumbered Australian troops finally managed to hold the weary Japanese on the Kodoka Trail, just thirty-two miles from Port Moresby. The Japanese offensive in the Pacific had reached its point of farthest advance.

There was time only for a sigh of relief. The 1st Marine Division had landed unopposed on Guadalcanal on August 7, setting in motion the first phase of the Marshall-King strategy for the Pacific. In the month since, that island almost by accident had become the linchpin in the Southwest Pacific.

Some thirty-six hours after the initial landings on Guadalcanal, a Japanese naval force of seven cruisers and a destroyer under cover of darkness attacked the Allied vessels screening the marine transport ships. In less than an hour, the Japanese with their superior night gunnery tactics had sunk four cruisers and two destroyers. Fearful of land-based bombers, however, Japanese Vice Admiral Mikawa Gunichi chose to withdraw rather than attack the hapless transports.

With their covering force lying in "Ironbottom Sound," the American transports hastily withdrew at noon the following day. Eleven thousand Marines on the island hunkered down, with only a four-day supply of ammunition and scant rations.

The Battle of Guadalcanal would rage for six months, a vortex for men and supplies. The fast destroyers of the "Tokyo Express" made repeated nighttime forays, landing thousands of Japanese reinforcements, then withdrawing before daylight. By December, the United States had 40,000 men and the Japanese 25,000 on Guadalcanal; an afterthought of an island had become a suppurating wound.

Preoccupied with TORCH, Marshall found himself unwillingly drawn to provide relief for the Southwest Pacific. The Navy had gravely underestimated its supply needs; disdainful of logistics, it had ignored that vital part of modern warfare to the peril of its first offensive. (Admiral

King reportedly said in the first months of the war, "I don't know what the hell this logistics is that Marshall is always talking about, but I want some of it.")

Hap Arnold, his treasured B-17 forces in Great Britain chivvied apart to beef up TORCH and to establish aerial superiority from Alaska to the Middle East, reminded the chief of staff, "Even though everyone agrees that success in the Pacific Theater will not win the war, we are planning to concentrate more airplanes there in spite of the very serious shortage which will exist in our North Africa operations."

Once of secondary priority, the Pacific theater had become a vast siphon sucking troops and weapons from TORCH and BOLERO.

Fearing yet another setback in the Pacific, President Roosevelt ordered the Joint Chiefs of Staff "to make sure that every possible weapon gets into that area to hold Guadalcanal." Shipping, planes, and an army division were already en route, the Joint Chiefs responded.

The president's order could not prevent MacArthur from transforming the Southwest Pacific into a domestic political issue. Inspired secretly by MacArthur, the Hearst and McCormick papers once more took up their anti-Roosevelt cudgels in October. Unleash MacArthur, the editorials shrilled, prompted by inspired reports from Brisbane. The Pacific stalemate was Roosevelt's fault; was he not an old navy man who favored a victory at sea to another MacArthur triumph? The division of the Pacific into two theaters had been arranged by Roosevelt to dilute the press attention and foil MacArthur's presidential prospects, they concluded.

Irritated by these MacArthur-inspired attacks on strategic policy, Marshall moved to set the record straight. He ordered the Army's public information office to release statements noting that the Joint Chiefs, not the Navy, had decided upon Guadalcanal. To Stimson he added that far from Roosevelt dividing the Pacific to frustrate MacArthur's political career, "I doubt if the president even knew of the subdivision at the time it was made." Roosevelt would not forget the courtesy.

Half a world away, the TORCH task forces converged on their targets. Off French Morocco, Patton puffed on the expensive Havana cigars he favored, and weighed the forecast calling for "fair to bad" surf conditions. At Oran, another of the generals recommended by Marshall, Lloyd R. Fredendall, planned a parachute drop to seize a vital airfield, while coordinating amphibious landings at five different points. Meanwhile, the Algiers plan turned on a deception. The understrength assault force was predominately American, and commanded by an American, this in hope of muting anti-British sentiment among the French defenders. Once the city was in Allied hands, the British troops and the task force commander, British Lieutenant General Kenneth A. N. Anderson, would disembark.

Everything was complicated by the presence of the French Army. No one in Allied circles knew—there was no shortage of partisans ready to offer predictions—just how those troops or their commanders would react to the invaders. This was Overseas France, part of the empire that lay beyond firm control of Vichy and its German masters. Invading American and British troops might be welcomed as liberators and allies, or attacked as an enemy invading Free French territory.

The Allies were landing on a foreign shore, landing without proper intelligence, landing with only a promise of support from the French arranged by Eisenhower's deputy commander, Mark Clark. On the night of October 21 / 22, Clark had secretly slipped ashore from the British submarine *Seraph* accompanied by a small staff and three British commandos. In an isolated villa overlooking the ocean sixty-five miles west of Algiers, Clark met secretly with Robert Murphy, the American consul-general in Casablanca, and a small group of Frenchmen Murphy had recruited.

The key figure there, Murphy told Clark, was General Charles Mast, deputy commander of the French XIX Corps. Mast was the covert representative in North Africa of General Henri Honoré Giraud, a one-legged hero from the first war who had escaped from German captivity in the second. Mast had organized a small pro-Giraud or anti-Vichy network of French Army officers Murphy believed capable of rallying Overseas France to the Allied cause.

Mast was running a great risk; he was, after all, collaborating with a representative of a nation about to invade a French colony. He wanted assurances first that the Allies were coming in sufficient strength to stay, that this was not a mere raid, and, second, that "perfidious Albion" would not play a major role. That insult French honor could not permit.

Satisfied by Clark's assurances and exaggerations, Mast pledged French military cooperation. In return, Mast asked that Giraud be named supreme commander of the Allied invasion force.

Now the negotiations got sticky. Clark and Murphy were under injunction to avoid any political commitments. In dispatching the jovial Murphy to North Africa two years before, President Roosevelt had instructed him not to "help anyone impose a government on the French people." Mast and Giraud were intent on just that. Certainly naming Giraud as supreme commander would make him the leading Free French political figure, and likely head of any liberation government.

Clark the suitor would make no promises. They parted, Mast to return to Algiers and Clark to rendezvous with the submarine, the question of French cooperation still unsettled.

More than two weeks later, they still did not know if they had won Giraud's hand. "The most complex operation in military history," as General T. T. Handy, chief of the Operations Division in Washington, had described it, rested on a gamble. Not only were there three landings in the west, but they had to be coordinated with a major British counter-attack in Egypt. The strategic concept called for a vast vise in North Africa, the jaws squeezing tight, then crushing Erwin Rommel's Afrika Korps in Tunisia.

A new British commander in Egypt, General Bernard Montgomery, had revitalized the Eighth Army since taking charge in August. The night after Clark met secretly with Mast, Montgomery's British, Australian, New Zealand, Indian, South African, Greek, and Free French units forced a hole in Rommel's lines at El Alamein, turned back brutal counterattacks, then bent the Germans into retreat. Once the British had faltered under pressure; now it was the German's turn. For the next two weeks, the Eighth Army pressed westward, dicing Rommel's Panzer divisions. By November 5, Montgomery's army had Rommel in full retreat, and had snared more than 30,000 prisoners. Delighted that Montgomery's victory would prevent Rommel from rushing troops westward to engage the Americans, Marshall cabled "a certain Naval Party" in London:

> Having been privileged to witness your courage and resolution on the day of the fall of Tobruk, I am unable to express to the full my delight over the news from the Middle East and my admiration for the British Army.

With one jaw of the great strategic vise closing on Rommel, TORCH lurched into motion on the night of November 7 / 8. Waiting in a dank cavern on Gibraltar for word from his task forces, Eisenhower wrote another in the series of personal letters to Marshall he had used since moving to London in June to privately vent his feelings.

The big question, Eisenhower wrote, was the reception they could expect from the badly splintered French. They were no further along, even after spiriting Giraud from France by submarine. Gambling for political leadership, Giraud still made cooperation conditional upon his appointment as supreme commander.

With or without Giraud, with or without the support of anti-Vichy elements in North Africa, Eisenhower wrote Marshall, they "must take the jump—whether the bottom contains a nice feather bed or a pile of brickbats!"

The first radio report from Patton's Western Task Force was meager, but encouraging. Seas capable of thirty-foot waves were strangely calm, more quiet, local residents said, than at any time in memory; two approaching storms that might have driven high surf onto the beaches of northwest Africa apparently canceled each other out. For the next few hours, the Americans landed easily. "The hand of the Lord was over us," Marshall would say later.

Divine intervention notwithstanding, the Moroccan landings went slowly. As the surf built, the clumsy plywood landing craft capsized in the rolling seas. Assault units were scattered up and down the coast, men and supplies hopelessly separated.

French resistance was sporadic, but sharp enough to further upset their timetables. The port of Safi would not fall until the afternoon of November 8, and it would be another thirty-six hours before the 2nd Armored Division overcame all opposition. At Fedallah, the harbor closest to Casablanca, the French Navy opened fire at close range upon the American ships offshore. It would take two days for the 3rd Infantry to slog its way to the outskirts of Casablanca, where a force of 4,000 pro-Vichy troops had dug in. The northernmost of Patton's landings, at Port Lyautey, encountered the most resistance; there even the French Air Force fought against the Americans. The garrison was to hold out for three days.

The Center Task Force off Oran had it no easier. French resistance, especially from naval units, was heavy. Giraud's underground had no influence here. The paratroop assault on the key airfields had dissipated when the inexperienced transport pilots scattered their planes in foul weather. Oran would not fall until noon on the 10th.

The Eastern Task Force under the temporary command of United States Major General Charles W. Ryder met a mixed reception. In the harbor of Algiers itself, the French navy bitterly resisted efforts to land U.S. Rangers. On flanking beaches where Mast and his Giraudists had taken command of military installations, the Americans landed unopposed. Twelve hours after the first landings, the Allies had captured Algiers, capital and administrative center of French North Africa.

In Washington, too, the generals waited for word from the landing beaches. The chief of staff declined to go to a Washington Redskins night football game on November 8, much to the irritation of his unknowing wife, who insisted he needed a break from work. Katherine instead went off in a huff with Hap and Eleanor Arnold, angry at her husband's vague explanation he could not be out of touch with the War Department.

In the middle of the game, Mrs. Marshall recalled, the loudspeaker commanded: "Stop the game! Important announcement!" The cheering faded away, the crowded stadium hushed. "The President of the United States of America announces the successful landing on the African coast of an American Expeditionary Force. This is our second front."

There was sudden bedlam, wave upon wave of cheers, Mrs. Marshall recalled. Eleven months after Pearl Harbor, after a wearying succession of defeats both in Europe and the Far East, the Allies "had wrested the offensive from the enemy and started the march toward ultimate victory."

The first reports suggested TORCH was a success, though hardly an elegant one. They were ashore, and there was sporadic fighting. The commander of the assault on Fort Lyautey, Major General Lucian K. Truscott, termed the landings "a hit and miss affair that would have spelled disaster against a well-armed enemy intent on resistance."

As the day wore on, the reports turned grim. Allied troops were slow to reach their objectives. Anti-Vichy Frenchmen, mostly Jews, fought pro-Vichy police and army units. Political factions fought in civil war. French North Africa was in turmoil, TORCH in jeopardy.

With resistance to the Allied landings stiffening and the casualty list growing, presidential envoy Robert Murphy learned that Admiral Jean François Darlan had flown unexpectedly from Vichy to Algiers.

The high-strung Murphy, seeing disaster for the Allies all about him, was desperate to end French fighting. Giraud had proved reluctant, but Darlan, the commander of all French armed forces in North Africa, might throw in with the Allies. An order from Darlan to cease fire, in any event, would have more legal force than a Giraud appeal. Given that, Murphy and later Eisenhower would overlook the admiral's ignoble career since 1940 and the fall of France.

As commander-in-chief of the French fleet, Darlan had wormed his way to the post of vice-president of the Council of Ministers in the Vichy government. In fact, he had run the government of the aged Marshal Pétain from February 1941 to April 1942. For fourteen months Darlan, a lifelong Anglophobe, had been a fervid collaborationist.

In one thing only had Darlan opposed Hitler. Out of national fervor, the admiral had not yielded his beloved fleet, anchored in Toulon, to the German Navy. That fleet—three battleships, eight cruisers, and a covey of supporting vessels—represented a great prize for either side: naval dominance in the Mediterranean.

Here on the morning of the invasion Darlan was unexpectedly in Algiers to see his son Alain, stricken with poliomyelitis. At Murphy's urging, Major General Mark Clark met Darlan and asked him to order an immediate cease-fire.

Through that Sunday Darlan stalled, exchanging messages with Marshal Pétain in Vichy; Pétain ordered continued resistance. French officers in North Africa, bound by personal oath to Pétain, vacillated between defending the sham of the Vichy government and casting their lot with the Allies. While they debated the requirements of honor, American and British troops were dying on the beaches.

Finally, late in the afternoon, Darlan threw in with the invaders, and as commander of French armed forces in North Africa ordered his troops to cease fire. Fighting stopped in Algiers immediately, but continued in Oran and Casablanca. In vital Tunisia, east of Algiers, the French commanders instead surrendered without resistance to a small force of Germans.

Though Clark badgered Darlan to call for a complete cease-fire, for thirty-six hours Darlan procrastinated. Not until Tuesday did he finally issue new orders to cease fire. It would be two days more before all resistance ended, and by then the British and American forces had lost the initiative. A frustrated Mark Clark growled to reporters, "the yellow-bellied sons of bitches" had made a deal.

Darlan had driven a hard bargain. He was to impose a cease-fire, then as high commissioner set up a civil administration in French North Africa. Darlan the turncoat would remain the personal representative of Marshal Pétain. At Clark's insistence, Giraud, no *capitulard* but hardly less reactionary, was named to head the armed forces, thus giving this new government a bi-partisan cast.

Press reaction in the United States to "the Darlan deal" was immediate and uniformly hostile; editorial opinion suggested "if we will make a deal with a Darlan in French territory, then presumably we will make one with a Goering in Germany or with a Matsuoka in Japan."

Stung by the intensity of the press reaction, Eisenhower cabled a long explanation of the Darlan deal to the Combined Chiefs of Staff. Asking that "no precipitate action at home upset the equilibrium we have been able to establish," Eisenhower pointed out that only Darlan had the personal authority to succeed Marshal Pétain and command the loyalty of the French armed forces.

Repudiating the deal would have grave consequences, Eisenhower warned. They could expect some active and a great deal of passive resistance from French army and navy units. Without French cooperation, they risked "stagnation of operations" and the need for additional troops. Any hope they had of bringing over to the Allies the French fleet anchored in Toulon Harbor would be lost.

Most professional army officers, certainly Marshall and Eisenhower among them, accepted the fact that in a democracy politics determined military strategy. But when Eisenhower, harried and anxious both, reversed cause and effect to use a military reason as sanction for a political expedient, Marshall felt compelled to support his field commander. The result was a public relations embarrassment.

Eisenhower was stunned by the intensity of the criticism leveled at him personally for the Darlan deal. He protested to British diplomat Harold Macmillan, "I can't understand why these long-haired, starry-eyed guys keep gunning for me. I'm no reactionary. Christ on the mountain! I'm as idealistic as hell."

Despite Eisenhower's plea, reaction in London was particularly hostile. Churchill felt compelled to warn FDR the Darlan deal "can only be a temporary expedient justifiable solely by the stress of battle. We must not overlook the serious political injury which may be done to our cause, not only in France but throughout Europe, by the feeling that we are ready to make terms with the local quislings."

Churchill added a rare injunction among these creatures of *realpolitik.* "There is above all our own moral position. We are fighting for international decency and Darlan is the antithesis of this." (Russian Ambassador Ivan Maisky relayed to Roosevelt Stalin's approval of the deal. They must use not only Darlan, but "even the Devil himself and his grandma.")

The furor in the press grew more heated. On November 17, the preeminent American political commentator Walter Lippmann wrote a private memorandum to Secretary of State Hull and General Marshall reminding them, "We are dealing with a man who betrayed the Allies in 1940, and then betrayed the French Republic, and has now betrayed the Germans." Two days later he used the memo as the basis for one of his widely syndicated newspaper columns. The United States, Lippmann charged, had miscalculated the political aspects, in large part because of "an unreasoning prejudice against General de Gaulle." That same day Marshall ordered his Intelligence section to adopt a more friendly policy toward Gaullist representatives in Washington. They had, after all, more accurately forecast events in North Africa than Murphy or Eisenhower.

The criticism mounting, Marshall felt compelled to step in before Eisenhower became a sacrificial lamb. Marshall urged Eisenhower to "leave the worries to us, and go ahead with your campaign" while he and Secretary of War Stimson put out fires at home.

In a confidential message to leading editors and broadcasting executives, Marshall took the unprecedented step of asking that they refrain from criticizing Eisenhower. "In any discussion of the current political situation in North Africa, the War Department requests that it be borne in mind that the prime consideration of General Eisenhower at the moment is the immediate defeat of the Axis forces now in that area, at the minimum cost of American lives." He asked that commentators and columnists defer critical comment until that task had been completed.

Late in November—the press still baying at the traffic with traitors— Marshall cabled Eisenhower for consent to release casualty figures. At a Washington press conference, Marshall noted that the American invasion forces had suffered only 1,800 casualties, 500 of these dead. Their planners had estimated the campaign to this point might cost them as many as 18,000 casualties. Thus the Darlan deal might be credited with saving them 16,200 casualties, Marshall argued.

At one of his periodic, off-the-record briefings for the handful of most influential Washington reporters, Marshall warned that continued criticism of Eisenhower would give the British an opening to demand that Eisenhower be replaced by a more experienced British commander. Were Eisenhower removed, it would be difficult, if not impossible, to put another American in command. Opponents of the Darlan deal were jeopardizing American prestige abroad, he stressed. One reporter who was to attend many of these confidential briefings recalled later, "I have never seen him so concerned as he was on this occasion."

The chief of staff was especially sensitive to implied criticism of Eisenhower from within the government. When the Department of State sought to remind Robert Murphy he was not to retain in office any Vichy official "to whom well founded objection might be taken," Marshall objected to the president. It appeared, he wrote, "to be directed at Darlan, the man to whom General Eisenhower had to look for immediate results in the Tunisian operation and in the matter of the French fleet." Marshall's influence was enough to kill the message.

The protests refused to die, despite the president's assurance at a press conference that the Darlan deal was "only a temporary expedient justified solely by the stress of battle." In Algiers, Darlan took to describing himself as a lemon the Allies would discard once he had been squeezed dry.

The price of Darlan's lemons fell sharply in the last week of November when the Germans occupied Toulon. Rather than make steam for North Africa, the fleet commanders chose instead to ignominiously scuttle their vessels. Darlan's dowry had disappeared. He had been unable to deliver Tunis to the Allies and now his fleet lay rusting in the mud of Toulon Harbor.

Rather more arrogant than his accomplishments warranted, Darlan made no effort to temper his politics. The pudgy admiral sought instead to proclaim himself head of state, the "repository of French sovereignty." He maintained the anti-Semitic decrees imposed by the Vichy government, meanwhile holding prisoner the Jews and Gaullists who had sided with the Allies on the day of the invasion.

Marshall cabled Eisenhower that there was strong sentiment in Washington for an end to the anti-Semitic decrees, in particular those requiring Jews to wear yellow armbands. Eisenhower wrested a statement from Darlan declaring himself in favor of "liberal government," but leaving the odious decrees standing. Darlan's excuse was that relaxation of the anti-Semitic laws would provoke the large Muslim population in French North Africa to revolt; that would force the Allies to divert troops from the battle with the Germans and Italians. Eisenhower dropped the matter.

The British Foreign Office was outraged with "this ridiculous declaration Roosevelt has put in the mouth of Darlan—without ever consulting us. . . . At present our policy is not being directed by State Department, but *by Gen. Marshall!*"

Marshall, the supposed author of the Darlan "liberalization" statement, was a good deal less confident than the Foreign Office supposed. To Elmer Davis, director of the Office of War Information, the chief of staff confessed, "I am very much worried over the terrific pressure being put on [Eisenhower]. . . ." Marshall also took every opportunity to buck up his gloomy protégé during this tumultuous period. The chief of staff wrote on December 8, "I want you to feel that you had not only my confidence but my deep sympathy in conducting a battle, organizing a fair slice of the continent, and at the same time being involved in probably the most complicated and highly supervised negotiations in history, considering the time element and other circumstances."

To regain momentum on the battlefield, Marshall advised Eisenhower to "delegate your international diplomatic problems to your subordinates and give your complete attention to the battle in Tunisia. . . ." His own anxiety unusually apparent, Marshall advised later, "You are doing an excellent job and I want you to feel free to give your exclusive attention to the battles, particularly as German intentions against your right flank seem evident."

The Darlan flirtation ended abruptly on Christmas Eve, when a twenty-year-old monarchist, Fernand Bonnier de La Chapelle, assassinated the admiral. Giraud succeeded Darlan, and launched a campaign to consolidate his position by putting the rival North African Gaullists in concentration camps. To an American who protested, a member of Eisenhower's staff snapped, "Art, old fellow, if you have nothing better to do in Africa than to worry about those Jews and Communists who helped us, why don't you go home?" Through callousness, through expedience, through military necessity, some part of the moral suasion Churchill had sought was lost.

The entire Darlan episode was to teach the chief of staff a keen lesson: Military expedience did not justify compromising the avowed principles for which they were at war. The government leaders and diplomats might trim their sails to the political winds; soldiers could not. Thereafter Marshall the soldier would circle wide around political issues.

This had been a year of lessons, and some accomplishments, a good year for the Allied cause. The Russians had held at Stalingrad, then counterattacked, encircling the entire German Sixth Army; in the spring the Soviets planned to launch their first offensive. The Americans and British had taken the offensive in both Europe and the Pacific, though their campaigns suffered a lack of men and materiel. Still, those were coming, in ever-increasing amounts.

Marshall now commanded an army of 5.4 million men, including his stepson Allen, a private at the Armored School at Fort Knox, Kentucky. More than a million of those young soldiers were already overseas, and they were sending additional divisions monthly. In the coming year the War Department would induct 3.6 million men, twenty times the size of the entire Army at the time Marshall became chief of staff just three and a half years earlier.

New weapons were coming from the assembly lines in prodigious quantities, Stimson pointed out with hardly disguised astonishment in his New Year's message. "Two years ago there was not enough ammunition in the country to supply our forces now overseas for a single day's fighting." Two years later the War Department was moving into its still incomplete new headquarters—the largest office building in the world—across the Potomac River from Washington adjacent to Fort Myer. Local wags dubbed it "Mammoth Cave, Washington, D.C." The Pentagon was so large that guides were said to get lost regularly.

The nation had weathered the parlous time. TORCH confirmed "the turning point in the war has at last been reached," President Roosevelt announced. It was not a time for exultation or premature celebration. "There is no time now for anything but fighting and working to win."

Marshall looked forward to the new year with guarded optimism. His letter accompanying a Christmas gift of a fifty-inch globe the War Department was sending to Winston Churchill noted, "The skies have cleared considerably since those dark weeks when you and your chiefs of staff first met with us a year ago. . . . Today the enemy faces our powerful companionship in arms which dooms his hopes and guarantees our victory."

CHAPTER

XX

The Wife's Legacy

The meeting was long overdue. The United States and Great Britain had been Allies for more than two years, yet, as George Marshall continually pointed out, they still lacked a coherent strategic plan for defeating the Axis. For the past year they had improvised, meeting German or Japanese threats with whatever they could scrape together, but plugging holes in a leaky dike was not a strategy.

Roosevelt first proposed in November 1942 that he, Churchill, and Stalin meet to plot a concerted political and military strategy. The Soviet leader scotched that plan, pleading that he could not leave Moscow when his armies were about to mount an offensive along the Don and Volga Rivers. In a pointed reply to Churchill's invitation, Stalin goaded, "I paid close attention to your communication that you and the Americans do not relax preparation along your south-eastern and southern coasts in order to keep the Germans pinned in the Pas de Calais etc. and that you are ready to take advantage of any favourable opportunity. I hope this does not mean that you changed your mind with regard to your promise given in Moscow to establish a second front in Western Europe in the spring of 1943." The second front question would color most of their discussions.

Even without Stalin's presence, Roosevelt and Churchill had much to discuss, most particularly where to use the armies they had massed in North Africa after the Germans and Italians were rolled up. The two government leaders had not met with their full military staffs since the Washington Conference a tumultuous year before. In those twelve months the Allies had staunched the tide of defeat and had gone over to the offensive.

By December 30 they had agreed to meet at Anfa, a seaside suburb of Casablanca in Morocco. A week later, Roosevelt summoned his chiefs of staff to discuss the upcoming meeting. FDR asked if he thought Marshall should go on to Moscow after the Casablanca Conference concluded.

"What would I be expected to accomplish there?"

First, he would give impetus to Russian morale, FDR replied disingenuously. Marshall, a soldier, could explain as a civilian could not just why the Western Allies had not opened a second front on the continent. "Stalin," the president added, "probably felt out of the picture as far as Great Britain and the United States were concerned and also that he has a feeling of loneliness."

To allay that, Roosevelt "said he was going to speak to Mr. Churchill about the advisability of informing Mr. Stalin that the United Nations were to continue on until they reach Berlin, and that their only terms would be unconditional surrender." Further, the president wanted to discuss with Churchill political questions relating to postwar disarmament, and to the possibility of a trilateral meeting in the summer. Roosevelt proposed that Marshall, the highest ranking American military officer, play a diplomat's part and relay the results to Stalin.

The president then turned to the upcoming conference in North Africa. Were they all "agreed that we should meet the British united in advocating a cross-channel operation?" FDR asked.

The question was somewhat embarrassing for Marshall. Marshall himself favored attacking the Brest peninsula. King gave token assent but increasingly urged greater effort in the Pacific, before the Japanese could consolidate their conquests. Neither man wanted to further operations in the Mediterranean; beyond that their planning staffs were divided.

For his part, Marshall continued, "the issue was purely one of logistics; that he was perfectly willing to take some tactical hazards or risks but that he felt we have no right to take logistical hazards."

From his conversations with Sir John Dill, Marshall knew the British chiefs preferred to extend Allied operations in the Mediterranean, leaving the cross-Channel invasion for a later date. Led by Alan Brooke, the Imperial General Staff argued the Allies could force the collapse of Italy and thereby make the Germans deploy more troops in that country. That, Churchill believed, would in turn impress Turkey, perhaps enough to tip that nation into the Allied camp. In addition, clearing the Mediterranean would reopen the vital convoy route to the East.

The likely targets in the Mediterranean were either Sicily or Sardinia, Marshall noted, but any operation would curtail what they could also send to the BOLERO build-up. America's arsenal of democracy was churning out unprecedented military supplies now, yet the dire shortage of available shipping wore on. U-boats had sunk 7.8 million tons in 1942, and even with shipyards working round the clock, planners still confronted a deficit for the year of 1.3 million tons. Great Britain was importing less than half of its prewar total of all goods, and far less than needed to meet even current military and civilian requirements.

His greatest worry about any operation in the Mediterranean, Marshall emphasized, was the loss of shipping. Their planners estimated a 20 percent loss of merchant tonnage involved in a Mediterranean invasion. Inevitably that would impact on Allied operations anywhere on the globe.

Were they to invade the Brest peninsula instead, as Marshall advocated, "the losses there will be in troops, but to state it cruelly, we could replace troops whereas a heavy loss in shipping . . . might completely destroy any opportunity for successful operations against the enemy in the near future."

King quickly dismissed Operation BRIMSTONE, the invasion of Sardinia. With Sicily, however, they could open the Suez Canal route to the East and shorten passage times required around Cape Horn. The effect would be as if they increased tonnage by as much as a third.

The president questioned the chances of the cross-Channel invasion, Marshall replying that he thought they could force their way ashore—in August at the earliest. The difficulty would come after the landings when German armor counterattacked.

Roosevelt was dubious. The trouble was that they were going to Casablanca without agreement among themselves about the next operation. At the conference, FDR warned, the British would have a plan and stick to it.

The British had thrashed out their differences amongst themselves, Marshall said, apparently settling on Sardinia and making agreement difficult. Sardinia would involve them in a deepening Mediterranean rather than a European war, Marshall insisted. They would pour men and materiel into operations that could only extend, not shorten the war.

Never far from mind in the Pentagon lurked the fear that delay in the Mediterranean furthered Imperial Britain's political aims: the longer Soviet Russia fought Germany alone, the weaker both nations would be, allowing "the British to enjoy their historic role of arbiter in the balance of power within continental Europe," as the head of the Strategy and Policy Group of the Operations Division, Albert Wedemeyer, argued.

American strategic goals, not to mention Marshall's ultimate destination, were still unsettled when the chief of staff, code-named "Braid," left Washington with Hap Arnold and Sir John Dill in a C-54 on the morning of January 9, 1943. Admiral King, Bill Somervell, and the two planners they were taking, Al Wedemeyer and Savvy Cooke, followed in a second plane. That night President Roosevelt, code-named "Admiral Q," and Harry Hopkins, "Mr. P," left Washington from a little used railroad siding beside the Bureau of Engraving for a more leisurely train trip to Miami.

Marshall and King flew ahead so as to have time to work out a compromise strategy with the Imperial General Staff, before Roosevelt and Churchill arrived at Casablanca. The two military transports hopped from Washington to Miami, to Puerto Rico, then on to Belem and Natal in Brazil, finally crossing the Atlantic to land eighteen and a half hours later in the former slave trading center of Bathurst, capital of the British colony of Gambia.

The following day the two transports flew on to Casablanca. Almost immediately Marshall and King discovered that the little meeting with "a very small staff" Roosevelt once envisioned had ballooned beyond recognition. The British had arrived not only with a full complement of planners but with a special communications ship anchored offshore that doubled as a floating library of preprepared strategic studies and maps.

The Americans had but two men, Wedemeyer and Cooke, to throw against such a formidable array. Things were starting badly for the chiefs of staff in this oasis four miles south of Casablanca.

The two delegations could hardly have asked for a more pleasant setting than the small and wealthy resort community dominated by the three-story Hotel Anfa. In the shadow of the modern hotel lay a clutch of well-appointed private villas, requisitioned for the use of the conferees. The president was to have Villa No. 2, Dar-es-Saada, a sumptuous home with its own swimming pool, well-tended garden, and improvised air-raid shelter.

The white hotel, built in the momentarily fashionable style to resemble the superstructure of an ocean liner, offered commanding views of the Atlantic shore just a mile to the west, and the mountains of Morocco to the east. As host for the conference—it was being held in a country garrisoned by Americans—the United States provided many of the amenities.

"The very smart ate their meals in the villas, and the more ordinary in the hotel," British diplomat Harold Macmillan wrote, tongue in cheek. "The whole thing was rather like the *Normandie* or the *Queen Mary*. However, the appointments were extremely well made. The whole thing was free, including most excellent food and quantities of drink. Even cigarettes, cigars, chewing gum, sweets, of which the Americans are very fond, and soap, shaving soap and razors—all these were freely distributed. . . ."

Around the hotel, General George Patton had thrown up a double circle of barbed wire amid the purple bougainvillea and blooming fruit trees. To that he added a ring of anti-aircraft guns, then posted a formidable portion of his 2nd Armored Division with machine guns to guard the newly created Anfa Camp. Patton may have been overly cautious, but three weeks earlier the Luftwaffe had raided Casablanca, a city believed still to be honeycombed with Axis spies. During their first night in camp, Roosevelt, Churchill, and their combined chiefs chatted through an air-raid alarm, the lights out, with only candles to illuminate the whiskey bottles. Though no bombs fell, Casablanca in this early African spring was all Roosevelt could have wanted. In just the last two days he had become the first president of the United States to fly in an airplane, the first to leave the country in wartime, and the first since Lincoln to visit a war zone. This journey to Casablanca, even if it was to be something of a vacation, came a good deal closer to his concept of a commander-in-chief's role in wartime than did his rattling about the White House.

Despite some criticism in the press, for most fathers were not granted such favors, the meeting at Casablanca served also as something of a family reunion. Captain Elliott Roosevelt flew in from his reconnaissance squadron in Algiers; artillery Lieutenant Hank Arnold and Signal Corps Sergeant Robert Hopkins came from mud-filled Algerian foxholes, Navy Lieutenant Franklin Roosevelt, Jr., from his destroyer patrolling the Atlantic. British Major Randolph Churchill similarly flew in from his Eighth Army posting.

Amid the incongruously fortified luxury of Anfa Camp, the American chiefs and their small staff held a preliminary meeting on the afternoon of January 13, 1943. The major problem, they agreed, was the need for a worldwide strategy, one that would determine the allocation of men and materiel. They feared the British would shy from the all-embracing strategy, preferring to approve only limited operations as opportunities arose. Marshall and King were prepared to concede a token operation in the Mediterranean once North Africa was cleared—after all, they had achieved some momentum in that theater—but they wanted to limit the commitment there. King proposed they first discuss with the British the available manpower and materiel, then the allocation between competing theaters of those resources.

The British too were meeting in a preliminary session. On the night of the 13th, Churchill warned his chiefs of staff "not to hurry or try to force agreement, but to take plenty of time," just as he would do with the president. "There was to be full discussion and no impatience—'the dripping of water on a stone,' " the prime minister called it.

The small American delegation was at a clear disadvantage when the first meeting of the Combined Chiefs of Staff opened the next day. The British had had long experience in consensus by committee, the Americans little. Furthermore, as one historian commented, "The customary American approach is to talk things out and then prepare a plan; the British approach is to have a plan ready and then talk things out—and it is also a British approach to have plans ready for all important foreseeable contingencies."

Somewhat ruefully, Admiral King later noted, "The Joint Chiefs of Staff found at Casablanca that every time they brought up a subject, the

British had a paper ready." The two American planners, Savvy Cooke and Al Wedemeyer, were finally buried under an avalanche of British studies.

The British were coming too with a plan they wanted to sell to the Americans. Churchill had given his chiefs a minimal slate of operations for 1943: Clear North Africa, then capture Sicily, retake Burma, and launch a preliminary invasion of France. While Brooke especially thought this too ambitious, he said nothing publicly. They "always present a solid front," Marshall observed, which was more than he, King, and Arnold could say.

The British also had a negotiating plan laid out. They intended to allow the Americans their say, then carefully, patiently pick it apart with paternal concern. King "would take a less jaundiced view of the rest of the world if he had been able to shoot his line about the Pacific and really get it off his chest. General Marshall, too, who has, and always has had, a strong feeling for China, was full of ideas about Burma, which it would be desirable to bring out into the light of day."

Marshall opened the first session with a statement arguing for a fixed allocation of resources between the Pacific and the European-Mediterranean theaters. He proposed allotting 70 percent of their resources—in effect, 70 percent of their effort—to Europe and dividing the balance between the Pacific and China-Burma-India theaters.

At present, they were devoting approximately 15 percent of their resources to the Pacific, Admiral King claimed his staff studies revealed. That proportion was not sufficient to prevent Japan from consolidating its holdings and thereby making its eventual defeat all the more difficult.

Forewarned by Dill, General Brooke replied with a diplomatic argument against committing too much to the Pacific. Brooke "expressed the admiration of the British Chiefs of Staff on the magnificent work of the U.S. Forces during the last twelve months after the early disasters of the war against Japan. At one time it seemed as if nothing would stem the tide of the Japanese, but the position now was very different. The Japanese were very definitely on a defensive basis and . . . worried about the situation of their European allies." In short, Brooke's unspoken subtext ran, they had done so well on so little there was no need to increase the allocation to the Pacific.

Brooke then shifted the discussion. First he warned that the shortage of merchant shipping was "a stranglehold on all offensive operations and unless we could effectively combat the U-boat menace, we might not be able to win the war." Then he began a review of the course of the war. Germany was failing, its allies disaffected, its manpower dwindling. "It seemed at least possible that the precarious internal situation of Germany might make it possible to achieve a final victory in the European theater before the end of 1943." If not this year, then they could "definitely" count on returning to the continent in 1944. (Brooke's estimate of the timing "let the cat out of the bag a little," Al Wedemeyer pointed out to Marshall.)

There were three means to defeat Hitler, Brooke continued: the Soviet Union's struggle in the East, supported in every way possible by the West; air bombardment; and, finally, amphibious operations against the continent.

The first two propositions they would settle upon easily. The Soviets were to receive as many convoys as possible and a fleet of requested bombers. The British and the American air forces would conduct round-the-clock bombing of continental targets.

The third proposal raised problems. While the Allies could pick their point of entry at will, they would be wise to select that spot where the enemy was least able to mass reinforcements. France had the advantage of a short sea crossing, Brooke conceded, but a staff study showed that the numerous rail lines permitted the Germans to move seven divisions simultaneously from the Russian front to the West in two weeks. The north-south lines meanwhile could handle no more than one division at a time. Moreover, the Italian railways were close to the coast and vulnerable to interdiction from the sea.

North Africa was they key, the precise British general argued. They could threaten a number of points in southern Europe, compelling the Germans to scatter forces all along the northern shore of the Mediterranean. "In this way we could probably give greater assistance to Russia than if we committed ourselves definitely to Northern France."

The actual blow, Brooke continued, should fall so as to knock faltering Italy out of the war, meanwhile waiting for "a crack in Germany in the late summer." Brooke was arguing for the strategies of a year before, as if the Allied successes had not changed the picture.

For the next two days the Americans sought to explain their positions. Usually content to leave the discussion to Marshall, Hap Arnold insisted they had to reach some decisions not only about operations in 1943, but the following year too. Otherwise, "owing to the time lag, our priorities in production might be wrongly decided."

In response, Air Marshal Sir Charles Portal seemed almost indifferent to the difficulties in scheduling production when they lacked a strategy. "Production plans could never follow strategy precisely since the situation changed so frequently in war. The best that could be hoped for was to take broad decisions on major questions and these would always be in the nature of compromises."

It was "impossible to map out a detailed plan for winning the war," Brooke added, "but Germany's position, if we knocked out Italy, would undoubtedly be most serious." The American argument had not been heard.

Brooke grew increasingly irritated at what appeared to be a stubborn American refusal to see reason, while Marshall patiently, coolly insisted that the British commit to an overall strategic concept. Marshall was willing to make concessions—some operation in the Mediterranean seemed a logical follow-on to the North African campaign—but he wanted something in return.

They had to decide what the "main plot" was to be, Marshall insisted on January 16. "Every diversion or side issue from the main plot acts as suction pump," he argued. The invasion of Sicily that the British proposed now—Churchill had refused "to be fobbed off with a sardine" (Sardinia)—appeared to be advantageous because of the excess number of troops in North Africa. But what part would the conquest of Sicily play in the overall strategy, he asked pointedly. What followed Sicily?

Ironically, Brooke too feared a suction-pump effect, one that extended operations in the Pacific would create. King, with Marshall's backing, had advocated a series of operations that would surely drain resources, especially landing craft, from the Mediterranean. Moreover, King and Marshall were pushing for expanded operations in Burma, first to open the single road into China, then to retake the entire country. Brooke could understand the Americans' desire to roll back the Japanese in the Pacific; he had no sympathy for their desire to aid Chiang Kai-shek, however. British respect for Chiang and the Chinese Army was minimal.

Drop by drop the water splashed upon the stone. Marshall—a man of "friendliness and honesty of purpose"—required time to weigh the British arguments, to be thoroughly convinced, a member of the British delegation noted. "He was not obstinate or rigid in his strategic views."

Admiral King was another matter. He was hot-tempered, and as committed to the Pacific as anyone among the British was wedded to the Mediterranean. King had scant tolerance, once exploding, "Those goddam British. Did you hear *that*?" Marshall instantly intervened. "Gentlemen, I think we'll take five minutes for a cigarette, and then we'll try a new approach." For eight days, the British delegation doggedly pushed its strategy, wearing American arguments away. When Brooke privately vented some of his own frustration, Air Marshal Portal calmly toyed with his pipe, counseling patience. "We are in the position of a testator who wished to leave the bulk of his fortune to his mistress. He must, however, leave something to his wife, and his problem is to decide how little he can in decency set apart for her."

While the Combined Chiefs of Staff groped for a compromise, Roosevelt and Churchill enjoyed a comparatively relaxed week. "There was a curious mixture of holiday and business," Harold Macmillan observed in his diary. "The charming Emperor of the West," President Roosevelt, was genial master of Villa No. 2. "There was a great deal of joking. . . .

There was a lot of bezique, an enormous quantity of highballs, talk by the hour, and a general atmosphere of extraordinary goodwill."

That goodwill did not extend to Macmillan's Red Emperor. Marshal Stalin radioed that a visit by General Marshall after the conference would serve no good purpose. Stalin wanted no alternatives to a second front, no excuses such an emissary would bring for not fulfilling Churchill's promise of the year before. The American delegation—all but Marshall—read Stalin's message as a personal slight, the secretary to the Joint Chiefs, Brigadier General John R. Deane, observed.

The military talks went slowly. On January 18, scheduled to present an agreed strategy to the president and prime minister at 5:00 p.m., the two delegations, nerves rubbed raw, were still far apart. The morning discussion grew heated.

To ease Brooke's fear of a Pacific suction pump, Marshall reiterated the Europe-first concept, adding a major concession. "He advocated an attack on the Continent but he was opposed to immobilizing a large force in the United Kingdom, awaiting an uncertain prospect, when they might be better engaged in offensive operations which are possible."

Marshall's statement seemingly ruled out transporting the North African veterans to Great Britain and holding them there to wait an indefinite German crack-up. Neither could those troops sit idle in North Africa. Marshall had opened the way for an operation in the Mediterranean.

Air Marshal Portal—who the Americans believed had the best mind among the British commanders—until now had left the presentation to Brooke. A thoughtful man, reserved in the manner Americans imagined all British to be, "Peter" Portal stepped in to summarize their position. First, he said, the British had always accepted that pressure should be maintained on Japan. "The British view was that for getting at Germany in the immediate future, the Mediterranean offered better prospects than Northern France. For this purpose they were advocating Mediterranean operations with amphibious forces while concentrating, so far as the United Kingdom was concerned, on building up a large heavy bomber force, which was the only form of force that could operate continuously against Germany."

Marshall replied he was most anxious to avoid "interminable operations in the Mediterranean." He wished northern France to be the scene of the main effort against Germany.

"It was impossible to say exactly where they should stop in the Mediterranean since we hoped to knock Italy out altogether," Portal replied. The British were inching away from Brooke's earlier assertion that they did not envision putting troops ashore in Italy, unless the Fascist government completely collapsed.

King reiterated the American position: "The real point at issue was to determine the balance between the effort to be put against Germany and against Japan, but we must have enough in the Pacific to maintain the initiative against the Japanese . . . gaining positions in readiness for the final offensive against Japan." Just as the British argued their two armies in North Africa should not remain idle once Rommel were defeated, so King insisted troops in the Pacific press the attack.

On one point King was tactlessly adamant: details of operations in the Pacific "must be left to the U.S. Chiefs of Staff, who were strategically responsible for the Pacific theater. He did not feel this was a question for a decision of the Combined Chiefs of Staff. The U.S. Chiefs of Staff had not been consulted before the British undertook operations in Madagascar and French Somaliland—nor did they expect to be; but the same considerations applied to the details of operations in the Pacific." That was non-negotiable, to Brooke's vexation.

Nearing adjournment for lunch, Marshall proposed they approve a series of Pacific operations "with the resources available in the theater."

Brooke was near despair as the morning meeting broke up. "It is no use, we shall never get agreement with them," he lamented to Sir John Dill.

Dill disagreed, pointing out Marshall's concessions could form the basis of agreement. How far would Brooke move to get a compromise, Dill asked.

Not an inch, Brooke replied.

"Oh yes, you will," Dill insisted, "You know that you must come to some agreement with the Americans and that you cannot bring the unsolved problem up to the prime minister and the president. You know as well as I do what a mess they would make of it."

Sir John Slessor, the Royal Air Force's chief planner, volunteered to try his hand at a compromise policy statement. Sitting in the hotel's rooftop restaurant, he scrawled a draft in a battered notebook:

> Operations in the Pacific and Far East shall continue with the forces allocated, with the object of maintaining pressure on Japan, retaining the initiative and attaining a position of readiness for the full-scale offensive against Japan by the United Nations as soon as Germany is defeated. These operations must be kept within such limits as will not, in the opinion of the Combined Chiefs of Staff, prejudice the capacity of the United Nations to take any opportunity that may present itself for the decisive defeat of Germany in 1943.

Handed hastily typed copies of the Slessor draft after lunch, Marshall and King stepped to one side of the room to pore over the document. Marshall made a few notes on the draft, then announced after a tense five minutes they could accept it—providing they added stipulations that the battle against the U-boat had first claim to their resources, and that the convoys to Russia were to continue.

Meeting with Roosevelt and Churchill that afternoon, Marshall as acting chairman of the Combined Chiefs asked Brooke to present their report.

"After seven days of argument," Brooke acknowledged with some relief, "definite progress had been made." They had agreed on a general strategic policy for 1943 that would:

(1) Make the submarine menace a first charge on United Nations resources;

(2) Concentrate on the defeat of Germany first;

(3) Undertake the conquest of Sicily;

(4) Continue to build troop strength and the number of landing craft in Great Britain;

(5) Launch a series of stepping-stone campaigns in the Solomons, the Marshalls, and at Truk in the Carolines;

(6) Invade Burma in December and open the Burma Road to China;

(7) Bomb Germany around the clock from bases in Great Britain; and

(8) Attempt to get Turkey to cast its lot with the Allies, and provide air bases to bomb the Rumanian oil fields.

There was a joint from the carcass for almost everybody. First Sea Lord Dudley Pound's nemesis, the U-boat, would be dealt with. The British chiefs collectively were reassured of the primacy of Europe. Churchill and Brooke got the Sicilian campaign they had advocated. Arnold and Portal won the brass ring of a bomber campaign. King would go home with a pledge of a larger share of resources in the Pacific and approval for three campaigns in which to use them. Marshall alone could not get what he most wanted—an invasion of France in 1943 or, in lieu of that, a comprehensive strategy for the defeat of Germany and Japan.

To allay suspicion that the British would defect from the Pacific, Churchill pledged "if and when Hitler breaks down, all of the British resources and effort will be turned toward the defeat of Japan. . . . [N]ot only are British interests involved, but her honor is engaged." President Roosevelt waved away Churchill's offer to enter into a treaty as unnecessary, but added it would be useful to have some sort of commitment from the Soviet Union to enter the Pacific War after Germany's defeat.

To Brooke's alarm, Churchill suddenly went off on another of his strategic fancies, asking that the Dodecanese Islands in the eastern Mediterranean be included as a possible target for invasion. Wedemeyer's hackles rose; once more the British appeared to be waging war only to preserve a postwar empire.

The agreements approved that afternoon covered only operations in the coming year. ROUNDUP was definitely out for 1943; they could not assemble enough landing craft fast enough after the Sicilian invasion.

Yet Sicily was the certain target, for all practical purposes selected months before when the president and prime minister settled upon the North African invasion. It was close, just 150 air miles from Tunis. The troops to mount the invasion would be available in North Africa, and opening the sea route through the Mediterranean would release the equivalent of 225 freighters for operations elsewhere. Sicily's loss could provoke wavering Italy to sue for peace; to avoid retreat, Hitler would be forced to garrison that nation with troops needed on the Russian front.

The plan was broad, so broad it would require tinkering as the year went on. By some tacit agreement—at least the minutes of the plenary session make no mention of it—no one raised the troubling question: what were they to do after Sicily? The Italian mainland beckoned just two and a half miles across the Straits of Messina, an obvious target, but an ever deeper commitment to peripheral operations in the Mediterranean. Leaving the follow-up operation unsettled, Marshall instead proposed they meet again as summer approached to make the necessary readjustments. Churchill agreed.

The president said little during the meeting, allowing Marshall to present the United States position. FDR's silence was another sign of the president's increasing confidence in his chief of staff. Eventually to earn what he considered "an extra-ordinary degree of independence," Marshall credited Harry Hopkins's unswerving support for convincing Roosevelt the chief of staff was to be relied upon.

Once begun, the decisions came quickly that Tuesday afternoon. The British were to play the Turkish hand, only keeping the United States informed. ROUNDUP too should be under British command, Roosevelt added, since the bulk of the troops would be British.

Churchill asked to defer appointment of a supreme commander but thought they might agree on a British officer to undertake planning of ROUNDUP. He too affirmed the general rule that command be held by an officer of the nation that furnished the majority of the forces engaged.

That done, he immediately reversed himself, surprising the Americans. In perhaps five weeks, he estimated, the six divisions of the British Eighth Army would cross into Tunisia. Even though the Commonwealth would then have some twelve divisions in North Africa to the United States' four, Churchill proposed that Eisenhower retain command. Harold Alexander, commander-in-chief of the British Middle East, would become deputy commander of the Allied ground forces under Eisenhower.

Just a week before, Eisenhower had flown from Algiers to Casablanca to meet with the president, fully expecting to be relieved of his command. His offensive had bogged down in the mud of the rainy season. His headquarters was frantic and inefficiently run, a British visitor noted. The general himself lacked self-confidence. "Eisenhower has such an exuberant and emotional temperament that he goes up and down very easily. . . ." His commanders lacked the necessary drive, his troops were inexperienced. He himself had made mistakes, most recently the appointment of a former Vichy minister of the interior as governor of Algeria; Darlan was dead, but fascism lived on under Eisenhower.

It was not an encouraging record. Both his wife in a letter and his aide at headquarters had warned him, as aide Harry Butcher put it, that "his neck is in a noose."

Eisenhower had made a favorable impression in a luncheon meeting with the president on January 16. He offered no apologies for the showing of his troops, or for his own political gaffes. He was learning. So were they.

That had boosted his standing somewhat, but more important was the chief of staff's continued sponsorship. (In a political sense, their fates were entwined. Eisenhower's performance reflected on Marshall's reputation and consequent effectiveness.) Still Roosevelt withheld his full endorsement. Pointing out that Eisenhower, a lieutenant general, would be formally outranked by his three British deputy commanders for ground, sea, and air, Marshall suggested Eisenhower get his fourth star. The president told General Marshall that "they would not promote Eisenhower until there was some damn good reason for doing it, that he was going to make it a rule that promotions should go to people who had done some fighting, that while Eisenhower had done a good job, he hasn't knocked the Germans out of Tunisia."

Privately, Brooke explained in his diary the surprising affirmation of a man he personally believed lacked the necessary tactical and strategic experience. Placing Alexander under Eisenhower,

> we were carrying out a move which could not help flattering and pleasing the Americans. . . .
>
> We were pushing Eisenhower up into the stratosphere and rarified atmosphere of a supreme commander, where he would be free to devote his time to the political and inter-allied problems, whilst we inserted under him one of our own commanders to deal with the military situations and to restore the necessary drive and co-ordination which had been so seriously lacking.

There were two other reasons for retaining Eisenhower, Brooke neglected to mention. The French under de Gaulle and Giraud could muster 250,000 troops in Africa and the Middle East, the equivalent of twelve divisions. They could be armed and trained, but no one believed either Giraud or de Gaulle would take orders from a British commanding officer. An American thus had to command in any theater where the French were employed.

Of the Americans, Eisenhower had proved himself most capable of melding British and American into a single staff, of achieving inter-Allied cooperation. Better Eisenhower the inexperienced than the devil they didn't know.

The agreement at Casablanca was illusory. Marshall still believed an invasion of France the key to victory in Europe. King gave lip service to the Europe-first strategy, but did everything possible to divert men and vital materiel to the Pacific. Arnold concerned himself almost entirely with building his bomber commands, convinced that first Germany, then Japan could be defeated by strategic bombing.

Despite their outward agreement, the British chiefs were equally split. Portal also thought they could bomb Germany into submission. First Sea Lord Admiral Dudley Pound focused his flagging energies—he was slowly dying of a brain tumor—on maintaining the continental blockade and defeating the submarine. Brooke placed his bet on a Mediterranean strategy intended to disperse the Germans, relieve the Russians, and open the door to France sometime in the unspecified future. Missing from all their plans was a sense of urgency that the Americans felt keenly. Public opinion in the United States would not permit the war in the Pacific to be long postponed.

While the Combined Chiefs of Staff put fine points to their plans, Roosevelt and Churchill sought to deal with a festering political problem: the wartime leadership of the Free French.

At the president's invitation, Giraud had attended the Casablanca Conference, meeting with both Roosevelt and the Combined Chiefs. On January 19 he had asked that the Allies reorganize and equip the French troops immobilized in North Africa. He estimated that he had cadre enough to form three armored and ten infantry divisions. Were he given the planes, the French could raise fifty fighter, thirty light bomber, and twenty transport squadrons.

The Combined Chiefs welcomed Giraud's offer, Marshall explaining, "It was not a question of whether to equip the French Army, but rather of how to carry it out. Availability of equipment was not the limiting factor, but transport." The French would be equipped entirely from American stocks, at the expense of American divisions.

Giraud was cooperative; Charles de Gaulle, still in London, was not. When Churchill asked him to fly to Casablanca, he stonily refused as a matter of honor to discuss French topics under the auspices of foreigners. "Here was our great hero, the winning horse that we had bred and trained in our stable," Harold Macmillan commented ruefully, "and when the great day came it refused to run at all."

Only after a vexed Churchill reminded de Gaulle that the Royal Treasury was paying his salary did the self-proclaimed leader of the Free French agree to make an appearance. Once there he raised a flurry of questions, finally suggesting creation of a Provisional Government with Giraud as head of the army, and he, de Gaulle, as political leader.

Roosevelt dismissed the proposal; he insisted they do nothing that would create a de facto French government-in-exile. The French people were to choose their own government after the war, not suffer one imposed by conquest.

On January 24, 1943, the last day of SYMBOL, the president and prime minister held a press conference in the garden of the president's villa adjacent to the hotel. Roosevelt was pleased with the results of their meetings and expansive in his good humor. They had met for ten days, world leaders discussing for the first time in history "the whole global picture," he told the semicircle of reporters sitting on the grass at his feet.

They had determined that "peace can only come to the world by the total elimination of German and Japanese war power. . . . The elimination of German, Japanese and Italian war power means the unconditional surrender by Germany, Italy and Japan. . . . It does not mean the destruction of the population of Germany, Italy, or Japan, but it does mean the destruction of the philosophies in those countries which are based on conquest and the subjugation of other people."

Not everyone at the conference favored the unconditional surrender concept, fearing it would prolong Axis resistance. Al Wedemeyer spoke so vehemently against it he thought it wise to tell Marshall he meant no disrespect. The chief of staff halted in his tracks, then lectured, "Wedemeyer, don't you ever fail to give me your unequivocal expression of views. You would do me a disservice if you did otherwise."

The SYMBOL conference adjourned, Marshall, King, and Somervell immediately flew from Casablanca to Eisenhower's headquarters in Algiers. Marshall made the trip ostensibly to discuss the new command arrangement proposed by Brooke, but an understandable curiosity surely impelled him to look over what had become the United States' largest overseas base. The chief of staff had, after all, worked since 1939 to create this massive military engine. Marshall would have been less than human had he not possessively thought of it as his creation, just as the selection of Eisenhower as its commander was also the chief of staff's doing.

Marshall's sense of pride showed. His "whole attitude toward Ike was almost that of father to son," noted Eisenhower's aide, Navy Commander Harry Butcher—though Marshall still could not bring himself to call him "Ike" as even the president and prime minister did.

As any father might, Marshall brought up Ike's health between visits to the front. A weeklong cold, a high temperature, and higher than normal blood pressure all suggested Eisenhower was not taking care of himself, Marshall insisted. "You're trying to do too much. You're making too many trips to the front. You ought to depend more on reports," he advised.

"Well, General," Ike retorted, "your headquarters are in Washington and yet you've come over here, and you've made several visits along the front to see for yourself."

Marshall looked at Eisenhower "rather fiercely," then said mildly, "I don't come to the field very often."

Between visits to the front, Marshall discussed with Eisenhower the performance of American troops in North Africa. Brooke had broadly hinted, more than once, at the British lack of confidence in the ability of the United States Army to produce combat-ready divisions. But for the light resistance from a portion of the French garrison, the TORCH landings might have been disastrous. Informally, Brooke and his planners urged that American training methods be discarded entirely and theirs substituted.

Marshall had a number of concerns about their performance, especially the lack of drive amongst his battlefield commanders. Once ashore, the American divisions had gathered themselves slowly, and moved cautiously rather than boldly. Eisenhower too was aware of British criticisms that the Americans had permitted a stalemate until the return of dry weather in the spring or until Bernard Montgomery's Eighth Army could crack the Germans on the east.

To tighten Eisenhower's control over corps and division commanders, Marshall suggested that Eisenhower take on a roving deputy, someone with rank enough to go into any headquarters and bring back information Eisenhower could trust. When Marshall casually suggested Major General Omar Bradley, then commanding the 28th Division in Florida, Eisenhower interrupted, "Go no further."

A West Point classmate of Eisenhower's, the quiet Bradley was much respected in the Army. As a newspaper reporter decided in the fall of 1942, Bradley was "solid and stable," not the colorful sort like MacArthur or Patton, but a man who "doesn't only command respect: he wins devotion." Marshall had refused numerous requests for Bradley's services, assuring him there would soon be a more interesting assignment than training a National Guard division. Marshall's recommendation to Eisenhower fulfilled the promise.

Eisenhower would need Bradley if they were to do their fair share in sweeping the Axis from Tunisia. The day before, the British Eighth Army under Bernard Montgomery had captured Tripoli; in another six days Monty's Desert Rats would cross the Libyan border into eastern Tunis. If Eisenhower's divisions vigorously pushed eastward, they would redeem themselves.

Marshall needed better performance from his army if he was to convince the British to undertake a cross-Channel operation. Eisenhower had the balance of the North African campaign and the Sicilian operation to prove the battlefield worth of the American soldier.

The two men discussed the new command arrangement proposed by Brooke. Marshall told Eisenhower he intended to press the president to grant him a fourth star. That rank would at least give him parity with his three British deputies; it would also make him one of just three four-star generals in the Army, along with Marshall himself and MacArthur.

Rank would help, but that alone could not end all of Eisenhower's problems. The new supreme commander was to discover that the British intended to hedge him in with a committee of deputy commanders. His own authority threatened, Marshall's principle of unified command undermined, Eisenhower would have to fight a running bureaucratic battle to maintain his leadership. As Marshall predicted, "He may think he has had troubles so far, including Darlan, but he will have so many before the war is over that Darlan will be nothing."

Marshall would have his share as well.

PART
III
THE VICTOR

C H A P T E R

XXI

A Very Vicious War

By February 1943, the vast military machine that George Marshall had created and the burgeoning arsenal that supplied it had gained a ponderous momentum. The previous year American industry had churned out $100 billion worth of military equipment; one of every three dollars spent in the United States was going into the war effort. Hardly an industry, hardly a company escaped the impact of world war. Once commonplace goods, from Coca-Cola to paperclips, became scarce. Rubber tires, nylons, and choice steaks were available only for an under-the-table premium to black marketeers. "Lucky Strike Green has gone to war," noted one of the most celebrated advertisements of the times, but virtually every manufacturer found a way to splash his product with khaki or battleship gray. Even Formfit trumpeted its brassieres "for the *support* you need these hectic days of added responsibility."

Formfit had more claim to patriotic support than many. Women *were* taking an active role in the war effort. Not only had 65,000 joined a newly created Women's Army Auxiliary Corps, the WAACs, but 5 million women had gone to work in war plants.

Unemployment virtually disappeared, and with it the vestiges of the Depression. Many—especially blacks from the South—had jobs for the first time in more than a decade.

Prosperity spurred public optimism, prompting a feeling that the war was all but won. Marshall feared that notion and the sense of complacency it fostered.

"We are just getting well started," the army chief of staff sternly warned. "The great battles lie ahead. We have yet to be proven in the agony of enduring heavy casualties, as well as the reverses that are inevitable in war. What we need now is a stoic determination to do everything in our power to overwhelm the enemy, cost what it may. . . ."

As the patriarch of America's mobilization, Marshall refused to hold out hope for an easy victory. When congressional blusterers and public sales promoted Alexander de Seversky's book and Walt Disney's film *Victory Through Air Power,* the chief of staff cautioned "against hasty conclusions or impromptu conceptions regarding the utilization of air power or any special weapon in the conduct of this war. . . . Your adversary may be hammered to his knees by bombing but he will recover unless the knockout blow is delivered by the ground army. . . ."

That army in the first months of 1943 numbered more than 5,000,000 men and women. One half million, including the first group of 100 women, were overseas—295,000 in the fast-swelling Mediterranean theater and 125,000 in the Pacific. Seventy thousand more were in Great Britain, far fewer than the 250,000 Marshall had planned to have poised for ROUNDUP by this time. The best Marshall could hope would be four divisions trained and equipped for the invasion of France by September and perhaps nineteen by year's end.

The small, close-knit Army Marshall had known all his life was no more. Over 1,000 men now wore a general's stars. In the three years of mobilization, the Army had spent $9.2 billion on construction of military bases, airfields, and industrial plants. They had employed as many as 1 million persons in construction; 350,000 were still throwing up barracks, including a carefully screened group at a rocky site in the Jemez Mountains of New Mexico called Los Alamos.

The army that had been hardly more than a border constabulary now had supply routes that stretched 59,000 miles, radiating from American ports to Australia, Persia, India, the British Isles, and Alaska.

No army had ever waged war on such a scale. Even the most routine tasks required extraordinary amounts of time. To make an inspection tour for the chief of staff after the Casablanca Conference, Al Wedemeyer traveled for seven weeks—through the Middle East, to Ceylon and India, then on to Kunming and Chungking, China. From there he flew by Clipper to Australia to meet with MacArthur. From Brisbane he visited the island battles in the Pacific, then Noumea and Canton Island, before finally taking off for Hawaii and the mainland.

American soldiers and airmen were scattered all about a world in which distances were measured not in miles but in days. Sidney was twenty-nine days by ship from San Francisco, Dutch Harbor nine days. Basra on the Persian Gulf lay seventy days by merchant ship from New York, Casablanca eighteen days. Even by airplane, it took seventy-three hours to fly from the West Coast to MacArthur's headquarters in Brisbane, twenty hours from Washington to Prestwick in Scotland.

Logistics governed Marshall's War Department. They determined global strategies. They set the timetables for campaigns in the field. The clamor for supplies never ceased. Great Britain, the Soviet Union, the Fighting

French, all had to be supplied, despite shipping shortages, despite aggressive submarine wolfpacks ranging the North Atlantic.

The submarine war known as the Battle of the North Atlantic had received the highest priority at Casablanca, for good reason. Through 1942 the U-boats were clearly winning the pivotal battle; the Germans had sunk over 1,000 merchant vessels, while losing but 106 submarines. Germany was putting U-boats to sea faster than the Allies could sink them. Meanwhile, British and American shipyards were unable to fully replace the lost merchant tonnage. By spring 1943 the U-boat had come close to strangling Great Britain's lifeline; imports were running less than half the prewar total of 50 million tons annually.

Unsatisfactory as that balance sheet read, Admiral King moved slowly to redress the imbalance of sinkings, stubbornly insisting on the prerogatives and independence of his service. King refused to cooperate with army pilots flying shore patrol, demanding the Navy have its own long-range air arm. Rather than risk British control, he resisted combined convoy escorts.

Furthermore, King disagreed with the British about the proper use of the bombers. He preferred that the long-range Liberators fly protective cover for convoys; the British advocated an offensive, search-and-destroy mission for the planes. While they wrangled, U-boat depredations reached record heights. On April 1, no longer replacing stocks of foodstuffs, the British cut the already meager meat ration for civilians by 14 percent.

Marshall prevailed on Arnold to yield control of the Liberator bombers that had provided air cover for the vital east-west convoys, turning them over to navy pilots trained by the Air Force. To meet Arnold's fears that King meant to divert the planes to the Pacific and create his own independent bomber force in that theater, Marshall asked King to cede long-range bombing duties to the Air Force.

On June 14, King wrote to Marshall accepting half the bargain, the Air Force's withdrawal from anti-submarine warfare, but saying nothing about his own long-range bombing designs. Arnold's and Marshall's suspicions grew, and for three weeks the memos traveled between the Pentagon and Main Navy on Constitution Avenue.

Some portion of King's resistance sprang from a fear of the future. The admiral was looking for bargaining tokens in a bureaucratic struggle he saw on the horizon. Younger officers in the army Air Forces were urging congressmen to press for the service's independent status—despite Arnold's efforts to suppress such agitation until the end of the war. Suspicious of air force intentions, King feared a separate, co-equal service would co-opt the Navy's air arm as well.

Not until July 3 did King yield on the bombing point and accept Marshall's offer of the Liberators. By then, Great Britain's Coastal Command, using improved radar and the decoded intercepts of German naval radio traffic, had dramatically turned the tables on the U-boat. By massing patrolling bombers and small escort carriers equipped with the radar, the British were able to sink fifteen U-boats in April and forty-one in the first three weeks of May. On May 22, the Germans broke off operations against the North Atlantic convoys. The Battle of the Atlantic had been won.

Slowly, grudgingly, the land war too was tipping in favor of the Allies. In New Guinea, the inadequately trained and equipped U.S. 32nd Infantry Division had bogged down in front of Buna, failing three times to pry out the Japanese defenders.

MacArthur fumed. In December 1942, he dispatched a new corps commander, Robert Eichelberger, with orders to remove the 32nd Division's commander, a friend of Marshall's from Tientsin, Major General E. Forrest Harding. (Marshall thoughtfully arranged Harding's transfer to the command of the important, if quiet, Canal Zone and Caribbean area.)

With MacArthur's order to "take Buna or don't come back alive," Eichelberger prodded the 32nd into renewed vigor. By the end of January, American and Australian forces had cleared all of Papuan New Guinea of the 15,000 Japanese defenders.

The Papuan campaign had been a close thing. Eichelberger saved MacArthur's reputation, resenting the fact that "the great hero went home without seeing Buna before, during or after the fight while permitting press articles from his GHQ to say he was leading his troops in battle." It had taken six months and 8,500 casualties, including 3,300 dead, to defeat disciplined Japanese troops who fought tenaciously, even when isolated and starving.

The 1st Marine Division's campaign on Guadalcanal was, if anything, even more viciously contested. The Japanese had continually reinforced the defenders with night runs of what came to be called the "Tokyo Express." From August through mid-November 1942 the two navies had fought a series of costly sea battles, the Americans only gradually gaining supremacy in the waters off the Solomons.

After five months of hard fighting, on December 9, the battle-weary Marines were withdrawn from Guadalcanal and replaced by two army divisions. The starving Japanese had no relief.

Its troops outnumbered three to one, unable to bear the losses suffered by the Tokyo Express, the Japanese High Command decided on the last day of 1942 to evacuate Guadalcanal. The Japanese withdrew to prepared positions, then evacuated 12,000 men as the Americans cautiously inched forward. On February 8, 1943, the last of the exhausted defenders slipped away aboard the destroyers that had brought them there, leaving the 100-by-20-mile island to the equally exhausted Americans.

The victory at Guadalcanal had cost the Americans 1,600 lives, the Japanese an estimated 10,000. In ships and airplanes, the losses had been equal, but the result was a strategic victory for the Allies. The United States and Australia could replace their losses in vessels and planes. Short of raw materials and industrial capacity, the Japanese could not.

With the end in sight on both Guadalcanal and New Guinea, Marshall proposed on December 1 that they proceed with the reduction of the major Japanese base at Rabaul on New Britain in the Bismarck archipelago. King was silent, for by the agreement reached in July 1942 overall command was to devolve upon MacArthur. Admiral William Halsey was to be relegated to a supporting role.

Just before Christmas Marshall again proposed to the Navy that strategic direction in the South Pacific pass to MacArthur. Still no response. Marshall advised Savvy Cooke that the Army would take no action to relieve Marines in Samoa as the Navy wanted until he got a reply.

Marshall's threat finally provoked a proposal from King's staff that the entire Pacific be placed under the strategic command of Admiral Chester Nimitz, the Navy's overall Pacific commander. Marshall's staff, in turn, replied that the subject of overall Pacific command was too snarled to be untangled immediately. The pressing problem, Marshall's planners replied, was the Southwestern area, where two strong-willed flag officers each insisted on his primacy.

Neither side would yield. If there were to be unified command in the Pacific, Marshall favored MacArthur for the post, King favored Nimitz.

Just as the chiefs of staff in Washington could not agree, so too their deputies in the Pacific squabbled about rival plans to take Rabaul. The dispute simmered at a personal level. MacArthur feared the Navy would steal his laurels; King and Nimitz feared MacArthur's desire to control naval vessels. "The feeling was so bitter and the prejudice was so great that the main thing was to get an agreement," Marshall said later. It was the only way to end "a war of personalities—a very vicious war."

To sort out the issues of jurisdictions, resources, and manpower, Marshall proposed a conference in Washington with representatives of the rival Pacific commanders.

The chief of staff was not in the capital when the conference convened on March 12. Instead, he had slipped off to Florida, "a rather tired-looking business man" attempting to overcome a cold that had laid him low for a week. The Marshalls rented a cottage on the ocean front in Miami Beach where the general intended to rest in the sunshine. The first evening, Marshall, wearing civilian clothes, was instructed by an officious Coast Guardsman to clear the beach. Marshall grumbled a protest; certainly a man could be outside his own home. Moments later, he was surrounded by a six-man patrol, and ordered inside. Didn't he know there was a war on, a petty officer repeatedly huffed. When they reached the cottage, light from the door fell on his face. "That is enough," he said quietly. "What is the reason for this ridiculous display? Does it take you and a patrol of six men to tell me that we are at war?"

The next day passing GIs and shoppers in a shoe store also recognized the tired man in battered fishing hat and sunglasses. The Marshalls retreated to their seaside cottage. "Your Dr. Jekyll and Mr. Hyde disguise is certainly working beautifully!" Katherine teased.

Marshall returned to Washington on March 14, where the Pacific strategy conference lay tangled in service politics. MacArthur wanted to clear out the Solomons, take Rabaul, then point northward toward the Philippines. Nimitz wanted his naval units in the Central Pacific to strike due west. Both commanders, and especially their pride-bound staffs, wanted the bulk of the resources. MacArthur was especially demanding; he had asked for an increase of one third in men and almost twice the number of planes ticketed for the theater.

The protests of the Washington planners moved MacArthur's air force commander, George Kenney, to sarcastic complaint:

> The army had an expert to tell us how tight manpower was and that, with the necessity to defeat Germany first, it was going to be extremely difficult to give us any troops. The navy expert pointed out that the German submarines were sinking shipping about as fast as it was being built and, accordingly, vessels to transport troops or supplies to the Far East were scarcer than hen's teeth. The air experts were the most pessimistic of all. They warned us that they had monthly commitments in Europe already that exceeded the factory output and that it was simply impossible "to pay dividends out of a deficit."

Despite the combat soldier's scorn for a desk-bound staff officer, the planners were correct. They had divisions enough in training, but lacked shipping to move them overseas and keep them supplied. Aircraft too were in short supply. The bulk of the strategic Eighth Air Force in Great Britain had transferred to North Africa, where it would fly 25,000 tactical sorties in the next two months. The remainder fell well below the force levels Hap Arnold and his strategic-bombing advocates considered necessary to crush Germany's industrial base. Aerial bombardment of German industry had also received a high priority at Casablanca, yet Bomber Command was starved for planes.

The critical shortage, as always, lay in shipping, especially with the increasing demands of North Africa. Eisenhower's American forces had swollen to 388,000, all of whom had to be continuously resupplied. Much of the shipping the War Department had managed to scrape together was on its way to the Japanese-held Aleutian Islands of foggy Attu and Kiska. By the end of the month, the North Pacific was an American ocean.

The practical demands of global war hardly deterred MacArthur or his congressional partisans. A small group of powerful Republican conservatives, including Michigan Senator Arthur Vandenberg, eyed the Southwest Pacific commander for their party's presidential nomination in 1944. As Vandenberg acknowledged to a *Time* magazine reporter, no Republican politician could beat Roosevelt, "but the people will really be voting for a commander in chief rather than for a president, and there are no credentials equal to MacArthur's upon that score."

The boomlet for MacArthur placed Marshall and Stimson in a difficult position. Army regulations forbade Regular Army officers from engaging in partisan politics; thus when Stimson pointedly brought this up at a press conference, he appeared to be muzzling MacArthur. At the same time, MacArthur needed the constant stroking of congratulatory messages from the president, praise and publicity that only boosted his political stock.

MacArthur and his supporters were ever alert for "enemies" in Washington who favored theaters other than the Southwest Pacific. Senator Vandenberg was especially sensitive to any slight rendered his man on a horse. More than once he questioned Marshall in Senate committee hearings about the president's role in determining strategy, implying Roosevelt was deliberately curbing MacArthur's genius. The chief of staff was never able to ignore national politics.

Nor service politics. To settle the command structure in the South Pacific, Marshall proposed a compromise: The Navy's Central Pacific offensive would be strengthened with another division and additional aircraft. In exchange, the Navy's "Bull" Halsey would be placed under MacArthur, with the understanding they would cooperate in parallel operations. Under pressure from the White House, King bought the agreement.

It was one of the better bargains struck. Gruff and pugnacious, Halsey got on well with the respectful MacArthur; by June, the two had conceived a canny three-pronged attack that brought Rabaul under constant air attack from two different directions. From this moment on, MacArthur became the master of the battlefield his advocates in Washington thought him.

Throughout the first months of 1943, Marshall also kept an especially keen eye on Eisenhower's developing Tunisian campaign. Two field armies, Bernard Montgomery's Eighth and Kenneth Anderson's First—

both under the command of a third British general, Harold Alexander—were to converge on Rommel's reinforced legions ranged along the Tunisian coast.

On the east, the first units of the British Eighth Army crossed from Libya into Tunisia on February 4. On the west, a combined force of British and American divisions under Anderson tightened the vise on Rommel against light opposition.

Ten days later, the Germans struck a roundhouse blow at the inexperienced American II Corps blocking the mountain passes leading to the Allied rear. Taking advantage of a welter of Allied poor intelligence, ineffectual command, and outright panic, Rommel directed drives by two German divisions that chewed up the American 1st Armored piecemeal and the 34th Infantry.

Portions of two American units broke and ran as the Germans pounded into Kasserine Pass, but Eisenhower and Alexander managed to shore up the line. Eight days after launching the attack, having driven more than 120 miles, Rommel was forced to call a halt. His weary troops could do no more against increased Allied resistance.

The Battle of Kasserine Pass was humiliating. The Germans overran American positions, sweeping up tanks and mounted guns, capturing a grand haul of trucks that would increase Rommel's mobility in the weeks to come, and taking more than 2,400 bewildered prisoners. It would take three weeks before the Americans could reorganize their front, and three more to reclaim the territory lost. Three divisions required extensive outfitting, including shipments of 5,400 trucks from the United States, rushed in less than three weeks with the rare cooperation of Admiral King. Eisenhower soberly radioed Marshall his assessment: "Our soldiers are learning rapidly, and while I still believe that many of the lessons we are forced to learn at the cost of lives could be learned at home, I assure you that the troops that come out of this campaign are going to be battle wise and tactically efficient."

The Battle of Kasserine Pass tempered American overconfidence and led to a reorganization of the command system. The battle also polarized Anglo-American relations. Kasserine Pass, said the British, proved the Americans' inability to train or lead battle-worthy troops. Senior British officers went so far as to recommend that American training methods be abandoned entirely in favor of British, a stinging blow to American pride. "Field Marshal Alexander was particularly bitter on this subject," Marshall said later, in an off-the-record interview. "One might even say he was actually contemptuous of the U.S. infantry and did not believe it could ever be an effective force against the Germans."

Marshall had his own, closely held explanation for the debacle in Tunisia, blaming it on the "stupid British generalship" that had continually fed small portions of the 1st Armored into the fight so they could be defeated in detail.

The American embarrassment at Kasserine was sobering. Putting national interests aside, Eisenhower asked that the British assign experienced combat officers as liaison with American divisions, in effect to sharpen the training. His once complacent troops "are now mad and ready to fight," Eisenhower assured Marshall. "All our people, from the very highest to the very lowest have learned that this is not a child's game and are ready and eager to get down to the fundamental business of profiting by the lessons they have learned and seeking from every possible source methods and means of perfecting their own battlefield efficiency."

By March 22, the Americans had essentially recaptured the territory lost to Rommel the month before. By then Rommel himself was home on sick leave, never to return to Africa and his drained Afrika Korps. The German and Italian troops he left behind under the command of Jürgen von Arnim were outnumbered two to one, and running out of maneuvering room. The Allies had a fourteen-to-one numerical superiority in operable tanks, an important advantage because American field commanders had been forced to discard the standard army theory that tanks should not engage tanks. Unless they did so, the Army was defenseless against German armor. The American anti-tank cannon was inadequate to pierce German armor; the vaunted "tank destroyer," a fast-moving truck mounting a cannon, was too thin-skinned. Combat remained the best teacher.

By and large the American equipment was "first class, and even as good or better than the German," one envious British journalist commented. Clothing and such personal equipment as mess gear were superior to the British, and "the Garand rifle and the officers' carbine were already regarded by many veterans as the best small arms on the front. As for their heavier equipment, it is doubtful if any army ever went to war so well supplied. The only general criticism might have been that there was too much of it. . . . It was the volume of the stuff, the intensity of the firepower that was so impressive."

Marshall expected this well-equipped army to perform creditably in the field. The chief of staff warned Eisenhower's aide-de-camp, Commander Harry Butcher, on a visit to Washington that "Ike's rise or fall depended on the outcome of the Tunisian battle. If Rommel & Co. are tossed into the sea, all quibbling, political or otherwise, will be lost in the shouting of the major victory."

The warning was not lost on Eisenhower. His first move was to replace the commander of the slow-moving II Corps with George Patton. Patton immediately clamped a disciplinarian's hand on the bruised corps. While

Montgomery's Eighth Army forced the Germans to withdraw westward from prepared positions along the Mareth Line, Patton's corps pressed eastward through the Tunisian mountains. The vise squeezed ever more tightly.

Fighting now on two fronts, the Germans and Italians retreated northward, one flank pinned to the coast to keep open an evacuation route. A week of hard fighting in the cold rain of a Tunisian spring forced the Axis troops into their last defensive positions in the hills stretching from Bizerte on the north to Enfidaville on the south, a distance of less than ninety miles.

Despite Allied dominance of the air, Montgomery and Anderson pursued methodically, tidying up the battlefield as they went.

British confidence in the ability of the American Army to fight did not run high. Alexander had repeatedly cautioned the impatient Patton to avoid pitched, indecisive battles where "we might get into trouble." The British held the American foot soldier in even less regard after the U.S. 34th Infantry Division failed in an attempt to drive to the coast and cut off the German rear. When the responsible British corps commander complained about the Americans' performance to reporters, the uncensored news stories received wide play in the United States.

Marshall now stepped in, radioing Eisenhower that the news stories of American soldiers left to mop up on the battlefields "created further unfortunate impressions to our national disadvantage." Admonishing Eisenhower to "watch this very closely," Marshall told him that reports from around the country "mark fall in prestige of American troops in minds of pressmen and in reaction of public."

The II Corps had not acquitted itself with particular distinction in its first combat assignment, the American commanders realized. But they were stunned when Field Marshal Alexander issued his plan VULCAN for the final offensive in North Africa. Alexander envisioned bringing the two British armies together and squeezing the Americans entirely out of the line.

From Washington, an alarmed George Marshall instructed Eisenhower to put his foot down "in this vital matter," not to yield "with unfortunate results as to national prestige."

Eisenhower flew to Alexander's headquarters. In a private meeting, he ordered the British general to give a sector of the front to the II Corps, now under Omar Bradley's command. Alexander resisted, arguing among other things that the American failure at Kasserine Pass deprived them of a share in the final glory.

For the first time Eisenhower repaid Marshall's belief in him. His authority challenged, Eisenhower sternly advised Alexander of the geopolitical realities. If the American public felt that its troops were not properly used in the European theater, there would be increased pressure to shift them to the Pacific, Eisenhower warned his British deputy. More important, before the war in Europe was won, the United States would supply the bulk of fighting forces; that made it imperative they gain confidence in their ability to face the Germans. Removing II Corps from the line would impair its future effectiveness and the confidence of American troops now training in the United States.

In the face of Eisenhower's direct order, Alexander reluctantly yielded, avoiding a test of Eisenhower's authority as supreme commander in the Mediterranean. The principle of combined command, so advocated by Marshall and his protégés, had survived its first real challenge.

At Bradley's suggestion, the four divisions of his corps took over the northernmost sector of the front, a hilly area more suited to mules than trucks, forty miles from the coast. To the scorned 34th, Bradley deliberately assigned a key objective, Hill 609; victory there would restore the disheartened unit's morale.

This last campaign in North Africa began on April 22, supported by overwhelming Allied air supremacy and command of the seas between the Tunisian coast and Sicily. For ten days von Arnim's defense lines bowed inward, but held. Then on May 1, the 34th struggled to the top of Hill 609, prizing the last defenders out, and beating off a series of furious counterattacks.

The Axis lines snapped under the weight of both ground and air attack on May 7. Bradley's II Corps captured Bizerte, hours after the British First Army secured Tunis. Penned in a small enclave on Cap Bon peninsula, pounded from the air and cut off from rescue or reinforcements, the remnants of two Axis armies, including the Afrika Korps, finally surrendered on May 13.

It was not an easy victory, though all the more a lift to Allied morale because of the difficulty. They had captured 275,000 Germans and dispirited Italians—more than the Russians had bagged at Stalingrad—but the North African campaign had been costly. British Empire, French, and American units had suffered 71,810 casualties since the TORCH landings, including almost 11,000 dead. American killed, wounded, and missing totaled 12,618. Moreover, it had taken the Allies six months to accomplish a task they had once estimated would be completed in weeks. The gritty defense led first by Rommel and then von Arnim had bought time for Germany, upsetting the Allies' timetable. The ragged remnants of von Arnim's army sitting in prisoner-of-war pens in Tunisia had scuttled any hope Marshall may have yet held for an invasion of France in 1943.

Still Marshall was pleased. In the final weeks of the campaign, American troops had acquitted themselves and American officers established they were capable combat commanders. They were blooded now, as the British put it, and they were fast learners. More than a little proud, Marshall wrote Eisenhower on May 6, "At the moment there seems to be nothing for me to say except to express deep satisfaction in the progress of affairs under your direction. . . . My interest is to give you what you need, support you in every way possible, and . . . to leave you free to go about the business of crushing the Germans and gaining us great victories."

For Roosevelt, Churchill, and their chiefs of staff the question was how to exploit the victory in North Africa. Sicily had been agreed upon— Patton was already at work on the invasion plan. Beyond that, they had only a vague agreement to knock Italy out of the war.

Two days after von Arnim's surrender in North Africa, Prime Minister Winston Churchill and his military planners were on their way to Washington to determine Italy's fate.

C H A P T E R

XXII

The Great Prize

The *Queen Mary* squatted in the mist off the tip of Staten Island, bow nosed into the swell as the prime minister's party transferred to the smaller harbor craft. The lighters pulled away from the towering hull, turning toward the dock where a special train waited, steam up, to carry them to Washington.

Winston Churchill, rejuvenated after a long siege of pneumonia, chatted affably in the cabin with the seventeen Wrens and six female secretaries he had insisted they take along. Field Marshal Brooke meanwhile peered through the mist, disappointed he could not see the Statue of Liberty and the towers of Manhattan.

Brooke did not look forward to the forthcoming meetings, in fact, hated the very thought of them. He anticipated hours of hard argument during long sessions with the American chiefs of staff. "It is all so maddening, as it is not difficult in this case to see that, unless our united efforts are directed to defeat Germany and hold Japan, the war may go on indefinitely." Brooke never doubted they had to push on in the Mediterranean, meanwhile preventing King from siphoning off resources for the Pacific.

The British delegation had devoted the six days of the voyage to ironing out proposals for the conference Churchill had code-named TRIDENT. The prime minister was anxious to capitalize on success in Sicily, now scheduled for July, "but no one could rest content with such a modest and even petty objective for our armies in the campaign of 1943." Italy proper, the Aegean Islands, even a landing on the Yugoslavian coast must follow. The prime minister and his chiefs of staff had finally agreed upon a strategy of invading Italy once Sicily fell, and forcing that nation from the Axis alliance.

For the first time in this series of international conferences, the Americans were coming prepared. Marshall had stressed at an early April meeting of the Joint Chiefs of Staff that they had to remain ahead of the British planners. To that end he reorganized the Operations Division of the War Department to make it more far-sighted, less concerned with putting out today's brush fires.

More importantly, the chief of staff had spent a good part of the three and a half months since the Casablanca Conference wooing the president to the cross-Channel strategy. Marshall had unlimbered all his arguments, even warning of "a most unfortunate diplomatic situation" should the Red Army be at the German border while the Americans and British were still mired in France.

American and British war aims differed, Marshall reminded Roosevelt. The Americans were concerned with a global war, one fought in both the Atlantic and Pacific theaters; the British considered the war to be essentially a European conflict. The Americans wanted to press the battle in Europe so as to turn to the Pacific quickly; the British felt no such urgency. "Their military objectives were conditioned upon political aspects of guaranteeing their post-war position—above all in the Mediterranean."

Victory in the Pacific, "no matter how long delayed, nor how completely accomplished by the United States," would restore Great Britain's role in the Far East. As a result, "they may be counted upon to perform the letter of their commitments in this connection, but they are traditionally expert at meeting the letter while avoiding the spirit of commitments, and such action in regard to British support of the war against Japan should always be kept in mind as a possibility," the Joint Chiefs warned in a pre-conference study paper.

On May 2, 1943, Marshall informed the president that the Joint Chiefs wanted to prevent any operations east of Sicily. Not only would such assaults delay the invasion of France, but a British presence in that region "can hardly fail to arouse Russian suspicions as to the future of the Dardanelles."

There were other reasons to avoid commitments east of Sicily, Marshall added. Public opinion in the United States demanded action in the Pacific; for most Americans the Japanese were *the* enemy. As the president himself knew, there was grumbling in congressional corridors that the British determined strategic policy, that America was doing Britain's dirty work; a Senate Foreign Affairs subcommittee had scheduled hearings for next week to investigate the charge.

Of all the operations the British might propose in the Mediterranean, Marshall advised, only Corsica or Sardinia were acceptable targets following the Sicily campaign. Either of those islands would serve as a staging area for a later invasion of southern France. An Allied occupation of Italy, on the other hand, would be "more of a liability than an asset," absorbing large numbers of troops and aircraft necessary for the cross-Channel invasion. If the British insisted on plunging into the eastern Mediterranean, Marshall recommended "they do it alone."

The president listened, then agreed with the Joint Chiefs, Marshall told Secretary of War Henry Stimson the next day. The Mediterranean was "a bad mess which we might just as well keep out of," FDR had decided. He favored transferring the troops now in North Africa to the British Isles, thus resuming the BOLERO build-up necessary for the invasion of France.

At least for the moment they held a united front. That was some relief, since Marshall would have to carry an even greater load than in prior strategy conferences. On the evening of May 9, Hap Arnold suffered a heart attack and was recuperating at Walter Reed Hospital.

TRIDENT opened on Wednesday, May 12, 1943, in the president's crowded office in the White House. They were in high spirits, for all morning Eisenhower's headquarters had been reporting the collapse of von Arnim's army in Tunisia. It was a great day of victory—in London church bells tolled an impromptu salute to the first successful campaign over the Germans since 1918—and a special moment for Brooke. Eleven months earlier they had been in this same room when word of the Tobruk disaster came. "And now!" Brooke exulted. "At last the first stage of my proposed strategy accomplished in spite of all the various factors that have been trying to prevent it."

The prime minister began the first session as the Americans had expected, advocating a Mediterranean strategy and a try at "the great prize" of Italy. While he "earnestly desired to undertake a full-scale invasion of the continent from the United Kingdom as soon as possible," Churchill insisted on "a plan offering reasonable prospects of success."

That cross-Channel operation could not be mounted until next spring, as long as a year away, Churchill continued. They could not let the battle against Germany fall solely to the Soviet Union for so long. They were already in Russia's debt and further idleness "would have a serious effect on relations with Russia, who was bearing such a disproportionate weight."

The president's response was larded with caution. He himself had always shrunk from the thought of putting large armies into Italy, he said from behind his knickknack-strewn desk. Whatever the operation undertaken in the Mediterranean, they would have surplus divisions out of action. Those troops should be transferred to the British Isles and placed in training for the invasion of France, Roosevelt suggested.

That operation, he agreed, could not be mounted this year, but two years of talking was enough. The invasion of France "should be decided upon definitely as an operation for the spring of 1944."

Certainly they must aid the Soviet Union, the president continued, but the Allied conquest of Italy would have the effect of freeing German troops to fight elsewhere. "I feel the most effective way of forcing

Germany to fight is by carrying out a cross-Channel operation," he insisted.

Marshall could not have been more pleased. As one British observer commented, "The Americans had done some very hard thinking, and Marshall was at the president's elbow to keep in his mind the high urgency of a second front." For the first time, Harry Hopkins acknowledged, the president could be left safely alone with the prime minister.

For the next twelve days in the paneled Board of Governors Room in the Federal Reserve Building, the two delegations argued their divergent strategies. The sessions were held amid an "unmistakable air of tension," General Hastings Ismay recalled. "The arguments went back and forth, and occasionally got so acrimonious that the junior staffs were bidden to leave the principals to continue the battle in secret session."

The meetings opened in disagreement. Marshall feared the Mediterranean gambit, yet also feared not pursuing the advantage that successive triumphs in North Africa and Sicily would offer. He compromised by suggesting an air campaign, rather than a landing, against Italy. The main thrust, he urged, was to be an invasion of northern France.

Brooke would have none of it. An air campaign alone would not knock Italy out of the war, he said. Only a land campaign could do that and thereby force the Germans to replace the Italian garrisons in the Balkans with perhaps twenty divisions from the Russian front. An invasion of France, on the other hand, was a risky business, Brooke argued. The British and American troops were comparatively inexperienced, and too few to do much more than force their way ashore and be penned in by hundreds of waiting German divisions.

Marshall hammered hard at the "vacuum in the Mediterranean which would preclude the assembly of sufficient forces in the United Kingdom to execute a successful cross-Channel operation. . . ." Further operations this year in the Mediterranean would bar until late 1944 any landing in France. That would, in turn, prolong the war in the Pacific, "which the people of the U.S. would not tolerate.

"We are now at the crossroads—if we were committed to the Mediterranean, except for air alone, it meant a prolonged struggle and one which was not acceptable to the United States. "This was "playing hardball," as the politicians on the Hill termed it; Marshall's threat to turn to the Pacific was deliberately implied and surely inferred.

Brooke gingerly backed away. The European war must be ended as fast as possible, he agreed, but to end operations in the Mediterranean would only prolong the war. Only there could they force Germany to divert enough troops to help the Soviet Union.

The divisions they could muster in the British Isles, he added, "would only be sufficient to hold a bridgehead and would not be large enough to debouch into the Continent. . . . No major operations would be possible until 1945 or 1946, since it must be remembered that in previous wars there had always been some eighty French divisions available on our side."

The Americans had no intention of waiting until 1945 to invade France. Such a timetable suggested the war in the Pacific raging into 1947 or 1948, far too long for public opinion to sustain.

The first meeting of the Combined Chiefs of Staff adjourned with the two groups far apart. Plainly aware of the new American resolve, Brooke wrote in his diary that evening: "I am thoroughly depressed with the prospects of our visit."

If Thursday's meeting was bad for the British, Friday was dreadful for the Americans. The commanders from the China–Burma–India theater, Field Marshal Archibald Wavell, Joe Stilwell, and Chennault, joined the Combined Chiefs to weigh proposed campaigns to retake Burma.

Wavell, a deliberate, cautious soldier, opened with a guarded fifteen-minute statement outlining the difficulties any attempt to establish a supply line to China entailed. The terrain was impossible, the jungles worse. There were few rail lines and those too small to handle the traffic. They had too few engineers and too few troops to guard the supply line. The monsoon limited operations. "Can't, can't, can't," Stilwell groused.

Stilwell followed with a shambling commentary that tumbled as much from his heart as from his head. Isolated from the West, the Chinese will to resist had deteriorated, he told the thirty men seated in the smoky boardroom. The fundamental need was to undertake offensive operations to open life-giving supply lines. "If a route supplying China could be made safe, everything else would follow; and conversely, if the route were lost, all of China would be lost."

Stilwell was nearly despondent. "Something must be done," he pleaded.

In diplomatic Washington, Joe Stilwell the field soldier was painfully uncomfortable. In wartime Chungking, he was beyond his depth— impatient with the convolutions of Chinese politics, blunt when protocol called for indirection. Stilwell's acidic temperament irritated the Chinese, especially when he demanded they use the army to counter the Japanese. Frustrated and out of favor, he scorned Chiang Kai-shek's alternative, a plan put forward by the commander of Chiang's air force, Major General Claire Chennault.

Chennault had become Stilwell's nemesis. A onetime high school teacher from Texas, Chennault had enlisted in the Army in 1917. He had gone on to flight school, discovering in flying all the excitement missing from the classroom. Chennault stayed in the service at the end of the war, transferring to the newly formed Army Aviation Corps in 1920. Among a group of young instructors at Maxwell Field—those who survived the cedar and canvas aircraft were destined for high command—Chennault became the expert in pursuit and fighter tactics.

The Air Corps was little interested, preferring the contrary notion that massed bomber fleets would be able to brush aside interceptors. His theories rejected, then grounded because of deafness, Chennault retired in 1936.

Former students at Maxwell Field who had flown in China recommended their old instructor to Chiang Kai-shek. For Chennault—a lanky, weatherbeaten romantic who saw himself as the knight errant—here was the ideal assignment: he was to build an air force to challenge the Japanese bombers flying unmolested through Chinese skies.

The champion of embattled China even had a fair lady. From the moment he first met her, Chennault was enthralled by Madame Chiang, the American-educated Mai-ling Soong. Ever after he considered her "a princess."

Even with his princess's favor, Chennault could not train Chinese pilots fast enough to overcome the Japanese advantage. Chiang instead wheedled 100 fighter planes from Hap Arnold's cache in early 1941, and permission to recruit American aviators to fly them in combat. Paid $750 a month, with $500 bonuses for each Japanese plane they shot down, those mercenaries became the American Flying Group, known colloquially as the Flying Tigers.

Chennault's cocky condottieri had since been reenlisted in the American Army as the 14th Air Force and beefed up. By mid-1942 Chennault was grandly claiming he could put the Japanese on the defensive, knock out the enemy's bomber force, and destroy his logistics network. All Chennault needed was 100 more fighters and 30 medium bombers; with that he guaranteed the defeat of Japan in China.

Generalissimo Chiang Kai-shek snatched up Chennault's plan: American pilots would bring victory without squandering any of the twenty-two Chinese divisions training with Stilwell. Those divisions then would be intact for the war to come, the war against the Communists once the Japanese were thrown out. It would be wisest, Chiang had long since concluded, to see that Chennault got the aviation fuel and spare parts necessary for a cheap victory.

To get those supplies, in effect to redirect the Allies' strategic priorities, Chiang turned to Chennault's princess, the forceful, winning Mai-ling Soong. In February 1943, ostensibly suffering from a skin condition brought on by nerves, Madame Chiang flew to the United States for treatment. Before entering the hospital, she lived as a guest at the White House, holding court in a blaze of favorable publicity.

Madame Chiang was even more than her husband a master of indirection, more than a match for the politicians with whom she dealt. Even the craggy Stimson came away impressed with that "most attractive and beguiling little lady," not yet aware just how persuasive she was.

Promoted by Madame Chiang, Chennault's "cheap" campaign appealed to both FDR and Harry Hopkins. Even if it was not successful, they reasoned, Chennault's option kept the skittish Chiang in harness. China was not yet a factor in the fighting, but FDR imagined a role for that nation as a peacekeeper in the postwar world.

Stilwell came to Washington aware he faced a difficult fight. Roosevelt had long held doubts about Stilwell's effectiveness, not for lack of victories, but for his shortcomings as a diplomat. The previous October, the president had dispatched an administrative assistant, Lauchlin Currie, to tell Marshall that Roosevelt wanted Stilwell relieved.

"He does, does he?" the chief of staff said coldly to the "little gnome-like man" sitting with one leg curled under him on the other side of the desk.

Yes, Currie replied.

"Is he sending you around to tell me?"

Currie nodded. He was.

"How long were you in China?" Marshall asked.

"Three weeks, sir," Currie responded.

Marshall said nothing, his frosty silence rebuke enough. An embarrassed Currie slipped out.

The president was not so easily put off. He wrote a memorandum suggesting to Marshall that Stilwell "would be more effective in some other field." Ordinarily such a presidential suggestion would be tantamount to a command, but Marshall bridled. First of all, Stilwell was a friend, one of the few men who called the chief of staff by his Christian name. (For Stilwell, Marshall had a special tolerance, once responding to a scathing Stilwell radiogram to the War Department, "I read your profane message and I sympathize with you in your reaction.")

In the second place, the chief of staff argued, an American had to lead those twenty-two Chinese divisions Stilwell was training if they were going to fight effectively. Marshall had last been in China in 1927, but remembered well enough the ineffective leadership of the ragged Chinese levies. They needed a combat soldier, preferably one who could command their respect; there was none better than Stilwell, certainly no one with his experience in China and his appreciation for the Chinese people themselves.

Roosevelt relented, but not without advising Marshall in a memorandum on March 8, 1943, that "Stilwell has exactly the wrong approach in dealing with Generalissimo Chiang . . . when he speaks of talking to him in sterner tones." Stilwell was to be reminded his relations with Chiang were as much diplomatic as military. "One cannot speak sternly to a man like that or exact commitments from him the way we might do from the Sultan of Morocco."

Lastly, the president wanted Chennault to have complete control over air operations. "Above all, I am depending on you to see that Chennault gets his chance to do what he believes he can do."

Ten days before TRIDENT opened, Stilwell himself was in Washington to argue his case. He came with a conservative alternative to Chennault's airpower panacea. Stilwell proposed he use his Chinese divisions to reopen the supply route through northern Burma to British India before attempting wider operations or Chennault's air strategy.

The plan was sound, but Stilwell bungled his presentation.

Perhaps it was shyness. Stilwell was, after all, a field soldier unused to such airy precincts. Perhaps it was fatigue. He *was* haggard. Perhaps it was the deeply ingrained sense that a soldier did not push his own cause, his biographer, Barbara Tuchman, has suggested. Perhaps it was simply tension, knowing the uphill struggle he faced. Whatever the reason, he sat hunched over in the president's office, his head down, Marshall said later, and "muttered something about China not fighting."

Aware he had muffed his great opportunity, Stilwell apologized to Marshall. The chief of staff merely ordered Stilwell to take a five-day holiday with his wife. Marshall would protect Stilwell's interests in Washington.

Roosevelt now renewed his effort to remove Stilwell. He wondered out loud if the China commander were ill, and might not that be a good reason to replace him? Marshall, disappointed in Stilwell's performance, defended him, as did Stimson in a calculated letter the next day. Stilwell had "the toughest task in the war . . . but is the only man I know who can carry that big job through."

On May 14, the president took another tack. He suggested to Marshall that military planners had not given sufficient consideration to the attrition of Japanese forces by bombing from China. In effect he was arguing the Chennault-Chiang position.

Marshall disagreed. As soon as Chennault's planes began imposing real damage, the Japanese would advance overland to capture his airfields, he insisted. Stilwell still had no forces capable of preventing that. Moreover, Marshall continued, there was the question of supplying Chennault's air forces. They could not fly enough tonnage over the Hump from India to China to supply both Chennault and Stilwell.

That afternoon, the Combined Chiefs and the Far East commanders met with Roosevelt in the White House to thrash out the future of the China–Burma–India theater. The British had no taste for a Burmese campaign, and little more for relieving the Chinese; they favored Chennault's air war as the cheapest alternative.

Once more Field Marshal Wavell painstakingly laid out the difficulties that confronted a land campaign in the theater, and again Stilwell stumbled over his feeling of inadequacy. "Ultimately the United Nations must meet the Japanese Army on the mainland of Asia," Stilwell argued. "To keep China in the war, it was essential they hold onto Yunnan province," the area that abutted the northern borders of Japanese-held Indochina and Burma. If Chennault's air forces proved too effective, the Japanese would be certain to attack the airfields they used in Yunnan. The Japanese had troops enough to move on Yunnan and its capital of Kunming; only the half-trained, ill-equipped divisions under Stilwell stood in the way.

It was a poor presentation. "Hard to say my piece," the dejected soldier conceded in his diary.

If Stilwell's and therefore Marshall's strategy had any chance before this, that faint opportunity went glimmering on that sweltering afternoon of May 14. Brooke judged Stilwell only a "stout-hearted fighter suitable to lead a brigade of Chinese scally-wags." The British had difficulty concealing their amusement, Chennault concluded.

Chennault was privately elated at Stilwell's poor showing. Happy with his own presentation, Chennault might have been surprised to learn that Brooke dismissed him too as "a fine fighting man, but of limited ability who added little of use to our discussions that day."

The president fantasized a compromise. Stilwell needed 2,700 tons of supplies a month to equip his troops, and Chennault 4,700 tons a month for the next four months to maintain his air effort. Airily ignoring the fact they had never shipped more than 2,400 tons in a month, FDR suggested a goal of 7,000 tons to be flown over the Himalayas from India to China. What would Chiang say if the tentative Burmese invasion were called off for lack of landing craft, Roosevelt asked.

He expected that operation, Stilwell replied. Without it he would feel deserted, and no alternative campaign in Sumatra or Malaya would assuage him. "The Chinese were suspicious of the British, and it would be necessary for the British to prove to them that they were in earnest."

Churchill bristled. "I am not prepared to undertake something foolish purely in order to placate the Chinese." There would be precious little support from that quarter.

In a short meeting after the conference broke up, Roosevelt asked Stilwell, "What do you think of the Generalissimo?"

"He's a vacillating, tricky, undependable old scoundrel, who never keeps his word," Stilwell snapped.

The president turned to Chennault. "What do you think?"

"Sir, I think the Generalissimo is one of the two or three greatest military and political leaders in the world today. He has never broken a commitment or promise made to me."

True or not, Chennault's was the correct answer, the response Roosevelt sought. The generalissimo might be an unreliable opportunist, as Stilwell said, but he was a head of state, and Roosevelt wanted Chiang's support in the postwar United Nations. Further, American public opinion favored the plucky Chinese; Madame Chiang, the president's charming guest, had wooed and won the American people.

At that moment, Stilwell became a marked man.

On Saturday morning, May 15, the Combined Chiefs met once more to discuss the cross-Channel invasion, the British chiefs arrayed against it, Marshall its ever more determined advocate. The British raised questions about the amount of air cover, about port capacity in the bridgehead area, and most of all about the number of German divisions the invasion force might confront.

The arguments were familiar by now. They all agreed that ROUNDUP, the invasion in strength, was essential, that "a strategy should be adopted which would produce the earliest possible successful invasion," as Air Marshal Sir Charles Portal said. The Americans noted the reservation.

The British argued operations in the Mediterranean were first necessary to drain German strength, the Americans favored a build-up in Great Britain "to give more strength to the blow," Portal continued.

They would not be able to build up sufficient forces in Great Britain if they continued operations in the Mediterranean, King responded. Operations there "would cause a vacuum into which our forces would be sucked."

"It must be remembered that this vacuum would suck in not only Allied forces, but also Axis forces," Portal rebutted.

They had to have a date certain, King said, otherwise valuable equipment, especially landing craft, would lie idle in Great Britain when it was needed in the Pacific.

Twice before they had begun the pre-invasion build-up in Great Britain, Marshall reminded them, only to have troops drawn off first for the invasion of North Africa and now for the invasion of Sicily. Unless the pre-invasion build-up were given priority over operations in the Mediterranean, the same thing would happen.

Neither side budged. Apprised of the deadlock, Stimson telephoned the president. "He told me he was coming to the conclusion that he would have to read the Riot Act to the other side and would have to be stiff." Stimson reminded Roosevelt: "the British are trying to arrange this matter so that Britain and America hold the leg for Stalin to skin the deer . . . a dangerous business for us at the end of the war. Stalin won't have much of an opinion of people who have done that and we will not be able to share much of the postwar world with him."

While the Combined Chiefs of Staff fought it out in the stuffy conference room at the Federal Reserve Building, at the far end of Constitution Avenue another problem for Marshall erupted.

Apparently tipped off by disgruntled military planners who doubted Britain's commitment to the war in the Far East, Kentucky Democrat Albert B. Chandler warned the Senate, "I should hate to envision a time after Germany becomes prostrate—as it is my belief that she will eventually—when we would be left entirely alone except for the loyal support of China, a magnificent people without arms, to fight the Japanese."

General MacArthur, "a magnificent American, and a real fighting man," must be reinforced, the senator urged. General Chennault, "the finest air officer in the world today," should receive the 500 aircraft he had told credulous correspondents he needed to win the war. "If we would send them to China we might be able to save those staunch, determined, Christian, God-fearing, good Chinese, the Generalissimo and his wife."

A subcommittee of the Senate Foreign Relations Committee had picked up the British scent just two days before TRIDENT opened. Despite Marshall's glowing testimony detailing their military progress, Republican Senator Arthur Vandenberg expressed his concern "about *who* makes our decisions and *how,* and about the British domination."

Political matters were never far from the minds of the Joint Chiefs of Staff, Marshall acknowledged, if only because the British position papers and discussions since the beginning of the war were influenced by political thinking. Yet they never discussed with the British Imperial General Staff political subjects. Their strategic decisions, he assured the senators, flowed only from military considerations.

Marshall's testimony in the closed session was not enough to silence the congressional criticism. A week later, Senator Chandler took the floor to argue once more for a Pacific-first strategy. An attack on northern France—the invasion Marshall sought above all else—"would be almost mass suicide," he insisted. Now that Germany was surrounded and had lost the initiative, they should turn to Japan. "If we attack Germany first, therefore, we shall suffer all the losses that it is possible for us to suffer, both in Europe and the Far East."

Maryland's Millard Tydings, aware that the British had prevailed at Casablanca, turned the argument from the global to the personal. He advised the Senate, "I am curious to know what, in their inner hearts and minds, General Marshall and Admiral King really think about it as trained and skilled military men, who have the responsibility of winning the war, not only in the Atlantic, but in the Pacific as well. . . . How much are political considerations in the international field influencing the better judgment of the experienced and seasoned Army and Navy men. . . ?"

The British at one hand, the president at the other. King and MacArthur, Stilwell and Chennault, not to mention fickle public opinion. Now the grandstanding of ambitious politicians undercut all his efforts. Marshall's close-kept anger exploded.

"This is a personal attack upon me. They are trying to destroy my character and reputation," he raged in a meeting with Secretary Stimson early on the morning of May 19.

Marshall was showing signs of strain, Stimson thought. Sternly, once more the colonel of artillery, he snapped, "General Marshall, it would be quite impossible for Senator Chandler to destroy or even in any degree impair your reputation or character, so let's drop this subject."

There was heartbeat's silence, then Stimson chuckled. His anger vented, Marshall smiled, then laughed. The moment had passed, but later that day the secretary acknowledged how much he worried about Marshall's physical condition and mental poise. On Marshall more than anybody in the government rested the fortunes of the United States in the war, Stimson wrote in his diary.

The public debate still rasped on Marshall's nerves as they resumed the conferences in the Federal Reserve Building. The Americans wanted to lay out an overall strategic plan, fitting operations to that concept. The British preferred the opportunistic method of old, shaping the strategic plan as they went.

"I find it hard even now not to look on your North Africa strategy with a jaundiced eye," Marshall told Brooke just before entering the boardroom.

"What strategy would you have preferred?"

"Cross-Channel operations for the liberation of France and an advance on Germany," Marshall answered. "We would finish the war quicker."

"Yes, probably," Brooke said dryly, "but not the way we hope to finish it!"

In a closed session that morning, the Combined Chiefs took the first steps to a solution. Marshall skimmed a British planners' study that seemed to suggest they could not amass by February 1944 enough troops to overwhelm German resistance in France the following spring. A few pages later, however, the paper also argued that further Mediterranean operations could tie up enough German strength to prevent the Wehrmacht from adequately reinforcing France when the Allies landed. The British planners estimated that by April 1, 1944, they would have as many as twenty-six and one-half divisions poised in Great Britain, enough to overcome the depleted German forces.

Another day of haggling moved the Americans closer to compromise. Marshall remained skeptical of British estimates of the casualties they would suffer or the need for additional troops to conclude any campaign in the Mediterranean. He feared the cost had been pegged too low, "since the wish might have been the father to the thought."

On Wednesday morning, May 19, they began to hammer out a plan. An invasion on April 1 was too early, Brooke hedged, because the Russian thaw would not be complete. Wait a month and the Soviet Army could launch a major offensive to pin German troops in the east. Marshall and King agreed to the delay.

At Marshall's suggestion, they once more cleared the room of their planners. The chief of staff was going to squeeze an agreement and he wanted no witnesses.

They had agreed on a firm date for ROUNDUP: May 1. Now Marshall was willing to extend a quid pro quo to the British—operations beyond Sicily "best calculated to eliminate Italy from the war and to contain the maximum number of German divisions." The decision would be made by Eisenhower, Marshall proposed, subject to the approval of the Combined Chiefs. Marshall was demanding veto power.

Wary of King's Pacific option or increased operations in far-off Burma, Brooke grudgingly settled for that half loaf. He agreed they would mass twenty-nine divisions for operations in France, including seven drawn from the Mediterranean. The draw down assured Marshall there could be no ever-expanding sideshow in the Mediterranean.

That night a thunderstorm cooled the humid city. The agreements would come quicker now that the air had cleared.

Thursday the 20th was given over entirely to the China–Burma–India theater. It was a very full day, according to Brooke, but in the end the British obtained virtually all they had sought. Marshall was dissatisfied, but without presidential backing, he could not overcome the hurdle of Stilwell's mumbling, tongue-tied report. "The President has gone over solid to the support of an air attack by Chennault as sufficient to secure China . . . ." Stimson grumbled in his diary.

Chennault was to get the largest portion of all tonnage flown over the Hump to Kunming. They also agreed to reopen the overland route, but left the date indefinite, and the operation itself therefore in limbo; Stilwell would do what he could without the supplies he needed to field a Chinese army.

The next day Admiral King held sway, delivering a hornbook lecture on Naval War College strategy. Navy doctrine held that to retake the Philippines they would have to first attack the Marianas and force the Japanese fleet to fight. Once the fleet was defeated, the Pacific would be an American pond; they could then starve Japan into submission.

King's speech had been honed on the skepticism of army planners. "It took me three months to educate Marshall about the importance of the Marianas, but any educated naval officer would have understood it," King said after the war.

The British feared King was not merely keeping pressure on in the Pacific, but intensifying the war there. They sought a clause requiring that future operations be ratified by the Combined Chiefs. King resisted, accepting only a weak substitute that gave the chiefs review of the effect any new operation in the Pacific might have elsewhere in the world.

Through the week they worked, dealing one after the other with the build-up of bombers in England, with air raids on the oil refineries at Ploesti in Rumania, rearming the French and supplying the Turks, with the U-boat campaign, and the proposed occupation of the Azores. Agreements came slowly, for one decision invariably affected two others.

Something was always in short supply, usually shipping, often landing craft, sometimes bombers or escort carriers. Between themselves the military men compromised, protecting favored plans as best they could. Marshall pressed the cross-Channel attack, King operations in the Pacific. Both air forces favored saturation bombing of Germany above all else. First Sea Lord Dudley Pound advocated primacy of the anti-U-boat campaign. Brooke plumped for the Mediterranean.

Agreement in hand, the Combined Chiefs presented themselves for examination at the White House on the afternoon of May 24. There the prime minister, to Brooke's consternation, "crashed in 'where angels fear to tread.' " Churchill insisted they take the toe and heel of the Italian boot after Sicily fell "and gain touch with the insurgents of the Balkan countries." Mention of the Balkans was enough to make Brooke cringe and Marshall bristle.

The prime minister did not want to leave the choice of the next Mediterranean operation to Eisenhower and the Combined Chiefs as their draft proposed. Sardinia was not an acceptable sequel to Sicily, Churchill insisted, waving his Cuban cigar about. Only with placating assurances that Eisenhower would be instructed to prepare operations that would oust Italy from the war did Churchill subside.

But not for long. In a last conference with the president, Churchill suddenly proposed that Marshall accompany him on an immediate trip to Eisenhower's headquarters. Without Marshall's presence, "if decisions were taken it might subsequently be thought that I had exerted an undue influence." The president agreed.

Informed the next morning, Marshall was put out. "He rather hated to be traded like a piece of baggage," he told Stimson. Furthermore, a long-planned trip with Ernest King to the South Pacific and MacArthur's headquarters would have to be postponed and a much-needed vacation with Katherine canceled. Stimson too was annoyed, he confided in his diary. The prime minister had placed another, and unnecessary, burden on "the strongest man there is in America, and Marshall is surely that today, the one on whom the fate of the war depends."

Neither man's irritation was to last long. They were too elated over the results of TRIDENT. Here at "one of the most historic military conferences of this war," Marshall had screwed from the reluctant British a firm date for the invasion of France. On that point he had finally prevailed.

Later that last day of TRIDENT, the president abruptly handed his chief of staff a new responsibility, suggesting Marshall and Churchill fly to North Africa together. They could discuss the communiqué informing Premier Stalin that the second front, promised for 1943, had been put off another year. They had discarded draft after draft until Churchill finally offered to make a fresh start while airborne to Newfoundland.

Marshall, the prime minister, and his chiefs of staff lifted off from Chesapeake Bay aboard the Boeing flying boat *Bristol* in a tepid summer rain. Churchill immediately settled into a private cabin to struggle with the sheaf of drafts of the communiqué to Stalin, made a stab or two, gave up, and turned them over to Marshall. The general thumbed through the drafts and decided to start afresh. Two hours later he turned over a clean-typed draft to the prime minister.

Marshall's message reported the decisions taken at TRIDENT, detailing the assistance to be furnished the Soviet Union: to step up the bombing of Germany and drain off fighters; to knock Italy out of the war and force Germany to spread its forces more thinly; and finally to resume the build-up of forces in the British Isles "at a rate to permit the full scale invasion of the continent to be launched at the peak of the great air offensive in the spring of 1944."

Churchill was impressed. Marshall's draft was precisely what he and the president had wanted, and it was written "with a clarity and comprehension not only of the military but of the political issues involved."

Until then, Churchill "had thought of Marshall as a rugged soldier and a magnificent organiser and builder of armies—the American Carnot. But now I saw he was a statesman with a penetrating and commanding view of the whole scene." As drafted by the chief of staff, the message eventually went to Stalin without change.

The 3,260-mile flight from Newfoundland to Gibraltar took seventeen hours. They slept the first portion, awakened only by a loud clap of lightning striking their airplane. For the balance of the flight, Marshall asked Churchill questions to deflect any discussion of future Mediterranean operations. Churchill enjoyed his "very agreeable" talks, lectures really, about the difference between impeachment in the United States and attainder in Great Britain, about Rudolf Hess's abortive mission to Scotland in 1941, about the abdication of Edward VIII.

They spent the second night in Gibraltar, visiting the governor's "special pet," a battery of eight guns sited in a gallery carved from the living rock. The British, who had poured an immense amount of effort and money into the project, filled with pride as Churchill and Marshall scanned the commanding field of fire. As they were climbing aboard their airplane once more, Marshall gently warned their host, "I admired your gallery, but we had one like it at Corregidor. The Japanese fired their artillery at the rock several hundred feet above it, and in two or three days blocked it off with an immense bank of rubble."

The traveling party flew the last leg of the journey in Churchill's converted Lancaster, arriving in Algiers on May 28. That evening they dined with Eisenhower, promoted at Marshall's insistence to full general, and his three British deputies for ground, air, and sea. After dinner they determined on an invasion of the small island of Pantelleria, lying between the Algerian coast and Sicily. Churchill and Brooke spent the time over coffee and cigarettes trying to persuade Eisenhower of the advantages of knocking Italy out of the war. "I still do not think that Marshall realizes this," Brooke wrote in his diary, "and I am quite certain that Eisenhower does not begin to realize the possibilities that lie ahead of us in this theater. . . ." In three different arguments Churchill sought to influence Eisenhower, upon whom the Combined Chiefs of Staff had rested responsibility for the choice of a follow-on to Sicily.

Churchill had correctly inferred that Eisenhower was wavering in favor of Italy. Once Sicily fell, Eisenhower would have over a million men standing idle while Italy beckoned, so close, and leached of the will to continue the fight. It appeared an easy target. Eisenhower proposed that if Sicily fell in a week, they immediately jump the Straits of Messina to the Italian toe.

The following day Brooke met privately with Eisenhower to argue that only the Soviet Army could produce decisive results in 1943. The British and Americans therefore should do everything they could to divert German troops from the Russian front, Brooke argued. He deliberately left open the question of how far north they should go in Italy; his vagueness rekindled fears in Eisenhower's mind of a bottomless Mediterranean pit.

Foreign Secretary Anthony Eden that afternoon aroused even more American suspicions. In a review of the Turkish situation, Eden noted that country would be much more friendly to the Allies "when our troops had reached the Balkan area."

Churchill scrambled to shove the cat back into the bag. "He was not advocating sending an army into the Balkans now or in the near future." Still he was not entirely disavowing a Balkans campaign. Once more Marshall was on his guard.

As if to pause to assess the damage, for the next two days they suspended their talks. Marshall used the time to inspect the American-held areas of Tunisia and to see the vast pens where a quarter-million German and Italian prisoners idled their days. Having tasted of the sweet victory, Marshall met in Algiers on June 3 to conclude the conference with Churchill and Brooke. The Eighth Army's Bernard Montgomery presented the staff plan for the capture of Sicily, a plan that made a greater impression on Marshall than did the man. Montgomery was narrow-minded, tactless, and lacking any appreciation of others' opinions. "It is most distressing that the Americans do not like him," Brooke wrote in his diary, "and it will always be a difficult matter to have him fighting in close proximity to them."

Despite Montgomery's poor impression, the last meeting ran smoothly— deceptively so since Marshall had decided to hold his peace when Churchill's imagination soared. The prime minister instantly interpreted that silence as agreement, happily concluding Marshall no longer opposed the conquest of Italy. Now both Marshall and Eisenhower had come round to his thinking, he concluded.

Churchill deceived himself. Marshall still favored only limited operations in Italy, no more than enough to tie up German troops and to perhaps force Italy from the war. As his assurance that operations would be limited, he insisted on the British-approved transfer of seven divisions from the Mediterranean to Great Britain. On that he had no intention of yielding.

With the end of the meetings, Marshall agreed to brief the British and American correspondents assigned to Eisenhower's headquarters at the St. Georges Hotel in Algiers. It was a press conference remembered as "an incredible performance" by one reporter who was present and "the most brilliant interview I ever attended in my life" by another. Word of it reached Washington quickly, adding to Marshall's already formidable reputation.

Seated at the head of a large mahogany table, Marshall suggested each of the thirty correspondents and photographers present ask all their questions at the beginning; he would then brief them on the "big picture." Each asked his question, Marshall looking at the correspondent, nodding once, then turning to the next. When all had asked their questions, some technical, some global in scale, the general leaned back in his chair, crossed his legs, pulled on an earlobe, and began a forty-minute exposition of the war. As he answered each correspondent's question, the chief of staff turned to the man who had asked it, fitting each answer into the global picture he was sketching. Again and again he stressed the difficulties of war in other theaters, attempting to combat what he had come to call "localitis," the tendency of commanders to think their theater the most important, the most in need of more men and materiel and the most difficult in which to fight a war. When he finished his theater by theater briefing, the men in the room sat stunned. Only when he rose to leave did the photographers rouse to snatch up their Speed Graflexes and shoot pictures.

Marshall returned to Washington in a C-54, on his own motion taking with him two awed enlisted men and a young second lieutenant who had been wounded in Tunisia. (At Marshall's request, his aide, Colonel Frank McCarthy, later called Walter Reed Hospital to find out how the three were doing.) Those young men were but three of the thousands of casualties the United States had already suffered. There would be more inevitably, and the responsibility would be his, always. George Catlett Marshall could never be far from the casualty lists.

CHAPTER

XXIII

Threshers

He was nearing the end of his term as chief of staff. In these four years since July 1939 and his appointment as acting chief of staff, George Marshall had raised and equipped an army and air force of almost 7 million men and women; in the last two years they had fielded fifty combat divisions. More were to come each month. His air force had grown thirty-five-fold, to 2 million men and more than 100,000 aircraft of all types.

In these same two years he had become the most powerful figure in the government after the president himself. No soldier since George Washington commanded such political influence and public respect as did this soldier of sober optimism. From his office in the outermost ring of the Pentagon flowed decisions or appeals to action that reached into every home in the nation: end the draft exemption for younger fathers; send a division to quell a race riot in Chicago; shift production priorities from aircraft to landing craft; grant deferments to hard-rock miners or men in other critical occupations; all that, and more, he decided, while managing the conduct of a war fought in theaters half a world apart.

Each Allied victory served to enhance a personal celebrity he found awkward, but a prestige that conferred on him even more authority to accomplish his aims. He was the architect and unflagging champion of coalition warfare, the man who had raised armies and armed allies. In less than two years those armies had rebounded from humbling defeat to help clear North Africa of the Axis; a million Allied troops now stood poised for further action, their assault on Sicily scheduled for July 10. In the Pacific, MacArthur and Nimitz steadily plucked off islands with strange names athwart the Japanese line of advance: Kiriwina and Woodlark, Sasvele, Baraulu, Rendova and Trobriand, Attu and Kiska. The war in the Pacific went slowly and was costly, but the Japanese were clearly on the defensive. In the Soviet Union, Red Army troops absorbed a major German attack on the central front, then launched a counterattack of their own on July 7, 1943. For two months Germans and Russians poured men and machines into this Kursk salient 140 miles south of Moscow until the greatest tank and air battles of the war ground up the Wehrmacht's last offensive in the east.

The United States had passed through its "military adolescence," and had "seized the initiative, the most vital factor in war," the chief of staff assured the nation in late June 1943. Now they had to guard against overconfidence.

In an era of prideful patriotism, there was little criticism of Marshall's accomplishment, and that easily brushed aside. To complaints of overspending, Marshall responded, ". . . I am profoundly grateful that for once in the history of the United States there is suggested the possibility that we may have too much of something or other with which to support our armies."

Moreover, the chief of staff added, he intended to continue to see that the American soldier was not limited in ammunition or in equipment, that he had sufficient training and medical care, "in other words, to see that for once in the history of this country he is given a fair break in the terrible business of making war." His sincerity and commitment only served to enhance the general's reputation.

Marshall's stature would reach such heights that, perhaps naturally enough, his name figured in speculation concerning the 1944 presidential campaign. "Gen. George Marshall may be unavailable because of his commitments and his sense of loyalty and duty, but just on the basis of personal merit can you think of a more desirable successor to President Roosevelt?" nationally syndicated columnist Westbrook Pegler wrote. Democratic Senator Edwin C. Johnson of Colorado followed with a speech on the floor of the Senate arguing "the Democratic Party owes it to the people to draft Gen. Marshall for President. He is not a candidate and he will emphatically say so, but no patriotic American from George Washington down can refuse such a call." Marshall, in Johnson's words "the man of this tragic hour," kept his embarrassed silence.

The Marshall-for-president boomlet finally petered out in the face of the candidate's silent antipathy. When Senator Johnson later complained that the chief of staff had not thanked him for putting his name forward, Marshall answered, "No, Senator, I certainly did not."

The prestige of American arms, something always to be protected, weighed constantly on Marshall. From prestige came the political leverage to pry concessions from allies, a lesson Marshall had learned from Black Jack Pershing in the first war. He concerned himself with everything from a scurrilous report that the Army was furnishing WAACs with contraceptives and prophylactics to whether Eisenhower's disposition of troops following British suggestions might have "unfortunate results as to national prestige." This concern for prestige, both national and personal, was to play a major role in the Sicilian campaign.

The landings on July 10, 1943, in the southeastern corner of Sicily had not gone well. There were problems of coordination between the services even before the first of the airborne troops—when challenged their countersign was to be "George Marshall"—landed in scattered clumps behind the invasion beaches. Intent upon strategic bombing, the air forces had provided "scandalously casual, careless and ineffective" air support, Major General Omar Bradley wrote later. The Luftwaffe played hob with the invasion fleet as it resupplied the beaches.

Lack of air supremacy complicated matters for the Allies. Put ashore from the largest naval force ever assembled, eight reinforced Allied divisions ran into determined opposition from veteran German units. The 15th Panzer Division punched through lightly armored American lines to threaten the landing beaches until supporting fire from naval vessels lying offshore drove the attackers off.

A second airborne attack went awry at night when U.S. Navy gunners opened up on the 144 transports carrying the paratroopers of the American 504th Regimental Combat Team. Casualties were heavy and the attack thwarted before it ever began. A third airborne attack by the British also aborted. By the end of the Sicilian campaign the future of airborne operations, which Marshall had backed wholeheartedly, was in serious doubt.

The Sicilian campaign, which Eisenhower had once suggested might be over in two weeks, settled down to a bitter slugging match. The Germans had concluded the island could not be held, but were determined to make the Allies pay dearly for it.

On the eastern or right flank of the Allied lines, British General Bernard Montgomery's four divisions bogged down at the base of Mount Etna. Without consulting his ally, Montgomery sent two divisions across the American front in a wild left hook thrown around the mountain. That move on D-plus-4 preempted a road designated for use by the Americans, squeezed them out of the line and left the American right flank hanging in mid-air. It was, Bradley complained later, "the most arrogant, egotistical, selfish and dangerous move in the whole of combined operations in World War II."

It was also futile. In the next several days of fighting, Montgomery's troops failed to dislodge the German and Italian defenders. The short route to Messina along the eastern shore of the triangular island was blocked.

On his own initiative, George Patton attacked northwesterly, along the coast toward meaningless Palermo, rather than due north to cut the island in half. Patton's 100-mile dash against light opposition from dispirited

Italian units produced the first major American victory of the Mediterranean war; only the extravagant headlines at home saved Patton from criticism or dismissal.

Eisenhower in far-off Algiers had lost control of the battlefield. The Allies were improvising their strategy, British and American generals scrambling for personal honors. On the east, the frustrated Montgomery settled into cautious habit, building up overwhelming forces before attacking. In the west, Patton rested in the royal palace at Palermo. In the center of the island, Bradley's two divisions probed for weaknesses, slugging hard against determined opposition.

To break the deadlock, Patton moved his rested Seventh Army eastward along the northern shore of the island toward the narrow Straits of Messina that separated Sicily from the mainland. Patton was openly racing Montgomery to capture both the city of Messina and the publicity. The Wehrmacht's crack Hermann Goering Division made it slow going for the ever more impatient Patton.

Patton's frustration exploded on August 3. Visiting a field hospital, he slapped a shell-shocked soldier across the face, then threw him out of the ward. "I don't want yellow-bellied bastards like him hiding their lousy cowardice around here, stinking up this place of honor," he barked.

A week later Patton visited another field hospital and encountered a second soldier suffering from shell shock. Patton pulled one of his ivory-handled pistols and waved it in the soldier's face. "You ought to be lined up against the wall and shot," he raged. "In fact, I ought to shoot you myself right now, God damn you." Instead, Patton slapped the soldier, then struck him with his fist. (Though reporters learned of the two incidents, they agreed not to file stories about them. Similarly Eisenhower protected Patton from the court-martial that striking an enlisted man required.)

Not until the night of August 10 did the Germans and those Italians still willing to fight begin an evacuation across the two miles of the Straits of Messina. Allied naval and air units inexplicably failed to interdict the exodus, a failure that could be laid to Eisenhower's doorstep in Algiers. For the next six days the Germans and remaining Italians methodically moved 110,000 men, 10,000 vehicles, and 17,000 tons of equipment to the mainland. Only then, thirty-nine days after the invasion, did Patton take Messina, a scant hour before Montgomery's first armored unit arrived.

That day Eisenhower's deputy, General Sir Harold Alexander, boastfully radioed Churchill that "the last German soldier [has been] flung out of Sicily." More accurately, Alexander might have reported that just three German divisions had carried the brunt of the fighting, skillfully holding up the Allies for five weeks, then escaping with few casualties to fight again. Allied coordination had been replaced by competition, planning by posturing. Sheer weight of numbers had crushed the Germans and Italians; the Allies had massed 500,000 men to the Axis' 200,000, the Italian majority of whom wanted only to go home. Even so, Sicily was dearly bought; the Germans actually suffered fewer dead than the Allies.

From the beginning, the Sicilian campaign produced a cocainelike euphoria in Washington and London. Normally sober men reacted oddly, perhaps because this was the first "European" territory to be reclaimed from the Axis. Moreover, the invasion on July 25 had brought down the tottering Mussolini government. Il Duce had fled to the Germans' protective custody while Italian emissaries secretly sought an armistice.

At the end of the campaign, Eisenhower wrote Marshall that Patton's vainglorious campaign would be considered "a model of swift conquest by future classes in the War College." Only hinting of the still secret slapping incidents, Eisenhower added that Patton "continues to exhibit some of those unfortunate personal traits of which you and I have always known. . . ." Eisenhower had quietly moved to bring Patton to heel, ordering him to apologize both to the men he had slapped and to the doctors, nurses, and patients who had seen the incidents.

Eisenhower believed Patton cured, he wrote Marshall, "not only because of his great personal loyalty to you and to me but because fundamentally he is so avid for recognition as a great military commander that he will ruthlessly suppress any habit of his own that will tend to jeopardize it." By not inquiring too closely, Marshall saved Patton to fight another day, though Patton would be denied any higher command. To the unassuming Omar Bradley, "the best all around combat leader" Eisenhower had met in the Army, would go command of the American troops invading France.

If they invaded. Once more Churchill the mercurial was blowing cold on the cross-Channel expedition, now renamed OVERLORD. He favored further action in the Mediterranean, alone if need be.

Unaware of Churchill's change of heart, on July 16 Marshall recommended to the Combined Chiefs of Staff that Eisenhower follow Sicily with an amphibious landing in the Naples area, well up the Italian boot. Marshall intended to deliver a quick punch that would knock Italy out of the war and capture Rome, then shift attention to the cross-Channel invasion. The Salerno landing site for Operation AVALANCHE was determined by the range of Allied fighters flying from Sicily; they were still 100 miles short of Rome and symbolic victory in Italy.

Churchill chose to interpret Marshall's proposal as a change of heart in favor of a full-bore Italian campaign. For his part, the prime minister told his chiefs of staff, the right strategy for 1944 was an Italian campaign "with option to attack westward in the south of France or northeastward towards Vienna, and meanwhile to procure the expulsion of the enemy from the Balkans and Greece." The twenty-seven divisions they had allocated for OVERLORD were not enough to do the job, he argued.

Churchill's change of heart was doubly aggravating to Marshall. Eisenhower wanted reinforcements to take advantage of Italy's precarious political situation; the Joint Chiefs of Staff had agreed to Eisenhower's request by diverting a troop convoy from Great Britain to Sicily. Worse still, the British Imperial General Staff unilaterally abrogated its TRIDENT agreement by freezing all British troops in the Mediterranean. Just as Marshall had feared, the build-up of forces for the cross-Channel operation was in jeopardy.

In response, on July 24 Marshall flatly refused to allocate further divisions to the Mediterranean. Additionally the Americans demanded that the British honor the TRIDENT decision to transfer seven British and American divisions to Great Britain and the BOLERO build-up.

The following day the chief of staff met with FDR to armor him against Churchill's supplications. The British strategy, Marshall argued, was based "on the speculation that a political or economic collapse, without a military invasion, can be brought about in the occupied territories, especially in the Balkans." If the British were wrong, Marshall pointed out, the war against the Axis would be a costly war of attrition. Still fixed on Japan as its major enemy, the American public would not long tolerate such a struggle in Europe; there would soon be questions about the president's conduct of the war, and a clamor to shift to the Pacific.

Once again their global strategy was in disarray, Churchill and the Imperial General Staff pulling the center of operations southward, Marshall tugging northward. Twice-promised and twice-delayed OVERLORD was again in question. Marshall moved to squelch the third repudiation.

American policy in the Mediterranean, the Joint Chiefs agreed in a Marshall-inspired position paper, called for the elimination of Italy from the war. Then they would establish bases on the mainland from which to bomb Germany and the Balkans. The capture of Italian Sardinia and French Corsica, and the supply of Balkan guerrillas would follow. In a preemptive rebuff to General Brooke, the American chiefs argued, "We must not jeopardize our sound overall strategy to exploit local successes in a generally accepted secondary theater, the Mediterranean, where logistical and terrain difficulties preclude decisive and final operations designed to reach the heart of Germany." If there were shortages of men or material, the paper proposed that OVERLORD have "an overriding priority."

The Balkans were unsuited to large-scale offensive operations, the U.S. planners continued, because of the mountainous terrain and poor transportation network. Only southern France offered a suitable area for

Mediterranean operations once Italy was knocked from the war, and an assault in that quarter was conceived only as a support for the cross-Channel invasion.

In short—and it would certainly be read in London that way—the Americans, Marshall, would tolerate no more diversions. They would endorse only limited operations in Italy, enough to knock Italy out of the war.

The result was strategic indecision. As an opposition member put it in the House of Commons, "The Allied High Command have approached the Italian mainland like an old man approaching a young bride, fascinated, sluggish and apprehensive."

To thrash out their differences, the president and prime minister agreed upon yet another meeting with their Combined Chiefs of Staff. This time they settled on the elegant suites of the plush hotel Château Frontenac overlooking the St. Lawrence River in Quebec.

The British delegates arrived on the *Queen Mary* in Halifax Harbor on August 9, 1943, as divided in their counsel as the Americans were finally firmly behind theirs. Once again Churchill was plumping for an invasion of Norway or an attack in far-off Malaya, plans the exasperated Brooke resisted as likely to estrange the Americans beyond reconciliation. The prime minister's sudden change of direction left Brooke the prime advocate of an opportunistic Mediterranean strategy, but down a queen even before play began.

Meanwhile, Marshall and Henry Stimson were stiffening the president's resolve for OVERLORD. Stimson argued the British wanted to leave the fighting on the continent to the Soviet Union. "To me, in the light of the post-war problems which we shall face, that attitude towards Russia seems terribly dangerous. We are pledged quite as clearly as Great Britain to the opening of a real second front. None of these methods of pinprick warfare can be counted on by us to fool Stalin into the belief that we have kept that pledge."

The time had come to put "our most commanding soldier" in charge of OVERLORD, said Stimson. "General Marshall already has a towering eminence of reputation as a tried soldier and as a broad-minded and skillful administrator." The British would be unable to criticize the choice since it was Churchill himself who had first suggested it a year earlier, Stimson reminded the president. Roosevelt had not accepted the offer then, but at least they had the prime minister on record.

Roosevelt was convinced. In a July 25 meeting with the Joint Chiefs of Staff, "The president went the whole hog" on OVERLORD, the delighted Stimson wrote in his diary.

The president, in fact, went even further. If the British scanted the cross-Channel attack, the Americans could carry it out themselves, he offered. In any event, Roosevelt said, "he was anxious to have American preponderance in the OVERLORD operation, starting from the first day of the assault. . . . Frankly, his reason for desiring American preponderance in force was to have the basis for insisting upon an American commander." Eisenhower was to make do with the forces he had in the Mediterranean, the president also decided; he wanted no operations into the Balkans.

They were committed. The following day, the chief of staff dispatched a memorandum to the White House assuring the president the United States would have ready for OVERLORD from one to four more divisions, 3,200 more combat planes, and considerably more support troops than the British. The supreme commander would be an American.

The Combined Chiefs of Staff opened their QUADRANT meetings in Quebec on August 14. From the first the Americans were "even more than usually unyielding," Brooke complained. The arguments of old only irritated the Americans, wrote Admiral Leahy in his diary. "British insistence on expanding the Italian operations provoked King to very undiplomatic language, to use a mild term."

Sunday, August 15, was a "gloomy and unpleasant day" for Brooke. He sought to appease the Americans, agreeing that the cross-Channel invasion should constitute the "major offensive for 1944." Brooke attempted to pose the Italian campaign as a precondition necessary for OVERLORD; the success of the cross-Channel operation would be better ensured if they advanced as far north in Italy as Milan and Turin. Such familiar arguments set Marshall's teeth on edge. During a later conversation with Sir John Dill, Marshall angrily threatened to resign if the British insisted upon any expansion in the Mediterranean.

Shortly before noon, the prime minister summoned Brooke to the governor-general's residence where Churchill was staying. Walking along the terrace overlooking the gray St. Lawrence River, Churchill abruptly asked Brooke how he would feel if command of OVERLORD went to Marshall. Brooke was crushed. Twice Churchill had promised him that he would lead the cross-Channel attack, most recently a month before.

Marshall would become supreme commander in Europe in exchange for the appointment of a Briton as supreme commander in Southeast Asia, Churchill explained. It was bitter medicine—to be supplanted by a man who could not grasp a strategic problem. Still, with what the prime minister called "soldierly dignity," Brooke responded that he "could not feel otherwise than disappointed." Neither the soldier's pain nor the politician's embarrassment would fade quickly.

Confronted with the fact that the United States would provide the bulk of the soldiers in northern Europe, Churchill had yielded to Roosevelt with what grace he could. Marshall was to become supreme commander in northern Europe and hold an advisory role in the Mediterranean. Eisenhower then would replace Marshall in Washington while command in the Mediterranean went to a Briton. That evening, the prime minister agreeably acknowledged in a confidential conversation with Marshall that he had also changed his mind about the chances of OVERLORD succeeding.

The British concession stood out in high relief the following day when Churchill received a message forwarded from the British Ambassador to Spain. Two emissaries from Marshal Pietro Badoglio, Mussolini's replacement as head of the Italian government, had approached him, the ambassador reported. Never long on martial spirit, depleted Italy apparently wanted to strike a separate peace with the Allies. The emissaries sought two concessions because of heavy German reinforcements in Italy: the Allies would invade the Italian mainland in force, and Italy would be allowed to fight alongside the welcome invaders to expel their former allies. Even unconditional surrender could be a surrender with honor.

With the end of the Sicilian campaign and looming elimination of Italy from the war, the need for a concerted strategy in Europe was all the more imperative. On Tuesday, August 17, the day Patton and Montgomery entered Messina, the Combined Chiefs of Staff met in a closed session to thresh out a European strategy.

The elliptical minutes of the closed-door session hardly suggest the stormy debates between American and British delegations and, more particularly, between Marshall and Brooke. Marshall yielded somewhat to British arguments that they take advantage of expected German weaknesses to press on north of Rome. In exchange, the British agreed to make OVERLORD the primary effort in Europe, with a target date of May 1, 1944. The cross-Channel operation was to have priority when there was a shortage of resources. Eisenhower in the Mediterranean would have to make do with the forces already allocated to him—unless the Combined Chiefs agreed to future reinforcements, a provision that would allow Brooke to press for greater effort in Italy, sometime in the future. "All our arguing has borne fruit and we have obtained quite fair results," the British general concluded.

Day by day they reviewed their strategic plans, revising here, reaffirming there. On August 19, the two sides agreed on the appointment of Lord Louis Mountbatten as supreme commander in Southeast Asia after Marshall rejected Churchill's nominee, Air Marshal Sir Sholto Douglas, for the post. "I would take every American out from under him if he was in command. He didn't like Americans and was very frank in saying it," Marshall explained later. He had conceived a model of Allied leadership based on mutual respect and cooperation. Eisenhower had followed it successfully. So would other theater commanders.

Similarly, Marshall's firm opinions shaped the choice of a deputy chief of staff for Mountbatten, Albert Wedemeyer, and a deputy commander,

Joseph Stilwell. Despite steady pressure from Chiang Kai-shek to have the critical Stilwell removed, despite Roosevelt's announced desire to replace him, Marshall and Stimson had loyally stood by him. Appointment as deputy commander in Southeast Asia would affirm Stilwell's position; Stilwell would simultaneously hold three posts: as Mountbatten's deputy, as Chiang's chief of staff, and as commander of American troops in the China–Burma–India theater.

With Mountbatten and Stilwell confirmed, Marshall excused himself from the meeting to inform T. V. Soong, the Chinese ambassador to the United States and Madame Chiang's brother. In undiplomatically blunt terms the chief of staff told the ambassador that China was expected to put troops into combat under Mountbatten and Stilwell "instead of confining themselves to lip service and letting someone else do that fighting."

On August 20, Marshall and Brooke opened a new subject, military relations with the Soviet Union. The Russians were stronger than ever before, Brooke noted, with ample reserves for further offensives before the winter's snows. Germany's allies, Rumania and Finland, were faltering; Hungary, like Italy, was seeking a separate peace. If those allies fell out, the Germans would be pressed to replace them on the Eastern Front, making the task of reinforcing Italy and France that much harder.

The Soviet Union's resurgence hardly came as a surprise to the Americans. Harry Hopkins was carrying in his briefcase a Joint Chiefs' strategic estimate that forecast Russia as the dominant power in postwar Europe. Great Britain alone would not be able to stand up to the Soviets, the estimate continued. Friendship with Moscow was crucial, the more so because Russian participation in the war against Japan would save American lives and end the war more quickly.

Marshall had another, more urgent concern at the moment. "It appeared that Russia was turning an increasingly hostile eye on the capitalistic world, of whom they were increasingly contemptuous. Their recent 'Second Front' announcement [implicitly critical of the Western nations for failing to invade France], no longer born of despair, was indicative of this attitude." Marshall wanted to know if Russia's attitude would affect the deployment of Allied forces, for example, "in the event of an overwhelming Russian success, would the Germans be likely to facilitate our entry into the country to repel the Russians?"

Brooke did not answer directly. Instead he suggested that the Soviet Union would demand a slice of Poland, at least a portion of the Baltic states and possible concessions in the Balkans. If it got those lands, "she [Russia] would be anxious to assist us in maintaining the peace of Europe."

Three days later, as Russian troops recaptured the gutted shell of the once great city of Kharkov, President Roosevelt asked the same question. Did the Chiefs of Staff have a study dealing with an emergency entrance onto the continent? He wanted United Nations troops to be ready to get to Berlin as soon as did the Russians, he told the chiefs.

Marshall seemingly interpreted the president's question as stemming not from some anxiety about Communist influence in Europe but from a desire for "prestige and ability to carry out the reorganization of Europe on an equal status with the Soviet Union." The capture of Berlin would be both a political and psychological victory; at least since March Marshall himself had worried about "a most unfortunate diplomatic situation" if the United States and Great Britain were bogged down in France while the Russians approached Germany. In any event, the Allies had an emergency plan to rush at least two divisions onto the continent within hours; one airborne division was to be ready to seize government buildings in Berlin.

Detail by detail the two delegations hammered out their plans for the defeat of the Axis in Europe, setting priorities, calculating the end of hostilities, and eying the world beyond. Most of the meetings were tense, the junior staffs dismissed while British and Americans blistered each other's plans. Bit by bit they concurred, first on a tentative plan for OVERLORD drafted by British Lieutenant General Frederick Morgan, then on two invasions of the Italian mainland, on a stepped-up bombing campaign against Germany, on plans to capture Sardinia and Corsica, then to invade southern France, on another to increase supplies to China and to launch a campaign during the dry season in northern Burma. Clause by careful clause they shaped an agreement.

The friction led to one lighter moment during the conference, when Lord Mountbatten sought the approval of the Combined chiefs for a new and unconventional weapon. British scientist Geoffrey Pyke, employed by Mountbatten's Combined Operations, had discovered that water mixed with sawdust when frozen produced a substance six times stronger than ice. Pyke proposed building 2,000-foot-long vessels of this "Pykrete" to provide floating, and virtually unsinkable, aircraft carriers. Excited by the discovery, Mountbatten insisted on demonstrating it to the Combined Chiefs.

Junior officers trundled a dripping block of ice and a block of Pykrete into the handsomely appointed conference room. Mountbatten handed an ax to Hap Arnold and urged him to have at the two blocks. Arnold noisily struck the ice, but wrenched his arm when the ax bounced off the Pykrete. Mountbatten then drew a service revolver and fired a shot at the impervious Pykrete, Lord Portal and Admiral King ducking as the bullet ricocheted between them.

In the hallway outside, one of the younger officers quipped, "First they argue, then they begin hitting each other, now they've started shooting."

The conference ended on August 24, 1943, and with it their "differences of opinion, stubbornness, stupidity, pettiness and pig-headedness." But if the arguments of Quebec were behind the president and his chief of staff, the stupidity, pettiness, and pigheadedness of Washington awaited their return.

At his regular press conference a week later, President Roosevelt announced the promotion of Dwight Eisenhower two ranks to permanent major general and the award of the Distinguished Service Medal for his service in North Africa. Almost as an afterthought, FDR added, "The other thing is that General Marshall's four-year term as chief of staff [ends] today. He of course will continue in office beyond the usual and customary four-year term. Outstanding service is the reason for continuing him in the office as chief of staff."

It was some measure of Marshall's reputation that news of his reappointment was overshadowed in the wire service reports by Eisenhower's promotion. It would have been news had he not been retained and the political repercussions even greater than they were when word of Marshall's appointment as supreme commander leaked to the press in the first week of September.

The chief of staff had returned to the Pentagon a quietly happy man, OVERLORD agreed to, a date set, and he to command this climactic operation of the war in Europe. Secretly Katherine Marshall began moving their personal goods from Quarters No. 1 at Fort Myer to Dodona Manor in Leesburg, then hired a cook and nurse for her daughter Molly's children. Marshall was relieved, his wife noted, "for he hated to leave for Europe with our domestic affairs unsettled."

Almost as if completing his stewardship, on the day of his reappointment Marshall turned over a copy of his second biennial report to Harry Hopkins. The 30,000-word report, written since May on weekends or during long airplane flights, was intended to put to rest all rumors and conjectures about the past two years, he told Hopkins. "Here is what we did and why we did it," Marshall said in an accompanying memorandum. "They may agree or may not but guesswork would no longer be involved and the public, I believe, will be better prepared to view the great battles to come with a better understanding of all that is involved."

Coincidentally released on the day the Italian surrender was announced, the report's assertion that the war was entering its final phase seemed prophetic. "The end is not clearly in sight," Marshall's text cautioned, "but victory is certain."

The report was "good reading," *The New York Times* decided; its text was like Marshall himself, said *Time* magazine with patriotic pride, "soldierly, sober, soundly optimistic." It sold widely in the United States and Great Britain; for perhaps the first time in history a government document appeared on best-seller lists.

The report's reception was some measure of the esteem in which public, press, and politicians alike held the chief of staff. His influence had grown steadily, quietly, to the point where his suggestions for appointments in the administration were given serious weight. Fearing he might be dropped from consideration as ambassador to the Soviet Union, Averell Harriman even asked Marshall not to recommend him to Roosevelt for another civilian position.

Paradoxically, Marshall might have wished for a little less prestige, a little less acclaim when word leaked that he was to go to London as supreme commander of the cross-Channel invasion. He could thank Admiral King for the resulting public outcry.

Ernest King opposed Marshall's shift to London and his probable replacement in Washington by Eisenhower. His objection, shared to some extent by Leahy and Arnold as well, was simple enough: why break up a winning team, he asked. King determined to see that did not happen.

Shortly after returning from Quebec, the chief of naval operations urged two members of a small group of journalists with whom he met confidentially in periodic off-the-record briefings to "help us out with articles and editorials saying how much Marshall is needed right here, and emphasizing what a good job he is doing."

Glen Perry of *The New York Sun* and the influential Marquis Child, columnist for the *St. Louis Post-Dispatch,* complied. As King had anticipated, other papers picked up the story until it took on a life of its own.

The unofficial but well-connected *Army and Navy Journal* followed in mid-September with an editorial scowling at unnamed but "powerful influences" that sought to remove the steadfast and effective Marshall as chief of staff. The publisher of the newspaper, John Callan O'Laughlin, a former treasurer of the Republican Party, then prevailed upon his old friend John J. Pershing to stick his oar in.

From his room at Walter Reed Hospital, the retired general of the armies wrote FDR urging that Marshall be retained as chief of staff. "To transfer him to a tactical command in a limited area, no matter how seemingly important, is to deprive ourselves of the benefit of his outstanding strategical ability and experience. I know of no one at all comparable to replace him as chief of staff."

The president's reply was full of man-to-man bluff heartiness:

"You are absolutely right about George Marshall—and yet, I think, you are wrong too! He is, as you say, far and away the most valuable man as chief of staff. But, as you know, the operations for which we are considering him are the biggest that we will conduct in this war. And, when the time comes, it will not be a mere limited area proposition, but I think the command will include the whole European theater. . . ."

Pleading that "it is only a fair thing to give George a chance in the field," the president concluded: "The best way I can express it is to tell you that I want George to be the Pershing of the second World War—and he cannot be that if we keep him here."

The controversy flashed through Congress. The ranking Republican members of the Senate Military Affairs Committee met confidentially with Secretary of War Stimson to vent their anxiety over the rumors of the general's reassignment. Marshall was needed in Washington, Senator Warren Austin assured Stimson. They relied on Marshall and "were able to carry controversial matters through with their colleagues if they could say that the measure in question had the approval of Marshall."

That afternoon at the White House, Stimson told Harry Hopkins that Marshall not only should be supreme commander in northwest Europe but should command the Mediterranean theater as well, all with the rank Pershing had held, general of the armies. Promotion and dual responsibility would give the new job a larger scope suitable for a man of Marshall's authority. The move, however, would require Pershing's consent, the two men agreed, otherwise Marshall would not assent. On the other hand, Marshall was about the only man Pershing would accept as his successor, they concluded.

Marshall was grateful for Stimson's double endorsement, but dubious that Churchill would consent to the unification of the two European theaters under one supreme commander. The prime minister also had an electorate to which he answered. Considerations of national pride figured on both sides of the ocean.

Marshall was correct. Reports in the British and American papers tickled Churchill to respond. He wired Hopkins that he had understood Marshall was to command OVERLORD, and would sit with the British chiefs from time to time, as Sir John Dill did in Washington, though "it would not fall to him to give decisions outside the sphere of OVERLORD." The British were not going to yield easily to Roosevelt's need for a command that would appear large enough for Marshall's talents.

Fueled by gossip, rumor, and political partisanship, opposition to Marshall's change of command grew ever more shrill. The strident *Washington Times-Herald* columnist Frank Waldrop informed his readers that Marshall was out of step with Roosevelt and Churchill when determining global strategy, and consequently was "on the skids." On September 20, a onetime isolationist from Illinois, Republican Jessie Sumner, charged in the House of Representatives that Marshall was being removed as chief of staff to appease the British "because he stood up for our American rights." Republican Paul Shafer inserted a short speech in the *Congressional Record* linking Marshall's transfer to a plot to convert "the War Department into a New Deal political W.P.A." Shafer fastened onto an article by the head of the Washington Bureau of Hearst's International News Service asserting that "a group of influential White House advisers" intended to "kick Marshall upstairs" and install Brehon Somervell in his place. Somervell then would become "an Army running mate for Mr. Roosevelt on a fourth-term ticket to offset the possible Republican nomination of Gen. Douglas MacArthur."

Throughout the "hullabaloo," as he termed it, Marshall declined to speak about his own transfer. He vigorously defended Somervell at a breakfast meeting with the ranking members of the House Military Affairs Committee. The assignment and promotion of all army officers was done without political consideration, he told the congressmen; Roosevelt accepted Marshall's and Stimson's recommendations with hardly a question. Yes, they could repeat his comments on the floor of the House.

Even the Germans managed to get involved. Allied monitors picked up a German propaganda broadcast from Paris reporting, "General George C. Marshall, the U.S. chief of staff, has been dismissed. President Roosevelt has taken over his command. This occurred two days ago, but has not yet been commented on in Washington." Marshall forwarded a transcript of the broadcast with a cover note asking, "Dear Harry: Are you responsible for pulling this fast one on me? G.C.M."

The president, not Hopkins, replied in a penciled note, "Dear George— Only true in part—I am now chief of staff *but* you are president. F.D.R."

Finally the firestorm passed, leaving the chief of staff's reputation permanently hardened and glazed. *Christian Science Monitor* reporter Richard Strout watched Marshall testify in Congress late in September, then wrote as T.R.B. in *The New Republic*:

> He is one of the most effective witnesses I ever followed. His testimony killed the bill. There were no false notes in his testimony, no mugging and gagging, nor the mawkish kind of deference and deprecation that so frequently go with a congressional hearing. Because he set a forthright tone, the members of the committee followed along on the same level too. He is not the military glamour type, like General MacArthur, and he is somewhat more articulate and practiced than General Eisenhower, able though the latter is. I don't know what his ideological convictions are (if any) and this may be a belated discovery on my part, but I think we have something pretty good in George Marshall.

Less than two weeks later, the man who had drafted the plan for OVERLORD arrived in Washington intent on getting the Americans finally to appoint a supreme commander for that operation. Time was short, seven months, and there were pending decisions only the supreme commander could make.

Lieutenant General Frederick Morgan was also job hunting when he met Marshall in his Pentagon office. Marshall had passed word to London that, if he assumed command of OVERLORD, he wanted to consider Morgan as his chief of staff. It would be the ideal choice. Freddie Morgan was, like Marshall, a consummate military planner; he certainly knew his own plan for the invasion. Moreover, Morgan had served with Canadian troops in the early days of the war in France, liked Americans—too much, some British staff members muttered—and admired both Eisenhower and Marshall.

The American welcomed Morgan "with the sweetest of smiles," then said, "I have heard the most unsatisfactory reports about you." Morgan's hopes crashed. "I hear you have taken no rest whatever for a long time, and that won't do. While you are over here I intend to see that you take leave, and the longer the better." Marshall arranged a short leave for the Briton and a tour of the Shenandoah Valley, following in the footsteps of Stonewall Jackson's columns.

Marshall was frank with Morgan, telling him there was some doubt in this first half of October about his taking command of OVERLORD. "There was an apparently insoluble problem of his succession as chief of staff in the States," Morgan recalled. There were personality conflicts within the services and questions about relationships with Congress. Further, Marshall appeared to be stepping down from command of the entire American Army to command in just one theater. Despite that, Marshall recommended they proceed as if he were to be supreme commander.

A later visit with the president confirmed Marshall's doubts. Morgan boldly asked for Marshall's services as supreme commander.

Roosevelt was dubious. "I doubt very much if General Marshall can be spared. . . ."

General Morgan was back where he had begun. He had a plan, but no commander. Worse yet, both British and American planners were clamoring to overhaul his invasion plan to suit their tactical prejudices. The grand strategy shaped in three conferences this year was close to unraveling.

More than OVERLORD was suddenly at stake. Marshal Stalin, who until now had declined to meet with Roosevelt and Churchill, cabled to suggest the three of them meet. Stalin, of course, would have his own agenda, both political and military. That agenda could shape the course of the war and with it the shape of the postwar world.

C H A P T E R

XXIV

A Rainbow Discerned

The Navy's newest battleship, crisp in its fresh paint, waited in Chesapeake Bay as the presidential yacht *Potomac* eased alongside. Aboard the massive warship with its sweeping decks, the Joint Chiefs of Staff watched the crew smartly run through its drills under the gimlet eye of Ernest King. "I never saw so much saluting in my life, not even at West Point!" a bemused Hap Arnold noted.

The three service chiefs had slipped secretly from Washington on the first leg of a journey that would take them to the president's first meeting with Premier Joseph Stalin in Tehran. This conference had been long in coming, and was all the more vital for having been postponed, yet a sailor's aversion to beginning a voyage on a Friday led the president to order their sailing delayed until Saturday, November 13. Better not to tempt fate. There was much at stake in Tehran—and before, at a preliminary meeting in Cairo with Churchill and China's Generalissimo Chiang Kai-shek.

The time had come, in the inelegant phrasing of the staff paper the planners had carried aboard the ponderous *Iowa*, to "fish or cut bait." Enough talk, the Joint Chiefs of Staff agreed, enough of Churchill's backing and filling, of his constant giving with the left hand and taking with the right. The invasion of France, thought settled at Quebec in August, was once again in question, jeopardized by a unilateral British attempt in September to seize the Dodecanese Islands in the eastern Mediterranean from the Italians.

That campaign had started modestly enough. At the prime minister's urging, the British commander in the Middle East, General Sir Henry Maitland Wilson, had put men ashore on three smaller islands before the Germans could take them. Meanwhile the Wehrmacht had taken the only prize worth the having in the Aegean Sea, the isle of Rhodes, and was threatening to oust the British from their precarious footholds on

Leros, Samos, and Cos. Churchill now wanted American aid to salvage the situation.

Eisenhower, stiffened by Marshall, had resisted diverting needed troops and landing craft from Italy; his refusal had precipitated what the prime minister called the most acute difference he would have with Eisenhower. Rebuffed the prime minister might be, still he remained firmly fixed on the eastern Mediterranean and what he perceived as golden opportunities to set the Balkans ablaze. Churchill determined to convene another meeting of the Combined Chiefs of Staff to persuade them to undo the Quebec decision of three months before giving the cross-Channel invasion priority. Preoccupied by his first meeting with Stalin, unwilling to renege on OVERLORD, President Roosevelt had agreed only reluctantly to meet once again with the prime minister.

The *Iowa*'s first sea passage was uneventful—after the second day when one of the destroyers in the battleship's screen accidentally unloosed a torpedo in the direction of the *Iowa*. The warship ponderously turned aside, the torpedo passing well astern before sinking harmlessly into the ocean.

The following day, the president and his chiefs of staff began working their transatlantic passage. In a series of meetings in the well-furnished confines of the captain's mess, they reaffirmed their global strategy, under Marshall's direction coordinating a war raging in the air over Germany, in the Mediterranean, in Burma, in China, and in both the Central and Southwest Pacific.

Much of the discussion concerned diplomatic issues Marshall considered the president's responsibility. The chiefs' problem, Marshall told his biographer, "was to be on guard that the military picture—meaning army, navy and air—was not completely disjointed by what I will call some irrelevant political gestures which were made without due thought to what was going on at the time. . . ."

Political questions were never far from mind, Marshall reiterated. "But we were very careful, exceedingly careful, never to discuss them with the British, and from that they took the [view] that we didn't observe those things at all." The chiefs "were not in any way putting our necks out as to political factors which were the business of the head of the state—the president—who happened also to be the commander-in-chief."

On November 15, the Joint Chiefs aboard *Iowa* began grappling with the geopolitical complexities of global war. The first, and to Marshall the most critical, was unification under a single supreme commander of both the invasion of France and a merged Mediterranean-Middle East theater. A supreme commander, intent on OVERLORD, would prevent further diversions from the cross-Channel build-up.

Leahy, Arnold, and King considered the post Marshall's by all rights, however loath they were personally to lose him in Washington. But only that joint command would appear to be a large enough responsibility for the man whose leadership stood him first among the chiefs; anything less would make Marshall "just another theater commander," Hap Arnold pointed out. In that case the shift would appear a demotion, especially if Eisenhower were to rotate back to Washington as acting chief of staff in Marshall's absence.

Marshall was the man for the task, his colleagues on the Joint Chiefs of Staff agreed. As supreme commander of all Allied troops in Europe and the Middle East, he could assure OVERLORD without distractions in the Mediterranean. And precisely for that reason, the prime minister was certain to object to unification of the two theaters.

The organization of a single command was more important to the chief of staff than who would fill that post. To seduce Churchill, Marshall proposed they nominate Sir John Dill as commander, though the bulk of the troops in the combined command would be American. That would place a Briton in the most prestigious of all commands, but a Briton committed to the cross-Channel invasion. Eisenhower would then stay in the Mediterranean, and Marshall remain in Washington.

The president had reservations about that ploy. Four days later, he convened the Joint Chiefs in the admiral's cabin for a hard-eyed review of the options open to them.

Like Marshall, Roosevelt wanted a single commander for all of Europe. Marshall's reason was strategic, a more efficient prosecution of the war. Roosevelt's reason was political, leadership of the alliance and pride of place in the postwar world.

The unwritten rule of coalition warfare held that the nation furnishing the most troops would name the commander. At that moment, the United States had more than twice the number of men under arms as did the British: 10.1 million to 4.5 million. Their overseas strengths were about the same, Marshall continued, but that would change. While the British had reached total mobilization, as many as fifty divisions were still to come from the United States. By January 1, 1944, Arnold added, the Air Force would have 12,000 operational planes, the British about 8,000. Those figures assured American command—if they chose to force the issue.

That decision the president put off, turning instead to a discussion of how they were to partition and occupy a defeated Germany. He did not like the present British plan to occupy the northwestern part of Germany while the United States took responsibility for France and Germany south of the Moselle River. "We do not want to be concerned with reconstituting France. France is a British 'baby,'" he stressed. "We should get out of France and Italy as soon as possible, letting the British and the French handle their own problem together." He was also opposed to putting an American army of occupation in either Italy or the Balkans.

The president personally envisioned an occupation army of a million Americans staying in Europe only two years; anything longer would upset the geopolitical balance. "We should not get roped into accepting any European sphere of influence," he cautioned the Joint Chiefs. As it had for more than a century, Europe was to balance between Great Britain and Russia.

Roosevelt proposed the United States take the northwestern portion of Germany, occupying an area that ran as far east as Berlin. That symbolic capital would be jointly occupied by British, American, and Soviet troops. There would "definitely be a race for Berlin," he added. "We may have to put the United States divisions into Berlin as soon as possible."

The assignment of the German occupation zones had flowed from longstanding logistical arrangements, Marshall explained. American troops were now billeted in the southwest of England, British and Canadian in the southeast. The plans for the invasion of France called for the Americans to occupy the right or southern half of the line, Commonwealth troops the left or northern portion. Once the invasion began, it would be hard to exchange their positions without snarling communications.

A northern zone of occupation was critical, the president insisted. Once there, the United States could have access to the great ports at Bremen and Hamburg, from where they could ship veteran divisions home as soon after the surrender as possible. Mindful of both "the longterm political and military advantages to the United States in occupying the northern area," the Joint Chiefs would later urge the president to press the matter with the prime minister.

Marshall had a more immediate problem than the postwar occupation of Germany: Churchill's enduring infatuation with the Balkans. The chief of staff wanted no part of that mountainous land. The conquest of the Balkans was not necessary to victory in Europe, while operations there would surely prolong the war, Marshall maintained. "The British might like to 'ditch' OVERLORD at this time in order to undertake operations in a country [Greece] with practically no communications," he warned FDR. "If they insist on any such proposal, we could say if they propose to do that we will pull out and go into the Pacific with all our forces."

Whatever the disagreements between these allies two and a half months into the fifth year of world war, the president and his chiefs of staff traveled with bright prospects for the future. The Soviet Union had blunted the German summer offensive, then rolled up the battered Wehrmacht with massive counterattacks. In the North Atlantic shipping losses had dwindled away as sea and air searchers hunted down the once mighty submarine wolfpacks. Over Germany, British and American bombers took heavy losses, but returned almost daily to shatter city after city. Sardinia and Corsica had fallen easily to guerrillas and small Allied forces. The Allies now held one third of Italy, and Mussolini was a refugee under German protection in northern Italy. Halfway around the world, the war against the Japanese was going equally well. Australian and American units had gained effective control of the New Guinea coast; the central Solomons and the Gilberts were free of Japanese troops.

Two fronts fared poorly. Eisenhower's armies had bogged down south of Rome, along the Volturno River. At the same time, British, Indian, and American troops, hampered by Burma's monsoon and jungle, had accomplished little to loosen the Japanese grip on the vital supply line to China. In addition, the British had suffered their reverse in the Dodecanese, tactically unimportant, the Americans argued, but humiliating for all that.

The prime minister and his Imperial General Staff were flying to Cairo and the SEXTANT conference determined to break the Italian stalemate and erase the embarrassment in the eastern Mediterranean. The Americans were arriving just as determined to aid the Chinese with an offensive in Burma.

Each delegation recognized they would not be able to do everything if they were to hold to the OVERLORD schedule, but neither intended to yield to the other. This third strategy conference of the year would be "the hottest one yet," gossip in Eisenhower's headquarters predicted.

Whatever they decided in Cairo, their Russian ally held veto power. Once a singleminded proponent of the cross-Channel invasion, Stalin had signaled a recent interest in expanded action in the Mediterranean, even if it meant a delay in OVERLORD. Marshall, who had relied on Soviet support for the invasion of France, now confronted the prospect of British and Soviet pressure for an increased Italian effort or, worse, an invasion of the Balkans. Either would force the cancelation of OVERLORD.

The chief of staff was uncomfortable on the defensive. What if the Russians, just sixty miles from the Polish border and forty from the Rumanian, asked the Allies to mount a pincers through the Balkans, the president had asked Marshall during one of their shipboard conferences.

We should offer air support only, Marshall replied, skittish of fighting a land war in the mountainous Balkans. It was a limp answer, for air support required constant liaison with the xenophobic Russians. Marshall suggested that a Soviet officer be included as an observer at the Combined Chiefs of Staffs meetings.

The American strategy was only partly settled as the delegation left the *Iowa* at Oran to fly to Tunis for a meeting with Dwight Eisenhower. While sightseeing about the still littered battlefield where Von Arnim had surrendered, the president casually announced that he wanted Marshall to be supreme commander. Eisenhower listened as Roosevelt explained a Briton would then have to take over the Mediterranean, just to balance matters, and that would put Eisenhower out of a job. Ike would return to Washington as acting chief of staff in Marshall's absence, Roosevelt continued. A gloomy Eisenhower, who had hoped he might be a field commander under Marshall, said nothing.

From Tunis, the presidential party flew on to Cairo and the plush Mena House Hotel where Churchill and Generalissimo Chiang waited. The modern resort—named after the founder of the first Egyptian dynasty—sat amid an incongruous barbed-wire compound within sight of the Great Pyramids at Giza. The hotel would serve as the meeting site while the dignitaries stayed in heavily guarded villas nearby.

SEXTANT, as Churchill had dubbed it, was to set the seal on Marshall and his reputation. In the course of the meetings, the general's longtime friend, Hap Arnold, watched the chief of staff "increasing in stature, in comparison with his fellows, as the days went by. He had more mature judgment, could see further into the future. What he said was said in a way that carried conviction. I am sure the president and the prime minister both felt the same, because each one called on him for advice and counsel at all hours of the day or night."

Marshall's first challenge was to transform President Roosevelt's improvised diplomatic policy regarding China into a coherent military campaign. The president desired to raise China's reputation, if not its actual contribution, to that of a great power. Doing so would enlist one quarter of the world's population in his gestating concept of a United Nations to keep the postwar peace. The key to that was prodding China into the offensive.

Chiang had been reluctant to fight. His levies were poorly equipped and poorly trained, he argued with some justification, even as he frustrated Joseph Stilwell's efforts to bring those troops up to scratch. What armaments he had received from the United States he preferred to husband for the postwar battle with the Chinese Communists for control of the nation. Other aid, especially food and monetary loans, had been siphoned away by successive layers of officialdom, each taking its ever larger bribe from an ever smaller fund.

The Americans recognized Chiang's reluctance to fight. Stilwell's radiograms had been candid. Moreover, presidential envoy Patrick J. Hurley, former secretary of war in the Hoover cabinet, had returned from Chungking to report: "It is advisable to consider with some skepticism the Chinese capacity, or readiness, to contribute materially to offensive warfare. It is advisable likewise to give consideration to the relative importance placed by the Chinese Central Government upon conserving its strength for maintenance of its postwar internal supremacy as against the more immediate objective of defeating Japan."

The British hardly troubled to mask their contempt for the Chinese or their impatience with American policy in China. "To the president," Churchill's physician and confidant Lord Moran wrote in his diary, "China means four hundred million people who are going to count in the world of tomorrow, but Winston thinks only of the colour of their skin; it is when he talks of India or China that you remember he is a Victorian."

Brooke, who understood less than he realized, treated the United States' China policy with a lofty disdain. "Marshall, like many Americans, had a romantic belief in the potential power of China." Romantic it may have been in 1924 when Lieutenant Colonel Marshall first arrived in Tientsin; two decades later he had no illusions, only a presidential directive. His task was to carry it out.

On November 23, 1943, the Cairo Conference opened with Lord Louis Mountbatten, supreme commander in Southeast Asia, proposing an operation to retake Burma. Troops from India, according to Mountbatten's plan, were to move eastward while Chinese forces moved westward, their pincers closing near the China-Burma border. (The American units to take part included a Marshall-sponsored Ranger group that would operate behind Japanese lines; the press was to make that unit famous under the name of "Merrill's Marauders.") Meanwhile, the British would mount an amphibious attack against the Andaman Islands 300 miles southwest of Rangoon to keep the Japanese fleet preoccupied.

In a plenary session after lunch, Marshall and King pressed for Mountbatten's plan, including the amphibious operation in the Andamans. King in particular argued for the Burmese campaign, convinced that it would open the way to China, and thereby make the Pacific War easier.

Brooke would hear none of it. Instead, he asked if the landing craft pledged to the attack on the Andamans might be diverted to the eastern Mediterranean, Churchill's favored theater. The meeting burst into a roiling argument. "Brooke got nasty and King got good and sore," the Anglophobic Stilwell delightedly wrote in his diary. "King almost climbed over the table at Brooke. God, he was mad. I wish he had socked him."

That evening, while the president entertained the generalissimo and Madame Chiang, Churchill and Marshall dined together. Through the long evening—the chief of staff would not leave until 2:00 a.m.—the two men discussed a variety of military operations; Marshall remained opposed to Churchill's great scheme to seize the island of Rhodes.

In the course of the evening's rambling discussion, Marshall angrily dismissed Churchill's sudden doubts about the ability of American troops in combat. When the prime minister insisted that two and a half U.S. divisions would be required against each German division, Marshall exploded. "I never want to hear this again." Chastened, the prime minister back-pedaled; he would not make that argument again.

Churchill resumed his campaign for the Rhodes attack the next morning, seeking to wear down Marshall as he did his own chiefs. As the chief of staff recalled,

> It got hotter and hotter. Finally Churchill grabbed his lapels . . . and he said, "His Majesty's Government can't have its troops standing idle. Muskets must flame," and more fine English like that. I said, "God forbid if I should try to dictate but . . . not one American soldier is going to die on [that] goddamned beach." The others were horrified, but they didn't want the operation and were willing for me to say it. Churchill never held this against me, but Ismay had to stay up with him all night.

Churchill also asked that sixty-eight LSTs scheduled to leave the Mediterranean for Great Britain and OVERLORD be held for an additional month. Those vessels would give Eisenhower the additional sea lift necessary to mount another amphibious end run and break the stalemate in Italy.

Wary of anything that might delay the invasion of France, fearful that holding the scarce LSTs in the Mediterranean would do just that, the American Joint Chiefs refused. In less than a day they had become deadlocked.

In the afternoon, the Combined Chiefs resumed discussion of Chinese participation in the Burmese campaign. The Nationalists temporized, cadging ever more tokens of Allied affection. First the Chinese insisted on the Andaman assault, for which they had few LSTs. Then they demanded shipments of additional supplies by air each month to equip troops for the Burmese campaign—on transports Hap Arnold did not have and would not get.

The Chinese recalcitrance provoked Marshall. Nowhere had China moved against the Japanese, and once more Chiang was asking his allies to carry China's water. Marshall resisted the blackmail, refusing to divert more transports to Southeast Asia. "There must be no misunderstanding about this," he added firmly.

General Shang Chen, chief of the Foreign Affairs Bureau of the National Military Council, protested. China had been promised supplies by air; China had "rights" in the matter.

Marshall grew cold with anger. "Now let me get this straight. You are talking about your 'rights' in this matter. I thought these were *American* planes, and *American* personnel, and *American* material. I don't understand what you mean by saying that we can or can't do thus and so."

Brooke stepped in with a series of sharp questions for General Shang, questions the Chinese general could not answer in Chiang Kai-shek's absence. The session wound down inconclusively, "a ghastly waste of time," Brooke scoffed.

"You're telling me," Marshall agreed.

The longer the discussion went on—they would return to it the following day with the generalissimo and his wife present—the less they seemed to accomplish. Chiang waffled in his support of the Burmese campaign, despite "George laying it on the line about U.S. planes, U.S. pilots, U.S. dough, etc." Stilwell thought it "a grand speech for the G-mo" to hear, but it changed nothing.

Not transport planes, but the shortage of the 300-foot-long LSTs was to shape world strategy. Even with production at capacity, the Allies had too few of those tank-landing ships with which to invade the Andamans, take Rhodes, mount another amphibious landing in Italy, and still hold to the OVERLORD timetable. Choices would have to be made.

Marshall hewed to the cross-Channel assault as the quickest way to end the war in Europe so that they could get on with it in the Pacific. He wanted no diversions.

The president had determined otherwise.

A month earlier FDR had complained to Marshall, ". . . Everything seems to go wrong [in China]. But the worst thing is that we are falling down on our promises every single time. We have not fulfilled one of them." Because the president intended to deliver on his pledge to Chiang of a supporting operation in the Andamans, Marshall had no room to maneuver. Chiang might be obdurate, his generals might be inept, his troops ill-prepared, but Marshall had to loyally support the Andaman Island diversion. The army chief of staff found himself caught between the scornful British and an adamant president.

On Thursday, November 25, they suspended their talks to celebrate the American holiday of Thanksgiving. That evening the president, toasting their unity, entertained Churchill while Marshall served as host to the Combined Chiefs. Marshall remembered it as "a merry party," a moment of fraternal warmth.

Those good feelings lasted only a bit longer than the last after-dinner brandy and cigar. The following day, just twenty-four hours before leaving for Tehran and talks with Premier Stalin, the Allies fell into deadlock.

Dwight Eisenhower proposed, first, that the Italian and eastern Mediterranean theaters be placed under a single commander. With adequate forces that commander could push his armies in Italy past Rome, as far north as the Po River. Without sufficient troops—a veiled reference to Churchill's Rhodes adventure—they would have to settle for just Rome and with it what Churchill called "the title deeds of Italy" before going on the defensive.

The British Middle East commander, General H. Maitland Wilson, just as predictably urged greater attention to the eastern Mediterranean. They should start with Rhodes, he argued; two brigades were all he needed for the task, Wilson estimated optimistically. Success on Rhodes would surely be enough to convince neutral Turkey to throw in with the Allies. Armed by the Allies, Turkey then could clear the Germans from the other Dodecanese islands and open the way to the Soviet Union through the Dardanelles.

That accomplished, Wilson continued with dogged optimism, they could shift attention to the islands of the Adriatic, picking them off one by one and supplying Marshal Tito's Yugoslavian guerrillas from there. "Operations in northern Yugoslavia would constitute a serious threat to the Germans' rear," Wilson insisted.

Despite their dislike of such "bush league tactics," the American response was mild. Speaking for the Joint Chiefs, Admiral Leahy tentatively accepted the British proposal for action in the eastern Mediterranean. This would serve as a basis for discussions with the Russians when they met in Tehran two days later.

As a tacit exchange, the Americans wanted British agreement to stage Operation BUCCANEER, the Andaman Islands invasion. It was a difficult moment for Marshall. They had not enough LSTs to mount operations in both the Andamans and the eastern Mediterranean yet keep favored OVERLORD on schedule. President Roosevelt's insistence that they promote Chiang's status was shaping global military strategy.

Brooke could only be elated. They were playing the Rhodes card, leading them inevitably into the Balkans, and delaying indefinitely the dangerous cross-Channel invasion—all for a token gesture in the Indian Ocean. Like a barrister nailing down his argument, Brooke stressed, "If the capture of Rhodes and Rome and Operation BUCCANEER were carried out, the date of OVERLORD must go back."

Marshall yielded gracefully. "He quite understood this point," the minutes of the meeting quote him. "He was of the opinion that it was essential to do Operation BUCCANEER, for the reasons that firstly, not only were the forces ready but the operation was acceptable to the Chinese; secondly, it was of vital importance to operations in the Pacific; and, thirdly, for political reasons it could not be interfered with."

Puffed with success, Brooke overplayed his hand. It might be necessary, he advised the Americans, to consider putting off the Andaman Islands assault in favor of throwing everything against Germany and "bringing the war as a whole to an end at the earliest possible date." Overreaching himself, Brooke had triggered what he would later call "the mother and father of a row."

His patience spent, Marshall lashed out. The United States had already contributed mightily to Europe, despite considerable public opinion in the States that Japan was the major enemy. Even today, "they had gone far to meet the British Chiefs of Staff views but the postponement of BUCCANEER they could not accept."

The chiefs went into executive session without aides present to thrash out their differences. Marshall staunchly argued for the Chinese option the president favored, forced to yield on OVERLORD. In the end, Brooke wrote in his diary that night, the British secured "most of the points we were after."

The two delegations would leave the next day for the first tripartite military discussions with only the semblance of an overarching strategy: northern and southern Europe were to be separate theaters; the Mediterranean and the Middle East would be joined, by unspoken agreement, under a Briton; Rhodes and the Dardanelles would be next in the Mediterranean; then they would foment revolt in the Balkans—though the Americans insisted on delaying formal approval of the invasion there. The date of the cross-Channel assault had been put off six weeks or more, perhaps long enough to make it questionable for 1944.

In effect, they were dealing the Soviet Union a veto power over strategy in Europe. If the Russians wanted immediate assistance in breaking into Poland and Rumania, as Marshall suspected, they might well ask for an invasion of the Balkans rather than OVERLORD. No matter Marshall's reservations about landing American armies in a mountainous land with few roads, a land unfavorable to the highly mobile divisions the chief of staff had created. Because the Americans and British could not agree, Stalin would cast the deciding vote.

Political considerations, never far from mind, pressed hard on them, Marshall acknowledged. The bred-in-the-bone indoctrination of the American soldier mandated supremacy of a civilian commander-in-chief over the military, and the geopolitical over the strategic. But as career diplomat John Davies noted in a discussion of policy conflicts at these international conferences, "Most American military men think of war as a soldier's job to be done. . . . Most of our officers want the job accomplished as soon as possible, with a minimum of fuss over international political and economic issues, which they regard as of secondary importance. Political and economic questions, they feel, can be discussed and decided after the defeat of the Axis." Marshall balanced constitutional obligation and military desire through the war.

The two delegations departed for Tehran and the EUREKA conference with Marshal Stalin on Saturday, November 27. After a seven-hour flight they landed in the capital of the young shah of Iran, the president traveling to the American Legation while his Joint Chiefs of Staff settled at the headquarters of the Persian Gulf Command six miles north of the city.

The following morning, the president met with the chiefs to review their position. If the Russians asked for immediate relief, what should they advise, Roosevelt asked.

Hoping to preserve even a belated OVERLORD, Marshall suggested

Eisenhower could push his armies northward in Italy, then split his forces to threaten France on the west and Austria through the Ljubljana Gap. They could also open small ports on the Adriatic to supply Tito's partisans in Yugoslavia, he added.

It was imperative they avoid fighting in too many places simultaneously. The threat was of scattering OVERLORD's men, supplies, and, most importantly, its shipping across the Mediterranean.

As the meeting broke up, the chief of staff asked the president if he would be needed further that day. With no meetings planned, Roosevelt thought it unlikely.

Marshall then decided to take a motor trip to visit the Soviet Union military zone. Hap Arnold agreed to go along. King declined in order to handle some correspondence.

Shortly after they drove off, Premier Stalin relayed an imperative warning that Axis agents in the city planned to assassinate the president. Stalin proposed that Roosevelt stay with him in the heavily guarded Russian compound and avoid traveling the dangerous streets. Delighted with the opportunity to deal with Stalin alone, Roosevelt promptly accepted.

Amid burly Russian servants armed with handguns, FDR and the man he privately called Uncle Joe, an American patrician and a Soviet revolutionary, met for the first time. Reaching up from his wheelchair, Roosevelt offered his hand to Stalin, dressed in a workaday gray-green uniform. "I am glad to see you. I have tried for a long time to bring this about."

The two men quickly skipped over the pleasantries to discuss the war against Hitler. Stalin abruptly suggested they call Churchill over from the British Legation and immediately get down to business rather than wait until the next day. Roosevelt agreed.

So it was that a chagrined George C. Marshall, sightseeing in the Russian zone, missed the most important strategy conference of the war.

This first plenary session of EUREKA convened around an oak table fashioned especially for the conference. Nine Britons, five Americans, and five Russians sat around the great round table as Stalin brusquely rumbled, "Now let us get down to business."

Roosevelt and Churchill laid out their contrary strategies, FDR pressing for the cross-Channel invasion, the prime minister urging the advantages of the Mediterranean. Rather quickly, Stalin settled the dispute.

Stalin's overriding concern was the balance of forces on the Eastern Front. The Soviet Army had 330 divisions, the Axis 260 divisions stretched from Leningrad to the Crimea. The Germans were bringing in reinforcements, enough so that Russian numerical superiority was ebbing. Stalin wanted military action in the West to pin down German units that might otherwise be transferred to the East.

The Italian campaign, he continued, was diversionary. If it was valuable in that it opened the Mediterranean to Allied shipping, the Alps were still "an almost insuperable barrier" to an invasion of Germany. "In the opinion of the Soviet military leaders, Hitler was endeavoring to retain as many Allied divisions as possible in Italy where no decision could be reached, and that the best method in the Soviet opinion was getting at the heart of Germany with an attack through northern or northwestern France and even through southern France."

Churchill was suddenly on the defensive. OVERLORD was absorbing most of their combined resources, he assured Stalin. They contemplated putting 1 million men on the continent in May, June, and July. Their Mediterranean operations were meant to be no more than a preliminary to the cross-Channel assault. Still, there were a million British or Empire troops in the Mediterranean, and Churchill wanted them gainfully employed—in Italy, in the Dodecanese, in Turkey, in the Adriatic. It was a rambling speech. Churchill, rasping through a chest cold, sought to persuade with argument since he could not convince with facts.

The Russian premier waved away the arguments with a sweep of his Latakia cigarette; a chain smoker, he would develop a fondness for American cigarettes as well as American strategy before the end of the conference. According to the minutes of the conference, "He questioned the wisdom of dispersing Allied forces for the various operations mentioned such as Turkey, the Adriatic and Southern France since there would be no direct connection between these scattered forces. He said he thought it would be better to take OVERLORD as the basis for all 1944 operations; that after the capture of Rome the troops thus relieved might be sent to Southern France, and in conjunction with forces operating from Corsica might eventually meet in France the main force of OVERLORD from the north."

Brooke was impressed with the Soviet premier. "He had a military brain of the very highest calibre. Never once in any of his statements did he make any strategic error." As a strategist, Stalin stood out among the three heads of government, Brooke noted. Roosevelt deferred on strategic matters to Marshall and Leahy, while Churchill, however brilliant he might be at a moment, was impulsive. (Marshall considered Churchill's planning "all wishing and guessing"; to the Combined Chiefs fell the burden of weaning him from "wildcat schemes.")

The following morning Brooke took up where Churchill had left off. In the first tripartite military meeting, the British general outlined for Marshal Kliment Voroshilov the campaigns they had under consideration: amphibious end runs to turn the German right flank in Italy and capture Rome; assistance to the Yugoslavian partisans; luring Turkey to abandon neutrality and offer the Allies air bases; then the capture of Rhodes. Because of the shortage of landing craft, to do all this would require retarding the date for OVERLORD. Furthermore, Brooke added, they had neither men nor landing craft to mount the major assault on southern France Premier Stalin had proposed the afternoon before. Marshall followed with a review of the logistical problems, stressing the Americans' choice of OVERLORD because it offered the shortest overseas transport route. Once they had taken a French port, the more than fifty divisions now training in the United States would be landed directly on the continent. The Allied problem was not men or materiel, Marshall added. It was the lack of merchant shipping, and especially the shortage of LSTs.

Marshall carefully avoided contradicting Brooke, a point the Russian commander apparently noted. "I wish to apologize for my failure to understand clearly," Voroshilov said through his interpreter, "but I am interested to know whether General Brooke, as chief of the Imperial General Staff, considered OVERLORD as important as General Marshall had indicated that he did. I would like General Brooke's opinion."

Neatly, with perfect courtesy, the Russian had pinned the Briton.

Brooke hedged. Yes, he considered the cross-Channel invasion vital, but added, "He knew the defenses of Northern France and did not wish to see the operation fail. In his opinion, under certain circumstances it was bound to fail."

Voroshilov brushed aside the argument. "Marshal Stalin and the Soviet General Staff attach great importance to OVERLORD and felt that the other operations in the Mediterranean can be regarded only as auxiliary operations."

Coldly, methodically, the Russian offered his own views: if the United States and Great Britain had the will, they could carry off the invasion, "and it would go down in history as one of our greatest victories."

He had no doubt the nine American divisions now in the United Kingdom could be doubled in number by the May 1 target date, that shipping would be found.

Small diversions in the Mediterranean were necessary to the success of OVERLORD, Voroshilov continued, but those operations must be planned to secure that assault, not delay or hinder it. Were they to go on the defensive in Italy, they could divert troops to the invasion of southern France. "Marshal Stalin does not insist on this but does insist on the execution of OVERLORD on the date already planned."

There were difficulties in staging the cross-Channel assault, Voroshilov acknowledged, but in recent offensives Soviet troops had successfully crossed several large rivers, including the broad Dnieper. Intense firepower and air superiority had been the key, he said.

"The difference between a river crossing, however wide," Marshall reminded the Russian, "and a landing from the ocean is that the failure of a river crossing is a reverse while the failure of a landing operation from the sea is a catastrophe, because failure in the latter case means the

almost utter destruction of the landing craft and personnel involved."
The lesson of the Dieppe raid had not been forgotten.

Voroshilov nodded, saying he appreciated Marshall's frankness.

"His [own] military education," Marshall continued, "had been based
on roads, rivers and railroads and . . . his war experience in France had
been concerned with the same. During the last two years, however, he
had been acquiring an education based on oceans and he had had to
learn all over again."

Before the war Marshall had never heard of any landing craft except
a rubber boat, he told the Russian. Now he thought of little else.

"If you think about it, you will do it," Voroshilov replied.

Marshall smiled. "That is a very good reply. I understand thoroughly."

At four o'clock that afternoon, the three heads of government and
their military staffs convened in the large hall of the Soviet Embassy for
the second plenary session of EUREKA. Forsaking his drab clothes of the
day before, Stalin was resplendent in a mustard-colored uniform with a
red stripe running down the pants leg. Churchill's doctor and confidant,
Lord Moran, wondered at the change, for the rumpled uniform of before
"fitted his blunt contempt for appearances; it seemed to scoff at all the
uniforms around him, with their five or six rows of meaningless deco-
rations."

Stalin's uniform suited his single-minded interest at the moment. After
Brooke, Marshall, and Voroshilov had summarized their morning meeting, the Soviet leader abruptly asked, "Who will be the commander in
this Operation OVERLORD?"

Taken aback by Stalin's peremptory question, the president and prime
minister stammered like young boys caught in a schoolyard prank. The
choice of a commander had not been decided, they admitted.

"Then nothing will come out of these operations," Stalin concluded
impatiently.

First Roosevelt, then Churchill attempted to soothe the premier. All
of the subsidiary commanders had been selected, the president assured
the Russian. The planning for the cross-Channel attack, under British
General Sir Frederick Morgan, was far advanced, Churchill added.

But Morgan might say they were ready to go and a newly arrived
supreme commander might disagree, Stalin pointed out. Inevitably that
would delay the attack. There must be one person in charge, he insisted
through his interpreter, and he wanted that man promptly charged with
both planning and execution.

That much Roosevelt and Churchill could grant. A commander would
be named within two weeks, Churchill pledged, before they completed
the suspended discussions in Cairo.

Clearly on the defensive, Churchill made yet another attempt to revive his favored Mediterranean strategy. Attacks in that theater would tie up German troops, assuring the success of the cross-Channel attack, he argued. In any case, they needed only a modest amphibious lift for two divisions.

Stalin would not be diverted. Despite the awkward pause for translations, there was no mistaking his intent. In the Mediterranean, he wanted an attack on southern France prior to OVERLORD, a plan first suggested by Dwight Eisenhower, then dropped for lack of support among the Combined Chiefs of Staff. Whatever else the Allies mounted must not interfere with the cross-Channel attack.

That left only the matter of timing. Roosevelt suggested May 1, certainly not later than May 15 or 20.

Churchill weakly protested, the rasp in his voice worse, "I cannot agree to that."

May, Stalin snapped. "There will be suitable weather in May."

Turning to the prime minister, the Soviet premier said he wished to ask Mr. Churchill an indiscreet question: "Do the British really believe in OVERLORD or are they only saying so to reassure the Russians?"

Glowering, biting hard on his cigar, Churchill responded that if the requirements for the invasion of France were met, "it was the duty of the British government to hurl every scrap of strength across the Channel."

That quickly OVERLORD had been settled. Twice they had promised the Soviets an invasion of France and twice they had reneged. Stalin would be put off no longer.

Marshall came away from the conference table quietly pleased, greatly impressed by the premier, "a strong leader, direct and practical." Such qualities appealed to the chief of staff. The best way to deal with Stalin was bluntly, Marshall discovered. The sixty-five-year-old premier was not a product of the Foreign Service, Marshall pointed out, but "a rough SOB who made his way by murder and everything else and should be talked to that way." Hap Arnold agreed, judging the man "apparently fearless, brilliant of mind," ruthless, and "a great leader."

In dealing with Marshall, Stalin openly displayed his appreciation of the general's long advocacy of OVERLORD. "He was agreeable, and in regard to me he made sort of semi-affectionate gesture. When we were in opposition [regarding the timing of the landings in southern France] he would stand with his hands on my shoulders," Marshall recalled for his biographer.

The British were less enthusiastic. Brooke, so certain of his strategic superiority, was furious. Seven hours of conferences, six of them with the wearying to-and-fro of interpreters, left the British chief of staff grumbling in his diary that he felt ready for "a lunatic asylum or a nursing home." As Churchill had feared, "A bloody lot has gone wrong."

The realities of a new world order pressed on Churchill. "There I sat," he later told Permanent Undersecretary for Foreign Affairs Alexander Cadogan, "with the great Russian bear on one side of me, with paws outstretched, and on the other side the great American buffalo, and between the two sat the poor little English donkey who was the only one . . . who knew the right way home."

Roosevelt was elated with the outcome of the meeting and confident about Stalin. "He gets things done, that man. He really keeps his eye on the ball he's aiming at," the president told his son, Elliott, that evening. "Whenever the PM argued for our invasion through the Balkans, it was quite obvious to everyone in the room what he really meant . . . keep the Red Army out of Austria and Rumania, even Hungary, if possible. Stalin knew it, I knew it, everybody knew it. . . ."

The following morning, the British and American military delegations met at the British Legation to draft a concise statement of their military plan in Europe for 1944. Once more the British argued for delaying the cross-Channel attack until June, and once more the Americans insisted on a May date.

The May 1 target date might be possible, Brooke countered, if they were to abandon the Andaman Islands attack and scatter the landing craft ticketed for that operation between the Aegean, the south of France, and OVERLORD itself.

The conversation grew heated, with Admiral Leahy waspishly asking Brooke if he believed the preconditions for the cross-Channel assault would ever arise unless the Germans collapsed beforehand.

They would, Brooke replied, providing the Germans were engaged on other fronts.

Compromising at every turn, they settled on a strategy to present to the president and prime minister:

(1) The campaign in Italy would press north of Rome, with landings on the coast turning the German right flank;

(2) They would mount ANVIL, the operation against the coast of southern France, timing it to coincide with OVERLORD; and

(3) The French invasions would take place in May.

Given their rule of unanimity, Marshall's absolute opposition to an attack on Rhodes left the Combined Chiefs deadlocked, unable to recommend that operation in their paper. Stubborn British resistance to the Andaman Islands operation similarly barred including that. Both would be referred to the president and prime minister for a decision.

At lunch in the Soviet Embassy on November 30, the president presented the three-part recommendation of the Combined Chiefs to Stalin. The Russian was hugely pleased, expansively pledging a Red Army offensive to coincide with OVERLORD. Once more he asked when the invasion commander would be selected.

Roosevelt, happy in his conviction that Stalin wanted to cooperate with his Western Allies, replied that the commander would be named in three or four days, immediately upon their return to Cairo. Later that afternoon, Stalin was informed unofficially, probably by Harry Hopkins, that the supreme commander would be Marshall.

"No wiser or more reassuring choice could be made," the premier said. Marshall's reputation had preceded him; indeed, he was "becoming a legendary figure even then," according to diplomat Charles Bohlen, the president's translator at Tehran.

The third and last plenary meeting late in the afternoon was short but decisive. Outvoted and wearying of the struggle, Churchill rallied to OVERLORD, urging it be delivered with "smashing force." Now assured of the long-desired second front, Stalin reiterated his earlier pledge: the Soviet Union would join the war on Japan once Germany was defeated.

During a final state dinner at the British Legation that night—among other things, they celebrated Churchill's sixty-ninth birthday with a succession of toasts—President Roosevelt radiated optimism. Concluding a pledge of lasting friendship among the Allies, FDR declared: "The rainbow, the traditional symbol of hope, could now for the first time, as a result of this conference, be discerned in the sky."

The following morning, the American chiefs of staff flew to Jerusalem to spend a moment out of war, tourists in the City of Peace. The following day, they departed for Cairo.

Once there, the rainbow so discernible in Tehran vanished.

This second Cairo Conference turned into a five-day debate about means to implement the Tehran manifesto. The Combined Chiefs of Staff were charged with finding sufficient landing craft for OVERLORD, now set for May 1944; the simultaneous ANVIL landing along the Côte d'Azur; amphibious flanking movement south of Rome; the Rhodes assault; and the Andaman Islands operation in the Indian Ocean.

With the British demanding at least a two-division assault in southern France, they simply would not have enough landing craft to go around and still meet the promised date for OVERLORD. Moreover, both British and American delegations were aware that two divisions was a bare minimum and no guarantee of success in southern France; they worried too that the planned three and one-half division assault on the beaches of Normandy was marginal.

First Marshall, then Arnold and Leahy grudgingly came to the conclusion that the Andaman Islands attack required too many LSTs needed elsewhere. Even with shipyards working overtime, "there were still not enough landing craft in sight," Marshall complained. Only King held out for the operation, but he was not so enthusiastic as to offer to divert landing craft from the Pacific to the Southeast Asian theater.

After three days of talks, on December 5 the president agreed that BUCCANEER had to be canceled. Marshall, never keen on the Andaman Islands attack, had prevailed in this last strategic disagreement with the president; from Cairo forward, military strategy in the West would be dictated by the chief of staff.

Roosevelt now wanted to be off—to the consternation of Brooke, who still hoped to get agreement on a plan for the eastern Mediterranean. Angrily the British general complained to his diary on December 3, "It all looks like some of the worst sharp practice that I have seen for some time." (Discussing that diary entry later, Brooke withdrew the allegation, "quite certain that the one thing that Marshall would never have tolerated was anything connected with 'sharp practice.' I have seldom met a straighter or more reliable man in my life.")

The British agenda notwithstanding, Roosevelt had one major decision yet to make: command of OVERLORD. He had promised Marshal Stalin his decision. It could wait no longer.

The president was indecisive. On Saturday, December 4, he dispatched Harry Hopkins before dinner to sound out Marshall. Sallow-faced and drawn, feeling the strain of these conferences, Hopkins told his friend, "The president was in some concern of mind" about the appointment.

Marshall could not discern from Hopkins's comments the president's attitude, though the general might have guessed. So long as the British refused to put the Mediterranean under a single European headquarters, Marshall's appointment as supreme commander would appear to be a demotion from his position as chief of staff. Roosevelt wanted no political sniping.

Marshall declined to comment on the appointment. ". . . I merely endeavored to make it clear that I would go along wholeheartedly with whatever decision the president made. He need have no fears regarding my personal reaction."

The president, who would have preferred his chief of staff make the decision, sent for Marshall at noon the following day.

They met alone. The president was reluctant to begin, raising a number of inconsequential matters before broaching the question. Finally he asked his chief of staff which post he preferred.

Marshall would not be drawn out. It was for the president to decide. "I just repeated again in as convincing language as I could that I wanted him to feel free to act in whatever way he felt was to the best interest of the country and to his satisfaction and not in any way to consider my feelings. I would cheerfully go whatever way he wanted me to go."

The president then decided, as he put it, on a "mathematical basis."

Eisenhower as chief of staff would have to become familiar with the Pacific theater and handle MacArthur, a jealous man under whom *Major* Eisenhower had once served. Ike would also have to learn to deal with a Congress impatient for the war's end. Eisenhower meanwhile had finally proved himself as supreme commander just as Marshall had in Washington. "The President decided he would be more comfortable if he kept Marshall at his elbow in Washington. . . ."

Roosevelt's decision was politically motivated, influenced by both national and international considerations. As Winston Churchill would later write, "It is not possible in a major war to divide military from political affairs. At the summit they are one." However much the chief of staff sought to put himself above the political, he had paradoxically become the one man politically acceptable to all. It would cost him the one command he most desired.

CHAPTER

XXV

Losses

The soldier who boarded the C-54 transport at the Cairo airport on Wednesday, December 8, 1943, revealed nothing of his feelings. No word, no facial expression suggested he had just lost the one posting he most coveted, command of the field armies he had created for the invasion of France. His aide and executive secretary, Lieutenant Colonel Frank McCarthy, saw no more than he had any other morning for the past three years. "If he would have shown emotion to anybody except his wife, I think he would have shown it to me," McCarthy later recalled. "He was really a stolid man. He was really a duty-bound man."

The commander-in-chief had made his decision; George Catlett Marshall would obey.

For all that, Marshall was leaving Cairo and SEXTANT with new standing in the councils of government. As *Time* magazine put it shortly before naming the chief of staff its Man of the Year later that month, "General Marshall has now attained the stature of a military statesman."

To some extent, Marshall's increased authority came at the expense of Winston Churchill. With the Soviets casting the deciding vote for OVERLORD, Marshall's plan, the American chief of staff had prevailed.

That decision made, the Imperial General Staff brimmed with the abiding confidence of true converts. At dinner on the last night in Cairo, Marshall, Dill, and Brooke each predicted Germany's defeat by March 1945. The prime minister himself tentatively estimated that Germany might quit before the end of 1944.

Marshall victorious was not returning to the United States with the president aboard the *Iowa*, but instead was to fly home via the Pacific. Marshall had twice considered visiting that theater and meeting with the prickly proud MacArthur, but had twice postponed the trip. Now that he was to continue as chief of staff, the delayed visit took on new importance. MacArthur was feeling neglected.

Marshall and a small party flew first to Ceylon, then on to Australia, that second leg a 3,400-mile, seventeen-hour flight over the ocean to Port Moresby. MacArthur was not there to meet the chief of staff, but instead was visiting a forward headquarters where subordinates were drawing plans for further landings in the Southwest Pacific. A MacArthur aide took Marshall shelling at the beach for part of a day, then on a careening Jeep chase after kangaroos. Ignoring MacArthur's snub, Marshall impatiently set out after his theater commander. On Goodenough Island off northern New Guinea, the two generals finally met.

They had not seen each other since MacArthur's retirement as army chief of staff in 1935. Marshall was then a little known colonel training the Illinois National Guard in Chicago, MacArthur a much decorated war hero retiring full of honors. Now Marshall was chief of staff and MacArthur just one of six American theater commanders. To a man of MacArthur's overweening pride, the role reversal was galling, the more so for his conviction that he and his theater were unfairly starved of men and materiel. MacArthur privately blamed the president and Pershing's "Chaumont crowd" for the perceived slights. He assumed too those "enemies" distrusted him in return, predicting Marshall would not meet privately with him. "He'll always find a way to have someone else present."

In fact, the two men did meet privately for what MacArthur acknowledged was a "long and frank discussion." According to the Southwest Pacific commander, Marshall told him that "Admiral King claimed the Pacific as the rightful domain of the navy; he seemed to regard the operations there as almost his own private war; he apparently felt that the only way to remove the blot on the navy disaster at Pearl Harbor was to have the navy command a great victory over Japan."

King was critical personally of MacArthur, Marshall supposedly told the theater commander, and King basked in the president's support. According to MacArthur, Leahy also was critical, and in many cases Hap Arnold as well. Marshall might agree the Southwest Pacific was starved for men and equipment, but there was little he could do; he was often outvoted three to one.

If, in fact, Marshall did say these things to MacArthur, he was uncharacteristically indiscreet. From the moment MacArthur left Corregidor to fetch up in Australia, a querulous rivalry had existed between him and the Navy. Marshall had sought constantly to mediate that dispute, but the Navy considered the Pacific War to be its responsibility and the Southeast Pacific commander no more than a vainglorious usurper. For their part, MacArthur and his fawning staff never lost an opportunity to criticize the bloody navy and Marine operations in the Central Pacific.

The interservice sniping grew increasingly hostile, especially in Washington. Marshall finally silenced King's criticisms of MacArthur at a meeting of the Joint Chiefs of Staff by pounding the table and thundering, "I will not have any meetings carried on with this hatred!"

Marshall had flown to the Southwest Pacific aware that its commander was "supersensitive about everything. He thought everybody had ulterior motives about everything." Mindful of MacArthur's tender ego, and his easily aroused suspicions, Marshall still could be sharply reproving. At one point in their discussion on Goodenough Island, MacArthur began a sentence with "My staff," only to have Marshall interrupt, "You don't have a staff, General. You have a court."

At lunch with MacArthur, the chief of staff reviewed the decisions taken at Cairo dealing with the Pacific theater. China no longer figured heavily in their plans, he told MacArthur; the assault on the Japanese homeland would come from the west. Despite British arguments that two campaigns would be mutually draining, the Americans were to continue the two-pronged advance of Admiral Chester Nimitz in the Central Pacific and MacArthur in the Southwest Pacific. Nimitz was to have first call on men and supplies for successive campaigns that would take the Marshall Islands in January, the Carolines in July, and the Marianas in October. Meanwhile, MacArthur was to clear New Guinea and the Solomons; they had not reached a decision about the Philippines attack MacArthur so ardently urged as a follow-on.

Marshall had fought stubbornly both at Joint Chiefs of Staff meetings in Washington and later at Cairo for the Southwest Pacific campaign, to give the Army a presence in the Pacific prior to the final assault on the Japanese homeland. He had done so despite the defection of Hap Arnold and his planners, who envisioned bombing Japan into submission with a new long-range bomber, the B-29. Marshall had not entirely prevailed in the meetings of the Joint Chiefs, but he had saved MacArthur's theater from becoming a forsaken backwater of the Pacific War. MacArthur was not especially appreciative.

Marshall stayed overnight with MacArthur on Goodenough Island, then flew to New Guinea. There he stopped over to visit the weary units that had been prying determined Japanese defenders from successive strongpoints along the northern coast of the island. He also toured the 116th Station Hospital where 600 patients were recovering from wounds, dysentery, and the skin infections they mockingly called "the crud." Second Lieutenant Doris Lieberman, the hospital dietitian, recalled the tall general in rumpled khakis shaking her hand and teasing, "A dietician will ruin the mess sergeants."

Lieberman, an unabashed civilian in uniform, was awed by the chief of staff. "He had a sparkle, a presence, very military. He was obviously interested in the hospital and what we were doing for the patients. He asked good questions; he knew that little segment of his army," she recalled fondly, forty years later.

After a brief stop in Hawaii, the chief of staff arrived in Washington three days before Christmas, carrying with him a planeload of wounded men who would make it home for the holidays. The general returned to share Christmas dinner in Leesburg and nostalgic memories of Mrs. Marshall's sons Clifton and Allen, then serving in Italy. For the family—Molly, her husband, and child joined them—it was a brief moment, a warming remembrance of more peaceful times before the chief of staff picked up his routine at the Pentagon.

The pace in the War Department had quickened, the vital Operations Division now routinely handling 500 messages a day. Picking up endorsements as they went, scores of those messages found their way to Marshall's desk each day, competing for his attention. The chief of staff necessarily dealt with them quickly, Colonel McCarthy remembered. "There was nothing except, 'Take this' and 'Do this' and so on and 'Yes, sir,' but always with great politeness. Never with humor, never with warmth but with correctness and politeness and you realized you were in the presence of a man who meant business." Only brusque dispatch made it possible to get through the increasing flow of papers, but it was strenuous work. "He was a demanding man, not in any disagreeable way, but you cared about him so much, and you wanted to see things go so well for him, that you felt tension within yourself which he didn't intend to induce—but it was there," McCarthy said.

If the chief of staff was demanding of others, he was no less hard on himself. As domestic gasoline supplies dwindled, Marshall determined to set an example of gas savings. He forsook his army limousine and driver in favor of driving himself to and from the Pentagon in his car. Washington newspapers periodically reported stories of the chief of staff giving rides to thunderstruck secretaries or enlisted men waiting in the rain or cold at bus stops.

As one secretary recalled, "When we reached the Pentagon we drove not up the usual entrance but to a private one; emerged from the car and went up in a private elevator into his private office and were escorted out by a colored attendant who vouched for us to the waiting guard.

"Needless to say we trod on air the rest of the morning. He is a very tall man with a kind voice and I've never seen such shiny shoes."

The very tall man with a kind voice commanded an army grown to the largest in American history, a force that would peak by the end of 1944 at 7.5 million men and women. Almost 4 million were overseas, half of those arrayed against Germany, half against Japan. Six divisions were fighting in Italy, eleven training for OVERLORD in Britain, and thirteen scattered on as many islands in the Southwest Pacific. Sixty more were in training or were authorized. The Air Force meanwhile had sent 12,400 planes overseas and the pace of aircraft production had increased to exceed 95,000 annually.

As large as this force was, it was less than half the number of divisions projected in the prewar Victory Program. The Army was depending on a dwindling manpower pool. Draft deferments had steadily mounted as essential industries sought to keep workers at the benches. To complicate Marshall's problem, both the Navy and Marines were for the first time relying on draftees.

The shortage of replacements would vex them until VE-Day, for even as his army grew, what Marshall later called "the terrible measure of casualties" also increased. The chief of staff took to sending graphic casualty charts in color to the president as a reminder of the human cost of implementing geopolitical policies. "I tried to keep before him all the time the casualty results *because you get hardened to these things and you have to be very careful to keep them always in the forefront of your mind.*"

Only the most rigorously disciplined man could have managed this vast engine of war. "Hired by the U.S. people to do a job," *Time* commented in its adulatory cover story about its Man of the Year, "he will be as good, as ruthless, as tough, as this job requires. There his ambitions stop. The U.S. people have learned why they trust General Marshall more than they have trusted any military man since George Washington: he is a *civis Americanus.*"

Yet even such a paragon could momentarily lose control.

Two days after Christmas, President Roosevelt ordered Secretary of War Henry Stimson to seize and operate the nation's strike-threatened railroads. Denied a wage hike, the railway brotherhoods had promised to tie up the nation's rail lines and with them the supply of war materials going overseas. Equally distressing to a chief of staff striving to supply tanks, trucks, and artillery to Allies and Army alike, the Steelworkers' Union also threatened a strike. It was as if the American public—including men granted draft exemptions because they worked in vital industries—believed the war already won.

Under the strain, Marshall exploded. On New Year's Eve, his sixty-third birthday, Marshall told the director of the Office of War Mobilization, James Byrnes, "He was sleepless with worry and that the strike had dashed his hopes that there would be a collapse in the Balkans. . . ." German propaganda making capital of this lack of national purpose in the United States had rallied the flagging Balkan states, Marshall said.

The chief of staff was so disturbed, Byrnes continued, that he had debated with himself "whether it was his duty to go on the radio, give his opinion and then resign."

Later that day, Byrnes arranged for Marshall to speak in a not-for-attribution briefing of newsmen representing twenty newspapers and radio networks. Marshall's anger was awesome, *Time* magazine reported. "He banged his white-knuckled fist on the desk, and although not a blasphemous man, he swore bitterly." The rail strike was "the damndest crime ever committed against America." It might cost the nation literally hundreds of thousands of lives, he raged.

The next day, the identity of the "high personage" who had so blistered the railway unions was revealed by the St. Petersburg, Florida, *Times.* Marshall found himself caught in a crossfire of praise and criticism. Liberal commentator I. F. Stone, among others, sharply scolded the chief of staff: ". . . this angry and exaggerated attack, made on vague grounds and under cover of an unmanly anonymity, bore the marks of an attempt to stir popular support for further anti-labor legislation or to make labor the scapegoat if coming invasions should prove costly or unsuccessful."

Weary and frustrated, the chief of staff had rashly spoken out. Unrepentant—the story appeared in his wife's published narrative *Together* three years later—Marshall nevertheless would not repeat that mistake.

Neither would he allow Dwight Eisenhower, his protégé and champion of OVERLORD, to succumb to fatigue as he had. Marshall had noted the signs of weariness in Eisenhower during the Cairo Conference and had ordered him immediately to take a few days off. Still concerned, Marshall prodded the supreme commander to enjoy a furlough in the United States before taking up command in England. When Eisenhower pleaded the press of work, Marshall put it in the form of a direct order.

Eisenhower arrived secretly in Washington on January 2 to be whisked about town in unmarked limousines, his insignia of rank removed. Eisenhower had a reunion with his wife, visited the Pentagon, then met with a handful of congressional leaders invited by Marshall to a private gathering at the elite Alibi Club on Capitol Hill. In a private railway car secured by the chief of staff, Eisenhower traveled with his wife to West Point to see his son, Cadet John Eisenhower. The couple traveled on to White Sulphur Springs, West Virginia, where the Eisenhowers rested for several days in a cottage at the posh Greenbrier Hotel, taken over by the Army as a convalescent hospital for the wounded. In all, the new supreme commander would spend two weeks relaxing in the United States before flying to London and command of OVERLORD.

In a series of talks at the Pentagon, Marshall and Eisenhower discussed new weapons programs, including rockets in which the chief of staff had become interested, and the development of a heavy tank capable of standing up to the Germans' best. They also reviewed the names of commanders Eisenhower would bring with him from the Mediterranean to Great Britain.

The choice of men was Eisenhower's, subject only to Marshall's cautionary comments. Many he had known during the first war. Others he had soldiered with in the peacetime Army. Still others—the redoubtable Omar Bradley and an aggressive division commander, J. Lawton Collins—had been instructors at the Infantry School under Marshall. Others, like Matthew Ridgway, had been on Marshall's War Department staff before rotating to field commands. Most of the senior commanders were identified as "Marshall's men," by inclination or training.

The troublesome appointment was that of George Patton; Washington columnist Drew Pearson had discovered the slapping incidents in Sicily. Eisenhower had persuaded reporters there to kill the story in August 1943, and there the matter had rested until the Sunday evening radio broadcast in November 1943 in which Pearson broke the story. The public outcry against a bullying general swirled for a month, putting both Marshall and Eisenhower on the defensive.

Marshall was already dubious about Patton's judgment, preferring other men for command of the individual armies and the overall ground war. Eisenhower disagreed. He wanted Patton, hot temper and all, and he assured the chief of staff that the volatile, offensive-minded Patton would always serve under the more even-handed Bradley. (Bradley's appointment as commander of all American troops in Great Britain dismayed Patton, who had coveted the assignment himself.)

Eisenhower prevailed, in part because it was the prerogative of any commander to pick his immediate subordinates, in part because Marshall preferred to tap as theater commanders men he trusted and allow them a free hand. In any event, Eisenhower's other choices were reassuring.

Two weeks in the United States left Eisenhower anxious to pick up his command in London. There was much to do in the five months before D-Day. He was already critical of the plan for the skimpy cross-Channel assault drawn up over the past year by General Sir Frederick Morgan. Like Morgan himself and the newly named ground commander for Commonwealth troops, Bernard Montgomery, Eisenhower wanted to increase the size of the projected three-division attack.

The constraint was the ever present shortage of landing craft. Montgomery proposed canceling ANVIL, the attack on southern France timed to coincide with the cross-Channel invasion; that would give them sufficient lift to increase the Normandy assault from three to five divisions. To Marshall, Montgomery's suggestion appeared to be yet another British effort to scuttle the Channel attack, for in his judgment, OVERLORD and ANVIL were interdependent. It was necessary to keep the German High Command on the alert for an attack from the south lest the Wehrmacht mass all its defenders in the Normandy vicinity. Once again, that plan was in question; what once seemed settled was still unsettled.

Meanwhile, Winston Churchill was stirring. From Tunis, where he was recuperating from pneumonia, the prime minister proposed an amphibious landing be made behind German lines, forty miles south of Rome.

In a cable to President Roosevelt, Churchill argued they needed only three weeks to mount the assault on the small port of Anzio. He asked to retain fifty-six LSTs in the Mediterranean for that time rather than send them immediately to Great Britain. "We cannot afford to go forward leaving [a] vast half-finished job behind us. . . . If this opportunity is not grasped we must expect the ruin of [the] Mediterranean campaign of 1944."

Once more Marshall took on the task of curbing the prime minister's appetite. "I doubt if I did anything better in the war than to keep Churchill on the main point (he always wanted to take the side shots). I was furious when he wanted to push us further in the Mediterranean," Marshall explained.

The three-week delay appeared minimal. In a reply carefully drafted by Marshall, the president agreed to the postponement, but only "on the basis OVERLORD remain the paramount operation and will be carried out on the date agreed to at Cairo and Teheran." To put a fine point on it, the Roosevelt-Marshall response added, "In view of the Soviet-British-American agreement reached in Teheran I cannot agree without Stalin's approval to any use of forces or equipment elsewhere that might delay or hazard the success of OVERLORD or ANVIL."

From Marrakesh where he had moved to continue his recuperation, the prime minister replied, "I thank God for this fine decision which engages us once again in whole hearted unity upon a great enterprise." The door to the Balkans had opened a crack.

It closed just as abruptly. Churchill's great enterprise faltered even as the first troops waded ashore at Anzio on January 22, 1944.

Though the campaign was the prime minister's hobby horse, because the troops involved would mainly be American, command fell to an American, Major General John P. Lucas. Lucas too was a Marshall protégé; the chief of staff considered the fifty-four-year-old Lucas a man of "military stature, prestige and experience." But Lucas was tired after leading the VI Corps during four months of grinding combat in rain and cold. He had come down from the bitter mountains of Italy, careworn and weary, convinced "wars should be fought in better country than this."

Lucas had serious reservations about Operation SHINGLE, the landing at the small coastal village of Anzio south of Rome. "They will end up putting me ashore with inadequate forces and get me in a serious jam. Then, who will take the blame?" he wrote in his diary. Mark Clark, Lucas's superior as commander of the American Fifth Army, also had doubts, but said nothing in the interest of Allied harmony. Churchill, Brooke, and Eisenhower's successor as commander in the Mediterranean, British General H. Maitland Wilson, were convinced SHINGLE would yield the great prize of Rome, and with it symbolic victory in Italy.

Lucas's 50,000 assault troops landed virtually unopposed, catching the Germans by surprise. Field Marshal Albert Kesselring coolly moved divisions to seal off the bridgehead, aided by Lucas's decision to dig in on his perimeter rather than strike boldly inland.

Guarding against a counterattack such as had imperiled the Salerno landings in September, Lucas lost the opportunity to seize the Alban Hills commanding the roads south of Rome. Not for a week would Lucas feel his units strong enough to move out from the perimeter, and by then it was too late. It would take almost six months to crack the German defenses and travel the forty miles from Anzio to Rome. In that six months, the Allied effort in Italy would become not a support for OVER-LORD and ANVIL but a drain, just as Marshall had feared. Unable to abandon their precarious foothold, the Allies turned tiny Anzio into the fourth busiest port in the world—largely supplied by the LSTs ticketed for OVERLORD.

Without the LSTs he needed for training his assault troops, Eisen-hower suggested to Marshall that OVERLORD be delayed to June. A post-ponement of thirty days would give them a month's additional LST production, Eisenhower argued. He was willing to forgo a month of favorable fighting weather in exchange for the reinforced landings. The Joint Chiefs of Staff agreed to the delay within a week.

On February 6, the prime minister cabled the president to ask, because of "the swiftly changing course of events," for an early meeting of the Combined Chiefs of Staff. Since the meeting could only be for the pur-pose of revising the OVERLORD-ANVIL compact, Marshall advised against it. King objected vehemently and profanely. Roosevelt rejected the prime minister's suggestion.

Additional assault vessels would be hard to come by. King would yield nothing from his large Pacific cache. Marshall confided to Sir John Dill who then informed London, as Marshall intended, "The U.S. Chiefs of Staff are engaged in a fresh battle regarding Pacific strategy. It really is the navy, and King in particular, *v.* the rest," Dill wrote to London. "King does not get any easier as time goes on. . . . He does not trust us a yard." Dill, who had once joked ruefully that he provided neutral ground upon which the Army and Navy could meet, added, "I believe his war with the U.S. Army is as bitter as his war with us."

King and his chief of staff, Savvy Cooke, suspected the British of deliberately underestimating the number of serviceable landing craft in the British Isles. To Eisenhower, who believed King was cooking his Pacific books, Marshall wrote that staff planners estimated there were in Europe more than enough vessels to mount a seven-division OVERLORD and a simultaneous two-division ANVIL.

Eisenhower, as commander on the ground, had the final decision, Marshall added, but the chief of staff wondered if Ike was not overly susceptible to Churchillian persuasion. "I merely wish to be certain that localitis is not developing and that pressures on you have not warped your judgment."

The failure at Anzio perhaps fixed a worm of doubt in Eisenhower's mind. The supreme commander would waver during February, trying to appease his mentor 3,000 miles away, yet gripped by the very "localitis" Marshall feared. Eisenhower had come around to the British position: OVERLORD must be strengthened with both a larger invasion force and a second assault in the south posed to keep German reinforcements from flowing into Normandy. Italy was the most likely place for that second attack, Ike now argued, the more so because the shortage of LSTs prevented ANVIL from posing a great enough threat. On March 9, Eisenhower informed Marshall they did not have enough vessels to simultaneously mount both OVERLORD and ANVIL.

As the messages rocketed back and forth across the Atlantic, Churchill grew restive with the role Sir John Dill was playing. A middleman, an "honest broker" as one historian described him, Dill's role was to interpret Americans to British, and vice versa. It was an awkward position made uncomfortable by Churchill's suspicion that Dill was too often taking the Yankees' part.

In mid-February, Marshall asked Secretary of War Stimson's special assistant, Harvey Bundy, for help. "We're in grave danger of losing Dill. The story is that the prime minister is getting tired of him and he wants to get somebody else, and that'd be very serious." To Bundy, an influential Boston lawyer in the years before the war, Marshall suggested that "an honorary degree from your friends at Harvard would impress the old man in England."

Bundy tried, but failed; Harvard would grant no quickie degrees nor call a special convocation to present an honorary doctorate.

"Try Yale," Marshall ordered.

As an old Eli, Bundy felt more secure. But even his alumnus status could not circumvent the problem of granting a degree without a ceremony. Instead, the university's president, Charles Seymour, proposed Dill be named the first winner of the recently created Charles P. Howland Award for contributions to international relations. Seymour offered to lay on a full-dress academic parade for the ceremony, and the Army's public relations staff arranged extensive press coverage. (Marshall later apologized to Seymour for encouraging photographers to take so many pictures.) Marshall went on to line up other degrees for his friend, always making sure that the publicity crossed the Atlantic.

Six weeks later, a smiling Marshall informed Bundy, "My underground tells me that the prime minister said, 'You know, that fellow must be doing quite a job.'" The honors-laden Dill would stay on.

He was needed. With Eisenhower in camp, Churchill and Brooke redoubled their arguments in favor of shattering the wearying stalemate in the mountain passes south of Rome. His Tehran pledges were forgotten; once again Churchill was arguing for decisive victory in Italy.

The campaign there had gone badly through the first months of the year. Bitter weather and the mountainous terrain favored the German defenders, tenacious veterans who had to be pried out of every ravine or crossroads barricade. It was hard going over treacherous terrain; the steep hills lining the two highways that led northward to Rome funneled all traffic into narrow shooting galleries for German artillery observers.

With Eisenhower's departure from Italy, the Allies had lost the cooperative spirit that had marked the North Africa campaign. Commanded now by "Jumbo" Wilson, the two Allied armies in Italy barely kept in touch with each other. Frustration had soured their joint enterprise. The British Eighth Army saw its desert glory slipping away, first in the winter snow, then in the mud and pelting rain of springtime Italy.

Meanwhile, half of the American Fifth Army huddled along the banks of the Rapido River, while sixty miles away the other half was penned in the Anzio beachhead, "a prison camp where the inmates fed themselves."

This was not the sort of war of movement for which Marshall had planned and for which he built his armies. No columns of tanks swept across inviting plains, no artillery-supported divisions punched through enemy lines, then poured into the rear. Instead, the chief of staff would have immediately recognized Italy 1944 as France 1918. When stepson Allen Brown wrote to grouse about the mud that had mired his 1st Armored Division, Marshall wrote, "That always appears to be the case in war, at least it was my experience in France; cold or rain and mud, high winds, or extreme heat and dust. We can but pray that this war will soon be over." (Shortly after, Pentagon officers objected to showing recruits a stark documentary produced by filmmaker John Huston on the fighting in Italy. Marshall personally overruled them, on the grounds that *The Battle of San Pietro* would help prepare them for the misery of combat.)

Waving away these difficulties of terrain and weather, Winston Churchill could not, *would not* turn his back on the Mediterranean. He had been the major advocate of an Italian campaign since the Casablanca Conference a year before. He had been the chief sponsor of the Anzio landings, and now, American planners feared, he intended to gut ANVIL in favor of an attack on northern Italy.

Churchill was a formidable advocate but he was forced to deal directly with Marshall, the man most determined to staunch the Italian drain. President Roosevelt no longer concerned himself with military questions; in this election year, Roosevelt had effectively placed global strategy in Marhsall's hands. Harry Hopkins could not intercede; the president's adviser was once more gravely ill, his recovery slowed by grief over the death of his eighteen-year-old son Stephen, killed in the Marshall Islands on the boy's first day in combat. Allied strategy would henceforth be settled between the British prime minister and the American chief of staff.

In a radio message to Marshall, Churchill complained that seven of the Allies' seasoned divisions had already been withdrawn from the Italian boot to be refitted for OVERLORD in the British Isles. "What I cannot bear is to agree beforehand to starve a battle or have to break it off just at the moment when success, after long efforts and heavy losses, may be in view."

Pleading, probing, arguing well into the spring of the year, Churchill pressed his military arguments upon Marshall.

> Dill tells me that you had expected me to support ANVIL more vigorously in view of my enthusiasm for it when it was first proposed by you at Teheran. Please do me the justice to remember that the situation is vastly changed. In November, we hoped to take Rome in January, and there were many signs that the enemy was ready to [retire] northward up the Italian peninsula. Instead of this, in spite of our great amphibious expedition, we are stuck where we are, and the enemy has brought down to the battle south of Rome the eight mobile divisions we should have hoped a full-scale ANVIL would have contained. Thus there has been cause for rejoicing as well as bitter disappointment.

Only the unquenchable optimism of a Churchill could turn stalemate into impending victory.

The two Allied armies in Italy reorganized their forces for a major offensive that would turn Churchill's wish into deed. On May 11, 1944, the Polish and British divisions of the Eighth Army opened the attack, the Royal Air Force bombing the abbey at Monte Cassino as Polish infantrymen cleaned out the town that lay at its feet. To the west, American and French troops crossed the Rapido River, pressing slowly northward toward the Anzio beachhead and Rome.

On May 23, the new commander at Anzio, Major General Lucian K. Truscott, Jr., sent his troops eastward against the ring of German units hemming in the beachhead. Two days later, they linked up with the Fifth Army driving northward. The fighting was harsh, their progress slow, but day by day the American pressed the Wehrmacht back toward the hills that dominated the roads to Rome.

A week later, Marshall arrived at his office to find a personal radio message from Mark Clark waiting for him. The chief of staff's favorite stepson, Second Lieutenant Allen Tupper Brown, had been killed in action.

The twenty-seven-year-old Brown had made his own way in the Army, his stepfather at some pains to keep their relationship hidden. Brown had enlisted as a private and had suffered the indignities of basic training before graduating Officers Candidate School like tens of thousands of other newly minted second lieutenants. Choosing the armored branch, he had become a replacement in the combat-hardened 1st Armored Division, a tank commander sobered by responsibility. "Mother," he had gently corrected Katherine in a letter scant days before, "there are no American 'boys' in Italy. They may have been boys when they arrived here, but they are all men now."

The loss was all the more painful for just the day before they had received a letter from Allen in which the young man had optimistically looked forward to the end of the war. A German sniper had stolen that future.

An hour after leaving for the Pentagon, Marshall returned to Quarters No. 1 to tell his wife of Allen's death on a muddy highway south of Rome. Behind the closed door of his wife's bedroom, the husband comforted the stricken mother.

Marshall would mourn as well. With no children of his own, the chief of staff had looked upon his stepson with paternal affection. "Allen was the apple of his eye," Marshall's aide, Frank McCarthy, remembered. Marshall felt Allen's death keenly, though he revealed nothing publicly. Instead he grieved privately, talking with friends who had also lost sons—among them Hopkins and the British Ambassador to the United States, Lord Halifax—or with Sir John Dill. In these first hours of grief, however, Marshall's concern was solely for Katherine, swathed at that moment in "a blessed numbness." Marshall promptly arranged for an air force plane to fly the two of them that afternoon to New York where Allen's wife and child lived.

The chief of staff needed no red-lined chart to remind him of the cost of war.

CHAPTER

XXVI

A Lesson in Geometry

Through the black hours past midnight and into the early morning of
June 6, they waited. In his advance headquarters at Portsmouth, Hampshire, Dwight Eisenhower tried to make small talk with his aide Harry
Butcher; their conversation finally lapsed into silence. Just hours before
the supreme commander had watched, with tears in his eyes, as the
groaning C-47s lumbered into the air bearing the Screaming Eagles of
the 101st Airborne toward the dark coast of the Cotentin peninsula. Below
the air fleets, schools of landing craft circled the transports filled with
burdened men to be gambled at dawn against grim odds. Eisenhower
had crammed into his pocket a statement he had written while he waited
in case the landings should fail: "The troops, the air and the Navy did
all that bravery and devotion to duty could do. If any blame or fault
attaches to the attempt it is mine alone."

   Three days earlier, a forbidding weather report had forced Eisenhower to postpone for twenty-four hours the cross-Channel invasion.
Naval commanders signaled back to port the advance units of their armada
of 6,000 vessels; there the troops waited, penned aboard ship, cramped,
bored, and apprehensive. On the following day, June 4, Eisenhower's
chief meteorologist, RAF Group Captain J. M. Stagg, predicted a break
in the gathering storm. Stagg foresaw thirty-six hours of clear weather,
a window of opportunity. Eisenhower had mulled his decision, to launch
now or postpone the cross-Channel attack for two weeks when the low
tide came next at dawn after a moonlight night. (The paratroops needed
moonlight for their night drop; a low tide would give assault troops and
landing craft wider beaches.) Waiting might bring them better weather
but it would surely take something from the assault troops' keen edge.
Eisenhower pondered for a minute, then two, and finally nodded toward
his deputy commanders. "O.K., let's go."

   To Marshall, Eisenhower radioed a coded advisory, "HALCYON plus 5 finally and definitely confirmed." D-Day, once projected for May 1, then postponed to June 1 to give Eisenhower another month's LST production, would fall on June 6.

Now the leaders of great armies could only wait for news in those predawn hours while the Allied fleets took up stations from Cabourg to Quinéville along the Calvados coast. As a thoughtful Henry Stimson wrote in his diary that night, this was one of the great moments in history, "perhaps the greatest and sharpest crisis that the world has ever had, and it has all focused together on tonight."

This had been a triumphal week. Allied troops had finally punched their way out of the Anzio beachhead and rumbled north toward Rome; even as Eisenhower saluted the C-47s droning into the darkness, Mark Clark was setting up his headquarters in Rome. The Allied armies in Italy had spent so much blood for the Eternal City, yet Rome's capture seemed overshadowed by an OVERLORD poised in the Channel ports.

In Washington, Marshall had been moody through the week, the tension he felt masking the pain of Allen's loss. The tightly wound chief of staff and the secretary of war, men usually in easy agreement, found themselves irritably snapping at each other about the overlapping responsibilities of the American Red Cross and the army Emergency Relief Organization. It was a petty squabble quickly forgotten in the satisfying news from Mark Clark on June 4 that Rome was theirs and German troops were blowing bridges as they retreated to a new defense line well north of the capital.

Marshall revealed no hint of excitement as the first Allied paratroops sprinkled down inland from the invasion beaches at 1:30 a.m. on June 6, French time. In Washington it was seven-thirty in the evening of June 5, and the chief of staff, in dress uniform, was due at the Russian Embassy where Ambassador Andre Gromyko would present him with the Order of Suvarov, the highest military decoration the Soviets awarded foreigners. That ceremony concluded, Marshall contrived to make his usual early escape to Fort Myer and bed. He had settled into an outward calm, explaining later, "Well, there was nothing I could do about it anymore. It was much better to get a good night's sleep and be ready for whatever the morning might bring."

H-Hour on the American landing beaches designated OMAHA and UTAH fell at 6:30 a.m. French time and 7:30 a.m. on the three British beaches. Offshore, nine battleships, 23 cruisers, and 175 destroyers and corvettes from a half-dozen nations trained their batteries on German fortifications while 4,000 landing craft churned toward the dim shore. People on the cliffs of Dover that day could hear faint booms as the far-off battleships let go their salvos, booms like some starter's cannon for a yacht race, one said. Overhead, echelon after echelon of fighters and bombers swept across the Channel to seek targets along the narrow roads of the Norman countryside; 11,000 aircraft that day flew in skies swept almost free of the Luftwaffe.

No man who saw the awesome fleets or the vast armies put ashore on June 6, 1944, would ever forget it. An arsenal of democracy had produced such stores that British ports had been unable to unload all the merchant vessels delivering supplies for OVERLORD. The United States, a nation whose Army had numbered 150,000 little more than four years earlier, was shipping that number of soldiers to Great Britain each month as the date of the invasion loomed.

The run-up to D-day had been bumpy. During landing exercises off the English coast at the end of April, German E-boats got in among the LSTs and sank three; 500 men were drowned. At the same time the British War Cabinet had raised questions about the pre-invasion plan to destroy the French rail system and thereby prevent the Germans from rapidly reinforcing their coastal defenses. The estimated death toll of 10,000, Churchill radioed Roosevelt, "may easily bring about a great revulsion in French feeling towards their approaching United States and British liberators."

Marshall was unmoved. "The people of France are being called upon to pay a price for their liberation but this price should not appear too high in the light of the necessity for victory in the coming operation. . . ." Eisenhower and his air commanders who favored the vital bombing plan should be left with complete freedom of action, Marshall stressed.

It was just that unwillingness to impose restrictions on Eisenhower that saved George Patton's career. Repeatedly warned by Eisenhower to avoid controversy since the slapping incidents, Patton had busied himself training his Third Army, posing too as the commander of a vast and mythical 1st United States Army Group invented to deceive German intelligence. He agreed to make a few polite comments at the opening of a service club near his headquarters, talking to an audience of some sixty civilians about Anglo-American cooperation. The subject was important "since it is the evident destiny of the British and Americans to rule the world, [and] the better we know each other the better job we will do."

Patton's comments made the British press the next morning, and the American papers the day after. In the United States, there was a public outcry; Patton the arrogant was disregarding the Russians, who were doing the bulk of the fighting just then.

Marshall himself radioed Eisenhower about the editorial and congressional backlash, adding that Patton's thoughtless comment had probably killed Senate confirmation of a new list of permanent promotions, Patton's included. "General Patton," *The Washington Post* noted in an editorial forwarded by Marshall to Eisenhower, "has progressed from simple assaults on individuals to collective assault on entire nationalities."

An exasperated Eisenhower vacillated on proper punishment. "Apparently he is unable to use reasonably good sense," he radioed Marshall. "I have grown weary of the trouble he constantly causes you and the War Department to say nothing of myself, that I am seriously contemplating the most drastic action."

"The decision is exclusively yours," Marshall replied. Patton, however, had experience fighting Erwin Rommel who would have command of the German defenders in Normandy, the chief of staff reminded Eisenhower. "Consider only OVERLORD and your own heavy burden of responsibility for its success." Eisenhower, his temper cooling, decided to retain Patton.

His career salvaged by Marshall's forbearance, Patton that day fumed impatiently in Great Britain as the 4,000 landing craft of OVERLORD churned toward the shingled shore. An hour and a half after the first landing craft dropped their ramps off OMAHA and UTAH beaches, Eisenhower reported to Marshall that preliminary indications were good. Air Marshal Sir Trafford Leigh-Mallory, who had gloomily predicted a 50 percent casualty rate among the paratroops, reported that this first phase of OVERLORD had gone well. Naval gunfire was apparently accurate, suppressing German counterfire. Eisenhower was optimistic. He had watched the men off, and had noted "the light of battle in their eyes."

An excited War Department duty officer rushed Eisenhower's first report to Quarters No. 1 in the early morning of June 6, Washington time. Katherine Marshall sleepily answered the insistent knock on the door but refused to wake her husband. The frustrated officer finally thrust the decoded message into her hands. Mrs. Marshall scanned it, then asked calmly, "And what would you have General Marshall do about it?" Deflated, the officer retreated and the general slept on.

Marshall reported to the Pentagon at his usual hour. He then spent much of that day signing thank-you notes for the hundreds of letters of condolence he had received after news of Allen's death was reported in the press. It was a way to pass the time while awaiting further reports from Eisenhower's temporary headquarters in Portsmouth.

This was a moment to frustrate later biographers; there is no record of Marshall's actions or feelings on this day of all days. Perhaps as he signed the letters he paused to wonder just what might have been had the president handed command of OVERLORD to him. He would have been less than human had he not felt some regret or anger, however deeply he had submerged it. Yet he revealed nothing, then or later. Perhaps he weighed the costs of their success as he relayed Eisenhower's intermittent reports that day to the White House. Perhaps he paused to think of Allen, dead on a rutted road to Rome, as President Roosevelt broadcast a D-Day prayer on a nationwide radio hookup: "Our sons, pride of our nation. . . . Lead them straight and true; give strength to their arms, stoutness to their hearts, steadfastness to their faith. They will need Thy blessings. Their road will be long and hard. For the enemy is strong. He may hurl back our forces. Success may not come with rushing speed, but we shall return again and again."

Success did not come with rushing speed in Normandy that day. The 4th Infantry Division had met little opposition on UTAH Beach and had pushed well inland with light casualties, Eisenhower reported. The 1st and 29th Divisions, however, had tougher going on OMAHA. For six hours the disorganized survivors of a withering German fire huddled on a strip of beach just ten yards wide. While the American troop commander, Omar Bradley, weighed abandoning the OMAHA assault, a squadron of U.S. Navy destroyers steamed close inshore and leveled its batteries on German strongpoints. That fire cleared first one, then a second pathway to the cliffs above the beaches; in his first report to Bradley, corps commander Leonard Gerow radioed, "Thank God for the U.S. Navy." The fight at OMAHA had been close run and costly; American dead there totaled 1,465, with another 5,000 wounded or missing in action.

Meanwhile, the British Second Army comprising British, Canadian, Polish, and Dutch units had had an easier time of it while landing. Once ashore, though, they had encountered stiffening resistance at the eastern end of the invasion beaches. Only by the narrowest of margins late in the afternoon did they beat back a German counterattack threatening to roll up the beachhead. That fight kept Lieutenant General Miles Dempsey's men from gaining their first day's objectives, and especially the crucial crossroads that was to open the way to Caen.

Still, they were in France. By nightfall, the Allies had landed 165,000 men, more than eight divisions, a force larger in size than the entire U.S. Army when Marshall took command in July 1939. Allied killed, wounded, and missing totaled 9,500.

Marshall might justifiably have taken some measure of pride in the day's accomplishment; as chief of staff he had made D-Day possible. The men who waded ashore had been drafted and trained according to his lights; they had been formed into military units, the smaller, more maneuverable three-regiment division, that had existed only on paper prior to Marshall's taking command; they were fighting using small unit tactics he had perfected during his tenure at the Infantry School. In large part, he had selected the field commanders and the planners, *his* army's very leadership. For all that, the chief of staff had had no hand in the tactical planning for OVERLORD.

He had put forward one plan, a bold, too bold, conception that sprang from a long-held fancy for the airborne divisions he had sponsored. The chief of staff suggested to Eisenhower they establish an airhead of massed airborne units around four airfields in the vicinity of EVREUX, west of Paris and eighty-five miles from the Calvados coast. "This plan appeals to me," he wrote Eisenhower in mid-February, "because I feel that it is a true vertical envelopment and would create such a strategic threat to the Germans that it would call for a major revision of their defensive plans."

The only argument against the plan, Marshall added, was "that we have never done anything like this before, and frankly, that reaction makes me tired."

Still the men shaping OVERLORD rejected Marshall's plan. The commander of the 82nd Airborne, Major General James Gavin, and Omar Bradley worried that the Evreux region was excellent tank country "and meeting with German armor would have been disastrous. It was a plan of great vision but totally unrealistic in terms of combat. . . . Washington never seemed to understand how vulnerable airborne was to tanks unless we were reinforced immediately," Gavin explained later.

Deferential, even somewhat defensive, Eisenhower gently broke the news to his mentor. "As I see it, the first requisite is for the expeditionary force to gain a firm and solid footing on the Continent and to secure at least one really good sheltered harbor." Despite Allied air superiority, the supreme allied commander noted, the Germans would mobilize forces large enough to keep beachhead and airhead from joining. That risked leaving the airborne "isolated and defeated in detail."

Eisenhower also sought to reassure Marshall that he had not been seized by that excess of caution which hampered a battlefield commander. "I instinctively dislike ever to uphold the conservative as opposed to the bold," he added, but this time he would do just that. Marshall's one tactical offering, a plan that would have given his favored airborne divisions the palm, was stillborn. The chief of staff said nothing more about the matter.

On an even more important point, Eisenhower in his growing self-confidence had crossed Marshall. From the Tehran Conference on, the chief of staff had insisted that ANVIL, the landings in southern France, coincide with the Normandy invasion. In that way, two Allied forces would place the Germans in the jaws of a giant nutcracker. But because of the landing craft shortage and the Anzio landings, the date of ANVIL had slipped steadily. Anzio stalemated and LSTs ticketed for OVERLORD still resupplying the beachhead, Eisenhower suggested in late January that ANVIL be canceled.

Marshall was irritated. The Combined Chiefs had agreed just weeks before that a seven-division assault in Normandy and a two-division landing in the south of France were possible on May 31 with the available reserves of landing craft. Yet once more, it seemed, no agreement was binding.

Marshall suspected that Eisenhower was unduly swayed by the British, particularly Bernard Montgomery, the crusty ground commander for

OVERLORD. In a letter to Eisenhower, Marshall ironically noted that "British and American chiefs of staff seem to have completely reversed themselves and we have become Mediterraneanites and they heavily pro-OVERLORD." Questioning Eisenhower's change of heart, Marshall wrote, "I will use my influence here to agree with your desires. I merely wish to be certain that localitis is not developing and that the pressures on you have not warped your judgment."

The criticism stung. In an immediate reply to "Dear General," the supreme commander sought to placate Marshall:

". . . I have occasionally had to modify slightly my own conceptions of the campaign in order to achieve a unity of purpose and effort. I think this is inescapable in Allied operations but I assure you that I have never yet failed to give you my own clear personal convictions about every project and plan in prospect. So far as I am aware, no one here has tried to urge me to present any particular view, nor do I believe that I am particularly affected by localitis."

Eisenhower dropped the other shoe. He proposed to Marshall that the invasion of southern France be postponed. So long as they had to supply the Anzio beachhead, that was the only way to scrounge enough LSTs for OVERLORD.

Marshall reluctantly bowed to logistical reality and acknowledged that a simultaneous OVERLORD / ANVIL was impossible; he suggested the southern invasion be rescheduled for July 10. To ensure that date, the chief of staff prevailed upon Ernest King to divert to the Mediterranean twenty-six of the scarce landing ship-tanks intended for the Pacific. King attached a binding condition. "We will not make this diversion which means a serious delay in the Pacific with the possibility of losing our momentum unless some sizable operation of the nature of ANVIL is on the books," Marshall wrote Eisenhower. The supreme commander could have the needed vessels, but only on condition they be used for an ANVIL landing immediately after OVERLORD.

Churchill might be finally coming around, "hardening very much" on the Normandy invasion, as Dill put it, but Brooke fretted, complaining the American chiefs were holding a pistol to his head: "Marshall is quite hopeless. . . . The strategy he advocates can only result in two months without any operations in the Mediterranean, just at the very moment when we require them most owing to the date of the cross-Channel operation."

Brooke clung obdurately to the notion that "our power should be utilized in the air and on the sea and that the Russians should do the land fighting." He would be the last to accept Marshall's strategic concept.

The Anzio breakout and the fall of Rome on June 4 settled nothing. While the Americans saw the capture of Rome as the end of the Italian campaign, Churchill and Brooke instead argued the German retreat opened unforeseen opportunities for new attacks toward Florence and the north. Churchill in particular remained keen on the "attractive prospects of advancing through the Ljubljana Gap into Austria and Hungary and striking at the heart of Germany from another direction." To Marshall's exasperation, they refused to let the matter drop.

Their persistence might have spoiled Marshall's flying visit to Great Britain and the invasion beaches, but for the excitement he felt. Ostensibly the trip—planned at the last minute—was to bring together the Combined Chiefs in case the landings failed and a decision to withdraw had to be made. In fact, it was born as much of the American chiefs' desire to see just what the labors of two and a half years had wrought.

Marshall's departure was delayed until the morning of June 8 by his attendance at a White House dinner for the premier of Poland, Stanislaw Mikolajczyk. It was some measure of Marshall's importance in wartime Washington that his presence was required at what was, for all practical purposes, a diplomatic dinner. It was another that White House secretary William D. Hassett, a longtime Washington functionary, wrote in his diary that night, "Wherever this man goes he inspires reverence— may God spare him."

Marshall, Arnold, and King flew by C-54 to Scotland on June 8, then rode by train to London in an unheated extra coach. The British chiefs were on hand at Euston Station to greet the travel-worn Americans, Admiral Sir Andrew Cunningham noting that "General Marshall was as charming as ever, and Admiral King as saturnine." The weary Americans were quickly on their way to Staines and a Tudor mansion twenty miles south of London, traveling through an idyllic spring countryside ripe with rhododendrons, poppies, and violets.

Reports from Normandy indicated that their build-up was going well. Ten divisions were ashore; more were en route. The big question was how the Germans would react. The Wehrmacht had seventeen understrength divisions in the invasion area, and dozens more within three days' travel. Were those reinforcements to join the battle in Normandy, it could be decisive.

The overall plan for the cross-Channel invasion had contemplated just this sort of situation. The landings were to be shrouded by an elaborate deception scheme, JAEL, intended to lead the Wehrmacht into believing that the invasion along the Calvados coast was but a feint; the main blow of the mythical 1st United States Army Group led by the respected George Patton would fall on the Pas de Calais. Hitler had more than enough divisions stationed along the Atlantic Wall to throw the invaders off their precarious ledge—if he used them immediately in a plan he called "Case Three." JAEL's deceptive radio traffic, its supposed fifty divisions under Patton's command, its fleets of dummy landing craft berthed in Channel ports, all were conceived to pin those Panzers in place until the beachhead had been expanded and reinforced. In Bletchley Park, Allied and British monitors listened for radio messages between German headquarters that would reveal their plans and especially the ominous Case Three, which committed 1,600 reserve Panzer tanks to the invasion beaches. There was no word yet; the Combined Chiefs of Staff could only wait.

The next morning, the chiefs joined the prime minister for a walkabout of Dwight Eisenhower's forward headquarters. Both Churchill and Marshall came away impressed with the supreme commander's war room and its elaborate maps marking the positions of each Allied and German regiment. Nothing on the maps, however, indicated if the German reserves were moving toward the invasion beaches or toward the threatened Pas de Calais.

Marshall found time to discuss with Eisenhower a number of subjects, including the speed of the build-up on the beach. Marshall also told Eisenhower he wanted combat troops promoted and decorated promptly, something he had learned from the French in the first war. (When the Republican minority leader in the House of Representatives came to question that policy, the chief of staff quoted Napoleon's dictum, "Give me enough ribbon to place on the tunics of my soldiers and I can conquer the world.")

Later that morning, they returned to London for a meeting of the Combined Chiefs of Staff in Churchill's bunker buried beneath Storey Gate. There they reviewed the global situation, King laying out their plans for the Central Pacific, Arnold adding his support for the air bases it would yield from which to attack Japan.

The British questioned the two-pronged strategy in the Pacific and especially MacArthur's Philippines thrust. Aware that MacArthur's denial would become a political issue at home, Marshall deflected the queries. The Combined Chiefs voted to solicit recommendations from both MacArthur and the Navy's Chester Nimitz, a harmless enough exercise.

On Sunday, June 11, the American chiefs played host at lunch in Staines for their British opposite numbers. Quickly they turned to the looming problem of future operations in the Mediterranean and the much debated invasion of southern France.

The Americans proposed that the Italian campaign halt at the foothills of the Apennines or, alternatively, along a line drawn from Pisa on the west coast to Rimini on the east. The British agreed, even if Brooke had reservations.

Once they reached that point, Brooke argued, they could mount ANVIL or some other landing in the south. The British proposed a number of alternatives: invasion of the Istrian peninsula and the port of Trieste; attack on the western coast of France aimed at securing the large port of Bordeaux; a landing at Sète on the south coast and a drive up the Rhone Valley; or ANVIL in the Toulon-Marseilles region.

Marshall held out for ANVIL but suggested they keep their options open; he wanted only an operation in the near future. Rather easily they agreed that various headquarters would draw plans for a three-division assault, with July 25 as the tentative D-Day, in no less than four target areas.

There was still no word from Erwin Rommel's headquarters or Hitler's *Oberkommando* on use of the reinforcements as they met once more in the underground war room at Storey Gate. The stuffy space was "heavy with tension and pipe and cigarette smoke combined with a faint aroma of good whiskey," a British staff officer recalled.

It was a frightful moment—there were those big red blobs on the war maps moving towards Normandy all the time. . . . Then Joan Bright [a secretary responsible for the ULTRA radio intercepts] knocked on the door, came in, and said there was a message which might interest us; she had just put it in the "Black Book." Brooke and Marshall went to have a look. They were all smiles. We looked at the ULTRA—and there it was: Hitler had canceled Case Three. We'd won—there might be very heavy battles, but we'd won.

Now they could visit the beachhead, carrying the news to the embattled commanders. That evening they joined Churchill and his close adviser, South African Field Marshal Jan Smuts, on a train that would take them to Portsmouth and a waiting destroyer. For all their years and experience, prime minister and Combined Chiefs were like Tom and Huck playing hooky, off on a forbidden rafting adventure with a delicious hint of danger.

At Portsmouth, they broke into two parties, British and American, each to visit its own invasion beaches across the crowded English Channel. Overhead, Hap Arnold noted smugly, 4,000 Allied planes flew that day without a single German in the sky; the Luftwaffe lacked the planes, pilots, and aviation fuel to be an effective force.

Aboard the destroyer *Thompson,* Marshall, King, Arnold, Eisenhower, and a clutch of aides approached OMAHA Beach. Transferring to an amphibious DUKW, they churned past the massive concrete caissons that had been towed across the Channel and anchored in the shelter of a reef of sunken ships to form a floating dock. Onto Beach EASY RED the vehicle rolled, then up the narrow road to the bluffs overlooking the Calvados coast.

Cameramen were on hand to record Marshall's first return to France since 1919, catching the chief of staff with a pistol strapped to his hip as he clambered out of the bathtub-shaped DUKW. Marshall was smiling broadly, a man fulfilled.

All about him was evidence of the Army he had built, from the tethered barrage balloons bobbing high overhead to the discarded equipment, shell casings, and C-ration cans underfoot. (The British never would get over the fact that Americans left such an untidy battlefield.) Even as the chiefs drove inland on the overcrowded country lanes toward Omar Bradley's headquarters, they passed elements of the ten divisions already ashore. Wherever they went, Eisenhower noted wryly, their presence appeared heartening to the troops—"possibly on the theory that the area is a safe one or the rank wouldn't be there."

The party toured the battlefields of the week past, stopping on Bradley's orders at the outskirts of Carentan. That vital crossroads town had fallen just the day before to the 101st Airborne and was still under harassing fire from German artillery.

Bradley and his corps commanders then briefed the visiting dignitaries at his headquarters in an apple orchard on the cliffs overlooking the invasion beaches. Lunch on the spartan C-rations at Bradley's headquarters followed, the brass washing off the road dust as best they could in a single basin filled from a jerrican.

A group of newsmen cornered them at the command post, columnist Ernie Pyle grousing they got little hard news. Eisenhower tried to fob them off, joking, "You're the people we're expecting news from." Marshall temporarily satisfied them by announcing that the invasion of Guam was at that moment under way.

Marshall and King returned to Portsmouth by destroyer, Arnold by light plane that afternoon. The chief of staff was generally pleased with their progress. He had noted some supply problems—probably no man in the Army had more experience or a keener eye than Marshall when it came to moving about large numbers of men and the necessary materiel. Still, the general cabled President Roosevelt later, "Eisenhower and his staff are cool and confident, carrying out an affair of incredible magnitude and complication with superlative efficiency." Some of Marshall's own enthusiasm leaked through in his estimate of the situation when he told the president, "I think we have these Huns at the top of the toboggan slide and the full crash of the Russian offensive should put the skids under them."

Once rejoined with Churchill, they ate dinner on the prime minister's train and Marshall dashed off a radiogram for Admiral Mountbatten in the far-off Southeast Asian theater:

"Today we visited the British and American armies on the soil of France. . . . We sailed through vast fleets of ships, with landing craft of many types pouring more and more men, vehicles, and stores ashore. . . . We wish to tell you at this moment in your arduous campaign that we realize that much of this remarkable technique and, therefore, the success of the venture, has its origin in developments effected by you and your staff of Combined Operations." It was signed in alphabetical order by Arnold, Brooke, Churchill, King, Marshall, and Smuts.

They returned to London about one in the morning of June 13, shortly after the first four of Hitler's vengeance weapons, the pilotless V-1 "buzz bombs," dropped on London. Two nights later, amid a barrage of 200 V-1s, one of the erratic rockets dropped a mile and a half from where the chiefs of staff were sleeping. The concussion knocked Hap Arnold out of bed.

For the next two days the Combined Chiefs met to review their global plans. Brooke and Marshall again crossed swords, this time over Stilwell's multiple responsibilities in the Southeast Asian theater. When Brooke proposed the jobs be split among three men, Marshall retorted that Stilwell was a fighter, the only one in the theater.

Brooke spun on his heel, breaking off the conversation "to save myself from rounding on him and irreparably damaging our relations." (The chief of the Imperial General Staff took what comfort he could from a commiserating letter by Sir John Dill, who wrote from Washington: "It is odd how that charming person Marshall can fly off the handle and be so infernally rude. Also he gets fixed ideas about things and people which it is almost impossible to argue.")

Brooke's haughty assurance was as nothing compared to the cool, overbearing attitude of Charles de Gaulle. Brooke merely believed himself the proponent of the proper military strategy; General Charles-André-Marie-Joseph de Gaulle, on the other hand, saw himself as the embodiment of an entire nation.

As D-Day neared, de Gaulle's sense of self-importance had grown apace. At de Gaulle's behest, a rump Consultative Assembly in Algiers had changed the name of the French National Committee of Liberation to Provisional Government of the French Republic. As head of the FNCL, de Gaulle considered himself the de facto president of France.

He alone considered it so. President Roosevelt still insisted that the French people choose their leader rather than have one thrust upon them by fiat. The president had complained to General Marshall that Eisenhower "evidently believes the fool newspaper stories that I am anti-de Gaulle, even the kind of story that says I hate him, et cetera, et cetera. All this, of course, is utter nonsense. I am perfectly willing to have de Gaulle made president, or emperor, or king or anything else so long as the action comes in an untrammeled and unforced way from the French people themselves."

De Gaulle found offense everywhere. Asked to join in a series of short announcements to be broadcast to Europe on D-Day, he was outraged by the order of the speeches: the king of Norway, the queen of the Netherlands, the grand duchess of Luxembourg, the prime minister of Holland, General Eisenhower, and then, finally, de Gaulle. The placement implied not only that de Gaulle was not a head of government, but that he was a soldier subordinate to Eisenhower. De Gaulle's refusal vexed Eisenhower, who assumed de Gaulle's backing would assure the cooperation of the French resistance. Only after much imploring did de Gaulle condescend to broadcast long after the others on the night of June 6. In retaliation, de Gaulle dispatched only 20 of the 180 bilingual officers who were to serve as liaison between the invading Allies and the French populace.

Marshall arrived in Great Britain coldly furious with the Frenchman and what he considered de Gaulle's "contemptible" actions. Marshall's opposition was based not on any objection to de Gaulle becoming the head of a future government of France. Instead, he feared for the well-being of the invasion itself. "The first thing Bradley told me in Normandy was that he [de Gaulle] had messed up their arrangements," Marshall recalled.

The chief of staff was traveling under orders from President Roosevelt to avoid any political discussion with either de Gaulle or Churchill. It was a close call. Once back in England, Marshall "raised the devil" with de Gaulle's chief of staff about the non-cooperation. To the elegant Foreign Secretary Anthony Eden, Marshall later raged that the Frenchman's actions were "outrageous" and "no sons of Iowa farmers would fight to put up statues of de Gaulle in France." When Eden persisted in defending de Gaulle's behavior, Marshall's temper flashed. As Stimson recounted the general's outburst, "He said he couldn't talk politics but he said he knew more about the army and he knew more about the people of the United States than Eden did and that if Eden went on in this way and things that had happened came out in the press in full . . . it would make a wave of indignation in the United States which would swamp the whole damn British Foreign Office."

Marshall, of course, *was* talking politics, and with a man who was not only foreign secretary but a leader in Parliament as well. The red-faced Eden, like Brooke before him, avoided argument by leaving the room. Perhaps it was tension, or anxiety about the fate of their armies on the still confined Normandy beachhead, but the man who had insisted on forging an alliance based on mutual tolerance was sorely testing the strength of the bond.

If the de Gaulle situation was likely to strain nerves, the unquiet question of ANVIL threatened to pop Marshall's safety valves. No issue so divided the two Western Allies, for no dispute was so hinged on differing concepts of the proper way to wage war—whether the peripheral, opportunistic strategy favored by Churchill and his Imperial General Staff, or the mass assault that crushed Germany's warmaking potential as Marshall advocated.

Each argument was grounded in national tradition. Through the years of Empire the British had relied on a puissant navy and small army to fight Queen Victoria's "little wars" here and there on two continents and a subcontinent. They had forsaken that overriding strategy during World War I and the result had been a carnage that seared their memory still. The United States, on the other hand, buttressed by its overwhelming productive capability, favored massing that force against an enemy's warmaking potential. Grant in the Civil War and Pershing in World War I had successfully used just those tactics.

Though he himself had rallied to OVERLOAD, the prime minister could not give up what he considered were the magnificent prizes to be had in the Mediterranean. Many of the ranking British planners also savored the prospect of a drive up the Italian boot, then a right wheel that would point Allied armies at Yugoslavia. Forcing the Ljubljana Gap, they insisted, they could drive on Zagreb or northward toward Austria. The biggest prize would be to place "Anglo-American forces on the Danube before the war came to an end," Air Marshal Sir John Slessor argued.*

If only to be fair, Marshall delayed his return to the United States to fly to Italy, so as to solicit the opinions of the senior military men there. On June 17 he met with the Mediterranean theater commander, "Jumbo" Wilson. The British commander urged they continue the land advance in Italy, coupling with it an amphibious landing on the Istrian peninsula that would leave them poised for an attack through the Ljubljana Gap.

Marshall demurred on the landing; it would mean the death of ANVIL. He stressed that a two-pronged attack in France was not only necessary but essential to gain the port facilities they needed in France. Forty or fifty divisions still in the United States could not be shipped to the war zone simply because they lacked the ports in which to land and resupply them, Marshall pointed out. ANVIL and the capture of Marseilles and Toulon on the Mediterranean shore were vital to maintaining pressure on the Germans in France.

Wilson was impressed with both Marshall's "masterly manner" and his arguments. The Mediterranean commanders "had no idea how Eisen-

---

*There were many more than British and American troops in Italy. If ever there was a United Nations military force, it was there, under the command of Field Marshal Sir Harold Alexander. Like Eisenhower, the easygoing Alexander found ways to bond disparate nationalities into a fighting force. At one time or another, he had troops from the British Isles, Canada, New Zealand, South Africa, India, Ceylon, the African colonies of Basutoland, Swaziland, and Bechaunaland, the islands of the Seychelles, Mauritius, Cyprus, and the Caribbean; from the United States, including the all-black 92nd Infantry Division and the Japanese-American 442nd Regimental Combat Team; French units composed of Algerians, Moroccans, Tunisians, Syrians, Lebanese, and Senegalese; a Polish division; a Brazilian division; and smaller units of Greeks, Belgians, Yugoslav irregulars, Italian partisans, and a Jewish Brigade recruited in Palestine.

hower was hampered by not having the ports, you see, and the extreme importance that Marseille would be to his future campaign against Germany." Further, the French divisions in Italy, anxious to liberate their homeland, wanted no part in a campaign in the Balkans. Because they would provide a significant portion of the southern invasion force, wherever it went, effectively the French held a veto power on further operations in that theater. "Once Marshall told me that," said Wilson, "I knew that strategically [ANVIL] was the only way."

There remained an additional problem, one that Churchill tended to wave aside as of no moment. Yet it was one that infantrymen clawing their way northward in Italy would never forget: the mountainous terrain favored the tenacious defenders. "None of us liked the offensive in Italy, really, against those mountains. It was a costly affair," Wilson later acknowledged.

The Ljubljana Gap offered only more of the same, a forbidding mountain pass threaded by a treacherous, two-lane road and a railroad that plunged into and out of a dozen tunnels along the route. A small group of defenders could hold off whole armies there, blowing the road and the tunnels as they retreated. Beyond this pass lay the eastern Alps and more mountain fighting. It would be the Italian campaign and worse.

The chief of staff reserved a portion of the following day for a personal mission. At the Anzio beachhead he visited the American Cemetery and the grave of his stepson near the flagpole. As workmen hacked out holes for the last of the 7,000 Americans who would be buried there, George Marshall stood quietly by the raw plot that sheltered the remains of Second Lieutenant Allen Tupper Brown. He spent a few moments there, swathed in a private sorrow, before returning to the still busy beach and a nearby airfield.

Allen's memory stirred restlessly. In an artillery spotter's light plane, Marshall flew toward Villetri in the Alban Hills, skimming just 300 feet above Highway 7 where Allen had died. He could see the road, the stone-pocked hills, the farms Allen had seen in his last hours, yet he still sought something, some solace in the Alban Hills.

Later that day at Fifth Army headquarters, Marshall talked with two members of Allen's tank crew and another tank commander from his son's company. The young officer still had Allen's map, "a much rumpled paper with various lines and objectives noted in crayon." The four of them, three young tankers and the chief of staff, pored over the map as the combat soldiers recalled Allen's last moments.

It was not enough. Once more Marshall flew back over the Alban Hills and Highway 7, following the map, with it locating the scene of Allen's last action. A tank column on the move, a young officer standing in the turret, the hatch thrown back the better to see. Then suddenly a sniper's bullet and the officer was dead in the dust of the Italian countryside. Marshall the soldier understood; Marshall the father grieved.

That evening Marshall dined with Mark Clark, once one of his tactical instructors at the Infantry School, now a three-star general in command of the American Fifth Army. Clark too urged that they press on in Italy and then into the Balkans. To do so, he proposed that ANVIL be given over solely to the French and that he keep the three American divisions slated for that operation. (Clark—"a very good soldier and very loyal," in Marshall's phrase—later would describe the decision not to cross the Alps as a great political mistake but remained silent at the time.) Marshall returned to Washington on June 22, determined to settle the Mediterranean strategy. Two days later Eisenhower radioed that a severe Channel storm, the worst in living memory, between June 19 and 24 had destroyed the artificial harbor at OMAHA Beach through which his armies were supplied. Deprived of supplies, he was necessarily slowing his advance. A large port was more vital than ever.

Marshall replied that the Joint Chiefs of Staff still insisted on ANVIL, instructing him to hold firm. The confident chief of staff then met with President Roosevelt at the White House in a short meeting that effectively settled Allied strategy as Marshall preferred.

The two of them, each for his own reasons, agreed on ANVIL. Marshall perceived a military necessity, a logistical problem to be solved, while the president in this election year foresaw a political liability. As Roosevelt candidly explained to Churchill, "Finally for purely political considerations over here I would never survive even a slight setback in OVERLORD if it were known that fairly large forces had been diverted to the Balkans."

Churchill was to make one more effort to abort the invasion of southern France. On June 28, he radioed a long argument against the invasion of southern France. Churchill's effort would fail, Brooke predicted. "We had led the Americans by the nose from Casablanca to Florence and it would not be easy to put this policy over on top of all that. They are so inclined to regard fresh ideas, to match new situations, as breaches of contract."

The invasion of southern France, Churchill went on, was a "bleak and sterile" campaign against superior German strength, one that offered little tactical support to OVERLORD. Worse, it would strip the Italian campaign of its momentum. To do the one meant the other.

The president's detailed reply, drafted by the Joint Chiefs of Staff, rejected Churchill's pleading. "The exploitation of OVERLORD, our victorious advances in Italy, an early assault on Southern France, combined with the Soviet drives to the west—all as envisaged at Teheran—will most surely serve to realize our object, the unconditional surrender of Germany." A change now would require Stalin's concurrence.

Roosevelt too was able to invoke the judgment of history. "At Teheran we agreed upon a definite plan of attack. That plan has gone well so far. Nothing has occurred to require any change. Now that we are fully involved in our major blow, history will never forgive us if we lost precious time and lives in indecision and debate. My dear friend, I beg of you, let us go ahead with our plan."

Against the firm American position, his troop strength vastly outnumbered in the field, the prime minister capitulated. "If you still press upon us the directive of your Chiefs of Staff to withdraw so many of your forces from the Italian campaign and leave all our hopes there dashed to the ground, his Majesty's Government, on the advice of their Chiefs of Staff, must enter a solemn protest. I need scarcely say that we shall do our best to make a success of anything that is undertaken."

Marshall had prevailed. As the president put it, borrowing from a remembered boyhood geometry lesson, "A straight line is the shortest distance between two points." George Marshall, the implacable logician, from now on was to determine the strategy of the war.

C H A P T E R
XXVII

End Game

Winston Churchill had impatiently waited weeks for this conference in Quebec. He confronted problems and needed answers only another conference with the president could provide. What part would the British Empire take in the Pacific once the fighting ended in Europe? How could they regain the initiative in Burma where a disease-riddled Indian Army hung on grimly? And what of the British Army in Italy; was it to be bled white in a stalemate?

The prime minister waved aside all objections. No matter that Stalin had declined to attend, pleading military responsibilities. No matter that Roosevelt, weary from a long trip to the Pacific in July, hesitated to take another so soon. Churchill proposed they return to the swank Château Frontenac on the bluff high above the St. Lawrence River for the conference code-named OCTAGON. In deference to their coalition, the president agreed.

The two government leaders and their military staffs met on September 11, 1944, as men of flourishing prospects. Their armies in northern France, now more than 2 million strong, had broken out of the Norman hedgerows to seize Paris on August 25. Then the armored columns had raced east and south to join the forces of ANVIL driving up the valley of the Rhone from the Côte d'Azur. Roosevelt and Churchill were meeting on the Plains of Abraham with France virtually free of Germans for the first time since June 1940.

While progress in Italy was less dramatic, the Germans were slowly giving ground. The British Eighth Army stood on the southern bank of the Marano River, the American Fifth Army probed in the Apennines. The terrain there favored the tenacious defenders, but Churchill was prepared to argue that the transfer of troops back from southern France would speed their progress and once more open the way to the Ljubljana Gap. Seeking a British-led victory, he refused to let the dream die.

On the Eastern Front relentless pressure from the Red Army had caved in the Axis. Bulgaria and Rumania abandoned the fight. The Russians stood on the Danube, the Balkans before them; Hungary and Czechoslovakia waited anxiously.

The three Allied fronts, Western, Eastern, and Italian, were closing the ring, as Churchill put it, squeezing Hitler's Third Reich into an ever smaller pocket. A joint American and British intelligence estimate went so far as to predict the end of the European war by December 1, or even sooner. The speed of their advance, faster even than the Panzers' progress in 1940, stirred elation, expectancy, and a feeling bordering on bewilderment, Churchill's cabinet secretary John Colville noted.

Half a world away, the twin prongs of the Allied offensive in the Pacific closed on the Japanese homeland. MacArthur looked northward, casting a covetous eye on the Philippines. In the Central Pacific, Saipan, Tinian, and Guam had fallen to the Army and Marines after a cave-by-cave battle in mid-August; those islands would provide airfields from which newly operational B-29s were to bomb Japan.

Though still powerful—army planners estimated the Japanese still had an army of 3.5 million to defend the home islands—the imperial war machine faltered. On June 19–20 in a massive air engagement American pilots dubbed the "Marianas Turkey Shoot," the Japanese lost 476 planes and three carriers to fewer than 30 Americans shot down. The First Air Fleet, the once proud victors at Pearl Harbor, would never again be a factor in the war.

Realists in Tokyo understood that the war had been lost. Acknowledging the looming disaster, on July 18, Hideki Tojo resigned his three posts as premier, war minister, and army chief of staff. The new government vowed to continue fighting, but a fatalistic recognition of the odds precluded optimism.

For the American Joint Chiefs of Staff, the question was where next in the increasingly vulnerable Japanese perimeter: the Philippines, Formosa, or, even more boldly, the Ryukyus? Marshall, Arnold, and Leahy favored the Philippines first; Ernest King favored a Navy-led assault on Formosa. King's obdurate stand prevented unanimity and a recommendation for action to the president.

Roosevelt—who now left military questions to his Joint Chiefs of Staff—had his eye fixed on the presidential elections just four months off. The Joint Chiefs' deadlock over Pacific strategy handed Roosevelt a grand opportunity to play the role of commander-in-chief for the voters. Summoning the two Pacific commanders, Douglas MacArthur and Admiral Chester Nimitz, to join him, the president embarked aboard the cruiser *Baltimore* for Hawaii in late July 1944.

Roosevelt's trip to Hawaii was as covertly political as it was overtly military. By casting himself in this military role as commander-in-chief, the president enhanced his reelection chances. At the same time, he subtly emphasized that the celebrated Douglas MacArthur, a onetime darkhorse for the GOP presidential nomination, was responsible to him as commander-in-chief. MacArthur took some satisfaction, perhaps, by arriving late in a limousine with siren blaring.

MacArthur and Nimitz sat down with the president in a private mansion overlooking Waikiki Beach to argue for their rival strategies in the Pacific. They stood far from agreement. Nimitz and the Navy—the shadow of Ernest King darkened all of Nimitz's arguments—urged bypassing the Philippines in favor of Formosa. MacArthur argued for just the opposite tack, with War Department backing. (Marshall judged MacArthur's arguments as much political as military. "MacArthur thought we never could explain to them if we by-passed them.")

On any other issue, Nimitz was a more than adequate opponent for MacArthur. Slight of figure, a man who eschewed publicity-seeking gestures, Nimitz had proved himself an astute naval tactician, perhaps the Navy's best. Ernest King tended to be suspicious of what he deemed the soft-spoken Nimitz's willingness to compromise with the Army, but that very quality had secured concessions in return, concessions the abrasive King could not win in Washington.

This time, however, MacArthur would have both logic and emotion on his side. Without the recapture of the Philippines first, any drive across the Central Pacific aimed at Formosa would have an exposed left flank, vulnerable to air attack from the islands. Moreover, the promise to the Philippine people must be kept; his personal honor was at stake, he insisted to the president.

When Roosevelt pointed out that reconquest of the islands would be costly, MacArthur disagreed. "Mr. President, my losses would not be heavy, any more than they have been in the past." Then he added an inferential criticism of the Marine commanders who had led the increasingly bloody island assaults in the Central Pacific: "The days of the frontal attack should be over. Modern infantry weapons are too deadly, and frontal assault is only for mediocre commanders. Good commanders do not turn in heavy losses."

Nimitz was overwhelmed. His argument favoring an attack on Formosa was Admiral King's, not his own; moreover, he himself tended to favor the Philippine thrust. He could not strongly advocate one strategy when a second was more appealing. The conference ended with the president grandly assuring MacArthur, "We will not bypass the Philippines."

In a welter of triumphal headlines, FDR the commander-in-chief returned to the mainland, renominated by acclamation, his vice-presidential running mate the dapper junior senator from Missouri, Harry S. Truman. Roosevelt was deftly campaigning without appearing to do so, probably the wisest course for a man seeking an unprecedented fourth term as president of the United States.

Though he sought to conserve his energy, the pace was taxing. The candidate who traveled to Quebec on September 11, 1944, tried to brush aside his fatigue with a joke. "Yes, I *am* tired," he told journalist John Gunther. "So would you be if you had spent the last five years pushing Winston uphill in a wheelbarrow."

To both Churchill, weary himself after five years of war, and the new first sea lord, Andrew Cunningham, the gaunt Franklin Roosevelt seemed frail, very frail. Churchill's secretary thought the president's eyes appeared glazed, even in the midst of conversation. Both president and prime minister—the latter recovering from his third bout of pneumonia since the beginning of the year—were ill more often and recovered more slowly than they once had.

Roosevelt and Churchill were not the only ones to feel the strain. Hopkins was bedridden with hemochromatosis in Washington once more, his recovery more and more problematical. The members of the British delegation were also distressed to see the once smartly turned out Sir John Dill for the first time in a year. "Dill was so seedy," Brooke wrote in his diary. He appeared to be wasting away, Brooke decided.

Dill's health had deteriorated. Hardly recovered from a hernia operation the year before, he now was dying of an intractable anemia. Refusing to go home, the field marshal instead quietly asked that Churchill's physician come to his aid if needed during the conference. Dill silently showed the doctor, Lord Moran, a crumpled piece of paper on which had been written the results of his last two blood tests. Moran concluded that the man who had served as the go-between nations in these years of unparalleled cooperation would soon be dead. "I wonder if he knows," the doctor mused.

The conference code-named OCTAGON marked the beginning of the end game. Until this point, such meetings had been dominated by military considerations; in those discussions Marshall had pushed through his strategic concept, gaining with it preeminence among the chiefs. From Second Quebec, largely given over to political issues, Marshall would play a new role in the coalition. The minutes of the meetings suggest Marshall spoke but little, and then usually as the broker of compromises.

For Churchill and Brooke, the first question at Second Quebec was the war in the Mediterranean and the campaign to follow on the success of the ANVIL landings in southern France. Until the last moment, the prime minister had resisted ANVIL. As late as August 9, just six days before the assault, Churchill had stormed about 10 Downing Street, railing that the United States was bullying Great Britain rather than acting as an equal partner. ANVIL, which Churchill had slyly renamed DRA-

GOON lest the name reveal the purpose of the landings, was wrong-headed, he insisted.

Churchill was never quite candid about the "soft underbelly," denying the difficulties of fighting in mountainous terrain, denying he wanted to put troops into the Balkans when that was precisely his intent. "Good God," he raged during a bedroom conference in early August, "can't you see that the Russians are spreading across Europe like a tide; they have invaded Poland, and there is nothing to prevent them from marching into Turkey and Greece!" In the face of that, ANVIL-DRAGOON was "sheer folly."

Despite Churchill, DRAGOON had gone forward. Under the command of Lieutenant General Alexander M. Patch, French and American troops had landed in the Cannes-Toulon area on August 15, forcing a bridgehead fifty-miles long on the first day. A week after the landings, Bordeaux fell; in another week, Marseilles and Toulon were in Allied hands. With them, Eisenhower had gained the port capacity necessary to supply his ammunition- and gasoline-short armies. By the time the Combined Chiefs of Staff gathered in Quebec, Marshall, the principal exponent of ANVIL, had been vindicated.

With DRAGOON safely launched, Marshall could afford to be magnanimous even when Field Marshal Alan Brooke came to the Château Frontenac urging the advantages of attacking Trieste and the Istrian peninsula. "It had not only a military value but also political value in view of the Russian advances in the Balkans," Brooke argued.

Without acknowledging Brooke's political argument, Marshall tacitly concurred. If not used in France, the six American divisions left in Italy might drive northeastward, around the base of the Alps, toward Vienna. In any event, they would not be withdrawn until the Germans had given up in Italy, Marshall promised.

The second big issue for the British delegation at Quebec involved securing American agreement to Great Britain's participation in the Pacific War. The issue was crucial to Churchill, who had vowed to restore the Empire.

The British had suffered considerable loss of prestige with the stunning defeats of 1941. Recovering and holding former colonies stretching from India to the South Pacific required that Great Britain refurbish its tarnished prestige. "We had to regain on the field of battle our rightful possessions in the Far East, and not have them handed back to us at the peace table."

At the first plenary meeting on September 13, Churchill immediately raised the subject. He firmly opposed any plan to bypass Singapore. Despite the fact that that fortress no longer held strategic value, it was "a great prize"—for the postwar Empire if not for the immediate defeat of Japan. Its recapture would avenge the humiliating surrender of 1942.

However much Marshall and his planners were pleased to have the British fighting in the Pacific theater, an emerging Roosevelt foreign policy would limit the employment of troops from the prewar colonial powers. American military planners "were trying to avoid the colonial thing throughout," Marshall recalled. The United States was not to recapture former colonies for the British, French, and Dutch. "I heard the president say that the French had made such a mess of Indo-China they ought not get any of it back."

The president's seemingly off-handed comment was as policy. To the end of the war, the chief of staff adamantly refused to use American troops solely for political ends. He also used his not-for-attribution press briefings to prompt public reassurances of that policy. As influential radio commentator Raymond Gram Swing noted in a nationwide broadcast privately inspired by Marshall, "We are not going to spend American lives and treasure in freeing imperial possessions from the Japanese and then turn them back to their prewar owners. . . . We see it as our assignment to bear the responsibility of defeating Japan and that we are prepared to do by ourselves."

Still Churchill pressed Marshall for a significant role in the Pacific. Army planners countered with a suggestion that the best use of British land forces was in northern India and Burma.

India and Burma would not suit Churchill. Drained by the need to garrison a restive India, Great Britain lacked the military manpower necessary to wage war on the Asian mainland—where there was little to be gained. The last of Britain's reserves had gone into combat the month before in Normandy. There would be no more, as Churchill acknowledged in a letter to Roosevelt. New levies would be sufficient only to replace casualties from this point on.

After six years of war, the prime minister stated in his opening remarks at Quebec, "The British empire effort in Europe, counted in terms of divisions in the field, was about equal to that of the United States. This was as it should be. He was proud that the British empire could claim equal partnership with their greatest ally, the United States, whom he regarded as the greatest military power in the world. The British empire effort had now reached its peak, whereas that of their ally was ever-increasing."

Short of divisions, Churchill instead offered the British battle fleet against the Japanese, to sail under an American commander. Behind Churchill's offer steamed the shadow of a much smaller Dutch fleet, for the exiled government of the Netherlands was equally intent on reclaiming its lost colonies in Dutch East Asia. Similarly, de Gaulle's Provisional Government of the French Republic, with British backing, had asked for an equivalent role in Indochina, and Portugal sought to recover Timor.

All but convinced that Japan could be defeated by a naval blockade alone, thus giving his navy the lion's share of the glory, Admiral King wanted no part of Churchill's proposal. The president, however, promptly accepted the British offer.

How would the British fleet be employed, Churchill pressed.

"My thought is to use it in any way possible," the president replied.

Admiral King tried to evade the problem. "The question was being actively studied."

The prime minister asked if it would not be better to replace battle-worn American vessels with new British ships.

Speaking for himself, the furious Admiral King could only say the matter was under examination.

"The offer of the British fleet has been made. Is it accepted?" Churchill pointedly asked the president.

"Yes," Roosevelt replied.

"Will you also let the British air force take part in the main operations," Churchill asked.

Arnold no less than King bridled. Air force planners now talked confidently of bombing Japan into submission; why should they share limited airfields, targets, and credit with the British?

Marshall immediately stepped in as conciliator. "Not so long ago we were crying for planes. Now we have a glut." Would not the British need their air forces in Southeast Asia and Malaya, he asked.

Once more Churchill spoke sweetly. "For the sake of good relations, on which so much depended in the future, it was of vital importance that the British should be given their fair share of the main operations against Japan. The United States had given us the most handsome assistance in the fight against Germany. It was only to be expected that the British Empire in return would give the United States all the help in their power towards defeating Japan."

Marshall and Arnold avoided direct response during the conference, pleading they lacked airfields. Hap Arnold suggested they would be lucky to transfer 1,500 of the 3,500 bombers in the European Theater of Operations. Marshall and Arnold sought to buy time, asking the British to furnish dates their long-range bombers could be available after the fall of Germany.

That evening, the American Joint Chiefs proved they were capable of quick decision—at least when it was in the best interest of the United States. The result was one of the pivotal decisions governing the Pacific War.

In the midst of a formal dinner sponsored by their Canadian hosts, the Joint Chiefs received copies of radiograms exchanged by Admirals Halsey and Nimitz earlier that day. Halsey reported his Third Fleet had mounted raids against the Carolines, Palaus, and the Philippines over the past three weeks, scaring up light opposition. The situation was "staggering, the lack of resistance amazing and fantastic," he wrote in his war diary. With an opportunistic eye, Halsey recommended canceling three preliminary assaults and striking directly at the heart of the Philippine archipelago, Leyte. Japanese aircraft were so few his carriers alone could support the landings, without the need for land-based planes flying from the southern anchor of the Philippines, Mindanao.

Nimitz responded with an offer to shift to MacArthur's command for use in the Philippines an amphibious fleet loading in Hawaii at that moment for an attack on Yap, the westernmost of the Caroline Islands. MacArthur's headquarters quickly accepted.

That exchange of cables was delivered to the Joint Chiefs during dinner in the Château Frontenac. The four American chiefs excused themselves from the table to huddle in an adjacent room for a brief conference. As Marshall noted in his final war report, it was not a difficult decision to make, though they were sharply redirecting the course of the war in the Pacific. The Carolines invasion was abandoned, so too an assault on Mindanao. Instead, MacArthur was to attack Leyte on October 20, accelerating the Pacific timetable by two months. Within ninety minutes of the cables' arrival in Quebec, the Pacific commanders had new orders in hand.

This dinner-table decision effectively ended any thought of bypassing the most important of the Philippine Islands, Luzon, with its capital city, Manila. Leyte would provide all the airfields they would need for an assault on the bigger island of Luzon. MacArthur would redeem his honor. Luzon's capture, in turn, would make unnecessary any invasion of the much tougher Formosa that Ernest King had so prized. (Aircraft on Luzon could interdict any Japanese fleet in the South China Sea.)

Each decision affected the next. The resolve to bypass Formosa had grave implications for their China policy, rendering negligible the forward Chinese air bases from which they had planned to bomb Formosa. Developments in the Pacific had also rendered the war in China militarily unimportant, however largely China figured in President Roosevelt's plans for a postwar organization of the United Nations.

Coincidentally, on September 16 Joe Stilwell radioed from Chungking a message detailing the deteriorating situation in eastern China. The generalissimo, despite his promise, refused to give Stilwell operational command of his armies. Instead, Chiang withdrew his armies as the Japanese advanced.

Three Japanese drives had swept the entire coastline of Chiang Kai-shek's troops, had opened a land corridor from Hanoi in Indochina to Peking and, most ominously, had captured an air base within range of Kunming's crucial supply depots for the Hump flights. Constantly retreating, the poorly led bulk of Chiang's troops had lost the will to fight. When they marched beyond their home province, they favored plunder of the peasants rather than fighting the disciplined Japanese.

The situation fast crumbling, Chiang and Flying Tiger commander Claire Chennault—who had assured Washington he could defend the lost bases with aircraft alone—urgently called for increased supply shipments. Even with those supplies, Chiang intended to withdraw; he would not use his troops in northern Burma to open the Ledo Road, the generalissimo informed Washington.

Provoked by Stilwell, the War Department drafted a hectoring message to Chiang. Marshall, who normally would have deleted the sharpest criticisms, instead forwarded the paper to President Roosevelt for his signature—a suggestion of the chief of staff's anger at Chiang's inaction. The message warned, in undiplomatically strong terms, that if the generalissimo refused to cooperate with Mountbatten in opening the land line to Burma, he would have to "accept the consequences and assume the personal responsibility."

The message recommended that to avert calamity, Chiang place his armies directly under Stilwell's command. That move would "fortify us in our decision and in the continued efforts the Unites States proposes to take to maintain and increase our aid to you."

To a delighted Stilwell fell the task of delivering the president's rebuke to Chiang two days after the OCTAGON conference ended. "The harpoon hit the little bugger right in the solar plexus and went right through him," Stilwell confided in his diary.

The Chinese puzzle set aside for the moment, OCTAGON ran its relatively placid way, largely devoted to Churchill's fear of the political dangers of divergence between the Allies. Marshall's draft of a statement to be released to the press by the president and prime minister at conference end noted, "[T]he only difficulty encountered at the Conference was the problem of providing employment for all the Allied forces who were eager to participate in the war against Japan. The difficulty had arisen as a result of the keenness of the competition to employ the maximum possible forces for the defeat of Japan."

Marshall the emerging diplomat assumed a new moral leadership at Second Quebec. The growing preponderance of American troops in the field would be matched by waxing American influence on the course of the war. That, Churchill feared, would warp the postwar world. "In Washington especially longer and wider views should have prevailed," he lamented.

Those views were longer than the prime minister realized. In July 1944, the Joint Chiefs of Staff forwarded to the secretary of state their confidential projection of the peace to come. Germany and Japan would be defeated, leaving the United States and the Soviet Union "the only military powers of the first magnitude." Because of their relative strength and geographic positions, neither could defeat the other, even if Great

Britain threw in with the United States. The British Empire, the Joint Chiefs predicted, "will emerge from the war having lost ground both economically and militarily." The United States would necessarily carry larger responsibilities in the postwar world.

George Marshall in this summer and fall of bright prospects found himself caught up with those responsibilities, and with them widening geopolitical concerns. He used one of his off-the-record press briefings to warn of the "follies of irresponsible criticism of Great Britain, stories which he said could only have a bad effect on morale of American soldiers fighting with their British allies." Congressmen and editors alike should avoid criticisms of Britain's relations with Ireland, of its refusal to immediately create a Jewish homeland in Palestine, and of Mountbatten's rumored failure to cooperate with Stilwell in China. At the urging of this man of "unrivaled reputation," the stories quickly died.

While Marshall accepted his role as a diplomat, domestic politics, especially the partisan jockeying that was the stuff of Washington life, vexed him. The irritation was all that much greater when Marshall found himself diverted by political matters from the business of winning the war.

If he had not dismissed it as a partisan thrust at President Roosevent, the chief of staff might have paid attention sooner to an undercurrent of unrest about the attack on Pearl Harbor two and a half years earlier. Memories of that debacle lurked still in Washington, even if Marshall himself considered the raid "water over the dam." There was nothing he could do now about the attack; there was a war to be won and fixing responsibility for the Pearl Harbor debacle a distraction from that task.

Others were not so single-minded. In late 1943, a number of Republicans—joined by anti-Roosevelt Democrats—began agitating for an open investigation of the December 7 attack. They hoped to pin blame or at least a charge of a cover-up on the president, and thereby embarass him prior to the November 1944 elections. Even inconclusive investigation of the December 7 attack would muddy the waters. The GOP would gain in either case.

The two commanders at Pearl Harbor, Rear Admiral Husband E. Kimmel and Lieutenant General Walter C. Short, had unwillingly retired from active duty in the wake of the attack. Marshall and Stimson had hoped that would settle the matter, but President Roosevelt insisted public opinion demanded more. The president proposed that the two officers request courts-martial, those trials to be held sometime after the war.

There the matter rested uneasily until the anti-Roosevelt coalition grasped at it late in 1943. Republican Senator Homer Ferguson of Michigan pushed a bill through Congress that would lift a two-year statute of limitations on courts-martial offenses and compel both the Army and Navy to secretly reinvestigate events surrounding the surprise attack.

The reinvestigations were to be held *in camera,* and nothing of the still vital MAGIC intelligence was to go on the record. Marshall and King feared that closely held secret would otherwise leak. Within that stricture Marshall sought to be fair, both to the concept of a thorough investigation and to the intimidated, futile General Short. "I gave no instructions about the army inquiry except that there must be no friend of mine on the board," Marshall acknowledged later.

There were none. Indeed, all three members of the board may have nursed a dislike of the chief of staff, one of the board's staff members noted. The president of the board, Lieutenant General George Grunert, had been relieved of a command at Marshall's insistence. A second member had been denied a lieutenant general's star, and a third had been replaced as commander of a regiment going overseas; both blamed Marshall. The three men selected had been tapped for the assignment merely because they were available, Marshall dryly explained.

From July through September both the army board and the parallel navy court of inquiry took testimony from the principal actors. During an off-the-record session on the first day of the army board's hearings, Marshall personally briefed the three members of the board about MAGIC. Because the Japanese still had not tumbled to the fact that their diplomatic, naval, and military codes had been cracked, radio intercepts continued to yield valuable intelligence, Marshall told the three-member panel.

Whether by his order or by the board's ruling, no hint of MAGIC entered the record. That would eventually lend an Alice in Wonderland touch to the proceedings. To provide an adequate defense, General Short's military counsel was permitted to view certain MAGIC materials during the course of the hearings, but not to discuss them with his client. Yet it was the scapegoat Short who most stood to gain from the knowledge.

Marshall's testimony before the army board was unstudied and matter-of-fact. When he could not remember details, he said as much, even when this hinted at his own failings. He made no effort to defend his actions in the days leading up to the attack, other than to say he believed Short had been adequately warned. "I feel that General Short was given a command instruction to put his command on the alert against a possible hostile attack by the Japanese. The command was not so alerted," he testified.

As the two service inquiries plodded on into September and October, Republicans in Congress picked up the issue of America's preparedness for war three years before. On the floor of the House on September 11, Representative Hugh Scott of Pennsylvania asked a series of penetrating, if rhetorical, questions about the Pearl Harbor attack. In particular Scott demanded, in the manner of outraged politicians, to know why the first investigation of the attack had blamed only Admiral Kimmel and

General Short, but turned a blind eye to possible culpability in Washington. GOP vice-presidential nominee John Bricker followed with an accusation that the White House was covering up details about "the disgraceful Pearl Harbor episode."

The White House was not. Marshall and King were.

For the past four years they had guarded MAGIC, their most closely held operational secret. Despite a widening circle of those with a "need to know"—some 16,000 were actively engaged in decoding Axis radio messages—despite cocktail party gossip in Washington, the secret had held. Any full-blown investigation of the Pearl Harbor attack ultimately threatened that unmatched source of information.

In a campaign speech on September 25, the Republican presidential nominee, New York Governor Thomas Dewey, blamed President Roosevelt for the nation's lack of preparedness at the outbreak of the war. "The simple truth is, of course, that my opponent's record is desperately bad. The price the American people have had to pay for that record is desperately high. This is not a record on which any man should seek the confidence of the American people."

Something about the tenor of Dewey's recent speeches or perhaps a shrill quality that had seeped into the Republican campaign disturbed Marshall. The campaign seemed to be growing more venomous as the Republicans lost ground. Dewey, who had begun with an assertion that the conduct of the war was not a partisan issue, now charged that MacArthur had been deprived of men and materiel in the Pacific because the general was a political threat to President Roosevelt.

Marshall was concerned with the campaign's direction. He had learned earlier that someone in the War or Navy Department—just who was never revealed—had informed Dewey's campaign advisers about MAGIC and the fact that Washington had advance warning that war was likely. Marshall believed Dewey planned to use that information publicly. If he did, he might turn the political tide, but he would simultaneously destroy the nation's most valuable source of military intelligence. Discussing it only with Admiral King, Marshall moved to stop Dewey's ploy.

The chief of staff did not know the Republican nominee well. Dewey, a former prosecutor, had publicly questioned Marshall and King about the course of the war at the National Governors Convention earlier in the year. Dewey's questions had been on point, the candidate demonstrating how much he knew about the conduct of the war, the two chiefs agreed; the session had been grueling. Since then, Dewey had talked to Marshall on the telephone, but if Marshall was aloof by nature, Dewey was personally stiff and formal. Between governor and chief of staff was no more than a formal acquaintance.

Unable to meet the governor in person without provoking questions from the press, the chief of staff dispatched a messenger in civilian clothes bearing a top secret letter "For Mr. Dewey's Eyes Only." The bearer, Colonel Carter W. Clarke of the Army's intelligence office, intercepted the Republican candidate in Tulsa on September 26, 1944.

Dewey was wary. He laid down the letter after reading the first two paragraphs, which asked him to read no further unless he agreed to keep its contents secret. Dewey "did not want his lips sealed on things that he already knew about Pearl Harbor, about facts already in his possession. . . ." Would Clarke care to discuss the matter with him? Clarke demurred; he had no such authority.

Curious yet suspicious, Dewey said he doubted Marshall, without presidential authority, would approach an opposition candidate. "Marshall does not do things like that. I am confident that Franklin Roosevelt is behind this whole thing."

Furthermore, the governor added, if the letter merely told him that the United States was reading Japanese codes and at least two were still in use, there was no point in his reading further. "Well, I know it, and Franklin Roosevelt knows all about it. He knew what was happening before Pearl Harbor and instead of being reelected he ought to be impeached." Dewey abruptly handed back Marshall's letter unread, offering to discuss the matter further when he returned to Albany in two days.

In Washington, Marshall relaxed the ground rules and sent Clarke to Albany for a second meeting. Dewey now insisted on a witness, "as he might later be charged with reading a letter different from the one he had really read." Dewey wriggled here and there, but knew he was caught. If he revealed, if he even hinted the United States had been reading the Japanese codes, he would leave himself open to charges of prolonging the war, of costing the lives of American boys. He could even guess that an outraged chief of staff, a man so avowedly apolitical that he did not even vote, would make the damning charge himself.

Roosevelt, according to Dewey, was "a traitor who had willingly or accidentally condemned more than a thousand American men, and most of the Pacific fleet, to a watery grave."

His rage could change nothing. The chief of staff had him check and mate. MAGIC remained a secret.

The final report of the army inquiry into the Pearl Harbor attack would not be as adroitly finessed. Delivered to Secretary of War Stimson on November 11, four days after President Roosevelt was reelected to a fourth term, the secret report laid the extent of the Pearl Harbor disaster primarily to two causes: Short's failure adequately to alert the garrison; and the War Department's "failure to keep him [Short] adequately informed as to the developments of the United States-Japanese negotiations, which in turn might have caused him to change from the inadequate alert to the adequate one."

The board's report criticized three officers: Short; Leonard "Gee" Gerow, at the time of Pearl Harbor the deputy chief of staff for War Plans in Washington; and the chief of staff himself. Marshall, the board concluded, had failed to keep his deputies fully informed. In the board's opinion, the chief of staff had also failed to keep Short abreast of negotiations with the Japanese and of "the probable outbreak of war at any time"—despite the alert of November 27. Furthermore, the panel concluded, Marshall had an "admitted lack of knowledge of the condition of readiness of the Hawaiian Command" after the alert was issued.

The secret report stung Marshall. For all the man's self-confidence and his aloofness, he too needed the approval of his colleagues. Now he was not only denied that token but criticized as well.

For three days, Marshall was despondent. A few months short of the mandatory retirement age of sixty-four, the chief of staff mulled immediate resignation. He told Stimson that "he thought his usefulness to the army had been destroyed by this board's report." Stimson impatiently waved aside Marshall's unspoken offer to step down. A fit of depression had temporarily affected his usually dependable judgment. Whether he acknowledged it or not, Marshall was "the one on whom the fate of the war depends."

The secretary of war favored immediate release of the army board's report, intending to couple it with a lawyerly vindication of the chief of staff. The president scotched that plan. At lunch at the White House on November 21, the president read the conclusion of the army report. When he came to the criticism of Marshall, Roosevelt muttered, "Why this is wicked. This is wicked."

Over lawyer Stimson's objections, Roosevelt insisted the separate army and navy reports be sealed. They might be opened after the war, if both Congress and the president approved.

The press releases issued by the Army and Navy spoke blandly of "errors of judgment," no more. Courts-martial were not indicated, Stimson and the new secretary of the navy, James Forrestal, said in separate statements.

Already infuriated by Roosevelt's reelection, Senator Ferguson lashed out. "How could it happen that our fleet could be sunk and our boys would be killed at Pearl Harbor without anyone's being to blame?" He demanded a full-dress Senate investigation, a probe Marshall feared might accidentally disclose the existence of MAGIC. Only White House agreement to cooperate in a postwar investigation deflected the Republican minority.

The attack on Pearl Harbor was to be a political time bomb ticking under Marshall's reputation through the rest of the war.

CHAPTER
XXVIII

The Winterkill

The winter would be long and harsh, a season of losses made the more bitter when compared to the succession of Allied victories in the first part of the year.

The setbacks began almost at the height of their success, on the day the OCTAGON conference closed. British General Bernard Montgomery on September 17, 1944, launched a three-division air drop in a daring attempt to turn the northern corner of the German lines in the Netherlands. Montgomery's plan, approved by Eisenhower, called for dropping parachute units to seize five successive bridges over canals and rivers, opening a way for a British armored corps to attack northward over the Rhine.

If the plan was bold, uncommonly so for the slow-footed Montgomery, it was also gravely flawed. Eisenhower, who might have modified the concept, instead ratified it. His approval was inspired in some measure by Marshall's continued advocacy of the highly trained paratroop divisions as a strike force. In addition, Eisenhower sought to mollify Montgomery with an opportunity to garner the sort of headlines that had heralded George Patton's dash across France the month before.

This time the Allies overreached themselves. Inadequate intelligence underreported the German defenders whose fierce counterattacks blunted MARKET-GARDEN from the first day. By September 25, Montgomery had acknowledged defeat and ordered the surviving paratroopers on the northern bank of the Rhine at Arnhem to withdraw. In all, 17,000 British, American, and Polish troops were casualties, more than the Allies had lost on D-Day.

Meanwhile, Patton's Third Army had rolled up against seventy-year-old forts in the vicinity of Metz, bogging down as supplies grew short and the weather worsened. Patton the armored commander found his infantrymen ensnared in a static battle, prying defenders from house to house through October. On Patton's right the southernmost of the American armies under Jacob Devers slogged into the Vosges Mountains, its pell-mell charge north from Marseilles now a muddy crawl. On Patton's left the American First Army under Courtney Hodges halted hard against the fortified *Westwall* near Aachen.

The crucial problem for Eisenhower's armies was supply. Artillery ammunition was rationed, and the gasoline stocks had dwindled to a two-day supply, all because of inadequate port facilities. A file of cargo vessels stood off the Normandy coast, waiting for a dock to open in one of the smaller Channel ports. The bottleneck was at its worst in early October, as Eisenhower's armies approached the 2.5 million mark; stevedores unloaded just one bottom while thirty-five other ships wallowed offshore for a week. The blockaded port at Antwerp grew ever more vital if Eisenhower's northern armies were to maintain pressure on the Germans.

Montgomery's troops had captured Antwerp with its port facilities intact on September 4, but bypassed German units still controlled the Scheldt estuary leading to the port.

Only with the failure of MARKET-GARDEN did Montgomery belatedly move to open the Channel. The first Allied convoy would not dock until November 28; by then winter was hard on the land and Eisenhower's offensive had frozen from the Netherlands to Switzerland.

At Eisenhower's request, the chief of staff flew to Europe on October 5 for a hasty inspection and search for a quick fix of their supply and manpower problems. Marshall was accompanied by former Senator and Supreme Court Associate Justice James Byrnes, now the director of war mobilization, and Thomas Handy, the assistant chief of staff for operations. Their presence was a token of the chief of staff's concern.

Marshall still exuded a sense of optimism when he arrived at Eisenhower's headquarters at the stone-cold Trianon Palace Hotel in Versailles. "It was apparent from the chief of staff's opening conversations that the chill which had caused us to revise our rosy September estimates on the end of the war had not yet filtered through to Washington and the War Department," Omar Bradley recalled. Later Bradley sought to temper Marshall's optimistic outlook; "I made it quite clear that the war could not be brought to an end by Christmas."

Marshall and Eisenhower privately discussed a number of incipient problems: repeated British urgings that a ground commander be named to coordinate the land battle; the shortages of ammunition, which had them flying artillery shells to Europe; and the fast-dwindling reserve of divisions training in the United States. (Only two remained to be assigned to a theater of war; after that, they would be training only replacements for casualties.)

Marshall remained confident. He was "like a breath of fresh air and, beyond doubt, his visit lifted our spirits and lent impetus to our planning for a November offensive," Bradley wrote.

The chief of staff was fulfilling the good commander's first obligation—to maintain morale. In fact, he had serious reservations about Bradley's new offensive to cross the Rhine. "I didn't see how he was going to do it myself."

Marshall and Bradley flew on to Montgomery's headquarters in Brussels on October 8, where the British commander insisted on a private conversation with the American chief of staff. As Montgomery recalled it, "I told him that since Eisenhower had himself taken personal command of the land battle . . . the armies had become separated nationally and not geographically." Careless of Marshall's reaction, Montgomery complained, "There was a lack of grip, and operational direction and control were lacking. Our operations had, in fact, become ragged and disjointed, and we had now got ourselves into a real mess."

Marshall was furious. "I came pretty near to blowing off out of turn," he recalled. The compulsion was to "whittle him down. And then I thought, now this is Eisenhower's business and not mine, and I had better not meddle, though it was very hard for me to restrain myself because I didn't think there was any logic in what he said but overwhelming egotism."

That afternoon the chief of staff discovered yet another rift in the coalition he had so painstakingly built. At Jacob Devers's army headquarters in eastern France, French General Jean de Lattre de Tassigny complained to Marshall about American corps commander Lucian Truscott. According to the hot-tempered de Lattre, Truscott had gotten the lion's share of the supplies, especially gasoline, and with it the lion's share of the victories. Aware of the French and American reporters listening with pencils poised, Marshall abruptly walked out of the meeting. It was shabby behavior for an Allied commander, Marshall thought. As he later explained to de Lattre, "You didn't have a leg to stand on. You celebrated all the way up the road. You were late on every damn thing and . . . you are critical of Truscott who is a fighter and not a talker."

During the next two days Marshall zigzagged northward through the cold rain, visiting corps and division headquarters, traveling once more over the embattled hills he first saw in the 1917–18 war. On the 11th he rode in an armored car across the German border near Aachen, savoring their impending victory until Bradley, fearing snipers, called a halt. The next day he visited a succession of corps and division headquarters. Many, most of the officers he met on this trip owed their commands to the sober man who had once hoped to lead them in the field. He was not their commander, but they were *his* army.

In all, he visited five army, eight corps, and sixteen division headquarters, and shook hands with the commanders and staffs of eight other divisions. As his biographer Forrest Pogue noted, Marshall reached out to the fighting men more on this trip than at any other time during the war. And always he had questions of the commanders. How was the winter clothing? What about the condition of their men? How about their morale? Were the new boots any good; why were they experiencing high rates of trench foot?

Marshall pointedly communicated his concern for the well-being of the line troops to Eisenhower. Remembering his own experiences with the mud of France during the first war, the chief of staff suggested that commanders take road trips with no visible signs of rank on their vehicles. Without preferential treatment, they would "find out for themselves what conditions actually are and take proper steps for correction of defects."

Though too busy to visit Madame Jouatte, his landlady from the first war, the chief of staff instructed Patton to see she was provided with supplies. Meanwhile he promised his commanders to tell their wives and families that he had seen them and to carry home personal greetings.

A week after landing at Le Bourget outside Paris, Marshall, Handy, and Byrnes were airborne once more for the United States. Between them, they had gained a clearer idea of the supply situation and an incipient manpower shortage. Byrnes had also come away convinced they could not yet give over to civilian production, no matter how politically popular that might be.

Marshall once more became the reproving father. On his return to the United States he pressed for even more war production. In a message to the Congress of Industrial Organizations convention, the chief of staff cautioned, "The very speed of our advance has created new production problems that demand herculean effort on the part of all our people in the months ahead." Specifically his armies needed more artillery and mortar ammunition, more tanks, more heavy trucks. "Every hour of delay means hundreds of lives and millions of money. A prodigious effort is being made by our Army. An equally prodigious effort must be made here at home."

Well into December, Marshall continued to stress the need for increased production, offering a cautionary lecture to a writer for *The New York Times Magazine:* "We have a stern duty here at home. There must be no let-up in our efforts. We must remember that the individual soldier will attach just as much importance to his life in the final week of this struggle as he does today, and if he feels that he is not being protected by the proper covering fire of bombs and artillery he will naturally blame the folks back home. And I don't think the folks at home want to have that blame rest on them."

The public clamor for conversion was premature. The war in Europe was not yet won, however optimistic things appeared. Following a strategic plan conceived in 1942 by Marshall and the War Plans Division, Eisenhower had mounted a broad campaign to close the Rhine. In launching multiple attacks toward that last water barrier to Germany, Eisenhower was setting up a grand double envelopment or pincers movement on the Ruhr Valley and its vital heavy industries.

In the south, Devers's French and American armies punctured German defenses and reached the Rhine, capturing Strasbourg. Amid the worst rains in fifty years, Patton's army took Metz, then clawed its way to the foot of the Siegfried Line. North of that city, however, the advances were meager; in alternating rain and snow storms, the American First and Ninth Armies managed to dig in on the frozen west bank of the Roer River. British efforts to reach the Rhine in the Netherlands were costly and slow going, Montgomery complaining he required a larger share of the available materiel.

In the East, the Russians too were stalled, their advance echelons dug into the rubble of Warsaw's eastern suburbs. Despite an uprising by the Polish underground army, embattled Warsaw would not fall until mid-January. Squeezed between Eastern and Western Fronts, battered at home by daily bombing raids, Germany still showed surprising resilience; the war in Europe would surely continue through the spring.

Marshall's worst fear had come to pass: they were locked in something like World War I's trench warfare, dogged by bad weather and hampered by supply shortages. The key was Antwerp; to mount an assault without first opening that port "would be to court failure," British planners warned.

The slowing of the war in Europe complicated Marshall's job considerably. Each success in the Pacific brought pressure on him to send even more resources to those theaters. On October 23, three days after Douglas MacArthur returned to the Philippines accompanied by a wave of exultant headlines, Marshall cabled Eisenhower to ask his opinion about ending the war in Europe before the new year. "Be frank with me," Marshall urged in concluding his message. "I will accept your decision."

Eisenhower could see no quick end to the war unless German morale collapsed. To undermine that will to resist, he recommended that the Allies modify their policy of unconditional surrender. Marshall forwarded Eisenhower's proposal to the White House, accompanying it with the draft of a conciliatory public announcement the Allies might use.

According to Omar Bradley, a weak and ailing President Roosevelt "now deferred almost completely to Marshall on military decisions involving our land forces on the Continent." True or not, it was some measure of Marshall's influence in the White House that the president, who had refused to compromise the unconditional surrender policy before, immediately adopted the proposal.

There it died. A statement now would appear as a sign of weakness, not generosity, Churchill replied. The Germans were not afraid of the treatment they might get from the British or Americans. "What they are afraid of is a Russian occupation, and a large proportion of their people being taken off to toil to death in Russia, or as they say, Siberia. Nothing that we can say will eradicate this deep seated fear."

Military questions Marshall might decide; political ones the president still reserved to himself. So it was that Marshall in mid-October confronted a personally distasteful task, the removal of a worthy officer for political reasons.

Frustrated by a succession of lost opportunities, Joseph Stilwell had asked Washington for an ultimatum to force Chiang Kai-shek into action. The result had been the Quebec harpoon. But Stilwell the soldier had miscalculated two factors. He had underestimated the generalissimo's canny instinct for survival, and he had ignored President Roosevelt's desire to have China raised to symbolic big power status in the postwar world.

A month after Quebec, Chiang extended a counteroffer to President Roosevelt. "Your policies will be executed without delay as soon as you relieve Stilwell and replace him with an officer better equipped to discharge his duties," the generalissimo promised.

Generals were more readily replaced than national leaders. President Roosevelt determined Stilwell would have to go.

Marshall defended his old friend as best he could in a meeting with the president at the White House on October 16. Always Stilwell's staunchest ally, the chief of staff was himself irritated at Chiang. The Chinese leader had no intention of fighting, believing the advance across the Pacific would spare him further effort, and leave him well enough armed to confront the Communists after the war. The generalissimo's backing and filling "betrayed me down the river," the chief of staff confided some years later.

But for Marshall and Secretary of War Stimson, every man's hand was turned against the too-blunt Stilwell: Roosevelt's ambassador, the back-slapping Patrick Hurley; Air Force General Claire Chennault; even British Chief of the Imperial General Staff Brooke had all urged Stilwell's replacement. "George C. Marshall continues to back me and if he didn't I would have tossed in my hand long ago," Stilwell wrote in his diary as early as November 1942.

For two years Marshall and Stimson had stayed the executioner's hand, convinced that if Stilwell were replaced, China's predicament would worsen. But their Pacific successes canceled any major role for China in the war against Japan. Thus there was no longer any military reason to keep Stilwell, the fighting general, in China.

That nation, however, figured still in Roosevelt's concept of a postwar United Nations organization. The president wanted Chiang confirmed in reputation if not in deed, and China elevated to the titular status of a major power. Stilwell the nettle would have to be plucked.

The ax fell, as Stilwell himself put it, on the afternoon of October 18. It was a mark of Marshall's personal concern for his old friend that he radioed Stilwell a "flash to prepare you for what now appears to be inevitable." Two and a quarter hours later, Marshall sent a second message informing Stilwell that the president had decided to recall him.

Stung, Stilwell left China and the Chinese people whom he so deeply admired without waiting to brief his successor, former War Department planner Albert C. Wedemeyer. He left under orders from the chief of staff that "if questioned, merely state that you have been ordered home and make no, repeat, no other statement or comment." Marshall wanted no inflammatory remarks from the outspoken Stilwell in the last days before the presidential election.

In fact, Marshall's warning came too late. Alerted that he would be soon removed, Stilwell had called in two reporters, Theodore White of *Time* magazine and Brooks Atkinson of *The New York Times,* and discussed the long file of cables leading to his dismissal. Stilwell's candor stunned White. "He wanted us to know, in the historian's phrase, 'the way it really was.'"

Atkinson's story on the front page of *The New York Times* described Chiang as "bewildered and alarmed by the rapidity with which China is falling apart." Casting aside the news reporter's usual stance of neutral objectivity, Atkinson continued:

> The decision to relieve General Stilwell represents the political triumph of a moribund, anti-democratic regime that is more concerned with maintaining its political supremacy than in driving the Japanese out of China. America is now committed . . . to support a regime that has become increasingly unpopular and distrusted in China, that maintains three secret police services and concentration camps for political prisoners, that stifles free speech and resists democratic forces.

White's equally scathing report never appeared. With the approval of publisher Henry R. Luce, *Time* instead ran a tendentious cover story critical of Stilwell's inability to get along with the generalissimo, and scoring the administration for what it termed inept handling of the China issue. *Time*'s story, the disillusioned White wrote later, was "so fanciful, so violently pro-Chiang Kai-shek that it could only mislead American opinion. . . ." Stilwell had begun a foreign policy dispute that would rage for almost three decades and destroy along the way scores of careers and reputations.

Marshall would suffer a second loss that month, a loss both personal and professional: the death of Jack Dill.

The field marshal had been slow to recover from the hernia operation a year earlier. His pernicious anemia resisted treatment, draining his strength even more. After the Quebec Conference, Marshall had arranged for Dill to stay at the army hospital in Hot Springs with Marshall's aide acting as nanny. But Dill's condition worsened and he was transferred hurriedly to Walter Reed Hospital.

The army doctors could do nothing; Dill slipped into a coma on November 2. Marshall paid a farewell visit to his friend the following afternoon, as Stilwell's plane was landing at National Airport. Field Marshal Sir John Dill died the same day.

Marshall felt Dill's death keenly. It was "a cruel blow to my husband," Katherine Marshall wrote, the chief of staff grieving the loss of "a close friend whom he admired and loved. . . ."

For Jack Dill as well, their friendship had meant much. "He really loved you, George," Lady Dill wrote Marshall "and your mutual affection meant a great deal to him. . . ." In the three years since coming to Washington, Dill had joined the small circle of men close to the chief of staff. Their relationship, as Marshall explained later, involved "a very intimate understanding of each other," founded on a trust possibly unique between international diplomats.

Early in his stay in Washington, Dill discovered that the president and prime minister often exchanged messages without Marshall's knowledge of the contents, though the letters might impact on military affairs. Through British channels, however, Dill would routinely get copies of those messages that concerned military affairs. "Then Dill would come over to my office, and I would get Mr. Roosevelt's message through Field Marshal Sir John Dill. Otherwise I wouldn't know what it was," Marshall recalled.

Marshall kept their arrangement secret. "I had to be very careful that nobody knew this—no one in the War Department—and certainly not the [British] Chiefs of Staff, because Dill would be destroyed in a minute if this was discovered."

Similarly, when the prime minister radioed the president, Dill made certain that Marshall knew of pertinent messages. It was unorthodox, but necessary, a way of circumventing what Marshall described as the president's penchant for secrecy about his conduct of government.

From such mutual trust had grown the deepest of friendships between the two men. To honor that friendship and the man himself, Marshall found a way around the regulation barring the burial of foreign soldiers in Arlington National Cemetery and fulfilled Dill's desire to be interred there. Marshall also personally arranged the military funeral and the solemn tribute of flying the American flags in the capital at half-mast the day of the burial.

A man who held his emotions tightly bound, Marshall vented his deep grief in a continuing series of acts honoring his friend. He persuaded Congress to pass a resolution of appreciation for Dill's efforts as chief of the British military mission. He wrote Churchill, who had considered removing Dill earlier that year, "Few will ever realize the debt our countries owe him for his unique and profound influence toward the cooperation of our forces. To be very frank and personal, I doubt if you or your cabinet associates fully realize the loss you have suffered and the U.S. also has suffered for that matter, in purely postwar adjustments, by his death."*

Marshall was to miss Dill keenly. The new representative of the Imperial General Staff in Washington, Field Marshal Sir Henry Maitland Wilson, could never take Dill's place—either in fact or in Marshall's heart. The former supreme commander in the Mediterranean, "Jumbo" Wilson was a Falstaffian figure, affable, an adroit diplomat, as good a choice as Churchill could have made. But Marshall could not welcome Wilson. ". . . Poor Wilson, quite evidently, was trying to imitate Dill with me, and I didn't rise to it very well, I'm afraid," Marshall acknowledged.

Just as tensions within the Allied coalition ratcheted tighter, the great friendship in Washington that might have eased the strain was no more. American and British friction would grow steadily in the last months of war.

For all of Marshall's influence, there were times when he could not control military matters in Washington. Despite his personal opposition, Congress in December 1944 approved a bill creating new five-star ranks for eight generals and admirals. In order of seniority, Leahy, Marshall, King, MacArthur, Nimitz, Eisenhower, Arnold, and "Bull" Halsey, named later, would hold ranks equivalent to field marshal.

The chief of staff had opposed the five-star rank when it was first proposed in November 1942 by Ernest King. Marshall disagreed with King's arguments that the individual service chiefs needed promotions in order to deal with the British. Even with fifth stars and a rank equivalent to field marshals, he and King would still be junior in seniority. Comparative rank, moreover, played no role in their dealings with the British; regardless of the number of stars they wore on their collars,

---

*As a last gesture, Marshall proposed that a lifesize equestrian statue of Dill be placed in Arlington, again circumventing regulations that banned statuary there. He helped to raise money for the bronze figure, and was there to see it dedicated in 1950. Dill's mounted figure sits eternally erect on the gently sloping hillside, looking over the graves toward the Potomac River, a friend's final tribute.

Marshall, King, and Leahy *were* the American chiefs, the men with whom the British had to deal.

The chief of staff had a second argument against the bill. "I didn't want to be beholden to Congress for any rank or anything of that kind. I wanted to be able to go in there with my skirts clean and with no personal ambitions concerned in it in any way, and I could get all I wanted with the rank I had."

As valid as those arguments might appear, Marshall had yet another reason to oppose the bill wending its way through Congress in mid-1944. Like other Pershing men, he knew that creation of five-star generals would dim the distinction of Pershing's unique title as general of the armies. Marshall wanted nothing to give offense to the ailing old soldier whose portrait hung in Marshall's office at the Pentagon.

Pressured by King and navy boosters in Congress, Roosevelt determined that his senior military commanders should have five stars. He easily persuaded Secretary of War Stimson, who secured Pershing's endorsement during a visit to the general at Walter Reed Hospital.

Marshall himself took no part in pushing the bill through Congress, contributing only the suggestion that the actual title to accompany this five-star rank be general of the army. That would leave Pershing still the only man to have been a general of the *armies*.

The rank was conferred on December 15, 1944, and celebrated in a toast to Marshall and Arnold at the Pentagon that afternoon.

At virtually the same time, Congress also acknowledged Marshall's pivotal role in prosecuting the war. The chief of staff would be sixty-four on the last day of the year, at the mandatory retirement age, unless it were waived. A bill that exempted Marshall from the Army's normal retirement age zipped through Congress.

These were to be Marshall's last moments of pleasure for a grim month. On December 16, 1944—the same day Eisenhower was notified of his promotion—two Panzer armies and supporting infantry units rumbled out of the thick ground fog to strike at a thinly defended portion of Allied lines in the Ardennes Forest of Belgium.

With a three-to-one superiority in men and a four-to-one advantage in tanks, the Panzer units led by ponderous Panther tanks staved in three American divisions, then burst into the rear. Hitler had gambled, his target not some short-range territorial gain but nothing less than the huge Allied stores and fuel dump at Liège, and the harbor at Antwerp that lay beyond. Were his two Panzer armies successful, they would drive a wedge between the British on the north and the Americans on the south. Perhaps, just perhaps, they could gain a stalemate in the West and sue for peace.

By the end of the first day, though neither side would know it for some time to come, Hitler's gamble had failed. American units on the northern edge of the attack bent, but held. Unable to open the gap wide, the Panzers were forced through a relatively small hole in the front, the angle of their attack deflected southward on the few available roads rather than westward.

The day following the attack, Eisenhower committed his reserve, sending armored divisions to the vital crossroads towns of St. Vith and Bastogne, and the 101st Airborne to Bastogne as well. Funneled south toward those two road junctions still in American hands, the German attack began to pile up.

At the same time, George Patton was organizing one of the more brilliant tactical maneuvers of the war, what his biographer termed "the sublime moment" of Patton's gaudy career. Well south of what Allied staff officers were now calling a bulge in the enemy lines, Patton's Third Army was attacking eastward, toward the Saar basin. In three days, he turned his army leftward, shifting his line of advance from east to north so as to strike at the left flank of the German attack. Patton's army was moving once more, a hound on the loose; the very size of the bulge made it a tempting, and vulnerable, target if they could lop it off at the base.

By December 20, Eisenhower had organized a defense that would turn a setback into a costly defeat for the dwindling Wehrmacht. Still, Eisenhower's battlefield decisions did not come rapidly enough to avert sharp criticism from the British. "Montgomery, Alan Brooke and Churchill all came at us like sharks at a shipwreck," Omar Bradley recalled.

Brooke had long disdained Eisenhower. The supreme commander, Brooke wrote in his diary on November 24, was "entirely detached and taking practically no part in the running of the war." Three days later he wrote, "Ike is incapable of running a land battle and it is all dependent on how well Monty can handle him. . . ." Brooke also sought to convince Churchill that "we must take the control out of Eisenhower's hands, and the best plan was to repeat what we did in Tunisia when we brought in Alex[ander] as deputy to Eisenhower to command the Land Forces for him."

Montgomery, who coveted that post of land commander, seized upon the Battle of the Bulge to argue for his elevation. Even as Eisenhower was ordering their counterattack, Montgomery was sending dark messages to London and SHAEF headquarters in Versailles, describing chaos at the front and panic in the American rear. Arguing that Bradley was not in control of the two American armies fighting on the northern shoulder of the Bulge, Montgomery proposed that he be appointed commander of all Allied forces north of the Bulge. In the meantime, he put his own units on the defensive, to await the Germans thirty miles from the point of their farthest advance.

Eisenhower's chief of staff, Walter Bedell Smith, agreed to Montgomery's command of the American units, and called Bradley. Bradley, in what he termed one of his biggest mistakes of the war, knuckled under. "Bedell, it's hard for me to object. Certainly if Monty's were an American command I would agreed with you entirely. It would be the logical thing to do."

Under pressure from his own staff, watching the German advance spread into his rear, Eisenhower agreed to a temporary command shift on the pretext that Bradley's communications with the northern sector were tenuous. The switch handed the British a political coup.

The German tide halted some eighteen miles from the Meuse and the waiting British units, the Panzers literally having run out of gas. In bitterly cold weather, the Germans began to withdraw, forced to swing around a Bastogne still held by the 101st Airborne, while Patton's attack from the south threatened to slice off the salient.

On December 22, with the issue still in doubt, Marshall sent Eisenhower Christmas greetings, praising him and concluding, "You have my complete confidence." Otherwise, Marshall held communications with Eisenhower to a minimum so as not to distract him during the battle. The president too remained calm. "Roosevelt didn't send a word to Eisenhower nor ask a question. In great stress Roosevelt was a strong man."

Eisenhower would hear from Marshall only with the crisis past, and the Panzer armies in retreat. Then it was to deal with a political issue.

The tide turning and Montgomery dropping pointed remarks to reporters, the British press took to portraying Montgomery as the man of the hour, the tactician who had saved the day. More than ever, the Battle of the Bulge had demonstrated the need for Montgomery as overall ground commander, London papers argued in editorials. (This was particularly galling to Bradley since Montgomery had ordered a retreat "to tidy up the lines." In defiance of the order, the aggressive American corps commander Joseph Collins ordered an armor division forward. The American 2nd Armored devastated the 2nd Panzer on December 25–26, draining the last strength from the German drive; still the cautious Montgomery refused to counterattack.)

Aware of the British news coverage and fearing a backlash in the equally chauvinistic American press, on December 30, Marshall cabled Eisenhower a fatherly admonition:

> My feeling is this: under no circumstances make any concessions of any kind whatsoever. You not only have our complete confidence but there would be a terrific resentment in this country following such action. I am not assuming that you had in mind such a concession. I just wish you to be certain of our attitude on this side. You are doing a fine job and go on and give them hell.

Supported by Marshall, Eisenhower took firm charge of the battle, realigning whole armies with decisive orders. Straightening out Montgomery would be harder.

The showdown came on the afternoon of December 30, with Marshall's warning cable in Eisenhower's pocket. Montgomery's chief of staff, Francis de Guingand, flew to Versailles to report that Montgomery would not attack the base of the salient on New Year's Day. Eisenhower was furious, insisting he had an earlier promise from Montgomery to launch a counterattack, that Montgomery's failure to attack would fritter away a golden opportunity to bag the exhausted Germans. Freddie de Guingand, diplomatic and well liked among the Americans, listened as Eisenhower pointed out that Bradley's position had become untenable, that Montgomery's comments to reporters threatened the confidence of Bradley's troops. "Monty himself had helped to create this crisis by his campaign for a land force commander," Eisenhower snapped.

Eisenhower then showed de Guingand a cable he was prepared to send to Marshall for delivery to the Combined Chiefs of Staff. The message was blunt: one of the two ranking Allied commanders on the Western Front, Eisenhower or Montgomery, would have to go.

De Guingand was stunned. He pleaded for a day's delay and time to talk to Montgomery. Eisenhower and his deputy supreme commander, British Air Marshal Arthur Tedder, relented only when Bedell Smith weighed in on de Guingand's behalf.

The diplomatic de Guingand, his usual affability rubbed raw by tension, flew to Montgomery's headquarters to explain to his disbelieving chief how tenuous his situation had become. Given the two-to-one preponderance of American over British troops, Montgomery would become expendable. The Combined Chiefs would be forced to side with Eisenhower.

Only when his chief of staff showed him a copy of Eisenhower's pending message to Marshall did Montgomery realize how close he was to professional suicide. Montgomery capitulated, sending a placating message to Eisenhower, and signing himself "Your very devoted subordinate, Monty."

The following day, Eisenhower dispatched new orders for Montgomery, rejecting his arguments in favor of a single powerful thrust into the Ruhr from his northern sector while the bulk of the American armies went on the defensive. Montgomery instead would return Bradley's First Army, temporarily retaining only the American Ninth Army. Eisenhower might have reassigned the Ninth as well but for a desire not to appear to be punishing Montgomery, and to avoid another draining battle with Churchill; Eisenhower acknowledged privately that "he was already exhausted in his struggle to block the British on overall ground command for Monty."

On that Eisenhower would not yield, he affirmed in his letter to Montgomery. "You disturb me by predictions of 'failure' unless your exact opinions in the matter of giving you command over Bradley are met in detail. I assure you that in this matter I can go no further."

Montgomery called a press conference on January 7 ostensibly to clarify the temporary command arrangement. In what de Guingand called a "what-a-good-boy-am-I" attitude, Montgomery told reporters that

> the whole Allied team rallied to meet the danger; national considerations were thrown overboard; General Eisenhower placed me in command of the whole Northern front. I employed the whole available power of the British Group of Armies. . . . It was put in with a bang, and today British divisions are fighting on both sides of American forces who have suffered a hard blow. This is a fine allied picture.

Finally, Montgomery added disingenuously, "The battle has been most interesting; I think possibly one of the most interesting and tricky battles I have ever handled, with great issues at stake."

The implication, and the press inference, was that a canny Montgomery had saved the situation and the British Army had rescued the hapless Americans. The American commanders who had managed the battle, Bradley and Patton, in particular, were enraged. Few British forces had been involved in the Battle of the Bulge at all; as the prime minister told Commons in an effort to correct the impression Montgomery had left, "The Americans have engaged thirty or forty men for every one we have engaged and have lost sixty to eighty men to every one of ours."

The Battle of the Bulge was costly to both sides. Army Intelligence estimated the Germans had lost as many as 250,000 men, including 36,000 captives. At the same time, the Americans had suffered some 77,700 battle casualties, the majority of these among infantrymen.

They could ill afford those losses. The shortages were acute. Eisenhower's seventy-three Allied divisions were seriously understrength, and confronting no fewer than seventy mauled but dangerous German divisions.

In Washington, an alarmed Secretary of War Henry Stimson proposed an accelerated draft call-up to create ten additional divisions by the fall of 1945 and the projected invasion of the Japanese main island of Honshu. Marshall objected on the grounds that it took almost two years to train a division from scratch, and the draftees were also needed in critical civilian industries.

The chief of staff told the secretary that "I opposed this to the point of resigning, and asked him to tell the president this." Stimson's proposal "would mean robbing us terribly" at home yet could not create fighting divisions quickly enough. In the face of Marshall's unrelenting opposition, Stimson shelved his proposition. They would hew to the ninety-division ceiling.

Marshall might have been forgiven a sense of satisfaction if he paused on the last day of the year, his sixty-fourth birthday, to ponder all they had accomplished. The toll in Europe had been high, a half-million casualties, of whom 90,000 were dead, but they were closing on the Rhine, poised for the long-planned double envelopment of Germany's industrial heartland in the Ruhr. The stalled Russian advance on the Eastern Front would resume in mid-January, putting more pressure on the Germans.

In the Pacific, too, they were tightening the drawstring around the bag. Although the Japanese Army of 3.5 million remained formidable, the Navy and Air Force had mastery of the seas and skies. *Kamikaze* pilots and suicide bombers were dangerous, but no match for B-29s, flying now from Saipan, bombing Japan at will.

Politically, the chief of staff might have taken some satisfaction as well. Their coalition was strained, but it had hung together. By stiffening Eisenhower, Marshall had made it possible for the supreme commander to snuff out Montgomery's bid for command of all Allied land forces.

For the moment he could be content, unaware that Winston Spencer Churchill meant to ride off to Malta on Montgomery's hobby horse.

CHAPTER

XXIX

The Argonauts

Once more he was airborne, once more flying to an international conference halfway around the world, once more the advocate of strategic plans his Allies rejected. How many times since 1940 had George Marshall carried this burden and how many times had he prevailed? In one sense the major conference to be set on the shore of the Black Sea at the Russian resort of Yalta would be easier than the preliminary meeting with the British on the Mediterranean island of Malta. Marshall's quarrel was not with the Russians but with the British.

The American delegation made its separate ways to Malta, the chief of staff landing in the Azores for a brief session with his old friend, newly named Secretary of State Edward Stettinius, Jr., replacing Cordell Hull. Reports of Soviet espionage activity on the West Coast had led Stettinius to wonder if the Russians would ask about the most secret A-bomb development at the Yalta Conference. Marshall advised they wait and see if the Soviets actually raised the issue; their response would necessarily depend upon the circumstances.

They had grown more wary of the Russian bear in recent weeks. Although Roosevelt had once hoped to end balance-of-power politics in European affairs, he realized now that the postwar world would be like the prewar in that regard. A week before sailing, the president had received a report from his ambassador in Moscow, Averell Harriman, pointing out that the Soviets were already bonding to the USSR those areas liberated by the Red Army in eastern Europe. A preoccupation with security had emerged as the overriding consideration of Soviet foreign policy, Harriman warned.

Even while preparing for a midwinter military offensive, Harriman added, the Russians were also employing "the wide variety of means at their disposal—occupation troops, secret police, local communist parties, labor unions, sympathetic leftist organizations, sponsored cultural societies, and economic pressure—to assure the establishment of regimes which, while maintaining an outward appearance of independence and of broad popular support, actually depend for their existence on groups responsible to all suggestions emanating from the Kremlin." Such realities the president would grapple with at the conference on the Black Sea.

Marshall's concerns at Yalta were less political than military. Specifically, he wanted the Soviet Union to confirm its pledge of the previous October that the Russians would enter the war against Japan three months after Germany surrendered.

That agreement was crucial, Marshall stressed in meetings with the president. The closer they had come to Japan in the last year, the more fierce the fighting, and the higher the number of casualties they took, Marshall pointed out. The Japanese *Sho* 3 and 4 plans called for an army of 3 million dedicated, even fanatic Japanese to meet the American invaders on the beaches. American planners reviewing OLYMPIC, the invasion of Kyushu, estimated that their casualties on this first of the Japanese home islands to be invaded would total 100,000. The casualty figure for the later invasion of Honshu and the Tokyo Plain, CORONET, could reach 250,000.

Marshall intended to prevent that, in part at least, by bringing the Soviet Union into the Far Eastern war. At peace with Japan now, the Soviet Union striking southward from Siberia could pin down as many as 1 million Japanese troops in Manchuria. The chief of staff had no more important strategic goal at the beginning of the new year, 1945.

But winning any concession from the Soviet Union would not be easy. Marshall's representative in Moscow, General John Deane, warned him of the ingrained Russian xenophobia. "They simply cannot understand giving without taking, and as a result even our giving is viewed with suspicion. Gratitude cannot be banked in the Soviet Union. Each transaction is complete in itself without regard to past favors."

Years of Lend-Lease counted for nothing, Deane added. Among other things he recommended that the United States insist on a quid pro quo when the Russians asked for more assistance than was necessary to win the war. Further, he urged that the United States "present proposals for collaboration that would be mutually beneficial and then leave the next move to them." Marshall intended to do just that.

The chief of staff had an equally serious matter to settle in preliminary meetings with the British chiefs of staff on Malta. Sir Alan Brooke and Churchill were coming to the island fortress in the middle of the Mediterranean Sea prepared for another confrontation with Marshall. The prime minister was determined to push through the appointment of a deputy ground commander in Europe, a man who could correct what Churchill considered to be the flaws in Eisenhower's final plan to end the war in Europe.

Marshall himself had doubts for the first time about the man he had chosen almost three years before to be supreme commander. They were nagging questions that could only be resolved in a face-to-face meeting before the Malta meetings. Marshall courteously radioed Eisenhower, "Would it be awkward for you to meet me in south of France . . . for one-day conference?"

Master and protégé met under leaden skies in the Château Valmonte, a villa fifty miles from Marseilles, on January 28, 1945. Relations between the two were clouded by questions surrounding Eisenhower's handling of the Ardennes battle, by his repeated calls for infantry reinforcements, and by Marshall's gnawing suspicion that Eisenhower was losing control of SHAEF.

The Eisenhower who greeted the chief of staff was certainly disheartened by the events of the last month, his confidence shaken. Brooke and Churchill had worn him down in repeated meetings, until Eisenhower agreed to the transfer of Field Marshal Sir Harold Alexander, from command of the Allied armies in Italy to be SHAEF deputy commander. The two had gotten on well in North Africa, when Alexander commanded the British armies under Eisenhower. Why not again?

If Eisenhower saw Alexander as a minister without portfolio, Marshall viewed the Britisher as an infantryman, a ground commander. Marshall immediately cautioned Eisenhower about "a weakening on your part under the heavy pressure of the press and British officialdom to get some high British military official into your general management of the ground forces."

Installing Churchill's favorite as deputy commander was problematic, Marshall advised. It meant that "the British had won a major point in getting control of ground operations in which their divisions of necessity will play such a minor part and, for the same reason, we are bound to suffer very heavy casualties." Then, too, Alexander "being who he is and our experience being what it has been, you would have great difficulty in offsetting the direct influence of the P.M." at SHAEF.

Eisenhower backed down on the appointment of a deputy commander. Still he had momentarily lost some token of Marshall's favor.

Eisenhower would lose even more ground by insisting upon reinforcements for the European theater, including a request for all of the remaining divisions then training in the United States. Future reinforcements, as Marshall pointed out, did nothing to improve the acute shortage of infantry replacements for those divisions already in combat. Eisenhower's staff had done a poor job of combing out infantry-trained supernumeraries in rear areas and sending them to the front.

Already seeking increased draft quotas and asking Congress too for authority to use eighteen-year-olds in combat, Marshall did not look kindly on the haphazard replacement plan devised by SHAEF. All that, plus the Ardennes setback, hinted that Eisenhower had lost his once sure grip on things. A French refusal in early January to obey orders to withdraw from Strasbourg and thereby shorten their lines was symptomatic. So too was Marshal Alphonse Juin's assertion that his eight divisions were too exhausted to fight on.

For much of that dreary Sunday afternoon—the day marking the official end of the Battle of the Bulge—Marshall reviewed Eisenhower's military plans for the coming months. Eisenhower planned a two-stage attack to clear the Wehrmacht from the west bank of the Rhine and secure his rear. That accomplished, he would launch a left-right combination punch to cross the last barrier into Germany with no less than sixty divisions. The major blow, directed by Montgomery, would be aimed at Berlin. That would be supported by a secondary effort under Bradley directed at the Ruhr. It was a cautious, methodical plan, just the sort Bernard Montgomery might have laid out.

Montgomery had not drawn this plan, however. Indeed, he was plumping for an alternative: command of a single, major thrust into the north, aimed generally toward Berlin. He proposed that they attack with no less than four armies made up of seventeen British and twenty American divisions, while the remaining forty-eight went over to the defensive. Under Montgomery's plan, they would put all their offensive resources into his northern offensive. Anything less, he insisted, risked failure on the brink of success.

Marshall was aware of British dissatisfaction with the Eisenhower plan, aware too that Montgomery, Brooke, and Churchill considered it further proof of the need for a deputy commander to oversee the ground war. Approving Eisenhower's plan meant rejecting the deputy. Approving the deputy probably meant modification of the plan.

After a long discussion dealing principally with casualty rates and finding replacements, Marshall decided to approve Eisenhower's two-stage plan to end the war: first to bring his armies up to the Rhine, then to cross at two separate points. As Eisenhower remembered the conversation, Marshall added in rather formal language: "I can, of course, uphold your position merely on the principle that these decisions fall within your sphere of responsibility. But your plan is so sound that I think it better for you to send General [Walter Bedell] Smith to Malta so that he may explain these matters in detail. Their logic will be convincing."

To reassure Eisenhower, now uncomfortably aware of the web Churchill had spun, Marshall promised, "As long as I'm chief of staff I'll never let them saddle you with the burden of an over-all ground commander."

Eisenhower was obviously relieved. "With General Marshall backing me up there would be no danger of interference with our developing plans." In a memo to the files, Eisenhower noted, "General Marshall will not agree to any proposal to set up a Ground commander-in-chief in this theater. If this is done, he says, he will not remain as chief of staff."

The two generals settled one further point. Eisenhower's promotion to five-star general opened the way for promotions below. To reward Bradley, leeched of divisions to reinforce Montgomery and denied credit by Montgomery's unjustifiable claim of restoring Allied lines in the Ardennes, Eisenhower asked that his old friend be granted a fourth star.

Marshall agreed to a horse trade: Eisenhower, in turn, was to support similar promotions for four others, including George Patton. Eisenhower concurred, though he considered one of Marshall's nominees, Jacob Devers, to be less than capable.

The following day Marshall flew from Marseilles to Malta, the tiny Mediterranean island that had withstood a German siege from 1940 to 1943. There on Suleiman the Magnificent's "accursed rock," where the Knights of the Order of St. John had beaten back the Ottoman invaders in 1565, Marshall intended to defeat his allies once and for all.

The Americans were coming to Malta reluctantly, and only at the repeated urgings of Winston Churchill. He had proposed Combined Chiefs of Staff discussions about the war against Japan and the use of Italian forces to beef up the weakened Allied fighting in northern Italy, but above all, the prime minister was anxious to reintroduce Eisenhower and Alexander with expectations of making a suitable match. That consummated, Churchill and Brooke believed, the single-thrust strategy in Germany would flow naturally from Alexander's desk.

The Combined Chiefs of Staff gathered in a drab conference room at Montgomery House. The British sat on one side of the table with Alan Brooke in the chair, the Americans squared off on the other, behind Marshall.

Bedell Smith represented Eisenhower at the Malta meetings, there specifically to present the two-thrust attack Marshall had approved earlier in the week at Marseilles. A former secretary of the U.S. Army General Staff during Marshall's first days as chief of staff, Smith was the perfect operations officer: bright, disciplined, and dedicated. If he had a flaw, it was a waspish temper with ulcer to match.

Coolly Smith laid out Eisenhower's plan, noting that time "had now become of great importance in view of the Russian advance." In two weeks the Red Army on three fronts had driven 200 miles to the Polish-German border, bypassing pockets of opposition, snaring hundreds of thousands of Germans in great hauls before the *Oberkommando* could shore up a defense line on the Oder River. Smith's implicit warning hung in the air: the Soviets might conquer Germany alone, leaving the Western Allies at a serious disadvantage in arranging the peace.

Smith reported that Eisenhower planned "to close the Rhine through its whole length"—a British expression that set Marshall's teeth on edge. By clearing the Wehrmacht from the entire west bank of the Rhine, Eisenhower would not have to divert troops to mop up in his rear. They simply lacked the large forces that would be necessary to defend their supply lines.

Closing the Rhine would free an additional twenty divisions for the Rhine crossings themselves. A northern assault would be made by thirty-six divisions initially, with a southern supporting operation "to be undertaken if at all possible."

Brooke warned of "a danger in putting too much into the southern effort and thereby weakening the main northern attack." A second assault would be fine, if it were close enough to be of immediate support to Montgomery's main push.

Marshall rejected that for two reasons. In a tactical sense, he argued, if the two assaults were so close together as to be directly supportive, they would also be more easily blunted by a single, large German force. Equally important, though he left it unstated, Marshall recognized that putting both forces into Montgomery's northern area would be sure to give the British the lion's share of the credit for the victory—even though the majority of his combat divisions would be American. Montgomery had already demonstrated his willingness to claim credit for others' accomplishments.

Still Brooke resisted. Bringing Allied troops to the Rhine along its entire length would necessarily slow Montgomery's attack on Germany, he argued. They had to speed up operations to keep pace with the Soviets.

Brooke was even less happy when Eisenhower wired his own intended assurances that night. He pledged to seize Rhine crossings in the north without waiting to mop up all German pockets of resistance west of the river. Fair enough, Brooke thought, but then the supreme commander added a conditional clause: "I will advance across the Rhine in the North with maximum strength and complete determination as soon as the situation in the South allows me to collect the necessary forces and do this without incurring unnecessary risks." They were right back where they had started.

At meetings on January 31, the British delegation hardly bothered to disguise its lack of faith in Eisenhower's judgment—not to mention his good faith. Eisenhower was not strong enough for the job, Brooke insisted. A deputy commander was the implicit solution.

Smith exploded. "Goddam it," he snapped at the stunned Brooke. "Let's have it out here and now."

What the hell did Brooke mean? Smith demanded.

Eisenhower paid too much attention to the counsels of his field commanders, notably Bradley and Patton, Brooke replied. The supreme commander was too easily swayed by the last man he saw—including George Marshall.

Eisenhower's cordiality did lead him to listen to his generals, Smith agreed. But that very quality had held their alliance together. If Brooke doubted Eisenhower's capacities, he could formally propose Eisenhower's relief.

Smith's challenge brought Brooke up short. He realized any move to impose a deputy ground commander would be vetoed instantly by Marshall; and the issue was no longer Eisenhower personally but future credit for winning the war in Europe.

The chief of staff was personally irritated when he learned Brooke feared Marshall's conversations with Eisenhower. If the British Chiefs of Staff were concerned about undue influence, Marshall replied, "they are not nearly as much worried as the American chiefs of staff are worried about the immediate pressures and influence of Mr. Churchill on General Eisenhower. The president practically never sees Eisenhower, never writes to him—that is at my advice because he is an Allied commander—and we are deeply concerned by the pressures of the prime minister and the fact of the proximity of the British chiefs of staff, so I think your worries are on the wrong foot."

The discussion became vehement, at times acrimonious, General Ismay recalled, putting the best face on it he could. "The closer one's personal relations, the more brutally frank one can be."

Frank they were. For attempting to subvert Eisenhower, Marshall excoriated Montgomery in an off-the-record session that cleared the air, even if it left Brooke outraged.

Despite the arguments, the Combined Chiefs managed to reach some decisions. Keen to assist the Red Army, Marshall agreed to a Russian request for supportive aerial bombings of urban areas in central and eastern Germany. Moreover, despite air force reservations about "morale bombing," the chief of staff agreed to American planes employing the long-standing British strategy of bombing through overcasts. In that way they could increase delivery of tonnage on urban targets, sewing confusion in the German rear, Marshall reasoned. (Within a week of the decision at Malta, 1,000 heavy bombers were to descend upon Berlin in a raid that killed 25,000 people; ten days later first British, then American bombers raided Dresden, obliterating 60 percent of that city and killing 35,000 to 70,000 civilians.)

Political realities determined other strategic decisions. On January 2 Roosevelt had reminded Churchill "of the difficulty of my getting involved in any operations in the Balkans that are not essential to the early defeat of Nazi Germany." Without American support, a despairing Churchill finally relinquished his dream. "Make no mistake," he told his private secretary John Colville, "All the Balkans, except Greece [where three

British divisions had landed], are going to be Bolshevised; and there is nothing I can do to prevent it. There is nothing I can do for poor Poland either."

At Malta a week later, Brooke gave Churchill's "soft underbelly" strategy its military burial. The field marshal quietly recommended the transfer of divisions from Italy to "the decisive Western Front. . . . There was now no question of operations aimed at the Ljubljana Gap and in any event the advance of the left wing of the Russian Army made such an operation no longer necessary." They agreed that two Canadian and three British divisions instead would be moved from the Mediterranean to reinforce Montgomery.

The conferees turned then to the Southeast Asian and Pacific theaters. In a move predicated on Roosevelt's unwillingness to help imperial powers regain their colonies, Marshall curtailed the use of American troops in Southeast Asia. Lord Mountbatten could employ them to clear Burma and thereby open the overland supply routes to China, but American troops were not to be used to free Malaya.

Together Marshall and King outlined their plans for the Pacific War. The next steps were the island of Okinawa in the Ryukyus and the Bonins, approximately 1,000 miles from Tokyo. Both would provide airfields from which to step up the bombing assault on industrial Japan. That softening up would precede the invasion of the Japanese homeland, tentatively set for September with a landing on Kyushu. They would invade the main island of Honshu and the Tokyo Plain in March 1946.

Throughout, they intended "to avoid full-scale land battles against Japanese forces, involving heavy casualties and slowing up the conduct of the campaign," Marshall and King assured the British delegation. The concept was to bypass strongholds, including Formosa; a rearmed Philippine Army and guerrillas were to mop up in those islands.

The Combined Chiefs of Staff had barely covered their agenda in the spare conference room at Montgomery House before the cruiser *Quincy* with the president of the United States on the quarterdeck steamed grandly into Valleta Harbor. Aboard HMS *Sirius* Churchill waved joyfully to the president as the *Quincy* moored across the channel. There would be few moments of pleasure for the prime minister in the days to come.

The last year had been hard on Roosevelt. Suffering from what his physician described as hypertensive heart failure, he was under orders to lose weight. He had lost thirty-five pounds, but the effect was startling to those seeing him after an absence. British General Hastings Ismay decided FDR was a very sick man; First Sea Lord Andrew Cunningham thought Roosevelt "very frail and worn out."

Meeting the president aboard the cruiser *Quincy* in the harbor at Valleta, both King and Marshall were stunned by Roosevelt's appearance. Normally a sea journey restored the man; this time the ten days on the Atlantic had done nothing so much as drain him further. He had suffered a cold for much of the passage. His face was wan and lined, his cloak hung loosely about his once broad shoulders. The two chiefs cut short their call, saying nothing, but exchanging looks of consternation as they went ashore.

Still, Secretary of State Stettinius—replacing the exhausted Cordell Hull—judged Roosevelt alert, more than equal to "the grueling give-and-take at the conference table with such powerful associates as Churchill and Stalin. . . ." Churchill too was tired, no longer buoyant; he had grumbled to his doctor for the past eight months about exhaustion, and Lord Moran concluded that his patient was "nearly burnt out."

Though the president left the running of the war to his chief of staff— Churchill grumbled to Moran that Roosevelt no longer took "intelligent interest" in military operations—there was little that Marshall could do to ease the president's burden at either Malta or Yalta. These conferences would be largely devoted to political matters: the postwar spheres of influence in Europe; the price of the Soviet Union's entry into the war against Japan; and the future status of Germany.

Most of the military questions on the table the two delegations settled in a two-hour plenary session on the evening of February 2 aboard the *Quincy*. Roosevelt and Churchill ratified the conclusions of the Combined Chiefs, leaving only one sticking point: British concern for the relief of liberated areas, particularly France and Italy. In both nations vigorous Communist parties had been keystones of the underground Resistance, achieving a respectability at the expense of rival parties discredited by their collaboration with Hitler and Mussolini. Strict rationing and continued privation in the months before election would only aid the Communists, the British argued. Rehabilitation of war-stricken Italy and France should begin immediately.

Marshall and King were concerned. Every shipload beyond already scheduled minimal rations of food, clothing, and fuel detracted from the "unqualified priority of beating Germany and Japan. . . . Any compromise almost certainly means prolongation of the war," they warned the president. Trusting Harry Hopkins's judgment, Marshall and King agreed to give the president's assistant power to arbitrate shipping quotas with the British.

The issue of Communist influence in postwar Europe would arise once more when Roosevelt and Churchill turned to the chiefs' proposals for Italy. The prime minister "attached great importance to a rapid follow-up of any withdrawal or of any surrender of the German forces in Italy. He felt it was essential that we should occupy as much of Austria as possible as it was undesirable that more of Western Europe than necessary should be occupied by the Russians." This was the first time Churchill openly raised the Russian specter in Allied councils.

Jabbing his Havana about him, the prime minister probed American intentions in China. Was not the president "somewhat disappointed at the results achieved by the Chinese, having regard to the tremendous American efforts which had been made to give them support"?

"Three generations of education and training would be required before China could become a serious factor" in world affairs, Roosevelt replied, virtually writing off the Chinese.

Marshall was the only one at the table to defend the Chinese. It was not so bleak as all that, he interposed. They now had the first well-trained Chinese divisions in China. They planned, ultimately, for that small Chinese Army to drive for the coast of the China Sea and a beachhead established by a powerful American landing force.

If the Americans were going to invade the mainland of China, Churchill wanted Great Britain to play a role—in the fighting, if necessary, in the peace, if possible. If they were to request British troops in China, the prime minister would certainly be prepared to consider it, he assured the Americans.

Admiral Leahy immediately demurred, protesting they had inadequate sealift to support the forces now in China. Marshall agreed; they could not increase troop strength in China until invading forces had captured a seaport.

These meetings on Malta ended inconclusively, their alliance strained by conflicting goals, Britain's focus on Europe and the United States' on the Pacific. For four often grim years they had been partners, allies; with victory in sight, they were partners still, but no longer allied.

The strained relationship troubled the president enough to make a placating gesture in Churchill's direction. In a brief meeting after the last plenary session, Roosevelt, Churchill, Marshall, and Brooke reconsidered the appointment of Field Marshal Alexander as Eisenhower's deputy. Roosevelt agreed to Alexander's transfer; Marshall insisted that the appointment be put off for six weeks. The delay would avert any hint that Alexander's appointment was a criticism of Eisenhower's handling of the Battle of the Bulge.

At midnight on February 2 / 3, the first of twenty-five transports carrying the British and American parties lifted off from the island's airport. At ten-minute intervals, the transports disappeared into the night sky, heading due east across the Aegean Sea, then northward, to follow the Dardanelles to their source in the Black Sea. Beyond lay Yalta, a pleasure dome for the vanished Russian nobility, and the conference Churchill had code-named ARGONAUT—because Jason had first sought the Golden Fleece in the kingdom of Colchis on the shores of the Black Sea.

From the airfield at Saki, they drove eighty miles to Yalta on the afternoon of February 3, the first part of their journey over snow-covered rolling hills. There was little pastoral serenity in the landscape, however. The Germans had retreated from here the year before, looting and burning as they withdrew. For the first time the president saw the gutted buildings, the carcasses of tanks and the splintered railway cars that marked the route of any twentieth-century army.

The journey into war along the winding road lined with stony-faced Russian troops ended for the presidential party five hours later at Livadia Palace, two miles south of the resort of Yalta. Built of white marble and limestone in 1911, the former summer palace of the last of the czars sat high on the cliffs 150 feet above the Black Sea. The Russians had selected furnishings from three Moscow hotels—guided by American Ambassador Averell Harriman's daughter, Kathleen—to refurbish the palace.

President Roosevelt took the czar's first-floor living quarters in a wing of the palace that overlooked the sea. Not far away stood the grand ballroom where the actual conferences would be held. The second floor, once the province of the czarina and her four daughters, housed the Joint Chiefs and a number of lesser lights. Marshall drew the Imperial bedroom, from where he ribbed King about his accommodations in the czarina's boudoir.

On Sunday, February 4, 1945, Roosevelt gathered the senior members of the American delegation for a review of their political position.

Two decisions by Roosevelt influenced Marshall's planning. First, the chief of staff had a free hand in Indochina so long as he did not make any "alignments with the French." France was not to reclaim its prewar colony with American help, FDR stressed.

More critical to Marshall, Ambassador Harriman reported that Stalin was likely to bring up the question of Russia's bounty for joining the Pacific War. The Soviets wanted the southern half of Sakhalin Island and the Kuriles, north of Hokkaido. They also wanted to maintain their dominance of Outer Mongolia and to obtain control of the railroad serving the port of Darien.

Roosevelt approved all but the Mongolian concession; on that he wanted to have Chiang Kái-shek's opinion. Marshall might well have breathed a small sigh of relief. The president's stance eased Marshall's major concern, securing the entry of the Soviet Union in the Pacific War.

That afternoon, Stalin and his foreign minister, the poker-faced Vyacheslav Molotov, paid a brief courtesy call upon the president at Livadia. Both Roosevelt and Stalin were in high spirits, buoyed by the war news. The two men bantered back and forth through their translators whether to bet that the Russians would capture Berlin before MacArthur's troops took Manila. Stalin was once more "Uncle" Joe.

Shortly after 5:00 p.m., the three delegations gathered in the palace ballroom. As he preferred, the president was seated first, waiting at the huge circular table for the others to join him. Stalin trooped in wearing his field marshal's uniform, at 5 feet 4 inches barely visible behind a squad of sturdy Russians carrying machine guns. More guards filled the balconies surrounding the room.

By prearrangement, Roosevelt chaired the first meeting, to be given over to statements of the military situation. Reading from a prepared text, pointing to large, prepared maps, Colonel General Aleksei I. Antonov for the next hour offered a detailed report on the Russian campaign of the last two weeks. Planned originally to begin at the end of the month when the weather was expected to improve, it had been launched on January 12 in low visibility with no air support "in view of the difficult circumstances on the Western Front in connection with the German attack in the Ardennes."

Massed artillery fire had crushed the German defenses; Russian troops broke into the rear and penned tens of thousands in isolated pockets that would be reduced piecemeal, Antonov reported. Some 400,000 Germans were casualties or prisoners. Forty-five divisions had been destroyed.

The survivors were forming on the east bank of the Oder River, reinforced by troops from the Western Front, from Italy and from central Germany. Antonov estimated that as many as fifty-six fresh German divisions could turn up on the Eastern Front. He predicted the *Oberkommando* would mass its strength to defend Berlin above all.

Marshal Stalin proposed closer coordination, for "when the Anglo-American armies were on the offensive in the West the Soviet armies were not ready and conversely." He suggested they mount a joint summer offensive.

Antonov wanted more immediate help, particularly attacks in the West and in Italy that would pin the Germans to those fronts, and the bombing of railroads to halt the transfer of eastern reinforcements.

Marshall followed with an extemporaneous summary of the Allied position, offering what Churchill described as "a brilliantly concise account of Anglo-American operations in the West." Secretary of State Stettinius judged Marshall's "one of the most magnificent presentations I have ever heard in my life. . . ."

Marshall had learned that the Russians appreciated blunt language. He had once advised Eisenhower to "approach them in simple Main Street Abilene style. They are rather cynically disposed toward the diplomatic phrasing of our compliments and seem almost to appreciate downright rough talk of which I give them a full measure."

Marshall was equally frank at Yalta. In some detail—numbers of divisions, men, tanks, and airplanes—he explained the pending strategy on the Western Front. The British 21st Army Group and the Ninth U.S. Army, still under Montgomery's command, would push the Germans back to the Rhine. Though they expected bridges to be demolished and upstream dam floodgates opened, five divisions employing rubber rafts and pontoon bridges were to cross the Rhine north of the Ruhr on a thirty-mile-wide front. Airborne troops would land on the eastern bank in a coordinated assault scheduled for March 1. Eisenhower had also laid on a secondary effort near Frankfurt that could be exploited if Montgomery's push failed.

The British and Americans had achieved numerical parity with the Germans, each with about eighty divisions on the line from Switzerland to Holland, Marshall stated. Whatever advantage the Allies had came from airpower, Churchill interjected. There they had an overwhelming preponderance.

Air operations against rail lines and oil refineries had gone well, Marshall continued. Several Panzer divisions transferring from the Western to the Eastern Front had been heavily hit by bombers, a subtle hint that the Western Allies were indeed assisting the Russians.

Stalin asked a series of probing questions regarding reserves, demonstrating a military acumen surprising for a onetime revolutionary six times arrested and exiled. How many tanks would the Allies use and what reserves did they have? What were the comparative strengths of the opposing forces?

Marshall answered in detail once more. According to Stettinius, Marshall's report "made a profound impression on the representatives of the Soviet Union."

Whatever the impression Marshall left, apparently the Soviets sensed British hostility. Brooke privately insisted that the great Russian offensive—they were now but forty miles from Berlin—had been made possible because Hitler had shifted troops from the east to the west in order to mount the Ardennes attack.

Confronting Brooke's antagonism, Stalin felt compelled to point out that the Soviet winter offensive had come about because the Soviets "felt it to be their duty as Allies to do it." There had been no bargaining, no pressure from Britain or the United States, merely Soviet goodwill. "The Soviet leaders," Stalin said with some asperity, "did not merely fulfill their obligations but were also prepared to fulfill their moral duty as far as possible."

Stalin did accede to more coordinated planning of their attacks, especially the coming summer offensive, "as he was not at all certain that the war would be over by that time."

Two hours and forty minutes after it began, the first plenary session concluded. Marshall would not take part in further sessions where the three heads of government discussed only political matters. His tasks were military ones.

At the suggestion of Marshal Stalin, on Monday, February 5, the three military delegations met as a strategic planning group for the first time. The Allied delegations looked on the meeting as a token of a new openness on the part of the usually tight-lipped Russians, a token too of a new world order.

The meeting at Koreiz Villa, where the Russians were quartered, began with the problem of coordinating their mutual offensives as to prevent the Germans from shifting reinforcements from one front to the other.

Marshall reiterated that the Western Allies had no superiority in numbers. Further, their supply line from the United States was both long and vulnerable to the V-bombs. Stalin had brushed that threat aside the day before, but Marshall had to keep in mind that a lucky strike could take out the Antwerp locks and with them their main source of supply. It was only with airpower that the Western Allies achieved superiority, Marshall reminded Antonov and his colleagues—and the use of airpower depended on good weather.

The Russians pointedly prodded Brooke and Marshall. Soviet operations in winter were planned on the supposition that bad weather would ground their air support. Massed artillery replaced bombers. "The Allies should bear this point in mind in planning their own operations," Air Marshal Sergei Khudyakov urged.

As spokesman for his delegation, Antonov asked if the Allies could prevent the Germans from pulling reinforcements out of Italy and transferring them to the Eastern Front. Brooke was forced to acknowledge they could not halt a slow leeching of as many as ten German divisions from the defensive line in the Po River Valley. Neither could they prevent transfers from Norway to the East. The Western Allies were unable to return the favor the Russians had extended in offering coordinated offensives.

Admiral Leahy raised the questions of closer liaison and drawing a bombing line between their mutual fronts. Antonov agreed to the need, adopting Leahy's suggestion that an overall coordinating committee be set up in Moscow.

Finally, Leahy asked for the Russian estimate of the end of the war in Europe. It was necessary for planning purposes, especially of shipping, Marshall interposed.

Antonov ducked, asserting he preferred not to make assumptions.

The Allies estimated the war's end no sooner than July 1 and no later than December 31, Marshall replied.

Antonov shrugged agreement: summer at the earliest, winter at the latest.

The meeting had been cordial, but inconclusive: Antonov was prohibited from making decisions without referring everything to Stalin. The next day's session was to go only a little better. The Americans and British sought reassurances that the Russians would attack on a broad front when the Western Allies attempted their Rhine journey. Although he was friendly, even responsive, given the authority the Supreme Soviet held over military affairs, Antonov could not be specific.

Neither could he give an exact date for the start of a summer offensive, Antonov told Marshall and Brooke. "The most difficult season was the second part of March and the month of April. This was the period when roads became impassable" with mud.

Would they be able to carry out any operation during that period, Marshall asked.

"If during this period operations in the West were carried out actively, the Soviets would take every possible action on the Eastern Front wherever this could be done."

It was just that time when they would attempt to cross the Rhine, Marshall pointed out.

Colonel General Antonov reassured Marshall that his armies would do everything possible to prevent the transfer of German forces from east to west during this period.

On the morning of February 8, the military staffs resumed their discussions of joint operations against Japan. Antonov almost offhandedly reiterated the October pledge to Ambassador Harriman that the Russians would commence operations in the Far East three months after Germany's surrender. "There have been no changes in the Soviet projected plan of operations in the Far East from those described to Mr. Harriman and General Deane in October." Marshall could breathe easier.

Between the end of that meeting and an afternoon session with Stalin, Roosevelt met hastily with his Joint Chiefs of Staff. No minutes were taken—it may have been no more than a hasty conversation in the former billiard room that served as the president's mess—but Marshall apparently briefed the president of Soviet intentions in the Far East. One of the prerequisites of the invasion plan stipulated Russian participation to keep the million-man Japanese Army in China tied down, Marshall reminded Roosevelt. It would be up to the president to secure Stalin's assent in that afternoon's meeting.

While the chief of staff waited anxiously, Roosevelt and Stalin hammered out a final agreement on Russia's entry into the Pacific War. The fighting in the Pacific was entering a new phase, Roosevelt noted. He "hoped it would not be necessary actually to invade the Japanese islands and would do so only if absolutely necessary." Still, they had to plan for stepped-up bombing of the Japanese homeland.

They needed additional bases in eastern Siberia from which to bomb Japan, the president stated. Stalin affably granted two. The Russian premier also agreed to allow American bombers to fly on missions over Germany out of Russian-held Budapest, and to permit an American strategic bombing survey team to look at bomb damage in areas liberated by the Red Army. If these were small gestures of an ally's support, they were gratefully accepted as possible harbingers of future cooperation.

Now it was Roosevelt's turn to offer a token of friendship. Responding to a Soviet request to buy surplus merchant vessels after the war, Roosevelt offered to seek congressional authority to transfer the bottoms on credit, without interest. "The British had never sold anything without commercial interest," Roosevelt added. "He had different ideas."

Stalin then raised the question of what he called the political conditions under which the USSR would enter the war against Japan. Roosevelt instantly assured the premier, "There would be no difficulty whatsoever in regard to the southern half of Sakhalin and the Kurile Islands going to Russia at the end of the war."

Other concessions had yet to be worked out. Granting rights to a warm-water port on the Manchurian coast and to Russian use of the Manchurian Railway depended on Chiang Kai-shek's agreement, the president noted. He had not had an opportunity to talk with Chiang.

Stalin was "an astute negotiator" and very clever, as Marshall put it. If these conditions were not met, the Soviet premier warned, "it would be difficult for him and Molotov to explain to the Soviet people why Russia was entering the war against Japan." If these political conditions were met, Stalin assured Roosevelt, "the people would understand the national interest involved and it would be very much easier to explain the decision to the Supreme Soviet."

Roosevelt was soothing but would yield nothing. "One of the difficulties in speaking to the Chinese was that anything said to them was known to the whole world in twenty-four hours." Since the Soviet Union and Japan were not at war, any hint that the Russians were weighing such a move could trigger a preemptive Japanese attack before the Russians were ready.

Stalin conceded the point. Though all of his conditions could not be met without Chiang's agreement, Stalin promised to guarantee the Supreme Soviet's approval of participation in the war against Japan. With that, the president had secured the great prize Marshall sought at Yalta.

Rather quickly the two men settled remaining questions in the Far East. Korea, for forty years Japanese, was to be a trusteeship while the people were prepared for self-government; the sooner the better, Stalin added. The premier approved too of Roosevelt's proposal that no foreign troops be stationed in that country.

Roosevelt also suggested a trusteeship in Indochina rather than return that colony to France. A trusteeship was fine, for "Indochina was a very important area," Stalin agreed.

China still presented problems, Roosevelt acknowledged, though General Wedemeyer and the new ambassador, Patrick Hurley, had made progress in bringing Chiang together with the Communists. Stalin admitted he was perplexed. "He did not understand why they did not get together since they should have a united front against the Japanese. He thought that for this purpose Chiang Kai-shek should assume leadership."

The following day, the last of the Yalta Conference, Roosevelt, Churchill, and their sometimes embattled military staffs moved to conclude their business. They approved a two-pronged attack over the Rhine that the Americans favored, but stipulated to the British insistence that Montgomery was to have the bulk of the striking force for his northernmost attack. The timing would be left to Eisenhower, as Marshall had urged.

During a final meeting with Marshall that afternoon, Colonel General Antonov reported Stalin's official concurrence in their combined Far Eastern strategy. Three months after the end of the war in Europe, the Soviet Union would be ready for war in the Far East. The Soviets, uncharacteristically, asked for military assistance; U.S. aid in defense of Kamchatka peninsula would be very useful, the Russians acknowledged. Breaking even further from their xenophobic tradition, they would prepare at least three bases in eastern Siberia and Kamchatka for American bombers operating against Japan. American survey teams could begin work immediately.

In exchange, Marshall arranged for vastly increased deliveries of C-47 transports for which the Soviets had asked, as many as 340 in the next year, more than double the Lend-Lease schedule.

If Marshall was generous to the Russians, they had been generous in turn. The chief of staff was delighted. Shortly before returning to the United States, Secretary of State Stettinius turned to Marshall on the steps of Livadia Palace and said, "General, I assume you are very eager to get back to your desk."

"Ed, for what we have got here, I would have stayed a month."

Brooke too was pleased. After dinner on the last night of the conference with Churchill, Marshall, and Alexander, the chief of the Imperial

General Staff unbent enough to write in his diary the conference "has on the whole been as satisfactory as could be hoped for, and certainly a most friendly one."

His golden prize firmly in hand, Marshall the Argonaut chose to delay his return to the United States to carry out an inspection of American troops in Italy. The visit was prompted by waspish comments from Representative Clare Boothe Luce, the wife of *Time* magazine publisher Henry Luce, who had earlier visited what she called "the forgotten front."

Marshall's visit was intended to prove that Mark Clark's Fifth Army was neither forgotten nor unappreciated. Informing Clark of his plans, the chief of staff had radioed, "Do not meet me at airport. I will come to your headquarters. No honors."

Clark courteously offered to meet his former commander. Marshall reiterated his instructions: "Don't meet me. No honors, repeat, no honors."

Nonetheless, when Marshall arrived at Clark's headquarters outside Florence, a large honor guard was drawn up in front of the building. Marshall scowled.

"Didn't you get my message?" he snapped at Clark.

"Yes, sir."

"Well?" he said through thin lips.

Clark suppressed a sinking feeling. "It will only take a few minutes and you'll not regret it."

Clark led the chief of staff—traveling overseas as a five-star general for the first time—to the head of the honor guard. Slowly Marshall's frown disappeared.

Lined up before him stood a squad of men from each of thirteen different fighting units: from the American 34th and the black 94th Divisions; from the Brazilian Expeditionary Force; from Scottish, Welsh, and Northern Irish regiments; from Punjabi, Newfoundland, Canadian, New Zealand, and South African units; from the Polish Corps; and from both Italian army and Italian partisan units. In addition, he had formed up nurses from five different countries, WACs, American Red Cross workers, and British women auxiliaries. Only two units were unrepresented; the French and the Japanese-American 442nd Infantry Regiment were fighting in southern France. Here in Italy was the true army of Allies.

The chief of staff's forbidding scowl had disappeared by the end of the pro forma inspection. Marshall told the relieved Clark he was glad his instructions had been ignored.

Where Marshall traveled, the press dutifully followed. For three days, making as many as fifteen stops between breakfast and dinner, he visited headquarters or spoke to grimy combat troops, climbed muddy trails to forward observation posts on the front, talking always of their contribution to the war effort. These "forgotten men" were holding down as many as twenty-seven German divisions in Italy, he reminded reporters; the lack of headlines did not diminish the importance of the Italian campaign in the European theater.

Once more he was seeing the war, not from a desk in remote Washington, not from an airplane flying serenely above the turmoil, not from a conference table in a cold ballroom in a former czar's palace, but in the field.

Here in the frozen mud of an Italian winter, there was a special satisfaction for him, a feeling of pride. These were his divisions, the armies he had created, the men and women who had prompted Winston Churchill that week to cable Jumbo Wilson in Washington: "Pray give General Marshall my warmest congratulations on the magnificent fighting and conduct of the American and Allied armies under General Eisenhower, and say what a joy it must be to him to see how the armies he called into being by his own genius have won immortal renown. He is the true 'organizer of victory.' "

C H A P T E R

XXX

The Battle Day Past

By the end of February 1945, an overwhelming Allied force pressed hard against the German border. Four million men, three quarters of them Americans, were massed into seven field armies composed of 53 infantry and 20 armored divisions, supported by more than 17,500 combat planes. The shattered Siegfried Line's West Wall lay behind them, the last defense, the rain-swollen Rhine River, ahead.

Even as Bernard Montgomery prepared a textbook-perfect crossing of that last barrier, an advance element of the U.S. 9th Armored Division on March 7 discovered a stone railroad bridge still standing in the winter mists over the Rhine River at Remagen. A company from the 27th Infantry Battalion dashed across the bridge while engineers cut electrical wires leading to planted explosives. By evening, elements of three divisions had followed them across the river.

Despite determined opposition, within days Bradley's Twelfth Army Group had forced a salient ten miles deep into the Rhineland. The German defense along the Rhine began to fall apart.

In the past six weeks, over one third of the Wehrmacht had disappeared. For the first time in the war, disciplined German regiments broke into disorderly retreat, fearful of being cut off on the west bank of the Rhine. George Patton wrote to his wife that he could smell the sweat of the Roman legions as he followed Caesar's road to the Rhine, and on March 23 sneaked a division across the river in boats, some seventy miles south of the Remagen riverhead. At a cost of just eight dead and twenty wounded, Patton had mounted the first amphibious crossing of the Rhine since Napoleon and given the Americans a second solid foothold across the river.

The following day, Montgomery opened his carefully prepared assault in the north. By the end of the month, three Allied armies stood poised for a last drive into the Third Reich. The grand strategy conceived in Marshall's insistence that the Allies destroy Germany's ability to make war had brought them to the brink of victory.

The succession of triumphant headlines in the United States fostered a mood of optimism as spring approached. Concerned that the public prematurely considered the war over, Marshall held another of his not-for-attribution press briefings, intended to dampen the rising excitement.

The press gathering in the chief of staff's office at the Pentagon took on the atmosphere of a papal audience. At no time had the general enjoyed as much respect as he did in this season of triumph. The questions were respectful, the chief of staff unchallenged. To one correspondent attending, Marshall was no longer "General" or "Chief of Staff," but simply "THE MAN." No one had a greater command of the situation "from the weather over Europe to the most minute gains made by the British in Burma." Marshall's caution was sobering, a reminder that victory in Europe was not the end of the war.

If Marshall feared anything, it was a public clamor for hasty demobilization now that the war in Europe was near an end. While the War Department had instituted an eighty-five-point requirement for discharge—combat troops counted twelve points for each child, five points for each campaign and medal, and a point for each month overseas—the public must not expect large-scale demobilization after VE-Day. Most of the troops in Europe would be shifted to the Pacific with Germany's surrender; some might not even get furloughs, Marshall warned.

Fighting in the Pacific would grow ever most costly as they neared the Japanese homeland, Marshall stressed. They had only to look at the newsreels of the savagery on Iwo Jima, ordered released by the usually close-hauled Admiral King as a reminder of the costs of war. The bloody footage foretold even more costly fighting once the United States invaded the Japanese home islands.

They would do all they could to hold down casualties, Marshall assured favored correspondents. The United States was "not going to spend American lives and treasure in freeing imperial possessions from the Japanese and then turn them back to their prewar owners."

For all their success, the chief of staff refused to relax discipline. No matter seemed too petty or too remote for immediate attention. Army divisions were not getting the publicity they deserved, Marshall complained. Had they been Marine divisions, he lectured Eisenhower in a letter, "every phase of a rather dramatic incident would have been spread throughout the United States." Marine press relations officers got results; the Army's did not—that a problem when they would be competing for scarce postwar appropriations. Further, Marshall wanted American commanders such as Omar Bradley and Courtney Hodges to receive newspaper attention "as a possible antidote for an overdose of Montgomery which is now coming into the country."

Hap Arnold's fourth heart attack in mid-January forced Marshall to address another problem. While there were deputies to step in—a brilliant brigadier general with a promising future, Laurence Kuter, had served at Yalta as Arnold's surrogate—air force staff weaknesses were palpable. Marshall ordered a reorganization of that staff to give its commander and Marshall himself more help. When Arnold returned to duty and his usual whirlwind schedule, Marshall could scold his old friend for not resting. "You are riding for a fall, doctor or no doctor," he remonstrated.

Their very success bred problems. In mid-February American and British bombers had struck the medieval city of Dresden; between 35,000 and 70,000 died in the resulting firestorm. Questions about the indiscriminate British "terror raid" bombing in Parliament impelled Secretary of War Henry Stimson to question an uneasy Marshall about the rationale for the raid and its results. Air force explanations about the choice of targets and the desire to aid the Russians by hammering transportation centers could not paper over the ultimate responsibility of the Combined Chiefs of Staff. They had approved indiscriminate area bombing as a strategic weapon in the first months after Pearl Harbor; their air forces had pursued that policy ever since, even if the Americans favored so-called precision bombing of specific targets. Dresden, like Hamburg and Berlin before, was the predictable result of that strategy.

"Making war in a democracy is not a bed of roses," Marshall groused in a letter to Eisenhower on March 6. Senator Robert Taft was fighting against the use of eighteen-year-olds in combat even as Douglas MacArthur clamored for more troops and rear-echelon commanders protested the conversion of their men to infantry replacements. "The combined circumstances could hardly present a more illogical pressure."

His spirits buoyed by the capture of the Ludendorff Bridge at Remagen, Eisenhower replied in an equally uncharacteristic, lighthearted tone: "Sometimes when I get tired of trying to arrange the blankets smoothly over the several prima donnas in the same bed I think no one person in the world can have so many illogical problems." Having read his chief's complaint, he "went right back to work with a grin," he wrote.

All these were minor problems compared to the increasing responsibility Marshall assumed in directing the war. For some months planners, "whether we like it or not," had grappled with "the fact that [the War Department] has a real interest in political matters of varying categories." Once the War Department had looked to the White House for guidance in political matters, but President Roosevelt was weary, his resilience and jaunty good humor gone. Moreover, he was preoccupied with postwar political questions, especially the organization of a United Nations; increasingly the president had referred matters pertaining to the conduct of the war to Marshall, regardless of their political quotient. "The entire responsibility was placed upon General Marshall, as chief of staff, and General Eisenhower, as theater commander," complained diplomat Robert Murphy. "Both of these army officers accepted this responsibility without complaint, then or afterward, but it was inevitable that they would regard Berlin from the military point of view."

In the eyes of the British, too, this was a damnable error.

Berlin had not originally figured in Eisenhower's plans. Western planners had long assumed the capital of the Third Reich would fall to the Red Army. As recently as February 5, Marshal Georgi Zhukov's armies stood on the banks of the Oder River, just fifty miles from Berlin. There the marshal, having outrun his supply lines, was forced to halt; though his troops forced a river crossing, German resistance held the attack in check.

With Germany pressed between Allied fronts just 250 miles apart and closing, Eisenhower and Omar Bradley conceived a new plan to bring the war to a close. Taking advantage of the American river crossings in the south, they decided to shift the main assault from Montgomery's 21st Army Group to Bradley's 12th Army Group.

Their reasoning was simple. "Barring an unlikely Russian reverse, Berlin would be in Russian hands long before we got there," Bradley explained after the war. Further, to target Berlin would mean halting progress elsewhere in order to force a crossing of the Elbe in the north. Even then Montgomery would confront poor tank terrain, a low, marshy plain crisscrossed with streams and canals. The battle to take Berlin would cost as many as 100,000 casualties, Bradley estimated, "a pretty stiff price to pay for a prestige objective."

That price was particularly high, Bradley continued, "when we've got to fall back and let the other fellow take over." The Allied occupation zones of a postwar Germany had been sketched at the second Quebec Conference by Roosevelt and Churchill, then settled at Yalta. Berlin, which itself would be divided into occupation sectors for each of the victorious Allies, was to be 100 miles inside the Soviet zone. Whatever territory the Western Allies took in that zone they had agreed to yield. "It seemed cruel and absurd to me to spend American lives or incur injuries to capture German territory which we would then turn back to the Russians," Bradley said later.

A prize more important than Berlin, in terms of winning the war, lay before them, Bradley argued. The Ruhr contained more than one half of Germany's industrial capacity; without it, the Germans would be forced to quit the fight. Moreover, the Wehrmacht's Army Group B was scraping together a defense in the Ruhr. Bagging them would end effective resistance in the West.

Eisenhower's decision was partly based on a personal factor: Bradley had loyally stood in Montgomery's shadow, and he deserved this opportunity. But there were also military factors; Army Intelligence had suggested that the last fanatical Nazi fighting units planned to retreat to fortified redoubts in the Austrian Alps and the mountains of Norway.

Both Eisenhower and Bradley "were early converts to the 'redoubt' gospel," as Bradley put it later. To prevent a bitter fight prying dedicated troops out of prepared positions—a battle that could well delay the shift of American divisions to the Pacific—Eisenhower drew a plan to cut the Wehrmacht's way into a southern redoubt. Bradley would drive boldly eastward to link up with Russians at the Elbe River. At the same time, Montgomery was to redirect a portion of his army north to Lubeck and the German-Danish border; that move would simultaneously block any German retreat into Norway and any Soviet conquest of Denmark.

Eisenhower's final plan involved an assault by seven armies with the heaviest blow given to Bradley in the center. The Ruhr was to be bagged by two converging American armies, Simpson's Ninth on the north and Hodges's First on the south. That accomplished, the Ninth, which had been under Montgomery's command since the beginning of the Battle of the Bulge, would once more revert to Bradley's control. Montgomery was to protect Bradley's northern flank, an order that abruptly cast the British commander in a supporting role for the rest of the war. The Eisenhower plan was balm for Bradley's old sores.

At a press conference in Paris on March 27, Eisenhower termed the Germans "a whipped enemy." Asked by a reporter who would get to Berlin first, Eisenhower pointed out that the Soviets had the closer army.

The following day, Eisenhower informed Montgomery of the revised plan. Berlin had "become, so far as I am concerned, nothing but a geographical location, and I have never been interested in these." Reciting the catechism of American military doctrine, Eisenhower added, "My purpose is to destroy the enemy's forces and his powers to resist."

According to the new plan, the main thrust, Bradley's, was to be along a line toward Leipzig and Dresden, with the intent of linking up with the Russians. Montgomery's armies to the north and Devers's to the south would press ahead as well, but to Bradley would go the honors. Bradley would have enough strength, Eisenhower assured Marshall, to move on Berlin as well if resistance was light and if the still stalled Red Army made no move to attack the capital.

That afternoon, Eisenhower received a cable from the chief of staff suggesting that Eisenhower take steps to coordinate a link-up with the Russians. The supreme commander took his cue, dispatching an unprecedented message directly to Marshal Stalin. He outlined his plans: first, encirclement of the Ruhr; then mopping up that pocket, probably by the end of April; then a drive eastward to link with the Soviets near Dresden; and finally, a drive to cut off German flight to the rumored southern redoubt.

The British chiefs of staff seethed—infuriated not only by Eisenhower's plan but by the fact that he had communicated it to Stalin without first consulting the Combined Chiefs. Alan Brooke immediately protested to Marshall, insisting they revert to the original plan. Montgomery must make the main thrust toward Berlin, Brooke argued; a major attack in the north would not only bag Berlin, but would simultaneously capture Germany's ports on the Baltic, snare the U-boat bases, and free Norwegian and Swedish shipping for Allied use.

Anticipating a negative response from Marshall, Churchill warned his chiefs that Americans were furnishing three quarters of the troops on the Western Front. In addition, the United States was producing some 45 percent of the world's armaments, and two thirds of all shipping. In such a new and unsettling world, the Americans, upstarts though they might be, however naive they might be, would have their way. Eisenhower's decisions were final authority on the battlefield.

Still Churchill made a token effort to reverse the supreme commander, radioing President Roosevelt about "these misunderstandings between the truest friends and comrades that ever fought side by side as allies."

Churchill tactfully complained that the British 21st Army Group was to be left in a "static condition." That argument ignored the fact that the original plan had as many as fifty American divisions go over to the defensive while Montgomery's twenty mounted their major attack.

There were geopolitical issues as well, Churchill continued. The Soviet armies would overrun all of Austria. "If they also take Berlin, will not their impression that they have been the overwhelming contributor to our common victory be unduly imprinted in their minds, and may this not lead them in a mood which will raise grave and formidable difficulties in the future?"

This was not the fulminating Churchill of old, but a decidedly junior partner raising feeble protest. Moreover, any arguments the prime minister might make were undercut by the immediate success of the Eisenhower plan. On Easter Sunday, April 1, elements of two American armies closed a pincers around the Ruhr, trapping more than 317,000 German troops. (The embattled Army Group B would surrender on April 18, giving Bradley a larger haul of prisoners than the Russians had taken at Stalingrad, or Eisenhower had bagged at the end of the Tunisian campaign.)

Aware that the chief of staff ran the war on the American side—Marshall would acknowledge only that the president "was saddling me with more responsibilities" as the war went on—Churchill added a postscript: "I need hardly say that I am quite willing that this message, which is my own personal message to you and not a staff communication, should be shown to General Marshall."

The chief of staff framed the president's reply, reading the text over the scrambler telephone to Roosevelt resting at Warm Springs. With serene resolve, Marshall deflected the prime minister's arguments. "The British army is given what seems to me very logical objectives on the northern flank. . . ."

> I appreciate your generous expressions of confidence in Eisenhower [Marshall wrote for FDR] and I have always been deeply appreciative of the backing you have given him and the fact that you yourself proposed him for this command. I regret that the phrasing of a formal discussion should have so disturbed you but I regret even more that at the moment of a great victory by our combined forces we should become involved in such unfortunate reactions.

Lest his message not be clear, Marshall reminded the Imperial General Staff that only Eisenhower was in a position to conduct the battle. The American Joint Chiefs—in truth, Marshall—discounted any "psychological and political advantages as would [sic] result from the possible capture of Berlin ahead of the Russians." The imperative consideration, a reflection of decades of Leavenworth doctrine, was the destruction and dismemberment of the German armed forces.

While Brooke grumbled about "that rude message," Churchill bowed to the reality of coalition warfare. "I regard the matter as closed," he radioed Roosevelt, "and to prove my sincerity will use one of my very few Latin quotations, *"Amantium irae amoris integratio est* [Lovers' quarrels always go with true love]."

Stern with the British, Marshall was just as firm with the Russians when he felt American integrity questioned. On April 4, 1945, he drafted a message to Premier Stalin for the president's signature pointedly rejecting the Russian's claim that the United States was negotiating secretly an end to the war. Stalin had learned—he never revealed how—that the American Office of Strategic Services representative in Bern, Allen Dulles, was negotiating a possible surrender of German forces in Italy. Concerned that the Germans would surrender to the Western Allies while continuing to fight the Soviets, a furious Stalin demanded that Russian representatives be present; they had agreed at Quebec not to hold surrender discussions unless representatives of all three nations were present.

Dulles and the *Schutzstaffeln* commander in Italy, General Karl Wolff, had met in Bern. Dulles, however, was wary of Wolff's claim to be able to end fighting in Italy, let alone elsewhere on the Western Front; Wolff was, after all, an SS general with no influence over the Wehrmacht. Thus there had technically been no "negotiations," only "discussions."

Expressing "astonishment" at Stalin's message, Marshall assured the Soviet premier no negotiations were held in Bern; it was only a meeting, with "no political implications whatever." Marshall-Roosevelt then indirectly reproached Stalin:

> . . . It would be one of the great tragedies of history if at the very moment of the victory, now within our grasp, such distrust, such lack of faith should prejudice the entire undertaking after the colossal losses of life, materiel and treasure involved. Frankly, I cannot avoid a feeling of bitter resentment toward your informers, whoever they are, for such vile misrepresentations of my actions or those of my trusted subordinates.

It was language that would have done Churchill proud; the prime minister immediately endorsed the Stalin reproof.

While the chief of staff and a small circle of advisers carried on the daily business of government, the president rested at Warm Springs. He worked only a few hours a day, swam often in the pool with other polio patients, and posed impatiently for a watercolor portrait. The rest and light workload helped; Roosevelt had regained some of his good humor, once more teasing his staff and his cook, retelling old jokes, visiting with his cousins and a close personal friend, Lucy Mercer Rutherfurd.

A few minutes before the end of a sitting on Thursday afternoon, April 12, in the Little White House, a restless FDR rubbed the back of his neck and complained softly of "a terrific headache." His arm flopped to his side. A heartbeat later he slumped in his chair, comatose.

Franklin Delano Roosevelt died of a cerebral hemorrhage two and a quarter hours later, at 3:35 in the afternoon, without ever regaining consciousness.

Word of the president's death went first to Mrs. Roosevelt in the White House. With impassive calm, she dictated a short message to be radioed by the War Department to the four Roosevelt sons in uniform: "Daddy slept away. He would expect you to carry on and finish your jobs."

At the same time, Stephen Early, the president's press secretary, located the vice president, relaxing with a glass of bourbon in the office of Speaker of the House Sam Rayburn. In a strained voice Early asked Harry S. Truman to come to the White House immediately. The unsuspecting Truman tossed down his drink and on a lark ducked his Secret Service escort by running through the basement of the Capitol.

Not until he reached the White House and was escorted to the family quarters on the second floor did the vice president realize something was amiss. Mrs. Roosevelt placed her arm around Truman's shoulder. "Harry, the president is dead."

Truman was stunned. It was a moment before he could ask, "Is there anything I can do for you?"

"Is there anything *we* can do for *you*?" Mrs. Roosevelt asked in return. "For you are the one in trouble now."

Though the nation would not learn of President Roosevelt's death for another half hour, word circulated quickly within the city's power structure. Informed of Mrs. Roosevelt's message, Marshall's sometime aide, Frank McCarthy, immediately drove to Fort Myer and Quarters No. 1. Less than an hour after the president's death, the chief of staff and his wife were on their way to pay their respects to Mrs. Roosevelt.

The usually bustling White House seemed subdued, Mrs. Marshall recalled. Reporters clustered in a hallway, too shocked to do much more than go through the motions of reporting the biggest story of their careers. While Mrs. Marshall waited outside, her husband was ushered into the Cabinet Room where the shaken vice president spoke briefly with him. Mrs. Roosevelt asked Marshall to make the funeral arrangements: the transport of the president's body to Washington, a White House funeral, and then the last journey to interment at Hyde Park. The Marshalls left as a solemn crowd began to gather in front of the White House, drawn as always at moments of crisis to the iron fence.

At the War Department, a member of Marshall's staff, H. Merrill Pasco, recalled, "There was sadness and great loss and just puzzlement as what in the world we were going to do with this new president who really didn't seem to us at that time to have any of the attributes of leadership. He had been a sort of picayunish, mean little investigator of excess spending in the Pentagon. And the feeling was what sort of leadership are we going to have?"

Marshall seemed impassive, displaying no outward emotion, Pasco recalled. The sense of loss was for a president, less for the man. The chief of staff had always considered FDR "a great war president" and "a great leader," but Marshall had deliberately kept his distance from the "obstinate Dutchman" who was president. Still, Marshall gave the impression he found Roosevelt, a man who could put aside or even evade difficult decisions, less appealing than Harry Hopkins, who tackled the thorniest issue directly.

At the War Department that night, the chief of staff made arrangements for the funeral of the man who had been president of the United States longer than any other. The basic plan and ceremonial rituals Marshall had personally worked and reworked for the pending funeral of his friend and mentor, John Pershing; Marshall's orderly, Master Sergeant James Powder, marched behind the flag-draped casket as it rode to the White House on Saturday, April 14, guarding his president one last time.

At 11:00 a.m. that day, the new president met for the first time with his Joint Chiefs and the secretaries of war and navy. It was a hard meeting for all of them. This second-term senator, a failed haberdasher said to be Kansas City political boss Tom Pendergast's man, could not be president, not yet. It was too soon. But he was, sworn in in this very Cabinet Room a day and a half before. Harry Truman humbly told the men who had brought the nation to the brink of victory "he was sure they understood the terrific burden which had been unloaded on him and how much help he would require."

For the next hour the military leaders briefed the president. Units of the U.S. Ninth Army had reached the Elbe River, just sixty-three miles from Berlin. Eisenhower had halted them there, waiting for the Red Army to link up. The American Seventh Army had entered Bavaria. The Soviets meanwhile had fought their way into Vienna and were taking on the bulk of the Wehrmacht outside Berlin. Army Intelligence estimated that no cohesive governmental, economic, or military structure would exist in the Third Reich after May 1, though fanatic Nazi troops would fight on in isolated pockets. Meanwhile, the British had broken through German defenses in northern Italy; the American Fifth Army was to begin clearing the Po River Valley today.

In the Pacific, MacArthur was mopping up isolated Japanese units in the Philippines. Two weeks before, the American Tenth Army had easily landed on the largest of the Ryukyu Islands, Okinawa, just 350 miles from Tokyo. The 20th Indian Division was advancing in Burma. Even the lagging Chinese had mounted the offensive Stilwell had urged a year earlier in the southern part of the country. Marshall's summary concluded with an estimate that it would take another six months to end the war in Europe and approximately eighteen months to defeat Japan. There was no mention made of the atomic bomb. Secretary of War Stimson the night before had only vaguely told the president about "a project looking to the development of a new explosive of almost unbelievable power."

Unsure of himself, Truman made just one immediate decision: to retain the Roosevelt cabinet, at least for the while, and the Joint Chiefs of Staff. Of the cabinet, he had personal doubts, in particular about Secretary of State Edward Stettinius, now next in line for the presidency. Others of Roosevelt's coterie Truman privately dismissed as "crackpots and the lunatic fringe."

The new president had no such doubts about the nation's military leadership. As chairman of the Senate committee monitoring the military mobilization, Truman had come to know and respect the Joint Chiefs—in particular the formal, correct George C. Marshall.

That Saturday afternoon, the Marshalls attended the simple funeral service at the White House. The following day Marshall and King flew to West Point, driving from there to Hyde Park, the president's beloved estate where he would be buried.

The interment service in the rose garden was crowded, Marshall and King barely able to see the grave beside the hemlock hedge. The Reverend George W. Anthony, rector of St. James's Episcopal Church in Hyde Park, the church where Roosevelt had served as a senior warden, read Hymn 411 from the *Episcopal Hymnal* in a voice Supreme Court Associate Justice Felix Frankfurter deemed of "unworldly authority and strangely powerful":

> Now the Laborer's Task is Done:
> Now the Battle Day is Past.
> Now upon the farther shore
>   Lands the voyager at last. . . .
> Father in Thy gracious keeping;
>   Leave we now our brother sleeping.

He had been president of the United States for twelve years, one month, and eight days. He had led the nation through Depression, restoring confidence in its institutions and in itself. He had shaped a New Deal with legislation that provided a measure of social security in America for the first time. He had reformed American industrial capacity, bending it to the needs of the Army and Navy, directing a massive military build-up to aid the nation's allies. Then he had led the country for more than four years at war. Suddenly he was gone.

Seventeen minutes after the rector began, Sergeant Powder's pallbearers eased the heavy casket into the ground. An honor guard loosed three volleys into the clear sky. A bugler sounded "Taps." The Roosevelt Years had ended.

On the train returning to Washington, the president's widow wrote a single thank-you note, addressing it in a trembling hand to George Marshall. Marshall, who disdained personal honors, thought enough of the note to share it with his wife.

> I want to tell you tonight how deeply I appreciate your kind thoughtfulness in all the arrangements made. My husband would have been grateful and I know it was all as he would have wished it. He always spoke of his trust in you and of his affection for you.

For Marshall, the most urgent matter was establishing a working relationship with the new president. Marshall had previously treated the Missouri senator deferentially, recognizing the political importance of the Truman Committee. Truman had been "a nuisance," according to

H. Merrill Pasco, an assistant secretary of the General Staff. "He wanted all sorts of information. We thought we had a war to fight; we didn't need to fight the Congress. It was important what he was doing, but it was just something extra for the staff to do that we wished we didn't have to do, but the general saw to it he got what he wanted."

The general's courtesy had inspired respect in return, and something bordering on affection—or at least as much affection as Marshall's austere manner permitted. The new president's military aide, Colonel Harry H. Vaughan, was soon telling reporters an anecdote about how Truman had pleaded for an active service assignment when the war began, only to be turned down. "This is a young man's war," Vaughan quoted the chief of staff.

Reminded by Truman that Marshall was older by four years, Marshall replied, "That's different. I'm a general and you are a colonel."

Marshall's influence upon the new president was not at first apparent. On Monday, April 23, Truman called a group together at the White House to discuss a scheduled meeting with Soviet Foreign Minister Vyacheslav Molotov, the implacable negotiator the Americans had nicknamed "Iron Pants." On his way to San Francisco and the organizing meeting of Roosevelt's United Nations, Molotov was to meet with Truman later that day to discuss the fate of Poland.

Truman had come to the White House as ill-prepared as any man for the task. President Roosevelt, who had conducted his own foreign policy with little recourse to the State Department, had neglected to brief Truman at any point since the election six months earlier. To prepare himself for the Molotov meeting, Truman had talked with a pessimistic Averell Harriman and then spent much of the weekend reading Yalta Conference documents.

What he read angered him. In violation of a strict interpretation of the Yalta Accords, the Soviet Union had installed a docile government in Poland dominated by its handpicked men. Truman insisted the Soviets honor the Yalta agreement, as vague as it was. "I intend to tell Molotov that in words of one syllable," he snapped.

Secretary of State Stettinius opened the April 23 meeting, reporting that Molotov adamantly insisted the Polish puppets be recognized as the de facto government of Poland and seated at the forthcoming San Francisco Conference. Though he didn't say it, that Russian insistence stemmed from Stalin's belief that "this war is not as in the past. Whoever occupies a territory also imposes on it his own social system. Everyone imposes his own system as far as his army can reach." Stalin intended to create an insulating band of nations along his western border, but his insistence on immediate recognition of the so-called Lublin government ran contrary to the agreement at Yalta that Poland was to have free elections.

The president opened the meeting with the peremptory comment that adherence to the Yalta agreement "so far had been a one-way street." That was to stop. If the Soviets pressed the Polish matter at San Francisco, "they could go to hell."

Alone of the men in the room, Henry Stimson urged moderation. Perhaps the Soviets were "being more realistic than we were in regard to their own security."

Long distrustful of the Russians, Admiral Leahy immediately countered. "He had left Yalta with the impression that the Soviet government had no intention of permitting a free government to operate in Poland. . . ." Leahy urged that the United States reiterate that "we stood for a free and independent Poland."

Stimson was distressed when he realized that he stood alone. "Then to my relief a brave man and a wise man spoke and he said that he, like me, was troubled and urged caution."

George Marshall might have remained silent. This was, after all, basically a political question, and the president had already announced he intended to take a firm position on the Polish issue. Then a succession of political advisers, including the secretaries of state and navy and the American ambassador to Moscow, had endorsed Truman's stand.

But the army chief of staff alone had responsibility for the military aspects of their policy. That special concern led him to be the most cautious of the men who spoke that day, according to the secretary of the navy, James Forrestal. The Russians were sensitive to slights, Marshall believed. Relations with the Soviets "were always delicate. They were always jealous, and it was very, very hard to preserve a coordinated association with them."

Marshall was keenly aware—as most in the room were not—of the increasing fury of Japanese resistance as they drew closer to the home islands. He was aware too of the planners' estimates that the invasion of Japan would cost as many as 250,000 American casualties.

As Forrestal put it, Marshall raised the issue on everyone's mind: securing "Soviet participation in the war against Japan *at a time when it would be useful to us.* The Russians had it within their power to delay their entry into the Far Eastern war until we had done all the dirty work." Marshall agreed with Stimson. The possibility of a break in relations with the Russians would be very serious.

Despite Marshall's concern, the president was to deliver a sharp lecture to the Soviet foreign minister. He warned that there was no chance of congressional approval of requested loans without public support. The Russians were to keep this in mind as they dictated the make-up of the Polish government. "All we were asking," he continued, "was that the Soviet government carry out the Crimea decision on Poland." An agreement had been reached and it "was for Marshal Stalin to carry out that agreement in accordance with his word."

Molotov sputtered in anger. "I have never been talked to like that in my life."

The president curtly dismissed the Russian. "Carry out your agreements and you won't get talked to like that."

Though he had rejected Marshall's counsel, the president's respect for the army chief of staff bordered on awe. Like Stimson, Harry Truman had brought away from his World War I tour in the field artillery treasured memories of great camaraderie and noble service in a just cause. To Harry Truman, onetime captain of Battery D, 129th Field Artillery Regiment, the Army embodied the virtues of patriotic sacrifice, of devotion to duty, and loyalty.

Perhaps it was sentimental, but George Catlett Marshall as chief of staff represented the finest qualities that Harry Truman's fondly remembered Army had to offer: selflessness, dedication, uncompromising integrity. Further, Truman believed Marshall had demonstrated his military leadership as the chief strategist both in Europe and the Pacific. The nation and what Truman came to call "the free world" owed Marshall "a debt of gratitude for his brilliant planning and masterly execution" in prosecuting that war.

With some coaching from the chief of staff, in a matter of days the president was to come around to Marshall's thinking. "General Marshall and I, in discussing each military phase, agreed that if we were to win the peace after winning the war, we had to have Russian help."

That peace was almost upon them. Eisenhower urged that Marshall make a quick trip to the European theater, "while we are still conducting a general offensive. You would be proud of the army you have produced. . . . In a short visit here you could see, in visible form, the fruits of much of your work over the past five years."

It was not to be. The death of President Roosevelt and the swift pace of the German collapse prevented Marshall from seeing for one last time the great armies he had brought into being. On April 25, patrols from the American 69th Infantry and the Russian 58th Guards Divisions made contact at the Elbe. Germany was severed in two.

Eisenhower still confronted problems. Throughout western Europe there were pockets of resistance, notably in Holland, Denmark, and Norway. Montgomery was slow in advancing to the northern coast, raising the possibility that Russian troops would occupy Denmark. "Our arrival at Lubeck before our Russian friends from Stettin would save a lot of argument later on," Churchill told his foreign minister. "There is no reason why the Russians should occupy Denmark, which is a country to be liberated and to have its sovereignty restored."

In the south, Patton's Third Army had reached the Czech border; Prague lay ahead with only disorganized German units defending that political prize. The British chiefs of staff sent a telegram to Marshall in

Washington noting the "remarkable political advantages derived from liberation of Prague and as much as possible of Czechoslovakia by U.S.-U.K. forces."

Forwarding the British message to Eisenhower, Marshall put thumbs down on the proposal: "Personally and aside from all logistic, tactical or strategical implications, I would be loath to hazard American lives for purely political purposes."

Eisenhower understood. There was no use expending American troops to take territory that the Russians could more readily take and territory they would have to surrender in any event. "I shall not attempt any move I deem militarily unwise merely to gain a political prize unless I receive specific orders from the Combined Chiefs of Staff," Eisenhower assured his mentor.

By the end of April, there was no longer any front in the West. Hitler lay dead in a bunker behind the Reich Chancellery, a suicide; his Thousand-Year-Reich had lasted five and a half years. Millions of displaced persons crowded the cratered roads, seeking escape from war. The last Russian offensive chewed up the remnants of ninety-three German divisions; almost a half million were swept into captivity, while other units scattered in flight westward, hoping to surrender to the Americans and British. Literally thousands of German prisoners docilely followed orders of a handful of army clerks herding them into holding pens. Trudging slowly past the stores of Allied equipment, ammunition, clothing, and food, one prisoner-of-war sullenly told a guard, "I know how you won. You piled up all the equipment and let it fall on us." It was an indirect tribute to George Marshall.

On May 6, the German chief of staff, General Alfred August Jodl, arrived at the three-story schoolhouse that served as SHAEF headquarters in Reims to discuss the final surrender with Eisenhower's chief of staff, Walter Bedell Smith. Jodl sought to stall, to give the 1.2 million Germans still fighting the Russians a last opportunity to avoid imprisonment in the East. The well-turned-out Jodl insisted that Allies would soon find themselves fighting the Russians, "and that if Germany were given time to evacuate as many troops and civilians as possible to the west there would be large resources available to help the Allies in the struggle against the Russians."

Smith threatened to close Allied lines if Jodl delayed any longer. Jodl capitulated. In a formal ceremony in the school's assembly hall, he signed the surrender document.

Moments later, Eisenhower dispatched his last war report to the Combined Chiefs of Staff in Washington: "The mission of this Allied Force was fulfilled at 0241, local time, May 7, 1945."

Across the nation crowds erupted into the streets, celebrating victory in Europe, civilians and servicemen alike swept up in momentary frenzy.

Churches were uncommonly filled at midday, the devout offering thanks. At the Pentagon, there was a pause, a sense of elation, H. Merrill Pasco recalled. Marshall was smiling, the door to his office left open for the well-wishers who came by: Hap Arnold, Bill Somervell, Robert Lovett, and a deeply grateful Henry Stimson.

"It was a relaxation," as Pasco described it. "There was great joy and elation, but the main thing was realizing we had to get meeting on the redeployment plan and get the troops from Europe to the Pacific. That was what the general immediately went to work on the next day."

Before then, there were courtesies to be extended. To Dwight Eisenhower, his protégé raised to supreme commander, Marshall radioed congratulations.

> . . . [S]ince the day of your arrival in England three years ago, you have been selfless in your actions, always sound and tolerant and altogether admirable in the courage and wisdom of your military decisions.

> You have made history, great history for the good of mankind and you have stood for all we hope for and admire in an officer of the United States Army. These are my tributes and my personal thanks.

Eisenhower's response brimmed with gratitude for the support the chief of staff had offered over the past three years. Marshall's place in the respect and affection of the army he had created was unparalleled, Eisenhower wrote. "Our army and our people have never been so deeply indebted to any other soldier. . . ."

To Winston Churchill, nemesis and friend, Marshall wrote of the "long and terrible road since the fall of France," of Allied meetings that proved the prime minister's "vast contribution to the reestablishment of a civilized peace in Europe. . . .

"Personally," Marshall continued, "I will cherish the friendship and confidence you gave me during the seemingly slow and tortuous progress to the greatest, the most complete victory in modern history."

Churchill's reply to the man he had called "the true organizer of victory" wryly recalled "the hard inside working of this terrific war." There was

> no one whose good opinion at the end of the struggle I value more than yours.
> It has not fallen to your lot to command the great armies. You have had to create them, organise them, and inspire them. Under your guiding hand the mighty and valiant formations which have

swept across France and Germany were brought into being and perfected in an amazing space of time. . . .

Beyond this, in shaping global strategy, Marshall had been "the mainspring of that marvelous organisation, the Combined Chiefs of Staff, whose conduct and relationship will ever be a model for the planning and supervision of Allied and Combined operations." The prime minister struck a truly Churchillian note in his concluding paragraph:

> There has grown in my breast through all these years of mental exertion a respect and admiration for your character and massive strength which has been a real comfort to your fellow-toilers, of whom I hope it will always be recorded that I was one.

They had achieved victory in Europe, in large part due to Marshall's unswerving direction. Secretary of War Henry Stimson, onetime soldier, sometime statesman, a man weathered by decades of public service, could only express his admiration: "I have seen a great many soldiers in my day and you, sir, are the finest soldier I have ever known."

It was a moment out of war. Ahead lay the Pacific—and the most awesome weapon in history.

C H A P T E R

XXXI

A Second Coming in Wrath

The moment of satisfaction was short-lived. Praised by *The New York Times* with Henry Stimson as "the architects of victory," George Marshall immediately turned his attention to the Pacific theater. Only half of the war had been won.

The redeployment of troops from Europe had already begun. Some 1.8 million men with the highest number of rotation points would be brought home for a series of carefully planned victory parades and discharges; the balance, 6 million soldiers, would be directed against Japan.

The margin was narrow, too narrow, Marshall fretted. The Japanese military numbered 4 million men overseas and an estimated 2.5 million garrisoned in the home islands. The United States would have barely sufficient forces to invade Japan, if the Imperial Army was prevented from transferring units from China back to Japan. The entry of the Soviet Union into the war was vital to prevent that reinforcement.

Overconfidence was a concern too. With Germany defeated, too many Americans believed that Japan, Japan of the Crackerjack toys, Japan of the buck-toothed, near-sighted, and obsequious, would collapse. "Waves of B-29s to cut an invasion path," headlines promised. Would it were so easy.

They had sent waves of B-29s over Japan since March. The Air Force estimated it could destroy Japan's industrial capacity by area bombing, the British strategy Americans had rejected in Europe in favor of so-called precision bombing. Japan's cities with their wood-and-paper housing were tempting targets.

On the night of March 9–10, B-29s flying from Guam had dropped 1,665 tons of incendiaries over Tokyo; a quarter of the city was destroyed in the resulting firestorm, a million people left homeless. More than 83,000 died in what the Japanese called "the raid of the fire wind," another

41,000 were injured. Nagoya, Osaka, and Kobe suffered in rapid order. In a single week, B-29s had seared a forty-square-mile swath across Japan.

Japan was failing, its economy slipping into paralysis. American air supremacy and unhindered submarine warfare had all but cut off the flow of vital raw materials from the outposts of the Greater East Asia Co-Prosperity Sphere. Oil refining had been reduced by 83 percent, airframe production by 60 percent. Without fuel, Japanese naval vessels hunkered in the mudflats of Tokyo Bay to become immobile artillery waiting for the invasion.

American naval planners argued that a tight blockade alone would bring Japan to its knees. Air force planners held that bombing would finish the job. Only Marshall insisted that invasion of the home islands would be necessary, pointing out the Japanese showed no sign of relenting.

If anything, Japan's resolve was stronger. A committee of the Japanese House of Peers forecast "twenty years of all-out war. . . . It should give just enough time for the Anglo-American warmongers to die off."

The Japanese were proving to be far tougher than expected. No matter how impossible his situation, the Nipponese soldier refused to surrender. Ten months after the end of organized resistance in the Marianas, stubborn Japanese on Guam, Tinian, and Saipan still ambushed unwary GIs. On Mindanao and on Negros, there remained pockets of unyielding holdouts; in the mountains of Luzon, MacArthur reported, 25,000 Japanese under General Yamashita fought on in a hopeless cause; they could neither escape nor even impede their enemy, yet they fought on, preferring starvation to surrender.

Others deliberately chose to sacrifice themselves. The first of the "Divine Wind," the *kamikaze* aircraft, had taken part in the Battle of Leyte Gulf the past October. The attacks had increased in March with the assault on Okinawa, where a new weapon, a manned, rocket-powered suicide bomb, also homed in on the invasion fleet. In the last three months, there had been 1,900 of these *kamikaze* attacks; they had sunk 26 American naval vessels and damaged 176 others.

The closer the Americans came to the home islands, the more desperate the fighting. Iwo Jima, a volcanic peak in a troubled ocean 750 miles from Tokyo, cost the Marines 6,000 dead; just 218 of the more than 20,000 Japanese defenders were alive after a month-long fight to clear the island.

Pondering the escalating casualty tolls, Marshall had earlier asked his Operations Division to consider the use of disabling gases in future campaigns. The chief of staff proposed the use of enough incapacitating gas to drive defenders from their bunkers or to keep the Japanese in gas masks for a week. That would leave them so weakened that the battle would be a walkover, Marshall suggested.

Marshall's willingness to consider the use of noxious gases, a violation of the Geneva Convention, was a reflection of his concern about the cost of ultimate victory. The use of gas risked public disapproval, the chief of staff acknowledged; nonetheless, the "character of the weapon was no less humane than phosphorus and flame throwers and need not be used against dense populations or civilians—merely against those last pockets of resistance which had to be wiped out but had no other military significance."

British protests shelved the plan. "The reason it was not used was chiefly the strong opposition of Churchill and the British. They were afraid that this would be the signal for the Germans to use gas against England," Marshall explained later.

Okinawa in the Ryukyu chain, just 350 miles south of Japan, was even more costly than Iwo Jima had been. The fighting there was savage; more than 12,000 Americans had died to take an island just sixty miles long. Another 36,631 were wounded. Ninety percent of the Japanese garrison, 109,000 determined troops, died defending an island where American advances were measured in feet per day.

The more desperate the Japanese position, the harder they seemed to fight. Taking the ferocity of the defenders into account, Marshall's planners now predicted 250,000 American casualties during the two-stage assault on Japan proper. That toll would be worse still if the Soviet Union did not tie down the elite Japanese Kwantung Army in Manchuria, Marshall warned British Foreign Secretary Anthony Eden in April.

The first stage of the invasion, an assault on the southernmost of the home islands, Kyushu, was tentatively set for December 1, 1945. This first attack, dubbed OLYMPIC, would be followed three months later by Operation CORONET, the invasion of the main island of Honshu.

Looking on the Pacific War with proprietary interest, Ernest King bridled at the command arrangement; Douglas MacArthur, an army man, was to command OLYMPIC-CORONET, selected by President Roosevelt the previous fall over the chief of naval operation's nominee, Admiral Chester Nimitz.

Admiral King would not yield graciously. He insisted that command of the fleet remain in naval hands. Marshall was alarmed; the Navy had insisted on divided responsibility at Leyte. The result was a near disaster. Ignoring MacArthur's protests, the naval commander, Bull Halsey, had left the transport fleet barely defended off the Leyte beaches, dispatching his main force to chase the will-of-the-wisp of every battleship admiral, a climactic sea battle. Only by the narrowest of margins did scratch naval forces left behind turn aside the main Japanese fleet before it could get in among the hapless transports.

There could be no repetition. "Control of the naval resources directly involved in putting the armies ashore is essential to the success of the operation and must be given to the commander having primary responsibility for the operation," Marshall stressed in a memorandum to King.

The chief of naval operations remained unyielding; he not only refused to let MacArthur command the amphibious assault, but he resisted designating an overall commander at all.

Within three days Marshall had forced a compromise upon King. MacArthur was to have overall command of CORONET, issuing orders in case of exigencies through the naval commander. If nothing else, the Navy could save face. Marshall never explained just how he compelled King to reason; the likelihood is that King feared a worse bargain if the chief of staff appealed to the president. After all, Truman was an army man, a reserve colonel. Worse still, Marshall had his ear and King did not.

Harry S. Truman, the unexpected president, had proved to be far more sound than many in Washington dared hope. He had taken command; unassuming as he might be, he *was* the president, and the Constitution, which he revered, vested authority in that office. "I am here to make decisions, and whether they prove right or wrong I am going to make them," Truman insisted to Foreign Minister Anthony Eden.

Truman's spunky confidence reassured Eden, that and the suggestion that the new president would rely on his chief of staff. Just four days after Truman was sworn in, British Ambassador Lord Halifax assured Churchill that Truman "venerates Marshall."

Marshall had almost incidentally earned Truman's respect during the early days of the mobilization, when he had ordered the War Department to cooperate with Truman and his Special Committee to Investigate the National Defense Program.

In the wrong hands, the Truman Committee might have proved an impediment to mobilization. Instead, the chairman scrutinized for waste the billions in defense expenditures with the same punctilious care he had devoted to the Fulton County, Missouri, road fund. The chief of staff might well have resisted the committee or, worse, embarrassed Truman by claiming the senator was impeding the all-important war effort. In fact, Marshall acknowledged the Congress's constitutional right to monitor defense appropriations and ask embarrassing questions, even when Truman turned up awkward, if local, scandals. Marshall also overcame Truman's long-held distaste for staff officers—"either West Pointers or from Dea' old Yale or H'va'd don'tche know"—in large part with confidential briefings of key senators.

In the end, Brehon Somervell estimated, the Truman Committee had saved the nation $15 billion without damaging the mobilization. The careful Harry Truman had come away with enough of a national reputation to garner for himself the vice-presidential nomination in 1944.

Given only a handful of perfunctory duties by FDR, Truman was unschooled in the issues or the responsibilities when he found himself thrust suddenly into the White House six months later. To newsmen he had known as a senator, he pleaded, "Boys, if you ever pray, pray for me now."

To such a man, a friendly face would be welcome, someone to be trusted, to rely upon as much as a president might depend upon any man. Truman found two: the army chief of staff, and a former crony from the Senate, Roosevelt's director of the Office of War Mobilization, the "assistant president for domestic affairs," James F. Byrnes.

Jaunty Jimmy Byrnes was a ferret of a politician, "able and conniving," Truman thought. "My, but he has a keen mind!" he marveled.

Born in rather humble circumstances, Byrnes had opportunistically learned shorthand in order to become a court reporter. Quickly enough he discovered he might be a lawyer himself. His career thereafter was luminous. As a congressman, then as a senator from South Carolina, as a Supreme Court associate justice, finally as Roosevelt's unofficial "assistant president," the prissy, fastidious Byrnes had repeatedly distinguished himself.

Once he might have hoped to be FDR's vice president, and perhaps even to succeed him. Roosevelt "played upon the ambitions of men as an artist would play upon the strings of a musical instrument," Byrnes later said bitterly. But passed over as a political liability to the ticket—Catholics, labor, and blacks were thought to be against him—Byrnes tasted the gall. He now served a junior colleague whom he had tutored in the ways of the Senate a decade before. Even appointment as secretary of state, which was soon to follow, could not expunge the sense that he had unjustly been deprived of the presidency.

It was to his old friend and mentor Byrnes that Harry Truman turned to handle the project the British called "Tube Alloys," Stimson referred to as "S-1," and the Army termed, after the location of its first office, "The Manhattan Engineer District." Byrnes was not only reliable but had followed the atomic bomb's progress since 1943 when he assumed responsibility for war mobilization.

Begun in August 1942, the project to build an atomic bomb by 1945 employed 150,000 people. Few of them knew what they were actually working on. Fewer still in Washington knew of the bomb program; Hap Arnold's deputy, the assistant chief of staff for air, did not learn of it until January 1945, when it became necessary to train the air crews that would drop the greatest weapon in the history of warfare.

On December 30, 1944, the officer in charge of the project, Major General Leslie Groves, informed Marshall that the first bomb, with a destructive power estimated at the equivalent of 10,000 tons of TNT, would be ready about August 1, 1945. The question was what to do with this awesome weapon.

First informed of the A-bomb on the evening of Roosevelt's death,

Harry Truman turned to consideration of the use of the bomb after an April 25 meeting with Stimson and Groves. (Marshall deliberately excused himself on the grounds that his presence would alert reporters to a good story.) Still feeling his way, the president on May 2 appointed an opaquely named Interim Committee to advise him about "the most terrible weapon known in human history, one bomb of which could destroy a whole city." Stimson was to be chairman of the committee, but the most influential member was the man who had the president's ear, his personal representative to the committee, James F. Byrnes.

The Interim Committee met for the first time in a day-long session at the Pentagon on May 31. The committee members were on unfamiliar ground; for the first time military men, Marshall and Stimson, "expressed the view that atomic energy could not be considered simply in terms of military weapons but must also be considered in terms of a new relationship of man to the universe."

The chief of staff was plainly disturbed about the nuclear bomb. On purely military grounds he favored use of the weapon to shorten the war. At the same time, he recognized what he called "primordial considerations."

"Don't ask *me* to make the decision," he told Assistant Secretary of War John J. McCloy.

In a May 29 conversation with Stimson and McCloy about concluding the war with minimum casualties on both sides, Marshall said that

> he thought these weapons might first be used against straight military objectives such as a large naval installation and then if no complete result was derived from the effect of that, he thought we ought to designate a number of large manufacturing areas from which the people would be warned to leave—telling the Japanese that we intended to destroy such centers. . . . We must offset by such warning methods the opprobrium which might follow from an ill-considered employment of such force.

Whatever Marshall's concerns, by the time the Interim Committee held its first meeting on May 31, "it seemed to be a foregone conclusion that the bomb would be used," said one of the sixteen participants in the meeting.

Marshall, in attendance though not formally a member of the committee, was troubled about the use of a weapon capable of leveling entire cities. Perhaps he recalled the furor surrounding the use of gas in the first war; perhaps he of all those attending the meeting best understood the meaning of casualty tolls in the tens of thousands.

In the interests of harmony between allies, the chief of staff also raised the question of informing the Soviet Union about the atomic bomb. Marshall discounted the sometimes tortuous problem of American-Soviet military dealings, attributing Russia's seemingly uncooperative attitude in military matters to its obsession with security. He wondered whether two Russian scientists might be invited to observe a planned test of the plutonium bomb in the forbidding desert of southwestern New Mexico.

Byrnes wanted no part of it. "If information were given to the Russians, even in general terms, Stalin would ask to be brought into the partnership," the president's personal representative said.

Groves had estimated that the Russians were twenty years from building their own bomb; Byrnes had no intention of helping them cut that lead time. He wanted secrecy.

From then on, the morning discussion "revolved around the question raised by Secretary Stimson as to whether there was any hope at all of using this development to get less barbarous relations with the Russians."

At lunch—the chief of staff had excused himself—Byrnes asked Ernest O. Lawrence, one of four leading scientists on the Manhattan District, to expand upon a morning suggestion that the bomb be used in a bloodless demonstration that would shock the Japanese into surrender.

J. Robert Oppenheimer, the head of the bomb development group in Los Alamos, New Mexico, was skeptical. What if the bomb were a dud, he asked. There were logistical difficulties to an unfettered test; the Japanese were not likely to allow a bomb to be exploded over Japan without trying to interrupt the test.

Byrnes himself performed the *coup de grâce* on the bloodless demonstration proposal: "If the Japanese were told that the bomb would be used on a given locality, they might bring our boys who were prisoners of war to that area." As abruptly as that, the notion of a warning demonstration of the nuclear bomb was throttled.

Byrnes presented the Interim Committee report to the president along with a deliberately attentuated estimate of American casualties in the battle for Japan. According to Byrnes, "The military experts informed us that, from the facts at their disposal, they believed our invasion would cost us a million casualties, to say nothing of those of our Allies and of the enemy."

The question of casualties was to figure heavily in the discussions of the next weeks over use of the nuclear bomb. MacArthur's planners forecast that more than 110,000 Americans would be killed or wounded in the preliminary Kyushu attack. MacArthur himself, fearing a high estimate would abort the operation he so coveted, assured Marshall it would be fewer. The invasion of the Tokyo Plain, however, "would have been a deadly thing," he acknowledged later. According to Marshall, that last assault "would take a million men for the landing and a million to hold it and . . . he thought such a landing would involve half a million casualties."

Two months earlier, Marshall had cautioned Stimson not to make a hasty judgment about the self-effacing man thrust into the White House. Whether Harry Truman were good or bad, Marshall advised a skeptical Stimson, "We shall not know what he is really like until the pressure begins to be felt."

That time had come.

The calendar for Monday, June 18, was crowded. In the morning Marshall welcomed Dwight Eisenhower to Washington as a returning hero, riding with him in the muggy heat at the head of a triumphant parade of European veterans who were to be discharged. The largest crowd ever to see a parade in the capital cheered Eisenhower and his wife as they rolled in the open Packard slowly up Pennsylvania Avenue. It was a joyful, tumultuous moment of triumph for the chief of staff and the man he had marked for history's ledger little more than three years before. This was Eisenhower's hour, but satisfying, so satisfying, to the man who had made it possible.

That afternoon the president convened a sober meeting of the Joint Chiefs of Staff at the White House. There was one item on the agenda: ending the war in the Far East.

At the president's request, Marshall opened the discussion with a justification of the agreed-upon next step, the invasion of Kyushu scheduled for November 1. No other target, not Formosa, not Korea, not the China coast, so clearly put the Japanese government on notice that the United States intended to prosecute the war to the end, he argued.

Privately, both King and Leahy had reservations. King had favored an attack on the mainland of China in order to create an unsinkable staging area for the invasion of Japan. He also believed that tightening the blockade around the home islands would force Japan to surrender without an invasion. Leahy was even more vigorously opposed to this OLYMPIC plan, even more certain that naval blockade and saturation bombing would end the war without the Army's involvement. Still, both had gone along with OLYMPIC on the grounds that *planning* was harmless, certain that Japan could be forced to surrender before the actual invasion.

Each of the chiefs of staff reflected the doctrines of his service. Leahy and King favored a sea blockade producing a naval victory in a naval theater. Arnold instead advocated air bombardment.

Marshall was dubious of both alternatives. "We had 100,000 people killed in Tokyo in one night [by] bombs and it had had seemingly no effect whatsoever." A naval blockade would prolong the war even as the American public showed signs of war weariness. Marshall's thinking too was shaped by army dogma holding that no enemy could be defeated until its army had been destroyed. The war against Germany had once more proved the thesis.

Marshall's alternative would be costly, Admiral Leahy warned. If the Kyushu operation suffered the 35 percent casualty rate they had incurred on Okinawa, Leahy predicted, they could expect 268,000 dead and wounded.

Aware that the president was concerned about expected casualties, Marshall came to the meeting with a message from MacArthur that minimized casualty estimates:

> I believe the operation prevents less hazards of excessive loss than any other that has been suggested and that its decisive effect will eventually save lives by eliminating wasteful operations of nondecisive character. . . . [S]ooner or later a decisive ground attack must be made. The hazard and loss will be greatly lessened if an attack is launched from Siberia sufficiently ahead of our target date to commit the enemy to major combat. I most earnestly recommend no change in OLYMPIC.

The president was not encouraged. The toll in the Pacific had been heavy and he wanted to avoid "an Okinawa from one end of Japan to the other."

The Russians might be poker-playing Harry Truman's ace in the hole. Would the Soviet Union's declaration of war against Japan be enough to shock the Japanese into surrender? And was the resulting increased Soviet influence in the Far East worth it?

Admiral King was lukewarm. Whatever advantage there might be to Russian participation—Truman spoke of saving 100,000 American lives by the Soviet Union's entry into the war in the Far East—the Russians were "not indispensable, and he [King] did not think we should go so far as to beg them to come in. While the cost of defeating Japan would be greater, there was no question in his mind but that we could handle it alone."

Alone of the chiefs of staff, Marshall urged the importance of Soviet participation to bring the war to an end. Furthermore, he noted dryly, the Soviet Union would march on Manchuria whenever the Soviet Union so desired.

With some reluctance, Truman ordered them to continue preparations for a Kyushu assault on November 1 and a Honshu landing four months later. He would give his final approval soon.

The bomb was now driving American policy, or its manufacture was. Early in the life of what they informally called "the Manhattan project," scientists had conceived of two forms of the bomb. One, made from uranium, was certain to work, the scientists said; it would be detonated by firing a "bullet" of atomic matter into a critical mass at the other end of the casing. The second form, constructed of plutonium, was more problematical. It depended upon fissionable material fired from the circumference of a sphere colliding in the center and going critical. It was this second, implosion bomb they were going to test in New Mexico.

The test was crucial. The scientists had refined plutonium enough for only two bombs, and processed uranium for one. The bombing strategy called for dropping two nuclear weapons, one to demonstrate the weapon's power to the Japanese, the second to prove that the United States had production capacity. Only that way, General Groves argued, would the bomb compel the obdurate Japanese to surrender.

This series of meetings wove together the American policies dealing with the conclusion of the war, employment of the A-bomb, and relations with the Soviet Union. Testing both men and ideas, they were tutorial sessions for a new president with no experience in foreign affairs who found himself about to set off to Germany and his first meeting with Winston Churchill and Joseph Stalin.

The conference at Potsdam, a relatively unscathed suburb of Berlin, was to be the last of the war. Code-named TERMINAL, it was largely a political meeting at which Stalin and Truman were to take each other's measure while shaping postwar Europe. Although the Joint Chiefs of Staff attended, the strategic decisions had already been made in Washington. By and large the chiefs spent their time coordinating contingency plans with their Soviet and British colleagues for the war in the Pacific. Great Britain anticipated immediately dispatching a sizable naval flotilla and a force of 300 bombers; the Red Army was already refitting, then transferring combat troops from Germany across two continents to the Manchurian border.

Stalin had selected the mosquito-infested former German movie colony along the shores of Lake Griebnitz in the Soviet zone at least in part for symbolic purposes. It was in Potsdam, in the elegant Sans Souci Palace, that Frederick the Great shaped the traditions of Prussian militarism which had led twice in a lifetime to German invasions of the Soviet Union and twice to German defeats.

On the afternoon of July 16, the American chiefs of staff met briefly with President Truman to discuss the comparatively short military agenda. Truman agreed with Marshall's proposals for a single commander in the Pacific—Marshall had secured the post for MacArthur—and American responsibility for strategy in that theater. The British participation in the fighting in the Pacific theater would be minimal; neither they nor the Russians were to share in the garrisoning of a defeated Japan. The British were to be consulted politely, patronized really; the decisions would be made in Washington.

Marshall and Arnold toured shattered Berlin that afternoon under skies that threatened rain. Their staff car with its military escort wound through the partially cleared streets, past the towering heaps of brick and wood that had once been stores and apartments, offices and homes. Hardly a building had been left untouched by the war. It was "terrible desolation," Arnold recalled, yet the inevitable refugees in forlorn hope straggled back on bicycles and pushcarts to live amid the filth of the unburied and of disinterred sewer lines. Here and there bedraggled workers, men and women, old and young, formed lines to pass broken bricks onto great piles of dusty rubble. What would it take to rebuild Berlin, Arnold asked rhetorically. Twenty, twenty-five years. He suggested it would be better to find a new site and start afresh.

Marshall and Arnold stopped their tour to visit the Reich Chancellery and Hitler's office, picking their way through the litter of the shell-pocked building. Scattered amid the documents strewn on the floor lay thousands of Iron Crosses never awarded. Adolf Hitler's large marble desk lay shattered. A number of ranking officials would pocket souvenirs; Marshall himself ended up with a small shard of marble from Hitler's desk.

The destruction was numbing. Marshall and Arnold retreated to the street and more damage. The Sieges-Allee, Victory Way, was a shambles. The few heroic statues that had survived the Russian shelling had been toppled by marauding Russian troops. The Tiergarten was barren, its gaunt trees broken or stripped, the once shaded park benches with their signs reading *Nicht für Juden* smashed. Berlin was no more. Marshall and Arnold found no comfort and little satisfaction in that.

At seven-thirty that evening, Secretary of War Henry Stimson received a cable from Washington. The plutonium bomb that scientists offhandedly described as "the gadget," sited on a tower 100 feet above the desert floor of the Jornada del Muerto in southwestern New Mexico, had momentarily turned the darkness before dawn into broad daylight. Stimson immediately told the president and Byrnes.

At noon the next day, July 17, Stimson told Marshall and Arnold of the successful test. With Assistant Secretary of War John J. McCloy, they discussed the timetable for use of the bomb and the question of targets. They agreed that the commander of the Air Force in the Pacific should choose the target from a list of four cities—Hiroshima, Kokura, Niigata, and Nagasaki—provided by Stimson. The bomb was not to be dropped before August 2, and not without a veiled warning issued from Washington.

With little dispute, the Combined Chiefs of Staff that afternoon settled on joint operations in the assault on Japan. Alan Brooke foresaw trouble ahead. "We want a greater share in the control of the strategy in the Pacific," he wrote in his diary, "and they are apparently reluctant to provide this share." British control, the Americans suspected, inevitably meant a diversion of effort from the main thrust to campaigns to free the former colonies, notably Singapore, Hong Kong, and Malaya. The Dutch and French too would certainly clamor for quick recovery of their colonies before native independence movements took root.

In "a very nice speech" the following day, Marshall diplomatically but firmly rebuffed the British on the question of control. As Brooke noted in his diary, "They would be prepared to discuss strategy but final decisions must rest with them. If the plan for the invasion of the Tokyo plain did not suit us, we could withhold our forces but they would still carry on." If that was the best the senior partner would yield, Brooke would accept graciously. Britain needed a presence in the Far East to reestablish the Empire's credibility among the native people.

On the evening of July 17, Churchill and Marshall dined alone, two old comrades near rest. Churchill was weary, and awaiting the results of a July 5 referendum on his ministry. The general election results had been withheld for three weeks to allow the soldiers' vote to be counted while the prime minister swung between optimism and the gloom of imminent retirement. Churchill confessed to his private secretary that he was overpowered by the end of a familiar order in Europe and the beginning of a new, "weighed down by responsibility and uncertainty." England was impotent, bled white by the war; Truman and Stalin would largely shape this new Europe.

For Churchill, Potsdam was a time of summation, of closure. To his personal physician, a pensive Churchill later that evening described Marshall as "the noblest Roman of them all. Congress always did what he advised. His work in training the American armies has been wonderful. I will pay tribute to it one day when the occasion offers."

In this golden moment of victory, Stalin too was personally generous in his estimate of the American chief of staff. After a dinner hosted by the British, Stalin puffed on a Churchillian cigar and pointed out Marshall across the table. "That is a man I admire. He is a good general. We have good generals in the Soviet Army, but so have you and the Americans. Only ours still lack breeding, and their manners are bad."

Stimson received more details about the New Mexico test on Wednesday, July 18. Light from the explosion had been visible for 250 miles, the blast heard for 40, Groves reported from Washington. The inference for the American delegation at Potsdam was that this was surely the club to stun the Japanese into surrender.

That moment was approaching. A succession of decoded radio intercepts revealed that the Japanese foreign minister had ordered his ambassador in Moscow to call on Molotov before the Soviets left for Potsdam. The ambassador was to inform Molotov that the emperor earnestly wished an end to the bloodshed. The ambassador was to state that Japan was ready to yield its conquered territory. This was not unconditional surrender, but Japan was wavering. One decisive blow, an atomic bomb whose blast could be seen 250 miles away, might push the Japanese to a decision.

Secretary Stimson forwarded the report from the atomic test site to Marshall, who was meeting with the Combined Chiefs of Staff. Marshall looked at it without emotion, then turned it face down on the table. Some moments later he suggested they go into executive session, clearing the room of all but the chiefs themselves. When they were alone, he announced in a matter-of-fact voice that the nuclear test on the desert called the Path of the Dead had been a complete success.

Privately, the British were shaken. Pug Ismay, often the genial broker in arguments between Yanks and Brits, felt revulsion. Admiral Cunningham, a man Marshall admired for his intellect, would come to regard the bomb's use as a mistake. Yet whatever their reservations, they said nothing; after all, it was the Americans who would have to bear the brunt of the assault and the casualties in the invasion of Japan.

That afternoon, a relaxed and affable George Marshall escorted the Combined Chiefs of Staff on a review of George Patton's old 2nd Armored Division, the largest of its kind in the world. Six hundred vehicles lined Unter der Linden for almost two miles; it was an unabashed display of the puissant American Army Marshall had created, an army that had turned the tide in the West.

"George was most friendly, almost gushing," Patton wrote his wife with discernible pride. A hero to the public, the fighting general with an ivory-handled pistol on each hip, Patton still craved his old friend's approval.

Alone for a moment that day, Arnold and Marshall talked about retirement. The war near its end, Arnold suggested, they did not have to pull quite so heavy a load. Better to let younger men have a chance. In short it was about time to retire, said Arnold, only too aware of his four heart attacks in the past three years.

But when Marshall agreed, Arnold scoffed. Marshall was too valuable to be retired. Arnold offered to bet five dollars the chief of staff would still be in office six months after Japan surrendered.

The tenor of the talks at Potsdam changed with word of the successful test of the plutonium bomb. Truman and Byrnes, his new secretary of state, took a harder attitude toward the Russians. Byrnes saw in the bomb a tool to minimize Soviet involvement in the Far East. Once the bomb were used, Byrnes told his personal secretary, "Japan will surrender and Russia will not get in so much on the kill, [and thereby gain] a position to press for claims against China." The bomb could effectively annul the Yalta agreement.

The president was hugely pleased when Stimson relayed a report from the scientists that the bomb had a yield of 15 to 20 kilotons, more than they had expected. He said "it gave him an entirely new feeling of confidence," Stimson wrote in his diary.

Churchill too was elated when the secretary of war showed him the scientists' report. "Stimson, what was gunpowder? Trivial. What was electricity? Meaningless. This atomic bomb is the second coming in wrath." Churchill advised telling the Soviets nothing more than the fact that they were working on an atomic weapon and would use it if and when it was successfully tested.

In formal meetings and informal conversations Stalin had pressed hard for a larger Soviet role in world affairs. In Poland, Bulgaria, Hungary, and Yugoslavia were newly installed governments sympathetic to the Russians—if not wholly controlled by them. In Austria and Czechoslovakia the Russians had feelers out. Moreover Stalin wanted a base in Turkey, and a presence in the Mediterranean. He proposed trusteeships for Korea, Hong Kong, and Indochina, all of which would give the USSR influence where none had existed. Some of the demands were bluff or bargaining chips, Truman realized, but there was no doubt the Russians meant to play a larger role in the postwar world than they had prior to 1939.

Truman determined to resist Soviet expansion. The major question, the president told Stimson on the morning of July 23, was how crucial Marshall believed Soviet participation in northern China to be.

Marshall declined to answer explicitly. This was effectively a political question, and Marshall did not meddle in matters political. Yes, Marshall had wanted the Russians in—they all had—so as to pin a significant portion of the Japanese Army along the Sino-Soviet border. That had worked even without the Soviets declaring war. Once the Russians started building up their forces along the border, the Japanese had been forced to counter. "Even if we went ahead in the war without the Russians," Marshall continued, "and compelled the Japanese to surrender to our terms, that would not prevent the Russians from marching into Manchuria anyhow and striking, thus permitting them to get virtually what they want in the surrender terms."

From the conversation and Marshall's diffidence, Stimson deduced that "Marshall felt, as I felt sure he would, that now with our new weapon we would not need the assistance of the Russians to conquer Japan."

The decision to drop the atomic bomb rested solely with the president. The targets had been selected. Marshall and Stimson had recommended the bomb be used. Churchill concurred, hours before he learned Labor had turned out his Conservative majority. Winston Churchill was once more in opposition; Labor Party leader Clement Attlee would become prime minister.

On the morning of July 25, Marshall forwarded the president's orders to the specially trained 509th Composite Group waiting on Tinian. The first bomb was to be dropped on either Hiroshima, Kokura, Niigata, or Nagasaki as soon after August 3 as weather conditions permitted visual bombing.

The target date was one week after the July 26 release of the Potsdam ultimatum demanding unconditional surrender, lest Japan suffer "complete and utter destruction." Signed by Truman, Churchill, and Chiang Kai-shek, the demand made no mention of an atomic bomb.

The Potsdam Proclamation called for the occupation of Japan—Marshall had already alerted Douglas MacArthur that it might "prove necessary to take action within the near future on the basis of Japanese capitulation, possibly before Russian entry"—and the reconstruction of the nation as a democracy. The document did nothing to clarify the status of the emperor.

The clock began running on the life of the target cities.

The Japanese response was equivocal. A single issue loomed: would they be permitted to keep the emperor? The proclamation gave no clue. After a heated discussion in the Imperial Cabinet between those who wanted to continue the war and those who sought peace, Prime Minister Kantaro Suzuki recommended, "We must *mokusatsu* it."

The Japanese response was ambiguous. *Mokusatsu* meant, literally, "to kill with silence." Suzuki himself said he wanted the word to convey "no comment," an equivocation that would give them time to explore through the Russians the future role of the emperor. American translators for the Foreign Broadcast Intelligence Service translated the word as "ignore." As "ignore," it was reported to the White House and in the American press.

The clock was ticking.

Marshall's work was done at Potsdam. With the president's permission he left Berlin for Washington on July 27. The president would stay on to resume diplomatic talks with Stalin and the new British prime minister, Clement Attlee.

Halfway around the world, the Pacific Air Force's stubby chief of staff, Major General Curtis E. LeMay, watched the weather plots. LeMay scrubbed the first mission set for August 4 due to cloud cover over the designated primary target, Hiroshima, seventh largest metropolitan area in Japan.

The next day's forecast was favorable. LeMay gave the order to proceed. On Tinian, the heavily laden B-29 *Enola Gay* lumbered into the air at 2:45 a.m. on Sunday, August 5, formed a V-formation with two escort planes, and disappeared into the night sky.

In Washington, fourteen hours behind Tinian time, the Pentagon waited for word about the mission. Groves by 3:00 p.m. was calling the duty officer in the communications room every fifteen minutes. The usually imperturbable Marshall also called after returning late in the afternoon to Fort Myer from Leesburg. Was there any word? No, he didn't want the duty officer to bother General Groves. "He has enough to think about without answering any unnecessary queries."

Marshall would call Colonel McCarthy, the secretary of the General Staff, at eleven-fifteen that Sunday night, this time to ask if they had received word of the strike. Fifteen minutes later Groves received a message from the mission: "Results clearcut, successful in all respects."

Groves's staff was elated. Prodded by Groves, McCarthy called Quarters No. 1 and woke the chief of staff to relay the news. Marshall merely said, "Thank you very much for calling me."

The next morning, Groves was waiting with an expanded report when Marshall and Arnold arrived at the Pentagon before 7:00 a.m. The explosive force of the uranium weapon dropped upon Hiroshima was apparently greater than the New Mexico bomb, Groves reported. The purple mushroom cloud, with flames swirling upward, had risen 40,000 feet above the stricken city. It was still visible from the observation planes 363 nautical miles away. Though dust obscured any observation of structural damage, it appeared the entire city had been torn apart, one observer reported.

Confronted by an elated Groves, Marshall soberly warned against any excessive celebration. The bomb, after all, meant a large number of civilian casualties. (The Japanese government's final estimate would place the death toll at 130,000.)

Groves replied he "was not thinking so much about those casualties as I was about the men who had made the Bataan death march."

In the hallway outside, Arnold slapped Groves on the back. "I am glad you said that. It's just the way I feel." Groves wanted to believe this was the real attitude of all those who made decisions in the Pentagon, Marshall included.

The Pentagon released a previously prepared statement announcing that a single atomic weapon had been dropped over Hiroshima. The statement quoted President Truman as warning, "We are now prepared to obliterate more rapidly and completely every productive enterprise the Japanese have above ground in any city. . . . Let there be no mistake; we shall completely destroy Japan's power to make war."

Japanese leaders had previously rejected the Potsdam ultimatum. "If they do not now accept our terms they may expect a rain of ruin from the air, the like of which has never been seen on this earth."

The first reaction in Japan was to dismiss the American announcement as propaganda. Some confirmation of the threat arrived in Tokyo the following morning, however, when the army General Staff received the chilling report: "The whole city of Hiroshima was destroyed instantly by a single bomb."

In Moscow, Ambassador Sato under urgent instructions finally gained an interview with newly returned Foreign Minister Molotov. Hopeful of a Soviet offer to mediate between Japan and the United States, Sato instead was brusquely handed a Soviet declaration of war effective the following day, August 8. Stalin had kept his promise to enter the Far Eastern war within three months of the end of hostilities in Europe.

The third and crushing blow fell on August 9. Rushed to the attack by Groves despite bad weather over Japan, a B-29 carrying a plutonium-type "Fat Man" bomb lifted off from Tinian. Its primary target was Kokura and the large military arsenal there. Three times "Bock's Car" flew in over the cloud-observed target and three times it droned away without dropping its bomb. After forty-five minutes, the pilot, Major Charles W. Sweeney, elected to try the secondary target, Nagasaki. Sweeney estimated he had fuel enough for one run.

Only at the last minute did the cloud cover over that city open, allowing the visual bombing run Sweeney's orders mandated. Although the bomb missed its aiming point by a mile and a half, almost half of the city was obliterated. At least 60,000 people died in Nagasaki that day.

There were questions raised almost immediately about the wisdom of the bombing strategy, in particular the drop of a second nuclear weapon. Marshall himself had no doubts:

> I think it was quite necessary to drop the bombs in order to shorten the war. There were hundreds and hundreds of thousands of American lives involved in this thing, as well as hundred [sic] of billions of money. They had been perfectly ruthless. We had notified them of the bomb. They didn't choose to believe that. And what they needed was shock action, and they got it. I think it was very wise to use it.

Because the bomb ended the war, its use was justifiable, he concluded.

The next day, August 10, Japan broadcast its acceptance of the Potsdam terms, so long as they did not prejudice the prerogatives of the emperor as sovereign. As a crowd gathered in front of the White House cheering and singing, a small group of cabinet officers met with the president to weigh the Japanese offer.

Byrnes worried about compromising the unconditional surrender formula. Leahy waved that aside, insisting that retention of the emperor was a minor matter compared to delaying victory. Stimson argued that the emperor was the only authority to compel the Japanese Army to surrender and prevent a score of battles to the end in China and the East Indies. The agreed-upon American response, hastily approved by Great Britain and the Soviet Union, stipulated that the emperor was to be under and responsive to the supreme commander of the allied forces.

For three days they waited while the Imperial Cabinet raged within, a growing peace camp arrayed against the die-hard militarists. Meanwhile conventional bombing of the home islands continued without challenge, and American planes dropped leaflets reporting the surrender offer to the Japanese people for the first time.

The hours dragged in Washington. "Never have I known time to pass so slowly!" James Byrnes complained.

Stimson too agonized. The longer the surrender was delayed, the closer the Soviets, who had invaded Manchuria, came to Japan. "It was of great importance to get the homeland into our hands before the Russians could put in any substantial claim to occupy and help rule it."

In Tokyo, the last of the War Party finally yielded to imperial authority. A tearful Emperor Hirohito himself, to save further loss of life, insisted upon acceptance of the American terms. A number of the discredited War Party would commit *seppuku* rather than submit.

Late on the night of August 14 the emperor nervously recorded a surrender message to be broadcast the following day. "The enemy," he informed his devoted subjects, "has begun to employ a new and most cruel bomb, the power of which to do damage is indeed incalculable, taking the toll of many innocent lives."

Three years, eight months, and eight days after the bombing of Pearl Harbor, World War II had ended.

PART
IV
THE STATESMAN

XXXII

The Chinese Midwife

George Marshall swung the road-worn family Plymouth into the circular driveway of their home in Leesburg, braked, and turned off the ignition. For a moment he sat quietly. Sitting beside her husband, Katherine Marshall sighed with pleasure. Though the fall was not her favorite season, this autumn and this homecoming were especially satisfying.

After forty-three years and nine months, George Catlett Marshall was once more a private citizen. In a deliberately simple ceremony at the Pentagon, Marshall, near tears, was released from duty as the chief of staff of the United States Army on November 26, 1945. One day later, he was beginning his long-anticipated retirement.

Once the president had decided that Dwight Eisenhower would take over for her husband, Marshall was a changed man, Katherine noted happily. A great load had been lifted from him. He smiled more often. He was even carefree at breakfast, idly weighing alternative plans for their retirement, for trips to Florida in the winter, and pheasant hunting at the cabin in Pinehurst. It would be that honeymoon they had never quite fitted in.

Katherine had packed their possessions at Quarters No. 1—including the resplendent dress uniform with its bold yellow sash laid away in an attic box after he had refused to wear it so long ago. Into crates went Marshall's books and the gifts ranging from a grotesque stuffed owl from who-could-remember to the exquisite antique sword presented by the Chinese ambassador, T. V. Soong. All that they would take with them; the Eisenhowers could keep the henhouse and chickens in the backyard at Fort Myer.

The couple stood for a few moments under the portico, savoring the Virginia countryside in the late afternoon sun. Perhaps the tall man took some satisfaction at that moment in what he had accomplished in the past six years: building a victorious army of 9 million men and women, equipped and supported with $167 billion he had requested of Congress. Perhaps he thought of the torrents of tanks, more than 88,000 built since 1940; of the 2.5 million Jeeps and trucks that made the United States Army, *his* army, the most mobile the world had known; of tens of thousands of howitzers, mortars, and anti-aircraft guns; of 12.6 million rifles and carbines, and 2 million machine guns. Perhaps he thought momentarily of the 129,000 combat aircraft he had ordered. Once there had been so few fighters and bombers, not enough to send even ten more B-17s to the Philippines in the first strained days of the war; four years later, Marshall's last act as chief of staff had been to sign an order condemning 2,500 obsolete B-17s to an Arizona scrapheap.

The tall man standing in front of his white Federal home in rural Virginia would have been less than human if he were not satisfied. "For the first time since assuming this office six years ago," he wrote the month before in his last biennial report to the secretary of war, "it is possible for me to report that the security of the United States of America is entirely in our hands."

He could take satisfaction in that, though it had been costly, this destruction of Hitler's Third Reich and Hirohito's Reign of Enlightened Peace. Two hundred thousand soldiers and airmen, including his own stepson, were dead; another 570,000 had been wounded. Millions more had seen combat, returning leeched of their youth, anxious only to get on with the rest of their lives. With them, Marshall felt a special closeness.

"It is impossible for the Nation to compensate for the services of a fighting man," he wrote with the memory of his own experience in the first war. "There is no pay scale that is high enough to buy the services of a single soldier during even a few minutes of the agony of combat, the physical miseries of the campaign, or of the extreme personal inconvenience of leaving his home to go out to the most unpleasant and dangerous spots on earth to serve his Nation."

For a somewhat embarrassed Marshall himself there had been ample rewards in these last months of service and no little acclaim. With the surrender of Japan and the end of fighting, dozens of personal letters of congratulations from heads of state, from field commanders, from other members of the Combined Chiefs of Staff, had poured into the Pentagon. Perhaps the most eloquent came from Marshall's frequent foe, Winston Churchill. Master of the English language that he was, the former prime minister had cabled to the organizer of victory a four-word message profound in its very simplicity: "Thank you very much."

Secretary of War Henry Stimson, whose career in public service dated to the administration of Theodore Roosevelt, had lauded the chief of staff he had come to consider a dear friend. "I have never seen a task of such magnitude performed by man." At Stimson's recommendation,

Congress was considering a bill to strike a special gold medal of appreciation for his efforts; only Ulysses S. Grant had received such an award before him. The president in announcing Marshall's retirement had publicly described him as "the greatest military man that this country ever produced—or any other country for that matter."

The Marshalls turned from the sunny yard, Katherine thinking it all so beautifully peaceful. It seemed a bright omen of their future.

They entered the house together. As Katherine started up the stairs, hoping to nap before dinner, the telephone rang. Marshall went to answer it.

The White House switchboard operator plugged the president in. Without preamble, Harry Truman announced, "General, I want you to go to China for me."

An hour later, Katherine came downstairs to find her husband stretched out on the chaise-longue on the sun porch listening to the three o'clock news broadcast. Standing in the doorway, she heard a newscaster announce that Patrick Hurley had resigned as ambassador to China. "President Truman has appointed General of the Army George C. Marshall as his special ambassadorial envoy to China. He will leave immediately."

Katherine stood dumbstruck. Her husband walked to her. "That phone call as we came in was from the president. I could not bear to tell you until you had had your rest."

It had happened just that suddenly. Without warning, Hurley, transformed into "a son of a bitch" in Truman's eyes, had abruptly resigned, complaining of Communists in the State Department hampering his efforts to shore up the government of Chiang Kai-shek. "A considerable section of our State Department is endeavoring to support communism generally as well as specifically in China," Hurley told wire service reporters. Republican Patrick Hurley had abruptly ended the wartime era of a bipartisan foreign policy.

Word of Hurley's resignation came over the clattering news wires in the White House basement. Secretary of Agriculture Clinton Anderson during a luncheon meeting with the cabinet proposed Marshall as a replacement. Secretary of the Navy James Forrestal agreed. Marshall's appointment would surely steal the headlines from Hurley's charges of Reds in the State Department.

The president was at first reluctant, explaining Marshall had earned his retirement. He briefly mulled the arguments, then put in the call to Leesburg.

Marshall had foreseen such calls to duty long before. Over a year before he had told the British ambassador, Lord Halifax, "When this war ends, there will have been no example in history of a nation as young as ours having such responsibility thrust upon it." The China mission was just

one of the unaccustomed burdens the United States would shoulder as
a world power.

Still the dutiful soldier, he could not shirk his share of that responsibility. For Marshall, there was no choice.

Katherine was furious. "There was the devil to pay" in the Marshall
home, the new presidential envoy later confessed to the president. Their
retirement had been snatched from them, Katherine stormed. She seethed
for some time, writing to her husband's sometime aide, Frank McCarthy,
"This assignment to China was a bitter blow. . . . I give a sickly smile
when people say how the country loves and admires my husband."

The next weeks would be as busy as any Marshall knew during the
war. Amid all the preparation for the mission to China, including drafting his own instructions from the president, Marshall found himself in
an awkward confrontation.

There had been a succession of military inquiries of the Pearl Harbor
attack, seven in all. All had been classified, and the findings heavily cen-
sored so as to protect the secret of MAGIC. To some extent the successive
reports were contradictory; certainly they were confusing. They had done
little to explain how the mightiest nation in the world had been humiliated in a surprise attack. Rumors of President Roosevelt's involvement
and of cover-ups swirled about Washington.

Marshall might have hoped the Pearl Harbor attack was behind him
after August 29, 1945, when Secretary of War Henry Stimson released
the long-classified report of the army board of inquiry investigating the
attack.

At the behest of Congress, the three-man army board had conducted
the most thorough inquiry to that moment.

The army Pearl Harbor board report, submitted in November 1944,
spread the blame for the disaster widely. The Grunert panel concluded,
among other things, that Marshall had failed to keep his staff properly
advised so they could act in his absence. Additionally, the chief of staff
had failed to keep the army commander in the islands, Lieutenant General Walter C. Short, fully informed of the worsening diplomatic situation. Finally, the board concluded that Marshall had been derelict for
failing to keep himself apprised of the Hawaiian Command's actual state
of alert in the month before the attack.

As commander-in-chief, President Roosevelt decided that the army
report, and a companion study by the Navy, were not to be released so
long as the war continued. The war over, both the army and navy reports
were made public. Stimson dismissed the army report's criticism of Marshall as "entirely unjustified." Rather, Stimson asserted, the chief of staff
had "acted with his usual great skill, energy and efficiency. . . ." President Truman agreed wholeheartedly.

The report would not be exorcised so easily. Marshall had acknowledged he did have responsibility for the actions of the General Staff, and for the failure to make certain that the army command in the Hawaiian Islands was on the alert. In mitigation, he explained later that he could not give each and every detail the attention it deserved in those chaotic days before the war.

Within a newspaper edition of the release of the army and navy reports, Republican stalwarts in both the House and Senate undertook to pull out this "skeleton in the Roosevelt Administration's closet. . . ." By pinning the debacle at Pearl Harbor upon *that* man, the Grand Old Party could exact repayment for four successive defeats at the polls, for more than twelve years of humiliation. At the same time, smearing Roosevelt would also aid Republican fortunes in the 1946 elections. What better way than to prove that FDR had deliberately led the nation into war? That he had deliberately provoked the Japanese to attack Pearl Harbor? That he had ordered vital information withheld from Pearl's defenders to make the attack even more costly and assure American retaliation?

The Republican agitation, magnified in the anti-Roosevelt press, stirred Senate Majority Leader Alben W. Barkley to co-opt the investigation. Barkley, a Kentucky Democrat, wanted no albatross hung around the neck of his party a scant year before the congressional elections of 1946. He sponsored a preemptive resolution calling for a "thorough, impartial and fearless inquiry. . . ." In practice, the subsequent inquiry rarely evoked those qualities.

The joint committee selected was made up of five senators and five representatives. Six of the ten were Democrats—this was a Democratic Congress—and four were Republicans. At least two of the Republicans, Senator Homer Ferguson of Michigan and Representative Frank Keefe of Wisconsin, intended to rattle the skeleton in Roosevelt's closet. Thus Marshall the determined non-partisan found himself uncomfortably caught up in a partisan political maelstrom.

On Thursday, December 6, 1945, Marshall appeared for the first time before the ten members of the Joint Committee on the Investigation of the Pearl Harbor Attack. One spectator that day recalled:

> We had other officials who came down, and the higher the official, the more aides he brought with him, particularly if he were in uniform. This particular day I was seated near the door where the spectators and witnesses would come into the committee room. General Marshall appeared very quietly and alone, while there was a witness on the stand. The minute he appeared in the doorway, everybody in the room stood up, and one of the newspapermen remarked—I think he put it in type—that the committee, all testimony, stopped when they saw everybody rise.

The former chief of staff recognized that "the investigation was intended to crucify Roosevelt, not to get me. There was no feeling in the War Department that we had anything to hide." Still, the questioning in the crowded Senate Caucus Room before the banks of newsreel cameras and the tireless still photographers was often hostile.

For the next week Marshall testified coolly, deferential, oblivious of the large audience in the marble-walled Caucus Room and the horde of reporters, occasionally wiping his brow under the hot Klieg lights the newsreel men had set up, otherwise bending not at all to the ordeal.

But ordeal it was.

Marshall was not the best witness in his own behalf. It was not his nature to defend himself; an officer, after all, took responsibility and suffered the consequences. Further, his memory for detail—where was he on the night of December 6, at what time did he go riding the following morning—was sometimes poor. He frequently answered questions tentatively: "My recollection is . . ." Often he confessed he could not remember. His testimony belied his wartime reputation for an uncanny memory and grasp of detail—but then Marshall, no less, no more than any other man, may have been blocking distasteful recollection.

He repeatedly acknowledged his own errors. In the last months before war came, he told the committee, he had discounted Pearl Harbor as a target, "inclined to feel that the hazards were too great and that they [the Japanese] would not risk it. . . ." He could not recall seeing General Short's message replying to the War Department alert of November 27. "The presumption must be that I did. In any event, that was my opportunity to intervene which I did not do."

Day after day, the questioning continued while a C-54 transport stood waiting for him at National Field. Each time Marshall entered the Caucus Room, the audience stood in respect. Each day, during the noon recess, Marshall drove to the Department of State or the White House to resolve questions about his mission to China.

The Democrats on the Pearl Harbor committee were brief and respectful, the frustrated Republicans more and more strident as their questioning continued through the week. Senator Ferguson grilled Marshall for more than nine hours over two and a half days, parsing each MAGIC intercept and War Department message, attempting to prove the late president withheld prior knowledge of the attack. Representative Keefe, a former prosecutor, followed, leading Marshall for another two days over similar ground. Marshall patiently answered each question courteously, but it was wearing.

Details of those tense days before Pearl Harbor escaped him. "May I say also, Mr. Keefe, at the risk of being unduly repetitious, that you gentlemen are bringing up things to me that have been, to a large extent, rubbed out by four years of global war. I have not investigated these things to refresh my memory until the past few days, and so I think it is not unduly remarkable that I would not remember the detailed conversations and the frequency of conferences [or] at which one we discussed this, and at which one we discussed that."

Marshall too was angry with the committee, but impotent. Of the time he spent testifying, he would later say with faint sarcasm, it had been "a *charming* week."

Still, when Marshall left the Caucus Room for the last time on December 13, the audience applauded. His reputation was untouched. The visibly tired man had conducted himself with dignified restraint through six days of testimony. He had accepted responsibility for his decisions, in particular his failure on the morning of December 7 to use the scrambler telephone to warn Short of the 1:00 p.m. deadline that day. In effect, he had stood on his record.

The committee's majority report ultimately exonerated political Washington—the president and his secretaries of state, war, and navy. The eight who signed the report concluded that the major fault lay in Hawaii, where General Short and Admiral Kimmel had failed properly to heed Washington's warnings. Those failures were, however, "errors of judgment and not derelictions of duty." As Marshall and Stimson had long planned, Short would be permitted to retire peacefully to his home in Dallas without court-martial.

The committee report found fault with the War Department's War Plans Division for failing to realize that Short had not ordered the proper alert. Further, War Plans and Intelligence had each failed to appreciate the importance of a series of MAGIC intercepts that might have tipped them off that Pearl was the target. Marshall had accepted responsibility for those lapses.

Beyond Kimmel and Short, the majority report faulted no one by name.

Though he signed the majority report, Representative Keefe also appended additional comments, specifically faulting the War and Navy Departments for not having their commands on a war footing. There too Marshall was responsible, the more so since he had been horseback riding along the Potomac, "outside of effective contact with his subordinates," at a crucial moment.

Republican Senators Ferguson and Owen Brewster of Maine were more partisan and more critical. Concluding a long minority report drafted in part by a rabid anti-Roosevelt newspaper columnist, John T. Flynn, the two laid "failure to perform the responsibilities indispensably essential to the defense of Pearl Harbor" upon Roosevelt, Stimson, Secretary of the Navy Frank Knox, Marshall, Stark, and the former head of War Plans, Leonard Gerow.

The immunity General George C. Marshall had known when the nation was at war had vanished.

The Chinese assignment promised worse. Marshall was to serve as President Truman's personal representative in China, charged with seeking an end to the civil war in that country, and encouraging a coalition government. The very choice of so prominent a representative invested considerable American prestige in the outcome. It also suggested the importance, and difficulty, of the task.

China had known no peace since 1911 and the revolution led by Sun Yat-sen. Sun's Kuomintang Party struggled to maintain its leadership, alternately cooperating and vying with a Chinese Communist Party and dozens of local warlords who tyrannized neighboring provinces. In 1927, Sun dead two years, a leader of the Kuomintang's right wing, General Chiang Kai-shek, seized leadership of the party. Chiang led his troops upon Shanghai, massacring left-wing members of the party and labor unionists, then organized a new government headquartered at Nanking, 150 miles up the Yangtze River from the coast.

A year later, Feng Yu-hsiang, the "Christian warlord" baptized by missionaries, captured Peiping and with it most of North China for the Kuomintang. The United States immediately recognized this new China despite its dubious legitimacy. At the end of 1928, the warlords ruling the Manchurian provinces threw in with Chiang and the Kuomintang. China was unified.

Chiang then moved on his former allies, dissident Communist armies roaming the south of China. Six years of fratricide would force the Communists, now led by Mao Tse-tung, into the 6,000-mile Long March. They would find haven in the city of Yenan in northwestern Shensi Province in October 1935.

Within two years, Chiang and Mao had agreed to suspend their quarrel in order to combat the marauding Japanese. From 1937 to the end of the war the two factions were wary partners. Sometimes they fought the Japanese, sometimes they fought each other. They squabbled always, maneuvering for postwar advantage. KMT-CCP relations, according to one observer, were marked by "chilly politeness at the top, mistrust and hostility at middle echelons, and a no-holds-barred contest on the local level."

Anointed at Franklin Roosevelt's insistence as one of the great powers, China had contributed little to the defeat of the Japanese. Rather than fight, Chiang had hoarded Lend-Lease supplies for the inevitable postwar struggle with the Communists. Mao's Communists had spent their time building political support among the peasants of the northern provinces—the sea in which his guerrilla fish would swim.

On March 1, 1945, Chiang invited the Communists to attend a national assembly to draft a constitution for a new Nationalist government. A week later Mao declined, dismissing the national assembly as "a congress of slaves" and demanded Chiang's ouster.

Under pressure from American Ambassador Patrick Hurley, the Kuomintang adopted a resolution legalizing all political parties and ostensibly ending one-party control of the army and the schools. While that May 19 resolution implied a beginning of Western-style democracy, it was a prerequisite to unification. The Communists headquartered in Yenan controlled over 10 percent of China and almost one quarter of that country's population.

Prodded by Hurley, Chiang invited Mao to Chungking on August 15 to confer on the "many international and internal problems" standing between them and unity. Mao accepted, and for six weeks the two men with Hurley's paternal intercession searched for a face-saving agreement. The key was the establishment of a Political Consultation Conference to be called in January 1946. That conference, open to all parties and non-party leaders, would implement the end of one-party rule, inaugurate constitutional government, and convene a national assembly. Leaving Chungking, Mao the Opaque permitted himself faint optimism. "There are great difficulties, but they can be overcome."

The amity would not last long. Within sixty days, there was fighting in eleven of China's twenty-eight provinces, Chiang's government reported. On November 5, Yenan radio charged that United States troops ostensibly in China to disarm the Japanese were assisting the Nationalists in skirmishes against the Communists. The commander of United States Forces in China, Albert Wedemeyer, conceded the point even as reports circulated in Washington that American troops might be withdrawn to avoid being drawn into the growing civil war.

Wedemeyer asked for instruction; his orders required he disarm the Japanese units in China until such time as the Nationalist government could do so unassisted. Wherever Communist troops vied to take the surrender, they inevitably clashed with American Marines. Significantly, Wedemeyer radioed, Chiang "will be unable to stabilize the situation in north China for months or perhaps even years unless a satisfactory settlement with the Chinese Communists is achieved and followed up realistically. . . ."

In response, Secretary of State Byrnes proposed they "try to force the Chinese government and the Chinese Communists to get together on a compromise basis, perhaps telling Generalissimo Chiang Kai-shek that we will stop the aid to his government unless he goes along with this."

Byrnes's suggestion was to become the core of Marshall's instructions as the president's special envoy. Marshall disliked the draft, claiming it was susceptible to misinterpretation. He asked to rewrite it. Over three days, at those moments when Marshall did not have to appear before the Pearl Harbor committee, the special envoy and Undersecretary of State Dean Acheson met to reconcile the differing proposals.

Acheson, tall, precisely groomed with his guardsman's mustache, a

sophisticated Washington lawyer of great influence, was to be acting secretary of state while James Byrnes was attending a conference of foreign
ministers in Moscow. A man not easily impressed, Acheson recalled the
striking presence of the retired chief of staff about this time: "His figure
conveyed intensity, which his voice, low, staccato, and incisive, reinforced. It compelled respect. It spread a sense of authority and of calm.
There was no military glamour about him and nothing of the martinet.
Yet to all of us he was always 'General Marshall.' The title fitted him as
though he had been baptized with it."

The general's instructions, Acheson wrote later, were shaped by an
overriding belief that the Chinese Communists were a "Trojan Horse"
through which the Soviets could dominate Chinese affairs. Marshall agreed
to do his best to secure concessions from both Chiang and Mao so that a
coalition government might be installed; the inducement was to be $500
million in economic and military aid to a united China. Marshall was also
to use United States Marines and the Navy to assist the transport of
Chinese Nationalist troops into Manchuria where unrepatriated Japanese still effectively governed.

There was one problem: what to do if Chiang refused to make concessions or refused to convene the national political conference that might
lead to a unity government? Should Marshall continue to assist the
Nationalists in taking control in the north? "This would mean that this
government would have to swallow its pride and much of its policy in
doing so," he pointed out.

The alternative, support of the Communists, was unthinkable. The
president settled on Chiang as "the proper instrument" to develop a
democracy and to further American policy in China. In the event that
Chiang refused to take reasonable steps to unification, ran an unwritten
codicil to Marshall's instructions, "it would still be necessary for the U.S.
government, through me, to back the National Government of the
Republic of China. . . ." Truman was effectively undermining his special
envoy. Once the clever Chiang realized Marshall had no power beyond
persuasion, there would be no incentive to yield any concessions to the
Communists.

Marshall made one last arrangement on Friday, December 14, before
departing for China. After meeting with the president, Marshall asked
Acheson to be his representative in Washington.

The following day, accompanied only by a newly selected military
attaché, Colonel Henry A. Byroade, and a State Department aide, James
R. Shepley, Marshall left for China. As the transport taxied down the
runway at National Airport, the head of the State Department's Far
Eastern desk, John Carter Vincent, turned to his ten-year-old boy. "Son,
there goes the bravest man in the world. He's going to try to unify China."

Marshall was returning to China for the first time since 1927 when he left Tientsin and the 15th Infantry Regiment garrisoned there. His almost three years in China hardly made him an expert on that embattled nation's political or cultural life, but, like Stilwell, he felt keenly the plight of the Chinese people and once prided himself on being able to get along in the language. He was then the perfect envoy: experienced, empathetic, and powerful.

The man who stepped from his C-54 at Shanghai's Kiangwan Airport five days before Christmas Day, 1945, was tired. MacArthur, seeing Marshall in Tokyo two days earlier for the first time since their one wartime meeting, thought the newly minted diplomat "had aged immeasurably since his visit to New Guinea. The former incisiveness and virility were gone. The war had apparently worn him down into a shadow of his former self."

That evening Wedemeyer and counselor to the embassy Walter S. Robertson met with Marshall in the general's suite at the once posh Cathay Hotel. "Many on the ground, and I was surely one of them," Robertson recalled, "thought that he'd been given an impossible directive . . . that there was no basis to hope that you could bring about a coalition government. They had no common ground for coalition, no common objective for China."

When Wedemeyer pointed out the difficulties, Marshall responded crossly, "I am going to accomplish my mission and you are going to help me." Wedemeyer was taken aback. What had happened to make his former chief so aloof, almost hostile, Wedemeyer wondered. He concluded, like MacArthur, that the war had taken its toll.

The next day Marshall flew to Nanking where he was met at the airport by Generalissimo Chiang Kai-shek. That evening the two men held their first conversations since the Cairo Conference.

The United States wanted a unified and peaceful China, Marshall explained to the impassive man disgruntled American troops in China had nicknamed "Chancre Jack." The head of a political party, Chiang was still a warlord, and accustomed to command. Though his authority was not absolute within the KMT Party, criticism irritated him, a fact he gave away by unconsciously crossing his leg and jiggling his foot.

"I indicated clearly to him that the American people would strongly disapprove any action on the part of their government which would involve them in the internal disputes of another nation," Marshall reported in the first of the 2,155 messages that would flow from his mission to Washington. He added "that the primary interest of the American people was in a peaceful world, and that in spite of their great friendship for the Chinese people they would not permit the president to maintain military aid in China and to extend economic assistance to China unless they saw positive evidence of success in the efforts being made to reach a peaceful solution of Chinese internal disputes."

Chiang—unfazed by the implicit threat of a suspension of United States aid—assured Marshall through clicking false teeth that the KMT's one-party government was just as anxious for peace. He blamed the Communists and the USSR for the sporadic fighting between them. The Soviets intended to create a puppet government in Manchuria under the Chinese Communists, Chiang stressed.

Marshall flew on to the wartime capital at Chungking where he set up headquarters for his mission in a Western-style villa called "Happiness Gardens." There Robertson, a former Virginia banker, told Marshall that he wanted to go home, that he had not seen his family in three years, that his children were growing up without him.

Marshall sighed. "I want to go home too," he told Robertson, explaining how the president had drafted him for yet another mission. "Here I am and you can't walk out on me."

As for the Robertson family, Marshall suggested, "Bring 'em out here." He reached into his pocket, took out an envelope, and jotted a message to Washington ordering the Robertson family sent out on the first plane. Three weeks later Walter Robertson met his wife and children at Chungking's airport.

Marshall's own problem was not so easily solved. He was homesick himself, he confessed to his goddaughter, Rose Page Wilson. "I long for personal freedom and my own home and simple pleasures. My shooting trips were all arranged for the winter along with the horseback rides on the lovely Pinehurst trails and a month in Florida at a luxurious cottage that had been placed at my disposal. But, here I am."

The president's special envoy began a round of meetings which representatives of six minority parties banded together as the Democratic League and with Chou En-lai, the urbane representative in Chungking of the Yenan Communists. Chou assured Marshall the CCP too wanted peace and a unified government, the basis of which they hoped to arrange at a Political Consultation Conference promised by Chiang.

Within days Marshall had a grasp of the basic political problem. Neither KMT nor CCP believed in the good faith of the other, each convinced the other wanted one-party rule. Furthermore, the Communists feared Chiang's secret police too much to lay down their arms until the CCP had a permanent voice in the coalition government and was assured of its continued existence. "This barrier of fear, distrust and suspicion between the rival parties has been the greatest obstacle to the realization of peace and unity in China," Marshall reported to Washington.

On January 7, 1945, Marshall convened the first meeting of a so-called Committee of Three, composed of himself as chairman; the Communist representative Chou En-lai; and the KMT's General Chang Chun, a longtime Chiang ally currently chairman of the Szechuan Provincial Government.

Chang was trustworthy, Marshall came to believe, but without real power. He deferred to his old military school comrade, Chiang Kai-shek, who in turn had to take into account the "CC Clique," a very influential, very conservative wing of the KMT headed by the intractable Chen brothers, Kou-fu and Li-fu. The two brothers had long held a succession of key posts in the Kuomintang Party and its shadow, the Nationalist government. They were implacably opposed to the Reds; Chen Li-fu as head of a secret police organization claimed to be personally responsible for the conversion of 20,000 Communists. Marshall, who met Chen Li-fu only once, had always to reckon with the CC Clique's anti-Communist militancy and the brothers' inflexibility.

Like Chang, Chou En-lai was an old campaigner, though he seemingly had more influence with his party leader, Mao Tse-tung, than did Chang with the generalissimo. A party stalwart, Chou had distinguished himself as a brilliant student both in China and in Europe, as a Communist Party organizer at home and abroad, as a political officer in the Red field army, finally as a diplomat dressed in an ill-made Western suit.

Though he was essentially a political figure, Chou helped to lead the Long March, and thereby had proved his doctrinaire and physical toughness. He earned Mao's lasting respect while rising to the rank of general. Through it all he remained less dogmatic, more flexible than Mao and the majority of the Central Committee, a diplomat willing to seek a political solution.

During the war, the CCP and KMT patched their differences enough to exchange representatives; the friendly Chou En-lai turned up in Chungking at the head of a small mission. The war over, Chou—who spoke good English—was the most logical Communist delegate to the truce talks.

Marshall confronted a number of sticking points when the Committee of Three met for the first time on January 7 to arrange a truce. The most pressing was control of Manchuria. The Nationalists charged that the Soviet Union was assisting the CCP in taking control of the vast lands north of the Great Wall. When Marshall stressed that the United States was committed to Nationalist government control over all of China, Chou smoothly gave ground.

The second pressing issue was control of two towns in the province of Jehol adjacent to Manchuria. The Communist Eighth Route Army had taken possession of the towns from the Japanese, and blocked a Nationalist Army from reaching Manchuria. In effect, the CCP served as a lookout while the Russians looted Manchurian factories of their Japanese-installed machinery.

Neither Chang nor Chou would yield claim to the two towns. Marshall personally appealed to Chiang Kai-shek, asking him to momentarily waive his rights in the matter. The generalissimo agreed to the issuance of a truce without referring to the disputed towns, in practical terms post-poning a dispute that might have otherwise sabotaged the agreement.

Intent on an initial success, Marshall finessed other issues, leaving them for an executive headquarters that was to be established in Peiping to arbitrate disputes relating to the truce. The Nationalists, the Communists, and the United States, in the role of arbitrator, would staff three-man teams dispatched from that headquarters to supervise the truce in various hot spots. On January 10, having secured prior agreement from both Chiang and Mao, the Committee of Three called for a cease-fire. Marshall had his first, vital agreement.

Creating a true coalition government would be more difficult. On the day the truce was announced, the Political Consultation Conference convened in Chungking for the purpose of drafting a new constitution for China. The conference could only recommend; each party's central committee held veto power over the proposals for a unified central government.

The American special envoy took no part in the deliberations of the Political Consultation Conference and refused to be an official liaison between the generalissimo and his fractionated opposition. To retain his independence, Marshall instead offered to serve unofficially as a go-between. In the meantime, Marshall suggested Chiang set up a temporary coalition government with himself as government head rather than party leader. It all would go down easier if he incorporated what Marshall called "a dose of American medicine," a Bill of Rights.

The lubricious generalissimo was nothing if not ameliorative; Chiang's opening address to the Political Consultation Conference contained a pledge of democratic rights to all Chinese, including freedom of speech, assembly, and association; equal legal status for all political parties; popular elections; and the release of all political prisoners.

While Chiang was overtly cooperative, he harbored private doubts. On February 2 he wrote in his diary, "Marshall has been dealing with the Communists for over a month now. Can it be that he has not yet understood the deceptive nature of Communist maneuvers?"

By the end of the month he was certain. "[M]ore and more he is being taken in by the Communists. The Americans tend to be naive and trusting. This is true even with so experienced a man as Marshall. . . ."

If Chiang had had any intention of honoring the Marshall recommendation of a Bill of Rights, the CC Clique did not. Within days there were reports of harassment of minority elements in the Political Consultation Conference, of beatings of Democratic League supporters in Chungking, and of meetings broken up by KMT bully boys. It would not be the last time Marshall would cope with benign acceptance of liberalization at one level of the Kuomintang and militant rejection at another. Chinese politics had always operated so.

Marshall's next task was to attempt to reorganize the Nationalist Army, integrating into it the 600,000 Communist regulars who took their orders only from the party's central committee. True integration, if it could be achieved, would end eighteen years of sporadic civil war.

Eleven days of hard bargaining salted with Marshall's judicial instruction—Chou and Chang took to calling the onetime American chief of staff "the professor"—eventually produced an agreement. Marshall hammered out a ratio of five Nationalist soldiers for every Communist, an end to puppet and warlord armies, and a limit on the size of the quasi-military police forces under the control of provincial governors. By terms of the agreement, the unified army was to be subservient to the central government, not to individual political parties.

Marshall made a major gesture to Chou, who seemed reluctant to accept immediate integration of the armies. Marshall suspected Chou was holding back, for fear of invidious comparison between his ragtag route armies and the carefully husbanded units of Chiang's army which Stilwell had trained during the war. Marshall offered to staff a school at which American troops could train selected Communist officers and men. Chou, and through him Mao, quickly accepted.

Clause by clause, the American ironed out a compromise, overcoming the covert but palpable opposition of conservative generals in the Nationalist Army. In the end, Marshall was reluctant to sign the hard-won unification agreement, insisting that publicity in the United States would naturally focus upon him while ignoring the contributions of Chang and Chou. That could lead, in turn, to potentially bad feelings in China, and the appearance that the American had dictated orders to a hapless ally. When both Chang and Chou insisted he sign as "adviser," Marshall relented.

"So if we are going to be hung, I will hang with you," he joked as he signed the agreement.

The military compact was signed on February 25, amid reports of a flare-up of bitter fighting between Communists and Nationalists in Manchuria. At the signing ceremony late that afternoon, General Chang praised Marshall with an exquisite courtesy that translates but awkwardly into English:

We owe so much to General Marshall for his advice as advisor to the Military Sub-Committee. The people in this country have created several titles for General Marshall. Certain people call General Marshall the midwife of the unification and peaceful reconstruction of China. Certain people call General Marshall the go-between of the Communist Party and the Government. Certain people call General Marshall the great ambassador of peace sent by the American government and the American people to China. I am of the opinion that no matter which you like best every one will suit General Marshall completely.

Marshall replied with a sober warning. "This agreement, I think, represents the great hope of China. I can only trust that its pages will not be soiled by a small group of irreconcilables who for a separate purpose would defeat the Chinese people in their overwhelming desire for peace and prosperity."

Manchuria, where as many as 800,000 Japanese troops were still under arms, remained a sore point. The Russians delayed their promised pullout, reluctant to withdraw to Outer Mongolia until they had gutted the country. Those delays allowed the CCP time to set up the machinery of local government, ready to take control when the Soviets did pull out. Marshall was unable to secure the cooperation of the Soviet ambassador to China to coordinate either the withdrawals or the repatriation of the remaining Japanese troops and dependents in Manchuria.

It was not an unalloyed success, but, in little more than three months, Marshall had fashioned the basis for agreement between the government and the Communists. They were tenuous pacts, shot through with mutual suspicion, but they were more than a succession of negotiators before him had been able to accomplish. In no small measure it was a token of Marshall's personal stature that he was able to propose a peace in the Middle Kingdom.

The Manchurian situation might bring it all crashing down, Marshall warned the president. It was too soon for optimism. Worse still, the Nationalist government, with or without liberalization, could not long survive given China's economic situation. Inflation was rampant. Profiteers with close connections to the KMT Party and to Chiang's government were skimming vast fortunes from speculations in rice and currency. Amid rampaging greed and price manipulations, the Chinese people endured near famine conditions.

With something resembling a truce in the offing, Marshall could take up the question of economic aid to the Chinese. It was time to return to Washington, Marshall radioed the president.

CHAPTER

XXXIII

The Tiger of Peace

He was going home, if only temporarily, and that was something for which to be thankful. Behind him he was leaving a volatile powder magazine, a cease-fire pasted together with "so many compromises on both sides," he acknowledged, "that I am in the awkward position of being obligated by pressure from both sides to stay on and maintain a balance between the mistrusts of the two parties. . . ."

As necessary as was his presence in China, he was also needed in Washington. Only there could he find solutions to China's endemic financial problems: runaway inflation amidst poverty, and a lack of investment capital. Despite widespread corruption within Chiang's circle—wartime American observers sarcastically termed the United States "Uncle Chump from over the Hump"—Marshall intended to revive negotiations for a $500 million loan which he had ordered suspended the previous December. He also intended to discuss with the Pentagon the transfer to China of surplus property scattered across the Pacific theater in warehouses and stockpiles.

The general was optimistic, if weary, as he climbed aboard his C-54 with the five stars painted on the tail for the five-day flight home on March 11. Just the day before, he had completed a week-long, 3,500-mile journey through ten cities in northern China. He had counseled and cajoled. He had sat through swirling folk dance performances in cold assembly halls, nibbling at fifteen-course dinners, cheered by tattered crowds carrying banners praising him as "Terror of the Evil-doers," "First Lord of the Warlords," and "Most Fairly [sic] Friend of China." Marshall also met for the first time Mao Tse-tung in the Communist capital of Yenan; Mao agreeably promised to fly to Nanking to meet with Chiang. Buoyed by his reception through the north, Marshall decided "there was every indication that affairs would clear up quickly and communications be reopened and normal life for the poor civilians actually gotten under way."

The general was deluding himself. "In common with many a touring leader," his biographer Forrest Pogue wrote, "Marshall was momentarily blinded by the friendly reception and did not fully see the realities of the situation."

The president's special envoy was not the only one to be momentarily blinded. Albert Wedemeyer, United States commander in the China theater, wrote Eisenhower that the former chief of staff had won the

> respect and admiration of all with whom he came in contact. His approach to the problems presented has been logical, first accomplishing cessation of hostilities, and now he is well on the way toward the successful implementation of a plan that will integrate military forces of the Central Government and the Communists. All of this has been accomplished in the background of intrigue, mistrust, selfish personalities, and oriental cunning. Really a stupendous accomplishment, and I doubt seriously whether any other person in the world could have done as much in so short a time.

Yet without Marshall's presence, Wedemeyer cautioned, the truce would go up the spout. Marshall's stature alone kept the factions in line. Peace in China depended on the former chief of staff.

From the hour of his arrival, the general's visit to Washington would be hectic. Marshall stepped from his C-54 to the ramp, kissed Katherine twice, briskly shook hands with the cluster of chilled dignitaries who had come to meet him, then rushed off in a limousine to report to the White House.

For four weeks Marshall ducked in and out of federal agencies, with the knowledgeable Dean Acheson's help mustering a considerable aid package: a new Lend-Lease program; $30 million in cotton credits; a $500 million loan from the Import-Export Bank; additional loans for transportation and communications equipment; transfer of a number of shallow-draft vessels that could steam in coastwise commerce; as well as a pledge of $475 million in aid over the next twenty months.

Amidst his appeals for money, he found himself summoned once more by the Joint Congressional Committee investigating the Pearl Harbor attack. Marshall spent another half-day on Capitol Hill, called to answer yet more questions about the events of December 6–7, 1941. It was like a half-recalled memory of his childhood, so far behind him.

In addition, there were personal matters to attend to. Marshall flew to Long Island to spend a day with Henry Stimson, retired finally to fearsome croquet matches and horseback riding on his estate, Highhold. He also paid a courtesy call on the eighty-eight-year-old Black Jack Pershing at Walter Reed Army Hospital. Meanwhile, he had to help Katherine pack for the 12,000-mile flight back to China.

Marshall had decided that Katherine was to return with him. Since their marriage in 1930, they had not been apart longer than five weeks. Three months in China had left him longing for her company and the comforts she provided. Though the climate in Chungking was harsh, he expected to move his headquarters to the far more pleasant Nanking from Chiang transferred the government back to the prewar capital. Nanking, with its large foreign colony, would be gracious, and an abundance of servants would make her life easier still. She would have plenty of time to work on the writing project she had started so as to fill her days.

For the Marshalls it was a strenuous pace, made all the more frantic by his need to return to China as soon as possible. The painstakingly knitted January truce was coming unraveled.

Chiang had imposed harsh restrictions on the travels of the three-member truce supervisory teams in Manchuria. KMT officials were also arresting Communist members of the truce teams, both in Mukden and Peiping. Without those monitors in the field settling disputes, the truce was in danger.

From Washington, Marshall instructed his deputy "to force the issue. . . . Face will be lost if the fighting develops more seriously in Manchuria and spreads south into Jehol. That will be serious consideration, not face."

The Russians too complicated matters. While Marshall's cease-fire agreement had granted the Nationalists sovereignty over Manchuria, access was another matter. Bound by no such agreement, the Russians denied the U.S. Navy use of the Manchurian port of Dairen to land Nationalist troops in Manchuria. The date for Russian withdrawal had twice come and gone, and still the Red Army, its looting of factories not yet complete, held its positions.

When the Soviets did finally begin their pullout, the Chinese Communists rushed in ahead of the KMT. The veteran route armies quickly consolidated their positions, refitting with the stores of arms and ammunition the Japanese had surrendered.

If the Soviet actions aided the CCP, they also strengthened the hand of the KMT's irreconcilables. What further proof was needed of Communist untrustworthiness than events in Manchuria?

Madame Chiang stoked Marshall's anxiety in an April 2 letter. "I feel that I should tell you frankly that your presence is vital if further deliberations take place. I hate to say 'I told you so' but even the short time you have been absent proves what I have repeatedly said to you—that China needs you."

Still it would be another ten days before the Marshalls were able to get away. The president's special envoy left on his private C-54 bearing a token of Congress's esteem; the Senate voted to make permanent his five-star rank. By terms of the bill the eight generals and admirals with that rank were to receive full salaries and benefits, and deemed to be on active duty until they died.

The Manchurian situation deteriorated even further while the Marshalls were flying across the Pacific. Within an hour of the Soviet withdrawal from Changchun, the heavily developed capital of Manchuria under the Japanese, CCP troops from two armies launched an attack on the ragtag Nationalist garrison. A clear violation of the truce, the attack drove the Nationalists from the city.

The fall of Changchun was to have serious consequences for his mission, Marshall later reported. "It made the victorious Communist generals in Manchuria over-confident and less amenable to compromise with the National government, but even more disastrous was the effect upon the government. . . . It greatly strengthened the hands of the ultra-reactionary groups in the government." The CC clique would criticize Marshall's prior advocacy of a truce, claiming the Communists had now amply demonstrated that they did not keep their agreements, just as the reactionaries had warned.

Changchun left the Communists well ahead in the race for control of Manchuria. Both the CCP and KMT were moving troops into the disputed territory, the Communists at full speed while the Nationalists, assisted by the Marines, plodded northward, fearing ambush at every village and river crossing.

Marshall landed in Chungking on April 19. He was gravely concerned; according to Frederick Gruin, *Time* magazine's correspondent, Marshall looked ten years older on his return.

With Madame Chiang serving as translator—the generalissimo did not understand Marshall's limited Chinese and spoke no English himself—Marshall immediately sought to break the looming impasse. In a private conference, Marshall pointed out that the government had been both "fatally provocative and at times inexcusably stupid" in impeding the truce teams; the Communists had seized their opportunity. To restore order, the Terror of Evildoers pressed for a reconciliation.

Chiang rejected "any compromise if the United States government continues to appease the Communists." Two days later, Chiang privately shifted blame for the impasse to Marshall. "If Marshall views the situation with any degree of objectivity, it is not difficult to see that neither the Soviet Union nor the Chinese Communists can be trusted. Yet Marshall refuses to abandon the policy of appeasement," he wrote in his personal diary.

On April 22, Marshall warned Chiang he would order American Marines to stop transporting Nationalist troops to Manchuria unless

Chiang agreed to resume negotiations immediately. The threat was merely more proof in Chiang's eyes that Marshall was thereby "forcing us to accept their proposals for appeasing the Communists. The fact is to appease the Communists at this time is to yield to the Soviet Union." Chiang would give no ground. He appeared firmly in the grasp of the CC clique.

The following day Marshall met with Chou En-lai, scolding the Communists, demanding they retract a charge that American pilots had strafed CCP troops in Manchuria. There was a new stridency in Chou, a man usually polite, often frank, who had even admitted at one point in earlier negotiations, "I cannot say that the position of our own side has always been rational. Perhaps we could have made a few more concessions."

Unruffled by Marshall's lecture, Chou responded to the American's demand with a series of his own: an immediate cease-fire, a revision of the agreed-upon proportion of Nationalist and Communist units in the new coalition army, and a halt to the movement of government troops into Manchuria.

With the "tired patience of Sisyphus, General Marshall began rolling his unwieldy stone uphill again," as Undersecretary of State Dean Acheson put it.

Chiang moved his capital from Chungking 750 air miles downstream on the Yangtze River to the old capital of Nanking. The diplomatic corps followed, the Marshalls taking up residence in the former home of the German ambassador on Ning Hai Road. The comfortable compound, probably the finest in Nanking, offered both living quarters and offices for the Marshalls and other members of the mission.

The next months would be taxing. Marshall was still the general, still in command, on top of everything. "Trying to brief General Marshall was like trying to teach an old bald eagle how to fly," said one ranking military officer about this time.

There was a more human quality about him, a sensitivity to the Chinese among whom he felt so at ease. "I probably have not properly represented the interests of the United States," he confessed to a civilian aide. "I feel that I am representing the Chinese people."

Chiang was not, Marshall came to realize. The generalissimo remained a warlord, not a national leader. "If Chiang had cared about or even had directed his attention to the woeful plight of the Chinese people—the masses—he could have knocked the props out from under Mao," Marshall said later.

Marshall and Chiang got along well, though the American had no illusion about the generalissimo's support. "Chiang's confidence in me may have been unbounded but it did not restrain him from disregarding my advice," Marshall noted wryly.

As Nanking's weather turned warm and miasmic, Marshall worried about its effect on Katherine. She accepted an invitation in July from Madame Chiang to visit with her and the generalissimo at their summer residence in the cooler mountains 250 miles to the west. The two women would become fast friends that summer in Kuling.

Marshall meanwhile stayed on in Nanking, fitting in as best he could the formidable journey to Kuling to see his wife. He would travel six and a half hours by, successively, plane, gunboat, and automobile, capping the trip perched in a sedan chair. If there was any redeeming aspect of the wearing trip, it was the two hours and more in the sedan chair. He could practice his Chinese with the bearers.

In May 1946, Dwight Eisenhower flew to Nanking, ostensibly on a trip as army chief of staff to investigate morale of American troops still in the Far East. In fact, Eisenhower was also serving as an emissary for President Truman.

The president had decided to replace his overly independent secretary of state, James Byrnes. Byrnes was going to become "quite ill" with stomach trouble about mid-year, Truman told Eisenhower. Eisenhower was to sound out Marshall's interest in the position.

The special envoy was more than agreeable to the assignment, Eisenhower recalled. "Great goodness, Eisenhower, I'd take any job in the world to get out of this one!" he blurted.

There was a problem with the timing. Marshall could not leave before September. He believed he could paste together a new truce and would need the additional time to be sure it held. The two men devised a code for use in case the president declared Byrnes stricken.

Marshall's new-found optimism that a truce was again possible stemmed from the Nationalists' recovery in Manchuria. Revitalized KMT troops were near to recapturing the Manchurian capital.

Chou, a middleman between hardliners in his own camp and the CC clique, reversed himself. He pressed Yenan to agree to a cease-fire: "During the last twenty years we have fought almost without stop, but also without any final settlement. I can declare without hesitation that even if we kept on fighting for twenty more years we still would not reach any solution. The fighting must stop!"

Circumstances suddenly favored a truce. The special envoy general had no leverage beyond his reputation when dealing with the Communists; they would listen only if the Nationalists appeared to hold the upper hand. But Marshall could invoke additional authority in dealing with the Nationalists—withholding economic loans and military aid, without which the government would ultimately fall.

This time Chiang resisted, believing he held the upper hand militarily. Marshall sought to point out that territorial conquest was not the same as victory. So long as the Communists held the bulk of their army in reserve, they were not defeated, he pointed out. Moreover, the more territory the KMT occupied, the thinner their forces would be, even while the Communists massed their armies.

The former chief of staff's tactical lessons went unheeded. Stiffened by the KMT Army and the irreconcilables, Chiang waved aside the general's warnings. The most Marshall could achieve was a fifteen-day cease-fire, then an extension of a week while he tried to find grounds for a permanent settlement.

The effort to negotiate was wearying. One side's offer provoked counteroffers or exceptions, all of which had to be debated. If he managed to hammer out agreement on one clause, Chiang or Chou introduced two more.

The Nationalists scorned his recommendation that they cooperate with the Communists, while Mao demanded that American aid to the Kuomintang dictatorial government be ended. Orchestrated demands for "all-out aid" by Chiang's emboldened partisans in the United States only hardened the CC Clique's resolve. In a personal note to Postmaster General Robert Hannegan, Marshall wrote, "You are accepted as an expert in politics, but, most confidentially, I suggest that you come out here and take a post-graduate course."

Marshall was "deathly tired," an aide commented, and growing discouraged. Katherine too was angry, bitterly complaining that her husband on the eve of retirement had been reduced to being "a messenger boy between the generalissimo and the Communists. . . ."

Marshall alone was driving the United States policy in China. According to former *Time* magazine correspondent Theodore White, "Never since the days of Roman proconsuls has a single man held in the name of a great republic such personal responsibility for security of its future and frontiers."

It would have been easier, though a contradiction to his instructions, to yield to Chiang. Marshall, however, doubted the Nationalists had the strength to secure a complete victory. The sheer numbers were against them. The Communists could field an army of more than 1 million disciplined regulars and another 400,000 guerrillas against the Nationalists' 3 million largely ill-trained troops.

On June 30, just hours before the makeshift truce was to expire, Marshall met with Chiang in a last effort to extend the cease-fire. He warned the generalissimo that statements issued by local commanders indicated the government had forsaken "democratic procedure and was pursuing a dictatorial policy of military force. I informed the generalissimo that the comparison with the army dictatorship in Japan, which led to the destruction of that nation, with the present procedure of the Chinese military leaders would be inevitable." The harsh lecture left Chiang near tears and quoting the Bible, Marshall reported to an aide.

Having delayed as long as he dared, the generalissimo agreed to order his armies to stand down, to shoot only if they were attacked. Pressed by Chou, Mao issued a similar order. Marshall had brought a tense quiet to northern China and Manchuria.

The special envoy was to get some assistance—and alienate a supporter—when he recommended John Leighton Stuart for the still vacant post of United States ambassador to China. He had earlier discussed the appointment with General Albert Wedemeyer, then changed his mind when the January truce soured. Marshall concluded that Wedemeyer, having served as Chiang Kai-shek's chief of staff during the war, would be perceived as too closely allied to the Nationalists to be acceptable to the Communists. In diplomacy, appearances were everything.

His heart set on the appointment, Wedemeyer was crushed. He later complained that Marshall, in effect, had given veto power over the appointment of a United States ambassador to the Communists. In the superheated atmosphere of the Cold War, it was a damning criticism.

The disappointed Wedemeyer concluded Marshall was "primarily a military man who had little knowledge of the complexities of the world conflict and no conception of the skill with which the Communists pervert great and noble aspirations for social justice. . . . Moreover, by the time he arrived in China on his fatal mission George Marshall was physically and mentally too worn out to appraise the situation correctly." Finally, Wedemeyer asserted, Marshall had been stricken with hubris, and "thought he could accomplish the impossible" by fusing the antagonistic Nationalists and Communists into a single government.

Marshall's nominee for the ambassadorship was at once an unlikely choice yet the perfect candidate. Born in China the son of a Presbyterian minister, like most missionary children, Stuart was sent to the United States to be educated. He returned to China at age twenty-nine, ordained a Presbyterian minister, committed to bringing Christian enlightenment to the Chinese people. In 1919 he became president of the church-affiliated Yenching University outside of Peking, serving there until Pearl Harbor. He spent the war under house arrest in Peking until he was asked by the Japanese to negotiate a separate peace with Chiang in July 1945.

Stuart at seventy was about to retire from the university when he met Marshall early in 1946. The special envoy was impressed with the churchman. Stuart not only spoke fluent Mandarin but had a deep appreciation of the Chinese people and culture. If he considered Chiang as the logical head of a coalition government, he was blind neither to the Nationalists' faults nor the Communists' virtues. Stuart's appointment would give Marshall credence in Chiang's eyes, Marshall believed.

In addition, Stuart brought to the post a special attribute as far as Washington was concerned: his longtime vice president at the university had been the missionary father of Henry Robinson Luce, the chairman of Time, Inc. A man convinced that the Lord had ordained his militant anti-communism, Luce the son was an immensely powerful force in the strident "China Lobby" advocating all-out American support for Chiang Kai-shek. Luce would be hard put to attack his father's devoted friend.

His nomination confirmed by the Senate on July 11, Stuart immediately pitched in. There was work enough for both him and Marshall as the Kuomintang clamped down on dissent within its camp. The murder of two members of the independent Democratic League and the closure of six opposition newspapers suggested that the Nationalists would not tolerate rival parties within the government.

When a peace delegation from Shanghai sought to see the generalissimo, it was set upon by a Nanking mob. For five hours, the assailants systematically beat the delegates, including a seventy-year-old woman. Marshall was livid.

Repeated incidents such as this, the general warned, were destroying both Chiang's and the government's prestige abroad. When the generalissimo blandly disclaimed any responsibility for the beatings, Marshall scolded him, "What you are saying is that your army is completely impotent and I can't swallow that at all."

A young Foreign Service officer assigned to the Nanking embassy watched the general's frustration mount during the summer. "Marshall is beginning to get the idea that he is being pushed around, made a fool of," John Melby noted in his diary, "and he doesn't like it at all. Nor is he a man to play a losing game. In short, he is about as angry as anyone I have ever seen."

Whatever moral high ground the Communists might have claimed that summer they lost with repeated attacks on the U.S. Marines assisting the Nationalists regain control of China as the truce of January stipulated. The low point came on July 29 when Communist guerrillas set upon a Marine supply convoy near Peiping, killing three Americans and wounding twelve. Marshall could gain no satisfaction; Chou privately admitted responsibility, yet publicly insisted the Kuomintang was at fault.

Yenan was repeating the familiar Communist pattern of seizing upon some incident, Marshall protested, embroidering it "without truth and accuracy to form the basis for an almost hysterical campaign of vituperation against the United States."

The fighting between Communists and Nationalists spread. Through August Marshall traveled back and forth between Nanking and Chiang's retreat in Kuling, trying to find an accommodation, trading concessions between the generalissimo and Chou En-lai, but never quite securing agreement on a new cease-fire.

On August 10, President Truman dispatched a letter to Chiang—drafted earlier by Marshall and Stuart—maintaining recent events had led him to conclude that "the selfish interests of extremist elements, both in the Kuomintang and the Communist Party, are obstructing the aspirations of the people of China." Truman warned that American generosity could not continue without genuine progress toward a peaceful settlement of China's problems.

Chiang called the bluff. In the middle of August he told Marshall he intended to mount a campaign to clear the northern provinces and Manchuria of Communists. Marshall replied with a blunt warning. They were near a general civil war that would blaze beyond Chiang's control.

Militarily, the situation in the north favored the Communists, Marshall cautioned. "I pointed out the Government had much to lose and little to gain from hostilities at this time, which might end in the collapse of the government and of the country's economy, and that it must be remembered that the long lines of communications in China and the bordering mountains favored the employment of Communist guerrilla tactics."

On the first anniversary of VJ-Day, Chiang issued a public statement blaming the Communists for both the worsening economy and the collapse of the truce. The Communists had refused to surrender the territories they held and "change into a peaceful, law-abiding political party and follow the democratic road to reconstruction," the statement asserted. If the Communists did not yield, Chiang threatened, "we must put down rebellions. . . ."

The Nationalists marched while Marshall and Stuart futilely shuttled back and forth, still seeking a compromise. In the middle of September, Marshall confidentially informed the president, "Dr. Stuart and I are stymied." From Shanghai, American reporter Waldo Drake telegraphed the fervently pro-Chiang *Los Angeles Times*, "Developments in China during the last week should wipe out any illusion that peace is likely to come to this unhappy land by any route other than military decision."

From Washington, Harry Truman wrote his beloved Bess in Independence, Missouri, "Looks like Marshall will fail in China."

Marshall had a final ploy to remind Chiang of his dependence upon American assistance. In August, the general ordered an embargo placed on munitions shipments to the Nationalists. They would continue to receive $900 million in non-lethal aid, principally trucks, bulldozers, and construction supplies, enough to provoke the Communists to charge that the United States had irrevocably sided with the Nationalists.

Chiang had husbanded ample stores from wartime Lend-Lease aid for just this moment. Nationalist forces began a march northward toward Kalgan, the largest city in Communist hands south of the Great Wall. As the Nationalist advance in the north gained momentum, Chou En-lai delivered an ultimatum to Marshall: If the Nationalists did not break off their offensive, the Chinese Communist Party would be "forced to presume that the government is thereby giving public announcement to a total national split. . . ."

Marshall was dispirited. The Nationalists, emboldened by their success in the field, believed victory near; they wanted no immediate truce while they negotiated. The Communists, on the other hand, needed a truce, even one that left them in a precarious military position should negotiations for a unity government fail.

On October 1, Marshall condemned both KMT and CCP strategies in a meeting with Communist representatives. They had each manipulated the negotiations, Marshall scolded—to the point that he could no longer continue as a middleman.

That same day the general wrote a memorandum to Chiang stating the same complaint. He concluded that unless they could find a basis for the termination of fighting without further delay, he could not serve as a go-between. He would then recommend to President Truman his recall and the end of the mission. It was a last threat, taken on his own initiative.

Explaining his reasoning to Dean Acheson, Marshall cabled that his participation in negotiations now would inevitably be judged "a cloak to the continued conduct of a military campaign.

> I am aware [he continued] of the delicacy of the position my communication to the generalissimo places the United States in in its relationship to the situation in the Far East but do not think our government can be a party to a course of questionable integrity in negotiations and I therefore felt that this fact must be made unmistakably clear to the government.

Marshall, commented the head of the State Department's Far Eastern desk, John Carter Vincent, was obviously angry. "He has virtually accused the government leaders of duplicity. . . . He clearly feels that his honor is at stake."

Truman did not flinch. With off-year congressional elections looming and Republicans asking the voters rhetorically, "Had enough?"; with wags charging "to err is Truman" and "I'm just mild about Harry"; the president chose not to meddle. Marshall was left to pursue what he considered the best policy.

Chiang's eventual reply all but convinced Marshall his mission was ended. Under the cover of Marshall's negotiations, Chiang was pressing the war against the Communists. Marshall did not intend to be used.

In a meeting with Chiang on October 4, Marshall dismissed the generalissimo's excuses. There could be no talks "at the point of a gun," Marshall insisted.

Chiang yielded to the threat of Marshall's recall on October 6, and offered a ten-day stand down. In that period, a five-man committee chaired by Dr. Stuart was to define the rules of Communist participation in a national assembly. This faint glimmer was snuffed out almost immediately by the Communist refusal so long as Kalgan and the gateway to Manchuria were threatened. In a letter from Communist headquarters in Shanghai, Chou dismissed the offer as merely a Nationalist subterfuge to gain time to reinforce the attack on Kalgan.

Marshall made a last effort, flying to Shanghai for a secret meeting with Chou on October 9. Over a three-hour midday meeting, the two men reviewed the situation. Chou finally presented a list of Communist requirements for a settlement. There was to be a permanent truce. The government was to break off its attack on Kalgan. Both CCP and KMT were to yield territorial gains made in China proper since the beginning of the year. The Communists, however, were not to give up the gains they had made in Manchuria.

The demands asked for everything and gave little, but they were a starting point.

On October 10, the thirty-fifth anniversary of Sun Yat-sen's 1911 revolution, Nationalist troops captured Kalgan and with it the invasion routes to Manchuria. To avoid being cut off, Communist troops retreated north and west throughout the northern provinces. That same day, the Nationalists announced the resumption of nationwide conscription; it was hardly the move of a government intent on winding down the war.

Chiang unilaterally announced on October 11 that the national assembly would convene on November 12 to write a new constitution. The number of seats for minority parties, including the Communists, were to be fixed by Chiang alone, not by negotiation as promised earlier. Claiming betrayal, Chou and representatives of the minority parties boycotted further peace talks.

When Chiang offered as a sweetener a cease-fire on October 16, the Communists rejected it. Still Marshall was able to induce them to discuss Chiang's proposal. Chou returned to Nanking; the two sides discussed peace while the fighting continued.

Even as the Nationalists drove into Manchuria, Marshall warned Chiang that while the victories were heady, they were also illusory. The Communists would continue to withdraw, avoiding a pitched battle. "While they had lost cities, they had not lost armies, nor was it likely they would," he pointed out. The Nationalists might even take Harbin, but it would stretch thin their lines of communication and open them to "endless trouble." Chiang was not listening.

Tentative peace talks in far-off China were not enough to save the Democrats at home, where the public, anxious for an end to war-induced austerities, handed the Republicans a landslide victory. The GOP picked up thirteen Senate and fifty-seven House seats, enough to organize both houses of Congress. Republican majorities on the Hill would sharply influence foreign policy.

Marshall was worn out. Confronting yet another round of proposal and counterproposal to even keep hope alive, Marshall groaned, "I can't go through it again. I am just too old and too tired for that."

On November 15 the national assembly convened, boycotted by the Communists and most other minority party members. That afternoon Chou called upon Marshall to say goodbye before returning to Yenan "for reorientation and new instructions."

Chou was regretful. "He felt very grateful for my personal efforts," Marshall reported to Washington. "He still had high respect for me personally, particularly since I had been confronted with even greater and more insurmountable difficulties since the end of the negotiations in June—for which I had his deepest sympathy."

Marshall asked Chou to "determine formally from the proper authorities at Yenan whether specifically they wished me personally to continue in my present position. I asked that his colleagues view the matter as a plain business proposition without regard to the Chinese consideration of 'face.' I was not interested in 'face.' " Marshall was making a last offer of assistance—or an effort to validate the futile efforts of the past eleven months. It was also an escape. If Yenan rejected him, he could go home, he told an American close to Chiang.

Discouraged, Marshall was uncharacteristically open with the small embassy staff. "I know Marshall now believes he made a mistake in ever thinking coalition was desirable or useful or possible," Melby wrote in his diary.

In conversation with an American public relations adviser hired by Chiang at Marshall's suggestion, the special envoy spread blame liberally. The Communists were clever negotiators, but riddled with suspicion. "They don't trust anybody." The Kuomintang was hardly better. The military was in control, firmly convinced the Communists would not honor any agreement reached. The reactionary CC Clique similarly believed that a coalition government was impossible since the Communists would deliberately disrupt the working arrangement.

If Marshall was resigned to the failure of his policy, as John Robinson Beal believed, he had little optimism for the Nationalists' future. "The Communists exist every place the government ain't," Beal, an adviser to Chiang, quoted the special envoy. Marshall also had questions about the Kuomintang's stability. "Since June, the government had been waging war on a constantly increasing scale, heavily absorbing government funds. These military expenditures served to increase inflation at the same time that the government was asking the United States for large loans."

Marshall was anything but diplomatic in rejecting those requests. "The army is draining 80 to 90 percent of the budget and if you think the U.S. taxpayer is going to step into the vacuum this creates, you can go to hell," he barked at KMT ministers.

With Madame Chiang acting as interpreter, on December 1 Marshall and Ambassador Stuart spent three hours in a last effort to persuade Chiang. This was no time for diplomatic courtesies; Marshall was plain-spoken.

The Nationalists' distrust of the Communists in the spring had been replaced in the fall by the Communists' suspicion of the government, he pointed out. "Even the most tolerant approaches of the national government, notably that represented by the generalissimo's eight-point proposal of October 16, had been neutralized by military action," Marshall stressed.

Moments later, Marshall spoke in English to Madame Chiang. "I will tell you something, but it is so strong, you may not want to translate it. Don't translate if it goes too far."

Addressing Chiang, he continued, "You have broken agreements, you have gone counter to plans. People have said you were a modern George Washington, but after these things they will never say it again."

Madame Chiang, a power in her own right, nodded. "I want him to hear it."

Chiang listened without expression, the only sign he was listening the characteristic bobbing of his foot when he was irritated.

The military expenditures, Marshall went on, were consuming as much as 90 percent of the government budget. Expenditures were outrunning income three or four to one, fueling massive inflation as the government printed ever more currency. The continuation of war risked a financial collapse that would imperil the KMT while creating a fertile field for the spread of communism. "The Communists were aware of the approaching crisis and this entered into their calculations in forming plans," he advised. The financial crisis, Marshall predicted, would come before military victory.

Marshall deliberately avoided discussion of what to him was a vital concern, the possibility of the KMT's collapse "and the evident growing disapproval of the people of the character of the local government, or misgovernment, that the Kuomintang was giving the country."

Chiang was not accustomed to advisers who contradicted his best laid plans. "His old foot went round and round and almost hit the ceiling," Marshall noted with perverse pleasure.

In a more than hour-long rebuttal, the generalissimo disagreed with Marshall, his false teeth clicking an obbligato. Her husband was convinced, Madame Chiang translated, that the Communists had never intended to cooperate. The CCP was controlled by the Soviet Union, whose purpose was to disrupt Chinese foreign policy. That could only be countered with a campaign to defeat the CCP; the Russians understood only strength. The Nationalists—their fortunes at high tide—could defeat the CCP armies in eight to ten months, well before any economic collapse. (At the same time, Chou En-lai was predicting that the unprecedented Kuomintang offensive would be shattered in six months and that "within a year there will be sweeping changes effective in China's over-all government and economic structure.")

The United States should redefine its China policy, casting its lot with the Nationalists "in light of the present situation." At the same time, the generalissimo remained open to suggestions of ways to open peaceful negotiations with the Communists.

Marshall's report of the unsatisfying interview led the president to give his envoy authority to shut down the mission. As paraphrased by Marshall's Washington liaison, Truman stated that "at such time as you felt the situation called for your return, all you had to do was to notify him how you wanted the matter handled and it would be done that way. . . . [T]he matter is yours and yours alone to determine."

Marshall wanted to go home. He declined an offer from Chiang to become an adviser to the reorganized government since he would be powerless to effect reforms. The question was where he could be of the most service, in China or in the United States. "The best way to defend against Communism," Marshall stressed, "was for the existing government of China to accomplish such reforms that it would gain the support of the people."

On January 3, 1947, Marshall learned that the president wanted his special envoy to return to Washington "for consultation on China and other matters." Marshall understood the implicit message; the president had decided to replace his secretary of state. Through Acheson, Marshall replied dryly, "My answer is in affirmative if that continues to be his desire. My personal reaction is something else."

Chiang Kai-shek and his wife met for a last conference with Marshall and Stuart on January 7. "That final conversation was one of dramatic intensity," the ambassador recalled. "The generalissimo renewed his invitation to General Marshall to continue his great service to China by acting as his supreme adviser. He pled with great earnestness, offering to give him all the power which he himself possessed and promising to cooperate with him to the utmost."

Marshall was moved but said nothing more than he appreciated the honor. The four shared a farewell dinner, Marshall, unlike his wife, having grown fond of the elaborate cuisine of North China.

Early the following day, Stuart drove with Marshall to Nanking Military Airport. On the way they discussed what American policy should be on China if peace negotiations failed. Stuart said he favored support of the government over the present drift or total withdrawal. Marshall pondered a moment, then agreed in principle. He was leaving China a tired man, frustrated, even angry, but still seeking a solution.

Standing on the snow-whitened tarmac before the C-54 with the five stars painted on its tail, Marshall informally said goodbye to the warmly bundled Stuart and the Chinese officials who had come to see off the Tiger of Peace. Chiang and his wife arrived in their new bulletproof Cadillac as the plane's engines turned over.

Marshall greeted Madame Chiang with courtly gravity. "Come back soon," she instructed. The Chiangs spent a brief moment of private farewell aboard the plane with Marshall, then the hatch was closed and army transport 49149 taxied to the runway. The "Most Fairly Friend" was going home.

As Marshall had arranged, the State Department released his final report, described as a "personal statement," an hour after his plane was airborne.

The statement was intended to bring public pressure to bear on both Nationalists and Communists. In it, Marshall described the obstacle to peace as mutual suspicion. Factors involved in the last breakdown of negotiations were, on the Nationalist side, "a dominant group of reactionaries who have been opposed, in my opinion, to almost every effort I have made to influence the formation of a genuine coalition government."

On the other side were "the dyed-in-the-wool Communists [who] do not hesitate at the most drastic measures to gain their end . . . and produce a situation that would facilitate the overthrow or collapse of the government without any regard to the immediate suffering of the people involved."

Extremists on both sides had time and again frustrated his efforts at a settlement, Marshall's statement continued. Irreconcilables within the KMT, "interested in the preservation of their own feudal control of China," had undercut the first truce the year before. "Though I speak as a soldier," Marshall added, "I must here also deplore the dominating influence of the military. Their dominance accentuates the weakness of civil government in China."

Marshall based his hopes for China upon those he called "liberals" in the government and the minority parties. That "splendid group of men," too few to exercise control, could under Chiang's leadership produce a unity government. On the Communist side too there were such liberals, "young men who have turned to the Communists in disgust at the corruption evident in the local governments—men who would put the interest of the Chinese people above ruthless measures to establish a Communist ideology in the immediate future."

The American press judged Marshall's unprecedented statement "a blistering plague on both your houses." In China, Chiang praised the statement as "friendly and constructive," while the CC Clique, those Marshall had referred to as "reactionaries," damned it. From Yenan, Chou En-lai approved the references to the reactionaries in the KMT, but expressed regret that "he did not point out that Chiang Kai-shek himself is the leader of this reactionary group."

Marshall's statement achieved nothing. The special envoy had spent a year, acquiring hard-earned diplomatic experience and deep understanding of Chinese politics, but he had failed. China was no closer to a coalition government, nor was the United States any closer to extricating itself. Marshall blamed himself. "I tried to please everyone," he commented later. "The result was that by the time I left, nobody trusted me."

It was a bitter lesson.

Within hours of the release of the China statement, the army transport plane yet to land in Hawaii, word of James Byrnes's resignation and Marshall's appointment leaked to White House reporters. Marshall would be sworn in three weeks later as secretary of state, the president's first counselor.

CHAPTER

XXXIV

Going to the Yar

The newly appointed secretary of state—his nomination unanimously confirmed by the Republican-dominated Foreign Relations Committee and the entire Senate in less than an hour—came to chilly Washington and the Department of State on January 21, 1947.

If Washington was familiar, George Marshall's new role required some adjustment. He was suddenly not just a governmental figure but a political figure as well. For a man who had followed the old army custom of never voting, it was damned uncomfortable. He did not lack ambition—without it he would never have become chief of staff—yet that desire did not extend to electoral office, or even to wielding power. After all, he had led an army of 8.2 million to victory. What more heady experience?

Marshall had tried to squelch the political rumors that raced his flight across the Pacific. Reporters meeting his plane in Hawaii two weeks before had asked if he would consider the presidency in 1948.

"I am an army officer and presumably will be secretary of state. And I am an Episcopalian." Beyond that, he had no comment.

The Hawaiian denials were to no avail. He was, according to *United States News*, assuming "the burden of reinforcing the peace he did so much to win. Beyond that, he automatically becomes a strong 1948 presidential prospect." With the vice-presidency vacant, by constitutional mandate he was also next in line for the White House; as secretary of state, he was effectively "a new style vice president, with powers and duties much broader than those usually associated with that office," the magazine concluded.

Although his appointment might be considered political—that he could not change—the new secretary had no intention of playing a partisan role. Met by a clutch of reporters at Washington's Union Station on the morning of January 21, Marshall volunteered,

I am assuming that the office of secretary of state, at least under present conditions, is nonpolitical and I am going to govern myself accordingly. I will never become involved in political matters, and therefore I cannot be considered a candidate for political office.

The popular conception that no matter what a man says he can be drafted as a candidate for some political office would be without any force with regard to me. I cannot be drafted for any political office.

The flat disclaimer cleared the air. Republicans in Congress could now support his program without fear they were creating a presidential candidate, James Reston wrote in *The New York Times*. David Lawrence, conservative publisher of *United States News*, concluded Marshall's railroad station announcement had "surrounded him with a prestige both inside and outside this country which no man in public office, not even President Truman, can command."

The reporters out of the way, Marshall turned to the officer sent to bring him to the White House, Lieutenant Colonel Marshall Carter.

"Do you know how the State Department operates?" Marshall asked the colonel.

"Yes, sir. I've been there eight or nine months," relied Carter, who had served as the Washington liaison for Marshall's China mission.

"Well then, you'd just better sit outside the door then with me and keep me out of trouble until I get my feet on the ground." Within two days Marshall had asked Carter if he had any civilian clothes. "It would look better if you wore them because you are going to stay with me." Just that quickly Marshall had decided upon, or, more accurately, adopted, a personal assistant.

Carter, thirty-eight, was an army brat, a graduate like his father and older brother of West Point. He had gone on to earn a master's degree with honors at Massachusetts Institute of Technology. He had spent the war in Washington, in the Operations Division, monitoring troop requirements. The work was prosaic but essential; Carter had performed with distinction and without complaint. Tireless, supple, and considered a brilliant staff worker, he had been transferred from the War Department to serve as the Washington contact for Marshall's China mission.

As he had earlier treated his former aide Frank McCarthy, discharged now from the service and soon to become a motion picture producer, so the secretary came to view Carter as a family member. Marshall granted few men such intimacy, though the general would call Carter by his last name throughout the five years they worked together.

Within an hour of arriving in Washington, George Catlett Marshall, clad in his one civilian suit, strode into the White House. As he made his way through the crowded lobby, he was greeted with spontaneous applause from White House staff members. In a brief ceremony, with Katherine and a beaming Harry Truman looking on, Marshall was sworn in by Chief Justice Fred Vinson as the fiftieth man to be secretary of state, and the first career military officer to hold the position.

Marshall's mettle would be tested quickly. He was coming to State with no overriding policy, with no personal agenda other than the most evident to a professional soldier who had weathered two world wars in his lifetime. "The only way to be sure of winning a third world war is to prevent it." All else was secondary.

The indoctrination of the new secretary of state began immediately. Marshall spent forty-five minutes with the president, then crossed to the adjacent State, War and Navy Building for a meeting with Undersecretary of State Dean Acheson. In that ornate structure, where forty-five years before, less one month, Second Lieutenant George C. Marshall had reported for duty, the new secretary of state began work. He would have been less than human if he had not paused to wonder about the very neatness of it all, beginning both his first and his last government job in the same building. He was lined and wiser now, and the years had left him 50 pounds heavier, at 200. His once sandy hair was silvered, the lean face drawn, grown lumpy, the flesh sagging beneath the chin. The eyes were the same, a piercing blue that riveted men in place.

Marshall's first move was to ask Acheson to stay on. The undersecretary was flattered; Marshall awed the sophisticated Acheson. Absent from his law firm for the past six years, Acheson agreed to stay for another six months. What did Marshall expect of him?

Acheson was to be his chief of staff; he, in fact, would run the State Department, coming to Marshall only when he needed help—"and his look indicated that that had better not be often."

Was there anything else?

"I shall expect of you," Marshall replied in measured language, "the most complete frankness, particularly about myself. I have no feelings except those I reserve for Mrs. Marshall."

The choice of Acheson, age fifty-four, was both necessary and apt. Acheson was a Washington insider, and if he dismissed most congressmen as beneath *his* consideration, the undersecretary and the president of the United States got along well together. The tall, patrician Acheson, a man of the Eastern establishment and wealth, and the plain-spoken Missourian were both hard-eyed students of politics, straightforward in their loyalties and salty in their antagonisms.

The experienced Acheson could guide Marshall through the host of international problems confronting his new department: the German and Austrian peace treaties had to be negotiated; France and Italy teetered on the brink of voting Communist; Great Britain was virtually bankrupt; divided Korea had to be unified; China—well, Marshall knew all about China. Despite a succession of one- to three-hour briefings he called his "Ten Commandments," Marshall could not hope to master more than a portion of it. He needed someone with a broad familiarity with the issues, and especially someone, like the acerbic Acheson, who understood just how the department functioned.

In his first weeks as secretary, Marshall found himself nearly overwhelmed by briefings and problems. "It is a little more than an endurance contest," he wrote Madame Chiang on February 5.

Still, these were rewarding weeks for a restored Marshall. Four days after the swearing-in ceremony, Acheson was writing the former secretary of state, Henry Stimson, "General Marshall has taken hold of this baffling institution with the calmness orderliness and vigor with which you are familiar."

He settled upon an easy schedule, arriving at his office at eight-thirty each morning. Lunch in the dining room next to his office was brief, often enough followed by a fifteen-minute nap on an army cot set up in the great walk-in safe in the secretary's office. After a day of briefings, he routinely left for Leesburg at four-thirty where he might find himself "dispatched to the roof to clean out the gutters, with the simple excuse that no other labor was obtainable," he wrote to the former British ambassador, Lord Halifax. "This was the action of the totalitarian government which kept me at work every evening when I returned at about 5:30. However, the physical labor really helped me to endure the mental torments of this confused situation and lack of time to assimilate the large amount of information required of me to act intelligently."

Marshall first tackled a thorough reorganization of his department. Marshall's predecessor, James Byrnes, had cared little about the convoluted bureaucracy. Absent at foreign ministers' meetings for 350 of his 562 days in office, Byrnes with his offhanded administrative style had driven Acheson, the acting secretary, to distraction and near resignation.

Acheson was delighted with Marshall's proposal. Power resided in the geographical desks, Far East, Latin America, Europe, headed by regional potentates who talked with each other only to wage jurisdictional war. It was a department grown encrusted with privilege and seniority, slow to respond, and ponderous with prerogatives.

In their first meeting on January 21, Marshall outlined a new structure, imposing a chain of command for the first time in departmental memory. He wanted Acheson to create a secretariat as Marshall once had in the War Department. Through that office and the undersecretary would come all papers to him. The secretariat staff—headed by another man drawn from the War Department, Colonel Carlisle Humel-

sine—would soon learn that he wanted concise reports with terse recommendations at the conclusion, and small boxes on the page, in which
he would initial his approval or rejection.

There were problems with strict adherence to the military model,
Acheson later told Marshall's biographer, Forrest Pogue. "I thought, as
distinct from the military services, the Department of State required at
all stages of the development of an idea the imprint of the secretary's
wishes, because these views would reflect the opinion of the Administration, of which the secretary and the under secretary were a part." Marshall would from time to time have to attend committee meetings, to
guide the discussions, Acheson advised. It would remain a distasteful
chore to the secretary.

Despite the militarylike structure of his department, Marshall's approach
to the work was not that of a soldier, Acheson discovered. Rather, it was
that of "a man who understood forms of public leadership and forces of
international friction. . . . [I]n the field of ideas, there hardly was less a
military mind than his."

Marshall first ordered that his department, tucked away in no less than
forty-six offices across Washington, move into a comparatively small
building erected in 1940 for the War Department in "Foggy Bottom."
New State at Twenty-first Street and Virginia Avenue Southwest, with
its 604 offices, was too small, but it was better than Old State. At least
this first new office building for the department since the administration
of Ulysses S. Grant was air-conditioned.

The Department of State, like most of official Washington, had grown
rapidly during the war. The fewer than 1,000 employees in 1939 and a
Foreign Service of 4,139 had grown by 1946 to 7,623 employees and
11,115 Foreign Service officers. With numbers had come a labyrinthine
bureaucracy that churned out few decisions and many reports. Robert
Lovett, the former undersecretary of war for air, compared the department's daily functions to the love life of an elephant: all important business was done at a very high level, any developments were accompanied
by tremendous trumpeting, and the results would not be forthcoming
for eighteen months.

Marshall intended no housecleaning. According to Colonel Carter, the
secretary treated those in the department as if they had the same moti-
vation, desire, and intelligence as he did. He did not want to tell people
how to do their tasks, but assumed they knew their jobs. When something went wrong, Marshall did not try to fix blame, but rather to fix the
problem.

There were those who could not, or would not adapt. With the assistance of Colonel Carter, Acheson grimly set to, often working against
the entrenched resistance of the department staff and the clubby Foreign Service. A succession of transfers and accepted resignations broke

the resisters; this would not be Cordell Hull's or James Byrnes's State Department.

A dinner guest at the Acheson home in the first months of 1947 marveled at the change in his host. "Dean spent a good deal of the time bubbling over with his enthusiasm, rapture almost, about General Marshall. He has admired him for a long time. But to work with him is such a joy that he can hardly talk about anything else," David Lilienthal noted.

Acheson was not the only employee of the State Department to feel the change. Up and down the halls, up and down the ranks, there was a new spirit. "At an early staff meeting, something was said regarding morale in the department," a newer member recalled. "Marshall replied, 'Gentlemen, it is my experience an enlisted man may have a morale problem. An officer is expected to take care of his own morale.'"

Shunning committee meetings, Marshall pressed staff members hard to come to conclusions. "Don't fight the problem. Decide it!" he insisted repeatedly. They were to make recommendations to him: "I don't want you fellows sitting around asking me what to do. I want you to tell me what to do." It was the well-honed military technique. Dean Rusk, a former officer in the War Department transferred to State, remembered Marshall as "a great teacher, by his own example and the remarks he made. . . . 'Gentlemen, let us not discuss this as a military problem; to do so turns it into a military problem.'"

Not everyone was pleased with the streamlined department. There were those who complained that the secretary of state was "rarely informed in detail on any aspect of the international situation. Some government officials who have attended conferences with him say they were astounded at how poorly briefed Marshall was." Fiorello LaGuardia, three times New York City mayor and director of the United Nations Relief and Rehabilitation Administration, "was amazed how little he knew of the food and agricultural organization, and of economics generally. . . ."

The secretary imposed a second significant reform within the department, creating a Policy Planning Staff to do long-range planning. The office was similar to the War Department panel he had established under Major General Stanley Embick. Its function was to permit State to attempt to plan ahead, to foresee diplomatic crises.

As head of the new Policy Planning Staff, Marshall selected George F. Kennan, a forty-three-year-old career officer in the Foreign Service. One of a group of six young diplomats who had specialized in Soviet studies since the early 1930s, Kennan had served in the State Department's "listening post" at Riga in Latvia before President Roosevelt recognized the Soviet Union. Kennan then spent five years in the reopened Moscow Embassy, followed by other diplomatic assignments. A scholarly sort, the balding Kennan had grown increasingly hostile to the Soviet government through the purge trials, the Red Army purge of the late 1930s, and the Stalin-Hitler pact. By war's end, his early romantic infatuation with Russian culture had evaporated, replaced by a deep suspicion of Stalin's expansive strategy.

The imposition of subservient Communist governments in North Korea, Hungary, Rumania, Bulgaria and, especially, Poland vexed Washington. Further, the Soviet Union was dragging its feet on withdrawing troops from northern Iran. The cordial relations of the war years had given way to mutual suspicion.

On February 9, 1946, Stalin proclaimed a new five-year industrial and armament production plan that would protect the USSR "against any eventuality." His speech clearly implied that international comity was "impossible under the present capitalist development of world econ-omy." Reflecting the gloomy mood in the winter of 1946–47, liberal Supreme Court Associate Justice William O. Douglas ominously termed the Stalin speech "the Declaration of World War III."

Nine days later, the press bannered the story of a defector from the Soviet Embassy in Ottawa who had disclosed details of a well-placed spy ring targeting the United States' atomic weapons research. Since pop-ular opinion held that friendly nations did not spy upon each other, this was obvious proof that the Soviet saw itself as an enemy of the United States.

Kennan was serving as chargé d'affaires in Moscow in February 1946 when the State Department requested an explication of the Soviet Union's growing uncooperativeness. Kennan, a testy man and not one to suffer fools in any event, exploded.

> For two years, I have been trying to persuade people in Washing-ton that the Stalin regime is the same regime we knew in the pre-war period, the same one that conducted the purges, the same one that concluded the Non-Aggression Pact with the Nazis—that its leaders are no friends of ours. I have tried to persuade Washington that dreams of a happy postwar collaboration with this regime are quite unreal; that our problem is deeper than that; that Stalin and his associates are now elated with their recent military and political successes and think they see favorable prospects for extending their political influence over all of Europe through the devices of infil-tration and subversion.

Kennan took the opportunity to write "a preposterously long tele-gram" of 5,540 words, what he thought of as a primer about the careers, nature, and ambitions of Soviet leaders. To his surprise, what would be called in Washington folklore "the long telegram" became required reading not only in the State Department but in the Pentagon as well.

For the first time in his life, Kennan wrote, he seemed to be on the same wavelength as his masters.

Kennan's thesis held that the current Soviet policy was not the product of Marxism, but was "centuries old," a neurotic, xenophobic view of world affairs, "traditional and instinctive." The Communists were only more insecure than the despots who preceded them. Marxist doctrine, "with its basic altruism of purpose," simply cloaked their instinctive fear of the outside world, "for the dictatorship without which they did not know how to rule, for cruelties they did not dare not to inflict, for sacrifices they felt bound to demand."

Wherever it was timely or promising, the Soviet Union would seek to expand, Kennan predicted, first in adjacent areas such as Iran and Turkey, later in a West subverted by national Communist parties subservient to Moscow. Finally, the pessimistic assessment continued, the Soviets would do everything possible to set the major Western powers against each other.

Confronted with force, and the readiness of an opponent to use it, the Soviet Union would back down. In a contest with the West, the Soviets were still the weaker force; success would depend on the degree of cohesion, firmness, and vigor the United States and its allies mustered, Kennan argued.

The new secretary of state had seen a copy of the long telegram while in China. By the time Marshall returned to Washington, the slight, physically unimpressive Kennan was counted a man influential well beyond his diplomatic rank. A member of the faculty of the National War College—the assignment of diplomats to that military finishing school had resulted from then Chief of Staff Marshall's urging—Kennan would become even more influential in shaping what was coming to be known as "the Cold War." As he put it in his memoirs, "My voice now carried." Marshall approved Acheson's selection of Kennan to head State's new Policy Planning Staff.

In the months that followed, Kennan too fell sway to Marshall's sense of duty and selflessness. In a heartfelt appreciation, Kennan later wrote that the man they addressed as "General" was "fully prepared to accept the responsibility of his own decisions, and did not put the blame on subordinates if the results turned out to be unfortunate. He valued the considered judgment of history; but for the day-to-day applause of contemporaries he had as little concern as for their criticisms."

Kennan had not yet moved to the Policy Planning Staff when Marshall's first crisis broke. Taking time from his preparation for a forthcoming foreign ministers' meeting in Moscow, Marshall was at Columbia University on Friday, February 21, to accept an honorary degree when the British Embassy telephoned.

Lord Inverchapel, explained his private secretary, had "a blue piece

of paper"—trade talk for a formal message from His Majesty's government—to be delivered to the secretary. Acheson arranged immediate
delivery of a carbon copy of the message, so as to have a response drafted
by the time Marshall returned on Monday.

There was not one, but two messages, the pair of them "shockers,"
Acheson wrote later. A virtually bankrupt Great Britain, after six years
of war and eighteen months of fitful recovery, could no longer sustain
its support of the Greek monarchy. Wracked by a Communist-led civil
war, its economy in tatters, Greece needed an immediate infusion of
$240 million and more in succeeding years if it was to survive as a West-
ern state. Turkey too needed funds to modernize its army and stimulate
economic development, though its needs were less pressing than Greece's.
Britain, no longer able to bear the burden, would end its aid in six weeks,
the blue paper cautioned.

It was as Kennan had forewarned. Two nations, adjacent to the Soviet
Union or to countries dominated by Moscow, were to be abandoned.
The Americans, as the British note hinted, would have to take up the
slack lest Greece and Turkey fall to the Communists.

By the time Marshall returned to his office on Monday, February 24,
Acheson's committee had waiting for him a summary of the situation,
an estimate of military aid needs, and an inventory of material on hand.
When later that morning Marshall met with Lord Inverchapel to formally accept the British message, the secretary had a clear idea of the
policy he would recommend to the president. Since he would be leaving
for the Moscow foreign ministers' meeting within a week, Marshall then
instructed Acheson to continue to take the lead on behalf of the nascent
program. Marshall, who had fought so hard to prevent the United States
from being drawn into the vortex at the eastern end of the Mediterranean, was about to recommend an involvement beyond any contemplated by Churchill in 1944.

The following day, Marshall secured the endorsement of immediate
aid from Secretary of War Robert Patterson; Secretary of the Navy James
Forrestal, a vigorous anti-Communist; and, finally, with Acheson making a crisp presentation in the White House, of President Truman.

Now came the difficult part, garnering support from congressional
leadership for the necessary legislation from the Republican-controlled
Congress. Happily planning to cut taxes 20 percent, Congress was little
inclined to take up Britain's burden.

On the morning of February 27, the president summoned Marshall
and Acheson to meet congressional leaders in the White House for what
a later occupant of the Oval Office would call a jawboning session.

They were met at Armageddon, Acheson later wrote. Truman opened
the meeting by briefly explaining the crisis Great Britain had thrust on
the United States. He had decided to extend aid to the two countries, he

announced to the bipartisan group, and he "hoped Congress would provide the means to make this aid timely and sufficient."

Marshall followed, reading a prepared statement explaining the rationale for the president's request. He read badly, as he always read prepared speeches, in a flat, barely inflected voice.

The secretary of state was concerned that Congress would deem the
proposed $400 million aid package a simple relief bill and would cut it
back as a refugee aid bill had been. He stressed immediately, "Our interest in Greece is by no means restricted to humanitarian or friendly
impulses."

Marshall's prepared statement was redolent with an emerging policy
of containment of the Soviet menace. A civil war in Greece, he warned
the legislators, would probably result in a Communist state under Soviet
control. Turkey would be threatened. "Soviet domination might thus
extend over the entire Middle East to the borders of India. The effect
of this over Hungary, Austria, Italy and France cannot be overestimated.
It is not alarmist to say that we are faced with the first crisis of a series
which might extend Soviet domination to Europe, the Middle East and
Asia."

No other nation could take up the slack, the secretary added, nor could
he assure them that $400 million would be enough. Nonetheless, "the
choice is between acting with energy or losing by default."

According to Joseph M. Jones, a member of the State Department's
public affairs office who sat in on the meeting, Marshall's matter-of-fact
statement fell flat with the legislators. Never flamboyant, Marshall had
avoided the anti-Communist rhetoric that excited, alarmed, or spurred
politicians to action in these days of growing nervousness about Soviet
global designs. He presumed the men in the president's office understood the sharpening East-West conflict, that they were patriotic, that
they wanted to do the right thing. In Marshall's opinion, fiery speeches
on the evils of communism merely provoked needless tension; publicly,
they complicated relations with the USSR. Further, Marshall was probably less reflexively anti-Soviet than the other men in the room, men who
could not, or did not consider the Soviet leaders former brothers-in-
arms.

The increasingly anxious Acheson—this was his crisis, after all—leaned
over to the secretary and asked in a low voice, "Is this a private fight or
can anyone get into it?" Marshall deferred to him. "Never have I spoken
under such a pressing sense that the issue was up to me alone," Acheson
wrote later.

The Soviets were poised to break out into three continents if Greece
or Turkey gave way, Acheson began. "Like apples in a barrel infected
by one rotten one, the corruption of Greece would infect Iran and all to
the east. It would also carry infection to Africa through Asia Minor and

Egypt, and to Europe through Italy and France. . . . We and we alone
were in a position to break up the play."

There was a long silence when Acheson finished. Then Arthur Vandenberg, Republican chairman of the Foreign Relations Committee, said
solemnly, "Mr. President, if you will say that to the Congress and the
country, I will support you and I believe that most of its members will
do the same."

Truman did more than that. Despite Marshall's effort to tone down
the anti-Communist rhetoric, the president delivered a stemwinder calculated to "scare hell out of the country." According to Truman, the
"All-Out Speech" was necessary to provoke Congress to action.

The United States was caught up in a global struggle "between alternative ways of life," the president proclaimed. "I believe," he continued
in a passage that would make it the most controversial address of his
presidency, "it *must* be the policy of the United States to support free
peoples who are resisting attempted subjugation by armed minorities or
by outside pressures." He asked Congress to appropriate $400 million
in Greek and Turkish aid, and authority to send both civil and military
advisers to the two nations. The congressional response as Truman walked
up the aisle to the doors at the rear of the House was restrained; the
importance of the speech and its marked departure from Roosevelt's
policy of international cooperation was clear and sobering.

There was opposition from both the political left and right. Conservative Republicans such as Representative Walter H. Judd of Minnesota, a
former medical missionary in China, asked, "If it is a wise policy to urge
. . . the government of China to unite with organized Communist minorities there, why is it a wise policy to assist the Greek government to fight
against the same sort of armed Communist minorities in Greece?" Liberals asked why the United States should aid a Greek government that
was both corrupt and authoritarian, or a Turkish government that had
refused to fight on the side of the Allies in the war.

It took more than three months before administration lobbyists could
satisfy the opposition and Congress passed what would be called the
"Truman Doctrine." The president's signature on May 22 fixed containment of Soviet advances as the cornerstone of American foreign relations.

While the president and Acheson shaped this marked departure in
American foreign policy, Marshall worked to master the issues that concerned State. He was still "going to school," preparing for the upcoming
foreign ministers' meeting in Moscow, he explained frankly in an executive session of the Senate Foreign Relations Committee.

Marshall's painstaking preparation, the genesis of wise counsel,
delighted the president. The secretary had none of Byrnes's self-impor-
tant posing, none of Byrnes's helter-skelter decision making. After seeing

Marshall on February 18, Truman wrote on his appointment list: "The more I see and talk to him the more certain I am he's the great one of the age. I am surely lucky to have his friendship and support."

The secretary of state left for the Moscow foreign ministers' meeting on March 5, traveling with a State Department cadre of eighty-four advisers, clerks, and supporting personnel. In Paris he would pick up another, John Foster Dulles, recommended at Marshall's request by Arthur Vandenberg, the Republican chairman of the Senate Foreign Relations Committee. Dulles's presence was a pledge of continued non-partisanship in foreign affairs.

Dulles had served as a virtual shadow foreign minister during the long Democratic tenure in the White House. A Wall Street lawyer with impeccable credentials, Dulles came from a family much experienced in international affairs. A brother, Allen, had headed the vital Bern listening post of the OSS during the war. A sister, Eleanor, perhaps the brightest of the Dulles offspring, was a respected economist specializing in foreign trade. If there was a Republican foreign policy establishment, the Dulles family was at the heart—some would say the soul—of it.

Born in 1888 the son of a Presbyterian minister, John Foster was more stolid than brilliant, scorned by one Wall Street wag as "Dull, Duller, Dulles." His sense of high moral purpose, enshrouding a sturdy patriotism, struck irritated colleagues as self-righteous and prissy; the British diplomat Lord Cadogan privately dismissed Dulles as "the wooliest type of useless pontificating American." If he was that, Dulles was also useful for reassuring Senate Republicans that American foreign policy remained bipartisan.

As his adviser in matters Russian, Marshall selected career diplomat Charles Bohlen, with his friend George Kennan one of the handful of Soviet experts in the Department of State. Born in comfortable surroundings, the handsome "Chip" Bohlen had spent summers with his family in Europe, drifting into the Foreign Service in 1929 after graduating from Harvard and working as an able body for a summer on a tramp steamer. In the years since joining the service, he had studied Russian, then had served in a variety of postings, including Tokyo at the time of Pearl Harbor. There he was imprisoned until exchanged in 1942. He had worked as Roosevelt's translator at Tehran and Yalta, then in the same capacity for Truman at Potsdam. Just forty-three, Bohlen was among the brightest luminaries of the Foreign Service, increasingly valued for his counsel on matters pertaining to the Soviet Union.

Marshall was to take a special liking to the engaging younger man, treating him, as one ranking diplomat put it, "like a son."

Marshall would need Dulles and Bohlen, according to *Time* magazine, which sent the secretary on his way with a pontificating cover story:

George Catlett Marshall is clearly a bigger man than his predecessor, Jimmy Byrnes. But is Marshall big enough for the gigantic task ahead of him?

He has many of the earmarks of real greatness. . . . He knows enough about war to know that it issues from and is conditioned by economics, politics and philosophy. His interest is as broad as the farthest ramifications of his job.

For all his qualifications, *Time* was dubious Marshall would be successful in the major agenda item in Moscow, drafting a German peace treaty. France feared a German economic recovery that would outpace its own. At the same time Great Britain wanted to meld its occupation zone more closely with that of the United States to save expenses. The Soviet Union wanted a strong centralized government for Germany; the United States, Britain, and France preferred a federation of states.

Marshall himself had no great expectation of success. "It would appear now to be extremely doubtful whether an actual treaty for Germany will be completed for consideration at this conference," he told reporters forthrightly. At best, he hoped to lay the groundwork for a future treaty, perhaps to get the Austrian pact on the table, he advised the Senate Foreign Relations Committee.

The secretary's C-54 landed in Paris on March 6, where he met with Premier Paul Ramadier and President Vincent Auriol. The two Frenchmen reiterated France's fear of a revitalized Germany, a fear that led the French to side often with the Russians at meetings of the Allied Control Council in Berlin. Marshall also sought to assure President Auriol that he appreciated the privations and the sufferings of his people and their consequences—a nod toward the looming electoral strength of the Communist Party in France.

In the first war, he had spent two years in France—"I was able to gauge the work of destruction wrought by the Germans and the sufferings and the courage of the French population." He had seen the ravages of the second war, reminding them gently that "the liberation of France was my great concern.

"I can tell you without boasting that among the men who are not Frenchmen I know as much as anyone else about the sufferings of this country, about its present situation and its worries." Marshall spoke candidly, at the end of the conversation assuring the two, "I am not a diplomat. I mean exactly what I say and there is no use trying to read between the lines because there is nothing to read there."

The following day he laid a wreath at the Tomb of the Unknown Soldier beneath the Arc de Triomphe. The brief ceremony in the damp chill of a Parisian winter stirred memories. For reporters, Marshall recalled the last time he had come to the Arc de Triomphe—riding on a horse. It was Bastille Day, 1919, and he was then a colonel on Pershing's staff, reveling in Paris's salute to the victorious armies of Marshal Foch.

Neither France nor the rest of Europe was cheering in March 1947. That winter, the worst in memory, had struck Europe hard. Victor and vanquished suffered equally with food production falling far behind demand. A severe shortage of housing had aggravated conditions. One third of Normandy's villages and towns had been destroyed in the fighting; nothing had been rebuilt. Similarly, block after block in London stood gap-toothed, with the bomb-gutted buildings cleared away.

Germany, where Marshall stopped for a briefing by European theater commander General Joseph T. McNarney, was even more desperate. City after city had been flattened by war, then stripped by the locusts of both Russian and French occupation forces in their respective zones. Amid a flourishing black market, with rocketing inflation, Germany had averted literal starvation in the last year only through $468 million in American and British aid. Life in the rubble of the Third Reich centered on survival; a gallows humor debate in Germany revolved around the best occupation zone to live in. "The Russians promise everything and do nothing. The Americans promise nothing and do everything. The British promise nothing and do nothing."

In Berlin, Marshall decided to add two more to his delegation: General Mark W. Clark, Allied high commissioner for Austria; and Lieutenant General Lucius D. Clay, the American military governor in Germany. A former instructor under Marshall at Benning's Infantry School, then an aggressive combat soldier, Clark had evolved into a strong-minded administrator and fiercely anti-Communist diplomat. The hard-driving Clay meanwhile had spent his war in the Pentagon, the second ranking man in G-4, as director of materiel responsible for all War Department procurement.

The briefings in Germany underlined what Marshall could see for himself. Germany was a great burden that would pull down all of Europe if it could not recover. There was a shortage of capital for investment and little hope of amassing more, Clay stressed. The USSR and France, in particular, were reluctant to deal with Germany in any way that brought a net profit to that nation. "We must realize that any transaction which brings a loss ostensibly to the US/UK zones of Germany today does, in fact, bring that loss to the US/UK Governments instead," since those two nations were underwriting the German economy.

Germany was bankrupt, unable to reestablish itself until its reparations debt was fixed, Clay continued. "We have to recognize that it is not Germany who is paying the penalty today, but rather the taxpayers of the United States and Great Britain and that we can unburden ourselves of this expense only by returning Germany to a satisfactory trading position or by abandoning her to chaos."

The Marshall party flew on to Moscow on March 9, met on a windy afternoon by the American ambassador, yet another army officer turned diplomat, Lieutenant General Walter Bedell Smith. Secretary to the army General Staff in 1940, Smith found himself reverting to an all-but-forgotten pattern. Marshall quickly took charge at the embassy, issuing terse orders, "I want you to do this and this," to which Smith replied, "Yes, Sir," while thinking to himself, "Here we go again."

While Marshall stayed at the embassy, Spasso House, most of the American delegation was housed at the fifteen-story Moskva Hotel on Manezh Naya Square, next to the American Embassy. The Russians had gone to some efforts to redecorate the hotel, to clean up the city, even to outfit waiters in the restaurants with new uniforms. It was a virtual Potemkin village, fabricated to put the best face on the economic recovery, the Americans discovered. The hotel rooms were cold, the restaurants overpriced, and the garbage uncollected in rank alleys just off the sparkling main avenues.

The Moscow Foreign Ministers' Conference opened the following day at the refurbished Aviation Industry Building, once one of the capital's most expensive restaurants, the Yar. Nostalgic czarist revelers remembered the song that warned:

> Sweetheart, don't go to the Yar.
> Don't throw your money away.
> Better to buy a guitar,
> And play on it all day.

Marshall settled into a routine: up at 8:00 a.m., dressing on alternative days in blue and gray suits with blue shirts and dark blue ties; then breakfast followed by a daily briefing at ten-thirty with the staff. Marshall fit in at least a twenty-minute walk before or after the 2:00 p.m. lunch, then left for the daily sessions of the conference.

International diplomacy was slow and frustrating, Marshall had learned in 600-plus meetings during his year in China. Through the wearying Moscow sessions—forty-four of them over a six-week period—Marshall sat erect, often with folded arms, listening to the translators. When he spoke, it was most often from notes, carefully read through the tortoise-shell reading glasses that perched precariously near the end of his nose. The effect was that of an accountant at his ledger or a contract attorney scrutinizing the last comma and period. Appearances notwithstanding, Marshall would be "the star of the conference" in the opinion of British journalist Henry Brandon.

The conference opened in the ornate main hall of the Aviation Industry Building with the foreign ministers flanked around a large table, one nation to a side. The Americans faced the Russians, Marshall flanked by Smith and Dulles; State Department Counselor Ben Cohen, diplomat Robert Murphy, and Mark Clark, hardliners all, were near at hand.

Vyacheslav Molotov once more represented the Soviet Union, his chin in his hand, the most experienced of them all, a veteran of foreign diplomacy since 1939 when he negotiated the Nazi-Soviet Pact. Given to rigid, doctrinaire statements, the expressionless Molotov was an unyielding negotiator, nor merely stubborn but rigid.

Molotov would insist, again and again, upon the Soviet position: the separation of the Ruhr with its war-making potential from Germany and four-power control of the area; de-Nazification; and, above all, the payment out of Germany's current production of $10 billion in war reparations.

On a third side sat the British delegation, headed by Foreign Minister Ernest Bevin. A veteran of the raucous labor movement and the even more rowdy Labor Party politics, Bevin had acquitted himself well in Churchill's wartime coalition cabinet. After the Labor Party's victory in 1945, Bevin was named foreign minister. Militant as only a Socialist can be in his opposition to communism, the seriously overweight Bevin was a man ponderous of thought and speech, but ever quick to defend the British Empire. He and Marshall in the next six weeks would often find themselves aligned against Molotov and the French foreign minister, Georges Bidault.

On the fourth side of the table sat the French, led by Bidault, a slight, even unprepossessing man who had been a leader of the wartime underground. Bidault's freedom to negotiate in Moscow was constrained. The coalition French government was squeezed between hostile Gaullists and Communists, who held one-third of the seats in the national assembly; Bidault was ever aware that a false step here would bring the government down and with it his preferred place.

Bidault was also hampered by express instructions to insist upon the separation of the Ruhr industrial area from Germany, a position that aligned him uncomfortably with the Soviet Union. Privately, the emotional Bidault sought to assure Marshall and Bevin that he favored their position, but what could he do? Marshall hid his impatience with Bidault, but cautioned him by telling of his own failure to please all sides in China. Marshall's open manner impressed the Frenchman. "He was unaffected and did not pretend to be infallible." Bidault recalled. "He would ask others for advice and could be unsure, even hesitant. But once he had made up his mind, nothing could have made him change it, not even the president of the United States in person."

Over the course of the meetings, Marshall would come around to the opinion that the United States confronted a hostile Soviet Union. According to Averell Harriman, U.S. ambassador to the Soviet Union from 1943 to 1946, the new secretary of state was slow to understand the Soviets' enduring hostility to the West; Marshall believed the wartime spirit of cooperation would extend to the business of making the peace.

On March 14, Marshall outlined the American position on Germany, urging that the new Germany be erected along democratic lines. Acknowledging that there were many definitions of "democracy"—he had spent no less than six hours thrashing out a definition with his senior advisers—Marshall offered a hornbook lecture:

> We believe that human beings have certain inalienable rights—that is, rights which may not be given or taken away. They include the right of every individual to develop his mind and his soul in the ways of his own choice, free of fear and coercion—provided only that he does not interfere with the rights of others. To us a society is not democratic if men who respect the rights of their fellow men are not free to express their own belief and convictions without fear that they may be snatched away from their home or family. To us a society is not free if law-abiding citizens live in fear of being denied the right to work or deprived of life, liberty and the pursuit of happiness.

To the American's regret, Marshall continued, the Allied Control Council sitting in Berlin had been unable to settle upon the guarantees necessary to assure political and economic freedom in Germany. He suggested that each of the states of a federated Germany adopt constitutional guarantees, a Bill of Rights. Further, the rights of political parties, of trade unions, of freedom of the press, of the right to travel freely should be guaranteed.

"We will never democratize Germany by the mere negative process of depriving the Nazis of their positions and influence. We must, rather, take an active part in the establishment of the essentials which I have outlined and proceed to restore the German economic and political life upon the foundation which they provide."

Marshall's commentary, wrote Bedell Smith, "was probably the most forthright statement on the rights of man ever made in Russia." Molotov remained unmoved; the Soviet Union was uninterested in "the generalities of democracy," he coldly stated.

Three days later, the four ministers turned to the economic organization of Germany. Molotov raked the Americans and British for creating the year before a joint economic region within their two occupation zones, charging it was no more than a cover to revivify the cartels and other trusts that had helped to foster the war.

Marshall spoke last that day, after Molotov and Bevin, after two sets of translations of both men. He diplomatically chided the Russian foreign minister: "But charges and countercharges get us nowhere except in the development of great differences. They do not solve our problems, they do complicate them."

The United States wanted to reunite Germany economically, making it possible for the industrial western zones to exchange their production for needed food from the heavily agricultural Soviet zone. The question was how to do that without giving the USSR a voice in management of the industrial Ruhr as it wanted.

That became tangled with the question of reparations. Day after day Molotov pressed for payment of $10 billion in reparations out of current production rather than waiting for the Germans to amass a surplus. Under the current Russian proposal, Marshall pointed out, continued German reparations to the Soviet Union would deprive a reunited Germany of the resources necessary to exist without aid from the United States. "We cannot accept a unified Germany under a procedure which in effect would mean that the American people would pay reparations to an ally."

Within the week, they were deadlocked. Marshall briefly tried to secure German and Austrian peace treaties, snarled in debates about frontiers, reparations, and assigning guilt for the war. That proved impossible, the ministers unable even to agree which of their wartime allies should be asked to participate in peace conferences.

By mutual agreement they shifted to the question of the form of government for a reunited Germany. Molotov argued for a strong central government, the three others for a weak federal system, Marshall countering that another autocratic Germany "would be a danger to the peace of the world."

The strong-weak debate masked another deep split between them. The Western allies feared a Germany with a strong central government would be more easily captured by a well-disciplined German Communist Party or with a rigged election as had Poland. Certainly aware of that fear, a grimly smiling Molotov proposed the German people be allowed to exercise a bit of democracy and vote for the form of government they wanted.

Bevin rose to the bait. Reminding his colleagues that twice in the century a strong central government in Germany had led the world to war, he stressed, "I can never be a party to a proposal for submitting the security of England to the judgment of the German people."

Wherever they turned, there was stalemate, Marshall reported to Washington. On reparations, on peace treaties, on the form of government, on the level of occupation forces in Germany, on the settlement of the German-Polish border, they were unable to move off center.

The pace of the conference was slow. In his second-floor bedroom in the embassy, Marshall read Harold Nicolson's *Congress of Vienna,* a far cry from the undemanding novels he had read in his fatigue in China. He found time for a matinée performance of the Bolshoi Ballet, where *première danseuse* Maya Plisetzkaya blew him a kiss in return for the basket of flowers he sent to her during her curtain call.

After five weeks of stalemate, Marshall came to the reluctant conclusion that Molotov had deliberately sought to delay any agreement, to string out the discussions as long as possible. Delay fostered economic disintegration in Germany, and enhanced the Communists' opportunities in the face of public unrest.

The conference near its inconclusive end, Marshall decided on a dramatic move to break the logjam before the next meeting of the foreign ministers in London. The secretary of state decided to pay a visit to Stalin, laagered as always behind the walls of the Kremlin. Perhaps he could pull an end run on the unrelenting Molotov.

Marshall had deferred the visiting diplomat's obligatory courtesy call on the host head of state, preferring to have something beyond courtesies to say. He did now.

They had been comrades in arms, after all, in what the Russians referred to as the Great Patriotic War. Moreover, Marshall suspected that however tough-minded Stalin was—the American had no doubt about the premier's negotiating abilities—Stalin might even hold him in some affection. (The Russian had once said of Marshall, "Military men make good politicians.") Based on that, Marshall might get agreement on the almost completed Austrian peace treaty, and demonstrate some concord among the four powers.

On the night of April 15, the secretary of state, the American ambassador, and translator Chip Bohlen followed a smartly turned-out colonel through a succession of reception rooms to the paneled conference room next to Stalin's private office. The premier—accompanied by Molotov, his Austrian peace treaty negotiator, and a translator—amiably greeted the American party, then took his usual place at the end of the table.

The Soviet leader, still wearing the mustard-colored uniform of a generalissimo, had aged in recent months, Bohlen thought. He appeared grayer, more careworn and weary. To Marshall he said disarmingly, "You look just the same as when I saw you last time, but I am just an old man." Throughout the hour and one-half interview he doodled wolf's heads with a colored pencil on a tablet of blue paper.

Marshall spoke at length, frankly, delivering what he later termed "almost brutal assaults," Stalin listening impassively to the translation. The war had ended, Marshall told Stalin, with the Soviet Union high in the regard of most Americans. Since then, the feelings of goodwill had been steadily dissipated. Marshall recounted a succession of Soviet moves that had, he said, alienated the American people and Congress since August 1945. Even tactfully stated then strained through a discreet translator, the statement was blunt.

Marshall told the premier that the United States did not intend to dismember Germany, but wished the exact opposite. The United States deeply desired economic unity, but feared a strong central government would constitute a real danger to the peace. Marshall was also concerned that the continued split between them might give "rise to a situation where the German people might be able to profit from the dissension among the allies."

Beyond the deadlock lay a larger issue, Marshall stressed. The European economy was near collapse. The United States was "frankly determined to do what we can to assist those countries which are suffering from economic deterioration which, if unchecked, might lead to economic collapse and the consequent elimination of any chance of democratic survival."

Stalin replied with his customary restraint. He had no more pity, sympathy, or love for the German people than did Marshall. "They had suffered too much from the Germans for any such sentiments to be conceivable." The Soviets wanted a strong central government for fear of "losing control of the instrument of German unity and handing it over to the militarists and chauvinists."

In "control" lay the American fears, for control meant Communist domination as in Poland, Hungary, and Rumania. That fear was emphasized when Stalin suggested there was a way out of their dispute: "Let the German people decide through a plebiscite what they wished." The Polish elections, the last under Communist supervision, had left much to be desired.

Reviewing the conference results, Stalin offered reassurances. "It is wrong to give so tragic an interpretation to our present disagreements."

These were like quarrels between family members, Stalin said, adding the dismaying comparison that the disputes over Germany at the conference were "only the first skirmishes and brushes of reconnaissance forces."

Agreement would come, the premier assured the Americans. "When people had exhausted themselves in dispute, they recognized the necessity for compromise." Stalin was confident. "We may agree the next time, or if not then, the time after that."

Marshall was dismayed by the lack of urgency in Stalin's comments. Molotov's intransigence at the conference table then did not flow from his personality but from Kremlin policy. There would be no progress made here.

According to Chip Bohlen, Marshall "came to the conclusion that Stalin, looking over Europe, saw that the best way to advance Soviet interests was to let matters drift. Economic conditions were bad. . . . This was the kind of crisis that Communism thrived on."

The concluding banquet in the hall of Catherine of Great in the Kremlin was short as such ceremonial dinners went. Bedell Smith marked the atmosphere as sober and quiet, but not hostile. "It would have been a pleasant evening had it not been for the general feeling of gloomy frustration on the Western side of the house," Smith wrote later.

The gloom persisted on the flight home. Marshall spent the time reviewing worsening economic conditions in Europe and considering an initiative "to prevent the complete breakdown of Western Europe."

Marshall accepted unblinking the fact that Moscow had not been a success. "It was the Moscow conference, I believe, which really rang down the Iron Curtain," said Robert Murphy, State Department adviser to Lucius Clay in Berlin.

Two days after returning to Washington and spending only a few hours with Katherine at their Pinehurst cabin, the secretary broadcast his report on the conference to the nation. Marshall recited "a melancholy catalog" of the disagreements, then reported Stalin's hint of future agreement. He hoped Stalin was correct, the secretary told his nationwide audience, but they had to hurry. "The patient is sinking while the doctors deliberate."

C H A P T E R

XXXV

A Fair Prospect of Success

The applause began at the far end of the maple- and elm-shrouded quadrangle. The sound rolled toward the platform on the steps of Memorial Church, swelling as the 8,000 in the audience recognized the tall man heading the column of men to be awarded honorary degrees this pleasant June morning. George Catlett Marshall had come to Harvard Yard for its 286th commencement, to be proclaimed a doctor of laws, *honoris causa.*

They were a distinguished group, the twelve honorees, among them poet T. S. Eliot, '10; physicist J. Robert Oppenheimer, '26; Mississippi newspaper editor W. Hodding Carter, Jr.; type designer William Dwiggins; naval architect William Gibbs; Frank L. Boyden, the revered headmaster of Deerfield Academy; and two friends of Marshall, former New York Senator James W. Wadsworth and General Omar Bradley. They were accomplished, they were already much honored, and they were overshadowed by the man in the three-piece gray suit, holding a Panama hat in his right hand as he marched past the rows of graduating seniors.

There in the shaded quadrangle, amid his faculty decked in somber medieval gowns and vibrant cowls, Harvard President James B. Conant read the citations, first in Latin, then in English. The last was Marshall's, the honorary degree, Conant announced, going to "an American to whom Freedom owes an enduring debt of gratitude, a soldier and statesman whose ability and character brook only one comparison in the history of this nation."

The graduates and their families rose in a sustained ovation. A sober Marshall said nothing, but bowed slightly, and accepted the leather-bound certificate.

Later that day, after lunch, in the custom of the university, a select number of speakers would give short addresses to new graduates and old alumni in Harvard Yard. Marshall had agreed to be one of those, but insisted his not be the major commencement address of the day. For all that, George Marshall, never a very effective speaker when reading a prepared address, was to give a speech that afternoon that Harvard has silently hoped succeeding honorees might match perhaps once a generation.

Fumbling with his reading glasses, Marshall began with a softly spoken thank you for the implied comparison to George Washington. "I am profoundly grateful—touched by the great distinction and honor and great compliment accorded me by the authorities of Harvard this morning. I am overwhelmed, as a matter of fact."

Then the secretary of state set his glasses on his nose, and began reading slowly, his voice intense, earnest. "I need not tell you that the world situation is very serious. . . ."

Marshall had not originally planned to speak at Harvard. He had declined Conant's invitations to accept an honorary degree in both 1945 and 1946; only at the last minute had he decided to accept a renewed offer this year. Marshall's calendar was full. He had no speech prepared and no particular reason to give one when invited once again to Harvard early in the year. That was to change in the days after his return from the Moscow Foreign Ministers' Conference.

On Tuesday, April 29, 1947, the secretary of state summoned scholarly George F. Kennan to his office at New State.

"Europe is in a mess," Marshall told Kennan. "Something will have to be done."

Privately, the secretary was gravely concerned about Soviet intentions in Europe. "It was my feeling that the Soviets were doing everything possible to achieve a complete breakdown in Europe," he explained later, "that is, they were doing anything they could think of to create greater turbulance. The major problem was how to counter this negative Soviet policy and restore the European economy."

Speed was critical, Marshall told Kennan. If State did not move soon, others in the cabinet or Congress would. Marshall instructed Kennan to draw up within the next two weeks a set of recommendations for a program to assist Europe. The secretary offered no specifics and only one bit of advice: "Avoid trivia."

This was no small assignment. Kennan had only rudimentary knowledge of the problem. Worse still, he had to contend with the national mood. A rebellious House of Representatives at that moment was hacking a $350 million foreign aid bill down to $200 million; State Department protests that the cut meant starvation and despair for 35 million people in Europe had been disregarded. Meanwhile the House Rules Committee had pigeonholed a $400 million aid program for Greece and Turkey called for by the Truman Doctrine. Foreign aid, or any program that did not produce tangible results, was out of favor, Marshall told Kennan.

The new head of the Policy Planning Staff had some precedents upon which to rely. First was the general's initial address as secretary of state, an informal speech at Princeton University before leaving for Moscow. Marshall had cautioned his audience, "Most of the other countries of the world find themselves exhausted economically, financially, physically. If the world is to get on its feet, if the productive facilities of the world are to be restored, if democratic processes in many countries are to resume their functioning, a strong lead and definite assistance from the United States will be necessary." That put the secretary on record as favoring American involvement in Europe's resuscitation.

An even more pointed augury followed in the first week of May. Undersecretary of State Dean Acheson substituted for President Truman at an annual gathering of businessmen at Delta State Teachers' College in Cleveland, Mississippi. Speaking in shirtsleeves to an audience fanning itself in a muggy gymnasium, the undersecretary delivered a speech frankly intended to shock the country, the administration, and the Congress into facing the growing European crisis.

Until "the various countries of the world get on their feet and become self-supporting, there can be no political or economic stability in the world and no lasting peace or prosperity for any of us," Acheson told the sweating businessmen. "Without outside aid, the process of recovery in many countries would take so long as to give rise to hopelessness and fear. In these conditions freedom and democracy and the independence of nations could not long survive, for hopeless and hungry people often resort to desperate measures."

News reports of the Acheson address irritated the chairman of the Senate Foreign Relations Committee. Arthur Vandenberg, a man of deliberate pace and considerable self-importance, disliked surprises. He certainly wanted no new foreign aid requests so late in the congressional term. In order to win Vandenberg over, Marshall invited him to the first of a series of confidential meetings at Blair House. There, across from the White House, the secretary solicited Vandenberg's opinions on the shape of foreign policy.

Arthur Vandenberg had come late to an international outlook. Appointed to the Senate in 1928, Vandenberg had for years been a Midwestern isolationist, a predictable vote taken for granted by both parties. However intelligent he might be, he was not an independent thinker. Only a world war could transform this former editor of the *Grand Rapids Herald* into an internationalist, from an obstructionist to a determined advocate of a bipartisan foreign policy. When in due course seniority and the Republican congressional victory of 1946 had set him up as chairman of the vital Foreign Relations Committee, Arthur Vandenberg became important to Marshall's plan, whatever it turned out to be.

The private meetings with the secretary of state and the undersecretary were an acknowledgment that Vandenberg's support was vital. But such men had their price. Vandenberg's was his insistence upon putting his stamp on any piece of major legislation that came through his committee; younger men in the State Department called it "the Vandenberg Amendment." That emendation—often drafted by those same young men—was the price of bipartisanship and his bellwether aye vote.

Vandenberg began this first meeting by challenging the idea of "opening the Treasury to every country in the world." Once the senator had sputtered to a halt, Marshall appealed to the high-minded national leader in Vandenberg. This was one of the greatest problems our people had ever faced, one that called for the widest national agreement, Marshall stressed. "Now as never before national unity depended upon a truly nonpartisan policy in the year of a presidential election. . . . The security of the country itself was the supreme consideration." By the end of the meeting, the senator was purring and Acheson was thinking about a "Vandenberg stamp" to whatever they proposed.

Harry Truman would not play a direct role in drafting the new policy, leaving that to Marshall and the State Department. The president's single contribution was to name it. "If we try to make this a Truman accomplishment, it will sink," he cautioned a White House adviser. "The Marshall Plan" would sound "a whole hell of a lot better in Congress."

To Marshall, indifferent to such public recognition, the president sternly ordered, "General, I want the plan to go down in history with your name on it. And don't give me any argument. I've made up my mind, and, remember, I'm your commander-in-chief."

A sense of urgency was growing even as Kennan groped for a policy in his State Department office next to Marshall's own. To an audience in London's Albert Hall, Winston Churchill, now leader of His Majesty's Loyal Opposition, asked rhetorically, "What is Europe now? It is a rubble heap, a charnel house, a breeding ground of pestilence and hate." As Churchill in 1940 had warned Franklin Roosevelt, bankrupt Great Britain neared "cruel privation" while the United States lost exports. Victor and vanquished would drag each other down. The European nations had to approach problems from a continental rather than a nationalistic angle.

In mid-May, Undersecretary of State for Economic Affairs William L. Clayton returned from Europe warning of impending collapse. Clayton drafted a gloomy memorandum that made its way to the secretary on May 28: "It is now obvious that we have grossly underestimated the destruction to the European economy by the war." French peasants were feeding grain to farm animals rather than sell it for paper francs they did not trust, while people in the cities were going hungry. Meanwhile, in Germany, caloric intake was half that necessary for factory workers.

Once head of the world's largest cotton brokerage, Clayton was keenly aware of the interdependence of national economies. His memorandum proposed substantial economic assistance to encourage European industry—a grant of "six to seven billion dollars worth of goods a year for three years."

There was nothing altruistic in hardheaded Will Clayton's approach. "Let us admit right off that our objective has as its background the needs and interests of the people of the United States. We need markets—big markets—in which to buy and sell."

Nor could Clayton be dismissed as simply another State Department "cookie-pusher." The word of a self-made Texas millionaire carried weight within the coalition of conservative Southern Democrats and Republicans that dominated the Senate. A prewar member of the isolationist "Liberty Lobby," Clayton had trimmed his course in the past ten years. Conservative in appearance—he still parted his hair in the middle then slicked it to the sides in a style popular five decades before—Clayton at sixty-seven had become something of a liberal in matters of trade policy.

While Clayton rang alarms in the corridors of New State, Acheson had meanwhile received the first draft of Kennan's policy planning paper. It was not a program for European aid so much as it was a collection of ideas for a plan; the foremost among them stressed that the initiative had to come from the Europeans. The Kennan study was less forceful than Clayton's memorandum, and more cautionary; it was the product of such intense debates within his small staff that Kennan one night excused himself to walk weeping around the building.

On May 28, Marshall met with Acheson, Clayton, Kennan, State Department Counselor Ben Cohen, and Chip Bohlen. In view of the situation, Marshall said in opening the discussion, they could not simply sit back and do nothing. What should they do?

Each man spoke in turn, Marshall listening, not committing himself. At the end, Marshall asked, "Are we safe in directing such a proposal to all of Europe? What will be the effect if the Soviets decide to come in?"

The consensus held that the United States should not bar the Soviets from participating, that they say nothing that would place the blame for dividing Europe upon the United States. "Play it straight," Kennan recommended.

Concerned about the timing and presentation of the plan, the secretary cautioned them against any leaks. Any new proposal for funding risked a crushing defeat in Congress. "It is easy to propose a great plan," he explained later, "but exceedingly difficult to manage the form and procedure so that it has a fair chance of political survival."

Marshall thanked the five men, then excused them. He announced no decision, keeping his opinions to himself until he had given it some thought. Apparently—there is no record—he discussed his ideas only with the president. The following day, Marshall told Acheson he had accepted an invitation from Harvard to receive an honorary degree and would probably have to give a short speech. Was this a good forum to say something about Europe? Acheson shook his head. Commencement speeches were a ritual to be endured without listening, he told the secretary. But a low-key forum was exactly what Marshall wanted. He turned to Bohlen, who served frequently as an aide, and asked him to draft a speech.

Using portions of both the Clayton and Kennan documents, then adding something of his own, Bohlen worked for two days. It was this draft that Marshall took with him as he and Katherine flew with Omar and Mary Bradley to Boston on June 4.

Bohlen had yet to learn Marshall's cadences and his style of speaking. Dissatisfied with the draft, Marshall reworked the text during the flight and again while staying at the Conants' home the next day. As an approving Harry Truman put it, the address was "a speech typical of the man . . . matter of fact and without oratorical flourishes."

The quadrangle was crowded with Harvard's old grads, the largest group ever, according to those who attended these annual affairs. Marshall read without any apparent emotion.

"I need not tell you gentlemen that the world situation is very serious. That must be apparent to all intelligent people." He then swiftly reviewed the situation in Europe, basing his brief comments on Will Clayton's memorandum.

"The breakdown of the business structure of Europe during the war was complete. Recovery has been seriously retarded by the fact that two years after the close of hostilities a peace settlement with Germany and Austria has not been agreed upon."

Production was niggardly, Marshall continued. Unable to buy goods they wanted, farmers were turning crop lands to grazing while people in the cities went hungry. Europe was forced to spend foreign credits on food, thereby slowing reconstruction.

Now came the warning, a hint to the resistant Congress. "The truth of the matter is that Europe's requirements for the next three or four years of foreign food and other essential products—principally from America—are so much greater than her present ability to pay that she must have substantial additional help or face economic, social and political deterioration of a very grave character."

Since the end of World War I, Marshall had watched, and sometimes opposed, those isolationists determined to turn the nation inward. How little they appreciated that in the twentieth century whatever loomed as a problem in Europe would eventually be America's. To them the secretary addressed his next comments: "Aside from the demoralizing effect on the world at large and the possibilities of disturbances arising as a result of the desperation of the people concerned, the consequences to the economy of the United States should be apparent to all. It is logical that the United States should do whatever it is able to do to assist in the return of normal economic health in the world, without which there can be no political stability and no assured peace."

Standing in the breeze-blown quadrangle on this day in late spring, Marshall then extended the offer that invested his speech with unparalleled generosity. "Our policy is directed not against any country or doctrine but against hunger, poverty, desperation and chaos. Its purpose should be the revival of a working economy in the world so as to permit the emergence of political and social conditions in which free institutions can exist." The Soviet Union and its dependencies could participate, if they chose to.

Marshall turned next to what President Truman considered the key section of the address, the new concept of formerly fierce competitors working together to foster economic recovery. "It is already evident that, before the United States government can proceed much further in its efforts to alleviate the situation and help start the European world on its way to recovery, there must be some agreement among the countries of Europe as to the requirements of the situation and the part those countries themselves will take in order to give proper effect to whatever action might be undertaken by this government."

Now came Kennan's contribution: the United States would not unilaterally draw up an aid package. "The initiative, I think, must come from Europe," Marshall suggested. "The role of this country should consist of friendly aid in the drafting of a European program and of later support of such a program so far as it may be practical for us to do so."

He was near the end. The program would require "a willingness on the part of our people to face up to the vast responsibility which history has clearly placed upon our country. . . ."

This last needed repeating, he felt. On the airplane to Boston, he had added what was for him a plea. America was insulated from a Europe of rubble, of cold, of hunger, too remote perhaps to grasp the urgency of the situation. "Yet the whole world's future hangs on a proper judgment, hangs on the realization of the American people of what can best be done, of what must be done." He paused, then conversationally added, "Thank you so very much."

The old grads rose to their feet, cheering the man more than the speech. Few seemed to realize that the address delivered in such flat cadences was charting a new course in American foreign policy, summoning a generosity of spirit that would animate American foreign policy for decades to come.

Still, the European reaction came with unexpected speed. Dean Acheson had contacted three British reporters on June 2, asking that they pay special attention to the secretary's address at Harvard on Thursday. BBC correspondent Leonard Miall decided to transmit excerpts from the advance text of the Harvard speech for the 9:00 p.m. news on June 5.

By chance, British Foreign Minister Ernest Bevin heard Miall's report of this "exceptionally important speech," and the broadcaster's comparison of it to "the grandeur of the original concept of Lend-Lease." Bevin wasted no time. The following morning he telephoned French Foreign Minister Georges Bidault, suggesting they convene a meeting to discuss Marshall's offer. Bevin then contacted Vyacheslav Molotov in Moscow, proposing that the three meet in Paris on June 23.

The Soviet bloc response was ambivalent. Both Poland and Czechoslovakia expressed interest in participating in the plan. The Soviet Union, however, was cool. On June 11, a commentator in *Pravda Ukraine* sneered, "From retail purchase of several European countries, Washington has conceived [a] design of wholesale purchase of [the] whole European continent."

Five days later, Moscow radio scored the proposal as an extension of the Truman Doctrine. Still—in a reflection of some debate within the Kremlin's councils—Moscow did not rule out participation in the plan. Molotov agreed to meet with Bevin and Bidault in Paris to discuss the Marshall proposal further.

In the meantime, Marshall dispatched Will Clayton to London to weigh Great Britain's special needs. Before he left, Marshall instructed him to make it quite clear to Bevin that the United States considered British management of the Ruhr's coal mines "pathetic." Coal was essential to recovery, and the United States would make no commitments to help Europe back on its feet unless coal production problems were quickly solved. The United States, he warned, could not wait while the Labor government fiddled "with socialization of coal mines; time does not permit of experimentation."

If this was not interference with the *internal* affairs of a friendly government, it was nonetheless meddling in the prerogatives of a sovereign nation. Yet with an earlier postwar loan from the United States fast running out and its financial reserves ebbing, Britain was in no position to complain.

On June 27, Molotov, Bidault, and Bevin met in Paris to weigh Marshall's proposal. Molotov backed and filled for the next week, uncharacteristically indecisive. He refused adamantly to list Soviet assets, to state Soviet needs or, most ominously, to allow a central European body to set priorities in disbursing the expected American aid.

Despite Bevin's warning that "debtors do not lay down conditions when seeking credits from potential creditors," Molotov spent the next week doing just that. He proposed that Italy and Germany be barred from the program. He suggested each of the former Allies list their own credit requirements, and put that figure to the United States. (Bevin would dismiss that notion with the comment, "In effect what you are asking the United States government to do is give us a blank check. If I were to go to Moscow with a blank check and ask you to sign it I wonder how far I would get at your end.")

The stone-faced Molotov held his cards close to the vest until the afternoon of July 2, 1947. In the midst of a discussion of the presentation of their dollar needs, an aide handed Molotov what was obviously a hastily decoded telegram. Molotov read it, then changed his debating stance. Moscow had reaffirmed Molotov's earlier position: the Soviet Union could not surrender its autonomy to joint planning. The Russians would not participate in the Marshall Plan.

The following day, Molotov withdrew. The plan "will lead to nothing good," he complained, but would "split Europe into two groups of states."

The Kremlin would also have a hand in that polarization. Czechoslovakia had earlier accepted the invitation to attend a meeting of Marshall Plan participants in Paris. On Stalin's orders, the Czechs, with a carefully balanced coalition government, abruptly withdrew. Similarly, Poland, which had privately indicated it would also attend, reversed itself, again on Stalin's insistence. From Moscow, Ambassador Walter Bedell Smith radioed Marshall that these moves constituted "a declaration of war by the Soviet Union on the immediate issue of the control of Europe."

By their sudden change in policy, the Soviets went far to end congressional doubts about the contemplated European Recovery Program and to assure its eventual passage. Large numbers of congressmen were dubious about aid to Communist Soviet Russia; Stalin's withdrawal abruptly mooted those reservations. Ironically, the Russians could have killed the Marshall Plan by joining it, said the former ambassador to the Soviet Union and now secretary of commerce, Averell Harriman.

If George Marshall was disappointed with the Soviet démarche, he gave no public sign. Over the next months, the secretary of state devoted intensifying efforts to securing passage of the European Recovery Program in Congress, leaving to an old friend and new undersecretary of state much of the responsibility for day-to-day administration of the State Department.

As he had planned since January, Dean Acheson was finally to leave the department and return to his law practice. To replace him, Marshall had wooed back to Washington Robert Abercrombie Lovett, former assistant secretary for air.

Like Henry Stimson, whom he deeply admired, like his friends Dean Acheson, Chip Bohlen, and Averell Harriman, Bob Lovett was at the very heart of the American establishment. The son of a Texas attorney who had become president of the Harriman railroad interests early in the century, Lovett was a child of privilege raised with a stringent sense of noblesse oblige. He had left Yale to enlist in the army Air Corps during the first war and had flown extensively in combat. Tapped for Yale's elite Skull and Bones while in the service, Lovett never completed his degree.

Tall and spare, with parchmentlike skin that made him appear forever sickly, the elegant Bob Lovett had courted and married equally elegant Adele Quartly Brown, daughter of one of the partners in the New York banking firm of Brown Brothers. He joined that firm, becoming a partner in 1926 at the age of thirty-one. Five years later, he figured prominently in the merger of Brown Brothers with his father's old firm, the Harriman investment interests.

A man of expensive tastes and a sometimes whimsical sense of humor, Lovett appeared to be effete and malleable. Those who judged him so did not make that mistake a second time; as Marshall noted, "There is iron in Lovett."

Called to Washington on the eve of the war, for five years he had served as assistant secretary of war for air, as responsible as any person for the vast increase in American airpower before 1945. He and the chief of staff had drawn close during those years, each recognizing in the other a kindred sense of public service.

At the end of the war, Lovett had resigned from the War Department and resumed his Wall Street career. He had not wanted to come back to Washington when President Truman first called him in February 1947. It would be difficult to disentangle himself from his partnership a second time, and he needed an operation on what he jokingly referred to as his "glass insides," a troublesome gallbladder.

Harry Truman could be persuasive, especially when he informed the banker that Marshall had insisted on bringing his "old copilot" down to Washington. Lovett could not refuse Marshall, particularly with Harriman and Acheson, another longstanding friend from Yale, telling him not to be a damn fool and to accept. Wall Street was all very well and good, but Washington was the great game today.

Lovett spent a month working beside Acheson in Washington, understudying the job of undersecretary of state. Within a matter of weeks he was referring to the war years as "the good old days." Nothing then seemed to present such momentous problems as those facing the United States in June 1947.

Kennan greeted Lovett on July 1 with a memorandum headed "Marshall 'Plan' " that began, "We have no plan." While France and Great Britain were pleased that the Soviets had opted out, they were sharply divided on Germany's participation. Thrice invaded in the last seventy-five years, France wanted a weak Germany; the British insisted that a weak Germany meant the continued support of that country's shattered economy.

The American military commander in Germany, Lieutenant General Lucius D. Clay, was to complicate matters further. A great-grandnephew of American statesman Henry Clay, the son of a United States senator, Clay had attended West Point, where he "ranked first in English and history but at the bottom in conduct and discipline." Headstrong and imperious, he had spent much of the war in charge of military procurement for the Army. In that post Clay had acquired such powerful friends as Bernard Baruch, Harry Hopkins, Henry Morgenthau, and, most importantly, James Byrnes. As secretary of state, Byrnes had been influential in securing the assignment of his wartime colleague as military commander in occupied Germany.

Beyond his profound distrust of the Russians, Clay worried most about Germany's woeful financial state. That nation's industrial base had to be rebuilt, if Germany was to get off the dole. In a letter to his former wartime chief, Clay cautioned that France, like the USSR, was fearful of a German economic recovery. A French veto could result in the United States subsidizing Germany indefinitely.

Hardly mollified by a noncommittal reply from Marshall, Clay convinced Secretary of War Kenneth Royall to speak out. Royall pointedly told a Washington press conference that he knew "of no agreement by the War Department or the State Department to consult with France before the promulgation of the plan to raise the level of industry in Western Germany."

French Foreign Minister Georges Bidault was furious, demanding an explanation. Further, France ominously announced it did not now find it convenient to take part in scheduled technical talks regarding economic recovery in Europe. The matter ended up on newly installed Undersecretary Lovett's desk.

Lovett was no more cowed by the Army than was Marshall. In a memorandum to Marshall, Lovett insisted, "The secretary of state with the responsibility for the conduct of American foreign policy by direction of the president, cannot be limited in foreign matters by any agreement with another department of this government without divesting him of the authority to carry out his responsibilities." The present situation,

Lovett pointed out, left the United States exposed to "a justified charge of duplicity and dishonest dealing."

For men such as Marshall and Lovett, such a circumstance was unbearable. On August 8, Marshall drew Royall aside at a cabinet meeting and firmly announced that General Clay would be welcome as an "adviser" at upcoming economic discussions in London. That much and no more. The War Department through Clay's military government— which Marshall contemplated ending—merely advised; the Department of State still made foreign policy. Marshall reported to Lovett that Royall "accepted my views."

Clay was furious. He threatened to resign, and to make his protest public. Marshall ignored him. After all, the military governor had threatened to resign "on frequent occasions in the past." Clay's past threats had regularly persuaded the former secretary of state, Clay's good friend James Byrnes, to yield whatever the proconsul wanted. A man of sterner stuff had called his bluff; Clay withdrew his resignation.

Clay was not the only insider seeking to redirect American foreign policy in these turbulent summer months of 1947. In its July number, the influential journal *Foreign Affairs* published an article dealing with "The Sources of Soviet Conduct." Attributed only to "X," the article carried an authoritative air, the pseudonym serving to underscore the author's presumed high office and thus the article's importance. Washingtonians considered the article an outline for a new, aggressively anti-Communist direction in American foreign policy.

Within short order, gossip had identified "X" as George Kennan, the State Department's new policy planner, the man whose office adjoined that of the secretary of state. Kennan had actually written the paper a year earlier as a briefing paper for Secretary of the Navy James Forrestal. Forrestal, who saw his a personal calling to expose the global menace of communism, had circulated copies of the Kennan paper among other administration policymakers. Marshall had read it while in China.

The "X" article advocated "a long-term, patient but firm and vigilant containment of Russian expansive tendencies." It was to be accomplished "by the adroit and vigilant application of counter-force at a series of constantly shifting geographical and political points, corresponding to the shifts and maneuvers of Soviet policy." What force, and how much, Kennan left vague in the article. (In his later biography, Kennan denied he intended to challenge any Soviet military threat by military means.)

The identification of Kennan as the bellicose "X" came as a sudden embarrassment. Marshall was shocked, Kennan wrote later. In the secretary's world, " 'planners don't talk.' The last thing he had expected was to see the name of the head of his new Planning Staff bandied about in the press as the author of a programmatical article—or an article hailed as programmatical—on the greatest of our problems of foreign policy.

He called me in, drew my attention to this anomaly, peered at me over his glasses with raised eyebrows (eyebrows before whose raising, I may say, better men than I had quailed), and waited for an answer. I explained the origins of the article, and pointed out that it had been duly cleared for publication by the competent official committee. This satisfied him."

Still, publication of the article in July had all the appearance of a quasi-official pronouncement by the government. It seemed to explain the rationale behind the Truman Doctrine announced in February. Further, Kennan's urging that the West be strengthened economically provided a hardheaded rationale to the Marshall Plan proposed just two weeks before at Harvard. Thus the European Recovery Program was coopted by a new form of international rivalry newspaper columnists had taken to calling "the Cold War."

Through the summer and fall delegates from the European countries meeting in Paris struggled to pull together a list of their economic needs even as their economic situation worsened. On September 12, the European planning committee delivered to Prime Minister Bevin a report calling for a four-year, $17 billion program. Sixteen countries and the occupied zones of West Germany would attempt with American aid to increase production in agriculture, fuel, and power, in transport and in machine tools. At the same time, they would strive to hold down inflation, develop mutual economic cooperation, and increase exports to the United States.

To mollify their satellites, the Soviets convened a September conference in Poland to discuss their own mutual aid plan. Opening the meeting, Andrei Zhdanov, a wartime hero considered "the savior of Leningrad" and then one of the more influential members of the Politburo, savaged "American imperialism" in a blistering speech. The United States was embarked with the Marshall Plan on "the enslavement of Europe," Zhdanov charged.

Zhdanov scored both the Truman Doctrine and the Marshall Plan as cunning efforts to subvert the freedom-loving governments of the nine-member Eastern bloc. The Marshall Plan would turn Europe into "the forty-ninth state of America."

On October 5, the Communist delegates released a formal communiqué disdaining the "Truman-Marshall Plan" as only

a farce, a European branch of the general world plan of political expansion being realized by the United States of America in all parts of the world. . . . The aggressors of yesterday—the capitalist tycoons of Germany and Japan—are being prepared by the United States of America for a new role, as tools of the imperialistic policy in Europe and Asia of the United States of America. . . .

In these conditions, the anti-imperialist democratic camp has to close its ranks . . . and work out its tactics against the chief forces of the imperialist camp. . . .

East and West were split.

A month later the American secretary of state gravely acknowledged the rift in testimony before the House Foreign Affairs Committee. "The war ended with the armies of the major allies meeting in the heart [of the European community]. The policies of three of them have been directed to the restoration of that European community. It is now clear that only one power, the Soviet Union, does not for its own reasons share this aim."

The growing international tension added its own urgency to the national campaign to pass the European Recovery Program in Congress. Back on Wall Street, Dean Acheson organized a Citizens' Committee for the Marshall Plan, enlisting former Assistant Secretary of War Robert Patterson as his co-chair. The president recruited Averell Harriman to rally internationally minded businessmen to the cause. Cabinet officers crisscrossed the country, making speeches in favor of the Marshall Plan. Chip Bohlen, now State Department counselor, was detailed to direct the public relations campaign supporting passage.

Throughout the winter and spring, well before the Senate took up the bill, Marshall campaigned for the European Recovery Act. He opened with an address to the Council on Foreign Relations and Chamber of Commerce in Chicago, challenging Colonel Robert McCormick's isolationist *Tribune* on its own turf. He followed with speeches to the steel-minded Pittsburgh Chamber of Commerce, to the National Cotton Council in Atlanta, to the National Farm Institute in Des Moines, and the Federal Council of Churches in Washington, D.C.

As the campaign wore on, his speeches would assume a harder edge. At the University of California in Berkeley, he spoke of "a world-wide struggle between freedom and tyranny, between the self-rule of the many as opposed to the dictatorship of the ruthless few." The following day at UCLA he was harsher still, warning the Italians that a Communist vote in their upcoming elections would be deemed a vote against Marshall Plan aid.

Yet Congress moved slowly, even when the president recalled it into special session on November 17. There was resentment and stubborn resistance. "We have seen in the past three months," protested isolation-minded Senator Robert A. Taft, "the development of a carefully planned propaganda for the Marshall Plan, stimulated by the State Department by widespread publicity and secret meetings of influential people in Washington and Hot Springs."

The most influential of those people was the secretary of state himself. A Gallup Poll reported that 63 percent of the American public judged

Marshall, after nine months in office, to be doing a good job. Another 20 percent rated his performance a fair job. In its cover story naming him Man of the Year for a second time, *Time* magazine maintained the secretary of state "was more a figure than an intimately known personality—a homely, reassuring man with compressed, unsmiling lips and deep-set, searching eyes. . . ."

Marshall's name attached to the European Recovery Program, as the president had predicted, was the surest guarantor of its passage. Confronting the leviathan, onetime Representative Hamilton Fish, a long-time Roosevelt nemesis, implored his former colleagues, "The Marshall Plan is not a sacred cow. It should not, and must not come before Congress surrounded by an aura of sanctity. There is nothing saintly about it, merely because it carries the name of General Marshall, who is no expert on either foreign affairs or European industrial production. . . . It should be analyzed and broken down in detail just as much as if it carried the name of Joe Zilch."

On Thursday, January 8, 1948, the secretary of state took the witness seat in the marble-paneled Senate Caucus Room before the Senate Foreign Relations Committee to open hearings on the proposed European Recovery Program. He spoke candidly, coolly, assuring the panel and the nation beyond, "This program will cost our country billions of dollars. It will impose a burden on the American taxpayer. It will require sacrifices today in order that we may enjoy security and peace tomorrow."

That was the challenge. He refused to minimize it, to make it politically palatable. George C. Marshall simply expected the senators facing him on the dais and the American public they represented to accept their responsibility.

The necessity was palpable, Marshall stressed. The war had destroyed "the vast and delicate mechanism by which European countries made their living." Steel mills, mines, rail lines, shipping, all were in a shambles. Moreover, "in the postwar period artificial and forcible reorientation to the Soviet Union of eastern European trade has deprived western Europe of sources of foodstuff and raw material from that area." The panel might infer that the pending legislation was also a blow against communism, a theme that would resonate through the hearings and floor debate.

The legislation would authorize a four and one-quarter year effort and an appropriation of $6.8 billion for the first fifteen months. That amount was not an " 'asking figure' based on anticipated reductions prior to approval," Marshall advised the committee. He did not intend to haggle. The total cost, which made senators swallow hard, was between $15.1 and $17.8 billion over the next four years.

After watching Marshall testify, *New York Times* reporter James Reston wrote, "He was clear. He was calm. He was patient and courteous. And yet he acted like a man who was determined to get substantially the Marshall Plan he wanted or, as is already rumored in the capital, retire at last to Leesburg."

Chairman Arthur Vandenberg was to parry the critics' attacks in the Senate, Marshall recalled. "He was just the whole show when we got to the actual movement of the thing." Encouraged by Lovett to cultivate Vandenberg during the previous months, Marshall had declined. "He assumed that the Senator was animated by the national interest and therefore required no cultivation by anyone."

Still, Marshall had paid heed to the influential chairman's wishes. The two men repeatedly at Blair House, in unpublicized meetings hammering out the legislation and the strategy to get it through Congress. Vandenberg, in fact, had come up with the necessary "stamp": asking not for the entire amount, but only for the first fifteen months' appropriation, $6.8 billion. In that way Congress could review Marshall Plan progress before appropriating further amounts. To the ponderous Vandenberg, the onetime isolationist, the often long-winded orator, Marshall gave full credit. "He was marvelous to work with, and fortunately, he thought I was."

Marshall would have a rougher time of it on January 12 when he appeared to open the hearings before the House Committee on Foreign Affairs. The House panel feared passage of the bill would result in an immediate tax hike, and worse, would be throwing bad money after good. Had not the Europeans wasted all the foreign aid given to them since the war?

Unlike Vandenberg, who secured a 13–0 committee vote in favor of the bill, the chairman on the House side, Charles A. Eaton of New Jersey, did not have a firm grip on his committee. Less vigorous than Vandenberg—he would turn eighty during the hearings—Eaton allowed committee members considerable latitude. Marshall was frequently on the defensive.

Democrat John Kee of West Virginia fretted about the administration of the Economic Recovery Program, Marshall assuring him that there would be few conflicts between the diplomats in State and the businessmen who would run the program. "If it comes to the worst . . . it would have to go to the president, who has the constitutional responsibility for all foreign policy."

The congressmen, Marshall reminded them, had to be careful not to introduce complications into the bill. "I have struggled with red tape most of my life. I have been generally on the receiving end, but in later years sometimes on the cutting end. . . . [I]t takes more knowledge and skill to cut red tape than any other particular endeavor I know in government."

Alabama Democrat Pete Jarman worried that "the door is open to Russia" to partake in the program.

Marshall agreed. "It is wide open." But the secretary repeatedly made clear he had little hope the Soviets would walk through. Europe was divided, with subject nations "behind the iron curtain." The Communists were "undermining and collapsing" independent governments "by infiltration and the influence of a few people. . . ." Once those efforts had been covert; now they were in the open.

"There was a tremendous effort by the Communists to overthrow the governments of Italy and France, and it was done in a very barefaced manner. It was remarkable. There was little effort to disguise the central, dominating fact of what that was all about."

In half a dozen responses, the secretary made it clear he had abandoned his wartime view of the Soviets as comrades. When Representative Mike Mansfield of Montana noted that "part of the reason behind this legislation before us is to contain communism," Marshall made no effort to correct him.

Marshall's was a sturdy performance, at once firmly anti-Communist yet welcoming the satellites' participation, generous in spirit yet businesslike in the management of the program. But if his testimony swayed some committee members, it roundly angered former Vice President Henry Wallace, well along in his independent campaign for the presidency.

Testifying before the Senate committee, Wallace charged that the generous spirit of the Harvard speech had been perverted. "ERP is the economic side of the bankrupt Truman doctrine. While it is being sold to the American people as a peaceful plan for cooperation and recovery, it will use the tax dollars of the American people for the benefit of private capitalists at home and abroad. It is a plan cloaked in decent language which is designed to suppress the democratic movements in Europe."

Marshall waited three weeks before responding offhandedly, dismissing Wallace with wry humor. "We are accused of an imperialistic policy in proposing the European Recovery Program, which was not conceived with any Machiavellian plot behind it; and to be more specific and personal, I am supposed to be the Shylock of Wall Street. I got that title on very limited capital."

The congressional hearings droned on for seven weeks. Then, on February 25, 1948, the unsteady coalition government of Czechoslovakia abruptly collapsed and Soviet-supported Communists rushed in to fill the vacuum. Arrests of dissidents and purges of opposition party members in Prague followed as the Communists tightened their grip on the hapless nation.

The abrupt collapse of Czech President Edvard Beneš's coalition government came as no surprise in official Washington. In a top secret briefing of the cabinet the previous November, Marshall had warned that the Soviets would eventually "clamp down completely on Czechoslovakia," since a coalition government in that nation "could too easily become a means of entry of really democratic forces into Eastern Europe in general."

Still, a sense of crisis gripped Washington. "We are faced with exactly the same situation with which Britain and France were faced in 1938–9 with Hitler," Harry Truman wrote his daughter Margaret. "Things look black."

A new sense of urgency raced through Washington. Three days later, Senator Vandenberg reported the European Recovery bill to the floor of an anxious Senate. In a 9,000-word address that he had worked over no less than seven times, Vandenberg reflected on a world he had once known that would return no more:

"It would be a far happier circumstance if we could close our eyes to reality, comfortably retire within our bastions, and dream of an isolated and prosperous peace. But that which was once our luxury would now become our folly. This is too plain to be persuasively denied in a fore-shortened, atomic world. We must take things as they are."

To the crowded Senate, to the gallery packed with family members, to the public beyond the Capitol, Vandenberg spoke of ideals and responsibilities. Concluding his address, he noted that the bill "is a plan for peace, stability and freedom. As such, it involves the clear self-interest of the United States. It can be the turning point in history for 100 years to come. If it fails, we have done our final best. If it succeeds, our children and our children's children will call us blessed."

Ignoring the rules, senators and gallery alike rose to cheer this man who had come late to wisdom. It was a climactic moment in the senator's public career. Vandenberg, said Marshall, had become "a full partner in the adventure. . . . But for his leadership and coordination in the Senate, the plan would not have succeeded."

The Senate began debate on the European Recovery Act amidst a sharp escalation in international tension. First the Czech crisis kept lights burning late at night in the State Department and White House. Then, at the request of the director of Army Intelligence, Lucius Clay, commanding general of U.S. Occupation Forces in Germany, whipped off a cable to be used in Congress so as to bolster the Army's request for a larger budget appropriation. Clay's cable was calculated to alarm purse-conscious representatives. "Within the last few weeks," Clay wrote, "I have felt a subtle change in Soviet attitude which I cannot define but which now gives me a feeling that it [war] may come with dramatic suddenness."

The next day the president asked, "Will Russia move first?" Even as the Pentagon went on the alert, an apprehensive Marshall counseled caution. This was a "world keg of dynamite—HST [Harry S. Truman] shouldn't start it," Marshall is quoted in the minutes of the meeting.

Leaked selectively by Secretary Forrestal, Clay's "war message" rang alarms around Washington. The secretary of the army asked the Atomic Energy Commission how long it would take to move nuclear weapons to the Mediterranean. On March 9, the chief of naval operations, Admiral Louis E. Denfeld, suggested that the American people be prepared for war. Four days later the Joint Chiefs handed Forrestal a hastily drawn war plan to counter a Soviet attack on western Europe and the Middle East.

In the midst of the alarm, the press reported that Czech Foreign Minister Jan Masaryk, the last pro-Western cabinet officer to retain his portfolio, fell or was thrown from his office window in the Cerninsky Palace on March 10. Masaryk's mysterious death in what Marshall publicly termed "a reign of terror" seemed to underscore the brutal nature of the enemy.

The war crisis swept everything before it. On March 16, the Central Intelligence Agency delivered to the White House a cautious estimate stating that war was not probable within sixty days. Beyond that the CIA was not prepared to go. That morning Forrestal noted in his diary, "Papers this morning full of rumors and portents of war."

Meanwhile, Truman's speech writers were drafting an address for him to deliver to a joint session of Congress on March 17. The president had determined to take advantage of the crisis to ask Congress to quickly adopt the European Recovery Program, a renewal of the draft, and universal military training.

Balancing between the needs of diplomacy and his own anger at Masaryk's death, Marshall sent Chip Bohlen to advise that the secretary preferred that Truman deliver a restrained speech. Best if there were no intemperate language, "no ringing phrases, nothing warlike or belligerent." The president was in a give-'em-hell mood, despite Marshall's warning that a bellicose speech might "pull the trigger."

Truman responded, "It is better to do that than to be caught, as we were in the last war, without having warned the Congress and the people."

Amidst the crisis, buttressed by a nationwide lobbying campaign, Vandenberg carried the fight for the recovery program on the floor of the Senate against the isolationist wing of his party. For every move to trim the size of the program, to hedge it with restrictions, Vandenberg, Marshall, Lovett, and a host of well-placed industrialists, including former President Herbert Hoover, countered. Opposition to the bill dwindled to a bare handful of irreconcilables.

After two weeks of debate, at five minutes past midnight on March 14, 1948, the Senate voted 69 to 17 to approve the program in essentially the form Marshall had first requested. (The administration did agree to a cut in the first year's budget to appease economy-minded senators.) Two days later the House Appropriations Committee reported the bill out with a due-pass recommendation to "reverse the trend of communism in Europe." On March 31, the full House shouted the bill through in a voice vote.

Born of enlightened self-interest, the European Recovery Program—the secretary of state never called it the "Marshall Plan"—was nurtured by crisis. Marshall had lent his prestige, then had played a major role in securing the votes necessary to beat back enviscerating amendments and secure passage. Of that he was immensely proud. "I worked on that as if I was running for the Senate or the presidency," he told his biographer, Forrest Pogue. "It was just a struggle from start to finish and that's what I am proud of, that we actually did that and put it over."

Within two weeks of Congress approving an initial $5.3 billion appropriation for European recovery, the freighter *John H. Quick* out of Galveston sailed with 9,000 tons of wheat, the first cargo of the Marshall Plan.

The United States had never appeared so great or so generous.

C H A P T E R

XXXVI

The Crowded Days

These were to be trying times for George Marshall. The clarity of their wartime goals had somehow become lost in the ambiguities of a restive peace. The great nineteenth-century dominions were breaking up all about them, erasing the maps of empire, making way for new world powers.

In Indochina, the French were fighting an increasingly bitter guerrilla war with the nationalistic Viet Minh. Marshall criticized France's "dangerously outmoded colonial outlook and method," instructed the American Embassy to urge the French to mediate, but added, "Frankly, we have no solution of problem to suggest." The French, rearmed with surplus American materiel, stubbornly fought on to reclaim their former colony of Vietnam.

In Greece, attacks by the Communist-supported guerrillas had the autocratic government reeling. Forced to choose between the two, the United States in the name of anti-communism found itself uncomfortably supporting an unpopular, unelected cadre of sometime Nazi collaborators. "We are in the awkward position at the moment of really having no Greek government to deal with," Lovett complained. American administrators were running the day-to-day affairs of the country. It was unsatisfactory, yet the alternative was chaos, special representative Mark Ethridge warned. "If Greece falls to communism the whole Near East and part of North Africa as well is certain to pass under Soviet influence."

In the Middle East, Jews and Arabs fought in the streets of Tel Aviv while Great Britain sought a way to divest itself of its increasingly fractious Palestine Mandate. Marshall's State Department worried that a proposed partition of the Holy Land into Jewish and Moslem states would antagonize the oil-rich Gulf states and surely provoke the Arabs to cut off the flow of vital oil to the West.

Meanwhile China slipped ever deeper into anarchy. Resurgent Communist troops drove Chiang's dispirited KMT divisions into slow retreat. In divided Korea, talks with the Russians to unify that nation had broken down. Neither the Soviets, who had taken the Japanese surrender north of the 38th parallel, nor the Americans, who governed in the South, could agree on which political groups would be permitted to take part in national elections. In India, Moslems battled Hindus, and both challenged the rule of Britain.

In Argentina, an avowed Fascist, Juan Perón, had come to power, gradually imposing a military dictatorship in the name of nationalism. Within the State Department there was debate whether to support or oppose the strutting Perón, who switched on and off his anti-American speeches as it suited his domestic political needs.

Here was a world turned upside down, yet Marshall remained the unruffled stalwart, an anchor to windward. When cabinet members demanded the United States talk tough to the Russians, the general reminded them they were "playing with fire while we have nothing with which to put it out."

Later he would recall "being pressed constantly" both while in Moscow and in Washington "to give the Russians hell. . . . At the time, my facilities for giving them hell—and I am a soldier and know something about the ability to give hell—were 1⅓ divisions over the entire United States. . . . We did not have enough to defend the air strip at Fairbanks."

The 12 million American men and women in uniform at war's end had shrunk by the time Marshall was sworn in as secretary of state to about 1.5 million. "It was no demobilization. It was a rout," Marshall commented with as much humor as he could muster. Once George Marshall had been hopeful about the future of Soviet–United States relations. Their common crusade against the forces of fascism and their ultimate victory could serve to bind them together. Moreover, a Soviet Union left shattered at war's end would be less adventurous, preoccupied with healing grave wounds to its economy.

The good feelings had evaporated during the wearying Moscow meetings in April 1947. The war in Europe had been over for twenty months when Marshall became secretary of state, yet peace treaties with Germany and Austria were hardly any closer to conclusion than they had been with the surrender of the German armed forces in May 1945.

Still Marshall hoped for another opportunity to restore good relations with the Soviet Union. When, in mid-1947, the Atomic Energy Commission proposed testing new nuclear weapons at Eniwetok Atoll in the Pacific, Marshall asked to have them postponed until the adjournment of the London meeting of the foreign ministers in November. An ill-timed atmospheric test would be "awkward," Marshall explained at a cabinet meeting. It would appear as saber rattling in the eyes of the already suspicious Soviets; there was also the risk of the tests unloosing an arms race. After the deadlock in Moscow in February, the London conference was critical. "That may be our last hope, that meeting," the secretary of state warned.

Across the nation, in the wake of postwar disappointment and seeming Soviet intransigence, virulent anti-communism had become the touchstone of patriotism. Keen on embarrassing the Democrats, Republicans charged that the establishment of Soviet satellites in Poland, the Balkans, and the onetime Baltic republics was due to subversion at home. Republican Speaker of the House Joe Martin early in 1947 promised to end "boring from within by subversionists high up in the government," particularly in the Department of State. Harry Truman scorned the Red-baiters and their "Communist bugaboo," but moved to preempt those Republicans who were happily flailing the Democrats as soft on communism. Truman effectively capitulated to the Red-hunters, hoping to placate the members of Congress most exercised about the Red menace. After all, he would need their later votes for the pending Turkey and Greece aid bill, as well as the European Recovery Program the State Department was then drafting.

Nine days after his speech before Congress detailing the Truman Doctrine for Greece and Turkey, the president promulgated Executive Order 9835. His fiat required a loyalty check of all 2 million federal employees; any derogatory evidence, regardless of how faulty or slight, was to be grounds for dismissal. The executive order would inspire a nationwide purge of those deemed suspect.

It was not enough. Republican Styles Bridges, chairman of the Senate Appropriations Committee, wrote Marshall in June 10, 1947, to complain that "there is a deliberate, calculated program being carried out not only to protect Communist personnel in high places [in the State Department] but to reduce security and intelligence protection to a nullity." The letter named nine employees of State whom the senators had deemed "a hazard to national security," and demanded they be summarily fired under terms that gave the secretary of state "absolute discretion."

Marshall refused; they had departmental procedures to screen out loyalty risks. Nevertheless, on June 27, the department reversed itself and, without hearings, summarily dismissed ten employees as "potential security risks." The department's statement alluded only vaguely to the employees' "indirect association" with representatives of foreign powers.

At a press conference dealing with the firings, a tight-lipped Marshall sought to minimize any danger that the truly innocent would be harmed. Still, he acknowledged that the first people dismissed had not had a "true hearing" such as the law demanded. They could not be told of the charges against them because those charges were based on "highly classified material" from another, unnamed department, the secretary explained. (That department was the Federal Bureau of Investigation.) To another questioner, Marshall conceded that he doubted the former employees would ever learn the true charges, even on appeal. They had been accused and that was sufficient in this new era of Communist-hunting.

The president had taken a political decision. Reluctantly or not, Marshall concurred; the alternative could only have been to resign.

Truman's appeasement whetted the appetites of hostile congressional committees. In January and February 1948, the House Appropriations Committee responded with an investigation of the State Department's security procedures. Marshall ordered his minions to cooperate, and turned over personnel files containing everything from unverified accusations to paranoid suspicions. The committee then spread them on the public record, erasing the names, but very effectively sullying the entire department. State would never quite recover; on the defensive, over the next five years the department would grapple with more than 600 "security" cases.

If the secretary of state was less than sensitive to these large issues of civil liberties, he was distracted. The scope of the problems confronting the department was as great as those he handled during the war, yet the nation lacked the national consensus of wartime. More than ever, Marshall took to conserving his energies, to focusing on work and Leesburg. He avoided as many of the formal social functions as a secretary of state might turn down and remain in diplomatic good graces. He preferred quiet dinners with such friends as Adele and Robert Lovett, Averell Harriman, and Lewis Douglas, once a member of the wartime shipping board, now, on Marshall's recommendation, ambassador to the Court of Saint James. Best of all were the quiet evenings spent at Dodona Manor with Katherine, who found the drier Leesburg climate better for her sinuses than Washington.

George Marshall remained a private man. He had repeatedly declined publishers' offers—some of them proposing million-dollar advances—for his memoirs. "His knowledge of people and events [was] too intimate for publication," he explained to Katherine. To write them would be to reopen all the arguments of the war, to wound former associates with harsh judgments of actions taken and not taken. He wanted no part of it.

Only a glimmer of his personality showed through even in the 1947 publication of Katherine's reminiscences of their life, *Together*. After her husband left for China, to fill her days Katherine had undertaken to arrange the scrapbooks she had been keeping since their marriage in 1930. From that came the idea for a book, anecdotal, affectionate, and, in dealing with Allen's death, undoubtedly therapeutic. But because the manuscript did reveal something of the man, Katherine was cautious.

She decided that her husband, when he returned from China, would determine whether the manuscript would ever be published. The book sold well.

His closest friends remained few, his personal aide during this period recalled. Frank McCoy and John McAuley Palmer, now long retired, stood out in Marshall Carter's memory. Only they and Leonard Nicholson, Marshall's long ago roommate at VMI who had inherited the *New Orleans Times-Picayune,* were on a first-name basis with the secretary. Men such as Omar Bradley were respected friends, so too Robert Lovett, but there was a sense of reserve, of formality that was not breached. These few knew him well, and only with these few did he reveal a sense of humor and a charming ability to tell tales about his youth. "The General was very reluctant to make close friends with anybody because he had all he needed with Mrs. Marshall and Madge and Molly and their children."

Old acquaintances could sometimes be trying. When Acheson complained that the influential capitalist Bernard Baruch was attempting to meddle in atomic policy, Marshall said that Baruch was all right "if you knew how to handle him." As an example, Marshall told Acheson, Baruch wanted his bust placed in the Army War College. "This wouldn't do; we have only Napoleon, Alexander and Caesar in there," he explained to Baruch. Not even Pershing occupied a niche.

The following day, Acheson silently handed the secretary an invitation he had just received in the mail. Acheson was invited to the unveiling of a bust of Baruch at the War College. "You certainly know how to handle him," Acheson teased.

"Yes," Marshall agreed. "And to top it off, it seems I am going to make a speech at the unveiling."

The undersecretary would have to tolerate but one more of these ceremonies for old men. On June 30, 1947, his promised six months up, a weary Dean Acheson stepped down, to be replaced by Marshall's old co-pilot, Robert A. Lovett. That final morning at New State, Marshall tersely informed Acheson that the president wished to discuss some last matters before Acheson left office. After an aimless conversation in the president's office, the surprised Acheson noticed through the window a clutch of his family and friends assembling in the Rose Garden. Before them, the president conferred the Award for Merit on Acheson. That was Truman's acknowledgment.

From Marshall, there was nothing. "No words of approval or disapproval of my service ever passed the General's lips. None were needed," Acheson wrote later.

Robert Lovett was to take over Acheson's desk, formally as the undersecretary of state, but in Marshall's frequent absences at international conferences serving as acting secretary. The two men were well matched, "almost like brothers," in the words of Marshall Carter. Lovett and Marshall dealt as peers, without disagreement. Lovett "absolutely revered" the secretary, who in turn had "total admiration and respect for Lovett." Between them they divided the work according to who was best suited for the task, Carter continued. "Something would come in and General Marshall would say, 'Well, I'll take care of this. I know Vandenberg.' Or he would say, 'Lovett, you take care of this.'"

With Lovett, George Marshall would once more confront that great, enduring conundrum that was their China policy—or lack of a policy.

By December 1946 and the end of the Marshall mission, Generalissimo Chiang Kai-shek's Nationalist troops appeared to be taking command in the civil war. Reverting to guerrilla tactics, Mao Tse-tung's Communist forces a month later began a series of raids on isolated Nationalist garrisons. Within weeks, the Nationalists, forced to protect scattered cities, found themselves on the defensive.

The initiative passed to the Communists. A succession of small offensives left the Reds dominant in Manchuria by the end of May 1947. Chiang was losing control. Inflation rates soared; prices of staples like rice, flour, and coal doubled. In villages across the country, hungry farmers staged rice riots. Profiteers manipulated currencies, driving the value of the yuan ever downward. Despite increased inducements, in particular the promise of food, army enlistments were scant. Students demonstrating in the streets of Shanghai, Peiping, and Nanking for an end to the civil war and improvement of the dire economy were set upon by Chiang's secret agents and brutally dispersed.

At the same time, an increasingly vociferous muster of men and organizations in the United States pressed harder for American aid to Chiang. The "China Lobby," as it would come to be known, was composed of men and women with strong emotional ties to a mythic China that no longer existed. Largely Republican in politics, these loosely linked people included China-born Henry R. Luce, publisher of the influential *Time-Life-Fortune* group of magazines; an array of conservative newspaper owners who believed Franklin Roosevelt had undermined Chiang by furnishing inadequate aid; and a handful of legislators, the most outspoken of whom was Representative Walter Judd, a Minnesota Republican who had served as a medical missionary in the Land of Ten Thousand Dragons. The acknowledged leader of the so-called China Lobby was Alfred Kohlberg, for thirty years an importer of Chinese embroidery, now organizing an American China Policy Association and a deceptively named Committee of One Million to lobby for aid to the Nationalists.

Increasingly strident, increasingly desperate as Chiang's fortunes waned, the China Lobby demanded immediate action. The political pressure on the White House to take some action grew.

More arms were not the answer, Marshall insisted in a meeting with the Nationalist ambassador in Washington, Wellington Koo. Chiang was "the worst advised military commander in history." When Koo nonetheless asked for an increase in military supplies, Marshall stared coldly at the elegantly turned out Koo. "He is losing about 40 percent of his supplies to the enemy," Marshall snapped. "If the percentage should reach 50 percent he will have to decide whether it is wise to continue to supply his troops."

The secretary was frankly perplexed. "I have tortured my brain and I can't now see the answer," he acknowledged in early June. The Joint Chiefs of Staff had weighed in with a recommendation for both military and economic assistance, a proposal Marshall judged neither realistic nor practical. As he radioed the American ambassador in China on July 6, "In the final analysis, the fundamental and lasting solution of China's problems must come from the Chinese themselves. The United States cannot initiate and carry out the solution of those problems and can only assist as conditions develop which give some beneficial results."

Harry Truman had an idea, though it was a politically expedient stopgap at best: a fact-finding mission. It would buy time for them while postponing delivery of any aid to Chiang.

In the first week of July, Marshall asked his former protégé in the War Department, Lieutenant General Albert Wedemeyer, if he would undertake that mission to China. Marshall understood he was hiring a committed partisan. Once Chiang's chief of staff, Wedemeyer had made no secret of his fervent anti-communism. Months before he had complained to Marshall that American policy in China was unrealistic; his opinion had not changed. Furthermore, Wedemeyer reminded the secretary, the Chinese Communists considered him, Wedemeyer, persona non grata. Marshall laughed away Wedemeyer's reservations, saying his own standing was hardly any better.

Privately Marshall considered Wedemeyer "a good man, but he developed an obsession about the Russians until he isn't rational on the subject," as he said later. For his part, Wedemeyer thought Marshall had "failed to understand the nature and aims of communism in general and of the Chinese Communists in particular."

Wedemeyer wondered about his appointment for years after submitting his report. It was unlike Marshall to gather sycophants around him, that Wedemeyer knew. In fact, the secretary of state was playing for time, temporarily stemming criticism of an aimless China policy by appointing a man close to the leaders of the vocal China Lobby. Should Wedemeyer's report be critical of the Nationalists—and he was honest enough to come to those conclusions independently—it would be tacit support for continued distancing. If the report came down for Chiang, it would give them leverage with those congressmen still unsure about the proper role for the United States in the Far East . . . when the president decided what that role should be.

Wedemeyer was to spend a month in China, gathering information from military and civilian figures alike, traveling from Mukden in the north to Shanghai in the south. Within days of arriving, he cabled Marshall that "the Nationalist Chinese are spiritually insolvent." The people had "lost confidence in their leaders." Public officials held office only to amass through graft what they could before the collapse came. The army had lost the will to fight, while the Communists displayed "excellent spirit, almost a fanatical fervor."

Just before Wedemeyer was to leave, Chiang invited him to address a joint meeting of the State Council and government ministers on August 22. Wedemeyer delivered an unvarnished lecture, pointing out the rampant corruption and inefficiency of the KMT government, and the lackluster effort of the Nationalist Army against the Communists. The war could not be won without the support of the Chinese people, long alienated, apathetic, and desirous only of peace, he admonished the shocked Chinese.

Two days later, preparing to fly from Nanking for the last time, Wedemeyer publicly recommended that the Nationalists "effect immediately drastic, far-reaching political and economic reforms. Promises will no longer suffice. Performance is absolutely necessary. It should be accepted that military force in itself will not eliminate communism."

Despite his gloomy findings while in China, the passionately anti-Communist Wedemeyer could not turn his back on the anti-Communist KMT. He recommended that the United States offer moral, advisory, and material support to the very Nationalist government he described in his report as corrupt, repressive, and incompetent. The alternative was to cede China to "a force presenting even greater dangers to world peace than did the Nazi militarists and the Japanese jingoists." However corrupt was Chiang, however undemocratic his government, an anti-Communist was surely better than a Communist.

Wedemeyer sought to ring the recommended assistance, in the form of a five-year plan funded by Congress, with various conditions. The most important required Chiang to ask the United Nations to take immediate action to effect a cease-fire in Manchuria, and then place that embattled province under United Nations trusteeship, or five-power control that would include the Soviet Union. As Wedemeyer imagined it, Manchuria then would serve as a buffer between the Soviets and their clients, the Chinese Communists.

Marshall was particularly troubled by the Manchurian recommendation, in effect, a proposal that an ally's territory be amputated. Moreover, the report was rife with undiplomatic, if accurate, criticisms of a friendly power. Words like "corrupt" and "reactionary" were not often found in diplomatic papers, nor allies described as "suffering increasingly from disintegration."

On September 25, 1947, Wedemeyer met briefly with President Truman at the White House, their conversation consisting of no more than pleasantries. The following day, Wedemeyer flew to Lake Success, New York, where Secretary of State Marshall was attending a meeting of the United Nations.

The two men had a "very gracious meeting," Wedemeyer recalled more than thirty-five years later. Marshall praised his work, then stated that "the gist of the report would be withheld for the time being. . . . He gave me no reason and I did not think the Secretary of State had to give me a reason. Marshall was very kind."

Marshall had decided to embargo the Wedemeyer report because the Manchurian recommendation raised a serious threat to other vital interests. Even as Wedemeyer presented his paper, the United States was attempting to blunt a Soviet-sponsored effort in the United Nations to investigate the ongoing civil war in Greece. The Russians might well ask if a trusteeship were in order for Manchuria, why not for Greece as well? Beating that down would be very difficult.

To the acutely suspicious China Lobby, the move to suppress a report by a staunch anti-Communist known to be sympathetic to the Nationalist regime appeared an ominous cover-up. Already suspect for his attempt the previous year to shape a coalition government in China, Marshall became a man to be watched carefully.

Meanwhile, the lobby scurried after those it judged responsible for the looming catastrophe. The first victim was an "Old China Hand," a former counselor in the Nanking embassy whom Kohlberg deemed an architect of the hands-off American policy. Congressional pressure on the White House led Marshall to approve the relief of John Carter Vincent as head of the Office of Far Eastern Affairs and reassignment as minister to Switzerland. The change in assignments appeased the department's Republican critics while keeping Vincent from harm's way. It was politically prudent, cowardly, and unavailing; the China Lobby now had the taste of blood in its mouth.

The last months of 1947 would be evil times for Chiang Kai-shek. Though his Nationalist Army ostensibly outnumbered the Communists by more than five to two, his troops continually gave ground in these months. Reluctantly, in November 1947, Marshall approved the use of American soldiers to train KMT units on Formosa. He also approved sending more advisers to reorganize the Nationalists' supply lines. That would be the limit of American intervention, Marshall determined.

On November 10, Marshall appeared in the Senate Caucus Room before a secret joint session of the House and Senate committees on foreign affairs to propose a $570 million aid program for China. The money was to pay for imports of cereals, rice, pharmaceuticals, cotton, and petroleum, Marshall told the legislators.

Fearful of the United States "getting sucked in" into a land war in Asia, Marshall asked no money for military aid. The secretary of state flatly opposed a recommendation of the Joint Chiefs of Staff that Chiang receive military aid "essential for the unification and stabilization of China." Marshall the soldier was personally taking the position that military aid would not remedy China's ailments.

Though he hardly thought himself a China expert, Marshall had more than a passing familiarity with the land and the people. He had spent three years in China in the 1920s and another just the year before. He understood warfare and he understood that the seriously overextended Nationalist Army had too few men to defend every possible target the Communists might choose in that vast land. Chiang might fortify the cities, but he could not prevent the Reds from sweeping across the empty steppes and forbidding mountains. Marshall and Lovett had earlier concluded that the Nationalists had more than enough surplus war materiel turned over to them since VJ-Day as American troops withdrew. Additional military assistance, short of actual intervention by American ground forces, would not be enough to help the Nationalists defeat the Communists, Marshall stressed in meetings with the president.

Caught up in partisan political squabbles between Democratic loyalists and the China Lobby's Republican supporters, Congress was to spend six months writing an aid bill—while Chiang's fortunes fell. The secretary of state made repeated trips up the Hill to testify, on February 20, 1948, delivering a plainly worded warning to the two foreign affairs committees:

"We have had many proposals for the government to support the Chinese military program. That is easy to say, but extraordinarily difficult and dangerous to do. It involves obligations and responsibilities on the part of government which I am convinced the American people would never knowingly accept."

The burden would be enormous, Marshall stressed. "The U.S. would have to be prepared virtually to take over the Chinese government and administer its economic, military and governmental affairs."

The United States, added Marshall, had given China $700 million in military Lend-Lease during the war, and at least an equal amount in military aid since VJ-Day. More would accomplish nothing, despite the Joint Chiefs' arguments that civilian aid would be wasted until the military situation improved.

Seated at the large table before the serried desks of the committee members, Marshall quietly, firmly admonished, "There is a tendency to feel that wherever the Communist influence is brought to bear, we should

immediately meet it, head on as it were. I think this would be a most
unwise procedure for the reason that we would be, in effect, handing
over the initiative to the Communists. They could, therefore, spread our
influence out so thin that it could be of no particular effectiveness at any
one point."

Congressman Judd would have none of it. With the support of Alfred
Kohlberg and a letter-writing campaign, Judd convinced the House of
Representatives to disregard the secretary of state. In addition to civilian
aid, the House inserted a clause calling for $150 million in military aid
to be administered by a U.S. mission stationed in China. Marshall's calm
counsel was drowned in anti-Communist hysteria.

The Senate, where Vandenberg insisted foreign policy be weighed on
a non-partisan basis, shied from similar pledges of military assistance.
More deliberative, less susceptible to momentary passions, the Senate
trimmed the money specifically earmarked for military assistance; it was
replaced by a $99 million fund to be used at the president's discretion
for military aid.

By April and passage of the China aid package, the Communists had
retaken Yenan and Mao's armies were operating south of the Yellow
River in central China. Steadily, inexorably, the government was dying.
The president of the American Chamber of Commerce in China wrote
privately to Wedemeyer that "we are no longer dealing with a government—we are dealing with a disorganized group of officials, incapable
or unwilling to assume responsibility in any degree."

Before the end of July 1948, Secretary of the Army Kenneth C. Royall
was asking if it was wise to continue sending military assistance to the
Nationalists; it would simply end up in the hands of the Communists.
Days later Marshall issued an order suspending military aid unless Chiang
dealt with the Chinese Reds.

Badly led and dispirited, the Nationalist armies reeled from debacle
to debacle through the summer and fall. Tsinan, the capital of Shantung
Province, fell in what Chiang himself acknowledged as "the greatest
disaster." Changchun, the capital of Manchuria, fell. The crucial communications and industrial center of Mukden fell. On November 5, the
American Embassy in Nanking began advising American citizens to leave
China.

A China aid bill not yet assured, the European Recovery Program still
creeping through Congress, Marshall picked up the next order of business—the second foreign ministers' meeting of the year. There was a
hint of fatigue in a letter he wrote to his sister-in-law, Charlotte Coles.
"I was counting up the other day and find that since January, '39 I have
had nineteen days of what might be called leave, although even then a
pouch from the War Department was almost a daily matter." In a hastily
dashed note to Hap Arnold, peacefully retired in northern California,

Marshall all but sighed. "You are, oh, so fortunate to be established as you are. Life for me is too difficult and filled with unpleasant tasks."

One of those unpleasant tasks was delivering public speeches, an obligation for a secretary of state intent upon enlisting public support for his policies. A week before the London Foreign Ministers' Conference scheduled for November 25, 1947, Marshall flew to Chicago with Adlai Stevenson, an alternate on the United Nations delegation to whom Marshall had offered the position of assistant secretary of state for public affairs. Stevenson, a Chicago lawyer then weighing a run for the governorship of Illinois, had regretfully turned Marshall down a month earlier.

Marshall and Stevenson spent the flight discussing politics and the recurring rumor that the secretary of state would be the Democratic candidate for president. The secretary dismissed "as conclusively and as briefly as one could possibly do it, any possibility of himself being considered. . . . And then we got on the subject of General Eisenhower and he explained . . . how he had counseled him to forsake any interest in politics or political preferment as inconsistent with the career of a professional soldier."

In his Chicago address, Marshall delivered a diplomatic warning and an appeal to the Soviet Union. Two of the great powers that had crushed Nazism, the secretary noted in a carefully worded speech, were seeking to rebuild shattered Europe. "Unfortunately it has become apparent that the third great power which contributed so much to the common victory evidently does not share that purpose. . . ." That divergence of purpose was the source of the present disputes between the United States and the Soviet Union.

Europe was a political and economic vacuum, Marshall read on. Contrary to Soviet claims, Washington did not intend to fill that vacuum with American power. If it did, Congress would not now be struggling to produce a plan to end European dependency on American aid.

The secretary of state then leveled a broadside: "Soviet officials and Communist groups elsewhere" were waging "a calculated campaign of vilification and distortion of American motives in foreign affairs. These opponents of recovery charge the United States with imperialistic design, aggressive purposes, and finally with a desire to provoke a third world war.

"I wish to state emphatically that there is no truth whatsoever in these charges, and I add that those who make them are fully aware of this fact."

In diplomatic terms, this was harsh talk, but Marshall was not through. The blame lay with the Russians.

Since the war, he continued, "the Soviet Union has in effect considerably expanded her frontiers. Since 1939 she has de facto annexed territory comprising an area of more than 280,000 square miles, with a population of some twenty-two million people." In the two years since the end of the war, these repeated, deliberate, provocative acts by the Soviet had cooled the once friendly American attitudes.

The issue now was the economic recovery of Germany. American taxpayers could not continue to support the German people indefinitely. "Germany must be made self-supporting as quickly as possible. With safeguards against any revival of German militarism and with measures to assure the utilization of the basic products of the Ruhr for the good of the European community as a whole, I believe that Europe and the world will be adequately protected against the danger of German domination."

Having issued the challenge, it was a determined George Marshall who was flying to London on the president's plane, "The Sacred Cow," a man intent upon a solution in Germany.

Seven months after the failure in Moscow, the American secretary of state was on his way to London with little expectation of success at this sixth conference of the Council of Foreign Ministers. There were too many issues separating them: German and Austrian reparations, even the size of the conference to draw up German and Austrian peace treaties.

Both sides professed a desire to reunite Germany, but neither wanted to do it on terms favorable to the other. From Moscow, *Pravda* condemned Marshall's Chicago call for restraint in international debate as "the clearest hypocrisy." The American was obviously "a proponent of the partition of Germany and transformation of the western zones into an anti-Soviet, anti-democratic coalition," the newspaper announced. It was not an auspicious omen.

London in that November of 1947 was gray and dank, a harbinger of yet another winter that would try already austere Britain. Marshall, however, was to be treated to a festive round of lunches and dinners hosted by a queue of wartime associates, including the king of England. Almost daily he would shuttle between the cool antagonism of an implacable international adversary and the warm comradeship of old campaigners. Admiral Cunningham looked thinner, Air Marshal Portal, unchanged. Brooke, the nemesis of yore, had aged, though he was in good spirits. Churchill, even out of office, was all brandy, cigars, and cascading conversation.

The day after his arrival, Marshall traveled to Oxford where his friend Lord Halifax, the former British ambassador to the United States, now the university's chancellor, had arranged to present him an honorary degree from All Souls College. Arrayed in the scarlet academic gown of a doctor of civil law—Marshall put aside his distaste for ostentation in deference to the customs of a 600-year-old university—the secretary listened as Halifax termed him "great architect of military strength and of victory, outstanding in devoted service both to your own country and to the world."

In London, Marshall and the American delegation worked at an apartment building on Grosvenor Square, near Eisenhower's former SHAEF headquarters and the American Embassy. According to Lucius Clay, commanding the American military government in Germany, "Marshall was in top form. . . . It was evident that he enjoyed developing any divergencies in viewpoint within the delegation so that they could be weighed in reaching his decisions."

If the ferret-eyed Clay was pleased with Marshall's apparently firm pro-German stance, John Foster Dulles was less enchanted. A Republican stalwart, he had been deliberately tapped for the American delegation as Senator Vandenberg's representative, an assurer of nonpartisanship. Dulles, long schooled in international relations, considered Marshall firmer and better organized, "a greater man" than former Secretary of State James Byrnes. Marshall was open-minded and shrewd in judging between competing claims when both were presented to him. Marshall's fault was a lack of diplomatic experience that sometimes led him to accept bad advice when only that was available, Dulles complained.

All their diplomatic experience told them they were negotiating from strength and could hold firm. A State Department briefing paper prepared by George Kennan earlier that month argued that "the political advance of the Communists in Western Europe has been at least temporarily halted. . . . The halt in the Communist advance is forcing Moscow to consolidate its hold on Eastern Europe. It will probably have to clamp down completely on Czechoslovakia."

According to Kennan, the Russians were even less inclined than before "to take their chances on a genuinely democratic, united Germany." A free Germany would be a disruptive influence on the Soviet bloc.

If the Soviets attempted to create a German state defenseless against Communist subversion, the United States would have "to make the best of a divided Germany. It will then be essential that we bring the western part of Germany into some acceptable relationship to the other western European countries."

The foreign ministers meeting each afternoon at Lancaster House were the same four as in Moscow: Molotov, the man they had privately nicknamed "Iron Pants,"; the short, unlettered Ernest Bevin, a lifetime trade unionist, once a radical who had led the 1927 General Strike; Georges Bidault, who kept a wary eye on the still influential French Communist Party; and Marshall himself.

The conference opened on November 25 with Marshall urging that they take up the long-postponed Austrian peace treaty. "It is necessary to come to agreement on something quickly to reassure the people of the world." Molotov rejected the proposal without acknowledging the reason: a peace treaty would mean the removal of Russian troops from Austria and the end of any Soviet influence in that country.

"The German question is more important than Austria and it should come first," Molotov insisted.

The next day, Molotov used his opening remarks to blast the reactionaries striving for an "imperialist peace" and the "enslavement" of other countries. Marshall mildly dismissed the allegation as "figments of propaganda," asserting that Molotov did not believe them himself.

The major sticking point for the conference was the question of the $10 billion in German reparations owed the Soviet Union as agreed upon at Yalta. Molotov continued to demand that money be paid immediately, from current production, as a condition of German reunification. The westerners wanted those reparations paid only after the German economy was minimally self-sufficient; otherwise the United States and Great Britain, already underwriting the German economy, would, in effect, pay Germany's debt to the Soviet Union.

The conference was to run on for seventeen sessions over three weeks, sessions marked more by posturing than international accommodation. By December 6, the three frustrated Western ministers were discussing among themselves adjournment of the conference. Bevin shrugged. It did not matter to the British if the breakdown came as a result of a procedural or substantive issue. A hardening Bidault concurred.

Marshall was dubious. American public opinion might immediately favor a break with the Soviet, he argued, "but I thought that on sober reflection of the implications that view would change. Therefore to me, it was important if a breakdown were to occur it be over [a] matter of substance, that is, something of real importance and that along with it there be clear evidence that we had done our best to go ahead with the business."

On Thursday, December 11, President Truman cabled his approval of Marshall's stance: "Your firm and constructive actions in London have my complete support. We are all with you. Warm regards. Harry Truman."

The following day, Molotov returned to the conference table to charge that the United States "was trying not only to enslave Germany by furnishing economic aid but also to make of Germany a strategic base against the democratic states of Europe."

Ignoring the notes members of his delegation passed to him with suggested replies, Marshall coolly rebutted. "It was evident that Molotov's remarks were not intended to be used as a basis for council discussion," ran the dry summary report to the president and Lovett. Instead, they "were intended solely for propaganda purposes." Molotov's speech, "considering that it was given before the Council of Foreign Ministers, reflected on the dignity of the government of the Soviet Union."

Marshall's sharp retort stung. Molotov visibly winced.

The conference was, for all purposes, at an end. It remained only to bury the corpse on Monday, December 15.

Molotov held firm, insisting that Germany immediately pay $10 billion in reparations. Bevin charged the Soviet Union was demanding black-mail as a condition to German and Austrian peace treaties. The current meetings, Bevin growled, had led him to wonder whether the Council of Foreign Ministers as a body could ever reach a settlement of the Ger-man and the European problem. Bevin looked about the table, waiting for a motion to adjourn.

Marshall proposed to end it, suggesting they adjourn since no real progress could be made in the face of Soviet intransigence.

The fifth and last Council of Foreign Ministers broke up without set-ting a date for future meetings.

The American secretary still had two plans he wanted to float. The following evening, with Molotov and the Soviet delegation already flying toward Moscow, Marshall met with Georges Bidault after dinner at the French Embassy. At Marshall's suggestion, the two men discussed France's joining with Britain and the United States in a single unified western zone of Germany. A combined zone would make economic recovery in the West easier, Marshall pointed out, even as it reduced the costs of the occupation.

In the early evening of the 17th, Marshall paid a courtesy call upon their nominal host, British Foreign Minister Ernest Bevin. Bevin was patently distracted, worried about the Soviet forces poised in Germany, unsure of Moscow's response. "There was no country on the Continent that had any confidence in the future," he told Marshall. What could the United States do?

Marshall declined to be specific. The only strategy he could think of was a military association somewhat like the earlier economic grouping then working its way through Congress as the European Recovery Pro-gram. It was up to the European nations to weigh their military resources against their defensive needs and then ask the United States to make up the difference with men and materiel. This was to be the first of a num-ber of conversations in which the general would press for what was to become the North Atlantic Treaty Organization. "I started NATO," Marshall later told his biographer, Forrest Pogue. "I got every living soul, one after the other, to talk to me personally on the thing and to get them stirred up to do this business."

Marshall was a troubled man as he flew home. He had given Lucius Clay permission to begin currency reform in the British and American zones, the area they were calling "Bizonia." While the new currency would prevent the Soviets from manipulating the value of the German mark, it would just as effectively divide East from West. Clay warned that the Russians could be expected to retaliate in some fashion, most likely in Berlin.

The secretary was returning to Washington as a year begun in optimism ended in sadness. He would arrive as *Time* magazine, for the second time, selected him its Man of the Year for 1947, "the man who offered hope to those who desperately needed it. . . ."

CHAPTER
XXXVII

Playing with Fire

Germany was to be the battleground.

With the collapse of the London Foreign Ministers' Conference in December, representatives of the United States, Great Britain, and France opened talks on February 23, 1948, to unify their occupation zones.

That same day, Edvard Beneš's coalition government of Czechoslovakia fell to a Communist coup. The nations of western Europe suddenly were alarmed by the apparently expansionist nature of Soviet policy. To angry Americans, the end of a democratic government in Czechoslovakia only proved the Russians harbored unlimited ambitions in Europe.

Marshall urged caution. "The situation is very, very serious," he told reporters, adding the next day, "The world is in the midst of a great crisis, inflamed by propaganda, misunderstanding, anger and fear."

By virtue of geography, industrial base, and population, hard-pressed Germany was vital to an economically rejuvenated western Europe. For that reason, on March 6, the conferees in London, joined by representatives from the Netherlands, Belgium, and Luxembourg, issued a statement calling for the unification of the American, British, and French occupation zones in Germany. Less than three years after the war, the victors were joining the vanquished to oppose the Soviet Union, ironically fulfilling Joseph Goebbels's prophecy hurled from the bunker behind the gutted Reichstag.

Stalin, after all, had anticipated as much. In January, he had privately informed Yugoslavian visitors that Germany was to remain divided. "The West will make Western Germany their own, and we shall turn Eastern Germany into our own state."

The wartime alliance was no more. The increasing polarization of East and West blocs prompted Harry Truman to appear before a joint session of Congress on March 17, 1948, and publicly condemn the Soviet Union as the great obstacle to peace. There were times in world history when it was far wiser to act than to hesitate, Truman told the legislators. This was one of them. *The New Republic*'s political columnist TRB commented, "Truman entered the chamber in a postwar atmosphere. He left it in a prewar atmosphere."

Marshall had sought to have Truman's speech toned down as unnecessarily provocative; as the president put it, his secretary of state feared this speech would "pull the trigger." But tough talk would be required to get congressional action on the three measures Truman wanted to counter Soviet belligerence: the Marshall Plan, still mired in committee; a temporary draft to extend selective service, due to expire at the end of the month; and, at Marshall's urging, a universal military training program for all young men turning eighteen.

The legislators listened uncomfortably. Universal military training (UMT), in particular, was unpopular, especially so with elections in November.

Disregarding congressional and popular opposition, Marshall had long favored universal military training. He had devoted a considerable portion of his last biennial report as chief of staff to urging that the nation adopt UMT, a concept advanced by his old friend John McAuley Palmer after World War I. That program would gradually build a trained reserve ready to be called up in an emergency; without being unduly provocative, passage of a UMT bill would demonstrate the nation's resolve to defend freedom around the world. At the moment, as Marshall had warned the cabinet in February, "We are playing with fire while we have nothing with which to put it out."

The secretary envisioned universal military training as a democracy's alternative to a large standing army. This would be a citizen army, a peacetime army, a deterrent. "Its purpose is to avoid war, not to provoke it," he explained to his goddaughter, Rose Page Wilson. The deterrence factor was vital. "The only way to be sure of winning a third world war is to prevent it," Marshall warned.

Four days after the president's speech, the secretary sought to move Congress by stressing the urgency of the situation. "Mankind is engaged once more in the age-old struggle between freedom and tyranny," Marshall noted with uncharacteristic harshness during his address at the University of California Los Angeles. "Nowhere is the issue more clearly drawn than in Europe. . . . [There] the Soviet Union and Communist parties of Europe will go to extreme lengths to defeat the recovery and revival of a strong, democratic and independent Europe."

That revival, Marshall added, could only take place with the adoption of a European Recovery Program and with the assurance that the United States would lend military support to its Western Allies. The secretary of state was sending unmistakable diplomatic signals to the capitals of Europe.

In Brussels, representatives of Great Britain, France, and the Benelux countries took their cue from Marshall's public endorsement of western European political union as "our great hope." On March 17, they signed a fifty-year mutual defense pact.

A Western bloc existed now in fact, ratified by solemn agreement. The Soviets responded on March 21 by abruptly walking out of the four-power Allied Control Council set up to govern Germany. Rift had become chasm.

A week later, the Soviets further retaliated by constricting traffic between the western zones and Berlin, 110 miles within the Soviet zone. Russian border guards were to demand that American personnel traveling through the Soviet zone present proof they were affiliated with the military administration in Berlin; that military freight travel only with a Soviet permit; and that all baggage traveling into Berlin be inspected by the Russians.

The regulations were unacceptable. Acceding to the Russian demands would, in effect, mean the Western Allies yielded any right of travel to Berlin by virtue of conquest or prior agreement. The United States, Britain, and France then would be in Berlin only because the Soviets permitted them to remain.

The West's position was tenuous. By a verbal agreement reached in 1945, the Western Allies had access to Berlin over the autobahn from Helmstadt and a single rail line, through Marienborn. Air safety requirements, however, had forced the four occupying powers to sign an explicit agreement plotting four air corridors between the western zones and Berlin. Those corridors would save the western portions of the city.

Incrementally, the Russians tightened the blockade on the city through April, constricting traffic here and there, and periodically interrupting telephone service with the West. The American representative on the Allied Control Council and commander of U.S. occupation forces, Lieutenant General Lucius Clay, attempted to run an armed train into Berlin only to see it switched onto a siding well into the Soviet zone. There it sat until Clay ordered the train's humiliating return to the West some days later.

Even as the Berlin crisis worsened, Marshall remained a calming influence in excitable Washington. At a May 7 White House meeting, Secretary of Defense James Forrestal pleaded for a massive increase of his department's budget for 1948–49. Opportunistic military planners, taking advantage of the crisis atmosphere, had constructed a wishful budget of $33 billion. Under pressure from the Bureau of the Budget, they had grudgingly trimmed it to $22 billion. Forrestal wanted all he could get, particularly for more new air force bombers.

Truman balked. The Bureau of the Budget estimated they could afford no more than $15 billion without adding to the already whopping national debt of $200 billion. Did General Marshall wish to comment?

The secretary of state was firm. "[T]he policy of this country was based upon the assumption that there would not be war and that we should not plunge into war preparations which would bring about the very thing we are taking these steps to prevent."

The Soviets, according to State Department estimates, would not move militarily against the West. The USSR still confronted a massive reconstruction from the war, and the Soviet people were war-weary. "In seeking control over foreign territories, Soviet leaders have a strong traditional preference for political means as opposed to direct military action."

Marshall would hew to that position throughout the year, despite alarms by more bellicose members of the administration that "there exists a continuing danger of war at any time."

The secretary dismissed such assessments; he had had more than a little skepticism about the quality of military intelligence. "Forrestal should plan on building his forces within a balanced national economy . . . the country could not and would not support a budget based on preparation for war." His belief had nothing to do with the international situation, but stemmed from a desire to avoid putting the nation on a wartime footing.

On June 7, the London conferees announced they would summon a constituent assembly to draft a constitution that would transform "Trizonia" into an independent, unoccupied West Germany. The Russian retaliation came on June 19, one day after the Western powers announced the introduction of their new Deutsche mark and with it currency reform. Claiming the Western Allies were engaging in economic imperialism, the Soviets suspended all passenger traffic between East and West, limited freight to one train per day, and closed the Helmstadt-to-Berlin autobahn. Barge traffic on the canals was interdicted. Power stations in the Soviet zone stopped supplying electricity to the western zones.

Only the air corridors remained open. Clay asked Washington for permission to ram a convoy through the autobahn using armed force if necessary. Marshall strongly opposed Clay's request. Militarily, their two battalions in West Berlin were no challenge to the nearby Soviet divisions, he pointed out. Their strength was political or moral, a position that would be instantly destroyed by the use of force. At Marshall's insistence, President Truman scotched Clay's proposal.

On his own initiative, Clay ordered all available air transport to begin supplying not only the American military personnel and their dependents, but all 2.5 million people living in the three western zones of Berlin as well. The first C-47 of the Berlin airlift landed at Templehof Airport on the morning of June 25, 1948.

That evening, Clay's political adviser, Robert Murphy, cabled Marshall to advise against a pullout. No matter that they could supply by air only one ninth of Berlin's daily food and fuel requirements. A retreat "would be the Munich of 1948," Murphy advised. He suggested that a force of B-29s be sent to Europe, to underline America's resolve to stay.

The following day, President Truman ordered the airlift increased and put on a regular basis. They would not be starved out of Berlin. As Marshall put it in a diplomatic message handed to the Soviet ambassador in Washington,

> The United States government categorically asserts that it is in occupation of its sector in Berlin with free access thereto as a matter of established right deriving from the defeat and surrender of Germany and confirmed by formal agreement among the principal Allies. It further declares that it will not be induced by threats, pressures or other actions to abandon these rights. It is hoped that the Soviet government entertains no doubts whatsoever on this point.

For the next 321 days, American C-47s and C-54s taking part in Operation VITTLES flew day and night from the western zones into Berlin's airports. Landing just three minutes apart, the more than 200 transports of the airlift kept Berlin alive. Though Russian fighters occasionally buzzed the slow-moving transports, the Soviets chose not to interrupt the airlift itself. Both sides were avoiding any confrontation that might escalate into shooting.

Murphy's request for the B-29s raised an ominous diplomatic problem for the secretary of state. For a week longer Marshall weighed the propaganda implications of the transfer of aircraft known to have dropped the atomic bombs on Japan. Sixty stationed in Great Britain and thirty more in Germany would all have a range sufficient to reach Moscow.

The redeployment was no more than "the atomic-age equivalent of gunboat diplomacy," a gesture. In the end, Marshall assented to the transfer of the bombers, on condition they went without atomic bombs.

Transfer of the B-29s also triggered an intramural fight within the administration. Given "atomic-capability," the Air Force now asked to take control of the atomic weapons as well. Secretary of Defense James Forrestal favored the shift. Marshall was opposed.

When an aide, Gordon Arneson, suggested to the general that they might use an atomic weapon to break the Berlin blockade, Marshall asked, "If we were to atomic bomb the Soviet Union, what targets would you choose? Would you bomb Leningrad with the Hermitage?"

Arneson conceded he might spare Leningrad.

"But if you're really serious about this, why is there any question?" Marshall suggested Arneson "go home and think about it."

The bomb was more than just another weapon. Its victims were women and children, entire cities. Its impact was as much political as it was military. Thus it was far too powerful to be handed over to the generals, the secretary argued in a private meeting with Truman. The decision to use it—not just in Germany, but anywhere—must remain with the constitutionally mandated civilian head of government.

Disdaining the Air Force's "glamour boys" and their infatuation with bombers, former artilleryman Truman wanted no convincing. As the president told Secretary of Defense James Forrestal in mid-July, Harry Truman did not intend "to have some dashing lieutenant colonel decide when would be the proper time to drop one."

Although he might be a moderating influence within the cabinet, the secretary of state took a hard-line position on Berlin. It was either that or "accepting the consequences of failure of the rest of our European policy," as he insisted in a July 19 cabinet meeting. Their policy of containment had been successful in Greece where the pro-Communist guerrillas were in retreat; and in France and Italy, where the voters had ultimately rejected Communist slates. Meanwhile, Stalin had his own problems keeping the Communist bloc in line; Marshal Tito had broken with Moscow and was leading Yugoslavia on its own path.

By the end of summer, Marshall was confident they had stemmed the Soviet tide. At lunch with a glum Harry Truman—who was seized by a "terrible feeling . . . that we are very close to war"—Marshall's steadying voice calmed the president. In Moscow, Marshall pointed out, Ambassador Bedell Smith was again talking to a more amenable Premier Stalin.

Smith might not be sanguine about the outcome; Stalin was implying the Berlin blockade would be lifted if the Western allies gave up their plan to merge their occupation zones into a unified West Germany. The price just then was too high, Chip Bohlen wrote. But Stalin might settle for less once he realized precisely how resolute the Americans were about continuing to supply Berlin through the cold German winter.

Marshall's optimism grew. "The Russians are retreating," he told Bevin and newly named French Foreign Minister Robert Schuman on September 21. "From now on, Berlin is the only foothold which they have against us; everywhere else, and particularly in Germany, they are losing ground. We have put Western Germany on its feet and we are engaged in bringing about its recovery in such a way that we can really say that we are on the road to victory."

Whatever their diplomatic successes, Marshall still drew critical fire. The Bucharest newspaper *Romania Libera* in February had compared him to a ventriloquist's dummy; in May, a Russian-controlled newspaper in East Berlin scored him as "a foe of peace."

At home too he was chastised both left and right. Former Roosevelt cabinet member Henry Wallace, running for the presidency on the left-of-center Progressive Party ticket, called upon Truman to fire Marshall.

Seeking the Republican nomination for the presidency, the staunchly conservative Ohio senator, Robert Taft, flayed Marshall as "still friendly to the Communists in China." Worse, Taft insisted in a stump speech, "Roosevelt, Truman and Marshall made and confirmed the agreements at Yalta which gave Eastern Germany and Czechoslovakia into Communist control."

The Republican chairman of the powerful House Ways and Means Committee, Harold Knutson, demanded Marshall be removed "if we would avert war." Marshall had been "a complete failure . . . pompous, self-opinionated in the extreme, vacillating and unpredictable." Writing in his weekly newspaper, the *Wadena Pioneer-Journal,* Knutson concluded, "It is tragic that the foreign affairs of our government are in the hands of two incompetents: Truman and Marshall."

Knutson was not known as a foreign policy expert, but columnist Walter Lippmann was. In early April, Lippmann weighed in with the opinion that Truman had given "no evidence of an ability to perform the functions of the commander in chief." Marshall, meanwhile, "has devoted such a large part of his time and energy to performing the work of a traveling ambassador that he has not had, and does not have, the whole of our foreign relations under his control."

The criticism Marshall took in some good humor. To an old friend he groused, "The finals of an adjourning Congress and the height of a presidential campaign do not help matters much from my point of view. The press and the radio I always have with me. God bless democracy!"

True, as Lippmann pointed out, Marshall was obliged to travel. In 1947 Marshall had been to the Moscow and London foreign ministers' conferences, and to Rio de Janiero for a meeting of the Pan-American nations. This year he was scheduled to attend a meeting of the United Nations General Assembly in Paris. But first he would have to travel to Bogotá, Colombia, and a conference that would create the region's first mutual defense pact.

Since 1939, when he made his first trip to Latin America, George Marshall had acquired substantial experience in the affairs of that often tempestuous region. His first South American visit, to Brazil, had laid the groundwork for that nation's active participation in World War II.

During the early years of the war, Marshall had diverted substantial amounts of vital military materiel to South American countries so as to overcome the considerable German influence in the region. By 1947, the colonels and generals, firmly addicted to U.S. aid, were clamoring for a Latin "Marshall Plan."

In August 1947, Marshall traveled with a large official party to Rio de Janiero and a conference intended to make permanent a treaty arrangement whereby an act of aggression against one Latin nation would be considered an act against all. The secretary of state found himself forced to an awkward stance: he had come to ask for a mutual defense pact, yet he had to report that there would be no reciprocal aid program for Latin America, no "Marshall Plan." The United States had only so much money to spend on foreign aid.

Despite his position, Marshall had been partially successful. In part the success stemmed from his tact, in part from a respected reputation that preceded him; there was even a horse show in his honor, "The General Marshall Trials."

Marshall's speech at the conference did no more than salve irritated Latin tempers. The United States did not have the resources to mount a Marshall Plan for Europe, meet its obligations in the Far East, and also support the Latin nations as they wished. In fact, the larger, wealthier countries of the region could carry some of the load, Marshall hinted. He asked that any economic questions be put over until the Bogotá meeting the following year.

The secretary's speech was sobering, but there was little these representatives of South American client nations could do. They needed American arms and American financial aid. Marshall's tact had only made the bitter medicine more palatable. The delegates agreed to strengthen their mutual assistance pact along lines Marshall proposed.

However modest the achievement appeared, it was significant. Marshall had sketched in Latin America the outline of the first of a series of mutual defense pacts the United States would soon write in Europe and Southeast Asia.

Six months later, the European Recovery Act awaiting final vote in the House of Representatives, the secretary of state flew to the Ninth International Conference of American States in Bogotá, Colombia.

Colombia was a troubled nation in that spring of 1948. The Central Intelligence Agency had reported that Communist agitators intended to stir trouble among Bogotá's eternally poor. The American ambassador warned that "Communists and left-wing liberals would endeavor to sabotage the Inter-American Conference in order to embarrass the Colombian government and create difficulties among American republics." Marshall decided Katherine would not accompany him on this trip.

Despite the rumors, Marshall refused to otherwise change his routine, to appear to be intimidated. He deliberately drove each morning from the private home in the expensive Chapinero district where the American delegation was staying to the embassy three blocks from the capitol in downtown Bogotá. He worked there until it was time to attend the meetings. Then, accompanied by Major Vernon ("Dick") Walters, his translator, he walked through the crowded streets to the capitol. Invariably, Marshall was recognized, storekeepers and shoppers applauding as he strode along the crowded sidewalks, some venturing to ask the smiling American secretary of state for his autograph. In fragmentary Spanish, recalled from his duty in the Philippines decades before, Marshall exchanged greetings with pedestrians. A man apparently at ease, he even stood in line at a postal substation in a five-and-dime store to buy souvenir stamps of his visit.

The threatened violence exploded on April 9. The secretary was at lunch when the embassy telephoned to inform Marshall Carter "that some guy by the name of Gaitan has been shot and killed downtown."

Dick Walters was stunned. "Oh, God, this is trouble," he said, putting his hands to his head. Jorge Eliecer Gaitan, a leader of the liberal opposition in the Colombian Senate, had a large and dedicated following. "If that is true, there is going to be a revolution or a civil war today."

Marshall Carter frowned. "Walters, you shouldn't make extreme statements like that in General Marshall's presence."

Within minutes they could hear scattered gunfire around the house. The two policemen assigned to guard the front door retreated inside. Two more from nearby streets joined them. The Americans among them had only a .38-caliber revolver brought by Marshall's resourceful aide, Sergeant C. J. George.

Bogotá was in turmoil. Incendiary squads were reported racing from government building to government building; black smoke columns smudged the sky over the central city. Rebels seized all eight radio stations, broadcasting impassioned appeals for revolution and justice. The Colombian Army, scattered across the countryside, had fewer than 600 soldiers stationed in the city and no immediate reinforcements available.

Mobs roamed the streets, attacking residences identified over the rebel-held radio stations. When Walters heard the excited rebels accuse the Americans of complicity in Gaitan's assassination and list their Chapinero residence as a target, the translator telephoned a friend at the Ministry of War to suggest they send troops to defend the secretary of state. Walters's friend dispatched a detachment of soldiers under the command of a young lieutenant.

Ignoring the clamor in the streets and the posting of the troops in front of the house, Marshall sat calmly in the living room, reading a paperback western. As it grew darker, the shooting swirled first toward, then away from the residence, Averell Harriman reporting its course from a balcony. Taking notice finally of the soldiers shivering in the cold night air, the secretary instructed Walters, "I would like to speak to the officer in charge of these men."

The Colombian lieutenant stiffly marched into the living room, helmet under his arm, clicked his heels and formally reported.

Speaking through Walters, Marshall asked, "Lieutenant Fonseca, how many men do you have?"

"Thirteen."

"But they are all at the front door," Marshall pointed out.

"Yes, sir."

"Well, what are you going to do if they come to the back door?"

"I don't know, sir."

Marshall smiled. "If I remember my small-unit tactics correctly, when you are defending a perimeter, what you do is to garrison that perimeter lightly and place a large, centrally located, mobile reserve at a point where it can move rapidly to any threatened point on the perimeter."

Lieutenant Fonseca was perplexed. "Yes, sir, but what shall I do?"

"Put one man at the front door, one man at the back door and all the others in the garage where they can keep warm tonight," the onetime instructor of infantry tactics advised. "That's the way the United States Army would handle it." For a brief, pleasant moment, he was a soldier once again.

Lieutenant Fonseca saluted, clicked his heels, and went off to reposition his troops. Marshall returned to his novel.

Through dinner and the balance of the evening, the American party listened to the radio, trying to deduce the course of the revolution. Not until eleven that night—Marshall calmly having retired—did the Colombian Army throw its full weight behind the elected government and recapture one by one the radio stations.

The city was quiet during the daylight hours of the next day, a Saturday. That night scattered sniper fire broke out once again, answered by heavy weapons as the army moved to squash the rebellion. Sunday too was quiet, Sunday night's sporadic warfare negligible.

The conference resumed on Monday in a boys' school not far from the ruined capitol. More than 1,000 were reported dead. Marshall's secretary, Mildred Asbjornson, recalled her fear when she saw truck after truck, with bodies carelessly heaped in the rear, drive by the embassy that morning. The central city resembled the ruins of Europe, General Ridgway noted, rubble spilling into the streets between smoke-blackened buildings.

Frightened by the turmoil in the city, agitated delegates repeatedly requested that the United States do something to restore order. Marshall mildly declined. When the Argentine foreign minister asked that the secretary of state order the 82nd Airborne Division to parachute into Bogotá, Marshall refused on the grounds that it would be an invasion of Colombian sovereignty. "This was a Colombian problem and the Colombians would have to take care of it."

In a speech to the unnerved delegates, Marshall noted, "This situation must not be judged on a local basis, however tragic the immediate results to the Colombian people. . . . It is the same definite pattern as occurrences which provoked strikes in France and Italy, and that is endeavoring to prejudice the situation in Italy, where elections will be held on April 18. . . . This is a world affair—not merely Colombian or Latin American."

Except for the timely action of William Douglas Pawley, the U.S. ambassador to Brazil, the conference might then have collapsed in a panic. Pawley instead dispatched his private DC-3 to Panama, giving the pilot $5,000 to purchase hams, turkeys, caviar, and pâté. He explained to a questioning secretary that the unnerved delegates would settle down to work if it appeared that life and its luxuries had resumed their normal course.

Pawley was correct in sizing up the temper of the delegates. His transport returned that same day with the provisions, the Americans hosted a lavish dinner that soothed jangled nerves, and on Tuesday they voted to continue the conference. Marshall meanwhile ordered the dispatch of 4,000 raincoats from Pentagon stocks for rain-soaked Colombian soldiers and food to feed American Embassy dependents.*

Because it resumed deliberations in the face of insurrection, the Bogotá conference ranked as an unqualified success. The delegates agreed to reconstitute the Pan American Union as the Organization of American States, to endorse peaceful settlement of disputes amongst the members, and to condemn all forms of totalitarian government, that last prompted by the revolt they had endured.

In Washington once more, Marshall picked up the routines of a weekday bachelor. During the week he stayed with Allen's widow and her six-year-old son in a tiny house in Georgetown; weekends he flew to Pinehurst or drove down to Leesburg to join Katherine. Normally solicitous of his wife's health, he was even more so in recent months; she was having trouble sleeping, a condition he decided was attributable to her smoking habit.

Even though he left his office at 4:30 p.m.—explaining to his secretary, Miss Asbjornson, that nobody ever had a serious thought after that hour—his days were crowded. When Katherine stayed in Leesburg, Marshall occasionally accepted dinner invitations from the Achesons or Lovetts. Those evenings he would unbend somewhat, revealing a warmth

---

*Forrest Pogue notes that in later years Lovett enjoyed recounting the aftermath. The Pentagon sent a bill for the raincoats and food to the State Department. Marshall returned it, saying it was more properly a Red Cross responsibility. By the time the Pentagon forwarded the bill to the Red Cross, Marshall was its president. "Once again he mulled over the charges and decided this time that they really should be settled by the Department of Defense. Then, declared Lovett with a perceptible twinkle, by the time the bill reached the Pentagon, new Secretary of Defense Marshall concluded that the papers were so tattered and worn that the bill would have to be paid by his new headquarters." See Pogue IV, pp. 391–92.

he otherwise masked, telling self-deprecating or wry anecdotes of his youth and military service.

In letters to friends he wistfully contemplated a more peaceful life. "All my instincts urge a quiet period of retrospect from Leesburg or Pinehurst," he wrote in June. In a note to Henry Stimson, he complained, "In all my Washington posts since 1938 I never seem to have a day of restful existence and apparently the pressures grow worse and worse." Marshall commiserated by letter with an equally occupied Dwight Eisenhower, "This is not an easy world to live in for people like you and myself."

His life was hemmed in by official responsibilities, and there was too little time for old friends and associates. On his California trip in the spring, he had been able to chat with Richard Wing, his former interpreter in China, only by inviting him to fly on "The Sacred Cow" from Berkeley to Los Angeles. There was no time to see Stimson, confined by arthritis to Highhold; not even time to reminisce with Leahy, only a few blocks away in the White House, who warned him that things at the Joint Chiefs of Staff "ain't like they used to be." Only the most pressing obligations—the funeral on July 16, 1948, of General of the Armies John J. Pershing—interrupted the round of State Department responsibilities.

Even medical exigencies yielded to public obligations. Late in June, both Marshall and his wife checked into Walter Reed Hospital for three-day physical examinations. The staff urologist, Colonel Clifford Kimbrough, discovered Marshall's right kidney palpably enlarged. Whether cyst or tumor, it would have to be monitored.

Driving in from Leesburg early on Monday mornings, Marshall periodically visited Walter Reed for check-ups. In September, Kimbrough's examination revealed the kidney had swollen to twice normal size. The organ would have to be removed entirely. Marshall chose to delay the operation until the conclusion of the October meetings of the United Nations General Assembly in Paris.

In an unrecorded meeting at the White House, Marshall apparently explained that he needed an operation soon and intended to retire in January when the president's first term came to an end. There would be no official announcement since news of his leaving might reflect badly on Truman's already difficult reelection campaign. Marshall told only a few friends. "It will be a great treat, beyond anything you can imagine, for me to be relieved of responsibility, and be free to pursue my own desires and family life," he wrote to actor Walter Huston, a sometime hunting and fishing companion.

Before that day, however, he had to deal with the sorest of those responsibilities, the one that gave him the most heartache, Palestine.

For twenty-five years Great Britain had uneasily administered the Holy

Land as a mandate for the League of Nations. Both Palestinian Arabs and Jewish immigrants claimed the land as their own; each could assert that Britain had pledged the arid country to them. The Jews relied on the November 1917 Balfour Declaration expressing sympathy for the creation of a Jewish national homeland. The Arabs pointed to a British White Paper, issued on the eve of World War II, proposing the creation of a joint Jewish-Arab state in 1949. In the meantime, the British suspended all Jewish immigration to Eretz Yisroel.

VJ-Day brought down on the Labor government of Clement Attlee a moral dilemma no White Paper could have anticipated. The stark photographs from the camps at Dachau, Buchenwald, and Auschwitz; the 200,000 Jewish survivors wandering between displaced person camps, seeking to emigrate; the unfathomable horror of 6 million dead, all worked to produce an international sympathy for the plight of the Jews. While the creation of a Jewish homeland took on a special urgency, Jews, Arabs, or both scuttled successive compromises intended to create that haven. Weary of it all, the Attlee government on April 2, 1947, turned the question of Palestine over to the United Nations.

Official Washington stood sharply divided on the Palestine question. Sensitive to the Jewish vote in large states like New York, Illinois, and California, elected officials, including President Truman, tended to favor the concept of a Jewish homeland.

The Pentagon and State Department were strongly opposed. According to a Joint Chiefs of Staff paper, American strategic interests in the Near and Middle East would suffer if the United States supported partition. "United States influence in the area would be curtailed to that which could be maintained by military force," the paper warned. Further, partition would mean conflict between Jew and Arab, and that would permit the Soviet Union to meddle in the area.

The Joint Chiefs worried that a U.S. policy that appeared to favor the Jews and partition would alienate the oil-rich Arab nations of the Middle East. The United States then would have to fight an "oil-starved" war. Thus the chiefs counted it of "great strategic importance to the United States to retain the good will of the Arab and Moslem states."

The director of the State Department's Office of Near Eastern and African Affairs, career diplomat Loy Henderson, wrote Marshall on September 22, 1947, to advise him against "any kind of a plan at this time for the partitioning of Palestine or for the setting up of a Jewish state in Palestine." Purportedly speaking for nearly every member of the Foreign Service or of the department who had worked to any appreciable extent on Near Eastern problems, Henderson asserted partition would require American enforcement, would sabotage American-Arab relations, and would fail because of Arab non-acceptance.

Harry Truman was undeterred. Even as Arab nations began moving troops toward the borders of Palestine, the president instructed the UN delegation to support partition. On November 29, 1947, the United States voted with the 33-to-13 majority of the United Nations General Assembly in favor of partition. The next day Arab forces attacked Jewish settlements; the underground Jewish army, Haganah, counterattacked.

Jettisoning its imperial baggage, Great Britain announced on December 15 that it would end supervision of the Palestine Mandate on May 15, 1948. State Department planner George F. Kennan's subsequent position paper warned that United States strategic interests in the Middle East and the Mediterranean had been severely prejudiced by American support for partition in the UN. Kennan foresaw the Jewish state going under unless the United States rendered aid or even sent troops. At the same time, the Russians would surely fish in muddied waters, offering their help to one or the other side, and thereby gaining a foothold in the area. Whatever happened, the Arabs would cut off the flow of oil to Europe and doom the pending Marshall Plan.

Former Wall Street banker turned Secretary of Defense James Forrestal weighed in two days later. Forrestal fancied himself an unflinching realist, not a man to be swayed by emotion. Arguing with presidential adviser Clark Clifford, who supported partition, the secretary of defense barked, "You just don't understand. There are 400,000 Jews and 40 million Arabs. Forty million Arabs are going to push 400,000 Jews into the sea. And that's all there is to it. Oil—that's the side we ought to be on."

State, Defense, the Joint Chiefs, the new Central Intelligence Agency, all had come down firmly against partition, against support of a Jewish homeland, for temporizing and, most important, for the continued flow of oil. The secretary of state would have to "grasp the nettle firmly" and persuade the president to withhold support from the Jewish militants pressing for a homeland.

Marshall needed no convincing. As long before as March 1944, as chief of staff he had appeared in an executive session of the Senate Foreign Relations Committee to testify against a resolution calling for immediate Jewish immigration into Palestine. Passage of the resolution, he told the committee, would alienate the Arabs and risk the supply of oil necessary for the war effort.

Four years later, he was once more to put his considerable prestige on the line. Kennan, Henderson, Lovett could provide a dozen diplomatic reasons why the United States should not come down on the side of a Jewish homeland. The Joint Chiefs offered another: it would take at least 100,000, perhaps three times that many troops, to maintain a truce in the Holy Land. They simply did not have the men to spare.

Even as the United Nations debated the Palestine question, the British deadline of May 15 rushed in on them. Marshall met with Moshe Shertok, the nominal foreign minister of the Jewish Agency, on the afternoon of Saturday, May 8.

The secretary of state did away with diplomatic tact in favor of frankness. Pointing to a map of Palestine on the wall of his office, he ticked off the poor strategic position of the proposed Jewish homeland. "Here you are surrounded by Arabs," he said, placing his hand over the Negev Desert. "And here in the Galilee, you are surrounded by other Arabs. You have Arab states all around you and your backs are to the sea."

Here was the man Churchill had called the architect of victory delivering a lecture on military strategy to a stubborn civilian determined to go to war. "Believe me, I am talking about things that I know," Marshall stressed. "You are sitting there in the coastal plains of Palestine while the Arabs hold the mountain ridges. I know you have some arms and your Haganah, but the Arabs have regular armies. They are well trained and they have heavy arms. How can you hope to hold out?"

Shertok could only shrug. There comes a time when a man must fight.

Marshall cautioned against overoptimism. "He wanted to warn us," Shertok said later, "against relying on the advice of our military people" who had enjoyed some initial victories against Arab irregulars the previous month. The Arab Legions poised in Trans-Jordan and the Egyptian Army were well trained by the British.

The situation was similar to his China experience, Marshall pointed out. Whenever he thought he had a truce arranged, one or the other side would score a victory and convince itself it had more to win on the field than in negotiation. The counsel of military men was suspect. "I told Mr. Shertok [Marshall reported] that they were taking a gamble. If the tide did turn adversely and they came running to us for help they should be placed clearly on notice now that there was no warrant to expect help from the United States, which had warned them of the grave risk they were running."

At four o'clock on the afternoon of Wednesday, May 12, the president joined his foreign policy advisers for a showdown on the Israel question. Two days earlier he had instructed his special counsel, Clark Clifford, to "prepare yourself and you be the lawyer for the position that we should recognize Israel. I am inclined to believe that General Marshall is probably opposed to it. . . ."

Harry Truman understood something of the sweep of history. However ill-prepared he had seemed in 1945 to be president of the United States, the onetime Missouri farm boy had spent much of his adult life reading history. It lent depth to his appreciation of the accidental moments when men had an opportunity to shape the sweep of events, to make history. For a man steeped in both Old and New Testaments, in chronicles of Imperial Rome, this was such an instant. Harry Truman might help to end 2,500 years of wandering by the Lord's chosen people, and do justice in the wake of the Holocaust.

In fact, Truman had already made up his mind. Clark Clifford was to be Israel's advocate, the president's advocate in the meeting. The meeting was not to convince Truman, but to bring his secretary of state to wisdom.

They assembled in a conference room at Blair House, Truman deferentially placing Marshall alone at his right hand. On the left Truman arranged Lovett and Clifford, the advisers; then the experts, David K. Niles of the White House staff, and Robert McClintock from the Department of State's Near East desk.

At the president's request, Lovett summarized the latest intelligence, of well-armed Arab Legions poised to strike at the Jewish lands defined by the UN's partition plan, of meager Haganah forces and ragtag irregulars digging in on rocky hilltops and barren crossroads.

Marshall followed, presenting over the next ten minutes the well-reasoned case against recognition: the disparity of forces; American need for oil lest, to use Forrestal's phrase, Detroit be forced to build cars with four-cylinder engines; the United States' long-term responsibilities and the shortage of military resources to carry them out.

Then it was Clifford's turn. He had prepared a lawyer's closing argument, summarizing all the reasons for recognition, then ending his fifteen-minute statement with "a ringing peroration."

In a guarded account for the files dictated immediately after the meeting, the secretary of state noted:

> I remarked to the president that, speaking objectively, I could not help but think that the suggestions made by Mr. Clifford were wrong. I thought that to adopt these suggestions would have precisely the opposite effect from that intended. . . . The transparent dodge to win a few votes would not in fact achieve this purpose. The great dignity of the office of President would be seriously diminished. The counsel offered by Mr. Clifford was based on domestic political considerations, while the problem which confronted us was international.

Were it not for domestic politics—November's presidential election in which the Jewish vote could be decisive in New York, Illinois, and California—Clifford would not even be at the meeting, Marshall lectured in "a righteous, goddamned Baptist tone."

"Mr. Clifford is here at my personal request," Truman said reproachfully. He had thought it wise to hear both sides.

The meeting was turning out badly, very badly. Truman attempted a bit of humor. "Well, General, it sounds to me as if even you might vote against me in November if I go ahead to recognize."

"Yes, Mr. President, and if in the election I was to vote, I would vote against the president."

Coming from Marshall, this was stinging reproval.

It appeared that Clifford had lost his case. After the meeting broke up, Truman apologized to his young counsel. "I didn't have any idea it would turn out this way." Both Truman and Clifford were upset, the adviser said later. Political considerations, whatever Marshall thought, were not a factor, Clifford said.

Later that evening, a disturbed Robert Lovett telephoned Clifford at the White House. Lovett was uneasy, he told the younger man. "We've got to straighten this out. It's going to lead to a breach between the president and General Marshall, and I'm afraid that Marshall could resign."

Lovett asked for help.

"There isn't anything I can do at this end," Clifford replied. "The thing for you to do is persuade General Marshall that he's wrong."

Clifford reported his conversation to the president. Truman's spirits revived. "I got the feeling from President Truman that he felt that Marshall just needed a little time."

On Thursday, May 13, Lovett called Clifford to report that Marshall had edged away from opposition to a Jewish state. Truman knew his man.

In George Catlett Marshall there ran strains of what historian Arthur Schlesinger, Jr., has called the universalist ideals of Woodrow Wilson idealism, of a world to be made better. These meshed with stories of Lee and Jackson, duty-bound to follow their conscience; of the southerner's romantic ties to a noble cause, however lost it might be. Ranged against these feelings of idealism, these character traits typical of Americans who came of age in the optimistic years before 1914, lay a pragmatic recognition of geopolitical realities, of lessons learned as a cadet at VMI and as a young officer in the first decades of the century. Two world wars— he had fought in one and led the second—had served to tamp down the idealism, but never quite extinguish it.

In a New Year's message to the president just five months earlier, Marshall had noted, "It seems to me in my relationship to you that invariably what we have tried to do has been without selfish national prejudices and for the general good of people all over the world."

They had that opportunity once more, to put aside national prejudice and do something for the general good, Marshall realized. In conversations at New State the following day, Lovett led a reassessment of their stance. Recognition of a Jewish Palestine lent only moral force to the new state; it did not mean they would have to send troops to defend Jews about to be driven into the sea. Oil was not truly a factor. If the

Arabs declined to sell to the United States, they would not also penalize Europe for an American recognition of a Jewish state. The Arabs needed the income.

One by one, Marshall's objections fell. Most important of all, the president had apparently chosen to give diplomatic recognition to the new Jewish state. Those who disagreed had two choices: they could carry out their duties, or they could resign. Marshall reportedly rejected the second with the advice, "No, gentlemen, you don't take a post of this sort and then resign when the man who has the constitutional responsibility to make decisions makes one you don't like."

At a lunch at the private F Street Club on Friday, May 14, Lovett and Clifford drafted the State Department's press release announcing American recognition of the new government. Lovett made a last effort to avert what he called the indecent haste in recognizing the new nation. Clifford simply explained that "the president was under unbearable pressure to recognize the Jewish state promptly." They finished just five hours before the British Mandate in Palestine came to an end at 6:00 p.m. Washington time that day.

The following morning at ten o'clock Washington time, the nation of Israel declared its independence. At that moment a representative of the new provisional government was presenting his credentials to waiting officials at the Department of State. His letter asked that the United States recognize the new nation and "welcome Israel into the community of nations." Eleven minutes later, the White House announced that the president had granted full and unconditional recognition. As Truman had insisted, the United States was the first nation to do so—even as Arab irregulars and the Jewish Haganah fought for control of Jerusalem and three Arab armies mobilized.

Recognition would not settle the Israeli question. Miffed State Department staff members leaked stories of a rift between the president and his secretary, of policies "formulated in a sort of no man's land, somewhere between the Democratic National Committee and the White House." On August 10, the president felt compelled to deny publicly that Marshall had threatened to resign.

Relations between the White House and the Department of State were strained as the campaign intensified. Marshall remained resolutely apolitical, certainly aware the president was considered an underdog to Republican nominee Thomas Dewey, yet unwilling to play a·partisan role. By mid-August, the president was summoning Undersecretary Lovett alone to the White House; there were some matters he could not discuss with Marshall because of political implications.

There were continuing embarrassments in dealing with the volatile Israeli question. In September, Marshall endorsed a peace proposal submitted earlier by the murdered United Nations mediator Count Folke

Bernadotte. Both sides were to accept a cease-fire, while each held onto the territory it then occupied.

The State Department had secured White House approval prior to releasing Marshall's statement. But the Bernadotte plan ran counter to the Democratic Party platform endorsing the borders of the original partition plan. The Jews, who had suffered setbacks in the initial fighting, were particularly opposed since the Bernadotte plan would result in lost territory. Pressure on the White House from Jewish voters was intense; one major backer wired: MARSHALL IS DOING PRESIDENT MORE HARM THAN ANYTHING I CAN THINK OF.

The election approaching, Clifford moved to keep the lid on. The State Department was ordered to do nothing that might embarrass the president. Truman asked Marshall, then preparing for a United Nations General Assembly meeting in Paris, to make no statement or take any action on the Palestine question without clearing it first with the White House. The American delegation found itself embarrassingly muzzled on a paramount issue of the conference.

The secretary of state, Mrs. Marshall, and a large delegation—including a doctor to monitor the general's condition—arrived for the Paris meetings of the General Assembly on September 20, 1948. Marshall had looked forward to this trip for some months. The Assembly's sessions would not be overly tiring; he and Katherine would find time for themselves.

This was a relaxed George Marshall, a man relishing the fast-approaching end of his final tour of duty. He was still firmly commanding the delegation, but he was more affable, less aloof. Despite security concerns in the face of rumored threats by Jewish terrorists on the secretary's life—Marshall Carter went about armed with a loaded pistol—the Marshalls and United States delegate Eleanor Roosevelt even slipped away for dinner at a small restaurant on the Left Bank.

The central figure at the Paris meetings, he fell into his usual routine of morning briefings with the delegation before they left for the daily meetings of the General Assembly. He arrived at the dilapidated Hôtel d'Iéna each morning early, "to get a better seat," he explained to an amused stenographer.

Delegates from other nations sought him out constantly. Where he had been criticized as distant at the Lake Success meetings, here in Paris he saw everyone, frequently over lunch at the American Embassy.

Marshall unbent—a little. Dean Rusk, then a member of the Department of State's supporting staff, recalled that Marshall "almost never complimented anyone until the working relationship ceased." Early one morning, an eyes-only cable from the president to the secretary came in. Because it required an immediate response, Rusk took the cable from the embassy code room, drafted a reply, then took them to the general's room. Marshall, in his bathrobe, read the messages, and approved. "Rusk, there are times when I think you are earning your pay." It was high praise coming from a man Rusk idealized.

In his first address to the General Assembly on September 23, Marshall urged early conclusion of peace treaties with Germany, Japan, and Austria; an end to fighting in Palestine and the admission of Trans-Jordan and Israel to UN membership; a unified Korea; termination of guerrilla war in Greece; and the early adoption of a system for control of atomic energy that would provide for the abolition of nuclear weapons.

Marshall carefully set aside two other issues for offstage discussions. First, there was Berlin and the question of bringing the blockade before the General Assembly for debate. More important to the secretary were his unceasing efforts to fashion a military alliance between the North Atlantic states.

In his opening speech, Marshall left to elliptical allusion the Berlin crisis, assuring the Assembly the United States wished to alleviate existing tensions. "But we will not compromise essential principles. We will under no circumstances barter away the rights and freedoms of other peoples."

Of the military pact, there was no public mention at all.

Marshall's encouragement of British Foreign Minister Ernest Bevin at the beginning of the year had led incrementally to the five-nation Brussels treaty in March. That fifty-year mutual defense pact, Marshall told the signers at the time, was essential to any wider arrangement in which the United States might play a part. In effect, Europe was creating a military parallel to the economic Marshall Plan. However poorly armed it might be at the moment, Europe was taking responsibility for its own defense.

At the end of March 1948, the National Security Council (NSC) rang in with a classified recommendation that the United States stand up to the advance of "Soviet-directed world communism." The NSC proposed supplying western European nations with arms and machine tools to standardize arms productions among the allies. The proposal neatly complemented the Brussels pact. Truman was delighted. "Our friends the Russkies understand only one language—how many divisions have you, actual or potential," he wrote in a draft of a speech never given.

The lines were hardening.

Lovett and Vandenberg then fit together Brussels treaty and NSC paper in a Senate resolution that called for regional defense agreements based on continuous mutual aid. With only four senators opposed, the Senate, in effect, was urging the president to proceed with regional defense pacts such as the Brussels group sought.

Stirred by the Czech coup and the Berlin blockade, a sense of urgency impelled Western diplomats. Beginning in July, an American delegation headed by Lovett met secretly in Washington with the ambassadors of Canada, Great Britain, France, and the Benelux nations to shape this North Atlantic defense alliance.

By the end of October, with an enthusiastic Marshall prodding from Paris, the compact was agreed upon. "Democracies," Marshall noted with satisfaction, "are slow starters, but when they do move they act with great force and resolution."

In Washington, meanwhile, President Truman fretted at that slow pace. He was facing long odds in his reelection bid; newspaper pundits and pollsters daily crowned Republican nominee Thomas Dewey victor. Looking for a bold stroke that would transform him into the peace candidate, Truman determined to send to Moscow his close friend, Chief Justice of the United States Fred M. Vinson. The mission was to dispel the "poisonous atmosphere of distrust" brought on by the Berlin blockade and to assure Premier Stalin of America's desire for peace.

Lovett, informed routinely by the White House, immediately protested. Such a move would undermine the secretary of state's authority, and certainly provoke him to resign immediately, Lovett warned. With that Truman abruptly canceled the Vinson mission.

In Paris, Marshall Carter had received a copy of the president's proposed announcement of Vinson's mission to Moscow. Carter dashed off a sharp reply beginning, "Never in the history of diplomatic bungling . . ."

Marshall killed that message with the admonition that one did not address the president in such a tone. Instead, the secretary cabled Washington to apologize for not keeping the president as well informed of developments as he might have. Marshall suggested he fly to Washington for a weekend conference.

The president agreed, dispatching his personal plane to fetch him. Marshall flew to Washington with only Sergeant George and the attentive, if unnecessary, doctor.

Marshall, Lovett, and Truman left no record of their meeting on Saturday, October 9. The secretary certainly detailed the negotiations over Germany and the evolving mutual defense compact. His biographer, Forrest Pogue, suggests he also reaffirmed his desire to leave the State Department after the election. If so, then Lovett probably indicated that he too would soon leave. They may have discussed a possible successor; Truman intended to ask Dean Acheson back.

The following day Marshall met with Secretary of Defense James Forrestal and Omar Bradley, chairman of the Joint Chiefs of Staff, to discuss the supply of arms to the North Atlantic nations. Those countries were apprehensive about the Soviets, "completely out of their skin, and sitting on their nerves." They needed a psychological lift, Marshall continued. Supplies for ground troops, even rifles, would have an electric effect, stimulating morale, he suggested.

Forrestal was frustrated. The president had fixed a defense budget of $14.4 billion for fiscal '49, the Joint Chiefs had brought their requests down to a still impossible $17.5 billion, and now Marshall wanted who knew how many billions to equip western Europe. Forrestal expected Truman to hold to the $14.4 billion ceiling. If he won reelection, he could then come back to Congress, after the election, for more money. If Dewey won, it would be his problem.

On his last day in Washington before returning to Europe, Marshall interrupted a meeting with Bradley to have a State Department photographer take their picture with the two-year-old son of Chip Bohlen on Marshall's knee. "This is how Charlie looked yesterday," he said when delivering the photograph in Paris to the Bohlens, who had not seen their son for more than a month.

Marshall would spend another six pleasant weeks based in Paris, taking trips on the weekends to show Katherine the World War I battlefields east and north of the city. For the secretary of state, these were weekends of nostalgic recall. His interpreter, Major Vernon Walters, was surprised Marshall remembered the location of cemeteries; Bohlen was similarly impressed that Marshall could recall telephone numbers from the first war.

Ostensibly they traveled incognito for security purposes; in fact, Marshall was recognized wherever they traveled. In Reims, Walters, Carter, and George in turn stood guard with a loaded pistol outside the Marshalls' hotel room in case Jewish terrorists attempted to make good an assassination threat.

From Reims they drove to Nancy, where Marshall asked Walters to inquire about his former landlady, Madame Jouatte. The woman was ninety, but still living in nearby Gondrecourt, Walters learned from the gendarmerie. They drove the next morning to the town and parked outside Madame Jouatte's home while Walters rang the bell.

The old woman who answered the door had heard on the radio that the American secretary of state had returned to the province for the first time since the *première guerre mondiale*.

"Oh, mon dieu, he is here, isn't he?" the old woman asked. In her excitement, she greeted Marshall with kisses on both cheeks.

They visited, Katherine meeting this woman of whom she had so often heard. Madame Jouatte assured her former boarder that George Patton had more than followed Marshall's orders to look her up four years before. Patton had not only delivered an entire truckload of scarce food but capped that by ordering an armored regiment to pass in review below her window.

In mid-October, the Marshalls flew on to Greece, where the secretary reviewed the course of the fratricidal guerrilla war with Lieutenant General James Van Fleet. The Greek Army was dispirited, weary of chasing the Communists into neighboring Albania only to see them return a month later, refitted and refreshed. Marshall concurred with Van Fleet's proposal that Greece's army be increased by 15,000 men. (Since he was secretary of state, not of defense, the punctilious Marshall was apologetic in forwarding the recommendation to Washington.)

The build-up of the Greek Army, coupled with the brutal repression of dissenters in the cities and with Joseph Stalin's orders from Moscow to close the guerrilla sanctuaries in Albania and Yugoslavia, would all work to suppress the civil war in the next twelve months.

From Greece, the Marshalls flew westward for a brief stop in Rome. Marshall held short talks with government figures, talks symbolic of Italy's importance to the new Atlantic union, according to Foreign Affairs Minister Carlo Sforza. Privately, Marshall wanted firm assurances that Italy would be able to contain the Communists, who had polled over a third of the vote in the last national elections. The following day, the Marshalls traveled to Castel Gondolfo for a thirty-minute visit with Pope Pius XII. From there they drove to the American cemetery at Anzio to visit Allen's grave.

The General Assembly was again meeting in Paris as the first returns from the American election began coming in on November 3. As predicted, the Republican nominee, Thomas Dewey, took an early lead, ostensibly on his way to a substantial victory. As the day wore on and later returns came in, President Truman's upset left many of the delegates in numbed surprise. When it was clear that Truman had been reelected, Marshall scrawled a brief telegram: "Congratulations on the greatest one-man victory in American history."

That afternoon, delegates buzzed with another surprise. The American delegation had announced that Secretary of State Marshall would retire at the end of President Truman's first term.

XXXVIII

Active Duty

His recuperation was slow, too slow, he fumed. Here he was, confined to Walter Reed by his doctor when he so wanted to spend Christmas at Pinehurst. The operation on December 7 had gone well, Colonel Clifford Kimbrough reported. Kimbrough had removed the right kidney with its non-malignant cyst. Now it was up to Marshall to mend.

It would not be so easily done. "The operation had taken a lot out of him," his personal aide, Marshall Carter, recalled. Furthermore, George Marshall made a poor patient. The considerable residual pain aside, he worried more about his wife. Katherine was struggling with an attack of shingles and, moreover, she had to entertain a house guest, the charming, redoubtable Mayling Soong, Madame Chiang Kai-shek.

Madame Chiang's visit was partly personal, partly diplomatic. She and Katherine had hit it off during the months Katherine spent in China the year before. They had exchanged gifts, three brocade gowns for Katherine, an electric polisher for the "Missimo," which she promised would give her home the most highly waxed floors in all of China. Quite naturally, when Madame Chiang came to the United States, the Marshalls invited her to stay with them.

The timing was unfortunate. Here he was, confined to a hospital bed while Madame Chiang waited at Dodona Manor for an invitation to call upon the president. The invitation would not come soon, Marshall knew.

Outwardly, the United States policy toward China had not changed. Yet the Kuomintang's situation was increasingly desperate, with the Communists marching from success to success. Despite American aid of almost $2.5 billion since the end of the war, the Nationalists were in full retreat. Chiang had already selected Taiwan as a bolthole if forced to abandon the mainland.

In Washington, the last hope faded. The State Department had prepared a report to the National Security Council on October 13 noting, it "is now abundantly clear that the Chiang–Kuomintang–National Government combination lacks the political dynamism to win out." Chiang might retain power only with "all-out aid . . . [that] amounts to overt intervention," the report concluded.

Harry Truman had no intention of sending more money to the "grafters and crooks" in China who had dipped so lavishly into the American aid. "I'll bet you that a billion dollars of it is in New York banks today," the president complained to one aide.

Help for China lay beyond the reach of the man fretting in a hospital bed at Walter Reed. Although Marshall had expected to spend Christmas at Pinehurst, he was not to be discharged until a few days before the New Year. Even then, it would be a while before he used the tree pruner that the Lovetts sent as a Christmas gift.

He mended slowly. His right side remained swollen and he could take only short walks around the property at Liscombe Lodge in Pinehurst. He was in no shape to manage foreign policy. It was time to retire.

On January 2, Marshall submitted a two-paragraph letter of resignation as secretary of state to the president. In it, he thanked Truman for his complete support, adding, "I shall never forget your kindness and I submit this resignation with affectionate regard and great respect." By prearrangement, the general would formally leave State on January 20 as Harry Truman was sworn in for a second term. Marshall would have completed exactly two years as secretary of state.

Truman considered only two men to replace Marshall. The general's logical successor, Bob Lovett, was quick to decline; he intended to retire with Marshall and return to Brown Brothers Harriman. Truman just as quickly turned once more to Dean Gooderham Acheson, who only eighteen months before had resigned as undersecretary of state to pick up his law practice at Covington, Burling and Rublee.

Truman's announcement on January 7 unleashed a flood of praise for Marshall, just three weeks short of concluding forty-seven years of public service. British Foreign Secretary Ernest Bevin paid tribute to Marshall as "one of the great United States Secretaries of State, to whom the world, and especially Europe owes a great debt." In a private letter, he added, "I personally, and the British people, will not forget all that you did for victory and in your present office for peace and world recovery." In an unusual front-page editorial, the chairman of the *News-Chronicle* in London termed Marshall "among the great names of contemporary history."

Acheson sent a handwritten letter with thoughts "hard to say but which I cannot leave unsaid. . . .

To say what makes greatness in a man is very difficult. But when one is close to it, one knows. Twice in my life that has happened to me: Once with Justice Holmes and once with you. Greatness is a quality of character and is not the result of circumstances. It has to do with grandeur and with completeness of character. . . . [I] shall take comfort in thinking from time to time that if what I am doing is what you would have done, then it meets the highest and surest test I know how to apply.

Harry Truman had his own way of expressing his gratitude. Concerned about Marshall's recuperation, he made a surprise inspection, flying to Pinehurst on the morning of January 12, 1949. Marshall was resting in bed when Truman arrived, but got up and put on a dressing gown. The two men talked for almost an hour—all personal stories, the president told curious reporters—before a reassured Truman returned to the White House in time for dinner.

Within days the president had arranged for the Marshalls to fly in his plane to Puerto Rico and a vacation at the guest quarters of the naval base at San Juan. Marshall's recovery speeded; there were bad days with continued swelling in the abdominal area, but he was back on his feet, he wrote to friends. Katherine's health too improved. She had finally begun to relax, easing her attack of shingles. They felt greatly restored when they boarded the president's plane on February 6 to fly to Washington and check-ups at Walter Reed.

Harry Truman would not rest there in his support of the man he considered the greatest living American. On March 1, the Army announced that George Marshall had been restored to the active list. The move was more than ceremonial. So as to avoid having a serving officer as secretary of state, Marshall had voluntarily gone on the retired list two years earlier. Congress had made the five-star ranks lifetime appointments; those holding them were considered as continuing on active duty even when retired, thus allowing them to draw salaries larger than the normal retirement pay. On active duty again, Marshall would also continue to receive the services of an aide, a secretary, and an orderly, an office in the Pentagon, and air transportation when needed.

Marshall's retirement was to reverberate through the cabinet. A deeply troubled man given to numbing depressions, Secretary of Defense James Forrestal considered Marshall a source of support in the cabinet. Marshall also stood with Forrestal in the secretary of defense's continuous effort to curb the air force appetite for ever-increasing appropriations. Moreover, Lovett, Marshall's undersecretary and one of Forrestal's closest friends, was also leaving.

It was more than the depressed Forrestal could bear. He talked to friends about retirement, began questioning himself and questioning decisions, ever uncertain. He was coming unraveled. Though admittedly weary, he burrowed into his office as if afraid to go home at night to an empty house.

On March 2, Truman accepted Forrestal's reluctantly tendered resignation as secretary of defense. Forrestal took it as a "dismissal under fire," especially when the president replaced him with Louis Johnson. Johnson was no more than a party hack, Forrestal cursed. Once the prewar assistant secretary of war, Johnson had been the largest fund-raiser for the Democratic Party during the past campaign.

When he learned of the switch at Defense, Marshall wrote a note of encouragement to Forrestal. To Johnson, well remembered for his ambitious political maneuvering in the prewar War Department, Marshall sent along an uncharacteristic bit of unsolicited advice—a letter perhaps written at the president's request. "I think your success will be dependent on your concentration on the actual job. . . . I felt then, and still think that you would have been one of the great outstanding figures of the war years if you had confined yourself to the job."

As if he sensed just how unlike him the gratuitous advice was, Marshall concluded with a faint explanation: "I have to ask you to pardon my frankness. I am deeply interested, naturally, in the military program and I have an earnest hope that you will give the country what is so urgently needed."

Forrestal no longer could give the country anything of himself. At Lovett's suggestion, the former secretary saw a psychiatrist. Forrestal then committed himself to Bethesda Naval Hospital for "involutional melancholia," raging against Communists, Jews, and the White House aides who had poisoned the president against him.

Sometime in the early morning hours of May 22, 1949, Forrestal tied one end of the belt of his dressing gown to a radiator, the other around his neck, and jumped from an unbarred window in the psychiatric ward at the naval hospital. Marshall was an honorary pallbearer at Forrestal's funeral in Arlington National Cemetery three days later.

Formally retired, Marshall remained informally a member of the Truman administration. In the next months the White House would often call confidentially for advice on a variety of foreign affairs and military issues. Less often did he speak out publicly, and then only on significant subjects in speeches either arranged, or approved by the White House.

Thus in the midst of Senate debate over ratification of the North Atlantic treaty, Marshall pressed for its adoption. Speaking at a black-tie dinner in New York commemorating the second anniversary of his Harvard speech, Marshall coupled military with economic strength:

"A feeling of security is essential to the future of Europe and to the world. Improved economy helps tremendously to that end but in the light of conditions as they exist today that alone is not enough. The Atlantic pact is significant of the future steps that are necessary to a restored Europe."

As the administration's representative, he met with the Republicans' John Foster Dulles to answer GOP fears of the Foreign Military Assistance Act. The $1.45 billion Truman had asked Congress to vote would make NATO a military reality, Marshall stressed. (In separate meetings at the Department of State, however, Marshall expressed concern that France's growing military involvement in Vietnam would impair its ability to meet its NATO commitments. That meant that inevitably the United States would have to boost its arms shipments to France.) At the same time, Marshall's steady opposition to further aid to China compelled the China Lobby to shift its efforts from the White House to the Congress.

Retired, Marshall still made time for the troops. The former chief of staff took it upon himself to drive from Pinehurst to the hamlet of Sanford, North Carolina, to talk with the wife of an air force sergeant who lived in an isolated cabin without telephone or electricity. Her husband, Early J. Snow, stationed in Okinawa, had reenlisted with the understanding he would be transferred to a post near his home. When the transfer was held up, he had written Marshall to solicit assistance. Eight days later, Sergeant Snow was on his way home. Asked whether Marshall had spoken to the Air Force about Snow's case, a public information officer said curtly, "Draw your own conclusions."

Similarly, on a tour with Marshall later, a reporter noted that he made time in a tightly scheduled day to talk to a man with whom he had served in World War I, and to chat easily with two amputees from the second war, joking about "their common experiences."

New York Times correspondent William S. White found Marshall later that year retired "only by courtesy." From eight o'clock until noon he worked in the four acres of gardens behind the white gates of Dodona Manor. In the afternoons he read, classics often, but increasingly the memoirs of his former wartime colleagues. Once a week Sergeant George drove him to the Pentagon, where Marshall's secretary had scheduled a list of men and women who wished to meet with the general. One did not inquire about the callers' identities. "The General has very strong notions about privacy," White reported.

There were frequent telephone calls and as many as fifty letters a day, often from people needing help, some from men who had served with him in France, in Tientsin, at Fort Benning. He answered each. He took pains to help the Sergeant Snows. Many of the telephone calls reported deaths of old comrades. They were, after all, of that age, Katherine said with a sad smile for a visitor.

Even in retirement, Marshall was formidable, the usually unabashed William White acknowledged. "The general wears a dark double-breasted suit of summer worsted. His face is so clean that it seems almost to gleam. His whitening hair, every strand of it, shines from the brushes. His brown, military oxford shoes tap the turf now and then. He is the epitome of formal courtesy, but the pale blue eyes search one with a probing, speculating force and it is very hard, sitting here with this remote, great gentleman under the trees, to ask just the questions one had intended to ask."

White came away from his afternoon interview in the garden at Dodona impressed by a sense of a man "to whom duty and honor are as real as the oak trees that stand with such sure strength about him here, a man convinced that, taking all in all, he has been right. . . ."

A man of duty and honor. It was just the sort Harry Truman had in mind once more for a new assignment. The president and the general had discussed it as early as Marshall's retirement from the Army in 1945 and again during the president's flying visit to Liscombe Lodge in March. Harry Truman wanted to nominate Marshall as president of the American Red Cross.

The offer was tempting; both he and Katherine held the Red Cross in high regard. Until now, Marshall had accepted only a handful of undemanding appointments with his retirement: a directorship of Pan American Airways; a trusteeship of the American Institute of Pacific Relations; membership on the American Battle Monuments Commission, a posting his mentor, John J. Pershing, had held before him.

The Red Cross was different. That quasi-public organization, chartered by Congress but privately funded, confronted serious problems. But the Red Cross, like the YMCA and a handful of other civic organizations that had aided the Army in past wars, held a special place in Marshall's affections.

Katherine would make the decision. "She had always been an active worker in the Red Cross," Marshall explained later, "and we agreed that this seemed by far the most satisfying work by contrast with the awful burdens of the war years. To us, the appointment offered too great an opportunity and challenge to be ignored. To head the Red Cross was a great honor." Marshall accepted.

The appointment would not come until September 22, 1949, when the outgoing president, Franklin D. Roosevelt's former law partner Basil O'Connor, finally stepped aside. It was then that Marshall found an organization dominated by a handful of powerful autocrats from New York and Boston, men and women of fixed habit, used to getting their way. Volunteers in the local regions across the country felt themselves ignored, their advice unwanted; they were merely to raise money and keep quiet, many complained.

Over the next months, Marshall would put reforms in place to broaden the organization's leadership and to give regional workers a larger voice in policy making. He traveled back and forth across the country, logging 35,000 air miles in a year, speaking publicly on behalf of the Red Cross and its humanitarian efforts, working privately to overhaul its organization. Understandably, he took a special interest in expansion of the Blood Bank and the Red Cross's services to the families of servicemen and women. In the end, he not only democratized the national federation but stoked the morale of once disheartened workers.

New York Times writer Gertrude Samuels traveled with Marshall on one of his first fact-finding tours for the organization. She watched as Marshall worked to familiarize himself with the problems of local officials. "Arms folded, legs crossed, a deep crease in his left cheek as he leans back to concentrate, immaculately clean from his thinning, silver-gray hair down to his gleaming black shoes, there is something startling about his intensity, as though he were memorizing or separating ideas."

Then he would begin to talk, to ask questions about fund-raising, about sources of volunteer workers. "His voice is gentle, prodding, husky. And as he talks his whole personality seems suddenly to change. His eyes warm and sparkle, his hands become volubly expressive as he gesticulates or brings his fingertips almost together."

This was, for Marshall, important work. Told by local businessmen that the Red Cross budget was too high, that it had not shrunk with the demobilization at war's end, Marshall pointed to the 110,000 men in veterans' hospitals, "60 per cent of whom are reported to be psychoneurotic.

"That's not my idea of demobilization."

The former chief of staff was still taking care of his troops.

While Marshall told reporters that he assumed the Red Cross was to be his "last public effort," he kept a weather eye on international affairs, and the ghost that would not rest, China.

On January 21, 1949, the day Dean Acheson was sworn in as secretary of state, Chiang turned over nominal control of the Nationalist Government and moved with his gold reserves to Formosa. There he would begin the work of turning that former Japanese possession into an offshore sanctuary for his fast-dwindling Nationalist Army.

As the Department of State put it, Chiang had squandered in just four years "greater military power than any ruler had ever had in the entire history of China." In doing so, he had been reduced to the status of "a refugee on a small island off the coast of China. . . ."

Like Marshall, Washington policymakers initially watched Chiang's defeat with a mixture of resignation and concern. The fall of Formosa to Chinese Communists, however, would be "seriously unfavorable," the Joint Chiefs of Staff concluded. The Navy even proposed that the United States be prepared to take over control of the island if Chiang's regime collapsed.

As time wore on, the panic abated. On February 3, the National Security Council recommended that the United States take a wait-and-see attitude. Four years of Nationalist bureaucracy and corruption since the war had not endeared Chiang to the people of Formosa. Native Taiwanese wanted the independence of their island, a Japanese colony since the settlement of the Sino-Japanese War in 1895.

The loss of Formosa posed a threat to the security of the United States, the Joint Chiefs stated in a second position paper. The major American base on Okinawa, the balance of the Ryukyu Island chain, and the Philippines, all would be endangered. Japanese shipping lanes to the Malay Peninsula's food and raw materials could be cut.

Serious that might be. Nonetheless, the report concluded, "the current disparity between our military strength and our many global obligations makes it inadvisable to undertake the employment of armed force in Formosa. . . ." As a national security asset, the Joint Chiefs ranked Formosa well below Iceland.

The relative unimportance of Formosa did not deter the members of the China Lobby and their friends in Congress. Bipartisanship was to founder here, on the rocks of China.

Republican critics, galled by the prospect of yet another four years of Democratic administration, maintained a drumfire of invective condemning Truman's China policy. "Leftwingers" were in control of that policy, Minnesota Representative Walter Judd charged in mid-January. "Our policy in Asia, in fact if not in words, has been one of abandonment of the Chinese government."

The criticism became ever more shrill. "The loss of China"—as if China were the United States' possession to lose—somehow proved that the State Department was "permeated by Reds and leftists," in the phrase of Maine Republican Representative Robert Hale. Acheson had gone along with the heresy of appeasement, charged the Republican floor leader in the Senate, Kenneth Wherry. The secretary of state had undercut Chiang's efforts to keep even a foothold on the mainland, New Hampshire Republican Senator Styles Bridges insisted.

As Chiang's grip slipped, the search for scapegoats began. Former Ambassador to China Patrick Hurley blamed Franklin D. Roosevelt— "America's failure in China today is the result of America's surrender of principles in the secret Yalta agreement." The young Massachusetts congressman John F. Kennedy scored the State Department's old China hands, the Yalta Accords, and George Catlett Marshall for Chiang's defeat. Republican Senator Owen Brewster of Maine put the responsibility squarely on Marshall. It was he who had imposed the fatal arms embargo on Chiang.

Still, Marshall's reputation insulated him from much of the immediate criticism. One of Chiang's agents in Washington cabled Formosa on

August 24, 1949: "In the past year I have been extremely patient with Marshall, but he hasn't changed his attitude in the slightest. But I feel it is advisable to continue to refrain from attacking him as an individual in order to avoid a direct break with the administration authorities."

In a move to counter the criticism and ease the anxieties of Democrats who would face the voters the following year, Acheson ordered the preparation of a review of recent American-Chinese relations. *United States Relations with China, 1944–1949*, was a compendium of 186 government documents, cables, and reports, including the suppressed Wedemeyer report.

Acheson argued for the release of the report, insisting it would silence the "primitives." Secretary of Defense Louis Johnson, a vigorous supporter of Chiang Kai-shek, pressed just as strenuously for its suppression. Release of the report would harm Chiang's reputation, Johnson insisted in a letter to the White House. President Truman backed Acheson. In an introductory letter to this "China White Paper," Acheson laid the blame for the successive failures in that country on Chiang's government:

> The unfortunate but inescapable fact is that the ominous result of the civil war in China was beyond the control of the government of the United States. Nothing that this country did or could have done within the reasonable limits of its capabilities could have changed that result; nothing that was left undone by this country has contributed to it. It was the product of internal Chinese forces, forces which this country tried to influence but could not. A decision was arrived at with China, if only a decision by default.

A man given to disciplined logic, Acheson had underestimated his critics. The 1,054-page White Paper only fired the China Lobby to harsher accusation. As the secretary ruefully put it, "The conclusion of the summary was unpalatable to believers in American omnipotence, to whom every goal unattained is explicable only by incompetence or treason."

Although his name occasionally figured in news accounts, Marshall remained aloof from the partisan battles bucketing about Washington. Instead, in the weeks immediately following the release of the White Paper, he vacationed with Katherine and Madame Chiang in the Adirondacks on the former estate of financier J. P. Morgan. Madame Chiang assured the press hers was a purely social visit. Years later she would remind Marshall of "the lovely leisurely life at Racquette Lake, the soft lapping waves on the side of the rowboat, and . . . the cool evenings in front of the roaring fires in the lounge, and best of all, the absence of 'musts.' No must to see people, no must to make speeches, no must to

smile when my facial muscles ache, and no must to race against time."
She would repay the Marshalls' hospitality by inviting them to dinner at
her New York City apartment before they saw the new hit musical *South
Pacific* the following month.

Meanwhile, Nationalist China failed. On October 1, 1949, Mao Tse-
tung proclaimed the People's Republic of China. Mao would serve as
chairman of the all-powerful central committee. The suave Chou En-lai
would double as premier and foreign minister.

Nine weeks later, Chiang extricated the remaining 300,000 Nationalist
troops from the mainland to his sanctuary on Formosa. From there,
Chiang proclaimed hollow defiance, promising to invade the mainland
and reclaim his rightful heritage. His strident supporters in the United
States demanded that the Truman administration provide the military
means, including American naval and air support if needed.

Acheson's "primitives" were to grow even more vociferous.

The United States in these early months of 1950 was sorely troubled,
a nation for the first time questioning itself and its newly preeminent
position in the world. On January 21, the president of the Carnegie
Endowment for International Peace, Alger Hiss, was convicted of per-
jury before a federal grand jury when he denied he had passed classified
documents to the Russians prior to 1937. Four days later, Acheson publicly reiterated his friendship with Hiss, a colleague in the prewar State
Department. "I do not intend to turn my back on Alger Hiss," he
announced. In effect, the secretary of state appeared to be supporting a
convicted Russian spy.

On February 3, Klaus Fuchs, a German-born physicist who had worked
on the atomic bomb in Great Britain, confessed in London he had passed
to the Soviet Union nuclear weapons information from the Manhattan
Project.

Less than a week later, the junior senator from Wisconsin, Joseph
McCarthy, gave a Lincoln Day speech before the Ohio County Republican Women's Club of Wheeling, West Virginia. McCarthy charged that
205 members of the Communist Party known to the secretary of state
"nevertheless are still working and shaping policy in the State Department." In effect, McCarthy was accusing Acheson of treason.

How else to explain the steady succession of Communist successes,
McCarthy asked in yet another forum, "unless we believe that men high
in this government are concerting to deliver us to disaster? This must be
the product of a great conspiracy on a scale so immense as to dwarf any
previous venture in the history of man."

The kindest estimate of Acheson, the senator told an April meeting of
the American Society of Newspaper Editors, "is that he is completely
incompetent."

If others ignored Marshall's former influence, the less restrained

McCarthy did not. It was "a pathetic thing" to give Marshall the State Department, the senator told the assembled editors. Marshall had been a great general, but he was "completely unfitted for the job" of secretary of state.

To many Americans, McCarthy's charges explained the otherwise unfathomable. The Republican right wing took up McCarthy's tarbrush. Acheson was nothing less than a "bad security risk," stormed Senator Kenneth Wherry of Nebraska. Would-be GOP presidential candidate Senator Robert Taft charged the Democrats were ignoring a "pro-communist group in the State Department who surrendered to every demand at Yalta and Potsdam and promoted at every opportunity the communist cause in China."

Word of spies, of deceit, only proved what many Americans suspected, that the Soviet Union was not to be trusted. But that threat could be managed, somehow contained. Spies, after all, could be rooted out by the FBI.

In the autumn of 1949, Americans suddenly confronted a Soviet threat far more fearful, far more threatening than a turncoat scientist. B-29s sampling the atmosphere on August 29 had picked up traces of radioactive dust in air samples. The Russians had detonated "Pumpkin," a plutonium bomb of advanced design, one similar to the weapon that had destroyed Nagasaki. The United States' monopoly on the atomic bomb had ended.

Word of the first radioactive air samples came as a shock to the small handful informed. Just a year before, a secret report to the president had estimated the Russians would not have a nuclear weapon until 1953, and Major General Leslie Groves, the strawboss on the Manhattan Project, publicly insisted the backward Soviet Union would not produce a bomb for at least fifteen years. They had miscalculated.

On September 23, 1949, President Truman stunned the nation with a terse announcement: "We have evidence that within recent weeks an atomic explosion occurred in the Soviet Union." The world would never be the same, and Americans never quite so secure as they had been. To the cabinet, Truman announced privately, "We are in a straight race with the Russians."

This would be an arms race of global scale. Four days after Truman's announcement of a Soviet nuclear weapon, Congress passed with large majorities the $1.3 billion Foreign Military Assistance Act that would transform NATO into a true military force. Even so, that military power was less important as an actual defense than as a psychological bulwark. Signaling the United States' commitment to western Europe, Truman prevailed upon a restive Dwight Eisenhower to resign as president of Columbia University and return to uniform as NATO's first commander.

The president was to take additional steps in coming months to implement his rearmament program.

The realization that the USSR had the atomic bomb impelled Truman to convene a small committee to weigh building a super bomb, one many times more powerful than the Hiroshima or Nagasaki weapons. Conceived in the midst of the Manhattan Project, the concept of a thermonuclear or hydrogen bomb had not advanced beyond theoretical studies. Actual development had been postponed in favor of amassing a large inventory of improved uranium and plutonium bombs.

All that was changed. Suddenly, the hydrogen bomb appeared "to have caught the imagination, both of congressional and of military people, as *the answer* to the problem posed by the Russian advance," grumbled nuclear physicist J. Robert Oppenheimer.

On March 10, 1950, Truman approved a crash program to develop the hydrogen bomb. In fact, the United States trailed at the outset of the race; five months earlier the Soviets had begun their own pursuit of a thermonuclear weapon.

This pell-mell rush to rearm vexed Marshall. "We should not place complete dependence on military and material power," he warned in a Memorial Day address from beside the Tomb of the Unknown Soldier at Arlington National Cemetery. "War is no longer just an evil. In this age it seems intolerable. . . . The victorious power will stand amidst its own ruins." He urged instead support of the United Nations, "where words can be used instead of bullets."

In less than three weeks, the United States would turn to the United Nations, seeking to use bullets in Korea rather than words.

CHAPTER

XXXIX

Positions Reversed

Harry Truman was angry, Missouri-spitting-mad angry. After five and a half years of working for peace, the United States found itself once more at war, he seethed. The fighting in Korea was not going well and his difficult secretary of defense was more obstacle than aid. Between Louis Johnson and that "play actor and bunco man" MacArthur, Harry S. Truman had major problems.

War had come suddenly, forewarned by intelligence sources, but unexpected for all that. The president had been vacationing at the family home in Independence, Missouri, when Deputy Secretary of State Dean Rusk called on the evening of Saturday, June 24, 1950. "Mr. President, I have very serious news. The North Koreans have invaded South Korea."

Rusk had only a few details. Led by tanks, 90,000 soldiers in the North Korean People's Army had crossed the 38th parallel dividing the peninsula into northern and southern halves. Members of the American Military Advisory Group reported their Republic of Korea troops had caved in and were retreating.

Returning to Washington aboard the *Independence* the following afternoon, that well-read student of history Harry Truman pondered the implications of the North Korean invasion of the South. The invasion of Korea reminded him of earlier attacks by totalitarian nations on Manchuria, on Ethiopia, on Austria. There the democracies had failed to act; the result had been World War II. Harry Truman "felt certain that if South Korea was allowed to fall, Communist leaders would be emboldened to override nations closer to our own shores."

Peculiarly, South Korea was more the property of its northern invaders than its American sponsors. To facilitate the Japanese surrender in 1945, then Colonel Dean Rusk had arbitrarily divided that vassal state at the 38th parallel. The United States would take the Japanese surrender in the South, the Soviet Union in the North. The division was to be temporary, until a joint trusteeship could be established and elections held.

Until this moment, Washington had nurtured only a nominal interest in South Korea. The South was not capable of being self-supporting, A. C. Wedemeyer had reported after a brief 1947 inspection on the way home from China. So long as the United States accepted responsibility for South Korea, the annual relief bill would be "substantially greater" than the proposed $137 million approved in 1948, he predicted.

At the same time, Truman's military advisers agreed that Korea was of no strategic importance to the United States. Wary of the costs of maintaining occupation troops, then Secretary of War Robert Patterson urged in May 1947 that the 50,000 Americans in that country be withdrawn. Marshall as secretary of state had considered Korea of some value, in a political sense, but only "if we can afford it, and find it possible to maintain it."

Marshall then recommended setting the two Koreas on the way to democracy by holding separate elections under United Nations supervision. In April 1948, voters in the South selected an arch-conservative Nationalist, the missionary-educated Syngman Rhee, as president of a Republic of Korea. By June 1949, the United States had withdrawn all but a 500-member military advisory group to train the fledgling South Korean Army.

North Korea followed suit with the election of a former guerrilla and former officer in the Red Army, Kim Il Sung, as first premier of the People's Republic of Korea. The Soviet Army too pulled out, but left behind a North Korean army George Marshall's State Department feared was far stronger than the South Korean.

Once Marshall retired from the Department of State at the beginning of 1949, only Rusk, by then a deputy secretary of state, thought Korea worth defending. In early 1949, MacArthur had publicly drawn America's defense line in the Far East as running from the Philippines north to Okinawa, on to the Japanese home islands, then north to Aleutians. Korea lay beyond the pale. The Joint Chiefs of Staff concurred. "The U.S. has little strategic interest in maintaining its present troops and bases in Korea." The National Security Council had recommended withdrawal in March 1949. As recently as January 1950, Secretary of State Dean Acheson told a National Press Club audience that neither South Korea nor Taiwan fell within the American defense perimeter.

Now, aboard the *Independence* flying over the Ohio River Valley, Harry Truman junked that wisdom. The Communists under Premier Kim Il Sung had invaded hapless South Korea. Truman was determined there would be no appeasement, no repetition of 1931, 1935, and 1938. The aggressor had to be stopped.

By Sunday night, the American military mission in Korea had provided a reasonably clear picture of the fighting. Led by Soviet-built T-34 tanks—the head of the American mission had earlier dismissed Korea as unfit for tank warfare—six columns of North Korean regulars and two amphibious units had knifed deep into the South. The inept Republic of Korea (ROK) Army was in retreat or routed. In Tokyo, the surprised supreme allied commander, Douglas MacArthur, airily dismissed it as a border incident, probably no more than a reconnaissance in force. "If Washington only will not hobble me I can handle it with one arm tied behind my back," he assured the visiting John Foster Dulles.

There was no doubt that the United States would intervene. An intelligence report furnished Rusk on the day after the invasion concluded: "The North Korean government is completely under Kremlin control and there is no possibility that the North Koreans acted without prior instruction from Moscow. The move against South Korea must therefore be considered a Soviet move."

At Lake Success, New York, the United Nations Security Council voted 9–0 to adopt an American-sponsored resolution fixing blame for the attack upon the North Koreans. The resolution also called for an immediate end to hostilities and the withdrawal of the invaders. The Soviets, boycotting the Security Council in protest of its failure to seat Red China in Chiang's stead, lost an opportunity to veto the condemnation. For what it was worth, international opinion now rested on the side of South Korea.

In meetings at Blair House over the next five days, President Truman approved orders committing American troops to defend South Korea. The White House also drafted a UN resolution that would commit member nations to eventually provide military units for an army under Douglas MacArthur's command. Throughout the immediate crisis, Truman frequently cautioned that United States military assistance was to be confined to South Korea, to the area below the 38th parallel.

Despite the introduction of American troops ferried from Japan, the situation in South Korea worsened. Ill-trained and out of shape, the American occupation troops fell in alongside the ROKs. Together, they retreated to a defensive perimeter set up at the toe of the peninsula centering on the port city of Pusan. On July 26, the commander of the retreating forces, Major General Walton Walker, issued a stand-or-die order; there would, there could be no further retreat.

With his battered troops penned in the stiffening Pusan Perimeter, Douglas MacArthur conceived his most brilliant military operation. Like some stumbling, bleeding prelim fighter, he had one last punch to throw— a wild, unexpected left hook to the head. One punch, and he was to turn the fight around.

In Washington, Harry Truman was seeking a similar political victory. Late in August 1950, the president ordered the White House opera-

tors—famous for their ability to track down people even far from telephones—to find the vacationing George Marshall on the shore of Lake
Superior. To Marshall, who had spent two weeks at Huron Mountain,
Michigan, fishing with Katherine, the messenger said only there was a
call waiting at the country store just down the road.

Over the pay phone, the store's studiously disinterested hangers-on
within earshot, Marshall tersely accepted yet another call to duty from
his president.

When he returned to Washington in two weeks, would he please come
by the White House, Harry Truman asked; there was something he
wanted to discuss with the general. He need say little more. Marshall
understood that Truman would ask him to return to the cabinet as secretary of defense.

Marshall was to accept, with some reluctance, though surely not without some sense of fitness, of coming full circle. After all, he could claim
to have been one of the major boosters, even fathers, of the unified
Department of Defense. It was somehow appropriate that he should be
asked to become the third man to head that department.

The concept of a single defense establishment had skittered about
Washington since the end of World War I. Though it made administrative sense, opposition from each of the prerogative-conscious services
had blocked serious consideration of the proposal. Competition for scarce
dollars in those years between the wars had prevented even a suggestion
of cooperation by beleaguered generals and admirals.

As army chief of staff, George Marshall had early on come to the conclusion that unification of the armed services into a single department
was desirable. Beginning in 1941, he periodically discussed the subject
with an unconvinced Ernest King before eventually bringing a unification proposal to the Joint Chiefs of Staff in May 1944. Fearful they might
lose control of the fleet's air arm and the Marine Corps, Admiral King
and his staff dug in their heels. In April 1945, over King's objection, a
special study group reporting to the Joint Chiefs of Staff nonetheless
recommended establishment of a single Department of National Defense.

Marshall in the next years was to be the leading advocate for unification. By May 1945, he had decided a single civilian secretary should replace
the secretaries of war and navy in the cabinet. He also wanted a strong
chairman to head the Joint Chiefs, thus discarding the collegial panel of
co-equals he had himself proposed in 1942. A single authority was necessary, Marshall testified before the Senate Committee on Military Affairs
two months after VJ-Day. The coming of peace made it extremely difficult to maintain the voluntary cooperation of the services. "With the end
of the war there is no longer a compelling necessity to reach at least
compromise agreements on major matters."

In addition to unification of the armed services, Marshall spoke out in favor of better intelligence coordination between the services. He advocated creation of a central intelligence agency in which the War, Navy, and State Departments would pool their information. "We should know as much as possible about the intent, as well as the military capabilities, of every country in the world. We must know the facts for our defense," he told the senators.

Marshall, the singular authority on matters military in Washington, easily impressed President Truman with the need for a Department of National Defense. (Truman, who still complained about the waste of duplicative procurement programs during the war, probably needed little convincing.) Still unification languished, blocked by navy influence in Congress. To break the impasse, at the end of 1945 Marshall recommended compromise with the Navy's stubborn insistence that the collegial Joint Chiefs be retained. It would mean giving up the idea of a single, powerful chairman, but Marshall urged, "Let us take the half loaf. It is my belief experience will ultimately give us the whole loaf."

It was still not enough. For more than a year, unification bills lay pigeonholed in congressional committee. Not until early 1947 did Truman press the Joint Chiefs and the rival military services to come up with a new bill. Marshall, by then secretary of state, played only a small role in passage of the omnibus National Security Act.

Marshall had one major criticism of the legislation: the proposed Central Intelligence Agency's powers "seemed almost limitless." Later he objected to putting direction of covert spy operations within the State Department; their inevitable discovery would damage State's reputation, he argued. He was not opposed to covert operations in themselves; indeed, he intended to have some control over them, and would eventually pick the first director of the euphemistically named Office of Policy Coordination to manage those "black" affairs, Eisenhower's former chief of staff, Walter Bedell Smith.

The half loaf of a National Security Act creating a single defense agency and a separate Central Intelligence Agency was finally signed into law on July 26, 1947. To reassure unyielding navy diehards, Truman appointed Secretary of the Navy James Forrestal as the first secretary of defense. Forrestal would serve until March 1949, when his dark furies overcame him and he was replaced by Louis Johnson.

Harry Truman would soon come to regret the Johnson appointment. The new secretary was a tough-minded lawyer and businessman who expected his orders to be executed without question. In short order he had alienated the prickly admirals by redlining money for a new supercarrier, the USS *United States,* in favor of appropriations for an untested air force bomber. With that single stroke Johnson took from the Navy its pride of place as the nation's first line of defense.

The resultant "Revolt of the Admirals" broke out in hearings before the House Appropriations Committee. Johnson raged as a parade of bemedaled admirals assailed the Pentagon budget, the bomber decision, and the secretary himself. A number of senior navy officers would see their careers summarily snuffed out in succeeding months, but, martyred, they won their point. Swallowing his pride, Truman bowed to congressional pressure and restored the supercarrier to the budget.

Johnson's behavior grew increasingly erratic in succeeding months. The secretary, ever ambitious and ever argumentative, careened about the capital, meddling in policy. Infatuated with bombers, Johnson argued publicly for preemptive first strikes and "preventative wars," pushing the Air Force's newly minted doctrine. Without consulting the White House, he authorized his secretary of the navy to give a public speech advocating that the United States become "the first aggressors for peace." United Nations allies, who had contributed troops to fight in Korea, worried about Johnson's seeming appetite for warfare.

When the State Department protested, Johnson complained of "the political domination of Defense in many ways by State." Johnson disrupted policy planning by barring military officers from dealing with planners from the State Department. He fumed about the White House influence of the contemptuous Dean Acheson—who privately dismissed Johnson as mentally ill. The chairman of the Joint Chiefs of Staff, Omar Bradley, came to agree with Acheson—"Unwittingly, Truman had replaced one mental case with another." Johnson had to go, Truman concluded.

On July 2, the war in Korea but a week old, the president and his daughter Margaret had motored across the Potomac to George Marshall's home in Leesburg. The two men talked privately, Truman explaining his problem with Johnson, Marshall assuring the president he was content in his retirement. However, Marshall added, he was a soldier. If his president called him back into service as secretary of defense, he would do his duty—at least for a limited time.

Truman explained that he was not ready to fire Johnson, but he did want Marshall to think about coming back to Washington. There they had left it.

The retired general did not want to return to Washington, he admitted to his goddaughter, Rose Page Wilson, "but when the President comes down and sits under our oaks and tells me of his difficulties, he has me at a disadvantage. . . ."

Marshall agreed to interrupt his retirement after Johnson precipitated yet another crisis. The White House learned that *U.S. News and World Report* was to reprint from an advance text a carping letter Douglas MacArthur had sent to the Veterans of Foreign Wars encampment. MacArthur's letter criticized administration policy in the Far East, in particular what he described as the timidity about Taiwan. "Nothing could be more fallacious than the threadbare argument by those who advocate appeasement and defeatism in the Pacific that if we defend Formosa we alienate continental Asia."

It was a strawman argument. Elements of the Seventh Fleet were patrolling the Strait of Formosa. As Acheson put it, "We *were* defending Formosa. . . . This seemed a very gratuitous crack at what had been the policies of the administration before the Korean War."

Truman personally instructed Johnson to order MacArthur to withdraw the letter. Suddenly indecisive, Johnson returned to the Pentagon, demurring, trying to find a way around the president's order. That afternoon, Truman dictated to Johnson the explicit message he wanted sent to MacArthur.

Still Johnson bridled. It would embarrass the president if he sent it, Johnson argued with Acheson, with Harriman, with anyone who might listen. MacArthur might even resign.

Truman placed his call to the Upper Peninsula of Michigan and the vacationing George Marshall. On September 6, the general visited the president at Blair House, across the street from a White House then undergoing substantial renovation. Johnson had to go, Truman told Marshall. And quickly.

"Mr. President, you have only to tell me what you want, and I'll do it. But I want you to think about the fact that my appointment may reflect upon you and your administration." The Hearst press, McCormick's *Chicago Tribune,* Roy Howard's string of newspapers, "they are still charging me with the downfall of Chiang's government in China. I want to help, not to hurt you."

Reporting the conversation in a letter to his wife, Truman added, "Can you think of anyone else saying that? I can't, and he's one of the *great.*" Marshall's appointment could not possibly hurt him, Truman stressed.

The following day Truman dispatched sometime ambassador-turned-troubleshooter Averell Harriman to brief Marshall in Leesburg. Harriman reported, "Wonder of wonders, Mrs. Marshall is for it!"

That last obstacle removed, Harry Truman asked a stricken Johnson for his letter of resignation. In tears, Johnson signed it, protesting to the end, "I didn't think you'd make me do it."

Marshall's confirmation would not be automatic. For one thing, the 1947 act creating the Department of Defense had stipulated the secretary not have served in the military in the previous ten years. As a five-star general, Marshall was still on active duty. That meant amending the law to remove this legal barrier, before his nomination was actually acted upon. Despite Marshall's reputation, there was some principled resistance among legislators to "the camel getting his nose under the tent," as California's Republican Senator William Knowland put it.

Greater trouble stemmed from an increasingly vociferous group of

Republican senators who had found militant anti-communism an effective club in this election year. Republicans sensitive to the China issue
chimed in, claiming Marshall's efforts in 1946 to bring about a truce
favored the Communists and undermined Chiang. Senator Joseph
McCarthy growled, "It should be remembered that as a diplomat Marshall did much to lose the war which as a soldier he had done so much
to win.

"Marshall," McCarthy told reporters, "should not be confirmed unless
and until he convinces the Senate that he has learned the facts of life
about communism, and that he will listen to MacArthur's advice rather
than Acheson's advice on the Far East."

McCarthy was not alone in his strident opposition to Marshall. During
the debate to amend the National Security Act, William E. Jenner,
Republican of Indiana, delivered a shrill, hour-long attack on the nom-
inee, on Secretary of State Dean Acheson ("the Communist-appeasing,
Communist-protecting betrayer of America"), and the United States' failed
China policy.

Jenner, facing reelection in 1952, raged against the Truman administration's "bloody tracks of treason." Marshall's nomination was Truman's newest "staggering swindle." Then, in a fury, Jenner shouted:
"General Marshall is not only willing, he is eager to play the role of a
front man, for traitors. The truth is this is no new role for him, for
General George C. Marshall is a living lie. . . ." In full cry, Jenner refused
to yield the floor to red-faced Democrat Scott Lucas, a longtime friend
of Marshall.

Jenner rumbled on. "It is tragic . . . that George Marshall is not enough
of a patriot to tell the American people the truth of what has happened,
and the terrifying story of what lies in store for us, instead of joining
hands once more with this criminal crowd of traitors and Communist
appeasers who, under the continuing influence and direction of Mr.
Truman and Mr. Acheson, are still selling America down the river."

Through Jenner's screed the Senate sat silent. When he finally concluded, Massachusetts Republican Leverett Saltonstall bolted to his feet.
Shaking, struggling to maintain his self-control, the courtly Saltonstall
restored what dignity he could to his house, his party, and the nominee.
"If there is any man whose public life has been above censure . . . it is
George C. Marshall. I wish I had the vocabulary to answer the statement
that the life of George Marshall is a lie because if ever there was a life
spent in the interest of our country, a life that is not a lie, it is the life of
George C. Marshall."

Informed later that day of Jenner's attack, Marshall said archly, "Jenner? Jenner? I do not believe I know the man."

The votes to amend the National Security Act to permit a military man to become secretary of defense were 220–105 in the House, and 47–21 in the Senate. Republicans furnished 20 of the nay votes in the upper House, 101 of the negative votes in the House of Representatives. The career of George Marshall, despite a lifetime of studied non-partisanship, had been twisted by politics and polemics into a partisan issue.

His nomination finally confirmed five days later by a Senate vote of 57–11, George Marshall returned to the E-ring of the Pentagon. He moved directly into the secretary's office, not bothering to change the furnishings, sitting down at Henry Stimson's old desk and promptly going to work.

Freed of the troublesome Louis Johnson, Chairman of the Joint Chiefs of Staff Omar Bradley breathed easier and welcomed his old boss from Fort Benning days. Secretary of State Dean Acheson was both pleased and somewhat embarrassed, for Marshall, senior in service, still insisted upon deferring in matters of protocol to Acheson, who now held the higher cabinet rank. Acheson found it a "harrowing experience" to have "his revered and beloved former chief" insist that Acheson enter rooms first, always stand or sit at the right, and be seated first.

Marshall's return immediately restored comity between State and Defense. Gone was Johnson with his anger and contumely. From their first meeting with the Joint Chiefs in the Pentagon's tightly guarded Map Room, Marshall sat alongside Acheson, across from the five military men facing them, a civilian. Despite his own five-star rank, Marshall was punctilious in leaving military decisions to the Joint Chiefs. He was no longer a soldier, but the civilian head of the massive defense establishment. Awash in this sudden amity, Acheson and Bradley even agreed to ban the phrases "from a purely military point of view" and "from a purely political or diplomatic point of view."

Marshall, who disliked the extended entourages of some officeholders, brought with him only his personal aide, Marshall Carter, when he picked up the Defense portfolio. The new secretary did want Robert Lovett again as his second, but hesitated to call once more. Lovett had been with Brown Brothers Harriman for just eighteen months, Marshall explained to Acheson, who was a good friend of Harriman's. Marshall debated with himself, then, at Acheson's prompting, called Lovett one morning at seven-thirty to ask him to return to Washington. Two days later, Lovett, who had repeatedly turned down Acheson's earlier offers to nominate him as ambassador to Great Britain, was at the Pentagon. The new deputy secretary of defense wryly acknowledged to friends, "There are two persons to whom I cannot say no: my wife and General Marshall."

Marshall's second appointment, assistant secretary of defense for manpower, was more controversial. It was, as Lovett put it, either a stroke of genius or the biggest mistake of his career. It was also indicative of Marshall's intention to find the best people possible, and to run Defense without regard to party.

Anna M. Rosenberg was as liberal in philosophy as Marshall and Lovett were conservative. Moreover, she was a Jew and a woman, an unrepentant New Dealer, not characteristics likely to endear her to a Congress in its current illiberal mood. Then forty-nine, small in stature, she was a smartly dressed torrent of energy. She had grown up in New York City, the daughter of a Hungarian immigrant; Rosenberg made her way into the new field of industrial relations, then branched out into the equally new business of public relations.

Her client list was impressive, but even more so was the woman herself. Marshall Carter recalled her with affection: "She was a great mediator. She had the happy faculty of understanding a problem before the people had expounded on what it was, and zeroed in on solutions. Most everybody who worked for her thought she walked on water."

Rosenberg had served in a succession of New Deal appointments, including the wartime War Manpower Commission. Both Roosevelt and Truman had sent her to Europe to look into military manpower problems. In the years since, she had been one of the few to endorse universal military training, a program Marshall steadily advocated, a program Congress and the public stridently opposed.

Rosenberg's confirmation by the Senate Armed Services Committee would become one of the uglier little episodes of the McCarthy era. Mistaken for another Anna Rosenberg, she would have to repeatedly attempt to prove that she had not been a member of the Communist Party during the 1930s. Anti-Semites leaped in. Then a number of doctors, obviously angry at Rosenberg's support for a national health insurance plan proposed by Truman two years earlier, saw fit to challenge her qualifications in letters to the committee.

Marshall ignored the critics. His decision made, he would not back down before the primitives. He called in chits. Eisenhower and Bedell Smith, who had worked with Rosenberg in 1944, wrote the committee in her support. James Byrnes and Bernard Baruch, both South Carolinians, weighed in on her behalf in conversations with Georgian Richard Russell, chairman of the committee.

Marshall, who avoided partisanship, had learned to play politics. In the end he won, just as he expected; the Senate voted her confirmation.

With this new team heading Defense, lingering problems found solutions. A Japanese peace treaty drafted by John Foster Dulles, then crippled by Johnson's cavils, got new life as Marshall endorsed Dulles's original draft. Marshall even overruled objections by the Joint Chiefs in order to conclude a treaty.

Marshall's prestige gave blessing to Acheson in negotiations with the French over the fledgling North Atlantic Treaty Organization. Thrice invaded in less than a century, France opposed German rearmament. Marshall quietly, persistently argued that without Germany, neither France alone nor NATO could prevent a fourth invasion. Eventually Marshall and Acheson would prevail.

If friendly persuasion failed, Marshall was capable of firmness. When Philippine President Elridio Quirino refused to fire two corrupt generals, Marshall bluntly told him that American military aid would be cut off. The generals were sent packing and the aid continued.

Most of Marshall's time as secretary, however, would be spent on the condition of the armed services. Successive tight budgets, then the unexpected war in Korea had left "the military situation worse than it had been in 1942," he told a reporter.

Marshall himself might have been responsible for that woeful state, wrote one critic, retired Admiral Arthur W. Radford, an advocate of major increases in military appropriations.

Truman had allowed the nation's defense posture to decline "to the dangerous point it reached in June, 1950," but Radford blamed Marshall, "in that he did not pay particular attention to the status of our forces." Busy with other responsibilities, Marshall had sought only universal military training in building a permanent defense establishment. "In the years when General Marshall might have tried to convince the president that our military strength was so dangerously low that it might invite attack, he elected not to do so."

If any of the blame was Marshall's, he would do much to remedy that in the next year by implementing a new policy, one that transformed George Kennan's concept of political containment into military dictum.

The new policy had been drafted for the National Security Council in April 1950, by yet another Wall Street banker who had come to Washington in the war years. Paul Nitze, the new director of the State Department's Policy Planning Staff, was an ardent anti-Communist, military-minded where his close friend and predecessor George Kennan was diplomatically oriented. Acheson turned to the tough-minded Nitze in the wake of the loss of China and the Soviet A-bomb explosion, instructing him to draft an overall review of American foreign and defense policies.

The result was NSC-68. This was the first unified military and diplomatic policy, intended "to wrest the initiative from the Soviet Union, confront it with convincing evidence of the determination and ability of the free world to frustrate the Kremlin design of a world dominated by its will."

Under NSC-68, the United States would meet force with force. Nitze, who recalled 1940 and the frantic attempt to build an air force, wanted no repetition. Thus NSC-68 called for the West to be armed and at the ready around the world. "A defeat of free institutions anywhere is a defeat everywhere," Nitze wrote.

NSC-68 advocated a massive "military shield behind which the free world can work to frustrate the Kremlin design." Cost estimates ran between $35 and $40 billion per year, a threefold increase in defense appropriations.

Intent to that moment on cutting the Pentagon budget, Louis Johnson had exploded in rage when NSC-68 was first discussed in March 1950. That placed Omar Bradley and the Joint Chiefs in the "rare, awkward and ironic situation" in which the quartet of military chiefs harmonized better with the secretary of state than the secretary of defense.

Six months later, Marshall must have experienced a sense of déjà vu. As a young officer he had studied American unpreparedness before the Spanish-American War. He had worried through the year-long build-up of Pershing's army while the fate of the Allies hung in the balance. He had presided over the largest peacetime military expansion in the nation's history, knowing all the while too little was coming too late. A decade later he once more confronted the issue of adequate military preparation in peacetime.

"The history of national defense in this country has been a succession of feasts and famines that have followed each other in demoralizing sequence," Marshall reminded Congress. "For a nation that prides itself on its logic, business precocity and its practical sense, we have given the world quite an opposite impression of these qualities when it came to the matter of national defense. Speaking frankly, I fear that we have given a demonstration somewhat of emotional instability."

Sound policy, NSC-68, would put an end to that, and create a large, permanent military establishment. In the next weeks Marshall worked to persuade the president to abandon his budget-cutting stance in favor of major military appropriations. Marshall proposed that over the next four years the military grow from 1.5 million to 3.2 million men and women in uniform.

Three months earlier, the budget-conscious Louis Johnson had only grudgingly approved 1952 goals of 10 army divisions, 281 navy warships, and 58 air wings. Under the admonition of NSC-68 and the prodding of George Marshall, those goals were revised upward to include 18 divisions, 397 combat ships, and 95 air wings.

What Averell Harriman called "a sour little war in Korea" had made a massive permanent defense establishment not only possible but imperative.

C H A P T E R

XL

Imperator

It would be a disaster or a miracle, a five-dollar bet to win $50,000, as he put it. His Eighth Army pressed into the Pusan Perimeter, General of the Army Douglas MacArthur threw the roundhouse punch that could turn the battle in his favor.

MacArthur's plan, Operation CHROMITE, was to land two hastily assembled divisions, the Marine 1st and the scratch 7th Infantry, near Seoul, well behind the advancing North Korean lines. The two divisions were to capture Seoul and its transportation hub, cutting the North Korean supply lines. At the same time, the troops pinned within the Pusan Perimeter were to force their way out, pressing the North Korean Army into a trap well below the 38th parallel.

MacArthur could not have picked a worse spot to land, one reason perhaps why the port was so lightly guarded. There were no beaches. The 32-foot tides at Inchon were among the worst in the world, at ebb exposing two miles or more of malodorous mudflats, at flood pounding against 12- to 16-foot-high sea walls. The troops would be landing not in open ground, but in a city that offered dozens of easily defended strongpoints.

Deliberately keeping details of his plans from the dubious Joint Chiefs in Washington, MacArthur sent the Marines ashore on September 15. Three days later the patchwork 7th landed. The two divisions forced their way into Seoul, eighteen miles inland, then began rolling up scattered North Korean resistance.

The North Koreans held their ground on the Pusan Perimeter, seemingly unaware of their peril. For a week the American and South Korean troops hammered at their encircling tormentors, finally breaking a hole through the ring on September 22. The once trapped Americans and ROKs poured through the breach, racing north and west to link with the Inchon beachhead.

"The swiftness and magnitude of the victory were mind-boggling," the chairman of the Joint Chiefs, Omar Bradley, later wrote. In a single stroke, MacArthur had turned defeat to victory, and reaffirmed his reputation as a military genius.

MacArthur's success posed the first problem for newly confirmed Secretary of Defense George Marshall. Just how far should they permit MacArthur to pursue the shattered North Korean Army? To that moment, official policy had been to halt at the 38th parallel, restoring the *status quo ante bellum*. That had been the ostensible purpose for which the United States was fighting.

To go beyond the parallel might be risky. Chip Bohlen and George Kennan, the department's two foremost Soviet experts, and Paul Nitze, chairman of the Policy Planning Staff, privately cautioned that the Kremlin would not permit a hostile regime in North Korea. Furthermore, they warned, any fighting close to the Sino-Korean border could bring the threatened Chinese Communists into the fight. The United States might find itself drawn into a land war in Asia.

But victory bred an appetite. California's William Knowland, so vigorous a member of the China Lobby that newsmen had dubbed him "the Senator from Formosa," thundered that to stop now would be appeasement. The former chairman of the Republican Party, Pennsylvania Representative Hugh Scott, Jr., charged the State Department intended to "cringe behind the 38th parallel." The GOP was certain to make capital of any failure by the Truman administration to press the victory home, conservative columnist David O. Lawrence concluded. The hounds were away and baying. "There's no stopping MacArthur now," Secretary of State Dean Acheson told his troubleshooter, Averell Harriman.

Harriman could only agree. "It would have taken a superhuman effort to say no. Psychologically, it was almost impossible not to go ahead and complete the job," he said later.

Acheson and Dean Rusk, the head of State's Far East desk, wanted to press northward. The 38th parallel had no political validity, insisted Rusk, the man who had drawn it in 1945. At the same time, MacArthur and the Joint Chiefs agreed that to prevent another invasion of the South, MacArthur would have to destroy the North Korean Army wherever it fled and even occupy North Korea.

The cautions of Bohlen, Kennan, and Nitze were overwhelmed by more aggressive men. The strong-willed president of South Korea, Syngman Rhee, notified Harry Truman that he would not be bound by any settlement that left Korea divided. Rhee implied his ROK troops would fight on, even if the Americans stopped at the parallel.

A National Security Council paper, NSC-81, attempted to meld the cautious and the bold. The document recommended unification of the two Koreas by election—if this could be done without bringing the Chinese or Soviets into play. While it contained no reference to stopping at the parallel, it required MacArthur to secure White House approval for operations north of that line. The densely worded document permitted MacArthur to cross the parallel, but instructed him to use only South Korean troops once he approached the border with China. Should his forces meet "major" Soviet or Chinese units, he was to break off contact immediately.

NSC-81 was all very artfully crafted. Too much so, one of the drafters, C. B. Marshall, said later. "I was full of awareness that we were kidding ourselves with the neatness of the phrasing." Approved by the president on September 11, NSC-81 formally shifted American war aims from preserving South Korea to destroying North Korea's warmaking potential and unifying the peninsula into a single nation.

There were two major snags in implementing that policy: China and MacArthur.

As the chairman of the Joint Chiefs later put it, they had "committed one cardinal sin. We seriously misjudged Chinese Communist reaction to our plans to cross the Thirty-eighth Parallel." MacArthur and the chiefs had ignored the recent quadrupling of Chinese troops in nearby Manchuria.

MacArthur's express orders, dispatched on September 27, stated baldly, "Your military objective is the destruction of the North Korean armed forces." That instruction was immediately hedged by restrictions imposed in NSC-81.

MacArthur was authorized to operate north of the 38th parallel, "provided that at the time of such operations there has been no entry into North Korea by major Soviet or Chinese Communist forces, no announcement of intended entry, nor a threat to counter our operations militarily in North Korea." His orders placed an overriding restraint on MacArthur: he was to do nothing to precipitate "a general war with Communist China."

MacArthur imperator was the second difficulty confronting Washington.

As SCAP, supreme commander of the allied powers, MacArthur churned with contradictions. A highhanded and autocratic personality, he had nevertheless imposed upon rigidly hierarchical Japan a political system that recognized civil liberties. Although he was greedy for power, he established meaningful local government in postwar Japan and broke the dominance of Tokyo over the lives of the average citizen. A conservative himself, he scored Japan's prewar reactionary governments and barred their members from power in postwar Japan. Demanding that the Japanese pay for their own occupation, at the same time he arranged for the United States to deliver $2 billion in relief to that country. Physically brave, even foolhardy, he repeatedly blamed others for his repeated political mistakes. Contemporaries praised his unusual grasp of geopolitics and world events, yet no commander so suffered from "localitis." He was considered an expert on the Far East, in particular on China, yet he had visited that country only twice, for nine weeks touring the coastal treaty ports as a young lieutenant in 1905, and for two days while conferring with Chiang on Formosa the month before.

MacArthur imperator was also headstrong, long since given to listening only to his wisest adviser, himself. As early as 1932 he had deliberately exceeded orders given to him by his civilian superiors, superseding constitutional mandate with his own judgment. Ordered merely to clear the bedraggled Bonus Marchers from the steps of the Capitol, he had deliberately sent his soldiers across the Eleventh Street bridge to level the marchers' shanty town on Anacostia Flats. Singlehandedly, Douglas MacArthur would tear out, root and branch, this "incipient revolution."

By the beginning of the war, MacArthur was exalted above any criticism. No investigation followed his abject failure to mount air patrols in the first hours of World War II and the consequent loss of his air force at Clark Field. Nor was he removed when he was outgeneraled by Masaharu Homma at Lingayen Gulf two weeks later. "I don't see why in hell Roosevelt didn't order Wainwright home and let MacArthur be a martyr," Harry Truman grumbled in his diary on June 17, 1945. The simple explanation was that the celebrated MacArthur's capture would have been a staggering blow to morale; he had to be rescued and his failures overlooked. Fed by the incessant press releases and his well-cultivated sense of the dramatic, MacArthur's reputation had swollen to such a point that he escaped censure after mounting unauthorized landings in the central and southern Philippines.

Nothing in the years since had dimmed either his self-confidence or his public reputation. During the war, interservice rivalries and Marshall as chief of staff had served to keep MacArthur somewhat in check. As proconsul in Japan, however, he grew increasingly autonomous of Washington, even contemptuous of those government figures who dared to question his actions.

By 1950, the strong-minded military men who had held MacArthur in harness—Ernest King, Chester Nimitz, Savvy Cooke, among them—were retired. The Joint Chiefs now were men junior in both years and military honors to their nominal subordinate in Tokyo. The chairman of the Joint Chiefs, Omar Bradley, had been a temporary major guarding Butte's copper mines in 1918 when Douglas MacArthur won his first star in France. Similarly, the army chief of staff, "Lightning" Joe Collins, had been a division commander on Guadalcanal when MacArthur was commanding the entire Southwest Pacific theater. Collins might be MacArthur's superior in the chain of command, but he was sixteen years younger than SCAP, who addressed him merely as "Joe." Air Force Chief of Staff Hoyt Vandenberg, class of 1923, had been a cadet when Mac-Arthur was superintendent at West Point.

MacArthur tended to condescend to his nominal superiors, sometimes even to lecture them. Bradley acknowledged in a later interview that the Joint Chiefs felt unable to deal with their commander in Tokyo. Collins agreed. "The success of Inchon was so great and the subsequent prestige of General MacArthur was so overpowering, that the chiefs hesitated thereafter to question later plans and decisions of the general, which should have been challenged."

Two days after MacArthur received his orders in Tokyo, news reports from Korea brought disturbing news. The ground commander of the Eighth Army, Major General Walton Walker, had seemingly told reporters he was going to halt at the parallel while awaiting authority to proceed from his nominal sponsors, the United Nations.

Secretary of Defense Marshall and Omar Bradley fired a carelessly drafted cable to MacArthur on September 29 advising, "We want you to feel unhampered tactically and strategically to proceed north of the parallel." Washington wanted no public discussion, no UN vote about crossing the 38th parallel, "but rather to find you have found it militarily necessary to do so."

MacArthur responded with gusto the following day. "Unless and until the enemy capitulates, I regard all of Korea open for our military operations." The 38th parallel would not be a restraint; MacArthur would seek to reunite Korea by force of arms.

Marshall inadvertently endorsed MacArthur's future plans by commending the Inchon strike in a handwritten personal letter on September 30. "Please accept my personal tribute to the courageous campaign you directed in Korea and the daring and perfect strategical operation which virtually terminated the struggle."

MacArthur replied in an expansive mood. "Thanks, George, for your fine message. It brings back vividly the memories of past wars and the complete coordination and perfect unity of cooperation which has always existed in our mutual relationships and martial endeavors. Again my deepest appreciation for your message and for your unfailing support."

Even as the United States was maneuvering a resolution through the UN General Assembly calling for the reunification of Korea, the Chinese were sending diplomatic signals of concern. India's ambassador to Peking, K. M. Panikkar, reported that a Chinese general had told him on September 25 that the "Chinese did not intend to sit back with folded hands and let the Americans come up to their border." A week later, Chou Enlai made the warning more explicit. If U.S. troops crossed the parallel, Chou told Panikkar, China would have to intervene.

Acheson waved off the warnings as "mere vaporings of a panicky Panikkar." MacArthur termed it a bluff, but reported the Chinese moving troops to the Korean border. With that, the Joint Chiefs, Marshall, and Truman settled upon a codicil to MacArthur's instructions on October 9. If his troops made contact with "major Chinese Communist units," he was to press the battle only so long as the forces then under his control offered a reasonable prospect of success. "In any case, you will obtain authorization from Washington prior to taking any military action against objectives in Chinese territory."

On October 10, the Chinese Foreign Ministry in Peking released a sharp warning: "The Chinese people cannot stand idly by with regard to such a serious situation—created by the invasion of Korea by the United States and its accomplice countries and to the dangerous trend toward extending the war." Four days later, units of the Chinese Fourth Field Army began crossing the Yalu River bridges at night and taking up positions in North Korea.

Unaware of the Chinese move, on October 15 an optimistic Douglas MacArthur flew to Wake Island for a meeting with Harry Truman. In some measure the meeting was born of politics, an attempt by the president to bask in the reflected glow of a winning general on the eve of off-year elections. In some measure it sprang from Truman's simple desire to meet finally with this so distant commander. MacArthur understood the first reason, but not the second; he arrived on Wake Island in a petulant mood.

Two ranking members of Truman's cabinet were significantly missing from the delegation that landed on October 15. Acheson had declined to go, pleading that "as I understood my duties, it was dealing with foreign powers, and although MacArthur seemed often to be such, I didn't think he ought to be recognized as that."

George Marshall also decided to remain in Washington. He explained that with Truman, MacArthur, Bradley, and Collins all at Wake Island, someone of authority should be at the Pentagon in case of emergency. Army Secretary Frank Pace attributed Marshall's absence to another reason—"General Marshall didn't think very much of General MacArthur . . . and vice versa." (According to one visitor, MacArthur similarly scorned Marshall, whose "fine patrician Virginia nose does not tolerate the daily smells of Asia.")

At Wake, MacArthur painted a bright picture for the president during their early morning meeting. Formal resistance north and south of the parallel would end by Thanksgiving. The North Koreans had only 100,000 poorly trained replacements, "and it goes against my grain to have to destroy them," SCAP told the president. "They are only fighting to save face."

MacArthur twice stated he expected to withdraw the Eighth Army to Japan by Christmas. The United Nations could hold elections by the 1st of the year. By January too he would even be able to give up a division for reassignment to the fledgling and undermanned North Atlantic Treaty Organization in Europe.

The conferees spent little time on the progress of the war. Reflecting their optimism, they instead discussed in some detail the postwar rehabilitation of Korea, north and south. Then Truman asked, "What are the chances for Chinese or Soviet interference?"

"Very little," MacArthur replied. The Chinese might be able to put 60,000 men across the Yalu River dividing China and North Korea. They had no air force, and without that support, if the Chinese tried to move south, "there would be the greatest slaughter," MacArthur predicted.

Before lunch, the conferees were back in the air.

Marshall was ambivalent when Secretary of the Army Frank Pace briefed him about the Wake Island meeting. Told the troops would be withdrawn to Japan by Christmas, Marshall frowned, his face deeply creased. "Pace, that's troublesome." The American people had not yet grasped the Cold War imperative of a permanent military presence around the world.

When Pace protested, Marshall reminded the younger man that he had not watched "people rush back to their civilian jobs and leave the tanks to rot in the Pacific and the military strength that was built up to fade away."

"Would you say I was naive if I said that the American people had learned their lesson?" Pace asked the Secretary.

"No, Pace. I wouldn't say you were naive. I'd say you were *incredibly* naive."

The war in Korea would shortly change all that. After three weeks of delay, during which MacArthur attempted to mount another amphibious operation in the rear of the fleeing North Koreans, SCAP impatiently hurled Eighth Army northward. To press the pursuit, MacArthur unilaterally removed all restrictions on the use of Americans and the British Commonwealth troops near the Chinese border.

Queried by the Joint Chiefs of Staff about his unilateral decision, MacArthur replied that his order was a matter of military necessity. ROK troops were not capable of pressing the battle home. Furthermore, his earlier instructions were not final, he argued, and Marshall's message of September 29 ("We want you to feel unhampered tactically and strategically to proceed north of the parallel") gave him all the latitude he needed. Lastly, he had discussed this at Wake Island.

MacArthur was straining. If his orders were not final, any changes to them were to come from Washington, not Tokyo, Bradley complained later. Marshall's order of the prior month had applied only to the region just north of the parallel, not to the area adjacent to the Chinese border. Finally, Bradley said, the question of American troops operating near the Chinese border had not been discussed at Wake.

Still, no one in Washington thought it wise to pull him up short, not Truman, not Marshall, not the Joint Chiefs, each for his own reasons. MacArthur had been proved right before. The war was going well; just two days earlier General Walker had suggested that ammunition ticketed for Pusan be delivered to dumps in Japan instead. Further, any change of MacArthur's orders would appear to be a criticism of the enormously popular SCAP two weeks before the elections. Truman would not do it for political reasons, and Marshall would not because of the excess of caution that had marked his relationship with MacArthur for decades. The chiefs either were in awe of MacArthur or feared his many friends in Congress.

The errors were piling up.

On the 25th, American and Korean units took Chinese prisoners after sharp battalion-level firefights. On the 26th, then again on the 28th, ROK regiments were mauled in fighting with well-disciplined Chinese units forty miles south of the Chinese border. More Chinese prisoners were brought to Pyongyang for interrogation. MacArthur's ever-fawning G-2, Major General Charles Willoughby, dismissed the reports of Chinese volunteers on the grounds that "the auspicious time for intervention has long since passed."

MacArthur was about to lose control, Omar Bradley wrote later. By October 29, the ROK drive up the east coast of the peninsula had been blunted, the entire II Corps routed. Two days later, a battalion from the American 8th Cavalry Regiment was surrounded, then decimated by Chinese troops. Walton Walker halted his attacks to reorganize his punctured front.

On November 3, the Joint Chiefs asked MacArthur for his assessment of the situation in Korea. In a soothing message, SCAP refused to concede the Chinese Communists had joined the battle in full force. He preferred to wait for developments before coming to any "hasty conclusions which might be premature."

Meanwhile MacArthur was laying out a plan he claimed would close out the war. His B-29s would be "flown to exhaustion if necessary," but he wanted every city, every communication link, every factory in North Korea flattened. The only exceptions were to be dams and power plants on the Yalu River that supplied Manchuria as well as North Korea with electricity.

MacArthur's preemptory move would unleash feelings in Washington that SCAP was not entirely to be trusted.

The air plan, forwarded routinely to Washington on November 6, alarmed Robert Lovett. The deputy secretary of defense was particularly disturbed by the inclusion of the two bridges over the Yalu linking Kim Il Sung's temporary capital, Sinŭiju, and Antung, Manchuria. Bombing the bridges violated the precautionary order of June 29 to stay clear of the Manchurian and Soviet borders. A World War I pilot and former undersecretary of war for air, Lovett did not like the plan at all. Precision bombing was a misnomer; there was a big risk that a stick of bombs might land in Antung. In addition, the Yalu was so shallow at that point it would soon freeze over; taking the bridges out would not seriously impede truck traffic.

With just three and a half hours left before the planes were to take off, Lovett called the State Department and learned that before they could bomb the bridges, the United States had agreed to consult with the British. The British, Acheson and Rusk informed the deputy secretary, were already skittish about provoking a general war in Asia. Lovett then telephoned Marshall at Leesburg. Marshall strongly advised that the bridges not be bombed unless a mass movement of Chinese Communists threatened the United Nations Command.

Contacted at his home in Independence, where he had gone to vote, the president ordered a postponement and asked for an explanation. After all, just two days earlier MacArthur was advising against hasty action; now he was proposing a major escalation in the war.

One hour and twenty minutes before the B-29s were to take off, the Joint Chiefs ordered the mission aborted. There was to be no bombing within five miles of the Chinese border. The cable also asked for an explanation of the need to bomb the bridges at Sinŭiju.

MacArthur was livid. For the first time the Joint Chiefs had scrubbed a theater commander's tactical order, certainly the first time *he* had ever been overruled. (In his later autobiography, MacArthur attributed the order to Marshall.) MacArthur wrote out a request for immediate relief, then easily permitted himself to be talked out of sending it on the ostensible grounds that "the army would not understand my leaving at such a critical moment, and might become demoralized and destroyed."

MacArthur fired a wrathful protest to the Joint Chiefs. "Men and material in large force are pouring across all bridges over the Yalu from Manchuria," his message began. He had planned an air strike to interdict the southbound flow of Chinese Communists to the front in some cases just fifty miles from the border.

"Every hour that this is postponed will be paid for dearly in American and other United Nations blood. . . . Under the gravest protest I can make, I am suspending this strike and carrying out your instructions." The air strike was entirely within the rules of war and his earlier instructions, MacArthur's cable continued. "I cannot overemphasize the disastrous effect, both physical and psychological, that will result from the restrictions which you are imposing."

The Joint Chiefs responded mildly, despite the fact that MacArthur's cable implied he would take orders only from the president. As Omar Bradley wrote later, the message, though not insubordinate, "was a grave insult to men who were his legal superiors, including George Marshall."

During an unusual night meeting on November 6, Marshall, Lovett, the Joint Chiefs, Acheson, and Rusk concluded that MacArthur's appeal should be granted. Bradley with hindsight would decide that the Joint Chiefs made the worst possible mistake by not dealing bluntly with MacArthur. Two factors held them back: the chiefs' standing policy of not interfering with a field commander, and the lack of reliable information about the Chinese threat.

Throughout, Marshall and the Joint Chiefs would hew to that policy of non-interference, though Marshall, for one, had doubts about MacArthur's troop dispositions. (MacArthur had violated a tactical tenet, and had divided his command. Walker's Eighth Army was separated from Ned Almond's X Corps by a north-south range of mountains that prevented them from supporting each other.) Still, Marshall, the only one among them with a military reputation strong enough to effectively challenge MacArthur, seemed bound in what Dean Acheson later described privately as a "curious quiescence."

Such punctiliousness would be costly. With the president's concurrence, MacArthur was granted permission the next day to take out the bridges along the Yalu. To protect MacArthur's command, they would risk widening the war.

Marshall in his curious quiescence as a civilian officer of the government deferred to the military Chiefs of Staff. He sent MacArthur a second "very personal and informal" message on November 7, hoping to ease the tension. Marshall was sensitive to MacArthur's problems leading a multinational army in mountainous combat during winter. "Everyone here, Defense, State, and the President, is intensely desirous of supporting you." Despite that, some limitations on his actions were necessary. "We are faced with an extremely grave international problem which could so easily lead to a world disaster."

MacArthur in turn thanked Marshall for his message, adding his "complete agreement with the basic concept of localizing, if possible, the Korean struggle."

That same day Truman and the Democrats suffered a stinging setback at the polls. While still retaining majorities, the Democrats lost twenty-eight seats in the House and five in the Senate. The Republican right, MacArthur's strongest supporters, did particularly well. Joseph McCarthy was credited with the ouster of two liberal senators who opposed his slash-and-burn style of politics. Republican Richard Nixon took California's open seat by Red-baiting his liberal opponent, Helen Gahagan Douglas. The results would inhibit Washington's decisions in the coming months when dealing with the supremely popular MacArthur.

Even as air force and navy planes began bombing the bridges over the Yalu on November 8, the Chinese were pulling their troops—MacArthur's headquarters estimated their numbers at 100,000—out of the line. Lacking solid intelligence, Tokyo assumed that the Chinese had suffered a black eye and had decided to take themselves out of the fight. A confident MacArthur responded by announcing in the press an all-out offensive to the Yalu that would conclude "the massive compression envelopment in North Korea against the new Red armies operating there" and unify the peninsula into "a nation of full sovereignty." Troops in Korea eagerly anticipated leaving bitterly cold "Frozen Chosin" for Tokyo by Christmas. Washington meanwhile weighed a British proposal to clear the north, then pull back from a disarmed buffer zone along the Manchurian border.

The crisis had eased. Marshall felt confident enough about the situation in Korea that he took time off to attend an Illinois-Ohio State football game in Champagne with Illinois Governor Adlai Stevenson on November 18.

The fantasy exploded on the night of November 25. Out of the snow-covered mountains of North Korea, 300,000 well-trained Chinese Communists descended upon Walton Walker's thinly scattered Eighth Army and Almond's independent X Corps. Within days, entire divisions were cut off, battalions and regiments hacked from the main body one by one, then decimated as they turned southward to fight their way toward safety.

At 6:15 a.m. on the morning of November 28, Washington time, a flustered Douglas MacArthur finally acknowledged to the Joint Chiefs of Staff that "we face an entirely new war." So confident of military victory just a few days before, the badly shaken MacArthur now advised Washington to "find their solution within the councils of the United Nations and chancellories of the world."

In what Robert Lovett scornfully termed "a posterity paper" written to shore up his reputation, a chastened MacArthur pleaded, "This command has done everything humanly possible within its capabilities but is now faced with conditions beyond its control and strength. . . . My plan for the immediate future is to pass from the offensive to the defensive. . . ."

That afternoon, the president called a meeting of the National Security Council. The participants were grim, uncomfortable with Acheson's admonition, "We are much closer to the danger of general war." China had backed the North Koreans, no doubt with the concurrence of the USSR, they reasoned. Despite the dangers, Acheson refused to buckle. They risked becoming the "greatest appeasers of all time" were they to abandon the South Koreans.

Vice President Alban Barkley was bitter. What about MacArthur's boastful assertions of getting the boys home by Christmas, he asked.

The Chinese Communist entry into the war had taken MacArthur completely by surprise, Bradley responded. No matter. Truman wanted nothing said or done that would cause MacArthur "to lose face before the enemy."

Marshall agreed. They should regard MacArthur's home-by-Christmas statement, Marshall said mildly, "as an embarrassment which we must get around in some manner." They had to get out in such a way as to salvage their honor.

The first problem was to contain the fighting, Marshall advised, for to become caught up in a war with China "would be to fall into a carefully laid Russian trap." The Chinese Communists could put more men into the Korean Peninsula, faster, than could the United States. The United States had to "avoid getting sewed up in Korea" and diverting troops needed in Europe. To limit the war, he also advised against taking up Chiang Kai-shek's offer of 33,000 Nationalist troops then in Taiwan, as MacArthur was urging.

Increasingly disturbed by the Joint Chiefs' inability to control their commander in the Far East, the next afternoon the president determined to monitor MacArthur more closely. He telephoned Marshall to order that copies of all Joint Chiefs' messages to SCAP be cleared with the White House.

Truman was to make an even more far-reaching decision shortly after the November 28 meeting. The United States was short of men, short of planes and tanks, short of naval vessels to mount an effective guard against Communist expansion in both Europe and Asia. Abandoning a Missouri farmer's bedrock desire to hold down the federal budget, he reversed himself and asked Congress for a $16.8 billion supplemental defense appropriation. Before the year was out, Truman was to more than triple the Pentagon's original budget for the next fiscal year.

In the meantime, they had to prevent retreat from becoming a rout in Korea. Somewhat skeptical of MacArthur's claims of outright disaster, the Joint Chiefs on November 29 asked about MacArthur's plans to consolidate a defense across the narrow waist of the peninsula. MacArthur dismissed the suggestion in a peremptory message Bradley termed "insulting." SCAP intended to pull his divided army into two beachheads from which they could be evacuated.

The Joint Chiefs were particularly worried about the exposed X Corps, whose forward elements thirty miles from the Chinese border were fighting for their survival. The chiefs strongly suggested MacArthur consolidate his bifurcated forces and minimize the threat posed by the Chinese Communists operating in the mountain range that separated X Corps and Eighth Army. Hoping to prompt a disciplined withdrawal to a predetermined line at the waist of the peninsula, Marshall added a sentence to the message advising MacArthur that he could ignore holding the northeast portion of Korea above the narrowed waist.

Suggestions, advisories. These special courtesies irritated some in the Pentagon. On December 3, the Army's deputy chief of staff for operations, Matthew Ridgway, approached Air Force Chief of Staff Hoyt Vandenberg, an old friend, and asked bluntly, "Why don't the Joint Chiefs send orders to MacArthur and *tell* him what to do?"

Vandenberg looked nonplussed. "What good would that do? He wouldn't obey the orders. What *can* we do?"

Ridgway exploded. "You can relieve any commander who won't obey the orders, can't you?" Puzzled, stunned, Vandenberg merely walked away.

MacArthur complicated matters with a series of self-serving statements to the press intended to explain away the looming defeat. On December 1, he charged that European governments—and, by extension, Washington—had a shortsighted preoccupation with NATO. To *The New York Times*'s Arthur Krock he stated that he had been advised to stop his troops short of the Chinese border. To *U.S. News and World Report* he complained that restrictions preventing his air force from pursuing Chinese jets into Manchuria were "an enormous handicap without precedent in military history."

Truman was livid. MacArthur's statement not only criticized presidential policy but offered a strong indication that SCAP would welcome a general war in Asia. "I should have relieved General MacArthur then and there," Truman wrote later. Instead, he ordered that any public statements dealing with foreign and military policy be cleared by Washington. The order applied to those in the field as well as those in Washington. The Joint Chiefs immediately sent MacArthur a copy of the order of December 5.

The military situation in Korea continued to deteriorate. MacArthur asked Washington for reinforcements "of the greatest magnitude" lest he be forced into a Pusan-like defensive perimeter once more. On Saturday evening, December 2, Harry Truman wrote in his intermittent diary that MacArthur is "in very serious trouble. We must get him out of it, if we can." Then underscoring the line for emphasis, he added: "It looks very bad."

The following day, the Joint Chiefs approved MacArthur's plan to retreat to beachheads if necessary. "We consider that the preservation of your forces is now the primary consideration."

Within the week, a gloom-ridden MacArthur had ordered the embattled X Corps withdrawn to the east coast port of Hungnam, from there to be evacuated by ship to Pusan.

The situation momentarily firmed. After a quick inspection tour of

Korea in early December, Army Chief of Staff Joe Collins returned to Washington convinced that they could hold despite MacArthur's pessimistic estimate. At the same time, the Chinese Communists, hampered by lengthening supply lines and subzero temperatures, coincidentally broke off pressure on Eighth Army positions along the 38th parallel. By December 10, the men of Foggy Bottom were wondering whether a cease-fire could be arranged on favorable conditions.

Two days before Christmas, the commander of the Eighth Army in Korea, Walton Walker, was killed in a traffic accident while on his way to the front. Matthew Ridgway, who as a company-grade officer had served with Marshall at Tientsin, flew to Tokyo to take command. Given the choice by MacArthur to stay or to withdraw, the forceful Ridgway elected to fight in Korea. He was to "turn the tide of battle like no other general in our military history."

As Ridgway took command in Korea, MacArthur cast the fate of the Eighth Army in apocalyptic terms: they faced annihilation or evacuation. The only alternative was to widen the war, blockading the coast of China, bombing China's industrial plants, and using Chiang Kai-shek's troops on Formosa in Korea and "against vulnerable areas of the Chinese mainland."

In a world of limited resources, MacArthur left no doubt where he believed those resources should be laid on. "I understand thoroughly the demand for European security and fully concur in doing everything possible in that sector, but not to the point of accepting defeat anywhere else—an acceptance which I am sure could not fail to insure later defeat in Europe itself." Regardless of national policy, MacArthur remained an Asia-first man. Two weeks later, Washington was to reject MacArthur's proposal to widen the war.

On New Year's Eve, 1950, Chinese Communist forces attacked the defensive line north of Seoul. ROK units in the center of the line gave way, forcing Ridgway to retreat to better defensive positions south of the parallel. They would surrender first Seoul, then Inchon, as they retreated to a river line they could defend.

MacArthur's spirits fell. On January 10 he cabled Washington that his orders needed clarification. He had insufficient strength to hold in Korea and still defend Japan, the great prize in Asia. Was he to withdraw from the one to defend the other?

His troops, he continued, were tired, "and their morale will become a serious threat to their battle efficiency unless the political basis upon which they are asked to trade life for time is clearly delineated...." (George Marshall looked dourly on the remark about morale, according to Dean Rusk. When a general complained about the morale of his men, it was time to consider his own, Marshall commented.)

Was it United States policy to maintain a military position in Korea,

MacArthur asked Washington. "... [U]nder the extraordinary limitations and conditions imposed upon the command in Korea its military position is untenable, but it can hold for any length of time up to its complete destruction if overriding political considerations so dictate."

Acheson was furious with yet another of MacArthur's "posterity papers," written to clear MacArthur of blame "if things went wrong but also ... putting the maximum pressure on Washington to reverse itself and adopt his proposals for widening the war against China." MacArthur was "incurably recalcitrant and basically disloyal to the purposes of his commander-in-chief," Acheson decided.

With MacArthur's message, they had reached their lowest point, Marshall said later. The charismatic, driving Ridgway was about to reverse the tide. Replacing five division commanders, Ridgway began refitting the battered remnants of the retreat from North Korea. Among other reforms, Ridgway would, with the backing of Marshall, Anna Rosenberg, and Truman, completely desegregate the Army; blacks would no longer be confined to segregated units.

The blooded Eighth Army, now fused with X Corps into a single command, had escaped the well-laid Chinese trap; having survived, it had found new spirit. By mid-January, visiting Army Chief of Staff Joe Collins radioed Washington: "Eighth Army in good shape and improving daily under Ridgway's leadership. Morale very satisfactory considering conditions. . . ." In a matter of days, Ridgway intended to counterattack.

Their estimate of the situation undermined whatever confidence the Department of Defense had left in Douglas MacArthur.

CHAPTER

XLI

The Shatter of Icons

The crisis had passed by the end of January 1951. Ridgway had stabilized the front some sixty miles south of the 38th parallel. There the bruised Chinese Communists broke off contact with the Eighth Army.

Just as Ridgway turned the situation around in Korea, the Truman administration began deliberating a vastly increased military budget. Over the next six months of this "great debate," as newsmen dubbed it, Marshall shaped United States military policy for another generation and incidentally created a permanent American arms industry brought into being by $50 billion and $60 billion annual budgets.

Ridgway's success, ironically, posed a problem for Marshall. The turnabout in Korea "dulled the public interest and urge as to the defense program." But the nation could not yet relax. "The best we can hope for, as I see it, is a prolonged tension rather than an all-out war ... during which we can build up our strength." The tension would last as long as ten years, he predicted.

"If we should get a complete agreement with the Soviets, we would be perfect fools to relax our military strength until we have evidence of good faith," Marshall insisted. With the passing of the crisis in Korea, "unfortunately, the tendency already is to relax. That's what we have to fight against."

By mid-February, Ridgway had launched a series of punishing counterattacks intended to grind up Chinese manpower. Back toward the parallel Ridgway's veterans slogged. Seoul changed hands, for the fourth time, on March 15.

Responding to pressure from United Nations allies, in particular from the British, the Truman administration began weighing the possibility of halting at or near the parallel. Accepting a stalemate would mean abandoning the earlier notion of reuniting North and South Korea, but might end the fighting.

On the day Seoul fell, the president of United Press, Hugh Baillie, asked MacArthur by cable how many men would be needed to garrison a line at the parallel. Ignoring the presidential order of December 5 requiring that policy statements be cleared in Washington, MacArthur wired Baillie he opposed any halt short of the "accomplishment of our mission in the unification of Korea."

Still wary of SCAP's prestige, no one in Washington moved to censure MacArthur for his out-of-policy comment. Instead, the Joint Chiefs merely informed MacArthur of an imminent presidential announcement stating that, "with clearing of bulk of South Korea of aggressors," the United Nations was now prepared to discuss conditions of a settlement in Korea. "Strong UN feeling persists that further diplomatic effort towards settlement should be made before any advance with major forces north of the Thirty-eighth Parallel."

Policy or no, MacArthur could not apparently end his military career in a stalemate. Acting as if he were unaware of the contemplated halt at the parallel, MacArthur replied with a demand that no further military restrictions be imposed upon him. Limitations on air and naval operations against the Chinese rendered it "completely inpracticable to attempt to clear North Korea."

On March 24, even as the State Department was securing the last approvals by UN members of a statement to be made to the Chinese, SCAP preempted the presidential initiative.

"Operations continue according to schedule and plan," MacArthur proclaimed in a public message. "We have now substantially cleared South Korea of organized forces"—though some 10,000 "stay-behind" guerrillas still roamed behind Ridgway's front.

More important, MacArthur continued, Red China had been revealed to be militarily impotent.

Even under the inhibitions which now restrict the activity of the United Nations forces and the corresponding military advantages which accrue to Red China, it has been shown its complete inability to accomplish by force of arms the conquest of Korea. The enemy, therefore, must by now be painfully aware that a decision of the United Nations to depart from its tolerant effort to contain the war to the area of Korea, through an expansion of our military operations to its coastal areas and interior bases, would doom Red China to the risk of imminent military collapse. . . .

Coming from a man who prided himself on his knowledge of the "oriental mind," MacArthur's was an exceedingly ill-considered statement. It was so clumsy, in fact, as to raise the suspicion in Washington that

SCAP was deliberately seeking to sabotage the president's UN initiative, and thereby to make foreign policy.

Having insulted Communist China, MacArthur had made certain Chairman Mao and Chou En-lai would reject any presidential offer to negotiate an end to the fighting.

Harry Truman was infuriated. MacArthur's "most extraordinary statement . . . was in open defiance of my orders as president and commander-in-chief. This was a challenge to the authority of the president under the Constitution." Truman would no longer tolerate MacArthur's insubordination. Lovett recommended MacArthur be removed immediately. Acheson agreed. Truman, having privately reached the same conclusion, nonetheless moved cautiously. For political reasons, he would need Marshall's and the Joint Chiefs' approval before sacking MacArthur—and they were undecided.

At Truman's orders, the Joint Chiefs dispensed only a gentle rap on the knuckles. SCAP was reminded merely of the presidential order of December 5 holding that policy statements were to be cleared with Washington.

Historian Joseph Goulden has uncovered another reason for Truman to relieve MacArthur. Days earlier, Truman read a sheaf of intercepted messages from Spanish and Portuguese diplomats in Tokyo in which they notified superiors in their vehemently anti-Communist governments that General MacArthur had told them he "was confident that he could transform the Korean War into a major conflict in which he could dispose of the 'Chinese Communist question' once and for all."

The intercepted messages established MacArthur's unwillingness to toe Truman's mark. Still, rather than reveal that the United States was eavesdropping on the diplomats of friendly governments, Harry Truman would wait until MacArthur furnished another good reason for his relief.

MacArthur's public challenge to the Red Chinese and Eighth Army's approach to the 38th parallel raised anew the question of how to end the war. To reassure nervous allies, and because "liberal opinion in the United States looked to General George C. Marshall as the one man in American public life who might bring MacArthur under control," the secretary on March 27 held his first press conference since taking up the Defense portfolio.

Marshall implied that the United States preferred a negotiated settlement rather than continued fighting. Ridgway would, in crossing the parallel, be governed by "the demands of security." Did that mean Ridgway could march to the Yalu, a reporter asked. "Such a move might prove to be a little extreme," Marshall replied, almost tongue-in-cheek.

Just as Marshall restored some sense of calm, a MacArthur partisan on April 5 roiled the waters once more.

A month earlier, House Minority Leader Joseph Martin of Massachusetts had forwarded to MacArthur a copy of a speech in which Martin advocated "unloosing Chiang." Martin proposed the United States assist Chiang in opening a second front against Red China by invading the mainland. He invited MacArthur's comments.

Deliberately challenging Truman's military policies and extension of the draft, Martin read MacArthur's response in the House. SCAP believed in "meeting force with maximum counter-force, as we have never failed to do in the past. Your view with respect to the utilization of the Chinese forces on Formosa is in conflict with neither logic nor this tradition."

MacArthur did not stop there:

It seems strangely difficult for some to realize that here in Asia is where the Communist conspirators have elected to make their play for global conquest, and that we have joined the issue thus raised on the battlefield; that here we fight Europe's war with arms while the diplomats there still fight it with words; that if we lose this war to Communism in Asia the fall of Europe is inevitable; win it and Europe most probably would avoid war and yet preserve freedom. As you pointed out, we must win. There is no substitute for victory.

The Martin letter was "the last straw. Rank insubordination," Truman slashed in his diary. "[O]ur big general in the Far East must be recalled." The president, a well-read student of American history, likened Mac-Arthur to Abraham Lincoln's nemesis, George B. McClellan. Lincoln finally had been compelled to fire his commander of the Army of the Potomac for making political statements to members of Congress and the press. Remembered too was McClellan's political ambition; dismissed, he ran against Lincoln for the presidency in 1864.

On Friday morning, April 6, prior to the cabinet meeting, Truman summoned his "Big Four"—Marshall, Acheson, Harriman, and Bradley—to a meeting. Still without revealing his own feelings, he polled the four men on MacArthur.

Acheson and Harriman favored dismissal. Bradley said he was unsure that MacArthur had clearly violated any direct order; he wanted to review the record.

Marshall advised caution for a different reason. Congress was considering their military budget, unprecedented in peacetime, and the renewed draft act. They hardly needed to give opponents more reason to fight the appropriation or the military policies behind it.

Marshall also raised the question of possible deleterious effects on troop morale should MacArthur be removed. He requested more time to ponder the situation.

Truman wanted a decision. He asked Marshall to review the entire file of messages between the Joint Chiefs and MacArthur for the past two years. "I knew the general very, very well," the president explained later. "We'd been through a lot together, and I knew how his mind worked, and there wasn't a doubt in the world in my mind that when he saw what I'd put up with, that he'd agree with me."

Because of Marshall's reputation for probity, his support was vital, Acheson warned. There was no doubt MacArthur deserved to be fired, but "if you relieve MacArthur, you will have the biggest fight of your Administration."

At the president's order, the four men met for two hours again that afternoon in Marshall's Pentagon office. Most of the time was spent discussing a Marshall proposal to summon MacArthur for consultations rather than to fire him. Acheson was strongly opposed to bringing MacArthur home under the "full panoply of his commands"; "the effect of MacArthur's histrionic abilities on civilians and of his prestige upon the military had been often enough demonstrated." Harriman and Bradley agreed with Acheson.

The following morning, Truman's "Big Four" met again with the president at the White House. The president was once more incensed by a MacArthur statement, this one printed in the April 5 issue of the conservative *Freeman* magazine. Asked by the editor why young ROK draftees were being released because the United States would not arm them, MacArthur had replied that the question "involves basic political decisions beyond my authority."

MacArthur's answer shifted responsibility to Washington. The decision not to arm the ROK draftees, in fact, had been based on MacArthur's own recommendation, and that because of the ROK's poor combat record.

The *Freeman* article hardened Acheson and Harriman in their conviction, while Marshall and Bradley found their position eroded even more. The two soldiers asked for more time to discuss the issue with the Joint Chiefs.

Both men were vexed, Bradley explained later. Marshall had agreed to serve as secretary of defense only until September, by which time the expanded military remobilization would be safely through Congress. He was tired, and his powers of recuperation were not good. Finally "approaching something like normal" late in December, he was stricken by a debilitating influenza that hung on and on through the winter.

Bradley too was a short-timer, with but four months remaining on his two-year term as chairman of the Joint Chiefs of Staff. MacArthur's relief would cause a great uproar on the political right; neither man wished to end his career under fire from the primitives.

In Marshall's case, there was another reason for caution. Though Marshall privately defended General MacArthur as "unquestionably one of the ablest military men in our history," Washington still remembered the long-whispered rumors of a Marshall-MacArthur rivalry. Bradley, of course, was one of Marshall's men. Neither wanted MacArthur's firing to appear to be the revenge of old and petty rivals.

Bradley was also concerned that the Joint Chiefs' decision not be construed as political. That "could lead to a drastic erosion in the standing of the JCS as objective advisers to any and all presidents."

On Sunday, April 8, Marshall met with the Joint Chiefs of Staff. "It was a sad and sober group of men that reported to Secretary Marshall in his office at 4:00 p.m. It was not easy to be a party to the dismissal of a distinguished soldier," Army Chief of Staff Joe Collins wrote later.

Sitting behind the carved wooden desk that John J. Pershing and Henry Stimson had used before him, Marshall polled the chiefs individually. Each speaking only from a military point of view, they unanimously recommended MacArthur's recall. None argued that MacArthur had clearly violated any lawful military order, to the relief of Bradley and Marshall. Both feared any legalistic charge that MacArthur had contravened military regulations, lest that provoke an embarrassing Billy Mitchell-like court-martial. Instead, the chiefs proposed MacArthur be relieved because:

1. MacArthur had repeatedly indicated he was "not in sympathy" with the effort to limit the conflict in Korea. The Joint Chiefs needed a commander more responsive to their orders.

2. He had subverted the president's effort to open negotiations with the Chinese.

3. The Joint Chiefs believed the military must be controlled by civilian authority. MacArthur's actions flouted that constitutional mandate.

Not until the following morning, when Truman met again with his Big Four, did Marshall reluctantly side with Acheson, Harriman, and the Joint Chiefs of Staff. Bradley, who by law had no vote on the Joint Chiefs, made it clear he too concurred by not expressing disagreement. Truman had his consensus.

For the first time the president told his advisers that he had already made up his mind to relieve MacArthur. Truman quickly accepted the chiefs' recommendation that Ridgway succeeded MacArthur in Tokyo. Lieutenant General James Van Fleet would take over as commander of the Eighth Army. MacArthur was to be accorded full military honors, Truman ordered; he was not coming home in disgrace.

Discussing a proposed public statement on MacArthur's relief, one Truman aide suggested that it contain a reference to the fact that Truman's action followed the unanimous advice of his principal military and civilian advisers. "Son, not tonight," Truman ruled. "Tonight I am taking this decision on my own responsibility as president of the United States and I want nobody to think I am sharing it with anybody else."

As they had anticipated, public reaction in the United States caused "quite an explosion . . . but I had to act," Truman wrote in his diary. By nine-thirty that morning in Washington, furious Republicans were meeting in Joe Martin's office in the Capitol, demanding a congressional investigation. Senator Robert Taft suggested Truman be impeached. Martin hastily telephoned key Democrats to arrange an invitation to MacArthur to address a joint session of the Congress.

Senator William Jenner opened the Senate that afternoon, raging that "this country is in the hands of a secret inner coterie which is directed by agents of the Soviet Union." To the applause of the crowded gallery, Jenner shrilled, "Our only choice is to impeach President Truman."

Glowering Joe McCarthy, himself well into alcoholism, charged that the recall was "a Communist victory won with the aid of bourbon and Benedictine." He too agreed "the son of a bitch should be impeached." California's new senator, Richard Nixon, sneered, "The happiest group in the country over General MacArthur's removal will be the Communists and their stooges."

On April 16, 1951, while an army band played "Auld Lang Syne," the door of Douglas MacArthur's Constellation closed and the plane taxied to the runway at Haneda Airport. Its engines revving, the *Bataan* began rolling, then lifted into the air toward home and a tumultuous welcome for the General of the Army Douglas MacArthur.

The following day, the MacArthurs drove past 100,000 cheering Hawaiian Islanders to a military cemetery where the general laid a commemorative wreath. The reception in San Francisco on the night of April 17 was more raucous. The hero home for the first time in fourteen years, MacArthur was greeted by crowds so large it took two hours to drive fifteen miles to their downtown hotel. The following day an estimated 300,000 people lined Market Street for a ticker-tape parade.

Bataan touched down at National Airport,Washington, at 12:35 a.m. on April 19. Waiting on the ramp stood the secretary of defense; Harry Truman's military aide, Major General Harry Vaughan; the Joint Chiefs; and Lieutenant General Jonathan Wainwright, MacArthur's former deputy.

MacArthur came down the ramp and reached first for Marshall's hand. "Hello, George," he said, smiling. "How are you?"

"Hello, General," Marshall replied, unsmiling.

MacArthur had barely shaken hands with the members of the greeting party when the excited crowd surged forward, engulfing them. It took fifteen minutes to get the dignitaries into limousines and to restore order.

"Seldom had a more unpopular man fired a more popular one," *Time* magazine concluded. Western Union estimated it delivered 75,000 telegrams to government officials in the first days after MacArthur's relief; ten to one they came down on MacArthur's behalf. Even those sent to the White House ran four and five to one in favor of the general.

The hero was to earn his greatest affirmation shortly after noon on April 19 when he appeared before a joint session of Congress. The crowded House chamber burst into prolonged cheers as the general worked his way through the packed aisles to the rostrum. Standing there, his uniform bare of medals and ribbons, he waited for the clamorous applause to subside.

His speech, written on *Bataan* while flying from Tokyo, was "one of the most impressive and divisive oratorical performances of recent American times," according to MacArthur's biographer, D. Clayton James. For more than a half-hour he held in thrall the Congress and a nation-wide television and radio audience.

As any debater will, MacArthur sought to stake out the high ground, claiming for himself both patriotism and humility. "I do not stand here as an advocate of any partisan cause, for the issues are fundamental and reach beyond the realm of partisan consideration. They must be resolved on the highest plane of national interest. . . . I address you with neither rancor nor bitterness in the fading twilight of life with but one purpose in mind, to serve my country."

The issues confronting the nation were global, MacArthur conceded. And while "there are those who claim our strength is inadequate to protect" both Asian and European allies, to MacArthur there was "no greater expression of defeatism." He would mention Europe no more, for Douglas MacArthur was a man of the Orient, heart and soul.

The war in Korea, MacArthur charged, wound on inconclusively because Washington refused to make the political decisions necessary for victory. MacArthur denied he was a warmonger. "I know war as few other men now living know it, and nothing to me is more revolting. . . . But once war is forced upon us, there is no other alternative than to apply every available means to bring it to a swift end. War's very object is victory—not prolonged indecision.

"In war, indeed, there can be no substitute for victory." There was thunderous applause from the Republican side and from the packed galleries.

MacArthur made no secret of his belief that America's future lay in the Far East. Ignoring the authoritarian nature of the government of Syngman Rhee, he praised the Korean people, who "have chosen to risk death rather than slavery. Their last words to me were 'Don't scuttle the Pacific.' " More applause from the Republican side.

Then, in a moving farewell, MacArthur spoke the lines that decades later retained the power to move men:

I am closing my fifty-two years of military service. When I joined the army, even before the turn of the century, it was the fulfillment of all of my boyish hopes and dreams. The world has turned over many times since I took the oath on the plain at West Point, and the hopes and dreams have all since vanished, but I still remember the refrain of one of the most popular barracks ballads of that day which proclaimed most proudly that old soldiers never die; they just fade away.

And like the old soldier of that ballad, I now close my military career and just fade away, an old soldier who tried to do his duty as God gave him the light to see that duty.

He paused, then lifted his hand in a half wave. "Goodby."

More than a few sought to stifle their tears amid the torrents of applause spilling from the galleries and the floor. Republicans were overjoyed, finding in the general something akin to religious exaltation. "We saw a great hunk of God in the flesh, and we heard the voice of God," boomed Missouri's Dewey Short. From New York former President Herbert Hoover judged MacArthur the very reincarnation of St. Paul.

Democrats were less enthused. Harry Truman dismissed the speech as "nothing but a bunch of damn bullshit." Dean Acheson scored it as bathetic.

Their opinions aside, the crowds and the national hysteria continued to swell. New York greeted MacArthur with the largest ticker-tape parade in history, saluted by millions along the nineteen-mile parade route. Later he would travel to Chicago and on to his boyhood home in Milwaukee, always to the cheers of enthusiastic crowds. MacArthur the hero offered America affirmation and a simple solution to an ever more complex world. Bags of adulatory mail, 150,000 letters and 20,000 telegrams, awaited his arrival at the Waldorf-Astoria Hotel in New York.

Pressed by MacArthur's partisans, the Senate Foreign Affairs and Armed Services Committees began joint hearings on the military situation in the Far East on Thursday, May 3, in the Senate Caucus Room. MacArthur would be the first witness, testifying behind closed doors. The mimeographed transcript, edited for military security reasons, would be released through the day to the press.

The GOP's old guard looked upon MacArthur as a club with which to bash Harry Truman's "no win" Asian policies. They would range widely and wildly in their questioning; more sophisticated Republicans would especially miss the moderating influence of Arthur Vandenberg in the coming weeks. Stricken six months earlier with a brain tumor, Vandenberg had died in Michigan on the day that MacArthur returned to the United States.

Greeted by the twenty-six committee members with bountiful praise and treated often with truckling deference, MacArthur was to testify for three days. Toying with a briar pipe, occasionally puffing it into life, he was the master, the twenty-six senators facing him pupils to be instructed in the elements of geopolitics and military affairs.

It went easily at first. Simple questions elicited long, sometimes windy lectures. The deferential senators gave him ample time to air his grievances, in particular about Washington's restrictions on his conduct of the war. In Korea, political considerations had outweighed military doctrine developed over the centuries, he complained.

So as not to appear to be standing alone, MacArthur claimed that the Joint Chiefs had endorsed four courses of action he had earlier recommended to win the war: economic blockade of China; naval blockade; air reconnaissance; and removal of the restrictions on the use of Chiang's armies.

MacArthur was less than forthright. The four proposals had been among sixteen contingencies they might take if the UN were forced to evacuate Korea. The list had been drawn up in a Joint Chiefs paper on January 12, during the very worst moments after the Chinese incursion. A copy had made its way to Tokyo for MacArthur's information.

In MacArthur's testimony four months later, proposals became firm plans. "The positions of the Joint Chiefs of Staff and my own so far as I know were practically identical," MacArthur assured the two committees.

"As far as I know, the JCS have never changed these recommendations. If they have, I have never been informed of it."

But if they had never been put into effect, Chairman Richard Russell of the Armed Services Committee commented, they must have been vetoed.

MacArthur would not blame the Joint Chiefs, admirable men and personal friends. "I hold them individually and collectively in the greatest esteem. If there has been any friction between us, I am not aware of it."

Responsibility for the veto lay elsewhere. "I have no knowledge of what happened to this study after it reached the Secretary of Defense. A decision putting this into effect never arrived."

The press had its lead and headline, wrong as they were, for the first day: Marshall had killed tough anti-Red measures.

MacArthur would admit no error himself. The division of his forces into two separate columns was justified; that tactical plan would have ended the war quickly had not the Chinese Communists come in. The failure to predict the Chinese entry into Korea was not his responsibility, but the Central Intelligence Agency's. The subsequent retreat—"a planned withdrawal from the beginning"—had been carried out with a minimum of casualties. Beside, had he been permitted to bomb the Chinese *before* they crossed the Yalu, they never would have entered the war. He would have bombed them even if it meant war between China and the United States.

Under questioning by the senior Republican, Styles Bridges of New Hampshire, MacArthur conceded the president had authority to relieve him. "The authority of the president to assign officers or to reassign them is complete and absolute. He does not have to give any reasons or anything else. That is inherent in our system."

But he had given no cause for his relief. "No more subordinate soldier has ever worn the American uniform."

MacArthur had criticisms of Truman's indecisive war, and of "fighting with no mission . . . which means that your accumulative losses are going to be staggering. It isn't just dust that is settling in Korea, Senator; it is American blood."

Informed that evening of MacArthur's comment, Marshall was upset. "A soldier can be very easily made to feel sorry for himself," he explained later, "particularly when he is in most disagreeable, unattractive, and dangerous localities, and particularly when he has been called upon to make a tremendous effort over a long period of time." MacArthur's statement threatened the morale of Ridgway's army.

It fell to younger Democratic members of the two committees to reduce MacArthur in size. Texas freshman Lyndon Johnson asked the general if his manpower requirements would mean raising the 3.4-million-man ceiling on the armed services or impact on the pending universal military training program. MacArthur pleaded ignorance. He had never given UMT "the slightest thought," he told the senators. "That problem did not fall within my responsibilities or authorities," he explained moments later.

Brien McMahon of Connecticut was unrelenting. "General, we are faced, are we not, with global problems in the ambitions of Communist Russia?"

"Unquestionably."

"You have given that problem a great deal of thought, I assume?"

MacArthur paused, then acknowledged he had, "with particular attention, of course, to my own theater."

Was it fair to say then he had no clear plan for a global defense if the USSR chose to make war on the United States?

"I have my own views, Senator, but they are not authoritative views, and I would not care to discuss them." Others, MacArthur said, had both the responsibility and the authority he lacked.

Having forced MacArthur to concede that his global views were only half-formed, McMahon pressed on. MacArthur had testified that he believed the Soviets would not come into the war in the Far East. "Suppose, General, you are wrong about that. You could be wrong about it, couldn't you?"

"Most assuredly."

If he happened to be wrong about the Soviets—as he had been about the Chinese earlier—"I want to find out how you propose in your own mind to defend the American nation against this war."

MacArthur was evasive. "That doesn't happen to be my responsibility, Senator. My responsibilities were in the Pacific, and the Joint Chiefs of Staff and the various agencies of this government are working day and night for an over-all solution to the global problem."

McMahon closed the trap. "General, I think you make the point very well that I want to make; that the Joint Chiefs of Staff and the president of the United States, the commander-in-chief, has [sic] to look at this thing on a global basis and a global defense.

"You, as a theater commander, by your own statement have not made that kind of study, and yet you advise us to push forward with a course of action that may involve us in that global conflict."

After twenty-three hours of testimony over three days, Douglas Arthur MacArthur stepped down. To the end he protested his innocence and his loyalty to the chain of command. To the end he insisted that the president, a civilian, had meddled in the conduct of the war, not that he, a soldier, had attempted to set national policy. To the end he maintained he was the most innocent of soldiers, operating in a vacuum of policy, his actions always in accord with instructions from the Joint Chiefs. He acknowledged no error and he insisted he did not know why he had been relieved.

The administration's rebuttal began on Monday morning, May 7, 1951, when Secretary of Defense Marshall took the oath in the Senate Caucus Room. MacArthur had made a "powerful impression" with his testimony, the press concluded. Marshall, an equally respected "old soldier," was to be the instant antidote.

Marshall acknowledged a certain discomfort in his role. This was "a very distressing necessity, a very distressing occasion," he told the joint committee. He was there in opposition to the views and actions of "a brother army officer, a man for whom I have tremendous respect as to his military capabilities and military performances and, from all I can learn, as to his administration of Japan."

Marshall sought, unsuccessfully, to confine his testimony to three issues at the heart of the dispute with MacArthur: the relationship of the military to the civilian; the chain of command; and the purported lack of a winning strategy in Korea.

Reading from a prepared statement, his voice flat, Marshall immediately denied that he or the president had ever overruled the Joint Chiefs of Staff as MacArthur hinted. "There have been, however, and continue to be basic differences of judgment between General MacArthur, on the one hand, and the president, the secretary of defense and the Joint Chiefs of Staff on the other hand."

The January 12 proposals MacArthur put forward as proof that he and the chiefs were in line had been merely tentative courses of action contingent upon forced retreat from the Korean Peninsula. None of these proposals had been disapproved by Marshall or "any higher authority." Instead, they were overtaken by favorable events and thus rendered unnecessary.

National policy in Korea, now as always, was to defeat the aggression from the North, without provoking a third world war, he continued. They had been successful; Ridgway and Van Fleet were then preparing limited assaults to push the front to easily defensible positions some fifty miles north of the parallel.

MacArthur, on the other hand, wanted to risk carrying the conflict to China and beyond, Marshall said. MacArthur would do it even at the expense of losing UN allies, wrecking the Western coalition, and exposing western Europe to attack by the Soviet Union.

There was a difference in responsibility between the Joint Chiefs and the secretary of defense, concerned with global security, and a theater commander, whose authority covered a narrow geographical area, Marshall continued. MacArthur had grown so far out of sympathy with national policy, set in Washington, that there was a grave doubt as to whether he could be trusted to make decisions in accordance with that policy. "In this situation, there was no other course but to relieve him."

The courtly Richard Russell, chairman of the Armed Forces Committee, asked about "unleashing Chiang." Marshall pointed out that the previous July, MacArthur himself had spurned the offer of Nationalist troops to fight in Korea "because of their ineffectiveness and lack of logistic support." Only in November, with the intervention of the Chinese Communists, did MacArthur change his mind and ask for them, Marshall continued. Based on their prior performance on the mainland and woeful equipment, the Joint Chiefs recommended Chiang's troops stay on Formosa.

On and on it went, for six wearying days, senatorial interest in the issues ebbing as Marshall calmly, carefully answered questions. At age seventy, he grew tired, especially late in the day. His voice was hoarse near the end. He had difficulty hearing questions, an infirmity that troubled him, and a name or two escaped him. Rarely did he express any emotion more than a certain sadness that he had to disagree with MacArthur in public.

They had but three choices, Marshall explained to the panel on the second day. They could expand the fighting as MacArthur had urged.

They could withdraw from Korea and sacrifice the people of that nation. Or with their vastly superior firepower they could fight deliberately to gain an advantage by inflicting severe casualties on the Chinese Communist forces. By depleting the Communists' trained cadre, they had the best chance of forcing negotiations to end the war satisfactorily.

Some in Washington, like MacArthur, had criticized this strategy as leading to stalemate, Marshall conceded. Then, reading from notes prepared after MacArthur testified, Marshall delivered the most impassioned statement that private man was capable of:

"For the last five years our supreme policy has been to curb Communist aggression, and, if possible, to avoid another world war in doing so. The execution of this policy has required extraordinary patience, firmness and determination in meeting and helping our allies to meet . . . challenges in Iran, Greece, Turkey, Trieste, Berlin and Indo-China, and finally Korea."

Once more he was the Marshall of old, the man of global vision, the architect of victory. No problem lay beyond his responsibility. "Year by year the United States has opposed these aggressions with courage and poise, and in each instance the threats were curbed or overcome without involving this government in a total war." This was a continuing struggle, one that might last much longer. There would not be a quick and decisive victory, short of another world war, he stressed. "This policy may seem costly, if maintained over a period of years, but those costs would not be comparable at all to what happens if we get involved in what you might call an atomic war."

Korea was only the latest challenge, "the most costly of all, for it involved the lives of our American troops." But throughout, the United States had resisted appeasement. "Korea is not the first time there have been complaints of stalemate, and it is not the first time that there have been demands for a quick and decisive solution," he reminded the senators. The Korean War had run on for ten months, but the Berlin crisis lasted almost fifteen before ending in "a notable victory." The guerrilla war in Greece had lasted for eighteen months before the Communists were defeated.

Pressed by Senator Russell, Marshall argued against war in China. Bombing would have little impact on a vast, largely preindustrial nation. Even heavy civilian casualty tolls would have small effect "in a country where human life is not put on the same standard of values that we have. . . ." The Japanese, after all, had not conquered despite fourteen years of fighting in China.

Marshall too could teach, but where MacArthur had been impatient with his questioners and anxious to get away, Marshall stayed the course. Again and again he argued that expansion of the war to China was not likely to lead to a quick decision. Furthermore, a looming defeat of Communist China raised "a very real possibility" of Soviet intervention. That, in turn, would immediately pose problems in defending Japan and leave Europe vulnerable to Soviet aggression. MacArthur, a theater commander, might ignore the global implications of his recommendations; the Joint Chiefs, the secretary of defense, and, above all, the president of the United States dared not.

Bridges of New Hampshire inadvertently opened up the second of the administration's defenses, the question of the chain of command. Alluding to MacArthur's letter to Congressman Martin, Bridges asked if a legislator wrote to a military man, was he not entitled to a frank reply?

"No, sir," Marshall replied firmly. Not from a commander advocating a position contrary to his commander-in-chief. "That goes contrary to my precepts and understanding as a soldier. . . ."

Nothing could be more important to a soldier. Half a century before, VMI Cadet George Catlett Marshall had learned the soldier's lessons of obedience, of responsibility. Those obligations applied to all, from the youngest of recruits to the most senior of generals.

"You preach loyalty all the time. You are dealing with an organization where a man receives an order from even a captain which leads to his death or his wound, and he has to obey that order. He doesn't debate it, he obeys it, and that has to be instinctive. Now, if the example at the top is contrary to that, then you have got a very serious situation."

Marshall himself had disagreed with presidential policy on at least two occasions: in the years before the fall of France when FDR pursued a go-slow policy on mobilization; then in 1942, with the invasion of North Africa. Each time he had followed orders; he had certainly kept his disagreements private.

Finally, after six wearying days, the committee concluded its questioning of the secretary. One by one the Joint Chiefs of Staff followed Marshall to the witness table. Bradley too would testify for six days, supporting Marshall's testimony, denying that the chiefs took MacArthur's position. For all of his testimony, nothing was more quoted than a comment in his opening statement on May 15 regarding MacArthur's desire to widen the war to China. "Frankly, in the opinion of the Joint Chiefs of Staff, this strategy would involve us in the wrong war, at the wrong place, at the wrong time, and with the wrong enemy."

If there was any doubt left—Bradley was, after all, a Marshall man— the three members of the Joint Chiefs put an end to it. Each testified for two days, and each agreed with Truman, Marshall, and Bradley. MacArthur was isolated.

As suddenly as the crowds had appeared, they disappeared. MacArthur might be a hero, but his ideas seemed perilous. For the first week, with MacArthur and Marshall testifying, "there was tremendous excitement," Bradley recalled. After that, it "became a great bore."

A number of things served to dampen the outcry. Like a forest fire, any public hysteria eventually burns itself out. Learning the price of "victory," the public declined to make the sacrifices MacArthur's war would demand. In addition, Marshall the accomplished soldier-diplomat had methodically buried MacArthur as a global strategist. Bradley's subsequent testimony threw dirt on the grave.

By the time Secretary of State Dean Acheson appeared to testify in early June, the committee members and the public alike had lost much of their interest in the old soldier who had taken up residence in Suite 37-A of the Waldorf-Astoria Hotel. Editors had moved the daily story on the hearings inside the paper; fewer and fewer readers bothered to search it out.

In the end, two months after MacArthur's testimony, Republican Charles W. Tobey of New Hampshire complained of "the utter futility of much that is going on here. . . . When we get all through Mr. MacArthur will still be deposed from his position, Mr. Marshall will still be the man in charge of the defense of this country, the Joint Chiefs of Staff will still be the same as they are now. . . ."

However futile the exercise had been, the hearings would have one disastrous effect; they sundered whatever restraints upon political debate remained in these years of anti-Red hysteria and fear.

Angered by Marshall's testimony, the man's quiet conviction and cool argument, Joseph McCarthy took the floor of the Senate on June 14, 1951, promising to expose "a conspiracy on a scale so immense as to dwarf any previous such venture in the history of man, a conspiracy of infamy so black that, when it is finally exposed, its principals shall be forever deserving of the maledictions of all honest men."

Speaking before a virtually empty chamber, McCarthy would hold the Senate floor for two and three-quarter hours that Thursday afternoon. The first-term senator droned from page to page of his prepared speech, charging George Marshall had shaped "the carefully planned retreat from victory."

The 169-page speech—actually appropriated from a book-length manuscript by Washington newspaperman Forrest Davis—reviewed the seemingly inexplicable rise of the Soviet Union as a world power during the war. McCarthy concluded, without ever using the word "treason," that Marshall and Acheson had duped a naive Harry Truman into repeatedly playing into Communist hands.

According to the Davis-McCarthy scenario of conspirators and turncoats, Marshall had fostered the rise of the Soviet Union for a decade. The onetime chief of staff had so easily fallen in with the Soviet Union's demand for a "second front now." He had fought against the North African invasion, then the Italian campaign advocated by Churchill and Mark Clark in favor of an invasion of France as Stalin wanted.

"It was Marshall, who, at Teheran, made common cause with Stalin on the strategy of the war in Europe and marched side by side with him thereafter." It was Marshall who had ordered the American military envoy in Moscow to get along with the Soviets, and to expedite Lend-Lease.

The audience in the galleries thinned, yet McCarthy growled on. Only a handful of senators spent any time in the chamber listening, and none bothered to challenge McCarthy. Inaccuracy heaped upon distortion, all unquestioned.

According to McCarthy, Marshall had ordered the Army not to establish a corridor into Berlin. It was Marshall too who had ordered American troops to permit the Russians to capture Berlin and Prague. Marshall, with the assistance of the since discredited Alger Hiss, had dictated the secret Yalta agreement by which the Soviet Union agreed to enter the war against Japan. He had done so "apparently indifferent to what should happen to the 2,000,000 riflemen he wanted to send ashore in Japan."

Marshall's deceits had continued in the postwar years, McCarthy went on. Marshall, with Acheson's aid, had "created the China policy which, destroying China, robbed us of a great and friendly ally, a buffer against the Soviet imperialism with which we are now at war."

Marshall had fixed the 38th parallel as the dividing line in Korea, McCarthy added. Marshall's strategy in Korea had "turned that war into a pointless slaughter, reversing the dictum of Von Clausewitz and every military theorist since him that the object of a war is not merely to kill but to impose your will on the enemy."

The McCarthy speech was, at heart, an elaboration of the Republican old guard's recurrent arguments that Roosevelt, Truman, Marshall, somebody, had abandoned the Far East in favor of Europe. In war, the United States had saved the Soviet Union from defeat, then in peacetime had ceded to the Communists the Orient. Capping it all, the removal of the revered Douglas MacArthur had stripped America of the last man powerful enough to stay the plot.

McCarthy heaped error upon error, all cloaked in pseudo-academic research and seemingly definitive documentation. It was a sham. The research was, at best, tendentious and incomplete, the documentation vague, and the quotations frequently edited to change their original meaning.

Near the end, his tone ever more shrill, McCarthy asked rhetorically:

What is the objective of the great conspiracy? I think it is clear from what has occurred and is now occurring: to diminish the United States in world affairs, to weaken us militarily, to confuse our spirit with talk of surrender in the Far East and to impair our will to resist evil. To what end? To the end that we shall be contained, frustrated and finally fall victim to Soviet intrigue from within and Russian military might from without.

The dinner hour closing in, McCarthy rushed to finish, literally ripping pages out of his text. Harry Truman was not master of his own house, McCarthy sputtered. The president was guided by a "larger conspiracy, the world-wide web of which has been spun from Moscow. It was Moscow, for example, which decreed that the United States should execute its loyal friend, the Republic of China. The executioners were that well-identified group headed by Acheson and George Catlett Marshall.

"How, if they would, can they break these ties, how return to simple allegiance to their native land? Can men sullied by their long and dreadful record afford us leadership in the world struggle with the enemy? How can a man whose every important act for years had contributed to the prosperity of the enemy reverse himself?"

He could not, McCarthy concluded, for George Catlett Marshall, like Shakespeare's Macbeth, was "in blood stepped in so far, that should I wade no more, returning were as tedious as go o'er."

The ignominious McCarthy era would hear no more defamatory speech. Marshall, beset by reporters, loftily refused to reply. When newspaper columnist Clayton Fritchey offered material for a rebuttal, Marshall declined politely. "I do appreciate that, but if I have to explain at this point that I am not a traitor to the United States, I hardly think it's worth it."

Though Marshall would not deign to reply, others rushed to rebut McCarthy. Adlai Stevenson, lately elected governor of Illinois, termed the speech a "hysterical form of putrid slander." A. C. Wedemeyer, who disagreed sharply with Marshall on the nation's China policy, rallied to his former superior. "Senator Joe McCarthy, who popularized the idea that Marshall was a 'second fronter' for sinister reasons, was absolutely wrong," the former War Department planner wrote. Marshall's World War II strategy conformed to sound principles, Wedemeyer stated. If he was to be faulted, it was only because he was tired in the postwar years and fell "easy prey to crypto-Communists or Communist-sympathizing sycophants. . . ."

Paul G. Hoffman, former director of the Marshall Plan in Europe and co-chairman of a committee to draft Dwight Eisenhower as the GOP presidential nominee in 1952, scored the McCarthy speech as "fantastically false." Marshall needed no defense from him, Hoffman said. Marshall's "record speaks for itself. It is a record of selfless devotion to his country that has been equalled by few and surpassed by no one since this Republic was founded."

Eisenhower himself impatiently brushed aside McCarthy's charges.

"Now look," he sternly lectured inquiring reporters later that year, "General Marshall is one of the patriots of this country. Anyone who has lived with him, has worked for him as I have, knows that he is a man of real selflessness."

McCarthy had his defenders, principally those identified with the China Lobby. The *Washington Times-Herald* dismissed critics of the speech as "kept columnists and newspaper errand boys." McCarthy apologists Brent Bozell and William F. Buckley, Jr., condoned character assassination in the service of partisan politics. While "Marshall's loyalty was not to be doubted in any reasonable quarters," they wrote, "to the extent that McCarthy, through his careful analysis of Marshall's record, has contributed to cutting Marshall down to size, he has performed a valuable service. . . ."

In the end, McCarthy's screed may have impelled the secretary of defense to resign, Marshall's biographer, Forrest Pogue, speculated. Marshall had originally agreed to serve through June, then had extended his term until Congress adopted the Cold War mobilization conceived in the pending military appropriation and draft bills.

Through the six months of the Great Debate, Dean Acheson's "least militant of soldiers" had lobbied vigorously for military preparedness, and especially for universal military training. Ignoring complaints of shortages in consumer goods, Marshall insisted that only the United States could provide both guns to defend western Europe and butter for American tables. "A cut of five percent in the European standard of living," Marshall pointed out, "meant the difference between white bread and black on the table, while in similar American homes such a cut would mean forgoing a radio or television."

Marshall pressed harder, even as the Korean War lurched toward a stalemate and negotiations with the North Koreans. The aging Bernard Baruch turned the dedication of an arch at VMI to be named after Marshall into a call for rearmament. "In our present situation," Baruch told the assembled cadets, "whatever is attempted on behalf of peace must fall short because of a lack of supporting military strength. We are trying to enforce a global doctrine of opposition to Communism with a military establishment that is sorely strained by the demands of only one theater."

House Speaker Sam Rayburn picked up the cudgel in Congress, warning that "winning a little battle in Korea had better not lull the American people to sleep, because I think we stand in the face of terrible danger and maybe the beginning of World War III."

Such alarms brought the Congress to heel. In June, Truman signed a misnamed Universal Military Training and Service Act. While the bill did not provide for *universal* military training, it extended the draft four years, lowered the draft age to eighteen and a half, increased the period of active duty to two years, and tacked on a six-year term in the inactive reserve.

By June 23, and the Soviet ambassador's call for a cease-fire in Korea, Marshall had doubled military strength to 2.9 million men and women. In three more months they would add another 500,000. In all, they had brought about a faster mobilization than Marshall had superintended during 1940–42.

George Marshall was past seventy and tired. During the MacArthur hearings he had several times said one name when he meant another. What others thought of as a humanizing foible had become for him a vexation; he had increasing trouble remembering names, even of people he knew well, he irritably told Acheson. His hearing seemed to be worse, a failing he considered an embarrassment for a public official. Katherine's health was only fair; furthermore, she had been sorely disturbed by the McCarthy speech. Besides, Lovett carried more and more of the burden at Defense, and could easily step in as secretary.

Leesburg beckoned.

C H A P T E R

XLII

Sunset

There would be no ceremony. After forty-nine years and eight months of service, on September 12, 1951, George Catlett Marshall intended only to drive home to Leesburg one last time. The retiring secretary of defense wanted no fuss made over his departure, his successor, Robert Lovett, told reporters. Marshall was leaving for what he wrote the president were "very personal reasons," without explaining further. Harry Truman accepted the resignation only with reluctance, he wrote in reply.

Marshall settled easily into a comfortable routine in Leesburg. At Truman's behest, Congress in 1948 had made the five-star rank a lifetime appointment. Though retired, Marshall thereby continued to draw his full salary. Carefully husbanded investments supplemented that. Marshall also retained an office at the Pentagon with a secretary to handle the hundreds of letters he received each month, and he had the services of his aide, C. J. George, and an orderly, Sergeant William Heffner. Marshall arranged for George, a World War II major who had taken a bust to master sergeant in order to stay in the Army at war's end, to be promoted to the rank of lieutenant colonel.

The quiet life of a small town in the Virginia countryside delighted Marshall. He ran errands, sometimes pushed a cart through the local market to do the family shopping, or stood in line at the post office to buy stamps. Two family dogs, summoned with a piercing whistle, followed him on walks.

His garden occupied him, though he no longer could do the heavy labor around Dodona Manor. He wrote letters to personal friends and former colleagues from a small vanity in the second-floor guest room. He read widely for his own pleasure, ranging from paperback westerns to old favorites like *Little Lord Fauntleroy* to the increasingly frequent memoirs of wartime colleagues. He himself would not write such a book. Indeed, he declined a publisher's offer of almost a million dollars. "I wouldn't take it," Marshall was quoted in *Time* magazine, "because the only thing I'd be able to add to the record would be personalities, and I don't want to do that." (Though he ordered his memoir of the first war destroyed, a copy survived, to be published finally in 1976.)

After traveling more than 1.5 million miles as army chief of staff and as a cabinet officer, Marshall welcomed the small world of Leesburg and the winters spent at the cottage on tree-lined Linden Road in the milder climate of Pinehurst, North Carolina.

In the beginning he still hunted, noting in a 1951 Christmas greeting to Adlai Stevenson that he had recently enjoyed some fine shooting. Still he was not as active as he had been. At Pinehurst, a resort popular among the quietly well-to-do, he followed the golf tourneys as a cart-borne spectator.

Marshall resisted efforts to draw him from that world. He declined Harry Truman's offer to reappoint him president of the American Red Cross. He did accept Truman's offer to name him chairman of the American Battle Monuments Commission, a less taxing assignment but personally satisfying. Like John J. Pershing before him, he was fulfilling an obligation to fallen comrades and their families.

He would take on few other responsibilities, none too taxing. He lent his name as a sponsor of the major organization in the China Lobby, the Committee of One Million. That drew a warm letter of thanks from Madame Chiang to her old friend "General Flicker." In 1955 he accepted an invitation to become a member of the Atlantic Union Committee, an organization dedicated to welding western Europe into political and economic union. And the onetime second lieutenant who had mapped the Pecos River area west of Del Rio served as a trustee of the National Geographic Society.

He was seen little in official Washington. In January 1952, he joined a small group for dinner at the British Embassy to honor the visiting Winston Churchill. The following month he slipped into the White House by a side door to visit the president; there was no announcement of the subject of their fifteen-minute discussion. In September, he and Katherine took a leisurely trip to Europe on the liner *United States,* the chairman of the Battle Monuments Commission off to inspect American military cemeteries in Europe. At Anzio they stole a private moment for Katherine to lay a bouquet of red roses on Allen's grave.

As quiet as his life was, controversy would nonetheless find him. In the election year of 1952, both parties had nominated men who counted Marshall a good friend, the Democrats Adlai Stevenson, the Republicans Dwight Eisenhower. Four years earlier Marshall had advised Eisenhower not to run. This time he was not consulted.

Still there was something of a father's pride in his comment when he told newsmen in Santa Barbara, California, where he and Katherine were vacationing, that the two candidates "are my boys. I sent Eisenhower to Europe. Governor Stevenson, with me when I was secretary of state, gave valuable assistance on both the United Nations and our program for economic aid to Europe." He himself would avoid having to choose by hewing to an old soldier's traditional practice of not voting.

During the campaign, Stevenson went out of his way to praise Marshall and score Senator McCarthy. Addressing the American Legion Convention on August 27, the Democratic standard-bearer asked rhetorically, "What can we say for the man who proclaims himself a patriot— and then for political or personal reasons attacks the patriotism of faithful public servants? I give you, as a shocking example, the attacks which have been made on the loyalty and the motives of our great wartime chief of staff, General Marshall. To me this is the type of 'patriotism' which is, in Dr. Johnson's phrase, the 'last refuge of scoundrels.' "

Eisenhower, who had earlier praised Marshall, stumbled in Wisconsin. Planning to deliver a speech in McCarthy's home state with a section strongly praising his former commander, Eisenhower deleted those comments under pressure from McCarthy and Wisconsin Governor Walter J. Kohler, Jr. When word of the deletion leaked to newsmen, Harry Truman was quick to rake Eisenhower for having "betrayed his principles" and "deserted his friends." Truman was also scornful since Eisenhower had earlier announced his endorsement of McCarthy—who sat on the platform while Eisenhower delivered the speech.

Marshall generously dismissed the Wisconsin incident. "Eisenhower was forced into a compromise, that's all it was," he told his goddaughter, Rose Page Wilson. Quoting Will Rogers, Marshall added, " 'There is no more independence in politics than there is in jail,' " (Similarly, when McCarthy later trotted out all but forgotten former Secretary of War Harry Woodring to assert that Marshall would "sell out his grandmother for personal advantage," Marshall was sympathetic. "Poor fellow. They used him." President Eisenhower was more angry. Queried by reporters, he strode from behind his desk and pounding his fist to palm snapped, "I think it is a sorry reward, at the end of at least fifty years' service to this country, to say that he is not a loyal, fine American and that he served only in order to advance his own personal ambitions.")

Eisenhower went on to post an overwhelming victory in the November general election. Marshall wrote to console Stevenson, assuring him he had fought a good fight. "You deserved far better of the electorate and you will be recognized increasingly as a truly great American."

Echoing the language of his speeches that Marshall had praised, Stevenson replied, "I have no regrets, except for the disappointment of my friends and supporters, and your letter alone would be sufficient regard for what I did and hoped to do better."

If Eisenhower had injured his old commander in bowing to McCarthy, the new president would atone for it many times over, Katherine insisted. The Marshalls were invited to the inauguration as members of the official party. Later they would often grace the guest list of White House dinners honoring visiting heads of state.

Despite friendship and frequent visits to the White House, Marshall claimed no special influence with the administration or with the man he now punctiliously addressed as "Mr. President." The retired general eschewed any political interest or involvement.

Other things occupied him. More and more he stood at gravesites in Arlington for the funerals of old comrades. Jonathan Wainwright, Ernest King, and Brehon Somervell among them.

In March 1953, Undersecretary of State Walter Bedell Smith proposed that Marshall head the American delegation to the June coronation of Queen Elizabeth II. Eisenhower made the appointment, ignoring political advisers who warned of McCarthy's continued attacks on Marshall for the loss of "a hundred million persons a year to international Communism."

Marshall was an apt choice to represent the United States in London. He had met both King George VI and his elder daughter during the war. A decade later, the highest ranking of all American soldiers was representing not only his president but those who had helped preserve Great Britain and make this ceremony possible: Franklin D. Roosevelt, stricken on the eve of victory; Harry Hopkins, Lord Root of the Matter, who had wasted to death early in 1946; Hap Arnold, dead in the Valley of the Moon, California, in January 1950; and tens of thousands of young men like Allen lying in cemeteries in strange lands.

Both Marshall and Katherine were delighted with the splendor and pomp of the occasion. Marshall was specially honored by his hosts. Just before the coronation in Westminster Abbey began, Omar Bradley recalled, first Winston Churchill, then Alan Brooke and Montgomery in their robes as Lords of the Realm pointedly turned out of the procession to shake Marshall's hand.

It was a grand celebration among old friends. There was a round of lunches with wartime colleagues and a day at the races with Churchill. He and Katherine spent time with Lady Mary Burghley, during the war the wife of the governor of the Bahamas where Marshall and Dill had once vacationed, now "my best friend over here," as the general wrote Truman.

A greater honor followed. On October 31, 1953, Marshall learned that he had been named the recipient of the Nobel Peace Prize. Nominated by former President Truman, among others, Marshall received the prize for his sponsorship of the European Recovery Program. He rose from a sickbed and month-long bout with the flu—he found it harder and harder to bounce back from these annual sieges—to hold an impromptu press conference in the living room of his Pinehurst cottage.

Regardless of the citation, he said in a hoarse voice, his greatest contribution to world peace "was in 1940 in the effort to persuade the administration and Congress to get under way with the preparations for the inevitable war. That was the hardest thing I ever did."

The award, Marshall told reporters, came as "a tribute to the whole American people." A number of people contributed to the plan, "the late Senator Vandenberg more than anyone else." His citation and the accompanying award of $33,840, thus was "unusual," he added, a contrast to the individual prize for literature, won that year by Winston Churchill.

The choice was widely applauded, except in the Soviet bloc. *Pravda* ran a satirical cartoon of a prognathous George Marshall, firebrand over one shoulder, dollar-sign insignia on the other sleeve, decked in a mask in the shape of a lamb's head.

The reporters gone, Marshall and Katherine spent two weeks recuperating from bronchial infections at Walter Reed. Confined there, he was unable to attend the White House dinner in honor of Queen Frederika of Greece. The queen instead visited him at the hospital.

To attend the Nobel ceremony in December, Marshall undertook a second sea voyage to Europe, hoping that the eight-day southern crossing to Naples would aid his recuperation. He traveled alone; Katherine did not feel up to the trip. Awed passengers on the *Andrea Doria* gave him a wide berth, until one approached to ask for an autograph. Marshall was more than gracious, the passenger recalled, "grateful for the momentary companionship. He complained that he was unhappy because no one came near him or talked to him. He was lonely."

Still weak from the influenza attack, Marshall husbanded his strength throughout the trip, preparing for the climactic banquet address he was to give.

Newsreels of the award ceremony before a glittering audience at Oslo University's Festival Hall caught Marshall as a seemingly weary man, the first professional soldier to be burdened by the responsibility of a Nobel Peace Prize. Just as Marshall was called to receive the medal, a small group of demonstrators in the balcony shouted: "Murderer! Murderer!" Described by police as members of Norway's ragged Communist Party, the protesters scattered over the audience below leaflets describing Marshall as "the man who decisively contributed to the atomic death of 100,000 people in Hiroshima and Nagasaki. . . ."

Even before members of Marshall's air crew, an embassy agriculture attaché, and police could grapple with the demonstrators, Norway's King Haakon VII rose to applaud the general. The entire audience followed, drowning out the protesters' shouts that "this is no peace candidate. Marshall go home!"

While fifty Communist protesters picketed outside the banquet hall the following night, Marshall in white tie and tails delivered his formal Nobel address.

"There has been considerable comment over the awarding of the Nobel Peace Prize for 1953 to a soldier," Marshall acknowledged. "I am afraid this does not seem as remarkable to me as it quite evidently appears to others. . . . The cost of war in human lives is constantly spread before me, written neatly in many ledgers whose columns are gravestones. I am deeply moved to find some means or method of avoiding another calamity of war."

For the moment, the means to peace included, paradoxically, arms. "A very strong military posture is vitally necessary today. How long it must continue I am not prepared to estimate, but I am sure that it is too narrow a basis on which to build a dependable, long-enduring peace."

That would take more, in particular, education of individuals and a change in national attitudes to foster international understanding. It would also require attention to the aspirations of the millions living under dreadful conditions "who have now come to a realization that they may aspire to a fair share of the God-given rights of human beings."

Marshall did not think highly of his Nobel address, written while he was ill. Yet the speech contained an insightful vision of the Western world's future challenge:

> We must present democracy as a force holding within itself the
> seeds of unlimited progress by the human race. By our actions we
> should make it clear that such a democracy is a means to a better
> way of life, together with a better understanding among nations.
> Tyranny inevitably must retire before the tremendous moral strength
> of the gospel of freedom and self-respect for the individual, but we
> have to recognize that these democratic principles do not flourish
> on empty stomachs and that people turn to false promises of dic-
> tators because they are hopeless and anything promises something
> better than the miserable existence that they endure.

Marshall returned to the United States still weak, still hoarse. He would never quite enjoy the best of health thereafter. He suffered a succession of minor illnesses—colds, bronchitis, a rash—his stays in the presidential suite at Walter Reed stretching out. His hearing worsened and he had trouble with his sense of balance. His limitations were more numerous, Marshall confessed in letters to friends.

He maintained a sense of humor. On the tenth anniversary of D-Day, he told inquiring White House newsmen his big worries now were "the blackbirds eating all my marigolds." He and Katherine did "a lot of gardening" he explained.

Nearing his seventy-fifth birthday, Marshall still struck *New York Times* writer Walter S. White as "rather like a finely coiled spring. The steel has bent a bit, become a bit less supple with the passing of the years. Still, it remains." Marshall appeared aloof, lofty, no man for small talk. It was Katherine, a "lady of subdued, relaxed gaiety," who softened the otherwise forbidding soldier.

To some who did not know him well, Marshall in retirement seemed venerable, a man still in command. One British guest recalled driving with the general to the country club in Leesburg for dinner; there Marshall's neighbors stood as he entered the club's dining room.

Some first-time visitors were awed despite themselves, perhaps by the signed photographs in the parlor from Queen Elizabeth and President Eisenhower, "Your Old Lieutenant"; perhaps by the expensive tapestries and paintings Madame Chiang had sent to Dodona Manor.

Visitors came often enough, both to Leesburg and Pinehurst. Omar Bradley came for a visit and golf. Marshall's stepgrandson Jimmie Winn stayed when his parents visited Japan. Queen Frederika brought her children, Crown Prince Constantine and daughter Sophia, to meet the man she considered Greece's protector.

He kept busy, for, after all, he was "absolutely all right from the neck up." Answering letters from well-wishers took time, and he spent some afternoons answering the questions of Forrest Pogue, the military historian selected to write his biography.

Occasionally he was consulted about military affairs. Interviewed on proposed reorganization of the Department of Defense, "the general made some very keen answers," Lieutenant Colonel George wrote Robert Lovett. "He reminisced quite a bit, almost entirely along lines of the importance of a unified and well coordinated team." Rather wryly Marshall noted for another interviewer, "Hindsight would be a valuable member of any cabinet."

The years grew harder. He took to using a cane on his afternoon walks with Katherine. Sergeant Heffner now made the daily run to pick up the mail in the civilian version of the Jeep Marshall so fancied. He had lately lost some weight and lacked energy, he wrote friends in May 1957.

In August 1958, Marshall checked into Walter Reed for the removal of a cyst on his face and for dental work. The short stay stretched out when he fell and cracked a rib. His concerned doctors discharged Marshall only after arranging for a medical corpsman to be on duty around-the-clock at Liscombe Lodge.

He was not well. Rose Wilson recalled visiting her godfather, sitting up in bed in his spartan bedroom, dressed in a dark blue Chinese dressing gown. Marshall was drawn, his skin pulled taut across his cheeks, his neatly brushed hair thinning, completely white. She was stunned. Her godfather, dear Colonel Marshall, was an old man.

She sat by his bed, holding his hand for long hours. "I have so much time now to remember," he told her. He recalled tobogganing with his father down Uniontown's steepest street. "What great sport that was!"

"Colonel Marshall," the woman replied, "I'm sorry your father didn't live long enough to know what a great son he had. He would have been very proud of you."

"Do you really think so?" Marshall asked. "I'd like to believe he would have approved of me."

Two weeks into the new year, the medical corpsman stationed outside Marshall's bedroom heard the strangled gasps of a man choking. Marshall had suffered a crippling stroke and had swallowed his tongue. The corpsman kept the general alive while an ambulance raced them to the Fort Bragg hospital nearby.

The stroke left him weakened and easily fatigued, but able to communicate. Even in sickness he clung to a sense of obligation. Responding to a request from *The Observer* (London), he dictated comments to be used in that newspaper's standing obituary for Winston Churchill. The prime minister, said the ailing general, was "a citizen of the world . . . a soldier, orator, author and statesman. Great was he in all . . . the perfect associate . . . dedicated to the principle that the right will prevail."

On February 18, Marshall suffered a second, more severe stroke. The hospital issued weekly bulletins and kept the White House informed of his condition. In March he was transferred to Walter Reed, but refused to oust cancer-stricken John Foster Dulles from the presidential suite. Sick herself, Katherine stayed in a guest cottage, always nearby, protecting her frail husband as best she could.

For a while Marshall seemed to rally, spending some of his time in a wheelchair, but slipping more and more often into the profound silence of the uncomprehending. Old comrades dropped by. Some he recognized and greeted in a whisper. With some he exchanged the stories of all old soldiers. His former orderly, retired Sergeant James W. Powder, came for a short visit, then stayed on at Marshall's request. Harry Truman visited. President Eisenhower came three times, once with Winston Churchill, himself eighty-four. Churchill merely stood in the doorway of the hospital room, watching with tears in his eyes the comatose man lying so small under the covers.

Marshall lost his sight, his hearing, his speech. He fell into a permanent coma, fed by tubes, but kept alive by dint of his strong physical constitution. His old doctor, Major General Morrison Stayer, who had helped Marshall beat the doctors in 1940, refused to come again. There was nothing medicine could do for the general.

Shortly after 6:00 p.m. on Friday, October 16, 1959, General of the

Army George Catlett Marshall, two and one-half months shy of his eightieth birthday, simply stopped breathing.

At his express order, there would be no state funeral. He who had planned the formal military funerals for Presidents Harding and Franklin Roosevelt, and for General of the Armies John J. Pershing, wanted no such elaborate ceremony for himself.

Instead, the honors would be simpler. At Eisenhower's order, flags flew at half-mast until the funeral. Marshall's body lay in state in the Bethlehem Chapel of the National Cathedral for twenty-four hours. Cadets from VMI joined the casket's honor guard traditionally composed of members of each of the services. Thousands shuffled quietly across the marble floor, past the casket, paying their respects.

The newspaper obituaries, long and prominent, struggled to take the measure of the man. Marshall had served his nation well. Born in 1880, when men easily recalled Lincoln and the Civil War, he had served ten presidents as a soldier and a diplomat. His career had carried him from the Philippines to the barren Oklahoma Territory, from a hellish war in France to service in strange, continually fascinating China. The perfect staff man, he had yearned for a troop command, only to become commander of the largest army his country would ever field.

Never the most brilliant student, or even the best read, he had steadily grown as a man and a soldier until he could be truly called a statesman. His world also grew, from Uniontown, Pennsylvania's few short blocks, to encompass the entire globe. In his lifetime, the United States transformed itself from an insular nation of thirty-eight states into a dominant world power. Marshall's own career paralleled much of that, and he would significantly shape many of the events in that history.

Over those years, he came to influence a generation of soldiers and scores of others who would hold high office long after his death. Some shared his military precepts, some his diplomatic vision. The best of them also emulated his concept of selfless service.

George Catlett Marshall exemplified in his lifetime all that was America's best—its sense of mission, of responsibility, of integrity, even nobility. The men and women in the small chapel at Fort Myer, Virginia, on this Tuesday in October understood what the nation had lost with that soldier's death.

The funeral on Tuesday, October 20, in the flower-filled chapel took just twenty minutes, the audience limited to a small list of invited guests. Some omitted asked to come, including Ambassador Robert Murphy, retired Lieutenant General Lucius Clay, and Sergeant Richard Wing, Marshall's orderly in China and in Moscow; all three were seated.

Canon Luther Miller of the National Cathedral, once Marshall's chaplain with the 15th Infantry at Tientsin and later chief of chaplains at the end of the war, presided over the brief Episcopal ceremony. President

Eisenhower and former President Truman, meeting for the first time in six years, sat side by side, their shared grief partially healing the rift between them. At Marshall's request, there was no eulogy.

The graveside service was equally brief. Marshall had asked for only a few honorary pallbearers: Sergeant Powder and his current orderly, Sergeant William Heffner; his wartime aide, Frank McCarthy, now a motion picture producer; Colonel George; Robert Lovett; and Walter Bedell Smith. Mrs. Marshall added a handful more, including retired Admiral Harold Stark and Omar Bradley. With Katherine, her daughter Molly, and Allen's widow, the men followed the coffin from the chapel to the green hillside below the Tomb of the Unknown Soldier not far from the equestrian statue of Marshall's friend, Sir John Dill.

Guests at the chapel heard first the honor guard's rifle volley reverberating among the tombstones, then a keening trumpet sounding "Taps."

NOTES

I have relied for guidance upon a handful of works by prior scholars. First, of course, are the four volumes of Forrest Pogue's official biography, *George C. Marshall*. Robert C. Dallek's *Franklin D. Roosevelt and American Foreign Policy, 1932–1945* similarly guided me in the paths of righteousness. James MacGregor Burns's *Roosevelt: The Soldier of Freedom* was a constant comfort. And for the complexities of big power diplomacy, I have leaned heavily on the unpublished official "History of the Joint Chiefs of Staff" written by Kenneth W. Condit, Walter S. Poole, James F. Schnabel, and Robert J. Watson. A copy of the draft manuscript is in the George C. Marshall Research Library (GCMRL), Lexington, Virginia.

Foreword

PAGE

xi   That civilized warrior: Wyden, p. 159.
xi   Perhaps he was: Winant, p. 134.
xi   I would trust: Harriman and Abel, p. 445.
xi   The combat soldier: Ridgway, *Soldier*, p. 126.
xi   I have seen: Acheson, *Sketches from Life*, p. 166.
xii Was still viewed: Wright and Bland, p. 150.
xii I have never: Bohlen, p. 268.
xii The greatest living: *New York Times*, October 17, 1959.
xii Primarily a military: Wedemeyer, p. 370.
xii Feet of clay: Pogue IV, p. 108.
xii A political general: Walter Trohan, "The Tragedy of George Marshall," *American Mercury* (March 1951), p. 271.
xiii I wonder: William Pfaff's comment is in the *Los Angeles Times*, July 8, 1988, part II, p. 7.
xiii Whether we shall ever: Alsop, p. 253.
xiii The lasting damage: Thomas Sowell, "How to Keep Good People Out of the Government," *Los Angeles Herald-Examiner*, July 28, 1988, p. A17.

Introduction: A Place in History

PAGE

5   Without considering: "The Story General Marshall Told Me," *U.S. News and World Report,* November 2, 1959, p. 52.

5   Withering vocabulary: Katherine Marshall, p. 109. Larry I. Bland, editor of the Marshall Papers, pointed out that Marshall extensively edited his wife's memoir, in effect making it his own.

6   If George Marshall: Ira C. Eaker is quoted in Coffey, p. 346.

6   Get results: Quoted in "Office of Chief of Staff Papers 1921–1942," Research notes by Miss E. D. Lejeune, GCMRL Xerox 3232.

7   You'd expect between old pals: General Laurence S. Kuter, "George C. Marshall, Architect of Air Power," *Air Force Magazine* (August 1978), quoted in Coffey, p. 209.

7   The best of a bad bargain: "Conversation with Secretary Marshall in His Office at the State Department, Wednesday Morning, July 23, 1947," in Robert E. Sherwood Papers, Houghton Library, Harvard University, archived as bMS Am 1947 (1899).

7   The most difficult: GCM to Robert E. Sherwood, February 25, 1947, in Sherwood Papers, bMS Am 1947 (548).

8   Nothing would come: Leahy, p. 208.

8   Hullabaloo: GCM to Sherwood, February 25, 1947. See Pogue III, pp. 266–278.

9   The best man: Roosevelt, *Rendezvous,* p. 348.

9   Marshall has got: Roosevelt, *Rendezvous,* p. 356.

9   His Majesty's Government: Pogue III, p. 307.

9   Not one American: *Ibid.* Such clashes may have influenced Roosevelt's decision to appoint Eisenhower. See Roosevelt, *Rendezvous,* p. 363.

9   Any soldier would prefer: Stimson and Bundy, p. 442.

9   Ike, you and I: Sherwood, p. 770.

9   *Newsweek* poll: December 7, 1943, reported by AP, December 2, 1943.

10 Has no "opposition": *Life,* January 3, 1944, p. 77.

10 Powerful forces: *Army and Navy Journal,* September 18, 1943.

10 It gave a false impression: Acheson, *Morning and Noon,* p. 165.

11 There is no point: Bill Henry, "Going My Way," *Los Angeles Times,* September 22, 1943.

11 You, Eisenhower: Buell, p. 426.

11 Almost official notice: Ambrose, *Supreme Commander,* p. 303.

11 I don't see: UPI dispatch to the *Los Angeles Herald-Examiner,* May 24, 1964.

12 He need have: GCM to Robert E. Sherwood, February 25, 1947, in Sherwood Papers.

12 Go along with it: Sherwood, p. 803.

13 It is for the President: *Ibid.*

13 On a mathematical basis: Stimson and Bundy, p. 442.

13 I feel I could not sleep: Sherwood, p. 803.

13 From the President: Marshall Library, Xerox 1339. The following

morning, Marshall retrieved the signed sheet from the code room, and added a postscript:

> Cairo, Dec. 7.43
> Dear Eisenhower. I thought you might like to have this as a memento. It was written very hurriedly by me as the final meeting broke up yesterday, the President signing it immediately. G.C.M.

Chapter I · A Very Simple Life

PAGE

17   Flicker: According to Pogue, Marshall's nickname is perhaps a corruption of the German word for freckles, *Flecke*. He attributed the name to Marshall's red hair.

17   I thought that: *Marshall Interviews*, p. 68.

17   Father was perfectly: *Marshall Interviews*, p. 43.

18   I suffered more: GCM to Rev. Bernard C. Newman, August 6, 1943, quoted in the *New York Herald Tribune*, September 24, 1943.

18   With short trousers: Catherine Armstrong to GCM, March 29, 1944, in *Papers*, I.

18   In this life: Pogue I, p. 17.

19   I was always: GCM to Mrs. Chester Davis, April 10, 1952, *Papers*, I.

19   Very famous hickory nut cakes: Pogue I, p. 27.

20   Squirted out into: Pogue I, p. 29.

20   She so soured me: Pogue I, p. 19.

20   Suffered very severely: Pogue I, p. 24.

21   If it was history: Pogue I, p. 22.

21   Bore a very heavy burden: GCM to Mrs. Davis, *Papers*, I.

21   Painful and humiliating: Pogue I, p. 35.

22   My father was rather contemptuous: Pogue I, p. 26.

22   It was a wonderful scene: GCM speech delivered at Uniontown, September 9, 1939, GCMRL.

24   I overheard Stuart: *Marshall Interviews*, p. 21.

24   The urgency to succeed: *Ibid.*

24   I send you my youngest: Pogue I, p. 42.

25   A lean and gawky cadet: General Johnson Hagood, quoted in Payne, p. 17.

25   I did not like school: GCM Uniontown speech, GCMRL.

26   To fight: Pogue I, p. 48, emphasis added.

27   I tried very hard: Pogue I, pp. 53–54.

28   Some of the airs: Pogue I, p. 55.

29   I was much in love: Pogue I, p. 56.

29   Made unkind: Rose Page Wilson, p. 175.

29   If commissioned: Pogue I, p. 63.

29   The old colored man: Pogue I, pp. 64–65. Pogue credits Marshall's father

PAGE

for continued lobbying that resulted in both Pennsylvania senators putting GCM on their list of young men recommended to take the exam.

30   Was catchy: GCM to "My Dear General Shipp," October 2, 1901, in *Papers*, I.

30   A very acceptable: *Ibid.*

Chapter II · The Long Years

31   The proximity: *Gazetteer*, p. 666.
31   Ill-suited to long: *Ibid.*
31   There isn't anything: Pogue I, p. 70.
31   About the wildest crowd: Pogue I, p. 74.
32   One day while working: *Statements*, 77th Congress.
32   It wasn't a time: Pogue I, p. 78.
32   In those far-off days: GCM to Clyde A. Benton, January 11, 1950, GCMRL.
32   A rather gloomy: *Ibid.*
33   As an immediate result: *Ibid.*
33   I remember: Pogue I, p. 81.
34   Burned almost black: Pogue I, p. 89.
34   The best one: *Ibid.*
35   He paid no attention: *Marshall Interviews*, p. 23.
36   Give the detail: Colonel A. L. Wagner to Brigadier General J. Franklin Bell, February 21, 1905, *Papers*, I.
36   I wondered: *Marshall Interviews*, p. 129.
36   And so I knew: *Ibid.*
37   I developed a position: *Ibid.*
37   Was the most thrilling: Associated Press Obituary Sketch 4025, November 1, 1958.
37   Learned how to learn: Pogue I, p. 101.
37   We were there: Pogue I, p. 100.
38   That two brothers: GCM speech, Air Corps Tactical School, Maxwell Field, Alabama, September 19, 1938, *Papers*, I.
38   Present to see the miracle: *Ibid.*
39   The human reactions: GCM speech, National Guard Association of Pennsylvania, October 13, 1939, *Papers*, I.
39   Rubbed each other: Manchester, p. 84.
39   On a shoestring: *Marshall Interviews*, p. 143.
40   They had taken me: *Marshall Interviews*, p. 141.
40   I turned out: GCM speech, Air Corps Tactical School, Maxwell Field, Alabama, September 19, 1938, *Papers*, I.
40   A few peaceful: GCM to General E. W. Nichols, February 3, 1912, *Papers*, I.
40   In any event: *Ibid.*
41   Develop the maneuver: *Marshall Interviews*, p. 137.

PAGE

41   The busiest man: *New York World,* August 17, 1912, quoted in *Papers,* I.
42   I am now paying: GCM to Nichols, July 4, 1913, *Papers,* I.
43   A courtly gentleman: *Marshall Interviews,* p. 150.
44   My company of infantry: Arnold, p. 44.
44   We pretty convincingly: GCM to Nichols, March 5, 1914, *Papers,* I.
44   A severe task: Pogue I, p. 123.
44   The greatest military genius: General Johnson Hagood, "Soldier," *Saturday Evening Post,* July 15, 1939, p. 62.
45   The lights are going out: Tuchman, *Guns,* p. 146.
46   The absolute stagnation: GCM to Nichols, October 4, 1915, *Papers,* I.
46   Now my dear fellow: Nichols to Marshall, n.d., *Papers,* I.
47   All the hot bloods: *Marshall Interviews,* p. 156.
47   This officer is well qualified: Hagood, "Soldier," p. 62.
48   The world must be made safe: Churchill, *The World Crisis,* pp. 700–03, describes the pursuit of Wilson from the British point of view.

Chapter III · Remarkably Gallant Fellows

Background material for this and the following chapter was drawn from Churchill, *The World Crisis;* Harbord; Pershing; *American Armies and Battlefields in Europe;* and Toland, *No Man's Land.*

49   The men seem: Marshall, *Memoirs,* p. 6.
49   The hell where youth: Siegfried Sassoon, "Suicide in Trenches."
50   The cost: Pogue I, p. 140.
51   Each seemed to feel, *Marshall Interviews,* p. 164.
51   They were such: Marshall, *Memoirs,* p. 3.
51   Especially well qualified: "Efficiency Report of G. C. Marshall, Jr., 1916," in *Papers,* I.
52   I have never seen: Marshall, *Memoirs,* p. 8.
53   Everyone seemed: *Marshall Interviews,* p. 170.
53   Personally got him up: Marshall, *Memoirs,* p. 13.
53   During the ensuing: *Ibid.,* p. 12.
54   To force the Germans: Pershing, I, p. 199.
54   A reverse: Marshall, *Memoirs,* p. 19.
55   We were "Exhibit A": *Ibid.,* p. 20.
56   Battles were inextricably: *Ibid.,* p. 32.
56   So picturesquely described: *Ibid.,* p. 33.
56   He just gave: *Marshall Interviews,* p. 175.
57   His eyes flashed: Benjamin F. Caffey to Forrest Pogue, January 14, 1961, GCMRL. Courtesy Larry Bland.
57   An inspired moment: *Marshall Interviews,* p. 176.
57   For like the only child: Marshall, *Memoirs,* p. 50.
58   Petted darlings: *Ibid.,* p. 21.

PAGE

58   I think General Pershing: *Marshall Interviews*, p. 185.

58   I was representing: *Ibid.*

59   Be left with us: Marshall, *Memoirs*, pp. 49–50. Three decades later, Marshall as chairman of the American Battle Monument Commission offered General Bordeaux's speech for the inscription on the memorial to the first men to die in the Normandy invasion, Pogue I, p. 156, notes.

59   A great mistake: *Marshall Interviews*, p. 189.

59   Had no business being: *Ibid.*

60   My God! Gas!: Marshall, *Memoirs*, p. 64.

60   This was the first: Marshall, *Memoirs*, p. 69.

61   The English army: Toland, *No Man's Land*, p. 57.

61   Assumed the proportions: Marshall, *Memoirs*, p. 76.

61   Infantry, artillery: Pershing, I, p. 373.

61   Temporarily jeopardizing: Marshall, *Memoirs*, p. 79.

62   When they began: *Ibid.*, p. 83.

62   The daily casualty lists: *Ibid.*

62   Feeling pretty seedy: *Ibid.*, p. 114.

63   Our troops: Pogue I, p. 166.

63   All felt that: Jean de Pierrefeu's remembrance is quoted in Churchill, p. 806.

Chapter IV · The Steamroller

64   When a high fly: Marshall, *Memoirs*, p. 108.

64   I am tired: Payne, p. 69.

64   Lt. Col. Marshall's: *Ibid.*

65   I had just enough champagne: Marshall, *Memoirs*, p. 111.

65   Bled white: Churchill, *The World Crisis*, p. 795.

66   He alone possessed: *Ibid.*, pp. 788–89.

66   Trials and tribulations: Marshall, *Memoirs*, p. 117.

67   Less frequent visits: *Ibid.*, p. 121.

67   The more serious: *Ibid.*, p. 129.

68   This enemy: Alden Brooks, quoted by Toland, *No Man's Land*, p. 322.

68   The history of the world: Frothingham, p. 286.

68   Wherever American troops: Marshall, *Memoirs*, p. 124.

68   The black day: Ludendorff, II, p. 683.

68   This virtually destroys: Pershing, II, p. 244.

69   Considerable sparring: *Ibid.*, p. 254.

69   To make a strong plea: Marshall, *Memoirs*, p. 125.

69   The high standard: *Ibid.*, p. 143.

70   To discuss with an old friend: *Ibid.*, p. 173.

70   One man sacrifices: *Ibid.*, p. 138.

71   Release and readjustment: *Ibid.*, p. 139.

71   That order for the Meuse: *Ibid.*

73   It was my fixed policy: *Ibid.*, p. 152.

PAGE

74   I rather feared: *Ibid.*, p. 156.
74   Despite the haste: *The United States Army in the World War, 1917–1919*, IX, p. 66.
74   Few people in England: Pershing, II, pp. 285–86.
76   Long and what must: Marshall, *Memoirs*, p. 162.
76   The propaganda: *Ibid.*, p. 163.
76   More a nervous: *Ibid.*, p. 166.
77   Everywhere on the battlefield: *Ibid.*, p. 167.
77   The fate: Quoted in Payne, p. 83.
78   A dangerous visionary: Callwell, II, pp. 134–35.
78   It would be a fatal: Toland, *No Man's Land*, p. 482.
78   Certain of our Allies: Marshall, *Memoirs*, p. 176.
79   A vain, ignorant: Toland, *No Man's Land*, p. 480.
79   A successor: *Ibid.*, p. 495.
79   Here was a commentary: Marshall, *Memoirs*, p. 183.
80   Staff officers: Johnson, p. 333.
80   It is General Pershing's desire: Marshall, *Memoirs*, p. 189.
81   MacArthur's paranoia: Manchester, p. 124.
81   Didn't have much patience: *Marshall Interviews*, p. 169.
82   A mild-looking: *New York Journal*, November 7, 1918, quoted in Payne, p. 91.
82   We had no thought: Marshall, *Memoirs*, p. 196.
83   My work is finished: Toland, *No Man's Land*, p. 575.

Chapter V · The Company of Generals

84   How would you like: Poque I, p. 196.
85   There is nothing romantic: "National Defense: The Business of Every Citizen," address at Brunswick, Md., November 6, 1938, GCMRL.
85   Hideous losses: Marshall, *Memoirs*, p. 31.
85   Ten minutes: Morison, *Turmoil and Tradition*, p. 550.
85   We had been friends: Marshall, *Memoirs*, p. 181.
85   The continuation of war: Quoted by Neumann, p. 14. Clemenceau was turning von Clausewitz's famous maxim on its head.
85   Americans would be fools: *The New Republic*, May 17, 1919, p. 3.
87   As long as I live: Rose Page Wilson, p. 30.
87   What a magnificent body: Marshall, *Memoirs*, p. 217.
87   Were so massive: *Ibid.*, p. 223.
87   For eight miles: *Ibid.*, p. 220.
88   I have never seen: *Marshall Interviews*, p. 218.
88   A voluptuous young Cuban: Rose Page Wilson, p. 11. Writing from memory, Wilson seemingly confused the time of this exchange. Some ten years later, MacArthur did keep a mistress in a Sixteenth Street apartment, according to Petillo, pp. 151–54.
89   Courtesy was one: Rose Page Wilson, pp. 268, 15, 21.

PAGE

89   He fetched: *Ibid.*, pp. 21–22.

89   George just naturally: *Ibid.*

89   Pershing led Jeff: *Ibid.*, p. 69.

90   A little girl: The poem was enclosed in GCM to Mrs. George C. Marshall [Sr.], March 7, 1921, and reprinted in *Papers*, I.

90   We both send: GCM to Pershing, December 13, 1920, *Papers*, I.

91   A master administrator: *Marshal Interviews*, p. 246.

91   In harmony with the genius: Pogue I, p. 206.

92   Profit by war experiences: *Infantry Journal*, XVIII (January 1921), pp. 34–37.

93   General Pershing had: *Marshall Interviews*, p. 90.

93   No, by God: *Ibid.*

93   General Pershing held: *Ibid.*

94   The war debt: "Address Before Headmasters Association—Boston," no date, but 1923, GCMRL.

Chapter VI · A Very Slow Thing to Improve

96   In the course of a tour: *Infantry Journal*, August 29, 1926, p. 171, cited in *Papers*, I. Larry I. Bland's notes there and Barbara Tuchman's *Stilwell*, pp. 30–51, 76–113, provide much of the background for this section.

97   Awfully nice house: Elizabeth C. Marshall to (Major) John C. Hughes, November 25, 1926, *Papers*, I.

98   A Chinese force: Ridgway, *Soldier*, p. 35.

98   Altogether, I find: GCM to Pershing, September 18, 1924, *Papers*, I.

98   Evidently my Chinese: GCM to Pershing, January 30, 1925, *Papers*, I.

99   With a fair degree: GCM to Pershing, April 22, 1925, *Papers*, I.

99   Now I can carry: GCM to John Hughes, July 18, 1925, *Papers*, I.

99   Stepping out: GCM to John Hines, June 25, 1925, *Papers*, I.

99   That farm home: GCM to Hines, ca. Christmas 1924, *Papers*, I.

99   During the last: GCM to Hines, June 6, 1925, *Papers*, I.

100   There has been: GCM to Pershing, December 26, 1926, *Papers*, I.

100   We all felt: Tuchman, *Stilwell*, p. 115.

100   All prance: *Ibid.*, p. 160.

101   As for me: GCM to Cocke, *Papers*, I.

102   The pleasantest house: GCM to Mrs. Thomas B. Coles, August 20, 1927, *Papers*, I.

102   A heart is a very slow thing: Elizabeth C. Marshall to Pershing, August 12, 1927, *Papers*, I.

102   I believe: Elizabeth C. Marshall to Mrs. Thomas B. Coles, September 6–7, 1927, *Papers*, I.

102   Just sort of picnicking: *Ibid.*

103   Spoke for a moment: Pogue I, p. 246.

103   Rose, I'm so lonely: Rose Page Wilson, p. 159.

PAGE

103   No one knows better: Pershing to GCM, October 6, 1927, *Papers*, I.

103   The truth is: GCM to Pershing, October 14, 1927, *Papers*, I.

104   She used to wear it: Rose Page Wilson, p. 160.

104   I thought I would explode: GCM to Major General Stephen J. Fuqua, November 25, 1932, *Papers*, I.

104   I have never forgotten: Stimson to GCM, January 21, 1928, *Papers*, I.

104   To the army: GCM to Stimson, December 22, 1927, *Papers*, I.

104   We bored: GCM to Major General Stuart Heintzelman, December 4, 1933, *Papers*, I.

105   [Benning] was magical: GCM to Fuqua, November 25, 1932, *Papers*, I.

105   A very special form: GCM, undated Infantry School lecture, *Papers*, I.

105   Picture the opening: *Ibid.* Marshall was not the only man to anticipate what would be called the blitzkrieg. The German Army staff was already at work developing those tactics. In Great Britain, Captain Basil Liddell Hart, in France an ignored Colonel Charles de Gaulle, and in the United States Lieutenant Colonel George S. Patton were all preaching the virtues of fast-moving armored columns in warfare. Marshall was virtually alone among the future Allied leaders to be in a position to transform theory into practice; it was probably one of his most significant contributions to the Allied cause, and one for which he has received scant credit.

105   I found: GCM to Heintzelman, December 18, 1933, *Papers*, I.

105   Expunge the bunk: *Ibid.*

106   Wicked memory: Katherine Marshall, p. 9.

106   Conspicuous: Pogue I, p. 258.

106   A genius: Tuchman, *Stilwell*, p. 157.

106   Move, shoot: *Ibid.*, p. 156.

106   The rudiments: Bradley, *A Soldier's Story*, pp. 19–20.

106   I hate: Rose Page Wilson, p. 163.

107   A very interesting officer: Katherine Marshall, p. 2. See also Pogue I, pp. 263–64. Details of Mrs. Marshall's life are from Pogue.

109   Tentatively engaged: Pogue I, p. 267.

109   I don't know: Marshall, *Together*, p. 3.

110   We hope: GCM to Pershing, October 1, 1930, *Papers*, I.

110   Any portion: GCM to Pershing, October 24, 1930, *Papers*, I.

110   In the new war: Eisenhower, *At Ease*, p. 195.

110   For duty with troops: "Special Order 96," April 25, 1931, in *Papers*, I.

111   Fine old sergeants: GCM to Pershing, December 3, 1931, *Papers*, I.

111   An unimportant station: Brigadier General Charles E. Kilbourne to Assistant Chief of Staff, November 4, 1932, in *Papers*, I.

111   At least keeps: GCM to Pershing, March 28, 1932, *Papers*, I.

111   Under his direction: "Report of the Infantry School for 1931–32," quoted in *Papers*, I.

Chapter VII · The Make

113   The essence of revolution: Schlesinger, *Crisis,* p. 264.

113   What a pitiful spectacle: *Ibid.*

113   Kind of amiable: Lippmann to Newton Baker, November 1931, quoted in Steel, p. 291.

113   We ate: Marshall, *Together,* p. 12.

114   As would a Southern: Pogue I, p. 273.

114   For the efficient: "Annual Inspection of Fort Screven, Ga., Fiscal Year 1933," by Major Thomas W. King, March 24, 1933, paragraph XXII, partially reprinted in *Papers,* I. This is apparently the only inspector general's report on Fort Screven that year, despite the undocumented contentions of Hunt, p. 161, that the post received a poor report.

114   In one week: Lippmann is quoted in Dallek, *Franklin D. Roosevelt,* p. 35.

115   A long wait: GCM to Pershing, July 11, 1933, *Papers,* I.

115   A splendid experience: *Ibid.*

115   The greatest social experiment: Pogue I, p. 280.

115   Pretty ruthless: GCM to Brigadier General George Grunert, December 5, 1938, *Papers,* I.

115   I made it: GCM to Major General George Van Horn Moseley, April 5, 1934, *Papers,* I.

116   Economic storm troops: Schlesinger, *Coming,* p. 339.

117   He has no superior: MacArthur to Keehn, September 28, 1933, *Papers,* I.

117   A very sympathetic: GCM to Pershing, November 12, 1933, *Papers,* I.

117   Those first months: Katherine Marshall, p. 18.

117   Well, Rosie: Rose Page Wilson, p. 199.

117   But the only trouble: GCM to Major Edwin F. Harding, February 26, 1935, *Papers,* I.

118   Our colored man: GCM to Pershing, September 8, 1935, *Papers,* I.

118   Two or three: GCM to Pershing, November 19, 1934, *Papers,* I.

118   I have had: *Ibid.*

119   Such letters: *Ibid.*

119   General Pershing asks: Franklin Delano Roosevelt Personal Papers, File 1604, Franklin Delano Roosevelt Library, Hyde Park, New York.

119   I can but wait: GCM to Pershing, June 10, 1935, *Papers,* I.

119   Outstanding man: Pogue I, p. 295. Military historian Pogue's charting of the intricacies of army politics is especially helpful. Pogue argues that MacArthur did not stall Marshall's promotion.

120   Every one: GCM to Pershing, December 27, 1935, *Papers,* I.

120   Heard from many: Katherine Marshall, p. 21.

120   Positively and definitely: Pogue I, p. 298.

121   All is in delightful: GCM to Major General Roy D. Keehn, March 25, 1937, *Papers,* I.

121   This matter: "Comments on C.C.C. Camp Inspections," undated, but June 1937, Vancouver Barracks, Washington, in *Papers,* I.

121   To help unblock: GCM to Captain Charles T. Lanham, August 28, 1936, *Papers*, I. In addition to Lanham, Marshall's correspondents during this period included Joseph Lawton Collins, Matthew Ridgway, Walton Walker, Terry de la Mesa Allen, and Mark W. Clark.

122   I am in splendid shape: GCM to Keehn, March 19, 1937, *Papers*, I.

123   Though no one wants: Major John S. Winslow to GCM, February 18, 1937, *Papers*, I.

123   An axis round: Goralski, p. 47.

124   A strategic trap: Steel, p. 339.

124   Abandoning the possibilities: GCM to John L. Cabell, April 20, 1937, *Papers*, I.

124   The two happiest years: Katherine Marshall, p. 24.

124   I am a country boy: GCM to Major General Frank R. McCoy, March 9, 1938, *Papers*, I.

124   The more prosaic: GCM to Leo A. Farrell, political editor of the *Atlanta Constitution*, March 26, 1938, *Papers*, I.

125   Much, a tremendous amount: GCM to Major Paul E. Peabody, April 6, 1937, *Papers*, I.

125   I am coming: GCM to Major Lloyd D. Brown, December 25, 1938, *Papers*, I.

125   We are so damned: GCM to Reed G. Landis, May 27, 1938, *Papers*, I.

Chapter VIII · The Last Lessons

126   Thank God, George: Katherine Marshall, p. 41.

127   I shall never: *Ibid.*

127   In the doorway: *Ibid.*, pp. 34–35. The orderly, who may well have saved the lives of the women, is identified only as "Private Jones" in Mrs. Marshall's book. The Marshalls met Jones at Vancouver Barracks when he was assigned, as a prisoner, to work in the brigadier's garden. Mrs. Marshall befriended him, learned he was to be given a dishonorable discharge, and asked her husband to intercede. Marshall succeeded, had Jones assigned as his orderly, and saw the court-martialed private eventually promoted to corporal, then sergeant.

128   Rumor is destroying: GCM to Pershing, September 26, 1938, *Papers*, I.

128   We never have: Speech, September 4, 1938, Clarksburg, West Virginia, *Papers*, I.

129   Peace with honor: *New York Times*, October 2, 1938.

129   A disaster of the first magnitude: Goralski, p. 73.

129   Sense of relief: Dallek, *Franklin D. Roosevelt*, p. 171.

129   Good man: Taylor, p. 185.

129   Only the beginning: Dallek, *Franklin D. Roosevelt*, p. 171.

129   Would be able: *Ibid.*, p. 172.

130   I fear: GCM to Keehn, October 15, 1938, *Papers*, I.

PAGE

130   A continuous matter: GCM to Colonel Frederick Palmer, December 8, 1938, *Papers,* I.

130   What are we going to do: Dallek, *Franklin D. Roosevelt,* p. 172.

130   Military victories: Speech, September 13, 1938, Maxwell Field, Alabama, *Papers,* I.

131   But in all these: Speech, March 3, 1939, *Papers,* I.

131   Did the major portion: *Marshall Interviews,* p. 87. The November 14 meeting is reconstructed from that source and from Pogue I, pp. 322–24; Blum, *Morgenthau Diaries,* pp. 46–49; Watson, pp. 130–43; and Dallek, *Franklin D. Roosevelt,* pp. 172–73.

132   The most pressing job: GCM to Stayer, October 18, 1938, *Papers,* I.

133   A tumultuous morning: GCM to Stayer, January 15, 1939, *Papers,* I.

133   I do not know: *Ibid.*

133   Harry Hopkins is described: Ickes, II, p. 508.

134   Something of the ill-fed horse: George Creel, quoted in *Current Biography 1941,* p. 406.

134   History's greatest spender: *Fortune* (June 1939), p. 53.

134   Too dumb: *Current Biography 1941,* p. 406.

134   He was generally: Sherwood, p. 1.

135   To impress Germany: Dallek, *Franklin D. Roosevelt,* p. 173.

136   We have lived: Lieutenant Colonel Truman Smith to GCM, November 20, 1938, cited in *Papers,* I.

136   It is five minutes: Dallek, *Franklin D. Roosevelt,* p. 184.

136   Nothing would so impress: Goralski, p. 83.

136   Cannot forever let pass: Dallek, *Franklin D. Roosevelt,* p. 179.

136   If Germany: *Ibid.,* p. 183.

137   Constant fear: *Ibid.,* p. 186.

137   Roosevelt put: *Ibid.,* p. 187.

138   My problem: Rose Page Wilson, p. 231.

138   While a brigadier: GCM to Leo A. Farrell, October 31, 1938, *Papers,* I.

138   My strength: *Ibid.*

139   Distasteful and I think: GCM to Major General William N. Haskell, January 30, 1939, *Papers,* I.

139   In very sketchy form: GCM to William M. Spencer, November 15, 1950, quoted in *Papers,* I.

139   Is that all right: Pogue I, p. 330.

139   I feel deeply honored: *Life,* January 3, 1944, p. 77.

139   The best of a bad bargain: "Conversation with Secretary Marshall in His Office at the State Department," July 23, 1947, in Robert E. Sherwood Papers, Houghton Library, Harvard University, bMS Am 1947 (1899).

140   I will need: GCM to Farrell, April 27, 1939, *Papers,* I.

Chapter IX · The Island Alone

143   Well, it's come: *Life,* January 3, 1944, p. 77.

144   That whole firmament: Blumenson, *The Patton Papers,* p. 944.

PAGE

144   I had not: Pogue II, p. 22.

144   Sorry state: "Conversation with Secretary Marshall in His Office at the State Department, July 23, 1947," in Robert E. Sherwood Papers, Houghton Library, Harvard University, bMS Am 1947 (1899).

144   I never haggled: Pogue II, p. 23.

145   I'm tired: Beschloss, pp. 199–200.

145   I would like: Perrett, p. 17.

145   This nation: FDR *Public Papers,* 1939 volume, p. 463.

147   That of a third-rate: Marshall, *The War Reports,* p. 16.

147   Time—time: L. C. Speers, "Our New Army Chief," *New York Times Magazine,* May 14, 1939, p. 17.

148   Have you noticed: Dallek, *Franklin D. Roosevelt,* p. 203. In the 1956 *Marshall Interviews,* p. 304, Marshall mentioned his "tragic feeling" that a prompt rearmament program in 1939 would have shortened the war by a year, while saving billions of dollars and 100,000 casualties.

148   There is no man: AP to the *Los Angeles Times,* October 28, 1939.

148   Everybody in town: Blum, *Morgenthau Diaries,* pp. 153–54.

148   Listen, Mr. Secretary: Pogue II, p. 22.

149   Nobody had: *Time,* May 8, 1939, p. 15.

149   I walk right: GCM to Malin Craig, September 19, 1939, in *Papers,* II, p. 59.

150   Marshall, officer: Associated Press "Obit Sketch 3130," June 15, 1944, by William Frye.

150   Beets no one: Katherine Marshall, p. 206.

150   Would do much: "Reminiscences of James T. Williams, Jr.," Oral History Research Office, Columbia University, 1957, pp. 917–18.

151   Whenever I find: GCM to General Green, July 5, 1940, *Papers,* II, p. 261.

151   We must be prepared: GCM to Brigadier General Lesley J. McNair, March 4, 1939, in *Papers,* I.

151   Events in Europe: Pogue II, p. 17.

151   If Europe blazes: *Military Establishment Appropriations Bill, 1941* (House of Representatives), p. 3.

152   The Army has never: Bernard Baruch to GCM, April 5, 1940, in GCMRL.

152   I feel culpable: *Marshall Interviews,* p. 574.

152   A turning point: Baruch, p. 278.

152   Before we become involved: *Military Establishment, Appropriations Bill for 1941* (Senate), p. 54.

152   I am more: *Ibid.*

153   General, I think: *Ibid.,* p. 65.

153   State for the record: *Ibid.,* p. 403.

153   Feeding the President: Blum, *Morgenthau Diaries,* p. 140.

154   Victory at all costs: *New York Times,* May 14, 1940, p. 1.

154   I don't scare: Pogue II, p. 29.

154   Stand right up: *Ibid.,* p. 30.

154   Well, I still think: The White House meeting is reconstructed from Pogue

Page

II, pp. 29–32; Dallek, *Franklin D. Roosevelt*, p. 221; and Blum, *Morgenthau Diaries*, pp. 142–49.

156   As you are no doubt: Churchill to Roosevelt, May 15, 1940, in Kimball, I, p. 37.

156   I know you can get: Pogue II, p. 32.

157   This is the end: Knightley, p. 231.

157   Militia of Dogberries: Calder, p. 92. According to recently declassified documents, Churchill was prepared to use poison gas against German invaders.

157   We shall defend: *New York Times*, June 5, 1940.

157   An armistice: See Shachtman, p. 248.

158   The almost incredible: Rosenman, IX, no. 58.

158   Has a tragic similarity: Blum, *Morgenthau Diaries*, p. 150.

158   If we were required: Pogue II, p. 53.

158   The tanks made: "Profiles: Chief of Staff," *The New Yorker*, October 26, 1940, p. 26.

158   Submitting: Blum, *Morgenthau Diaries*, p. 150.

158   Required to meet: Hall, p. 132.

159   Splendid stabilizer: Pogue II, p. 35.

159   France has lost: Kersaudy, p. 51.

160   Catspaw: Burns, p. 38.

160   Everybody is running: Henry L. Stimson Diaries, Manuscripts and Archives, Sterling Memorial Library, Yale University, New Haven, Conn., June 19, 1940. See also Murphy, *The Brandeis-Frankfurter Connection*, pp. 195–204.

160   Not once but many: Baruch, p. 277.

160   A small clique: Reprinted in *The New York Times*, June 21, 1940, p. 4.

160   Would sell out: Harry Woodring to Bob Harris, June 23, 1954, inserted in the *Congressional Record*, Vol. C, part 10, p. 12960, by Senator Joseph McCarthy, August 2, 1954. Woodring seems to have come late to that harsh opinion. *Papers*, II, p. 633, notes a chatty exchange of letters between Woodring and Marshall *sixteen months* after Woodring was replaced.

161   A New England conscience: Morison, *Turmoil*, p. 559.

161   I never heard: Ibid., p. 506.

162   Critical attention: *Ibid.*

162   The door: *Ibid.*, p. 499.

162   Always anxious: Stimson Diaries, July 22, 1940.

162   The wisdom: "Reminiscences of James T. Williams, Jr.," Oral History Research Office, Columbia University, 1957, p. 920.

162   It will be made: *Ibid.*

163   Their selection: James H. Hagerty, "Stimson and Knox Disowned by Party," *New York Times*, June 21, 1940, p. 4.

163   So give me your hand: Translated in Jullian, p. 23.

Chapter X · The Most Businesslike Manner

PAGE

164 But all reports: Stimson Diaries, July 24, 1940.

165 Two months ago: Smith, *Thomas E. Dewey*, p. 304.

165 A great many: *Marshall Interviews*, p. 300.

165 Why is this: Coffey, p. 209. On the eve of Pearl Harbor, the Air Corps was four times its 1939 size, with 11,000 aircraft of all types.

166 Then there was plenty: Pogue II, p. 193.

166 "Attacked" for inactivity: Sherwood, p. 157.

167 Chinaman's chance: Morison, *Turmoil*, p. 480.

167 One of the most stupid: *Ibid.*, p. 480 fn., emphasis added.

168 The only fair: Stimson and Bundy, p. 346. See also Watson, pp. 189–196, for details based on Grenville Clark's manuscript memoirs.

168 I would have defeated: Pogue II, p. 58.

168 Owing to the lower: Pershing, II, p. 228. When capably led, all-black units performed creditably, Pershing noted. See p. 117.

168 Darkey soldier: GCM to Mrs. Egbert Armstrong, May 16, 1941, in *Papers*, I. Marshall had no patience for those, including Mrs. Roosevelt, who agitated for full integration of the Army. On September 4, 1941, he wrote a note to Assistant Secretary of War John J. McCloy, pointing out that Communists had taken up this cause. See GCMRL Xerox 3232, p. 5.

169 White cooks: GCM to Charles Lawrence, November 5, 1941, GCMRL.

169 It has been: *Second Supplemental Hearings*, p. 17.

169 The Army played: Pogue II, p. 58.

169 We've got to: Associated Press dispatch to the *Los Angeles Times*, August 1, 1940. Churchill had secretly promised FDR he would never surrender the fleet.

170 We cannot afford: *Selective Compulsory*, p. 102.

170 The weeks have come: *Second Supplemental Hearings*, pp. 21–22.

171 Of course, General: *Ibid.*

172 An historic muster: Phillips, *The 1940s*, p. 72.

173 I was a little ashamed: Pogue II, p. 66.

173 And he did it well: Stimson Diaries, September 27, 1940.

174 One does acquire: *Promotion*, p. 12.

174 I was accused: Pogue II, p. 97.

175 Ruthless: Pogue II, p. 461, n. 29.

175 The President just laughs: Pogue II, p. 99.

176 Several men: Stimson Diaries, September 21, 1940.

176 I have been absolutely: GCM to "Dear Roosevelt," December 22, 1941, *Papers*, I.

176 At last they: Eichelberger, *Our Jungle Road*, p. xviii.

177 I tell you: Pogue II, p. 461.

177 Monotonous drilling: Marshall's speech at Trinity College on June 15, 1941, is in *Papers*, I.

178 I am interested: Pogue II, p. 110.

PAGE

178   Some warmed-over: Pogue II, p. 113.
178   The President: Katherine Marshall, p. 79.
179   Addressed to you: Sherwood, p. 191.
180   I did not think: Kimball, p. 81.
180   It is now: Stimson Diaries, December 19, 1940.
180   This emergency: Stimson Diaries, December 16, 1940.

Chapter XI · The Common Law Alliance

181   Was one of the most important: Churchill, *Their Finest Hour,* p. 554.
181   Expanding to the utmost: Kimball, I, p. 108.
182   The best immediate: Rosenman, IX, No. 149.
182   With that neighborly: Sherwood, p. 225. Churchill had proposed the United States loan Great Britain destroyers for convoy duty in the December 7 message; FDR was merely broadening the concept to include all war goods.
182   The Nazi masters: Rosenman, IX, pp. 633 ff. Sherwood, p. 226, attributes the ringing "arsenal of democracy" phrase to Harry Hopkins.
183   In times like these: Burns, pp. 34–35.
183   The result of lend-lease: Perrett, p. 75.
183   Most unsordid: Churchill, *Their Finest Hour,* p. 569.
183   Declaration of economic war: Stimson and Bundy, p. 360. The United States would produce $50 billion worth of goods under the act.
183   A ripping speech: Stimson Diaries, March 2, 1941.
184   An endless chain: Katherine Marshall, p. 80.
185   Been through hell: Truman, I, p. 185.
186   Goddam contrary cuss: Miller, *Plain Speaking,* p. 180.
186   Every ten cents: *Ibid.,* p. 172.
186   No military man: *Ibid.*
186   It seems to me: Pogue II, p. 108.
186   I got to know: Miller, *Plain Speaking,* p. 178.
187   Should the United States: *Pearl Harbor Attack,* XV, Exhibit 15, pp. 1485–1542.
187   That we would stand: Watson, pp. 124–25.
188   There can be no doubt: "History of the Joint Chiefs of Staff," Section III, Chapter I, ms. p. 7, GCMRL Xerox 1561. From at least 1924 on, military planning in the event of a two-ocean war called for a Europe-first strategy, planners ceding temporary possession of the Philippines, Wake, and Guam to the Japanese until their recapture. See "Joint Planning Committee to Joint Board, March 12, 1924," in GCMRL Xerox 2567.
188   An ever present possibility: "Joint Army and Navy Basic War Plans," Joint Planning Committee to Joint Board, April 9, 1940, GCMRL.
189   First, that America: "Introduction," dated July 17, 1941, by President Roosevelt, in Rosenman, IX.

PAGE

189   Alone, the British Commonwealth: Joint Board 325, Serial 670, December 21, 1940, quoted in "History of the Joint Chiefs," ms. p. 28, GCMRL Xerox 1561.

190   British leadership: *Ibid.* This memorandum, apparently never printed in full, clearly establishes that American military leaders understood geopolitical realities, despite the contrary assertions of such Commonwealth historians as A. J. P. Taylor and Chester Wilmot.

190   I don't feel: Pogue II, p. 128.

190   Strategic thinking muddled: Slessor, p. 349.

191   Provided the highest: Sherwood, p. 273.

191   One last desperate: *New York Times,* April 24, 1941.

192   Every possible assistance: Rosenman, IX, pp. 181 ff.

192   The naval thinking: "Conversation with Secretary Marshall in His Office at the State Department, July 23, 1947," in Robert E. Sherwood Papers, Houghton Library, Harvard Library, bMS Am 1947 (1899). Not until spring 1943 did the Navy move to reorganize its logistical system, according to Buell, pp. 405 ff.

193   Most valuable: Eisenhower, *Crusade,* p. 163. The other four were the bulldozer, the 2½-ton truck, the C-47 transport, and the amphibious DUWK.

193   At the dead center: Paul Robinett Diary, January 2, 1941, GCMRL.

193   The most self-contained: *Ibid.,* January 5, 1941.

194   He would seem: "Reminiscences of James T. Williams, Jr.," Oral History Research Office, Columbia University, p. 919.

194   Nothing irritates: Robinett Diary, February 14, 1941.

194   Would never fight: Author's interview with A. C. Wedemeyer, USA Ret., in Pacific Palisades, California, August 1, 1983.

194   That long-legged major: Wedemeyer, p. 62.

194   That blue-eyed major: "The Reminiscences of General Anthony C. McAuliffe," Oral History Research Office, Columbia University, 1963, p. 67.

195   Very severe: *Ibid.*

195   No one was willing: *Ibid.,* p. 49.

195   And they didn't call: *Ibid.,* p. 47.

195   Were almost sure: *Ibid.,* p. 50.

195   Jesus, man: Pogue II, p. 292.

195   Resent our suggestions: Robinett Diary, January 5, 1941.

195   Golden streak of imagination: *Ibid.*

195   A consummate Army politician: Robinett Diary, January 16, 1941.

196   I often shudder: Bradley and Blair, p. 92.

Chapter XII · The Summer's Storms

In addition to the sources cited, William R. Emerson's essay "F.D.R.," in May, *The Ultimate Decision,* and Feis, *The Road to Pearl Harbor,* were helpful.

PAGE

198   A minimum of one month: Stimson Diaries, June 23, 1941.

198   Formidable only: "Assistant Chief of Staff, G-2, to War Plans Division, July 3, 1941," in *Pearl Harbor Attack,* XXVI, p. 1412.

198   Were wise enough: "Minutes of Secretary of War Conference," June 23, 1941, GCMRL, cited in Pogue II, p. 72.

198   In the first place: GCM to Stimson, August 29, 1941, quoted in Watson, p. 329.

199   The only thing: Sherwood, p. 342.

199   The estimates: *House of Representatives . . . Second Supplemental Appropriation Bill for 1942,* I, p. 15.

200   We certainly: *Second Supplemental,* I, p. 24.

200   Clearcut strategic estimate: Cline, p. 60.

200   The intrigues: Wedemeyer, p. 79.

201   Prevention of the disruption: "Joint Board Estimate of United States Over-all Production Requirements," September 11, 1941, in GCMRL.

201   *While holding Japan: Ibid.* The italics are those of Marshall and Stark, who signed the estimate.

201   Naval and air forces: *Ibid.*

202   Was very worried: Author's telephone interview with Dean Rusk, November 25, 1980.

202   His efforts: Katherine Marshall, p. 91. Since Marshall himself closely edited and, in places, rewrote the manuscript, it may be assumed this is a self-evaluation.

202   The virtual demobilization: *Ibid.,* p. 92.

203   Only a small portion: "Biennial Report of the Chief of Staff of the United States Army, July 1, 1939 to June 30, 1941 to the Secretary of War," reprinted in Marshall, *The War Reports,* p. 29.

204   Worst of all: Associated Press dispatch to the *Los Angeles Times,* July 4, 1941.

204   Do not come: *Los Angeles Times,* July 4, 1941.

204   Undoubtedly we shall need: *New York Times,* July 5, 1941.

204   We certainly are: *New York Times,* July 7, 1941.

204   A gigantic conspiracy: Burns, p. 120.

205   Again afraid: Sherwood, p. 367.

205   Of all the men: "Reminiscences of James T. Williams, Jr.," Oral History Research Office, Columbia University, 1957, pp. 918–19.

206   In forty years: Pogue II, p. 148.

207   It may clarify: *Retention of Reserve Components,* p. 5.

207   We have seen: *Ibid.,* p. 8.

208   Blow us back: Martin, p. 96.

208   Willing to risk: Pogue II, p. 153.

208   You put the case: *Marshall Interviews,* p. 276–77. See also James W. Wadsworth to GCM, August 25, 1941, GCMRL.

209   If I can only: Sherwood, p. 281.

209   Were based on: *Providing for the National Defense,* pp. 3 ff.

209   I think it would: *Ibid.,* p. 33.

PAGE

212   To some: Stark's letter is quoted in Buell, p. 139.
213   Watch and see: Roosevelt and Brough, p. 292.
213   I think the best: Pogue II, p. 142.
213   Charm and real: Colville, *Winston Churchill*, p. 181.
213   But Britain: Roosevelt and Brough, p. 293.
214   The Americans must: *Ibid.*, p. 294.
214   Deeply moving: Churchill, *The Grand Alliance*, p. 384.
214   That these military: "British-American Cooperation, Department of State Memo of Conversation," August 11, 1941, by Sumner Welles, quoted in "History of the Joint Chiefs of Staff," Section III, GCMRL Xerox 1561.
215   To take countermeasures: Sherwood, p. 354.
215   Be almost decisive: *Ibid.*, p. 355.
215   It seemed likely: Gwyer, III, p. 127.
216   The exact status: Elliott Roosevelt, *As He Saw It*, p. 23.
216   So resplendent: Roosevelt and Brough, p. 293.

Chapter XIII · *Oranges, Purples, and Rainbows*

218   I shall run: Prange, et al., *At Dawn*, p. 10.
218   To launch: *Ibid.*, pp. 16–17.
220   A new order: *FRUS: Japan, 1931–1941*, II, pp. 165–66.
220   Intricate rat's nest: *Pearl Harbor Attack*, XXXV, p. 392.
221   In view of abnormal: Associated Press dispatch to the *Los Angeles Times*, October 9, 1940.
222   When a big house: Prange, et al., *At Dawn*, p. 6.
222   I wish to declare: Goralski, p. 146.
222   Excellent shape: Pogue II, p. 170, citing the *Honolulu Advertiser*, March 6, 1940.
222   To protect the base: Pogue II, p. 170.
222   Dangers envisaged: *Pearl Harbor Attack*, III, p. 1058.
222   Seed corn: GCM to Stark in *Pearl Harbor Attack*, XXXII, p. 556. The best study of American political and military policy in the Pacific is Pomeroy, *Pacific Outpost*.
223   There can be: Pogue II, p. 172.
223   In the past: *Pearl Harbor Attack*, III, p. 1061.
223   Machine gun outfits: Hoehling, p. 47. See also Prange, et al., pp. 53–54.
223   Impression of the Hawaiian problem: GCM to Short, February 7, 1941, reprinted in *Pearl Harbor Attack*, XXVII, p. 17.
224   Old Army: *Ibid.*
224   The hazards: *Pearl Harbor Attack*, III, p. 1086.
224   With our heavy: Stimson Diaries, April 23, 1941.
224   It would be: *Pearl Harbor Attack*, XV, p. 1635.
224   Just as one carrier: Prange, et al., p. 124, quoting a Short press conference.
224   Here in Hawaii: *Honolulu Star-Bulletin*, April 7, 1941.

PAGE

225 Many drifting straws: Churchill to Roosevelt, February 15, 1941, in Kimball, I, p. 135.

225 This region: Goralski, p. 148.

225 We shall attain: Far East Military Tribunal, cited by Prange, et al., p. 741.

226 We will endeavor: *Pearl Harbor Attack,* XII, p. 2.

227 The Japs are: Roosevelt to Ickes, July 1, 1941, quoted in Feis, *The Road,* pp. 206–07.

227 Policy of force: *Ibid.*

227 CNO and COS: *Pearl Harbor Attack,* XIV, p. 1327.

228 Field marshal: Pershing to John Callan O'Laughlin, June 10, 1937, quoted by Petillo, p. 276, n. 68.

228 Provide an adequate: MacArthur's letter to GCM is quoted in Manchester, p. 208.

228 I hold: MacArthur to Steve Early, March 21, 1941, as quoted by Petillo, p. 196. See also James, *Years,* I, pp. 585 ff.

228 In all discussions: Watson to MacArthur, April 15, 1941, quoted in Petillo, p. 197.

228 Marshall incidentally: Stimson Diaries, May 21, 1941. From the entry, it is not clear when Marshall discussed MacArthur's role. In a letter to MacArthur, Marshall said they first discussed it about March 20, 1941.

229 It was decided: GCM to MacArthur, June 20, 1941, GCMRL. Just who held up the MacArthur appointment remains unclear. Those who believe there was a feud between MacArthur and Marshall blame the chief of staff; see Lee and Henschel, p. 121, for example. MacArthur's *Reminiscences,* p. 108, misdates Marshall's reply.

229 Given the rank: MacArthur, p. 109, blaming "the bureaucracy."

230 I think Stimson: Unpublished "Reminiscences of Harvey H. Bundy," interviews conducted in 1958–60 in Boston by Saul Benison and Frank Safford, Oral History Research Office, Columbia University, p. 259.

230 Lay more in their temperaments: Pogue II, p. 185.

230 Secret plans: Hunt, p. 211.

231 Complete jubilation: MacArthur to John Callan O'Laughlin, October 6, 1941, cited in Petillo, p. 199.

231 Overconfidence: James, *Years,* I, p. 609.

231 "Citadel" notion: Manchester, p. 215. See also Petillo, pp. 199–201, and Pogue II, pp. 186–88.

232 War Department calling: The anecdote is retold by Katherine Marshall, pp. 125–26.

233 The case: Steel, p. 391.

233 The British, for example: Pogue II, p. 77.

233 To sound: "Morale of the Country, Notes on the Lippmann-Lindley Theory," September 22, 1941, in GCMRL, Research File, Chief of Staff, Xerox 235, Victory Program. The Victory Program stated flatly: "We must prepare to fight Germany by actually coming to grips with and defeating her ground forces and definitely breaking her will to combat."

234 A new Chinese: Karnow, p. 13. Significantly, Henry Luce, whose publications then and later stirred so much sentiment in favor of Chiang, was born in China, the son of missionaries.

234 With God's help: *Ibid.*

234 Will function: Associated Press dispatch to the *Los Angeles Times*, August 21, 1941.

234 To hell: *Life* is quoted in Pogue II, p. 155. The *Nation* poll by Harold Lavine is in the August 19, 1941, issue.

234 Quite tragic: GCM to Bernard Baruch, August 19, 1941, quoted in Pogue II, p. 155.

235 Misinformed individuals: Associated Press dispatch to the *Los Angeles Times*, September 15, 1941.

235 While the troops: GCM "Memorandum for the President," September 6, 1941, GCMRL.

235 Dear George: FDR to GCM, September 23, 1941, GCMRL.

235 The Task Force: Prange, et al., p. 332. The complete text of the 700-page document is in *Pearl Harbor Attack*, XIII, pp. 431 ff. Because of the international dateline, Tokyo is twenty hours later than Honolulu. The 7:00 a.m. December 7 zero hour was 4:00 a.m. Monday, December 8, in Tokyo.

Chapter XIV · The Throw of the Die

236 Action by Japan: *FRUS: Japan, 1931–1941*, II, p. 701, quoted in Feis, *The Road*, p. 298.

236 Because of our state: GCM to the Navy Court of Inquiry, reprinted in *Pearl Harbor Attack*, XXXII, p. 560.

236 Calculated risk: Brereton, p. 8.

237 Now that I: *The Magic Background to Pearl Harbor*, Nomura to Togo, October 22, 1941.

237 At the present time: Prange, et al., *At Dawn*, p. 337.

237 Minor concessions: "Minutes of the Joint Board," November 3, 1941, quoted in Pogue II, p. 196.

237 Strain every nerve: Dallek, *Roosevelt*, p. 305.

237 Last effort: Togo to Nomura, November 4, 1941, Telegram No. 725 in *The Magic Background to Pearl Harbor*.

238 Because of various: *Pearl Harbor Attack*, XII, p. 100.

238 Would be out of the question: Dallek, *Roosevelt*, p. 306, citing *FRUS: Japan, 1931–1941*, II, pp. 715–19.

238 The United States: Sherrod, "Secret Conference with General Marshall," in Brown and Bruner, p. 40. Sherrod's notes of the conference, addressed to David Hulburd, November 15, 1941, are in *Papers*, II, pp. 676–79. Those of Ernest K. Lindley of *Newsweek* are in GCMRL.

240 The Grand Strategy: Sherrod to Hulburd, November 15, 1941, in *Papers*, II, p. 676. Questioned in 1949 about his November 1941 remarks, Mar-

PAGE

shall acknowledged his misplaced faith. See GCM to Hanson Baldwin, September 21, 1949, in GCMRL. Marshall apparently did not recall that, on November 28, 1941, the United States ambassador to the Soviet Union cast cold water on the idea of using Soviet airfields. See the Stimson Diaries for that date.

240   To stay there: Pogue II, p. 216. See also Katherine Marshall, p. 98.

240   After that: *Pearl Harbor Attack,* XII, p. 165.

240   TOP SECRET: *Pearl Harbor Attack,* XIV, p. 1405.

241   It seems to me: Roosevelt to Churchill, November 24, 1941, in Kimball, I, p. 276.

241   The Japanese are: Cordell Hull's diary is quoted in Millis, *This Is Pearl,* p. 236.

241   These fellows mean: *Pearl Harbor Attack,* III, p. 1148.

241   For the Japanese: Stimson Diaries, November 25, 1941.

242   The first Japanese: *Pearl Harbor Attack,* III, p. 1149.

242   Actual hostilities: Pogue II, p. 207.

242   Fairly blew up: Stimson Diaries, November 26, 1941. Actually, the convoy sighted south of Formosa was headed for Thailand, Malaya, and Singapore. Other convoys were en route, undetected, to Tarawa and Makin Islands in the Gilberts, to Wake Island, to Guam; and within days to Borneo and the Philippines.

243   The moment the Japanese: *Pearl Harbor Attack,* III, p. 1246.

243   To kick the whole thing: Stimson Diaries, November 26, 1941.

243   Possible at any: Dallek, *Roosevelt,* p. 308.

243   Any peaceful nation: Pogue II, p. 206.

243   But Hull remained: Nomura to Togo, November 26, 1941, in *Pearl Harbor Attack,* XII, p. 182.

243   A very tense: Stimson Diaries, November 27, 1941.

243   I have washed: *Ibid.*

243   To be on the *qui vive:* Stimson deposition in *Pearl Harbor Attack,* XI, p. 5423.

244   Negotiations with the Japanese: *Pearl Harbor Attack,* XI, p. 5424, and Pogue II, p. 209. MacArthur's supporters and Pearl Harbor revisionists sometimes omit the crucial last sentence. See Manchester, p. 223, and Toland, *Infamy,* pp. 6–7.

244   Prior to hostile: *Pearl Harbor Attack,* XI, p. 5424 (emphasis added). The "do-don't" nature of the warning, to use General Short's description, was a case of too many cooks. In contrast, the War Department on June 17, 1940, acted with precision in responding to rumors of an attack on Pearl Harbor.

244   The large numbers: *Ibid.*

244   However unjustified: *Pearl Harbor Attack,* III, p. 1173.

244   The most essential: "Memorandum for the President," signed by GCM and Stark, November 27, 1941, in GCMRL. The same is in *Pearl Harbor Attack,* XXVII, p. 15.

245   This dispatch: *Pearl Harbor Attack,* XIV, p. 1406.

PAGE

245   The Secretary of War: "SECRET Radiogram," GCM to MacArthur, November 28, 1941, GCMRL.

245   *Higashi no kaze ame:* Prange, et al., *At Dawn,* p. 360.

245   Humiliating proposal: Togo to Nomura, November 28, 1941, in *Pearl Harbor Attack,* XII, p. 195.

246   With the permission: Toland, *But Not in Shame,* p. 29.

247   Our empire has decided: Prange, et al., *At Dawn,* p. 433.

247   *Niitaka yama nobore:* Prange, et al., *At Dawn,* p. 445.

247   Should Japan: *Pearl Harbor Attack,* XII, p. 200.

247   Now stand ruptured: *Pearl Harbor Attack,* XII, p. 204.

248   Perhaps his position: Stimson Diaries, December 1, 1941.

248   Something is going: Prange, et al., *At Dawn,* p. 457.

248   Thanksgiving failed: Secret "Memorandum for the Chief of Naval Operations," December 2, 1941, GCMRL.

248   I want to know: GCM to "Dear Marley," November 26, 1941, GCMRL.

248   Anyone who stays: "Memorandum for Colonel Smith," November 6, 1941, filed under "Thompson, Charles R.," in GCMRL.

249   Nothing more unpatriotic: Stimson Diaries, December 4, 1941.

249   If this is a blackfish: Prange, et al., *At Dawn,* p. 463. They had stumbled upon a Japanese scout submarine.

249   As the morning: Stimson Diaries, December 6, 1941.

250   The situation: *Pearl Harbor Attack,* XII, pp. 238–39.

250   The rise and fall: Prange, et al., *At Dawn,* p. 472. The signal was inspired by that sent by Admiral Togo at Tsushima in 1905, Japan's greatest sea victory: "On this one battle rests the fate of our nation. Let every man do his utmost." See Prange, et al., *At Dawn,* p. 445. Of course, both owe something to Nelson's signal at Trafalgar.

250   Give thought: *Pearl Harbor Attack,* XIV, p. 1420.

251   This son of man: Dallek, *Roosevelt,* p. 309.

251   It is the immutable: "Memorandum," *Pearl Harbor Attack Report,* pp. 213–16. The Japanese invasion of China was purportedly a move to restore peace between the three feuding factions in the Chinese civil war. Hence China's "failure."

252   This means war: *Pearl Harbor Attack,* X, pp. 4461–69.

252   Required action: *Pearl Harbor Attack,* II, pp. 5543.

253   It certainly looked: Prange, et al., *At Dawn,* p. 475.

253   In coping: *Pearl Harbor Attack Report,* p. 223, n. 309, and *Pearl Harbor Attack,* XII, p. 245.

254   The Japanese were: *Pearl Harbor Attack,* IX, p. 4517. On Marshall's ride, see *Pearl Harbor Attack,* III, p. 1108, and Rose Page Wilson, p. 245.

254   A most important message: *Pearl Harbor Attack,* XI, pp. 5175–76. Marshall's morning ride has become a part of the Pearl Harbor myth, his official biographer notes. Significantly, he points out that the president, Stimson, Knox, Hull, Stark, the two military intelligence chiefs, and the chiefs of war plans for both services saw the message at least a half-hour before Marshall, but sounded no alarm. Alone of everyone in Washing-

PAGE

ton, he sent an alert that last morning. The *assumption* is that had he seen the Fourteen-Part Message sooner, he would have acted sooner.

254   Everything in MAGIC: Stimson Diaries, December 7, 1941.

255   The Honolulu radio: Prange, et al., *At Dawn*, p. 487.

255   Some definite significance: *Pearl Harbor Attack Report*, p. 224.

255   The Japanese are: *Ibid.*

256   If there is any question: *Pearl Harbor Attack*, XI, p. 5273.

257   The biggest sightings: Prange, et al., *At Dawn*, p. 500.

Chapter XV · The Sword Drawn

259   This is no drill: Prange, et al., *At Dawn*, p. 517.

259   Just the kind: Sherwood, p. 431.

260   Shocked disbelief: Prange, et al., *At Dawn*, p. 555.

260   I suppose it was: Alsop, p. 238. Alsop had the story second or third hand. Still, it is as close to an explanation for Stark's otherwise unexplained dismissal as we have. Were Stark dismissed for his failure to prevent the Pearl Harbor attack, then the equally culpable Marshall too should have been relieved. Stark's successor, Admiral Ernest J. King, believed Stark was "sacrificed to political expediency," according to King and Muirhead, p. 356.

260   My God: Prange, et al., *At Dawn*, p. 556.

261   We're now in the fog: "The Reminiscences of Harvey H. Bundy," Oral History Research Office, Columbia University, 1961, p. 209.

261   What's this about Japan: Burns, p. 163.

261   Yesterday comma: Marjorie Hunter, "Grace Tully, 83, a Secretary to Franklin Roosevelt, Dies." *New York Times*, June 16, 1984.

261   They were careless: Rose Page Wilson, p. 246.

261   Four hours: *Ibid.* The first air raids on northern Luzon did come four hours after word of Pearl reached Manila. Whatever hope MacArthur had of defending the Philippines until relief could come from the United States probably ended in those first minutes of war.

262   "Marauder"-"Murderer": Coffey, p. 246.

262   We should: Stimson Diaries, December 8, 1941.

262   Thanked him: *Ibid.*

263   He spent his whole: Bundy Oral History, p. 184. See also *Marshall Interviews*, pp. 408–09.

263   A sort of graduate school: Eisenhower, *At Ease*, p. 173.

264   The chief says: Eisenhower, *Crusade*, p. 14.

264   What should be: *Ibid.*, p. 18.

264   Filipino wards: *Ibid.*, p. 21.

264   General: *Ibid.*

265   An eye that seemed: Ambrose, *Eisenhower*, I, p. 134.

267   Reality and new facts: Churchill to Roosevelt, December 9, 1941, reprinted in Kimball, I, p. 283.

268   The war against Japan: "Record of Staff Conferences on 19 Dec. 41, Churchill and Beaverbrook with British C.O.S.," cited in unpublished "The War Against Germany and Her Satellites," Chapter II, GCMRL Xerox 1561.

268   The realisation: "Memo by British C.O.S., sub 'American-British Strategy,' Doc. W.W.-1, 22 Dec. 41," from the files of Joint Chiefs of Staff Historical Section, GCMRL.

269   Did not foresee: "The War Against Germany and Her Satellites," Chapter II, p. 70, citing the British minutes of the White House meeting. Churchill apparently had in mind the notion of a relatively small, twelve-division landing force applying a *coup de grâce* to a Germany in collapse.

269   The prime minister: Roosevelt and Brough, p. 306.

270   At least he provided: Ismay, p. 244. Another British officer was stunned to discover that the "dislike existing between the American Army and Navy was . . . carried to extraordinary lengths." See Cunningham, pp. 466–67.

270   They could examine: Halifax, p. 260. See also *Marshall Interviews,* pp. 379–80.

271   This country: Dill to Brooke, December 28, 1941, quoted in Bryant, *Turn,* p. 233.

271   I cannot help reflecting: Sherwood, p. 444.

272   This country has not: Bryant, *Turn,* pp. 234.

272   One of his major: Pogue II, p. 275. The description here of Marshall pushing through the concept of the unified commander is based on Pogue's.

272   I am convinced: Sherwood, p. 455.

273   What the devil: Pogue II, p. 280. The British point of view is stated in Kirby, *Singapore,* I, pp. 264–66.

274   Accept the responsibilities: Pogue II, p. 287.

275   Motivated more largely: Stanley D. Embick, unpublished notes written December 29, 1941, for discussion with the chief of staff, GCMRL. Churchill judged Embick unduly alarmist. See *Grand Alliance,* p. 515.

275   The Limeys: White, *Stilwell Papers,* p. 16.

275   The ineffectual bleeding: *Ibid.,* p. 23.

276   Too much anti-British: [John P. Sutherland], "The Story Gen. Marshall Told Me," *U.S. News and World Report,* Nov. 2, 1959, p. 5.

276   Nobody knows: Tuchman, *Stilwell,* p. 231. The estimates of shipping troops are drawn from an unpublished "Memorandum for the President" dated December 26, 1941, on the subject of "North Africa," signed by "Chief of Staff" in GCMRL.

276   Failure in this: Pogue II, p. 288. See also the unpublished minutes, "Meeting of President with Sec-War, Sec-Navy and U.S. Chiefs of Staff, White House, 28 Dec. 41," GCMRL.

276   Considered it very important: Pogue II, p. 288.

Chapter XVI · The Pacific Deeps

In addition to the works cited below, Ronald H. Spector, *Eagle Against the Sun;*
Louis M. Morton, *The Fall of the Philippines;* and D. Clayton James, *The Years of
MacArthur,* Vol. II, proved invaluable.

PAGE

277   The darkest: Katherine Marshall, p. 104.

277   I was listening: *Ibid.,* pp. 109–10.

278   Some kind of organization: Pogue II, p. 293.

278   Not a voting: Pogue II, p. 295.

279   One of the most: Pogue II, p. 297.

279   Entirely impersonal: *Marshall Interviews,* p. 395.

280   But you are chief: *Ibid.,* p. 396.

280   Time—even days: "Minutes, Chiefs of Staff Meeting," January 11, 1942, in GCMRL.

281   Certain inconsistencies: Stimson Diaries, January 14, 1942. See also Pogue II, pp. 357–60.

281   Would be more: Stimson Diaries, January 14, 1942.

282   Crazy scheme: *The Stilwell Papers,* January 1, 1942. See Tuchman, *Stilwell,* p. 309.

282   Me? No, thank you: *The Stilwell Papers,* January 1, 1942.

282   An ignorant, illiterate: White, *In Search of History,* p. 134.

282   Joe, you have: Tuchman, *Stilwell,* p. 311.

282   I'd go: Stimson Diaries, January 13, 1942.

283   Looking like the wrath of God: *Providence Journal* editorial, May 20, 1942, quoted in Tuchman, *Stilwell,* p. 382.

283   I claim: Tuchman, *Stilwell,* p. 385.

283   Ships! Ships!: Eisenhower, *Diaries,* p. 12.

284   We were out-shipped: Lohbeck, p. 164.

284   All maneuvering: MacArthur to Marshall, January 23, 1942, is quoted in Friend, *Between Two Empires,* p. 215.

297   Most flamboyant: Eisenhower, *Diaries,* January 23, 1942.

297   As big a baby: *Ibid.,* January 19, 1942.

297   The public has: *Ibid.,* March 19, 1942.

297   There was money: Severeid, p. 215. See also Blum, *V Was for Victory,* pp. 92–117.

297   Great men around: Severeid, p. 217.

298   Heroic conduct: MacArthur, *Reminiscences,* p. 147. The true reason for the award was in the citation's last sentence, noting MacArthur had "confirmed the faith of the American people in their armed forces."

298   Will meet with: Quoted in Pogue II, p. 254.

298   Magniloquent communiques: Stimson Diaries, February 8, 1942. See also Stimson and Bundy, p. 398.

298   Flood of communications: Eisenhower, *Diaries,* p. 46.

298   A brave garrison: Stimson and Bundy, p. 400.

298   So long as the flag: *Ibid.,* pp. 402–03.

PAGE

298   I immediately discarded: Pogue II, pp. 247–48.
299   The greatest disaster: Sherwood, p. 501.
299   Supporting supplies: *Ibid.*, p. 502.
299   Well, I got: Eisenhower, *Diaries*, p. 48.
300   Definite plans: Kimball, I, pp. 398–99.
301   The navy wants: Eisenhower, *Diaries*, p. 48.
301   War Department is: *The Stilwell Papers*, January 1, 1942.
301   If I get through: Manchester, pp. 293–94.
301   The President: Burns, p. 209.
302   God help you all: Wainwright, p. 79.
302   I have not communicated: Morton, p. 458.
303   Hardihood, courage: Wainwright, p. 90. A generous Wainwright later
        termed the message "encouraging."
303   Please say: *Ibid.*, pp. 122–23.
303   Poor Wainwright!: Eisenhower, *Diaries*, p. 54.
303   Wainwright's actions: Pogue II, p. 258.
303   The Gibraltar: *New York Times*, July 24, 1932, p. 3E.

Chapter XVII · Modicum's Success

Hayes, *The History of the Joint Chiefs of Staff in World War II: The War Against Japan*, and Matloff and Snell, *Strategic Planning for Coalition Warfare, 1941–42*, provided background information for this chapter.

PAGE

304   But meanwhile: Churchill to Roosevelt, March 4, 1942, in Kimball, I,
        pp. 381–84.
304   Defensive operation: Stimson Diaries, March 8, 1942.
305   Anger cannot win: Eisenhower, *Diaries*, p. 52.
305   Had a rather rambunctious: Stimson Diaries, March 23, 1942.
305   Wildest kind: Stimson Diaries, March 25, 1942.
305   His cigarette-holder: Pogue II, p. 305.
307   I want to be sure: Coffey, p. 264.
307   Mark this day: Stimson Diaries, April 1, 1942.
307   Put Hopkins to bed: Sherwood, p. 531. Wedemeyer, pp. 97 ff., provided
        details of the MODICUM trip.
308   Hectic scenes: *Marshall Interviews*, p. 586.
308   Brooke made: Sherwood, p. 523.
309   A pleasant and easy: Bryant, *Turn of the Tide*, p. 354.
309   He had old-fashioned ideas: Ismay is quoted in Sulzberger, p. 936. Brooke
        judged MacArthur a more astute geopolitician than Marshall.
309   Yes, but not the way: Bryant, *Turn*, p. 28.
309   How can I get: Leasor, p. 130. See also Ferguson, pp. 149 ff.
310   A good general: Bryant, *Turn*, p. 358.
310   I asked him: *Ibid.*, p. 359. Reporting Brooke's criticism, Samuel Eliot

Morison, p. 30, added, "General Marshall has adopted a policy of dignified silence about these war controversies, so I cannot quote him; but I am confident that his strategic ideas did not stop at the water-edge; that he had a very definite concept of land strategy—namely, the double envelopment of the Ruhr which was actually carried out in 1945 against the strong objections of Field Marshals Brooke and Montgomery."

310   The plans are fraught: *Ibid.*

311   Offensive action: Bryant, *Turn*, p. 355.

311   The shadow: Leasor, p. 190 fn.

311   I think we could: Interview of Lord Ismay, October 18, 1960, by Forrest C. Pogue, GCMRL.

311   Our American friends: Ismay, pp. 249–50.

311   The time of action: Associated Press dispatch to the *Los Angeles Times*, April 19, 1942.

312   Whether General MacArthur: Churchill to Roosevelt, April 29, 1942, in Kimball, I, p. 478.

312   It is realized: GCM to CinCSWPA [MacArthur], May 3, 1942, GCMRL.

313   We must remember: Memo, Chief of Staff for President, May 6, 1942, GCMRL. Marshall inadvertently refers to SLEDGEHAMMER as BOLERO in the quoted paragraph.

313   I do not want: FDR for Marshall, May 6, 1942, GCMRL. See also Matloff and Snell, pp. 218–19.

314   This is home: Katherine Marshall, p. 118.

314   How in hell: Eisenhower, *Diaries*, p. 54.

315   It may interest: Compton, *Atomic Quest*, pp. 166–67.

315   Before our very institutions: Author's interview with Dean Rusk, November 25, 1982.

316   Reasonably certain: Interpreter Samuel H. Cross's notes on the meeting are reprinted in Sherwood, pp. 562–63. See also Stoler's excellent analysis of the Molotov mission, pp. 40–51.

317   What do you want: "Memorandum for the Record, Interview, General George C. Marshall with Col. L. M. Guyer and Col. C. H. Donnelly," February 11, 1949, GCMRL.

317   Was a little vague: Sherwood, p. 568, quoting Hopkins's notes.

318   The chiefs of staff: Standley and Ageton, p. 241.

318   The Soviets could not: Dallek, *Franklin D. Roosevelt*, p. 344. The Russians apparently knew this before Molotov set out for Washington. The Soviet ambassador to Great Britain, Ivan M. Maisky, wrote in his later *Memoirs*, p. 280, "It will be seen that there was no sentimentality in Marshall's arguments. They bore a strictly business-like, military character."

318   Throughout the Pacific: United Press dispatch to the *Los Angeles Times*, May 30, 1942.

Chapter XVIII · Lighting the Torch

PAGE

320   The faces that are not: Sherwood, p. 590.

320   Discouragement and new proposals: Stimson Diaries, June 19, 1942.

322   Seemed to have agreed: Wedemeyer, p. 132.

322   Was going to jump: Stimson Diaries, June 17, 1942.

322   Were pretty well: Bryant, *Turn*, p. 324.

322   Can we afford: Churchill's note is quoted in *ibid.*, pp. 327–28.

322   Had taken up GYMNAST: Stimson Diaries, June 21, 1942.

323   We failed to see: Pogue II, p. 330.

323   Tobruk has surrendered: Burns, p. 235.

323   Defeat is one thing: Churchill, *Hinge*, p. 383.

323   What can we do: Burns, p. 235.

323   It is a terrible thing: Pogue II, p. 333.

324   The British Army: Wedemeyer, p. 132.

324   I always feel: Bryant, *Turn*, p. 329.

324   A major effort: Wedemeyer, pp. 148–49.

324   A perfect oilcan: Moran, p. 121.

324   Operations in Western Europe: Draft included in memo "General Smith for CofS," June 21, 1942, quoted in Matloff and Snell, p. 243.

325   The president was: Stimson Diaries, June 22, 1942.

325   You're wrong: Bryant, *Turn*, p. 333. See also Churchill, *Hinge*, p. 387.

325   No responsible British: Churchill to Roosevelt, July 8, 1942, reprinted in Kimball, I, p. 520. Soviet writers have been critical of the decision not to open a second front in France in 1942. See, for example, Maisky, pp. 278–88. Stoler, pp. 52–66, has a compelling analysis of the differing geopolitical goals of Roosevelt, Churchill, and Stalin.

326   The U.S. should turn: Matloff and Snell, p. 268, quoting the minutes of the JCS meeting of July 10, 1942.

327   Would do anything: Buell, p. 216. Buell's source is probably notes of conversations between King and his earlier biographer. Marshall's "basic trouble," said King, "was that like all Army officers he knew nothing about sea power and very little about air power." See Buell, p. 217.

327   At the behest: Stimson Diaries, October 30, 1942.

328   Both indecisive: "Memo, CofS, COMINCH, and CNO for President, 10 Jul 42," quoted in Matloff and Snell, p. 269.

328   Fatuous defeatist position: Stimson Diaries, July 12, 1942. Stimson later described the Pacific shift as a bluff, and one he somewhat rued. See Stimson and Bundy, p. 425.

328   Something of a red herring: Hayes, p. 152.

328   Taking up your dishes: Stimson Diaries, July 15, 1942.

329   Fish or cut bait: Sherwood, p. 600.

329   Everything points: Churchill, *Hinge*, p. 440.

329   My main point: Sherwood, p. 602.

329   A queer party: Bryant, *Turn*, p. 341.

PAGE

330 Tough, intensive grind: Eisenhower to Brigadier General Spencer Akin, June 19, 1942, quoted in Ambrose, *Eisenhower,* I, p. 154.

330 The men who: Eisenhower recounts this anecdote in *At Ease,* p. 249.

331 I certainly do intend: Eisenhower, *Crusade,* p. 51.

331 We would lick: Casey, p. 90.

331 His faculty for getting: Rose Page Wilson, p. 378.

331 It's a big job: Eisenhower, *Diaries,* p. 62.

331 It looks as if: Clark, p. 19.

332 I opened the door: Truscott, p. 49.

332 The British: Eisenhower, *Diaries,* p. 73.

333 It's no use: Leasor, p. 173. Marshall remembered the comment, later repeating it to S. E. Morison.

333 Blackest day: Butcher, p. 29.

333 The least harmful diversion: Pogue II, p. 346.

333 A defensive, encircling line: "Memo, U.S. CsofS for Br CsofS, 24 July 42," quoted in Matloff and Snell, p. 280.

334 They didn't want: Pogue II, p. 347.

334 The Americans had gone: Bryant, *Turn,* p. 428.

334 All was therefore agreed: Churchill, *Hinge,* p. 448.

335 It would be agreeable: Sherwood, p. 615. There is a somewhat different wording in Kimball, I, p. 523. On Marshall as commander of the invasion, see Truscott, p. 43, and Butcher, p. 12.

335 Neither of them: Clark, p. 37.

335 Discussion: "Note drawn up by General de Gaulle's office after his interview with the Heads of the American Army and Navy, July 23, 1942," in de Gaulle, *War Memoirs,* II, part 2, p. 26.

335 That TORCH would be: Matloff and Snell, p. 238, quoting a "Memo, Gen Smith for JCS, 1 Aug 42."

Chapter XIX · A Pile of Brickbats

In addition to the sources cited below, Butler and Gwyer, *Grand Strategy,* IV; *The Eisenhower Diaries;* Jackson, *The North African Campaign;* and Spector, *Eagle Against the Sun,* proved useful.

338 British son-of-a-bitch: Ismay, p. 263.

338 I truly believe: Hobbs, p. 59.

338 Blooded: Lucius DuBignon Clay's Oral History, Micro III, Oral History Research Office, Columbia University, p. 314. In an interview with the author on August 1, 1983, retired Lieutenant General Albert Wedemeyer dismissed this experience factor as "a matter of degree." Only the British Eighth Army, a relatively small force, had any more combat experience as a unit than did the green American divisions.

338 Unfortunately: DDE to GCM, October 7, 1942, reprinted in Hobbs, p. 45.

338 Please make it: Pogue II, p. 402. Marshall added in a 1956 interview, "However, when I found we had to have more time and it came afterward, he never said a word. He was very courageous." The Democrats lost nine Senate and forty-five House seats while retaining their majorities.

339 A somewhat raw job: "Former Naval Person to President," August 4, 1942, in Kimball, I, p. 553.

339 Just why the president: Pogue II, p. 400, quoting "GCM to Dwight David Eisenhower," August 14, 1942.

339 The transatlantic essay contest: Butcher, p. 83.

340 The hearts of the Americans: Kennedy, p. 261.

340 Immediate and artificial: Arnold, p. 322. According to Ambrose, *Supreme Commander,* p. 67, Marshall would go to his grave convinced that TORCH had been "a mistake."

340 Just a God damned mess: Bullitt, p. 559. See also Butcher, p. 58.

340 A fair chance: Clark, p. 44.

340 It was better: Blumenson, *The Patton Papers,* p. 83.

341 I shall try: Hobbs, p. 25.

341 Whenever I'm tempted: *Ibid.,* p. 52.

341 Frankest possible basis: Ambrose, *Supreme Commander,* pp. 103–04.

341 When you disagree: *Ibid.,* p. 104.

341 A failure of SLEDGEHAMMER: "Minutes, Combined Chiefs of Staff Meeting, August 28, 1942," GCMRL.

342 Hurrah, etc.: Kimball, I, p. 592.

342 King never lets up: Stimson Diaries, September 3, 1942. One British observer in Washington commented with some astonishment, "The violence of inter-service rivalry in the United States in those days had to be seen to be believed and was an appreciable handicap to their war effort." See Slessor, p. 494.

343 Gives me the impression: Coffey, p. 289, quoting Arnold's diary.

344 I don't know: Griffith, p. 30.

344 Even though everyone: Arnold to Chief of Staff, August 21, 1942, quoted in Pogue II, p. 385.

344 To make sure: Hayes, p. 191. See also Griffith, p. 180.

344 I doubt if the president: Stimson Diaries, October 29, 1942.

345 Help anyone impose: Murphy, p. 102.

345 The most complex: Handy is quoted in Sherwood, p. 648.

346 Having been privileged: Marshall to Churchill via Commanding General, U.S. Forces, London, November 6, 1942, in GCMRL Box 61, Folder 1.

346 Must take the jump: Eisenhower to GCM, printed in Hobbs, p. 59.

346 The hand of the Lord: GCM address to the National Association of Manufacturers, New York City, December 4, 1942, in De Weerd, p. 219.

347 Stop the game!: Katherine Marshall, p. 130.

348 A hit and miss affair: Truscott is quoted in Samuel E. Morison, *History,* II, p. 123.

PAGE

349   The yellow-bellied sons of bitches: Schoenbrun, p. 224.

349   If we will make: Sherwood, p. 651.

349   No precipitate action: Eisenhower, *Crusade,* p. 109. To protect codes used, both Eisenhower and Sherwood were required to paraphrase this message. Sherwood has a fuller version, p. 652, of what he described as "an eloquent plea."

349   I can't understand: Macmillan, p. 174.

349   Can only be: "Former Naval Person to President Roosevelt Personal and Secret," November 17, 1942, in Kimball, II, p. 7.

350   Even the Devil: Sherwood, p. 651.

350   We are dealing: Steel, p. 401.

350   Leave the worries: Pogue II, p. 420.

350   In any discussion: Viorst, pp. 122–23.

351   I have never: Ambrose, *Eisenhower,* I, p. 209, attributes the quote to "one of Marshall's aides." His earlier *Supreme Commander,* p. 132, attributes the comment to a "reporter who was there."

351   To whom well founded objection: Pratt, II, p. 562.

351   Only a temporary expedient: *New York Times,* November 18, 1942. A month later, Roosevelt was still striving for a token to throw to critics. The apparently overlooked minutes of the Casablanca Conference note that on January 17, 1943, "The President stated that he felt the whole Jewish problem should be studied very carefully and that progress should be definitely planned. In other words, the number of Jews engaged in the practice of the professions (law, medicine, etc.) should be definitely limited to the percentage that the Jewish population in North Africa bears to the whole of the North African population. Such a plan would therefore permit the Jews to engage in the professions, at the same time would not permit them to overcrowd the professions, and would present an unanswerable argument that they were being given their full rights. To the foregoing, General Nogues [resident general in Morocco and a member of the governing council] agreed generally, stating at the same time that it would be a sad thing for the French to win the war merely to open the way for the Jews to control the professions and the business world of North Africa. The President stated that his plan would further eliminate the specific and understandable complaints which the Germans bore towards the Jews in Germany, namely, that while they represented a small part of the population, over 50 percent of the lawyers, doctors, school teachers, college professors, etc., in Germany, were Jews." See *FRUS: Casablanca, 1943,* II, p. 608.

351   This ridiculous declaration: Cadogan, p. 499.

351   I am very much worried: Pogue II, p. 422.

352   I want you to feel: Marshall to Eisenhower, No. 63, quoted in *ibid.*

352   Delegate your international: Ambrose, *Supreme Commander,* p. 148.

352   You are doing: Marshall to Eisenhower, December 22, 1942, quoted in Pogue II, p. 423.

352   Art, old fellow: Schoenbrun, p. 231.

PAGE

353   Two years ago: "Army Confident, Stimson Says," *Los Angeles Times*, January 1, 1943.

353   The turning point: Dallek, *Franklin D. Roosevelt*, p. 373.

353   The skies have cleared: Pogue II, p. 427.

Chapter XX · The Wife's Legacy

In addition to the sources cited below, Butler and Guyer, *Grand Strategy*, and Hayes, *History*, pp. 278 ff., proved valuable.

354   I paid close: See "Formal Naval Person to President, Personal and Most Secret," December 2, 1942, in *FRUS: The Conferences at Washington and Casablanca, 1943*, II, p. 494.

355   What would I: *FRUS: The Conferences at Washington and Casablanca, 1943*, II, p. 506. Brigadier General J. R. Deane's paraphrastic notes furnish the only account of this meeting.

355   The issue was purely: *Ibid.*

356   The losses there: *Ibid.*

356   The British to enjoy: Pogue III, p. 11. In an interview with the author in 1983, General Wedemeyer denied he was anti-British. "All of my troubles with the British [stemmed from] their failure to go along with me in planning to cross the Channel. I wanted to go over there in the summer of '43 while the bulk of German forces were concentrated in Russia."

357   A very small staff: Roosevelt to Churchill, December 12, 1942, in *FRUS: Casablanca, 1943*, II, p. 494.

357   The very smart: Macmillan, p. 193.

358   Not to hurry: Bryant, *Turn*, p. 544.

358   The customary American: Colonel L. M. Guyer, in Chapter V of "United States Joint Chiefs of Staff: The War Against Germany and Her Satellites, 1938—August 15, 1943," Unpublished manuscript, p. 179, in GCMRL Xerox 1561.

358   The Joint Chiefs: *Ibid.*, p. 180.

359   Always present. *Ibid.*

359   Would take a less: Manuscript Diary of General Sir Ian Jacob, January 14, 1943, quoted in Bryant, *Turn*, p. 544.

359   Expressed the admiration: *FRUS: Casablanca, 1943*, II, p. 537.

359   A stranglehold: *Ibid.*

359   It seemed at least: *FRUS: Casablanca, 1943*, II, p. 538.

360   Let the cat out: Wedemeyer, pp. 177–78.

360   In this way: *FRUS: Casablanca, 1943*, II, p. 580.

360   Owing to the time lag: *Ibid.*

360   Production plans: *Ibid.*

360   Impossible to map: *Ibid.*

361   Main plot: *FRUS: Casablanca, 1943*, II, p. 583.

PAGE

361   To be fobbed off: Eisenhower, *Allies,* p. 221.

361   Friendliness and honesty: Kennedy, p. 283.

361   Those goddam British: Ferguson, p. 265. Wedemeyer considered Admiral King "the strongest man on the U.S. Joint Chiefs of Staff. He had a keen, analytical mind. He was incisive and direct in his approach to the solution of a problem." See Wedemeyer, p. 184.

361   We are in the position: Tedder, p. 389.

361   There was a curious mixture: Macmillan, pp. 193–94.

362   He advocated: *FRUS: Casablanca, 1943,* II, p. 618.

362   The British view: *FRUS: Casablanca, 1943,* II, p. 619.

363   It is no use: Bryant, *Turn,* p. 550.

363   Operations in the Pacific: Slessor, p. 446.

364   After seven days: *FRUS: Casablanca, 1943,* II, p. 628.

364   If and when Hitler: *FRUS: Casablanca, 1943,* II, p. 629.

365   An extra-ordinary degree: Robert E. Sherwood, "Conversation with Secretary Marshall in His Office at the State Department, Wednesday Morning, July 23, 1947," typescript in Houghton Library, Harvard University, bMS Am 1947 (1899).

366   Eisenhower has: Manuscript diary of Sir Ian Jacob, January 1, 1943, quoted in Ambrose, *Eisenhower,* I, p. 218.

366   His neck is in a noose: Ambrose, *Eisenhower,* I, p. 217.

366   They would not promote: Sherwood, p. 689.

366   We were carrying: Bryant, *Turn,* p. 556.

367   It was not a question: *FRUS: Casablanca, 1943,* II, p. 653.

368   Here was our great hero: Macmillan, p. 198.

368   The whole global picture: *FRUS: Casablanca, 1943,* II, p. 727.

368   Peace can only come: *FRUS: Casablanca, 1943,* II, p. 727. The "unconditional surrender formula," announced without warning by Roosevelt, had been discussed at Casablanca, Churchill even getting the War Cabinet's approval of the concept. See *ibid.,* p. 635 fn., and Pogue III, pp. 32–35.

368   Wedemeyer, don't you ever: Wedemeyer, p. 187.

368   Whole attitude toward Ike: Butcher, p. 247.

369   You're trying: Eisenhower, *At Ease,* p. 260.

369   Go no further: *Ibid.,* p. 261.

369   Solid and stable: Bradley and Blair, p. 111.

370   He may think: Butcher, p. 248. See also Hobbs, p. 100.

Chapter XXI · A Very Vicious War

Among other sources the author relied on John S. D. Eisenhower's *Allies.* Statistics in this chapter are drawn from Wedemeyer, p. 212; Matloff and Snell, pp. 354–55; *FRUS: Casablanca, 1943,* II, pp. 795–96; and Marshall's *Biennial Report of the Chief of Staff of the United States Army, July 1, 1941 to June 30, 1943 to the Secretary of War,* pp. 104 ff.

PAGE

373   For the *support:* Formfit's ad is quoted Blum, *V Was for Victory*, p. 100. Details for this section are taken from that book and from Perrett's *Days of Sadness.*

373   We are just getting: "Report to the Nation, Conference of State Governors, Columbus, Ohio, June 21, 1943," in De Weerd, p. 223.

374   Against hasty conclusions: *Ibid.*, p. 224.

375   Details on the controversy are taken from Pogue III, pp. 160–78; Buell, pp. 282–99; and King and Whitehill, pp. 464–71.

376   Take Buna: Manchester, p. 375. Spector concludes that MacArthur's "insistence on pressing forward with repeated frontal attacks by poorly supported infantry against a heavily dug-in enemy was reminiscent of the worst generalship of the First World War. It might have ended in the same futile slaughter had not the Japanese finally collapsed due to starvation." See Spector, *Eagle Against the Sun*, p. 217.

376   The great hero: Eichelberger, p. 64.

377   The feeling was so bitter: Pogue III, p. 168.

377   A rather tired-looking: Katherine Marshall, pp. 140–41.

378   The army had: Kenney, p. 211.

379   But the people: *Time*, April 26, 1943.

380   Our soldiers: Eisenhower to Marshall, February 15, 1942, quoted in Ambrose, *Supreme*, p. 172.

380   Field Marshal Alexander: "Conversation with Secretary Marshall in His Office at the State Department, Wednesday Morning, July 23, 1947," Robert E. Sherwood Papers, Houghton Library, Harvard University, bMS Am 1947 (1899).

380   Stupid British generalship: *Ibid.* The general responsible, Sir Kenneth Anderson, was transferred in June 1943.

381   Are now mad: Ambrose, *Supreme*, p. 174.

381   First Class: Moorehead, p. 650.

381   Ike's rise or fall: Butcher, p. 278.

382   We might get into trouble: Eisenhower to Marshall, March 29, 1942, in Hobbs, p. 107.

382   Created further unfortunate: GCM to Eisenhower, April 14, 1943, quoted in Pogue II, pp. 188–89.

382   In this vital matter: Bradley and Blair, p. 151.

384   At the moment: Pogue III, p. 190.

Chapter XXII · The Great Prize

In addition to the books cited, Butler and Gwyer, *Grand Strategy*, IV, and Dallek, *Franklin D. Roosevelt and American Foreign Policy*, proved useful.

385   It is all so maddening: Bryant, *Turn*, p. 500.

385   But no one: Prime Minister Churchill to President Roosevelt, April 5, 1943, in *FRUS: The Conferences at Washington and Quebec, 1943*, p. 13.

PAGE

386   A most unfortunate: "Memorandum for General Handy," dictated by GCM, March 30, 1943, classified "Super-Secret," in GCMRL, reel 56, no. 2003.

386   Their military objectives: Colonel E. A. Peterson, Unpublished manuscript of Chapter VIII, "The United States Joint Chiefs of Staff: The War Against Germany and Her Satellites," GCMRL Xerox 1561, p. 158.

386   No matter how long delayed: "Current British Policy and Strategy in Relationship to that of the United States," May 3, 1943, quoted in *ibid.*, pp. 158–59.

386   Can hardly fail: *Ibid.*, p. 165.

386   More of a liability: *Ibid.*

387   A bad mess: Stimson Diaries, May 3, 1943.

387   And now!: Bryant, *Turn*, p. 503.

387   The great prize: *FRUS: Washington, 1943*, p. 25.

387   Earnestly desired: *FRUS: Washington, 1943*, p. 27.

387   Should be decided: *FRUS: Washington, 1943*, p. 30.

387   I feel: Paraphrased in *FRUS: Washington, 1943*, p. 32.

388   The Americans had done: Moran, p. 102.

388   Unmistakable air: Ismay, pp. 269, 298.

388   Vacuum in the Mediterranean: *FRUS: Washington, 1943*, p. 44.

388   Would only be sufficient: *FRUS: Washington, 1943*, p. 45.

389   I am thoroughly: Bryant, *Turn*, p. 504.

389   Can't, can't, can't: Tuchman, *Stilwell*, p. 474.

389   If a route: *FRUS: Washington, 1943*, p. 62.

390   A princess: Chennault's diary is quoted in Tuchman, *Stilwell*, p. 277.

390   Most attractive: Stimson Diaries, February 23, 1943.

391   He does, does he: Tuchman, *Stilwell*, p. 416.

391   Would be more effective: Franklin Delano Roosevelt, *Personal Correspondence*, II, p. 1350.

391   I read your profane: Tuchman, *Stilwell*, p. 442.

391   Stilwell has: "Memorandum for George Marshall," March 8, 1943, signed "F.D.R." in GCMRL.

391   One cannot speak: *Ibid.*

392   Muttered something: Stimson Diaries, May 3, 1943.

392   The toughest task: Henry L. Stimson to "My Dear Mr. President," May 3, 1943, appended to the Stimson Diaries for that date.

392   Ultimately the United: *FRUS: Washington, 1943*, p. 72.

393   Hard to say: Tuchman, *Stilwell*, p. 474.

393   Stout-hearted fighter: Bryant, *Turn*, pp. 505–06.

393   A fine fighting man: *Ibid.*, p. 506.

393   The Chinese were suspicious: *FRUS: Washington, 1943*, p. 75.

393   What do you think: Chennault, p. 226.

394   A strategy: *FRUS: Washington, 1943*, p. 83.

394   He told me: Stimson Diaries, May 17, 1943.

394   I should hate: *Congressional Record*, April 16, 1943, pp. 3454 ff.

395   About *who* makes: Minutes, Joint Chiefs of Staff, 79th Meeting, May 10,

PAGE

1943, item 7, microprinted in *Records of the Joint Chiefs of Staff* (University Microfilms).

395 Would be almost mass suicide: *Congressional Record*, May 17, 1943, p. 4512.

395 I am curious: *Ibid.*, p. 4518.

395 This is a personal attack: Stimson Diaries, May 19, 1943.

396 I find it hard: Bryant, *Turn*, p. 508.

396 Since the wish: *FRUS: Washington, 1943*, p. 102. "The British Plan for the Defeat of the Axis Powers in Europe," dated May 17, 1943, is in this volume, pp. 261–72.

397 Best calculated: *Ibid.*

397 The President has: Stimson Diaries, May 21, 1943.

397 It took me three: Buell, p. 337.

398 Crashed in: Bryant, *Turn*, p. 153.

398 And gain touch: *FRUS: Washington, 1943*, p. 194.

398 If decisions were taken: Churchill, *Hinge*, p. 811.

398 He rather hated: Stimson Diaries, May 25, 1943.

398 The strongest man: *Ibid.*

398 One of the most: *Biennial Report of the Chief of Staff of the United States Army, July 1, 1943 to June 30, 1943*, p. 157.

399 At a rate to permit: "Present Aerial Person to President Roosevelt," May 26, 1943, in Kimball, II, p. 218.

399 With a clarity: Churchill, *Hinge of Fate*, pp. 812–13. Lazare-Nicolas-Marguerite Carnot as minister of war from 1793 to 1797 raised and equipped fourteen armies to defend Revolutionary France against foreign intervention.

399 Very agreeable: *Ibid.*, p. 814. See also Pogue III, p. 215.

399 I admired: Churchill, *Hinge of Fate*, p. 815.

400 I still do not think: Bryant, *Turn*, p. 633.

400 When our troops, *Ibid.*, p. 826.

400 It is most distressing: *Ibid.*, p. 525.

401 An incredible performance: W. Richard Bruner, "Three Generals," in Brown and Brumer, p. 77.

401 The most brilliant: "Vignettes of America's No. 1 Soldier," *Reader's Digest* (January 1944), p. 71.

401 Localitis: Butcher, p. 324.

Chapter XXIII · Threshers

403 Military adolescence: *Vital Speeches of the Day*, August 15, 1943, pp. 659 ff.

403 I am profoundly: *Vital Speeches of the Day*, October 1, 1943, p. 761.

403 Gen. George Marshall: Pegler's column was printed in the *Los Angeles Times*, October 22, 1943.

403 The Democratic Party: *New York Times*, November 27, 1943.

403 No, Senator: Katherine Marshall, p. 158.

404   Unfortunate results: GCM to Eisenhower, April 14, 1943, in GCMRL.

404   Scandalously casual: Bradley and Blair, p. 178.

404   The most arrogant: *Ibid.*, p. 188.

405   I don't want: *Ibid.*, p. 195.

405   You ought to be: *Ibid.*, p. 197.

405   The last German: Alexander is quoted in Grigg, p. 95.

406   A model: Eisenhower to Marshall, August 24, 1943, reprinted in Hobbs, p. 121.

406   The best all around: Eisenhower to GCM, September 6, 1943, in *ibid.*, p. 123.

406   With option: Howard, p. 45.

407   On the speculation: Colonel W. E. Todd, deputy chief, S&P, to AC of S, OPD, "Special JCS Meeting of July 26, 1943," in GCMRL.

407   We must not jeopardize: "Strategic Concept for the Defeat of the Axis in Europe," August 9, 1943, in *FRUS: The Conferences at Washington and Quebec, 1943*, p. 473.

408   The Allied High Command: Aneurin Bevan is quoted in Higgins, *Soft Underbelly*, p. 89.

408   To me, in the light: Stimson to FDR, August 10, 1943, reprinted in *FRUS: Washington, 1943*, p. 497.

408   The president went: Stimson Diaries, August 10, 1943.

408   He was anxious: "Minutes of Meeting Held at the White House Between the President and the Chiefs of Staff on 10 August 1943 at 1415," reprinted in *FRUS: Washington, 1943*, pp. 498 ff.

409   Even more than usually: Bryant, *Turn*, p. 575.

409   British insistence: Leahy, p. 175.

409   Gloomy and unpleasant: Bryant, *Turn*, p. 577.

409   Major offensive: *FRUS: Washington, 1943*, p. 864.

409   Soldierly dignity: Quoted in Bryant, *Turn*, p. 578, fn.

409   Could not feel: *Ibid.* Brooke's opinion of Marshall is here, his opinion of Mountbatten in Ziegler, p. 220.

410   All our arguing: Bryant, *Turn*, p. 581. The text of the agreement is printed in *FRUS: Washington, 1943*, pp. 1024 ff.

410   I would take: Pogue III, p. 258.

411   Instead of confining: Stimson Diaries, September 6, 1943.

411   It appeared: *FRUS: Washington, 1943*, p. 911.

412   Prestige and ability: Wedemeyer, p. 245. Various writers have implied that the Americans were political innocents when considering the Soviet Union's postwar aims. Kolko, *Politics*, pp. 28–30, argues that the existence of the RANKIN plan instead "reflected a political sophistication no less intense than that of the English. . . ."

412   A most unfortunate: GCM "Memorandum for General Handy," March 30, 1943, classified "Super-Secret," in GCMRL.

412   First they argue: Ball, p. 29.

412   Differences of opinion: Bryant, *Turn*, p. 588.

412   The other thing: *Roosevelt Presidential Press Conferences*, XXII, pp. 80–81.

PAGE

413   For he hated: Katherine Marshall, p. 164.

413   Here is what: GCM "Memorandum for Mr. Harry Hopkins," September 1, 1943, GCMRL.

413   The end is not: Associated Press dispatch to the *Los Angeles Times*, September 8, 1943.

413   Good reading: *New York Times*, September 12, 1943.

413   Soldierly: *Time*, September 13, 1943, p. 22.

414   Help us out: Buell, p. 410. See also Perry, p. 213.

414   Powerful influences: Sherwood, p. 768.

414   To transfer: Pershing to Roosevelt, September 16, 1943, reprinted in Katherine Marshall, pp. 156–57.

414   You are absolutely: FDR to Pershing, September 20, 1943, is in Katherine Marshall, p. 157.

415   Were able to carry: Stimson Diaries, September 15, 1943.

415   It would not fall: Churchill to Hopkins, September 26, 1943, reprinted in *FRUS: Washington, 1943*, p. 830.

415   On the skids: United Press dispatch to the *Los Angeles Times*, September 20, 1943.

415   Because he stood up: *Congressional Record*, 78th Congress, 1st Session, p. 7682.

415   The War Department: *Congressional Record*, 78th Congress, 1st Session, p. A3987.

415   A group of influential: *Congressional Record*, 78th Congress, 1st Session, p. A4001.

416   Hullabaloo: GCM to Robert E. Sherwood, February 25, 1947, in Robert E. Sherwood Papers, Houghton Library, Harvard University, bMS Am 1947 (548).

416   General George: Sherwood, p. 761.

416   He is one: T.R.B. (Richard L. Strout) is in *The New Republic*, October 4, 1943.

417   With the sweetest: Morgan, p. 193.

417   There was an apparently: *Ibid.*, p. 194.

417   I doubt very much: *Ibid.*, p. 201.

Chapter XXIV · A Rainbow Discerned

418   I never saw: Arnold, p. 454.

418   Fish or cut bait: Draft memorandum, Chief of Staff for President, November 8, 1943, "Conduct of the European War," GCMRL.

419   Was to be: Pogue III, p. 315.

420   Just another theater: Matloff, *Strategic Planning*, p. 277.

420   We do not want: *FRUS: The Conferences at Cairo and Tehran, 1943*, p. 254.

421   We should not get: *FRUS: Cairo, 1943*, p. 259.

421   Definitely be a race: *Ibid.* The proposal for joint occupation is in a mem-

PAGE

orandum written by T.T.H[andy], November 19, 1943, in GCMRL, Verifax 1349.

421   The longterm political: "Appendix D" to GCMRL Xerox 2025, undated draft memo to the president from the Joint Chiefs of Staff.

421   The British might like: *FRUS: Cairo, 1943*, p. 259. George VI on October 14, 1943, wrote the agreeable Churchill, "What we want to see is Greece & Yugoslavia liberated; then Turkey may come in with us & maybe we shall see the 3 Great Powers, Great Britain, U.S.A. & U.S.S.R. fighting together on the same front!!" See Wheeler-Bennett, *King George VI*, p. 595.

422   Hottest one: Butcher, p. 442.

423   Increasing in stature: Arnold, p. 462.

423   It is advisable: Hurley to FDR, November 20, 1943, in *FRUS: Cairo, 1943*, p. 265.

424   To the president: Moran, *Churchill*, p. 140.

424   Marshall, like many: Bryant, *Turn*, p. 600.

424   Brooke got nasty: *Stilwell Papers*, p. 245.

424   I never want: "Interview, General George C. Marshall with Col. L. M. Guyer and Col. C. H. Donnelly," GCMRL, p. 1.

425   It got hotter: *Marshall Interviews*, p. 586.

425   There must be no misunderstanding: *FRUS: Cairo, 1943*, p. 343.

425   Now let me get: *Stilwell Papers*, p. 255.

425   A ghastly waste: Bryant, *Triumph*, p. 81.

426   George laying it: *Stilwell Papers*, p. 246.

426   Everything seems: Dallek, *Franklin D. Roosevelt*, p. 425.

426   A merry party: Pogue III, p. 307.

426   The title deeds: Sherwood, p. 775.

427   Operations in northern: *FRUS: Cairo, 1943*, p. 362.

427   Bush league tactics: Ambassador John Winant's comment is quoted in Beitzell, p. 291.

427   If the capture: *FRUS: Cairo, 1943*, p. 364.

427   The mother and father: Bryant, *Triumph*, p. 57.

427   They had gone far: *FRUS: Cairo, 1943*, pp. 364-65.

428   Most of the points: Bryant, *Triumph*, p. 84.

428   Most American military: Matloff, p. 287.

429   I am glad: Burns, p. 407.

429   Now let us: Roosevelt and Brough, p. 352.

430   An almost insuperable barrier, *FRUS: Tehran, 1943*, p. 490.

430   He questioned the wisdom: *FRUS: Tehran, 1943*, p. 494.

430   He had a military brain: Bryant, *Triumph*, p. 90.

430   All wishing and guessing: Moran, p. 834.

431   I wish to apologize: *FRUS: Tehran, 1943*, p. 524.

431   Marshal Stalin: *FRUS: Tehran, 1943*, p. 525.

431   The difference between: *FRUS: Tehran, 1943*, pp. 527-28.

432   Fitted his blunt: Moran, *Churchill*, p. 147.

432   Who will be: *FRUS: Tehran, 1943*, pp. 535 and 541.

PAGE

433   I cannot agree: *FRUS: Tehran, 1943*, p. 547.
433   Do the British: *FRUS: Tehran, 1943*, p. 539.
433   A strong leader: Katherine Marshall, p. 167.
433   A rough SOB: Pogue III, p. 313.
433   Apparently fearless: Arnold, p. 168.
433   He was agreeable: Pogue III, p. 313.
433   A lunatic asylum: Bryant, *Triumph*, p. 93.
433   A bloody lot: Moran, *Churchill*, p. 145.
434   There I sat: Cadogan, p. 582.
434   He gets things done: Roosevelt and Brough, p. 356.
435   No wiser: Sherwood, p. 791.
435   Becoming a legendary: Bohlen, p. 149.
435   Smashing force: *FRUS: Tehran, 1943*, p. 577.
435   The rainbow: Matloff, p. 367.
435   There were still: *Biennial Report, 1934–1945*, p. 30. A week after the close of SEXTANT, King assigned twenty-six more LSTs to OVERLORD and forty-six more to ANVIL; they provided the barest margin for success.
436   It all looks: Bryant, *Triumph*, p. 104.
436   The president was: Sherwood, p. 803.
436   I merely endeavored: *Ibid.*, quoting GCM to Sherwood, February 25, 1947.
436   I just repeated: *Marshall Interviews*, p. 315. In 1956, he told a magazine correspondent, "Of course I would have preferred the appointment." See *Newsweek*, January 2, 1956.
436   Mathematical basis: Stimson and Bundy, p. 442.
437   The President decided: *Ibid.* Sherwood, who talked to more than ten principals about Roosevelt's decision, concluded, "No one will ever know just what finally went on in Roosevelt's complex mind to determine his decision." See p. xiv.
437   It is not possible: Churchill, *Grand Alliance*, p. 28.

Chapter XXV · Losses

438   If he would: Interview with Frank McCarthy, Beverly Hills, California, January 7, 1981.
438   General Marshall has: *Time*, December 27, 1943, p. 17.
439   He'll always find: Hunt, p. 314.
439   Long and frank: MacArthur, p. 183.
439   Admiral King claimed: *Ibid.*
440   I will not: Stimson Diaries, November 22, 1944.
440   Supersensitive: Pogue II, p. 375.
440   My staff: Manchester, p. 407.
440   A dietician will: Conversation with Mrs. Doris Lieberman Fleischman of Malibu, California, July 1985.

PAGE

441   There was nothing: McCarthy interview, January 7, 1981.

441   When we reached: Katherine Marshall, p. 181.

442   The terrible measure: GCM to Forrest Pogue, February 11, 1957, quoted in Pogue III, p. 316.

442   I tried to keep: *Ibid.* (emphasis in original).

442   Hired by: *Time,* January 3, 1944, p. 16. The poll of newsmen was reported by United Press, May 2, 1944. See too Perry, p. 227.

442   He was sleepless: Byrnes, *All in One Lifetime,* p. 201.

442   He banged: *Time,* January 3, 1944.

442   The damndest crime: Perrett, p. 308.

443   This angry: I. F. Stone, "Marshall and the Second Front," *The Nation,* January 15, 1944, p. 63.

445   We cannot afford: Kimball, II, p. 633.

445   I doubt if I: Pogue III, p. 331.

445   On the basis: Kimball, II, p. 636.

445   I thank God: *Ibid.,* p. 638.

445   Military stature: Blumenson, *Anzio,* p. 59.

445   Wars should be fought: *Ibid.*

445   They will end up: Blumenson, "General Lucas at Anzio," in Greenfield, *Command Decisions,* p. 335.

446   The swiftly changing: Kimball, II, p. 705.

446   The U.S. Chiefs: Bryant, *Triumph,* pp. 146–47.

446   I merely wish: Pogue III, p. 335.

447   Honest broker: Pogue III, p. 336.

447   We're in grave danger: "The Reminiscences of Harvey H. Bundy," interviews 1958–60 in Boston by Saul Benison and Frank Safford, Oral History Research Office, Columbia University, 1961, pp. 201–05.

447   My underground: *Ibid.*

448   A prison camp: German propaganda broadcast quoted in Severeid, pp. 393–94.

448   That always appears: GCM to Allen Tupper Brown, March 1, 1944, quoted in Pogue III, p. 344.

449   What I cannot: Churchill to GCM, April 16, 1944, quoted in Churchill, *Closing the Ring,* pp. 513–14.

449   Dill tells me: *Ibid.*

450   Mother, there are: Katherine Marshall, p. 195.

450   Allen was the apple: Interview with Frank McCarthy, January 7, 1981.

450   A blessed numbness: Katherine Marshall, p. 195.

Chapter XXVI · *A Lesson in Geometry*

Among other sources used in this chapter were Bradley and Blair, *A General's Life;* Hastings, *Overlord;* Harrison, *Cross-Channel Attack;* and Schoenbrun, *Soldiers of the Night.*

PAGE

451 The troops, the air: Ambrose, *Eisenhower*, I, p. 309.

451 O.K., let's go: *Ibid.*, p. 308.

451 Halcyon plus 5: Pogue III, p. 388.

452 Perhaps the greatest: Stimson Diaries, June 5, 1944.

452 Well, there was nothing: Bohlen, p. 259.

453 May easily bring: Kimball, II, p. 122.

453 The people of France: "Memorandum for the President," enclosed in McNarney to Marshall, May 10, 1944, GCMRL.

453 Since it is: Ambrose, *Supreme Commander*, p. 342.

453 General Patton: Pogue III, p. 384.

454 Apparently he is: Ambrose, *Supreme Commander*, p. 343.

454 The decision: *Ibid.*, p. 344.

454 The light of battle: Butcher, p. 568.

454 And what would you: Bohlen, p. 259.

454 Our sons: Burns, p. 476.

455 Thank God: Bradley and Blair, p. 251.

455 This plan appeals: Hobbs, p. 141.

456 And meeting with: Alexander Cochran, "Night Jump over Normandy," *Military History* (August 1984), p. 37.

456 As I see it: Ambrose, *Supreme Commander*, p. 397.

457 British and American: GCM to Eisenhower, February 7, 1944, GCMRL.

457 I have occasionally: Eisenhower to GCM, February 8, 1944, GCMRL.

457 We will not: GCM to Eisenhower, March 25, 1944, GCMRL.

457 Hardening very much: Sir John Dill to GCM, March 12, 1944, GCMRL.

457 Marshall is quite: Bryant, *Triumph*, p. 177.

457 Our power should: Leasor, p. 234.

458 Attractive prospects: Churchill, *Triumph*, p. 61.

458 Wherever this man: Hassett, p. 249.

458 General Marshall: Cunningham, p. 605.

459 Give me enough ribbon: Associated Press dispatch to the *Los Angeles Times*, June 16, 1944.

460 Heavy with tension: Lieutenant Colonel Sir Ronald Evelyn Wingate, quoted in Brown, *Bodyguard*, p. 687.

461 . Possibly on the theory: Eisenhower, *Crusade*, p. 254.

461 You're the people: Butcher, p. 579.

461 Eisenhower and his staff: Ambrose, *Supreme Commander*, p. 424.

461 I think we: GCM to FDR, June 14, 1944, quoted in Pogue III, p. 391.

461 Today we visited: Churchill, *Triumph*, pp. 13–14.

462 To save myself: Bryant, *Triumph*, p. 218.

462 It is odd: Dill to Brooke, July 7, 1944, quoted in *Ibid.*, p. 218, n. 2.

462 Evidently believes: Roosevelt to GCM, June 2, 1944, quoted in Pogue III, p. 398.

463 The first thing: Pogue III, p. 400. De Gaulle apparently never warmed to Marshall either, though he credited him as "the animating spirit of a war effort and a military strategy of global dimensions." See his *War Memoirs*, II, Part 1, p. 240.

PAGE

463   Raised the devil: Pogue III, p. 400.

463   No sons of Iowa: Stimson Diaries, June 15, 1944.

463   He said he couldn't: Stimson Diaries, June 22, 1944.

464   Anglo-American forces: Slessor, p. 587.

464   Masterly manner: Pogue III, p. 406.

465   None of us: *Ibid.*

465   A much rumpled: GCM to Mrs. Madge Brown, June 23, 1944, quoted in Pogue III, p. 404.

465   A very good: Pogue III, p. 404. Clark was not the only one to criticize the decision not to try the Balkan campaign. See, for example, Wilmot, pp. 452 ff., Churchill, *Triumph and Tragedy,* pp. 65 ff., and Baldwin. The criticism, however, seems to be founded on postwar anti-Red feeling, and the notion that a move into the Balkans would have preempted the Soviet Union from imposing Communist governments in these captured nations. The critics seem to overlook the fact that the Allies, battling stubborn German resistance, were still far from the Yugoslavian border when ANVIL was launched on August 17. Before the end of the month Rumania had surrendered, Bulgaria had sued for peace, the Soviet Army had entered Transylvania and eastern Hungary and had occupied Bucharest. By mid-September, the Reds stood on Poland's border with Czechoslovakia. Two weeks later they had advanced to the northern and eastern borders of Yugoslavia. For a defense of ANVIL, see Maurice Matloff, "The Anvil Decision: Crossroads of Strategy," in Greenfield, *Command Decisions,* pp. 384 ff., and Morison, *Strategy and Compromise,* pp. 54–57.

466   Finally for purely: Roosevelt to Churchill, June 29, 1944, in Kimball, III, p. 223.

466   We had led: Kennedy, p. 334.

466   Bleak and sterile: Churchill to Roosevelt, June 28, 1944, in Kimball, III, p. 217.

466   The exploitation: Roosevelt to Churchill, June 29, 1944, in *ibid.,* pp. 221 ff.

467   If you still press: *Ibid.,* p. 229.

467   A straight line: *Ibid.,* p. 232.

Chapter XXVII · End Game

Perrett's *Days of Sadness, Years of Triumph;* Colville's *The Fringes of Power;* and MacArthur's *Reminiscences* provided background on this period.

470   MacArthur thought: *Marshall Interviews,* p. 532.

470   Mr. President: Manchester, p. 426.

470   We will not: Burns, p. 489.

471   Yes, I *am:* Gunther, *Roosevelt,* p. 10.

471   Dill was so: Bryant, *Triumph,* p. 277 fn.

PAGE

471   I wonder: Moran, *Churchill*, p. 190.

472   Good God: *Ibid.*, p. 173. Churchill's assurance he did not wish to put Anglo-American forces into the Balkans is in *FRUS: Tehran, 1943*, p. 543, reporting a meeting between Roosevelt, Churchill, and Stalin on November 29, 1943. He had earlier given the same assurance to Henry Stimson on August 10, 1943. See *FRUS: The Washington and Quebec Conferences, 1943*, p. 498.

472   It had not only: Minutes of the Meeting of the Combined Chiefs of Staff, September 12, 1944, in *FRUS: Quebec, 1944*, p. 303. Churchill argued the same point to the president the next day: "An added reason for this right-handed movement was the rapid encroachment of the Russians into the Balkans and the consequent dangerous spread of Russian influence in this area. He preferred to get into Vienna before the Russians did as he did not know what Russia's policy would be after she took it." *Ibid.*, p. 314.

472   We had to: Churchill, *Triumph*, p. 153.

473   Were trying to avoid: *Marshall Interviews*, p. 531. But see the Joint Chiefs of Staff to the Secretary of State, August 29, 1944, in *FRUS: Quebec, 1944*, p. 252–53, stating, "[W]e should recognize, in so far as they are consistent with our national policies, the French desires concerning Indo-China."

473   We are not: Nicholas, p. 528.

473   The British empire: *FRUS: Quebec, 1944*, p. 313.

474   My thought is: *FRUS: Quebec, 1944*, p. 317.

474   The offer: Churchill, *Triumph*, p. 154.

474   Not so long ago: *Ibid.*

474   For the sake: *Ibid.*, p. 155.

475   Staggering: Falk, *Decision at Leyte*, p. 27.

476   Accept the consequences: Roosevelt to Chiang, September 16, 1944, but erroneously dated February 16, 1944, in *Joint Committee on the Military Situation in the Far East*, pp. 2867–68.

476   The harpoon hit: Tuchman, *Stilwell*, p. 631.

476   The only difficulty: GCMRL.

476   In Washington: Churchill, *Triumph*, p. 455.

476   The only military: JCS Paper 973, July 28, 1944, GCMRL.

477   Follies of irresponsible: Nicholas, p. 332.

477   Water over the dam: "Proceedings Before the Army Pearl Harbor Board," in *Hearings Before the Joint Committee on the Investigation of the Pearl Harbor Attack*, XXXII, p. 545.

478   I gave no: Pogue III, p. 429.

478   I feel: *Pearl Harbor Attack*, III, p. 1334.

479   The disgraceful: Smith, *Dewey*, p. 426.

479   The simple truth: *New York Times*, September 25, 1944, p. 15.

480   For Mr. Dewey's: *Pearl Harbor Attack*, III, pp. 1128.

480   Did not want: Unpublished "Statement for Record of Participation of Brig. Gen. Carter W. Clarke, GSC in the Transmittal of Letters from

PAGE

Gen. George C. Marshall to Gov. Thomas E. Dewey the Latter Part of
September 1944," p. 3, to be found in the National Archives, Record
Group No. 457, SRH-043.

480   Marshall does not: *Ibid.*
480   As he might: *Ibid.,* p. 6.
480   A traitor who: Smith, *Dewey,* p. 429.
480   Failure to keep: *Pearl Harbor Attack,* XXXIX, pp. 175–76.
481   The probable outbreak: *Ibid.,* p. 144.
481   He thought: Stimson Diaries, November 14, 1944.
481   The one on whom: Stimson Diaries, May 25, 1943.
481   Why this is wicked: Stimson Diaries, November 21, 1944. The navy report
       swiped at Admiral Stark, but blamed no one for the debacle at Pearl
       Harbor. The inference then is that the Army was at fault, Prange, Gold-
       stein, and Dillon point out in *At Dawn We Slept,* p. 657.
481   How could it happen: *New York Times,* December 2, 1944.

Chapter XXVIII · The Winterkill

In addition to the sources cited, Weigley's *Eisenhower's Lieutenants;* MacDonald's
The Mighty Endeavor; and Ambrose's *Eisenhower,* I, provided background for this
chapter.

483   It was apparent: Bradley, p. 429.
483   I made it: Bradley and Blair, p. 338.
484   I didn't see: *Marshall Interviews,* p. 317.
484   I told him: Montgomery, *Memoirs,* p. 254.
484   I came pretty near: *Marshall Interviews,* p. 316.
484   You didn't have: *Ibid.,* p. 305.
484   Find out for themselves: Ambrose, *Supreme Commander,* p. 537.
485   The very speed: *New York Times,* November 22, 1944, p. 1.
485   We have a stern: *New York Times Magazine,* December 21, 1944, p.30.
486   Would be to court failure: Ellis and Warhurst, p. 138.
486   Be frank with me: GCM to Eisenhower, quoted in Ambrose, *Supreme,* p.
       543.
486   Now deferred: Bradley and Blair, p. 361.
487   What they are afraid of: Churchill to FDR, November 24, 1944, in Kim-
       ball, III, pp. 408–09.
487   Your policies: Chiang to FDR of September 25, 1944, is quoted in Leahy,
       p. 271.
487   Betrayed me: *Marshall Interviews,* p. 571.
487   George C. Marshall continues: *The Stilwell Papers,* p. 169.
488   A flash: GCM to Stilwell, October 18, 1942, in *Stilwell's Personal File,* p.
       2512.
488   If questioned: GCM to Stilwell, October 20, 1944, in *ibid.*
488   He wanted us: White, *In Search of History,* p. 176.
488   Bewildered and alarmed: *New York Times,* October 31, 1944.

PAGE

488   So fanciful: White, *In Search*, p. 206.

489   A cruel blow: Katherine Marshall, p. 214.

489   He really loved you: Pogue III, p. 483, quoting Janet Dill to GCM, December 22, 1944.

489   A very intimate: Pogue III, p. 379.

489   Then Dill would come: *Ibid.*, p. 380.

490   Few will ever realize: GCM to Churchill, November 7, 1944, quoted in Pogue III, p. 482.

490   Poor Wilson: *Marshall Interviews*, p. 504.

491   I didn't want: *Ibid.*, pp. 419–20.

492   The sublime moment: Martin Blumenson is quoted in Bradley and Blair, p. 359, without a source.

492   Montgomery, Alan Brooke: *Ibid.*, p. 360.

492   Entirely detached: Bryant, *Triumph*, p. 338.

492   We must take: *Ibid.*, p. 341.

493   Bedell, it's hard: Bradley and Blair, p. 364.

493   You have my complete confidence: Ambrose, *Supreme*, p. 567.

493   Roosevelt didn't: Pogue III, p. 486.

493   To tidy up: Bradley and Blair, p. 369.

493   My feeling: GCM to Eisenhower, December 30, 1944, in GCMRL.

494   Monty himself: de Guingand, pp. 106 ff.

494   Your very devoted: Montgomery, *Memoirs*, p. 319.

494   He was already: Bradley, p. 492.

495   You disturb me: Montgomery, *Memoirs*, p. 320.

495   What-a-good-boy: de Guingand, p. 434.

495   The whole Allied team: Montgomery, *Memoirs*, p. 279.

495   The Americans: Churchill is quoted in Weigley, *Eisenhower's Lieutenants*, p. 565.

495   I opposed this: *Marshall Interviews*, p. 555.

Chapter XXIX · The Argonauts

497   The wide variety: Harriman to Stettinius, January 10, 1945, is in *FRUS: The Conferences at Malta and Yalta, 1945*, p. 450.

498   They simply cannot: Pogue III, p. 530, quoting Deane to GCM, December 2, 1944.

498   Present proposals: *Ibid.*

499   Would it be awkward : GCM to Eisenhower, January 17, 1945, GCMRL.

499   A weakening: Harry Butcher's unpublished diary is quoted in David Eisenhower, *Eisenhower: At War*, p. 616.

499   The British had won: GCM to Eisenhower is quoted in Ambrose, *Supreme Commander*, p. 582.

500   I can, of course: Eisenhower, *Crusade*, p. 372.

500   As long as: Quoted in Clemens, p. 100.

500   With General Marshall: Eisenhower, *Crusade*, p. 372.

PAGE

500   General Marshall will not: *Eisenhower Papers*, IV, p. 2460.

501   Had now become: *FRUS: Malta, 1945*, p. 471.

502   To be undertaken: *Ibid.*

502   A danger in putting: *FRUS: Malta, 1945*, p. 472.

502   I will advance: Bryant, *Triumph*, pp. 394–95.

502   Goddam it: Ambrose, *Supreme*, p. 586.

503   They are not nearly: *Marshall Interviews*, p. 505.

503   The closer: Ismay, p. 385.

503   Morale bombing: Greenfield, *American Strategy*, pp. 115–18, has a summary of the arguments. He concludes these "were nonetheless terror raids." *The United States Strategic Bombing Survey: Summary Report*, p. 5, noted that American claims of "pin point" bombing were inflated. Only one in five aimed bombs fell within 1,000 feet of the target. The survey estimated 305,000 German civilians were killed and 780,000 injured in Allied bombing and 20 percent of that nation's dwellings made uninhabitable.

503   Of the difficulty: FDR to Churchill, January 2, 1945, in Kimball, III, p. 490.

503   Make no mistake: Colville, *Fringes*, p. 555.

504   The decisive: *FRUS: Malta, 1945*, p. 486.

504   To avoid full-scale: *FRUS: Malta, 1945*, p. 518.

504   Very frail: Cunningham, p. 627. Lord Moran predicted that Roosevelt had only a few months to live.

505   The grueling give-and-take: Stettinius, *Roosevelt*, p. 73.

505   Nearly burnt out: Moran, p. ix.

505   Intelligent interest: *Ibid.*, p. 243.

505   Unqualified priority: Joint Chiefs to the President, January 30, 1945, in *FRUS: Malta, 1945*, p. 535.

505   Attached great importance: *FRUS: Malta, 1945*, p. 543.

506   Somewhat disappointed: *FRUS: Malta, 1945*, p. 544.

507   Alignments with the French: *FRUS: Malta, 1945*, p. 566.

508   In view of the difficult: *FRUS: Malta, 1945*, p. 579.

508   When the Anglo-American armies: *FRUS: Malta, 1945*, p. 578.

508   A brilliantly concise: Churchill, *Triumph*, p. 349.

508   One of the most magnificent: Stettinius, *Diaries*, p. 238.

508   Approach them: GCM to Eisenhower, January 17, 1945, GCMRL.

509   Made a profound impression: Stettinius, *Roosevelt*, p. 107.

509   Felt it to be: *FRUS: Malta, 1945*, p. 586.

509   The Soviet leaders: Clemens, p. 127.

510   And he was not: *Ibid.*

510   The Allies should bear: *FRUS: Malta, 1945*, p. 603.

511   The most difficult season: *FRUS: Malta, 1945*, p. 646.

511   There have been no changes: *FRUS: Malta, 1945*, p. 758.

512   Hoped it would not be: *FRUS: Malta, 1945*, p. 766. Just after his inauguration Roosevelt had flatly told his son James, "They'll never make that landing on Japan." See *Los Angeles Times*, March 4, 1983, p. 6.

PAGE

512   The British had never: *FRUS: Malta, 1945,* p. 768.

512   An astute negotiator: *Marshall Interviews,* p. 313.

512   It would be difficult: *FRUS: Malta, 1945,* p. 769.

513   Indochina was: *FRUS: Malta, 1945,* p. 770. The president added that "the Indochinese were people of small stature, like the Javanese and Burmese and were not warlike."

513   General, I assume: Alger Hiss, "Two Yalta Myths," *The Nation,* January 23, 1982, p. 69.

514   Has on the whole: Bryant, *Triumph,* p. 411. Three weeks later, Douglas MacArthur inadvertently ratified the Yalta pact when he urged that the United States obtain a commitment from the Russians to battle the Japanese in Manchuria so "as to pin down a very large part of the Japanese army." See *Forrestal Diaries,* p. 38.

514   The forgotten front: Blumenson, *Mark Clark,* p. 239.

514   Do not meet me: Clark, *Calculated Risk,* p. 423.

515   Pray give: Katherine Marshall, p. 236.

Chapter XXX · The Battle Day Past

517   THE MAN: Perry, p. 310.

517   Not going to spend: Radio commentator Raymond Gram Swing is quoted in Nicholas, p. 528.

517   Every phase: Ambrose, *Supreme Commander,* p. 621.

518   As a possible antidote: Pogue III, p. 553.

518   You are riding: Arnold, p. 548.

518   Making war: GCM to Eisenhower, March 6, 1945, GCMRL.

518   Sometimes when I: Ambrose, *Supreme,* p. 620.

518   Whether we like it: Major General Craig to Lieutenant General Handy, February 3, 1945, quoted in Cline, p. 313.

519   The entire responsibility: Murphy, *Diplomat,* p. 229.

519   Barring an unlikely: Bradley and Blair, p. 417.

519   A pretty stiff price: Bradley, p. 535

519   It seemed cruel: Bradley and Blair, p. 418.

520   Were early converts: *Ibid.*

520   A whipped enemy: David Eisenhower, *Eisenhower: At War,* p. 739.

520   Berlin had become: Eisenhower to Montgomery, March 31, 1945, quoted in Toland, *The Last 100 Days,* p. 325.

521   These misunderstandings: WSC to FDR, April 1, 1945, in Kimball, III, p. 604.

522   Was saddling me: *Marshall Interviews,* p. 386.

522   The British Army: FDR to WSC, April 3, 1945, in Kimball, III, pp. 608–09.

522   Psychological and political: Ambrose, *Eisenhower,* I, p. 395.

522   That rude message: Quoted in Gavin, *On to Berlin,* p. 342.

522   I regard: WSC to FDR, April 5, 1945, in Kimball, III, p. 612.

PAGE

523   Negotiations . . . discussions: Roosevelt to Stalin, April 4, 1945, in Kimball, III, p. 611. GCM acknowledged authorship of this diplomatic note in *Marshall Interviews*, p. 384.

523   A terrific headache: Burns, p. 600.

523   Daddy slept away: Pogue III, p. 557.

524   Harry, the President: Truman, *Memoirs*, I, p. 15.

524   There was sadness: Interview with H. Merrill Pasco of Richmond, Virginia, December 9, 1986.

524   A great war president: Alsop, p. 245.

524   A great leader: *New York Times*, April 13, 1945, p. 10.

524   Obstinate Dutchman: Cadogan, p. 620.

525   He was sure: Daniels, p. 262.

525   A project looking: Truman, *Memoirs*, I, p. 20. Details of Marshall's briefing are contained in Marshall's "Memorandum for the President," April 2, 1945, in GCMRL Box 91, Folder 32.

525   Crackpots: Cochran, p. 120.

526   Unworldly authority: Baker, p. 411.

526   I want to tell: Katherine Marshall, p. 245.

526   A nuisance: Interview with H. Merrill Pasco of Richmond, Virginia, November 4, 1986.

527   A young man's war: Associated Press dispatch to the *Los Angeles Times*, April 19, 1945.

527   I intend to tell: Harriman and Abel, p. 440.

527   This war is not: Stalin's comment to Marshal Tito is quoted by William Pfaff in the *Los Angeles Times*, January 8, 1982.

528   So far had been: Forrestal, p. 50.

528   He had left Yalta: *Ibid.*, p. 51.

528   Then to my relief: Stimson Diaries, April 23, 1945.

528   Were always delicate: Nelson, p. 58.

528   Soviet participation: Bohlen's minutes are in Forrestal, p. 51 (italics in the original).

528   All we were asking: Truman, I, pp. 98–99.

529   The free world: *Ibid.*, p. 262.

529   General Marshall and I: *Ibid.*, p. 274.

529   While we are still: Eisenhower to GCM, April 15, 1945, in Hobbs, p.223.

529   Our arrival: Ambrose, *Supreme*, p. 653.

530   Remarkable political advantages: *Ibid.*

530   Personally: GCM to Eisenhower, April 28, 1945, GCMRL.

530   I shall not attempt: Eisenhower to GCM, April 29, 1945, GCMRL.

530   I know how: Conversation with Leonard Leader, Los Angeles, California, November 17,1981.

530   And that if Germany were given: Botting, p. 87.

530   The mission: *Ibid.*, p. 91.

531   It was a relaxation: Interview with H. Merrill Pasco, December 9, 1986.

531   Since the day: Pogue III, p. 583–84.

PAGE

531   Our army: Pogue III, p. 584.
531   Long and terrible road: GCM to Winston Churchill, May 9, 1945, GCMRL.
531   The true organizer: Churchill to GCM, March 30, 1945, GCMRL.
531   The hard inside working: Churchill to GCM, May 17, 1945, GCMRL.
532   I have seen: Stimson Diaries, May 8, 1945.

Chapter XXXI · A Second Coming in Wrath

533   The architects of victory: *New York Times,* May 9, 1945, p. 22.
533   Waves of B-29s: *Los Angeles Times,* June 23, 1946.
533   The raid of the fire wind: Larrabee, p. 619.
534   Twenty years: Associated Press dispatch to the *Los Angeles Times*, April 6, 1945.
535   Character of the weapon: "Memorandum of Conversation with General Marshall, May 29, 1945—11:45 a.m." in GCMRL Verifax 2798. The United States also had deadly biological weapons ready. See the *Los Angeles Times*, January 1, 1987, p. 16.
535   The reason: Lilienthal, p. 199.
535   Control of the naval resources: Memorandum for the Commander-in-Chief, U.S. Fleet, Subject: Operation OLYMPIC, May 17, 1945, GCMRL. MacArthur's partisans were certain Marshall was scheming to take command of CORONET himself. See Hunt, pp. 374–76, and Eichelberger, pp. 229–30.
536   I am here: Eden, p. 621.
536   Venerates Marshall: Churchill, *Triumph,* p. 481.
536   Either West Pointers: Truman, *Dear Bess,* p. 487.
537   Boys, if you ever: Truman, *Memoirs,* I, p. 17.
537   Able and conniving: Messer, p. 71.
537   Played upon: *Ibid.,* p. 11.
538   The most terrible: Stimson, "Decision," p. 99.
538   Expressed the view: *Ibid.,* p. 100. Marshall later told David Lilienthal, "Stimson wrote a good article about it, but he generously took a greater share of the responsibility than was fair." See Lilienthal's *Journal,* II, p. 198.
538   Primordial considerations: Pogue IV, p. 530, n. 30.
538   He thought these weapons: "Memorandum of Conversation with General Marshall, May 29, 1945—11:45 a.m." in GCMRL Verifax 2798.
538   It seemed to be: Wyden, p. 158, quoting Arthur Compton.
539   If information: "Notes of the Interim Committee Meeting, Thursday, 31 May 1945," GCMRL 1482 / 196, p. 11.
539   Revolved around: Morton, "Decision," p. 497.
539   If the Japanese: Wyden, p. 161. See also "Notes of the Interim Committee Meeting, Thursday, 31 May 1945," GCMRL 1482 / 196, p. 14.
539   The military experts: Byrnes, *Speaking Frankly,* p. 262. In organizing the

defense of the home islands, the national slogan was "A hundred million die together." Imperial Navy General Staff Directive 31 stipulated: "All war preparations will be carried out in the spirit of suicide attacks and the total national manpower will be united into a fighting force that can furnish the necessary manpower for the coordinated war plans of the army and navy." See Spurr, pp. 135–36. A former president of the Japan Medical Society in 1983 noted, "When one considers the possibility that the Japanese military would have sacrificed the entire nation if it were not for the atomic bomb attack, then this bomb might be described as having saved Japan." See Paul Jacobs, "A-Bomb Spared Lives, Doctor Says," *Los Angeles Times*, August 5, 1983. A contrary view is in Barton J. Bernstein, "The Myth of Lives Saved by A-Bombs," *Los Angeles Times*, pp. E1, 2; or Bernstein, "A Postwar Myth."

539   Would have been a deadly thing: Eichelberger, p. 300. Eichelberger wrote later, after inspecting the invasion beaches, "Through the years I have been inclined to believe that I should have a very grateful attitude towards the atomic bomb and its use at Hiroshima and Nagasaki. . . . The Japanese defenses were almost impregnable and the defenders would have been well disciplined and fanatical," p. 310, n. 15.

540   Would take a million: Daniels, p. 281. Other Truman estimates are in Fleming, I, p. 297 (200,000 Americans, 400,000 Japanese), and Lamont, p. 331 (250,000 American dead, 500,000 wounded). The totals are not necessarily contradictory in that Truman may have been dealing with different cohorts: the dead from both sides, all casualties, or only American casualties (dead). Henry Stimson said he was told that total American casualties for OLYMPIC and CORONET might be as high as one million. See Stimson, "Decision," p. 102, and Bernstein.

540   We shall not know: Stimson Diaries, April 13, 1945.

540   We had 100,000: *Marshall Interviews*, p. 389.

541   I believe: From General MacArthur to General Marshall, June 18, 1945, GCMRL. In a bald attempt to rewrite the record, MacArthur later wrote, "From my viewpoint, any intervention by Russia during 1945 was not required." See *Reminiscences*, p. 301. By 1964 and the publication of his autobiography however, the Cold War had intervened.

541   An Okinawa from one end: Wyden, p. 172.

541   Not indispensable: *FRUS: The Conference at Berlin*, I, p. 902.

543   Terrible desolation: Arnold, p. 583.

543   We want: Bryant, *Triumph*, p. 474.

544   A very nice speech: *Ibid.*

544   They would be prepared: Bryant, *Triumph*, p. 475.

544   Weighed down: Colville, *Fringes*, p. 599.

544   The noblest Roman: Moran, p. 292.

544   That is a man: Birse, *Memoirs*, p. 209.

545   George was almost: Blumenson, *The Patton Papers*, p. 731.

545   Japan will surrender: Messer, p. 105.

546   It gave him: Stimson Diaries, July 21, 1945.

546   Stimson, what was gunpowder: Wyden, p. 224.
546   Even if we went: Stimson Diaries, July 23, 1945.
547   Complete and utter: *New York Times,* July 27, 1945.
547   Prove necessary: Cline, p. 348.
547   We must *mokusatsu:* Wyden, p. 211. The War Department was aware by the end of June that "the Japanese believe . . . that unconditional surrender would be the equivalent of national extinction, and there are as yet no indications that they are ready to accept such terms."
548   He has enough: Groves, p. 320.
548   Results clearcut: *Ibid.,* p. 322.
548   Was not thinking: Groves, p. 324. The toll reached 130,000 dead.
548   We are now prepared: *New York Times,* August 7, 1945, p. 2.
548   The whole city: Butow, *Japan's Decision,* p. 151.
549   I think it was: *Marshall Interviews,* p. 391. Marshall did acknowledge they had overlooked the shock value. See Lilienthal, p. 198.
550   Never have I known: Byrnes, *All in One Lifetime,* p. 305.
550   It was of great importance: Stimson Diaries, August 10, 1945.
550   The enemy has begun: Wyden, p. 305.

Chapter XXXII · The Chinese Midwife

554   For the first time: Marshall, *Biennial,* 1945, p. 3.
554   It is impossible: GCM is quoted in Snyder, *The War,* p. 505.
554   Thank you very much: Winston Churchill to GCM, August 9, 1945, GCMRL.
554   I have never seen: Katherine Marshall, p. 251.
555   The greatest military man: *New York Times,* November 21, 1945, p. 4.
555   General, I want: Truman, *Memoirs,* II, p. 86.
555   President Truman has: Katherine Marshall, p. 282.
555   That phone call: *Ibid.*
555   A son of a bitch: Donovan, *Conflict,* p. 149.
555   A considerable section: Associated Press dispatch to the *Los Angeles Times,* November 28, 1945.
555   When this war ends: Halifax, p. 293.
556   There was the devil: Truman, *Memoirs,* II, p. 86.
556   This assignment: Katherine T. Marshall to Frank McCarthy, December 30, 1945, quoted in Pogue IV, p. 30.
556   Entirely unjustified: Associated Press dispatch to the *Los Angeles Times,* August 30, 1945.
557   Skeleton: Prange, et al., *At Dawn,* p. 675.
557   Thorough, impartial: *Ibid.,* p. 676.
557   We had other: "Reminiscences of James T. Williams, Jr.," Oral History Research Office, Columbia University, p. 926.
558   The investigation was intended: Pogue II, p. 431. In an earlier interview, however, Marshall spoke of "the Pearl Harbor investigation *against*

         me [emphasis added] after the war was over." See *Marshall Interviews,* February 11, 1957, p. 377.

558   My recollection is: See, for example *Pearl Harbor Attack,* III, pp. 1108–09.

558   Inclined to feel: *Pearl Harbor Attack,* III, p. 1086.

558   The presumption: *Pearl Harbor Attack,* III, p. 1141.

558   May I say also: *Pearl Harbor Attack,* III, pp. 1406–07.

559   A *charming* week: William S. White, "Mr. George C. Marshall of Leesburg, Va.," *New York Times Magazine,* August 7, 1949, p. 78

559   Errors of judgment: *Investigation of the Pearl Harbor Attack, Report,* p. 252.

559   Failure to perform: *Ibid.,* p. 266H.

560   Chilly politeness: *Marshall's Mission to China,* I, pp. xv–xvi.

561   Many international: *China and U.S. Far East Policy* (Washington: Congressional Quarterly, 1947), p. 38. See also National Security Council 34, on "United States Policy Toward China," October 13, 1948. A copy is available at GCMRL as Xerox 1574.

561   There are great: *New York Times,* October 12, 1945.

561   Will be unable: *China White Paper,* p. 131. Wedemeyer met in Tokyo with MacArthur and Admiral Raymond P. Spruance, the three concurring that this was an opportune moment to fuse the rival factions in one government. "Later, when it became unpopular to have seemed to advocate any such unification, all three authors of the joint statement reacted in their characteristic fashion: MacArthur denied having signed it, Wedemeyer straddled the issue, and Spruance declared, 'We meant exactly what we said.' "—E. J. Kahn, Jr., *The China Hands,* p. 176.

561   Try to force: *Forrestal Diaries,* p. 123.

562   His figure: Acheson, *Sketches,* p. 147.

562   A "Trojan Horse": Acheson, *Present,* p. 198.

562   This would mean: *FRUS: 1945,* VII, pp. 767 ff.

562   The proper instrument: Donovan, *Conflict,* p. 152.

562   It would still: *FRUS: 1945,* VII, p. 770.

562   Son, there goes: Kahn, *China Hands,* p. 184.

563   Had aged immeasurably: MacArthur, *Reminiscences,* p. 320.

563   Many on the ground: "The Reminiscences of Walter S. Robertson," Oral History Research Office, Columbia University, p. 9.

563   I am going: Wedemeyer, p. 363. Stilwell in retirement agreed with Wedemeyer that Marshall would not be successful, snorting, "George Marshall can't walk on water." See Tuchman, *Stilwell,* p. 673. On the other hand, Stalin commented that if anyone could untangle the Chinese knot, it was Marshall, according to Byrnes, *Speaking Frankly,* p. 228.

563   I indicated clearly: *Marshall's Mission to China,* I, p. 6.

564   I want to go: Robertson Oral History, p. 3.

564   I long for personal: Rose Page Wilson, p. 314.

564   This barrier: *Marshall's Mission,* I, p. 7.

566   A dose of American medicine: Pogue IV, p. 89.

566   Marshall has been dealing: Furuya, p. 865.

PAGE

566   More and more: *Ibid.*
567   So if we are going: *Marshall's Mission*, II, p. 262.
567   We owe so much: *Ibid.*, p. 288.
568   This agreement: *Ibid.*, p. 290.

Chapter XXXIII · The Tiger of Peace

569   So many compromises: Pogue IV, p. 99, quoting GCM to Frank McCarthy, February 22, 1946.
569   Terror of the Evildoers: *Time*, March 25, 1946, p. 30.
569   There was every: *FRUS: 1946*, X, p. 510.
570   In common with many: Pogue IV, p. 102.
570   Respect and admiration: Pogue IV, p. 106.
571   To force the issue: Pogue IV, p. 109.
571   I feel that I: Madame Chiang to GCM, April 2, 1946, GCMRL.
572   It made the victorious: *Marshall's Mission*, I, p. 99.
572   Fatally provocative: *Ibid.*, p. 101.
572   Any compromise: Chiang's diary for April 19, 1946, is quoted in Furuya, p. 875.
572   If Marshall views: Furuya, p. 876.
573   Forcing us to accept: *Ibid.*
573   I cannot say: Wilson, *Zhou Enlai*, p. 169.
573   Tired patience: Acheson, *Present*, p. 204.
573   Trying to brief: Kubek, p. 327. Kubek thinks this a criticism.
573   I probably: Beal, p. 23.
573   If Chiang: Rose Page Wilson, p. 377.
573   Chiang's confidence: *Ibid.*
574   Quite ill: Dwight D. Eisenhower oral history, Vol. I, pp. 39 ff., Eisenhower Administration Project, Oral History Research Office, Columbia University.
574   During the last: Wilson, *Zhou Enlai*, p. 170.
575   All-out aid: Truman, *Memoirs*, II, p. 81.
575   You are accepted: GCM to Hannegan, June 5, 1946, GCMRL.
575   Deathly tired: Melby, p. 164.
575   A messenger boy: Beal, p. 156.
575   Never since the days: Beal, pp. 328–29, quoting an article in *The New Republic*.
575   Democratic procedure: *Marshall's Mission*, I, p. 174.
576   Primarily a military: Wedemeyer, p. 370.
577   What you are saying: *Marshall Interviews*, p. 539.
577   Marshall is beginning: Melby, p. 128.
577   Without truth: *Marshall's Mission*, I, p. 444.
577   The selfish interests: Truman to Chiang, August 10, 1946, in *Marshall's Mission*, II, pp. 381–82.
578   I pointed out: *Marshall's Mission*, I, p. 208.

PAGE

578   Change into: *Marshall's Mission,* II, pp. 385–86.

578   Dr. Stuart and I: Truman, *Memoirs,* II, p. 86.

578   Developments in China: *Los Angeles Times,* September 14, 1946.

578   Looks like Marshall: *Dear Bess,* p. 538.

578   Forced to presume: Chou to GCM, September 30, 1946, in *Marshall's Mission,* II, p. 413.

579   A cloak: Acheson, *Present,* p. 208.

579   He has virtually accused: *Ibid.*

579   At the point, Truman, *Memoirs,* II, p. 87.

580   While they had lost: *White Paper,* p. 202.

581   I can't go: Melby, p. 161.

581   For reorientation: Beal, p. 283.

581   He felt: *Marshall's Mission,* I, pp. 375–76.

581   Determine formally: *Ibid.,* p. 377.

581   I know Marshall: Melby, p. 173.

581   They don't trust: Beal, p. 292.

581   The Communists exist: *Ibid.*

581   Since June: *Marshall's Mission,* I, p. 379.

581   The army: Beal, p. 293.

582   Even the most tolerant: *Marshall's Mission,* I, p. 405.

582   I will tell: *Marshall Interviews,* p. 571.

582   The Communists were aware: *Marshall's Mission,* I, p. 406.

582   His old foot: Beal, p. 313.

583   Within a year: *New York Times,* December 19, 1946.

583   At such time: Pogue IV, p. 139.

583   The best way: Beal, p. 339.

583   For consultation: Pogue IV, p. 144.

583   My answer: Acheson, *Present,* p. 210.

583   That final conversation: *U.S. News and World Report,* October 1, 1954, p. 45.

584   Come back soon: *Time,* January 20, 1947, p. 34.

584   A dominant group: *Marshall's Mission,* II, pp. 522 ff.

584   A blistering plague: United Press dispatch to the *Los Angeles Times,* January 8, 1947.

585   Friendly and constructive: *New York Times,* January 13, 1947.

585   He did not: *New York Times,* January 15, 1947.

585   I tried to please: Bidault, p. 144.

Chapter XXXIV · *Going to the Yar*

586   I am an army officer: *Newsweek,* January 20, 1947, p. 25.

586   The burden: *United States News,* January 17, 1947, p. 50.

587   I am assuming: *Christian Science Monitor,* January 22, 1947.

587   Surrounded him: Pogue IV, p. 145.

587   Do you know: Interview with Marshall Carter, March 9, 1988.

PAGE

588 The only way: Robert E. Sherwood radio address, April 29, 1951, over the Mutual Broadcasting System under the auspices of the Committee on the Present Danger.

588 And his look: Acheson, *Sketches*, p. 154.

589 It is a little more: GCM to Madame Chiang Kai-shek, February 5, 1947, GCMRL.

589 General Marshall has: Isaacson and Thomas, p. 391.

589 Dispatched to the roof: GCM to "Dear Lord Halifax," February 5, 1947, GCMRL.

590 I thought: Pogue IV, p. 148.

590 A man who understood: *Ibid.*

590 The love life of an elephant: Lovett's analogy is in Ferrell, *American Diplomacy*, p. 18. Ferrell's volume on Marshall in the American Secretaries of State series furnished the figures on the department's growth.

591 Dean spent: Lilienthal, II, p. 159.

591 At an early: Interview with Dean Rusk, November 25, 1980.

591 Don't fight: Acheson, *Present*, p. 737.

591 I don't want you: Author's interview with Dean Rusk, November 25, 1980.

591 A great teacher: *Ibid.*

591 Rarely informed: Donald Robinson, "Secretary of State Marshall," *American Mercury* (July 1948), p. 38.

591 Was amazed: Berle, p. 578. On the other hand, Adlai Stevenson found Marshall "precise and accurate about those matters which one wouldn't have thought were within his area of interest or particular competence. . . ." See *The Papers of Adlai Stevenson*, p. 443.

592 Against any eventuality: *Forrestal Diaries*, p. 134.

592 The Declaration of World War III: *Ibid.*

592 For two years: George Kennan, "Flashbacks," p. 58.

592 A preposterously long telegram: *Ibid.*

593 Centuries old: Kennan, *Memoirs*, pp. 547–59, has a copy of the telegram.

593 My voice: *Ibid.*, p. 295.

593 Fully prepared: Kennan in "Letters to the Times," *New York Times*, October 18, 1959.

593 A blue piece: Acheson, *Present*, p. 217.

595 Hoped Congress: Truman, *Memoirs*, II, p. 127.

595 Our interest: Pogue IV, p. 164.

595 The choice: Vandenberg, p. 339.

595 Is this a private fight: Jones, p. 139.

595 Never have I: Acheson, *Present*, p. 219.

596 Mr. President: *Ibid.*

596 Scare hell: Ferrell, *Marshall*, p. 81.

596 Between alternative ways: *Los Angeles Times*, March 13, 1947.

596 If it is a wise policy: Ferrell, *Marshall*, p. 91.

597 The more I see: Ferrell, *Off the Record*, p. 109.

597 Dull, Duller: Smith, *Thomas E. Dewey*, p. 47.

PAGE

597   The wooliest: Cadogan, p. 462.

597   Like a son: "Reminiscences of James T. Williams, Jr.," Oral History
        Research Office, Columbia University.

598   George Catlett Marshall: *Time*, March 10, 1947, p. 25.

598   It would appear: *Los Angeles Times*, March 6, 1947.

598   I was able to gauge: *FRUS: 1947*, II, p. 193.

598   I am not a diplomat: *FRUS: 1947*, II p. 195.

599   The Russians promise: Botting, p. 226.

599   We must realize: Clay to GCM, May 2, 1947, in Clay, *Papers*, I, pp. 347–
        49.

600   I want you: Pogue IV, p. 180.

600   Sweetheart don't go: *Time*, March 17, 1947, p. 27.

600   The star of the conference: Brandon, p. 38.

601   He was unaffected: Bidault, p. 144.

602   We believe: *World Report*, April 1, 1947, p. 47.

602   Was probably: Smith, *My Three Years*, p. 220.

602   The generalities: *FRUS: 1947*, II, p. 252.

603   But charges: *World Report*, April 1, 1947, p. 44.

603   We cannot accept: *Ibid.*, p. 45.

603   Would be a danger: United Press dispatch to the *Los Angeles Times*, April
        8, 1947.

603   I can never: *Ibid.*

604   Military men make: Brandon, p. 38.

604   You just look: Yergin, p. 300.

604   Almost brutal assaults: *Marshall Interviews*, p. 314.

605   Rise to a situation: *FRUS: 1947*, II, p. 339.

605   Frankly determined: *FRUS: 1947*, II, p. 340.

605   They had suffered: *FRUS: 1947*, II, p. 342.

605   Let the German people: *Ibid.*

605   It is wrong: Smith, *My Three Years*, p. 221.

605   Only the first skirmishes: *FRUS: 1947*, II, pp. 343–44.

605   We may agree: Bohlen, p. 263.

605   Came to the conclusion: *Ibid.*

606   It would have been: Smith, *My Three Years*, p. 229.

606   To prevent: Bohlen, p. 263.

606   It was the Moscow: Murphy, *Diplomat*, p. 307.

606   A melancholy catalog: James Reston in *The New York Times*, April 29,
        1947.

606   The patient is sinking: *Current History* (June 1947), p. 592.

Chapter XXXV · A Fair Prospect of Success

607   An American: *Harvard Magazine* (May–June 1987), p. 84.

608   I am profoundly: *Ibid.*

608   Europe is in a mess: Kennan, *Memoirs*, pp. 325–26.

PAGE

608   It was my feeling: Price, p. 395.

608   Avoid trivia: *Ibid.*, p. 326.

609   Most of the other: Jones, p. 108.

609   The various countries: *Ibid.*, p. 276.

610   Opening the Treasury: Acheson, *Present*, p. 230.

610   If we try: Isaacson and Thomas, p. 410.

610   General, I want: Miller, *Plain Speaking*, p. 14.

610   What is Europe: Cochran, p. 191.

610   Cruel privation: Kimball, I, p. 109.

610   It is now obvious: Acheson, *Present*, pp. 230–31.

611   Six to seven billion: *Ibid.*, p. 231.

611   Let us admit: Mee, *Marshall Plan*, p. 79.

611   Are we safe: Price, p. 24.

611   Play it straight: Jones, p. 253.

611   It is easy: Price, p. 25, citing a 1954 memorandum from GCM to the author.

612   A speech typical: Truman, *Memoirs*, II, p. 138.

612   I need not tell: A text of the Harvard address is in Jones, pp. 281–84.

613   Yet the whole world's future: Pogue IV, p. 214, has Marshall's appended comments.

614   Exceptionally important: Pogue IV, p. 217.

614   From retail purchase: Pogue IV, p. 220.

614   Pathetic: Gimbel, *Origins*, p. 210.

615   Debtors do not: Mee, *Marshall Plan*, p. 131.

615   In effect: *Ibid.*, p. 134.

615   Will lead to nothing: *FRUS: 1947*, III, p. 308.

615   A declaration of war: *FRUS: 1947*, III, p. 327.

616   There is iron: Payne, p. 321.

616   Glass insides: Isaacson and Thomas, p. 417.

616   Old copilot: *Ibid.*

617   Marshall Plan: *Ibid.*, p. 420.

617   Ranked first: Yergin, p. 373.

617   Of no agreement: Mee, *Marshall Plan*, p. 174.

617   The secretary of state: *Ibid.*, pp. 176–77.

618   Accepted my views: Gimbel, *Origins*, p. 243.

618   A long-term, patient: "X" [George F. Kennan], "The Sources of Soviet Conduct, *Foreign Affairs*, XXV (July 1947), pp. 566–82.

618   Planners don't talk: Kennan, p. 356.

619   American imperialism: "How Russia Fights Marshall Plan," *U.S. News— World Report*, January 16, 1948, pp. 68 ff.

619   Truman-Marshall Plan: *World Report*, October 27, 1947, p. 34. There is a more graceful rendering in Mee, p. 210.

620   The war ended: Gimbel, *Origins*, p. 139.

620   A world-wide struggle: *Los Angeles Times*, March 20, 1948.

620   We have seen: *Marshall's Plan*, p. 273.

621   Was more a figure: *Time*, January 5, 1948, p. 19.

PAGE

621   The Marshall Plan: *United States Foreign Policy for a Post-War Recovery Program*, Part II, p. 1322.
621   This program: *Post-War Recovery Program*, p. 1.
622   He was clear: *New York Times,* January 9, 1948.
622   He was just: *Marshall Interviews,* pp. 491–92.
622   He assumed: Acheson, *Present,* p. 270.
622   He was marvelous: *Marshall Interviews,* p. 492.
622   If it comes: *United States Foreign Policy for a Post-War Recovery Program,* Part I, p. 46.
622   I have struggled: *Ibid.,* p. 84.
623   The door is open: *Ibid.,* p. 65.
623   Behind the iron: *Ibid.,* Part II, p. 2039.
623   Undermining: *Ibid.,* p. 2019.
623   There was a tremendous: *Ibid.,* Part I, p. 42.
623   Part of the reason: *Ibid.,* p. 76.
623   ERP is the economic: *Ibid.,* Part II, pp. 1585, 1593.
623   We are accused: *Universal Military Training,* p. 23.
624   Clamp down completely: Yergin, p. 346. Marshall was apparently relying on a Kennan briefing paper.
624   We are faced: Yergin, p. 349. Davenport, pp. 408–09, suggests that Truman and Marshall had written off Czechoslovakia the previous fall.
624   It would be a far: Vandenberg, p. 390.
624   Is a plan for peace: *Ibid.,* pp. 391–92.
624   A full partner: Price, p. 65.
624   Within the last few: Clay, II, p. 568.
624   Will Russia move: Isaacson and Thomas, p. 440.
625   A reign of terror: Associated Press dispatch to the *Los Angeles Times,* March 11, 1948.
625   Papers this morning: Forrestal, p. 394.
625   No ringing phrases: Isaacson and Thomas, p. 441.
625   It is better: Yergin, p. 353.
626   Reverse the trend: Mee, *Marshall Plan,* p. 245.
626   I worked on that: *Marshall Interviews,* pp. 520–21.

Chapter XXXVI · The Crowded Days

627   Dangerously outmoded: GCM to Embassy in France, *FRUS: 1947,* VI, pp. 67–68.
627   We are in the awkward position: Yergin, p. 292.
627   If Greece falls: *FRUS: 1947,* V, p. 17.
628   Playing with fire: *The Forrestal Diaries,* p. 373.
628   Being pressed: Sparrow, p. 380.
628   It was no demobilization: Hodgson, p. 22.
628   Awkward: Lilienthal, *Journals,* II, p. 213.
629   Boring from within: Donovan, *Conflict,* p. 293.

PAGE

629 There is a deliberate: Quoted in McCarthy's *America's Retreat*, p. 8.

629 Potential security: Caute, p. 304. The ten were subsequently permitted to resign without prejudice "in order to avoid a possible injustice to them."

629 True hearing: Bert Andrews, "Federal Loyalty Check is No. 1 Topic in Capital," *New York Herald Tribune*, November 8, 1947.

630 His knowledge: Draft "Foreword" of the *Together* manuscript, GCMRL.

631 The General was: Carter interview, March 18, 1988.

631 If you knew how: Lilienthal, II, p. 258.

631 No words: Acheson, *Sketches*, p. 161.

632 Almost like brothers: Carter interview, March 9, 1988.

633 The worst advised: May, *China Scapegoat*, p. 159.

633 I have tortured: Lilienthal, II, p. 201.

633 In the final analysis: *White Paper: U.S. Relations with China*, p. 252.

633 A good man: *Marshall Interviews*, p. 562.

633 Failed to understand: Wedemeyer, p. 376.

634 The Nationalist Chinese: Stueck, p. 35.

634 Effect immediately: *White Paper*, pp. 257–58.

634 A force presenting: *Ibid.*, p. 767.

635 Suffering increasingly: *Ibid.*, p. 773.

635 Very gracious: Interview with Albert C. Wedemeyer, August 1, 1983.

636 Getting sucked in: May, *Truman Administration*, p. 32.

636 Essential for the unification: "Report to the National Security Council by the Secretary of the Army, July 26, 1948," in GCMRL Xerox 1574.

636 We have had: *White Paper*, pp. 380 ff.

637 We are no longer: Stueck, p. 95.

637 The greatest disaster: *New York Times*, October 11, 1947.

637 I was counting up: GCM to Charlotte Coles, November 13, 1947, GCMRL.

638 You are, oh, so fortunate: GCM to Arnold, October 27, 1947, GCMRL.

638 As conclusively: *Letters of Adlai E. Stevenson*, p. 412.

638 Unfortunately, it has: Marshall's text is reprinted in *Vital Speeches of the Day*, December 1, 1947, pp. 98–101.

639 The clearest hypocrisy: Associated Press dispatch to the *Los Angeles Times*, November 24, 1947.

640 Great architect: Associated Press dispatch to the *Los Angeles Times*, November 23, 1947.

640 Marshall was in: Clay, *Decision*, pp. 344–45.

640 A greater man: Sulzberger, p. 368.

640 The political advance: "Resume of the World Situation," Policy Planning Staff Paper 13, November 6, 1947, GCMRL.

640 It is necessary: United Press dispatch to the *Los Angeles Times*, November 26, 1947.

641 Imperialist peace: Quotations from the conference are taken from *FRUS: 1947*, II, pp. 700 ff.

641 Figments of propaganda: United Press dispatch to the *Los Angeles Times*, November 27, 1947.

641 But I thought: *FRUS: 1947*, II, p. 754.

PAGE

641   Your firm: *FRUS: 1947*, II, p. 764.
641   Was trying not only: *FRUS: 1947*, II, p. 767.
641   It was evident: *FRUS: 1947*, II, p. 767. See also p. 769.
642   There was no country: Bohlen, p. 266, placing the conversation at a luncheon.
642   I started NATO: *Marshall Interviews*, p. 525.
643   The man who offered: *Time*, January 5, 1948, p. 1R.

Chapter XXXVII · Playing with Fire

644   The situation: United Press dispatch to the *Los Angeles Times*, March 10, 1948.
644   The world: Associated Press dispatch to the *Los Angeles Times*, March 11, 1948.
644   The West: Djilas, p. 153.
645   Truman entered: Strout, p. 62.
645   Pull the trigger: Pogue IV, p. 299.
645   We are playing: *The Forrestal Diaries*, p. 373.
645   Its purpose: Rose Page Wilson, p. 296.
645   The only way: Attributed to GCM by Robert E. Sherwood in a Mutual Broadcasting System radio address, April 29, 1951. The script is in the Houghton Library, Harvard.
645   Mankind is engaged: *Los Angeles Times*, March 21, 1948.
646   Our great hope: United Press dispatch to the *Los Angeles Times*, February 14, 1948.
647   The policy of this country: *The Forrestal Diaries*, p. 432.
647   In seeking control: "Report by the National Security Council on U.S. Objectives with Respect to the USSR. . . ." November 23, 1948, p. 6, GCMRL.
647   Forrestal should plan: "Secretary Marshall's Views," Unsigned Department of State document internally dated November 1948, GCMRL.
648   Would be the Munich: Botting, p. 308.
648   The United States government: Ferrell, *George C. Marshall*, p. 140.
648   The atomic-age equivalent: Herken, p. 258.
648   If we were: *Ibid.*, p. 262.
649   Glamour boys: Ferrell, *Off the Record*, p. 134.
649   To have some dashing: *The Forrestal Diaries*, p. 458.
649   Accepting the consequences: *The Forrestal Diaries*, p. 459.
649   Terrible feeling: Ferrell, *Off the Record*, p. 149.
649   The Russians: *FRUS: 1948*, II, p. 1178.
649   A ventriloquist's dummy: Associated Press dispatch to the *Los Angeles Times*, February 16, 1948.
649   A foe of peace: Associated Press dispatch to the *Los Angeles Times*, May 14, 1948.

PAGE

650   Still friendly: Associated Press dispatch to the *Los Angeles Times*, April 4, 1948.

650   If we would avert: Associated Press dispatch to the *Los Angeles Times*, March 29, 1948, quoting the Wadena *Pioneer-Journal.*

650   No evidence: *Los Angeles Times*, April 3, 1948.

650   The finals: GCM to Spencer L. Carter, June 14, 1948, GCMRL.

651   Communists and left-wing liberals: Pogue IV, p. 386.

652   That some guy: Walters, p. 152.

652   Oh, God: Author's interview with Marshall Carter, March 9, 1988.

652   If that is true: Walters, p. 152.

652   I would like: *Ibid.*, p. 154. The name of the officer, Jaime Fonseca, is in GCM to Lieutenant General German Ocampo, April 23, 1948, GCMRL.

653   That's the way: Carter interview, March 9, 1988.

653   This was a Colombian: Walters, p. 164.

653   This situation: United Press dispatch to the *Los Angeles Times*, April 13, 1948.

655   All my instincts: GCM to Spencer L. Carter, June 14, 1948, GCMRL.

655   In all my Washington: GCM to Henry L. Stimson, May 7, 1948, GCMRL.

655   This is not: GCM to Dwight D. Eisenhower, June 3, 1948, GCMRL.

655   Ain't like: Leahy to GCM, May 11, 1948, GCMRL.

655   It will be: GCM to Walter Huston, September 2, 1948, GCMRL.

656   United States influence: Condit, *History*, p. 87.

656   Any kind of a plan: Grose, p. 245.

657   You just don't understand: Isaacson and Thomas, p. 452.

657   Grasp the nettle: Paraphrased from *The Forrestal Diaries*, p. 367.

658   Here you are surrounded: *FRUS: 1948*, V, pp. 940–41.

658   He wanted to warn: Grose, p. 287.

658   I told Mr. Shertok: *FRUS: 1948*, V, p. 972.

658   Prepare yourself: Francis L. Loewenheim, "Recognition of Israel in 1948 No Sure Thing," *Los Angeles Herald-Examiner*, May 15, 1988. Marshall's summary of the meeting is in *FRUS: 1948*, V, pp. 972–73.

659   A ringing peroration: *FRUS: 1948*, V, p. 973.

659   I remarked: Grose, p. 291.

659   A righteous: Daniels, p. 319.

660   Well, General: Grose, p. 291.

660   I didn't have: Loewenheim, "Recognition."

660   We've got to straighten: Isaacson and Thomas, p. 452.

660   It seems to me: GCM to "My dear Mr. President," December 20, 1947, GCMRL.

661   No, gentlemen: Interview with Dean Rusk, November 25, 1980.

661   The president was under: Grose, p. 293.

661   Welcome Israel: *Ibid.*

661   Formulated in: Joseph Alsop column in the *Los Angeles Times*, June 1, 1948.

662   MARSHALL IS DOING: Snetsinger, p. 126.

PAGE

662   To get a better: *Newsweek*, November 1, 1948, p. 30.
662   Almost never complimented: Interview with Dean Rusk, November 25, 1980.
663   But we will not: *Vital Speeches of the Day*, October 1, 1948, p. 757.
663   Soviet-directed: NSC 7, March 30, 1948, GCMRL.
663   Our friends: Ferrell, *Off the Record*, p. 133.
664   Democracies are slow: Smith, *My Three Years*, p. 197.
664   Poisonous atmosphere: Druks, p. 189.
664   Never in the history: Pogue IV, p. 407.
664   Completely out: *The Forrestal Diaries*, p. 500.
665   This is how: Bohlen, p. 270.
665   Oh, mon dieu: Walters, p. 182.
666   Congratulations: *Ibid.*, p. 149.

Chapter XXXVIII · Active Duty

667   The operation: Interview with Marshall Carter, March 9, 1988
668   Is now abundantly clear: "A Report to the National Security Council by the Department of State on United States Policy Toward China, October 13, 1948," p. 12, GCMRL Xerox 1574.
668   I'll bet you: Lilienthal, II, p. 525.
668   I shall never forget: GCM to the President, January 2, 1949, GCMRL.
668   One of the great: *New York Times*, January 8, 1949.
668   I personally: Bevin to GCM, January 14, 1949, GCMRL.
668   Among the great names: *New York Times*, January 8, 1949.
668   Hard to say: Acheson to GCM, January 10, 1947 [sic], GCMRL.
670   Dismissal under fire: *The Forrestal Diaries*, p. 533.
670   I think your success: GCM to Louis Johnson, March 12, 1949, GCMRL.
670   Involutional melancholia: Isaacson and Thomas, p. 470.
670   A feeling of security: *Vital Speeches of the Day*, June 15, 1949, p. 518.
671   Draw your own: Associated Press dispatch to the *Los Angeles Times*, March 23, 1949.
671   Their common experiences: Gertrude Samuels, "Touring with Marshall of the Red Cross," *New York Times Magazine*, February 16, 1950, p. 30.
671   Only by courtesy: William S. White, "Mr. George C. Marshall of Leesburg, Va.," *New York Times Magazine*, August 7, 1949, p. 7.
672   To whom duty: *Ibid.*
672   She had always: Samuels, p. 27.
673   Arms folded: *Ibid.*, p. 28.
673   60 percent: *Ibid.*
673   Greater military power: Department of State *Bulletin*, January 23, 1950, p. 113.
673   Seriously unfavorable: *FRUS: 1949*, IX, p. 261.

PAGE

674 The current disparity: Joint Chiefs of Staff, "Memorandum for the Secretary of Defense," February 10, 1949, in *FRUS: 1949*, IX, pp. 284–86.

674 Our policy: Donovan, *Tumultuous Years*, p. 75.

674 The loss of China: *Ibid.*

674 America's failure in China: *Ibid.*, p. 77.

675 In the past year: Koen, p. 256, n. 18.

675 The unfortunate but inescapable: *White Paper*, p. xvi.

675 The conclusion: Acheson, *Present*, p. 303.

675 The lovely leisurely: Madame Chiang to Dear General, August 1, 1950, GCMRL.

676 I do not intend: Acheson, *Present*, p. 360.

676 Nevertheless are still: Reeves, p. 224.

676 Unless we believe: Isaacson and Thomas, p. 466.

676 Is that he is: Associated Press dispatch to the *Los Angeles Times*, April 21, 1950.

677 A pathetic thing: *Ibid.*

677 Bad security risk: Steel, p. 467.

677 Pro-communist group: *Ibid.*

677 We have evidence: *New York Times*, September 24, 1949.

677 We are in a straight race: Herken, p. 303.

678 To have caught: *Ibid.*, p. 307.

678 We should not: *New York Times*, May 31, 1950.

Chapter XXXIX · Positions Reversed

679 Play actor: Ferrell, *Off the Record*, p. 47.

679 Mr. President: Goulden, p. 48.

679 Felt certain: Truman, *Memoirs*, II, p. 379.

680 Substantially greater: *Los Angeles Times*, May 2, 1951.

680 If we can afford it: *Military Situation in the Far East*, Hearings Before the Committee on Armed Services and the Committee on Foreign Relations, 82nd Congress, 1st Session, Senate, I, p. 373.

680 The U.S. has little: National Security Council Report to the President, NSC-68/2, p. 13, GCMRL Xerox 1574.

681 If Washington only: Goulden, p. 53.

681 The North Korean government: Schoenbaum, p. 211.

682 With the end: *Congressional Digest* (December 1945), p. 304.

683 We should know: *New York Times*, October 19, 1945.

683 Let us take: "Reminiscences of James T. Williams, Jr.," Oral History Research Office, Columbia University, p. 932. Thirty-nine years later, events proved Marshall correct. President Reagan signed legislation making the chairman of the Joint Chiefs of Staff the principal military adviser to the president. As Marshall had recommended, the four military chiefs of staff were to be subordinate to the chairman. See *The New York Times*, October 2, 1986.

PAGE

683   Seemed almost limitless: Prados, p. 6. Information on the Eberstadt and Lovett role came from an interview with former CIA general counsel Lawrence R. Houston, July 29, 1982. Houston wrote the actual language of the bill.

684   Preventative wars: Hanson Baldwin in *The New York Times,* September 1, 1950.

684   The first aggressors: Stone, p. 92, quoting *The New York Times,* August 26, 1950.

684   The political domination: Millis, *Arms,* p. 235.

684   Unwittingly, Truman: Bradley and Blair, p. 503.

684   But when the President: Rose Page Wilson, p. 343.

684   Nothing could be more: Goulden, p. 160.

685   We *were* defending: *Ibid.* (Italics in original).

685   Mr. President: Ferrell, *Off the Record,* p. 189, quoting a letter from Truman to his wife, September 7, 1950.

685   Wonder of wonders: Truman, *Dear Bess,* p. 562.

685   I didn't think: Goulden, p. 163.

685   The camel: *Time,* September 25, 1950, p. 20.

686   It should be remembered: *New York Times,* September 14, 1950.

686   The Communist-appeasing: *Congressional Record,* September 15, 1950, pp. 14913–14.

686   Jenner? Jenner?: Pogue IV, p. 428.

687   Harrowing experience: Acheson, *Present,* p. 441.

687   From a purely military: Acheson, *Sketches,* p. 163.

687   There are two persons: Paraphrased from Edward B. Lockett, "Again the Marshall-Lovett Team," *New York Times Magazine,* October 29, 1950, p. 12.

688   She was a great mediator: Carter interview, March 9, 1988.

689   The military situation: *Life,* December 18, 1950.

689   To the dangerous point: Radford, pp. 218–19.

689   To wrest the initiative: NSC-68/2, September 30, 1950, GCMRL Xerox 1574, p. 6.

690   A defeat of free: NSC-68, April 30, 1950, GCMRL Xerox 1574.

690   Rare, awkward: Bradley and Blair, p. 519.

690   The history: *New York Times,* November 25, 1950.

690   A sour little war: Goulden, p. xv.

Chapter XL · Imperator

692   The swiftness: Bradley and Blair, p. 556.

692   To cringe behind: Donovan, *Tumultuous,* p. 277.

692   There's no stopping: Isaacson and Thomas, p. 532.

692   It would have taken: Donovan, *Nemesis,* p. 85.

693   I was full: Isaacson and Thomas, p. 532.

693   Committed one cardinal: Bradley and Blair, p. 561.

PAGE

693   Your military objective: *Ibid.*, p. 563.

694   Incipient revolution: Davis, p. 349.

694   I don't see why: Ferrell, *Off the Record*, p. 47.

695   The success of Inchon: James, III, p. 485.

695   We want you to feel: GCM to MacArthur, September 29, 1950, GCMRL Xerox 2566.

695   Unless and until: MacArthur to GCM, September 30, 1950, GCMRL.

695   Please accept: GCM to MacArthur, September 30, 1950, GCMRL.

695   Thanks, George: MacArthur to GCM, October 1, 1950, GCMRL.

695   Chinese did not: Isaacson and Thomas, p. 533.

695   Mere vaporings: *Ibid.* In his later *Korean War*, Acheson is less flippant. He describes Chou's words as a warning, "not to be disregarded, but, on the other hand, not an authoritative statement of policy" (p. 55).

696   Major Chinese Communist units: Truman, *Memoirs*, II, p. 413.

696   The Chinese people: Bradley and Blair, p. 571.

696   As I understood: Goulden, p. 264.

696   General Marshall didn't think: *Ibid.*

696   Fine patrician: *Ibid.*, p. 188, giving no source.

696   And it goes against: "Substance of Statements Made at Wake Island Conference on 15 October 1950," GCMRL Xerox 2566.

697   Pace, that's troublesome: Pace's oral history is quoted in Goulden, p. 273.

698   The auspicious time: Goulden, p. 288.

698   Hasty conclusions: Bradley and Blair, p. 583.

698   Flown to exhaustion: Goulden, p. 298.

699   The army would not understand: MacArthur, *Reminiscences*, p. 421.

699   Men and material: Truman, II, pp. 427–28.

700   Was a grave insult: Bradley and Blair, p. 585.

700   Curious quiescence: Isaacson and Thomas, p. 538.

700   Very personal: James, III, p. 523.

700   Complete agreement: *Ibid.*

701   The massive compression: *New York Times*, November 24, 1950.

701   We face: James, III, p. 536.

701   A posterity paper: Isaacson and Thomas, p. 536.

701   This command: James, III, p. 536.

701   We are much closer: *FRUS: 1950*, VII, pp. 1242 ff.

702   Would be to fall: *Ibid.*

702   Insulting: Goulden, p. 387.

703   Why don't: Ridgway, *Korean War*, pp. 61–62.

703   An enormous handicap: *U.S. News and World Report*, dated December 8, but on newsstands December 1, 1950.

703   I should have relieved: Truman, *Memoirs*, II, p. 437.

703   Of the greatest magnitude: Pogue IV, p. 466.

703   Is in very serious trouble: Ferrell, *Off the Record*, p. 202.

703   We consider: Blair, *Forgotten War*, p. 529.

704   Turn the tide of battle: Bradley and Blair, p. 608.

PAGE

704 Against vulnerable allies: James, III, p. 550.
704 And their morale: *FRUS: 1950*, VII, pp. 56–57.
705 If things went wrong: Acheson, *Present*, p. 515.
705 Eighth Army in good shape: Donovan, *Tumultuous*, p. 349.

Chapter XLI · The Shatter of Icons

706 Dulled the public interest: *U.S. News and World Report*, April 13, 1951, pp. 24 ff.
707 Accomplishment of our mission: Donovan, *Nemesis*, p. 149.
707 With clearing: Schnabel and Watson, III, Part I, p. 525.
707 Operations continue: James, III, p. 586.
708 Most extraordinary statement: Truman, *Memoirs*, II, p. 501.
708 Was confident: Goulden, p. 477.
708 Liberal opinion: Stone, *Hidden*, p. 272.
708 The demands of security: *New York Times*, March 28, 1951.
709 Meeting force: *Military Situation*, p. 3544.
709 The last straw: Ferrell, *Off the Record*, p. 210.
710 I knew the general: Miller, *Plain Speaking*, p. 328.
710 If you relieve: Blair, *Forgotten War*, p. 784.
710 Full panoply: Acheson, *Present*, p. 521.
710 Involves basic: Truman, *Memoirs*, II, p. 510.
710 Approaching something: GCM to John Leighton Stuart, December 29, 1950, GCMRL.
710 Unquestionably one of the ablest: Rose Page Wilson, p. 350.
711 Could lead: Bradley and Blair, p. 633.
711 It was a sad: Collins, *War in Peacetime*, p. 283.
711 Not in sympathy: *Ibid.*, p. 284.
711 Son, not tonight: Heller, *Truman White House*, p. 157.
712 Quite an explosion: Ferrell, *Off the Record*, p. 211.
712 This country is in: *New York Times*, April 13, 1951.
712 A Communist victory: Goulden, p. 499.
712 The happiest group: *Los Angeles Times*, April 13, 1952.
712 Hello, George: Bradley and Blair, p. 639.
712 Seldom had: *Time*, April 23, 1951, p. 24.
713 One of the most: James, III, p. 613.
713 I do not stand here: *New York Times*, April 20, 1951.
714 We saw: James, III, p. 616.
714 Nothing but a bunch: Miller, *Plain Speaking*, p. 337.
715 The positions: *Military Situation*, I, pp. 13–14.
716 A soldier can: *U.S. News and World Report*, May 18, 1951, p. 117.
716 General, we are faced: *Military Situation*, I, pp. 75 ff.
717 Powerful impression: United Press dispatch to the *Los Angeles Times*, May 7, 1951.
717 A very distressing: *Military Situation*, I, pp. 323 ff.

PAGE

720   Frankly, in the opinion: *Ibid.*, II, p. 732.

720   There was tremendous: Bradley and Blair, p. 640.

721   The utter futility: Collins, p. 292.

721   A conspiracy: *Congressional Record*, June 14, 1951, p. 6602. The speech
       is reprinted, with some emendations, in McCarthy's *America's Retreat from
       Victory*. The attribution of the authorship to Davis is in Reeves, pp. 373–
       74.

722   It was Marshall: *Congressional Record*, p. 6602.

722   Apparently indifferent: *Congressional Record*, p. 6572.

722   Created the China policy: *Congressional Record*, p. 6602.

722   What is the objective: *Ibid.*

723   Larger conspiracy: *Congressional Record*, p. 6603.

723   I do appreciate that: David Ignatius, "They Don't Make Them Like George
       Marshall Anymore," *Washington Post Weekly Edition*, June 8, 1987, p. 25.

723   Hysterical form: Reeves, p. 372.

723   Senator Joe: Wedemeyer, p. 154.

723   Easy prey: *Ibid.*, p. 370.

723   Fantastically false: *New York Times*, August 20, 1952.

724   Now look: *Newsweek*, September 1, 1952.

724   Kept columnists: Reeves, p. 372.

724   Marshall's loyalty: Buckley and Bozell, p. 392.

724   Least militant: Acheson, *Present*, p. 559.

724   In our present situation: Associated Press dispatch to the *Los Angeles
       Times*, May 16, 1951.

724   Winning a little battle: Stone, p. 273.

Chapter XLII · Sunset

Forrest Pogue's *George C. Marshall: Statesman, 1945–1959* provided a number
of details about Marshall's last years.

726   Very personal reasons: *Time*, September 24, 1951.

726   I wouldn't: *Ibid.*

728   Are my boys: United Press dispatch to the *Los Angeles Times*, August 30,
       1952.

728   What can we say: *Papers of Adlai Stevenson*, IV, p. 50.

728   Betrayed his principles: Donovan, *Tumultuous*, p. 400.

728   Eisenhower was forced: Rose Page Wilson, p. 371.

728   Sell out his grandmother: *Congressional Record*, August 3, 1954, p. 12960.

728   Poor fellow: Pogue IV, p. 497.

728   I think: *New York Times*, August 4, 1954.

728   You deserved far better: GCM to Adlai Stevenson, November 7, 1952,
       GCMRL.

729   A hundred million persons: *Reporter*, January 5, 1954.

729   My best friend: Pogue IV, p. 503.

PAGE

730   Was in 1940: United Press to the *Los Angeles Times,* November 1, 1953.

730   A tribute to: Associated Press to the *Los Angeles Times,* November 29, 1953.

730   Grateful for the momentary: Tess Jaksohn, Los Angeles, to the author, January 6, 1981.

730   Murderer!: Associated Press to the *Los Angeles Times,* December 11, 1953.

731   This is no peace: *Ibid.*

731   There has been: Marshall's Nobel Prize speech is reprinted as "Essentials to Peace," *Social Research* (Spring 1954), pp. 1–10.

731   The blackbirds: Associated Press dispatch to the *Los Angeles Times,* June 5, 1954.

732   Rather like: White, "Marshall at 75: The General Revisited," *New York Times Magazine,* December 25, 1955.

732   Your old Lieutenant: James Fulton to President Eisenhower, August 19, 1957, GCMRL.

732   Absolutely all right: White, "Marshall at 75."

732   The general made: George to Lovett, March 12, 1958, GCMRL.

732   Hindsight would be: *Saturday Review of Literature,* June 1, 1957.

733   I have so much time: Rose Page Wilson, p. 388.

733   A citizen: GCM to the *Observer* (London), January 28, 1959, GCMRL.

BIBLIOGRAPHY

Citations in the notes are by author and, if needed, short title. The exception is the ongoing series of Marshall's papers, edited by Larry I. Bland, et al., which is cited as *Papers*.

Acheson, Dean, *Fragments of My Fleece* (New York: W. W. Norton, 1971).
———, "Homage to General Marshall," *The Reporter*, November 26, 1959, p. 25.
———, *The Korean War* (New York: W. W. Norton, 1971).
———, *Morning and Noon* (Boston: Houghton Mifflin, 1965).
———, *Present at the Creation* (New York: W. W. Norton, 1969).
———, *Sketches from Life* (New York: Harper & Brothers, 1959).
Adams, Henry H., *Harry Hopkins* (New York: G. P. Putnam's Sons, 1977).
Alperovitz, Gar, *Atomic Diplomacy: Hiroshima and Potsdam,* expanded, updated edition (New York: Penguin, 1985).
Alsop, Joseph, *FDR 1882–1945: A Centenary Remembrance* (New York: Viking Press, 1982).
Ambrose, Stephen E., *Eisenhower*, Vol. I (New York: Simon & Schuster, 1983).
———, *Eisenhower and Berlin, 1945: The Decision to Halt at the Elbe* (New York: W. W. Norton, 1967).
———, *Supreme Commander: The War Years of General Dwight D. Eisenhower* (Garden City, N.Y.: Doubleday & Co., 1969).
American Armies and Battlefields in Europe: A History, Guide, and Reference Book (Washington, D.C.: Government Printing Office, 1938).
Anderson, Jack, with James Boyd, *Confessions of a Muckraker* (New York: Random House, 1979).
Andrews, Robert Hardy, *A Corner of Chicago* (Boston: Little, Brown, 1963).
Arkes, Hadley, *Bureaucracy, the Marshall Plan and the National Interest* (Princeton, N.J.: Princeton University Press, 1972).
Armstrong, Anne, *Unconditional Surrender* (Rutgers, N.J.: Rutgers University Press, 1961).
Arnold, Henry A., *Global Mission* (New York: Harper & Brothers, 1949).
Bachrack, Stanley D., *The Committee of One Million* (New York: Columbia University Press, 1976).
Baker, Leonard, *Brandeis and Frankfurter: A Dual Biography* (New York: Harper & Row, 1984).
Baldwin, Hanson, *Great Mistakes of the War* (New York: Harper & Brothers, 1950).
Ball, George W. *The Past Has Another Pattern* (New York: W. W. Norton, 1982).

Bamford, James, *The Puzzle Palace* (Boston: Houghton Mifflin, 1982).

Bartlett, Bruce R., *Cover-Up: The Politics Of Pearl Harbor, 1941–1946* (New Rochelle, N.Y.: Arlington House, 1978).

Baruch, Bernard, *The Public Years* (New York: Holt, Rinehart & Winston, 1960).

Beitzell, Robert, *The Uneasy Alliance* (New York: Alfred A. Knopf, 1972).

Berle, Adolf A., *Navigating the Rapids* (New York: Harcourt Brace Jovanovich, 1973).

Bernstein, Barton, "A Postwar Myth: 500,000 U.S. Lives Saved," *Bulletin of the Atomic Scientists* (June–July 1986), pp. 38–40.

Bernstein, Irving, *The Lean Years* (Boston: Houghton Mifflin, 1960).

Beschloss, Michael R., *Kennedy and Roosevelt: The Uneasy Alliance* (New York: W. W. Norton, 1980).

Bidault, Georges, *Resistance* (New York: Frederick Praeger, 1967).

Biennial Report of the Chief of Staff of the United States Army, July 1, 1941 to June 30, 1943 to the Secretary of War (Washington, D.C.: Government Printing Office, 1943).

Birse, A. H., *Memoirs of an Interpreter* (London: Michael Joseph, 1967).

Blair, Clay, *The Forgotten War* (New York: Times Books, 1987).

———, *Ridgway's Paratroopers* (Garden City, N.Y.: Doubleday & Co., 1985).

Blum, John Morton, *From the Morgenthau Diaries: Years of Urgency, 1938–1941* (Boston: Houghton Mifflin, 1965).

———, *V Was for Victory* (New York: Harvest/HBJ, 1976).

Blumenson, Martin, *Anzio: The Gamble That Failed* (Philadelphia: J. B. Lippincott, 1963).

———, *Mark Clark* (New York: Congdon & Weed, 1984).

———, *Patton: The Man Behind the Legend* (New York: William Morrow, 1985).

———, *The Patton Papers*, Vols. I and II (Boston: Houghton Mifflin, 1974).

Bohlen, Charles, *Witness to History, 1929–1969* (New York: W. W. Norton, 1973).

Botting, Kenneth, *From the Ruins of the Reich* (New York: Crown, 1985).

Bradley, Omar N., *A Soldier's Story* (Chicago: Rand McNally, 1951).

———, and Clay Blair, *A General's Life* (New York: Simon & Schuster, 1983).

Brandon, Henry, *Special Relationships* (New York: Atheneum, 1988).

Brereton, Lewis H., *The Brereton Diaries* (New York: William Morrow, 1946).

Brown, Anthony Cave, *Bodyguard of Lies* (New York: Harper & Row, 1975).

———, *The Last Hero: Wild Bill Donovan* (New York: Times Books, 1982).

Brown, David, and W. Richard Brumer, *I Can Tell It Now* (New York: E. P. Dutton, 1964).

Bryant, Arthur, *Triumph in the West* (Garden City, N.Y.: Doubleday & Co., 1959).

———, *The Turn of the Tide* (Garden City, N.Y.: Doubleday & Co., 1957).

Buckley, William F., Jr., and Brent Bozell, *McCarthy and His Enemies* (Chicago: Henry Regnery Co., 1954).

Buell, Thomas B., *Master of Sea Power* (Boston: Little, Brown, 1980).

Bullard, Robert L. *Personalities and Reminiscences of the War* (Garden City, N.Y.: Doubleday, Page, 1925).

Bullitt, William, *For the President, Personal and Secret* (Boston: Houghton Mifflin, 1972).

Burns, James MacGregor, *Roosevelt: The Soldier of Freedom* (New York: Harcourt Brace Jovanovich, 1970).

Bush, Vannevar, *Modern Arms and Free Men* (New York: Simon & Schuster, 1949).

Butcher, Harry C., *My Three Years with Eisenhower* (New York: Simon & Schuster, 1946).

Butler, J. R. M., and M. A. Gwyer, *Grand Strategy*, Vols. III and IV (London: Her Majesty's Stationery Office, 1964).

Butow, Robert J. C., *Japan's Decision to Surrender* (Stanford, Calif.: Stanford University Press, 1954).

———, *Tojo and the Coming of War* (Princeton, N.J.: Princeton University Press, 1961).

Byrnes, James F., *All in One Lifetime* (New York: Harper & Brothers, 1958).

———, *Speaking Frankly* (New York: Harper & Brothers, 1947).

Cadogan, Sir Alexander, *The Diaries of Sir Alexander Cadogan, O. M., 1938–1945*, edited by David Dilkes (New York: G. P. Putnam's Sons, 1972).

Calder, Angus, *Revolutionary Empire* (New York: E. P. Dutton, 1981).

Callwell, Major-General Sir C. E., *Field-Marshall Sir Henry Wilson*, Vol. II (London: Cassell, 1927).

Caraley, Demetrios, *The Politics of Military Unification* (New York: Columbia University Press, 1966).

Carlyle, Margaret, ed., *Documents on International Affairs, 1947–48* (London: Oxford University Press, 1952).

Casey, Lord, *Personal Experience, 1939–1945* (London: Constable & Co., 1962).

Catton, Bruce, *The War Lords of Washington* (New York: Harcourt, Brace & Co., 1948).

Caute, David, *The Great Fear: The Anti-Communist Purge Under Truman and Eisenhower* (New York: Simon & Schuster, 1978).

Chandler, Alfred D., Jr., ed., *The Papers of Dwight David Eisenhower: The War Years* (Baltimore: Johns Hopkins Press, 1970).

Chennault, Claire Lee, *Way of a Fighter: The Memoirs of Claire Lee Chennault*, edited by Robert Hotz (New York: G. P. Putnam's Sons, 1949).

China and United States Far Eastern Policy (Washington, D.C.: Congressional Quarterly, 1967).

Churchill, Winston S., *Closing the Ring* (Boston: Houghton Mifflin, 1951).

———, *The Grand Alliance* (Boston: Houghton Mifflin, 1950).

———, *The Hinge of Fate* (Boston: Houghton Mifflin, 1960).

———, *Their Finest Hour* (Boston: Houghton Mifflin, 1949).

———, *The World Crisis* (New York: Charles Scribner's Sons, 1942).

———, *Triumph and Tragedy* (Boston: Houghton Mifflin, 1953).

Clark, Mark W., *Calculated Risk* (New York: Harper & Brothers, 1950).

Clay, Lucius D., *Decision in Germany* (Garden City, N.Y.: Doubleday & Co., 1950).

———, *The Papers of General Lucius D. Clay*, edited by Jean Edward Smith, Vols. I and II (Bloomington, Ind.: Indiana University Press, 1974).

Clemens, Diane Shaver, *Yalta* (New York: Oxford University Press, 1970).

Cline, Ray S., *Washington Command Post: The Operations Division* (Washington, D.C.: Department of the Army, 1960).

Cochran, Bert, *Harry Truman and the Crisis Presidency* (New York: Funk & Wagnalls, 1973).

Coffey, Thomas M., *Hap* (New York: Viking Press, 1982).

Cole, Wayne S. *America First: The Battle Against Intervention* (Madison, Wisc.: University of Wisconsin Press, 1953).

Collins, J. Lawton, *War in Peacetime: The History and Lessons of Korea* (Boston: Houghton Mifflin, 1969).

Colville, John, *Winston Churchill and His Inner Circle* (New York: Wyndham Books, 1981).

———, *The Fringes of Power* (New York: W. W. Norton, 1985).

Compton, Arthur H., *Atomic Quest* (New York: Oxford University Press, 1956).

Compton, Karl, "If the Atomic Bomb Had Not Been Used," *Atlantic Monthly* (December 1946), pp. 54–56.

Condit, Kenneth W., "U.S. Joint Chiefs of Staff, The Joint Chiefs of Staff and National Policy, 1947–1949," Historical Division, Joint Secretariat, Joint Chiefs of Staff, Unpublished manuscript in the Marshall Library.

———, *The History of the Joint Chiefs of Staff: The Joint Chiefs of Staff and National Policy*, Vol. II (Wilmington, Del.: Michael Glazier, 1979).

Corson, William R., *The Armies of Ignorance* (New York: Dial Press, 1977).

Cunningham, Andrew B., *A Sailor's Odyssey* (London: Hutchinson, 1951).

Dallek, Robert, *The American Style of Foreign Policy* (New York: Alfred A. Knopf, 1983).

———, *Franklin D. Roosevelt and American Foreign Policy, 1932–1945* (New York: Oxford University Press, 1979).

Danchev, Alex, *Very Special Relationship* (London: Brassey's Defence Publishers, 1986).

Daniels, Jonathan, *The Man of Independence* (Philadelphia: J. B. Lippincott, 1950).

Davenport, Marcia, *Too Strong for Fantasy*, reprint edition (New York: Avon 1979).

Davis, Kenneth S., *FDR: The New York Years, 1928–1932* (New York: Random House, 1985).

Davison, W. Phillips, *The Berlin Blockade* (Princeton, N.J.: Princeton University Press, 1958).

Dawson, Raymond H., *Foreign Policy and Domestic Politics* (Chapel Hill, N.C.: University of North Carolina Press, 1959).

de Gaulle, Charles, *War Memoirs: Unity, 1942–44, Documents*, Vol. II, Parts 1 and 2 (London: Weidenfeld & Nicolson, 1959).

———, *War Memoirs: Salvation, 1944–46*, Vol. III (London: Weidenfeld & Nicolson, 1960).

de Guingand, Sir Francis, *Operation Victory* (London: Hodder & Stoughton, 1947).

De Weerd, H. A., *Selected Speeches and Statements of General of the Army George C. Marshall* (Washington, D.C.: Infantry Journal, 1945).

Deane, John R., *The Strange Alliance* (New York: Viking Press, 1947).

Dear Bess : The Letters from Harry to Bess Truman, edited by Robert H. Ferrell (New York: W. W. Norton, 1983).

Djilas, Milovan, *Conversations with Stalin* (New York: Harcourt, Brace & World, 1962).

Donovan, Robert, *Conflict and Crisis* (New York: W. W. Norton, 1977).

———, *Tumultuous Years* (New York: W. W. Norton, 1982).

dos Passos, John, *1919* (New York: Harcourt Brace, 1932).

Douglas, Lord Sholto, with Robert Wright, *Combat and Command: The Story of an Airman in Two World Wars* (New York: Simon & Schuster, 1966).

Druks, Herbert, *The United States and Israel, 1945–1973* (New York: R. Speller, 1979).

Dulles, Allen, *The Secret Surrender* (New York: Harper & Row, 1966).

Dulles, Foster Rhea, *American Policy Toward Communist China, 1949–1969* (New York: Thomas Y. Crowell, 1972).

Eden, Anthony, *The Reckoning: The Memoirs of Anthony Eden, Earl of Avon* (Boston: Houghton Mifflin, 1965).

Eichelberger, Robert L., *Dear Miss Em*, edited by Jay Luvaas (Westport, Conn.: Greenwood Press, 1972).

———, *Our Jungle Road to Tokyo* (New York: Viking Press, 1950).

Eisenhower, David, *Eisenhower: At War 1943–1945* (New York: Random House, 1986).

Eisenhower, Dwight D., *At Ease: Stories I Tell to Friends* (Garden City, N.Y.: Doubleday & Co., 1967).

———, *Crusade in Europe* (Garden City, N.Y.: Doubleday & Co., 1948).

———, *Crusade in Europe*, enlarged edition (New York: Da Capo Press, 1977).

———, *The Eisenhower Diaries*, edited by Robert H. Ferrell (New York: W. W. Norton, 1981).

Eisenhower, John S. D., *Allies: Pearl Harbor to D-Day* (Garden City, N.Y.: Doubleday & Co., 1982).

———, *The Bitter Woods* (New York: G. P. Putnam's Sons, 1969).

Ellis, John, *Cassino: The Hollow Victory* (New York: McGraw-Hill, 1986).

Ellis, Major L. F., with Lieutenant Colonel A. E. Warhurst, *Victory in the West*, Vol. II, *The Defeat of Germany* (London: Her Majesty's Stationery Office, 1968).

Fairbank, John King, *The United States and the People's Republic of China*, 4th ed. (Cambridge, Mass.: Harvard University Press, 1979).

Falk, Stanley L., *Decision at Leyte* (New York: W. W. Norton, 1966).

Farwell, Byron, *Queen Victoria's Little Wars*, reprint edition (New York: W. W. Norton, 1985).

Feis, Herbert, *The Road to Pearl Harbor* (Princeton, N.J.: Princeton University Press, 1950).

Ferguson, Bernard, *The Watery Maze: The Story of Combined Operations* (London: Collins, 1961).

Ferrell, Robert H., *American Diplomacy* (New York: W. W. Norton, 1975).

———, *George C. Marshall: The American Secretaries of State and Their Diplomacy*, Vol. XV (New York: Cooper Square Publishers, 1966).

———, *Harry S. Truman and the Modern American Presidency* (Boston: Little, Brown, 1983).

———, *Off the Record: The Private Papers of Harry S. Truman* (New York: Harper & Row, 1980).

Foreign Relations of the United States, various years (Washington, D.C.: Government Printing Office). Cited as *FRUS*.

Foreign Relations of the United States, Diplomatic Papers: The Conference at Berlin, Vols. I–II (Washington, D.C.: Government Printing Office, 1960).

Foreign Relations of the United States, Diplomatic Papers: The Conference at Quebec, 1944 (Washington, D.C.: Government Printing Office, 1972).

Foreign Relations of the United States, Diplomatic Papers: The Conferences at Cairo and Tehran, 1943 (Washington, D.C.: Government Printing Office, 1961).

Foreign Relations of the United States, Diplomatic Papers: The Conferences at Malta and Yalta, 1945 (Washington, D.C.: Government Printing Office, 1955).

Foreign Relations of the United States, Diplomatic Papers: The Conferences at Washington and Casablanca, 1943, Vols. I–II, (Washington, D.C.: Government Printing Office, 1968).

Foreign Relations of the United States, Diplomatic Papers: The Conferences at Washington and Quebec, 1943 (Washington, D.C.: Government Printing Office, 1970).

Foreign Relations of the United States, Japan, 1931–1941 (Washington, D.C.: Government Printing Office, 1943).

Forrestal, James, *The Forrestal Diaries,* edited by Walter Millis (New York: Viking Press, 1951).

Friend, Theodore, *Between Two Empires* (New Haven: Yale University Press, 1965).

Frothingham, Thomas G., *The American Reinforcement in the World War* (Garden City, N.Y.: Doubleday, Page & Co., 1927).

Funk, Arthur, *The Politics of Torch* (Lawrence, Kans.: University of Kansas Press, 1974).

Furuya, Keiji, *Chiang Kai-Shek: His Life and Times* (New York: St. John's University, 1981).

Gavin, James M., *On to Berlin: Battles of an Airborne Commander, 1943–1946* (New York: Viking Press, 1978).

Gazetteer of the Philippine Islands, Senate Document 280 (Washington, D.C.: Government Printing Office, 1900).

George C. Marshall Interviews and Reminiscences for Forrest C. Pogue: Transcripts and Notes, 1956–57, edited by Larry I. Bland (Lexington, Va.: George C. Marshall Research Foundation, 1986). Cited as *Marshall Interviews.*

Gimbel, John, *The American Occupation of Germany* (Stanford, Calif.: Stanford University Press, 1968).

———, *The Origins of the Marshall Plan* (Stanford, Calif.: Stanford University Press, 1976).

Goebbels, Josef, *The Goebbels Diaries: 1939–1941,* translated and edited by Fred Taylor (New York: G. P. Putnam's Sons, 1983).

Goldman, Eric F., *The Crucial Decade—and After,* reprint edition (New York: Vintage, 1960).

Goralski, Robert, *World War II Almanac: 1931–1945* (New York: G. P. Putnam's Sons, 1981).

Goulden, Joseph C., *Korea: The Untold Story of the War* (New York: Times Books, 1982).

Greenfield, Kent Roberts, ed., *Command Decisions* (Washington, D.C.: Department of the Army, 1960).

Greenstein, Fred I., *The Hidden-Hand Presidency* (New York: Basic Books, 1982).

Grew, Joseph C., *Turbulent Era,* Vol. II (Boston: Houghton Mifflin, 1952).

Grigg, John, *1943: The Victory That Never Was* (New York: Hill & Wang, 1980).

Grose, Peter, *Israel in the Mind of America* (New York: Alfred A. Knopf, 1983).

Groves, Leslie M., *Now It Can Be Told* (New York: Da Capo Press, 1962).

Gunther, John, *Roosevelt in Retrospect* (New York: Harper & Brothers, 1950).

Gwyer, M. A., *Grand Strategy,* Vol. III (London: Her Majesty's Stationery Office, 1964).

Halifax, The Earl of, *Fullness of Days* (London: Collins, 1957).

Hall, Hessel D., *North American Supply* (London: Her Majesty's Stationery Office, 1955).

Harbord, James G., *The American Army in France, 1917–1919* (Boston: Little, Brown, 1936).

——, *Leaves from a War Diary* (New York: Dodd, Mead, 1926).

Harriman, W. Averell, *America and Russia in a Changing World: A Half Century of Personal Obligation* (Garden City, N.Y.: Doubleday, 1971).

Hassett, William, *Off the Record with F.D.R.* (New Brunswick, N.J.: Rutgers University Press, 1958).

Hayes, Grace Person, *The History of the Joint Chiefs of Staff in World War II: The War Against Japan* (Annapolis, Md.: Naval Institute Press, 1982).

Heller, Francis H., ed., *The Korean War: A 25-Year Perspective* (Lawrence, Kans: Regents' Press of Kansas, 1977).

——, *The Truman White House* (Lawrence, Kans.: Regents' Press of Kansas, 1980).

Hemingway, Ernest, *By-Line: Ernest Hemingway*, edited by William White (New York: Simon & Schuster, 1967).

Herken, Gregg, *The Winning Weapon* (New York: Alfred A. Knopf, 1983).

Higgins, Trumbull, *Korea and the Fall of MacArthur* (New York: Oxford University Press, 1960).

——, *Soft Underbelly* (New York: The Macmillan Company, 1968).

Hiss, Alger, *Recollections of a Life* (New York: Seaver, 1988).

"History of the Joint Chiefs of Staff: The War Against Germany and Her Satellites," Unpublished manuscript filed in George C. Marshall Research Library, Lexington, Va., as Xerox nos. 1561 and 2567.

Hobbs, Joseph Patrick, ed., *Dear General: Eisenhower's Wartime Letters to Marshall* (Baltimore: Johns Hopkins Press, 1971).

Hodgson, Geoffrey, *America in Our Time* (New York: Viking Press, 1978).

Hoehling, A. A., *The Week Before Pearl Harbor* (New York: W. W. Norton, 1963).

Hoffman, Erik P., and Fredric J. Fleron, Jr., *The Conduct of Soviet Foreign Policy* (New York: Aldine Publishing Co., 1980).

Hogan, Michael J., *The Marshall Plan* (Cambridge, Eng.: Cambridge University Press, 1987).

Horne, Alistair, *The Price of Glory: Verdun 1916*, reprint edition (Harmondsworth, Middlesex: Penguin Books, 1964).

Hotz, Robert, ed., *Way of a Fighter: Claire Lee Chennault* (New York: G. P. Putnam's Sons, 1949).

House of Representatives, Subcommittee, Committee on Appropriations, on Consideration of the Second Supplemental Appropriation Bill for 1942, 77th Congress, 1st Session (Washington, D.C.: Government Printing Office, 1941).

Howard, Michael, *The Mediterranean Strategy in the Second World War* (London: Weidenfeld & Nicolson, 1968).

Hull, Cordell, *The Memoirs of Cordell Hull*, Vols. I and II (New York: The Macmillan Company, 1948).

Hunt, Frazier, *The Untold Story of Douglas MacArthur* (New York: Devin-Adair, 1954).

Ickes, Harold L., *The Secret Diary of Harold L. Ickes* (New York: Simon & Schuster, 1954).

Investigation of Far Eastern Policy, United States Senate, Committee on Foreign Relations, 79th Congress, 2nd Session, 1945, in *United States–China Relations,* 92nd Congress, 1st Session, 1973 (Washington, D.C.: Government Printing Office, 1973), pp. 96 ff.

Investigation of the Pearl Harbor Attack, Report of the Joint Committee on the Investigation of the Pearl Harbor Attack, Congress of the United States, 79th Congress, 2nd Session, Senate Document No. 244. (Washington, D.C.: Government Printing Office, 1946).

Irving, David, *The War Between the Generals* (New York: Congdon & Lattes, 1981).

Isaacson, Walter, and Evan Thomas, *The Wise Men* (New York: Simon & Schuster, 1986).

Ismay, General Sir Hastings, *The Memoirs of General Lord Ismay* (New York: Viking Press, 1960).

Jackson, W. G. F., *The North African Campaign* (London: B. T. Batsford, 1975).

James, D. Clayton, *The Years of MacArthur,* Vols. I–III (Boston: Houghton Mifflin, 1970–85).

Johnson, Thomas M., *Without Censor: New Light on Our Greatest World War Battles* (Indianapolis, Ind.: Bobbs-Merrill, 1928).

Jones, Joseph M., *The Fifteen Weeks* (New York: Viking Press, 1955).

Jullian, Marcel, *The Battle of Britain,* reprint edition (New York: Fawcett-Crest, 1968).

Kahn, E. J., Jr., *Far-Flung and Footloose* (New York: G. P. Putnam's Sons, 1979).

———, *The China Hands* (New York: Viking Press, 1975).

Karnow, Stanley, *Vietnam: A History* (New York: Viking Press, 1983).

Kendrick, Alexander, *Prime Time,* reprint edition (New York: Avon, 1970).

Kennan, George, "Flashbacks," *The New Yorker,* February 25, 1985.

———, *Memoirs, 1925–1950* (Boston: Little, Brown, 1967).

Kennedy, Sir John, *The Business of War* (New York: William Morrow, 1958).

Kenney, George, *General Kenney Reports* (New York: Duell, Sloan & Pearce, 1949).

Kersaudy, François, *Churchill and de Gaulle* (New York: Atheneum, 1982).

Kimball, Warren F., ed., *Churchill and Roosevelt: The Complete Correspondence,* Vols. I–III (Princeton, N.J.: Princeton University Press, 1984).

Kimmel, Husband, E., *Admiral Kimmel's Story* (Chicago: Henry Regnery Co., 1955).

King, Ernest J., and Walter Muir Whitehead, *Fleet Admiral King: A Naval Record* (New York: W. W. Norton, 1952).

Kirby, S. Woodburn, *Singapore: The Chain of Disaster* (London: Cassell & Co., 1971).

———, *The War Against Japan,* Vols. I and II (London: Her Majesty's Stationery Office, 1957, 1958).

Kluger, Richard, *The Paper* (New York: Alfred A. Knopf, 1986).

Knightley, Phillip, *The First Casualty* (New York: Harcourt Brace Jovanovich, 1975).

Koen, Ross Y., *The China Lobby in American Politics* (New York: Octagon Books, 1974).

Kolko, Gabriel, *The Politics of War* (New York: Random House, 1968).

———, Joyce, and Gabriel Kolko, *The Limits of Power* (New York: Harper & Row, 1972).

Kubek, Anthony, *How the Far East Was Lost* (New York: Twin Circle Publishing Co., 1972).

Kurzman, Dan, *Day of the Bomb* (New York: McGraw-Hill, 1986).

Lamont, Lansing, *Day of Trinity* (New York: Atheneum, 1985).

Lane, Frederic C., Blanche D. Coll, Gerald J. Fischer, and David B. Tyler, *Ships for Victory* (Baltimore: Johns Hopkins Press, 1951).

Langer, William L., and O. Everett Gleason, *The Undeclared War, 1940–1941* (New York: Harper & Brothers, 1953).

Larrabee, Eric, *Commander-in-Chief* (New York: Harper & Row, 1987).

Lash, Joseph, *Love, Eleanor* (Garden City, N.Y.: Doubleday & Co., 1982).

———, *A World of Love* (Garden City, N.Y.: Doubleday & Co., 1984).

Latham, Earl, *The Communist Controversy in Washington* (Cambridge, Mass.: Harvard University Press, 1966).

Layton, Edwin T., with Roger Pineau and John Costello, *"And I Was There"* (New York: William Morrow, 1986).

Leahy, Fleet Admiral William, *I Was There* (New York: Whittlesey House, 1950).

Leasor, James, *War at the Top, Based On the War Experiences of General Sir Leslie Hollis* (London: Michael Joseph, 1959).

Lee, Clark, and Richard Henschel, *Douglas MacArthur* (New York: Henry Holt & Co., 1952).

Letters of Adlai E. Stevenson, The, edited by John Bartlow Martin (Boston: Little, Brown, 1973).

Lewin, Ronald, *The American Magic,* reprint edition (London and New York: Penguin, 1983).

Liebling, A. J., *Liebling Abroad* (New York: Wideview Books, 1981).

Lilienthal, David E., *Journals of David E. Lilienthal,* Vol. II (New York: Harper & Row, 1964).

Lohbeck, Don, *Patrick J. Hurley* (Chicago: Henry Regnery Co., 1956).

Lowenheim, Francis L., Harold D. Langley, and Manfred Jonas, *Roosevelt and Churchill: Their Secret Wartime Correspondence* (New York: Saturday Review Press, 1975).

Ludendorff, General Erich, *My War Memories,* Vols. I and II (London: Hutchinson, n.d.).

Lyons, Leonard, "Truman's Last Night," in Jerry D. Lewis, ed., *The Great Columnists* (New York: Collier Books, 1965).

MacArthur, Douglas A., *Reminiscences* (New York: McGraw-Hill, 1964).

Macmillan, Harold, *The Blast of War* (New York: Harper & Row, 1967).

MacVane, John, *On the Air in World War II* (New York: William Morrow, 1979).

McCarthy, Joseph, *America's Retreat from Victory* (New York: Devin-Adair, 1951).

McFarland, Keith, D., *Harry H. Woodring* (Lawrence, Kans.: University Press of Kansas, 1975).

McLellan, David S., *Dean Acheson* (New York: Dodd, Mead, 1975).

Magic Background to Pearl Harbor, The (Washington, D.C.: Department of the Army, 1980).

Maisky, Ivan M., *Memoirs of a Soviet Ambassador: The War 1939–1942* (New York: Charles Scribner's Sons, 1967).

Manchester, William, *American Caesar,* reprint edition (New York: Dell, 1978).

Marshall, George C., *Memoirs of My Services in the World War, 1917–1918* (Boston: Houghton Mifflin, 1976).

———, *The War Reports of General of the Army George C. Marshall . . . to the Secretary of War* (Philadelphia and New York: J. B. Lippincott, 1947).

Marshall Interviews: see *George C. Marshall Interviews.*

Marshall, Katherine Tupper, *Together* (New York: Tupper & Love, 1946).

Marshall's Mission to China: December 1945–January 1947, introduction by Lyman P. Van Slyke, Vols. I and II (Arlington, Va.: University Publications of America, 1976).

Martin, Joseph, *My First Fifty Years in Politics* (New York: McGraw-Hill, 1960).

Matloff, Maurice, *Strategic Planning for Coalition Warfare, 1943–1944, United States Army in World War II* (Washington, D.C.: Office of the Chief of Military History, Department of the Army, 1959).

———, and Edwin M. Snell, *Strategic Planning for Coalition Warfare, 1941–42, United States Army in World War II* (Washington, D.C.: Office of the Chief of Military History, Department of the Army, 1953).

May, Ernest R., *The Truman Administration and China, 1945–1949* (Philadelphia: J. B. Lippincott, 1975).

———, ed., *The Ultimate Decision* (New York: George Braziller, 1960).

May, Gene, *China Scapegoat* (Washington, D.C.: New Republic Books, 1979).

Mee, Charles L., Jr., *The Marshall Plan* (New York: Simon & Schuster, 1984).

———, *Meeting at Potsdam,* reprint edition (New York: Dell, 1975).

Melby, John, *The Mandate of Heaven* (Toronto: University of Toronto, 1968).

Messer, Robert L., *The End of an Alliance* (Chapel Hill, N.C.: University of North Carolina Press, 1982).

Michel, Henri, *The Second World War,* translated by Douglas Parmee (Bergenfield, N.J.: Andre Deutsch, 1975).

Military Establishment Appropriations Bill, 1941, Hearings Before the Military Appropriations Subcommittee, Committee on Appropriations, House of Representatives (Washington, D.C.: Government Printing Office, 1940).

Military Establishment Appropriations Bill for 1941, Hearings Before the Subcommittee of the Committee on Appropriations, United States Senate (Washington, D.C.: Government Printing Office, 1940).

Military Situation in the Far East, Hearings Before the Committee on Armed Services and the Committee on Foreign Relations, 82nd Congress, 1st Session (Washington, D.C.: Government Printing Office, 1951).

Miller, Merle, *Ike the Soldier: As They Knew Him* (New York: G. P. Putnam's Sons, 1987).

———, *Plain Speaking,* reprint edition (New York: Berkley Books, 1974).

Millis, Walter, *Arms and the State* (New York: 20th Century Fund, 1958).

———, *This Is Pearl* (New York: William Morrow, 1947).

Montgomery of Alamein, Field Marshal the Viscount Bernard, *Memoirs* (Cleveland: World Publishing Co., 1958).

Moran, Lord, *Churchill: Taken From the Diaries of Lord Moran* (Boston: Houghton Mifflin, 1966).

Moorehead, Alan, *The March to Tunis,* reprint edition (New York: Dell, 1968).

Morgan, Sir Frederick. *Overture to Overlord* (Garden City, N.Y.: Doubleday & Co., 1950).

Morison, Elting E., *Turmoil and Tradition: A Study in the Life and Times of Henry L. Stimson* (Boston: Houghton Mifflin, 1960).

Morison, Samuel Eliot, *History of United States Naval Operations in World War II*, revised edition (Boston: Little, Brown, 1954–65).

———, *Strategy and Compromise* (Boston: Little, Brown, 1958).

Morton, Louis. *The Fall of the Philippines* (Washington, D.C.: Office of the Chief of Military History, Department of the Army, 1953).

Murphy, Bruce Allen, *The Brandeis/Frankfurter Connection* (New York: Oxford University Press, 1982).

Murphy, Robert, *Diplomat Among Warriors* (Garden City, N.Y.: Doubleday & Co., 1964).

Nelson, James, ed., *General Eisenhower on the Military Churchill: A Conversation with Alistair Cooke* (New York: W. W. Norton, 1970).

Neumann, William L., *After Victory* (New York: Harper & Row, 1967).

Nicholas, H. G., ed., *Washington Despatches: Weekly Political Reports from the British Embassy* (Chicago: University of Chicago Press, 1981).

Overy, R. J., *The Air War: 1939–1945* (New York: Stein & Day, 1980).

Paige, Glenn D., *The Korean Decision* (New York: Free Press, 1968).

Papers of George Catlett Marshall, The, Larry I. Bland, Sharon Ritenour, et al., eds., Vols. I and II (Baltimore and London: Johns Hopkins University Press, 1981, 1986). Cited as *Papers.*

Parton, James, *Air Force Spoken Here* (Bethesda, Md.: Adler & Adler, 1986).

Paule, Gerald, *The War and Colonel Warden* (New York: Alfred A. Knopf, 1963).

Payne, Robert, *The Marshall Story* (Englewood Cliffs, N.J.: Prentice-Hall, 1951).

Pearl Harbor Attack, Hearings Before the Joint Committee on the Investigation of the Pearl Harbor Attack, Congress of the United States, 79th Congress, 1st Session (Washington, D.C.: Government Printing Office, 1946).

Pentagon Papers, The: The Defense Department History of United States Decision-making on Vietnam, Vol. I (Boston: Beacon Press, 1971).

Perrett, Geoffrey, *Days of Sadness, Years of Triumph: The American People 1939–1945* (New York: Simon & Schuster, 1973).

Perry, Glen C. H., *"Dear Bart": Washington Views of World War II* (Westport, Conn.: Greenwood Press, 1982).

Pershing, John J., *My Experiences in the World War,* Vols. I and II (New York: Frederick Stokes, 1931).

Peterson, Colonel E. A., "United States Joint Chiefs of Staff, The War Against Germany and Her Satellites, 1938 to August 15, 1943," Unpublished manuscript in the George C. Marshall Research Library, Xerox 1561.

Peterson, Edward N., *The American Occupation of Germany: Retreat to Victory* (Detroit: Wayne State University Press, 1977).

Petillo, Carol Morris, *Douglas MacArthur: The Philippine Years* (Bloomington, Ind.: Indiana University Press, 1981).

Phillips, Cabel, *The 1940s: Decade of Triumph and Trouble* (New York: The Macmillan Company, 1975).

Pogue, Forrest C., *George C. Marshall: Education of a General* (New York: Viking Press, 1963). Cited as Pogue I.

————, *George C. Marshall: Ordeal and Hope* (New York: Viking Press, 1966). Cited as Pogue II.

————, *George C. Marshall: Organizer of Victory* (New York: Viking Press, 1973). Cited as Pogue III.

————, *George C. Marshall: Statesman, 1945–1959* (New York: Viking Press, 1987). Cited as Pogue IV.

————, *The Supreme Command* (Washington, D.C.: Office of the Chief of Military History, Department of the Army, 1954).

Pomeroy, Earl S., *Pacific Outpost: American Strategy in Guam and Micronesia* (Stanford, Calif.: Stanford University Press, 1951).

Poole, Walter S., "Extracts from the Joint Chiefs of Staff and National Policy, Vol. IV, 1950–52," Unpublished manuscript from the Historical Division, Joint Secretariat, Joint Chiefs of Staff, archived in the George C. Marshall Research Library as Xerox 2573.

Powers, Thomas, *The Man Who Kept the Secrets* (New York: Alfred A. Knopf, 1979).

Prados, John, *The Soviet Estimate* (New York: Dial Press, 1982).

Prange, Gordon W., in collaboration with Donald M. Goldstein and Katherine V. Dillon, *At Dawn We Slept: The Untold Story of Pearl Harbor* (New York: McGraw-Hill, 1981).

————, with Donald M. Goldstein and Katherine V. Dillon, *Pearl Harbor: The Verdict of History* (New York: McGraw-Hill, 1985).

Price, Harry Bayard, *The Marshall Plan and Its Meaning* (Ithaca, N.Y.: Cornell University Press, 1955).

Promotion of Promotion-List Officers of the Army, Committee on Military Affairs, House of Representatives, 76th Congress, 2nd Session, April 9, 1940 (Washington, D.C.: Government Printing Ofice, 1940).

Providing for the National Defense by Removing Restrictions on Numbers and Length of Service of Draftees, Hearings Before the House of Representatives Committee on Military Affairs, on Consideration of HJ Res. 217, etc., 77th Congress, 1st Session, July 22, 1941 (Washington, D.C.: Government Printing Office, 1941).

Public Papers of the Presidents, The: Harry S. Truman, 8 vols. (Washington, D.C.: Government Printing Office, 1957–61).

Radford, Admiral Arthur W., *From Pearl Harbor to Vietnam* (Stanford, Calif.: Hoover Institution Press, 1980).

Records of the Joint Chiefs of Staff (Frederick, Md.: University Publications of America, 1982).

Reeves, Thomas C., *The Life and Times of Joe McCarthy* (New York: Stein & Day, 1981).

Retention of Members and Units of Active Reserve Components in Active Military Service Beyond Twelve Months, Hearings Before the Senate Committee on Military Affairs (Washington, D.C.: Government Printing Office, 1941).

Retention of Reserve Components and Selectees in Military Service Beyond Twelve Months, Hearings Before the Committee on Military Affairs, United States Senate, July 17, 1941 (Washington, D.C.: Government Printing Office, 1941).

Ridgway, Matthew B., *The Korean War* (Garden City, N.Y.: Doubleday & Co., 1967).

————, as told to Harold H. Martin, *Soldier* (New York: Harper & Brothers, 1956).

Roberts, Chalmers, *First Rough Draft* (New York: Frederick Praeger, 1973).

Roosevelt, Elliott, *As He Saw It* (New York: Duell, Sloan & Pearce, 1946).

————, and James Brough, *A Rendezvous with Destiny* (New York: G. P. Putnam's Sons, 1975).

Roosevelt, Franklin Delano, *Personal Correspondence*, Vols. I and II, edited by Elliott Roosevelt (New York: Duell, Sloan & Pearce, 1950).

Roosevelt Presidential Press Conferences, Vols. XVII, XXII (New York: Da Capo Press, 1972).

Rosenman, Samuel L., ed., *The Public Papers and Addresses of Franklin D. Roosevelt*, Vol. IX (New York: The Macmillan Company, 1941).

Rovere, Richard, *Senator Joe McCarthy* (New York: Harcourt, Brace, 1959).

Salisbury, Harrison, *The 100 Days*, reprint edition (New York: Avon, 1970).

Sayre, Francis Bowes, *Glad Adventure* (New York: The Macmillan Company, 1957).

Schlesinger, Arthur M., Jr., *The Coming of the New Deal* (Boston: Houghton Mifflin, 1958).

————, *The Crisis of the Old Order, 1919–1933* (Boston: Houghton Mifflin, 1957).

Schnabel, James F., and Robert J. Watson, "The History of the Joint Chiefs of Staff: The Joint Chiefs of Staff and National Policy, The Korean War, Part I," Historical Division, Joint Secretariat, Joint Chiefs of Staff, April 12, 1978, filed as Xerox 2571 in the George C. Marshall Research Library, Lexington, Va.

Schoenbaum, Thomas J., *Waging Peace and War* (New York: Simon & Schuster, 1988).

Schoenbrun, David, *Soldiers of the Night* (New York: E. P. Dutton, 1980).

Schultz, Duane, *Hero of Bataan* (New York: St. Martin's Press, 1981).

Second Supplemental National Defense Appropriations Bill for 1941, Hearings Before the Subcommittee of the Committee on Appropriations, United States Senate (Washington, D.C.: Government Printing Office, 1940).

Selective Compulsory Training and Service, Hearings Before the Committee on Military Affairs, House of Representatives (Washington, D.C.: Government Printing Office, 1940).

Severeid, Eric, *Not So Wild a Dream*, reprint edition (New York: Atheneum, 1978).

Shachtman, Tom, *The Phony War, 1939–1940* (New York: Harper & Row, 1982).

Shaplen, Robert, *A Turning Wheel* (New York: Random House, 1980).

Sherwood, Robert E., *Roosevelt and Hopkins* (New York: Harper & Brothers, 1948).

Slessor, Sir John, *The Central Blue* (London: Cassell & Co., 1956; New York: Frederick Praeger, 1957).

Smith, R. Elberton, *The Army and Economic Planning* (Washington, D.C.: Department of the Army, 1959).

Smith, Richard Norton, *Thomas E. Dewey and His Times* (New York: Simon & Schuster, 1982).

————, *An Uncommon Man: The Triumph of Herbert Hoover* (New York: Simon & Schuster, 1984).

Smith, Walter Bedell, *My Three Years in Moscow* (Philadelphia: J. B. Lippincott, 1950).

Snell, John L., ed., *The Meaning of Yalta* (Baton Rouge, La.: Louisiana State University Press, 1956).

Snetsinger, John, *Truman, the Jewish Vote, and the Creation of Israel* (Stanford, Calif.: Hoover Institution Press, 1974).

Sparrow, John C., *History of Personnel Demobilization in the United States Army* (Washington, D.C.: Department of the Army, 1951).

Spector, Ronald H., *United States Army in Vietnam: Advice and Support* (Washington, D.C.: Center of Military History, United States Army, 1983).

———, *Eagle Against the Sun* (New York: The Free Press, 1985).

Spurr, Russell, *A Glorious Way to Die* (New York: Newmarket Press, 1981).

Standley, William H., and Arthur A. Ageton, *American Ambassador to Russia* (Chicago: Henry Regnery Co., 1955).

State Department Policy Planning Staff Papers, The, introduction by Anna Kasten Nelson, Vols. I and II (New York: Garland Publishing Co., 1983).

Statements Before the House of Representatives Committee on Military Affairs, 77th Congress, 1st Session, July 22, 1941, on Consideration of . . . Joint Resolutions Declaring a National Emergency (Washington, D.C.: Government Printing Office, 1941).

Steel, Ronald, *Walter Lippmann and the American Century* (Boston: Little, Brown, 1980).

Stettinius, Edward R., Jr., *The Diaries of Edward R. Stettinius, Jr., 1943–1946,* edited by Thomas M. Campbell and George C. Herring, reprint edition (New York: New Viewpoints, 1975).

———, *Lend-Lease: Weapon for Victory* (New York: The Macmillan Company, 1944).

———, *Roosevelt and the Russians: The Yalta Conference* (Garden City, N.Y.: Doubleday, 1949).

Stilwell's Personal File: China-Burma-India, 1942–1944, edited by Riley Sunderland and Charles F. Romanus (Wilmington, Del.: Scholarly Resources, Inc., 1976).

Stimson, Henry L., "The Decision to Use the Bomb," *Harpers* (February 1947).

———, Diaries (Manuscripts and Archives, Sterling Memorial Library, Yale University, New Haven, Conn.).

———, and McGeorge Bundy, *On Active Service in Peace and War* (New York: Harper & Brothers, 1948).

Stoler, Mark A., "The 'Pacific-First' Alternative in American World War II Strategy," *International History Review,* II (1980), pp. 432–52.

———, *The Politics of the Second Front* (Westport, Conn.: Greenwood Press, 1977).

Stone, I. F., *The Hidden History of the Korean War* (New York: Monthly Review Press, 1952).

Stone, Norman, *Hitler* (Boston: Little, Brown, 1980).

Strauss, Lewis L., *Men and Decisions* (Garden City, N.Y.: Doubleday & Co., 1962).

Strout, Richard L., *TRB* (New York: The Macmillan Company, 1979).

Stueck, William, *The Wedemeyer Mission* (Athens, Ga.: University of Georgia Press, 1984).

Sulzberger, Cyrus, *A Long Row of Candles* (New York: The Macmillan Company, 1969).

Swanberg , W. A., *Luce and His Empire,* reprint edition (New York: Dell, 1973).

Taylor, A. J. P., *The Origins of the Second World War*, reprint edition (New York: Premier Books, 1963).

Taylor, Telford, "Day of Infamy, Decades of Doubt," *New York Times Magazine*, April 29, 1984, pp. 106 ff.

Tedder, Lord, *With Prejudice* (Boston: Little, Brown, 1967).

Terraine, John, *To Win a War* (Garden City, N.Y.: Doubleday & Co, 1981).

Theobald, Rear Admiral Robert A., *The Final Secret of Pearl Harbor* (New York: Devin-Adair, 1954).

Theoharis, Athan G., *The Yalta Myths* (Columbia, Mo.: University of Missouri Press, 1970).

Thorne, Christopher, *Allies of a Kind* (New York: Oxford University Press, 1978).

Togo, Shigenori, *The Cause of Japan* (New York: Simon & Schuster, 1956).

Toland, John, *But Not in Shame*, reprint edition (New York: Signet, 1961).

———, *Infamy* (Garden City, N.Y.: Doubleday & Co., 1982).

———, *No Man's Land* (Garden City, N.Y.: Doubleday & Co., 1980).

Trohan, Walter, *Political Animals* (Garden City, N.Y.: Doubleday & Co., 1975).

Troy, Thomas F., *Donovan and the CIA* (Frederick, Md.: University Publications, 1981).

Truman, Harry S., *Memoirs*, Vols. I–II, reprint edition (New York: New American Library, 1965).

Truscott, Lucian K., *Command Missions* (New York: E. P. Dutton, 1954).

Tuchman, Barbara W., *The Guns of August*, reprint edition (New York: Bantam Books, 1976).

———, *Stilwell and the American Experience in China, 1911–1945*, reprint edition (New York: Bantam Books, 1972).

———, *The Zimmermann Telegram*, reprint edition (New York: Dell, 1965).

Tully, Grace, *F.D.R., My Boss* (New York: Scribners, 1949).

United States Army in the World War, 1917–1919, The, IX (Washington, D.C.: Department of the Army, 1948).

United States Foreign Policy for a Post-War Recovery Program, Hearings Before the Committee on Foreign Affairs, House of Representatives, 80th Congress, 1st and 2nd Sessions, Parts I and II (Washington, D.C.: Government Printing Office, 1948).

United States Strategic Bombing Survey: Summary Report (European War) and *The Effects of Strategic Bombing on the German War Economy,* Vol. III (Washington, D.C.: Government Printing Office, 1945).

Universal Military Training, Hearings Before the Senate Committee on the Armed Services, 80th Congress, 2nd Session (Washington, D.C.: Government Printing Office, 1948).

Vandenberg, Arthur H., *The Private Papers of Senator Vandenberg,* edited by Arthur Vandenberg, Jr., and Joe Alex Morris (Boston: Houghton Mifflin Co., 1952).

Viorst, Milton, *Hostile Allies* (New York: The Macmillan Company, 1965).

Wainwright, Jonathan, *General Wainwright's Story,* edited by Robert Considine (Garden City, N.Y.: Doubleday & Co., 1946).

Walters, Vernon, *Silent Missions* (Garden City, N.Y.: Doubleday & Co., 1978).

Watson, Mark S., *The United States Army in World War II, Chief of Staff: Prewar Plans and Preparations* (Washington, D.C.: Office of the Chief of Military History, Department of the Army, 1950).

Wedemeyer, Albert C., *Wedemeyer Reports!* (New York: Henry Holt, 1958).

Weigley, Russell F., *Eisenhower's Lieutenants* (Bloomington, Ind.: Indiana University Press, 1981).

———, *Towards an American Army* (New York: Columbia University Press, 1962).

Weintraub, Stanley, *A Stillness Heard Round the World* (New York: E. P. Dutton, 1985).

Wendt, Lloyd, *Chicago Tribune: The Rise of a Great American Newspaper* (Chicago: Rand McNally, 1979).

Werth, Alexander, *Russia at War* (New York: E. P. Dutton, 1964).

Wheeler, Burton K., *Yankee from the West* (Garden City, N.Y.: Doubleday & Co., 1962).

Wheeler-Bennett, John W., *King George VI, His Life and Reign* (New York: St. Martin's Press, 1958).

[White Paper] *United States Relations with China with Special Reference to the Period 1944–1949* (Washington, D.C.: Government Printing Office, August, 1949).

White, Theodore H., *In Search of History*, reprint edition (New York: Warner Books, 1979).

———, ed., *The Stilwell Papers* (New York: Sloane, 1948).

Whiting, Allen S., *China Crosses the Yalu* (New York: The Macmillan Company, 1960).

Wilmot, Chester, *The Struggle for Europe*, reprint edition (London: Fontana, 1959).

Wilson, Dick, *Zhou Enlai* (New York: Viking Press, 1984).

Wilson, Edmund, *The Thirties*, reprint edition (New York: Washington Square Press, 1980).

Wilson, Harold, *Chariot of Israel* (New York: W. W. Norton, 1982).

Wilson, Rose Page, *General Marshall Remembered* (Englewood Cliffs, N.J.: Prentice-Hall, 1968).

Wilson, Theodore, *The First Summit* (Boston: Houghton Mifflin, 1969).

Winant, John G., *Letter from Grosvenor Square* (Boston: Houghton Mifflin, 1947).

Wright, C. Ben, and Larry I. Bland, "Russian Expert: The Diplomatic Career of George F. Kennan" (Unpublished typescript courtesy of Larry I. Bland, GCMRL).

Wyden, Peter, *Day One*, reprint edition (New York: Warner Books, 1985).

Yergin, Daniel, *Shattered Peace* (Boston: Houghton Mifflin, 1978).

Young, Lucien, *The Real Hawaii* (New York: Doubleday & McClure, 1899).

Ziegler, Philip, *Mountbatten* (New York: Alfred A. Knopf, 1985).

INDEX

Acheson, Dean, 631, 664, 673, 686, 724, 725
  China aid and, 570
  in departure from State Department, 615–17,
    631
  on European economic crisis, 609
  and fall of Chiang, 674–76
  Greek and Turkish aid and, 594–96
  Johnson's conflicts with, 684
  Korean War and, 680, 692, 695–96, 699–701,
    705, 708–9
  MacArthur's conflicts with, 685
  on MacArthur's congressional address, 714
  MacArthur's relief and, 708–11
  McCarthy's attacks on, 721–23
  Marshall admired by, 591
  Marshall Plan and, 611–12, 614, 620
  Marshall's China mission and, 561–62, 570,
    573, 579, 583
  on Marshall's management of State Depart-
    ment, 589–91, 593
  Marshall's relationship with, 687
  Marshall's reliance on, 588–89
  on Marshall's retirement, 668–69
  Marshall's State Department appointment and,
    588
  NATO and, 689
  Red-baiting and, 676
Adams, Alva, 152, 204
Afrika Korps, German, 323
  TORCH and, 346
  in Tunisian campaign, 381, 383
Agriculture Department, U.S., 114
Air Corps, U.S., 125, 146–47, 193, 684
  ARCADIA and, 275
  atomic-capability of, 648
  blacks turned away from, 169
  plans for expansion of, 129–32, 135, 140,
    165–66, 171
  war strategy planning by, 201
Alexander, Sir Harold, 365–66, 464n, 499, 501,
    506, 513
  Sicilian invasion and, 405
  in Tunisian campaign, 380, 383
Algiers, Allied assault on, 341, 344, 347
Allied Control Council, 598, 602, 646
Almond, Edward M., 701
America First, 165, 210
America First Research Bureau, 204
American Battle Monuments Commission, 672,
    727
American-British Conversations (ABC-1), 190–
    91, 201
American Chamber of Commerce, 637
American China Policy Association, 632

American Expeditionary Forces (AEF), 50, 55,
    57, 67, 86, 88, 91
American Institute of Pacific Relations, 672
American Legion, 728
American Red Cross, 452, 727
  Marshall's appointment to, 672
  Marshall's management of, 672–73
American Society of Newspaper Editors, 676
Andaman Island invasion, see BUCCANEER
Anderson, Clinton, 555
Anderson, Kenneth A. N., 344
  in Tunisian campaign, 379–80, 382
Anfa Camp, 357–58
Anschluss, 153
Anthony, George W., 526
Antonov, Aleksei I., ARGONAUT and, 508,
    510–11, 513
Antwerp, capture of, 483, 486
ANVIL, 444–46, 459, 468
  Churchill on, 448–49, 466–67, 471
  Eisenhower on, 456–57, 464–65, 472
  EUREKA on, 434
  SEXTANT on, 435
  troops committed to, 446
  U.S.-British dispute over, 463–67, 471
Anzio assault, 444–47
Anzio breakout, 457
ARCADIA (Washington Conference), 267–76,
    282, 308
  Churchill's six-point strategy presented at,
    268–69
  Combined Chiefs of Staff established at, 274–
    75
  Europe-first strategy accepted at, 269, 272,
    275
  Marshall's unified field command plans at,
    272–74
  on war production, 274
Ardennes, German offensive in, 491–92, 499–
    501, 508–9
Argentina, 628
ARGONAUT (Yalta Conference), 497–98, 505,
    506–14, 518
  on Soviet entrance into Pacific War, 507, 511–
    13
  on war-ending offensive, 510
Army, French, 45, 53
  casualties of, 50, 53, 56, 66
  Fourth, 80
  in Meuse-Argonne offensive, 75, 77
  Moroccan Divisions of, 68
  mutiny in, 177
  on St. Mihiel front, 60–61
  in St. Mihiel offensive, 73

Army, French (*continued*)
  Second, 68–69
Army, U.S.:
  balanced-force budget of 132–35, 165
  blacks in, 168–69
  CCC and, 114–16, 134
  debates over size of, 233
  desegregation of, 705
  domestic anti-riot activities of, 112–13
  in maneuvers with National Guard, 40–41
  Marshall's biennial reports on state of, 203–4,
    207, 209, 413, 554
  Marshall's decision on career in, 22–24, 27
  Marshall's mobilization plan for, 154–58
  Marshall's officer's commission in, 29–30
  Marshall's reorganization of, 278–79
  Marshall's retirement from, 553–55
  Marshall's selection of junior leadership of,
    176–77
  Marshall's selection of senior leadership of,
    175–76
  need for expansion of, 147–48
  pay in, 32, 113
  Pearl Harbor attack investigated by, 478, 480–
    81, 556–57
  Philippine insurrection and, 31–34
  postwar demobilizations of, 91–94, 112, 517,
    628
  promotion and retirement reforms in, 174–75
  readiness of, 51, 192
  Senate consideration of appropriations for,
    152–53
  Signal Intelligence Service of, 220
  size of, 374, 441–42
  in Solomon Islands campaign, 327
  Texas-Mexican border maneuvers of, 40
  threatened demobilization of, 202–3
  war strategy planning by, 200
  see also specific units
Army Air Force, U.S., *see* Air Corps, U.S.
Army and Navy Club, 33, 42–43
Army and Navy Journal, 119, 414
Army Group B, German, 520
Army Group Center, German, 197
Army Reorganization Act, 94, 116, 144
Army School of the Line, 36
Army Staff College, 37
Army War College, 37
  Marshall's lectureship at, 101–4
Arneson, Gordon, 648
Arnim, Jürgen von, 422
  in Tunisian campaign, 381, 383, 387
Arnold, Eleanor, 347
Arnold, Hank, 358
Arnold, Henry "Hap," 3, 5–6, 158, 231, 305,
    347, 390, 418, 420, 458–59, 469, 531
  appointment of supreme commander and, 419
  ARCADIA and, 274–75
  in Army reorganization, 278–79
  Atlantic Conference and, 210–11, 215
  atomic bomb and, 543, 548
  in Batangas maneuvers, 44
  Battle of the North Atlantic and, 375
  Berlin toured by, 542–43
  death of, 729
  on ending war in Far East, 540
  EUREKA and, 429, 433
  Europe-first strategy and, 304
  and expansion of Air Corps, 130–31
  five-star rank of, 490–91

  illnesses of, 518
  MacArthur's conflicts with, 439
  Marshall's friendship with, 5–7, 45
  OCTAGON and, 474
  OVERLORD and, 11, 414, 460–62
  QUADRANT and, 412
  in reinforcing Philippines, 249–50
  retirement of, 545, 637–38
  SEXTANT and, 423, 425, 435
  Solomon Islands campaign and, 342–44
  SYMBOL and, 356, 359–60, 364, 367
  TRIDENT and, 387
  in War Department mobilization, 193
Asbjornson, Mildred, 653
Atkinson, Brooks, 488
Atlanta Constitution, 138, 140
Atlantic Charter, 217, 275
Atlantic Conference (Placentia Bay Conference),
    210–17
  British strategy to defeat Germany and Italy
    presented at, 215–16
  British vs. U.S. preparation for, 216–17
  results of, 217
Atlantic Union Committee, 727
atomic bomb, 321, 525, 537–43
  Berlin crisis and, 648
  building of, 6
  casualties caused by, 548
  invasion of Japan vs., 539–40
  Japanese surrender and, 545
  proposed demonstration of, 539
  selection of targets for, 543
  Soviet development of, 677–78
  testing of, 542–46
Atomic Energy Commission, 625, 628
atomic weapons, civilian vs. military control of,
    648–49
Attlee, Clement, 546
  on partition of Palestine, 656
  TERMINAL and, 547
Auchinleck, Claude, 204
Auriol, Vincent, 598
Austin, Warren, 415
Australia, 265
  Japanese bombing of, 299
  MacArthur's transfer to, 300–301
Australian, British, Dutch, American (ABDA)
    command, 272, 274, 299–300
Austria:
  peace treaty with, 603, 612, 639–42, 663
  reparations of, 639
AVALANCHE, 406–8, 422, 447–48
  EUREKA on, 429–30

Bach, Johann Sebastian, 6
Badoglio, Pietro, 410
Baillie, Hugh, 707
Baker, Newton, 91
Balfour Declaration, 656
Bali, Japanese invasion of, 299
Balkan campaign, 400, 421–22, 445, 503–4
Barbarossa, Operation, 197–98
Barkley, Alben W., 557, 701
Baruch, Bernard, 93, 152, 234–35, 617, 631, 688
Bataan, Japanese assault on, 302
Batangas maneuvers, 43–44
Bay of Bengal, Japanese offensive in, 309
BBC, 614
Beal, John Robinson, 581
Beardall, John R., 253

Beaverbrook, Max, 274
Belgium, fall of, 153–54
Bell, J. Franklin, 36–37, 43–44, 47, 50–52, 85
Belleau Wood, German attack at, 63
Beneš, Edvard, 623, 644
Benning Revolution, 106
Berlin:
    battle for, 519–22, 525
    Marshall's tour of, 542–43
    occupation of, 519
Berlin crisis, 646–49, 663–64, 719
    airlift during, 647–48
Berlin offensive, 500
Bernadotte, Folke, 661–62
Bevin, Ernest, 663
    Berlin crisis and, 649
    London Foreign Ministers' Conference and,
        640–42
    Marshall Plan and, 614–15, 619
    on Marshall's retirement, 668
    Moscow Foreign Ministers' Conference and,
        601, 603
Bidault, Georges:
    London Foreign Ministers' Conference and,
        640–42
    Marshall Plan and, 614, 617
    Moscow Foreign Ministers' Conference and,
        601
Biddle, Francis, 159
Bizonia, 642
Blanchard, Mrs., 108
Bliss, Tasker, 41
Boeing Aircraft Company, 232
Bogotá Inter-American Conference, 650–54
Bohlen, Charles "Chip," 665
    background of, 597
    Czech crisis and, 625
    Korean War and, 692
    Marshall Plan and, 611–12, 620
    Moscow Foreign Ministers' Conference and,
        597, 604–6
BOLERO, 306, 313, 317, 321–22, 328–29, 331,
        336, 340, 344, 355, 387, 407
Bolshoi Ballet, 604
BONIFACE, 191
Bonnet, Georges, 136
Bonnier de La Chapelle, Fernand, 352
Bonus Expeditionary Force, 112–13, 694
Bordeaux, Paul-Emile, 58–59
Borneo, Japanese attack of, 277
Borodin, Mikhail, 101
Boxer Rebellion, 96
Boyden, Frank L., 607
Bozell, Brent, 724
Braddock, Edward, 18
Bradley, Omar, 6, 151, 369–70, 486, 500, 502,
        518, 607, 631, 684, 687, 729, 735
    Battle of the Bulge and, 493–95
    congressional testimony of, 720–21
    in difficulties with MacArthur, 694–95
    end of war estimate of, 483
    Infantry School instructorship of, 106
    Korean War and, 692–93, 695–98, 700, 702,
        720
    on Marshall, 484
    NATO and, 664–65
    NSC-68 and, 690
    in OVERLORD, 443–44, 455–56, 461, 463
    promotion to four stars for, 501
    in Rhine offensive, 516

    on sacking MacArthur, 709–11
    Sicilian invasion and, 404–6
    in Tunisian campaign, 382–83
    War Department mobilization and, 196
    war-ending plan of, 519–20
Brandon, Henry, 600
Bratton, Rufus:
    Pacific command alerts and, 255–56
    U.S.-Japanese negotiations and, 248, 250,
        253–56
Brewster, Andre, 87
Brewster, Owen, 559, 674
Bricker, John, 479
Bridges, Styles, 629, 674, 716, 720
Bright, Joan, 460
BRIMSTONE, 356
Britain, Battle of, 164, 169, 173, 191
British Chiefs of Staff, 458
    on Czechoslovakia, 529–30
    Malta Conference and, 498, 503
    OVERLORD and, 415, 457
    SEXTANT and, 427
    SYMBOL and, 359, 367
    TRIDENT and, 394
Brooke, Sir Alan, 321–22, 325, 329, 370, 462–
        63, 487, 639, 729
    ANVIL and, 459, 466
    Anzio assault and, 445, 447–48
    ARCADIA and, 271
    ARGONAUT and, 509–11, 513–14
    AVALANCHE and, 407, 409, 411, 447–48
    background of, 308
    Eisenhower criticized by, 492, 499–500, 502–3
    on Eisenhower's war-ending plan, 521–22
    ETO conferences and, 333–34
    EUREKA and, 430–34
    on follow-ons to Sicilian invasion, 400
    Malta Conference and, 498, 501–4, 506
    MODICUM and, 308–11
    OCTAGON and, 471–72
    OVERLORD and, 409–10, 457
    QUADRANT and, 408, 409–10
    SEXTANT and, 424–25, 427–28, 436, 438
    on SLEDGEHAMMER and ROUNDUP, 310–
        11
    SYMBOL and, 355, 359–64, 366–68
    TERMINAL and, 543–44
    Tobruk defeat and, 324
    TORCH and, 340, 369
    TRIDENT and, 385, 387–89, 393, 396–98
    Tunisian campaign and, 387
Brown, Allen (stepson), 109, 111, 118, 159, 352,
        441, 448, 666, 727, 729
    death of, 450, 452, 454, 465–66
Brown, Clifton, Jr. (stepson), 109, 441
Brown, Clifton S., 108–9
Brown Brothers, 616
Brown Brothers Harriman, 668, 687
Brussels treaty, 663
Bryan, William Jennings, 23, 47, 234
Bryden, William, 193
BUCCANEER:
    EUREKA on, 434
    SEXTANT on, 424, 426–27, 435–36
Buck, Pearl, 234
Buckley, William F., Jr., 724
Bulge, Battle of the, 492–95, 506
    casualties of, 495
    end of, 500
Bulkeley, John D., 301

Bullard, Robert L., 59–60, 63–64
Bullitt, William C., 129
Bundy, Charles, 255
Bundy, Harvey, 230, 447
Bureau of the Budget, 646–47
Burghley, Lady Mary, 729
Burke, Edward R., 167, 172
Burma, Allied invasion of, 364
Burma campaign, 283, 422, 525
  Chiang's participation in, 389–90, 476
  SEXTANT on, 424–26
  TRIDENT on, 389, 392–94, 397
Bush, Vannevar, 321
Butcher, Henry, 366, 369, 381, 451
Byrnes, James F., 138, 152, 167, 174, 442, 483, 485, 688
  atomic bomb and, 537–39, 543, 545
  Clay's friendship with, 617–18
  draft extension and, 206
  Japanese surrender and, 549
  Marshall compared with, 596, 598, 640
  Marshall's China mission and, 561–62
  resignation of, 585
  State Department managed by, 589, 591
  Truman's reliance on, 537
  Truman's replacement of, 574, 583
Byroade, Henry A., 562

Cadogan, Sir Alexander, 434, 597
  Atlantic Conference and, 211, 215
Cairo Conference, see SEXTANT
Calapan, Marshall's posting in, 31–32
Cambrun, Jacques de, 78
Camp Leonard Wood, waste in construction of, 185
Canada, TORCH and, 340
Cannon, Clarence, 200
Cantigny, battle for, 62–63
Carnegie Endowment for International Peace, 676
Carolines invasion, 475
Carrazana, Venustiano, 46
Carter, Marshall, 587, 590, 631–32, 652, 662, 664–65, 667, 687–88
Carter, W. Hodding, Jr., 607
Casablanca Conference, see SYMBOL
Casablanca landings, 341–42, 346–47
CC Clique, 565–66, 572–75, 581, 585
Central Intelligence Agency (CIA), 625, 651, 657, 683
  Korean War and, 715
Central Pacific offensive, 440
  successes of, 402
  TRIDENT on, 397
  see also Solomon Islands campaign
Central Republic Bank, 92
Chamberlain, Neville, 136, 153–54
  Hitler's territorial demands and, 128–29
Chandler, Albert B., 394–96
Chang Chun, 564–65, 567–68
Changchun, fall of, 572
Chang Tso-lin, 97–98
Château-Thierry, German attack at, 63
Chen Kou-fu, 565
Chen Li-fu, 565
Chennault, Claire, 11, 476, 487
  background of, 389–90
  "cheap" campaign of, 390–93, 397
  congressional allies of, 395
  TRIDENT and, 389, 392–93, 397

Chiang Kai-shek, 101, 123, 234, 237, 252, 283, 411, 628, 681, 694
  ARGONAUT and, 507, 512
  Burma campaign and, 389–90, 476
  Chennault's "cheap" campaign and, 390–93
  constantly retreating troops of, 475–76
  fall of, 667–68, 673–76, 685–86
  in flight to Taiwan, 667, 673–76
  Japanese isolation of, 220
  Korean War and, 702, 704, 709, 715, 718
  loss of power by, 632, 635–37
  Mao's negotiations with, 560–61
  Marshall's China mission and, 555, 560, 562–66, 568, 571–85
  Marshall's criticisms of, 633
  press on, 488
  Roosevelt's commitment to, 281
  Roosevelt's warnings to, 476, 487
  SEXTANT and, 418, 423–27
  Stilwell's dislike of, 282
  SYMBOL on, 361
  Wedemeyer's China mission and, 633–34
Chiang Kai-shek, Madame, 390–91, 393–94, 411, 424, 589, 667, 675–76, 727, 732
  Marshall's China mission and, 571–72, 574, 582–84
Chicago Chamber of Commerce, 620
Chicago *Daily News*, 160
Chicago *Tribune*, 116–17, 175, 249, 620, 685
Child, Marquis, 414
China, Nationalist, see China, Republic of; Formosa; Kuomintang
China, People's Republic of (PRC):
  Korean War and, 692–93, 695–705, 706–9, 715–16, 718–20
  proclamation of, 676
China, Republic of, 265
  ARGONAUT on, 507, 512–13
  Burma campaign and, 389, 392–94 397
  congressional allies of, 395
  financial problems of, 569
  Japanese war with, 123–24, 136, 219–21, 234
  Lend-Lease aid to, 560, 570, 575, 578, 581–82, 636
  Malta Conference on, 506
  Marshall's command in, 95–102
  Marshall's mission to, 555–56, 558, 560–85, 587
  Nationalists vs. Communists in, 561–68, 570–85, 596, 628, 632–37, 667–68
  rapid deterioration of, 475–76
  Roosevelt's policy on, 281, 487–88, 506, 512–13, 560, 632
  SEXTANT on, 423–28
  Soviet claims on, 507, 512, 546
  Stilwell's mission to, 282–83
  SYMBOL on, 361
  U.S. aid to, 237
  U.S.-Japanese negotiations on, 238, 240–41, 243, 246, 250–52
  Wedemeyer mission to, 633–35
  see also, Formosa; Kuomintang; Manchuria
China Lobby, 577, 632, 671, 692, 727
  on fall of Chiang, 674–75
  on KMT aid, 636
  McCarthy defended by, 724
  Wedemeyer's China mission and, 633, 635
Chinese Communist Party (CCP), 560–61, 596, 628, 632–37, 667

Formosa and, 673
Marshall's China mission and, 562–68, 570–84
Wedemeyer's China mission and, 633–34
see also China, People's Republic of
Chou En-lai, 676
Korean War and, 695, 708
Marshall's China mission and, 564–65, 567, 573–81, 585
Christian Science Monitor, 416
CHROMITE, 691–92
Chrysler, Tank Arsenal of, 185
Churchill, Randolph, 358
Churchill, Winston, 87, 134, 154, 162, 300, 303, 307, 312, 319–20, 417, 437, 489, 494, 496, 515, 529, 535–36, 554, 594, 639, 658, 721, 727, 729
ANVIL and, 448–49, 466–67, 471
Anzio assault and, 444–45
appointment of supreme commander and, 420
ARCADIA and, 267–69, 273–76
ARGONAUT and, 506–9, 513–14
Atlantic Conference and, 210–17
atomic bomb and, 321, 546
AVALANCHE and, 406–7, 447–48
Balkan campaign and, 421, 445, 503–4
on Battle of the Bulge, 495
BOLERO and, 322
Darlan deal and, 349–50, 352
death of, 733
on Dill's death, 490
Dodecanese campaign and, 418–19
Eisenhower criticized by, 492, 499–500, 503
Eisenhower's meetings with, 399–401
on Eisenhower's war-ending plan, 521–22
electoral threats to government of, 325, 328
EUREKA and, 4–5, 429–30, 432–35
on European economic crisis, 610
on follow-ons to Sicilian invasion, 400–401
on German occupation and partition, 421
and German offensive against Soviet Union, 198–99
German surrender and, 523, 531–32
GYMNAST and, 276, 322
on Hitler's territorial demands, 129
invasion of England anticipated by, 157
on Japanese threat, 225
Lend-Lease and, 183–84
Malta Conference and, 498, 501, 504–6
Marshall respected by, 544
on Marshall's unified field command plan, 273–74
Mediterranean strategy of, 7, 9
MODICUM and, 308–9, 311
Nobel Prize awarded to, 730
OCTAGON and, 468–69, 471–74, 476
opportunistic strategy of, 463–65
OVERLORD and, 8, 406–9, 415, 419, 445–47, 449, 453, 457, 459–62, 464
Pearl Harbor attack and, 261
QUADRANT and, 408–9
on Roosevelt's reelection, 179–80
Roosevelt's relationship with, 269
second front issue and, 398–99
SEXTANT and, 11, 418, 422–26, 438
Sicilian invasion and, 365, 405
on SLEDGEHAMMER and ROUNDUP, 308–9, 311, 325–26
on surrender of Singapore, 299
SYMBOL and, 354–55, 357–59, 361–68
TERMINAL and, 542, 544

on territorial concessions to Soviet Union, 316
Tobruk defeat and, 323–24
TORCH and, 334, 338–39, 341–42, 349–50, 352–53
TRIDENT and, 385, 387–88, 393, 398
Tunisian campaign and, 384
on unconditional surrender, 487
U.S. aid requested by, 156, 158, 181–82, 304
U.S.-British alliance announced by, 271–72
U.S.-Japanese negotiations and, 241
war declared against Japan by, 267
Citizens' Committee for the Marshall Plan, 620
City of Flint incident, 148
Civilian Conservation Corps (CCC), 114–16, 121, 125, 133–35, 176
Civilian Military Education Fund, 113
Clark, Grenville, 167–68, 176
Clark, Mark W., 263, 331, 335, 445, 449, 452, 466, 599, 721
Marshall's meetings with, 514
Moscow Foreign Ministers' Conference and, 601
TORCH and, 345–46, 348–49
Clarke, Carter W., 480
Clausewitz, Karl von, 722
Clay, Henry, 617
Clay, Lucius D., 606, 734
on bankruptcy of Germany, 599–600
Berlin crisis and, 646–48
Czech crisis and, 624
German currency reform and, 642–43
London Foreign Ministers' Conference and, 640
Marshall Plan and, 617–18
Clayton, William L.:
on European economic crisis, 610–12
Marshall Plan and, 614
Clemenceau, Georges, 56, 65–66, 78, 83, 85, 227n
Clifford, Clark, 657–61
Cocke, William H., 101–2
Cohan, George M., 50
Cohen, Benjamin V.:
Marshall Plan and, 611
Moscow Foreign Ministers' Conference and, 601
Cold Harbor, siege of, 54
Cold War, 619
Coles, Charlotte (sister-in-law), 637
Coles, Sally (aunt), 39
Collins, J. Lawton "Lightning Joe," 151
in difficulties with MacArthur, 694–95
Korean War and, 696, 704–5
in OVERLORD, 443
on sacking MacArthur, 711
Colombia, insurrection in, 652–54
Colorado Saloon, 33
Colville, John, 469, 503–4
Combined Chiefs of Staff, 299, 422, 433, 456, 462, 494, 518
atomic bomb and, 545
AVALANCHE and, 406
BOLERO and, 306
Darlan deal and, 349
on Eisenhower's war-ending plan, 521
establishment of, 274–75
EUREKA and, 434
German surrender and, 532
Malta Conference and, 501, 503–5
OCTAGON and, 472

Combined Chiefs of Staff (*continued*)
OVERLORD and, 446, 458–60
QUADRANT and, 408–10, 412
SEXTANT and, 425–26, 435
SYMBOL and, 358, 361, 363–64, 369
TERMINAL and, 543, 545
TORCH and, 334
TRIDENT and, 389, 392, 394, 396–98
in war-ending plan, 530
Command and General Staff School, 151
Commerce Department, U.S., 134
Committee of One Million, 632, 727
Committee of Three, 564–66
Communists:
alleged infiltration of State Department by,
555
in Greek civil war, 594–95, 627, 635, 649,
665–66, 719
postwar influence of, 505–6
see also China, People's Republic of; Chinese
Communist Party; Soviet Union
Conant, James B., 607–8, 612
conferences, wartime:
listing of, 211*n*
see also specific conferences
Congress, U.S., 13, 41, 46, 77, 84, 127, 134, 146,
184, 196, 242, 417, 527, 608, 730
Air Corps expansion and, 131–32
on Army pay, 113
CCC and, 114
Churchill's announcement of U.S.-British alliance to, 271–72
conscription and, 167, 169–72, 202–10, 234,
499
on Dill's death, 490
and expansion of Air Corps, 166, 171
on fall of Chiang, 674
five-star rank approved by, 490–91
and funding for Protective Mobilization Force,
170–71
and Greek and Turkish aid, 594–96
isolationism of, 123–24, 136
Joint Committee on the Investigation of the
Pearl Harbor Attack of, 557–59, 570
on KMT aid, 636–37
Korean War and, 702, 714–25
Lend-Lease and, 182–83, 185, 199–200
MacArthur's address to, 713–14
MacArthur's allies in, 297, 379, 395, 698, 700,
709, 712, 714
MacArthur's testimony before, 715–18, 725
Marshall honored by, 669, 726
Marshall Plan and, 610–12, 615, 620–26,
637–38, 642, 645
Marshall's balanced-force budget and, 165
and Marshall's biennial reports on state of
Army, 203–4
Marshall's mobilization plan and, 156–58
Marshall's officer's commission confirmed by,
30
on Marshall's promotion to five stars, 572
Marshall's relationship with, 10, 544, 587
on munitions sales to Britain, 159, 173
NATO and, 665, 677
Neutrality Act repeal and, 147–48
NSC-68 and, 690
OVERLORD and, 8
Pearl Harbor attack investigations and, 260*n*,
266, 477–79, 481, 556–59, 570

on post-World War I Army demobilization,
91–94, 112
Red-baiting and, 629–30
Republican electoral success in, 581
restrictive immigration laws adopted by, 94
Spanish-American War and, 26
UMT and, 724–25
war against Imperial Germany declared by, 48,
51
Wedemeyer's China mission and, 634
see also House of Representatives, U.S.; Senate,
U.S.
Congressional Record, 415
Congress of Industrial Organizations, 485
Congress of Vienna (Nicolson), 604
Connally, Tom, 136–37
Connecticut, Army and National Guard maneu-
vers in, 40–41
Conner, Fox, 67, 69, 80–81, 91, 110, 263–66,
330
Constantine, Crown Prince of Greece, 732
Cooke, Charles M. "Savvy," 326–27, 694
OVERLORD and, 446
Solomon Islands campaign and, 377
SYMBOL and, 356–57, 359
CORONET, 498, 535–36
Corregidor, Japanese shelling of, 302–3
Coughlin, Charles, 146, 164
Council of National Defense, 48
Council on Foreign Relations, 620
Covington, Burling and Rublee, 668
Craig, Malin, 34, 119–20, 122, 124–25, 133, 147,
149, 175, 192
Air Corps expansion and, 130–32
balanced-force concept pressed by, 135
retirement of, 126, 137–38, 143
Cross, Samuel, 317
Cunningham, Lord Andrew, 458, 471, 504, 545,
639
Currie, Lauchlin, 391
Curtin, John, 300, 312
Czechoslovakia:
British Chiefs of Staff on, 529–30
collapse of coalition government of, 623–25,
644
Hitler's territorial claims on, 128–29
Marshall Plan and, 614–15

Daladier, Edouard, Hitler's territorial demands
and, 128–29
Darlan, Alain, 348
Darlan, Jean François, 348–52, 366, 370
Darlan deal, 349–52
Davies, John, 428
Davis, Elmer, 351–52
Davis, Forrest, 721
Dawes, Charles G., 92–93
Deane, John R., 362, 498, 511
Defense Department, U.S., 670, 732
Marshall's appointment to, 682–87
Marshall's management of, 687–88
Marshall's resignation from, 726
on partition of Palestine, 656–57
unification of armed services into, 682–83
de Gaulle, Charles, 159, 350, 473
D-Day message of, 462–63
ETO conferences and, 335
Marshall's conflicts with, 463
Marshall's meetings with, 335

OVERLORD and, 462–63
SYMBOL and, 367–68
Delta State Teachers' College, Acheson's speech at, 609
Democratic League, 564, 566, 577
Dempsey, Miles, 455
Denfeld, Louis E., 625
Denmark, German invasion of, 151
Dern, George, 127
  Marshall's promotion to brigadier general and, 118–20
de Seversky, Alexander, 374
Devers, Jacob, 263, 483–84, 486, 501
Dewey, John, 116
Dewey, Thomas, 479–80, 661, 664, 666
DeWitt, John L., 137
Díaz, Porfirio, 40
Dieppe raid, OVERLORD vs., 431–32
Dill, Sir John, 305, 308–9, 334, 415, 450, 735
  appointment of supreme commander and, 420
  ARCADIA and, 269–73
  Atlantic Conference, 211, 213, 216
  death of, 489–90
  honors presented to, 447
  illnesses of, 471
  Marshall's relationship with, 213, 269–71, 489–90
  OVERLORD and, 446, 457
  QUADRANT and, 409
  SEXTANT and, 438
  SYMBOL and, 355–56, 359, 363
Dill, Lady Nancy, 270, 489
Disney, Walt, 374
Dodecanese campaign, 418–19, 422
  Rhodes offensive in, 424–27, 435
Dodona Manor, 150, 313–14
Doolittle, James H., 312
Douglas, Helen Gahagan, 700
Douglas, Lewis, 630
Douglas, Sir Sholto, 410
Douglas, William O., 592
Downey, Sheridan, 207
DRAGOON, *see* ANVIL
Drake, Waldo, 578
Dresden, bombing of, 518
Drum, Hugh, 70–72, 81, 92, 95
  chief of staff appointment sought by, 137–39
  Marshall's conflicts with, 280–82
Dulles, Allen, 522–23, 597
Dulles, John Foster, 165, 733
  background of, 597
  Japanese peace treaty and, 688
  Korean War and, 681
  London Foreign Ministers' Conference and, 640
  Moscow Foreign Ministers' Conference and, 597, 601
  NATO and, 671
Dunkirk evacuation, 155, 157–58
E. I. duPont powderworks, 155
Dutch East Indies, 265
  Japanese offensive in, 225, 277
  U.S.-Japanese negotiations on, 240
Dwiggins, William, 607

Eaker, Ira, 6
Early, Stephen, 228–29, 523
Eastman, George, 22
EASY RED, Beach, 460

Eaton, Charles A., 622
Eden, Anthony, 400, 463, 535–36
Edward VIII, King of England, 399
Eichelberger, Robert L., 176, 376
18th Infantry Regiment, U.S., 52, 60–61
Eighth Air Force, U.S., 378
Eighth Army, British, 320, 322–23, 339, 346, 365, 369–70, 449, 468
  Sicilian invasion and, 400
  in Tunisian campaign, 379–80, 382
Eighth Army, U.S., 691, 695, 701–2, 704–5, 706, 708, 711
8th Cavalry Regiment, U.S., 698
VIII Corps, U.S., 84
8th Infantry Division, U.S., 248
  Marshall's command in, 111, 113–15
Eighth Route Army, Chinese Communist, 565
82nd Airborne Division, U.S., 456, 653
Eisenhower, Dwight D., 6, 110, 299, 315, 335, 403–4, 409–10, 414, 416–17, 420, 433, 485, 496, 508–9, 515, 517–19, 553, 640, 655, 683, 688, 732–33
  ANVIL and, 456–57, 464–65, 472
  and appointing OVERLORD commander, 437
  appointment of supreme commander and, 422–23
  Ardennes assault and, 491–92
  AVALANCHE and, 406–7, 422
  background of, 263–64
  Battle of the Bulge and, 492–95
  BOLERO and, 306, 331
  and bombing component of OVERLORD, 453
  China mission of, 574
  Churchill's meetings with, 399–401
  commanders for OVERLORD selected by, 443–44
  on crumbling defenses of Philippines, 283, 297–300, 303
  Darlan deal and, 349–52
  de Gaulle and, 462–63
  Dodecanese campaign and, 419
  ETO command given to, 329–31
  at ETO conferences, 332–33
  EUREKA and, 429
  five-star rank of, 490–91
  on follow-ons to Sicilian invasion, 400–401
  forward headquarters of, 459
  German surrender and, 530–31
  and launching of OVERLORD, 451–52
  MacArthur's conflicts with, 297–98
  on McCarthy, 723–24, 728–29
  Malta Conference and, 498, 502–3, 506
  manpower replacement plan of, 499–500
  MARKET-GARDEN and, 482
  Marshall compared with, 10–11
  Marshall described by, 278
  Marshall's attitude toward, 368–69
  Marshall's China Mission and, 570
  Marshall's death and, 734
  Marshall's doubts about, 499
  at Marshall's funeral, 735
  Marshall's meetings with, 499–501, 503
  and Marshall's plan for OVERLORD, 455–56
  Montgomery's criticisms of, 484, 492, 500
  NATO appointment of, 677
  need for deputy commander for, 502–3, 506
  on OVERLORD-ANVIL simultaneity, 447, 456–57
  OVERLORD battlefields toured by, 460–61

Eisenhower, Dwight D. (*continued*)
  OVERLORD command given to, 9, 12–13
  OVERLORD delayed by, 446–47
  OVERLORD reports of, 454–56, 466
  on Patton controversies, 453–54
  in planning unified field commands, 272
  political ambitions of, 638
  presidential campaign of, 723, 727–28
  procurement problems of, 314
  Rhine offensive and, 486, 513
  Roosevelt's promotion of, 413
  on Roosevelt's redividing theater responsibili-
    ties, 301
  SEXTANT and, 426, 443
  Sicilian invasion and, 404–6
  supply problems of, 483, 485
  SYMBOL and, 365–68
  temper of, 305
  TORCH and, 334, 337–41, 345–46, 349–52,
    369
  TRIDENT on, 397–98
  Tunisian campaign of, 379–84, 387
  on unconditional surrender, 486
  victory parade for, 540
  war-ending plan of, 500–501, 519–22, 525,
    529–30
  War Plans appointment of, 264–66
Eisenhower, John, 443
El Alamein, Montgomery's victory at, 346
Eliecer Gaitan, Jorge, 652
Eliot, T. S., 607
Elizabeth II, Queen of England, 732
  coronation of, 729
Ely, Hanson, 101
Embick, Stanley D., 130, 200, 275, 591
Emergency Relief Organization, 452
Enola Gay, 547
Ethiopia, Italian invasion of, 123–24, 129
Ethridge, Mark, 627
EUREKA (Teheran Conference), 3–4, 8–9, 418,
  426, 428–35
  on AVALANCHE, 429–30
  on OVERLORD, 428–35
Europe:
  economic crisis of, 599–600, 605–6, 608–13,
    638
  Marshall's tour of, 39–40
  postwar Communist influence in, 505–6
  predictions on end of war in, 510–11, 525
  World War II casualties of, 496
European Recovery Program, *see* Marshall Plan
European Theater of Operations (ETO), 5, 13
  Eisenhower appointed commander of, 329–31
  Roosevelt's options presented on, 333
  ROUNDUP and, 332–34
  SLEDGEHAMMER and, 332–33
  TORCH and, 334–35
Executive Order 9835, 629

Far East Air Force, U.S., 231
Farley, James A., 138–39
Farrell, Leo A., 138, 140
Federal Bureau of Investigation (FBI), 248, 297,
  677
Federal Council of Churches, 620
Federal Emergency Relief Administration, 134
Feng Yu-hsiang, 97, 560
Ferguson, Homer, 477, 481, 557–59
Fifteenth Army, Japanese, 283

15th Infantry Regiment, U.S., 563, 734
  Marshall's command of, 95–102
15th Panzer Division, German, 404
Fifth Army, U.S., 445, 448, 449, 465–66, 468,
  514, 525
58th Guards Division, Soviet, 529
Fire Island, N.Y., Marshall's family rescued
  from, 127–28
1st Armored Division, U.S., 448, 450
  in Tunisian campaign, 380–81
First Army, British, 383
First Army, U.S., 79–81, 280, 483, 494, 520
  Marshall's transfer to, 69–70
1st Infantry Division, U.S., 52, 55, 57–59, 455
  casualties of, 59, 62–63, 64–65, 67–68, 78
  German attacks on, 58, 61–62
  Marshall's command of, 124
  Marshall's departure from, 66–67
  in Meuse-Argonne offensive, 78
  Picardy defended by, 61–62
  and recapture of Sedan, 81
  on St. Mihiel front, 60–61
1st Marine Division, U.S., 204–5, 326, 343, 376,
  691
1st United States Army Group, 453, 458
Fish, Hamilton, 204, 621
504th Regimental Combat Team, U.S., 404
509th Composite Group, U.S., 547
Flanders' field, Battle of, 50
Flying Tigers, 390
Flynn, John T., 559
Foch, Ferdinand, 65–67, 338, 599
  attempt to relieve Pershing by, 78–79
  counterattacks planned by, 68
  Meuse-Argonne offensive and, 70, 73–74, 76
  Pershing's conflicts with, 68–69, 78–79
  and recapture of Sedan, 80
  St. Mihiel offensive and, 68–69
  truce negotiations and, 82–83
Fonseca, Lieutenant, 652–53
Foreign Affairs, 618
Foreign Broadcast Intelligence Service, 547
Foreign Legion, French, 56
Foreign Military Assistance Act, 671, 677
Foreign Office, British, 351, 463
Formosa, 694
  Chiang's flight to, 667, 673–76
  King's call for invasion of, 475
  MacArthur on, 684–85
  Nimitz's call for invasion of, 470
  see also China, Republic of; Kuomintang
Forrestal, James, 481, 528, 555, 594, 618, 683
  budget increase requests of, 646–47
  on control of atomic weapons, 648
  Czech crisis and, 625
  Marshall's retirement and, 669
  NATO and, 664–65
  on partition of Palestine, 657, 659
  resignation of, 670
  suicide of, 670
Fort Benning Infantry School, Marshall as assis-
  tant commandant at, 104–8, 110–11
Fort Clark, 34
Fort Crockett, Marshall's posting at, 42
Fort Douglas, Marshall's posting at, 47
Fort Leavenworth:
  Command and General Staff School at, 151
  Infantry and Cavalry School at, 35–39
  Marshall's instructorship at, 38
Fort Logan Roots, Marshall's posting at, 41–42

Fort McKinley:
  Marshall's posting at, 42–45
  Officers' Club at, 43
Fort Moultrie, Marshall's command at, 115–16
Fort Myer, 30, 38, 89
Fort Necessity, 18
Fort Reno, Marshall's posting at, 34–36
Fort Screven, Marshall's command at, 111, 113–15
Fort Snelling, Marshall's posting at, 42
Fortune, 146, 632
42nd Infantry Division, U.S., 64, 81
XLVI Panzer Corps, German, 191
Foulois, Benjamin D., 38, 64
442nd Infantry Regiment, U.S., 514
IV Corps, U.S., 130
Fourth Field Army, Chinese Communist, 696
4th Infantry Regiment, U.S., 41–43, 455
4th Marine Regiment, U.S., 230
France, 47
  Allied invasion of, *see* OVERLORD
  bankruptcy of, 610–11
  Berlin crisis and, 646
  British distrust of, 65–66
  German invasion of, 155–57, 159, 165
  and German invasion of Poland, 143, 145
  and German occupation and partition, 420
  on German peace treaty, 598
  Hitler's territorial demands and, 128–29, 136
  Indochinese war of, 627
  Marshall Plan and, 614–15, 617
  Marshall's posting in, 52–85
  Pershing's conflicts with commanders of, 54–55, 58–59
  prisoners captured by, 56
  rehabilitation of, 505
  unified Allied command and, 65–66
  U.S. sales of munitions to, 146, 153, 161, 165
  war damages in, 599
  World War I casualties of, 50, 53, 56
France, Vichy:
  anti-Semitic decrees of, 351
  TORCH and, 340, 344–49
Franco, Francisco, 123
Franco-Prussian War, 66
Frankfurter, Felix, 160–61, 526
Franklin, Benjamin, 21
Fredendall, Lloyd R., 344
Frederick II (the Great), King of Prussia, 542
Frederika, Queen of Greece, 730, 732
Freeman, 710
Freeman, Sir Wilfrid, 211
French, Edward, 256–57
Frick, Henry Clay, 21
Friedensturm, 67
Friedman, William F., 220, 248, 251
Fritchey, Clayton, 723
Fuchida, Mitsuo, 258
Fuchikami, Tadao, 257
Fuchs, Klaus, 676

Gavin, James, 456
Genda, Minoru, 219, 226–27, 245
"General Marshall Trials, The," 651
General Service and Staff College, 36
Geneva Convention, 535
George, C. J., 652, 664–65, 671, 732, 735
George VI, King of England, 729
Germany, Imperial:
  attacks on 1st Infantry Division by, 58, 61–62

Belleau Wood and Château-Thierry attacks of, 63
  casualties of, 66
  collapse of, 82
  in general retreat, 80
  Meuse-Argonne offensive and, 75–78
  on St. Mihiel front, 60–61
  St. Mihiel offensive and, 72–73
  spring offensives of, 65–67
  U-boat threat of, 47–48
  U.S. declaration of war against, 48, 51
Germany, Nazi, 5, 7, 187
  in alliance with Japan and Italy, 220–21, 238, 259
  Allied invasion of, 516–17, 519–21, 525, 529
  Allied morale bombings of, 503
  Ardennes offensive of, 491–92, 499–501, 508–9
  Battle of the North Atlantic and, 375–76
  bomber campaign against, 364
  casualties of, 198
  Eisenhower's plan to end war with, 500–501, 519–22, 525, 529–30
  France invaded by, 155–57, 159, 165
  Norway and Denmark invaded by, 151
  occupation and partition of, 420–21
  Poland invaded by, 143, 145–47, 149
  reaction to OVERLORD of, 458–60
  rearmament of, 123
  Sicilian invasion and, 404–6
  southern redoubt of, 520–21
  Soviet non-aggression pact with, 143
  Soviet offensive against, 352, 402–3, 509–10
  Soviet offensive of, 197–99, 316, 320
  surrender of, 522–23, 530–33
  SYMBOL on, 359–60, 362–64, 367–68
  TORCH and, 337–39, 346, 348, 351–52
  TRIDENT on, 385, 387–88, 394, 396–97
Germany, Occupied:
  bankruptcy of, 599–600, 611, 617
  currency reform in, 642–43, 647
  economic organization of, 602–3
  form of government for, 603
  London Foreign Ministers' Conference on, 639, 641
  Marshall Plan and, 614–15, 617, 619
  Moscow Foreign Ministers' Conference on, 598, 601–6
  peace treaty with, 598, 612, 639, 642, 663
  reparations of, 603, 639, 641–42
  reunification of, 639, 641
  unifying French, British, and U.S. zones of, 642, 644, 647, 649
  war damages in, 599
Gerow, Leonard "Gee," 255, 299, 559
  Pearl Harbor attack and, 481
  Philippine alerts and, 256
  U.S.-Japanese negotiations and, 249–50
  warning to MacArthur drafted by, 242–44
Gibbs, William, 607
Giraud, Henri Honoré, 345–48, 352, 367
Goebbels, Joseph, 644
Goering, Hermann, 164
Good Earth, The (Buck), 234
Goulden, Joseph, 708
Grand Rapids *Herald*, 609
Grant, Ulysses S., 92, 464, 555, 590
Grant, Walter S., 67, 71, 73
Great Britain, 4, 47, 52–54
  anticipated invasion of, 157

Great Britain (continued)
  bankruptcy of, 610
  Battle of the North Atlantic and, 375–76
  Berlin crisis and, 646
  casualties of, 50, 56, 61, 65–66, 311
  command responsibilities of, 300
  French distrust of, 65–66
  German bankruptcy and, 599–600
  and German invasion of Poland, 143, 145
  and German occupation and partition, 420–21
  on German peace treaty, 598
  Greek civil war and, 594
  Hitler's territorial demands and, 128–29
  India and, 628
  JCS postwar projections on, 476–77
  Korean War and, 699–701, 706
  Lend-Lease aid to, 182–85, 191–92, 198, 233,
    262
  and Marshall's biennial reports on state of
    Army, 204
  Marshall's posting of, 87
  merchant losses of, 213
  Meuse-Argonne offensive and, 76
  OVERLORD and, 7
  Pacific theater participation of, 472–74, 542–
    44
  Palestine Mandate of, 627, 655, 657, 661
  Pershing's conflicts with commanders of, 54–
    55
  scientific research and intelligence data
    exchanged with, 191
  Tobruk surrender of, 323–24
  TORCH and, 337–41, 344–46, 348, 351
  Turkish aid and, 594
  unified staff command with, 65–66, 272–74
  U.S. meetings on joint operations with, 187–
    91
  U.S. sales of munitions to, 146, 153, 155–56,
    158–61, 164–65, 172–73
  World War I casualties of, 50, 56, 61
Great Depression, 113, 117, 176, 187, 526
Greater East Asia Co-Prosperity Sphere, 219,
  222, 226, 534
Greece:
  Communist-led civil war in, 594–95, 627, 635,
    649, 665–66, 719
  fall of, 191
  Italian invasion repelled by, 180
  U.S. aid to, 594–96, 608, 629
Grew, Joseph, 222, 236, 246
Grey, Sir Edward, 45
Gromyko, Andre, 452
Groves, Leslie R., 315, 677
  atomic bomb and, 537–39, 542, 544, 547–48
Gruin, Frederick, 572
Grunert, George, 478, 556
Guadalcanal, Battle of, 343–44, 376–79
Guam:
  Allied invasion of, 461
  Marshall on Japanese threat to, 242
Guderian, Heinz, 155–56
Guingand, Francis de, 494
Gulf of Siam, Japanese threat in, 254
Gunichi, Mikawa, 343
Gunther, John, 471
GYMNAST, 276, 282, 284, 311, 322, 333

Haakon VII, King of Norway, 730
Hagood, Johnson, 44, 47, 118
Haig, Douglas, 61, 66, 67

Haile Selassie, 124
Hale, Robert, 674
Halifax, Lord, 450, 536, 555, 589, 639–40
Halsey, William "Bull," 377, 379, 474–75, 490,
  535
Handy, Thomas, 483, 485
Handy, T. T., 345
Hannegan, Robert, 575
Harbord, James, 93, 95
Harding, E. Forrest, 106, 376
Harding, Warren G., 92–93, 734
Harriman, Averell, 211, 414, 497–98, 602, 616,
  630, 685, 687
  ARGONAUT and, 507, 511
  Bogotá Inter-American Conference and, 652
  Korean War and, 690, 692
  Marshall Plan and, 615, 620
  on sacking MacArthur, 709–11
Harriman, Kathleen, 507
Harvard University:
  Marshall honored by, 607–8, 612
  Marshall's speech at, 608, 612–14
Hassett, William D., 458
Hay, John, 26
Hayden, Carl, 153
Headmasters Association, 94
Hearst, William Randolph, 116
Heffner, William, 726, 732, 735
Henderson, Loy, 656–57
Henderson, Peter, 22
Henderson & Company, 22
Herron, Charles D., 120, 223
Hertling, Georg von, 68
Hess, Rudolf, 399
Hill 609, 383
Hines, John, 89, 95
  Marshall's China command and, 99–100
Hirohito, Emperor of Japan, 550, 554
Hiroshima, atomic bomb dropped on, 547–48
Hiss, Alger, 676
Hitler, Adolf, 7, 79, 116, 123, 143, 157, 160, 165,
  204, 215, 247, 267, 505, 543, 554
  Ardennes assault and, 492
  Darlan's opposition to, 348
  death of, 530
  Marshall's mobilization plan and, 155
  military budget of, 136
  in negotiation with Japan, 225–26
  Operation Barbarossa of, 197–98
  Operation Sealion of, 180
  OVERLORD and, 458, 460
  Pearl Harbor attack and, 259
  Pétain's collaboration with, 280
  Sicilian invasion and, 365
  territorial demands of, 128–29, 136–37
  U.S. Air Corps expansion and, 131
Hobart, Alice Tisdale, 234
Hodges, Courtney, 45, 483, 518, 520
Hoffman, Paul G., 723
Hollis, Sir Leslie, 311
Holmes, Oliver Wendell, 669
Holocaust, 656, 659
Homma, Masaharu, 694
Hoover, Herbert, 112–13, 160, 625, 714
Hopkins, Harry, 3–4, 131, 305, 450, 524
  and appointing OVERLORD commander,
    435, 436
  ARCADIA and, 269, 274
  and Army promotion and retirement reform,
    175

Atlantic Conference, 211, 215
background of, 133
BOLERO and, 329
on Chennault's "cheap" campaign, 391
death of, 729
Europe-first strategy and, 307
and German offensive against Soviet Union, 199
illnesses of, 148–49, 153, 448–49, 471
Lend-Lease and, 184
Marshall's balanced-force budget and, 134–35
and Marshall's biennial reports on state of Army, 413
Marshall's chief of staff appointment and, 139, 144
Marshall's friendship with, 7, 12, 135
MODICUM and, 307–9, 311–12
need for preparedness stressed by, 135–36
OVERLORD and, 9, 12–13, 415–16
on Pacific military priorities, 299
Pearl Harbor attack and, 259
QUADRANT and, 411
Roosevelt-Molotov meetings and, 317–18
Roosevelt's relationship with, 133–34
SYMBOL and, 356, 365
TRIDENT and, 388
and U.S. aid to Britain, 164
U.S.-Japanese negotiations and, 251–52, 253n
Hopkins, Robert, 358
Hopkins, Stephen, 449
House, Edward, 239n
House of Representatives, U.S., 10, 153
    Appropriations Committee of, 151, 626, 630, 684
    Foreign Affairs Committee of, 620, 622
    Military Affairs Committee of, 29, 170, 174, 209–10, 416
    Rules Committee of, 608
    Ways and Means Committee of, 650
    see also Congress, U.S.
Howard, Roy, 685
Howell, Fannie, 18
Hudson, Mr. and Mrs. Tom, 107
Huerta, Victoriano, 46
Hughes, Charles Evans, 179
Hughes, John, 99
Hugo, Jean, 55
Hull, Cordell, 161, 173, 187, 221, 242, 497, 505, 591
    Darlan deal and, 350
    U.S.-Japanese negotiations and, 236–38, 241–43, 245–46, 250–55
    on U.S. readiness for Japanese attack, 241
Humelsine, Carlisle, 589–90
Hurley, Patrick J., 284, 300, 423, 487, 513, 561
    on fall of Chiang, 674
    Marshall's China mission and, 555
Huston, Walter, 655
hydrogen bomb, 678

Import-Export Bank, 570
India, Great Britain and, 628
Indochina:
    ARGONAUT on, 507, 513
    French war in, 627
    Japanese offensive in, 224–26, 229
    U.S.-Japanese negotiations on, 238, 240–41, 243, 246, 250–52
Industrial Revolution, 18

Infantry and Cavalry School, 35–39
    Marshall's enrollment at, 36–39
Infantry Journal, 92, 96
Interim Committee, 538–39
Interior Department, U.S., 114
International News Service, 415–16
Inverchapel, Lord, 593–94
Ironsides, Sir Edmund, 157
Ismay, Hastings "Pug," 309, 311, 322, 324–25, 425, 504
    atomic bomb and, 545
    GYMNAST and, 325
    Malta Conference and, 503
    TRIDENT and, 388
Israel, 663
    independence declared by, 661
    UN peace proposal for, 661–62
    U.S. recognition of, 658–61
Italy, 7
    in alliance with Germany and Japan, 220–21, 238, 259
    attempted invasion of Greece by, 180
    Ethiopia invaded by, 123–24, 129
    Marshall's inspection of U.S. troops in, 514–15
    rehabilitation of, 505
    Sicilian invasion and, 365, 404–6
    surrender of, 410, 413
    surrender of German forces in, 522–23
    SYMBOL on, 360, 362, 365, 368
    TORCH and, 339, 351
    TRIDENT on, 385–88, 397–98
Iwo Jima, 517
    casualties of, 534–35

Jackson, Robert H., 131
Jackson, Thomas "Stonewall," 24–25, 39, 44, 417, 660
JAEL, 458–59
James, D. Clayton, 713
Japan, 5, 160
    in alliance with Germany and Italy, 220–21, 238, 259
    atomic bomb and, 538–39, 542, 545–49
    Bali invaded by, 299
    Bataan assault of, 302
    Bay of Bengal offensive of, 309
    Borneo attacked by, 277
    breaking diplomatic code of, 220–21
    Burma campaign and, 392–93
    Chennault's "cheap" campaign against, 390–93, 397
    Chinese war with, 123–24, 136, 219–21, 234
    Churchill's declaration of war against, 267
    Corregidor shelled by, 302–2
    diplomatic initiatives by, 237–38
    Doolittle's bombing raid over, 312
    Dutch East Indies attacked by, 225, 277
    gas used against, 534–35.
    Indochina offensive of, 224–26, 229
    JCS on ending war with, 540–41
    Korea annexed by, 42
    Manchuria invaded by, 129
    Marshall's visit to, 45
    OCTAGON on, 472–74, 476
    offensives planned by, 203, 224–27
    peace treaty with, 663, 688
    Philippine aggression threatened by, 173, 236, 239, 242, 248–50
    Philippine-based bombers as threat to, 239–40

Japan (*continued*)
 Philippines attacked by, 261–62, 264–66, 277, 283–303, 320
 Philippines lost by, 525
 planned Allied invasion of, 495, 498, 504, 517, 528, 533–36, 539–40, 544
 Portuguese Timor invaded by, 299
 Potsdam ultimatum to, 547–49
 Solomon Islands campaign and, 327–28, 342–43, 376–77
 Soviet entry into war against, 498, 505, 507, 511–13, 528, 533, 540, 542, 546, 549–50
 Soviet neutrality treaty with, 226
 surrender of, 544–45, 547, 549–50, 554
 SYMBOL on, 359, 361–64, 367–68
 TRIDENT on, 385–86, 392–93, 397
 U.S. bombing of, 512, 533–34, 550
 U.S. embargoes against, 219, 221, 227, 229
 U.S. negotiations with, 236–47, 250–55, 481
 U.S. occupation of, 547, 693–95
 U.S. readiness for attack by, 241–43
 warnings about threat of, 225, 236, 240–44
Jarman, Pete, 623
Jeanne d'Arc, Saint, 54
Jenner, William E., 686, 712
Jewish Agency, 658
Jodl, Alfred August, 530
Johnson, Edwin C., 403
Johnson, Hiram, 137, 204, 206
Johnson, Louis, 126–27, 129–30, 132, 144, 148, 160–61, 670, 688
 balanced-force concept pressed by, 135
 and fall of Chiang, 675
 Korean War and, 679
 Marshall's chief of staff appointment and, 138
 Marshall's mobilization plan and, 154
 on NSC-68, 690
 resignation of, 685, 687
 Truman's dissatisfaction with, 683–85
Johnson, Lyndon, 716
Johnson, Thomas, 80
Joint Chiefs of Staff (JCS), 5, 326, 395, 469, 522, 655
 on aid to Chiang, 633, 636
 ANVIL and, 466
 appointment of supreme commander and, 419–20
 ARCADIA and, 275
 ARGONAUT and, 507, 511
 on atomic bomb, 538–39
 AVALANCHE and, 407
 and creation of Defense Department, 682–83
 Czech crisis and, 625
 in difficulties with MacArthur, 694–95, 702
 on ending war in Far East, 540–41
 EUREKA and, 418, 428
 on Formosa, 673–74
 on German occupation and partition, 421
 Japanese peace treaty and, 688
 Korean War and, 680, 691–92, 696–703, 707–8, 710–12, 715, 717–18, 720
 MacArthur's relief and, 708, 710–11
 Marshall's relationship with, 687
 Marshall's reorganization of, 279–80
 NATO and, 665
 NSC-68 and, 690
 OCTAGON and, 474–75
 OVERLORD and, 408, 446, 457, 460–62
 on partition of Palestine, 656–57

 on peace to come, 476–77
 second front issue and, 318
 SEXTANT and, 425, 427–28
 Solomon Islands campaign and, 328, 342, 344
 SYMBOL and, 358–59, 363
 TERMINAL and, 542
 on Tobruk defeat, 324
 TRIDENT and, 386–87
 Truman's respect for, 525
Jones, Joseph M., 595
Jouatte, Madame, 55, 485, 665
Judd, Walter H., 596, 632, 637, 674
Juin, Alphonse, 500
JUPITER, 311, 322

Kalgan, Nationalist drive to, 578–79
Karl I, Emperor of Austria, 77
Kasserine Pass, Battle of, 380–81
Kee, John, 622
Keefe, Frank, 557–59
Keehn, Roy D., 116–17, 130
Kennan, George F., 689
 on European economic crisis, 608–11
 and Greek and Turkish aid, 594
 Korean War and, 692
 Marshall Plan and, 610–13
 on partition of Palestine, 657
 on Soviet Union, 591–93, 618, 640
 "X" article of, 618–19
Kennedy, John F., 172, 674
Kennedy, Joseph, 145, 172
Kenney, George, 378
Kerensky, Alexander, 59
Kesselring, Albert, 445–46
Khudyakov, Sergei, 510
Kimbrough, Clifford, 655, 667
Kim Il Sung, 680, 698
Kimmel, Husband E., 249
 Japanese embargoes and, 227
 Pearl Harbor alerts issued to, 245, 257
 Pearl Harbor attack and, 477–79, 559
 Pearl Harbor defenses and, 224
 relief of, 266
King, Campbell, 59, 110–11
King, Edward P., 302
King, Ernest, 5, 10–11, 305, 326, 335–36, 395, 398, 418, 458–59, 469, 517, 682, 694, 729
 appointment of supreme commander and, 419
 ARCADIA and, 273
 ARGONAUT and, 507
 Atlantic Conference and, 210, 212–13, 215–16
 Battle of the North Atlantic and, 375
 BOLERO and, 329
 COMINCH appointment of, 266
 on ending war in Far East, 540–41
 ETO conferences and, 332
 EUREKA and, 429
 Europe-first strategy and, 304, 307
 five-star rank of, 490–91
 and investigations of Pearl Harbor attack, 479
 MacArthur's conflicts with, 439–40
 Malta Conference and, 504–5
 and Marshall's reorganization of JCS, 279–80
 Nimitz and, 470
 OCTAGON and, 474–75
 OLYMPIC-CORONET and, 535–36
 OVERLORD and, 414, 446, 460–62
 Pacific theater interests of, 310

Philippine crisis and, 284
at Roosevelt's funeral, 526
second front issue and, 316
SEXTANT and, 424, 435–36
Solomon Islands campaign and, 327–28, 342–43, 377
SYMBOL and, 355–59, 361–64, 367–68
TORCH and, 334
TRIDENT and, 394, 396–98
KMT, *see* Kuomintang
Knowland, William, 685, 692
Knox, Frank, 148, 160–61, 163, 180, 187, 305, 559
    Pearl Harbor attack and, 259, 266
    on Pearl Harbor defenses, 222
    U.S.-Japanese negotiations and, 252, 254
    on U.S. readiness for Japanese attack, 241
Knox, Philander, 29
Knutson, Harold, 650
Kohlberg, Alfred, 632, 635
Kohler, Walter J., Jr., 728
Konoye, Fumimaro, Prince of Japan, 219, 221, 236–37
Koo, Wellington, 633
Korea, 663
    ARGONAUT on, 513
    Japanese annexation of, 42
    Marshall's visit to, 45
    post–World War II division of, 679–80
    reunification of, 695, 706
    U.S. vs. Soviet Union on, 628
Korea, People's Republic of (North), 680
Korea, Republic of (South), 680–81
Korean War, 679–81, 684, 689–721
    cease-fire negotiations in, 704, 707–8, 724–25
    Chinese entrance into, 701–2
    CHROMITE in, 691–92
    MacArthur's air plan in, 698–701
    stalemate in, 706–7, 719, 724
    Wake Island meeting during, 696–97
Kramer, Alwin D., 251–53
Krock, Arthur, 703
Krueger, Walter, 137
Kuomintang (KMT), 97–98, 101, 560–61, 596, 628, 632–37
    lobbying campaign for, 632
    Marshall's China mission and, 562–68, 570–84
    U.S. aid for, 635–37, 667, 671
    Wedemeyer's China mission and, 633–34
    see also China, Republic of; Formosa
Kurusu, Saburo, 238–40, 243
Kuter, Laurence, 165, 518

Labor Department, U.S., 114
LaGuardia, Fiorello, 591
Landon, Alfred, 160
Latin America, Marshall Plan for, 650–51
Lattre de Tassigny, Jean de, 484
Lawrence, David O., 587, 692
Lawrence, Ernest O., 539
League of Nations, 85–86, 116, 129
Leahy, William D., 8, 11, 409, 655
    appointment of supreme commander and, 419
    ARGONAUT and, 510
    background of, 279–80
    on ending war in Far East, 540–41
    EUREKA and, 430, 434
    five-star rank of, 490–91

Japanese surrender and, 549
MacArthur's conflicts with, 439
Malta Conference and, 506
OVERLORD and, 414
on Poland, 528
SEXTANT and, 427, 435
Lee, Robert E., 21, 25, 660
Leigh-Mallory, Sir Trafford, 454
Lejeune, John A., 69
LeMay, Curtis E., 547
Lend-Lease, 271, 282, 722
    to China, 560, 570, 575, 578, 581–82, 636
    Congress and, 182–83, 185, 199–200
    to Great Britain, 182–85, 191–92, 198, 233, 262
    to Soviet Union, 198–200, 312, 316–18, 320, 498, 513
Lend-Lease Act, 204
Leyte Gulf, Battle of, 475, 534–35
Liberty Lobby, 611
Lieberman, Doris, 440
Liebling, A. J., 158
Life, 10, 234, 632
Liggett, Hunter, 45, 79, 81–82, 85
Lilienthal, David, 591
Lincoln, Abraham, 709, 734
Lindbergh, Charles A., 146, 164–65, 191
Lindemann, F. A., 211
Lindley, Ernest K., 233
Lindsay, Catherine, 21
Lindsay, Judge, 21
Lippmann, Walter, 113–14, 124, 233, 350, 650
Lloyd George, David, 85
Lockard, Joseph L., 257
London:
    1919 Victory Parade in, 87
    war damages in, 599
London Foreign Ministers' Conference, 628–29, 638–42, 644
    on Austrian peace treaty, 640–41
    on Occupied Germany, 639, 641
Long, Huey, 120n
"long telegram," 592–93
Los Angeles Times, 578
Lost Battalion, 77–78
Lovett, Adele Quartly, 616, 630
Lovett, Robert, 161–62, 531, 590, 627, 630, 654n, 668, 687–88, 725, 732, 735
    Acheson replaced by, 616–17, 631
    background of, 616
    in departure from State Department, 669
    on KMT aid, 636
    Korean War and, 698–701, 708
    London Foreign Ministers' Conference and, 641
    on MacArthur's relief, 708
    Marshall Plan and, 617–18, 622, 625
    Marshall replaced by, 726
    Marshall respected by, 687
    Marshall's relationship with, 631–32
    NATO and, 663–64
    on partition of Palestine, 657, 659–61
    Vinson's Soviet mission and, 664
Lucas, John P., 445–46
Lucas, Scott, 686
Luce, Clare Boothe, 514
Luce, Henry Robinson, 234, 488, 576–77, 632
Ludendorff, Erich, 61, 63, 66–68, 75, 77, 79,
157

Lusitania, sinking of, 47
Luxembourg, fall of, 153–54
Luzon, capture of, 475

MacArthur, Arthur, 301
MacArthur, Douglas, 5–6, 13, 64, 88, 137–38,
   146, 221, 264, 333, 336, 369–70, 374, 398,
   416, 479, 490, 508, 518, 534
  air plan of, 698–701
  and appointing OVERLORD commander, 437
  Battle of Leyte Gulf and, 475
  CCC and, 116
  Central Pacific offensive and, 402
  congressional address of, 713–14
  congressional allies of, 297, 379, 395, 698, 700,
   709, 712, 714
  congressional testimony of, 715–18, 725
  contradictory nature of, 693–94
  in defense of Philippines, 236, 261–62, 265,
   284–303
  domestic rebellions suppressed by, 112–13
  in evacuation from Philippines, 299–303
  on Formosa, 684–85
  Japanese occupation and, 547
  Korean War and, 679–81, 691–705, 707–9,
   713–21, 725
  Marshall's China mission and, 563
  Marshall's meetings with, 438–40
  Marshall's promotion to brigadier general and,
   119
  Marshall's relationship with, 39, 230, 312
  Marshall's 33rd Division command and, 117
  Medal of Honor awarded to, 298
  Navy's conflicts with, 439–40
  OLYMPIC-CORONET and, 535–36, 539–40
  overconfidence of, 231–32
  Pacific theater interests of, 310
  paranoia ascribed to, 81
  Philippine retreat of, 277, 284–98
  Philippines retaken by, 459, 470, 486, 525
  presidential ambitions of, 10
  press and, 703, 710, 712–13, 715, 717
  RAINBOW-5 criticized by, 231–32
  recalled to active duty, 227–31
  recapture of Philippines urged by, 305, 312
  and recapture of Sedan, 81
  reinforcements sought by, 305, 312–13
  reputation of, 694
  Roosevelt's conflicts with, 119*n*–20*n*
  Roosevelt's Hawaiian visit and, 469–70
  sacking of, 708–13, 716, 722
  self-confidence of, 694
  Solomon Islands campaign and, 326–27, 342–
   44, 376–79
  Stimson's conflicts with, 230
  supreme Pacific theater command given to,
   542
  transfered to Australia, 300–301
  Truman policy criticized by, 684, 716
  Truman's conflicts with, 703, 708–9
  USAFFE command given to, 229
  Wake Island meeting and, 696
  warning on imminent Japanese attack issued
   to, 242–45, 257, 261
MacArthur, Jean, 301
McAuliffe, Anthony, 194–95
McCarthy, Frank, 5, 438, 441, 450, 524, 548,
  556, 587, 735
McCarthy, Joseph, 700

Eisenhower on, 723–24, 728–9
  Korean War and, 722
  on MacArthur's relief, 712, 722
  Marshall attacked by, 721–25, 728–29
  on Marshall's Defense Department nomina-
   tion, 686
  Red-baiting by, 676–77
McClellan, George B., 709
McClintock, Robert, 659
McCloy, John J., 161, 177, 205
  atomic bomb and, 538, 543
McCormick, Robert W., 116–17, 175, 620, 685
McCoy, Frances, 117
McCoy, Frank R., 117, 120, 176, 631
McKinley, William, 23, 29
McMahon, Brien, 716–17
Macmillan, Harold:
  Darlan deal and, 349
  SYMBOL and, 357, 361–62, 368
McNair, Lesley J., 151
  in Army reorganization, 278–79
McNarney, Joseph T., 195, 331, 599
  in War Department management, 278–79
Madero, Francisco, 40
MAGIC, 203, 220–21, 237, 242, 245, 248, 253*n*,
  254, 259, 321, 558–59
  Pearl Harbor attack and, 478–79, 481
  secrecy of, 256, 478–81, 556
Malay Peninsula, planned Japanese offensive on,
  225
Malta Conference, 497–98, 501–6
  on Communist influence in postwar Europe,
   505–6
  on Eisenhower's war-ending plan, 501–2
  on necessity for deputy commander for Eisen-
   hower, 502–3, 506
  on Southeast Asian and Pacific theaters, 504
Manchester, William, 39, 81
Manchuria:
  Communist domination of, 632
  Japanese invasion of, 129
  Marshall's visit to, 45
  Nationalists vs. Communists in, 565, 567–68,
   571–74, 578, 580
  Wedemeyer's China mission and, 634–35
Manhattan Project, 537, 676–78
  two bombs conceived by, 541–42
  see also atomic bomb
Manila, Marshall's posting in, 33
Manley, Chesly, 249
Mansfield, Mike, 623
Mansfield, Richard, 109
Mao Tse-tung, 676
  Chiang's negotiations with, 560–61
  Korean War and, 708
  Marshall's China mission and, 562, 565–67,
   569, 573, 575–76
  military successes of, 632, 637
March, Peyton, 90–93
Marianas campaign, 397
Marianas Turkey Shoot, 469
Marine Corps, U.S.:
  drafting by, 442
  KMT supported by, 577
  press relations of, 517
  see also specific units
MARKET-GARDEN, 482–83
Marne, Battle of the, 49, 63, 68
Marne, Second Battle of the, 67–68

Marshall, C. B., 693
Marshall, Elizabeth Carter Coles "Lily" (first
    wife), 35, 40, 45, 51–52, 87–88, 108, 111,
    122
  background of, 28
  death of, 103–4, 106
  European tour of, 39–40
  heart condition of, 90, 102
  honeymoon of, 30
  hospitalization of, 102–3
  Marshall's China command and, 95–97, 99,
    102
  Marshall's courtship and winning of, 28–30
  Marshall's devotion to, 89
  Marshall's domestic life with, 88–89
  Marshall's faithfulness to, 33
  Marshall's Fort Leavenworth posting and, 37–
    39
  Marshall's Fort Reno posting and, 34
  Marshall's Philippine postings and, 32–33, 42
  Marshall's 33rd Division command and, 117
Marshall, George Catlett, Jr.:
  aging of, 563, 572
  aloofness of, 6–7, 25–27, 93, 270, 479, 481,
    675
  ambition of, 36–37, 40, 45–46, 270, 442, 586
  austere manner of, 5
  celebrity of, 402
  competitiveness of, 37
  confidence of, 5, 27
  courteousness of, 89
  curiosity of, 60
  death of, 734
  decisiveness of, 277
  depressions of, 117–18
  diplomacy of, 8–9
  education of, 20–21, 23–28
  finances of, 21, 24, 86, 669, 726
  fishing enjoyed by, 121, 124
  frankness of, 170, 186, 207, 509, 601, 604–5,
    670
  funeral of, 734–35
  gossip disliked by, 88–89
  global vision of, 5–6
  heritage of, 17–18, 20
  horseback riding enjoyed by, 33, 45, 87, 99–
    100, 105, 111, 118, 122, 202, 254, 270
  hunting enjoyed by, 45, 109, 111, 118, 727
  idealism of, 660
  illnesses and injuries of, 25–26, 44–45, 62–64,
    74, 87, 107, 121–22, 132–33, 232, 655,
    667–69, 710, 725, 730–33
  insight of, 6
  leadership of, 6–7, 10, 32
  loneliness of, 105, 107
  matter-of-fact manner of, 310
  medals and honors received by, 84, 166, 442,
    452, 555, 593, 607–8, 621, 643, 669, 726,
    729–31
  memoirs of, 95
  memory of, 194–95
  musical talent of, 18
  nervous tic of, 85, 107
  nicknames of, 17–18, 74, 727
  organizational skills of, 8
  paternalism of, 121
  personal heroes of, 21, 39
  physical appearance of, 5, 17–18, 25–26, 32,
    87, 100, 108, 588, 671–72

  poetry written by, 90
  political influence of, 402, 414
  popularity of, 620–21
  pragmatism of, 100, 660
  prestige of, 9–10, 689
  public confidence in, 10
  reading interests of, 671, 726
  reputation of, 40, 43–44, 110, 170, 401, 403,
    413, 416, 423, 435, 477, 481, 559, 651,
    674, 685, 700, 710
  respect commanded by, 402
  self-confidence of, 5, 27, 481
  self-control of, 277–78
  selflessness of, 270, 593, 724
  self-satisfaction of, 554
  sense of duty of, 593
  sense of humor of, 731–32
  sports enjoyed by, 27, 45, 100, 111, 122, 178–
    79, 727
  stolidity of, 438
  success drive of, 24, 26
  tactfulness of, 651
  temper of, 5–6, 57, 235, 305, 395–96, 442–43,
    463
  writing style of, 203
Marshall, George Catlett, Sr. (father), 35
  death of, 39
  genealogy of, 17, 20–21
  Marshall's childhood and, 17–22
  Marshall's education and, 23
  Marshall's officer's commission and, 29
Marshall, John, 17
Marshall, Katherine Boyce Tupper Brown (sec-
    ond wife), 8, 111, 127, 184, 277–78, 398,
    413, 443, 526, 651
  background of, 108–9
  on Dill's death, 489
  Dodona Manor purchased by, 313–14
  illnesses of, 654, 667, 669, 725, 730, 733
  injuries of, 240, 253n
  Marshall's China mission and, 555–56, 570–
    75, 583
  Marshall's courtship of, 109
  Marshall's 1st Division command and, 124
  Marshall's first meeting with, 107–8
  Marshall's Fort Moultrie command and, 115–
    16
  Marshall's Fort Screven posting and, 113–14
  at Marshall's funeral, 735
  Marshall's leisure time with, 149–50, 178–79,
    240, 314, 377–78, 553, 555, 606, 630, 662,
    665–66, 675, 682
  Marshall's promotion to brigadier general and,
    120–21
  Marshall's retirement and, 553, 671–72, 727–
    30, 732
  Marshall's State Department appointment and,
    588
  Marshall's Vancouver Barracks command and,
    120–21
  OVERLORD and, 454
  reminiscences of, *see Together*
  on son's death, 450
  TORCH and, 347
  wedding of, 109–10
Marshall, Laura Emily Bradford (mother), 35
  Marshall's childhood and, 19–21, 24
  Marshall's education and, 24
Marshall, Marie (sister), 19, 106

7

Marshall, Stuart (brother), 19, 21, 23–24, 27, 29, 37
Marshall Plan, 610–15, 617–26, 629, 637–38, 642, 645, 657, 663, 723, 729–30
  announcement of, 612–14
  European reaction to, 614–15
  for Latin America, 650–51
  lobbying campaign for, 620, 625
  Marshall's congressional testimony on, 621–23
  Paris meeting on, 619
Martha, Princess of Norway, 182
Martin, Frederick L., 222–23
Martin, Joseph W., 629
  draft extension and, 208
  Korean War and, 709, 720
  on MacArthur's relief, 712
Marwitz, General von der, 77
Marxism, 593
Masaryk, Jan, death of, 625
Massachusetts State Militia, Marshall's training of, 40
Mast, Charles, 345–47
Matsuoka, Yosuke, 220, 222, 225–26
Max, Prince of Baden, 79
Maxwell Field, 130–31
May, Andrew J., 174
Melby, John, Marshall's China mission and, 577, 581
Memoirs of My Service in the World War (Marshall), 95
Metz, Patton in, 482–83, 486
Meuse-Argonne offensive, 70–78
  casualties of, 76–78
  deployment of troops for, 71–75
Miall, Leonard, 614
Midway, Battle of, 321
Mikolajczyk, Stanislaw, 458
Miles, Sherman, 245
  U.S.-Japanese negotiations and, 249–50, 253–56
Miller, Luther, 734
Mills, Ogden, 86
Mitchell, Billy, 711
MODICUM (London mission), 307–13
Moley, Raymond, 114
Molotov, Vyacheslav M., 549
  ARGONAUT and, 507, 512
  London Foreign Ministers' Conference and, 640–42
  Marshall Plan and, 614–15
  Moscow Foreign Ministers' Conference and, 601–5
  on Poland, 527–29
  Roosevelt's meetings with, 316–19
Monroe Doctrine, 188
Monte Cassino, bombing of, 449
Monfauçon heights, battle for, 75–76
Montgomery, Bernard Law, 369–70, 410, 456–57, 496, 501, 504, 509, 729
  Battle of the Bulge and, 492–95
  Eisenhower criticized by, 484, 492, 500
  MARKET-GARDEN and, 482–83
  OVERLORD and, 444
  press on, 493–95, 518
  Rhine offensive and, 486, 513, 516
  Sicilian invasion and, 400, 404–5
  TORCH and, 346
  Tunisian campaign and, 379–80, 382
  war-ending plan and, 502, 519–21
Moore, Richard C., 193

Moran, Lord, 424, 432, 471
Morgan, Sir Frederick, 412, 416–17, 432, 444
Morgan, J. P., 675
J. P. Morgan and Company, 51, 86
Morgenthau, Henry, 131, 139, 148, 617
  background of, 153
  British aid requests and, 158
  Marshall's mobilization plan and, 154–55
  Roosevelt's relationship with, 153
Morrison, John, 36
Morrow, Dwight, 86
Moscow Foreign Ministers' Conference, 597, 600–606, 608
  on Occupied Germany, 598, 601–6
Moseley, George Van Horn, 118
Mothers for America, 210
Mountbatten, Lord Louis, 309–10, 332, 334, 461, 476–77, 504
  QUADRANT and, 412
  SEXTANT and, 424
  Southeast Asian command given to, 410
Munich crisis, 129
Murphy, Robert, 519, 734
  Berlin crisis and, 648
  Darlan deal and, 351
  Moscow Foreign Ministers' Conference and, 601, 606
  TORCH and, 345, 348, 350–51
Mussolini, Benito, 123, 137, 156, 406, 410, 422, 505

Nagasaki, atomic bomb dropped on, 549
Nagumo, Chuichi, 238
  Pearl Harbor attack of, 247, 250
Nason, Virginia, 6, 194
Nation, 234
National Cotton Council, 620
National Defense Act, 48
National Farm Institute, 620
National Geographic Society, 727
National Governors Convention, 479
National Guard:
  in maneuvers with Army, 40–41
  see also specific units
National Guard Association, 116
National Press Club, 680
National Security Act, 683, 686–87
National Security Council (NSC), 663, 689
  and fall of Chiang, 667–68
  Formosa and, 674
  Korean War and, 680, 692, 701
Navy, U.S., 166, 673
  in Battle of Midway, 321
  Central Pacific offensive of, 379
  drafting by, 442
  OP-20-G of, 220
  readiness of, 192
  in Solomon Islands campaign, 326–27, 342–44, 377
Navy Department, U.S., 184, 279
  Johnson's conflicts with, 683
  MacArthur's conflicts with, 439–40
  Pearl Harbor attack investigated by, 478, 481, 556–57, 559
  on Pearl Harbor defenses, 222–23
  in planning joint operations with British, 188–90
  war strategy planning by, 200–202
Netherlands, fall of, 153–54

Neutrality Act, 123–24, 135, 145–46, 159
  congressional repeal of, 147–48
New Deal, 13, 526
New Orleans Times-Picayune, 25, 631
New Republic, 85, 416, 645
News-Chronicle (London), 668
Newsweek, 9–10
New York Mirror, 138
New York State Relief Administration, 134
New York Sun, 414
New York Times, 147, 172, 204, 413, 488, 533,
  587, 621–22, 671, 703, 732
New York Times Magazine, 485
New York Tribune, 93
New York World, 41
Nichols, Edward W., 40, 42, 46, 51
Nicholson, Leonard Kimball "Nick," 25–27, 631
Nicolson, Harold, 604
Niebuhr, Reinhold, 116
Niles, David K., 659
Nimitz, Chester, 459, 474–75, 490, 694
  Central Pacific offensive and, 402, 440
  invasion of Formosa promoted by, 470
  OLYMPIC-CORONET and, 535
  Roosevelt's Hawaiian visit and, 469–70
  Solomon Islands campaign and, 326, 342,
    377–78
XIX Corps, French, 345
94th Infantry Division, U.S., 514
92nd Infantry Division, U.S., 168
9th Armored Division, U.S., 516
Ninth Army, U.S., 494, 509, 520, 525
Ninth International Conference of American
  States, 651–54
Nitze, Paul, 689–90, 692
Nixon, Richard, 700, 712
Nobel Peace Prize, 729–31
Nomura, Kichisaburo, 221–22
  in negotiations with U.S., 237–40, 243, 245,
    250–51, 253–54
Non-Partisan Committee for Peace Through
  Revision of the Neutrality Act, 146
Normandy invasion, *see* OVERLORD
North Atlantic, Battle of the, 375–76
  TRIDENT on, 397–98
North Atlantic Treaty Organization (NATO),
  642, 663–65, 666, 677, 689, 697, 703
  Senate debate on, 663, 670–71
Norway, German invasion of, 151
NSC-81, 692–93
NSC-68, 689–90
Nye, Gerald P., 171

Observer (London), 733
O'Connor, Basil, 672
OCTAGON (Quebec Conference), 468–69,
  471–76, 482
  on British participation in Pacific War, 472–74
Office of Strategic Services (OSS), 522, 597
Office of War Mobilization, 442, 537
Officers Reserve Corps, U.S., 47
Oil for the Lamps of China (Hobart), 234
Okinawa:
  assault on, 504, 525, 534–35
  casualties of, 535
O'Laughlin, John Callan, 119, 414
Oliphant, Herman, 131
OLYMPIC, 498, 535–36, 539–40
OMAHA Beach, 452, 454–55, 460, 466
O'Mahoney, Joseph, 169

101st Airborne Division, U.S., 451, 461, 492–93
129th Field Artillery Regiment, U.S., 529
Oppenheimer, J. Robert, 539, 607, 678
Oran, Allied assault on, 341
Organization of American States, 654
Oshina, Baron, 247
Ostrava, Hitler's claims on, 128
Ouida, 56
Oumansky, Constantine A., 198
Outerbridge, William W., 257
Outline of History (Wells), 307
OVERLORD, 5, 7–8, 406–10, 421–22, 438, 443,
  451–67
  appointing commander of, 8–13, 408–9, 414–
    17, 419–20, 432, 435, 436–37
  bombing component of, 453–54
  casualties of, 453–55
  deception schemes for, 458–60
  Dieppe raid vs., 431–32
  Eisenhower's commanders for, 443–44
  Eisenhower's reports on, 454–56, 466
  EUREKA on, 428–35
  German reaction to, 458–60
  JCS tour of battlefields of, 460–62
  landing exercises for, 453
  launching of, 451–52
  Marshall's plan for, 455–56
  QUADRANT on, 408–11
  SEXTANT on, 425–28, 435–37
  SHINGLE and, 444–47
  troops committed to, 441, 446, 449
  U.S. landing beaches in, 452, 454–55, 460, 466

Pace, Frank, 696–97
Pacific Theater of Operations, 5, 13, 310
  British participation in, 472–74, 542–44
  MacArthur appointed supreme commander
    of, 542
  Malta Conference on, 504
  TERMINAL on, 542–44
Palestine, partition of, 627, 655–63
Palmer, John McAuley, 89, 91, 102, 631, 645
Panama, alerts issued to, 255, 257, 261
Pan American Airways, 672
Panikkar, K. M., 695
Papuan campaign, 376
Paris:
  fall of, 159
  Marshall's visits to, 598–99
  meeting on Marshall Plan in, 619
  1919 Victory Parade in, 86–87
  UN meeting in, 662–64, 666
Paris Peace Conference, 76, 85
Parker, Frank, 81
Pasco, H. Merrill, 524, 527, 531
Passchendaele, Battle of, 66
Patch, Andrew M., 472
Patterson, Cissy, 175
Patterson, Robert A., 161–62, 176–77, 205, 594,
  620, 680
Patton, George S., Jr., 6, 53–54, 144, 151, 176,
  305, 323, 369, 410, 502, 529, 545, 665
  Battle of the Bulge and, 492–93, 495
  controversies stirred by, 453–54
  in Metz, 482–83, 486
  OVERLORD and, 444, 453–54, 458
  promotion to four stars for, 501
  in Rhine offensive, 486, 516
  in St. Mihiel offensive, 72
  Sicilian invasion and, 384, 404–6

Patton, George S., Jr. (*continued*)
  SYMBOL and, 357
  TORCH and, 337, 340, 344, 346–47
  In Tunisian campaign, 381–82
Pawley, William Douglas, 654
Pearl Harbor:
  alerts issued to, 240–41, 244–45, 255–58
  Japanese submarine sightings near, 256–57
  reviews of defenses of, 222–24
Pearl Harbor attack, 5, 255–58
  as campaign issue, 479–80
  casualties of, 260
  consequences of, 259–62, 264–67
  investigations of, 260*n*, 266, 477–79, 481, 556–59, 570
  planning of, 218–19, 222, 226–27, 235, 245, 247
  Tokyo-Berlin exchange prior to, 247–48
Pearson, Drew, 444
Pecos River area, Marshall's mapping of, 34–35
Pegler, Westbrook, 403
Peiping-to-Mukden railroad, 96
Pendergast, Tom, 525
Pennsylvania National Guard, Marshall's training of, 38–39
Percival, Arthur, 299
Perón, Juan, 628
Perry, Glen, 414
Pershing, John J., 46, 50–51, 53–54, 64, 111, 115, 122, 124, 149, 152, 165, 196, 205, 228, 264, 403, 464, 570–71, 599, 631, 672, 690, 711, 727, 734
  on blacks in Army, 168
  in conflict with French and British commanders, 54–55, 58–59
  five-star rank and, 491
  Foch's attempted sacking of, 78–79
  Foch's conflicts with, 68–69, 78–79
  funeral of, 524, 655
  and Lily Marshall's illness and death, 102–3
  Ludendorff's offensives and, 61
  March's conflicts with, 90–92
  Marshall as aide to, 84–95
  Marshall's chief of staff appointment and, 128, 138–39, 144
  Marshall's China command and, 98–100
  Marshall's confrontations with, 56–57, 93, 132, 155
  Marshall's off-duty relationship with, 89–90, 95
  Marshall's posting at headquarters of, 66–85
  Marshall's promotion to brigadier general and, 118–20
  on Marshall's recommendations for promotions, 176
  Marshall's respect for, 88
  Marshall's second wedding and, 110
  memoirs of, 110
  Meuse-Argonne offensive and, 71–73, 75–78
  on need for standing Army, 91–92
  OVERLORD and, 414–15
  and recapture of Sedan, 80
  retirement of, 95
  St. Mihiel offensive and, 67–70, 73
  Siebert relieved by, 59
  and taking of Cantigny, 62
  unified Allied command and, 65
Pétain, Henri Philippe, 55, 61, 74, 157, 159
  Battle of the Marne and, 63, 68
  in collaboration with Hitler, 280

German spring offensives and, 65–66
  TORCH and, 348–49
Petersburg, siege of, 54
Peyton, "Buster," 27
Philippines, 124, 469
  air reinforcements sent to, 231
  alerts issued to, 240–44, 255–57
  crumbling U.S. defenses in, 283–303
  freedom granted to, 33–34
  insurrection in, 27, 29, 31–34
  Japanese attack of, 261–62, 264–66, 277, 283–303, 320
  Japanese conquest of, 320
  Japanese threat to, 173, 236, 239, 242, 248–50
  MacArthur's calls for recapture of, 305, 312
  MacArthur's evacuation from, 299–303
  MacArthur's return to, 459, 470, 486, 525
  Marshall's dependence on bombers in, 239–40
  Marshall's postings in, 30–34, 42–46
  recapture of, 470, 474–75, 525
  Spanish-American War and, 26
Phillips, Cabell, 172
Phony War, 151
Picardy:
  Allied offensive, 50, 53
  1st Infantry defense of, 61–62
Pittsburgh Chamber of Commerce, 620
Pius XII, Pope, 666
Placentia Bay Conference, *see* Atlantic Conference
Plan Dog, 190, 201, 267
Plattsburg Officers Training Camps, 50–52
Plisetzkaya, Maya, 604
Pogue, Forrest, 27, 334, 485, 570, 590, 626, 642, 654*n*, 664, 724, 732
Poindexter, Joseph B., 260
Poland:
  German invasion of, 143, 145–47, 149
  Hitler's territorial demands on, 136–37
  Marshall Plan and, 614
  revised borders of, 4
  Soviet invasion of, 146–47
  Truman-Molotov meeting on, 527–29
Political Consultation Conference, 561, 564, 566
Portal, Sir Charles, 639
  QUADRANT and, 412
  SYMBOL and, 360–62, 364, 367
  TRIDENT and, 394
Portland Chamber of Commerce, 122
Portuguese Timor, Japanese invasion of, 299
Potsdam Conference, *see* TERMINAL
Potsdam Proclamation, 547–49
Pound, Sir Dudley, 211
  SYMBOL and, 364
  TRIDENT and, 398
Powder, James H., 524–26, 733, 735
Pravda, 639
Pravda Ukraine, 614
Presidio, Marshall's posting at, 47
press:
  on battle for Cantigny, 63
  on Chiang, 488
  on Connecticut maneuvers, 41
  Darlan deal and, 349–50
  on deployment of troops for Meuse-Argonne offensive, 74–75
  on Korean War, 707
  MacArthur and, 703, 710, 712–13, 715, 717
  on Marshall Plan, 621–22

on Marshall's appointment as commander of OVERLORD, 414–16
on Marshall's appointment to State Department, 586–87
and Marshall's biennial reports on state of Army, 204, 207
Marshall's chief of staff appointment and, 138–39, 144
Marshall's China mission and, 584
on Marshall's death, 734
on Meuse-Argonne offensive, 76–77
on Montgomery, 493–95, 518
on Moscow Foreign Ministers' Conference, 597–98
on OVERLORD, 8, 13
on Pearl Harbor investigations, 557, 559
Prince of Wales, sinking of, 217
Princeton University, Marshall's speech at, 609
Principles of War (Foch), 66
Protective Mobilization Force, 166–67, 170–71
Purchasing Commission, British, 173
Pyke, Geoffrey, 412
Pykrete, 412
Pyle, Ernie, 461

QUADRANT (Quebec Conference), 8, 408–13
on OVERLORD, 408–11
on relations with Soviet Union, 411–12
on Southeast Asian command, 410–11
Quebec conferences:
of 1943, *see* QUADRANT
of 1944, *see* OCTAGON
Quezon, Manuel, 298
Quirino, Elpidio, 689

Rabaul offensive, 377–79
Radford, Arthur W., 689
rail strike, Marshall's concern about, 442–43
RAINBOW-5, 231–32, 267
RAINBOW plans, 188–89
Ramadier, Paul, 598
Rayburn, Sam, 204
draft extension and, 205–6
Red-baiting, 629–30, 700
of McCarthy, 676–77
Remagen, capture of Ludendorff Bridge at, 518
Reminiscences (MacArthur), 261*n*
Repington, Charles, 74–75
Reston, James, 587, 621–22
Revolt of the Admirals, 683–84
Reynard, Paul, 157
Reynolds Metals, 185
Rhee, Syngman, 680, 692, 713
Rhine offensive, 484, 486, 500–502, 509, 511, 513, 516
Rhodes campaign, SEXTANT on, 424–27, 435
Ribbentrop, Joachim von, 247
Ridgway, Matthew B., 653
Korean War and, 703–5, 706–7, 716, 718
MacArthur replaced by, 711
Marshall's China command and, 98, 101
in OVERLORD, 444
Rio Conference, 650–51
Roberts, Owen J., 266
Robertson, Walter S., 563–64
Robertson, Sir William, 307
Robinett, Paul, 193–95
Rogers, Will, 728
Romagne, American Cemetary at, 85
Romania Libera, 649

Rome, Allied capture of, 452, 457–58
Rommel, Erwin, 320, 323–24, 363, 454
GYMNAST and, 325, 333
OVERLORD and, 460
TORCH and, 339, 346
in Tunisian campaign, 380–81, 383
Roosevelt, Eleanor, 524, 526, 662
Roosevelt, Elliott, 9, 211–13, 358, 434
Roosevelt, Franklin D., 113, 123–24, 127, 200, 225, 235, 303, 305–6, 309, 320, 379, 395, 411, 442, 489, 497, 535, 591, 596–97, 610, 649–50, 672, 688, 694, 720, 729, 734
Air Corps expansion pressed by, 129–32, 135, 140, 165–66
ANVIL and, 466–67
Anzio assault and, 444–45
appointment OVERLORD commander and, 9, 12–13, 432, 435, 436–37
appointment of supreme commander and, 420, 422–23
ARCADIA and, 267–69, 273–75
ARGONAUT and, 498, 507–8, 511–13
and Army promotion and retirement reform, 175
Atlantic Conference and, 210–17
atomic bomb and, 321
Balkan campaign and, 503
Battle of Britain and, 164
Battle of the Bulge and, 493
BOLERO and, 306, 313, 328–29
British arms sales and, 159
CCC and, 114, 116
on Chennault's "cheap" campaign, 391–92, 397
Chiang warned by, 476, 487
China policy of, 281, 487–88, 506, 512–13, 560, 632
Churchill's congressional address and, 271
Churchill's pleas for aid to, 181–82
Churchill's relationship with, 269
conscription and, 166–69, 172, 205–9
Darlan deal and, 349
D-Day prayer of, 454–55
death of, 523–24, 529, 537
de Gaulle and, 462
on Eisenhower's war-ending plan, 521–22
ETO conferences and, 333
EUREKA and, 3–4, 8–9, 418, 428–30, 432–35
Europe-first strategy and, 304, 307
on expansion of Army, 147–48
Far East policy of, 173
Fireside Chats of, 114
five-star rank and, 491
funeral of, 524–26
on German occupation and partition, 421
and German offensive against Soviet Union, 198–99
German surrender negotiations and, 523
GYMNAST and, 276, 325
Hawaiian visit of, 469–70
Hitler's aggression and, 136–37
Hopkins's relationship with, 133–34
illnesses of, 486, 504–5
and investigations of Pearl Harbor attack, 556–59
and Japanese attack of Philippines, 266
Japanese embargoes and, 219, 221, 227
on joint operations with British, 187–91
Leahy and, 279–80

Roosevelt, Franklin D. (*continued*)
  Lend-Lease aid and, 182–83, 191–92
  MacArthur's conflicts with, 119*n*–20*n*
  MacArthur's popularity and, 297–98
  MacArthur's recall to active duty and, 228
  and MacArthur's requests for reinforcements, 313
  McCarthy's attacks on, 722
  Malta Conference and, 504–6
  Marshall appointed chief of staff by, 7, 139–40, 144
  Marshall retained as chief of staff by, 413–14
  Marshall's access to, 149
  Marshall's balanced-force budget and, 132, 135
  and Marshall's biennial reports on state of Army, 204
  Marshall's confrontations with, 132, 154–55
  Marshall's mobilization plan and, 154–58
  Marshall's promotion to brigadier general and, 119
  Marshall's relationship with, 12, 144–45
  MODICUM and, 307, 309, 311, 313
  Molotov's meetings with, 316–19
  Morgenthau's relationship with, 153
  in negotiations with Japan, 237–38, 240–44, 246, 250–52
  OCTAGON and, 468, 471, 473–76
  OVERLORD and, 8–9, 12–13, 408–9, 414–17, 419, 453, 454–55, 461
  Pearl Harbor attack and, 259–61, 266, 477, 479–81
  Pearl Harbor defenses and, 224
  Philippine crisis and, 284–99
  presidential campaigns of, 4, 145, 159–61, 164–65, 179–80, 448, 469–71, 479–80
  QUADRANT and, 408–9, 411–13
  and recapture of Philippines, 470
  second front issue and, 316–18
  self-confidence of, 13
  SEXTANT and, 3–4, 11–13, 423–24, 426–28, 436
  Solomon Islands campaign and, 328, 344
  state of national emergency declared by, 147
  SYMBOL and, 354–58, 361–67
  on territorial concessions to Soviet Union, 316
  theater responsibilities reshuffled by, 300–301, 304
  Tobruk defeat and, 323–24
  TORCH and, 334–36, 338–42, 345, 347, 349, 353
  TRIDENT and, 386–88, 392–94, 397–98
  Truman's responsibilities under, 536–37
  Tunisian campaign and, 384
  UN planned by, 275
  U.S. military aid to Britain and, 172–73
  on U.S. readiness for Japanese attack, 241–42
  war declaration and, 261
  weariness of, 518–19
Roosevelt, Franklin D., Jr., 172, 358
Roosevelt, Theodore, 12, 554
Roosevelt, Theodore, Jr., 56
Root, Elihu, 161
Rosenberg, Anna M., 688, 705
Rosenman, Sam, 139
Roughriders, 51
ROUNDUP, 306, 308–11, 313, 322, 326, 332–34, 336, 365, 374
  Solomon Islands campaign and, 327
  TRIDENT on, 394, 397

Rowell, Frank, 137
Royal Air Force, British, 191, 449
Royall, Kenneth C.:
  on KMT aid, 637
  Marshall Plan and, 617–18
Ruhr offensive, 519–21
Runyon, Damon, 82
Rusk, Dean, 202
  Korean War and, 679–80, 692, 699–700
  on Marshall's management of State Department, 591
  UN Paris meeting and, 662–63
Russell, Richard, 688, 715, 718–19
Russo-Japanese War, 42, 45
Rutherford, Lucy Mercer, 523
Ryder, Charles W., 347

St. Louis *Post-Dispatch*, 414
St. Mihiel:
  Allied offensive at, 66–73
  1st Infantry Division on front at, 60–61
  release and readjustment of units after, 71–75
St. Petersburg *Times*, 443
St. Peter's Episcopal Church, 17–18
Salerno landing, *see* AVALANCHE
Saltonstall, Leverett, 686
Samuels, Gertrude, 673
San Francisco Conference, 527–28
San Juan Hill, 51
Sato, Ambassador, 549
Schlesinger, Arthur, Jr., 660
Schuman, Robert, 649
Scott, Hugh, Jr., 478–79, 692
Sealion, Operation, 180
2nd Armored Division, U.S., 305, 323, 347, 357, 545
Second Army, British, 455
II Corps, South Korean, 698
II Corps, U.S., 380–83
2nd Infantry Division, U.S., 63, 68–69
Second Supplemental Appropriation Act, 174
Sedan, Allied recapture of, 80–82
Selective Service Act, 169–72, 204, 206, 208–9
Senate, U.S., 314, 537, 577
  Appropriations Committee of, 170–71, 629
  Armed Services Committee of, 688, 714–15, 718
  Army appropriations considered by, 152–53
  Foreign Relations Committee of, 136–37, 204, 386, 395, 586, 596–98, 609–10, 621, 657, 714–15, 718
  League of Nations rejected by, 86
  Military Affairs Committee of, 10–11, 91, 94, 206–8, 415, 682
  NATO and, 663, 670–71
  Pacific-first proponents in, 394–96
  Special Committee to Investigate the National Defense Program of, 10, 186–87, 526, 536
  see also Congress, U.S.
Seoul, fall of, 707
Seventh Army, U.S., 405, 525
Seventh Fleet, U.S., 685
7th Infantry Division, U.S., 691
77th Infantry Division, U.S., 77, 81
Sevareid, Eric, 297
SEXTANT (Cairo Conference), 3–4, 11–13, 308, 418, 422–28, 438, 443
  on ANVIL, 435
  on Burma campaign, 424–26
  on China, 423–28

on OVERLORD, 425–28, 435–37
on Rhodes campaign, 424–27, 435
second half of, 3–4, 435–37
Seymour, Charles, 447
Sforza, Carlo, 666
Shafer, Paul, 415
Shang Chen, 425
Shang-hai, student riots in, 99
Shannon, Jimmy, 85
Shenandoah campaign, 24, 39
Shepley, James R., 562
Sheridan, Philip, 159
Sherrod, Robert, 240
Shertok, Moshe, 657–58
Sherwood, Robert, 134, 182, 192, 267, 299
SHINGLE, 444–47
Shipp, Scott, 24–27, 29–30, 35
Sho plans, 498
Short, Dewey, 714
Short, Walter Campbell:
    Japanese embargoes and, 227
    Pearl Harbor attack and, 477–80, 556, 558–59
    Pearl Harbor defenses and, 223–24
    relief of, 266
    warnings on imminent Japanese attack issued
        to, 244–45, 250, 257, 261
Sibert, William L., 51–53, 55–57, 59
Sicilian invasion, 370, 384, 402, 404–6
    casualties of, 404, 406
    discussions of follow-ons to, 400–401
    SYMBOL on, 361, 364–65
    TRIDENT on, 385–86, 388, 394
Signal Corps, U.S., 40
Signal Corps School, 38
Simpson, William, 520
Sims, William S., 212
Singapore, British surrender of, 299
16th Infantry Regiment, U.S., 52, 58
Sixth Army, German, 352
VI Corps, U.S., 117, 445
69th Infantry Division, U.S., 529
SLEDGEHAMMER, 306–11, 313, 323, 325–26,
    329, 340–41
    Churchill's opposition to, 325–26
    Eisenhower's drafting of, 332–33
Slessor, Sir John, 363, 464
Smith, Lee, 20
Smith, Walter Bedell, 151, 158, 264, 331, 335,
    500, 683, 688, 729, 735
    Battle of the Bulge and, 492–94
    Berlin crisis and, 649
    in German surrender negotiations, 530
    Malta Conference and, 501–3
    Marshall Plan and, 615
    Moscow Foreign Ministers' Conference and,
        600–602, 606
    in War Department mobilization, 193
Smuts, Jan, 460, 462
Snow, Early J., 671
Soldiers and Statesmen (Robertson), 307
Solomon Islands campaign, 326–28, 342–44,
    364, 422
    Battle of Guadalcanal in, 343–44, 376–79
    casualties of, 377
    Rabaul offensive in, 377–79
Somervell, Brehon, 263, 314, 416, 531, 536, 729
    in Army reorganization, 278
    SYMBOL and, 356, 368
Somme, Battle of the, 49–50, 66
Soong, T. V., 411, 553

Sophia, Princess of Greece, 732
"Sources of Soviet Conduct, The" (Kennan), 618
Southeast Asian Theater:
    Malta Conference on, 504
    QUADRANT on, 410–11
southwestern Texas desert, Marshall's mapping
    of, 34
Southwest Pacific campaign, 440
Soviet Union, 4, 123, 303
    aerial bombings in support of, 503
    ARCADIA and, 275
    atomic bomb and, 539, 542, 546, 677–78
    Berlin crisis and, 646–48
    casualties of, 198
    Chinese claims of, 507, 512, 546
    and collapse of Czech coalition government,
        623–25, 644
    containment policy toward, 595–96, 623
    on currency reform, 647
    entrance into war against Japan by, 498, 505,
        507, 511–13, 528, 533, 540, 542, 546,
        549–50
    expansionism of, 546, 592–93, 618, 638–40,
        644
    German non-aggression pact with, 143
    on German occupation and partition, 421
    German offensive of, 352, 402–3, 509–10
    German offensives against, 197–99, 316, 320
    on German peace treaty, 598
    Greece and Turkey threatened by, 594–96
    on Greek civil war, 635
    Japanese neutrality treaty with, 226
    in Japanese surrender negotiations, 544–45,
        547, 549
    JCS postwar projections on, 476
    Kennan on, 591–93, 618, 640
    Korea and, 628
    Korean War and, 681, 692–93, 697, 701–2,
        706, 716–18, 720
    Lend-Lease aid to, 198–200, 312, 316–18,
        320, 498, 513
    Marshall Plan and, 613–15, 619–21, 623, 638
    Marshall's China mission and, 564–65, 568,
        571–73, 582–83
    mutual suspicions between U.S. and, 592
    NSC-68 on, 689–90
    Poland invaded by, 146–47
    proposed Vinson mission to, 664
    QUADRANT on relations with, 411–12
    reparations demanded by, 603, 641–42
    second front issue and, 316–19
    SLEDGEHAMMER and, 306–7
    SYMBOL on, 360
    TRIDENT and, 386–88, 396
    in war-ending plan, 519–21, 525, 529–30
    Wedemeyer's China mission and, 634
Spain, TORCH and, 337, 339–40
Spanish-American War, 26–27, 43, 51, 165, 188,
    690
Spanish Civil War, 123–24
Squier, George O., 38, 40
SS *Robin Moor*, sinking of, 191
Stagg, J. M., 451
Stalin, Joseph, 12, 204, 417, 436, 466, 644, 664,
    666, 721–22
    ARGONAUT and, 507–13
    atomic bomb and, 539
    Berlin crisis and, 649
    calls for second front by, 309
    Eisenhower's war-ending plan and, 521–22

Stalin, Joseph (continued)
   EUREKA and, 4–5, 418, 426, 428–35
   expansion of, 592
   and German offensive against Soviet Union,
      197, 199
   German surrender negotiations and, 522–23
   Marshall admired by, 544
   Marshall Plan and, 615
   Moscow Foreign Ministers' Conference and,
      604–6
   OCTAGON and, 468
   OVERLORD and, 7–8, 13
   on Poland, 528
   second front issue and, 317, 354, 362, 398–99,
      408
   SEXTANT and, 422
   SYMBOL and, 354–55, 362
   TERMINAL and, 542, 544, 546–47
   TORCH and, 339
   TRIDENT and, 394
   in war against Japan, 549
Stark, Harold, 149, 159, 166, 180, 192, 221, 248,
      279, 559, 735
   alerts issued to Pacific commanders by, 245,
      255–56
   ARCADIA and, 273
   Atlantic Conference and, 210–12, 215–16
   on Japanese embargoes, 227
   Pearl Harbor attack and, 259–60, 266
   Pearl Harbor defenses and, 222, 224
   Philippine crisis and, 284
   in planning joint operations with British, 187–
      90
   U.S.-Japanese negotiations and, 236–37, 240–
      44, 251–52
   on U.S. readiness for Japanese attack, 241
State Department, U.S., 123, 275, 527, 608,
      654n, 680, 687
   Acheson's departure from, 615–17, 631
   alleged Communist infiltration of, 555
   Berlin crisis and, 647
   Czech crisis and, 624
   Darlan deal and, 351
   on fall of Chiang, 667–68, 673–74
   Johnson's conflicts with, 684
   Korean War and, 692, 699, 707
   Marshall Plan and, 610–11, 620, 622, 629
   Marshall's appointment to, 586–88
   Marshall's China mission and, 558, 562, 579
   Marshall's management of, 589–91, 593
   Marshall's resignation from, 668–70
   on partition of Palestine, 656–57, 661–62
   Policy Planning Staff of, 591
   Red-baiting and, 629–30, 676–77
   size of, 590
Stayer, Morrison C., 107, 132–33, 139, 232, 733
Steelworkers' Union, 442
Stettinius, Edward, Jr., 86, 159, 240, 497, 525
   ARGONAUT and, 508–9, 513
   Malta Conference and, 505
   on Poland, 527
Stevenson, Adlai, 638, 701, 723
   presidential campaign of, 727–28
Stilwell, Joseph, 5–6, 11, 134, 275, 331, 395, 462,
      475–76, 487, 563
   Chennault's "cheap" campaign and, 390–93
   China mission of, 282–83
   GYMNAST and, 276
   Infantry School instructorship of, 106
   Marshall's China command and, 100–101

   Marshall's friendship with, 100–101, 106
   relief of, 488
   SEXTANT and, 423–24, 426
   TRIDENT and, 389, 392–94, 397
Stilwell, Winifred, 100, 282
Stimson, Henry L., 41, 104, 178, 180, 187, 204,
      234, 242, 248–50, 257, 305–6, 353, 379,
      392, 395–96, 398, 411, 442, 447, 463, 518,
      525, 529, 570, 589, 616, 687, 711
   and aid to Soviet Union, 198
   atomic bomb and, 537–39, 543–46
   background of, 160–61
   Battle of Britain and, 164
   China policy and, 281–82
   Churchill's congressional address and, 271
   conscription and, 167–69, 172, 205, 495–96
   on crumbling defenses of Philippines, 283, 298
   Darlan deal and, 350
   Europe-first strategy and, 304, 307
   German surrender and, 531–33
   GYMNAST and, 322, 325
   illnesses of, 655
   and investigations of Pearl Harbor attack, 556,
      559
   and Japanese attack of Philippines, 262, 266
   Japanese surrender and, 549
   on leaking of Victory Program, 249
   Lend-Lease aid and, 183
   MacArthur's conflicts with, 230
   MacArthur's recall to active duty and, 228–29
   MacArthur's seduction of, 231–32
   Marshall accessible to, 194
   Marshall praised by, 554–55
   on Marshall's management of War Depart-
      ment, 263
   on Marshall's recommendations for promo-
      tions, 176–77
   Marshall's relationship with, 162
   and Marshall's reorganization of JCS, 280
   in negotiations with Japan, 236, 242–43, 246,
      250, 254–55
   OVERLORD and, 9, 12–13, 415, 452
   Pearl Harbor attack and, 260, 266, 477, 480–
      81
   Pearl Harbor defenses and, 222, 224
   on Poland, 528
   QUADRANT and, 408
   Solomon Islands campaign and, 327–28
   TERMINAL and, 546
   TRIDENT and, 387, 394
   on U.S. readiness for Japanese attack, 241
   war declaration and, 261
   War Department appointment of, 160–63
   War Department mobilization and, 193
   warning to MacArthur issued by, 243–45
Stone, Harlan F., 143, 271
Stone, I. F., 443
Straight, Willard, 86
Strout, Richard, 416
Stuart, Eliza (aunt), 20, 25
Stuart, John Leighton:
   background of, 576–77
   Marshall's China mission and, 576–78, 580,
      582–84
Sudentenland, Hitler's claims on, 128
Summerall, Charles F., 104
Sumner, Jessie, 415
Sun Yat-sen, 97, 101, 560, 580
Sutherland, Richard, 297
Suzuki, Kantaro, 547

Sweeney, Charles W., 549
Swing, Raymond Gram, 473
Swope, Herbert Bayard, 93
SYMBOL (Casablanca Conference), 354–68,
    378, 395, 448
  British proposals at, 359–62
  operations discussed at, 361, 363–64
  on Sicilian invasion, 361, 364–65
  on submarine warfare, 375
  on unconditional surrender, 368
  U.S. position at, 360–63

Taft, Robert A., 162, 518, 620, 650, 677, 712
Taft, William Howard, 33, 51, 104, 161
Taiwan, *see* Formosa
Tariff Commission, 88
Taylor, Maxwell, 151
Tedder, Arthur, 494
Teheran Conference, *see* EUREKA
Ten-Point Plan, 243, 245, 250
Tenth Army, U.S., 525
X Corps, U.S., 701–3, 705
10th Pennsylvania Infantry, 22–23, 26–27
TERMINAL (Potsdam Conference), 542–47
  atomic bomb and, 544–45
Texas-Mexican border:
  Army maneuvers on, 40
  campaign on, 51
Third Army, U.S., 264, 453, 482, 492, 529
III Corps, U.S., 75–76
Third Fleet, U.S., 474
3rd Infantry Division, U.S., 63
  Marshall's command of, 120–22
Third Punic War, 9
13th Infantry Regiment, U.S., 42
30th Infantry Regiment, U.S., 31–33
34th Infantry Division, U.S., 514
  in Tunisian campaign, 380, 382–83
32nd Infantry Division, U.S., 376
33rd National Guard Division, Marshall's com-
    mand of, 116–18
Thomason, R. Ewing, 170
Thompson, Andy, 19–22, 25, 35
308th Infantry Regiment, U.S., 77
Time, 234, 240, 379, 413, 438, 442, 488, 514,
    572, 575, 597–98, 621, 632, 643, 727
Time, Inc., 577
Times (London), 74–75
Tito (Josip Broz), 7, 427, 429, 649
Tobruk, British surrender at, 323–24
Together (Katherine Marshall), 443, 630–31
Togo, Shigenori, 245, 250
Tojo, Hideki, 219, 225, 469
  U.S.-Japanese negotiations and, 237, 246–47
Tokyo, bombing of, 533–34, 540
Topeka Capital, 160
TORCH, 334–36, 337–53, 383
  casualties of, 348, 350
  Darlan deal and, 349–52
  Marshall's criticisms of, 369
  success of, 347
Trade and Navigation, Treaty of, 219
TRB, 645
Treasury Department, U.S., 183, 221
TRIDENT (Washington Conference), 385–99,
    407
  on Burma campaign, 389, 392–94, 397
  decisions taken up at, 399
  results of, 398
  Sicilian invasion and, 385–86, 388, 394

Tripartite Pact, 220–21, 238, 259
Trizonia, 647
Trotsky, Leon, 59
Truman, Bess, 578, 685
Truman, Harry S., 10, 153, 470, 609, 616, 650,
    688, 694, 727, 729, 733
  atomic bomb and, 537–39, 543, 545–46, 548
  Berlin crisis and, 647–48
  Byrnes removed by, 574, 583
  China aid and, 668
  on civilian vs. military control of atomic weap-
    ons, 649
  CORONET and, 536
  duties performed for Roosevelt by, 536–37
  Eisenhower denounced by, 728
  on ending war in Far East, 540
  and fall of Chiang, 675
  on Forrestal's budget requests, 646
  and Greek and Turkish aid, 594, 596
  and investigations of Pearl Harbor, 556
  Israel recognized by, 661
  Japanese surrender and, 549
  Johnson's conflicts with, 683–85
  Korean War and, 679–81, 689, 692, 696–700,
    702–3, 705–9, 714, 716–18, 720
  London Foreign Ministers' Conference and,
    641
  MacArthur sacked by, 708–12, 716
  MacArthur's conflicts with, 703, 708–9
  on MacArthur's congressional address, 714
  MacArthur's criticisms of, 684, 716
  McCarthy's attacks on, 721–23
  Marshall appointed head of American Red
    Cross by, 672
  Marshall appointed to Defense Department
    by, 682–87
  Marshall Plan and, 610, 612–13, 620–21, 625
  Marshall respected and admired by, 525, 597,
    669, 685
  Marshall's China mission and, 555–56, 560,
    562, 564, 569–70, 572, 574, 577–79, 583
  at Marshall's funeral, 735
  Marshall's relationship with, 186, 526–27, 529,
    536–37
  and Marshall's resignation from Defense
    Department, 726
  and Marshall's resignation from State Depart-
    ment, 668–70
  Marshall's State Department appointment and,
    588
  Marshall's successor chosen by, 668
  military procurement investigated by, 185–87
  NATO and, 663–65
  on partition of Palestine, 656–61
  on Poland, 527–29
  Red-baiting and, 629–30
  reelection campaign of, 655, 659–60, 662, 664,
    666
  Roosevelt's death and, 523–24
  on Soviet atomic bomb development, 677–78
  on Soviet clamp down on Czechoslovakia,
    624–25
  Soviet expansionism and, 546
  Soviet Union condemned by, 644–45
  TERMINAL and, 542, 544–47
  UMT and, 645, 724
  Vinson's Soviet mission and, 664
  Wedemeyer's China mission and, 633–35
Truman, Margaret, 624, 684
Truman Committee, 10, 186–87, 526, 536

Truman Doctrine, 596, 608, 614, 619, 623, 629
Truscott, Lucian K., Jr., 332, 348, 449, 484
Tsushima, Battle of, 250
Tuberculosis and Health Association, 133–34
Tuchman, Barbara, 392
Tully, Grace, 260–61
Tunisian campaign, 379–84, 387
  Battle of Kasserine Pass in, 380–81
  casualties of, 383
  prisoners taken in, 383
Turkey:
  SYMBOL on, 364–65
  U.S. aid to, 594–96, 608, 629
12th Army Group, U.S., 519
20th Infantry Division, Indian, 525
28th Infantry Regiment, U.S., 52, 67–68
  in attack on Cantigny, 62–63
21st Army Group, British, 509, 519, 521
24th Infantry Regiment, U.S., Marshall's command of, 40, 110–11
29th Infantry Division, U.S., 455
27th Infantry Battalion, U.S., 516
26th Infantry Regiment, U.S., 52
Tydings, Millard, 395
Tyler, Kermit, 257

ULTRA, 191, 460
Under Two Flags (Ouida), 56
Uniontown, Pa.:
  Marshall's visits to, 35
  Marshall's youth in, 17–23
United Nations, 4, 635, 678, 680, 728
  General Assembly of, 655, 657, 659, 662
  Israel peace proposal of, 661–62
  Korean War and, 681, 695–96, 699, 701, 706–8, 715, 718
  Paris meeting of, 662–64, 666
  on partition of Palestine, 657, 659, 662
  Relief and Rehabilitation Administration of, 591
  Roosevelt's planning for, 275
  San Francisco meeting of, 527–28
  Security Council of, 681
  Wedemeyer's China mission and, 634
United Nations Declaration, 281
United Press, 707
United Services Organization (USO), 178
United States Army Forces in the Far East (USAFFE), 229
United States News, 586–87
United States Relations with China, 1944–1949, 675
United States Steel Exporting Co., 159
universal military training (UMT), 645, 688–89, 716, 724–25
Universal Military Training and Service Act, 724
Uranium Committee, 321
U.S. News and World Report, 684, 703
USS Housatonic, sinking of, 48
USS Niblack, U-boats fired on by, 191
UTAH Beach, 452, 454–55

Vancouver Barracks, Marshall's command at, 120–22
Vandenberg, Arthur, 379, 395, 596
  background of, 609–10
  death of, 714
  on KMT aid, 637
  London Foreign Ministers' Conference and, 640

Marshall Plan and, 610, 622, 624–25, 730
Moscow Foreign Ministers' Conference and, 597
NATO and, 663
Vandenberg, Hoyt, 695, 703
Van Fleet, James, 666, 711, 718
Vaughan, Harry H., 527, 712
Versailles Treaty, 110, 116, 123
Veterans of Foreign Wars, 684
Vicksburg, siege of, 54
Victoria, Queen of England, 464
Victory Program, 200–202, 249, 263, 314, 442
Victory Through Air Power (de Seversky), 374
Viet Minh, 627
Villa, Francisco, 46
Vincent, John Carter, 562, 579, 584, 635
Vinson, Fred M., 588, 664
Virginia Military Institute (VMI), 13, 21
  Confederate tradition of, 24–26
  hazing at, 26
  Marshall's attendance at, 23–28
  superintendency offered to Marshall by, 101–2
VITTLES, 648
Voroshilov, Kliment, 430–32
VULCAN, 382

Wadena Pioneer Journal, 650
Wadsworth, James W., 91, 93, 167, 172, 607
  draft extension and, 208, 210
Wainwright, Jonathan, 301–3, 712, 729
Wake Island, Marshall on Japanese threat to, 242
Wake Island meeting, 696–97
Waldrop, Frank, 415
Walker, Walton, 681, 695, 698, 701, 704
Wallace, Henry, 623, 650
Walters, Vernon "Dick," 651–52, 665
War College, 125
Ward, Orlando, 151
War Department, U.S., 40, 59, 64, 91, 92, 118, 134, 147
  atomic bomb and, 548
  CCC and, 115–16
  Chiang warned by, 476
  Darlan deal and, 350
  Department of the East of, 50–51
  draft extension and, 207
  and expansion of Air Corps, 130–31
  expenditures of, 315
  General Staff of, 195
  and German offensive against Soviet Union, 198
  Lend-Lease and, 183–84
  logistics and, 374–75
  Marshall's management of, 150–51, 192–96, 263, 278–79, 441–42, 589
  Marshall's promotion to brigadier general and, 119
  mismanagement of supplies by, 51
  Pearl Harbor attack and, 480, 559
  on Pearl Harbor defenses, 223
  in planning joint operations with British, 188–90
  Roosevelt's death and, 524
  Stimson's appointment to, 160–63
  TORCH and, 340
  Truman Committee and, 187
  Victory Program of, 200–202, 249, 263, 314, 442

War Plans Division of, 124, 126–27
see also Defense Department, U.S.
War Manpower Commission, 688
War Plan Orange, 298, 303
War Plan White, 112, 118
Washington, George, 18, 150, 272, 402–3, 442
Washington conferences:
  of 1941, *see* ARCADIA
  of 1943, *see* TRIDENT
Washington *News*, 113
Washington Post, 233, 453
Washington *Times-Herald*, 175, 249, 253n, 415, 724
Watson, Edwin, 228
Wavell, Sir Archibald, 204, 272–74
  TRIDENT and, 389, 392
Wedemeyer, Albert, 194, 324, 374, 410–11, 488, 513, 561, 637, 680, 723
  China mission of, 633–35
  Marshall's China mission and, 563, 570, 576
  MODICUM and, 307, 309
  SYMBOL and, 356–57, 359, 364–65, 368
  Victory Program of, 200–202
Welles, Sumner, 263
  Atlantic Conference and, 211, 214–15
Wells, H. G., 307
Wesson, Charles "Bull," 195
Western Desert Force, British, 180
West Point, 23
  Marshall's address to graduating class at, 318
Wheeler, Burton K., 183, 249
Wherry, Kenneth, 234, 674, 677
White, Theodore, 282, 488, 575
White, William S., 671–72, 732
Whittlesey, Charles, 77–78
Wilhelm II, Kaiser, 80, 82
Wilhelmina, Queen of the Netherlands, 232
Wilkinson, Theodore, 253
Williams, E. J., 43
Willkie, Wendell, 171, 179
Willoughby, Charles, 698
Wilson, Sir Henry Maitland "Jumbo," 78–79, 418, 448, 464–65, 490, 515
  Anzio assault and, 445
  SEXTANT and, 426–27
Wilson, Rose Page (goddaughter), 88–90, 564, 645, 684, 728, 732–33
  Lily Marshall's death and, 103–4, 106
  Marshall's chief of staff appointment and, 138
  Marshall's 33rd Division command and, 117
Wilson, Woodrow, 91, 168, 179, 239n, 660
  convalescence of, 88

neutrality of, 45–48
peace negotiations and, 76–79, 85–86
Winant, John G., 250
Wing, Richard, 655, 734
Winn, James, Jr. (son-in-law), 184
Winn, Jimmie (stepgrandson), 732
Winn, Molly Brown (stepdaughter), 107, 109, 111, 113, 118, 122, 127, 149, 184, 413, 441, 631, 735
Wise, John, 29
Wolff, Karl, 522–23
Women's Army Auxiliary Corps (WAACS), 373, 403–4
Wood, Leonard, 40–41
Woodring, Harry H., 116, 126–27, 129, 131–32, 143, 144, 159
  dismissal of, 160
  Marshall's chief of staff appointment and, 138
  Marshall's mobilization plan and, 154
  Neutrality Act repeal and, 148
Workers and Soldiers Committees, 82
Works Progress Administration (WPA), 6, 132–34
World War I, 36
  casualties of, 50, 53, 56, 61
  costs of, 85
  final battles of, 79–82
World War II:
  casualties of, 496, 554
  end of, 550
  predictions on end of, 469, 510–11, 525
Wright, Orville, 38, 64
Wright brothers, 38
Wright Flyers, 38
Wu Pei-fu, 97

"X" article, 618–19

Yalta Conference, *see* ARGONAUT
Yamamoto, Isoroku, 259
  Pearl Harbor attack planned by, 218–19, 226, 235, 247
  war strategy of, 218–19
Yamashita, General, 534
Yap, attack on, 475
Yeaton, Ivan, 199
Yugoslavia, fall of, 191

Zhdanov, Andrei, 619–20
Zhukov, Georgi, 519
Zimmermann, Arthur, 48